Fodor's

NEW ENGLAND

Welcome to New England

New England's distinctive sights and landscapes make it a classic American destination. Vermont's and New Hampshire's blazing fall foliage, Connecticut's Colonial towns, and Maine's rocky coast are just a few regional icons. Massachusetts, home to Boston's stirring Revolutionary-era sites, is one of many places where history comes alive. You can sample the good life, too, with visits to Newport's Gilded Age mansions in Rhode Island or a stay in a sleek country inn. Enjoy nature's bounty, whether you're skiing, hiking, or simply taking in a magnificent view.

TOP REASONS TO GO

★ **Fall Foliage:** Scenic drives and walks reveal America's best festival of colors.

★ **History:** The Freedom Trail, Mystic Seaport, and more preserve a fascinating past.

★ **Small Towns:** A perfect day includes strolling a town green and locavore dining.

★ **The Coast:** Towering lighthouses and pristine beaches, plus whale-watching and sailing.

★ **Outdoor Fun:** Top draws are Acadia National Park, Cape Cod, and the Appalachian Trail.

★ **Regional Food:** Maine lobster and blueberries, Vermont maple syrup and cheese.

Contents

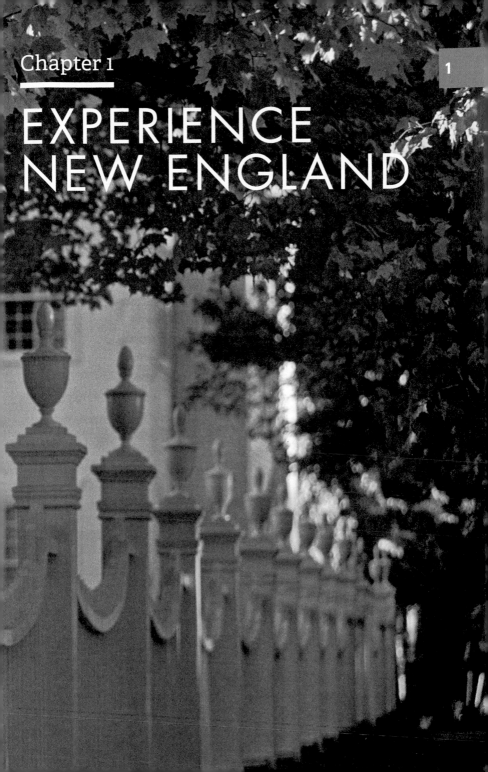

Chapter 1

EXPERIENCE NEW ENGLAND

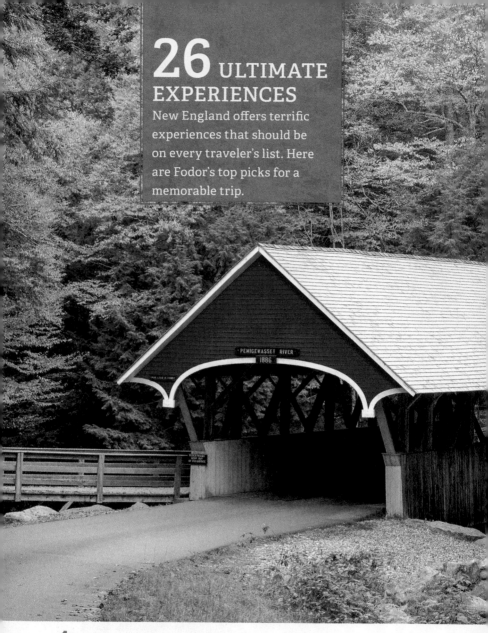

26 ULTIMATE EXPERIENCES

New England offers terrific experiences that should be on every traveler's list. Here are Fodor's top picks for a memorable trip.

1 Count Covered Bridges

There are 54 of these iconic American symbols still in use in New Hampshire. In fact, the Cornish-Windsor Bridge (1866), which spans the Connecticut River between Cornish, NH, and Windsor, VT, is New England's only covered bridge that connects two states, the country's longest wooden bridge, and the world's longest two-span covered bridge. *(Ch. 10)*

2 Drive Down to "P-town"

Lively, historical, colorful, busy, sometimes silly, Provincetown is full of inns, restaurants, shops, galleries, and nightlife. If you're on the Cape, visiting P-town is a pleasant day trip or a longer stay. *(Ch. 5)*

3 Boating on Lake Champlain

The 107-mile-long lake is hugely popular for recreation—especially boating. You can rent numerous types of vessels, take lessons, or, cruise aboard *Spirit of Ethan Allen*, the lake's only "floating restaurant." *(Ch. 9)*

4 Have a Maine Lobster

A trip to Maine isn't complete without a meal featuring the official state crustacean. Whether you choose a classic lobster dinner, a bowl of lobster stew, or a lobster roll, bring your appetite. *(Ch. 12)*

5 Visit the Ocean State

Known as "The Ocean State" for a reason, Rhode Island's south coast is replete with long strips of powdery white sand facing great swells of the Atlantic Ocean just beckoning you to dive in. *(Ch. 8)*

6 Hike Mt. Monadnock

At 3,165 feet, Mt. Monadnock looms over the New Hampshire town of Jaffrey. The only way to reach the summit is by foot, and the miles of trails attract well over 100,000 hikers each year. *(Ch. 10)*

7 Climb Aboard a Whaler at Mystic Seaport

Mystic Seaport is home to more than 60 buildings in this re-created 19th-century village, and a number of historic vessels including the *Charles W. Morgan*, the last of the wooden whaling ships. *(Ch. 7)*

8 Explore Acadia National Park

At New England's only national park, drive or bike the 27-mile Park Loop Road, climb the 1,530 summit of Cadillac Mountain, or explore 45 miles of carriage roads. *(Ch. 12)*

9 Dinosaurs in Connecticut

Check out Yale Peabody Museum's "Great Hall of Dinosaurs" before heading north to Rocky Hill and Dinosaur State Park—one of North America's largest dinosaur track sites. *(Ch. 7)*

10 Ferry Over to Block Island

Just 12 miles off Rhode Island's south coast, this laid-back island has 17 miles of sandy beaches, the 200-foot-high Mohegan Bluffs, the tranquil Great Salt Pond, and the charming town of New Shoreham. *(Ch. 8)*

11 Boating on Lake Winnipesaukee

At 182 miles around, you won't run out of space or adventures at New Hampshire's largest lake. Boats rentals are available to explore more than 250 islands, and there are numerous waterfront restaurants. *(Ch. 10)*

12 Vintage Steam Trains

The 12-mile round-trip journey along the picturesque Connecticut River will delight the whole family—particularly because the train's 1920s-era coaches are pulled by a vintage steam locomotive. *(Ch. 7)*

13 The Beautiful Berkshires

The "far west" of Massachusetts is green, mountainous, and scattered with interesting towns and villages tucked into pretty valleys. There are outdoor activities, artist enclaves, and excellent leaf-peeping. *(Ch. 6)*

14 Visit a Working Farm

Several Vermont farmers welcome visitors for a day, overnight, or a few days. Guests can help with chores like collecting eggs, milking cows, feeding sheep, picking veggies, or baking bread. *(Ch. 9)*

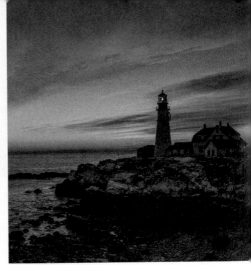

15 Historic and Hip Portland

Old Port has eclectic restaurants, boutiques, and high-end apartments, while the Arts District has the Portland Museum of Art. The Eastern Promenade has a 2-mile paved trail at the water's edge. *(Ch. 12)*

16 Whaling (and Lizzie Borden)

New Bedford was the world's most important whaling port in the 1800s. Visit the town's whaling museum, then tour the Lizzie Borden Bed & Breakfast … the "creep factor" is real. *(Ch. 4)*

17 Try Your Luck at a Mega-casino

Foxwoods and Mohegan Sun are 15 minutes apart in southeastern Connecticut. Both have slot machines, gaming tables, restaurants, shops, hotels, and a full schedule of events. *(Ch. 7)*

18 Ski Vermont

The Green Mountains form the spine of Vermont, and snuggled in and around all of the peaks are nearly two-dozen major ski resorts, including Sugarbush, Snow, Stratton, and Stowe. *(Ch. 9)*

19 Take a Walk Around Providence

Enjoy restaurants, beautifully restored Colonial homes, picturesque universities, the magnificent Museum of Art, RISD, and, if your timing is right, WaterFire. *(Ch. 8)*

20 See How "the other half" Lived in Newport

America's wealthiest families summered here in the 19th century. Many of the mansions have been beautifully preserved and are open to the public for tours. *(Ch. 8)*

21 Cruise on a Windjammer

Pretty Camden Harbor and nearby Rockland are home ports for a fleet of owner-operated schooners that take guests on voyages around Maine's rugged coast, peninsulas, and islands. *(Ch. 12)*

22 Go Back in Time

Plimoth Plantation is a living-history museum that replicates one of the country's original settlements. Old Sturbridge Village, another living-history museum, re-creates rural New England life. *(Ch. 4, 6)*

23 Walk Boston's Freedom Trail

Boston's Freedom Trail is a 2½-mile-long marked path that links 16 historical landmarks, starting at the Boston Common and ending at the Bunker Hill Monument and USS *Constitution*. *(Ch. 4)*

24 Vermont Sugar Shacks

There are about 1,500 sugarhouses in Vermont. In 2017 those shacks produced about 2 million gallons of syrup, or about half of all maple syrup consumed in the United States. *(Ch. 9)*

25 Wend Your Way Through the White Mountains

Mt. Washington (6,288 feet) is the highest peak in New Hampshire and the northeastern U.S. There are great views, but it's cold and windy even in mid-summer. *(Ch. 10)*

26 Treat Yo'self at Ben & Jerry's

At the Ben & Jerry's Factory in Waterbury, take the half-hour guided factory tour to watch ice cream being made, then mosey over to the Scoop Shop for a treat. *(Ch. 9)*

WHAT'S WHERE

1 Boston. Massachusetts's capital city is also New England's hub. Boston's many universities lend it a cosmopolitan air, yet its blue-collar roots are still visible. This is the cradle of American democracy, a place where soaring skyscrapers cast shadows on Colonial graveyards.

2 Cape Cod, Nantucket, and Martha's Vineyard. Great beaches, delicious seafood, and artsy shopping districts fill scenic Cape Cod, chic Martha's Vineyard, and remote Nantucket.

3 The Berkshires and Western Massachusetts. The mountainous Berkshires live up to the storybook image of rural New England while supporting a thriving arts scene. Farther east, the Pioneer Valley is home to a string of historic settlements.

4 Connecticut. The bustling southwest contrasts with the Quiet Corner in the northeast, known as an antiquing destination. Small villages line the southeastern coast, within reach of a pair of casinos. The Connecticut River Valley and Litchfield Hills boast grand old inns, rolling farmlands, and state parks.

5 Rhode Island. The smallest New England state is home to great sailing and glitzy mansions in Newport. South County has sparsely populated beaches and fertile countryside; scenic Block Island is a short ferry ride away.

6 Vermont. Vermont has farms, freshly starched towns and small cities, quiet country lanes, and bustling ski resorts. The Green Mountain state is synonymous with cheese and maple syrup, and its billboard-free back roads may be the most scenic in the region.

7 New Hampshire. Portsmouth is the star of the state's 18-mile coastline. The Lakes Region is a popular summertime escape, and the White Mountains' dramatic vistas attract photographers and adventurous hikers farther north.

8 Inland Maine. The largest New England state's rugged interior—including the Western Lakes and vast North Woods regions—attracts skiers, hikers, campers, anglers, and other outdoors enthusiasts.

9 The Maine Coast. Classic villages, rocky shorelines, and picturesque Main Streets draw scores of vacationers to Maine. Acadia National Park is where majestic mountains meet the coast; Bar Harbor is the park's gateway town.

New England's Best Seafood Shacks

BITE INTO MAINE, CAPE ELIZABETH, ME

Since 2008, this spot has been serving up high-quality lobster rolls—locally sourced, never-frozen meat—no matter the season. The traditional lobster roll is one of the best, but the contemporary twists make the trip worth it, and the LBT (Lobster Bacon and Tomato) sandwich is sheer heaven.

AUNT CARRIE'S, NARRAGANSETT, RI

Local lore states that this modest clam shack is where New Englanders first came up with the brilliant idea of frying fresh clams into cakes in the early 1920s. Since then, this joint has been serving up seafood, including traditional Rhode Island shore dinners—clam chowder, steamers, clam cakes, coleslaw, fried flounder, French fries, and sometimes a lobster for good measure.

ABBOTT'S LOBSTER IN THE ROUGH, NOANK, CT

Nestled on the banks of the storied Mystic River, Abbott's Lobster in the Rough has been serving delicious seafood dishes since 1947. Plan enough time to appreciate the view while enjoying the stuffed clams and pitch-perfect lobster rolls. And remember, the shack is BYOB.

CAPTAIN SCOTT'S LOBSTER DOCK, NEW LONDON, CT

Often touted as New London's best kept secret, Captain Scott's is a little off the beaten path, but it's worth it for the tasty Rhode Island Clam Chowder and piping hot clam fritters, not to mention a thick lobster bisque that will leave you swooning.

TWO LIGHTS LOBSTER SHACK, CAPE ELIZA-BETH, ME

You'd be hard-pressed to find a more stunning view than the panorama that spreads out across the ocean from this classic Maine seafood shack. Flanked by the historic twin lighthouses for which it is named, this shack has been serving up seafood since the 1920s.

FIVE ISLANDS LOBSTER, GEORGETOWN, ME

Located on a lively working wharf overlooking Sheepscot Bay, this seafood spot welcomes hungry folks with its delicious seafood and stunning views. The family-friendly atmosphere extends to the menu, which also has options for diners not entirely keen on seafood.

FLO'S CLAM SHACK AND DRIVE-IN, PORTSMOUTH, RI

The original Flo's Clam Shack got its start in 1936 when the owner set up shop in a chicken coup and began serving its signature fresh, juicy fried clams. Flo's has been wiped out by five massive hurricanes since its inception but has somehow always managed to keep on trucking, serving up the same heavenly seafood that keeps locals and visitors coming back time and time again.

ARNOLD'S LOBSTER AND CLAM BAR, EASTHAM, MA

This legendary spot serves up generous portions of traditional fried and fresh seafood dishes along with hearty baked potatoes, a raw bar, and fresh salads. There's a kid-friendly menu, on-site minigolf, and an ice-cream stand.

BOB LOBSTER, NEWBURYPORT, MA

A trip to Plum Island isn't complete unless you grab a bite to eat at this local favorite, which got its start as a local seafood market. The menu always includes homemade seafood pies, creamy seafood chowders loaded with fresh meat, and a to-die-for lobster mac-n-cheese.

CLAM BOX OF IPSWICH, IPSWICH, MA

Since 1938, this unmistakable saltbox shack—bright, red-and-white-striped awnings and unique architectural shape—has been a go-to spot for locals and visitors alike. The fried clams are an institution, but you also can't go wrong tucking into one of their seafood rolls or homemade coleslaw.

Buy Local: 10 Popular New England Souvenirs

ANTIQUES & COLLECTIBLES

Collectibles and antiques abound from cities like Boston (Charles Street), Providence (Wickenden Street), and Portland (Old Port District) to towns like Woodbury and Middlebury, CT; Chester, VT; Essex, MA; and Wells, ME. New Hampshire's Route 4 is known as Antique Alley, and in May, July, and September, there's Massachusetts's Brimfield Antiques & Collectibles Show.

JAMS & PRESERVES

Pick up strawberry preserves, apple butter, cranberry sauce, or blueberry jam at farmers' markets or country stores like Old Wethersfield (CT), Brown & Hopkins (RI), Wayside (MA), Old Country Store & Museum (NH), East Boothbay (ME), or the Vermont Country Store.

MOCCASINS

Maine shoemakers craft some of the best moccasins, and Quoddy, known for its custom, made-to-order moccasins, deck shoes, and boots, is one of the best. Reach out while you're Down East or back at home. The wait for your shoes is worth it. Ditto with Wassookeag, another great Maine maker of bespoke footwear.

CANVAS BAGS

Nothing says durability like canvas; nothing says coastal New England like sailing. Portland-based Sea Bags has creative, rope-handled totes made from recycled sails. Port Canvas in Arundel, Maine, also hand-crafts sporty, customizable canvas totes and duffels—perfect for lugging your souvenirs home.

MAPLE SYRUP

Each spring, sugarhouses tap their maple trees and boil the resultant sap down into syrup. Although it takes about 40 gallons of sap to make 1 gallon of syrup, locally made varieties are readily available— Grades A and B and in light, medium, and dark (for baking only) shades of amber. The best known states are New Hampshire and Vermont, which, by the way, has its own strict grading system.

TOYS

Vermont Teddy Bears are guaranteed for life; there's even a hospital for Teddy emergencies! Vermont's Real Good Toys makes finely crafted dollhouses and miniature accessories. New Hampshire's Annalee Dolls are distinctive, cute, and collectible—especially the holiday ones.

YARN & KNITWEAR

The wares of independent spinners and knitters can be found throughout the region. Noteworthy companies include Bartlettyarns, Inc., which has been in Maine since 1821; Rhode Island's North Light Fibers; and Maine's Swans Island Company.

FLANNEL WOOLENS

New England's textile industry declined in the 1920s and '30s, but Vermont's Johnson Woolen Mills is still going strong. The warm, soft, and often boldly checked flannel shirts, jackets, capes, wraps, scarves, hats, and even undies sold in its factory store and elsewhere are splurge-worthy classics.

CRAFT BEER & CIDER

New England's brewing history includes one of America's oldest outfits, Rhode Island's Narragansett (1890) and some of the nation's first craft breweries: Maine's D.L. Geary (1983) and Massachusetts's Boston Beer Company (1984) of Sam Adams fame. There are smaller breweries in every state, including cideries— hard or not. Notable cideries include Maine's Urban Farm Fermentory and Vermont's family-friendly Cold Hollow.

LOBSTER

Seafood markets, lobster pounds, and even some independent lobstermen sell lobster to go. As soon as you buy them, you have 48 hours (max) to cook them, and lobsters must be kept sedated (i.e., lightly chilled) but alive, with claws rubber-banded, until then. Another option: ask about shipping or look into online pack-and-ship retailers like Maine Lobster Now, The Lobster Guy, and Lobsters New England.

New England's Most Picturesque Towns

BRISTOL, RI
Tucked between Providence and Newport, this small New England town has a lot to offer in the way of history, but its charm lies chiefly in its breathtaking scenery and well-preserved, historic architecture, comprised of picture perfect Colonial, 19th-century, and Gilded Age buildings.

WOODSTOCK, VT
This quintessential Vermont town is ridiculously, wonderfully picturesque—classic covered bridges, local cheese makers, cider mills, working farms and orchards, sugar shacks, meandering brick streets, and a town center that is straight out of a Norman Rockwell painting.

KENT, CT
Located in the northwest corner of Connecticut, the historic town of Kent is a lively mix of art galleries, shops, and restaurants. There are also great outdoor destinations like Kent Falls State Park, home to the state's tallest waterfall, and the Appalachian Trail's longest river walk.

SIASCONSET, MA
This tiny Nantucket town gives visitors exactly what they want—sweeping panoramas of the Atlantic and Sankaty Head Light, rows of classic New England saltbox houses, delightfully overflowing gardens chock-full of beach peas and roses enclosed in white picket fences, and scenic coastal walks.

EASTPORT, ME
Most of Maine's visitors don't make it past the Mid-Coast, but Down East Maine is more than worth the hike, if only to pay a visit to Eastport, a picturesque seaside town with historic architecture situated on pristine Moose Island. A world apart, Eastport prides itself on its fishing and lobstering industries, excellent local arts scene, and vibrant indigenous community.

DAMARISCOTTA, ME

Just north of Wiscasset, this often overlooked village is surrounded by salt marsh preserves and oyster beds. The village's historic brick architecture and quaint but vibrant Main Street overlooks the harbor where the annual and delightfully oddball Pumpkinfest and Regatta takes place.

NEWBURYPORT, MA

First settled by Europeans in 1635, this seaside town has immaculate red brick streets and a vibrant working harbor that delivers that quintessential, New England feel. Classic seafood shacks, charming taverns with Old World flair, and a bevy of upscale specialty boutiques add to the charm.

CAMDEN, ME

With its brick architecture and Victorian mansions, Maine doesn't get any more picturesque than this village. Situated in the heart of the Mid-Coast, the town's working harbor is surrounded by rolling, mountains that cascades seamlessly down to the water's edge.

ESSEX, CT

On the southwestern bank of the beautiful Connecticut River lies Essex, a quaint New England town scattered with cozy inns and taverns and historical architecture that are best explored on foot. With a picture-perfect harbor, a historic working steam train, and a delightfully eclectic cluster of buildings, Essex has a lot to offer in the way of small town charm.

KEENE, NH

Stunning brick streets, charming maple farms, quaint storefronts, classic covered bridges, gorgeous nature preserves, and a college town vibe combine to create the quintessential New England experience. Keene, the darling of New Hampshire's southwestern Monadnock Region, even has a white clapboard church with a soaring spire.

New England's Best Beaches

FOOTBRIDGE BEACH, OGUNQUIT, ME

This spot offers excellent swimming, beach combing, and bodysurfing opportunities, as well as a boat launch for kayaks, small boats, and standup paddleboards. Typically less crowded than neighboring Ogunquit Beach, it's reached by crossing a foot bridge that runs over the Ogunquit River.

HAMMONASSET BEACH, MADISON, CT

At about 2 miles long, Connecticut's largest beach beckons day-trippers and campers to its shore for superb birding, swimming, and sandy strolls on the charming wooden boardwalk. There are also picnic spots, bike trails, great fishing, and the Meigs Point Nature Center.

EAST BEACH, MARTHA'S VINEYARD, MA

Located between Cape Pogue Wildlife Refuge and Wasque Reservation on Chappaquiddick Island, East Beach—also known as Leland Beach—is a popular spot for surf fishing. The half-mile beach is also an excellent spot for birding, swimming, and peaceful sunset walks, but there is an entrance fee.

GOOSE ROCKS BEACH, KENNEBUNKPORT, ME

A wildly popular beach in warmer months and equally as beautiful in the offseason, Goose Rocks Beach is treasured for its long stretch of clean sand and close proximity to town. Parking can be tough in the high season and permits are required, but it's well worth the headache to get up early and snatch a spot for a glorious day in the sun at this picture-perfect beach.

WALLIS SANDS STATE BEACH, RYE, NH

This family-friendly swimmers' beach has bright white sand, a picnic area, a store, and beautiful views of the Isles of Shoals.

EAST MATUNUCK STATE BEACH, SOUTH KINGSTOWN, RI

With well over 100 acres of sandy shoreline, this popular beach on Block Island Sound has everything you need for a perfect seaside outing with the whole family, including a beach pavilion with changing rooms, a concession stand, and a lifeguard tower.

SAND BAR STATE PARK, MILTON, VT

Vermont is not known for its beaches, but its plethora of lakes means that there are actually quite a few beaches worth checking out. This 2,000-foot-long beach remains shallow well out from shore, making it a perfect spot for families with young kids.

Sand Beach, Acadia, ME.

NAUSET LIGHT BEACH, EASTHAM, MA

Adjacent to Coast Guard Beach, this long, sandy beach is backed by tall dunes, frilly grass, and heathland. The trail to the Three Sisters lighthouses takes you through a pitch-pine forest. Parking can fill up quickly in the summer, so get here early or you may have to swim elsewhere.

PEMAQUID BEACH, NEW HARBOR, ME

Although not as long as the beach at nearby Reid State Park, Pemaquid Beach is a draw for families and couples looking for a quintessential beach day complete with an umbrella, sand bucket, and ice cream, all of which can be rented or purchased from the kiosk near the changing facilities and community center.

HAMPTON BEACH STATE PARK, HAMPTON, NH

The Granite State's ocean shore is short, but this state park along historic Route 1 takes full advantage of the space it has. In addition to swimming and fishing, there are campsites with full hookups for RVs, as well as an amphitheater with a band shell for outdoor concerts.

PLUM ISLAND BEACH, NEWBURYPORT, MA

Officially known as Newbury Beach, this pristine stretch of sand has excellent fishing, swimming, and birdwatching opportunities.

RACE POINT BEACH, PROVINCETOWN, MA

Designated by President Kennedy as part of Cape Cod National Seashore in 1961, this sandy beach is well known for its strong currents, which makes it great for surfers and serious swimmers. Its location on the Seashore's extreme northern side also makes it an excellent spot for sunbathing.

New England's Historical Sites: Beyond Revolutionary

FREEDOM TRAIL, BOSTON, MA

The iconic, red-lined, 2½-mile trail features 16 historical sites, including the Old South Meeting House, where the Sons of Liberty organized their Tea Party, and Old North Church, where those two fateful lanterns were hung. Across the Charles River in Charlestown are the USS *Constitution* (aka Old Ironsides) and the Bunker Hill Monument.

PORTLAND HEAD LIGHT, CAPE ELIZABETH, ME

Built in 1791, this 80-foot lighthouse is one of New England's most picturesque in any season. The keeper's quarters (operational 1891–1989) house a seasonally-open museum and gift shop; surrounding Fort William Park, site of an army fort between 1872 and 1964, is open year-round.

MAINE MARITIME MUSEUM, BATH, ME

The museum's permanent exhibits cover it all from Bath Iron Works' role in building the nation's navy to a collection of more than 100 small wooden water crafts. In warmer months, board the 1906 schooner, the *Mary E.*, for sails with docents.

STRAWBERY BANKE, PORTSMOUTH, NH

Located in downtown Portsmouth, the seasonally open, 10-acre living-history complex has docents in period garb portraying tavern keepers, merchants, artisans, and other everyday folk, and more than 35 structures dating from the 17th to 20th centuries.

SHELBURNE MUSEUM, SHELBURNE, VT

Nothing says "Vermont" like a big red barn, and the museum has two really big, really red barns that house American fine, folk, and decorative art as well as vintage toys, hats, decoys, and firearms. There's a vintage carousel, miniature circus-parade figurines in the Circus Building, and more than 200 horse-drawn vehicles. There's even an old Lake Champlain steamship.

MYSTIC SEAPORT MUSEUM, MYSTIC, CT
The year-round Seaport Village contains sloops, schooners, tugboats, and other historic vessels that are open for tours, sails, and hands-on maritime experiences. Exhibits have intriguing seafaring themes and there's a planetarium. Don't miss the *Charles W. Morgan*, an 1841 whaling ship.

MARK TWAIN HOUSE AND MUSEUM, HARTFORD, CT
Twain penned classics such as T*he Adventures of Tom Sawyer* and *A Connecticut Yankee in King Arthur's Court* here, and exhibits showcase the writer's storied life. If you have the time, plan a visit to the neighboring Harriet Beecher Stowe Center (combination tickets are available).

PLIMOTH PLANTATION, PLYMOUTH, MA
Role players—portraying actual 1620s Plymouth Colony settlers—attend to 17th-century life at this bayside village. There's a longhouse where Native Americans showcase early Wampanoag culture. *The Mayflower II* is a replica of the ship that carried the Pilgrims to the New World.

CLIFF WALK, NEWPORT, RI
The 3½-mile trail is hair-raising in spots, and the amazing views along either side are distracting, so wander with care. There are 10 mansions open to the public for touring, including the Italian Palazzo-style The Breakers; Rosecliff, modeled on a Versailles garden retreat; and The Elms, a French Chateau-style confection.

LEXINGTON AND CONCORD, MA
These two towns embody the American spirit. Minute Man National Historic Park, site of the first official Revolutionary War battle, is bookended by visitor centers in Lincoln, just outside Lexington, and Concord. In Concord, visit the Ralph Waldo Emerson House, Thoreau Farm, Waldon Pond, or Orchard House, where Louisa May Alcott wrote *Little Women*.

New England's Outdoor Activities

SKI THE REAL VERMONT
Just shy of the U.S.-Canadian border, some of Vermont's best ski slopes can be found in the northern Green Mountains at Jay Peak, with an elevation reaching almost 4,000 feet. The surrounding area boasts a massive network of trails, a top-notch resort, and the most snow in eastern North America.

GO SAILING IN NEWPORT
Often touted as one of the world's prime sailing capitals, Newport, Rhode Island's port is filled to the brim with rigs, including the America's Cup fleet. Numerous boats can be chartered for day trips or longer journeys, or you can try your hand at sailing a boat yourself.

HORSEBACK RIDING IN CONNECTICUT
Located on a narrow peninsula in Long Island Sound, Bluff Point State Park has more than 800 acres that appeal to equestrians looking for moderate rides through varying landscapes. The 3.6-mile Coastal Reserve Trail offers fantastic views of the Long Island Sound.

VISIT LAKE CHAMPLAIN
Leaf peeping and Vermont are virtually synonymous, but most visitors don't think about taking in the Green Mountain State's stunning fall foliage from out on the water. Best accessed from Burlington, you can rent a standup paddleboard to explore the lake while surrounded by majestic mountains covered in thick forests that put on a colorful display. Far from the constant flow of leaf-peeping traffic, you'll feel like nature is putting on a show for you in every direction that you paddle.

GO SURFING IN MAINE
Surfing isn't exactly what comes to mind when considering a visit to the Pine Tree State, but serious surfers know that Maine's Reid State Park has some of the East Coast's most dramatic breakers. Those who brave Maine's notoriously chilly coastal waters are rewarded with a steady flow of billowing white caps and swelling combers epic enough to send any diehard surfer howling "akaw!"

HIKE THE APPALACHIAN TRAIL
This is a bucket list item for most hardcore trekkers, but tackling the entire length of America's most notorious hiking trail is nothing short of a commitment. Featuring more miles above treeline than any other state, New Hampshire's 161-mile leg is one of the route's most challenging and rewarding stretches, with steep inclines leading to stunning alpine tundra and breathtaking panoramic views.

Go on a Leaf Peeping Cycle Tour along the Stowe Bike Path, VT.

KAYAKING ON THE ALLAGASH WILDERNESS WATERWAY

The 92-mile-long series of rivers, streams, ponds, and lakes that comprises northern Maine's Allagash Wilderness Waterway ribbon their way through the delicate, tundralike landscape of the Northern Woods. The waterway remains fairly rustic with limited resources along the route, which seems to be one of the major draws.

BIKING THE CAPE COD RAIL TRAIL

Passing through six Cape Cod towns, the Cape Cod Rail Trail covers an impressive 22 miles of paved trails. The reliably level terrain allows feasibly attainable long-distance excursions along the coastal landscape in a single day for all levels. During the winter months, exchange your wheels for skis to enjoy some of the Cape's best cross-country skiing.

TAKE A LEAF-PEEPING CYCLE TOUR

With its many nature preserves, green spaces, and hiking trails, Vermont shines in every season, but autumn may be its finest. You'd be hard-pressed to find a lovelier stroll through an autumnal Vermont landscape than in the charming village of Stowe, which is home to the Stowe Recreational Path, a paved, 5½-mile greenway that leads you to picture-perfect village and mountain views.

EXPLORE ACADIA NATIONAL PARK

Boasting around 160 miles of pristine coastal hiking trails and an extensive network of meandering carriage roads peppered with charming stone bridges, America's oldest national park offers bountiful opportunities to experience the raw, natural beauty of Maine's coast.

New England with Kids

Favorite destinations for family vacations in New England include Boston, Cape Cod, the White Mountains, Mystic and southeastern Connecticut, and coastal Maine—but, in general, the entire region has plenty to offer families. Throughout New England, you'll have no problem finding reasonably priced, kid-friendly hotels and family-style restaurants, as well as museums, beaches, parks, planetariums, and lighthouses.

Each New England state has specific requirements regarding age and weight requirements for children in car seats and for whether you can smoke in a car with children as passengers. If you will need a car seat, make sure your rental-car agency has one or bring your own. Many airlines won't charge if you check your car seat, or there are numerous travel options like the Mifold or BumbleBum.

LODGING

New England has many family-oriented resorts with lively children's programs. Farms that accept guests can be great fun for children. Rental houses and apartments abound, particularly around ski areas. In the off-season, these can be especially economical, because most have kitchens—saving you the expense of restaurant dining for some or all meals.

Most hotels in New England allow children under a certain age to stay in their parents' room at no extra charge, but others charge for them as extra adults; be sure to find out the cutoff age. Bed-and-breakfasts and historic inns are not always suitable for kids, and many flat-out refuse to accommodate them. In Maine, only hotels and inns with five or fewer rooms can put age restrictions on children.

Most lodgings that welcome infants and small children will provide a crib or cot, but remember to provide notice so that one will be available for you. Many family resorts make special accommodations for small children during meals.

MASSACHUSETTS
Children's Museum, Boston.
Make bubbles, climb through a maze, and while away the hours in the "Adventure Zone" at this fun museum just for tykes in Downtown Boston. A special play area for those under three lets them run around in a safe environment. There are seasonal festivals throughout the year.

Magic Wings Butterfly Conservatory & Gardens, Deerfield.
Almost 4,000 free-flying native and tropical butterflies are the star attraction here, contained within an 8,000-square-foot glassed enclosure that keeps the temperature upward of 80°F year-round. Relax around the Japanese koi pond on one of numerous benches and watch the kids chase the colorful creatures as they flit about. Or walk outside to the Iron Butterfly Outdoor Gardens, where flowers attract still more butterflies.

Massachusetts Audubon Wellfleet Bay Wildlife Sanctuary, South Wellfleet.
With its numerous programs and its beautiful salt-marsh surroundings, this is a favorite stop for Cape vacationers year-round. Five miles of nature trails weave throughout the sanctuary's 1,100 acres of marsh, beach, and woods. If you're careful and quiet, you may be able to get close to sunbathing seals or birds like the great blue heron. Naturalists are on hand for guided walks and lectures.

Plimoth Plantation, Plymouth.
Want to know what life was like in Colonial America? A visit to this living-history museum is like stepping into a time machine and zooming back to the year 1627. Guides dress in period costume and act like early-17th-century Pilgrims.

CONNECTICUT

Connecticut Science Center, Hartford. With unique, high-quality, and highly interactive exhibits, this science center is a must. It's geared toward older kids, but there is a kids space for the under-seven set. There's also a 3-D theater.

Dinosaur State Park, Rocky Hill. Dinosaur lovers can explore a 200-million-year-old fossil trackway, take in interactive exhibits, and even cast a dinosaur footprint to take home.

Mystic Aquarium and Institute for Exploration, Mystic. This aquarium and research institute is one of only four North American facilities to feature endangered Steller sea lions; it's also home to New England's only beluga whale. You'll also see African penguins, harbor seals, graceful sea horses, Pacific octopuses, and sand tiger sharks—kids can even touch a cownose ray. Nearby Mystic Seaport is another great attraction for families.

RHODE ISLAND

Block Island. Hop on the ferry at Port Judith and head to Block Island for an easy and scenic bike ride or just to spend the day at one of its many gorgeous, and often uncrowded, beaches.

Providence Children's Museum. Aimed at children ages 1–11, PCM explores arts, culture, history, and science. Exhibits are based on the developmental needs of children and embrace a wide range of learning styles.

Roger Williams Park and Zoo, Providence. Home to more than 100 species of animals from around the world, Roger Williams Park has more than 40 acres to explore. One highlight is Marco Polo's Adventure Trek, with camels, moon bears, snow leopards, red crowned cranes, and red pandas. Look for interactive educational programs.

VERMONT

ECHO Leahy Center for Lake Champlain, Burlington. Lots of activities and hands-on exhibits make learning about the geology and ecology of Lake Champlain an engaging experience.

Montshire Museum of Science, Norwich. This interactive museum uses more than 60 hands-on exhibits to explore nature and technology. The building sits amid 110 acres of nature trails and woodlands, where live animals roam freely.

Shelburne Farms, Shelburne. This working dairy farm is also an educational and cultural resource center. Visitors can watch artisans make the farm's famous cheddar cheese from the milk of more than 100 purebred and registered Brown Swiss cows. A children's farmyard and walking trails round out the experience.

NEW HAMPSHIRE

Hampton Beach. This seaside diversion draws families to its almost Coney Island–like fun. Along the boardwalk, kids enjoy arcade games, parasailing, live music, and an annual children's festival. They can even learn how saltwater taffy is made.

Lake Winnipesaukee, Weirs Beach. The largest lake in the state, Lake Winnipesaukee provides plenty of family-friendly fun. Base yourself in Weirs Beach and the kids can swim, play arcade games, cruise the lake, take a scenic railroad along the shoreline, and even see a drive-in movie.

SEE Science Center, Manchester. For kids who love LEGO, the models of old Manchester and the millyard are sure to impress. There are also rotating exhibits and science demonstrations.

MAINE

Acadia National Park, Mount Desert Island. Head out on a whale- and puffin-watching trip from Bar Harbor, drive up scenic Cadillac Mountain, swim at Echo Lake Beach, hike one of the many easy trails, and don't forget to sample some wild blueberry pie.

Coastal Maine Botanical Garden, Boothbay. The "children's garden" is a wonderland of stone sculptures, rope bridges, small teahouselike structures with grass roofs, and even a hedge maze. Children and adults alike adore the separate woodland fairy area.

Maine Narrow Gauge Railroad Museum, Portland. For train fans, check out the scenic rides on these narrow-gauge trains. In the winter, they have Polar Express-themed trips.

NEW ENGLAND BEST BETS

Fodor's writers and editors have chosen our favorites to help you plan. Search individual chapters for more recommendations.

🍴 RESTAURANTS

BEST UPSCALE (*$$$$*)

Chillingsworth, *$$$$*, *Ch. 5*

Honey Road, *$$$$*, *Ch. 9*

L'Espalier, *$$$$*, *Ch. 4*

Max Downtown, *$$$*, *Ch. 7*

Mistral, *$$$$*, *Ch. 4*

No. 9 Park, *$$$$*, *Ch. 4*

Union League Café, *$$$$*, *Ch. 7*

BEST MID-RANGE (*$$–$$$*)

Buca's Tuscan Roadhouse, *$$$*, *Ch. 5*

Bolster, Snow and Co., *$$$*, *Ch. 12*

The Dorset Inn, *$$$*, *Ch. 9*

Harvest, *$$$*, *Ch. 4*

Hen of the Wood, *$$$*, *Ch. 9*

In Good Company, *$$*, *Ch. 12*

Mary's at Baldwin Creek, *$$*, *Ch. 9*

Myers + Chang, *$$*, *Ch. 4*

Northern Union, *$$$*, *Ch. 12*

Peasant, *$$$*, *Ch. 9*

The Pointe, *$$$*, *Ch. 5*

Toro, *$$$*, *Ch. 4*

Union, *$$$*, *Ch. 12*

BEST BUDGET (*$–$$*)

Bee and Thistle Inn, *$$*, *Ch. 7*

Chef Wayne's Big Mamou, *$*, *Ch. 6*

Coyote Flaco, *$*, *Ch. 6*

Down Home Kitchen, *$*, *Ch. 9*

Nick's on Broadway, *$$*, *Ch. 8*

Olympia Tea Room, *$$*, *Ch. 8*

Otis, *$$*, *Ch. 10*

Prohibition Pig, *$*, *Ch. 9*

Provender, *$* *Ch. 8*

Three Penny Taproom, *$*, *Ch. 9*

LOCAL FAVORITE

Al Forno, *$$$*, *Ch. 8*

Antico Forno, *$$*, *Ch. 4*

Area Four, *$$*, *Ch. 4*

Giulia, *$$$*, *Ch. 4*

Judie's, *$$*, *Ch. 6*

La Cucina Sul Mare, *$$$*, *Ch. 5*

Newcastle Publick House, *$$*, *Ch. 12*

Peter Havens, *$$$*, *Ch. 9*

BEST LOBSTER

Little Red Schoolhouse, *$$*, *Ch. 10*

Moscungus Bay Lobster Co., *$$*, *Ch. 12*

Young's Lobster Pound, *$$$*, *Ch. 12*

BEST FOR SEAFOOD

Atlantic Fish Co., *$$$*, *Ch. 4*

Bitter End, *$$*, *Ch. 12*

C Salt Wine Bar & Grille, *$$$*, *Ch. 5*

Daily Catch, *$$*, *Ch. 4*

Fore Street, *$$$*, *Ch. 12*

Row 34, *$$$*, *Ch. 10*

Saltie Girl, *$$$*, *Ch. 4*

The Tides Beach Club Restaurant, *$$$*, *Ch. 12*

Woodman's of Essex, *$$*, *Ch. 4*

BEST OYSTERS

18 Central Oyster Bar and Grill, *$$$*, *Ch. 12*

Eventide Oyster Co., *$*, *Ch. 12*

Matunuck Oyster Bar, *$$*, *Ch. 8*

Naked Oyster Bistro & Raw Bar, *$$$*, *Ch. 5*

Neptune Oyster, *$$$*, *Ch. 4*

Pearl Restaurant & Oyster Bar, *$$*, *Ch. 10*

Shade Eatery at Higgins Beach, *$$*, *Ch. 12*

Wicked Oyster, *$$$*, *Ch. 5*

BEST NONSEAFOOD SPOT

22 Bowen's Wine Bar & Grille, *$$$$*, *Ch. 8*

Base Camp, *$$*, *Ch. 10*

Brazilian Grill, *$$$*, *Ch. 5*

Grill 23 & Bar, *$$$$*, *Ch. 4*

Havana, *$$*, *Ch. 12*

Long Grain, *$*, *Ch. 12*

Luca's Mediterranean Café, *$$*, *Ch. 10*

Mami, *$*, *Ch. 12*

Primo, *$$$$*, *Ch. 12*

Student Prince, *$$*, *Ch. 6*

Sweet Cheeks Q, *$$*, *Ch. 4*

BEST FAMILY-FRIENDLY DINING

Abbott's Lobster in the Rough, *$$*, *Ch. 7*

Aunt Carrie's, *$$*, *Ch. 8*

Flour Bakery + Café, *$*, *Ch. 4*

Woodford Food and Beverage, *$$*, *Ch. 12*

BEST DINING WITH A VIEW

Castle Hill Inn, *$$$$*, *Ch. 8*

Clarke Cooke House, *$$$$*, *Ch. 8*

George's of Galilee, *$$*, *Ch. 8*

The Mill at Simon Pearce, *$$$*, *Ch. 9*

Ocean Restaurant, *$$$$*, *Ch. 12*

Pier 77 Restaurant, *$$$*, *Ch. 12*

BEST OUTDOOR DINING

The Canteen, *$*, *Ch. 5*

Straight Wharf, *$$$$*, *Ch. 5*

Tavern on Main, *$$$*, *Ch. 7*

The White Horse, *$$*, *Ch. 7*

🛏 HOTELS

BEST VIEWS

Atlantic Breeze Suites, *$$*, *Ch. 10*

Hill Farm Inn, *$$*, *Ch. 9*

The Inn at Stonington, *$$*, *Ch. 7*

Inn on the Sound, *$$*, *Ch. 5*

A Little Inn on Pleasant Bay, *$$$*, *Ch. 5*

Mt. Philo Inn, *$$$*, *Ch. 9*

Ocean House, *$$$$*, *Ch. 8*

Royal Sonesta Boston, *$$$*, *Ch. 4*

BEST BUDGET (*$–$$*)

Alpamayo, *$$*, *Ch. 6*

The Danforth, *$$*, *Ch. 12*

The Homestead Inn, *$*, *Ch. 7*

Hotel on North, *$*, *Ch. 6*

The Inn on Putney Road, *$*, *Ch. 9*

Omni Providence, *$*, *Ch. 8*

River Bend Farm, *$*, *Ch. 6*

Sugar Hill Inn, *$$*, *Ch. 10*

BEST MID-RANGE (*$$–$$$*)

Bernerhof Inn, *$$*, *Ch. 10*

Brass Key, *$$$*, *Ch. 5*

The Break, *$$*, *Ch. 8*

Crowne Pointe Historic Inn and Spa, *$$*, *Ch. 5*

The Francis, *$$$*, *Ch. 12*

The Hanover Inn, *$$$*, *Ch. 10*

Inn by the Bandstand, *$$$*, *Ch. 10*

Lambert's Cove Inn, *$$*, *Ch. 5*

Norumbega Inn, *$$$*, *Ch. 12*

Omni Mount Washington Hotel, *$$$*, *Ch. 10*

The Press Hotel, *$$$*, *Ch. 12*

Stage Neck Inn, *$$$*, *Ch. 12*

State Road Restaurant, *$$$*, *Ch. 5*

Wilburton Inn, *$$*, *Ch. 9*

The Woodstock Inn and Resort, *$$$*, *Ch. 9*

BEST LUXURY (*$$$$*)

Bretton Arms Dining Room, *$$$$*, *Ch. 10*

Delamar Greenwich Harbor Hotel, *$$$*, *Ch. 7*

Earth at Hidden Pond, *$$$$*, *Ch. 12*

Grace Mayflower Inn & Spa, *$$$$*, *Ch. 7*

Hob Knob, *$$$$*, *Ch. 5*

Pickering House, *$$$$*, *Ch. 10*

The Pitcher Inn, *$$$$*, *Ch. 9*

Twin Farms, *$$$$*, *Ch. 9*

The Wauwinet, *$$$$*, *Ch. 5*

Wentworth by the Sea, *$$$$*, *Ch. 10*

West Street Hotel, *$$$$*, *Ch. 12*

Winvian, *$$$$*, *Ch. 7*

BEST NEW ENGLAND CHARM

Adair Country Inn and Restaurant, *$$$*, *Ch. 10*

The Atlantic Inn, *$$*, *Ch. 8*

Bedford Village Inn, *$$*, *Ch. 10*

Blueberry Hill Inn, *$$*, *Ch. 9*

The Hancock Inn, *$$*, *Ch. 10.*

The Inn at Pleasant Lake, *$$*, *Ch. 9*

The Inn on Putney Road, *$$*, *Ch. 9*

The Manor on Golden Pond, *$$*, *Ch. 10*

The Notchland Inn, *$$$*, *Ch. 10*

Spring House Hotel, *$$$*, *Ch. 8*

BEST FOR FAMILIES

Basin Harbor Resort & Boat Club, *$$*, *Ch. 9*

Colonnade, *$$*, *Ch. 4*

Even'tide, *$*, *Ch. 5*

Kimpton Nine Zero, *$$*, *Ch. 4*

The Nantucket Hotel and Resort, *$$$$*, *Ch. 5*

Old Sea Pines Inn, *$*, *Ch. 5*

Samoset Resort, *$$$*, *Ch. 12*

Smugglers' Notch Resort, *$$$*, *Ch. 9*

Trapp Family Lodge, *$$$*, *Ch. 9*

Weekapaug Inn, *$$$$*, *Ch. 8*

Wequassett Inn Resort and Golf Club, *$$$$*, *Ch. 5*

Winnetu Oceanside Resort, *$$$$*, *Ch. 5*

BEST LOCATION

Anchor-In, *$$$*, *Ch. 5*

Blair Hill Inn, *$$$*, *Ch. 11*

Capt. Farris House, *$$*, *Ch. 5*

Eliot Hotel, *$$*, *Ch. 4*

Harborside Inn, *$$*, *Ch. 4*

Stowe Mountain Lodge, *$$*, *Ch. 9*

Taj Boston, *$$*, *Ch. 4*

BEST B&B

Amelia Payson House, *$$*, *Ch. 4*

Castle Manor Inn, *$*, *Ch. 4*

The Fan House Bed and Breakfast, *$$*, *Ch. 9*

Gateways Inn and Restaurant, *$$$*, *Ch. 6*

Gryphon House, *$$$*, *Ch. 4*

Honeysuckle Hill, *$*, *Ch. 5*

The Inn at Kent Falls, *$$*, *Ch. 7*

Kennebec Inn Bed and Breakfast, *$$*, *Ch. 12*

Liberty Hill Inn, *$*, *Ch. 5*

Peacock House, *$*, *Ch. 12*

BEST HISTORIC

The Belfry Inn, *$*, *Ch. 5*

Captain Freeman Inn, *$$*, *Ch. 5*

The Chanler at Cliff Walk, *$$$$*, *Ch. 8*

Chatham Gables Inn, *$$$*, *Ch. 5*

Grace Vanderbilt, *$$$$*, *Ch. 8*

Harbor Light Inn, *$*, *Ch. 4*

The Inn at Shelburne Farms, *$*, *Ch. 9*

Inn at Weathersfield, *$$*, *Ch. 9*

Omni Parker House, *$$$*, *Ch. 4*

New England Today

CONNECTICUT

Connecticut has long been a melting pot, attracting immigrants who landed in New York or Boston and then sought work outside the city or simply yearned for life in the "country." Longtime Connecticut Yankees, celebrated authors and artists, and successful businesspeople blend easily with continuing generations of immigrants. Their hard work has contributed to the state's highest per-capita income in the nation (per 2010 census). The founders saw "The Constitution State" as the model for our national government. Today's Connecticut voters often vote Democratic for national offices but fluctuate between the parties for state and municipal officeholders. Small manufacturers and defense contractors have been mainstays of Connecticut's economy since colonial days, supplying brass buttons for Revolutionary War and Civil War uniforms and Colt 45s to tame the Wild West. Today's workers build airplane engines, helicopters, and submarines. In between, bright minds came up with the cotton gin, the Erector Set and the Frisbee! Connecticut residents are definitely sports enthusiasts despite having no home professional teams. Half root for the Boston Red Sox and New England Patriots; the others root for the New York Yankees and Giants—or the Mets and Jets. That said, UConn's basketball teams, both men's and women's, are the greatest!

MASSACHUSETTS

The Commonwealth of Massachusetts, New England's most populous state, is often just seen through the lens of its capital city, Boston, with good reason. It's home to the majority of the state's population. As a whole, the majority blue state (though it has a Republican governor) is doing well. The unemployment rate as of July 2018 was at 3½%, while the rest of the country was at 4.1%, though the inflation rate, especially in Greater Boston, was among the highest in the nation.

Fans from all five states follow Massachusetts's sports teams as if they were their own. Boston is home to three of the region's four major sports teams—Red Sox baseball, Bruins hockey, and Celtics basketball. The New England Patriots (football) play in the small suburb of Foxboro, about 30 miles southwest of Downtown Boston. The city is also home to the Boston Marathon, New England's largest sporting event and the world's oldest annual marathon. Held each spring, it attracts more than 500,000 spectators and more than 30,000 competitors.

MAINE

In recent decades, Maine's Congressional delegation has often been 50–50—half Democrat and Republican, and half male and female, which somewhat resembles the makeup of the state. Voters legalized recreational marijuana in 2016, but regulatory snags have delayed opening of retail pot shops (expected by spring 2019). Since 2000, Somali immigration has generated both tensions and welcome cultural diversity in Lewiston and Portland. As paper mills shutter, farming is on the upswing, while the billion-dollar tourism industry struggles to find enough workers yet fuels rising real estate prices and rents in popular destinations.

NEW HAMPSHIRE

With its state motto of "Live Free or Die" and a long-running political reputation as one of the nation's swingiest—albeit slightly left of center—states, New Hampshire marches to its own drummer. The fifth smallest—and 10th least populous—state in America maintains a fierce libertarian streak, collects neither sales tax or income tax, and each presidential year holds the country's first primary. Like the rest of northern New England, ruggedly mountainous New Hampshire is characterized by a mostly rural, heavily wooded topography that gives way to more densely populated small cities and suburbs only in its southeastern corner. Relatively prosperous, with the seventh-highest median household income in the country, New Hampshire has also enjoyed slow but steady growth in recent years, lagging behind only Massachusetts in population growth since 2010 among New England's six states.

RHODE ISLAND

It may be one of the smallest states, but Rhode Island is actually the country's second most densely populated state. Providence, the capital city, is a college town with a young vibe. To the north, descendants of French Canadian, Italian, and Irish workers who arrived during the birth of the American Industrial Revolution populate the cities and towns. Democrats have held sway over Rhode Island politics since the 1930s with a few notable exceptions. The revered Senator Claiborne Pell and John Chafee were Republicans, for example, as was Mayor "Buddy" Cianci of Providence, who was convicted on RICO charges and served four years in prison. Rhode Island was the birthplace of the American Industrial Revolution, and manufacturing has always been the predominant influence on the state's economy. Jewelry, silverware, machinery, and textiles have always been important local products, and Galilee continues to be a busy commercial fishing port. Today, the state ranks as the 9th best economy in the country. Boston is only an hour away from just about any town in Rhode Island, so the Red Sox, Patriots, and Bruins are like local teams—so much so that Pawtucket has the PawSox AAA baseball team and the Providence Bruins are an affiliate of the Boston ice hockey champs. And don't

forget sailing. Newport was home to the America's Cup Race for more than a century—and it's still a wonderful place to hoist a sail. Rhode Islanders drop the "r" in most words—or replace it with "ah"—but then add an "r" to the end of other words, like "bannaner" or "lawr" (particularly if it precedes "office"). They also pronounce "o" as "aw," as in "horse"—remember, don't pronounce the "r"! Basically, it's a hangover ("hang-ovah") of colonial English influenced by waves of Italian, Irish, Portuguese, and French Canadian immigrants. Still today, some 20% of the state's residents speak a language other than English in the home.

VERMONT

Few states are more proud of its rugged, independent, and liberal spirit than Vermont. From Ethan Allen to Bernie Sanders, Vermonters have never been afraid to follow a different drumbeat and be outspoken about it. This is perhaps never more on display than in the state's long-standing protection of the environment that borders on obsession. It's one of only four states than ban billboards, and strict regulations on land use and development makes many towns and villages appear as if pulled from Norman Rockwell paintings. During fall, the peak tourist season, the landscape literally takes your breath away with an array of fiery reds, golds, oranges, and bronze bursting from the hills and valleys. Cities are few and far between, with Burlington topping out at just 42,000 people, but a robust cultural and arts scene thrives throughout the state, thanks to the abundance of colleges, collectives, and individual artists that continually draw inspiration from the Vermont spirit and beauty. Locals and tourists do the same on the ski slopes, hiking trails, bike paths, and swimming holes, and there's plenty for all.

What to Read and Watch Before Your Trip

LOBSTERMAN BY DAHLOV IPCAR

Dahlov Ipcar, a native New Englander, is best remembered as a writer and illustrator of children's books, many of which took place in her home state of Maine. One such classic is *Lobsterman*, which portrays the day in the life of a lobsterman and his son as they work along the coast of Maine.

IT BY STEPHEN KING

You won't find Derry, Maine on any map, but you can visit it via a number of chilling tales courtesy of horror writer Stephen King, including his 1986 novel *It*, which follows a group of friends who try to kill a monster that terrorizes their town.

WE HAVE ALWAYS LIVED IN THE CASTLE BY SHIRLEY JACKSON

Merricat Blackwood lives in isolation on her family's estate with her sister Constance and their infirm Uncle Julian. When an estranged cousin arrives, the already uneasy state of the Blackwood home is thrown into disarray.

LITTLE WOMEN BY LOUISA MAY ALCOTT

Published in 1868, the book has remained a beloved coming of age story loosely based on the author's own life. The story follows four sisters—Meg, Jo, Beth, and Amy—and their mother after the family patriarch, having lost all of his money, must leave their Massachusetts's home to act as a pastor during the Civil War.

THE SECRET HISTORY BY DONNA TARTT

Richard leaves his working class, California home behind in order to attend a liberal arts college in Vermont. Once there he falls in with a privileged group of classics students. But beneath the group's veneer of charm and sophistication is a dark, violent secret.

JAWS

The movie that singlehandedly invented the summer blockbuster also happens to be the reason you jump out of your skin when a bit of seaweed brushes against your leg at the beach. In this all-time classic, the resort town of Amity Beach (filmed on Martha's Vineyard) is terrorized by an insatiable, man-eating, great white shark.

THE IRON GIANT

This charming animated film tells the story of Hogarth, a young boy who befriends a giant robot after it crashes in Maine. When a paranoid government agent tries to destroy the giant, Hogarth enlists help to save the gentle-hearted automaton.

THE DEPARTED

Martin Scorsese's remake is a twisty crime drama set against the backdrop of Boston's criminal underworld. When both the police and the mob discover they have a rat among them, the infiltrators have to race against the clock in order to uncover the other's identity.

GOOD WILL HUNTING

Will Hunting is a mathematical genius with a troubled past. An MIT professor offers to help him avoid jail time if he studies mathematics and starts seeing a therapist. Through his therapy sessions with Dr. Sean Maguire, Will comes to terms with the trauma of his past and learns how to keep himself from sabotaging his future.

WHITE CHRISTMAS

This holiday classic, brimming with good cheer and the iconic music of Irving Berlin, follows a song and dance team and a pair of performing sisters as they travel to a Vermont inn where they've been booked to perform over Christmas. The inn, owned by their old army commander, is on the verge of failure, so they stage a nationally televised yuletide extravaganza in order to save it.

Chapter 2

TRAVEL SMART NEW ENGLAND

Updated by
Jane E. Zarem

★ **CAPITALS**
Hartford, CT; Augusta, ME; Boston, MA; Concord, NH; Providence, RI; Montpelier, VT

👫 **POPULATION**
14,727,584

💬 **LANGUAGE**
English

€ **CURRENCY**
US Dollar

📠 **AREA CODES**
CT: 203, 475, 860, 959; ME: 207; MA: 413, 339, 351, 508, 617, 774, 781, 857, and 978; NH: 603; RI: 401; VT: 802

⚠ **EMERGENCIES**
911

🚗 **DRIVING**
On the right

⚡ **ELECTRICITY**
120–240 v/60 cycles; plugs have two or three rectangular prongs

🕐 **TIME**
Eastern Time
(same as New York)

🌐 **WEB RESOURCES**
www.visitnewengland.com; newengland.com/category/travel/

New England: Know Before You Go

New England has its share of regional character, color, and flavor—not to mention a few geographical and seasonal challenges. Here are some tips that will enrich your trip and ease your travels.

IT'S WICKED GOOD TO LEARN SOME LINGO.

To avoid seeming like a chowdah-head (aka "chowder head" aka "idiot"), brush up on some basic dialect. Want a big, long sandwich? Order a grinder, not a sub or a hero, and wash it down with a frappe or a tonic, not a milk shake or soda. At the hotel, grab the clickah (clicker) to change the TV station. At the supermarket, grab a carriage to shop for picnic sundries. If people direct you to a rotary, they mean traffic circle. And, even if you're traveling north toward, say, Bar Harbor, you're headed Down East.

YOU CAN'T ALWAYS GET THEAH FROM HEAH.

As this famous regional saying implies, the shortest distance between two points isn't always a straight—or single—line. Finding the real New England means driving (and getting lost on) its scenic byways. And GPS and cell-phone service will be disrupted, especially up north, so pack road maps or an atlas. There are a few places where you won't need a car, though. Cities, particularly Boston, have great public transit options to, within, and around them. Block Island, Nantucket, and Martha's Vineyard are bike friendly and have good taxi and/or shuttle services. In Acadia National Park, you'll have to trade your car for hiking boots, a bike, or a carriage (an actual horse and buggy, not a shopping cart).

DON'T FORGET THE DRAMAMINE.

Elevations aren't as dramatic as those out west, but car sickness is possible on drives through the Green or White mountains. Even south, amid the gentler terrain of Massachusetts's Berkshires or Connecticut's Litchfield Hills, roads ribbon up, down, and around—just as they do along rugged, often-precipitous stretches of Atlantic coast.

SMALL TOWNS RULE.

You might have to dig a little deeper to sightsee here, but it's worth it. Most villages have a Colonial- or Revolutionary-era homestead or site, small museum or historical society, and time-honored tavern or country store. And it's not just Boston and New Haven that have photo-worthy commons (open spaces once used for grazing livestock and around which towns were built). You can find traditional greens in many small towns, from Woodstock, Vermont, to Bethel, Maine.

EVEN THE BIG CITIES HERE ARE RELATIVELY SMALL.

Boston, the region's largest city, has just about 650,000 people; the next biggest, Worcester, Massachusetts, has just over 180,000. Still, most cities have thriving cultural scenes; several are major university towns (New Haven, Providence, Burlington) and/or are steeped in history (Portland). Regardless, you can allow less time for urban explorations and more time for losing yourself in the bucolic settings.

THE BEST FOODS ARE WHOLESOME, HEARTY BASICS.

Field-or-fishing-boat-to-table is the norm, with abundant local produce and seafood that includes lobster; quahogs or other clams; bay or sea scallops; and pollack, hake, haddock, or cod (the latter two might appear on local menus as "scrod"). In Maine, lobster-roll meat is dressed in mayonnaise; in Connecticut, it's drizzled with melted butter. Chowder is creamy, except in Rhode Island, where it has a clear but flavorful broth, and Connecticut, where it might be made with milk and contain bacon. Boston has its famous baked beans and cream pies (made with cream or custard); Rhode Island has its johnnycakes (fried cornmeal patties). Everywhere, though, maple syrup adorns shaved ice (or snow!) and ice cream as well as pancakes; breakfast home fries are griddled and seasoned just so; and craft beer and cider pair well with boiled dinners and Yankee pot roast. Be sure to try a Moxie, an "energizing," regionally unique tonic (aka soda).

IN THE LAND OF THE COUNTRY INN, IT'S BEST TO BOOK AHEAD.

Although there are abundant chain hotels and several large, notable Victorians—seaside and near the slopes—smaller inns, often historical and privately owned, are among the best lodgings. Loads of charm and lower room counts make booking ahead essential, especially during peak seasons, when there might also be a two-night minimum. And "peak seasons" vary. Leaf-peeping season is roughly late September to mid-October in Maine, New Hampshire, and Vermont and mid- to late October in Connecticut, Massachusetts, and Rhode Island. In the southern ski areas, the season runs December through March; up north it might be November through April or even May.

THE ATLANTIC IS COLD UP HERE.

Even in late August, ocean temperatures off Maine and New Hampshire only climb to the upper 50s or lower 60s—still limb-numbingly chilly. Wet suits (and water shoes for rockier shores) are musts. Temperatures are warmer near Boston and points south, where the Atlantic's summer highs are in the mid-60s to mid-or-upper 70s. Obviously, the farther north you go, the shorter the beach season, with some properties reducing their hours or shuttering entirely between Labor Day and Memorial Day or July 4.

WHEN IT COMES TO PARKLAND, THE STATES HAVE IT.

Although much of New England is woodsy, the entire region has only one national park (Acadia) and just two national forests (Green Mountain and White Mountain). That said, there are plenty of opportunities to hike, canoe, kayak, mountain bike, camp, and otherwise embrace the outdoors in the plethora of park or recreation/wilderness areas overseen by each state.

SOME OF THE FLIES BITE.

First, it's the black flies, whose bites leave red, itchy welts. May through June is the season, which is particularly notorious in Maine. Then, in July, it's the deer flies. Summer also sees greenhead flies (aka saltmarsh greenheads) in some coastal areas. On hikes, use insect repellent and wear clothing that covers your arms and legs.

And don't forget to check for ticks. The disease they're known to carry was named after a New England town: Lyme, Connecticut.

THE PEOPLE ARE WARM AND WELCOMING

The idea of the self-reliant, thrifty, and often stoic New England Yankee has taken on almost mythic proportions in American folklore, but in some parts of New England—especially in rural Maine, New Hampshire, and Vermont—there still is some truth to this image, which shouldn't come as a surprise. You need to be independent if you farm an isolated field, live in the middle of a vast forest, or work a fishing boat miles off the coast. As in any part of the country, there are stark differences between the city mice and the country mice of New England. Both, however, are usually well educated and fiercely proud of the region, its rugged beauty, and its contributions to the nation.

SPORTS IS A RELIGION

This is Sox, and Pats country. New England Fans follow Massachusetts's sports teams as if they were their own. Boston is home to three of the region's four major sports teams—Red Sox baseball, Bruins hockey, and Celtics basketball. The New England Patriots (football) play in the small suburb of Foxboro, about 30 miles southwest of Downtown Boston. The city is also home to the Boston Marathon, New England's largest sporting event and the world's oldest annual marathon.

Getting Here and Around

✈ Air Travel

Most travelers visiting New England use a major gateway, such as Boston, Providence, Hartford/Springfield, Manchester, or even New York City or Albany, and then rent a car to explore the region. The New England states form a fairly compact region, with few important destinations more than six hours apart by car. It's costly and generally impractical to fly within New England, the exceptions being the island resort destinations of Martha's Vineyard and Nantucket in Massachusetts and Block Island in Rhode Island, which have regular air service from Boston and a few regional airports.

Boston's Logan Airport is one of the nation's most important domestic and international airports, with direct flights arriving from all over North America and abroad. New England's other major airports receive few international flights (mostly from Canada) but receive many direct domestic flights from East Coast and Midwest destinations and, to a lesser extent, from the western United States. Some sample flying times to Boston are: 2½ hours from Chicago, 6½ hours from London, and 6 hours from Los Angeles. Times from other U.S. cities are similar, if slightly shorter, to Albany and Hartford, assuming you can find direct flights.

AIRPORTS

The main gateway to New England is Boston's Logan International Airport (BOS). Bradley International Airport (BDL), in Windsor Locks, Connecticut (12 miles north of Hartford), is convenient to Western Massachusetts and much of Connecticut. T. F. Green International Airport (PVD), just outside Providence, Rhode Island, and Manchester Boston Regional Airport (MHT), in New Hampshire, are other major airports—and alternative approaches to Boston, which

is a one-hour drive from each. Additional New England airports served by major carriers include Portland International Jetport (PWM) in Maine and Burlington International Airport (BTV) in Vermont.

Other convenient airports are Albany International Airport (ALB) in Albany, New York, near Western Massachusetts and Vermont; Westchester County Airport (HPN) in White Plains, New York, near Southern Connecticut; Bangor International Airport (BGR) in Bangor, Maine; and Barnstable Municipal Airport in Hyannis, Massachusetts. You can access Nantucket and Martha's Vineyard via ferries from Hyannis or fly directly to each island's airport.

FLIGHTS

American, Delta, JetBlue, Southwest, and United serve airports in Albany, Boston, Hartford, Manchester, Portland, Providence, and (except Southwest) Westchester County. Spirit flies into Boston. Cape Air, a regional carrier, serves various New England airports in Maine, New Hampshire, Vermont, and Massachusetts—including those on Cape Cod and the islands. New England Airlines serves Block Island with regularly scheduled flights to and from Westerly, Rhode Island.

⛴ Boat Travel

Principal ferry routes in New England connect New Bedford on the mainland and Cape Cod with Martha's Vineyard and Nantucket, Boston with Provincetown, Providence with Newport, Newport and Point Judith with Block Island, and Connecticut with Block Island and New York's Long Island. Other ferry routes provide access to islands off the Maine coast and across Lake Champlain between Vermont and upstate New York. International service between Portland,

Travel Times from Boston

TO	BY AIR	BY CAR	BY BUS	BY TRAIN
Acadia National Park (ME)	1 hour	5 hours	not applicable	not applicable
Burlington, VT	no direct flight	3½ hours	4½–5 hours	8¾ hours
Hartford, CT	no direct flight	1¾ hours	2–2¾ hours	4–4½ hours
New York, NY	¾–1 hour	4 hours	4½–7 hours	3½–4¼ hours
Portland, ME	no direct flight	2 hours	2¼ hours	2½ hours
Providence, RI	no direct flight	1 hour	1 hour	½–¾ hour
Provincetown, MA	½ hour	2¼ hours	3–3½ hours	not applicable

Yarmouth, and Bar Harbor in Maine and Nova Scotia is also available. With the exception of the Lake Champlain ferries—which are first-come, first-served—reservations are advisable for cars.

🚌 Bus Travel

With fares starting at just $1 if you reserve early enough, BoltBus buses equipped with Wi-Fi and electrical outlets serve Boston, New Haven, New York, Philadelphia, and Washington, D.C. Megabus also offers low fares, and its buses (also with Wi-Fi) serve New York City and many other points on the East Coast. Both BoltBus and Megabus use Boston's South Station.

Once in New England, regional bus service is relatively extensive. It can be a handy and affordable means of getting around, as buses travel many routes that trains do not. Concord Coach buses connect Boston with Concord, New Hampshire, and Portland and Bangor, Maine; the company also operates a route between New York City and Portland. C&J buses (with Wi-Fi) serve Dover, Durham, and Portsmouth, New Hampshire, and Newburyport, Massachusetts; C&J also provides service to New York City. Both Concord and C&J leave from Boston's South Station, which is connected to the Amtrak rail station, and from Logan Airport.

Within Rhode Island, Rhode Island Public Transit Authority (RIPTA) runs buses throughout the state for $2 per ride or $6 per day regardless of the distance.

🚗 Car Travel

New England is best explored by car. Inland, especially in Western Massachusetts, Vermont, New Hampshire, and Maine, public transportation options are limited; a car is almost essential. Coastal areas can get congested in summer, especially the roads to and from Cape Cod. Cars are a nuisance in Boston; parking can be hard to find or expensive there, in Providence, and near the beach in resort towns along the coast. Interstate 95 enters New England at the New York border, follows the Connecticut shoreline, and then heads north to Providence, Boston, and Portland before ending at the Canadian border in Calais, Maine. Interstate 90, the Massachusetts Turnpike, is a toll road that goes across the state from the New York border (near Albany) to Boston. If you rent a

Getting Here and Around

car at Logan International Airport, allow plenty of time to return it—as much as an hour to be on the safe side.

GASOLINE

Gas stations are easy to find along major highways and throughout the region. Prices vary from station to station within any city and from state to state. The majority have self-serve pumps that accept credit or debit cards.

PARKING

In Boston and other large cities, finding street parking can be time-consuming and nerve-wracking. Your best bet is to park in a garage, but rates in large cities can top $30 a day. In smaller cities, street parking is usually simpler, though parking garages are still convenient and, for the most part, reasonably priced. Pay attention to signs: some cities allow only residents to park on certain streets. In most small towns, parking is not a problem—though some beach and lake parking areas are reserved for those with resident stickers.

ROAD CONDITIONS

Major state and U.S. routes are generally well maintained, with snowplows at the ready during the winter to salt and plow road surfaces soon after the flakes begin to fall. Traffic is heaviest around Boston, Hartford, and New Haven, especially during rush hour. Secondary state routes and rural roads can be a mixed bag; Route 1, for example, is well maintained; but traffic is stop-and-go and can get tied up in even the smallest coastal towns.

ROADSIDE EMERGENCIES

Throughout New England, call ☎ 911 for any travel emergency. For breakdowns, call a towing service.

RULES OF THE ROAD

Throughout the region, you're permitted to make a right turn on a red light except where posted. Be alert for one-way streets in congested cities like Boston and Providence.

Boston motorists are notorious for driving aggressively. Streets in the Boston area are confusing, so GPS can be very helpful.

You will encounter many traffic circles or rotaries in New England, especially in the Boston area. Cars entering traffic circles must yield to cars that are already in the circle. Some rotaries have two lanes, which complicates things. If you plan to leave the rotary at the next exit, stay in the right lane. When changing lanes in a rotary or on any two-lane road, carefully check your mirrors to ensure you don't sideswipe a driver coming along behind you.

State laws require drivers and passengers to wear seat belts at all times. The age and weight requirements for safety seats for children vary from state to state; the Governors Highway Safety Association's website lists the requirements for each.

CAR RENTAL

Major airports serving the region all have on-site car-rental agencies. A few train or bus stations have one or two car-rental agencies on-site, as well.

Rates at Boston's Logan Airport begin at around $50 per day and $300 per week for an economy car with air-conditioning, automatic transmission, and unlimited mileage. The same car might go for around $60 per day and $175 per week at a smaller airport, such as Providence's. These rates do not include state tax on car rentals, which varies depending on the airport but generally runs 12%–15%. It usually costs less to rent a car away from an airport, but be sure to consider how easy or difficult it may be to get to that off-airport location with luggage.

Most agencies won't rent to drivers under the age of 21, and several major agencies won't rent to anyone under 25 or over the age of 75. When picking up a rental car, non-U.S. residents need a voucher for any prepaid reservation made in their home country, a passport, a driver's license, and a travel policy that covers each driver. Logan Airport is spread out and usually congested; if returning a rental vehicle there, allow plenty of time to do so before heading to your flight.

Ⓜ Subway Travel

The Massachusetts Bay Transportation Authority (MBTA)—known as "the T"—operates subways, buses, and trolleys along five connecting lines in Boston, as well as many bus and several rail commuter lines that reach nearby suburbs and cities. Subways and buses operate from about 5:30 am to about 1 am, with limited late-night service. A 24-hour hotline and the MBTA website have specific information on routes, schedules, fares, wheelchair access, and other matters. Free maps are available at the MBTA's Park Street Station information stand, open daily from 7 am to 10 pm. The MBTA website has a useful trip planner tool.

"Inbound" trains head into the city center (Park Street Station) and "outbound" trains head away from it. If you get on the Red Line at South Station, the train heading toward Alewife (Cambridge) is inbound. But once you reach Park Street, the train becomes outbound. Similarly, the Green Line to Fenway Park would be the Boston College or Cleveland Circle train. Large maps prominently posted at each station show the line(s) that serve it, with each stop marked; small maps are overhead

in each car. Free 24-hour shuttle buses connect Airport Blue Line Station with all airline terminals. Shuttle Bus 22 runs between the subway and Terminals A and B, and Shuttle Bus 33 runs between the subway and Terminals C and E. *See the Boston chapter for fare information.*

Ⓣ Train Travel

Amtrak offers frequent daily service along its Northeast Corridor route from Washington, D.C., Philadelphia, and New York to Boston, with stops in Connecticut and Rhode Island. Amtrak's high-speed Acela trains link Boston and Washington, with stops at New York, Philadelphia, and other cities along the way. The *Downeaster* connects Boston and Brunswick, Maine, with stops in coastal New Hampshire and Portland.

Other Amtrak services include the *Vermonter* between Washington, D.C., and St. Albans, Vermont (via New York City); the *Ethan Allen Express* between New York and Rutland, Vermont (via Albany, NY); and the *Lake Shore Limited* between Boston and Chicago, which stops at Pittsfield, Springfield, Worcester, and Framingham in Massachusetts.

Several commuter services are handy for travelers. The Massachusetts Bay Transportation Authority (MBTA) operates within Boston and connects the city with outlying areas on the north and south shores of the state. Metro-North Railroad's New Haven Line offers service from New York City along the Connecticut coast up to New Haven, with spur lines north to New Canaan, Danbury, and Waterbury. Also in Connecticut, Shore Line East serves coastal towns between New Haven and New London.

Before You Go

🌐 Passports

American travelers never need a passport to travel domestically. Non-American travelers always need a valid passport to visit any of the states in New England.

Visas

For international travelers, a tourism visa is required for traveling to New England and the rest of the United States.

✏️ Immunizations

No specific immunizations or vaccinations are required for visits to New England.

📅 When to Go

All six New England states are year-round destinations. Winter is popular with skiers, summer draws beach lovers, and fall delights those who love the bursts of autumnal color. Spring can also be a great time, with sugar shacks transforming maple sap into all sorts of tasty things. You'll probably want to avoid rural areas during mud season (April) and black fly season (mid-May to mid-June).

Memorial Day sets off the great migration to the beaches and the mountains, and summer begins in earnest on July 4. Those who want to drive to Cape Cod in July or August, beware: on Friday and Sunday, weekenders clog the overburdened U.S. 6. The same applies to the Maine Coast and its feeder roads, Interstate 95 and U.S. 1.

In the fall, a rainbow of reds, oranges, yellows, purples, and other vibrant hues emerges. The first scarlet and gold colors appear in mid-September in northern areas; "peak" color occurs at different times from year to year. Generally, it's best to visit the northern reaches in late September and early October and move south as October progresses.

CLIMATE

In winter, coastal New England is cold and damp; inland temperatures may be lower, but generally drier conditions make them easier to bear. Snowfall is heaviest in the interior mountains and can range up to several hundred inches per year in northern Maine, New Hampshire, and Vermont. Spring is often windy and rainy; in some years it feels as if winter tumbles directly into summer. Coastal areas can be quite humid in summer, while inland, particularly at higher elevations, there's a prevalence of cool summer nights. Autumn temperatures can be mild even into October.

The winter sports season typically runs from Thanksgiving through April, weather permitting; holidays are the most crowded. Most of the season's snow tends to come in March, so if you want to ski on fresh, natural powder, plan accordingly. To increase your odds, choose a ski area in the northern part of the state. Many lifts start at 8 or 9 am, with ticket windows opening a half-hour earlier, so plan to hit the slopes early, and then take a mid-morning break when lines get longer and head out again when others come in for lunch.

During summertime, many ski resorts reinvent themselves as prime destinations for golfers, zipline and canopy tours, mountain bikers, and weddings. Other summer visitors come to enjoy hiking trails, climbing walls, aquatic centers, chairlift and horseback rides, and festivals.

Tours

🍴 Culinary

The Connecticut Wine Trail celebrates more than 25 statewide wineries. Download a trail map from the website and start your wine-tasting adventure. ⊕ *www.ctwine.com*

Maine Food for Thought. Guided tours take you to six of Portland's best restaurants for a sampling of their dishes and discussions about the importance of the farm-to-table movement in Maine. ☎ *207/405–0482* ⊕ *www.mainefoodfor-thought.com.*

Portsmouth Eats. On White Table, Best of Portsmouth, and Sweets and Treats walking tours—mostly on weekends—you get to taste the culinary delights of four or five establishments in New Hampshire's coastal city. ☎ *603/571–3287* ⊕ *www.portsmouth-eats.com* ✉ *From $32.*

👁 General Interest

New England Vacation Tours. This versatile company conducts everything from packages that include flights and tours in luxury coaches to ones that involve cruises and sightseeing excursions on land. All transportation is covered, and every detail is attended to. You can also create a completely customized itinerary to take you wherever your heart desires—the people here are very easy to work with. ☎ *800/742–7669* ⊕ *www.newenglandva-cationtours.com* ✉ *Call for prices.*

Northeast Unlimited Tours. As the name indicates, Northeast Unlimited's range of itineraries includes New England. The eight-day Taste of New England tour, for example, hits all the highlights from Boston to Maine. ☎ *800/759–6820* ⊕ *www.newenglandtours.com* ✉ *From $1959.*

Wolfe Adventures & Tours. Wolfe specializes in tours for groups, including families. New England tours include Boston, Newport, the White Mountains, Vermont farms, maritime adventures, Cape Cod, and more. ☎ *888/449–6533* ⊕ *wolfe-tours.com* ✉ *Call for prices.*

🎭 Performing Arts

The Connecticut Art Trail lists 14 Connecticut museums containing the work of Connecticut's artists, the landscapes that inspired them, and other related sites. ⊕ *www.arttrail.org.*

🏃 Sports and the Outdoors

BICYCLING
Urban Adventours. This bike shop in downtown Boston conducts guided bicycle tours of the city, Cambridge, and surrounding towns. For example, the ambitious 26-mile Paul Revere tour traces the patriot's famous ride. ☎ *617/670–0637* ⊕ *www.urbanadven-tours.com* ✉ *From $55.*

SKIING
North East Action Sports. Based in Rhode Island, day trips are offered to Sunday River, ME; Killington, VT; Stowe, VT; Mount Snow, VT; Stratton, VT; Okemo, VT; and Bretton Woods and Cannon in NH. Private groups are available. ☎ *844–754-7776* ⊕ *neactionsports.com*

Ski 93 Trips. Individual and group ski trips are offered to ski resorts in Maine, Vermont, and New Hampshire. ☎ *800/451–1830* ⊕ *ski93trips.com*

Essentials

🍴 Dining

Although certain ingredients and preparations are common to the region as a whole, New England's cuisine varies greatly from place to place. Urban centers like Boston, Providence, New Haven, and Portland—and upscale resort areas such as the Berkshires, Martha's Vineyard, and Nantucket—have stellar restaurants, many of them with culinary luminaries at the helm and a reputation for creative—and occasionally daring—menus.

Elsewhere, restaurant food tends more toward the simple, traditional, and conservative. Towns and cities have a variety of international restaurants, especially excellent Italian, French, Japanese, Indian, and Thai eateries. There are also many diners serving burgers and other comfort food—a few serve breakfast all day.

The proximity to the ocean accounts for the abundance of very fresh seafood, and the area's numerous boutique dairy, meat, and vegetable suppliers account for other choice ingredients. Menus in upscale and tourism-driven communities often note which Vermont dairy or Berkshires farm a particular goat cheese or heirloom tomato came from.

MEALS AND MEALTIMES
For an early breakfast, pick places that cater to a working clientele. City, town, and roadside establishments specializing in breakfast for early workers often open their doors at 5 or 6 am. At country inns, breakfast is seldom served before 8 am; if you need to get an earlier start, ask ahead of time. Lunch generally runs 11 am–2:30 pm; dinner is usually served 6–9 pm, with early-bird specials sometimes beginning at 5. Only in larger cities will you find dinner available much later than 9 pm. Many restaurants in New England close Monday and sometimes Sunday or Tuesday, although this is never true in resort areas during high season. However, resort-town eateries often shut down completely in the off-season.

PAYING
Credit cards are accepted for meals throughout New England in all but the most modest establishments. *Prices in the reviews are the average cost of a main course at dinner or, if dinner is not served, at lunch.*

RESERVATIONS AND DRESS
It's a good idea to make a reservation if you can. We specifically mention them only when reservations are essential—there's no other way you'll ever get a table—or when they are not accepted. For popular restaurants, book as far ahead as you can and reconfirm as soon as you arrive. Large parties should always call ahead to check the reservations policy. We mention dress only when men are required to wear a jacket or a jacket and tie.

WINE, BEER, AND SPIRITS
New England is no stranger to microbrews. The granddaddy of New England's independent breweries is the Boston Beer Company, maker of Samuel Adams. Following the Sam Adams lead in offering hearty English-style ales and special seasonal brews are breweries such as Vermont's Long Trail, Maine's Shipyard, and New Hampshire's Smuttynose Brewing Co. Green Mountain Cidery makes Woodchuck Hard Cider in Middlebury, Vermont.

New England is beginning to earn some respect as a wine-producing region. Cabernet Franc, Vidal, Riesling, and other grape varieties capable of withstanding the region's harsher winters and relatively shorter growing season compared to California and other leading areas have been the basis of promising enterprises such as Rhode Island's Sakonnet Vineyards and Connecticut's

Hopkins Vineyard (part of the Connecticut Wine Trail). Even Vermont is getting into the act with the Snow Farm Vineyard in the Lake Champlain Islands and Boyden Valley Winery in Cambridge.

Although a patchwork of state and local regulations affect the hours and locations of places that sell alcoholic beverages (e.g., Massachusetts bans "happy hour"), New England licensing laws are fairly liberal. State-owned or franchised stores sell hard liquor in New Hampshire, Maine, and Vermont. Many travelers have found that New Hampshire offers the region's lowest prices due to the lack of a sales tax; look for state-run liquor "supermarkets" on interstates in the southern part of the state—but keep in mind that it's illegal to take untaxed liquor across state lines. A bottle or two isn't a problem, but undercover cops are on the lookout for anyone transporting a huge stash.

➕ Health and Safety

Lyme disease, so named for its having been first reported in the town of Lyme, Connecticut, is a potentially debilitating disease carried by deer ticks. They thrive in dry, brush-covered areas, particularly in coastal areas. Always use insect repellent: the potential for outbreaks of Lyme disease makes it imperative that you protect yourself from ticks from early spring through summer and into fall. To prevent bites, wear light-color clothing and tuck pant legs into socks. Look for black ticks about the size of a pinhead around hairlines and the warmest parts of the body. If you have been bitten, consult a physician—especially if you see the telltale bull's-eye bite pattern. Flu-like symptoms often accompany a Lyme infection. Early treatment is imperative.

New England's most annoying insect pests are black flies and mosquitoes. The former are a phenomenon of late spring and early summer and are generally a problem only in densely wooded areas of the far north. Mosquitoes, however, are a nuisance just about everywhere. The best protection against both pests is repellent containing DEET; if you're camping in the woods during black fly season, you'll also want to use fine mesh screening in eating and sleeping areas and even wear mesh headgear. One pest particular to coastal areas, especially salt marshes, is the greenhead fly, which has a nasty bite and is hard to kill. It is best repelled by a liberal application of Avon Skin So Soft or a similar product.

Coastal waters attract seafood lovers who enjoy harvesting their own clams, mussels, and even lobsters; permits are required, and casual harvesting of lobsters is strictly forbidden. Amateur clammers should be aware that New England shellfish beds are periodically visited by red tides, during which microorganisms can render shellfish poisonous. To keep abreast of the situation, inquire when you apply for a license (usually at town halls or police stations) and pay attention to red tide postings as you travel.

Rural New England is one of the country's safest regions. In cities—Boston, in particular—observe the usual precautions: avoid out-of-the-way or poorly lighted areas at night; clutch handbags close to your body and don't let them out of your sight; and be on your guard in subways and on buses, not only during the deserted wee hours but also during crowded rush hours, when pickpockets may be at work. Keep your valuables in the hotel or room safe. When using an ATM, choose a busy, well-lighted place such as bank lobbies.

Essentials

If your vehicle breaks down in a rural area, pull as far off the road as possible, tie a handkerchief to your radio antenna (use flares at night—check if your rental agency can provide them), and stay in your car with the doors locked until help arrives. Don't pick up hitchhikers. If you're planning to leave a car overnight to make use of off-road trails or camping facilities, look for a supervised parking area whenever possible. Cars left at trailhead parking lots are a target for theft or vandalism.

Throughout New England, the universal telephone number for all emergencies is 911.

Lodging

In New England, you can bed down in a basic chain hotel or a luxurious grande dame; but unless you're staying in a city, this is really bed-and-breakfast land. Charming—and sometimes historic—inns, small hotels, and bed-and-breakfasts dot the region and provide a glimpse of local life. *Hotel prices are the lowest cost of a standard double room in high season.*

APARTMENT AND HOUSE RENTALS

You are most likely to find a house, apartment, or condo rental in areas of New England where ownership of second homes is common, such as beach resorts and ski country. Home-exchange directories sometimes list rentals alongside exchanges. Another good bet is to contact real-estate agents in the area in which you are interested, or check VRBO or Airbnb.

BED-AND-BREAKFASTS

In many less touristy areas, bed-and-breakfasts offer an affordable, homey alternative to chain properties. In most major towns, expect to pay about the same or more for a historic inn. Many of the region's finest restaurants are attached to country inns, so you often don't have to go far for the best meal in town. Quite a few inns serve substantial breakfasts.

HOTELS

Major hotel and motel chains are amply represented in New England. The region is also liberally supplied with small, independent motels.

Reservations are always a good idea, particularly in summer and winter resort areas; at college towns in September and at graduation time in spring; and at areas renowned for autumn foliage. Most hotels and motels will hold your reservation until 6 pm; call ahead if you plan to arrive late. All will hold a late reservation for you if you guarantee it with your credit card.

In Vermont and in Boston, Massachusetts, all hotels are no-smoking by state law; elsewhere, smoking is allowed only in designated guest rooms. All lodgings listed have private baths unless otherwise noted.

$ Money

It costs a bit more to travel in most of New England than it does in the rest of the country, the most costly areas being Boston and coastal resort towns. You'll also find some posh inns and restaurants in the Berkshires, in northwestern Connecticut, and in parts of Vermont and New Hampshire. ATMs are plentiful, and large-denomination bills (as well as credit cards) are readily accepted in tourist destinations during the high season.

CREDIT CARDS

Major credit cards are readily accepted throughout New England, though at small businesses in rural areas you may encounter difficulties or the acceptance of only MasterCard or Visa.

Tipping Guidelines for New England

Bartender	$1 to $5 per round of drinks
Bellhop	$1 or $2 per bag
Hotel Concierge	$5 or more, if he or she performs a service for you
Hotel Doorman	$1 or $2 if he helps you get a cab
Hotel Maid	$2 to $5 a day depending on the level of the hotel
Hotel Room-Service Waiter	$2 to $5 per delivery, even if a service charge has been added
Porter at Airport or Train Station	$1 per bag
Skycap at Airport	$2 or $3 per bag checked
Taxi Driver	15% to 20%, but round up the fare to the next dollar amount
Tour Guide	15% of the cost of the tour
Valet Parking Attendant	$3 to $5, but only when you get your car
Waiter	15% to 20%, with 20% being the norm at high-end restaurants; nothing additional if a service charge is added to the bill
Other Attendants	Restroom attendants in expensive restaurants expect some small change or $1. Tip coat-check personnel at least $1 or $2 per item checked unless there is a fee, then nothing.

 Packing

The principal rule of weather in New England is that there are no rules. A cold, foggy spring morning often warms to a bright, 60°F afternoon. A summer breeze can suddenly turn chilly, and rain often appears with little warning. Thus, the best advice on how to dress is to layer your clothing; that way, you can peel off or add garments as needed for comfort. Even in summer, you should bring long pants, a sweater or two, and a light jacket, for evenings are often chilly, and sea spray can make things cool. Showers are frequent, so pack a waterproof windbreaker or raincoat and umbrella.

Casual sportswear—walking shoes and jeans or khakis—will take you almost everywhere, but swimsuits and bare feet will not. Shirts and shoes are required attire at even the most casual venues. Dress in restaurants is generally casual, except at some of the distinguished restaurants in Boston, Newport, Maine coastal towns (such as Kennebunkport), a few inns in the Berkshires, and in Litchfield and Fairfield counties in Connecticut. Upscale resorts, at the very least, will require men to wear long pants and collared shirts at dinner, and jeans are often frowned upon.

In summer, bring a hat and sunscreen. You can bring or buy insect repellent. If you find yourself in walking in wooded areas, near brush, or around foliage from early spring through fall, be sure to check your body for ticks, which can cause Lyme disease if not removed.

Great Itineraries

Whether it's your first trip to New England or you vacation here every year, these itineraries will help you explore charming seaside towns and bustling cities, eat at cutting-edge restaurants and the best seafood shacks, and experience both popular spots and hidden gems. Mix and match the itineraries, or use them as a jumping-off point for your own adventure.

Cape Cod Beaches and Villages, 7 Days

Cape Cod can be all things to all visitors, with quiet villages and lively resorts, gentle bay-side wavelets and crashing surf. A car is the best way to meander along Massachusetts's beach-lined, arm-shape peninsula, but in busy town centers—such as Falmouth, Hyannis, Chatham, and Provincetown—you can get around quite easily on foot. Keep in mind that Cape-bound traffic is particularly bad on Friday late afternoon–evening and Saturday morning–afternoon (most house rentals are Saturday to Saturday), and traffic in the other direction is rough on Sunday, especially in the afternoon. Cross as early in the day as possible or wait until well after rush hour. For most visitors, time at the beach is key, but there is plenty to do and see once you've had enough sun and surf or if the weather doesn't cooperate. And about those beaches: be prepared to pay for day passes—most beach parking lots charge a sometimes-hefty fee.

Fly in: Logan International Airport (BOS), Boston

Fly out: Logan International Airport (BOS), Boston

DAY 1: HYANNIS
The best way to spend a week on the Cape is to pick a central location and use it as a launching point to explore. Begin by crossing the Bourne Bridge and head east on U.S. 6 toward Hyannis: make this centrally located, larger town your headquarters.

The crowded Mid Cape is a center of activity, and its heart is **Hyannis.** Here you can cruise around the harbor or go on a deep-sea fishing trip. There are shops and restaurants along Main Street and plenty of kid-friendly amusements. Fans of John F. Kennedy shouldn't miss the museum in his honor. End the day with a concert at the **Cape Cod Melody Tent** (open seasonally) or the Cotuit Center for the Arts.

Logistics: 72 miles; via I–90 W, I–93 S, Rte. 3 S, U.S. 6 E, and Rte. 132 S; 1½ hours from Logan airport.

DAY 2: FALMOUTH
For your first excursion, wander along Route 28 until you reach **Falmouth** in the Upper Cape. Here you can stroll around the village green, duck into some of the historic houses, and stop at the Waquoit Bay National Estuarine Research Reserve for a walk along the barrier beach. Take some time to check out the village of **Woods Hole,** a center for international marine research, and the year-round ferry port for Martha's Vineyard. A small aquarium has regional sea-life exhibits and touch tanks. If you have extra time, head north to the lovely old town of **Sandwich,** known for the **Sandwich Glass Museum,** and the beautiful grounds and collection of antique cars at **Heritage Museums and Gardens.**

Logistics: 21 miles; via Rte. 28 N; 48 minutes, starting in Hyannis.

DAY 3: BARNSTABLE, YARMOUTH PORT, DENNIS
Spend your day exploring the northern reaches of the Mid Cape with a drive along scenic Route 6A, which passes through the charming, slow-paced villages of **Barnstable, Yarmouth Port,**

and **Dennis.** There are beaches and salt marshes, antiques shops and galleries, and old cemeteries along this route. Yarmouth Port's **Bass Hole Boardwalk** makes for a particularly beautiful stroll. In Dennis there are historic houses to tour, and the **Cape Cod Museum of Art** merits a stop. End the day by climbing 30-foot Scargo Tower to watch the sun set. At night you can catch a film at the Cape Cinema, on the grounds of the **Cape Playhouse.**

If you're traveling with kids, spend some time in the southern sections of Yarmouth and Dennis, where Route 28 passes by countless amusement centers and miniature-golf courses.

Logistics: 9 miles; via Rte. 6A E; 20 minutes, starting in Hyannis.

DAY 4: CHATHAM

Chatham, with its handsome Main Street, is a perfect destination for strolling, shopping, and dining. A trip to the nearby **Monomoy Islands** is a must for bird-watchers and nature lovers. Back in town, you can watch glassblowing at the **Chatham Glass Company,** visit the **Atwood House Museum,** and drive over to take in the view from **Chatham Light.**

Logistics: 19½ miles; via U.S. 6 E; 35 minutes, starting in Hyannis.

DAY 5: CAPE COD NATIONAL SEASHORE

On Day 5, leave your Hyannis hub and head for the farther reaches of Cape Cod. Take U.S. 6 east, before making a slight detour onto the less commercial end of Route 28. On the way north toward Orleans you'll drive past sailboat-speckled views of Pleasant Bay.

Stop in Eastham at the Cape Cod National Seashore's **Salt Pond Visitor Center.** Take time to stroll along one of the beaches—there are more than 40 miles of pristine sand from which to choose—or bike on the many picturesque trails. Head slightly farther north to historic **Marconi Station,** which was the landing point for the transatlantic telegraph early in the 20th century, or park your car in **Wellfleet**'s historic downtown area, where you'll find a bounty of intriguing shops and galleries. It's also worth walking the short but stunning White Cedar Swamp Trail. Continue on to Provincetown to spend two nights at the tip of the Cape.

Logistics: 47 miles; via U.S. 6 E; 1¼ hours, starting in Hyannis.

DAYS 6 AND 7: PROVINCETOWN

Bustling **Provincetown** sits at the very end of the Cape, and there's a lot to see and do here. You can park the car and

Great Itineraries

forget about it until you leave town, as everything is easily walkable. Catch a whale-watching boat and take a trolley tour through town, or bike through the **Cape Cod National Seashore** on its miles of trails. Climb the **Pilgrim Monument** for a spectacular view of the area—on an exceptionally clear day you can see the Boston skyline. Visit museums, shops, and art galleries, or spend the afternoon swimming and sunning on the beaches at **Herring Cove** or **Race Point.**

Logistics: 116 miles; via U.S. 6 W, Rte. 3 N and I-93 N; 2½ hours, starting in Provincetown and ending in Boston.

New Haven, Boston, and Providence in 5 days

These three cities all have some of the best dining the northeast has to offer, and each makes a case for having the finest Italian cuisine in the region, leaving you to judge whose cuisine reigns supreme. In addition, history buffs can get their fill while exploring New England's Colonial and maritime past.

Fly in: Bradley International Airport (BDA), Hartford

Fly out: Logan International Airport (BOS), Boston

DAY 1: NEW HAVEN
Start your journey in **New Haven,** Connecticut. The Constitution State's second-largest city is home to **Yale University,** named for British shipping merchant Elihu Yale. Take an hour-long walking tour with one of the university's guides and feast your eyes on the iconic Gothic-style structures that adorn the campus. After you've worked up an appetite, a stop for New Haven–style pizza is a must. Less than a mile from campus are two institutions known for thin-crust pies cooked

in brick ovens: **Pepe's Pizzeria** and **Sally's Apizza.** For the burger enthusiast, there's **Louis' Lunch** on Crown Street. Don't ask for ketchup; it's been taboo here since they opened in 1895. Spend your first night in New Haven.

Logistics: 53 miles; via I-91 S; 1 hour starting at Bradley airport.

DAY 2: NEW HAVEN TO PROVIDENCE
On your second day, get an early start, and head north on Interstate 95 to make your way toward Providence, Rhode Island. There are plenty of small towns bursting with New England's maritime history along Connecticut's shoreline. Stop in Niantic, New London, or **Stonington** and explore the region's rich seafaring history. If you're planning on making one stop on the way to Rhode Island, the seaside village of **Mystic** is worth at least a half day to explore the seaport or to take a boat out on the water. **Mystic Seaport,** with its nearly 500 ships and more than 60 preserved historic buildings, will transport you back to 19th-century New England. For those looking to try their luck at a game of chance, take a slight detour north on Interstate 395 to either of Connecticut's two casinos, **Foxwoods Resort Casino** or **Mohegan Sun.** Overnight in Providence or in any of the seaside towns along the way.

Logistics: 103 miles; via I-95 N; 1 hour 45 minutes, starting in New Haven.

DAY 3: PROVIDENCE
Rhode Island's capital holds treasures like **Benefit Street,** with its Federal-era homes, and the **RISD Museum of Art** at the Rhode Island School of Design. Be sure to savor a knockout Italian meal on Atwells Avenue in **Federal Hill—Pane e Vino** is a popular choice. For dessert, it's hard to top the cannoli at **Scialo Bros. Bakery.** If you're visiting in early June,

sample authentic eats from all over Italy, while live music fills the streets, during the Federal Hill Stroll. On summer nights, catch a Paw Sox baseball game at McCoy Stadium in the neighboring town of **Pawtucket,** home of the beloved Triple-A farm team for the Boston Red Sox. Also in the warmer months, typically late May–early November, Providence hosts **WaterFire,** a public celebration of art and performance. The festival's 100 bonfires on the rivers of downtown Providence attracts tens of thousands of viewers each year for the popular event. Spend the night in a downtown Providence hotel for easy access to sights and restaurants.

DAYS 4 AND 5: BOSTON

A short drive north on Interstate 95 will bring you to **Boston,** New England's cultural and commercial hub. To savor Boston's centuries-old ties to the sea, take a half-day stroll past **Faneuil Hall** and **Quincy Market** or a boat tour of the harbor (you can even head out on a whale-watching tour from here). In Boston, famous buildings such as Faneuil Hall are not merely civic landmarks, but national icons. From the **Boston Common,** the 2.5-mile **Freedom Trail** links treasures of America's struggle for independence, such as the **USS *Constitution*** (better

known as "Old Ironsides") and **Old North Church** (of "one if by land, two if by sea" fame). Be sure to walk the gas-lighted streets of **Beacon Hill,** too. Boston's **North End** is the oldest residential neighborhood in the city, and has great dining options like **Antico Forno,** which offers pizza baked in a wood-burning brick oven.

The following day, either explore the massive **Museum of Fine Arts** and the grand boulevards and shops of **Back Bay,** or visit colorful **Cambridge,** home of **Harvard University** and the **Massachusetts Institute of Technology (MIT).** Lively **Harvard Square** is a perfect place to do some people-watching or catch a street performance; the **All Star Sandwich Bar** is an excellent choice for lunch. For an experience unique to the Boston area, head a few miles south of the city along U.S. 1 to Dorchester's **Boston Bowl** to cap off your trip with candlepin bowling. Here, at all hours of the night, Bay Staters play a smaller version of 10-pin bowling that uses balls weighing less than 3 pounds and allows participants to bowl three balls per frame instead of two.

Logistics: 50 miles; via I–95 N and I–93 N; 1 hour, starting in Providence.

Great Itineraries

Massachusetts, New Hampshire, and Maine, 7 Days

Revel in the coast beauty of three New England states—Massachusetts, New Hampshire, and Maine—on the path from the region's largest city, Boston, to the its highest peak, Mt. Washington. An assortment of New England's treasures are at your fingertips as you negotiate the ins and outs of the jagged northeastern coastline, before ascending the heights of the White Mountains.

Fly in: Logan International Airport (BOS), Boston

Fly out: Logan International Airport (BOS), Boston

DAY 1: THE NORTH SHORE AND NEW HAMPSHIRE COAST

After flying into Boston, pick up a rental car and head for the North Shore of Massachusetts. In **Salem,** the **Peabody Essex Museum** and the **Salem Maritime National Historic Site** chronicle the evolution of the country's early shipping fortunes. Spend some time exploring more of the North Shore, including the old fishing port of **Gloucester,** and **Rockport,** a great place to find that seascape rendered in oils. **Newburyport,** with its Federal-style shipowners' homes, is home to the **Parker River National Wildlife Refuge,** beloved by birders and beach walkers.

New Hampshire fronts the Atlantic for a scant 18 miles, but its coastal landmarks range from honky-tonk **Hampton Beach** to quiet **Odiorne Point State Park** in Rye and urbane and historic Portsmouth, where pre-Revolutionary high society built Georgian- and Federal-style mansions—visit a few at the **Strawbery Banke Museum.** Stay

the night in **Portsmouth** at the centrally located **Ale House Inn.**

Logistics: 64 miles; via I–95 N; 1 hour 10 minutes, starting at Logan airport.

DAY 2: THE YORKS

Much of the appeal of the Maine Coast lies in geographical contrast—from its long stretches of swimming and walking beaches in the south to the rugged, rocky cliffs in the north. As the shoreline physically evolves, each town along the way reveals a slightly different character, starting with **York.**

In **York Village** take a leisurely stroll through the buildings of the **Museums of Old York** getting a glimpse of 18th-century life in this gentrified town. Spend time wandering between shops or walking nature trails and beaches around York Harbor. There are several grand lodging options here, most with views of the harbor. If you prefer a livelier pace, continue on to **York Beach,** a haven for families with plenty of entertainment venues. Stop at Fox's Lobster House after visiting **Nubble Light** for a seaside lunch or dinner.

Logistics: 10 miles; via I–95 N; 15 minutes, starting in Portsmouth.

DAY 3: OGUNQUIT AND THE KENNEBUNKS

For well over a century, **Ogunquit** has been a favorite vacation spot for those looking to combine the natural beauty of the ocean with a sophisticated environment. Take a morning walk along the Marginal Way to see the waves crashing against the rocks. In **Perkins Cove,** have lunch, stroll the shopping areas, or sign on with a lobster-boat cruise to learn about Maine's most important fishery— the state's lobster industry satisfies more than 90% of the world's appetite.

Head north to the Kennebunks, allowing at least two hours to wander through the shops and historic homes of Dock Square in **Kennebunkport.** This is an ideal place to rent a bike and ramble around backstreets, head out Ocean Avenue past large mansions, or ride to one of several beaches to relax awhile. Spend your third night in Kennebunkport.

Logistics: 22 miles; via I–95 N and Rte. 9 E; 30 minutes, starting in York.

DAYS 4 AND 5: PORTLAND

If you have time, you can easily spend several days in **Portland,** Maine's largest city, exploring its historic neighborhoods, shopping and eating in the **Old Port,** or visiting one of several excellent museums. A brief side trip to **Cape Elizabeth** takes you to **Portland Head Light,** Maine's first lighthouse, which was commissioned by George Washington in 1787. The lighthouse is on the grounds of Fort Williams Park and is an excellent place for a picnic; be sure to spend some time wandering the ample grounds. There are also excellent walking trails (and views) at nearby Two Lights State Park. If you want to take a boat tour while in Portland, get a ticket for Casco Bay Lines and see some of the islands that dot the bay. Spend two nights in Portland.

Logistics: 28 miles; via I–95 N; 40 minutes, starting in Kennebunkport.

DAY 6: BRETTON WOODS

Wake up early and drive to **Bretton Woods,** New Hampshire where you will spend nights six and seven. The driving time from Portland to Bretton Woods is approximately three hours, due to windy two-lane mountain roads. Drive northwest along U.S. 302 toward Sebago Lake, a popular water-sports area in the summer, and continue on toward the time-honored New England towns of Naples and Bridgton. Just 15 miles from the border of New Hampshire, and nearing Crawford Notch, U.S. 302 begins to thread through New Hampshire's **White Mountains,** passing

beneath brooding **Mt. Washington** before arriving in Bretton Woods.

Logistics: 98 miles; via Rte. 113 N and U.S. 302 W; 3 hours, starting from Portland.

DAY 7: THE WHITE MOUNTAINS

In Bretton Woods, the **Mount Washington Cog Railway** chugs to the summit, and the **Omni Mount Washington Resort** recalls the glory days of White Mountain resorts. Beloved winter activities here include snowshoeing and skiing on the grounds; you can even zip-line. Afterward, defrost with a cup of steaming hot cider while checking out vintage photos of the International Monetary Conference (held here in 1944), or head to the Cave, a Prohibition-era speakeasy, for a drink.

Logistics: 159 miles; via I–93 S; 2½ hours, starting at the Omni Mount Washington Resort and ending in Boston.

Great Itineraries

Maine's Northern Coast: Portland to Acadia National Park, 6 Days

Lighthouses, beaches, lobster rolls, and water sports—Maine's northern coast has something for everyone. Quaint seaside villages and towns line the shore as U.S. 1 winds its way toward the easternmost swath of land in the United States at Quoddy Head State Park. Antiquing is a major draw, so keep an eye out for roadside shops crammed with gems. Maine's only national park, Acadia, is a highlight of the tour, drawing more than 2 million visitors per year.

Fly in: Portland International Jetport (PWM), Portland

Fly out: Bangor International Airport, (BGR), Bangor

DAY 1: PORTLAND TO BRUNSWICK

Use Maine's maritime capital as your jumping-off point to head farther up the Maine Coast, or, as Mainers call it, "Down East." Plan to spend half of your first day in Portland, then head to Brunswick for the night.

Portland shows off its restored waterfront at the **Old Port.** From there, before you depart, you can grab a bite at either of two classic Maine eateries: **Gilbert's Chowder House** or **Becky's Diner,** or check out what's new in the buzzy restaurant scene here. For a peek at the freshest catch of the day, wander over to the **Harbor Fish Market,** a Portland institution since 1968, and gaze upon Maine lobsters and other delectable seafood. Two lighthouses on nearby **Cape Elizabeth, Two Lights** and **Portland Head,** still stand vigil.

Following U.S. 1, travel northeast along the ragged, island-strewn coast of Down East Maine and make your first stop at the retail outlets of **Freeport,** home of **L.L. Bean.** Almost 3 million people visit the massive flagship store every year, where you can find everything from outerwear to camping equipment. Just 10 miles north of Freeport on U.S. 1, **Brunswick** is home to the campus of **Bowdoin College,** the superb **Bowdoin College Museum of Art,** and also features a superb coastline for kayaking. Plan for dinner and an overnight in Bath.

Logistics: 30 miles; via U.S. 1 N; 30 minutes from Portland airport.

DAY 2: BATH

In **Bath,** Maine's shipbuilding capital, tour the **Maine Maritime Museum,** stopping for lunch on the waterfront. Check out the boutiques and antiques shops, or take in the plenitude of beautiful homes. From here it's a 30-minute detour down Route 127 to Georgetown Island and Reid State Park, where you will find a quiet beach lining Sheepscot Bay—and maybe even a sand dollar or two to take home, if you arrive at low tide. For a stunning vista, make your way to Griffith Head.

Drive north and reconnect with U.S. 1. Continue through the towns of **Wiscasset and Damariscotta,** where you may find yourself pulling over to stop at the outdoor flea markets and intriguing antiques shops that line the road. Another hour from here is **Rockland,** where you'll spend your second night.

Logistics: 52 miles; via U.S. 1 N; 1 hour 15 minutes, starting in Brunswick.

DAY 3: ROCKLAND, CAMDEN, AND CASTINE

From Rockland, spend the day cruising on a majestic schooner or reserve a tee time at Somerset Resorts' 18-hole championship course that overlooks the

Rockland Harbor. If you're an art lover, save some time for Rockland's **Farnsworth Art Museum,** the **Wyeth Center,** and the **Maine Center for Contemporary Art.**

In **Camden** and **Castine,** exquisite inns occupy homes built from inland Maine's gold and timber. Camden is an ideal place to stay overnight as you make your way closer to Acadia National Park; it is a beautiful seaside town with hundreds of boats bobbing in the harbor, immaculately kept antique homes, streets lined with boutiques and specialty stores, and restaurants serving lobster at every turn. The modest hills (by Maine standards, anyway) of nearby Mt. Battie offer good hiking and a great spot from which to picnic and view the surrounding area. It is also one of the hubs for the beloved and historic windjammer fleet—there is no better way to see the area than from the deck of one of these graceful beauties.

Logistics: 62 miles; via U.S. 1 N and Rte. 166 S; 1½ hours, starting in Rockland.

DAYS 4 AND 5: MOUNT DESERT ISLAND AND ACADIA NATIONAL PARK

On Day 4, head out early for **Bar Harbor** and plan to spend two nights here, using the bustling village as jumping-off

point for the park—Bar Harbor is less than 5 miles from the entrance to **Mount Desert Island**'s 27-mile Park Loop Road. Spend at least a day exploring **Acadia National Park,** Maine's only national park and its most popular tourist destination. Enjoy the island's natural beauty by kayaking its coast, biking the 45-mile, historic, unpaved, carriage-road system, and driving to the summit of **Cadillac Mountain** for a stunning panorama.

Logistics: 52 miles; via Rte. 166 N, U.S. 1 N and Rte. 3 E; 1¼ hours, starting in Castine.

DAY 6: BAR HARBOR TO QUODDY HEAD STATE PARK

About 100 miles farther along U.S. 1 and "Way Down East" is Quoddy Head State Park in Lubec, Maine. Here, on the easternmost tip of land in the United States, sits the **West Quoddy Head Light,** one of 60 lighthouses that dot Maine's rugged coastline. Depending on the time of year (and your willingness to get up very early), you may be lucky enough to catch the East Coast's first sunrise here.

Logistics: 103 miles; via U.S. 1 N; 2½ hours, starting in Bar Harbor. From the park, it is 119 miles (2½ hours) to the Bangor airport via Rte. 9 W.

Great Itineraries

Connecticut Wineries and Rhode Island Mansions, 5 Days

Travel through the Lower Connecticut River Valley as you meander toward the eastern section of the state's Wine Trail. While you sample varietals from the area's best wineries, get a taste of New England's literary and maritime history along the way. Stay overnight in seaside Mystic, another highlight, and then finish your tour by gawking at Newport's grand mansions and strolling the gorgeous Cliff Walk.

Fly in: Bradley International Airport (BGR), Hartford

Fly out: T.F. Green Airport (PVD), Warwick

DAY 1: HARTFORD

Start your journey in **Hartford,** Connecticut. The **Mark Twain House and Museum,** which Samuel Clemens and his wife built in the city's Victorian neighborhood of Nook Farm, is adjacent to the **Harriet Beecher Stowe Center,** which is also worth a visit. Downtown, you can visit the Nutmeg State's ornate **State Capitol** and the **Wadsworth Atheneum Museum of Art,** which houses fine Impressionist and Hudson River School paintings. Sports fans, take note: the **Naismith Memorial Basketball Hall of Fame** is only a quick detour up Interstate 91, in **Springfield,** Massachusetts, where Dr. James Naismith invented basketball in 1891. Spend your first night in Hartford.

DAY 2: CONNECTICUT RIVER VALLEY AND SOUTHEASTERN SHORE

Just a half-hour southeast of Hartford along Route 2 is your first wine stop, Priam Vineyards, in Colchester. Sample any of the boutique wines

before bearing south on Route 149 to explore the centuries-old river towns of **East Haddam,** Chester, and **Essex.** In East Haddam, stop at Gillette Castle State Park—with its medieval-style stone mansion built for to actor William Gillette—before crossing the Connecticut River on the historic (since 1769), eight-car Hadlyme-Chester ferry (April–November). In Essex, take a ride on the **Essex Steam Train**—the 12-mile excursion showcases the area's well-preserved countryside. (You can also return to Essex via riverboat.)

Continue on to **Mystic,** where the days of wooden ships and whaling adventures live on at **Mystic Seaport.** This world-class museum offers a peek into the past with restored vessels, historic buildings, figureheads, ship carvings, and much more. Spend your second night in Mystic.

Logistics: 60 miles; via Rte. 2 E; 1 hour, starting in Hartford (not including stops).

DAY 3: CONNECTICUT WINE TRAIL

A patchwork of six wineries—the heart of the eastern section of the **Connecticut Wine Trail**—sit in the southeastern corner of the state. Taste through the portfolio at each of the picturesque vineyards until you find the perfect bottle to take home; many wineries offer self-guided walks through peaceful vineyards, allowing you to roam on your own. **Stonington Vineyards** has daily guided tours, and Jonathan Edwards Winery, farther inland in North Stonington, is a serene setting for picnics. Cap off the day by crossing the state line into Rhode Island and spend the night in **Watch Hill.** You can wander the grounds of the **Watch Hill Lighthouse;** in its museum, open midweek afternoons in summer, you can see the original Fresnel lens, a binnacle, mariners' sea chests, and

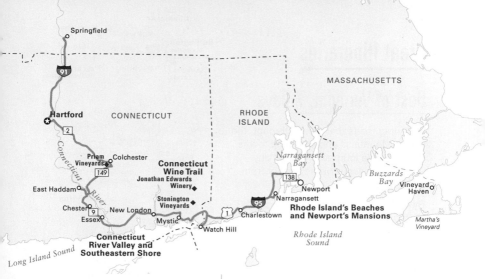

historical documents and photos about the lighthouse and the area.

Logistics: 13½ miles; via U.S. 1 N; 25 minutes, starting in Mystic (not including stops).

DAYS 4 AND 5: RHODE ISLAND'S BEACHES AND NEWPORT'S MANSIONS

En route to Newport along U.S. 1 from **Watch Hill,** sandy beaches dot the coast from Misquamicut and Weekapaug to **Charlestown** and **Narragansett.** If it's summer and the weather is fine, spend the afternoon at the beach before continuing on to **Newport.** Despite its Colonial downtown and seaside parks, to most people Newport means mansions—the most opulent enclave of private homes ever built in the United States. Turn-of-the-20th-century "summer cottages" such as the **Breakers** and **Marble House** are must-sees. Embark on the scenic **Cliff Walk** for remarkable views of these great houses on one side and the Atlantic Ocean on the other. Newport's downtown is excellent for window-shopping, and there are plenty of places to enjoy fresh seafood.

Newport is known to many as the sailing capital of the East Coast, and you may get the best feel for it from the deck of a schooner cruising its famous harbor. Tours generally last around 90 minutes, and some offer beverages and snacks. Tennis enthusiasts can visit the **International Tennis Hall of Fame,** which, along with exhibits focusing on the legends of the game, has a unique interior designed by architect Stanford White. You can easily spend a few days exploring Newport.

Logistics: 39½ miles; via U.S. 1 N; 1 hour, starting in Watch Hill. From Newport, it is 26 miles (30 minutes) to T.F. Green Airport via RI 138 W and RI 4 N.

■TIP➔ **T.F. Green Airport (PVD) is less than 20 minutes by car from Providence.** There's also commuter rail service on the MBTA between the two. If you have some time, or even an extra evening, consider spending it in Rhode Island's largest city. There's a thriving arts scene, an impressive restaurant scene including some of the best Italian food on Atwells Avenue in Federal Hill, and landmark hotel's like Providence Biltmore, which opened in 1922. If you're lucky enough to be in town on a Saturday night when WaterFire is on, you'll be left dumbstruck.

Great Itineraries

Best of Vermont, 7 Days

Following roads that weave through the Green Mountains and charming towns, this 200-mile journey is ideal at any time of year and covers Vermont from top to bottom.

Fly in: Bradley International Airport (BDL), Hartford

Fly out: Burlington International Airport (BTV), Burlington

DAY 1: BRATTLEBORO

Artsy **Brattleboro** is the perfect place to begin a tour of Vermont, and it's worth taking a day to do some shopping and exploring. Catch a movie at the Art Deco **Latchis Theatre,** browse in a bookstore, or simply grab a cup of joe and people-watch. For dinner, make a reservation well in advance at tiny **T.J. Buckley's,** one of the best restaurants in the state. Spend your first night in Brattleboro.

Logistics: 78 miles; via I–91 N; 1 hour and 15 minutes from Bradley airport.

DAYS 2–4: KILLINGTON

Depart Brattleboro heading west on Route 9 and link up with Route 100 in Wilmington. As you travel north along the eastern edge of **Green Mountain National Forest,** you'll pass a plethora of panoramic overlooks and delightful ski towns. Stop to snap a photo, or take a moment to peruse the selection at a funky general store, as you make your way toward gigantic Killington Peak. Spend the next three nights in **Killington,** the largest ski resort in Vermont, and an outdoor playground year-round. A tip for skiers: one of the closest places to the slopes to stay is **The Mountain Top Inn & Resort.**

Wake up early to carve the mountain's fresh powder in winter. Nonskiers can still enjoy the snow, whether at the

tubing park, on a snowmobile adventure, or in snowshoes on one of several trails. In summer, long after the ground has thawed, those trails are opened to mountain bikers and hikers. For a more leisurely activity, try your hand at the 18-hole disc-golf course. The excellent Grand Spa is also a lovely way to spend the day.

Logistics: 94 miles; via Rte. 9 W, Rte. 100 N, 2½ hours, starting in Brattleboro.

DAY 5: KILLINGTON TO BURLINGTON

Continue on Route 100 north until you reach Hancock, then head west on Route 125. Welcome to the land of poet Robert Frost, who spent almost 40 years living in Vermont, summering in the nearby tiny mountain town of Ripton, where he wrote numerous poems. Plaques along the 1.2-mile **Robert Frost Interpretive Trail,** a quiet woodland walk that takes about 30 minutes, display commemorative quotes from his poems, including his classic, "The Road Not Taken." After your stroll, head north on U.S. 7 until you hit Burlington.

Burlington, Vermont's largest city and home to the **University of Vermont,** is located on the eastern shore of Lake Champlain. Bustling in the summer and fall, the **Burlington Farmers' Market** is filled with everything from organic meats and cheeses to freshly cut flowers and maple syrup. Spend the night in Burlington. In the evening, check out **Nectar's,** where the band Phish played their first bar gig, or wander into any of the many other pubs and cafés that attract local musicians.

Logistics: 84 miles; via Rte. 100 N, Rte. 125 W, and U.S. 7 N; 2½ hours, starting in Killington.

DAY 6: SHELBURNE AND LAKE CHAMPLAIN

On your second day in Burlington, you can take a day trip south to the **Magic Hat Brewing Company**; established in 1994, it was at the forefront of Vermont's microbrewery explosion. Take a free half-hour guided or self-guided tour of the Artifactory (even dogs are welcome), and fill a growler from one of the 48 taps pumping out year-round, seasonal, and experimental brews. A stone's throw down U.S. 7, in **Shelburne,** is family-friendly **Shelburne Farms.** Watch the process of making cheese from start to finish, or wander the gorgeous 1,400-acre estate designed by Frederick Law Olmsted, co-designer of New York's Central Park. The grounds overlook beautiful **Lake Champlain** and make the perfect setting for a picnic. In winter Shelburne Farms offers sleigh rides and other themed activities; if you're visiting in late July, don't miss the **Vermont Cheesemakers Festival,** showcasing more than 200 varieties of

cheese crafted by 40 local purveyors. If you can't get enough, you can opt to spend the night here.

Logistics: 3.6 miles, via U.S. 7 to Magic Hat; another 3.4 miles to Shelburne Farms; 40 minutes round-trip altogether.

DAY 7: STOWE

A 30-minute drive down Interstate 89 from Burlington reunites you with Route 100 in the town of Waterbury. Head north in the direction of Stowe, and in under 2 miles you can make the obligatory pit stop at **Ben & Jerry's Ice Cream Factory.** The factory tour offers a lively behind-the-scenes look at how their ice cream is made; at the end of the tour, you get to taste limited-release creations only available at the factory before voting on your favorites.

Next, set out for the village of **Stowe.** Its proximity to Mt. Mansfield (Vermont's highest peak at 4,395 feet) has made Stowe a popular ski destination since the 1930s. If there's snow on the ground, hit the slopes, hitch a ride on a one-horse open sleigh, or simply put your feet up by the fire and enjoy a Heady Topper (an unfiltered, hoppy, American Double IPA beloved by beer aficionados the world over). In warmer weather, pop into the cute shops and art galleries that line the town's main street and sample some of the finest cheddar cheese and maple syrup that Vermont has to offer. Rejuvenate yourself at **Topnotch Resort,** which offers more than 100 different treatments. Spend your final night here.

Logistics: 36 miles; via I–89 S and Rte. 100 N; 45 minutes, starting in Burlington. From Stowe to the Burlington airport: 33 miles; via Rte. 100 and I–89 N; 41 minutes.

On The Calendar

January

Jackson Invitational Snow Sculpting Competition, Jackson, New Hampshire. Started in 2000, the free event takes places at Black Mountain Ski and features more than 12 teams carving intricate snow sculptures. ⊕ *www.jacksonnh.com*

Sun Wine and Food Fest, Uncasville, Connecticut. This four-day festival, Connecticut's largest wine and food event, takes place at Mohegan Sun and features tastings, chef appearances, and cooking demonstrations. ⊕ *mohegansun.com*

February

Newport Winter Festival, Newport, Rhode Island. Billed as "New England's Largest Winter Extravaganza," the annual event features more than 150 events that range from food and music to a Chili Cook-Off. ⊕ *www.newportwinterfestival.com*

Winter Carnival, Dartmouth, New Hampshire. Started in 1911, Dartmouth's winter festival celebrates the season with races, polar bear plunges, and snow sculpture contests. ⊕ *students.dartmouth.edu/ collis/traditions-events/winter-carnival*

March

Connecticut Spring Antiques Show, Hartford, Connecticut. Started in 1973, this antiques show is the premier destination for collectors of early American furniture and decorative arts. ⊕ *www.ctspringantiquesshow.com*

April

Vermont Maple Festival, St. Albans, Vermont. This weekend is all about syrup. There's a pancake breakfast, a carnival and parade, and, of course, plenty of yummy maple treats. ⊕ *vtmaplefestival.org*

May

Brimfield Antique and Collectible Shows, Brimfield, Massachusetts. Operating since the 1950s, Brimfield welcomes thousands of visitors for a weeklong antique and flea market extravaganza every May, July, and September. ⊕ *www.brimfieldshow.com*

WaterFire, Providence, Rhode Island. Late May through early November, more than 80 bonfires are lit on the city's three rivers on select weekends. ⊕ *waterfire.org*

June

Elephant's Trunk Country Flea Market, New Milford, Connecticut. Open every Sunday from late March through mid-Decemeber since 1976, Elephant's Trunk features antiques, up-cyclers, farm stands, food stalls, and vendors of all kinds. ⊕ *www. etflea.com*

Festival of Historic Homes, Providence, Rhode Island. Hosted by the Providence Preservation Society, the festival highlights the city's historic neighborhoods, architecture, and history. ⊕ *ppsri.org*

Jacob's Pillow Dance Festival, Beckett, Massachusetts. The festival, which takes place mid-June through August, features more than 350 free performances, talks, tours, exhibits, community events, and classes. ⊕ *www.jacobspillow.org*

Strolling of the Heifers, Brattleboro, Vermont. An annual local food-focused festival that includes a parade of about 100 cows dressed in their Sunday best. ⊕ *www. strollingoftheheifers.com*

July

Chowderfest, Boston, Massachusetts. Thousands gather at City Hall Plaza for the annual chowder cook-off, which is part of Harborfest, Boston's yearly festivities centered on Independence Day. ⊕ *www.bostonharborfest.com*

Sailfest, New London, Connecticut. A weekend of fireworks, music on multiple stages, more than 200 vendors lining the streets, and boat cruises. ⊕ *sailfest.org*

Vermont Cheesemakers Festival, Shelburne, Vermont. Artisanal cheeses and local beer and wine highlight this daylong festival that features samples of more than 200 cheese varieties from 40 local cheese makers. ⊕ *www.vtcheesefest.com*

August

Maine Antiques Fair, Union, Maine. Maine's largest antiques festival features vendors from more than 20 states. ⊕ *maineantiquesfestival.com*

Maine Lobster Festival, Rockland, Maine. Stuff your face with lobster tails and claws during this "lobstravaganza" that puts almost 20,000 pounds of delicious crustacean at your finger tips. ⊕ *www.mainelobsterfestival.com*

Wilton Blueberry Festival, Wilton, Maine. You can pick your own wild blueberries and sample baked goods from pancakes to pies at the annual festival. ⊕ *www.wiltonbbf.com*

September

The Big E, West Springfield, Massachusetts. Also known as The Eastern States Exposition, this is the eastern seaboard's largest agricultural event and the country's seventh-largest fair. ⊕ *www.thebige.com*

October

Fryeburg Fair, Fryeburg, Maine. Established in 1851, traditional fair highlights include horse, ox, and tractor pulling; animal, craft, and art exhibits; sheepdog trials; cooking contests; flower shows; a farm equipment museum; demonstrations; and food, food, food. ⊕ *www.fryeburgfair.org*

New Hampshire Pumpkin Festival, Laconia, New Hampshire. Formerly located in Keene, the newly renamed and relocated festival (as of 2015) tries to outdo itself each October for most lighted pumpkins. ⊕ *www.nhpumpkinfestival.com*

Wellfleet OysterFest, Wellfleet, Massachusetts. A family-friendly weekend that celebrates the town's famous mollusk with food, art, and music. ⊕ *www.wellfleetoysterfest.org*

November

America's Hometown Thanksgiving Celebration, Plymouth, Massachusetts. Celebrated the weekend before Thanksgiving in the holiday's birthplace, this event focuses on history, Americana, Pilgrims, and Native Americans. ⊕ *usathanksgiving.com*

December

Inn to Inn Holiday Cookie Tour, White Mountains, New Hampshire. This self-guided tour includes sweet treats, copious Christmas decorations, and charming winter scenes. ⊕ *www.countryinnsinthewhitemountains.com*

Winter Wassail Weekend, Woodstock, Vermont. The annual fete features a parade with holiday-costume clad horses and riders, live music, house tours, kids' activities, and a Wassail Feast. ⊕ *www.woodstockvt.com*

Contacts

VISITOR INFO

Connecticut Office of Tourism. ☎ *888/288–4748* ⊕ *www.ctvisit.com.* **Greater Boston Convention & Visitors Bureau.** ☎ *888/733–2678* ⊕ *www.bostonusa.com.* **Maine Office of Tourism.** ☎ *888/624–6345* ⊕ *www.visitmaine.com.* **Massachusetts Office of Travel and Tourism.** ☎ *800/227–6277, 617/973–8500* ⊕ *www.massvacation.com.* **New Hampshire Division of Travel and Tourism Development.** ☎ *800/386–4664* ⊕ *www.visitnh.gov.* **Rhode Island Tourism Division.** ☎ *800/556–2484* ⊕ *www.visitrhodeisland.com.* **Vermont Department of Tourism and Marketing.** ☎ *800/837–6668* ⊕ *www.vermontvacation.com.*

ONLINE RESOURCES

Online Info New England Today. ⊕ *newengland.com/category/travel.* **Visit New England.** ⊕ *www.visitnewengland.com.*

 Air Travel

AIRPORTS

Albany International Airport. ✉ *737 Albany Shaker Rd., Albany* ✈ *7 miles northwest of Albany in Latham* ☎ *518/242–2200* ⊕ *www.albanyairport.com.* **Bangor International Airport.** ✉ *287 Godfrey Blvd., Bangor* ☎ *207/992–4600* ⊕ *www.flybangor.com.* **Barnstable Municipal Airport.** ✉ *480*

Barnstable Rd., Hyannis ☎ *508/775–2020* ⊕ *www.town.barnstable.ma.us/airport.* **Bradley International Airport.** ✉ *Schoephoester Rd., Windsor Locks* ☎ *860/292–2000* ⊕ *www.bradleyairport.com.* **Burlington International Airport.** ✉ *1200 Airport Dr., South Burlington* ☎ *802/863–2874* ⊕ *www.btv.aero.* **Logan International Airport.** ✉ *1 Harborside Dr., Boston* ☎ *800/235–6426* ⊕ *www.massport.com/logan-airport* Ⓜ *Blue, silver.* **Manchester-Boston Regional Airport.** ✉ *1 Airport Rd., Manchester* ☎ *603/624–6539* ⊕ *www.flymanchester.com.* **Martha's Vineyard Airport.** ✉ *71 Airport Rd., West Tisbury* ☎ *508/693–7022* ⊕ *www.mvyairport.com.* **Nantucket Memorial Airport.** ✉ *14 Airport Rd., Nantucket* ☎ *508/325–5300* ⊕ *www.nantucketairport.com.* **Portland International Jetport.** ✉ *1001 Westbrook St., Portland* ☎ *207/874–8877* ⊕ *www.portlandjetport.org.* **T.F. Green International Airport.** ✉ *2000 Post Rd., Warwick* ☎ *401/691–2471* ⊕ *www.pvdairport.com.* **Westchester County Airport.** ✉ *240 Airport Rd., White Plains* ☎ *914/995–4860* ⊕ *airport.westchestergov.com.*

AIRLINE CONTACTS

Cape Air. ☎ *800/227–3247* ⊕ *www.capeair.com.* **New England Airlines.** ☎ *800/243–2460* ⊕ *www.block-island.com/nea.*

 Bus Travel

BoltBus. ☎ *877/265–8287* ⊕ *www.boltbus.com.* **C&J.** ☎ *800/258–7111* ⊕ *www.ridecj.com.* **Concord Coach Lines.** ☎ *800/639–3317* ⊕ *concordcoachlines.com.* **Peter Pan Bus Lines.** ☎ *800/343–9999* ⊕ *www.peterpanbus.com.* **Rhode Island Public Transit Authority.** ☎ *401/781–9400* ⊕ *www.ripta.com.*

🚗 **Car Travel**

Governors Highway Safety Association. ☎ *202/789–0942* ⊕ *www.ghsa.org/html/stateinfo/laws/childsafety_laws.html.*

🚆 **Train Travel**

Amtrak. ☎ *800/872–7245* ⊕ *www.amtrak.com.* **Massachusetts Bay Transportation Authority (MBTA).** ☎ *617/222–3200* ⊕ *www.mbta.com.* **Metro-North Railroad.** ☎ *511 within New York State, 877/690–5114 from Connecticut* ⊕ *www.mta.info/mnr.* **Shore Line East.** ☎ *877/287–4337* ⊕ *www.shorelineeast.com.*

🛏 **Lodging**

New England Inns & Resorts Association. ☎ *603/964–6689* ⊕ *www.newenglandinnsandresorts.com.*

Chapter 3

BEST FALL FOLIAGE DRIVES

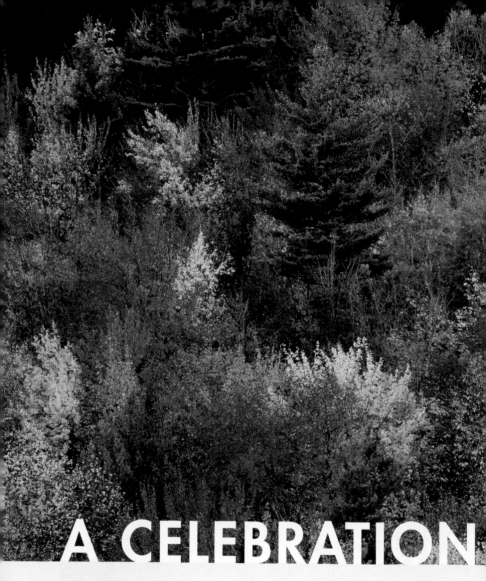

A CELEBRATION

Picture this: one scarlet maple offset by the stark white spire of a country church, a whole hillside of brilliant foliage foregrounded by a vintage barn or perhaps a covered bridge that straddles a cobalt river. Such iconic scenes have launched a thousand postcards and turned New England into the ultimate fall destination for leaf peepers.

OF COLOR

Mother Nature, of course, puts on an annual autumn performance elsewhere, but this one is a showstopper. Like the landscape, the mix of deciduous (leaf-shedding) trees is remarkably varied here and creates a broader than usual palette. New England's abundant evergreens lend contrast, making the display even more vivid. Every September and October, leaf peepers arrive to cruise along country lanes, join outdoor adventures, or simply stroll on town greens.

Did you know the brilliant shades actually lurk in the leaves all year long? Leaves contain three pigments. The green chlorophyll, so dominant in summer that it obscures the red anthocyanins and orangey yellow carotenoids, decreases in fall and reveals a crayon box of color.

Above, Vermont's Green Mountains are multicolored in the fall (and often white in winter).

PREDICTING THE PEAK

AVERAGE FOLIAGE PEAK
- ■ October 1–7
- ■ October 7–14
- □ October 14–21
- □ October 21–Later

LOCATION

Pinning down precisely when colors will appear remains an inexact science, although location plays a major role. Typically, the transformation begins in the highest and northernmost parts of New England in mid-September, then moves steadily into lower altitudes and southern sectors throughout October.

For trip planning, think in terms of regions rather than states. In Maine (a huge state that runs north–south) leaf color can peak anytime from the fourth week of September to the third week of October, depending on the locale.

WEATHER

Early September weather is another deciding factor. From the foliage aficionado's perspective, the ideal scenario is calm, temperate days capped by nights that are cool but still above freezing. If the weather is too warm, it delays the onset of the season. If it's too dry or windy, the leaves shrivel up or blow off.

COLOR CHECK RESOURCES

Curious about current conditions? In season, each state maintains a dedicated website reporting on foliage conditions. Weather Channel has peak viewing maps and Foliage Network uses a network of spotters to chart changes.

- ■ Connecticut: ☎ 800/282–6863
  ⊕ www.ct.gov/dep
- ■ Foliage Network:
  ⊕ www.foliagenetwork.com
- ■ Maine: ☎ 888/624–6345
  ⊕ www.mainefoliage.com
- ■ Massachusetts: ☎ 800/227–6277
  ⊕ www.massvacation.com
- ■ New Hampshire: ☎ 800/258–3608
  ⊕ www.visitnh.gov
- ■ Rhode Island: ☎ 800/556–2484
  ⊕ www.visitrhodeisland.com
- ■ Vermont: ☎ 800/837–6668
  ⊕ www.vermontvacation.com
- ■ Weather Channel:
  ⊕ www.weather.com

TOP TREES FOR COLOR

A **American Beech.** This tree's smooth, steel-gray trunk is crowned with gold, copper, and bronze-tinted leaves in autumn, giving it a metallic sheen. Though the elliptical leaves sometimes hang on all winter, its "fruit" goes fast because beechnuts are a popular snack for birds, squirrels, and even bears.

B **Northern Red Oak.** The upside of oaks is that they retain their fall shading until late in the season—the downside is that, for most species, that color is a boring brown. Happily, the northern red isn't like other members of the oak family. Its elongated, flame-shaped leaves turn fiery crimson and incandescent orange.

C **Quaking Aspen.** Eyes and ears both prove useful when identifying this aspen. Look for small, ovate leaves that usually become almost flaxen. Or listen for the leaves' quake: a sound, audible in even a gentle breeze, which the U.S. Forest Service likens to that made by "thousands of fluttering butterfly wings."

D **Sugar Maple.** The leaf of the largest North American maple species is so lovely that Canada put it on its national flag. Each generally has five multi-pointed lobes—plus enough anthocyanin to produce a deep red color. The tree itself produces plentiful sap and is the cornerstone of New England's syrup industry.

E **White Ash.** This tall tree typically grows to between 65 to 100 feet. Baseball enthusiasts admire the wood (which is used to craft bats); while foliage fans admire the compound leaves, each consisting of five to nine slightly serrated, tapering leaflets. They range in hue from burgundy and purple to amber.

F **White Birch.** A papery, light, bright bark makes this slender hardwood easily recognizable. Centuries ago, Native Americans used birch wood to make everything from canoes to medicinal teas. Today's photographers know the bark also makes great pictures since it provides a sharp contrast to the tree's vibrant yellow leaves.

FANTASTIC FALL ITINERARY

The Berkshires

Fall is the perfect time to visit New England—country roads wind through dense forests exploding into reds, oranges, yellows, and purples. For inspiration, here is an itinerary for the truly ambitious that links the most stunning foliage areas; choose a section to explore more closely. Like autumn itself, this route works its way south from northern Vermont into Connecticut, with one or two days in each area.

VERMONT

Northwest Vermont

In Burlington, the elms will be turning colors on the University of Vermont campus. You can ride the ferry across Lake Champlain for great views of Vermont's Green Mountains and New York's Adirondacks. After visiting the resort town of Stowe, detour off Route 100 beneath the cliffs of Smugglers' Notch. The north country's palette unfolds in Newport, where the blue waters of Lake Memphremagog reflect the foliage.

Northeast Kingdom

After a side trip along Lake Willoughby, explore St. Johnsbury, where the Fairbanks Museum and St. Johnsbury Athenaeum reveal Victorian tastes in art and natural-history collecting. In Peacham, stock up for a picnic at the Peacham Store.

NEW HAMPSHIRE

White Mountains and Lakes Region

In New Hampshire, Interstate 93 narrows as it winds through craggy Franconia Notch. Get off the interstate for the sinuous Kancamagus Highway portion of Route 112 that passes through the mountains to Conway. In Center Harbor, in the Lakes Region, you can ride the *MS Mount Washington* for views of the Lake Winnipesaukee shoreline, or ascend to Moultonborough's Castle in the Clouds for a falcon's-eye look at the colors.

Mt. Monadnock

In Hanover, stroll the leafy campus of Dartmouth College, then go for a drive nearby around Lake Sunapee. Several trails climb Mt. Monadnock, near Jaffrey Center, and the surrounding countryside abounds with deciduous forests.

⇨ For local drives perfect for an afternoon, also see our Fall Foliage Drive Spotlights on Western Massachusetts, Connecticut, Rhode Island, Vermont, New Hampshire, and Inland Maine.

THE MOOSE IS LOOSE!

Take "Moose Crossing" signs seriously because things won't end well if you hit an animal that stands six feet tall and weighs 1,200 pounds. Some 75,000 reside in northern New England. To search out these ungainly creatures in the wild, consider an organized moose safari in northern New Hampshire or Maine.

MASSACHUSETTS
The Mohawk Trail

In Shelburne Falls, Massachusetts, the Bridge of Flowers displays the last of autumn's blossoms. Follow the Mohawk Trail section of Route 2 as it ascends into the Berkshire Hills—and stop to take in the view at the hairpin turn just east of North Adams (or drive up Mt. Greylock, the tallest peak in New England, for more stunning vistas). In Williamstown, the Clark Art Institute houses a collection of impressionist works.

The Berkshires

The scenery around Lenox, Stockbridge, and Great Barrington has long attracted the talented and the wealthy. Near U.S. 7, you can visit the homes of novelist Edith Wharton (the Mount, in Lenox), sculptor Daniel Chester French (Chesterwood, in Stockbridge), and diplomat Joseph Choate (Naumkeag, in Stockbridge).

CONNECTICUT
The Litchfield Hills

This area of Connecticut combines the feel of upcountry New England with exclusive urban polish. The wooded shores of Lake Waramaug are home to country inns and wineries in pretty towns. Litchfield has a perfect village green—an idealized New England town center.

FOLIAGE PHOTO HINT

Don't just snap the big panoramic views. Look for single, brilliantly colored trees with interesting elements nearby, like a weathered gray stone wall or a freshly painted white church. These images are often more evocative than big blobs of color or panoramic shots.

LEAF PEEPER PLANNER

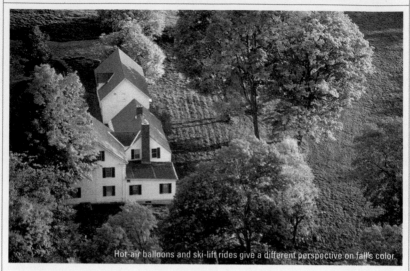

Hot-air balloons and ski-lift rides give a different perspective on fall's color.

Enjoying fall doesn't necessarily require a multistate road trip. If you are short on time (or energy), a simple autumnal stroll might be just the ticket: many state parks even offer free short ranger-led rambles.

HIKE AND BIKE ON A TOUR

You can sign on for foliage-focused hiking holidays with **Country Walkers** (☎ 800/234–6900 ⊕ www.countrywalkers.com) and **Boundless Journeys** (☎ 800/941–8010 ⊕ www.boundlessjourneys.com); or cycling ones with **Discovery Bike Tours** (☎ 800/257–2226 ⊕ www.discoverybik-etours.com) and **VBT Bicycling Vacations** (☎ 800/245–3868, ⊕ www.vbt.com). Individual state tourism boards list similar operators elsewhere.

SOAR ABOVE THE CROWDS

New Hampshire's Cannon Mountain (☎ 603/823–8800 ⊕ www.cannonmt.com) is only one of several New England ski resorts that provides gondola or aerial tram rides during foliage season. Area hot-air balloon operators, like **Balloons of Vermont, LLC** (☎ 802/369–0213 ⊕ www.balloonsofvermont.com), help you take it in from the top.

ROOM AT THE INN?

Accommodations fill quickly in autumn. Vermont's top lodgings sell out months in advance for the first two weeks in October. So book early and expect a two-night minimum stay requirement. If you can't find a quaint inn, try basing yourself at a B&B or off-season ski resort. Also, be prepared for some sticker shock; if you can travel midweek, you'll often save quite a bit.

RIDE THE RAILS OR THE CURRENT

Board the **Essex Steam Train** for a ride through the Connecticut countryside (☎ 800/377–3987 ⊕ www.essexsteam-train.com) or float through northern Rhode Island on the **Blackstone Valley Explorer** riverboat (☎ 401/724–2200 ⊕ www.rivertourblackstone.com).

MASSACHUSETTS FALL FOLIAGE DRIVE

When fall foliage season arrives, the Berkshires are the place to appreciate the autumnal grandeur. Winding roads lined with dramatic trees ablaze—notably maples, birches, and beeches—pass alongside meadows, pasture, farmland, mountains, rivers, and lakes.

Begin in **North Adams**, a city transformed by art, and spend some time at the **Massachusetts Museum of Contemporary Art** (MASS MoCA). Stop by one or two of downtown's smaller art galleries, before checking out the Porches Inn, a row of eye-catching multihue Victorians. Just west of downtown off Route 2, the Notch Road leads into the **Mt. Greylock State Reservation**, ambling upward to the summit. At 3,491 feet, it's the state's highest point and affords expansive views of the countryside. Hike any of the many trails throughout the park, picnic at the peak, or stay for a meal at the rustic **Bascom Lodge**. Continue your descent on the Notch Road to Rockwell Road to exit the park and join Route 7 South.

BEST TIME TO GO

Peak season for leaf viewing in the Berkshires generally happens in mid-October. Trees growing near waterways—and they are plentiful in the area—tend to have more vibrant colors that peak a bit sooner. The state regularly updates fall foliage information by phone and online (☎ 800/632–8038 ⊕ www.massvacation.com).

PLANNING YOUR TIME

This scenic loop is only about 35 miles, but you could easily spend the day leisurely exploring the circuit.

Follow Route 7 South into the small town center of Lanesborough, where you'll turn left onto Summer Street. Horse farms and wide-open pastures make up the landscape, with distant mountain peaks hovering grandly in the background. If you want to pick your own apples, take a 1½-mile detour off Summer Street and stop at **Lakeview Orchard**.

Summer Street continues to tiny Berkshire Village, where you'll pick up Route 8 heading back toward North Adams. Running parallel to Route 8 from Lanesborough to Adams, is the paved **Ashuwillticook Rail Trail** for biking and walking. Right in the midst of two mountain ranges, the trail abuts wetlands, mixed woodland (including beech, birch, and maple trees), the Hoosac River, and the Cheshire Reservoir. In Cheshire, **Whitney's Farm Market** is busy on fall weekends with pony rides, pumpkin picking, a corn maze, and hayrides; plus it sells baked goods like the pumpkin whoopie pie.

Continuing on Route 8, you'll start to leave farm country as you make your way back to North Adams. Once a part of its much larger neighbor, the town of Adams still has active mills and the **Susan B. Anthony Birthplace Museum**. The 1817 Federal home of her birth has been fully restored.

3

Best Fall Foliage Drives MASSACHUSETTS FALL FOLIAGE DRIVE

NEED A BREAK?

Bascom Lodge. Built in the 1930s, this mountaintop lodge retains its rustic charm with comfortable, no-frills lodging and a restaurant in a stunning setting. ⊠ *Mt. Greylock State Reservation, Adams* ☎ *413/743–1591* ⊕ *www.bascomlodge.net* ⊘ *Closed Nov.–May.*

Lakeview Orchard. Here you can pick your own bushel of apples (and other fall fruit) and sip on freshly pressed cider. The friendly farmers also sell homemade pies and pastries, but make sure to sample their singular (and superb) cider doughnuts. ⊠ *94 Old Cheshire Rd., Lanesborough* ☎ *413/448–6009* ⊕ *www. lakevieworchard.com.*

Whitney's Farm Market. Whitney's Farm has a large market with baked goods and a deli; you can also pick your own seasonal fruit. The fun Pumpkin Fest takes place on weekends, mid-September–October. ⊠ *1775 S. State Rd., Cheshire* ☎ *413/442–4749* ⊕ *www. whitneysfarm.com.*

CONNECTICUT FALL FOLIAGE DRIVE

Tucked into the heart of Litchfield County, the crossroads village of New Preston perches above a 20-foot waterfall on the Aspetuck River. Just north of here you'll find Lake Waramaug nestled in the rolling foothills and, to the east, Mt. Tom—both ablaze with rich color every fall.

Start in New Milford and stroll along historic Main Street. Here you'll find one of the longest town greens in the state, as well as many shops, galleries, and restaurants within a short walk. Hop in the car and drive south on Main Street, then turn left to head north on wooded Route 202. About 4 miles north of the green, you'll find the **Hunt Hill Farm**. The former property of the late Skitch Henderson, long-time musical director of the NBC Orchestra and founder of the New York Pops, the farm consists of a gallery, cooking school, shop, and cafe housed in the buildings of two farms, which date to the 1800s. Continue north on Route 202 to the junction of Route 45 and follow signs for Lake Waramaug.

BEST TIME TO GO

Peak foliage in Connecticut occurs early October–early November, according to the state's Department of Energy and Environmental Protection. In season, the website (⊕ www.ct.gov/deep/foliage) includes daily updates on leaf color. Hope for a wet spring, warmer fall days, and cool (but not too cool) fall nights for the most dramatic display.

PLANNING YOUR TIME

It's less than 30 miles from New Milford to the center of Litchfield, but with stops at Hunt Hill Farm, Lake Waramaug, and Mt. Tom you could easily spend half the day enjoying the scenery.

Route 45 will bring you through the tiny village center of New Preston; stop here for a bit of shopping at **Dawn Hill Antiques**. Continue on 45 north to Lake Waramaug. The 8-mile drive around the lake is stunning in autumn with the fiery foliage of red maples, rusty brown oaks, and yellow birches reflected in the water. The beach area of **Lake Waramaug State Park**, about halfway around the lake, is a great place for a picnic, or even a quick dip on a warm fall day. **Hopkins Vineyard** is open daily for tastings; head to its Hayloft Wine Bar to enjoy a glass of wine and the spectacular lake views.

After completing a loop of Lake Waramaug, head back to Route 202 North toward Litchfield. Another excellent leaf-peeping locale is **Mt. Tom State Park**, about 4 miles or so from the junction of Routes 45 and 202. Here you can hike the mile-long trail to the summit and climb to the top of a stone tower that provides 360-degree views of the countryside's colors—the vibrant reds of the sugar maples are always among the most dazzling. After your hike, continue north on Route 202, ending your journey in the quintessential New England town of Litchfield. Peruse the shops and galleries in the town center and end the day with a dinner at the chic **West Street Grill**.

NEED A BREAK?

Dawn Hill Antiques. This shop is filled with mainly Swedish antiques selected by the owners on their regular trips to Europe. ⊠ *11 Main St., New Preston* ☎ *860/868–0066* ⊕ *dawnhillantiques.com.*

Hopkins Vineyard. This winery produces more than 13 different wines, from sparkling to dessert. Tastings are available, and a wine bar in the hayloft with views of the lake serves a fine cheese-and-pâté board. ⊠ *25 Hopkins Rd., off N. Shore Rd., New Preston* ☎ *860/868–7954* ⊕ *www.hopkinsvineyard.com* ⚲ *Tours $20.*

West Street Grill. This sophisticated dining room on the town green is the place to see and be seen. It's the perfect spot for a casual lunch or formal dinner. The house-made ice creams and sorbets are amazing. ⊠ *43 West St.* ☎ *860/567–3885* ⊕ *www.weststreetgrill.com.*

3

Best Fall Foliage Drives

CONNECTICUT FALL FOLIAGE DRIVE

RHODE ISLAND FALL FOLIAGE DRIVE

The Rhode Island State Tree is the red maple, whose leaves turn to shades of gold, purple, and scarlet in fall.

This tiny state is also home to such diverse species as scarlet oak, white oak, northern red oak, yellow birch, gray birch, ash, and black cherry. Pine forests dominate the southern woodlands, so the most dramatic leaf peeping is in the northern and western regions. Along the way, you'll find dense forests, rolling meadows with centuries-old stone walls, an occasional orchard or pumpkin patch, and archetypal New England country stores.

This tour through the state's quieter corners begins in Providence, where you can stroll across **Brown University's** dignified campus of handsome academic buildings and towering shade trees. Drive north from Providence on Route 122 and then Route 114 north for about 9 miles to Cumberland, a small town with undulating woodland crowned by a canopy of sugar maple, scarlet oak, and birch trees. Stop at **Diamond Hill Vineyards,** whose grapevines and apple trees yield an intriguing selection of wines, including some sweet varieties made from fruits and berries grown on-site—perfect on a cool October day.

BEST TIME TO GO

Foliage peaks in most of Rhode Island in the second and third weeks of October, beginning in the northwestern corner and moving south toward the coast. Color can last more than two weeks in years without big storms but with plenty of cool, crisp autumn nights. If you don't have long to linger, check out the stunning views from Prospect Terrace Park, on Providence's East Side, or head for the Southeastern Coast and take a walk along the rural trails of Tiverton's Weetamoo Woods and Little Compton's Wilbour Woods.

The rest of the tour meanders through some of Rhode Island's most pastoral countryside. Drive west about 12 miles on Route 116 to Greenville, turning west on U.S. 44 for 7 miles to the hamlet of Chepachet, where Colonial and Victorian buildings contain antiques shops and quirky stores. Don't miss **Brown & Hopkins Country Store,** one of the country's oldest continuously operating general stores—complete with a nostalgia-inducing candy counter—or the **Tavern on Main,** a restaurant in a rambling 18th-century building that some say is haunted.

Follow U.S. 44 west 5 miles to the burst of changing colors in **Pulaski Memorial Recreation Area.** Turn left onto Route 94 and follow this for about 13 miles to Route 102, then continue southeast another 20 miles to Exeter. This mostly undeveloped route from Chepachet to Exeter is lined with pristine hardwood forests, with an abundance of red maple, white oak, beech, elm, and poplar trees.

From Route 102, continue east to Wickford, a Colonial seaport whose pretty harbor opens to Narragansett Bay. The town's oak- and beech-shaded lanes are perfect for a late-afternoon stroll among the galleries and boutiques.

The drive totals about 80 miles and takes 4–8 hours, depending on stops.

3

Best Fall Foliage Drives RHODE ISLAND FALL FOLIAGE DRIVE

NEED A BREAK?

Brown & Hopkins Country Store. Opened in 1809, this store carries candles, reproduction antiques, penny candy, and handmade soaps. ⊠ 1179 Putnam Pike, Chepachet ☎ 401/568–4830 ⊕ www. brownandhopkins.com.

Diamond Hill Vineyards. This winery produces Pinot Noir from grapes grown on-site, as well as wines made from local apples, blueberries, and other fruit. ⊠ 3145 Diamond Hill Rd., Cumberland ☎ 401/333–2751 ⊕ www. diamondhillvineyards. com ☑ Free.

Tavern on Main. For lunch, try the homemade seafood stuffies or the lobster roll. ⊠ 1157 Putnam Pike, Chepachet ☎ 401/710–9788 ⊕ www. tavernonmainri.com.

Pulaski Memorial Recreation Area. The 100 acre recreation area has fishing, picnic spots, easy hiking trails, and the 13 acre Peck Pond. ⊠ 151 Pulaski Rd., Chepachet ☎ 401/568–2085 ⊕ www.riparks.com.

VERMONT FALL FOLIAGE DRIVE

Nearly 80% of Vermont is forested, with cities few and far between. The state's interior is a rural playground for leaf peepers, and it's widely considered to exhibit the most intense range of colors anywhere on the continent. Its tiny towns and hamlets—the few distractions from the dark reds, yellows, oranges, and russets—are as pristine as nature itself.

Begin this drive in Manchester Village, along the old-fashioned, well-to-do homes lining Main Street, and continue south to Arlington, North Bennington, and Old Bennington. Stop just a mile south along Route 7A at **Hildene**. The 412 acres of explorable grounds at the estate of Abraham Lincoln's son are ablaze with color, and the views over the Battenkill Valley are as good as any you can find. Drive south another mile along 7A to the **Equinox Valley Nursery,** where you can sample delicious apple cider and doughnuts amid views of the arresting countryside. A few more miles south along 7A is the small town of Arlington.

BEST TIME TO GO

Late September and early October are the times to go, with the southern area peaking about a week later than the north. Remember to book hotels in advance. The state has a Fall Foliage Hotline and an online interactive map (☎ 802/828–3239 ⊕ www. foliage-vermont.com).

PLANNING YOUR TIME

The drive from Manchester to Bennington outlined here takes just 30 minutes, but a relaxed pace is best suited to taking in all the sights.

From Route 7A in Arlington you can take two adventurous and stunning detours. One is pure foliage: follow Route 313 west a few miles to the New York State border for more beautiful views. Or head east 1 mile to East Arlington, where there's a delightful chocolate emporium. (You can continue even farther east from this spot to Kelly Stand Road leading into the Green Mountains—a little-known route that can't be beat.) Back on 7A South in Arlington, stop at the **Cheese House,** the delightfully cheesy roadside attraction.

Farther south in Shaftsbury is **Clear Brook Farm,** a brilliant place for fresh produce and pumpkins. Robert Frost spent much of his life in South Shaftsbury, and you can learn about his life at his former home, the **Stone House.** From South Shaftsbury take Route 67 through North Bennington and continue on to Route 67A in Old Bennington. Ride the elevator up the 306-foot-high **Bennington Battle Monument** to survey the season's progress across four states. Back down from the clouds, walk a few serene blocks to the cemetery of the **Old First Church,** where Robert Frost is buried, and contemplate his autumnal poem, "Nothing Gold Can Stay."

NEED A BREAK?

The Cheese House. Get your Vermont cheddar fix at this shop shaped like a cheese wheel. It also sells maple syrup, chocolate, wine, and other local products and gifts. ⊠ *5187 Rte. 7A, Arlington* ☎ *802/375–9033* ⊕ *www. thevermontcheese-house.com* ⊠ *Free.*

Clear Brook Farm. Set on more than 25 acres, this certified organic farm sells its own produce, in addition to plants, baked goods, and other seasonal treats. ⊠ *47 Hidden Valley Rd., Manchester* ☎ *802/442–4273* ⊕ *www.clearbrook-farm.com.*

Equinox Valley Nursery. This nursery carries fresh produce, seasonal snacks, cider doughnuts, and is full of family-friendly fall activities: a corn maze, hayrides, and pumpkin carving. Kids especially will appreciate the 300-odd scarecrows scattered throughout the property. ⊠ *1158 Main St., Manchester* ☎ *802/362–2610* ⊕ *www. equinoxvalleynursery. com* ⊠ *Free.*

NEW HAMPSHIRE FALL FOLIAGE DRIVE

Quaint villages graced with green commons, white town halls, and covered bridges: southwestern New Hampshire is dominated by the imposing rocky summit of Mt. Monadnock and the brilliant colors of autumn. Kancamagus Highway is another classic foliage route, but for more solitude and less traffic, try this more accessible route that peaks a few weeks later than the state's far north.

The Granite State is the second-most-forested state in the nation; by Columbus Day the colors of the leaves of its maple, birch, elm, oak, beech, and ash trees range from green to gold, purple to red, and orange to auburn. Routes 12, 101, 202, and 124 compose a loop around **Mt. Monadnock**. Start on the picturesque Main Street in Keene with a stop for coffee at Prime Roast; for New Hampshire–made products, take a walk on Main Street or detour west on Route 9 to reach **Stonewall Farm** for something more country.

BEST TIME TO GO

The best time to view foliage in southern New Hampshire is generally early October, but it can vary by up to four weeks. For updates about leaf changes, visit the Foliage Tracker page on the website of Visit New Hampshire (☎ 800/258–3608 ⊕ www.visitnh.gov).

PLANNING YOUR TIME

Expect to travel about 55 miles. The journey can take up to a full day if you stop to explore along the way.

From Keene, travel east on Route 101 through Dublin. In **Peterborough**, browse the local stores like the Peterborough Basket Company—the country's oldest continuously operating basket manufacturer in the country—whose attitudes and selections mirror the state's independent spirit.

Then turn south on Route 202 toward Jaffrey Village. Just west on Route 124, in historic Jaffrey Center, be sure to visit the **Meeting House Cemetery,** where author Willa Cather is buried. One side trip, 4 miles south on Route 202, leads to the majestic **Cathedral of the Pines** in Rindge, one of the best places in the region for foliage viewing because evergreens offset the brilliant shades of red.

Heading west on Route 124, you can take Dublin Road to the main entrance of **Monadnock State Park** or continue along to the Old Toll Road parking area for one of the most popular routes up the mountain, the **Halfway House Trail**. All the hiking trails have great views, including the area's many lakes. Continuing on Route 124, head southwest on Fitzwilliam Road to Fitzwilliam. If you have time, pop into **Bloomin' Antiques** to browse their selection of fine art and unusual antiques. If you need a bite to eat before heading back to Keene along Route 12, stop by **The Fitzwilliam Inn**, which was once a stagecoach stop.

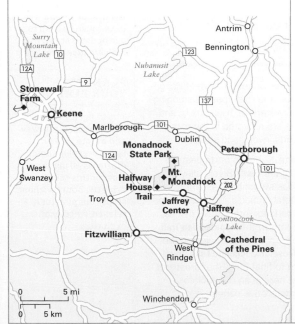

NEED A BREAK?

Stonewall Farm.
The only working dairy farm in the region open to the public, Stonewall is open daily and presents an active schedule of events, including maple sugaring and seasonal horse-drawn hayrides. Walking trails wind throughout the farm. There's fine hiking in good weather, and in winter you can borrow snowshoes for free. Young children love the discovery room, and the interactive greenhouse is geared for all ages. ⊠ 242 Chesterfield Rd., Keene ☎ 603/357–7278 ⊕ www.stonewallfarm. org.

Bloomin' Antiques.
Fine art and unusual antiques. ⊠ 3 Templeton Pike, Village Green, Fitzwilliam ☎ 603/585–6688 ⊕ www.bloominantiques.com.

The Fitzwilliam Inn.
The dinner-only menu features burgers, sandwiches, and salads. And, there are 10 rooms in case you want to stay the night. ⊠ Town Common, 62 Rte.119, Fitzwilliam ☎ 603/585–9000 ⊕ www.fitzwilliaminn. com.

3

Best Fall Foliage Drives NEW HAMPSHIRE FALL FOLIAGE DRIVE

INLAND MAINE FALL FOLIAGE DRIVE

Swaths of pine, spruce, and fir trees offset the red, orange, and yellow of maples and birches along this popular foliage drive through western Maine's mountains, but hardwoods largely dominate the landscape.

Wending its way to the four-season resort town of Rangeley, near its northern terminus, the route passes stunning overlooks, forest-lined lakes, waterfalls, hiking trails, and a state park. Mountain vistas are reflected in the many (often connected) lakes, ponds, rivers, and streams.

From U.S. 2 in Mexico, Route 17 heads north past old homesteads and fields along the Swift River Valley before making a mountainous switchback ascent to **Height of Land,** the drive's literal pinnacle. The must-stop overlook here has off-road parking, interpretive panels, stone seating, and a short path to the **Appalachian Trail.** On a clear day, you can look west to mountains on the New Hampshire border. **Mooselookmeguntic Lake** and **Upper Richardson Lake** seem to float amid the forestland below. A few miles north of here is an overlook for Rangeley Lake, also with interpretive panels.

BEST TIME TO GO

Fall color usually peaks in the Rangeley area in the first or second week of October. Get fall foliage updates at ⊕ *www. mainefoliage.com.*

PLANNING YOUR TIME

The Rangeley Lakes National Scenic Byway and a state byway (⊕ *www.exploremaine. org/byways*) make up most of this 58-mile drive (1½ hours without stops), but plan for a relaxed, full day of exploring.

In tiny, welcoming Oquossoc, where Routes 17 and 4 meet, stop at the **Gingerbread House Restaurant** for breakfast or lunch, or for just baked goods or an ice cream. The hamlet is also home to the **Rangeley Outdoor Sporting Heritage Museum,** where you can learn why visitors have come here to fish, hunt, and enjoy the outdoors since the mid-1800s. The trailhead for Bald Mountain, a popular hike, is just outside the village.

Rangeley, 7 miles east on Route 4, has restaurants, inns, a waterfront park, and outdoorsy shops. The countryside sweeps into view along public hiking trails at the 175-acre **Wilhelm Reich Museum.** There's also hiking at Rangeley Lakes Trail Center on Saddleback Mountain.

The road to **Rangeley Lake State Park** is accessible from both Routes 4 and 17, as is the **Appalachian Trail.** Overhanging foliage frames waterfalls at the scenic rest areas at each end of the drive: at Coos Canyon on Route 17 en route to Height of Land, and at Smalls Falls on Route 4 near Madrid, the terminus. Both spots have swimming holes, several falls, and paths with views of their drops. Coos Canyon is along the Swift River, a destination for recreational gold panning. You can rent or buy panning equipment at Coos Canyon Rock and Gift, across from its namesake. It also sells sandwiches and snacks.

3

Best Fall Foliage Drives INLAND MAINE FALL FOLIAGE DRIVE

NEED A BREAK?

Rangeley Lakes Heritage Trust. The trust protects about 13,000 acres of land in the Rangeley Lakes area. Both online and at its Oquossoc office, the trust has maps and descriptions of its 32 miles of recreational trails and access roads, along with information about fishing, hunting, snowmobiling, picnicking, and other outdoor activities. ⊠ 52 Carry Rd., Oquossoc ☎ 207/864–7311 ⊕ www. rlht.org.

Wilhelm Reich Museum. This museum showcases the life and work of controversial physician-scientist Wilhelm Reich (1897–1957). There are magnificent views from the observatory, and great trails throughout the 175-acre property. ⊠ 19 Orgonon Circle, off Rte. 4, Rangeley ☎ 207/864–3443 ⊕ www.wilhelmreich-trust.org ⊅ Museum $6, grounds free.

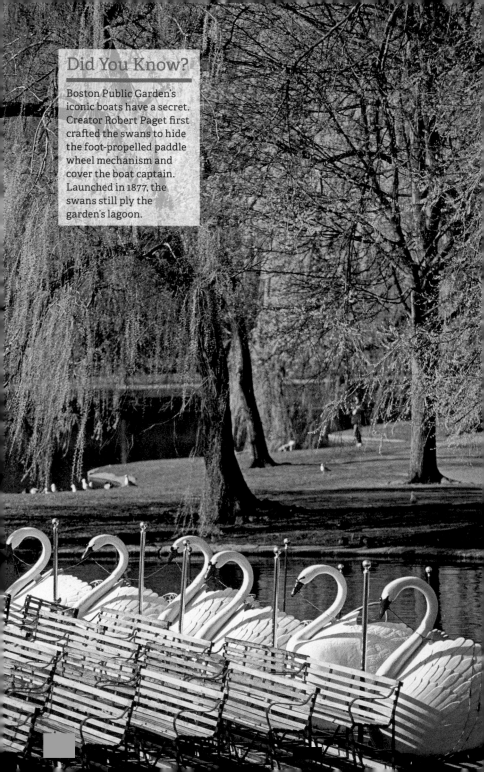

Did You Know?

Boston Public Garden's iconic boats have a secret. Creator Robert Paget first crafted the swans to hide the foot-propelled paddle wheel mechanism and cover the boat captain. Launched in 1877, the swans still ply the garden's lagoon.

Chapter 4

BOSTON AND ENVIRONS

Updated by
Kim MacKinnon

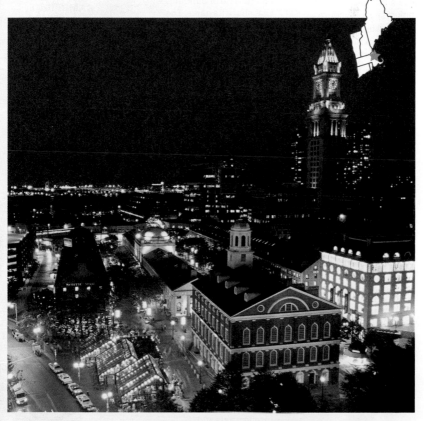

⊙ Sights	🍴 Restaurants	🛏 Hotels	🛍 Shopping	🍸 Nightlife
★★★★★	★★★★★	★★★★★	★★★★★	★★★★★

WELCOME TO BOSTON AND ENVIRONS

TOP REASONS TO GO

★ **Freedom's Ring:** Walk through America's early history on the 2½-mile Freedom Trail that snakes through town.

★ **Ivy-Draped Campus:** Hang in Harvard Square like a collegian or hit the university's museums: the Sackler (ancient art), the Botanical Museum, the Peabody (archaeology), and the Natural History Museum.

★ **Posh Purchases:** Strap on some stilettos and join the quest for fashionable finds on Newbury Street, Boston's answer to Manhattan's 5th Avenue.

★ **Sacred Ground:** Root for (or boo) the Red Sox at baseball's most hallowed shrine, Fenway Park.

★ **Tea Time:** Interact with the city's history at the Boston Tea Party Ships & Museum: greet reenactors and explore replicas of the ships at the actual spot where the tea met the sea.

1 **Beacon Hill, Boston Common, and the Old West End.** The Brahmins' old stomping ground has many landmarks. The Old West End has the Museum of Science and TD Garden.

2 **Government Center and the North End.** The Government Center area is home to Faneuil Hall and the trio of buildings that share its name. The small North End is full of history.

3 **Charlestown.** Charlestown's Freedom Trail sights can't be missed. The Bunker Hill Monument is a towering tribute to a pivotal 1775 battle; the USS *Constitution* highlights the neighborhood's naval heritage.

4 **Downtown.** This mazelike section of central Boston encompasses the Financial District and Downtown Crossing.

5 **The Back Bay.** Back Bay's upscale shops, restaurants, and lodgings sit alongside attractions like the Public Garden and Public Library.

6 **The Fenway.** Fenway Park, the Museum of Fine Arts, and the Isabella Stewart Gardner Museum are here.

7 **Cambridge.** Cambridge has long been a haven for intellectuals and iconoclasts.

There's history and culture around every bend in Boston—skyscrapers nestle next to historic hotels, while modern marketplaces line the antique cobblestone streets. But to Bostonians, living in a city that blends yesterday and today is just another day in their beloved Beantown.

It's difficult to fit Boston into a stereotype because of the city's many layers. The deepest is the historical one, the place where musket-bearing revolutionaries vowed to hang together or hang separately. The next tier, a dense spread of Brahmin fortune and fortitude, might be labeled the Hub. It was this elite caste of Boston society, descended from wealthy English Protestants who first settled the state, that funded and patronized the city's universities and cultural institutions, gaining Boston the label "the Athens of America" and felt only pride in the slogan "Banned in Boston." Over that layer lies Beantown, home to the Red Sox faithful and the raucous Bruins fans who crowded the old Boston "*Gah*-den"; this is the city whose ethnic loyalties account for its many distinct neighborhoods. Crowning these layers are the students who converge on the area's universities and colleges every fall.

Planning

WHEN TO GO
Summer brings reliable sunshine, sailboats to Boston Harbor, concerts to the Esplanade, and café tables to assorted sidewalks. If you're dreaming of a classic shore vacation, summer is prime.

Weather-wise, late spring and fall are the optimal times to visit Boston. Aside from mild temperatures, the former offers blooming gardens throughout the city and the latter sees the surrounding countryside ablaze with brilliantly colored foliage. At both times expect crowds.

Autumn attracts hordes of leaf peepers, and more than 250,000 students flood into the area each September, then pull out in May and June. Hotels and restaurants fill up quickly on move-in, move-out, and graduation weekends.

Winters are cold and windy.

RESTAURANTS
In a city synonymous with tradition, Boston chefs have spent recent years rewriting culinary history. The stuffy, wood-paneled formality is gone; the endless renditions of chowdah, lobster, and cod have retired. A crop of young chefs has ascended, opening small, upscale neighborhood spots that use New England ingredients to delicious effect.

Traditional eats can still be found (Durgin-Park remains as the best place to get baked beans), but many diners now gravitate toward innovative food in understated environs. Whether you're looking for casual French, down-home Southern cooking, some of the best sushi in the country, or Vietnamese *banh mi* sandwiches, Boston restaurants are ready to deliver. The fish and shellfish brought in from nearby shores continue to inform the regional cuisine: expect to see several seafood options on local menus, but don't expect them to be boiled or dumped into the lobster stew that JFK loved. Instead, you might be offered swordfish with salsa verde, cornmeal-crusted scallops, or lobster cassoulet with black truffles.

In many ways, though, Boston remains solidly skeptical of trends. If you close your eyes in the North End, Boston's Little Italy, you can easily imagine you're in Rome circa 1955. And over in the university culture of Cambridge, places like Henrietta's Table and Oleana espoused the locavore and slow-food movements before they became buzzwords. *Restaurant reviews have been shortened. For full information, visit Fodors.com.*

What It Costs

$	$$	$$$	$$$$
AT DINNER			
under $18	$18–$24	$25–$35	over $35

HOTELS

At one time great lodging was scarce in Boston. If you were a persnickety blue blood in town to visit relatives, you checked into the Charles or the old Ritz on Newbury. If you were a parent in town to see your kid graduate from one of the city's many universities, you suffered through a stay at a run-down chain. And if you were a young couple in town for a little romance, well, you could just forget it. A dearth of suitable rooms practically defined Boston. Oh, how things have changed.

In the early 2000s, Boston finally got wise to modernization, and a rush of new construction took the local hotel scene by storm. Sleek, boutique

accommodations began inviting guests to Cambridge and Downtown, areas once relegated to alumni and business traveler sets. New, megaluxury lodgings like the Mandarin Oriental and the Taj (the latter, in that old Ritz spot) infiltrated posh Back Bay, while high-end, hipster-friendly spots like the W Boston and Ames are drawing visitors to up-and-coming areas Downtown. Even mostly residential areas like the South End now draw discerning boarders, thanks to the revamped Chandler and the nearby Inn@ St. Botolph.

Speaking of revamped, it seems that nearly every hotel in town just got a face-lift. From spruced-up decor (good-bye, grandma's bedspread; hello, puffy white duvets) to hopping restaurant-bars to new spas and fitness centers, Boston's lodgings are feeling the competitive heat and acting accordingly. You don't just get a room anymore—you get an experience.

Many properties have stellar week-end deals, so you may be able to try an upscale Fodor's Choice even if you thought it was out of your budget. *Hotel reviews have been shortened. For full information, visit Fodors.com.*

What It Costs

$	$$	$$$	$$$$
FOR TWO PEOPLE			
under $200	$200–$299	$300–$399	over $399

PERFORMING ARTS

Boston's cultural attractions are a bracing mix of old-world aesthetics and new-world experimentation. At the classical end of the spectrum, revered institutions like the Museum of Fine Arts, the Boston Symphony Orchestra and Boston Pops, and the Isabella Stewart Gardner Museum offer refined experiences. For less reverential attitudes toward the arts, the Institute of Contemporary Art (ICA) features edgy electronic concerts, and graffiti and multimedia exhibitions. Museums like the MFA, the Gardner, and the ICA also host special shows and festivals in strikingly handsome performance spaces.

ACTIVITIES

Everything you've heard about the zeal of Boston fans is true; you cheer, and you pray, and you root some more. "Red Sox Nation" witnessed a miracle in 2004, with the reverse of the curse and the team's first World Series victory since 1918.

Then in 2007 and 2013 they proved it wasn't just a fluke with two more Series wins. In 2008 the Celtics ended their 18-year NBA championship drought with a victory over longtime rivals the LA Lakers. And five-time champions the New England Patriots are still a force to be reckoned with.

Bostonians' fervor for sports is equally evident in their leisure-time activities. Harsh winters keep locals wrapped up for months, only to emerge at the earliest sign of oncoming spring. Once the mercury tops freezing and the snows begin to melt, Boston's extensive parks, paths, woods, and waterways teem with sun worshippers and athletes.

Except when frozen over, the waterways coursing through the city serve as a playground for boaters of all stripes. All types of pleasure craft, with the exception of inflatables, are allowed from the Charles River and Inner Harbor to North Washington Street on the waters of Boston Harbor, Dorchester inner and outer bays, and the Neponset River from the Granite Avenue Bridge to Dorchester Bay.

SHOPPING

Boston's shops are generally open Monday through Saturday from 10 or 11 until 6 or 7 and Sunday noon to 5. Many stay open until 8 pm one night a week, usually Thursday. Malls are open Monday through Saturday from 9 or 10 until 8 or 9 and Sunday noon to 6.

Boston's shops and department stores lie concentrated in the area bounded by Quincy Market, the Back Bay, and Downtown, with plenty of bargains in the Downtown Crossing area. The South End's gentrification creates its own kind of consumerist milieus, from housewares shops to avant-garde art galleries. In Cambridge you can find many shops around Harvard and Central squares, with independent boutiques migrating west along Massachusetts Avenue ("Mass Ave.") toward Porter Square and beyond.

PLANNING YOUR TIME

If you have a couple of days, hit Boston's highlights—Beacon Hill, the Freedom Trail, and the Public Garden—the first day, and then check out the Museum of Fine Arts or the Isabella Stewart Gardner Museum the morning of the second day. Reserve day two's afternoon for an excursion to Harvard or shopping on Newbury Street.

GETTING HERE AND AROUND
AIR TRAVEL

Boston's major airport, Logan International (BOS), is across the harbor from Downtown, about 2 miles outside the city center, and can be reached by taxi, water taxi, or bus/subway via MBTA's Silver or Blue line. Logan has four passenger terminals, identified by letters A, B, C, and E. A free airport shuttle runs between the terminals and airport hotels. Some airlines use different terminals for international and domestic flights; most international flights arrive at Terminal E. A visitor center in Terminal C offers tourist information. T.F. Green Airport, in Providence, Rhode Island, and the Manchester Boston Regional Airport in Manchester, New Hampshire, are both about an hour from Boston.

AIRPORT INFORMATION Logan International Airport (Boston) ⊠ *I–90 east to Ted Williams Tunnel, Boston* ☎ *800/235–6426* ⊕ *www.massport.com/logan-airport* Ⓜ *Airport.* **Manchester Boston Regional Airport** ⊠ *Off I–293N/Rte. 101W, Exit 13,*

Manchester ☎ 603/624–6539 ⊕ www.
flymanchester.com. **T.F. Green Airport**
✉ 2000 Post Rd., off I-95, Exit 13, Warwick ☎ 401/691–2471⊕ www.pvdairport.
com.

CAR TRAVEL

In a place where roads often evolved
from cow paths, driving is no simple
task. A surfeit of one-way streets and
inconsistent signage add to the confu-
sion. Street parking is hard to come by,
as much of it is resident-permit-only.
Your own car is helpful if you're taking
side trips, but for exploring the city it will
only be a burden. Also, Bostonians give
terrible directions, since few of them
actually drive.

PUBLIC TRANSIT

The "T," as the Massachusetts Bay Transportation Authority's subway system is
nicknamed, is the cornerstone of an efficient, far-reaching public transit network
that also includes aboveground trains,
buses, and ferries. Its five color-coded
lines will put you within a block of almost
anywhere you want to go. Subways operate from about 5:30 am to 12:30 am, as
do buses, which crisscross the city and
reach into suburbia.

A standard adult subway fare is $2.25
with a CharlieCard or $2.75 with a ticket
or cash. For buses it's $1.70 with a Char-
lieCard or $2 with a ticket or cash (more
if you are using an Inner or Outer Express
bus). Commuter rail and ferry fares vary
by route; yet all options charge seniors
and students reduced prices, and kids
under 11 ride free with a paying adult.
Contact the MBTA (☎ 617/222–3200,
800/392–6100 ⊕ www.mbta.com) for
schedules, routes, and rates.

TAXI TRAVEL

Cabs are available 24/7. Rides within the
city cost $2.60 for the first 1/7 mile and
40¢ for each 1/7 mile thereafter (tolls,
where applicable, are extra).

VISITOR INFORMATION

Contact the city and state tourism
offices for details about seasonal events,
discount passes, trip planning, and
attraction information. The National Park
Service has a Boston office for Boston's
historic sites that provides maps and
directions. The Welcome Center and Boston Common Visitor Information Center
offer general information. The Cambridge
Tourism Office's information booth is in
Harvard Square, near the main entrance
to the Harvard T stop.

**CONTACTS Boston Common Visitor Informa-
tion Center** ✉ Downtown ☎ 617/536–4100
⊕ www.bostonusa.com/visit/planyourtrip/
resources/vic. **Cambridge Tourism Visitor
Booth** ✉ 0 Harvard Sq., Harvard Square
☎ 800/862–5678, 617/441–2884 ⊕ www.
cambridge-usa.org. **Greater Boston
Convention and Visitors Bureau** ✉ Back
Bay ☎ 888/733–2678, 617/536–4100
⊕ www.bostonusa.com. **Massachusetts
Office of Travel and Tourism** ✉ Downtown
☎ 800/227–6277, 617/973–8500 ⊕ www.
massvacation.com. **National Parks Service
Visitor Center** ✉ Faneuil Hall, Downtown
☎ 617/242–5642 ⊕ www.nps.gov/bost.

ONLINE RESOURCES

Boston.com, home of the Boston Globe
online, has news and feature articles,
ample travel information, and links to
towns throughout Massachusetts. The
Bostonian Society (⊕ bostonhistory.
org) answers some frequently asked
questions about Beantown history on its
website. The iBoston (⊕ www.iboston.
org) page has wonderful photographs of
architecturally and historically important buildings. The Improper Bostonian
(⊕ www.improper.com) and WickedLo-
cal (⊕ www.wickedlocal.com) provide
a more relaxed (and irreverent) take on
Boston news and information.

Beacon Hill, Boston Common, and the Old West End

Past and present home of the old-money elite, contender for the "Most Beautiful" award among the city's neighborhoods, and hallowed address for many literary lights, Beacon Hill is Boston at its most Bostonian. The redbrick elegance of its narrow streets sends you back to the 19th century just as surely as if you had stumbled into a time machine. But Beacon Hill residents would never make the social faux pas of being out-of-date. The neighborhood is home to hip boutiques and trendy restaurants frequented by young, affluent professionals rather than DAR (Daughters of the American Revolution) matrons.

Beacon Hill

 ### Sights

Central Burying Ground

CEMETERY | The Central Burying Ground may seem an odd feature for a public park, but remember that in 1756, when the land was set aside, this was a lonely corner of the Common. It's the final resting place of Tories and Patriots alike, as well as many British casualties of the Battle of Bunker Hill. The most famous person buried here is Gilbert Stuart, the portraitist best known for his likenesses of George and Martha Washington; he died a poor man in 1828. The Burying Ground is open daily 9 to 5. ☒ *Boylston St. near Tremont, Beacon Hill* ⊕ *www.cityofboston.gov/parks/hbgi/CentralBuryingCentral.asp* Ⓜ *Park St., Boylston.*

Louisburg Square

NEIGHBORHOOD | One of Beacon Hill's most charming corners, Louisburg Square (proper Bostonians always pronounce the "s") was an 1840s model for a town-house development that was never built on the Hill because of space restrictions. Today, the grassy square, enclosed by a wrought-iron fence, belongs collectively to the owners of the houses facing it. The statue at the north end of the green is of Columbus, the one at the south end of Aristides the Just; both were donated in 1850 by a Greek merchant who lived on the square. The houses, most of which are now divided into apartments and condominiums, have seen their share of famous tenants, including author and critic William Dean Howells at Nos. 4 and 16, and the Alcotts at No. 10 (Louisa May not only lived but also died here, on the day of her father's funeral). In 1852 the singer Jenny Lind was married in the parlor of No. 20. Louisburg Square is also the current home of former U.S. secretary of state John Kerry.

There's a legend that Louisburg Square was the location of the Rev. William Blaxton's spring, although there's no water there today. Blaxton, or Blackstone, was one of the first Bostonians, having come to the Shawmut Peninsula in the mid-1620s. When the Puritans, who had settled in Charlestown, found their water supply inadequate, Blaxton invited them to move across the river, where he assured them they would find an "excellent spring." Just a few years later, he sold them all but 6 acres of the peninsula he had bought from the Native Americans and decamped to Rhode Island, seeking greater seclusion; a plaque at 50 Beacon Street commemorates him. ☒ *Between Mt. Vernon and Pickney Sts., Beacon Hill* Ⓜ *Park St.*

★ Massachusetts State House

BUILDING | FAMILY | On July 4, 1795, the surviving fathers of the Revolution were on hand to enshrine the ideals of their new Commonwealth in a graceful seat of government designed by Charles Bulfinch. Governor Samuel Adams and Paul Revere laid the cornerstone; Revere would later roll the copper sheathing for the dome.

Bulfinch's neoclassical design is poised between Georgian and Federal; its finest features are the delicate Corinthian columns of the portico, the graceful pediment and window arches, and the vast yet visually weightless golden dome (gilded in 1874 and again in 1997). During World War II the dome was painted gray so that it would not reflect moonlight during blackouts and thereby offer a target to anticipated Axis bombers. It's capped with a pinecone, a symbol of the importance of pinewood, which was integral to the construction of Boston's early houses and churches; it also serves as a reminder of the state's early connection to Maine, once part of Massachusetts.

Inside the building are Doric Hall, with its statuary and portraits; the Hall of Flags, where an exhibit shows the battle flags from all the wars in which Massachusetts regiments have participated; the Great Hall, an open space used for state functions that houses 351 flags from the cities and towns of Massachusetts; the governor's office; and the chambers of the House and Senate. The Great Hall contains a giant, modernistic clock designed by New York artist R.M. Fischer. Its installation in 1986 at a cost of $100,000 was roundly slammed as a symbol of legislative extravagance. There's also a wealth of statuary, including figures of Horace Mann, Daniel Webster, and a youthful-looking President John F. Kennedy in full stride. Just outside Doric Hall is *Hear Us,* a series of six bronze busts honoring the contributions of women to public life in Massachusetts. But perhaps the best-known piece of artwork in the building is the carved wooden *Sacred Cod,* mounted in the Old State House in 1784 as a symbol of the commonwealth's maritime wealth. It was moved, with much fanfare, to Bulfinch's structure in 1798. By 1895, when it was hung in the new House chambers, the representatives had begun to consider the Cod their unofficial mascot—so much so that when *Harvard*

Did You Know?

Beacon Hill's north slope played a key part in African American history. A community of free blacks lived here in the 1800s; many worshipped at the African Meeting House, established in 1805 and still standing. It came to be known as the "Black Faneuil Hall" for the fervent antislavery activism that started within its walls.

Lampoon wags "codnapped" it in 1933, the House refused to meet in session until the fish was returned, three days later. You can take a guided tour or do a self-guided tour. ✉ *Beacon St. between Hancock and Bowdoin Sts., Beacon Hill* ☎ *617/727–3676* ⊕ *www.sec.state. ma.us/trs/trsidx.htm* 🎟 *Free* ⊗ *Closed weekends* Ⓜ *Park St.*

Museum of African American History

MUSEUM | FAMILY | Ever since runaway slave Crispus Attucks became one of the famous victims of the Boston Massacre of 1770, the African American community of Boston has played an important part in the city's history. Throughout the 19th century, abolition was the cause célèbre for Boston's intellectual elite, and during that time, blacks came to thrive in neighborhoods throughout the city. The Museum of African American History was established in 1964 to promote this history. The umbrella organization includes a trio of historic sites: the Abiel Smith School, the first public school in the nation built specifically for black children; the African Meeting House, where in 1832 the New England Anti-Slavery Society was formed under the leadership of William Lloyd Garrison; and the African Meeting House on the island of Nantucket, off the coast of Cape Cod. Park Service personnel lead tours of the **Black Heritage Trail**, starting from the Shaw Memorial

Beacon Hill,
Boston Common,
and the Old West End

KEY

1 *Exploring Sights*
1 *Restaurants*
1 *Hotels*
Ⓣ *Subway station*
- - *Freedom Trail*
- - *Black Heritage Trail*

on Boston Common. The museum is the site of activities, including lectures, children's storytelling, and concerts focusing on black composers. ⊠ *46 Joy St., Beacon Hill* ☎ *617/725–0022* ⊕ *maah.org* 🎫 *$10* ⊙ *Closed Sun.* Ⓜ *Park St.*

🍴 Restaurants

Lala Rokh

$$$ | **MIDDLE EASTERN** | A rotating gallery of Persian art adorns the walls of this pearl-gray eatery specializing in home-style Iranian dishes. Along with classics such as *fesejan,* duck leg in a satiny pomegranate-walnut sauce, you'll find brain fritters, smoky eggplant puree, *pollo* (rice dishes), kebabs, and richly spiced lamb stews, including one seasoned with dried lime. **Known for**: authentic Persian cuisine; home-style dishes; exotic, yet approachable, seasonings. 💲 *Average main: $26* ⊠ *97 Mt. Vernon St., Beacon Hill* ☎ *617/720–5511* ⊕ *www.lalarokh. com* ⊙ *No lunch* Ⓜ *Charles/MGH.*

★ No. 9 Park

$$$$ | **EUROPEAN** | The stellar cuisine at chef Barbara Lynch's first restaurant continues to draw plenty of well-deserved attention from its place in the shadow of the State House's golden dome. Settle into the plush but unpretentious dining room and indulge in pumpkin risotto with rare lamb or the memorably rich prune-stuffed gnocchi drizzled with bits of foie gras, the latter of which is always offered even if you don't see it on the menu. **Known for:** upscale French-Italian dishes; polished service; prune-stuffed gnocchi with foie gras. 💲 *Average main: $46* ⊠ *9 Park St., Beacon Hill* ☎ *617/742–9991* ⊕ *www.no9park.com* Ⓜ *Park St.*

Hotels

Beacon Hill Hotel & Bistro

$ | **HOTEL** | This home away from home—or, rather, full-service version of home where you hardly have to lift a finger—is within walking distance of the Public Garden, Back Bay, Government Center, and the river Esplanade. **Pros:** free Wi-Fi; many nearby shops and restaurants; executive-chef Lucas Sousa's decadent Sunday brunch at the ground-floor bistro. **Cons:** neighborhood parking is nonexistent; the rooms are somewhat small; no room service. 💲 *Rooms from: $199* ⊠ *25 Charles St., Beacon Hill* ☎ *617/723–7575* ⊕ *www.beaconhillhotel.com* 🛏 *13 rooms* �🍴 *No meals* Ⓜ *Arlington, Charles/MGH.*

★ Liberty Hotel Boston

$$$ | **HOTEL** | Since it opened in late 2007, the buzz surrounding the chic Liberty—formerly Boston's Charles Street Jail—was at first deafening, with bankers, tech geeks, foreign playboys, and fashionistas all scrambling to call it their own; a few years later, the Liberty has evolved into what is part retreat, part nightclub. **Pros:** Lydia Shire's popular restaurant Scampo is on the first floor; bustling nightlife; proximity to the Esplanade and Beacon Hill. **Cons:** loud in-house nightlife; long waits at bars and restaurants; parking is expensive. 💲 *Rooms from: $369* ⊠ *215 Charles St., Beacon Hill* ☎ *617/224–4000* ⊕ *www.libertyhotel.com* 🛏 *298 rooms* �🍴 *No meals* Ⓜ *Charles/MGH.*

XV Beacon

$$$$ | **HOTEL** | The 1903 Beaux Arts exterior of the city's first small luxury boutique hotel is a study in sophistication and elegance. **Pros:** hotel's modern steak-house Mooo provides 24-hour room service; courtesy Lexus car service; dogs of any size welcome for no fee; complimentary Wi-Fi. **Cons:** some rooms are small; can be expensive on weekends during peak months (May, June, September, October); no view from classic rooms. 💲 *Rooms from: $575* ⊠ *15 Beacon St., Beacon Hill* ☎ *617/670–1500, 877/982–3226* ⊕ *www.xvbeacon.com* 🛏 *63 rooms* �`🍴 *No meals* Ⓜ *Government Center, Park St.*

● Nightlife

BARS

Cheers

BARS/PUBS | The upstairs pub—dismantled in England, shipped to Boston, and reassembled—later became the inspiration for the now-classic TV series *Cheers*. Enjoy a quality burger at the model bar of the Hollywood set and imagine Sam and Diane walking in the door and calling your name. ■ **TIP→ You'll find many a tourist in Cheers, but locals tend to stay away to avoid the crowds.** ✉ *Hampshire House, 84 Beacon St., Beacon Hill* ☎ *617/227–9605* ⊕ *www.cheersboston.com* Ⓜ *Arlington, Park St., Charles/MGH.*

★ The Sevens Ale House

BARS/PUBS | Serving beer and wine, this classic dive bar is an easygoing alternative to Beacon Hill's tony stuffiness, with its dark tones, simple bar setup, well-peppered dartboard, perfectly poured pints, and decent wines. It's pleasantly untrendy. ✉ *77 Charles St., Beacon Hill* ☎ *617/523–9074* Ⓜ *Charles/MGH.*

● Performing Arts

MUSIC

Hatch Memorial Shell

CONCERTS | On the bank of the Charles River, this wonderful acoustic shell, 100 feet wide and wood inlaid, is home to Boston Pops' famous July 4 concert and dozens of other free summer classical-orchestra concerts, Zumba dance shows, and other events. Local radio stations air music shows and festivals here from April through October. Friday Flicks, often animated for children, are screened at sunset. ✉ *Off Storrow Dr. at embankment, Beacon Hill* ☎ *617/626–1250* Ⓜ *Charles/MGH, Arlington.*

ORCHESTRAS AND CHAMBER MUSIC

Boston Pops

MUSIC | Under the agile baton of Keith Lockhart, Boston Pops (largely Boston Symphony musicians) perform a bracing blend of American standards, movie themes, and contemporary vocal numbers (with top-tier guests) during May and June at Symphony Hall, plus 40 festive holiday-season concerts. Outdoor concerts on July 3 and 4 at the Hatch Memorial Shell are followed by concerts at Boston Symphony Orchestra's summer home, Tanglewood in Lenox, Massachusetts, in July and August. The free outdoor concerts are packed; be sure to arrive early with blankets, folding chairs, and a picnic. ☎ *617/266–1492, 888/266–1200 box office* ⊕ *www.bso.org.*

● Shopping

CLOTHING AND SHOES

Crush Boutique

CLOTHING | Step down to this subterranean shop to find weekend casual outfits, jeans, silky shifts, and even party-girl attire. You'll also find affordable jewelry and handbags to dress up any ensemble. Crush's Newbury Street shop (between Fairfield and Gloucester Streets) has a more LA vibe to it. ✉ *131 Charles St., Beacon Hill* ☎ *617/720–0010* ⊕ *www.shopcrushboutique.com* Ⓜ *Charles/MGH.*

Helen's Leather Shop

SHOES/LUGGAGE/LEATHER GOODS | Channel your inner cowgirl (or-boy) at this family-owned shop specializing in Western wear, including hand-tooled boots embroidered, dyed, and crafted from leather and exotic skins. Choose from half a dozen brands of boots (Lucchese, Nocona, Dan Post, Tony Lama, Justin, and Frye); then browse through the leather sandals, jackets, briefcases, luggage, and accessories. ✉ *110 Charles St., Beacon Hill* ☎ *617/742–2077* ⊕ *www.helensleather.com* Ⓜ *Charles/MGH.*

MAJOR SHOPPING DISTRICT

Charles Street

SHOPPING NEIGHBORHOODS | Pretty Charles Street, running north to south, abounds with top-notch antiques stores such as Eugene Galleries and Devonia, as well as plenty of independently owned fashion boutiques and home-goods stores whose prices reflect their high Beacon Hill rents. River Street, parallel to Charles Street, is also an excellent source for antiques. Both are easy walks from the Charles Street T stop on the Red Line. ⊠ *Beacon Hill* Ⓜ *Charles/MGH.*

Boston Common

◉ Sights

★ Boston Common

CITY PARK | FAMILY | Nothing is more central to Boston than the Common, the oldest public park in the United States and undoubtedly the largest and most famous of the town commons around which New England settlements were traditionally arranged. Dating from 1634, Boston Common started as 50 acres where the freemen of Boston could graze their cattle. (Cows were banned in 1830.) Latin names are affixed to many of the Common's trees; it was once expected that proper Boston schoolchildren be able to translate them.

On Tremont Street near Boylston stands the 1888 **Boston Massacre Memorial;** the sculpted hand of one of the victims has a distinct shine from years of sightseers' caresses. The Common's highest ground, near the park's Parkman Bandstand, was once called Flagstaff Hill. It's now surmounted by the **Soldiers and Sailors Monument,** honoring Civil War troops. The Common's only body of water is the **Frog Pond,** a tame and frog-free concrete depression used as a children's wading pool and spray fountain during steamy summer days and for ice-skating in winter. It marks the original site of a natural pond that inspired Edgar Allan Poe to call Bostonians "Frogpondians." In 1848 a gushing fountain of piped-in water was created to inaugurate Boston's municipal water system.

On the Beacon Street side of the Common sits the splendidly restored **Robert Gould Shaw 54th Regiment Memorial,** executed in deep-relief bronze by Augustus Saint-Gaudens in 1897. It commemorates the 54th Massachusetts Regiment, the first Civil War unit made up of free black people, led by the young Brahmin Robert Gould Shaw. He and half of his troops died in an assault on South Carolina's Ft. Wagner; their story inspired the 1989 movie *Glory.* The monument—first intended to depict only Shaw until his abolitionist family demanded it honor his regiment as well—figures in works by the poets John Berryman and Robert Lowell, both of whom lived on the north slope of Beacon Hill in the 1940s. This magnificent memorial makes a fitting first stop on the Black Heritage Trail. ⊠ *Bounded by Beacon, Charles, Tremont, and Park Sts., Beacon Hill* ⊕ *www.boston.gov/parks/boston-common* Ⓜ *Park St., Boylston.*

The Old West End

A few decades ago this district—separated from Beacon Hill by Cambridge Street—resembled a typical medieval city: thoroughfares that twisted and turned, maddening one-way lanes, and streets that were a veritable hive of people. Today little remains of the *old* Old West End except for a few brick tenements and a handful of monuments, including the first house built for Harrison Gray Otis. The biggest surviving structures with any real history are two public institutions, Massachusetts General Hospital and the former Suffolk County Jail, which dates from 1849. The onetime prison is now part of the luxurious, and wryly named, Liberty Hotel. Here you'll also find TD Banknorth Garden, the home away from home for loyal Bruins and Celtics fans. In addition, the innovative Museum of Science is one of the neighborhood's more modern attractions. The newest addition to the skyline here is the Leonard P. Zakim Bunker Hill Bridge, which spans the Charles River just across from the TD Banknorth Garden.

◉ Sights

★ Museum of Science

COLLEGE | FAMILY | With 15-foot lightning bolts in the Theater of Electricity and a 20-foot-long *Tyrannosaurus rex* model, this is just the place to ignite any child's scientific curiosity. More than 550 exhibits cover astronomy, astrophysics, anthropology, medical progress, computers, and the organic and inorganic earth sciences. Children learn the physics behind everyday play activities such as swinging and bumping up and down on a teeter-totter in the "Science in the Park" exhibit. The perennial favorite, "Dinosaurs: Modeling the Mesozoic," lets kids become paleontologists and examine dinosaur bones, fossils, and tracks. The Charles Hayden Planetarium produces exciting programs on astronomical discoveries. The museum also includes the Mugar Omni Theater, a five-story dome screen. The huge projection allows the audience to practically experience the action on-screen. Try to get tickets in advance online or by phone. ⊠ *Science Park at Charles River Dam, Old West End* ☎ *617/723–2500* ⊕ *www.mos. org* ⊠ *$25* Ⓜ *Science Park.*

The Sports Museum

MUSEUM | FAMILY | The fifth and sixth levels of the TD Garden house the Sports Museum of New England, where displays of memorabilia and photographs showcase local sports history and legends. Take a tour of the locker and interview rooms (off-season only), test your sports knowledge with interactive games, and see how you stand up to life-size statues of heroes Carl Yastrzemski and Larry Bird. Call ahead to confirm open hours because it closes often for events. ⊠ *TD Garden, 100 Legends Way, Old West End* ⊹ *Use west premium seating entrance* ☎ *617/624–1234* ⊕ *www.sportsmuseum. org* ⊠ *$15* Ⓜ *North Station.*

TD Garden

SPORTS VENUE | FAMILY | Diehards may still moan about the loss of the old Boston Garden, a much more intimate venue than this mammoth facility, which opened in 1995. Regardless, the home of the Celtics (basketball) and Bruins (hockey) is still known as the good old Garden and its air-conditioning, comfier seats, improved food selection, 1,200-vehicle parking garage, and nearly double number of bathrooms, has won grudging acceptance. The Garden also serves as a concert venue, featuring big-name acts, like Justin Timberlake and U2. On occasion, there are public-skating events in winter; call ahead for information. ⊠ *100 Legends Way, Old West End* ☎ *617/624–1050* ⊕ *www.tdgarden.com* Ⓜ *North Station.*

◉ Performing Arts

TD Garden

CONCERTS | New England's largest sports and entertainment arena, the TD Garden hosts concerts by big-name artists (Adele, Red Hot Chili Peppers, Katy Perry, Ed Sheeran, Imagine Dragons, and Kendrick Lamar to name a few) and special events (WWE, Disney On Ice, Harlem Globetrotters). The Garden is also home to NHL's Boston Bruins and NBA's Boston Celtics. ⊠ *100 Legends Way, Old West End* ☎ *617/624–1000 event info line* ⊕ *www.tdgarden.com* Ⓜ *North Station.*

◉ Activities

BASKETBALL
Boston Celtics

BASKETBALL | One of the most storied franchises in the National Basketball Association, the Boston Celtics have won the NBA championship 17 times since 1957, more than any other team in the league. The last title came in 2008, after a solid defeat of longtime rivals (the LA Lakers) ended an 18-year championship dry spell. Basketball season runs from late October to April, and playoffs last until mid-June. ⊠ *TD Garden, 100 Legends Way, Old West End* ☎ *866/423–5849* ⊕ *www.celtics.com* Ⓜ *North Station.*

4

Boston and Environs BEACON HILL, BOSTON COMMON, AND THE OLD WEST END

Government Center and the North End

This is a section of town Bostonians love to hate. Not only does Government Center house what they can't fight—City Hall—but it also contains some of the bleakest architecture since the advent of poured concrete. But though the stark, treeless plain surrounding City Hall has been roundly jeered, the expanse is enlivened by feisty political rallies, free summer concerts, and the occasional festival.

Government Center

Sights

★ Faneuil Hall

HISTORIC SITE | FAMILY | Faneuil Hall has always sat in the middle of Boston's main marketplace and, to be clear, the single building facing Congress Street is the real Faneuil Hall, though locals often give that name to all five buildings in this shopping complex. Bostonians pronounce it *Fan*-yoo'uhl or *Fan*-yuhl. It was erected in 1742, the gift of wealthy merchant Peter Faneuil, who wanted the hall to serve as both a place for town meetings and a public market. It burned in 1761 and was immediately reconstructed according to the original plan of its designer, the Scottish portrait painter John Smibert (who lies in the Granary Burying Ground). In 1763 the political leader James Otis helped inaugurate the era that culminated in American independence when he dedicated the rebuilt hall to the cause of liberty.

In 1772 Samuel Adams stood here and first suggested that Massachusetts and the other colonies organize a Committee of Correspondence to maintain semiclandestine lines of communication in the face of hardening British repression. In later years the hall again lived up to Otis's dedication when the abolitionists Wendell Phillips and Charles Sumner pleaded for support from its podium. The tradition continues to this day: in presidential-election years the hall is the site of debates between contenders in the Massachusetts primary.

Faneuil Hall was substantially enlarged and remodeled in 1805 according to a Greek Revival design of the noted architect Charles Bulfinch; this is the building you see today. Its purposes remain the same: the balconied Great Hall is available to citizens' groups on presentation of a request signed by a required number of responsible parties; it also plays host to regular concerts.

Inside Faneuil Hall are dozens of paintings of famous Americans, including the mural *Webster's Reply to Hayne* and Gilbert Stuart's portrait of Washington at Dorchester Heights. Park rangers give informational talks about the history and importance of Faneuil Hall every half hour. There are interactive displays about Boston sights and National Park Service rangers at the visitor center on the first floor can provide maps and other information.

On the building's top floors are the headquarters and museum and library of the **Ancient & Honorable Artillery Company of Massachusetts,** which is free to visit. Founded in 1638, it's the oldest militia in the Western Hemisphere, and the third oldest in the world, after the Swiss Guard and the Honorable Artillery Company of London. The museum is open weekdays 9 to 3.

When such men as Andrew Jackson and Daniel Webster debated the future of the Republic here, the fragrances of bacon and snuff—sold by merchants in **Quincy Market** across the road—greeted their noses. Today the aroma of coffee wafts through the hall from a snack bar. The shops at ground level sell New England bric-a-brac. ⊠ *Faneuil Hall Sq., Government Center* ☎ *617/523–1300*

⊕ www.nps.gov/bost/learn/historyc-
ulture/fh.htm 🖼 Free Ⓜ Government
Center, Aquarium, State.

Haymarket
MARKET | Loud, self-promoting vendors
pack this exuberant maze of a marketplace at Marshall and Blackstone Streets
on Friday and Saturday from dawn to
dusk (most vendors are usually gone
by 5). Pushcart vendors hawk fruits and
vegetables against a backdrop of fish,
meat, and cheese shops. The accumu-
lation of debris left every evening has
been celebrated in a whimsical 1976
public-arts project—Mags Harries's *Asa-
roton,* a Greek word meaning "unswept
floors"—consisting of bronze fruit peels
and other detritus smashed into pave-
ment. Another Harries piece, a bronze
depiction of a gathering of stray gloves,
tumbles down between the escalators in
the Porter Square T station in Cambridge.
At Creek Square, near the Haymarket,
is the **Boston Stone.** Set into a brick wall,
this was allegedly a marker used as
milepost zero in measuring distances
from Boston. ⊠ *Marshall and Blackstone
Sts., Government Center* ☉ *Closed Sun.–
Thurs.* Ⓜ *Government Center.*

New England Holocaust Memorial
MEMORIAL | Located at the north end of
Union Park, the Holocaust Memorial is
the work of Stanley Saitowitz, whose
design was selected through an international competition; the finished memorial was dedicated in 1995. During the
day the six 50-foot-high glass-and-steel
towers seem at odds with the 18th-cen-
tury streetscape of Blackstone Square
behind it; at night, they glow like ghosts
while manufactured steam from grates
in the granite base makes for a particularly haunting scene. Recollections by
Holocaust survivors are set into the
glass-and-granite walls; the upper levels
of the towers are etched with 6 million
numbers in random sequence, symbol-
izing the Jewish victims of the Nazi
horror. ⊠ *Union St. near Hanover St.,
Government Center* ☎ *617/457–8755*

⊕ www.nehm.org Ⓜ Haymarket, Government Center, State.

★ **Quincy Market**
LOCAL INTEREST | FAMILY | The market
consists of three block-long annexes:
Quincy Market, North Market, and **South
Market.** The structures were designed in
1826 to alleviate the cramped conditions
of Faneuil Hall and clean up the refuse
that collected in Town Dock, the pond
behind it. The central structure has kept
its traditional market-stall layout, but the
stalls now purvey international and specialty foods: sushi, frozen yogurt, bagels,
calzones, sausage-on-a-stick, Chinese
noodles, barbecue, and baklava, plus
all the boutique chocolate-chip cookies
your heart desires. Along the arcades
on either side of the Central Market are
vendors selling sweatshirts, photographs
of Boston, and arts and crafts—some
schlocky, some not—alongside a couple
of patioed bars and restaurants. The
North and South markets house a mix-
ture of chain stores and specialty boutiques. Quintessential Boston remains
here only in Durgin-Park, opened in 1826
and known for its plain interior, brassy
waitresses, and large portions of traditional New England fare. ⊠ *Bordered by
Clinton, Commercial, and Chatham Sts.,
Government Center* ☎ *617/523–1300*
⊕ www.quincy-market.com Ⓜ Government Center, Aquarium, State.

🍽 Restaurants

Durgin-Park Market Dining Room
$$ | AMERICAN | You should be hungry
enough to cope with enormous portions,
yet not so hungry you can't tolerate a
long wait (or sharing a table with others).
Durgin-Park was serving its same hearty
New England fare (Indian pudding, baked
beans, corned beef and cabbage, and
a prime rib that hangs over the edge of
the plate) back when Faneuil Hall was
a working market instead of a tourist
attraction. **Known for:** solid, Yankee clas-
sics; purposely brusk waitstaff; huge

4

Boston and Environs GOVERNMENT CENTER AND THE NORTH END

Continued on page 112

FOLLOW THE REDBRICK ROAD

BOSTON'S FREEDOM TRAIL

by Mike Nalepa

Paul Revere

Paul Revere's ride

Benjamin Franklin

Samuel Adams

John Hancock

The Freedom Trail is more than a collection of historic sites related to the American Revolution or a suggested itinerary connecting Boston's unique neighborhoods. It's a chance to walk in the footsteps of our forefathers—literally, by following a crimson path on public sidewalks—and pay tribute to the figures all school kids know, like Paul Revere, John Hancock, and Ben Franklin. In history-proud Boston, past and present intersect before your eyes not as a re-creation but as living history accessible to all.

Boston played a key role in the dramatic events leading up to the American Revolution. Many of the founding fathers called the city home, and many of the initial meetings and actions that sparked the fight against the British took place here. In one day, you can visit Faneuil Hall—the "Cradle of Liberty"—where outraged colonial radicals met to oppose British authority; the site of the incendiary Boston Massacre; and the Old North Church, where lanterns hung to signal Paul Revere on his thrilling midnight ride. Colonists may have originally landed in Jamestown and Plymouth, but if you really want to see where America began, come to Boston.

Boston Common, Founder's Statue

🌐 www.nps.gov/bost
🌐 www.thefreedomtrail.org

☎ 617/242–5642

✉ Admission to the Freedom Trail itself is free. Several museum sites charge for admission. However, most attractions are free monuments, parks, and landmarks.

The 1729 Old South Meeting House, where many protesters gathered during the American Revolution.

PLANNING YOUR TRAIL TRIP

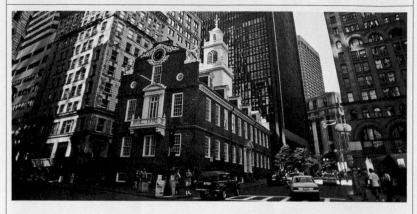

THE ROUTE

The 2½-mi Freedom Trail begins at Boston Common, winds through Downtown, Government Center, and the North End, and ends in Charlestown at the USS *Constitution*. The entire Freedom Trail is marked by a red line on the sidewalk; it's made of paint or brick at various points on the Trail. ⇨ *For more information on Freedom Trail sites, see listings in Neighborhood chapters.*

GETTING HERE AND BACK

The route starts near the Park Street T stop. When you've completed the Freedom Trail, head for the nearby Charlestown water shuttle, which goes directly to the downtown area. For schedules and maps, visit ⊕ *www.mbta.com.*

TIMING

If you're stopping at a few (or all) of the 16 sites, it takes a full day to complete the route comfortably. ■TIP→ **If you have children in tow, you may want to split the trail into two or more days.**

VISITOR CENTERS

There are Freedom Trail information centers in Boston Common (Tremont Street), at 15 State Street (near the Old State House), and at the Charlestown Navy Yard Visitor Center (in Building 5).

TOURS

The National Park Service's free 90-minute Freedom Trail walking tours begin at the Boston National Historical Park Visitor Center at 15 State Street and cover sites from the Old South Meeting House to the Old North Church. Check online for times; it's a good idea to show up at least 30 minutes early, as the popular tours are limited to 30 people.

Half-hour tours of the USS *Constitution* are offered Tuesday through Sunday. Note that visitors to the ship must go through security screening.

FUEL UP

The trail winds through the heart of Downtown Boston, so finding a quick bite or a nice sit-down meal isn't difficult. Quincy Market, near Faneuil Hall, is packed with cafés and eateries. Another good lunch choice is one of the North End's wonderful Italian restaurants.

WHAT'S NEARBY

For a short break from revolutionary history, be sure to check out the major attractions nearby, including the Boston Public Garden, New England Aquarium, and Union Oyster House.

Above: In front of the Old State House a cobblestone circle marks the site of the Boston Massacre.

TOP SIGHTS

Benjamin Franklin Statue

Boston Common

The Granary Burial Grounds

Faneuil Hall

Park Street Church

Old North Church

Bunker Hill Monument

BOSTON COMMON TO FANEUIL HALL

Old State House

GOVERNMENT CENTER

Cambridge St.

0 — 100 yards
0 — 100 meters

Clinton St.

Hancock St.

Joy St.

Bowdoin St.

Somerset St.

Court St.

Faneuil Hall

Boston National Historic Park Visitor Center

Chatham St.

State House

BEACON HILL

Mt. Vernon St.

King's Chapel and Burying Ground

Old State House

Boston Massacre Site

State St.

India St.

Walnut St.

School St.

Old Corner Bookstore

Kilby St.

Milk St.

Broad St.

Granary Burying Ground

Beacon St.

Park St.

Ben Franklin Statue

Washington St.

Old South Meeting House

Congress St.

Devonshire St.

Arch St.

Federal St.

Franklin St.

Boston Common

Park Street Church

PARK ST.

Start: near the Park Street T stop.

Freedom Trail Foundation Center Information

KEY

--- *Freedom Trail*

Many of the Freedom Trail sites between Boston Common and the North End are close together. Walking this 1-mile segment of the trail makes for a pleasant morning.

THE ROUTE

Begin at ★ **Boston Common,** then head for the **State House,** Boston's finest example of Federal architecture. Several blocks away is the **Park Street Church,** whose 217-foot steeple is considered to be the most beautiful in New England. The church was actually founded in 1809, and it played a key role in the movement to abolish slavery.

Reposing in the church's shadows is the ★ **Granary Burying Ground,** final resting

place of Samuel Adams, John Hancock, and Paul Revere. A short stroll to Downtown brings you to **King's Chapel,** founded in 1686 by King James II for the Church of England.

Follow the trail past the **Benjamin Franklin statue** to the **Old Corner Bookstore** site, where Hawthorne, Emerson, and Longfellow were published. Nearby is the **Old South Meeting House,** where arguments in 1773 led to the Boston Tea Party. Overlooking the site of the Boston Massacre is the city's oldest public building, the **Old State House,** a Georgian beauty. In 1770 the Boston Massacre occurred directly in front of here—look for the commemorative stone circle.

Cross the plaza to ★ **Faneuil Hall** and explore

where Samuel Adams railed against "taxation without representation." ■TIP→ A good mid-trail break is the shops and eateries of **Faneuil Hall Marketplace,** which includes Quincy Market.

Old Corner Book Store Site

★ = **Fodor's** Choice ★ = Highly Recommended ℃ = Family Friendly

NORTH END TO CHARLESTOWN

USS Constitution

Freedom Trail sites between Faneuil Hall and Charlestown are more spread out along 1½ miles. The sites here, though more difficult to reach, are certainly worth the walk.

Bunker Hill Monument

Water Shuttle Dock

1st Ave.

USS Constitution

Boston National Historic Park Visitor Center

End: In Charlestown head for the nearby water shuttle, which takes you downtown

CHARLESTOWN

0   100 yards
0   100 meters

Charlestown Bridge

NORTH END

Commercial St.

Copp's Hill Burying Ground

Charter St.

Hull St.

Snowhill St.

Salem St.

Tileston St.

Old North Church

Prince St.

Margin St.

Endicott St.

Pierce-Hichborn House

Paul Revere House

Hanover St.

North St.

Richmond St.

John F. Fitzgerald Surface Rd.

Cross St.

GOVERNMENT CENTER

Clinton St.

Faneuil Hall

State St.

THE ROUTE

When you depart Faneuil Hall, follow the red stripe to the North End, Boston's Little Italy.

The ☾ **Paul Revere House** takes you back 200 years—here are the hero's own saddlebags, a toddy warmer, and a pine cradle made from a molasses cask. It's also air-conditioned in the summer, so try to stop here in mid-afternoon to escape the heat. Next to the Paul Revere House is one of the city's oldest brick buildings, the **Pierce-Hichborn House.**

Next, peek inside a place guaranteed to trigger a wave of patriotism: the ★ **Old North Church** of "One if by land, two if by sea" fame. Then head toward **Copp's Hill Burying Ground,** where you can view graves from the late

17th century through the early 19th century. Afterward, cross the bridge over the Charles and check out that revered icon, the ☾ **USS Constitution,** "Old Ironsides." You'll need about an hour for a visit, so plan accordingly.

The perfect ending to the trail? A walk to the top of the ☾ **Bunker Hill Monument** for the incomparable vistas. The hill was the site of one of the first battles of the Revolutionary War. Though the colonial rebels actually lost, they inflicted large casualties on the better-trained British, proving themselves against the empire.

Paul Revere House

Government Center and the North End

KEY

- ❶ Sights
- ❶ Restaurants
- Ⓣ Subway station
- – – Freedom Trail

portions. ⑤ *Average main: $20* ✉ *340 Faneuil Hall Market Pl., North Market Bldg., Government Center* ☎ *617/227–2038* ⊕ *www.durginparkrestaurant.com* Ⓜ *Government Center.*

Union Oyster House

$$$ | **SEAFOOD** | Established in 1826, this is Boston's oldest continuing restaurant, and a must-see destination. Eat what Daniel Webster had—oysters on the half shell at the ground-floor raw bar, which is the oldest part of the restaurant and still the best. **Known for:** oldest Boston restaurant; long waits on weekends; oysters. ⑤ *Average main: $28* ✉ *41 Union St., Government Center* ☎ *617/227–2750* ⊕ *www.unionoysterhouse.com* Ⓜ *Haymarket.*

ⓨ Nightlife

BARS
Black Rose

BARS/PUBS | Hung with 20 bright county banners, decorated with pictures of Ireland and portraits of Samuel Beckett, Lady Gregory, and James Joyce, the Rose draws as many tourists as locals. Friendly Irish bartenders serve up pints, blarney, and far more Irish whiskeys (42) than Scotches (14). Nightly shows by traditional Irish and contemporary musicians confirm its abiding Gaelic good cheer, or *craic*. ✉ *160 State St., Government Center* ☎ *617/742–2286* ⊕ *www.blackroseboston.com* Ⓜ *Aquarium, State.*

⬤ Shopping

FOOD
★ Boston Public Market

FOOD/CANDY | Opened in 2015, this indoor, year-round market houses nearly four dozen vendors of locally sourced comestibles and goods that run the gamut from meats, cheeses, and eggs to fresh-picked produce, prepared foods, and New England-made wool and carved wooden bowls. The Boston Public Market Kitchen, which runs cooking demos,

lectures, and educational programs, is also located here. ✉ *100 Hanover St., Government Center* ⊕ *bostonpublicmarket.org* Ⓜ *Haymarket/Government Center.*

MAJOR SHOPPING DISTRICT
Faneuil Hall Marketplace

SHOPPING NEIGHBORHOODS | This complex is both huge and hugely popular (drawing 18 million people a year), but not necessarily unique—most of its independent shops have given way to Banana Republic, Urban Outfitters, and other chains. Founded in 1742 as a market for crops and livestock, the place has plenty of history and offers one of the area's great à la carte casual dining experiences (Quincy Market). Pushcarts sell everything from apparel to jewelry to candy to Boston souvenirs, and buskers perform crowd-pleasing feats such as break dancing. ✉ *Bounded by Congress St., Atlantic Ave., the Waterfront, and Government Center, Government Center* ☎ *617/523–1300* ⊕ *www.faneuilhallmarketplace.com* Ⓜ *Government Center.*

The North End

The warren of small streets on the northeast side of Government Center is the North End, Boston's Little Italy. In the 17th century the North End *was* Boston, as much of the rest of the peninsula was still under water or had yet to be cleared. Here the town grew rich for a century and a half before the birth of American independence. The quarter's dwindling ethnic character lingers along Salem or Hanover Street, where you can still hear people speaking with Abruzzese accents.

⊙ Sights

Copp's Hill Burying Ground

CEMETERY | An ancient and melancholy air hovers like a fine mist over this Colonial-era burial ground. The North End graveyard incorporates four cemeteries established between 1660 and 1819.

Near the Charter Street gate is the tomb of the Mather family, the dynasty of church divines (Cotton and Increase were the most famous sons) who held sway in Boston during the heyday of the old theocracy. Also buried here is Robert Newman, who crept into the steeple of the Old North Church to hang the lanterns warning of the British attack the night of Paul Revere's ride. Look for the tombstone of Captain Daniel Malcolm; it's pockmarked with musket-ball fire from British soldiers, who used the stones for target practice. Across the street at 44 Hull is the **narrowest house in Boston**—it's a mere 10 feet across. ⊠ *Intersection of Hull and Snowhill Sts., North End* ⊕ *www.cityofboston.gov/ parks/hbgi/CoppsHill.asp* Ⓜ *North Station.*

Hanover Street

NEIGHBORHOOD | FAMILY | This is the North End's main thoroughfare, along with the smaller and narrower Salem Street. It was named for the ruling dynasty of 18th- and 19th-century England; the label was retained after the Revolution, despite a flurry of patriotic renaming (King Street became State Street, for example). Hanover's business center is thick with restaurants, pastry shops, and Italian cafés; on weekends, Italian immigrants who have moved to the suburbs return to share an espresso with old friends and maybe catch a soccer game broadcast via satellite. Hanover is one of Boston's oldest public roads, once the site of the residences of the Rev. Cotton Mather and the Colonial-era patriot Dr. Joseph Warren, as well as a small dry-goods store run by Eben D. Jordan—who went on to launch the Jordan Marsh department stores. ⊠ *Between Commercial and Congress Sts., North End* Ⓜ *Haymarket, North Station.*

★ Old North Church

BUILDING | At one end of the **Paul Revere Mall** is a church famous not only for being the oldest standing church building in Boston (built in 1723) but for housing the two lanterns that glimmered from its steeple on the night of April 18, 1775. This is Christ, or Old North, Church, where Paul Revere and the young sexton Robert Newman managed that night to signal the departure by water of the British regulars to Lexington and Concord.

Although William Price designed the structure after studying Christopher Wren's London churches, Old North—which still has an active Episcopal congregation (including descendants of the Reveres)—is an impressive building in its own right. Inside, note the gallery and the graceful arrangement of pews; the bust of George Washington, pronounced by the Marquis de Lafayette to be the truest likeness of the general he ever saw; the brass chandeliers, made in Amsterdam in 1700 and installed here in 1724; and the clock, the oldest still running in an American public building. Try to visit when changes are rung on the bells, after the 11 am Sunday service; they bear the inscription, "We are the first ring of bells cast for the British Empire in North America." On the Sunday closest to April 18, descendants of the patriots reenact the raising of the lanterns in the church belfry during a special evening service. Visitors are welcome to drop in, but to see the bell-ringing chamber and the crypts, take the 30-minute behind-the-scenes tour.

Behind the church is the **Washington Memorial Garden,** where volunteers cultivate a plot devoted to plants and flowers favored in the 18th century. ⊠ *193 Salem St., North End* ☎ *617/858–8231* ⊕ *www. oldnorth.com* ✉ *$3 suggested donation; $6 behind-the-scenes tour* Ⓜ *Haymarket, North Station.*

Paul Revere House

HOUSE | FAMILY | Originally on the site was the parsonage of the Second Church of Boston, home to the Rev. Increase Mather, the Second Church's minister. Mather's house burned in the great fire of 1676, and the house that Revere was to occupy was built on its location about four years later, nearly 100 years before Revere's 1775 midnight ride through Middlesex County. Revere owned it from 1770 until 1800, although he lived there for only 10 years and rented it out for the next two decades. Pre-1900 photographs show it as a shabby warren of storefronts and apartments. The clapboard sheathing is a replacement, but 90% of the framework is original; note the Elizabethan-style overhang and leaded windowpanes. A few Revere furnishings are on display here, and just gazing at his silverwork—much more of which is displayed at the Museum of Fine Arts—brings the man alive. Special events are scheduled throughout the year, many designed with children in mind.

The immediate neighborhood also has Revere associations. The little park in North Square is named after Rachel Revere, his second wife, and the adjacent brick **Pierce-Hichborn House** once belonged to relatives of Revere. The garden connecting the Revere house and the Pierce-Hichborn House is planted with flowers and medicinal herbs favored in Revere's day. ⊠ *19 North Sq., North End* ☏ *617/523–2338* ⊕ *www.paulreverehouse.org* ⌦ *$5 (cash only)* ⊗ *Closed Mon. Jan.–Mar.* Ⓜ *Haymarket, Aquarium, Government Center.*

🍴 Restaurants

★ Antico Forno
$$ | ITALIAN | Many of the menu choices here come from the eponymous wood-burning brick oven, which turns out surprisingly delicate pizzas simply topped with tomato and fresh buffalo mozzarella. Though its pizzas receive top billing, Antico excels at a variety of Italian country dishes, like veal parmigiana, osso buco with pork shanks, chicken saltimbocca, and handmade pastas; the specialty, gnocchi, is rich and creamy but light. **Known for:** wood-fired, brick-oven pizza; Italian country classics; casual, jovial atmosphere. Ⓢ *Average main: $18*

⊠ *93 Salem St., North End* ☏ *617/723–6733* ⊕ *www.anticofornoboston.com* Ⓜ *Haymarket.*

Bricco
$$$$ | ITALIAN | A sophisticated but unpretentious enclave of nouveau Italian, Bricco has carved out quite a following. And no wonder: the handmade pastas alone are argument for a reservation. **Known for:** sophisticated Italian classics; dark, elegant atmosphere; pillowy homemade pastas. Ⓢ *Average main: $38* ⊠ *241 Hanover St., North End* ☏ *617/248–6800* ⊗ *No lunch* Ⓜ *Haymarket.*

★ Daily Catch
$$ | SEAFOOD | You've just got to love this shoebox-size place—for the noise, the intimacy, the complete absence of pretense, and, above all, the food, which proved so popular, it spawned two other locations (one in Brookline and another in Boston's Seaport area). With garlic and olive oil forming the foundation for almost every dish, this cheerful, bustling spot specializes in calamari, black squid-ink pastas, and linguine with clam sauce, all served in the skillets in which they were cooked, hot from the stove. **Known for:** garlic-rich preparations; luscious seafood skillet pastas; intimate, elbow-to-elbow dining. Ⓢ *Average main: $21* ⊠ *323 Hanover St., North End* ☏ *617/523–8567* ⊕ *thedailycatch.com* ⊟ *No credit cards* Ⓜ *Haymarket.*

★ Neptune Oyster
$$$ | SEAFOOD | This *piccolo* oyster bar, the first of its kind in the neighborhood, has only 22 chairs, but the long marble bar adorned with mirrors has extra seating for 15 more patrons, who can watch the oyster shuckers deftly undo handfuls of more than a dozen different kinds of bivalves to savor as an appetizer or on a *plateau di frutti di mare,* a gleaming tower of oysters and other raw-bar items piled over ice that you can order from the slip of paper they pass out listing each day's crustacean options. Dishes change seasonally, but a couple of year-round

favorites include the North End Cioppino (fish stew) and the signature lobster roll that, hot or cold, overflows with meat. **Known for**: casual setting; Italian-style seafood; generously packed lobster roll. $ *Average main: $30* ⊠ *63 Salem St., North End* ☎ *617/742–3474* ⊕ *www. neptuneoyster.com* Ⓜ *Haymarket.*

Nightlife

CAFÉS AND COFFEEHOUSES
★ Caffe Vittoria
CAFES—NIGHTLIFE | The glorious matriarch of North End cafés, glistening with marble-topped tables, mirrors, and shiny machines, lets you glimpse *la dolce vita* on Hanover Street as baristas pump steaming espresso machines from 7 am until midnight. Skip the frenzy at tourist trap Mike's Pastry next door; relax as you sip caffe latte or grappa and nibble authentic gelati and pastries—tiramisu, sfogliatelle, cannoli. Cash only, *per favore.* ⊠ *290–296 Hanover St., North End* ☎ *617/227–7606* ⊕ *www.caffevittoria.com* Ⓜ *Haymarket.*

Shopping

BOOKS
I Am Books
BOOKS/STATIONERY | Once you've eaten your fill of pasta and cannoli, nourish your noggin at this independent, Italian American bookstore, where you'll find more than 1,200 titles in English and Italian. In addition to books written in Italian, including many children's books like Dr. Seuss, you'll find books devoted to Italian cooking, art, history, language, literature, and more, along with Italian comic books, magazines, ceramics, and fragrances. ⊠ *189 North St., North End* ☎ *857/263–7665* ⊕ *www.iambooksboston.com.*

CLOTHING
★ Shake the Tree
SPECIALTY STORES | Irresistible defines this one-stop shop brimming with an eclectic array of strappy dresses and tops, unique body products, bags, fun jewelry, gifts, and home items that you never knew you needed. ⊠ *67 Salem St., North End* ☎ *617/742–0484* ⊕ *www.shakethetreeboston.com* Ⓜ *Haymarket.*

Charlestown

Boston started here. Charlestown was a thriving settlement a year before Colonials headed across the Charles River at William Blaxton's invitation to found the city proper. Today the district's attractions include two of the most visible—and vertical—monuments in Boston: the Bunker Hill Monument, which commemorates the grisly battle that became a symbol of patriotic resistance against the British, and the USS *Constitution,* whose masts continue to tower over the waterfront where she was built more than 200 years ago.

Sights

★ Bunker Hill Monument
MEMORIAL | Three misunderstandings surround this famous monument. First, the Battle of Bunker Hill was actually fought on Breed's Hill, which is where the monument sits today. (The real Bunker Hill is about ½ mile to the north of the monument; it's slightly taller than Breed's Hill.) Bunker was the originally planned locale for the battle, and for that reason its name stuck. Second, although the battle is generally considered a Colonial success, the Americans lost. It was a Pyrrhic victory for the British Redcoats, who sacrificed nearly half of their 2,200 men; American casualties numbered 400 to 600. And third: the famous war cry "Don't fire until you see the whites of their eyes" may never have been uttered by American colonel William Prescott or General Israel Putnam, but if either one did shout it, he was quoting an old Prussian command made necessary by the notorious inaccuracy of the musket. No matter. The Americans did employ a

deadly delayed-action strategy on June 17, 1775, and conclusively proved themselves worthy fighters, capable of defeating the forces of the British Empire.

Among the dead were the brilliant young American doctor and political activist Joseph Warren, recently commissioned as a major general but fighting as a private, and the British major John Pitcairn, who two months before had led the Redcoats into Lexington. Pitcairn is believed to be buried in the crypt of Old North Church.

In 1823 the committee formed to construct a monument on the site of the battle chose the form of an Egyptian obelisk. Architect Solomon Willard designed a 221-foot-tall granite obelisk, a tremendous feat of engineering for its day. The Marquis de Lafayette laid the cornerstone of the monument in 1825, but because of a lack of funds, it wasn't dedicated until 1843. Daniel Webster's stirring words at the ceremony commemorating the laying of its cornerstone have gone down in history: "Let it rise! Let it rise, till it meets the sun in his coming. Let the earliest light of the morning gild it, and parting day linger and play upon its summit."

The monument's zenith is reached by a flight of 294 steps. There's no elevator, but the views from the observatory are worth the effort of the arduous climb. From April through June, due to high numbers, all visitors who wish to climb must first obtain a pass from the Bunker Hill Museum at 43 Monument Square. Climbing passes are free, but limited in number and offered on a first-come, first-served basis. The museum's artifacts and exhibits tell the story of the battle, while a detailed diorama shows the action in miniature. ✉ *Monument Sq., Charlestown* ☎ *617/242–5641* ⊕ *www.nps.gov/bost/historyculture/bhm.htm* 🎫 *Free* Ⓜ *Community College.*

★ **USS** *Constitution*

MILITARY SITE | **FAMILY** | Better known as "Old Ironsides," the USS *Constitution* rides proudly at anchor in her berth at the Charlestown Navy Yard. The oldest commissioned ship in the U.S. fleet is a battlewagon of the old school, of the days of "wooden ships and iron men"—when she and her crew of 200 succeeded at the perilous task of asserting the sovereignty of an improbable new nation. Every July 4, she's towed out for a turnabout in Boston Harbor, the very place her keel was laid in 1797.

The venerable craft has narrowly escaped the scrap heap several times in her long history. She was launched on October 21, 1797, as part of the nation's fledgling navy. Her hull was made of live oak, the toughest wood grown in North America; her bottom was sheathed in copper, provided by Paul Revere at a nominal cost. Her principal service was during Thomas Jefferson's campaign against the Barbary pirates, off the coast of North Africa, and in the War of 1812. In 42 engagements her record was 42–0.

The nickname "Old Ironsides" was acquired during the War of 1812, when shots from the British warship *Guerrière* appeared to bounce off her hull. Talk of scrapping the ship began as early as 1830, but she was saved by a public campaign sparked by Oliver Wendell Holmes's poem "Old Ironsides." She underwent a major restoration in the early 1990s. Today she continues, the oldest commissioned warship afloat in the world, to be a part of the U.S. Navy.

The navy personnel who look after the *Constitution* maintain a 24-hour watch. Instead of taking the T, you can get closer to the ship by taking MBTA Bus 93 to Chelsea Street from Haymarket. Or you can take the Boston Harbor Cruise water shuttle from Long Wharf to Pier 4. ✉ *Charlestown Navy Yard, 55 Constitution Rd., Charlestown* ☎ *617/242–7511* ⊕ *www.navy.mil/local/constitution* 🎫 *Free* Ⓜ *North Station.*

Nightlife

BARS

★ Warren Tavern

BARS/PUBS | This venerable Colonial-era watering hole, rebuilt in 1780, was frequented by Paul Revere; even George Washington had a few drinks here. Today tourists and locals stop by for a glass and passable grub en route to the historic Navy Yard. Try the house-made potato chips with your ale of choice. ⊠ *2 Pleasant St., Charlestown* ☎ *617/241–8142* ⊕ *www.warrentavern.com* Ⓜ *Community College.*

Downtown

Boston's commercial and financial districts—the area commonly called Downtown—are in a maze of streets that seem to have been laid out with little logic; they are village lanes now lined with modern 40-story office towers. Just as the Great Fire of 1872 swept the old Financial District clear, the Downtown construction in more recent times has obliterated many of the buildings where 19th-century Boston businessmen sat in front of their rolltop desks. Yet historic sites remain tucked among the skyscrapers; a number of them have been linked together to make up a fascinating section of the Freedom Trail.

The area is bordered by State Street on the north and by South Station and Chinatown on the south. Tremont Street and the Common form the west boundary, and the harbor wharves the eastern edge. Locals navigate the tangle of thoroughfares in between, but few of them manage to give intelligible directions, so carry a map.

◉ Sights

★ Boston Tea Party Ships & Museum

LOCAL INTEREST | FAMILY | This lively museum offers an interactive look at the past in a place as close as possible to the actual spot where the Boston Tea Party took place on December 16, 1773. Situated at the Congress Street Bridge where Griffin's Wharf once was, visitors can check out *The Beaver II*, a historic reproduction of one of the ships forcibly boarded and unloaded the night Boston Harbor became a teapot, along with a reproduction of the *Eleanor*, another of the ships (the third ship, the *Dartmouth*, is under construction with no firm date set for opening). The museum is big on visitor engagement. Actors in period costumes greet patrons, assign them a Colonial persona, and then ask a few people to heave boxes of tea into the water. Inside, there are 3-D holograms, talking portraits, and even the Robinson Half Tea Chest, one of two original tea chests known to exist. Outside, you can explore the replicas of the ships, meet reenactors, or drink a cup of tea in Abigail's Tea Room, which has one of the best views around. ⊠ *Fort Point Channel at Congress St. Bridge, Downtown* ⊕ *www.bostonteapartyship.com* ☎ *$30 (check website for discounts)* Ⓜ *South Station.*

★ Children's Museum

MUSEUM | FAMILY | The country's second-oldest children's museum has always been ahead of the curve with creative hands-on exhibits, cultural diversity, and problem solving. Some of the most popular stops are also the simplest, like the bubble-making machinery and the two-story climbing maze. At the Japanese House you're invited to take off your shoes and step inside a two-story silk merchant's home from Kyoto. The "Boston Black" exhibit stimulates dialogue about ethnicity and community, and children can dig, climb, and build at the Construction Zone. In the toddler PlaySpace, children under three can run free in a safe environment. There's also a full schedule of special exhibits, festivals, and performances. ⊠ *308 Congress St., Downtown* ☎ *617/426–6500* ⊕ *www. bostonchildrensmuseum.org* ☎ *$17, Fri. 5–9 $1* Ⓜ *South Station.*

★ New England Aquarium

ZOO | FAMILY | With one of the world's largest ocean-reef tanks in the world and exhibits covering every sea creature imaginable, this aquarium is a must for anyone curious about life under and around the sea. Its glass-and-steel exterior is constructed to mimic fish scales, and seals bark outside. Inside the main facility you'll see penguins, sea otters, sharks, and other exotic sea creatures—more than 30,000 animals, with 800 different species. The real showstopper, though, is the four-story, 200,000-gallon ocean-reef tank. Ramps winding around the tank lead to the top level and allow you to view the inhabitants from many vantage points. Up top, the Yawkey Coral Reef Center features a seven-tank exhibit gallery that gives a close-up look at animals that might not be easily seen on the reef. Don't miss the five-times-a-day feedings; each lasts nearly an hour and takes divers 24 feet into the tank. ⊠ *1 Central Wharf, between Central and Milk Sts., Downtown* ☎ *617/973-5200* ⊕ *www.neaq.org* ✆ *$28, IMAX $10* Ⓜ *Aquarium, State.*

Old South Meeting House

HISTORIC SITE | FAMILY | This is the second-oldest church building in Boston, and were it not for Longfellow's celebration of the Old North in "Paul Revere's Ride," it might well be the most famous. Today, visitors can learn about its history through exhibits and audio programs. Some of the fiercest of the town meetings that led to the Revolution were held here, culminating in the gathering of December 16, 1773, which was called by Samuel Adams to confront the crisis of three ships, laden with dutiable tea, anchored at Griffin's Wharf. The activists wanted the tea returned to England, but the governor would not permit it—and the rest is history. The Voices of Protest exhibit celebrates Old South as a forum for free speech from Revolutionary days to the present. ⊠ *310 Washington St.,* *Downtown* ☎ *617/482-6439* ⊕ *www.old-southmeetinghouse.org* ✆ *$6* Ⓜ *State, Downtown Crossing.*

Rowes Wharf

MARINA | Take a Beacon Hill redbrick town house, blow it up to the nth power, and you get this 15-story Skidmore, Owings & Merrill extravaganza from 1987, one of the more welcome additions to the Boston Harbor skyline. From under the complex's gateway six-story arch, you can get great views of Boston Harbor and the yachts docked at the marina. Water shuttles pull up here from Logan Airport—a gorgeous way to enter the city. A windswept stroll along the Harborwalk waterfront promenade at dusk makes for an unforgettable sunset on clear days. ⊠ *Atlantic Ave. south of India Wharf, Waterfront* Ⓜ *Aquarium.*

U.S. Custom House

BUILDING | This 1847 structure resembles a Greek Revival temple that appears to have sprouted a tower. It's just that. This is the work of architects Ammi Young and Isaiah Rogers—at least, the bottom part is. The tower was added in 1915, at which time the Custom House became Boston's tallest building. It remains one of the most visible and best-loved structures in the city's skyline. To appreciate the grafting job, go inside and look at the domed rotunda. The outer surface of that dome was once the roof of the building, but now the dome is embedded in the base of the tower. You can visit the 26th-floor observation deck ($7) at 2 pm and 6 pm (except for Friday). You must show up promptly to be admitted. The magnificent Rotunda Room sports maritime prints and antique artifacts, courtesy of the Peabody Essex Museum in Salem. ⊠ *3 McKinley Sq., Downtown* ☎ *617/310-6300* ✆ *$7* Ⓜ *State, Aquarium.*

Downtown and South Boston

KEY

- ① Sights
- ① Restaurants
- ① Hotels
- Ⓣ Subway station
- --- Freedom Trail

Sights ▶

1 Boston Tea Party Ships & Museum	**F3**
2 Children's Museum	**F3**
3 Institute of Contemporary Art	**H3**
4 New England Aquarium	**F1**
5 Old South Meeting House	**C1**
6 Rowes Wharf	**F1**
7 U.S. Custom House	**E1**

Restaurants ▶

1 o ya	**D3**

Hotels ▶

1 Ames Boston Hotel	**C1**
2 Battery Wharf Hotel	**F1**
3 Harborside Inn	**E1**
4 Kimpton Nine Zero Hotel	**C1**
5 The Langham, Boston	**D2**
6 Omni Parker House	**C1**
7 Revere Hotel	**A3**

Restaurants

★ o ya

$$$$ | **JAPANESE** | Despite its side-street location and hidden door, o ya isn't exactly a secret: dining critics from the *New York Times, Bon Appetit,* and *Food & Wine* have all named this tiny, improvisational sushi spot among the best in the country, so much so, it now has a branch in Manhattan. Chef Tim Cushman's small-plate menu features squid-ink bubbles, homemade potato chips, and foie gras, along with dozens of other dishes, some paying homage to New England, like the wild Maine uni toast with truffled honey and local smoked bluefish with wasabi vinaigrette. **Known for**: creative small-plate Japanese; mind-blowing omakase. ⑤ *Average main: $60* ✉ *9 East St., Downtown* ☎ *617/654–9900* ⊕ *o-ya.restaurant/o-ya-boston* ⊙ *Closed Sun. and Mon. No lunch* Ⓜ *South Station.*

Hotels

Ames Boston Hotel

$$$ | **HOTEL** | Located in the iconic Ames Building, this 15-story hotel is now part of the Curio Collection by Hilton. **Pros:** Molton Brown bath products; complimentary bicycles; great proximity to the Freedom Trail and Beacon Hill. **Cons:** far from South End and Back Bay shopping; no swimming pool or spa; parking is expensive. ⑤ *Rooms from: $375* ✉ *1 Court St., Downtown* ☎ *617/979–8100* ⊕ *www.ameshotel.com* ⇨ *114 rooms* ⑩ *No meals* Ⓜ *State, Government Center.*

Battery Wharf Hotel

$$$$ | **HOTEL** | **FAMILY** | One of the growing number of lodgings clustered along Boston's ever-expanding Harborwalk—a pretty pedestrian path that runs from Charlestown to Dorchester—the Battery Wharf Hotel looks more like a gated community than a chain hotel. **Pros:** walking distance to more than 80 world-class restaurants; on site Exhale Spa has discounted spa services and fitness classes for hotel guests; great North End location; water taxi stand on-site. **Cons:** far from Newbury Street and South End shopping; 15- to 20-minute walk to nearest T stations; hotel is in two separate buildings. ⑤ *Rooms from: $499* ✉ *3 Battery Wharf, North End* ☎ *617/657–1834* ⊕ *www.batterywharfhotelboston.com* ⇨ *150 rooms* ⑩ *No meals* Ⓜ *Haymarket, North Station.*

★ Harborside Inn

$$ | **HOTEL** | With rates that are considerably lower than most Waterfront hotels—as low as $119 in the off-season—this hotel with an understated charm is an exceptional value. **Pros:** free Wi-Fi; close to Quincy Market and the New England Aquarium; nearby water taxi. **Cons:** the area might be too touristy for some leisure travelers; no turndown service; no valet. ⑤ *Rooms from: $250* ✉ *185 State St., Downtown* ☎ *617/723–7500, 888/723–7565* ⊕ *harborsideinnboston.com* ⇨ *116 rooms* ⑩ *No meals* Ⓜ *Aquarium.*

★ Kimpton Nine Zero

$$ | **HOTEL** | **FAMILY** | If it's all about location, the Kimpton Nine Zero can't be beat. **Pros:** pet- and kid-friendly; lobby wine tasting every evening (from 5 to 6); Atelier Bloem bath products. **Cons:** smallish rooms; high parking fees; small gyms. ⑤ *Rooms from: $249* ✉ *90 Tremont St., Downtown* ☎ *617/772–5800, 866/906–9090* ⊕ *www.ninezero.com* ⇨ *185 rooms* ⑩ *Free breakfast* Ⓜ *Park St., Government Center.*

The Langham, Boston

$$$ | **HOTEL** | This 1922 Renaissance Revival landmark (the former Federal Reserve Building) strikes an admirable balance between historic, old-world charm and sleek, modern appointments. **Pros:** ideal Downtown location for business travelers; fabulous Sunday brunch and Saturday Chocolate Bar at Café Fleuri; guests enjoy special deals at the Chuan Body + Soul spa. **Cons:** downtown location feels remote on weekends; pricey during the week; expensive valet parking. Ⓢ *Rooms from: $395* ✉ *250 Franklin St., Downtown* ☎ *617/451–1900* ⊕ *www.boston. langhamhotels.com* ⤳ *335 rooms* ⑩ *No meals* Ⓜ *South Station.*

Omni Parker House

$$$ | **HOTEL** | **FAMILY** | If any hotel says "Boston," it's this one, where JFK proposed to Jackie, and Charles Dickens gave his first reading of "A Christmas Carol"; there's more than a century and a half of rich and varied history within these walls. **Pros:** overflowing with history; great location on the Freedom Trail; newly renovated public areas. **Cons:** small rooms, some of which are a bit dark; thin-walled rooms can be noisy; area parking is very expensive. Ⓢ *Rooms from: $339* ✉ *60 School St., Downtown* ☎ *617/227–8600*, *800/843–6664* ⊕ *www.omniparkerhouse. com* ⤳ *567 rooms* ⑩ *No meals* Ⓜ *Government Center, Park St.*

★ Revere Hotel

$$ | **HOTEL** | The Revere Hotel experienced a $28 million renovation in 2017, and the stylish spot now embraces New England history, but with a twist. **Pros:** rooftop pool and bar has amazing city views; balconies in every room; ideal location where Back Bay meets Downtown Boston. **Cons:** expensive parking; elevators can get congested; no three-meal restaurant on-site. Ⓢ *Rooms from: $249* ✉ *200 Stuart St., Downtown* ☎ *617/482–1800* ⊕ *www.reverehotel.com* ⤳ *356 rooms* ⑩ *No meals* Ⓜ *Arlington.*

Nightlife

BARS

★ Beantown Pub

BARS/PUBS | Right on the Freedom Trail, this is the only pub in Boston where you can enjoy a Sam Adams lager while pondering the grave of that Founding Father himself. It's a fine place to watch multiple sports events, shoot pool, or people-watch. The standard pub menu, available until 2 am, includes great burgers, soups, salads, mains, and sandwiches, many

named after local heroes and patriots buried in the Granary Burying Ground (founded 1660) across the street— Mother Goose, Paul Revere, John Hancock, Robert Treat Paine, and yes, Mr. Adams (Cajun chicken with Vermont cheddar). ✉ *100 Tremont St., Downtown* ☎ *617/426–0111* ⊕ *www.beantownpub. com* Ⓜ *Park St., Downtown Crossing.*

★ Drink

BARS/PUBS | This area favorite lounge in a brick Fort Point Channel warehouse offers a short beer, wine, and food list, but no cocktail menu. Patrons rely on the highly knowledgeable bartenders to concoct libations on the spot according to drinkers' preferences. The space has an underground, modern speakeasy feel. Chat with the bartender to create your perfect drink; hint: if you like creative Manhattans, ask for a "Fort Point." ✉ *348 Congress St., Fort Point, South Boston* ☎ *617/695–1806* ⊕ *drinkfortpoint.com* Ⓜ *South Station.*

GAY AND LESBIAN

★ Jacque's Cabaret

CABARET | There's nothing traditional about Jacque's Cabaret, an institution for more than 60 years. Nightly drag-queen shows draw bachelorette parties and locals looking to swill cocktails from plastic cups. Be sure to make reservations if you're going in a group, and don't show up late; they may give your table away if you aren't seated before showtime. Because of a long-running licensing dispute with sleepy Bay Villagers, the whole carnival shuts down nightly at midnight. ✉ *79 Broadway, Theater District* ☎ *617/426–8902* ⊕ *www.jacques-cabaret.com* Ⓜ *Arlington.*

🎭 Performing Arts

THEATERS

★ Boch Center

THEATER | Formerly the Citi Performing Arts Center, the renamed Boch Center is a performance-space complex dedicated to large-scale productions (at the former

Wang Theater) and more intimate shows (at the Shubert and Colonial theaters). Expect big names (Steely Dan, Diana Ross, Radiolab, Brian Wilson), nationally touring Broadway shows, hot comedians, and occasional ballets. ⊠ *270 Tremont St., Theater District* ☎ *617/482–9393 general Boch Center, 866/348–9738 Shubert Theatre* ⊕ *www.bochcenter.org* Ⓜ *Boylston.*

Boston Opera House

THEATER | The meticulously renovated 2,700-seat, Beaux Arts building has been lavished with $35 million worth of gold leaf, lush carpeting, and rococo ornamentation. It features lavish musical productions such as *Newsies, Kinky Boots,* and Boston Ballet's *The Nutcracker.* ⊠ *539 Washington St., Downtown* ☎ *617/259–3400* ⊕ *www.bostonoperahouse.com* Ⓜ *Boylston, Chinatown, Downtown Crossing, Park St.*

★ Cutler Majestic Theatre at Emerson College

THEATER | This handsome 1903 Beaux Arts-style theater, now linked to Emerson's adjacent communications college, has a tastefully restored and extravagantly gilt interior, where it hosts a dazzling array of professional and student productions including dance, drama, opera, comedy, and musicals. ⊠ *219 Tremont St., Theater District* ☎ *617/824–8000* ⊕ *cutlermajestic.org* Ⓜ *Boylston.*

 Activities

BOATING

Boston Harbor Cruises

PARK—SPORTS-OUTDOORS | Boston Harbor Cruises offers ferries to the Harbor Islands from Long Wharf (Downtown) with limited service in spring and fall. Service expands in June with additional departures from Hingham and Hull to six island destinations. High-speed catamarans run daily from May through mid-October and cost $19.95 round-trip. Other islands can be reached by the free interisland water shuttles that depart

from Georges Island. ⊠ *Long Wharf, Waterfront* ☎ *617/227–4321* ⊕ *www. bostonharborcruises.com* Ⓜ *Aquarium.*

HOCKEY

Boston Bruins

HOCKEY | Boston's hockey team is on the ice from September until April, frequently on Thursday and Saturday evenings. Playoffs last through early June. ⊠ *TD Garden, 100 Legends Way, Old West End* ☎ *617/624–2327* ⊕ *www.bostonbruins. com* Ⓜ *North Station.*

PARKS AND BEACHES

★ Boston Harbor Islands National Park Area

PARK—SPORTS-OUTDOORS | **FAMILY** | Comprising 34 islands and peninsulas, the Boston Harbor Islands National Park Area is something of a hidden gem for nature lovers and history buffs, with miles of lightly traveled trails and shoreline and several little-visited historic sites to explore. The focal point of the national park is 39-acre Georges Island, where you'll find the partially restored pre–Civil War Ft. Warren that once held Confederate prisoners. Other islands worth visiting include Peddocks Island, which holds the remains of Ft. Andrews, and Spectacle Island, a popular destination for swimming (with lifeguards). Lovells, Peddocks, Grape, and Bumpkin islands all allow camping with a permit from late June through Labor Day. Peddocks also has yurts available. Pets and alcohol are not allowed on the Harbor Islands. ⊠ *Visitor Pavilion, 191 W. Atlantic Ave., Downtown* ☎ *617/223–8666* ⊕ *www. bostonharborislands.org* Ⓜ *Aquarium.*

Rose Fitzgerald Kennedy Greenway

PARK—SPORTS-OUTDOORS | The Rose Fitzgerald Kennedy Greenway is a gorgeous 1½-mile-long ribbon of parks boasting fountains, organically maintained lawns and landscapes, hundreds of trees, and chairs, tables, and umbrellas for the public's use. It stretches from the North End (New Sudbury and Cross Streets) to Chinatown (Kneeland and Hudson Streets), curving through the heart of Downtown, just a few blocks from the harbor in most places. The Conservancy, a nonprofit foundation, operates, maintains, and programs the park with more than 350 events each year, including concerts, exercise classes, and farmers' and artisan markets. A mobile food program features more than 20 food trucks and carts operating seasonally in several locations on the Greenway, with the heart of the activity at Dewey Square Park. Kids will love the one-of-a-kind carousel with 36 seats featuring 14 characters native to the Boston area, including a lobster, rabbit, grasshopper, and falcon. ⊠ *Downtown* ☎ *617/292–0020* ⊕ *www.rosekennedygreenway.org* Ⓜ *South Station, North Station, Aquarium, Haymarket.*

Shopping

BOOKS

Brattle Book Shop

BOOKS/STATIONERY | The late George Gloss built this into Boston's best used- and rare-book shop. Today his son Kenneth fields queries from passionate book lovers. If the book you want is out of print, Brattle has it or can probably find it. The store has been in operation since 1825. ⊠ *9 West St., Downtown* ☎ *617/542–0210, 800/447–9595* ⊕ *www.brattlebookshop.com* Ⓜ *Downtown Crossing.*

South Boston

The landfill project that became South Boston—known as "Southie" and not to be confused with the South End—isn't a true streetcar suburb; its expansion predates the era of commuting. Some of the brick bowfront residences along East Broadway in City Point date from the 1840s and 1850s, but the neighborhood really came into its own with the influx of Irish around 1900, and Irish Americans still hold sway here. Southie is a Celtic enclave, as the raucous annual St. Patrick's Day parade attests.

Sights

★ Institute of Contemporary Art

MUSEUM | Housed in a breathtaking cantilevered edifice that juts out over the Boston waterfront, the ICA moved to this site in 2006 as part of a massive reinvention that has made the museum one of Boston's most exciting attractions. Since its founding in 1936, the institute has cultivated its cutting-edge status: it's played host to works by Edvard Munch, Egon Schiele, and Oskar Kokoschka. Early in their careers, Andy Warhol, Robert Rauschenberg, and Roy Lichtenstein each mounted pivotal exhibitions here. The ICA's permanent collection showcases work by contemporary artists featured in ICA exhibitions, many at seminal moments in their careers. ⊠ *25 Harbor Shore Dr., Waterfront* ☎ *617/478–3100* ⊕ *www.icaboston.org* ⊠ *$15, free Thurs. 5–9, free for families last Sat. of month (except Dec.)* ⊘ *Closed Mon.* Ⓜ *Courthouse.*

Back Bay and the Fenway

In the folklore of American neighborhoods, the Back Bay stands as a symbol of propriety and high social standing. Before the 1850s it really was a bay, a tidal flat that formed the south bank of a distended Charles River. The filling in of land along the isthmus that joined Boston to the mainland (the Neck) began in 1850, and resulted in the creation of the South End. To the north a narrow causeway called the Mill Dam (later Beacon Street) was built in 1814 to separate the Back Bay from the Charles. By the late 1800s Bostonians had filled in the shallows to as far as the marshland known as the Fenway, and the original 783-acre peninsula had been expanded by about 450 acres. Thus the waters of Back Bay became the neighborhood of Back Bay.

Heavily influenced by the then-recent rebuilding of Paris according to the plans of Baron Georges-Eugène Haussmann, the Back Bay planners created thoroughfares that resemble Parisian boulevards. Almost immediately, fashionable families began to decamp from Beacon Hill and South End and establish themselves in the Back Bay's brick and brownstone row houses. By 1900 the streets between the Public Garden and Massachusetts Avenue had become the smartest, most desirable neighborhood in all of Boston.

Today the area retains its posh spirit, but mansions are no longer the main draw. Locals and tourists flock to the commercial streets of Boylston and Newbury to shop at boutiques, galleries, and the usual mall stores. Many of the bars and restaurants have patio seating and bay windows. The Boston Public Library, Symphony Hall, and numerous churches ensure that high culture is not lost amid the frenzy of consumerism.

Back Bay

Sights

★ Boston Public Garden
GARDEN | FAMILY | America's oldest botanical garden, the Public Garden is replete with gorgeous formal plantings. Keep in mind that the Boston Public Garden and Boston Common (not Commons!) are two separate entities with different histories and purposes and a distinct boundary between them at Charles Street. The central feature of the Public Garden is its irregularly shaped pond, intended to appear, from any vantage point along its banks, much larger than its nearly 4 acres. The pond has been famous since 1877 for its foot-pedal-powered (by a captain) **Swan Boats** (⊕ *swanboats.com*), which make leisurely cruises during warm months. The dominant work among the park's statuary is Thomas Ball's equestrian **George Washington** (1869), which faces

the head of Commonwealth Avenue at the Arlington Street gate, but follow the children quack-quacking along the pathway between the pond and the park entrance at Charles and Beacon Streets to the *Make Way for Ducklings* bronzes sculpted by Nancy Schön, a tribute to the 1941 classic children's story by Robert McCloskey. ⊠ *Bounded by Arlington, Boylston, Charles, and Beacon Sts., Back Bay* ☎ *617/522–1966 Swan Boats* ⊕ *friendsofthepublicgarden.org* 🚢 *Swan Boats $4* Ⓜ *Arlington.*

★ Boston Public Library
BUILDING | FAMILY | This venerable institution is a handsome temple to literature and a valuable research library, but you don't need a library card to enjoy the magnificent art. The library offers free art and architecture tours daily. The corridor leading from the annex opens onto the Renaissance-style **courtyard**—an exact copy of the one in Rome's Palazzo della Cancelleria—around which the original library is built. A covered arcade furnished with chairs rings a fountain; you can bring books or lunch into the courtyard, which is open all the hours the library is open, and escape the bustle of the city. Beyond the courtyard is the main entrance hall of the 1895 building, with its immense stone lions by Louis St. Gaudens, vaulted ceiling, and marble staircase. The corridor at the top of the stairs leads to **Bates Hall,** one of Boston's most sumptuous interior spaces. This is the main reference reading room, 218 feet long with a barrel-arch ceiling 50 feet high. ⊠ *700 Boylston St., at Copley Sq., Back Bay* ☎ *617/536–5400* ⊕ *www.bpl. org* Ⓜ *Copley.*

Esplanade
PROMENADE | FAMILY | Near the corner of Beacon and Arlington Streets, the Arthur Fiedler Footbridge crosses Storrow Drive to the 3-mile-long Esplanade and the **Hatch Memorial Shell.** The free concerts here in summer include the Boston Pops' immensely popular televised July 4 performance. For shows like this,

Back Bay, the Fenway, and Kenmore Square

0	275 yards
0	250 meters

Sights ▶

1 Boston Public Garden...	E1
2 Boston Public Library....	D2
3 Esplanade	E1
4 Fenway Park	A2
5 Isabella Stewart Gardner Museum	B3
6 Museum of Fine Arts ...	B3
7 Newbury Street..........	E1
8 Trinity Church	E2

Restaurants ▶

1 Atlantic Fish Co..........	D2
2 Eastern Standard Kitchen and Drinks..............	A2
3 Flour Bakery + Café	C2
4 Franklin Cafe	F3
5 Grill 23 & Bar............	E2
6 L'Espalier..............	D2
7 Mistral	E2
8 Myers+Chang...........	F3
9 Oishii Boston...........	F3
10 Saltie Girl	D1
11 Sonsie................	C2
12 Sweet Cheeks Q.........	A3
13 Toro...................	E3
14 Troquet on South.......	H2

Hotels ▶

1 Charlesmark Hotel	D2
2 The Colonnade Hotel ...	D2
3 Eliot Hotel	B2
4 Fairmont Copley Plaza..	E2
5 Gryphon House..........	B2
6 Hotel Commonwealth...	B2
7 Inn@St. Botolph........	D3
8 Mandarin Oriental, Boston..............	D2
9 Taj Boston Hotel.......	E1

KEY

- 1 Sights
- 1 Restaurants
- 1 Hotels
- Ⓣ Subway station
- – – Freedom Trail

Bostonians haul lawn chairs and blankets to the lawn in front of the shell; bring a takeout lunch from a nearby restaurant, find an empty spot—no mean feat, so come early—and you'll feel right at home. An impressive stone bust of the late maestro Arthur Fiedler watches over the walkers, joggers, picnickers, and sunbathers who fill the Esplanade's paths on pleasant days. Here, too, is the turn-of-the-20th-century **Union Boat Club Boathouse,** headquarters for the country's oldest private rowing club. ⊠ *Back Bay* ⊕ *www.esplanadeassociation.org.*

★ Museum of Fine Arts

MUSEUM | FAMILY | The MFA's collection of approximately 450,000 objects was built from a core of paintings and sculpture from the Boston Athenæum, historical portraits from the city of Boston, and donations by area universities. The MFA has more than 70 works by John Single-ton Copley; major paintings by Winslow Homer, John Singer Sargent, Fitz Henry Lane, and Edward Hopper; and a wealth of American works ranging from native New England folk art and Colonial portraiture to New York abstract expressionism of the 1950s and 1960s.

More than 30 galleries contain the MFA's European painting and sculpture collection, dating from the 11th century to the 20th. Contemporary art has a dynamic home in the MFA's dramatic I.M. Pei–designed building. ⊠ *465 Huntington Ave., The Fenway* ☎ *617/267–9300* ⊕ *www.mfa.org* 🎫 *$25 (good for 2 days in a 10-day period)* Ⓜ *Museum.*

Newbury Street

NEIGHBORHOOD | Eight-block-long Newbury Street has been compared to New York's 5th Avenue, and certainly this is the city's poshest shopping area, with branches of Chanel, Diane von Furstenberg, Burberry, Kate Spade, Marc Jacobs, and other top names in fashion. But here the pricey boutiques are more intimate than grand, and people live above the trendy restaurants and ubiquitous hair salons, giving

the place a neighborhood feel. Toward the Massachusetts Avenue end, cafés proliferate and the stores get funkier, ending with Newbury Comics and Urban Outfitters. ⊠ *From Arlington St. to Massachusetts Ave., Back Bay* ⊕ *www. newbury-st.com* Ⓜ *Hynes, Copley.*

★ Trinity Church

BUILDING | In his 1877 masterpiece, architect Henry Hobson Richardson brought his Romanesque Revival style to maturity; all the aesthetic elements for which he was famous come together magnificently—bold polychromatic masonry, careful arrangement of masses, sumptuously carved interior wood-work—in this crowning centerpiece of Copley Square. A full appreciation of its architecture requires an understanding of the logistical problems of building it here. The Back Bay is a reclaimed wetland with a high water table. Bedrock, or at least stable glacial till, lies far beneath wet clay. Like all older Back Bay build-ings, Trinity Church sits on submerged wooden pilings. But its central tower weighs 9,500 tons, and most of the 4,500 pilings beneath the building are under that tremendous central mass. The pilings are checked regularly for sinkage by means of a hatch in the basement. For a nice respite, try to catch one of the Friday organ concerts beginning at 12:15. The 11:15 Sunday service is usually followed by a free guided tour. ⊠ *206 Clarendon St., Back Bay* ☎ *617/536–0944* ⊕ *trinitychurchboston.org* 🎫 *Entrance free, guided and self-guided tours Tues.– Fri., $7* Ⓜ *Copley.*

🍴 Restaurants

★ Atlantic Fish Co

$$$ | SEAFOOD | Designed to look like an ocean vessel with gorgeous wood finishes and nautical artwork, this local seafood restaurant delivers first-class fish, so fresh that the extensive menus are printed daily to reflect the day's catch, served broiled, baked, blackened, fried, grilled, or pan-seared. Unsnap your starched napkin and begin with a platter of chilled seafood (lobster, littlenecks, oysters, crab, and shrimp), followed by any one of the specialties ranging from whole-bellied fried Ipswich clams to pan-seared bass with lobster ravioli in an unctuous lobster cream sauce. **Known for:** elegant seafood; solicitous service in a lux atmosphere. $ Average main: $31 ⊠ 761 Boylston St., Back Bay ☎ 617/267–4000 ⊕ www.atlanticfish.com Ⓜ Copley.

★ Eastern Standard Kitchen and Drinks

$$$ | AMERICAN | A vivid red awning beckons patrons of this spacious brasserie-style restaurant with menus for breakfast, lunch, midday, dinner, and late night (until 1:30 am). The bar area and red banquettes fill most nights with Boston's power players (members of the Red Sox management are known to stop in), thirtysomethings, and students from the nearby universities all noshing on raw-bar specialties and comfort dishes such as lamb-sausage rigatoni, steak frites, and burgers. **Known for:** brasserie fare; terrific craft cocktails; Parisian-style decor. $ Average main: $25 ⊠ 528 Commonwealth Ave., Kenmore Square ☎ 617/532–9100 ⊕ www.easternstandardboston.com Ⓜ Kenmore.

★ Flour Bakery + Café

$ | AMERICAN | FAMILY | When folks need coffee, a great sandwich, or an irresistible sweet, like a pecan sticky bun, lemon tart, or double chocolate cookie—or just a place to sit and chat—they come to one of owner Joanne Chang's seven Flour bakeries, including this one in the South End. A communal table in the middle acts as a gathering spot, around which diners enjoy morning pastries, homemade soups, hearty bean and grain salads, and specialty sandwiches like grilled chicken with Brie, roasted peppers, caramelized onions, and arugula, or a BLT with applewood-smoked bacon. **Known for:** scrumptious sweets; delicious salads and sandwiches; laid-back setting. $ Average main: $9 ⊠ 1595 Washington St., South End ☎ 617/267–4300 ⊕ www. flourbakery.com Ⓜ Massachusetts Ave.

The Franklin Café

$$ | AMERICAN | With a full menu served until 1:30 pm, this place has jumped to the head of the class by keeping things simple yet effective, from the well-crafted cocktails to the homey cuisine: think skillet-smoked mussels, succulent turkey meat loaf, and braised beef brisket with roasted vegetables. The vibe tends to feel more like a bar than a restaurant (hence the many bartender awards), so be forewarned that it can get loud and the wait for a table (there are only seven booths and two tables) can be long. **Known for:** gastropub fare; neighborhood feel; open late. $ Average main: $20 ⊠ 278 Shawmut Ave., South End ☎ 617/350–0010 ⊕ www.franklincafe. com ☾ No lunch Ⓜ Union Park.

★ Grill 23 & Bar

$$$$ | STEAKHOUSE | Pinstripe suits, dark paneling, Persian rugs, and waiters in white jackets give this single-location steak house a posh tone, and the kitchen places a premium on seasonal, organic ingredients and sustainable and humanely raised meats—and leave room for dessert. Two bars, a big, buzzing one overlooking Berkeley Street and a quieter, smaller one on the second floor by the cozy fireplace, serve excellent drinks, specialty Scotches, and bar bites, along with the full menu. **Known for:** nonchain steak-house status; excellent meats; party-dress vibe. $ Average main: $40 ⊠ 161 Berkeley St., Back Bay ☎ 617/542–2255 ⊕ grill23.com ☾ No lunch Ⓜ Back Bay/South End.

★ L'Espalier

$$$$ | FRENCH | Adjacent to the Mandarin Oriental Hotel, this elegant French restaurant, with floor-to-ceiling windows and modern decor, is the sort of place where locals come to splurge with either a five- or eight-course tasting menu, including a vegetarian one. Chef-owner Frank McClelland's dishes—from caviar

and roasted foie gras to beef sirloin and smoked Maine lobster—are as delicious as they are artful and often include ingredients harvested that morning from McClelland's own farm. **Known for:** masterful French cuisine; sumptuous cheese trolley; special-occasion atmosphere. ⑤ *Average main: $98* ✉ *774 Boylston St., Back Bay* ☎ *617/262–3023* ⊕ *www.lespalier.com* Ⓜ *Copley.*

★ Mistral

$$$$ | **FRENCH** | Boston's fashionable set flocks to this long-popular South End restaurant with polished service and upscale yet unpretentious French-Mediterranean cuisine with fail-safe favorites like tuna tartare, duck with cherries, and French Dover sole. The seasonally tweaked menu rarely changes—but no one's complaining; a luxurious à la carte brunch is served on Sunday. **Known for:** sophisticated Mediterranean cuisine; superb service; white-cloth, country French decor. ⑤ *Average main: $36* ✉ *223 Columbus Ave., South End* ☎ *617/867–9300* ⊕ *mistralbistro.com* ☾ *No lunch* Ⓜ *Back Bay.*

★ Myers + Chang

$$ | **CHINESE** | Pink and orange dragon decals cover the windows of this all-day Chinese café, where Joanne Chang (of Flour bakery fame) taps her familial cooking roots to create shareable platters of creative dumplings, wok-charred udon noodles, and stir-fries brimming with fresh ingredients and plenty of hot chili peppers, garlic, fresh herbs, crushed peanuts, and lime. The staff is young and fun, and the crowd generally follows suit. **Known for:** Asian soul food; fabulous cocktails; punchy decor. ⑤ *Average main: $18* ✉ *1145 Washington St., South End* ☎ *617/542–5200* ⊕ *www.myersandchang.com* Ⓜ *Back Bay.*

Oishii Boston

$$$ | **JAPANESE** | Although the entrance to this superb sushi restaurant may elude you, simply follow the crowds of raw-fish fans streaming into the sleek, gray, industrial space, to find edible aquatic enchantment in the form of tuna tartare with caviar and crispy shallots tempura, lobster maki in a daikon radish wrapper, and seafood risotto in a sizzling hot pot. The vibe is stylish and so are the diners. **Known for:** high-end Japanese sushi; quiet atmosphere; minimalist decor. ⑤ *Average main: $35* ✉ *1166 Washington St., South End* ☎ *617/482–8868* ⊕ *www.oishiiboston.com* ☾ *Closed Mon.* Ⓜ *East Berkeley.*

★ Saltie Girl

$$$ | **SEAFOOD** | Step into this snug Back Bay raw bar specializing in snappy cocktails and luscious preparations of all things seafood and you'll fall hook, line, and sinker for everything on the menu, including platters of fresh-shucked oysters on crushed ice, torched salmon belly with charred avocado, smoked fish that would make a New York deli owner proud, seafood-topped toasts, and arguably the best warm lobster roll in the city, a butter-drenched affair overflowing with fresh lobster meat. Rounding out the menu and decorating the restaurant's walls are 80-plus tins of domestic and imported gourmet fish and shellfish (including caviar!) served in all their oily goodness with bread, butter, smoked salt, lemon, and sweet pepper jam. **Known for:** yummy seafood tapas; huge tinned seafood selection; big, buttery, warm lobster roll. ⑤ *Average main: $25* ✉ *281 Dartmouth St., Back Bay* ☎ *617/267–0691* *saltiegirl.com.*

Sonsie

$$$ | **AMERICAN** | Café society blossoms along Newbury Street, particularly at Sonsie (a favorite haunt of the Patriot's Tom Brady), where a well-heeled crowd sips coffee up front or angles for places at the bar. Lunch and dinner dishes veer toward basic bistro fare with an American twist such as kale Caesar salad with grilled chicken and pan-roasted salmon with potatoes, chard, and beet "ketchup." The restaurant is a terrific place for weekend brunch, when the light pours through the long windows, and is at its most vibrant in warm weather, when the open doors make for colorful people-watching. **Known for:** American bistro favorites; sceney vibe; Sunday brunch. $ *Average main: $25* ✉ *327 Newbury St., Back Bay* ☎ *617/351–2500* ⊕ *sonsieboston.com* Ⓜ *Hynes.*

★ Sweet Cheeks Q

$$ | SOUTHERN | Red Sox fans, foodies, and Fenway residents flock to this meat-lover's mecca, where Texas-style barbecue is the name of the game. Hefty slabs of dry-rubbed heritage pork, great northern beef brisket, and plump chickens cook low and slow in a jumbo black smoker then come to the table heaped on a tray lined with butcher paper, along with homemade sweet pickles, shaved onion, and your choice of "hot scoops" (collard greens, mac 'n' cheese) or "cold scoops" (coleslaw, potato salad). **Known for:** finger-licking barbecue; scrumptious sides; jeans and T-shirt atmosphere. $ *Average main: $22* ✉ *1381 Boylston St., The Fenway* ☎ *617/266–1300* ⊕ *www.sweetcheeksq.com* ▭ *No credit cards* Ⓜ *Fenway.*

★ Toro

$$$ | SPANISH | The opening buzz from chefs Ken Oringer and Jamie Bissonnette's tapas joint, which now has an outpost in Manhattan, still remains loud—for good reason. Small plates such as grilled corn with aioli and cotija cheese are hefty enough to make a meal out of a few, or you can share the regular or vegetarian paella with a group. **Known for:** excellent traditional tapas; cozy, small dining room; cult following. $ *Average main: $35* ✉ *1704 Washington St., South End* ☎ *617/536–4300* ⊕ *www.toro-restaurant.com* Ⓜ *Massachusetts Ave.*

★ Troquet on South

$$$$ | FRENCH FUSION | Despite having what might well be Boston's longest wine list, with nearly 500 vintages (more than 50 of which are available by the glass), plus an interactive Champagne cart, this French fusion spot flies somewhat under the radar. Still, locals know that Troquet offers all the ingredients for a lovely and delectable evening: a generous space for drinking and dining, a knowledgeable yet unpretentious staff, and decadent fare, beginning with chewy rolls and farm-churned butter scooped from a bucket, and entrées like roasted suckling pig and rosy duck with lentils and mandarin. **Known for:** exceptional wine selection; mouthwatering bistro fare; excellent cheese cart. $ *Average main: $42* ✉ *107 South St., Theater District* ☎ *617/695–9463* ⊕ *troquetboston.com* ☾ *No lunch Sat. Closed Sun.* Ⓜ *Boylston.*

Hotels

Charlesmark Hotel

$ | HOTEL | Hipsters and romantics who'd rather spend their cash on a great meal than a hotel bill have put this late-19th-century former residential row house on the map. **Pros:** fantastic price for the location; free Wi-Fi; all rooms have safes and refrigerators. **Cons:** some might feel crowded by compact rooms and hallways; no valet; no turndown service. $ *Rooms from: $169* ✉ *655 Boylston St., Back Bay* ☎ *617/247–1212* ⊕ *www.thecharlesmarkhotel.com* ⇥ *40 rooms* �ⓘ⊘⎮ *Free breakfast* Ⓜ *Copley.*

The Colonnade Hotel

$$ | HOTEL | FAMILY | The Colonnade showcases clean, modern environs injected with hues of khaki, chocolate, and chrome. **Pros:** roof-deck pool; across from Prudential Center shopping; close to Hynes Convention Center. **Cons:** Huntington Avenue can get clogged with rush-hour traffic; on summer days the pool is packed by 11 am; parking is expensive. $ *Rooms from: $260* ✉ *120 Huntington Ave., Back Bay* ☎ *617/424–7000, 800/962–3030* ⊕ *www.colonnadehotel.com* ⇥ *294 rooms* ⓘ⊘⎮ *No meals* Ⓜ *Back Bay, Prudential Center.*

★ Eliot Hotel

$$ | HOTEL | One of the city's best small hotels is on posh Commonwealth Avenue, modeled after Paris's epic Champs-Élysées, and it expertly merges the old blue-blood Boston aesthetic with modern flair (like contemporary rugs mingling with crystal chandeliers); everyone from well-heeled Sox fans to traveling CEOs to tony college parents have noticed. **Pros:** great location near Fenway and Newbury Street; top-notch restaurant; pet-friendly; beautiful rooms. **Cons:** very expensive; some complain of elevator noise; parking is expensive. ⑤ *Rooms from: $285 ⌧ 370 Commonwealth Ave., Back Bay* ☎ *617/267–1607, 800/443–5468* ⊕ *www.eliothotel.com* ⤴ *95 rooms* �“⊙❙ *No meals* Ⓜ *Hynes.*

★ Fairmont Copley Plaza

$$$ | **HOTELHOTEL** | **FAMILY** | Past guests, including one Judy Garland, felt at home in this decadent, unabashedly romantic hotel that underwent a $20 million renovation in early 2012. **Pros:** prime Back Bay location, centrally located in Copley Square; luxurious gym; 24-hour daily in-room dining. **Cons:** small bathrooms; charge for Internet access (no charge on Fairmont President's Club level); due to the historical nature, room sizes vary greatly. ⑤ *Rooms from: $359 ⌧ 138 St. James Ave., Back Bay* ☎ *617/267–5300, 866/540–4417* ⊕ *www.fairmont.com/copley-plaza-boston* ⤴ *383 rooms* ❙⊙❙ *No meals* Ⓜ *Copley, Back Bay.*

★ Inn@St. Botolph

$$ | **B&B/INN** | **FAMILY** | The posh yet homey 16-room Inn@St. Botolph follows a groundbreaking new hotel model—no front desk, no restaurant, no keys, and no valet (there is, however, an office on-site that is staffed 24/7). **Pros:** guests get 25% off meals at Columbus Hospital Group restaurants; free Wi-Fi; free transit to select restaurants. **Cons:** DIY parking; no traditional front desk check-in services; may be too "off the beaten path" for some. ⑤ *Rooms from: $279 ⌧ 99 St. Botolph St., Back Bay* ☎ *617/236–8099* ⊕ *www.innatstbotolph.com* ⤴ *16 rooms* ❙⊙❙ *Free breakfast* Ⓜ *Prudential.*

Mandarin Oriental, Boston

$$$$ | **HOTEL** | With too many amenities to list, the 148-room hotel has helped redefine luxury in town (pay attention, Ritz and Four Seasons) since opening in 2008. **Pros:** amazing service; very quiet; good-size rooms. **Cons:** small fitness center; rates are exorbitant; valet parking is expensive. ⑤ *Rooms from: $595 ⌧ 776 Boylston St., Back Bay* ☎ *617/535–8888* ⊕ *www.mandarinoriental.com/boston* ⤴ *150 rooms* ❙⊙❙ *No meals* Ⓜ *Prudential, Copley, Back Bay.*

Taj Boston Hotel

$$ | **HOTEL** | **FAMILY** | Standing guard at the corner of fashionable Newbury Street and the Public Garden, the old-school elegant Taj features plush new robes and towels in guest rooms, new carpets, Molton Brown bath amenities, and vibrant floral displays in the lobby. **Pros:** white-glove service; amazing views; proximity to shopping, dining, and the park. **Cons:** all this luxury will cost you; rooms on the 16th floor are under the roof-deck party space; guest rooms need an update. ⑤ *Rooms from: $279 ⌧ 15 Arlington St., Back Bay* ☎ *617/536–5700* ⊕ *www.thetajboston.com* ⤴ *315 rooms* ❙⊙❙ *No meals* Ⓜ *Arlington.*

Nightlife

BARS

★ JJ Foley's Cafe

BARS/PUBS | Family-owned and-operated since 1909, JJ Foley's Cafe (or "Foley's," as regulars call it) is one of the most authentic Irish bars in Boston. There's an intimate dining room, as well as a more casual bar area where everyone from former Boston mayors to Justin Timberlake have enjoyed a pint. The pub food is great; order a sky-high plate of nachos if you dare. ■TIP➔ **Don't mistake this Foley's with the JJ Foley's Bar & Grill in Downtown Boston; despite similar names, the South End Foley's is the real thing.** ⌧ *117 E. Berkeley St., South End* ☎ *617/728–9101* ⊕ *www.jjfoleyscafe.com* Ⓜ *Tufts Medical Center.*

★ Sonsie

BARS/PUBS | The crowd spilling through French doors onto the sidewalk café in warm weather consists of trendy cosmopolitans, fun-loving professionals, local sports celebs, and scenesters. Founding owner-chef Bill Poirier's offerings of contemporary Americana have been a Back Bay standout for 20 years. The sophisticated jazz-rock soundtrack remains at a civilized volume as you dine, sip, and people-watch. Hungry? There's breakfast after 9, with specialty coffees from a Presse espresso coffee-bar, a weekday lunch, weekend brunches from 11 to 3:30 pm, and daily dinner and late-night menus until 12:30 am. ⊠ 327 Newbury St., Back Bay ☎ 617/351–2500 ⊕ sonsieboston.com Ⓜ Hynes.

MUSIC CLUBS
★ Beehive

MUSIC CLUBS | An underground bohemian bistro featuring delicious food, libations, and live music nightly, the Beehive is nestled under the historic Cyclorama building. The performers might play jazz, blues, R&B, reggae, or Latin music while patrons enjoy craft cocktails and wines. Dine on Mediterranean meze platters, daily special pastas, and comfort entrées. If jazz is your jam, don't miss the weekend jazz brunch from 10 am to 3 pm; Sunday nights feature blues. ⊠ 541 Tremont St., South End ☎ 617/423–0069 ⊕ www.beehiveboston.com Ⓜ Back Bay.

★ Darryl's Corner Bar & Kitchen

CAFES—NIGHTLIFE | This longtime neighborhood soul-food and jazz hangout still looks spiffy, and features real Southern cooking and live bands nearly nightly at light cover charges. Come for glorified chicken and waffles on Wednesday, and on Sunday there is a blues brunch starting at 10:30 am. Theatergoers receive dining discounts. ⊠ 604 Columbus Ave., South End ☎ 617/536–1100 ⊕ www.dcbkboston.com Ⓜ Massachusetts Ave.

★ Wally's Café

MUSIC CLUBS | A rare gem for jazz and blues fans, Wally's Café, founded in 1947, is the oldest continuously operating family-owned jazz club in America. Patrons may see nostalgic stars like Branford Marsalis or Esperanza Spalding drop by, because the place is internationally renowned for its steady stream of heated performances by local bands and guests. Wally's diverse crowd attracts regulars from the South End and Roxbury, and music-hungry students, especially from Berklee College of Music. It's jammed every night of the year and there's never a cover. Monday it's blues and Thursday it's Latin jazz. Daily jam sessions run from 6 to 9 pm; bring your horn! Arrive early if you want a seat, because the line can be brutal. ⊠ 427 Massachusetts Ave., South End ☎ 617/424–1408 ⊕ www.wallyscafe.com ⊡ Free Ⓜ Massachusetts Ave., Symphony.

⊕ Performing Arts

CONCERT SERIES
★ Boston Public Library

CONCERTS | Completed in 1895, the Central Library in Copley Square's McKim building is known for its classical serenity and elegance, and includes Bates Hall's majestic barrel-arched ceiling, John Singer Sargent murals, and an interior courtyard that plays host to the summer Concerts in the Courtyard series (June through August, Wednesday at 6 pm, Friday at 12:30 pm). There are also free daily Art and Architecture tours. The Central Library's Johnson building, reopened to the public in July 2016 after a multiyear renovation, is an open and vibrant space, while the new Newsfeed Cafe is home to a WGBH satellite radio and television studio that features live tapings of shows like Boston Public Radio, hosted by Jim Braude and Margery Eagan. ⊠ 700 Boylston St., Copley Sq., Back Bay ☎ 617/536–5400 ⊕ www.bpl.org Ⓜ Copley.

DANCE
Boston Ballet
DANCE | The city's premier dance company performs at the Boston Opera House. Shows have included *Romeo & Juliet*, classic Balanchine, and *La Sylphide*. And, of course, if you're visiting during the holidays, be sure to score seats to the *Nutcracker*. ✉ *19 Clarendon St., South End* ☎ *617/695–6955* ⊕ *www.bostonballet.org* Ⓜ *Back Bay.*

Activities

BICYCLING
Back Bay Bicycles
BICYCLING | Road bikes rent here for $45 per day (weekly rates are also available). City bikes rent for $35. ✉ *362 Commonwealth Ave., Back Bay* ☎ *617/247–2336* ⊕ *www.papa-wheelies.com.*

Community Bicycle Supply
BICYCLING | This South End place rents cycles from April through October. The $25 daily rate also includes a helmet and lock. ✉ *496 Tremont St., at E. Berkeley St., South End* ☎ *617/542–8623* ⊕ *www.communitybicycle.com* Ⓜ *Back Bay.*

RUNNING
★ Boston Marathon
RUNNING | Every Patriots' Day (the third Monday in April), fans gather along the Hopkinton-to-Boston route of the Boston Marathon to cheer on more than 25,000 runners from all over the world. The race ends near Copley Square in the Back Bay. ✉ *Copley Sq., Back Bay* ⊕ *www.baa.org* Ⓜ *Copley, Arlington.*

Shopping

MAJOR SHOPPING DISTRICTS
Boylston Street
SHOPPING NEIGHBORHOODS | Parallel to Newbury Street is Boylston Street, where you'll find a few standout shops such as Pompanoosuc Mills (handcrafted furnishing) scattered among the other chains and restaurants. ✉ *Back Bay* Ⓜ *Back Bay.*

Copley Place
STORE/MALL | Two modern structures dominate Copley Square—the **John Hancock Tower** off the southeast corner and the even more assertive Copley Place skyscraper on the southwest. An upscale, glass-and-brass urban mall built between 1980 and 1984, Copley Place includes two major hotels: the high-rise Westin and the Marriott Copley Place. Dozens of shops, restaurants, and offices are attractively grouped on several levels, surrounding bright, open indoor spaces. ✉ *100 Huntington Ave., Back Bay* ⊕ *www.simon.com/mall/copley-place* Ⓜ *Copley.*

Newbury Street
SHOPPING NEIGHBORHOODS | Boston's version of LA's Rodeo Drive, all of Newbury Street is a shoppers' paradise, from high-end names such as Brooks Brothers to tiny specialty shops such as Ball and Buck. Upscale clothing stores, up-to-the-minute art galleries, and dazzling jewelers line the street near the Public Garden. As you head toward Massachusetts Avenue, Newbury gets funkier and the cacophony builds, with skateboarders zipping through traffic and garbage-pail drummers burning licks outside hip boutiques. The big-name stores run from Arlington Street to the Prudential Center. ✉ *Back Bay* ⊕ *www.newbury-st.com* Ⓜ *Arlington, Copley, Hynes.*

Prudential Center
SHOPPING NEIGHBORHOODS | A skywalk connects Copley Place to the Prudential Center. The Pru, as it's often called, contains popular chain stores such as Ann Taylor and Sephora and is anchored by Saks Fifth Avenue and Lord and Taylor. ✉ *800 Boylston St., Back Bay* ☎ *800/746–7778* ⊕ *www.prudentialcenter.com* Ⓜ *Prudential.*

South End
SHOPPING NEIGHBORHOODS | Independent stores, galleries and restaurants, chic home furnishings, and gift shops line Tremont Street, starting at Berkeley Street. The MBTA's Silver Line bus runs through the

South End. ⊠ *South End* ⊕ *www.south-end-boston.com* Ⓜ *Back Bay.*

ART GALLERIES
Copley Society of Art

ART GALLERIES | After more than a century, this nonprofit membership organization continues to present the works of well-known and aspiring New England artists, as well as out-of-town and foreign members. ⊠ *158 Newbury St., Back Bay* ☎ *617/536–5049* ⊕ *www.copleysociety. org* Ⓜ *Copley.*

CLOTHING
Alan Bilzerian

CLOTHING | Satisfying the Euro crowd, this store sells luxe men's and women's clothing by such fashion darlings as Yohji Yamamoto and Ann Demeulemeester. ⊠ *34 Newbury St., Back Bay* ☎ *617/536–1001* ⊕ *www.alanbilzerian. com* Ⓜ *Arlington.*

Anne Fontaine

CLOTHING | You can never have too many white shirts—especially if they're designed by this Parisienne. The simple, sophisticated designs are mostly executed in cotton and priced at $295 and up. Complete your outfit with the store's selection of sleek skirts, slacks, and accessories; the store also carries dresses and outerwear. ⊠ *280 Boylston St., Back Bay* ☎ *617/423–0366* ⊕ *www. annefontaine.com* Ⓜ *Arlington, Boylston.*

CRAFTS
★ Society of Arts & Crafts

CRAFTS | More than a century old, this is the country's oldest nonprofit crafts organization. In addition to selling a fine assortment of ceramics, jewelry, glass, woodwork, and furniture from a rotating roster of more than 400 of the country's finest artists, the soaring space sponsors free art exhibits, and a featured artist in residence, who you can see working in the studio. ⊠ *100 Pier 4, Suite 200, Back Bay* ⊹ *Above Ocean Prime restaurant on 2nd fl.* ☎ *617/266–1810* ⊕ *www.societyof-crafts.org* Ⓜ *Silver Line MBTA to Court St. station.*

THRIFT SHOPS
★ Bobby from Boston

OUTLET/DISCOUNT STORES | For years this hidden gem was kept on the down low—but the word's out about this two-room space filled with one-of-a-kind finds. Although the items are mostly menswear, there are bargains for females, too. ⊠ *19 Thayer St., South End* ☎ *617/423–9299* ⊕ *www.bobbyfrombostonvintage. com* Ⓜ *Back Bay, Prudential.*

★ Boomerangs–Special Edition

CLOTHING | Stepping into this cozy secondhand boutique feels like you could be in the salon of a very wealthy couple, who just happen to be unloading their cache of designer clothes and housewares. Jade satin flats, beaded Armani tops, and vintage dresses and jewelry—all at a fraction of their original cost—are the sorts of treats you'll find sharing space with menswear, books, and silver-plated serving dishes. Area residents and businesses donate these treasures with all proceeds going to AIDS Action Committee. The branches in Cambridge, Jamaica Plain, and West Roxbury have much more downscale pickings. ⊠ *1407 Washington St., South End* ☎ *617/456–0996* ⊕ *shopboomerangs.org.*

TOYS
Tadpole

TOYS | This is a treasure trove of board games, dolls, trucks, blocks, books, and every other necessity for a kid's toy chest. Stock up on baby gear and essentials as well. ⊠ *58 Clarendon St., South End* ☎ *617/778–1788* ⊕ *www.shoptad-pole.com* Ⓜ *Back Bay.*

The Fenway and Kenmore Square

The marshland known as the Back Bay Fens gave this section of Boston its name, but two quirky institutions give it its character: Fenway Park, home of Boston's beloved Red Sox, and the Isabella

Stewart Gardner Museum, the legacy of a high-living Brahmin who attended a concert at Symphony Hall in 1912 wearing a headband that read, "Oh, You Red Sox." Not far from the Gardner is another major cultural magnet: the Museum of Fine Arts. Kenmore Square, a favorite haunt for Boston University students, adds a bit of funky flavor to the mix.

◉ Sights

★ Fenway Park

SPORTS VENUE | For 86 years, the Boston Red Sox suffered a World Series dry spell, a streak of bad luck that fans attributed to the "Curse of the Bambino," which, stories have it, struck the team in 1920 when they sold Babe Ruth (the "Bambino") to the New York Yankees. All that changed in 2004, when a maverick squad broke the curse in a thrilling seven-game series against the team's nemesis in the series semifinals. This win against the Yankees was followed by a four-game sweep of St. Louis in the finals. Boston, and its citizens' ingrained sense of pessimism, hasn't been the same since. The repeat World Series win in 2007, and again in 2013, cemented Bostonians' sense that the universe had finally begun working correctly and made Red Sox caps the residents' semiofficial uniform. ⊠ *4 Jersey St., between Van Ness and Lansdowne Sts., The Fenway* ☎ *877/733–7699 box office, 617/226–6666 tours* ⊕ *www.redsox.com* 🎫 *Tours $20* Ⓜ *Kenmore.*

★ Isabella Stewart Gardner Museum

MUSEUM | A spirited society woman, Isabella Stewart came in 1860 from New York to marry John Lowell Gardner, one of Boston's leading citizens. She built a Venetian palazzo to hold her collected arts in one of Boston's newest neighborhoods. Her will stipulated that the building remain exactly as she left it—paintings, furniture, and the smallest object in a hall cabinet—and that is as it has remained. The palazzo includes such

New England's Favorite Team

New England Patriots. Boston has been building a football dynasty over the past decade, starting with the Patriots' victory against the St. Louis Rams in the 2002 Super Bowl. Coach Bill Belichick and quarterback Tom Brady then brought the team four more championship rings in 2004, 2005, 2014, and 2017. Exhibition games begin in August, and the season runs through the playoffs in January. ⊠ *Gillette Stadium, Rte. 1, off I–95 Exit 9, Foxborough* ☎ *508/543–1776 Ticketmaster* ⊕ *www.patriots.com* Ⓜ *Gillette Stadium.*

masterpieces as Titian's *Europa,* Giotto's *Presentation of Christ in the Temple,* Piero della Francesca's *Hercules,* and John Singer Sargent's *El Jaleo.* Spanish leather panels, Renaissance hooded fireplaces, and Gothic tapestries accent salons; eight balconies adorn the majestic Venetian courtyard. There's a Raphael Room, Spanish Cloister, Gothic Room, Chinese Loggia, and a magnificent Tapestry Room for concerts. On March 18, 1990, thieves disguised as police officers stole 12 works, including Vermeer's *The Concert.* None of the art has been recovered, and because Mrs. Gardner's will prohibited substituting other works for any stolen art, empty expanses of wall identify spots where the paintings once hung. The popular RISE Music Series features pop, rock, and hip-hop artists, while the STIR is an adventurous mix of contemporary art, music, and performance. ■ TIP→ **A quirk of the museum's admission policy waives entrance fees to anyone named Isabella and on your birthday.** ⊠ *25 Evans Way, The Fenway* ☎ *617/566–1401* ⊕ *www.gardnermuseum.org* 🎫 *$15* ⊗ *Closed Tues.* Ⓜ *Museum.*

Hotels

★ **Gryphon House**

$$$ | B&B/INN | The staff in this value-packed, four-story 19th-century brownstone is helpful and friendly, and the suites are thematically decorated: one evokes rustic Italy; another is inspired by neo-Gothic art. **Pros:** elegant suites are lush and spacious; gas fireplaces in all rooms; free Wi-Fi. **Cons:** may be too fussy for some; no elevator; no wheelchair access. ⑤ *Rooms from: $300* ⊠ *9 Bay State Rd., Kenmore Square* ☎ *617/375–9003, 877/375–9003* ⊕ *www.innboston. com* ⌁ *8 suites* ⎟⊙⎟ *Free breakfast* Ⓜ *Kenmore.*

★ **Hotel Commonwealth**

$$$ | HOTEL | Luxury and service without pretense make this hip spot a solid choice. **Pros:** down bedding; perfect locale for Red Sox fans; happening bar scene at Eastern Standard; free Wi-Fi. **Cons:** area is absolutely mobbed during Sox games; small gym; pricey rates. ⑤ *Rooms from: $399* ⊠ *500 Commonwealth Ave., Kenmore Square* ☎ *617/933–5000, 866/784–4000* ⊕ *www. hotelcommonwealth.com* ⌁ *245 rooms* ⎟⊙⎟ *No meals* Ⓜ *Kenmore.*

 Activities

BASEBALL
See the Fenway Park listing in Sights.

PARKS AND BEACHES
★ **Arnold Arboretum**
PARK—SPORTS-OUTDOORS | FAMILY | The sumptuously landscaped Arnold Arboretum is open all year to walkers, nature lovers, and joggers. Volunteer docents give free walking tours in spring, summer, and fall. ⊠ *125 Arborway, Jamaica Plain* ☎ *617/524–1718* ⊕ *www.arboretum.harvard.edu* Ⓜ *Forest Hills.*

★ **Emerald Necklace**
PARK—SPORTS-OUTDOORS | FAMILY | The six large public parks known as Boston's Emerald Necklace stretch 7 miles from the Back Bay Fens to Franklin Park in Dorchester, and include Arnold Arboretum, Jamaica Pond, Olmsted Park, and the Riverway. The linear parks, designed by master landscape architect Frederick Law Olmsted more than 100 years ago, remain a well-groomed urban masterpiece. ⊠ *Boston* ⊕ *www.emeraldnecklace.org.*

Cambridge

Across the Charles River is the uberliberal academic enclave of Cambridge. The city is punctuated at one end by the funky tech-noids of MIT and at the other by the grand academic fortress that is Harvard University. Civic life connects the two camps into an urban stew of 100,000 residents who represent nearly every nationality in the world, work at every kind of job from tenured professor to taxi driver, and are passionate about living on this side of the river.

The Charles River is the Cantabrigians' backyard, and there's virtually no place in Cambridge more than a 10-minute walk from its banks. Strolling, running, or biking here is one of the great pleasures of Cambridge, and views include graceful bridges, the distant Boston skyline, crew teams rowing through the calm water, and the elegant spires of Harvard soaring into the sky.

No visit to Cambridge is complete without an afternoon in Harvard Square. It's home to every variation of the human condition; Nobel laureates, homeless buskers, trust-fund babies, and working-class Joes mill around the same piece of real estate. Walk down Brattle Street past Henry Wadsworth Longfellow's house. Farther along Massachusetts Avenue is Central Square, an ethnic melting pot of people and restaurants. Ten minutes more brings you to MIT, with its eclectic architecture from postwar pedestrian to Frank Gehry's futuristic fantasyland. In addition to providing a

Cambridge

Sights ▶

1 Harvard Art Museums .. **C2**
2 Harvard Museum of
Natural History............ **C1**
3 Harvard Square............ **C2**
4 Harvard University **B1**

5 Longfellow House-
Washington's
Headquarters **A2**
6 Massachusetts Institute
of Technology............. **H3**
7 Peabody Museum of
Archaeology &
Ethnology.................... **C1**

Restaurants ▶

1 All Star Sandwich Bar .. **F1**
2 Area Four **H2**
3 Giulia **B1**
4 Harvest......................... **C2**
5 Oleana **G1**
6 Orinoco **C3**

Hotels ▶

1 Charles Hotel............. **B3**
2 Royal Sonesta Boston.. **H2**

KEY

1 Sights
1 Restaurants
1 Hotels
🕐 Subway station

MASSACHUSETTS
INSTITUTE OF
TECHNOLOGY

HARVARD
UNIVERSITY

RADCLIFFE
COLLEGE

Charles River

0   500 yards
0   500 meters

stellar view, the Massachusetts Avenue Bridge, spanning the Charles from Cambridge to Boston, is also notorious in MIT lore for its Smoot measurements.

Sights

★ Harvard Art Museums

MUSEUM | In late 2014, the combined collections of the Busch-Reisinger, Fogg, and Arthur M. Sackler museums were united under one glorious, mostly glass roof, under the umbrella name Harvard Art Museums. Housed in a facility designed by award-winning architect Renzo Piano, the 204,000-square-foot museum is spread over seven levels, allowing more of Harvard's 250,000-piece art collection to be seen in one place. Highlights include American and European paintings, sculptures, and decorative arts from the Fogg Museum; and works by German expressionists, materials related to the Bauhaus, and postwar contemporary art from German-speaking Europe from the Busch-Reisinger Museum. In addition to the gallery spaces, there's a 300-seat theater, a café, plus conservation and research labs. ⊠ 32 Quincy St., Harvard Square 🕾 617/495–9400 ⊕ www.harvardartmuseums.org 🎟 $15 Ⓜ Harvard.

★ Harvard Museum of Natural History

MUSEUM | FAMILY | The Harvard Museum of Natural History (which exhibits specimens from the Museum of Comparative Zoology, Harvard University Herbaria, and the Mineralogical and Geological Museum) displays some 12,000 specimens, including dinosaurs, rare minerals, hundreds of mammals and birds, and Harvard's world-famous Blaschka Glass Flowers. The museum combines historic exhibits drawn from the university's vast collections with new and changing multimedia exhibitions such as New England Forests and Mollusks: Shelled Masters of the Marine Realm, and the renovated Earth & Planetary Sciences gallery. ⊠ 26 Oxford St., Harvard Square 🕾 617/495–3045 ⊕ www.hmnh.harvard.edu 🎟 $12; ticket includes admission to adjacent Peabody Museum Ⓜ Harvard.

★ Harvard Square

NEIGHBORHOOD | FAMILY | Tides of students, tourists, political-cause proponents, and bizarre street creatures are all part of the nonstop pedestrian flow at this most celebrated of Cambridge crossroads.

Harvard Square is where Massachusetts Avenue, coming from Boston, turns and widens into a triangle broad enough to accommodate a brick peninsula (above the T station). The restored 1928 kiosk in the center of the square once served as the entrance to the MBTA station. Harvard Yard, with its lecture halls, residential houses, libraries, and museums, is one long border of the square; the other three are composed of clusters of banks and a wide variety of restaurants and shops.

On an average afternoon you'll hear earnest conversations in dozens of foreign languages; see every kind of youthful uniform from Goth to impeccable prep; wander by street musicians playing Andean flutes, and doing excellent Stevie Wonder or Edith Piaf imitations; and watch an outdoor game of pickup chess between a street-tough kid and an older gent wearing a beret. An afternoon in the square is people-watching raised to high art.

The historic buildings are worth noting. It's a thrill to walk though the big brick-and-wrought-iron gates to Harvard Yard on up to Widener Library, the University's flagship library. More than 50 miles of bookshelves snake around six stories aboveground and four stories below, holding more than 3 million volumes. The imposing neoclassical structure was designed by one of the nation's first major African American architects, Julian Abele.

Across Garden Street, through an ornamental arch, is **Cambridge Common,** decreed a public pasture in 1631. It's

Did You Know?

The Harvard Museum of Natural History's collection includes 21 million specimens, but only a small sample is on display. An active lecture and family program means there's plenty of opportunity to interact with another local species—the Harvard researcher.

said that under a large tree that once stood in this meadow George Washington took command of the Continental Army on July 3, 1775. A stone memorial now marks the site of the "Washington Elm." Also on the Common is the Irish Famine Memorial by Derry artist Maurice Herron, unveiled in 1997 to coincide with the 150th anniversary of "Black '47," the deadliest year of the potato famine. At the center of the Common a large memorial commemorates the Union soldiers who lost their lives in the Civil War. On the far side of the Common is a fantastic park. ⊠ *Harvard Square* ⊕ *www. harvardsquare.com* Ⓜ *Harvard.*

Harvard University

COLLEGE | The tree-studded, shady, and redbrick expanse of **Harvard Yard**—the very center of Harvard University—has weathered the footsteps of Harvard students for hundreds of years. In 1636 the Great and General Court of the Massachusetts Bay Colony voted funds to establish the colony's first college, and a year later chose Cambridge as the site. Named in 1639 for John Harvard, a young Charlestown clergyman who died in 1638 and left the college his entire library and half his estate, Harvard remained the only college in the New World until 1693, by which time it was firmly established as a respected center of learning. Local wags refer to Harvard as WGU—World's Greatest University— and it's certainly the oldest and most famous American university.

Although the college dates from the 17th century, the oldest buildings in Harvard Yard are from the 18th century (though you'll sometimes see archaeologists digging here for evidence of older structures). Together the buildings chronicle American architecture from the Colonial era to the present. **Holden Chapel,** completed in 1744, is a Georgian gem. The graceful **University Hall** was designed in 1815 by Charles Bulfinch. An 1884 statue of John Harvard by Daniel Chester French stands outside;

ironically for a school with the motto of "Veritas" ("Truth"), the model for the statue was a member of the class of 1882 and not Harvard himself. **Sever Hall,** completed in 1880 and designed by Henry Hobson Richardson, represents the Romanesque revival that was followed by the neoclassical (note the pillared facade of Widener Library) and the neo-Georgian, represented by the sumptuous brick houses along the Charles River, many of which are now undergraduate residences. **Memorial Church,** a graceful steepled edifice of modified Colonial Revival design, was dedicated in 1932. Just north of the Yard is **Memorial Hall,** completed in 1878 as a memorial to Harvard men who died in the Union cause; it's High Victorian both inside and out. It also contains the 1,166-seat Sanders Theatre, which serves as the university's largest lecture hall, site of year-round concerts by students and professionals, and the venue for the festive Christmas Revels.

Many of Harvard's cultural and scholarly facilities are important sights in themselves, but most campus buildings, other than museums and concert halls, are off-limits to the general public.

The **Harvard Information Center,** in the Smith Campus Centre, has a small exhibit space, distributes maps of the university area, and offers free student-led tours of Harvard Yard. The tour doesn't include visits to museums, and it doesn't take you into campus buildings, but it provides a fine orientation. The information center is open year-round (except during spring recess and other semester breaks). From the end of June through August, guides offer tours every half hour; however, it's best to call ahead to confirm times. ⊠ *Bounded by Massachusetts Ave. and Mt. Auburn, Holyoke, and Dunster Sts., 1350 Massachusetts Ave., Harvard Square* ☎ *617/495–1573 Information Center* ⊕ *www.harvard.edu* Ⓜ *Harvard.*

Longfellow House-Washington's Headquarters

HOUSE | Henry Wadsworth Longfellow, the poet whose stirring tales of the Village Blacksmith, Evangeline, Hiawatha, and Paul Revere's midnight ride thrilled 19th-century America, once lived in this elegant mansion. One of several original Tory Row homes on Brattle Street, the house was built in 1759 by John Vassall Jr., and George Washington lived (and slept!) here during the Siege of Boston from July 1775 to April 1776. Longfellow first boarded here in 1837 and later received the house as a gift from his father-in-law on his marriage to Frances Appleton, who burned to death here in an accident in 1861. For 45 years Longfellow wrote his famous verses here and filled the house with the exuberant spirit of his own work and that of his literary circle, which included Ralph Waldo Emerson, Nathaniel Hawthorne, and Charles Sumner, an abolitionist senator. Longfellow died in 1882, but his presence in the house lives on—from the Longfellow family furniture to the wallpaper to the books on the shelves (many of the poet's own). The home is preserved and run by the National Park Service; guided tours of the house are offered May through October. The formal garden is the perfect place to relax; the grounds are open year-round. Longfellow Park, across the street, is the place to stand to take photos of the house. The park was created to preserve the view immortalized in the poet's "To the River Charles." ✉ 105 Brattle St., Harvard Square ☎ 617/876–4491 ⊕ www.nps. gov/long ✎ Free Ⓜ Harvard.

Massachusetts Institute of Technology

COLLEGE | Founded in 1861, MIT moved to Cambridge from Copley Square in the Back Bay in 1916. Once dissed as "the factory," particularly by its Ivy League neighbor, Harvard University, MIT mints graduates that are the sharp blades on the edge of the information revolution. It's perennially in the top five of U.S. News and World Report's college rankings. It has long since fulfilled the predictions of its founder, the geologist William Barton Rogers, that it would surpass "the universities of the land in the accuracy and the extent of its teachings in all branches of positive science." Its emphasis shifted in the 1930s from practical engineering and mechanics to the outer limits of scientific fields.

Architecture is important at MIT. Although the original buildings were obviously designed by and for scientists, many represent pioneering designs of their times. The **Kresge Auditorium,** designed by Eero Saarinen, with a curving roof and unusual thrust, rests on three, instead of four, points. The nondenominational **MIT Chapel,** a circular Saarinen design, is lighted primarily by a roof oculus that focuses natural light on the altar and by reflections from the water in a small surrounding moat; it's topped by an aluminum sculpture by Theodore Roszak. The serpentine **Baker House,** now a dormitory, was designed in 1947 by the Finnish architect Alvar Aalto in such a way as to provide every room with a view of the Charles River. Sculptures by Henry Moore and other notable artists dot the campus. The latest addition is the Green Center, punctuated by the splash of color that is Sol LeWitt's 5,500-square-foot mosaic floor.

The East Campus, which has grown around the university's original neoclassical buildings of 1916, also has outstanding modern architecture and sculpture, including the stark high-rise **Green Building** by I. M. Pei, housing the Earth Science Center. Just outside is Alexander Calder's giant stabile (a stationary mobile) The Big Sail. Another Pei work on the East Campus is the **Wiesner Building,** designed in 1985, which houses the **List Visual Arts Center.** Architect Frank Gehry made his mark on the campus with the cockeyed, improbable **Ray & Maria Stata Center,** a complex of buildings on Vassar Street. The center houses computer, artificial intelligence, and information systems laboratories, and is reputedly as confusing to navigate on the inside as it is to follow on the outside. East Campus's **Great Dome,** which looms over neoclassical Killian Court, has often been the target of student "hacks" and has at various times supported a telephone booth with a ringing phone, a life-size statue of a cow, and a campus police cruiser. Nearby, the domed **Rogers Building** has earned unusual notoriety as the center of a series of hallways and tunnels dubbed "the infinite corridor." Twice each winter the sun's path lines up perfectly with the corridor's axis, and at dusk students line the third-floor hallway to watch the sun set through the westernmost window. The phenomenon is known as "MIT-henge."

MIT maintains an information center in the Rogers Building, and offers free tours of the campus weekdays at 11 and 3. Check the schedule, as the tours are often suspended during school holidays. General hours for the information center are weekdays 9 to 5. ⊠ *77 Massachusetts Ave., Kendall Square* ☎ *617/253–4795* ⊕ *www.mit.edu* Ⓜ *Kendall/MIT.*

Peabody Museum of Archaeology & Ethnology

MUSEUM | With one of the world's outstanding anthropological collections, the Peabody focuses on Native American and Central and South American cultures. The Hall of the North American Indian is particularly outstanding, with art, textiles, and models of traditional dwellings from across the continent. The Mesoamerican room juxtaposes ancient relief carvings and weavings with contemporary works from the Maya and other peoples. ⊠ *11 Divinity Ave., Harvard Square* ☎ *617/496–1027* ⊕ *www.peabody.harvard.edu* Ⓜ *Harvard.*

🍴 Restaurants

All Star Sandwich Bar

$ | AMERICAN | This brightly colored place with about a dozen tables turns out fresh, high-quality sandwiches all served with coleslaw, dill pickle, and a smile. Beyond multiple beef burgers, you'll find classics like crispy, overstuffed Reubens and the famous Atomic Meatloaf Meltdown, which has been highlighted on a number of foodie networks. **Known for:** chef-quality sandwiches; creative combinations; simple setting. Ⓢ *Average main: $12* ⊠ *1245 Cambridge St., Cambridge* ☎ *617/868–3065* ⊕ *www.allstarsandwichbar.com* Ⓜ *Central/Inman.*

★ **Area Four**

$$ | MODERN AMERICAN | A bona fide hit from day one, everything at this glass-enclosed eatery in the avant-garde Technology Square area is scrumptious—from the morning sticky buns and excellent dark coffee at the café to the wood-fire-oven-cooked food in the dining room; blistered pizzas (try the clam-bacon one), mac and cheese served in your own skillet, and crackly skinned chicken best enjoyed with a side of market veggies, like charred greens with miso and candied peanuts. You will find only local, seasonal, and sustainable cooking here. **Known for:** crisp, blistered pizzas; market-fresh salads and mains; relaxed feel. Ⓢ *Average main: $18* ⊠ *500 Technology Sq., Cambridge* ☎ *617/758–4444* ⊕ *www.areafour.com.*

★ **Giulia**

$$$ | ITALIAN | With exposed brick walls and soft lighting, this welcoming Italian restaurant has a back communal pasta table that doubles as a counter that the kitchen uses for rolling out superlative pastas. Just as delicious are the various antipasti, as well as mains like the house-made sausage with fennel risotto. If you don't (or can't get) a reservation on a preferred night, give your name to the hostess and grab a drink (or two) at the bar or up the street; chances are

you'll get seated sooner or later. **Known for:** excellent Italian food; silky pastas; warm, softly-lit space. $ *Average main: $28* ✉ *1682 Massachusetts Ave., Harvard Square* ☎ *617/441–2800* ⊕ *www.giuliarestaurant.com* ⊗ *Closed Sun.*

★ Harvest

$$$ | AMERICAN | Once a favorite of former Cambridge resident Julia Child, this sophisticated shrine to New England cuisine remains a perennial go-to spot for Harvard students when their parents are in town. The seasonal menu could feature Cape scallop crudo, fresh pasta with braised veal and pesto, or fresh Cape lobster with lemon hollandaise. **Known for:** elegant New England cuisine; expansive wine list; pretty patio dining area. $ *Average main: $34* ✉ *44 Brattle St., on walkway, Cambridge* ☎ *617/868–2255* ⊕ *harvestcambridge.com* Ⓜ *Harvard.*

★ Oleana

$$$ | MEDITERRANEAN | With three restaurants (Sofra in Cambridge and Sarma in Somerville) and two cookbooks to her name, chef-owner Ana Sortun continues to bewitch area diners with her intricately spiced eastern Mediterranean meze (small plates) made with fresh-picked produce from her husband's nearby Siena Farms. Oleana's menu changes often, but look for the hot, crispy-fried mussels starter and Sultan's Delight (tamarind-glazed beef with smoky eggplant puree) along with Turkish-spiced lamb and lemon chicken. **Known for:** eastern Mediterranean menu; mouthwatering small plates; deft use of spices. $ *Average main: $27* ✉ *134 Hampshire St., Cambridge* ☎ *617/661–0505* ⊕ *www.oleanarestaurant.com* ⊗ *No lunch* Ⓜ *Central.*

★ Orinoco

$ | LATIN AMERICAN | Don't miss this red clapboard, Latin American restaurant located down an alleyway in Harvard Square. Owner Andres Banger's dream to bring bountiful plates of superfresh family fare from his home country of Venezuela to Cambridge (as well as Brookline and the South End) rewards diners with delectable, palm-sized *arepas,* or crispy, hot, corn-flour pockets stuffed with beans, cheese, chicken, or pork; *pabellon criollo,* moist shredded beef with stewed beans, rice, and plantains; and red chili adobo–marinated, charred *pollo* (chicken). **Known for:** Venezuelan specialties; generous portions; great value. $ *Average main: $17* ✉ *56 JFK St., Harvard Square* ☎ *617/354–6900* ⊕ *www.orinocokitchen.com* ▭ *No credit cards* ⊗ *Closed Mon.*

Hotels

★ Charles Hotel

$$$ | HOTEL | FAMILY | It used to be that the Charles was *the* place to stay in Cambridge, and while other luxury hotels have since arrived to give it a little healthy competition, this Harvard Square staple is standing strong. **Pros:** two blocks from the T Red Line to Boston; on-site jazz club and hip Noir bar; on-site 4,000-square-foot Corbu Spa & Salon. **Cons:** luxury comes at a price; restricted pool hours for children; coffee pots and tea kettles are available by request only. $ *Rooms from: $399* ✉ *1 Bennett St., Cambridge* ☎ *617/864–1200, 800/882–1818* ⊕ *www.charleshotel.com* ⚲ *295 rooms* ⦿ *No meals* Ⓜ *Harvard.*

★ Royal Sonesta Boston

$$$ | HOTEL | FAMILY | Right next to the Charles River, the certified-green Sonesta has one of the best city skylines and sunset views in Boston. **Pros:** walk to Museum of Science and T to Downtown Boston; complimentary shuttle to Cambridge-area attractions; nice pool. **Cons:** parking is not free; river-view guest rooms have much better view than Cambridge-view rooms; ArtBar's fire pits are first come, first served. $ *Rooms from: $379* ✉ *40 Edwin Land Blvd., off Memorial Dr., Cambridge* ☎ *617/806–4200, 800/766–3782* ⊕ *www.sonesta.com/boston* ⚲ *400 rooms* ⦿ *No meals* Ⓜ *Lechmere.*

Nightlife

BARS

★ Middlesex Lounge

BARS/PUBS | For those looking to avoid the ubersceney clubs of Boston's Theater District, the Middlesex is a welcoming, laid-back club for all sorts of people looking to dance the night away. Rolling settees, movable in varied seating configurations for trivia, games, and nerd nights, are usually cleared by 9 pm, when a $10 cover kicks in for DJs spinning crowd-pleasing EDM and hip-hop. Feed on small plates and pressed sandwiches. The lounge is only open Thursday through Saturday, 7 pm–2 am. ⊠ *315 Massachusetts Ave., Cambridge* ☎ *617/868–6739* ⊕ *www.middlesexlounge.us* Ⓜ *Central.*

★ Toad

BARS/PUBS | Bands, beers, and burgers sum up this amiable little Porter Square club attached to Christopher's. The bar is maple, the toads ceramic. Nightly music comes in many a stripe, and usually in double bills at 7 and 10 pm. Check out Sunday spins after 5 pm: bring your own vinyl. Twelve taps, Toad T-shirts, and never a cover charge: what's not to like? ⊠ *1912 Massachusetts Ave., Cambridge* ☎ *617/497–4950 recording* ⊕ *www.toadcambridge.com* Ⓜ *Porter.*

MUSIC CLUBS

★ Cantab Lounge

MUSIC CLUBS | This place hums every night with live bands cranking out rhythm and blues, soul, funk, rock, or bluegrass. The theme-driven bar hosts open-mike performers (Monday) bluegrass (Tuesday), poetry slams (Wednesday), and soul and funk (Thursday). Its diverse twenties-to-forties crowd is friendly and informal, and loves to get up and dance. ⊠ *738 Massachusetts Ave., Cambridge* ☎ *617/354–2685* ⊕ *www.cantab-lounge.com* Ⓜ *Central.*

★ Middle East & ZuZu Restaurant & Nightclub

MUSIC CLUBS | This nightclub has balanced its kebab-and-falafel menu with three ever-active performance spaces to carve its niche as one of New England's most eclectic alternative-rock venues. National and local acts vie for the large upstairs and cavernous downstairs rooms, while intimate combos play ZuZu's and the tiny Corner. Phenoms like the Mighty Mighty Bosstones got their start here. Music-world celebs drop by when playing in town. There's also belly dancing, folk, jazz, country-rock, and dancing at ZuZu. Nightly shows at 8 pm usually run $10 to $20. ⊠ *472–480 Massachusetts Ave., Cambridge* ☎ *617/497–0576, 617/864–3278 recorded line* ⊕ *www.mideastoffers.com* Ⓜ *Central.*

The Sinclair

MUSIC CLUBS | Bringing a long-awaited sophisticated rock music and dining venue to Harvard Square, The Sinclair's adventurous, near-nightly lineup of indie rock—with enticing flings into world, electronica, and jazz—often sells out. Its adjacent but quite separate restaurant and bar, with wanderlusty train and highway decor, serious beverage list, creative mixology, and cuisine inspired by regional Americana, is proving to be a winning formula. Accommodating 500, here's a party made to order for transient, academic, and streetwise grown-ups. ⊠ *52 Church St., Harvard Square* ☎ *617/547–5200* ⊕ *www.sinclaircambridge.com* Ⓜ *Harvard.*

⊕ Performing Arts

MUSIC

★ Sanders Theatre

CONCERTS | This gilt-wood jewel box of a stage is the preferred venue for many of Boston's classical orchestras and the home of Harvard University's many ensembles. The 180-degree stage design and superb acoustics afford intimacy and crystal projection. A favorite of folk, jazz, and world-music performers, the 1,000-seat Sanders hosts the holiday favorite, *Christmas Revels,* a traditional participatory Yule celebration. Winston Churchill, Martin Luther King, Wynton Marsalis, Leonard Bernstein, and Oprah Winfrey have lectured at this famed seat of oratory and music. ⊠ *Harvard University, 45 Quincy St., Harvard Sq., Cambridge* ☎ *617/496–2222 box office* ⊕ *www.fas.harvard.edu/~memhall/sanders.html* Ⓜ *Harvard.*

THEATER

★ American Repertory Theater

THEATER | Founded by Robert Brustein and since 2009 under the helm of Tony Award–winning director Diane Paulus, the ART is one of America's most celebrated regional theaters, winning Tonys for Broadway originals *All the Way* and *Once* and revivals of *The Glass Menagerie, Pippin,* and *The Gershwins' Porgy and Bess.* The ART often premieres new works and seeks to expand the boundaries of theater through productions such as *Waitress, Finding Neverland,* and *Natasha, Pierre & The Great Comet of 1812* among others. The Loeb Drama Center, home of the ART, houses two theaters: the Mainstage and The Ex, a smaller black box often staging productions by the irreverent Harvard-Radcliffe Dramatic Club. OBERON, the ART's "club theater" with flexible stage design, engages young audiences in immersive theater (and has attracted national acclaim for its groundbreaking model), like Paulus's "disco-ball and hustle queen" extravaganza, *The Donkey Show,* every Saturday night. ⊠ *64 Brattle St., Harvard Sq., Cambridge* ☎ *617/547–8300* ⊕ *americanrepertorytheater.org* Ⓜ *Harvard.*

Activities

BOATING

Charles River Canoe & Kayak Center

BOATING | From May through mid-November you can rent a canoe, kayak,

paddleboard, rowboat, or rowing shell from Charles River Canoe & Kayak Center. The center also offers a variety of canoeing and kayaking classes for all skill levels as well as organized group outings and tours. ⊠ *2401 Commonwealth Ave., Newton* ☎ *617/965–5110* ⊕ *www.paddleboston.com.*

★ Head of the Charles Regatta

BOATING | In mid-October about 400,000 spectators turn out to cheer the more than 11,000 male and female athletes who come from all over the world to compete in the annual Head of the Charles Regatta, which in 2014 marked its 50th anniversary. Crowds line the banks of the Charles River with blankets and beer (although the police disapprove of the latter), cheering on their favorite teams and generally using the weekend as an excuse to party. Limited free parking is available, but the chances of finding an open space close to the race route are slim; take public transportation if you can. During the event, free shuttles run between the start and end point of the race route on both sides of the river. ⊠ *Banks of the Charles River, Harvard Square* ☎ *617/868–6200* ⊕ *www.hocr.org* Ⓜ *Harvard, Central.*

Shopping

ANTIQUES

Cambridge Antique Market

ANTIQUES/COLLECTIBLES | Off the beaten track, this antiques hot spot has a selection bordering on overwhelming: five floors of goods from over 150 dealers ranging from 19th-century furniture to vintage clothing, much of it reasonably priced. Head to the basement for a large selection of secondhand bikes. For those with four wheels, a parking lot sits next to the building. ⊠ *201 Monsignor O'Brien Hwy., Cambridge* ☎ *617/868–9655* ⊕ *www.marketantique.com* Ⓜ *Lechmere.*

Many of the local University teams row on the Charles River.

BOOKS
★ Harvard Coop Society
BOOKS/STATIONERY | Begun in 1882 as a nonprofit service for students and faculty, the Coop is now managed by Barnes & Noble College, a separate entity that manages college campus bookstores. In addition to books and textbooks (many discounted), school supplies, clothes, and accessories plastered with the Harvard emblem are sold here, as well as basic housewares geared toward dorm dwellers. If you're looking for a public restroom, you'll find it here. ⊠ *1400 Massachusetts Ave., Cambridge* ☎ *617/499–2000* ⊕ *store. thecoop.com* Ⓜ *Harvard.*

MAJOR SHOPPING DISTRICTS
Brattle Street
SHOPPING NEIGHBORHOODS | A handful of chains and independent boutiques are clustered on Brattle Street. ⊠ *Behind Harvard Sq., Cambridge* Ⓜ *Harvard.*

Harvard Square
SHOPPING NEIGHBORHOODS | Harvard Square takes up just a few blocks but holds more than 150 stores selling clothes, books, records, furnishings, and specialty items. ⊠ *Cambridge* Ⓜ *Harvard.*

Porter Square
SHOPPING NEIGHBORHOODS | This spot in north Cambridge has distinctive clothing stores, as well as crafts shops, coffee shops, natural-foods stores, restaurants, and bars with live music. ⊠ *West on Massachusetts Ave. from Harvard Sq., Cambridge* Ⓜ *Porter Square.*

SPECIALTY STORES
★ Leavitt & Peirce
GIFTS/SOUVENIRS | A throwback to another era, this storied tobacco shop has been in the same location since 1883, when it served as a clubby gathering spot for young Harvard men, who puffed away while playing pool on the back billiard tables. While Harvard oars, hockey sticks, and photos still adorn the ivy-green walls, the store now caters to a broader clientele in search of quality smoking items, toiletries, chess and checker sets, and small gift items, such as beer steins. Don't miss the four chess tables

on the second level, where you can rent pieces for $2 an hour (checkers and backgammon are available, too). ✉ *1316 Massachusetts Ave., Harvard Square* ☎ *617/547–0576* ⊕ *www.leavitt-peirce. com* Ⓜ *Harvard.*

TOYS

The World's Only Curious George Store

TOYS | FAMILY | Decorated with tropical plants, a fake hut, and tot-size chairs, and equipped with puzzles, toys, activity sets, and books of all kinds for all ages, this store is a wonderland for kids and a parent's salvation on a rainy day. ✉ *Harvard Sq., 1 JFK St., Cambridge* ☎ *617/547–4500* ⊕ *thecuriousgeorgestore.com* Ⓜ *Harvard.*

Side Trips from Boston

Lexington

16 miles northwest of Boston.

Incensed against the British, American colonials burst into action in Lexington in April 1775. On April 18, patriot leader Paul Revere alerted the town that British soldiers were approaching. The next day, as the British advance troops arrived in Lexington on their march toward Concord, the Minutemen were waiting to confront the redcoats in what became the first skirmish of the Revolutionary War.

These first military encounters of the American Revolution are very much a part of present-day Lexington, a modern suburban town that sprawls out from the historic sites near its center. Although the downtown area is generally lively, with ice-cream and coffee shops, boutiques, and a great little movie theater, the town becomes especially animated each Patriots' Day (April 19 but celebrated on the third Monday in April), when costume-clad groups re-create the Minutemen's battle maneuvers and Paul Revere rides again.

To learn more about the city and the 1775 clash, stop by the **Lexington Visitor Center.**

GETTING HERE AND AROUND

Massachusetts Bay Transportation Authority (MBTA) operates bus service in the greater Boston area and serves Lexington.

TOURS

CONTACTS **Liberty Ride** ✉ *1875 Massachusetts Ave.* ☎ *339/223–5623* ⊕ *www. tourlexington.us/liberty-ride-trolley-tours.*

VISITOR INFORMATION

CONTACTS **Lexington Visitors Center** ✉ *1875 Massachusetts Ave.* ☎ *781/862–1450* ⊕ *www.lexingtonchamber.org.*

Sights

Battle Green

CITY PARK | It was on this 2-acre triangle of land, on April 19, 1775, that the first confrontation between British soldiers, who were marching from Boston toward Concord, and the Colonial militia known as the Minutemen took place. The Minutemen—so called because they were able to prepare themselves at a moment's notice—were led by Captain John Parker, whose role in the American Revolution is commemorated in Henry Hudson Kitson's renowned 1900 *Minuteman* statue. Facing downtown Lexington at the tip of Battle Green, the statue's in a traffic island, and therefore makes for a difficult photo op. ✉ *Junction of Massachusetts Ave. and Bedford St.* 🎫 *Free.*

Buckman Tavern

BUILDING | While waiting for the arrival of the British on the morning of April 19, 1775, the Minutemen gathered at this 1690 tavern. A half-hour tour takes in the tavern's seven rooms, which have been restored to the way they looked in the 1770s. Among the items on display is an old front door with a hole made by a British musket ball. ✉ *1 Bedford St.* ☎ *781/862–5598* ⊕ *www.lexingtonhistory.org* 🎫 *From $8* ⊗ *Closed Oct. 31–Apr.*

Hancock-Clarke House

HOUSE | On April 18, 1775, Paul Revere came here to warn patriots John Hancock and Sam Adams (who were staying at the house while attending the Provincial Congress in nearby Concord) of the advance of British troops. Hancock and Adams, on whose heads the British king had put a price, fled to avoid capture. The house, a parsonage built in 1698, is a 10-minute walk from Lexington Common. Inside is the Treasures of the Revolution exhibit, and outside, a Colonial herb garden. ⊠ *36 Hancock St.* ☏ *781/861–0928* ⊕ *www.lexingtonhistory.org* ✉ *From $8* ⊙ *Closed Oct. 31–Apr.*

Minute Man National Historical Park

NATIONAL/STATE PARK | FAMILY | West of Lexington's center stretches this 1,000-acre park that also extends into nearby Lincoln and Concord. Begin your park visit at the **Minute Man Visitor Center** in Lexington to see the free multimedia presentation, "The Road to Revolution," a captivating introduction to the events of April 1775. Staffed by costumed park volunteers, the Whittemore House has a hands-on "Try on 1775!" exhibit where kids can wear Colonial clothing and gather ingredients for a meal. Continuing along Highway 2A toward Concord, you pass the point where Revere's midnight ride ended with his capture by the British; it's marked with a boulder and plaque, as well as an enclosure with wayside exhibits. You can also visit the 1732 **Hartwell Tavern,** a restored drover's (driver's) tavern staffed by park employees in period costume; they frequently demonstrate musket firing, militia drills, and talk about life in Colonial Massachusetts. ⊠ *Rte. 2A, ¼ mile west of Rte. 128* ☏ *978/369–6993* ⊕ *www.nps.gov/mima.*

Munroe Tavern

BUILDING | As April 19, 1775, dragged on, British forces met fierce resistance in Concord. Dazed and demoralized after the battle at Concord's Old North Bridge, the British backtracked and regrouped at this 1695 tavern 1 mile east of Lexington Common, while the Munroe family hid in nearby woods. The troops then retreated through what is now the town of Arlington. After a bloody battle there, they returned to Boston. Tours of the tavern last about 30 minutes. ⊠ *1332 Massachusetts Ave.* ☏ *781/862–0295* ⊕ *www. lexingtonhistory.org* ✉ *From $8* ⊙ *Closed weekdays Apr. and May.*

The Scottish Rite Masonic Museum & Library

MUSEUM | View artifacts from all facets of American life, put in social and political context. Specializing in the history of American Freemasonry and Fraternalism, the changing exhibits and lectures also focus on local events leading up to April 1775 and illustrate Revolutionary-era life through everyday objects such as blacksmithing tools, bloodletting paraphernalia, and dental instruments, including a "tooth key" used to extract teeth. ⊠ *33 Marrett Rd., Rte. 2A at Massachusetts Ave.* ☏ *781/861–6559* ⊕ *www.srmml.org* ✉ *Donations accepted.*

Concord

About 10 miles west of Lexington, 21 miles northwest of Boston.

The Concord of today is a modern suburb with a busy center filled with arty shops, places to eat, and (recalling the literary history made here) old bookstores. Autumn lovers, take note: Concord is a great place to start a fall foliage tour. From Boston, head west along Route 2 to Concord, and then continue on to find harvest stands and apple picking around Harvard and Stow.

GETTING HERE AND AROUND

The MBTA runs buses to Concord. On the MBTA Commuter Rail, Concord is a 40-minute ride on the Fitchburg Line, which departs from Boston's North Station.

VISITOR INFORMATION

CONTACTS Concord Visitor Center ⊠ *58 Main St.* ☏ *978/369–3120* ⊕ *www.concordchamberofcommerce.org.*

Sights

Concord Museum

MUSEUM | FAMILY | The original contents of Emerson's private study, as well as the world's largest collection of Thoreau artifacts, reside in this 1930 Colonial Revival building just east of the town center. The museum provides a good overview of the town's history, from its original American Indian settlement to the present. Highlights include American Indian artifacts, furnishings from Thoreau's Walden Pond cabin (there's a replica of the cabin itself on the museum's lawn), and one of the two lanterns hung at Boston's Old North Church to signal that the British were coming by sea. If you've brought children, ask for a free family activity pack. ✉ *200 Lexington Rd., GPS address is 53 Cambridge Tpke.* ☎ *978/369–9763* ⊕ *www.concordmuseum.org* 💲 *$10.*

Louisa May Alcott's Orchard House

HOUSE | The dark brown exterior of Louisa May Alcott's family home sharply contrasts with the light, wit, and energy so much in evidence within. Named for the apple orchard that once surrounded it, Orchard House was the Alcott family home from 1857 to 1877. Here Louisa wrote *Little Women,* based in part on her life with her three sisters; and her father, Bronson, founded the Concord School of Philosophy—the building remains behind the house. Because Orchard House had just one owner after the Alcotts left, and because it became a museum in 1911, more than 80% of the original furnishings remain, including the semicircular shelf-desk where Louisa wrote *Little Women.* ✉ *399 Lexington Rd.* ☎ *978/369–4118* ⊕ *www.louisamayalcott.org* 💲 *$10.*

Old Manse

HOUSE | The Reverend William Emerson, grandfather of Ralph Waldo Emerson, watched rebels and Redcoats battle from behind his home, which was within sight of the Old North Bridge. The house, built in 1770, was occupied continuously by the Emerson family for almost two centuries, except for a 3½-year period during which Nathaniel Hawthorne rented it. Furnishings date from the late 18th century. Tours run throughout the day and last 45 minutes, but call ahead to check. Don't whip out your camera, however: photography is prohibited inside the house. Grounds are open year-round sunrise–sunset. ✉ *269 Monument St.* ☎ *978/369–3909* ⊕ *www.thetrust-ees.org/places-to-visit/greater-boston/old-manse.html* 💲 *Grounds free; house tours $10* ⊙ *House closed Tues.*

Old North Bridge

BRIDGE/TUNNEL | A half mile from Concord center, at this bridge, the Concord Minutemen turned the tables on the British on the morning of April 19, 1775. The Americans didn't fire first, but when two of their own fell dead from a Redcoat volley, Major John Buttrick of Concord roared, "Fire, fellow soldiers, for God's sake, fire." The Minutemen released volley after volley, and the Redcoats fled. Daniel Chester French's famous statue *The Minuteman* (1875) honors the country's first freedom fighters. The lovely wooded surroundings give a sense of what the landscape was like in more rural times. Guests who take the Liberty Ride trolley tour from Lexington Center will be treated to a quick stop at the bridge. ✉ *Concord* ⊕ *www.nps.gov/mima.*

Ralph Waldo Emerson House

HOUSE | The 19th-century essayist and poet Ralph Waldo Emerson lived briefly in the Old Manse in 1834–35, then moved to this home, where he lived until his death in 1882. Here he wrote the *Essays.* Except for artifacts from Emerson's study, now at the nearby Concord Museum, the Emerson House furnishings have been preserved as the writer left them, down to his hat resting on the newel post. You must join one of the half-hour-long tours to see the interior. ✉ *28 Cambridge Tpke., at Lexington Rd.* ☎ *978/369–2236* ⊕ *www.nps.gov/nr/travel/massachusetts_conservation/ralph_waldo_emerson_house.html* 💲 *$9*

KEY

🛈 *Sights*

🛈 *Restaurants*

🕒 *Closed Nov.–mid-Apr., and Mon.–Wed. mid-Apr.–Oct.* ☞ *Call ahead for tour-scheduling information.*

Sleepy Hollow Cemetery

CEMETERY | This garden cemetery on the National Registry of Historic Places served as a place of inspiration and a final resting place for American literary greats like Louisa May Alcott, Ralph Waldo Emerson, Henry David Thoreau, and Nathaniel Hawthorne. Each Memorial Day Alcott's grave is decorated in commemoration of her death. ⊠ *Bedford St. (Rte. 62), 24 Court La. and Bedford St.* ⊕ *1 block east of Monument Sq. in Concord*☎ *978/318–3233.*

★ Walden Pond

BUILDING | For lovers of Early American literature, a trip to Concord isn't complete without a pilgrimage to Henry David Thoreau's most famous residence.

Here, in 1845, at age 28, Thoreau moved into a one-room cabin—built for $28.12—on the shore of this 100-foot-deep kettle hole formed by the retreat of an ancient glacier. Living alone for the next two years, Thoreau discovered the benefits of solitude and the beauties of nature. *Walden,* published in 1854, is a mixture of philosophy, nature writing, and proto-ecology. The site of the original house is staked out in stone. A full-size, authentically furnished replica of the cabin stands about ½ mile from the original site, near the Walden Pond State Reservation parking lot. During the summer, don't be shocked if you aren't allowed entrance: Walden Pond has a visitor capacity. ⊠ *915 Walden St. (Rte. 126)* ⊕ *To get to Walden Pond State Reservation from center of Concord—a trip of only 1½ miles—take Concord's Main St. a block west from Monument*

Retrace Henry David Thoreau's steps at Walden Pond.

Sq., turn left onto Walden St., and head for intersection of Rtes. 2 and 126. Cross over Rte. 2 onto Hwy. 126, heading south for ½ mile ☎ *978/369–3254* ⊕ *www.mass.gov/locations/walden-pond-state-reservation* ✉ *Free, $8 for vehicles with Massachusetts plates, $15 for vehicles with non-Massachusetts plates* ☞ *No dogs allowed.*

The Wayside
HOUSE | Nathaniel Hawthorne lived at the Old Manse in 1842–45, working on stories and sketches; he then moved to Salem (where he wrote *The Scarlet Letter*) and later to Lenox (*The House of the Seven Gables*). In 1852 he returned to Concord, bought this rambling structure called The Wayside, and lived here until his death in 1864. The home certainly appealed to literary types: the subsequent owner of The Wayside, Margaret Sidney, wrote the children's book *Five Little Peppers and How They Grew* (1881), and before Hawthorne moved in, the Alcotts lived here, from 1845 to 1848. An exhibit center, in the former barn, provides information about the Wayside authors and links them to major events in American history. Hawthorne's tower-study, with his stand-up writing desk, is substantially as he left it. ✉ *455 Lexington Rd.* ☎ *978/318–7863* ⊕ *www.nps.gov/nr/travel/pwwmh/ma47.htm* ✉ *$7* ⊗ *Closed Tues., Wed., and in winter.*

Restaurants

Main Streets Market & Cafe
$$ | AMERICAN | Cyclists, families, and sightseers pack into this brick building, which was used to store munitions during the Revolutionary War. Wood floors and blackboard menus add a touch of nostalgia, but the extensive menu includes many modern hits. **Known for:** live music six nights a week; summertime ice cream counter; open early for breakfast. ⑤ *Average main: $18* ✉ *42 Main St.* ☎ *978/369–9948* ⊕ *www.mainstreetsmarketandcafe.com* ▭ *No credit cards.*

The North Shore

The slice of Massachusetts's Atlantic Coast known as the North Shore extends past Boston to the Cape Ann region just shy of the New Hampshire border. In addition to miles of woods and beaches, the North Shore's highlights include Marblehead, a classic New England sea town; Salem, which thrives on a history of witches, writers, and maritime trades; Gloucester, the oldest seaport in America; Rockport, rich with crafts shops and artists' studios; and a handful of typical New England towns in between. Bustling during the short summer season and breathtaking during the autumn foliage, the North Shore is calmer (and colder) between November and June. ■TIP→ **Many restaurants, inns, and attractions operate on reduced hours during the off-season.**

Marblehead

17 miles north of Boston.

Marblehead, with its narrow and winding streets, beautifully preserved clapboard homes, sea captains' mansions, and harbor, looks much as it must have when it was founded in 1629 by fishermen from Cornwall and the Channel Islands. One of New England's premier sailing capitals, Marblehead attracts boats from along the Eastern Seaboard each July during Race Week—first held in 1889. Parking in town can be difficult; lots at the end of Front Street or on State Street by the Landing restaurant are the best options.

VISITOR INFORMATION

CONTACTS Marblehead Chamber of Commerce Information Booth ✉ *131 Essex St.* ☎ *781/631–2868* ⊕ *www.marblehead-chamber.org.*

◉ Sights

Abbot Hall

MUSEUM | The town's Victorian-era municipal building, built in 1876, displays Archibald Willard's painting *The Spirit of '76.* Many visitors, familiar since childhood with this image of the three Revolutionary veterans with fife, drum, and flag, are surprised to find the original in an otherwise unassuming town hall. Also on-site is a small naval museum exploring Marblehead's maritime past. ✉ *188 Washington St.* ☎ *781/631–0528 town clerk* ✇ *Free.*

Fort Sewall

CITY PARK | Magnificent views of Marblehead, of the harbor, the Misery Islands, and the Atlantic are best enjoyed from this fort built in 1644 atop the rocky cliffs of the harbor. Used as a defense against the French in 1742 as well as during the War of 1812, Ft. Sewall is today open to the public as community parkland. Barracks and underground quarters can still be seen, and Revolutionary War reenactments by members of the modern-day Glover's Marblehead Regiment are staged at the fort annually. ✉ *End of Front St.* ☎ *781/631–0000 town hall* ✇ *Free.*

The 1768 Jeremiah Lee Mansion

HOUSE | Marblehead's 18th-century high society is exemplified in this mansion run by the Marblehead Museum. Colonel Lee was the wealthiest merchant and ship owner in Massachusetts in 1768, and although few original furnishings remain, the unique hand-painted wallpaper and fine collection of traditional North Shore furniture provide clues to the life of an American gentleman. Across the street at the main museum (open year-round), the J.O.J. Frost Gallery & Carolyn Lynch Education Center pays tribute to the town's talented 19th-century native son. ✉ *161 Washington St.* ☎ *781/631–1768* ⊕ *www.marbleheadmuseum.org/properties/lee-mansion* ✇ *$10* ⊘ *Closed Sun. and Mon.*

Restaurants

The Landing

$ | SEAFOOD | Decorated in nautical blues and whites, this pleasant restaurant sits right on Marblehead harbor, with a deck that's nearly in the water. The restaurant offers classic New England fare like clam chowder and broiled scrod, and serves brunch on Sunday. **Known for:** waterside dining; classic New England menu; local feel. $ *Average main: $12* ⌧ *81 Front St.* ☎ *781/639–1266* ⊕ *www.thelandingrestaurant.com* ⊟ *No credit cards.*

Hotels

★ Harbor Light Inn

$ | B&B/INN | Housed in a pair of adjoining 18th-century mansions in the heart of Old Town Marblehead, this elegant inn, which is now honored as one of the Distinguished Inns of New England, features many rooms with canopy beds, brick fireplaces, and Jacuzzis. **Pros:** beautiful location; tavern with pub grub; outdoor swimming pool. **Cons:** confusing town to navigate; Jacuzzis are loud; two-night minimum stay on weekends during high season; prices spike in high season. $ *Rooms from: $179* ⌧ *58 Washington St.* ☎ *781/631–2186* ⊕ *www.harborlightinn.com* ⇌ *23 rooms* ⋈ *Free breakfast.*

Salem

16 miles northeast of Boston, 4 miles west of Marblehead.

Known for years as the Witch City, Salem is redefining itself. Though numerous witch-related attractions and shops still draw tourists, there's much more to the city. First, a bit on its bewitched past....

The witchcraft hysteria emerged from the trials of 1692, when several Salem-area girls fell ill and accused the townspeople of casting spells on them. More than 150 men and women were charged with practicing witchcraft, a

crime punishable by death. After the trials later that year, 19 people were hanged and one man was crushed to death.

Though the witch trials might have built Salem's infamy, it'd be a mistake to ignore the town's rich maritime and creative traditions, which played integral roles in the country's evolution. Frigates out of Salem opened the Far East trade routes and generated the wealth that created America's first millionaires. Among its native talents are writer Nathaniel Hawthorne, the intellectual Peabody sisters, navigator Nathaniel Bowditch, and architect Samuel McIntire. This creative spirit is today celebrated in Salem's internationally recognized museums, waterfront shops and restaurants, galleries, and wide common.

To learn more on the area, stop by the **Regional Visitor's Center.** Innovatively designed in the Old Salem Armory, the center has exhibits, a 27-minute film, maps, and a gift shop.

VISITOR INFORMATION

CONTACTS Destination Salem ⌧ *81 Washington St., Suite 204* ☎ *978/744–3663, 877/725–3662* ⊕ *www.salem.org.* **Salem Visitor Center** ⌧ *2 New Liberty St.* ☎ *978/740–1650* ⊕ *www.nps.gov/ner/sama.*

Sights

House of the Seven Gables

HOUSE | Immortalized in Nathaniel Hawthorne's classic novel, this site is itself a historic treasure. Built in 1668 and also known as the Turner-Ingersoll Mansion, the house includes the famous secret staircase, a re-creation of Hepzibah's cent shop from *The House of Seven Gables,* and some of the finest Georgian interiors in the country. Also on the property is the small house where Hawthorne was born in 1804; built in 1750, it was moved from its original location a few blocks away. ⌧ *115 Derby St.* ☎ *978/744–0991* ⊕ *www.7gables.org* ⌧ *$15.*

The First Witch Trial

It was in Danvers, not Salem, that the first witch trial was held, originating with the family of Samuel Parris, a minister who moved to the area in 1680 from Barbados, bringing with him two slaves, including one named Tituba. In 1691 Samuel's daughter, Betty, and niece, Abigail, began having "fits." Tituba, who had told Betty and Abigail stories of magic and witchcraft from her homeland, baked a "witch cake" to identify the witches who were harming the girls. The girls in turn accused Tituba of witchcraft. After three days of "questioning," which included beatings from Samuel and a promise from him to free her if she cooperated, Tituba confessed to meeting the devil (in the form of a black hog or dog). She also claimed there were other witches in the village, confirming the girls' accusations against Sarah Good and Sarah Osborne, but she refused to name any others. Tituba's trial prompted the frenzy that led to the deaths of 20 accused "witches."

★ Peabody Essex Museum

MUSEUM | Salem's world-class museum celebrates superlative works from around the globe and across time, including American art and architecture, Asian export art, photography, maritime art and history, as well as Native American, Oceanic, and African art. Its 30 galleries, housed in a contemplative blend of modern design, represent a diverse range of styles; exhibits include pieces ranging from American decorative and seamen's art to an interactive Art & Nature Center and photography. While there be sure to tour the Yin Yu Tang house. This fabulous 200-year-old house dates to the Qing Dynasty (1644–1911) of China. The museum brought it over from China in sections and reassembled it here. ☒ *East India Sq.* ☎ *978/745–9500, 866/745–1876* ⊕ *www.pem.org* ☎ *$20* ⊘ *Closed Mon.*

Salem Maritime National Historic Site

LIGHTHOUSE | Near Derby Wharf, this 9¼-acre site focuses on Salem's heritage as a major seaport with a thriving overseas trade. It includes the 1762 home of Elias Derby, America's first millionaire; the 1819 Custom House, made famous in Nathaniel Hawthorne's *The Scarlet Letter*; and a replica of the *Friendship,* a 171-foot, three-masted 1797 merchant vessel. There's also an active lighthouse dating from 1871, as well as the nation's last surviving 18th-century wharves. Newer to the site is the 1770 Pedrick Store House, moved from nearby Marblehead and reassembled right on Derby Wharf; the two-story structure once played a vital role in the lucrative merchant seaside trade. ☒ *193 Derby St.* ☎ *978/740–1650 visitor center* ⊕ *www.nps.gov/sama/index.htm* ☎ *Free with the exception of the film "Salem Witch Hunt."*

Salem Witch Museum

MUSEUM | An informative and fun introduction to the 1692 witchcraft hysteria, this museum has a 15-minute guided tour through their exhibit, "Witches: Evolving Perceptions," that describes witch hunts through the years. ☒ *19½ Washington Sq. N* ☎ *978/744–1692* ⊕ *www.salemwitchmuseum.com* ☎ *$12.*

🍴 Restaurants

Finz Seafood & Grill

$$ | SEAFOOD | This contemporary seafood restaurant on Salem Harbor treats patrons to prime canal views. Seafood

potpie and lobster rolls highlight the lunch menu, while sesame-crusted tuna or steamed lobster are dinner favorites. **Known for:** outdoor seating; classic New England seafood; canal-side views. ⑤ *Average main: $21* ✉ *76 Wharf St.* ☎ *978/744–8485*⊕ *www.hipfinz.com.*

Hotels

★ Amelia Payson House

$$ | B&B/INN | Built in 1845, this Greek Revival house is a comfortable bed-and-breakfast near all the historic attractions. **Pros:** fireplaces in each room; outdoor lounge with a fire pit; on-site parking. **Cons:** no children under 12; hard to get reservations. ⑤ *Rooms from: $200* ✉ *16 Winter St.* ☎ *978/744–8304* ⊕ *www. ameliapaysonhouse.com* ↪ *3 rooms* ⦿| *Free breakfast.*

The Hawthorne Hotel

$ | HOTEL | Elegantly restored, this full-service landmark hotel celebrates the town's most famous writer and is within walking distance from the town common, museums, and waterfront. **Pros:** lovely, historic lobby; free parking available behind hotel; free Wi-Fi. **Cons:** many rooms are small; no swimming pool; no spa. ⑤ *Rooms from: $179* ✉ *18 Washington Sq. W* ☎ *978/744–4080, 800/729–7829* ⊕ *www.hawthornehotel. com* ↪ *93 rooms (89 in main building, 4 in guesthouse)* ⦿| *No meals* ↪ *$30 charge per room per night for pets.*

Performing Arts

THEATER

Cry Innocent: The People versus Bridget Bishop

THEATER | This show, the longest continuously running play north of Boston, transports audience members to Bridget Bishop's witchcraft hearing of 1692. After hearing historical testimonies, the audience cross-examines the witnesses and decides whether to send Bridget to trial or not. Actors respond in character revealing much about the Puritan frame of mind. Each show is different and allows audience members to play their "part" in history. ✉ *Old Town Hall, 32 Derby Sq.* ☎ *978/810–2588* ⊕ *www. historyalivesalem.com* ✉ *$25.*

Gloucester

37 miles northeast of Boston, 8 miles northeast of Manchester-by-the-Sea.

On Gloucester's fine seaside promenade is a famous statue of a man steering a ship's wheel, his eyes searching the horizon. The statue, which honors those who go down to the sea in ships, was commissioned by the town citizens in celebration of Gloucester's 300th anniversary in 1923. The oldest seaport in the nation (with some of the North Shore's best beaches) is still a major fishing port. Sebastian Junger's 1997 book *A Perfect Storm* was an account of the fate of the *Andrea Gail*, a Gloucester fishing boat caught in the storm of the century in October 1991. In 2000 the book was made into a movie, filmed on location in Gloucester.

VISITOR INFORMATION

CONTACTS Cape Ann Chamber of Commerce ✉ *33 Commercial St.* ☎ *978/283–1601*⊕ *www.capeannchamber.com.*

Sights

Cape Ann Museum

NEIGHBORHOOD | The Cape Ann Museum celebrates the art, history, and culture of Cape Ann. The museum's collections include fine art from the 19th century to the present, artifacts from the fishing, maritime, and granite-quarrying industries, as well as textiles, furniture, a library-archives, and two historic houses. ✉ *27 Pleasant St.* ☎ *978/283–0455* ⊕ *www.capeannmuseum.org* ✉ *$12* ⊘ *Closed Mon.*

Hammond Castle Museum

MUSEUM | Inventor John Hays Hammond Jr. built this structure in 1926 to resemble a "medieval" stone castle. Hammond is credited with more than 500 patents, including remote control via radio waves. The museum contains medieval-style furnishings and paintings, and the Great Hall houses an impressive 8,200-pipe organ. From the castle you can see Norman's Woe Rock, made famous by Longfellow in his poem "The Wreck of the Hesperus." ⊠ *80 Hesperus Ave., south side of Gloucester off Rte. 127* ☎ *978/283–2080, 978/283–2080* ⊕ *www.hammondcastle.org* ⊠ *$12* ⊙ *Closed Mon. and in winter.*

Rocky Neck

HISTORIC SITE | On a peninsula within Gloucester's working harbor, the town's creative side thrives in this neighborhood, one of the oldest continuously working artists' colonies in the United States. Its alumni include Winslow Homer, Maurice Prendergast, Jane Peter, and Cecilia Beaux. Call for winter hours. ⊠ *6 Wonson St.* ☎ *978/515–7005* ⊕ *www.rockyneckartcolony.org.*

 Beaches

Gloucester has some of the best beaches on the North Shore. From Memorial Day through mid-September, parking costs $25 on weekdays and $30 on weekends, when the lots often fill by 10 am.

Good Harbor Beach

BEACH—SIGHT | This beach has calm, waveless waters and soft sand, and is surrounded by grassy dunes, making it perfect any time of year. In summer (June, July, and August), it is lifeguard patrolled, handicap accessible, and there is a snack bar if you don't feel like packing in food. The restrooms and showers are wheelchair accessible, and you can pick up beach toys at the concessions. On weekdays parking is plentiful, but the lot fills by 10 am on weekends. In June, green flies can be bothersome. **Amenities:** food and drink; lifeguards; parking (fee); showers; toilets. **Best for:** swimming; walking. ⊠ *Gloucester* ⊹ *Clearly signposted from Rte. 127A* ⊕ *gloucester-ma.gov* ⊠ *Parking $25 per car; $30 on weekends and holidays.*

Long Beach

BEACH—SIGHT | Just as its name implies, this soft-sand beach that is half in Rockport, half in Gloucester is long, and it's also broad. It draws crowds from the houses that border it, particularly on weekends. Pay attention to the tide schedule, or you may find there's no beach to sit on. Cape Ann Motor Inn is nearby. Parking is very limited. Don't even think of parking on neighborhood streets if you don't have a town parking sticker—you will be towed. However, there is a lot on the Gloucester side. **Amenities:** none. **Best for:** swimming; walking. ⊠ *Off Rte. 127A on Gloucester-Rockport town line, Off Rockport Rd.*

Wingaersheek Beach

BEACH—SIGHT | With white sand and dunes, Wingaersheek Beach is a well-protected cove with both a beach side and a boat side. The white Annisquam lighthouse is in the bay. The beach is known for its miles of white sand and calm waters. On weekends arrive early. The parking lot generally fills up by midmorning. It's handicap accessible and beach wheelchairs are available on request. **Amenities:** food and drink; parking (fee); toilets. **Best for:** swimming; walking. ⊠ *232 Atlantic St.* ⊹ *Take Rte. 128 N to Exit 13* ⊕ *gloucester-ma.gov* ⊠ *Limited parking, $25 per car; $30 on weekends and holidays.*

Restaurants

The Franklin Cafe

$$ | **AMERICAN** | This contemporary nightspot offers bistro-style chicken, roast cod, and steak frites, perfect for the late-night crowd (it's open until midnight during the summer). Live music is on tap every Thursday evening. **Known for:** open late; friendly vibe; moderate prices. ⑤ *Average main: $20* ✉ *118 Main St.* ☎ *978/283–7888* ⊕ *www.franklincapeann.com* ☽ *No lunch.*

Passports

$ | **ECLECTIC** | **FAMILY** | In the heart of Downtown Gloucester, Passports serves up a modern take on classic New England seafood. The fried oysters and house haddock are favorites here, and there's always local art hanging on the walls for patrons to buy. **Known for:** seafood dishes like fried oysters; warm, fresh popovers; great, central location. ⑤ *Average main: $15* ✉ *110 Main St.* ☎ *978/281–3680.*

Hotels

Cape Ann's Marina Resort & Spa

$ | **RESORT** | **FAMILY** | This year-round hotel less than a mile from downtown Gloucester comes alive in summer. **Pros:** free Wi-Fi; full marina; indoor pool and Jacuzzi with poolside bar. **Cons:** hotel surrounded by parking lots; price hike during summer; bar area can be loud in summer. ⑤ *Rooms from: $117* ✉ *75 Essex Ave.* ☎ *978/283–2116, 800/626–7660* ⊕ *www.capeannmarina.com* ⇆ *31 rooms* ⍾❶ *No meals.*

★ Castle Manor Inn

$ | **B&B/INN** | With original woodwork and cozy fireplaces, this restored 1900 Victorian inn perfectly captures the Cape Ann aesthetic. **Pros:** discount parking passes to the local beaches; historic; close to Gloucester's beaches. **Cons:** closes for the winter; roads in the area can be windy and confusing; may be too intimate for some travelers. ⑤ *Rooms from: $150* ✉ *141 Essex Ave.* ☎ *978/515–7386* ⊕ *www.castlemanorinn.com* ⇆ *26 rooms* ⍾❶ *No meals.*

Rockport

41 miles northeast of Boston, 4 miles northeast of Gloucester on Rte. 127.

Rockport, at the very tip of Cape Ann, derives its name from the local granite formations. Many Boston-area structures are made of stone cut from its long-gone quarries. Today the town is a tourist center with a well-marked, centralized downtown that is easy to navigate and access on foot. Unlike typical tourist-trap landmarks, Rockport's shops sell quality arts, clothing, and gifts, and its restaurants serve seafood or home-baked cookies rather than fast food. Walk past shops and colorful clapboard houses to the end of Bearskin Neck for an impressive view of the Atlantic Ocean and the old, weather-beaten lobster shack known as Motif No. 1 because of its popularity as a subject for amateur painters and photographers.

VISITOR INFORMATION

CONTACTS Rockport Visitor Center ✉ *170 Main St.* ☎ *978/283–1601* ⊕ *www.rockportusa.com.*

Restaurants

Brackett's Ocean View

$$ | **SEAFOOD** | A big bay window in this quiet, homey restaurant provides an excellent view across Sandy Bay. The menu includes chowders, fish cakes, and other seafood dishes. **Known for:** seafood. ⑤ *Average main: $18* ✉ *25 Main St.* ☎ *978/546–2797* ⊕ *www.bracketts.com* ☽ *Closed Columbus Day–mid-Apr.*

Hotels

Bearskin Neck Motor Lodge

$ | **HOTEL** | **FAMILY** | Near the end of Bearskin Neck, this small brick-and-shingle motel offers guests the best of both worlds: beautiful, oceanfront rooms, as well as easy access to shopping and restaurants. **Pros:** all rooms have balconies and unobstructed ocean views; central location; mini-refrigerators in rooms. **Cons:** lots of summertime tourists; heavy "classic motel" vibe; high prices in summer. ⑤ *Rooms from: $145* ✉ *64 Bearskin Neck* ☎ *978/546–6677, 877/507–6272* ⊕ *www.bearskinneckmotorlodge.com* ⊗ *Closed early Dec.–Mar.* ☞ *8 rooms* ❍❘ *No meals.*

Essex

35 miles northeast of Boston, 12 miles west of Rockport.

The small seafaring town of Essex, once an important shipbuilding center, is surrounded by salt marshes and is filled with antiques stores and seafood restaurants.

GETTING HERE AND AROUND
Head west out of Cape Ann on Rte. 128, turning north on Rte. 133.

VISITOR INFORMATION
CONTACTS Escape to Essex
⊕ *www.visitessexma.com.*

Sights

Essex Shipbuilding Museum
MUSEUM | FAMILY | At what is still an active shipyard, this museum chronicles over 300 years of wooden shipbuilding. Essex launched approximately 4,000 vessels, most of them two-masted fishing schooners for the Gloucester fleet. The museum offers shipbuilding demonstrations, events, and self- and fully guided tours. The collection includes ship models on loan from the Smithsonian, as well as the 83-foot *Evelina M. Goulart*—one of only seven remaining Essex-built schooners. ✉ *66 Main St. (Rte. 133)* ☎ *978/768–7541* ⊕ *www. essexshipbuildingmuseum.org* ☞ *Tours from $7* ⊗ *Closed Mon. and Tues.*

❍ Restaurants

★ Woodman's of Essex
$$ | SEAFOOD | FAMILY | According to local legend, this is where Lawrence "Chubby" Woodman invented the first fried clam back in 1916. Today this sprawling wooden shack with indoor booths and outdoor picnic tables is *the* place for seafood in the rough. **Known for:** fried clams; gluten-free options; open year-round; the popular "down-river" lobster combo plate. ⑤ *Average main: $18* ✉ *121 Main St. (Rte. 133)* ☎ *978/768–2559, 800/649–1773* ⊕ *www.woodmans.com.*

South of Boston

People from all over the world travel south of Boston to visit Plymouth for a glimpse into the country's earliest beginnings. The two main stops are the Plimoth Plantation, which re-creates the everyday life of the Pilgrims; and the *Mayflower II,* which gives you an idea of how frightening the journey across the Atlantic must have been. As you may guess, November in Plymouth brings special events focused on Thanksgiving.

Adams National Historic Park
MEMORIAL | FAMILY | Take a guided tour of the birthplace and homes of Presidents John Adams and his son John Quincy Adams, as well as the Stone Library and Adams Crypt, where the Adams presidents and their wives are buried in Quincy's Church of the Presidents. Tours begin at the NPS Visitor Center and Bookstore at 1250 Hancock Street, with trolley transportation to all sites. Get your parking validated adjacent to the visitor center on Saville Road. ✉ *135 Adams St., Quincy* ☎ *617/770–1175, 617/773–1177 park headquarters* ⊕ *www.nps.gov/adam/index.htm* ☞ *$15* ⊗ *Closed Dec.–Mar.*

Plymouth

40 miles south of Boston.

On December 26, 1620, 102 weary men, women, and children disembarked from the *Mayflower* to found the first permanent European settlement north of Virginia. Today Plymouth is characterized by narrow streets, clapboard mansions, shops, antiques stores, and a scenic waterfront. To mark Thanksgiving, the town holds a parade, historic-house tours, and other activities. Historic statues dot the town, including depictions of William Bradford, Pilgrim leader and governor of Plymouth Colony for more than 30 years, on Water Street; a Pilgrim maiden in Brewster Gardens; and Massasoit, the Wampanoag chief who helped the Pilgrims survive, on Carver Street.

VISITOR INFORMATION
CONTACTS Plymouth Visitor Information Center ⊠ *130 Water St., at Rte. 44* ☎ *508/747–7525, 800/872–1620* ⊕ *www. seeplymouth.com.*

 Sights

National Monument to the Forefathers
MEMORIAL | The largest freestanding granite statue in the United States, this allegorical monument stands high on an 11-acre hilltop site. Designed by Hammet Billings of Boston in 1854 and dedicated in 1889, it depicts Faith, surrounded by Liberty, Morality, Justice, Law, and Education, and includes scenes from the Pilgrims' early days in Plymouth. ⊠ *Allerton St.* ⊕ *www.seeplymouth.com.*

Pilgrim Hall Museum
MUSEUM | FAMILY | From the waterfront sights, it's a short walk to one of the country's oldest public museums. Established in 1824, Pilgrim Hall Museum transports you back to the time of the Pilgrims' landing with objects carried by those weary travelers to the New World. Historic items on display include a carved chest, a remarkably well-preserved

wicker cradle, Myles Standish's sword, and John Alden's Bible. ⊠ *75 Court St. (Rte. 3A)* ☎ *508/746–1620* ⊕ *www. pilgrimhall.org* ⊠ *$12* ⊙ *Closed Jan.*

★ Plimoth Plantation
MUSEUM VILLAGE | FAMILY | Against the backdrop of the Atlantic Ocean, and 3 miles south of downtown Plymouth, this living museum shares the rich, interwoven story of the Plymouth Colony and the Wampanoag homeland through engaging daily programs and special events. A 1620s Pilgrim village has been carefully re-created, from the thatch roofs, cramped quarters, and open fireplaces to the long-horned livestock. Throw away your preconception of white collars and funny hats; through ongoing research, the Plimoth staff has developed a portrait of the Pilgrims that's more complex than the dour folk in school textbooks. Listen to the accents of the "residents," who never break out of character. Feel free to engage them in conversation about their life. Don't worry, 21st-century museum educators are on hand to help answer any questions you have as well. On the Wampanoag homesite meet native people speaking from a modern perspective of the traditions, lifeways, and culture of Eastern Woodlands Indigenous people. Note that there's not a lot of shade here in summer. ⊠ *137 Warren Ave. (Rte. 3A)* ☎ *508/746–1622* ⊕ *www.plimoth.org* ⊠ *$28* ⊙ *Closed late-Nov.–mid-Mar.*

Plymouth Rock
MEMORIAL | FAMILY | This landmark rock, just a few dozen yards from the *Mayflower II,* is popularly believed to have been the Pilgrims' stepping-stone when they left the ship. Given the stone's unimpressive appearance—it's little more than a boulder—and dubious authenticity (as explained on a nearby plaque), the grand canopy overhead seems a trifle ostentatious. Still, more than a million people a year come to visit this world-famous symbol of courage and faith. ⊠ *Water St.* ⊕ *www.mass.gov/locations/ pilgrim-memorial-state-park.*

⦿ Restaurants

Blue-eyed Crab Grille & Raw Bar
$$ | SEAFOOD | FAMILY | Grab a seat on the outside deck overlooking the water at this friendly, somewhat funky (plastic fish dangling from the ceiling), fresh-fish shack. Enjoy Caribbean cocktails on the patio, or hang out in the colorful dining room. **Known for:** views of the water; funky decor; tropical cocktails. ⑤ *Average main: $22* ⊠ *170 Water St.* ☎ *508/747–6776* ⊕ *www.blue-eyedcrab. com* ⊟ *No credit cards.*

New Bedford

45 miles southwest of Plymouth, 50 miles south of Boston.

In 1652 colonists from Plymouth settled in the area that now includes the city of New Bedford. The city has a long maritime tradition, beginning as a shipbuilding center and small whaling port in the late 1700s. By the mid-1800s it had developed into a center of North American whaling. Today New Bedford has the largest fishing fleet on the East Coast. Although much of the town is industrial, the restored historic district near the water is a delight. It was here that Herman Melville set his masterpiece, *Moby-Dick*, a novel about whaling.

⦿ Sights

New Bedford Whaling Museum
MUSEUM | FAMILY | Established in 1903, this is the world's largest museum of its kind. A highlight is the skeleton of a 66-foot blue whale, one of only three on view anywhere. An interactive exhibit lets you listen to the underwater sounds of whales, dolphins, and other sea life—plus the sounds of a thunderstorm and a whale-watching boat—as a whale might hear them. You can also peruse the collection of scrimshaw, visit exhibits on regional history, and climb aboard an 89-foot, half-scale model of the 1826 whaling ship *Lagoda*—the world's largest ship model. A small chapel across the street from the museum is the one described in *Moby-Dick.* ⊠ *18 Johnny Cake Hill* ☎ *508/997–0046* ⊕ *www.whalingmuseum.org* ⊠ *$14.*

Rotch-Jones-Duff House & Garden Museum
MUSEUM | The only whaling-era mansion on its original grounds open to the public, the Rotch-Jones-Duff (RJD) House and Garden Museum chronicles the economic, social, and political evolution of the city. Originally built in 1834, the Greek Revival mansion, which is located on a full city block of gardens a half-mile south of downtown, tells the story of the three prominent families who called it home in the 1800s. The museum is filled with elegant furnishings from the era, including a mahogany piano, a massive marble-top sideboard, and portraits of the house's occupants. A free self-guided audio tour is available. ⊠ *396 County St.* ☎ *508/997–1401* ⊕ *www.rjdmuseum.org* ⊠ *$6.*

Chapter 5

CAPE COD, MARTHA'S VINEYARD, AND NANTUCKET

Updated by
Laura V. Scheel

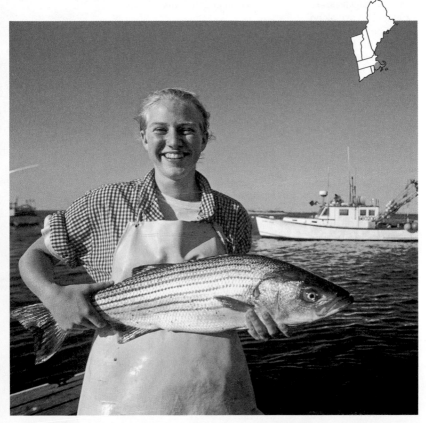

⊙ Sights	🍴 Restaurants	🛏 Hotels	🛍 Shopping	🍸 Nightlife
★★☆☆☆	★★★★☆	★★★★☆	★★★★☆	★★☆☆☆

WELCOME TO CAPE COD, MARTHA'S VINEYARD, AND NANTUCKET

TOP REASONS TO GO

★ **Beaches:** Cape Cod's picturesque beaches are the ultimate reason to go. The high sand dunes, gorgeous sunsets, and never-ending sea will get you every time.

★ **Visiting Lighthouses:** Lighthouses rise along Cape Cod's coast like architectural exclamation points. Highlights include Eastham's beautiful Nauset Light and Chatham and Nobska Lights for their spectacular views.

★ **Biking the Trails:** Martha's Vineyard and Nantucket each have dedicated bike paths, but the Cape Cod Rail Trail from South Dennis to south Wellfleet (with a spur out to Chatham) is the definitive route, with over 25 miles of relatively flat terrain.

★ **Setting Sail:** Area tour operators offer everything from sunset schooner cruises to charter fishing expeditions. Whale-watching adventures are popular mid-April–October.

★ **Browsing the Galleries:** The Cape was a prominent art colony in the 19th century, and today it has a number of galleries.

1 Sandwich. Heritage and Sandwich Glass museums.

2 Falmouth. The family-friendly Old Silver Beach.

3 Hyannis. The Cape's unofficial capital.

4 Barnstable. West Barnstable, Cotuit, Marston Mills, Osterville, Centerville, and Hyannis.

5 Yarmouth. South and West Yarmouth, and Yarmouthport.

6 Dennis. Museums and B&Bs.

7 Brewster. Rich in conservation lands and state parks.

8 Harwich. Boats of all shapes and sizes anchor in the harbors.

9 Chatham. A quietly posh seaside resort.

10 Orleans. Beautiful homes and beaches.

11 Eastham. A town full of hidden treasures.

12 Wellfleet. World-renowned for its oysters.

13 Truro. Home to high dunes, estuaries, and vineyards.

14 Provincetown. Fun-loving town at the Cape's tip.

15 Martha's Vineyard. 7 miles off the Cape's southwest tip.

16 Nantucket. 30 miles south of Hyannis.

0   6 mi

0   6 km

Plymouth Bay

Plimouth Plantation

3A

3

Provincetown

14

Long Point

North Truro

LOWER
CAPE

Truro

13

Cape Cod
National
Seashore

Wellfleet

12   6   South
Wellfleet

Wellfleet
Harbor

North
Eastham

11   Eastham

CAPE COD

Cape Cod Bay

Sagamore

Buzzards
Bay

v2

Bourne

Sandwich

East Sandwich

Monument
Beach

West Barnstable

Marstons
Mills

Pocasset

UPPER
CAPE

Forestdale

North
Falmouth

130

Centerville

151

28

West
Falmouth

almouth

28

East Falmouth

Teaticket

Cotuit

Mashpee
National
Wildlife Refuge

Woods Hole

6

6A

6A

Yarmouth
Port

Yarmouth

Dennis

4

Barnstable

Osterville

Hyannis

Hyannis Port

East Dennis

Dennis

28

132

6

5

MID
CAPE

South
Dennis

Dennis
Port

3

S. Yarmouth

Brewster   7

East Orleans

Orleans

East Orleans

10

South Orleans

Long
Pond

6

East Harwich

9   Chatham

8   West Chatham

28   Harwich Port

Harwich

Monomoy
Nat'l Wildlife Refuge

MONOMOY
ISLAND

Monomoy Point

Nantucket Sound

Great Point

Vineyard
Haven

Oak Bluffs

15

Edgartown

W. Tisbury

MARTHA'S
VINEYARD

CHAPPAQUIDDICK
ISLAND

TUCKERNUCK
ISLAND

NANTUCKET

Nantucket

16

Sankaty Head

Siasconset

Even if you haven't visited Cape Cod and islands, you can likely—and accurately—imagine "sand dunes and salty air, quaint little villages here and there." As that 1950s Patti Page song promises, "you're sure to fall in love with old Cape Cod."

Cape Codders are fiercely protective of the environment. Despite some occasionally rampant development, planners have been careful to preserve nature and encourage responsible, eco-conscious building. Nearly 30% of the Cape's 412 square miles is protected from development, and another 35% has not yet been developed (on Nantucket and Martha's Vineyard, percentages of protected land are far higher). Opportunities for sports and recreation abound, as the region is rife with biking and hiking trails, serene beaches, and waterways for boating and fishing. One somewhat controversial potential development has been a large-scale "wind farm" in Nantucket Sound, comprising some 130 turbines, each about 260 feet tall and several miles offshore.

The area is also rich in history. Many don't realize that the Pilgrims landed here first: in November 1620, the lost and travel-weary sailors dropped anchor in what is now Provincetown Harbor and spent five weeks here, scouring the area for food and possible settlement. Were it not for the aid of the resident Native Americans, the strangers would barely have survived. Even so, they set sail again for fairer lands, ending up across Cape Cod Bay in Plymouth.

Virtually every period style of residential American architecture is well represented on Cape Cod, including—of course—that seminal form named for the region, the Cape Cod–style house. These low, 1½-story domiciles with clapboard or shingle siding—more traditionally the latter in these parts—and gable roofs have been a fixture throughout Cape Cod since the late 17th century. You'll also find grand Georgian and Federal mansions from the Colonial era, as well as handsome Greek Revival, Italianate, and Second Empire houses that date to Victorian times. Many of the most prominent residences were built for ship captains and sea merchants. In recent decades, the region has seen an influx of angular, glassy, contemporary homes, many with soaring windows and skylights, and massive wraparound porches that take advantage of their enviable sea views.

MAJOR REGIONS

The Cape is divided into four major areas and is shaped roughly like an arm bent at the elbow: the **Upper Cape** (the shoulder); the **Mid Cape** (the upper arm); the **Lower Cape** (the bicep and forearm); and the **Outer Cape** (the wrist and hand). Each of the Cape's 15 towns are further broken up into smaller villages.

The Upper Cape (closest to the bridges) has the oldest towns like **Sandwich** and **Falmouth,** plus fine beaches and fascinating little museums. The Mid Cape has sophisticated Colonial-era hamlets but also motels and miniature golf courses. There's **Barnstable, Dennis,** and **Yarmouth,** as well as **Hyannis,** the Cape's unofficial capital. The Lower Cape consists of **Brewster, Chatham, Harwich,** and **Orleans.**

Here you'll find casual clam shacks, lovely lighthouses, funky art galleries, and stellar natural attractions. **Eastham, Wellfleet, Truro,** and **Provincetown** populate the narrow forearm of the Outer Cape, which is famous for sand dunes, crashing surf, and scrubby pines.

The islands, **Martha's Vineyard** and **Nantucket,** lie to the south. Martha's Vineyard is about 7 miles off the Cape's southwest tip, while Nantucket is some 30 miles south of Hyannis. Both are connected to the Cape by ferries, and both also have air service.

Planning

WHEN TO GO

The Cape and islands teem with activity during high season: roughly late June to Labor Day. If you're dreaming of a classic shore vacation, this is prime time. However, along with the dream come daunting crowds and high costs. Fall has begun to rival summer in popularity, at least on weekends through late October, when the weather is temperate and the scenery remarkable. Many restaurants, shops, and hotels remain open in winter, too, making the area desirable even during the coldest months. The region enjoys fairly moderate weather most of the year, with highs typically in the upper 70s and 80s in summer, and in the upper 30s and lower 40s in winter. Snow and rain are not uncommon during the cooler months, and it can be windy any time.

PLANNING YOUR TIME

The region can be enjoyed for a few days or a few weeks, depending on the nature of your trip. As the towns are all quite distinct on Cape Cod, it's best to organize your trip based on your interests: an outdoors enthusiast would want to head to the National Seashore region, for example; those who prefer shopping and amusements would do better in the Mid-Cape area. As one Fodors.com forum member noted, the Cape is generally "not something to see ... instead, people go to spend a few days or weeks, relax, go to the beach ... that sort of thing." A day trip to Nantucket to wander its historic downtown is manageable; several days is best to appreciate Martha's Vineyard's diversity.

Numerous towns on the Cape have weekly beach and lawn concerts, pancake breakfasts, art shows, and more. The Cape Week Section of the *Cape Cod Times* is a great source for information to help plan your days, as is the local Chamber of Commerce.

AIR TRAVEL

The major air gateways are Boston's Logan International Airport and Providence's T. F. Green International Airport. Most major airlines fly to Boston; several fly to Providence; even fewer fly directly to the Cape and islands, and many of those flights are seasonal. Smaller municipal airports are in Barnstable, Martha's Vineyard, Nantucket, and Provincetown.

CAR TRAVEL

Cape Cod is easily reached from Boston via Route 3 and from Providence via Interstate 195. Once you cross Cape Cod Canal, you can follow U.S. 6. Without any traffic, it takes about an hour to 90 minutes to reach the canal from either Boston or Providence. Allow an extra 30–60 minutes' travel time in peak periods.

Parking, in general, can be a challenge in summer, especially in congested downtowns and at popular beaches. If you can walk, bike, carpool, or cab it somewhere, do so. But unless you are planning to focus your attention on a single community, you'll probably need a car on the Cape. Authorities on both Nantucket and Martha's Vineyard strongly encourage visitors to leave their cars on the mainland: taking a vehicle onto the island ferries is expensive and requires reservations (another option is renting upon arrival), and there is ample and efficient transportation once you arrive.

FERRY TRAVEL

Martha's Vineyard and Nantucket are easily reached by passenger ferries (traditional and high-speed boats) from several Cape towns; farther afield one can get a seasonal ferry from Plymouth, MA; New Bedford, CT; Highlands, New Jersey; and Manhattan. Ferries to Provincetown embark from Boston and Plymouth. Some services run year-round, while others are seasonal. Even parking for the ferries must be reserved during the busy season, but passenger reservations are rarely necessary. Trip times vary from as little as 45 minutes to about two hours and run $8.50–$39 one-way; bicycles can be taken aboard many ferries for $4, while cars cost $43.50–$68 one-way (reservations required and very limited).

TRAIN TRAVEL

The seasonal *Cape Flyer* only runs on weekends (Friday–Sunday) from Boston's South Station, Memorial Day–Labor Day. The 2½-hour trip makes stops in Braintree, Middleborough, Buzzards Bay, and Hyannis. Round-trip fare from Boston is $40; bring your bike for no extra fee. Kids 11 and under ride free with adult.

CONTACT Cape Flyer ⊠ *Hyannis Transportation Center, 215 Iyannough Rd., Barnstable* ☎ *508/775–8504* ⊕ *www. capeflyer.com.*

RESTAURANTS

Cape Cod kitchens have long been closely associated with seafood: the waters off the Cape and islands yield a bounty of lobsters, clams, oysters, scallops, and myriad fish that make their way onto local menus. In addition to the region's strong Portuguese influence, globally inspired and contemporary fare commonly turn up among restaurant offerings. Also gaining in popularity is the use of locally, and often organically, raised produce, meat, and dairy.

Note that ordering an expensive lobster dinner may push your meal into a higher price category than this guide's price range shows for the restaurant. You can indulge in fresh local seafood and clambakes at seat-yourself shanties for a lower price than at their fine-dining counterparts. *Restaurant reviews have been shortened. For full information, visit Fodors.com.*

HOTELS

B&Bs are king in the Cape, so you can bed down in a former sea captain's home or even a converted church. However, there are also a few larger resorts and even a handful of chain hotels. You'll want to make reservations for inns well in advance during peak summer periods. Smoking is prohibited in all Massachusetts hotels. *Hotel reviews have been shortened. For full information, visit Fodors.com.*

CONDO AND HOUSE RENTALS

Many travelers to the Cape and the islands rent a house if they're going to stay for a week or longer. Many local real-estate agencies deal with rentals. Be sure to book a property well in advance of your trip: prime properties are often rented out to the same people year after year. Expect rentals on both Martha's Vineyard and Nantucket to be significantly higher than those on the Cape, simply because there are fewer options.

What It Costs			
$	$$	$$$	$$$$
RESTAURANTS			
under $18	$18–$24	$25–$35	over $35
HOTELS			
under $200	$200–$299	$300–$399	over $399

Sandwich

3 miles east of Sagamore Bridge, 11 miles west of Barnstable.

★ The oldest town on Cape Cod, Sandwich was established in 1637 by some of the Plymouth Pilgrims and incorporated on March 6, 1638. Today, it is a well-preserved, quintessential New England village with a white-columned town hall and streets lined with 18th- and 19th-century houses.

VISITOR INFORMATION

CONTACTS Sandwich Chamber of Commerce ⊠ *Sandwich Center* ☎ *508/833–9755* ⊕ *www.sandwichchamber.com.*

Sights

★ Heritage Museums and Gardens

CAROUSEL | FAMILY | These 100 beautifully landscaped acres overlooking the upper end of Shawme Pond are one of the region's top draws. Paths crisscross the grounds, which include gardens planted with hostas, heather, herbs, and fruit trees. Rhododendrons are in full glory mid-May–mid-June, and daylilies reach their peak mid-July–early August. In 1967, pharmaceuticals magnate Josiah K. Lilly III purchased the estate and turned it into a nonprofit museum. One highlight is the reproduction Shaker Round Barn, which showcases classic and historic cars— including a 1919 Pierce-Arrow, a 1915 Milburn Light Electric, a 1911 Stanley Steamer, and a 1930 yellow-and-green Duesenberg built for movie star Gary Cooper. The art museum has an extraordinary collection of New England folk art, including paintings, weather vanes, Nantucket baskets, and scrimshaw. Both adults and children can enjoy riding on a Coney Island–style carousel dating to the early 20th century. Other features include Hidden Hollow, an outdoor activity center for families with children.

A shuttle bus, equipped with a wheelchair lift and space to stow baby strollers, transports visitors on certain days. In summer, concerts are held in the gardens, often on Wednesday or Saturday evening or on Sunday afternoon. The center of the complex is about ¾ mile on foot from the in-town end of Shawme Pond. ⊠ *67 Grove St., Sandwich Center* ☎ *508/888–3300* ⊕ *www.heritagemuseumsandgardens.org* 🎫 *$18.*

Sandwich Boardwalk

BEACH—SIGHT | FAMILY | The long sweep of Cape Cod Bay stretches out around the beach at the end of the Sandwich Boardwalk, where a platform provides fine views, especially at sunset. You can look out toward Sandy Neck, Wellfleet, and Provincetown or toward the white cliffs beyond Sagamore. Near this mostly rocky beach are dunes covered with rugosa roses, which have a delicious fragrance; this is a good place for birding. The creeks running through the salt marsh make for great canoeing. From the town center it's about a mile to the boardwalk; cross Route 6A on Jarves Street, and at its end turn left, then right, and continue to the boardwalk parking lot. ⊠ *End of Jarves St., Sandwich Center.*

Sandwich Glass Museum

HISTORIC SITE | Shimmering glass was manufactured here nearly two centuries ago, and the Sandwich Glass Museum shows you what the factory looked like in its heyday. There's an "ingredient room" showcasing a wide spectrum of glass colors, along with the minerals added to the sand to obtain them, and an outstanding collection of blown and pressed glass in many shapes and hues. Large lamps, vases, and pitchers are impressive, as are the hundreds of candlesticks on display. There are glass-blowing demonstrations daily 10–3. The extensive gift shop sells some handsome reproductions, including some made by local and national artisans. Also home to the Sandwich Historical Society, the museum hosts historic walking tours on certain days June–October. ⊠ *129 Main St., Sandwich Center* ☎ *508/888–0251* ⊕ *www.sandwichglassmuseum.org* 🎫 *$10* ⏱ *Closed Jan.; Mon. and Tues. Feb. and Mar.*

Cape Cod

KEY

- Beaches
- Cape Cod Bike Trail
- Ferry

8 mi

8 km

TO BOSTON

Green Harbor
Duxbury
Kingston
Plymouth

Race Point Beach

Province Lands

CAPE COD
Provincetown

Herring Cove Beach

Long Point Light

Long point

Cape Cod Bay

White Horse Beach
Manomet
Manomet Beach
Ellisville
Nameloc Heights

Head of the Meadow Beach
Highland Light
North Truro
Truro Vineyards of Cape Cod
Truro

Cahoon Hollow Beach
South Wellfleet
Marconi Station
Wellfleet
Massachusetts Audubon Wellfleet
Bay Wildlife Sanctuary

Nauset Light
Nauset Light Beach
Coast Guard Beach
Salt Pond Visitor Center
North Eastham
Eastham
Wellfleet Harbor

East Orleans
Orleans
South Orleans

Nauset Beach

First Encounter Beach
Skaket Beach
Nickerson State Park
Brewster
E. Dennis
South Dennis
Dennis

Corporation Beach

Dennis
Yarmouth
Sandy Neck Light
Sandy Neck

Sandy Neck Beach
Scusset Beach Reservation
Sandwich
E. Sandwich

Sagamore
Buzzards Bay
Monument Beach
Pocasset

Heritage Plantation
Museums and Gardens Massachusetts

Myles Standish State Forest
South Carver

W. Barnstable
Marstons Mills
Barnstable

Military Reservation
Forestdale

Centerville
Osterville
Cotuit

Craigville Beach

Hyannis
Hyannis Port

S. Yarmouth
West Dennis Beach
Kalmus Park Beach

Dennis Port

Harwich
East Harwich
West Chatham
Chatham
Chatham Light

Harding's Beach

South Orleans
East Harwich

Monomoy National Wildlife Refuge

MONOMOY ISLAND

Monomoy Point

Nantucket Sound

TO NANTUCKET

Mashpee National Wildlife Refuge

Waquoit Bay National Estuarine Research Reserve

North Falmouth
West Falmouth
Teaticket
East Falmouth
Falmouth

Grews Pond
Old Silver Beach

Woods Hole
Nobska Light

MARTHA'S VINEYARD

NAUSHON ISLAND

Buzzards Bay

Restaurants

Pilot House
$$$ | **SEAFOOD** | Views of the bustling Cape Cod Canal abound from this casual spot's enviable waterside perch. Seafood is the main catch here, particularly pleasing eaten alfresco under an umbrella or by the fire pit. **Known for:** great views of the canal; daily live music; local seafood. $ *Average main: $25* ✉ *14 Gallo Rd., Sandwich Center* ☎ *508/888–8889* ⊕ *www.pilothousecapecod.com* ⊙ *Closed Mon. and Tues. Nov.–Apr.*

Hotels

★ Belfry Inne & Bistro
$ | **B&B/INN** | This sophisticated complex comprises a 1901 former church (the Abbey), an ornate wood-frame 1882 Victorian (the Painted Lady), and an 1827 Federal-style house (the Village House), and the theme in each is a nod to the buildings' respective histories—the Painted Lady's charmingly appointed guest rooms, for example, are named after former inhabitants. **Pros:** great in-town location; bright, beautiful, and spacious rooms; dramatic architecture. **Cons:** some steep stairs; not suited for families; some rooms can be on the smaller side. $ *Rooms from: $189* ✉ *6 Jarves St., Sandwich Center* ☎ *508/888–8550, 800/844–4542* ⊕ *www.belfryinn.com* ⇥ *23 rooms* ⦿ *Free breakfast.*

Isaiah Jones Homestead Bed & Breakfast
$$ | **B&B/INN** | Expect extraordinary service in an equally stellar setting—graceful lines and high ceilings, authentic period antiques and moody stained glass—at this venerable Victorian. **Pros:** easy walk to town center; beautiful grounds; elegant surroundings. **Cons:** some steep stairs. $ *Rooms from: $229* ✉ *165 Main St., Sandwich Center* ☎ *508/888–9115, 800/526–1625* ⊕ *www.isaiahjones.com* ⇥ *7 rooms* ⦿ *Free breakfast.*

Nightlife

British Beer Company
BARS/PUBS | This traditional British "public house" has a great menu that includes fish, ribs, and pizza. Entertainment options throughout the week include karaoke, trivia night, and a variety of bands that perform Thursday–Saturday. There are two other Cape locations in Falmouth and Hyannis. ✉ *46 Rte. 6A* ☎ *508/833–9590* ⊕ *www.britishbeer.com.*

Shopping

Downtown Sandwich has quite a few specialty shops, as well as several good antiques co-ops, boutiques, and galleries. Along Route 6A, you'll find more of the same, just spread out along the miles.

★ Titcomb's Bookshop
BOOKS/STATIONERY | You'll find used, rare, and new books here, including a large collection of Americana. There's also an extensive selection of children's books. Look for frequent author events and book signings. ✉ *432 Rte. 6A, East Sandwich* ☎ *508/888–2331* ⊕ *www. titcombsbookshop.com.*

Falmouth

15 miles south of Bourne Bridge, 20 miles south of Sandwich.

Falmouth, the Cape's second-largest town, was settled in 1660. Today it is largely suburban, with a mix of old and new developments and a sizable year-round population. Many residents commute to other towns on the Cape, to southeastern Massachusetts, and even to Boston. The town has a quaint downtown area, with a typically old New England village green and a shop-lined Main Street. South of town center, Falmouth faces Nantucket Sound and has several often-crowded beaches popular with families. To the east, the Falmouth Heights neighborhood mixes inns,

B&Bs, and private homes, nestled close together on residential streets leading to the sea. Bustling Grand Avenue, the main drag in Falmouth Heights, hugs the shore and the beach.

The village of Woods Hole, part of Falmouth, is home to several major scientific institutions—the National Marine Fisheries Service, the Marine Biological Laboratory (MBL), the Woods Hole Oceanographic Institution, and the U.S. Geological Survey's Branch of Marine Geology—and is a departure point for ferries to Martha's Vineyard.

GETTING HERE AND AROUND

Heading from the Bourne Bridge toward Falmouth, County Road and Route 28A are prettier alternatives to Route 28, and Sippewisset Road meanders near Buzzards Bay between West Falmouth and Woods Hole. If you're coming from Falmouth to Woods Hole, either ride your bicycle down the straight and flat Shining Sea Trail or take the Cape Cod Regional Transit Authority's WHOOSH trolley. In summer, the basically one-street village overflows with thousands of visiting scientists, students, and tourists heading to the islands. Parking, limited to a relatively small number of metered spots on the street, can be nearly impossible.

CONTACTS Cape Cod Regional Transit Authority ☎ *800/352–7155* ⊕ *www.capecodtransit.org.*

VISITOR INFORMATION

CONTACTS Falmouth Chamber of Commerce and Visitor Center ☎ *508/548–8500, 800/526–8532* ⊕ *www.falmouthchamber.com.*

Sights

Nobska Light

LIGHTHOUSE | This imposing lighthouse has spectacular views from its base of the nearby Elizabeth Islands and of Martha's Vineyard, across Vineyard Sound. The 42-foot cast-iron tower, lined with brick, was built in 1876 with a stationary light. It shines red to indicate dangerous waters or white for safe passage. Friends of Nobska Light, a nonprofit group, has been carefully restoring the structure (it is hoped that lighthouse keeper's house will be finished by 2020), and tours are once again offered on Tuesday and Thursday in July and August, 10 am–2 pm. The grounds are open dawn to dusk for sightseeing, though parking is very limited. Best to arrive by bike along the scenic bike path. ⚠ **Tour times are not guaranteed and depend on both weather and volunteer availability.** ⊠ *233 Nobska Rd., Woods Hole* ⊕ *www.friendsofnobska.org/* ⟋ *Free.*

Ocean Science Exhibit Center

COLLEGE | FAMILY | Here visitors can get a glimpse of the extraordinary scientific marine research that goes on within the Woods Hole Oceanographic Institute. Climb inside a replica of *Alvin*, the submersible that dove thousands of feet deep to explore the wreck of the *Titanic*. Other exhibits show footage of the rich life at vast depths of the ocean. Scientists give informative lectures on a regular basis in July and August. ⊠ *15 School St., Woods Hole* ☎ *508/289–2663* ⊕ *www.whoi.edu/main/ocean-science-exhibit-center* ⟋ *$3 suggested donation* ☉ *Closed Jan.–mid-Apr.*

Waquoit Bay National Estuarine Research Reserve

BEACH—SIGHT | FAMILY | Encompassing 3,000 acres of estuaries, woodlands, salt marshes, and barrier beaches, this research reserve is a good place for walking, kayaking, fishing, and birding. In July and August, there are nature programs for families, including an outdoor lecture series on Tuesday evening. **South Cape Beach** is part of the reserve; you can lie out on the sand or join one of the interpretive walks. **Flat Pond Trail** runs through several different habitats, including fresh- and saltwater marshes. You can reach **Washburn Island** on your own by boat, or by joining a Saturday-morning tour; it offers 330 acres of pine barrens

and trails, swimming, and 10 wilderness campsites (an advance reservation and permit are required). ✉ *149 Rte. 28, Waquoit Village ✣ 3 miles west of Mashpee rotary* ☎ *508/457–0495* ⊕ *www.waquoitbayreserve.org* 💲 *Free; daily parking fee for beach.*

★ Woods Hole Science Aquarium

ZOO | FAMILY | This impressive facility displays numerous large tanks and many more smaller ones filled with regional fish and shellfish. Rooms are small, but they are crammed with stuff to see. Magnifying glasses and a dissecting scope help you examine marine life. Several hands-on pools hold banded lobsters, crabs, snails, starfish, and other creatures. The stars of the show are two harbor seals, on view in the outdoor pool near the entrance; watch their feedings, most days, at 11 and 4. ✉ *166 Water St., Woods Hole* ☎ *508/495–2001* ⊕ *aquarium.nefsc.noaa.gov* 💲 *Free* ☉ *Closed Sun. and Mon.*

Beaches

Old Silver Beach

BEACH—SIGHT | FAMILY | This long, beautiful crescent of soft white sand is anchored by the Sea Crest Beach Resort at one end. It's especially good for small children because a sandbar keeps it shallow at the southern end and creates tidal pools full of crabs and minnows. Very popular, this beach has its share of crowds on nice, sunny days. **Amenities:** food and drink; lifeguards; parking (fee); showers; toilets. **Best for:** swimming; walking. ✉ *296 Quaker Rd., North Falmouth* ⊕ *www.falmouthmass.us* 💲 *$20 daily parking.*

Restaurants

★ C Salt Wine Bar & Grille

$$$ | AMERICAN | With an open kitchen that turns out some excellent and artful dishes, this tiny place keeps its tables full and its guests happy (reservations strongly recommended). Fine service by a friendly and knowledgeable staff adds greatly to the overall atmosphere. **Known for:** raw oyster selection; notable wine list; creative seafood. 💲 *Average main: $32* ✉ *75 Davis Straits (Rte. 28)* ☎ *774/763–2954* ⊕ *www.csaltfalmouth.com.*

The Clam Shack

$ | SEAFOOD | Fried clams are crisp and fresh at this basic seafood joint right on Falmouth Harbor; the meaty lobster roll and the fish 'n' chips platter are good choices, too. Place your order at the counter, and then take your tray to the picnic tables on the roof deck for the best views. **Known for:** clam strips; crowds; waterfront perch. 💲 *Average main: $16* ✉ *227 Clinton Ave., Falmouth Harbor* ☎ *508/540–7758* ▭ *No credit cards* ☉ *Closed early Sept.–mid-May.*

★ La Cucina Sul Mare

$$$ | ITALIAN | Northern Italian and Mediterranean cooking distinguish this classy, popular place. Make sure to come hungry—portions here are huge—and expect a long wait during prime hours in season (reservations are accepted only for parties of five-plus); however, you can use the call-ahead wait list to get a jump on the line. **Known for:** zuppa de pesce; boisterous atmosphere; attentive service. 💲 *Average main: $27* ✉ *237 Main St., Falmouth Center* ☎ *508/548–5600* ⊕ *www.lacucinasulmare.com.*

Hotels

The Captain's Manor Inn

$$ | B&B/INN | With its expansive landscaped grounds ringed by a wrought-iron fence, this elegant 1849 Italianate inn with a wraparound porch and grand foyer resembles a private estate. **Pros:** easy walk to town center; elegant setting; ample grounds make you feel worlds away from the hustle and bustle. **Cons:** not for those with small children; long stairway to second-floor rooms; not for those traveling on a budget. 💲 *Rooms from: $289* ✉ *27 W. Main St., Falmouth Center* ☎ *508/388–7336* www.captainsmanorinn.com ⤳ 7 rooms ¶⊙¶ Free breakfast.

★ Inn on the Sound

$$ | B&B/INN | At this understated and serene but stylish inn, perched on a bluff overlooking Vineyard Sound, common areas include an art-laden living room with a boulder fireplace and water views, oversize windows, and modern white couches; a bistrolike breakfast room; and a porch with more stunning water views. **Pros:** grand water views; elegant setting; easy walk to beach. **Cons:** not an in-town location; not for those with small children. ⑤ *Rooms from: $289* ✉ *313 Grand Ave., Falmouth Heights* ☏ *508/457–9666, 800/564–9668* ⊕ *www.innonthesound. com* ⤳ *11 rooms* ¶⊙¶ *Free breakfast.*

Woods Hole Passage

$$ | B&B/INN | FAMILY | A century-old carriage house and barn have been converted into a romantic showcase with more than 2 acres that include beautiful gardens; when you want to explore outside the grounds, hop on the town trolley, which runs right by the inn. **Pros:** family-friendly; easy walk to beach; extremely helpful innkeepers; Martha's Vineyard ferry is five minutes away. **Cons:** not an in-town location; some steep stairs. ⑤ *Rooms from: $229* ✉ *186 Woods Hole Rd., Woods Hole* ☏ *508/548–9575, 800/790–8976* ⊕ *www. woodsholepassage.com* ⤳ *5 rooms* ¶⊙¶ *Free breakfast.*

 Activities

BASEBALL

The Cape Cod Baseball League, begun in 1885, is an invitational league of college players that counts Carlton Fisk, Ron Darling, Mo Vaughn, Nomar Garciaparra, and the late Thurman Munson as alumni. Considered the country's best summer league, it's scouted by every major-league team. The 10 teams of the Cape Cod Baseball League play a 44-game season mid-June–mid-August; games held at all 10 fields are free.

Falmouth Commodores

BASEBALL/SOFTBALL | FAMILY | The Falmouth Commodores of the collegiate Cape Cod Baseball League play their home games at Guv Fuller Field, mid-June–mid-August. Players and coaches lead youth baseball clinics in June and July. ✉ *790 Main St., Falmouth Center* ⊕ *www.falmouthcommodores.com* ✉ *Free.*

BIKING

★ Shining Sea Bikeway

BICYCLING | The wonderful Shining Sea Bikeway is almost 11 miles of paved bike path through four of Falmouth's villages, running from Woods Hole to North Falmouth. It follows the shore of Buzzards Bay, providing water views, and dips into oak and pine woods; a detour onto Church Street takes you to Nobska Light. A brochure is available at the trailheads. If you're taking your bike to Martha's Vineyard, park in one of Falmouth's Steamship Authority lots and ride to the ferry. Free shuttles from Falmouth to the Woods Hole ferry dock have bike carriers. There's also a parking area near Depot Avenue, on County Road at the other end. ✉ *Falmouth.*

FISHING

Eastman's Sport & Tackle

FISHING | Freshwater ponds are good for perch, pickerel, trout, and more; get the required license (along with rental gear) at Eastman's Sport & Tackle. It's a good resource if you are looking for local guides. ■ **TIP→ Anglers over the age of 16 will also need a saltwater fishing license.** ✉ *783 Main St., Falmouth Center* ☏ *508/548–6900* ⊕ *www.eastmanstackle.com.*

 Shopping

Falmouth Village has an easily walkable and attractive Main Street, lined with specialty shops—you won't find major chain stores here—and an assortment of good restaurants. The pretty Marine Park is home to many events, including an impressive Thursday afternoon Farmers' Market held mid-May–mid-October, noon to 6.

Bean & Cod

FOOD/CANDY | This specialty food shop sells cheeses, breads, great sandwiches, and picnic fixings, along with coffees and teas. They also pack and ship gift baskets. ⊠ *140 Main St., Falmouth Center* ☎ *508/548–8840.*

Hyannis

23 miles east of the Bourne Bridge, 21 miles northeast of Falmouth.

Perhaps best known for its association with the Kennedy clan, the Hyannis area was also a vacation site for President Ulysses S. Grant in 1874 and later for President Grover Cleveland. A bustling year-round hub of activity, Hyannis has the Cape's largest concentration of businesses, shops, malls, hotels and motels, restaurants, and entertainment venues.

GETTING HERE AND AROUND

There's plenty of public parking around town, on both sides of Main Street as well as in several public parking lots. The island ferry companies have designated parking lots ($15–$20 daily fee in summer season) with free shuttles to the docks. Hyannis is the Cape's transit hub and is served by a number of bus routes.

VISITOR INFORMATION

CONTACTS Hyannis Chamber of Commerce ☎ *508/775–2201* ⊕ *www.hyannis.com.*

 Sights

Cape Cod Maritime Museum

MUSEUM | **FAMILY** | This waterfront museum stands as testament and tribute to the bustle of the harbor that it overlooks. Changing maritime art exhibits, classes on boatbuilding and other nautical arts, and an active boatbuilding shop all highlight the importance of the sea, in past and present alike. Take a harbor sail on the historic replica Crosby Catboat *Sarah*, and learn "dead reckoning"—real navigation without the aid of modern technology. ⊠ *135 South St., Hyannis Harbor* ☎ *508/775–1723* ⊕ *www.capecodmaritimemuseum.org* ⊠ *$6* ⊙ *Closed Mon.*

John F. Kennedy Hyannis Museum

LIBRARY | In Main Street's Old Town Hall, this museum explores JFK's Cape years (1934–63) through enlarged and annotated photographs culled from the archives of the JFK Library near Boston, as well as a seven-minute video narrated by Walter Cronkite. Changing exhibits focus on various members of the family at different stages of their life and career. Events include lectures, book signings, and speaking engagements by those with close connections to the family, both past and present. Expansion is underway in 2018 to incorporate an auditorium and media center to further educational and community activities. ⊠ *397 Main St.* ☎ *508/790–3077* ⊕ *www. jfkhyannismuseum.org* ⊠ *$12.*

 Beaches

Kalmus Park Beach

BEACH—SIGHT | **FAMILY** | This wide, sandy beach has an area set aside for windsurfers and a sheltered area that's good for kids. It's a great spot for watching boats go in and out of the harbor. **Amenities:** food and drink; lifeguards; parking (fee); showers; toilets. **Best for:** swimming; walking; windsurfing. ⊠ *End of Ocean St., Hyannis Harbor* ⊕ *www.townofbarnstable.us* ⊠ *Parking $20.*

 Restaurants

★ Brazilian Grill

$$$ | **BRAZILIAN** | At this all-you-can-eat churrascaria, waiters continually circulate through the dining room offering more than a dozen grilled meats—beef, pork, chicken, sausage, and the beloved Brazilian chicken hearts on large, swordlike skewers. The massive buffet is laden with soups, salads, and side dishes, including plantains, rice, and beans

Cape Cod Clam Shacks

Cape Codders have been clamming for generations, and the iconic mollusks are a celebrated part of the culture here. Classic clam shacks are known for their bountiful baskets of crispy fried clams, which, according to Cape Codders, should always be ordered "whole"—that is, with the bellies. Fried clams are never the only item on the menu: a typical menu also includes clam chowder, lobster rolls, fried fish, scallops, shrimp, coleslaw, fries, potato salad, and other nonseafood items. The quintessential experience usually involves ordering at one window, picking up at another, and eating at a picnic table—hopefully one with a beach or harbor view! A few of our favorites on Cape Cod include the Clam Shack in Falmouth,

JT's Seafood in Brewster, Captain Frosty's in Dennis, Mac's Seafood in Wellfleet, Arnold's Lobster & Clam Bar in Eastham, and the Lobster Pot in Provincetown The Bite in Menemsha on Martha's Vineyard is also worth a try.

If you're interested in learning how to try recreational clamming, put on your clamdiggers, grab your rake and basket, and head to the local town hall to get your license and any other necessary information. You can also take a class, like the ones offered by the Barnstable Association for Recreational Shellfishing (⊕ www.shellfishing.org), or check in with the local shellfish warden to find out about any organized clamming excursions.

(vegetarians could happily eat from the buffet). **Known for:** grilled meats, Brazilian style; loud and festive atmosphere; homemade flan. ⑤ *Average main: $35* ✉ *680 Main St., West End* ☎ *508/771–0109* ⊕ *www.braziliangrill-capecod.com* ⊘ *No lunch weekends.*

★ Naked Oyster Bistro & Raw Bar
$$$ | ECLECTIC | More than 1,000 oysters are eaten here on an average summer weekend, a good deal of them procured near daily from the restaurant's own oyster farm in nearby Barnstable. You'll always find close to two dozen raw and "dressed" oyster dishes; there's also a nice range of nonoyster entrées, salads, and appetizers. **Known for:** oyster stew; locally sourced ingredients; oysters, oysters, oysters. ⑤ *Average main: $29* ✉ *410 Main St.* ☎ *508/778–6500* ⊕ *www.nakedoyster.com* ⊘ *Closed Sun. mid-Oct.–mid-Apr.*

Roadhouse Café
$$$ | ECLECTIC | Candlelight flickers off the white-linen tablecloths and dark-wood

wainscoting in the main dining room, while the more casual bistro has a large mahogany bar and a lighter-fare menu. Listen to excellent straight-ahead jazz on Monday night year-round in the bistro; weekend nights feature a piano bar. **Known for:** seafood fra diavolo; live music year-round; sophisticated yet casual ambience. ⑤ *Average main: $28* ✉ *488 South St.* ☎ *508/775–2386* ⊕ *www.roadhousecafe.com* ⊘ *No lunch.*

Hotels

★ Anchor-In
$$$ | HOTEL | Most rooms at this small-scale motel on the north end of Hyannis Harbor have harbor views and small balconies overlooking the water, and its simple street-side appearance belies its spacious and immaculate accommodations, extensive grounds, and warm, B&B-style personal service from Lisa and Skip Simpson. **Pros:** easy walk to downtown; great harbor views; well-appointed rooms. **Cons:** no elevator—second-floor

rooms accessed via stairs; not for the budget-minded; crowded area. $ *Rooms from: $329* ✉ *1 South St., Hyannis Harbor* ☎ *508/775–0357* ⊕ *www.anchorin. com* ⇌ *42 rooms* ⦿ *Free breakfast.*

SeaCoast Inn

$ | **HOTEL** | While the rooms at this hotel are basic, it's conveniently located between downtown and the harbor—look for the abundantly blooming window boxes. **Pros:** rooms are big and very clean; reasonable rates; walk to beaches, downtown, and ferries. **Cons:** not a scenic location; no great views; midway between town and harbor. $ *Rooms from: $159* ✉ *33 Ocean St., Downtown* ☎ *508/775–3828* ⊕ *www. seacoastcapecod.com* ⊗ *Closed Nov.– Mar.* ⇌ *26 rooms* ⦿ *No meals.*

Performing Arts

Cape Cod Melody Tent

CONCERTS | **FAMILY** | In 1950, actress Gertrude Lawrence and her husband, producer-manager Richard Aldrich, opened the Cape Cod Melody Tent to showcase Broadway musicals and concerts. Today, it's the region's top venue for pop concerts and comedy shows. Performers who have played here in the round include the Indigo Girls, Lyle Lovett, Tony Bennett, Diana Krall, and Crosby, Stills & Nash. The Tent also holds a children's theater series in July and August, Wednesday at 11 am. ✉ *21 W. Main St., West End* ☎ *508/775–5630* ⊕ *www.melodytent.org.*

Activities

BASEBALL

Hyannis Harbor Hawks

BASEBALL/SOFTBALL | **FAMILY** | The Hyannis Harbor Hawks of the collegiate Cape Cod Baseball League play home games at McKeon Park mid-June–mid-August. Interested 5- to 17-year-olds can sign up with the Youth Baseball Academy. ✉ *McKeon Park, High School Rd.* ☎ *508/420–0962* ⊕ *www.harborhawks.org.*

Shopping

Main Street in downtown Hyannis has gradually become gentrified in recent years and is now one of the top shopping destinations on the Cape, buzzing with several art galleries and antiques shops, numerous clothiers, and a slew of other, mostly independent, boutiques and gift emporia. You'll also find quite a few restaurants along this walkable stretch, including several cafés that are nice for a cup of coffee or a light snack. Heading through the villages of Barnstable along Route 6A, you'll find no shortage of intriguing art galleries and rustic antiques shops.

Christmas Tree Shops

SPECIALTY STORES | This Cape mainstay—the chain originated here—is a bargain shoppers' haven. Take home Cape souvenirs at a great discount along with just about anything you might need (or not need) to decorate your home. There are multiple locations throughout the Cape, from the Sagamore Bridge to Orleans. ✉ *655 Iyanough Rd.* ☎ *508/778–5521* ⊕ *www.christmastreeshops.com.*

HyArts Artist Shanties

ART GALLERIES | Located on a boardwalk that parallels the Hyannis Harbor, seven artist shanties host a rotating slate of Cape Cod-based artists. Work ranges from photography and paintings to handmade jewelry, ceramics, and wood carving. ✉ *Hyannis Harbor, 152–160 Ocean St., Hyannis Harbor* ☎ *508/862–4990* ⊕ *hyartsdistrict.com/visual-arts/art-shanties/artists.*

Barnstable

4 miles north of Hyannis.

With nearly 50,000 year-round residents, Barnstable is the largest town on the Cape. It's also the second oldest, founded in 1639. You can get a feeling for its age in Barnstable Village, on and near Main Street (Route 6A), a lovely area of large old homes.

GETTING HERE AND AROUND

Most people drive to Barnstable via Route 6 or Route 6A. The Cape Cod Regional Transit Authority operates the Barnstable Villager, a small bus that travels from Barnstable to Hyannis. Service is daily late June–Labor Day; buses run about every hour.

Beaches

Sandy Neck Beach

BEACH—SIGHT | FAMILY | Sandy Neck Beach stretches some 6 miles across a peninsula that ends at **Sandy Neck Light.** The beach is one of the Cape's most beautiful—dunes, sand, and bay spread endlessly east, west, and north. The marsh used to be harvested for salt hay; now it's a haven for birds, which are out and about in the greatest numbers in morning and evening. The lighthouse, standing a few feet from the eroding shoreline at the tip of the neck, has been out of commission since 1952. It was built in 1857 to replace an 1827 light, and it used to run on acetylene gas. As you travel east along Route 6A from Sandwich, Sandy Neck Road is just before the Barnstable line, although the beach itself is in West Barnstable. **Amenities:** food and drink; lifeguards; parking (fee); showers; toilets. **Best for:** sunset; swimming; walking. ⊠ Sandy Neck Rd., West Barnstable 🅿 Parking $20.

Restaurants

Barnstable Restaurant & Tavern

$$ | AMERICAN | This handsome old building right in the village center, across from the courthouse, holds both a formal restaurant and a more relaxed tavern; dine street-side on the brick patio in nice weather. Fresh seafood dishes and the chef's rich pasta dishes are local favorites. **Known for:** Tavern burger; Friday-night live music on the patio; local seafood. ⑤ Average main: $19 ⊠ 3176 Rte. 6A ☎ 508/362–2355 ⊕ www.barnstablerestaurant.com.

Hotels

★**Honeysuckle Hill**

$ | B&B/INN | There are plenty of thoughtful touches at this 1810 Queen Anne–style cottage: fresh flowers in every room, lavish breakfasts, refrigerators stocked with beverages, and beach chairs with umbrellas (perfect for nearby Sandy Neck Beach); there's even an outdoor hot tub and shower. **Pros:** lush gardens on the grounds; tasteful, large rooms; very short drive to Sandy Neck Beach. **Cons:** most rooms are accessed via steep stairs; no water views; not an in-town location. ⑤ Rooms from: $199 ⊠ 591 Rte. 6A, West Barnstable ☎ 508/362–8418, 866/444–5522 ⊕ www.honeysucklehill.com ⇨ 5 rooms ⑩ Free breakfast.

Yarmouth

Yarmouth Port is 3 miles east of Barnstable Village; West Yarmouth is 2 miles east of Hyannis.

Once known as Mattacheese, or "the planting lands," Yarmouth was settled in 1639 by farmers from the Plymouth Bay Colony. By then the Cape had begun a thriving maritime industry, and men turned to the sea to make their fortunes. Many impressive sea captains' houses—some now B&Bs and museums—still line enchanting Route 6A and nearby side streets, and Yarmouth Port has some real old-time stores in town. West Yarmouth has a very different atmosphere, stretched on busy commercial Route 28 south of Yarmouth Port.

GETTING HERE AND AROUND

Route 6A is the main route to Yarmouth Port, and there are lovely streets heading north toward the water and through hidden residential areas filled with beautiful old homes. West Yarmouth lies in the midst of busy Route 28, between Hyannis and South Yarmouth. If you want to avoid this road entirely, a sensible option is to take speedy U.S. 6 to the exit nearest what you want to visit and then cut south across the interior. If you must travel the Route 28 area, take Buck Island Road, which runs north of and parallel to much of the busy route in West and South Yarmouth. Like West Yarmouth, South Yarmouth has a stretch of blight and overdevelopment on Route 28, but it also has some nice beaches that are good for families. Avoid Route 28 if you aim to get anywhere quickly.

VISITOR INFORMATION

CONTACTS Yarmouth Chamber of Commerce ☎ 508/778–1008, 800/732–1008 ⊕ www.yarmouthcapecod.com.

 ## Sights

Bass Hole Boardwalk

BEACH—SIGHT | FAMILY | Taking in one of Yarmouth Port's most beautiful areas, Bass Hole Boardwalk extends over a swampy creek, crosses salt marshes, and winds around vegetated wetlands and upland woods. Gray's Beach is a little crescent of sand with still water that's good for kids inside the roped-in swimming area. At the end of the boardwalk, benches provide a place to relax and look out over abundant marsh life and, across the creek, the beautiful, sandy shores of Dennis's Chapin Beach. At low tide you can walk out on the flats for almost a mile. ⊠ Center St., near Gray's Beach parking lot, Yarmouth Port.

Edward Gorey House

LOCAL INTEREST | Explore the eccentric doodlings and offbeat humor of the late acclaimed artist and illustrator. Regularly changing exhibitions, arranged in the downstairs rooms of Gorey's former home, include drawings of his oddball characters and reveal the mysterious psyche of the sometimes dark but always playful illustrator. ⊠ 8 Strawberry La., Yarmouth Port ☎ 508/362–3909 ⊕ www.edwardgoreyhouse.org 🎟 $8 ⊗ Closed Jan.–mid-Apr.

 ## Restaurants

★ Inaho

$$$ | JAPANESE | Yuji Watanabe, chef-owner of the Cape's best Japanese restaurant, makes early-morning journeys to Boston's fish markets to shop for the freshest local catch, and the resulting selection of sushi and sashimi is vast and artful. The serene and simple Japanese garden out back has a traditional koi pond. **Known for:** chef's tasting menu; moody lighting; seafood tempura. ⑤ Average main: $31 ⊠ 157 Main St., Yarmouth Port ☎ 508/362–5522 ⊗ Closed Sun. No lunch.

The Optimist Café

$ | BRITISH | From the outside, this bold Gothic Victorian looks like something out of a Brothers Grimm tale, with its steeply pitched roof, fanciful turrets, frilly gingerbread trim, and deep rose-and-green paint job. There is a great selection for breakfast (served all day) and lunch, featuring traditional English fare like smoked fish dishes, curries, scones, and crumpets. **Known for:** hearty ploughman's lunch; proper afternoon tea; eclectic surroundings. ⑤ Average main: $11 ⊠ 134 Rte. 6A, Yarmouth Port ☎ 508/362–1024 ⊕ www.optimistcafe.com ⊗ No dinner.

 ## Hotels

Bayside Resort

$$ | HOTEL | FAMILY | A bit more upscale than most properties along Route 28, the Bayside overlooks pristine salt marshes and Lewis Bay, and although it's not right on the water, there's a small beach and a large outdoor pool with a café (there's also an indoor pool). **Pros:** ideal for families with children; close to attractions of busy Route 28; views of the water. **Cons:** no beach swimming; not for those seeking intimate surroundings; public areas can be noisy. ⑤ Rooms from: $259 ⊠ 225 Rte. 28, West Yarmouth ☎ 508/775–5669, 800/243–1114 ⊕ www.baysideresort.com ⇴ 128 rooms ⧉ Free breakfast.

★ **Capt. Farris House**

$$ | B&B/INN | A short hop off congested Route 28 sits this imposing 1845 Greek Revival home. **Pros:** beautiful grounds; ideal location for exploring Mid Cape area; close to area restaurants and attractions. **Cons:** no elevator; not close to the beach; not for those with small children. ⑤ *Rooms from: $210* ✉ *308 Old Main St., Bass River Village* ☎ *508/760–2818* ⊕ *www.captainfarris.com* ⌐ *9 rooms* ⑩ *Free breakfast.*

★ **The Inn at Cape Cod**

$$ | B&B/INN | A stately Greek Revival building with imposing columns, the inn has one of the most dramatic facades of any house on the Cape; it sits near the Botanical Trails and has its own fine gardens, patios, and tree-shaded lawns. **Pros:** elegant lodging; close to attractions; serene surroundings. **Cons:** no water views or direct beach access; some steep stairs; not for small children. ⑤ *Rooms from: $299* ✉ *4 Summer St., Yarmouth Port* ☎ *508/375–0590, 800/850–7301* ⊕ *www.innatcapecod.com* ⌐ *9 rooms* ⑩ *Free breakfast.*

★ **Liberty Hill Inn**

$ | B&B/INN | Smartly and traditionally furnished common areas—including the high-ceiling parlor, the formal dining room, and the wraparound porch—are a major draw to this dignified 1825 Greek Revival house. **Pros:** tasteful surroundings; beautiful grounds; extravagant homemade breakfast. **Cons:** some steep stairs; some bathrooms have only small shower stalls; not a waterfront location. ⑤ *Rooms from: $195* ✉ *77 Rte. 6A, Yarmouth Port* ☎ *508/362–3976* ⊕ *www. libertyhillinn.com* ⊗ *Closed Feb.–mid-Mar.* ⌐ *9 rooms* ⑩ *Free breakfast.*

Nightlife

Oliver's & Planck's Tavern

BARS/PUBS | Fish tanks illuminate this friendly bar, which hosts live music on most summer nights. There's also a midweek trivia night. ✉ *6 Bray Farm Rd., off*

Rte. 6A, Yarmouth Port ☎ *508/362–6062* ⊕ *www.oliverscapecod.com.*

Performing Arts

Cultural Center of Cape Cod

ART GALLERIES—ARTS | This lively center plays host to a full schedule of art openings and exhibits, workshops, readings, various performances, and great live music. ✉ *307 Old Main St., South Yarmouth* ☎ *508/394–7100* ⊕ *www.cultural-center.org.*

🛍 Shopping

If you're heading along Route 6A, expect to see a multitude of art galleries, craft and antiques stores, specialty shops, and boutiques that adhere to the modest and subdued aesthetics demanded by the Historic Commission. Over on Route 28, though, there are no building codes or rules on good taste; there you'll find larger stores that can advertise their wares with flashy signage, selling souvenirs, T-shirts, and other fun vacation goodies.

Just Picked

GIFTS/SOUVENIRS | In the buildings that made up the very first Christmas Tree Shop franchise, this Cape Cod-focused shop features local artisans and crafters who fill its shelves with a stunning variety of home, garden, food, and gift items. ✉ *13 Willow St., Yarmouth Port* ☎ *508/362–0207* ⊕ *justpickedgifts.com.*

🏃 Activities

BASEBALL

Yarmouth-Dennis Red Sox

BASEBALL/SOFTBALL | FAMILY | The Yarmouth-Dennis Red Sox of the collegiate Cape Cod Baseball League play home games at Dennis-Yarmouth High School's Red Wilson Field, mid-June–mid-August. Baseball clinics for girls and boys age five and up run throughout the season. ✉ *Dennis-Yarmouth High School, 210 Station Ave., South Yarmouth* ☎ *508/394–9387* ⊕ *www.ydredsox.org.*

Dennis

Dennis Village is 4 miles east of Yarmouth Port; West Dennis is 1 mile east of South Yarmouth.

The back streets of Dennis Village still retain the Colonial charm of their seafaring days. The town, which was incorporated in 1793, was named for the Reverend Josiah Dennis. There were 379 sea captains living here when fishing, salt making, and shipbuilding were the main industries, and the elegant houses they constructed—now museums and B&Bs—still line the streets.

GETTING HERE AND AROUND

Route 6A is also known as Main Street as it passes through Dennis Village. If you're driving between West Dennis and Harwich, Lower County Road is a more scenic alternative to overdeveloped Route 28: it gives you occasional glimpses of the sea between the cottages and beachfront hotels.

VISITOR INFORMATION

CONTACTS Dennis Chamber of Commerce
☎ *508/398–3568, 508/398–3568*
⊕ *www.dennischamber.com.*

 Sights

★ Cape Cod Museum of Art

ARTS VENUE | This multiple-gallery museum on the grounds of the Cape Playhouse has a permanent collection of more than 850 works by important Cape-associated artists such as Hans Hoffman, William Paxton, and Charles Hawthorne; Hawthorne was the founder of America's first artists' colony in 1899 in Provincetown. Rich in cultural programming, changing exhibits, special events, workshops, and classes are held throughout the year. ⊠ *60 Hope La.* ☎ *508/385–4477* ⊕ *www.ccmoa.org* ☜ *$9.*

Scargo Tower

BUILDING | On a clear day, you'll have unbeatable views of Scargo Lake, Dennis Village's scattered houses below, Cape Cod Bay, and distant Provincetown from the top of this tower. A wooden tower built on this site in 1874 was one of the Cape's first tourist attractions; visitors would pay 5¢ to climb to the top for the views. That tower burned down, and the present all-stone 30-foot tower was built in 1901 to replace it. Winding stairs bring you to the top; don't forget to read the unsightly but amusing graffiti on the way up. Expect crowds at sunrise and sunset. ⊠ *Scargo Hill Rd., off Rte. 6A or Old Bass River Rd.* ☜ *Free.*

 Beaches

Parking at all Dennis beaches is $25 per day in season ($30 on weekends and holidays) for nonresidents.

Corporation Beach

BEACH—SIGHT | FAMILY | Once a privately owned packet landing, this is a beautiful crescent of white sand backed by low dunes on Cape Cod Bay. Between the upper parking lot and the beach, the DPM Surfside Grill, operated by the same owners of local staple Dennis Public Market, serves great sandwiches, grill favorites, fried seafood, and other seafood classics as well as drinks, snacks, and ice cream allowing your beach day to last a little longer. **Amenities:** food and drink; lifeguards; parking (fee); showers; toilets. **Best for:** sunset; swimming; walking. ⊠ *Corporation Rd.* ☜ *Parking $25 weekdays, $30 weekends/holidays.*

West Dennis Beach

BEACH—SIGHT | FAMILY | This is one of the best beaches on the south shore (Nantucket Sound), with the crowds to prove it. A breakwater was started here in 1837 in an effort to protect the mouth of Bass River, but that was abandoned when a sandbar formed on the shore side. It's a long, wide, and popular sandy beach, stretching for 1½ miles, with marshland and the Bass River across from it. **Amenities:** food and drink; lifeguards; parking (fee); toilets. **Best**

for: swimming; walking; windsurfing. ⊠ *Lighthouse Rd., off Lower County Rd., West Dennis* ⌂ *Parking $25 weekdays, $30 weekends/holidays.*

Restaurants

Captain Frosty's

$ | SEAFOOD | FAMILY | A great stop after the beach, this modest joint has a regular menu of seafood classics like fried clams and fish 'n' chips supplemented by specials posted on the board and a counter where you order and take a number written on a French-fries box. There's seating inside as well as outside on a shady brick patio. **Known for:** classic fried seafood platters; soft-serve ice cream and frappes; chaotic parking lot during high season. $ *Average main: $15* ⊠ *219 Rte. 6A* ☎ *508/385–8548* ⊕ *www.captainfrosty.com* ☉ *Closed early Sept.–mid-Apr.*

FIN Cape Cod

$$$ | SEAFOOD | As the name suggests, seafood is the star here, from salmon to red snapper, halibut to tuna, and all very recently caught in Atlantic waters. Two floors of seating in an antique home make for an eclectic setting aglow with candlelight in the company of many satisfied diners. **Known for:** oyster chowder with smoked bacon; attentive and knowledgeable service; extensive wine list. $ *Average main: $28* ⊠ *800 Main St., off Rt. 6A* ☎ *508/385–2096* ⊕ *fincapecod.com* ☉ *Closed Sun. and Mon.*

The Oyster Company

$$$ | SEAFOOD | Supplies pour in from the restaurant's own oyster farm in the bay, though oysters (and clams) from other towns are well represented and can be had a variety of ways—raw on the half shell is the best way to enjoy these superfresh bivalves. It's a fun place all around, with great food and a boisterous atmosphere. **Known for:** $1.25 oysters til 6:30; the "Red Sox" martini (among other fanciful martinis); locally sourced food. $ *Average main:*

$26 ⊠ *202 Depot St., Dennis Port* ☎ *508/398–4600* ⊕ *www.theoystercompany.com.*

Hotels

★ Isaiah Hall B&B Inn

$ | B&B/INN | Lilacs and pink roses trail the white-picket fence outside this 1857 Greek Revival farmhouse on a quiet residential road near the bay, where innkeepers Jerry and Judy Neal set the scene for a romantic getaway with guest rooms that have country antiques, floral-print wallpapers, fluffy quilts, and Priscilla curtains. **Pros:** beautiful grounds; near beaches and attractions. **Cons:** not for those with children under seven; some very steep steps; some rooms are on the small side. $ *Rooms from: $175* ⊠ *152 Whig St.* ☎ *508/385–9928* ⊕ *www.isaiahhallinn.com* ⇨ *12 rooms* ❍ *Free breakfast.*

Nightlife

Harvest Gallery Wine Bar

WINE BARS—NIGHTLIFE | Near the Cape Playhouse, this friendly place has an extensive wine list, a good variety of hors d'oeuvres and other nibbles, eclectic artwork, and live music. ⊠ *776 Main St.* ☎ *508/385–2444* ⊕ *www.harvestgallerywinebar.com.*

Performing Arts

★ Cape Playhouse

THEATER | FAMILY | For Broadway-style dramas, comedies, and musicals, attend a production at the Cape Playhouse, the country's oldest professional summer theater. In 1927 Raymond Moore, who had been working with a theatrical troupe in Provincetown, bought an 1838 Unitarian meetinghouse and converted it into a theater. The opening performance was *The Guardsman,* starring Basil Rathbone. Other stars who performed here in the early days—some in their professional stage debuts—include Bette Davis (who first worked here as an usher), Gregory Peck, Lana Turner, Ginger Rogers, Humphrey Bogart, Tallulah Bankhead, and Henry Fonda, who appeared with his then-unknown 20-year-old daughter, Jane. Behind-the-scenes tours are available. The playhouse offers children's theater on Friday mornings in July and August. The 20-acre property includes a restaurant, the Cape Cod Museum of Art, and the Cape Cinema. ⊠ *820 Rte. 6A* ☏ *508/385–3911, 877/385–3911* ⊕ *www. capeplayhouse.com.*

 ## Activities

BICYCLING
You can pick up the Cape's premier bike path, the more than 25-mile **Cape Cod Rail Trail** (⊕ *www.mass.gov/dcr*), at several points; continuing expansion has now extended to South Yarmouth, with plans to reach further west to Barnstable. Though it is possible, riding the entire trail in a single day doesn't do justice to its sights and side trips. Many cyclists, especially those with small kids, prefer the piecemeal method because they can relax and enjoy the sights—and not turn their legs to jelly in the process.

There is ample parking at the lot off Route 134 south of U.S. 6, near Theophilus Smith Road in South Dennis, and it ends at the post office in South Wellfleet. Access points in Brewster are Long Pond Road, Underpass Road, and Nickerson State Park. There's also a spur off the trail that goes to Chatham.

A guidebook published by the Dennis Chamber of Commerce includes bike tours and maps. You can rent bikes from a number of places along the Cape Cod Rail Trail.

Brewster

7 miles northeast of Dennis, 20 miles east of Sandwich.

Brewster's location on Cape Cod Bay makes it a perfect place to learn about the region's ecology. The Cape Cod Museum of Natural History is here, and the area is rich in conservation lands, state parks, forests, freshwater ponds, and brackish marshes. When the tide is low in Cape Cod Bay, you can stroll the beaches and explore tidal pools up to 2 miles from the shore on the Brewster flats.

GETTING HERE AND AROUND
Brewster—6 miles north of Chatham and 5 miles west of Orleans—is spread along Route 6A. Take it slow through the town limits, not just in honor of the speed limit, but to appreciate the abundant display of grand old homes, fanciful rose arbors, antiques shops, and countless historic details that make this one of the region's prettiest towns.

VISITOR INFORMATION
CONTACTS Brewster Chamber of Commerce ☏ *508/896–3500* ⊕ *www.brewster-capecod.org.*

 ## Sights

Brewster Store
LOCAL INTEREST | Built in 1852 as a church, this local landmark has been a typical New England general store since 1866, with such essentials as daily newspapers, penny candy, groceries, and benches out front for conversation. It specializes in oil lamps and antique lanterns of all types. Out back, the Brewster Scoop serves ice cream mid-June–early September. Upstairs, memorabilia from antique toys to World War II bond posters is displayed. Downstairs there's a working antique nickelodeon; locals warm themselves by the old coal stove in colder months. ⊠ *1935 Rte. 6A* ☏ *508/896–3744* ⊕ *www. brewsterstore.com.*

Learn more about the Cape's marshlands, forests, and ponds at the Cape Cod Museum of Natural History in neighboring Brewster.

★ Cape Cod Museum of Natural History

MUSEUM | FAMILY | A short drive west from the heart of Brewster, this spacious museum and its pristine grounds include a shop, a natural-history library, and exhibits such as a working beehive and a pond- and sea-life room with live specimens. Walking trails wind through 80 acres of forest, marshland, and ponds, all rich in birds and other wildlife. The exhibit hall upstairs has a wall display of aerial photographs documenting the process by which the famous Chatham sandbar was split in two. In summer there are guided field walks, nature programs, and art classes for preschoolers through ninth graders. ⊠ *869 Rte. 6A, West Brewster* ☎ *508/896–3867* ⊕ *www.ccmnh.org* ⌦ *$15.*

Nickerson State Park

FOREST | FAMILY | These 1,961 acres were once part of a vast estate belonging to Roland C. Nickerson, son of Samuel Nickerson, a Chatham native who founded the First National Bank of Chicago. Roland and his wife, Addie, lavishly entertained such visitors as President Grover Cleveland at their private beach and hunting lodge in English country-house style, with coachmen dressed in tails and top hats and a bugler announcing carriages entering the front gates. In 1934 Addie donated the land for the state park in memory of Roland and their son, who died during the 1918 flu epidemic.

The park consists of acres of oak, pitch-pine, hemlock, and spruce forest speckled with seven freshwater kettle ponds formed by glaciers. Some ponds are stocked with trout for fishing. You can swim, canoe, sail, and kayak in the ponds, and bicycle along 8 miles of paved trails that have access to the Cape Cod Rail Trail. Bird-watchers seek out the thrushes, wrens, warblers, woodpeckers, finches, larks, cormorants, great blue herons, hawks, owls, and ospreys. Red foxes and white-tailed deer are occasionally spotted in the woods. The over 400 campsites are extremely popular: reservations are necessary. ⊠ *3488 Rte. 6A, East Brewster* ☎ *508/896–3491* ⊕ *www.mass.*

gov/eea/agencies/dcr *$8 parking (MA resident), $15 (nonresident) Memorial Day–Oct.*

🍴 Restaurants

Brewster Fish House

$$$ | **SEAFOOD** | There is nothing ordinary about the menu here: seafood selections range from just off the boat scallops to tuna, local oysters, and octopus. It can be noisy and it's always crowded in summer, but it's worth the wait. **Known for:** artful seafood presentations; sophisticated atmosphere; locally sourced ingredients. $ *Average main: $30* ✉ *2208 Rte. 6A* ☎ *508/896–7867* ⊕ *www.brewsterfishhouse.com.*

★ Chillingsworth

$$$$ | **FRENCH** | One of the crown jewels of Cape restaurants, Chillingsworth combines formal presentation with an excellent French menu. The seven-course prix fixe includes an appetizer, soup, salad, sorbet, entrée, "amusements," and dessert, plus coffee or tea, while the less expensive à la carte options for lunch, dinner, and Sunday brunch are served in the more casual, patio-style Chill's Bistro. **Known for:** one of the best restaurants on the Cape; prix-fixe menu; located at the historic 300-year-old estate. $ *Average main: $70* ✉ *2449 Rte. 6A, East Brewster* ☎ *508/896–3640* ⊕ *www.chillingsworth. com* ☽ *No dinner Sun. and Mon. Closed Thanksgiving–mid-May.*

JT's Seafood

$$ | **SEAFOOD** | **FAMILY** | Fresh and ample portions of fried seafood take center stage at this casual joint, which is very popular with families. Place your order at the counter and sit inside or out; be sure to save room for ice cream. **Known for:** fried clams; hot lobster rolls; clam chowder. $ *Average main: $19* ✉ *2689 Rte. 6A* ☎ *508/896–3355* ⊕ *www.jt-seafood.com* ☽ *Closed mid-Oct.–mid-Apr.*

🏨 Hotels

★ Captain Freeman Inn

$$ | **B&B/INN** | Named for the sea captain who had the home built in 1866, this gracious inn retains its aged elegance with original ornate plaster ceiling medallions, marble fireplaces, and sturdy yet graceful construction. **Pros:** authentic historic lodging with modern amenities; it's a short walk to Breakwater Beach on the bay, even shorter to the ice-cream shop next to the Brewster General Store; extravagant breakfast and afternoon tea. **Cons:** not for those with children; not a waterfront location; most rooms upstairs. $ *Rooms from: $259* ✉ *15 Breakwater Rd.* ☎ *508/896–7481* ⊕ *www.captainfreemaninn.com* ⇄ *10 rooms* ❘⊙❘ *Free breakfast.*

★ Old Sea Pines Inn

$ | **B&B/INN** | **FAMILY** | With its white-column portico and wraparound veranda overlooking a broad lawn, Old Sea Pines, which housed a "charm and personality" school in the early 1900s, resembles a vintage summer estate. **Pros:** welcomes families; beautiful grounds; reasonable rates. **Cons:** no TV in main building; steep stairway to upper floors; not for those looking for upscale design; family suites have shared baths. $ *Rooms from: $170* ✉ *2553 Rte. 6A* ☎ *508/896–6114* ⊕ *www.oldseapinesinn. com* ☽ *Limited room availability Nov.–Apr.* ⇄ *24 rooms* ❘⊙❘ *Free breakfast.*

🎭 Performing Arts

MUSIC

Brewster Town-band Concerts

CONCERTS | **FAMILY** | Sunday evenings by the bay are filled with the sounds of the town-band concerts, held in the gazebo on the grounds of Drummer Boy Park. Bring your beach chairs, blankets, and a picnic for a lovely evening outing. The park is about ½ mile west of the Cape Cod Museum of Natural History, on the western side of Brewster. ✉ *Drummer Boy Park, Rte. 6A, West Brewster* *Free.*

THEATER
Cape Cod Repertory Theatre Co.
THEATER | FAMILY | Several impressive productions, from original works to the classics, are staged every year in this indoor Arts and Crafts–style theater set way back in the woods. There are mesmerizing outdoor shows for kids offered on weekday mornings during the summer, as well as hour-long puppet shows. ⊠ *3299 Rte. 6A, west of Nickerson State Park, East Brewster* ☎ *508/896–1888* ⊕ *www.caperep.org* ☉ *Closed Dec.–Apr.*

 Activities

BASEBALL
Brewster Whitecaps
BASEBALL/SOFTBALL | FAMILY | The Brewster Whitecaps of the collegiate Cape Cod Baseball League play home games mid-June–mid-August. Kids 6–13 can sign up for fun clinics led by the players. ⊠ *Stony Brook Elementary School, 384 Underpass Rd.* ☎ *508/896–8500* ⊕ *www.brewsterwhitecaps.com.*

🛍 Shopping

With Brewster's abundant historic and natural appeal, it's no surprise that shoppers will benefit from the bounty of antiques shops, art galleries, and specialty shops here.

★ Brewster Book Store
BOOKS/STATIONERY | FAMILY | A special place, Brewster Book Store is filled to the rafters with all manner of books by local and international authors, with an extensive fiction selection and kids' section. Author signings and children's story times take place year-round. ⊠ *2648 Rte. 6A, East Brewster* ☎ *508/896–6543, 800/823–6543* ⊕ *www.brewsterbookstore.com.*

Harwich

6 miles south of Brewster, 5 miles east of Dennis.

The Cape's famous cranberry industry took off in Harwich in 1844, when Alvin Cahoon was its principal grower. Today you'll still find working cranberry bogs throughout Harwich. Three naturally sheltered harbors on Nantucket Sound make the town, like its English namesake, popular with boaters. You'll find dozens of elegant sailboats and elaborate yachts in Harwich's harbors, plus plenty of charter fishing boats. Every August the town pays celebratory homage to its large boating population with a grand regatta, Sails Around the Cape.

GETTING HERE AND AROUND
The center of Harwich, 6 miles south of Brewster, is easily accessed off Exit 10 of U.S. 6. It sits right at the crossroads of several roads that branch off to various towns. Route 39, which becomes Main Street in town, leads to Orleans; Bank Street, next to the Brooks Free Library, is the most direct route to Harwich Port.

VISITOR INFORMATION
CONTACTS Harwich Chamber of Commerce ⊠ *Harwich Port* ☎ *508/432–1600, 800/442–7942* ⊕ *www.harwichcc.com.*

 Restaurants

★ Buca's Tuscan Roadhouse
$$$ | ITALIAN | This romantic roadhouse near the Chatham border, adorned with tiny white lights, wine bottles, and warm-hue walls, might just transport you to Italy—and if it doesn't, the fantastic food certainly will. There are always excellent specials added to the menu; in the fall and winter, look for value-priced entrées. **Known for:** authentic Italian food; atmosphere; crowds: make reservations. ⑤ *Average main: $34* ⊠ *4 Depot Rd.* ☎ *508/432–6900* ⊕ *www.bucasroadhouse.com* ☉ *No lunch.*

★ **Cape Sea Grille**

$$$ | AMERICAN | This chef-owned gem with distant sea views uses what's locally available as the inspiration for an ever-changing and creative menu that's complemented by a vibrant, welcoming atmosphere. There are also generous wine, martini, and drink lists. **Known for:** inviting atmosphere; inventive seafood entrées; three-course sunset dinner specials before 6 pm. $ *Average main: $34* ⊠ *31 Sea St., Harwich Port* ☎ *508/432-4745* ⊕ *www.capeseagrille. com* ⊗ *Closed Tues.*

Hotels

★ **Wequassett Inn Resort and Golf Club**

$$$$ | RESORT | FAMILY | On 22 acres of shaded landscape partially surrounded by Pleasant Bay, 20 Cape-style cottages and an attractive hotel make up this traditionally elegant resort by the sea. **Pros:** attentive service; activities and programs for all ages; babysitting services and full children's program. **Cons:** rates are very steep; not an in-town location; isolated area. $ *Rooms from: $595* ⊠ *2173 Orleans Rd. (Rte. 28)* ☎ *508/432-5400, 800/225-7125* ⊕ *www.wequassett.com* ⊗ *Closed Nov.–Mar.* ↝ *122 rooms* ⍩ *No meals.*

Winstead Village Inn

$$$$ | B&B/INN | With its graceful columns and welcoming front veranda, the regal Winstead Inn sits along a quiet street; many of the rooms have a view of the heated, outdoor saltwater pool, a real oasis with potted palms, fountains, and flowers. **Pros:** spacious, elegant rooms; pretty pool area; beach access. **Cons:** numerous stairs; not for those on a budget; not a waterfront location. $ *Rooms from: $410* ⊠ *114 Parallel St.* ☎ *508/432-4444, 800/870-4405* ⊕ *www. winsteadinn.com* ⊗ *Closed Nov.–Easter* ↝ *15 rooms* ⍩ *Free breakfast.*

Activities

BASEBALL

Harwich Mariners

BASEBALL/SOFTBALL | FAMILY | The Harwich Mariners of the collegiate Cape Cod Baseball League play home games at Whitehouse Field on Oak Street mid-June–mid-August. The team leads a youth clinic for boys and girls. ⊠ *Whitehouse Field, 75 Oak St.* ☎ *508/432-2000* ⊕ *www.harwichmariners.org.*

Shopping

Harwich Port has a busy little Main Street area lined with shops and restaurants, though the majority of Harwich is somewhat rural with little in the way of a dense shopping area. In East Harwich, on the way to Orleans, is a large commercial center with a large grocery store, drug stores, and a few other options.

Cape Cod Lavender Farm

LOCAL SPECIALTIES | Cape Cod Lavender Farm consists of some 14,000 lavender plants, making it one of the largest such farms on the East Coast. Harvest (best for visits) is usually around mid-June–July, when you'll see acres and acres of stunning purple waves. The farm sells soaps and bath salts, candles, potpourri, marmalade, lemonade, and many other lavender-infused goods. Keep your eyes peeled for its sign (on the right) as you're driving south on Route 124—it's easy to miss. ⊠ *Corner of Rte. 124 and Weston Woods Rd., off U.S. 6, Exit 10* ☎ *508/432-8397* ⊕ *www.capecodlavenderfarm.com.*

Chatham

5 miles east of Harwich.

At the bent elbow of the Cape, with water nearly surrounding it, Chatham has all the charm of a quietly posh seaside resort, with plenty of shops but none of the crass commercialism that plagues some other towns on the Cape. The town has gray-shingle houses—many improbably large and grandiose—with tidy awnings and cheerful flower gardens, an attractive Main Street with crafts and antiques stores alongside dapper cafés, and a five-and-dime. Although it can get crowded in high season—and even on weekends during shoulder seasons—Chatham remains a true New England village.

VISITOR INFORMATION
CONTACTS Chatham Chamber of Commerce ☎ *508/945–5199, 800/715–5567* ⊕ *www.chathaminfo.com.*

Sights

Atwood House Museum
HOUSE | Built by sea captain Joseph C. Atwood in 1752, this museum has a gambrel roof, hand-hewn floor planks, an old kitchen with a wide hearth and a beehive oven, and some antique dolls and toys. The New Gallery displays portraits of local sea captains. The Joseph C. Lincoln Room has the manuscripts, first editions, and mementos of the Chatham writer, and antique tools are displayed in a room in the basement. There's also a local commercial fishing gallery. The 1974 Durand Wing has collections of seashells from around the world, as well as threaded Sandwich glass, Parian-ware figures, unglazed porcelain vases, figurines, and busts. In a remodeled freight shed are the stunning and provocative murals (1932–45) by Alice Stallknecht Wight portraying religious scenes in Chatham settings. On the grounds are an herb garden, the old turret and lens from the Chatham Light, and a simple camp house rescued from eroding North Beach. ⊠ *347 Stage Harbor Rd., West Chatham* ☎ *508/945–2493* ⊕ *www.chathamhistoricalsociety.org* ☑ *$10* ⊗ *Closed Nov.–May (special events scheduled in off-season).*

Chatham Light
LIGHTHOUSE | The view from this lighthouse—of the harbor, the sandbars, and the ocean beyond—justifies the crowds. The lighthouse is especially dramatic on a foggy night, as the beacon's light pierces the mist. Coin-operated telescopes allow a close look at the famous "Chatham Break," the result of a fierce 1987 nor'easter that blasted a channel through a barrier beach just off the coast. The U.S. Coast Guard auxiliary, which supervises the lighthouse, offers free tours May–October on most Wednesdays; otherwise, the interior is off-limits. There is free parking in front of the lighthouse—the 30-minute limit is strictly monitored. ⊠ *Main St., near Bridge St., West Chatham* ☎ *508/945–3830* ⊕ *www.uscg.mil/d1/staChatham* ☑ *Free.*

Fish Pier
LOCAL INTEREST | **FAMILY** | Smells and sights are abundant here; keep an eye out for the many lingering seals who are hoping for a free meal. The unloading of the boats is a big local event, drawing crowds who watch it all from an observation deck. From their fishing grounds 3–100 miles offshore, fishermen bring in haddock, cod, flounder, lobster, halibut, and pollack, which are packed in ice and shipped to New York and Boston or sold at the fish market here. Also here is *The Provider,* a monument to the town's fishing industry, showing a hand pulling a fish-filled net from the sea. ⊠ *54 Barcliff Rd. Ext., North Chatham* ⊕ *www.chatham-ma.gov/chatham-fish-pier* ☑ *Free.*

★ Monomoy National Wildlife Refuge
BEACH—SIGHT | This 2,500-acre preserve includes the Monomoy Islands, a fragile 9-mile-long barrier-beach area south of Chatham. A haven for bird-watchers,

the refuge is an important stop along the North Atlantic Flyway for migratory waterfowl and shorebirds—peak migration times are May and late July. It also provides nesting and resting grounds for 285 species, including gulls—great black-backed, herring, and laughing—and several tern species. White-tailed deer wander the islands, and harbor and gray seals frequent the shores in winter. The only structure on the islands is the **South Monomoy Lighthouse,** built in 1849. The visitor center offers maps and some guided walks in the summer. ⊠ *Wikis Way, Morris Island* ☎ *508/945–0594* ⊕ *www. fws.gov/refuge/Monomoy* ⊠ *Free.*

 Beaches

Harding's Beach

BEACH—SIGHT | FAMILY | West of Chatham center, on the calmer and warmer waters of Nantucket Sound, Harding's Beach is very popular with families. It can get crowded, so plan to arrive earlier or later in the day. **Amenities:** food and drink; lifeguards; parking (fee); showers; toilets. **Best for:** swimming; walking; windsurfing. ⊠ *Harding's Beach Rd., off Barn Hill Rd., West Chatham* ⊠ *Parking $20.*

 Restaurants

Del Mar Bar and Bistro

$$$ | ECLECTIC | Fanciful cocktails, an intriguing menu, live music, and daily blackboard specials make this a popular Chatham spot. There's also a changing tapas menu for quick bites at the bar. **Known for:** wood-fired meals; live jazz; intriguing specials. ⓢ *Average main: $26* ⊠ *907 Rte. 28* ☎ *508/945–9988* ⊕ *www. delmarbistro.com* ⊗ *No lunch.*

Impudent Oyster

$$$ | SEAFOOD | This cozy, festive tavern is a great place for a romantic meal or dinner with the kids, and the menu offers light burgers and sandwiches, as well as more-substantial fare. It's always packed, and there's not a ton of seating,

so reserve on weekends. **Known for:** spicy local mussels with chorizo; local favorite dining spot; oysters Rockefeller. ⓢ *Average main: $31* ⊠ *15 Chatham Bars Ave.* ☎ *508/945–3545* ⊕ *www. theimpudentoyster.com.*

 Hotels

★ Chatham Gables Inn

$$$ | B&B/INN | The embodiment of understated elegance, this 1839 former sea captain's home shines in the simple beauty of 19th-century craftsmanship in gleaming wide-plank floors, and graceful molding and wainscoting. **Pros:** exquisite historic lodging; 10-minute walk to town and beach; exceptional service. **Cons:** not a waterfront location; not for those traveling with small children; not an in-town location. ⓢ *Rooms from: $325* ⊠ *364 Old Harbor Rd.* ☎ *508/945–5859* ⊕ *www.chathamgablesinn.com* ⌁ *8 rooms* ⦿ *Free breakfast.*

The Hawthorne

$$ | HOTEL | Beyond the Hawthorne's modest roadside appearance extends a private beach overlooking Pleasant Bay, the Atlantic, and Chatham Harbor. **Pros:** fresh-brewed coffee and complimentary morning newspapers in the lobby; easy access to nearby attractions and activities; pretty reasonable for the area; there's a fire pit on the beach with plenty of wood on hand. **Cons:** rooms are pretty standard motel fare though clean and comfortable; 10- to 15-minute walk to town center; some dated decor. ⓢ *Rooms from: $275* ⊠ *196 Shore Rd.* ☎ *508/945–0372* ⊕ *www.thehawthorne. com* ⊗ *Closed late Oct.–mid-May* ⌁ *26 rooms, 1 cottage* ⦿ *No meals.*

 Nightlife

Chatham Squire

BARS/PUBS | Boasting four bars (including a raw bar), this is a rollicking year-round local hangout, drawing a young crowd to the bar side and a mixed crowd of locals to the restaurant. There's live entertainment on weekends. ⊠ *487 Main St.* ☎ *508/945–0945* ⊕ *www.thesquire.com.*

Activities

BASEBALL

Chatham Anglers

BASEBALL/SOFTBALL | FAMILY | Chatham Anglers baseball games are great free entertainment by the collegiate-level players in the Cape Cod Baseball League. Clinics for aspiring 6- to 17-year-olds are led by the team. ⊠ *Veterans' Field, Main and Depot Sts., near rotary* ☎ *508/996–5004* ⊕ *www.chathamanglers.com.*

📋 Shopping

Chatham Jam and Jelly Shop

FOOD/CANDY | This shop sells delicious concoctions like rose-petal jelly, apple-lavender chutney, and wild beach plum jelly, as well as all the old standbys. All preserves are made on-site in small batches, and about 75 of the 120-plus varieties are available for sampling (which is encouraged). ⊠ *16 Seaquanset Rd., at Rte. 28, West Chatham* ☎ *508/945–3052* ⊕ *www.chathamjamandjellyshop.com.*

★ Yankee Ingenuity

GIFTS/SOUVENIRS | Here you'll find a varied selection of unique jewelry and lamps and a wide assortment of unusual, beautiful trinkets at reasonable prices (especially for Chatham). ⊠ *525 Main St.* ☎ *508/945–1288* ⊕ *www.yankee-ingenuity.com.*

Orleans

8 miles north of Chatham, 35 miles east of Sagamore Bridge.

Orleans has a long heritage in fishing and seafaring, and many beautifully preserved homes from the Colonial era can still be seen in the small village of East Orleans, home of the town's Historical Society and Museum. In other areas of town, such as down by Rock Harbor, more modestly grand homes stand near the water's edge.

GETTING HERE AND AROUND

Downtown Orleans, 8 miles north of Chatham, is a kind of extended triangle made by Route 28, Route 6A, and Main Street. Main Street crosses Route 28 as it makes its way east toward the lovely enclave of East Orleans and Nauset Beach. Heading west, Main Street blends into Rock Harbor Road, which makes its journey all the way to Cape Cod Bay. A bus connecting Hyannis and Orleans serves the Lower Cape region. Year-round transport on the Flex service goes from Harwich to Provincetown, serving the towns of Brewster, Orleans, Eastham, Wellfleet, and Truro along the way.

VISITOR INFORMATION

CONTACTS Orleans Chamber of Commerce ☎ *508/255–1386, 508/255–1386* ⊕ *orleanscapecod.org.*

Sights

Rock Harbor

BEACH—SIGHT | FAMILY | This harbor was the site of a War of 1812 skirmish in which the Orleans militia kept a British warship from docking. In the 19th century Orleans had an active saltworks, and a flourishing packet service between Rock Harbor and Boston developed. Today it's the base of charter-fishing and party boats in season, as well as of a small commercial fishing fleet. Sunsets over the harbor are spectacular, and it's a great place to watch the boats float past. Parking is free. ⊠ *Rock Harbor Rd.*

🏖 Beaches

There is a daily parking fee for both beaches mid-June–Labor Day. Keep your parking ticket: it can be used at any Orleans beach for that calendar date, including the two freshwater ponds in town. The increased presence of great white sharks in the area (they dine on the massive seal population) seems to be both a tourist boon and a concern. It's not unusual to hear the blare of lifeguard whistles followed by orders to exit the water until the coast is clear. Best tip: don't swim with the seals.

Nauset Beach

BEACH—SIGHT | FAMILY | This town-managed beach—not to be confused with Nauset Light Beach on the National Seashore—is a 10-mile sweep of sandy ocean beach with low dunes and large waves good for bodysurfing or board surfing. Despite its size, the massive parking lot often fills up on sunny days; arrive quite early or in the late afternoon if you want to claim a spot. The beach gets extremely crowded in summer; unless you walk a ways, expect to feel very close to your neighbors on the sand. **Amenities:** food and drink; lifeguards; parking (fee); showers; toilets. **Best for:** sunrise; surfing; swimming; walking. ⊠ *Beach Rd., Nauset Heights* ☎ *508/240–3780* ⊠ *Parking $20 mid-June–Labor Day.*

Skaket Beach

BEACH—SIGHT | FAMILY | On Cape Cod Bay, Skaket Beach is a sandy stretch with calm, warm water good for children. When the tide is out, you can walk seemingly endlessly on the sandy flats. The parking lot fills up fast on hot July and August days; try to arrive before 11 or after 2. The many tide pools make this a favorite spot for families. Sunsets here draw a good crowd. **Amenities:** food and drink; lifeguards; parking (fee); showers; toilets. **Best for:** sunset; swimming; walking. ⊠ *Skaket Beach Rd.* ☎ *508/240–3775* ⊠ *Parking $20 mid-June–Labor Day.*

Restaurants

Land Ho!

$$ | AMERICAN | Tried-and-true tavern fare is the rule at Orleans's flagship local restaurant. The scene is usually fun and boisterous; dozens of homemade wooden signs heralding local businesses hang from the rafters above the red-checker tablecloths. **Known for:** daily blackboard specials; thriving local bar scene; sea clam pie. $ *Average main: $21* ⊠ *38 Cove Rd.* ☎ *508/255–5165* ⊕ *www.land-ho.com.*

Mahoney's Atlantic Bar and Grill

$$$ | ECLECTIC | This always-hopping downtown spot serves commendable dinner fare and draws big crowds for cocktails and appetizers. The bar is long and comfortable, and is a good spot to dine if there are no tables available. **Known for:** seafood bouillabaisse; specialty cocktails; lively local hangout. $ *Average main: $27* ⊠ *28 Main St.* ☎ *508/255–5505* ⊕ *www.mahoneysatlantic.com* ☽ *No lunch.*

Hotels

★ A Little Inn on Pleasant Bay

$$$ | B&B/INN | This gorgeously decorated inn occupies a 1798 building on a bluff beside a cranberry bog, and many of the rooms look clear out to the bay for which it's named (others face the lush gardens)—there's even a small private beach with its own dock. **Pros:** great water views; abundant buffet breakfast; spacious baths. **Cons:** not an in-town location; not for those traveling with small children. $ *Rooms from: $355* ⊠ *654 S. Orleans Rd., South Orleans* ☎ *508/255–0780, 888/332–3351* ⊕ *www.alittleinnonpleasantbay.com* ☽ *Closed Oct.–mid-May* ⏎ *9 rooms* ⏐◯⏐ *Free breakfast.*

Ship's Knees Inn

$$ | B&B/INN | Giving a generous nod to its name and its 19th-century heritage, this inn is full of nautical and historic touches: seaside artwork and furnishings, steeply pitched roof lines, wide-plank floors, antiques, and a good deal of painted furniture. **Pros:** short walk to beach; beautifully maintained property; pool. **Cons:** two rooms share a bath; some steep stairs; not for those traveling with small children. $ *Rooms from: $220* ⊠ *186 Beach Rd.* ☎ *508/255–1312* ⊕ *www.shipskneesinn.com* ⏎ *17 rooms, 1 apartment* ⏐◯⏐ *Free breakfast.*

Activities

BASEBALL

Orleans Firebirds

BASEBALL/SOFTBALL | FAMILY | The Orleans Firebirds of the collegiate Cape Cod Baseball League play home games at Eldredge Park mid-June–mid-August. Kids can sign up for daily clinics with the players. ⊠ *Eldredge Park, Rte. 28 at Eldredge Pkwy.* ☎ *508/255–0793* ⊕ *www.orleansfirebirds.com* ▣ *Free.*

BOATING AND FISHING

Many of Orleans's freshwater ponds offer good fishing for perch, pickerel, trout, and more. Anglers will need a license for both fresh and saltwater fishing. Pleasant Bay is ideal and popular for boating as well as kayaking.

Arey's Pond Boat Yard

BOATING | There's a sailing school here offering individual and group lessons. The company also rents sailboats, kayaks, row boats, and standup paddleboards. ⊠ *45 Arey's La., off Rte. 28, South Orleans* ☎ *508/255–0994* ⊕ *www. areyspondboatyard.com.*

Goose Hummock Shop

FISHING | Fishing licenses and gear are available at the Goose Hummock Shop, which also rents powerboats, canoes, paddleboards, and kayaks. Lessons and tours are available. ⊠ *15 Rte. 6A* ☎ *508/255–0455* ⊕ *www.goose.com.*

Eastham

3 miles north of Orleans, 6 miles south of Wellfleet.

Often overlooked on the speedy drive up toward Provincetown on Route 6, Eastham is a town full of hidden treasures. Unlike other towns on the Cape, it has no official town center or Main Street; the highway bisects it, and the town touches both Cape Cod Bay and the Atlantic. Amid the gas stations, convenience stores, restaurants, and large motel complexes, Eastham's wealth of natural beauty takes a little exploring to find.

GETTING HERE AND AROUND

Eastham's main drag is busy Route 6, which gives visitors no feel for the town's natural beauty. It's hard to get lost in Eastham, which is about 3 miles north of Orleans. You're never more than a few miles from the road ending at a beach. Take the time to meander about and see what's off the highway on both the bay and ocean sides.

VISITOR INFORMATION

CONTACTS Eastham Chamber of Commerce ☎ *508/240–7211* ⊕ *www.easthamchamber.com.*

 Sights

★ **Cape Cod National Seashore**

INFO CENTER | FAMILY | The region's most expansive national treasure, Cape Cod National Seashore was established in 1961 by President John F. Kennedy, for whom Cape Cod was home and haven. The 27,000-acre park, extending from Chatham to Provincetown, protects 30 miles of superb beaches; great rolling dunes; swamps, marshes, and wetlands; and pitch-pine and scrub-oak forest. Self-guided nature trails, as well as biking and horse trails, lace through these landscapes. Hiking trails lead to a red-maple swamp, Nauset Marsh, and to Salt Pond; the Buttonbush Trail is a nature path for people with vision impairments. A hike or bike ride to Coast Guard Beach leads to a turnout looking out over marsh and sea. A section of the cliff here was washed away in 1990, revealing the remains of a prehistoric dwelling. The National Seashore has two visitor centers, one in Eastham and one in Provincetown.

Salt Pond Visitor Center, at the southern end of the Cape, offers guided walks, boat tours, demonstrations, and lectures mid-April–Thanksgiving, as well as evening beach walks, campfire talks, and other programs (many are free) in summer. The center includes a museum with displays on whaling and the old saltworks, as well as early Cape Cod artifacts including scrimshaw, the journal that Mrs. Penniman kept while on a whaling voyage with her husband, and some of the Pennimans' possessions, such as their tea service and the captain's top hat. An air-conditioned auditorium shows films on geology, sea rescues, whaling, Henry David Thoreau, and Guglielmo Marconi. ⊠ *Salt Pond Visitor Center, 50 Doane Rd.* ☎ *508/255–3421 for Salt Pond Visitor Center* ⊕ *www.nps.gov/caco* ⌦ *Free.*

★ Fort Hill Area

NATURE PRESERVE | The road to the Cape Cod National Seashore's Ft. Hill area ends at a parking area with a lovely view of old farmland traced with stone fences that rolls gently down to Nauset Marsh. The marsh winds around brilliant green grasses and makes its way to the ocean beyond; it is one of the more dramatic views on the Cape. Appreciated by bird-watchers and nature photographers, trails pass through wetlands and to Skiff Hill, an overlook with benches and informative plaques that quote Samuel de Champlain's account of the area from when he moored off Nauset Marsh in 1605. Also on Skiff Hill is Indian Rock, a large boulder moved to the hill from the marsh below. Once used by the local Nauset tribe as a sharpening stone, the rock is cut with deep grooves and smoothed in circles where ax heads were whetted. Trails are open from dawn to dusk. ⊠ *Fort Hill Rd., off U.S. 6* ⊕ *www.nps.gov/caco/index.htm* ⌦ *Free.*

Nauset Light

LOCAL INTEREST | Moved 350 feet back from its perch at cliff's edge in 1996, this much-photographed red-and-white lighthouse tops the bluff where the Three Sisters Lighthouses once stood. (The Sisters themselves can be seen in a little landlocked park surrounded by trees; they're reached by paved walkways off Nauset Light Beach's parking lot.) How

the lighthouses got there is a long story. In 1838 three brick lighthouses were built 150 feet apart on the bluffs in Eastham overlooking a particularly dangerous area of shoals (shifting underwater sandbars). In 1892, after the eroding cliff dropped the towers into the ocean, they were replaced with three wooden towers. In 1918, two were moved away, as was the third in 1923. Eventually the National Park Service acquired the Three Sisters and brought them together in the inland park, where they would be safe. Lectures on and guided tours of the lighthouses (free, donations accepted) are conducted Sunday early May–October, as well as Tuesday and Wednesday in July and August. ⊠ *Ocean View Dr. and Cable Rd.* ☎ *508/240–2612* ⊕ *www. nausetlight.org* ⌦ *Free.*

⛱ Beaches

Coast Guard Beach

BEACH—SIGHT | FAMILY | Coast Guard Beach, part of the National Seashore, is a long beach backed by low grass and heathland. A handsome former Coast Guard station is also here, though it's not open to the public. The beach has a very small parking lot that fills up early, so park at the Salt Pond Visitor Center or at the lot up Doane Road from the center and take the free shuttle to the beach. At high tide the size of the beach shrinks considerably, so watch your blanket. ■TIP→ **Daily parking is $20; the annual seashore pass grants access to all six national park beaches and costs the same as three days of parking. Amenities:** lifeguards; parking (fee); showers; toilets. **Best for:** sunrise; surfing; swimming; walking. ⊠ *Off Ocean View Dr.* ⊕ *www.nps.gov/ caco/index.htm* ⌦ *Parking $20.*

First Encounter Beach

BEACH—SIGHT | FAMILY | A great spot for watching sunsets over Cape Cod Bay, First Encounter Beach is rich in history. Near the parking lot, a bronze marker commemorates the first encounter

196

between local Native Americans and passengers from the *Mayflower,* led by Captain Myles Standish, who explored the entire area for five weeks in 1620 before moving on to Plymouth. The beach is popular with families who favor its warmer, calmer waters and tide pools. **Amenities:** parking (fee); showers; toilets. **Best for:** sunset; swimming; walking; windsurfing. ⊠ *End of Samoset Rd., off Rte. 6* 🚗 *Parking $20.*

★ **Nauset Light Beach**
BEACH—SIGHT | Adjacent to Coast Guard Beach, this long, sandy beach is backed by tall dunes, frilly grasses, and heathland. The trail to the Three Sisters lighthouses takes you through a pitch-pine forest. Parking here fills up very quickly in summer; plan to arrive early or you may have to go elsewhere. ■**TIP**→ **Daily parking is $20; the annual seashore pass grants access to all six national park beaches and costs the same as three days of parking.** **Amenities:** lifeguards; parking (fee); showers; toilets. **Best for:** sunrise; surfing; swimming; walking. ⊠ *Off Ocean View Dr.* ⊕ *www.nps.gov/caco/index.htm* 🚗 *Parking $20.*

 Restaurants

Arnold's Lobster & Clam Bar
$$ | **SEAFOOD** | **FAMILY** | You can't miss this hot spot on the side of Route 6: look for the riot of colorful flowers lining the road and the patient folks waiting in long lines for fried seafood and other fixings. Unusual for a clam shack like this is the full bar, offering beer, wine, mixed drinks, and the house specialty: margaritas. **Known for:** lobster rolls and fried clams; ice cream from Richardson's Dairy Farm; pirate-themed minigolf. ⑤ *Average main: $21* ⊠ *3580 Rte. 6* 🕾 *508/255–2575* ⊕ *www.arnoldsrestaurant.com* ▤ *No credit cards* ⊗ *Closed mid-Oct.–Apr.*

Fairway Restaurant and Pizzeria
$$ | **ITALIAN** | **FAMILY** | The friendly, family-run Fairway specializes in Italian comfort food but also has a very popular

breakfast. Attached to the Hole in One Donut Shop—a favorite among locals for early-morning coffee and exceptional doughnuts and muffins—the Fairway puts a jar of crayons on every paper-covered table and sells its own brand of root beer. **Known for:** hearty pizza; homemade dessert; eggplant Parmesan. ⑤ *Average main: $18* ⊠ *4295 Rte. 6, North Eastham* 🕾 *508/255–3893* ⊕ *www.fairwaycapecod.com* ⊗ *No lunch.*

 Hotels

★ **Fort Hill Bed and Breakfast**
$$ | **B&B/INN** | This enchanting, adults-only B&B is in an 1864 Greek Revival farmhouse nestled in the tranquil Ft. Hill area—the only lodging within the National Seashore—which is minutes off busy U.S. 6, but steps away from quiet, secluded trails that wind through cedar forests, fields crisscrossed by old stone fences, and a red-maple swamp. **Pros:** pastoral setting; close to nature trails; private and elegant lodging. **Cons:** not for those traveling with children; need to make reservations far in advance; only three rooms. ⑤ *Rooms from: $290* ⊠ *75 Fort Hill Rd.* 🕾 *508/240–2870* ⊕ *www.forthillbedandbreakfast.com* ⊗ *Closed mid-Oct.–May* 🛏 *2 suites, 1 cottage* ⦿l *Free breakfast.*

★ **Whalewalk Inn & Spa**
$$ | **B&B/INN** | Set amid 3 landscaped acres, this 1830 whaling master's home has wide-plank pine floors, fireplaces, and 19th-century country antiques that provide historical appeal. **Pros:** beautiful grounds; elegantly appointed rooms; decadent spa treatments. **Cons:** not for those traveling with small children; no water views; not an in-town location. ⑤ *Rooms from: $230* ⊠ *220 Bridge Rd.* 🕾 *508/255–0617, 800/440–1281* ⊕ *www.whalewalkinn.com* ⊗ *Closed Dec.–Mar.* 🛏 *16 rooms* ⦿l *Free breakfast.*

Wellfleet and South Wellfleet

6 miles north of Eastham, 13 miles southeast of Provincetown.

★ Still famous for its world-renowned and succulent namesake oysters, Wellfleet is today a tranquil community; many artists and writers call it home. Less than 2 miles wide, it's one of the most attractively developed Cape resort towns, with a number of fine restaurants, historic houses, and art galleries, and a good old Main Street in the village proper.

GETTING HERE AND AROUND

Like many Cape Cod towns, Wellfleet is spread out on either side of U.S. 6. Wellfleet Village is on the bay side, about 3 miles north of the entrance to Marconi Beach. Main Street makes its way past several businesses. A left turn will take you toward the harbor along Commercial Street, which is full of shops and galleries. The center of Wellfleet is quite compact, so it's best to leave your car in one of the public parking areas and take off on foot.

For a scenic loop through a classic Cape landscape near Wellfleet's Atlantic beaches—with scrub and pines on the left, heathland meeting cliffs and ocean below on the right—take LeCount Hollow Road just north of the Marconi Station turnoff. All the beaches on this strip rest at the bottom of a tall grass-covered dune, which lends dramatic character to this outermost shore. Winter storms continue to drastically alter the dunescape; don't be surprised to find a precipitous descent to area beaches.

Some beaches are restricted in the busy summer season to locals and long-term renters; the Beach Sticker Office issues permits so you can visit (you need a proof-of-stay form).

VISITOR INFORMATION

Sights

Marconi Station

HISTORIC SITE | On the Atlantic side of the Cape is the site of the first transatlantic wireless station erected on the U.S. mainland. It was from here on January 18, 1903, that Italian radio and wireless-telegraphy pioneer Guglielmo Marconi sent the first American wireless message to Europe: "most cordial greetings and good wishes" from President Theodore Roosevelt to King Edward VII of England. There's a lookout deck that offers a vantage point of both the Atlantic and Cape Cod Bay. Off the parking lot, a 1½-mile trail and boardwalk lead through the Atlantic White Cedar Swamp, one of the most beautiful trails on the seashore; free maps and guides are available at the trailhead. Marconi Beach, south of the Marconi Station on Marconi Beach Road, is one of the National Seashore's lovely ocean beaches. ✉ *Marconi Site Rd., South Wellfleet* ☎ *508/349–3785* ⊕ *www. nps.gov/caco* ⌧ *Free.*

★ Massachusetts Audubon Wellfleet Bay Wildlife Sanctuary

NATURE PRESERVE | **FAMILY** | Encompassing nearly 1,000 acres, this reserve is home to more than 250 species of birds. The jewel of the Massachusetts Audubon Society, the sanctuary is a superb place for walking, birding, and watching the sun set over the salt marsh and bay. The **Esther Underwood Johnson Nature Center** contains two 700-gallon aquariums that offer an up-close look at marine life common to the region's tidal flats and marshlands. From the center you can hike five short nature trails, including a fascinating boardwalk trail that leads over a salt marsh to a small beach, or you can wander through the butterfly garden. ⊠ *291 U.S. 6, South Wellfleet* ☎ *508/349–2615* ⊕ *www.massaudubon. org/wellfleetbay* 🖼 *$8.*

Beaches

Extensive storm-induced erosion has made the cliffs to most of Wellfleet's ocean beaches quite steep, so be prepared for a taxing trek up and down the dune slope. Only the Cape Cod National Seashore beach at Marconi has steps; some have handrails to aid in the descent.

Though this does not apply to the beaches listed in this section, access to several Wellfleet beaches requires resident or temporary resident parking stickers (this includes saltwater and freshwater ponds) in season only, from the last week of June through Labor Day. For the rest of the year anyone can visit these beaches for free. ■ **TIP→ Note that people arriving on foot or by bicycle, or after 5 pm, can visit the beaches at any time; the sticker is for parking only.**

Cahoon Hollow Beach

BEACH—SIGHT | The restaurant and music club on top of the dune are the main attractions at Cahoon Hollow Beach, which tends to draw younger and slightly rowdier crowds. It's a big Sunday-afternoon party place. The Beachcomber restaurant has paid parking, which is reimbursed when you buy something to eat or drink. Erosion has made getting to the beach a steep climb. **Amenities:** food and drink; lifeguards; parking (fee); toilets. **Best for:** partiers; surfing; swimming; walking. ⊠ *Ocean View Dr., Greater Wellfleet* 🖼 *Parking $20.*

★ Marconi Beach

BEACH—SIGHT | Marconi Beach, part of the Cape Cod National Seashore, is accessed via a very long and steep series of stairs lead down to the beach. It's also popular with both surfers and surf casters looking for striped bass or bluefish. Erosion from fierce storms has compromised beach access. ■ **TIP→ Daily parking is $20; the annual seashore pass grants access to all six national park beaches and costs the same as three days of parking.** **Amenities:** lifeguards; parking (fee); showers; toilets. **Best for:** sunrise; surfing; swimming; walking. ⊠ *Marconi Beach Rd., off U.S. 6, South Wellfleet* ⊕ *www.nps.gov/caco* 🖼 *Parking $20.*

White Crest Beach

BEACH—SIGHT | White Crest Beach is a prime surfer hangout where the dudes often spend more time waiting for waves than actually riding them. If you're up to the challenge, join one of the spontaneous volleyball games. The other challenge will be working your way down (and then up) to the water: Mother Nature and her fury have made this a steep trek. **Amenities:** lifeguards; parking (fee); toilets. **Best for:** sunrise; surfing; swimming; walking. ⊠ *Ocean View Dr., Greater Wellfleet* 🖼 *Parking $30.*

Restaurants

Mac's Seafood

$$ | **SEAFOOD** | **FAMILY** | Right at Wellfleet Harbor, this ambitious little spot serves some of the freshest seafood around. You can always sit along the pier and soak up the great water views while you chow down on a vast variety of local fish dishes, plus globe-trotting fare like sushi, grilled-scallop burritos, and linguiça sausage sandwiches. **Known for:** excellent sushi; lobster mashed potatoes; local oysters. ⑤ *Average main: $22* ⊠ *Wellfleet Town Pier, 265 Commercial St., Wellfleet Harbor* ☎ *508/349–9611* ⊕ *www.macsseafood.com* ⊙ *Closed mid-Sept.–late May.*

Moby Dick's

$$ | **SEAFOOD** | **FAMILY** | A meal at this good-natured, rough-hewn fish shack with a hypernautical theme is an absolute Cape Cod tradition for some people. Bring your own libations, and if you need to kill time (the lines are sometimes daunting), stop inside Moby's Cargo, the bustling gift shop next door. **Known for:** the Nantucket Bucket—a pound of whole-belly Monomoy steamers, a pound of native mussels, and corn on the cob served in a bucket; lobster bisque; friendly international staff. ⑤ *Average main: $20* ⊠ *3225 Rte. 6, Greater Wellfleet* ☎ *508/349–9795* ⊕ *www.mobydicksrestaurant.com* ⊗ *Closed mid-Oct.–Apr.*

PB Boulangerie Bistro

$$$ | **FRENCH** | Once a clam shack, this bistro has found new life and caused a serious sensation in this seaside town selling just-baked breads and succulent pastries—by early morning (even in off-season) the line snakes down the ramp and into the parking lot. There's outdoor and indoor seating for breakfast and dinner; the latter attracts a multitude of eager patrons in search of the finer flavors of this French kitchen. **Known for:** succulent French pastries; fresh bread; authentic French experience. ⑤ *Average main: $35* ⊠ *15 LeCount Hollow Rd., South Wellfleet* ☎ *508/349–1600* ⊕ *www. pbboulangeriebistro.com* ⊗ *Closed Mon. and Tues. and Jan. No lunch.*

★ Wicked Oyster

$$$ | **AMERICAN** | For some of the most innovative fare in Wellfleet, secure a table in this 18th-century clapboard house, known for taking the local catch to flavorful new heights. Breakfast is a favorite here; there's also an outstanding wine list. **Known for:** oyster stew; duck spring rolls; local favorite for breakfast and dinner. ⑤ *Average main: $27* ⊠ *50 Main St., Downtown Wellfleet* ☎ *508/349–3455* ⊕ *www.thewickedo.com* ⊗ *No lunch July and Aug. No dinner Tues. and Wed.*

Winslow's Tavern

$$ | **SEAFOOD** | This 1805 Federal-style captain's house contains five dining rooms; try for a table on the patio overlooking the center of town. The kitchen specializes in bistro-inspired seafood, mostly with American and Mediterranean preparations. **Known for:** daily oyster happy hour; ideal perch on Main Street; lobster tacos.

⑤ *Average main: $24* ⊠ *316 Main St., Downtown Wellfleet* ☎ *508/349–6450* ⊕ *www.winslowstavern.com* ⊗ *Closed Mon. and mid-Oct.–mid-May.*

 ## Hotels

Even'tide

$ | **HOTEL** | **FAMILY** | Long a summer favorite, this peaceful motel is set back from the main road, surrounded by 5 acres of trees and lawns, which include a 60-foot indoor pool. **Pros:** short drive or bike ride to Wellfleet's beaches; suites are a bargain for families; direct access to Cape Cod Rail Trail. **Cons:** need a car to get downtown; motel-style rooms. ⑤ *Rooms from: $169* ⊠ *650 Rte. 6, South Wellfleet* ☎ *508/349–3410, 800/368–0007* ⊕ *www.eventidemotel.com* ⊗ *Closed mid-Oct.–Apr.* ⤵ *31 units, 10 cottages* ❖| *No meals* ⌖ *1- or 2-wk minimum for cottages in summer.*

Holden Inn

$ | **B&B/INN** | If you're watching your budget, try this no-frills place on a tree-shaded street just outside the town center but within walking distance of several galleries and restaurants—the main house's screened front porch with rockers is a good place to relax after a day of exploring. **Pros:** rock-bottom prices; excellent in-town location; good for solo travelers. **Cons:** old-fashioned feel; many units share a bath; no credit cards. ⑤ *Rooms from: $130* ⊠ *140 Commercial St., Downtown Wellfleet* ☎ *508/349–3450* ⊕ *www.theholdeninn.com* ⊟ *No credit cards* ⊗ *Closed Nov.–Apr.* ⤵ *24 rooms* ❖| *No meals.*

Performing Arts

FILM

★ Wellfleet Drive-In Theater

FILM | **FAMILY** | A classic Cape experience is the Wellfleet Drive-In Theater, located near the Eastham town line. Regulars spend the night in style: chairs, blankets, and picnic baskets. Films start at dusk nightly May–September, and there's also a standard indoor cinema with four screens, a miniature-golf course, and a bar and grill. It's also the home of the beloved Wellfleet Flea Market, held weekends late spring–mid-October. ⊠ *51 U.S. 6, South Wellfleet* ☎ *508/349-7176* ⊕ *www.wellfleetcinemas.com.*

THEATER
Wellfleet Harbor Actors Theater
THEATER | The well-regarded Wellfleet Harbor Actors Theater continues its tradition, since 1985, of producing provocative, often edgy, world premieres of American plays, satires, farces, and black comedies in its mid-May–late-September season. In July and August there are productions aimed for kids, held under a white tent. From October to April, opera lovers can watch performances from the Met, live in HD. ⊠ *2357 U.S. 6, Greater Wellfleet* ☎ *508/349-9428* ⊕ *www.what.org.*

Activities

BOATING
Jack's Boat Rental
BOATING | Jack's rents canoes, kayaks, pedal boats, sailboats, surfboards, boogie boards, and sailboards. Delivery is available for three-plus-day rentals for a fee. ⊠ *2616 Rte. 6, at Cahoon Hollow Rd., Greater Wellfleet* ☎ *508/349-9808, 508/349-7553* ⊕ *www.jacksboatrental.com.*

Shopping

Downtown Wellfleet is best approached on foot; along the way you'll find many art galleries and clothing boutiques. You'll pay a handsome premium for fresh fruits, vegetables, and flowers behind the Town Hall at Hatch's—but what a beautiful display. There's also the Wellfleet Marketplace for groceries, books, beer, and wine. In the height of summer, the price is worth not having to drive 15 miles to Orleans. The

Wednesday-morning Wellfleet Farmers' Market, held behind the Congregational Church (200 Main Street), is a fine place to fill your basket with local food. The Wellfleet Flea Market draws people from all over the Cape who drive the distance to find bargains.

FLEA MARKET
Wellfleet Flea Market
OUTDOOR/FLEA/GREEN MARKETS | The giant Wellfleet Flea Market sets up shop in the parking lot of the Wellfleet Drive-In Theater mid-April–June, September, and October, weekends and holiday Mondays 8–4; July and August, Wednesday, Thursday, weekends, and holiday Mondays 8–4. You'll find antiques, cosmetics, kitchen supplies, socks, old advertising posters, books, plants, trinkets, and plenty more among the many vendors. A snack bar and playground keep fatigue at bay. ⊠ *51 Rte. 6, South Wellfleet* ☎ *508/349-0541* ⊕ *www.wellfleetcinemas.com/flea-market.*

Truro

13 miles north of Eastham, 9½ miles southeast of Provincetown.

Today Truro is a town of high dunes, estuaries, and rivers fringed by grasses, rolling moors, and houses sheltered in tiny valleys. It's a popular retreat for artists, writers, politicos, and numerous vacationing psychoanalysts. Edward Hopper summered here from 1930 to 1967, finding the Cape light ideal for his austere brand of realism. One of the largest towns on the Cape in terms of land area—almost 43 square miles—it's also the smallest in population, with about 1,400 year-round residents. Truro is also the Cape's narrowest town, and from a high perch you can see the Atlantic Ocean on one side and Cape Cod Bay on the other.

If you thought neighboring Wellfleet's downtown area was small, wait till you

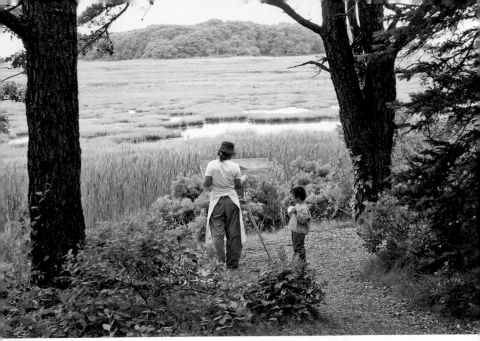

Artists and birders flock to the Wellfleet Bay Wildlife Sanctuary, protected by the Massachusetts Audubon Society.

see (or don't see) Truro's. It consists of a post office, a town hall, and a shop or two—you'll know it by the sign that says "Downtown Truro" at a little plaza entrance. Truro also has a library, a firehouse, and a police station, but that's about all. The North Truro section contains most of the town's accommodations, either along U.S. 6 or fronting the bay along Route 6A, just south of the Provincetown border. Many people who live or vacation in Truro choose it for its easygoing, quiet personality and lack of development—and its proximity to the excitement and commerce of Provincetown.

Settled in 1697, Truro has had several names during its long history. It was originally called Pamet after the local Native Americans, but in 1705 the name was changed to Dangerfield in response to all the sailing mishaps off its shores. "Truroe" was the final choice, named for a Cornish town that homesick settlers thought it resembled; the final "e" was eventually dropped. The town relied on the sea for its income: whaling, shipbuilding, and cod fishing were the main industries.

GETTING HERE AND AROUND

Truro sits near the end of Cape Cod, just 2 miles north of Wellfleet. U.S. 6 is the way most people reach Truro, though the real beauty of the town lies farther afield on back roads that lead to either Cape Cod Bay or the Atlantic. The Cape is fairly narrow here, so you will never find yourself hopelessly lost.

The Provincetown/North Truro Shuttle, run by the Cape Cod Regional Transit Authority, provides a much-needed transportation boost. Traveling along Route 6A, it stops wherever a passenger requests; it runs every 30 minutes and can carry bicycles.

Sights

Highland House Museum

BUILDING | Home to the Truro Historical Society, the 1907 Highland House was once a grand summer hotel in its time, boasting of many private rooms, meals, and even one shared indoor bathroom. Now a museum, each season a new exhibition heralds Truro's rich history;

upstairs you can see how early settlers lived and the unique industries they created to survive. There is also a room dedicated to Edward and Jo Hopper and their art and lives in Truro. Throughout the summer, talks, live music events, and children's programs are offered. ✉ *6 Highland Light Rd., North Truro* 🕾 *508/487–3397* ⊕ *www.trurohistorical-society.org* ✆ *$7* ⊙ *Closed Oct.–May.*

Highland Light

LIGHTHOUSE | Truly a breathtaking sight, this is the Cape's oldest lighthouse. The first light on this site, powered by 24 whale-oil lamps, began warning ships of Truro's treacherous sandbars in 1797— the dreaded Peaked Hills Bars, to the north, had claimed hundreds of ships. The current light, a 66-foot tower built in 1857, is powered by two 1,000-watt bulbs reflected by a huge Fresnel lens; its beacon is visible for more than 20 miles.

One of four active lighthouses on the Outer Cape, Highland Light has the distinction of being listed in the National Register of Historic Places. Henry David Thoreau used it as a stopover in his travels across the Cape's backside (as the Atlantic side is called). Twenty-five-minute tours of the lighthouse are given daily in summer; especially grand are the special full-moon tours. ✉ *27 Highland Light Rd., North Truro* 🕾 *508/487–3397* ⊕ *www. capecodlight.org* ✆ *From $4* ⊙ *Closed mid-Oct.–mid-May.*

★ Truro Vineyards of Cape Cod

WINERY/DISTILLERY | Owned and operated by the Roberts family, this vineyard has greatly stepped up production, and has begun experimenting with some new varieties. The vineyard makes several notable blends, both red and white. It also makes a red table wine that's flavored with cranberries and known for its unusual bottle, shaped like a lighthouse. Free tours are given daily at 1 and 3, Memorial Day–Columbus Day; tastings are available throughout the day. There is also an aged rum and gin

distillery on the property, South Hollow Spirits, which produces organic spirits; tours and tastings available. There are many excellent wine and food events scheduled throughout the summer. It's a great place to picnic, and there's a resident food truck on-site. ✉ *Rte. 6A, North Truro* 🕾 *508/487–6200* ⊕ *www. trurovineyardsofcapecod.com* ✆ *Free.*

 Performing Arts

Payomet Performing Arts Center of Truro

ARTS CENTERS | **FAMILY** | From mid-June through late September, the Payomet Performing Arts Center of Truro presents a wide range of concerts, plays, films, music, and classes inside a big tent at Cape Cod National Seashore. Past performers have included the Cape Cod Opera, Patty Larkin, and the Shakespeare on the Cape troupe. There's also a kids' summer stage, featuring children's entertainment. ✉ *29 Old Dewline Rd., North Truro* 🕾 *508/487–5400* ⊕ *www.payomet.org.*

Provincetown

9 miles northwest of Wellfleet, 62 miles from Sagamore Bridge.

Many people know that the Pilgrims stopped here at the curved tip of Cape Cod before proceeding to Plymouth. Historical records suggest that an earlier visitor, Thorvald, brother of Viking Leif Erikson, came ashore here in AD 1004 to repair the keel of his boat and consequently named the area Kjalarness, or Cape of the Keel. In 1602, Bartholomew Gosnold came to Provincetown and named the area Cape Cod after the abundant codfish he found in the local waters.

Incorporated as a town in 1727, Provincetown was for many decades a bustling seaport, with fishing and whaling as its major industries. In the late 19th century, groups of Portuguese fishermen and whalers began to settle here, lending their expertise and culture to an already cosmopolitan town. Fishing is still an important source of income for many Provincetown locals, but today the town ranks among the world's leading whale-watching—rather than whale-hunting—outposts.

Artists began to arrive in the late 1890s to take advantage of the unusual Cape Cod light; in fact, Provincetown is the nation's oldest continuous art colony. By 1916, with five art schools flourishing here, painters' easels were nearly as common as shells on the beach. This bohemian community, along with the availability of inexpensive summer lodgings, attracted young rebels, as well as writers like John Reed (*Ten Days That Shook the World*) and Mary Heaton Vorse (*Footnote to Folly*), who in 1915 began the Cape's first significant theater group, the Provincetown Players. The young, then unknown Eugene O'Neill joined them in 1916, when his *Bound East for Cardiff* premiered in a tiny wharf-side East End fish house.

America's original gay resort, Provincetown today is as appealing to artists as it is to gay and lesbian—as well as straight—tourists. The awareness brought by the AIDS crisis and, more recently, Massachusetts's legalization of same-sex marriage, has turned the town into the most visibly gay vacation community in America.

GETTING HERE AND AROUND

You're at the end of the line here, which means driving to Provincetown in the height of summer often means slogging through slow traffic. Congestion is heaviest around Wellfleet and it can be slow going. Driving the 3 miles of Provincetown's main downtown thoroughfare, Commercial Street, in season could take forever. No matter, there are plenty of pretty vistas on the way along U.S. 6 and Route 6A. Parking is not one of Provincetown's better amenities (there are two large, paid central parking lots if you can

find a space), so bike and foot are the best and most popular ways to explore the downtown area. But Provincetown can also be reached by air (year-round via Cape Air from Boston) or ferry (multiple options from Boston in season).

The Provincetown/North Truro Shuttle, run by the Cape Cod Regional Transit Authority, provides a much-needed seasonal transportation boost in season (mid-June–mid-September). Once in Provincetown, the shuttle heads up Bradford Street, with alternating trips to Herring Cove Beach, Race Point Beach, Pilgrim Park, and the Provincetown Airport. Bikes are accommodated.

BUS CONTACTS Cape Cod Regional Transit Authority ☎ 800/352–7155 ⊕ *www.capecodtransit.org.*

VISITOR INFORMATION

CONTACTS Provincetown Business Guild ✉ *Downtown Center* ☎ *508/487–2313, 800/637–8696* ⊕ *www.ptown.org.* **Provincetown Chamber of Commerce** ✉ *Downtown Center* ☎ *508/487–3424* ⊕ *www.ptownchamber.com.*

Sights

★ Commercial Street

LOCAL INTEREST | Take a casual stroll by the many architectural styles—Greek Revival, Victorian, Second Empire, and Gothic, to name a few—used in the design of the impressive houses for wealthy sea captains and merchants. The Provincetown Historical Society's walking-tour pamphlet is available for $1 at many shops. The center of town is where you'll find the crowds and the best people-watching, especially if you try to find an empty spot on the benches in front of the exquisitely renovated Town Hall. The East End has a number of nationally renowned galleries; the West End has a number of small inns with neat lawns and elaborate gardens. There is one-way vehicle traffic on this street, though pedestrians dominate the pavement, particularly in July and August.

Commercial Street runs parallel to the water, so there is always a patch of sand close at hand, should you need a break. ⊠ *Provincetown.*

Pilgrim Monument

BUILDING | The first thing you'll see in Provincetown is this grandiose edifice, somewhat out of proportion to the rest of the low-rise town. The monument commemorates the Pilgrims' first landing in the New World and their signing of the Mayflower Compact (the first Colonial American rules of self-governance) before they set off to explore the mainland. Climb the 116 steps and 60 short ramps of the 252-foot-high tower for a panoramic view—dunes on one side, harbor on the other, and the entire bay side of Cape Cod beyond. At the tower's base is a museum of Lower Cape and Provincetown history, with exhibits on whaling, shipwrecks, and scrimshaw. ⊠ *1 High Pole Hill Rd., Downtown Center* ☎ *508/487–1310* ⊕ *www.pilgrim-monument.org* ⊠ *$12.*

★ Province Lands Visitor Center

NATIONAL/STATE PARK | Part of the Cape Cod National Seashore, the Province Lands stretch from High Head in Truro to the tip of Provincetown and are scattered with ponds, cranberry bogs, and scrub. More than 7 miles of bike and walking trails lace through forests of stunted pines, beech, and oak and across desertlike expanses of rolling dunes. At the visitor center you'll find short films on local geology and exhibits on the life of the dunes and the shore. You can also pick up information on guided walks, birding trips, lectures, and other programs, as well as on the Province Lands' pristine beaches, Race Point and Herring Cove, and walking, biking, and horse trails. Don't miss the awe-inspiring panoramic view of the dunes and the surrounding ocean from the observation deck. This terrain provides optimal conditions for the deer tick, which can cause Lyme disease, so use extra caution. ⊠ *Race Point Rd.,*

east of U.S. 6, Greater Provincetown ☎ *508/487–1256* ⊕ *www.nps.gov/caco* ⊠ *Free.*

★ Provincetown Art Association and Museum

LOCAL INTEREST | Founded in 1914 to collect and exhibit the works of artists with Provincetown connections, this facility has a 1,650-piece permanent collection, displayed in changing exhibitions that mix up-and-comers with established 20th-century figures like Milton Avery, Philip Evergood, William Gropper, Charles Hawthorne, Robert Motherwell, Claes Oldenburg, Man Ray, John Singer Sargent, Andy Warhol, and Agnes Weinrich. A stunning contemporary wing has greatly expanded the exhibit space. The museum store carries books of local interest, including works by or about area artists and authors, as well as posters, crafts, cards, and gift items. Art classes (single day and longer) offer the opportunity to study under such talents as Hilda Neily, Selina Trieff, and Doug Ritter. ⊠ *460 Commercial St., East End* ☎ *508/487–1750* ⊕ *www.paam.org* ⊠ *$10* ⊙ *Closed Mon.–Wed. Oct.–May.*

Beaches

Herring Cove Beach

BEACH—SIGHT | **FAMILY** | Herring Cove Beach is relatively calm and warm for a National Seashore beach, but it's not as pretty as some because its parking lot isn't hidden behind dunes. It's close to town, so in warm weather it's always crowded. The lot to the right of the bathhouse is a great place to watch the sunset. ■**TIP➜ Daily parking is $20; the annual seashore pass grants access to all six national park beaches and costs the same as three days of parking. Amenities:** food and drink; lifeguards; parking (fee); toilets; showers. **Best for:** sunset; swimming; walking. ⊠ *Provincetown* ⊕ *www.nps.gov/caco* ⊠ *Parking $20.*

★ Race Point Beach

BEACH—SIGHT | **FAMILY** | Race Point Beach, one of the Cape Cod National Seashore beaches in Provincetown, has a wide swath of sand stretching far off into the distance around the point and Coast Guard station. Because of its position facing north, the beach gets sun all day long. Keep an eye out for whales offshore; it's also a popular fishing spot. ■ TIP→ **Daily parking is $20; the annual seashore pass grants access to all six national park beaches and costs the same as three days of parking. Amenities:** lifeguards; parking (fee); showers; toilets. **Best for:** sunrise; sunset; surfing; swimming; walking. ⊠ *Race Point Rd., east of U.S. 6* ☎ *508/487–1256* ⊕ *www.nps.gov/caco/index.htm* 🅿 *Parking $20.*

🍴 Restaurants

★ The Canteen

$ | **AMERICAN** | Bustling from breakfast until 11 pm, this casual spot specializes in remaking classics like grilled cheese with delicious ingredients like mushrooms, chickpeas, and cucumbers. Order at the counter, then grab a seat at one of the picnic tables street-side or in a little shady grove out back; there's also a large beer menu, a good selection of wines, and delicious house-made lemonade and iced tea. **Known for:** hot or cold lobster rolls; cod banh mi (Vietnamese sandwich); great atmosphere out back. ⑤ *Average main: $12* ⊠ *225 Commercial St., Downtown Center* ☎ *508/487–3800* ⊕ *www.thecanteenptown.com.*

Lobster Pot

$$$ | **SEAFOOD** | Provincetown's Lobster Pot is fit to do battle with all the lobster shanties anywhere (and everywhere) else on the Cape; although it's often jammed with tourists, the crowds reflect the generally high quality. The hardworking kitchen turns out classic New England cooking: lobsters, generous and filling seafood platters, and some of the best chowder around. **Known for:** locally award-winning clam chowder; local icon; extensive menu. ⑤ *Average main: $27* ⊠ *321 Commercial St., Downtown Center* ☎ *508/487–0842* ⊕ *www.ptownlobsterpot.com* ⊗ *Closed Jan.*

★ The Mews Restaurant & Cafe

$$$ | **AMERICAN** | This perennial favorite with magnificent harbor views focuses on seafood and grilled meats with a cross-cultural flair (there's also a lighter bistro menu for smaller appetites). The view of the bay from the bar is nearly perfect, and the gentle lighting makes this a romantic spot to have a drink. **Known for:** waterfront setting; ambience; Sunday brunch (May–October). ⑤ *Average main: $27* ⊠ *429 Commercial St., East End* ☎ *508/487–1500* ⊕ *www.mews.com.*

Napi's

$$$ | **ECLECTIC** | The food and the interior share a penchant for unusual, striking juxtapositions—a classical sculpture in front of an abstract canvas, for instance, or cod amandine and Brazilian-style shrimp (sautéed with garlic, herbs, and lime). The local art collection on display here is worthy and significant; Napi has been collecting gems for many, many years. **Known for:** international flavors; clam chowder; ample vegetarian options. ⑤ *Average main: $28* ⊠ *7 Freeman St., Downtown Center* ☎ *508/487–1145* ⊕ *www.napisptown.com* ⊗ *No lunch May–Sept.*

★ The Pointe

$$$ | **AMERICAN** | Inside the snazzy Crowne Pointe Inn, this intimate, casually handsome restaurant occupies the parlor and sunroom of a grand sea captain's mansion. The kitchen serves finely crafted, healthful, modern American food, and there's a substantial wine list, with well over a hundred selections to choose from. **Known for:** superb service; cocktails in the lounge; truffle popcorn. ⑤ *Average main: $27* ⊠ *Crowne Pointe Inn, 82 Bradford St., Downtown Center* ☎ *508/487–2365* ⊕ *www.provincetown-restaurant.com* ⊗ *No lunch.*

Red Inn

$$$ | **AMERICAN** | Inside the striking red house on P-town's West End (also an enchanting B&B with rooms starting at $305), the Red Inn is perhaps even better known as one of the Outer Cape's most romantic dining destinations—the views are simply stunning. The menu changes with the season, but always features the freshest local seafood and dishes like lamb chops seasoned with spices. **Known for:** exquisite location; raw bar happy hour; Sunday jazz brunch. ⑤ *Average main: $34* ✉ *15 Commercial St., West End* ☎ *508/487–7334* ⊕ *www. theredinn.com* ☉ *Closed Jan.–mid-Apr.*

Hotels

Anchor Inn

$$$ | **B&B/INN** | This regal, turreted beach house in the heart of Provincetown enjoys a wonderful location just steps from bars, shops, and restaurants. **Pros:** unobstructed water views; near the action; sleek and luxurious style. **Cons:** not for those with kids under 18; some rooms can be noisy; Downtown location can be a bit hectic. ⑤ *Rooms from: $305* ✉ *175 Commercial St., Downtown Center* ☎ *508/487–0432, 800/858–2657* ⊕ *www.anchorinnbeachhouse.com* ⌖ *23 rooms* ❍ *Free breakfast.*

★ Brass Key

$$$ | **B&B/INN** | One of the Cape's most luxurious small resorts, this meticulously kept year-round getaway comprises a beautifully restored main house— originally a sea captain's home built in 1828—and several other carefully groomed buildings and cottages all centered around a beautifully landscaped pool area. **Pros:** ultraposh rooms; beautiful and secluded grounds; pool on-site. **Cons:** among the highest rates in town; not for those with children; significant minimum-stay requirements in summer. ⑤ *Rooms from: $349* ✉ *67 Bradford St., Downtown Center* ☎ *508/487–9005, 800/842–9858*

⊕ *www.brasskey.com* ⌖ *43 rooms* ❍ *Free breakfast* ☞ *Pets are only allowed in certain rooms.*

★ Crowne Pointe Historic Inn and Spa

$$ | **B&B/INN** | Created meticulously from six different buildings, this inn hasn't a single detail left unattended—period furniture and antiques fill common areas and guest rooms; a queen-size bed is the smallest you'll find, dressed in 300-thread-count linens; treats are left on the pillow for nightly turndown service; and there's complimentary wine and cheese in the afternoon. **Pros:** great on-site amenities like the full-service Shui Spa and the excellent Bistro at Crowne Pointe; posh and luxurious room decor; professional and well-trained staff. **Cons:** among the highest rates in town; significant minimum-stay requirements in summer. ⑤ *Rooms from: $269* ✉ *82 Bradford St., Downtown Center* ☎ *508/487–6767, 877/276–9631* ⊕ *www.crownepointe. com* ⌖ *40 rooms* ❍ *Free breakfast.*

Eben House

$$ | **B&B/INN** | A rigorous interior renovation in 2015 on this 1776 property— among the oldest of the few remaining brick colonials in town—took it from sad to chic. **Pros:** simple, stunning interior design; exceptional service; complimentary parking. **Cons:** some rooms accessed via steep stairs; on busy road. ⑤ *Rooms from: $200* ✉ *90 Bradford St., Downtown Center* ☎ *508/487–0386* ⊕ *www.eben- house.com* ☉ *Closed weekdays Nov.– Apr.* ⌖ *14 rooms* ❍ *Free breakfast.*

Harbor Hotel Provincetown

$ | **HOTEL** | Directly across the street from the bay, this former drab and run-down property on the eastern edge of town has been transformed into a hip and sleek hotel, whose lively vibe is evident in the poolside bar, outdoor fire pit, and Whaler's Lounge, which is home to movie nights, live music, cocktails, and food. **Pros:** hotel is on the shuttle stop to town; great views and easy access to bay beach; great amenities like free bicycles. **Cons:** very long walk to town center; bay-view rooms closed in winter. ⑤ *Rooms from: $179* ⊠ *698 Commercial St., Greater Provincetown* ☎ *800/422–4224* ⊕ *www.harborhotelptown.com* ⛵ *129 rooms* ⦿ *No meals.*

Salt House Inn

$ | **B&B/INN** | Though one side of this aged beauty sits right on busy Conwell Street, the interior is all serenity, bathed in white, an ideal backdrop for the brilliant wood floors, statement furniture, and art pieces—think Colonial farmhouse with a decidedly modern and hip edge. **Pros:** in-town location, walk to everything; on-site concierge service is extremely helpful without being intrusive; on-site complimentary parking. **Cons:** some rooms are quite small; some rooms extremely close to the road; some rooms with detached (but private) bathroom. ⑤ *Rooms from: $170* ⊠ *6 Conwell St., Downtown Center* ☎ *508/487–1911* ⊕ *www.salthouseinn. com* ⊘ *Closed Nov.–Mar.* ⛵ *15 rooms* ⦿ *Free breakfast.*

★ White Porch Inn

$$ | **B&B/INN** | This sterling, light-filled B&B offers a soothing respite from the bustle of town; opt for one of the carriage-house rooms for even more seclusion. **Pros:** a selection of wines and small bites are set out each afternoon for guests; steps from East End shopping and dining; enthusiastic and friendly staff. **Cons:** somewhat long walk to West End shopping and businesses; not for those with children; limited parking. ⑤ *Rooms from: $299* ⊠ *7 Johnson St., Downtown Center* ☎ *508/364–2549, 508/487–0592* ⊕ *www. whiteporchinn.com* ⊟ *No credit cards* ⛵ *10 rooms* ⦿ *Free breakfast.*

ⓨ Nightlife

Provincetown is a party town. While the nightclub scene is decidedly gay, in most venues there is a clear "straight-friendly" welcome.

BARS

Governor Bradford Restaurant

BARS/PUBS | If you think the Governor Bradford looks a bit like a locals' dive bar, that wouldn't be too far from the truth: it's dark and rustic, and lacks the glittering lights of some of the other town nightspots. It's on a busy corner of Commercial and Standish Streets, where you can sit at tables with windows open to the street or inside at the long bar. Late-night fun includes drag karaoke, a great time and wildly popular; downstairs are multiple pool tables, darts, and a jukebox. ⊠ *312 Commercial St., Downtown Center* ☎ *508/487–2781.*

Paramount

DANCE CLUBS | Part of the Crown & Anchor complex of entertainment options, the Paramount is the hotel's main nightlife venue, offering poolside dancing to skilled DJs—including many names from the top international dance scene—on many nights. It's also host to cabaret performances and live theater. Next door is a video bar and a male-only leather bar, The Vault. Cover charges vary. ⊠ *247 Commercial St., Downtown Center* ☎ *508/487–1430* ⊕ *www.onlyatthecrown. com/paramount.*

ⓝ Performing Arts

During the busy summer season, hawkers in full-on drag or wearing very little at all compete with the din on Commercial Street to announce showtimes of the evening's performances. Pick your pleasure: dancing poolside at a few big nightclubs; watching talented drag performers strut their stuff; enjoying excellent live theater; strolling between art galleries; or sipping colorful cocktails at the water's edge. Much of the summer entertainment is first-class, drawing top Broadway and cabaret performers from New York City and beyond, offered at prices that would be a bargain back home.

THEATER

The Art House

CONCERTS | Every season showcases a powerhouse of performances. Hot tickets include the Broadway @ concert series, hosted by pianist Seth Rudestsky, with such previous guests as Neil Patrick Harris and David Burtka, Matthew Broderick and Sarah Jessica Parker, Sam Harris, and Lea DeLaria. Other acts, like beloved drag queen Varla Jean Merman and the Well-Strung Quartet, light up the stage every summer. ⊠ *214 Commercial St., Downtown Center* ☎ *508/487–9222* ⊕ *www.ptownarthouse.com.*

Post Office Cafe & Cabaret

MUSIC | Downstairs, it's a lively place for breakfast and lunch, with tables looking out onto Commercial Street. Upstairs, you can expect even jauntier—and often playfully raunchy—entertainment in the nightly cabaret offerings. ⊠ *303 Commercial St., Downtown Center* ☎ *508/487–0006* ⊕ *www.postofficecabaret.com.*

The Provincetown Theater

DANCE | This year-round venue provides excellent theater, showcasing many new works, as well as more unusual fare. In addition, there are dance performances, readings by playwrights, and workshops. ⊠ *238 Bradford St., East End* ☎ *508/487–7487* ⊕ *www.provincetowntheater.org.*

 Activities

TOURS

★ Art's Dune Tours

TOUR—SPORTS | Art's Dune Tours has been taking eager passengers into the dunes of Province Lands since 1946. A bumpy but controlled ride (about one hour) transports you through sometimes surreal sandy vistas peppered with beach grass, along a shoreline patrolled by seagulls and sandpipers. Head out at sunset for a stunning ride, available with or without a clambake feast; on Sunday there is a special Race Point Lighthouse Tour. ⊠ *4 Standish St., Downtown Center* ☎ *508/487–1950, 800/894–1951* ⊕ *www.artsdunetours.com* ⊠ *From $28.*

WHALE-WATCHING

★ Dolphin Fleet

WHALE-WATCHING | **FAMILY** | Tours are led by scientists from the Center for Coastal Studies in Provincetown, who provide commentary while collecting data on the whales they've been monitoring for years. They know many of them by name and will tell you about their habits and histories. These trips are most often exciting and incredibly thrilling with close-up encounters. ■**TIP→ Look for discount coupons in local free brochures and publications.** ⊠ *Chamber of Commerce Bldg., MacMillan Wharf, Downtown Center* ☎ *508/240–3636, 800/826–9300* ⊕ *www.whalewatch.com* ⊠ *From $52.*

⊙ Shopping

Provincetown shopping can be artistic, sophisticated, whimsical, and even downright tawdry—a perfect reflection of the town's very character. There is also a wide selection of touristy schlock. You'll find exquisite original art galleries primarily on the east end but also next to taffy and fudge shops, high-end home decor and designer clothing boutiques next to tattoo parlors and T-shirt shops, and even boutiques specializing in alternative interests (think leather and adult novelties). Most shopping is concentrated along Commercial Street.

ART GALLERIES

★ Julie Heller Gallery

ART GALLERIES | Julie Heller Gallery has contemporary artists as well as some Provincetown icons. The gallery has works from the Sol Wilson and Milton Avery estates, as well as from such greats as Robert Motherwell, Agnes Weinrich, and Blanche Lazzell. There's another location at 465 Commercial Street. ⊠ *2 Gosnold St., Downtown Center* ☎ *508/487–2169* ⊕ *www.juliehellergallery.com.*

The Schoolhouse Gallery

ART GALLERIES | The Schoolhouse Gallery, in an 1844 former school, shows the works of more than 50 local and national artists (modern and contemporary), as well as that of printmakers and photographers. ⊠ *494 Commercial St., East End* ☎ *508/487–4800* ⊕ *www. galleryschoolhouse.com.*

SPECIALTY STORES

Marine Specialties

SPECIALTY STORES | Marine Specialties is full of treasures, knickknacks, and clothing. Here you can purchase some very reasonably priced casual- and military-style clothing, as well as seashells, marine supplies, stained-glass lamps, candles, rubber sharks (you get the idea), and prints of old advertisements. ⊠ *235 Commercial St., Downtown Center* ☎ *508/487–1730.*

Tim's Used Books

BOOKS/STATIONERY | Set back off the street at the end of a wooden walkway, Tim's Used Books is packed with volumes of volumes—rooms of used-but-in-good-shape books, including some rare and out-of-print texts. It's a great place to lose track of time. ⊠ *242 Commercial St., Downtown Center* ☎ *508/487–0005.*

Martha's Vineyard

Far less developed than Cape Cod—thanks to a few local conservation organizations—yet more cosmopolitan than neighboring Nantucket, Martha's Vineyard is an island with a double life. From Memorial Day through Labor Day, the quieter (some might say the real) Vineyard quickens into a vibrant, star-studded place.

The busy main port, Vineyard Haven, welcomes day-trippers fresh off ferries and private yachts to browse in its array of shops. Oak Bluffs, where pizza and ice-cream emporiums reign supreme, has the air of a Victorian boardwalk.

Edgartown is flooded with seekers of chic who wander tiny streets that hold boutiques, stately whaling captains' homes, and charming inns.

Summer regulars have included a host of celebrities over the years, among them Oprah Winfrey, Carly Simon, Ted Danson, Spike Lee, and Diane Sawyer; former president Barack Obama and his family vacationed here nearly every summer of his two terms in the Oval Office. If you're planning to stay overnight on a summer weekend, be sure to make reservations well in advance; spring is not too early. Things stay busy on September and October weekends, a favorite time for weddings, but begin to slow down soon after. In many ways the Vineyard's off-season persona is even more appealing than its summer self, with more time to linger over pastoral and ocean vistas, free from the throngs of cars, bicycles, and mopeds.

GETTING ORIENTED

The island is roughly triangular, measuring about 20 miles east to west and 10 miles north to south. The west end of the Vineyard, known as Up-Island—from the nautical expression of going "up" in degrees of longitude as you sail west—is more rural and wild than the eastern Down-Island end, comprising Vineyard Haven, Oak Bluffs, and Edgartown.

Vineyard Haven (Tisbury). One of the island's busiest towns, Vineyard Haven sees ferry traffic all year long. A fairly compact downtown area keeps most shopping and dining options within easy reach.

Oak Bluffs. Once a Methodist campground, Oak Bluffs is a little less refined than the other towns. It has a vibrant vacation vibe, with lots of nightlife, dining, and shopping.

Edgartown. Dominated by the impeccably kept homes of 19th-century sea captains, Edgartown has a sense of sophistication. There's great history here, and several museums tell the story.

Martha's Vineyard

KEY
- Beaches
- Bike Trail
- Ferry

TO HYANNIS

TO QUONSET POINT

Nantucket Sound

TO NANTUCKET (SUMMER ONLY)

TO FALMOUTH

Cape Poge

Cape Poge Wildlife Refuge

Cape Poge Bay

East Beach

Mytoi

Chappaquiddick Island

Wasque Point

Edgartown Harbor

Edgartown Lighthouse

Katama Bay

Wasque Beach

TO FALMOUTH

TO WOODS HOLE

TO NEW BEDFORD

TO FALMOUTH

TO WOODS HOLE

East Chop Lighthouse

Oak Bluffs

Flying Horses Carousel

Oak Bluffs Campground

Oak Bluffs Beach

Joseph A. Sylvia State Beach

Beach Rd.

Sengekontacket Pond

County Rd.

Tisbury Town Beach

Beach Rd.

Lagoon Pond

Mass Audubon's Felix Neck Wildlife Sanctuary

Havisa Rd.

Edgartown

Chappaquiddick Rd.

Katama Rd.

Katama (South Beach)

South Katama Beach

Herring Creek

STATE FOREST

Airport Rd.

Vineyard Rd.

Edgartown-West Tisbury Rd.

Airport

Oyster Pond

Edgartown Great Pond

TO NEW BEDFORD

TO NORTH KINGSTOWN, RI

Lake Tashmoo Town Beach

Owen Park Beach

Vineyard Haven (Tisbury)

Lake Tashmoo

Lambert's Cove Rd.

Lambert's Cove Beach (restricted)

Edgartown

Stoney Hill Rd.

MANUEL F. CORRELLUS

Old County Rd.

Sepiessa Point Reservation

Tisbury Great Pond

Long Point Beach

ATLANTIC OCEAN

Vineyard Sound

Indian Hill Rd.

Polly Hill Arboretum

West Tisbury

State Rd.

South Rd.

Tea La.

Lucy Vincent Beach (restricted)

Middle Rd.

North Rd.

Menemsha Beach

Menemsha

Chilmark

Menemsha Pond

State Rd.

Squibnocket Pond

Menemsha Harbor

Lobsterville Beach

Gay Head Lighthouse

Aquinnah

Moshup Trail

Squibnocket Beach (restricted)

Aquinnah Cliffs

Moshup Beach

Philbin Beach (restricted)

4 miles

6 km

0

Chappaquiddick Island. Take the tiny ferry from Edgartown to explore Chappaquiddick Island's vast nature preserves. It's a favorite place for bird-watchers and anglers.

West Tisbury. There's beautiful farm country out this way, and the 1859 Grange Hall is still the center of action. During the warmer months, don't miss the bountiful West Tisbury Farmers' Market.

Menemsha. An active fishing harbor, Menemsha is known for its splendid sunsets. There are a few shops and galleries, and a couple of excellent take-out spots for the freshest of seafood.

Aquinnah. Known until recently as Gay Head, Aquinnah is famous for its grand and dramatic red clay cliffs, as well as the resident lighthouse.

AIR TRAVEL

Cape Air has regular, year-round flight service to the island from Hyannis, Boston, and Providence's T.F. Green Airport and seasonal service (starting mid-June) from White Plains, NY (including a bus transfer to and from Manhattan). Jet-Blue provides seasonal nonstop service from New York–JFK.

BUS TRAVEL

Once on the island, the Martha's Vineyard Transit Authority (VTA) provides regular service to all six towns on the island, including stops at all ferry landings and the airport. The buses can accommodate a limited number of bicycles, and the island has an excellent network of well-maintained bike trails. The VTA also has free in-town shuttle-bus routes in Edgartown and Vineyard Haven. You can also get around by bicycle (rentals are available) and by taxi (an expensive option).

BUS CONTACTS Martha's Vineyard Transit Authority (*VTA*) ☎ *508/693–9940* ⊕ *www.vineyardtransit.com.*

CAR TRAVEL

Although traffic can be bad during the season, it can be handy to have a car in order to see all of Martha's Vineyard and travel freely. Instead of bringing one over on the Steamship Authority ferry from Woods Hole (the only ferry service that transports cars—expensively), it's sometimes easier and more economical to rent one once you're on the island for a few days of exploring, particularly during the busy season when car reservations on the ferry are hard to come by. Don't expect a bargain for on-island rentals either; you'll pay about $180 per day for a Jeep. The island does its best to discourage extra automobile traffic.

CONTACTS A-A Island Auto Rental ⊠ *5 Corners, 4 Water St., Vineyard Haven* ☎ *508/696–5300* ⊕ *www.mvautorental. com.* **Sun 'n' Fun Rentals** ⊠ *28 Lake Ave., Oak Bluffs* ☎ *508/693–5457* ⊕ *www.sunnfunrentals.com.*

FERRY TRAVEL

The Steamship Authority is the main ferry (operating year-round) heading to Martha's Vineyard from Woods Hole. Other ferries leave from Falmouth Harbor (Island Queen); North Kingstown, RI (Vineyard Fast Ferry); Hyannis (Hy-Line); New Bedford (Seastreak); New York City (Seastreak, seasonally).

VISITOR INFORMATION

CONTACTS Martha's Vineyard Chamber of Commerce ☎ *508/693–0085, 800/505–4815* ⊕ *www.mvy.com.*

Vineyard Haven (Tisbury)

7 miles southeast of Woods Hole, 3½ miles west of Oak Bluffs, 8 miles northwest of Edgartown.

Most people call this town Vineyard Haven because of the name of the port where ferries arrive, but its official name is Tisbury. Not as high-toned as Edgartown or as honky-tonk as Oak Bluffs, Vineyard Haven blends the past and present with a touch of the bohemian. Visitors step off the ferry right into the bustle of the harbor, one block from the shops and restaurants of Main Street.

GETTING HERE AND AROUND

Vineyard Haven sees ferry traffic year-round, so this port town is always active. If you're traveling without a car, you can get around by taxi or the white buses run by Martha's Vineyard Transit Authority. Bike, scooter, and car rentals are also possibilities. Much of the downtown area is easily explored on foot, and a good number of the lodgings are within reach. Vineyard Haven is 3½ miles west of Oak Bluffs.

Beaches

Lake Tashmoo Town Beach

BEACH—SIGHT | FAMILY | Swimmers have access to the warm, relatively shallow, brackish Lake Tashmoo from this beach—or cooler, gentler Vineyard Sound. It's a favorite spot for surf casters. **Amenities:** lifeguards; parking (no fee); toilets. **Best for:** sunset; swimming. ⊠ *End of Herring Creek Rd.*

Owen Park Beach

BEACH—SIGHT | FAMILY | This small, sandy harbor beach is just steps away from the ferry terminal in Vineyard Haven, making it a great spot to catch some last rays before heading home. **Amenities:** lifeguards; toilets. **Best for:** swimming. ⊠ *Off Main St.*

Tisbury Town Beach

BEACH—SIGHT | This public beach is next to the Vineyard Haven Yacht Club. It is only accessed by foot or bike: no parking here. But it's a nice place for a picnic. **Amenities:** none. **Best for:** swimming. ⊠ *End of Owen Little Way, off Main St.*

Restaurants

Beach Road

$$$ | SEAFOOD | With its ample windows looking out to the serene lagoon, lofted ceilings, and mellow globe lighting held aloft by sturdy ropes, the decor aptly reflects the kitchen's "sea-to-table" theme for its seasonally inspired and locally sourced offerings. The massive bar is a popular spot for dining and cocktails; despite town bylaws forbidding hard liquor, there is a creative and unusual selection of alcohol concoctions. **Known for:** $1 nightly oyster happy hour; intriguing small plates; elegant farmhouse atmosphere. ⑤ *Average main: $28* ⊠ *79 Beach Rd.* ☎ *508/693–8582* ⊕ *www.beachroadmv.com.*

Black Dog Tavern

$$$ | AMERICAN | FAMILY | This island landmark—more popular with tourists than locals—lies just steps from the ferry terminal in Vineyard Haven. The dining room—roaring fireplace, dark-wood walls, maritime memorabilia, and a grand view of the water—makes everyone feel so at home; there's additional seating on the patio when the weather allows. **Known for:** menu featuring local fish, chowders, and chops; hour-long wait for breakfast in July and August; welcoming atmosphere. ⑤ *Average main: $25* ⊠ *20 Beach St. Ext.* ☎ *508/693–9223* ⊕ *www.theblackdog. com* ⊙ *No dinner Sun.–Wed. Oct.–May.*

🛏 Hotels

Crocker House Inn

$$$$ | B&B/INN | This casual 1890 farmhouse-style inn is tucked into a quiet lane off Main Street, minutes from the ferries and Owen Park Beach. **Pros:** great owners; short walk from town; easygoing vibe. **Cons:** not for those with small children; books up quickly in summer. ⑤ *Rooms from: $450* ⊠ *12 Crocker Ave.* ☎ *508/693–1151, 800/772–0206* ⊕ *www.crockerhouseinn.com* ⊸ *8 rooms* ⊙ *Free breakfast.*

Mansion House

$$$ | HOTEL | There has been a hostelry on this Main Street site just above Vineyard Haven Harbor since 1794, but it was updated in 2003 to include an indoor pool and well-provisioned health club. **Pros:** on-site spa; steps from shopping and ferry; light-filled rooms. **Cons:** location can be a little noisy; not historic. $ *Rooms from: $309* ⊠ *9 Main St.* 🕾 *509/693–2200, 800/332–4112* ⊕ *www.mvmansionhouse.com* ⇨ *40 rooms* ⦿ *Free breakfast.*

Performing Arts

THEATER
Vineyard Playhouse

FILM | The Vineyard Playhouse has a year-round schedule of professional productions. From mid-June through early September, a troupe performs drama, classics, and comedies on the air-conditioned main stage. Summer Shakespeare and other productions take place at the natural amphitheater at Tashmoo Overlook on State Road in Vineyard Haven—bring insect repellent and a blanket or lawn chair. The theater is wheelchair accessible and provides hearing devices. ⊠ *24 Church St.* 🕾 *508/696–6300* ⊕ *mv-playhouse.org/theater/.*

Shopping

Vineyard Haven has a nice concentration of shopping along Main Street, which is intersected with several shorter streets that also hold shops of interest. Conveniently, since many people arrive by ferry without their vehicles, the majority of shopping is easily accessible right from the ferry docks. You won't find any large-scale chain stores here—rather, a good variety of upscale clothing shops, galleries, and other independently owned businesses selling everything from kitchen ware to luxury bath products.

Bunch of Grapes Bookstore

BOOKS/STATIONERY | Bunch of Grapes Bookstore is an excellent independent, with eager and knowledgeable booksellers and a varied selection of new books for adults and children. It also sponsors book signings. ⊠ *35 Main St.* 🕾 *508/693–2291* ⊕ *www.bunchofgrapes.com.*

★ **Rainy Day**

CRAFTS | As the name suggests, Rainy Day carries gifts and amusements perfect for one of the island's gloomy afternoons when you just need a warm, dry diversion. You'll find toys, crafts, cards, soaps, home accessories, gifts, and more. ⊠ *66 Main St.* 🕾 *508/693–1830* ⊕ *www.rainydaymv.com.*

Tuck and Holand

CRAFTS | Nationally renowned for its distinctive, hand-sculpted metal weather vanes, Tuck and Holand has a studio gallery a 10-minute walk from downtown. Here you can examine Anthony Holand and the late Travis Tuck's otherworldly creations, including copper Martha's Vineyard wall maps, school-of-bluefish chandeliers, and the signature custom weather vanes. ⊠ *275 State Rd.* 🕾 *508/693–3914, 888/693–3914* ⊕ *www.tuckandholand.com.*

Oak Bluffs

3½ miles east of Vineyard Haven.

Circuit Avenue is the bustling center of the Oak Bluffs action, with most of the town's shops, bars, and restaurants. Colorful gingerbread-trimmed guesthouses and food and souvenir joints enliven Oak Bluffs Harbor, once the setting for several grand hotels. This small town is more high-spirited than haute, more fun than refined. ■**TIP**➜ **Look for the yellow tourist information booth at the bottom of Circuit Avenue. It's open June–mid-October and is staffed with helpful folks from the area.**

GETTING HERE AND AROUND
Oak Bluff is the terminal for seasonal ferries. If you have a car, it's best to find a space and leave it while you walk, bike, or take the white buses operated by Martha's Vineyard Transit Authority.

Sights

East Chop Lighthouse

LIGHTHOUSE | This lighthouse was built out of cast iron in 1876 to replace an 1828 tower (used as part of a semaphore system) that burned down. The 40-foot structure stands high atop a 79-foot bluff with spectacular views of Nantucket Sound. Open Sunday evenings at sunset (from 6 pm) in summer. ⊠ *E. Chop Dr.* ☎ *508/627–4441* ⊕ *www. mvmuseum.org* 🎫 *$5.*

Flying Horses Carousel

CAROUSEL | **FAMILY** | A National Historic Landmark, this is the nation's oldest continuously operating merry-go-round. Handcrafted in 1876—the horses have real horsehair and glass eyes—and brought from Coney Island in 1884, the ride gives children a taste of entertainment from an era before smartphones. ⊠ *15 Lake Ave.* ☎ *508/693–9481* ⊕ *www. mvpreservation.org* 🎫 *$3.*

★ Oak Bluffs Campground

BUILDING | This 34-acre warren of streets is tightly packed with more than 300 gaily painted Carpenter Gothic Victorian cottages with wedding-cake trim; they date mainly to the 1860s and '70s, when visitors coming for Methodist revivalist services began to lease lots and build houses for summer use. As you wander through this fairy-tale setting, imagine it on a balmy summer evening, lighted by the warm glow of paper lanterns hung from every cottage porch. This describes the scene on Illumination Night at the end of the Camp Meeting season, which is attended these days by some fourth- and fifth-generation cottagers—and newcomers: some houses do change hands, and some are rented. Attendees mark the occasion as they have for more than a century, with lights, song, and open houses for families and friends. Ninety-minute tours of the area are conducted at 11 am on Tuesday and Thursday in July and August; join Community Sings on Wednesday evenings. ⊠ *Off Circuit Ave.*

☎ *508/693–0525* ⊕ *www.mvcma.org* 🎫 *Tour $12.*

Beaches

Joseph A. Sylvia State Beach

BEACH—SIGHT | **FAMILY** | This 2-mile-long sandy beach has a view of Cape Cod across Nantucket Sound. Occasional food vendors and calm, warm waters make it a popular spot for families. Arrive early or late in high summer: the parking spots fill up quickly. It's best to bike, walk, or take the shuttle here. **Amenities:** parking (no fee). **Best for:** swimming. ⊠ *Off Beach Rd., between Oak Bluffs and Edgartown.*

Restaurants

Red Cat Kitchen

$$$$ | **SEAFOOD** | Standing at nearly 6½ feet tall and covered with colorful tattoos, chef-owner Ben Deforest turns out an extraordinary array of dishes—chorizo-stuffed local calamari, crab and wild mushroom risotto, or truffle arancini—from a tiny kitchen visible from the dining room. Regulars love the funky artwork, thundering tunes, and the irreverent spirit of the place, but no question here: it's the food that keeps them coming back. **Known for:** frequently changing (sometimes daily) seasonal-based menu; crispy Brussels sprouts; ample portions. ⑤ *Average main: $42* ⊠ *14 Kennebec Ave.* ☎ *508/696–6040* ⊕ *www.redcatkitchen. com* ◷ *Closed Nov.–Mar.*

Sweet Life Café

$$$$ | **AMERICAN** | Housed in a charming Victorian house, this island favorite's warm hues, low lighting, and handsome antique furniture will make you feel like you've entered someone's home. The cooking is more sophisticated than home style, however: dishes are prepared in inventive ways and change often with the seasons. **Known for:** superb desserts; outdoor dining by candlelight in a shrub-enclosed

Sacred to the Wampanoag Tribe, the red-hued Aquinnah Cliffs are a popular attraction on Martha's Vineyard.

garden; locally sourced food. $ Average main: $37 ⌧ 63 Upper Circuit Ave. ☎ 508/696–0200 ⊕ www.sweetlifemv. com ⊙ Closed Jan.–Mar. No lunch.

Hotels

Madison Inn

$$ | **B&B/INN** | While this stylish little inn doesn't have the high prices of nearby hotels, it does have all the amenities you need including coffee and tea available all day and night, and complimentary snack basket in each room. **Pros:** extremely reasonable rates; location is right in town and everything is walkable; sophisticated lodging. **Cons:** no parking; some rooms on the small side. $ Rooms from: $205 ⌧ 18 Kennebec Ave. ☎ 508/693–2760, 800/564–2760 ⊕ www.madisoninnmv. com ⊙ Closed Nov.–mid-Apr. ⇴ 15 rooms ⦿ No meals.

Pequot Hotel

$$ | **B&B/INN** | In this casual cedar-shingle inn on a tree-lined street, the first floor has a wide porch with rocking chairs—perfect for enjoying coffee or tea with the

cookies that are set out in the afternoon—and there's a small breakfast room where you can help yourself to bagels, muffins, and cereal in the morning. **Pros:** the bustle of downtown Oak Bluffs is a pleasant five-minute walk past Carpenter Gothic houses, and it's one block from the beaches that line Oak Bluffs–Edgartown Road; reasonable rates; charmingly offbeat. **Cons:** some rooms are small; some rooms with no TV. $ Rooms from: $225 ⌧ 19 Pequot Ave. ☎ 508/693–5087, 800/947–8704 ⊕ www.pequothotel.com ⊙ Closed mid-Oct.–Apr. ⇴ 31 rooms, 1 apartment ⦿ Free breakfast.

Nightlife

Lampost Bar & Nightclub

BARS/PUBS | The Lampost is a good, old-fashioned neighborhood bar with a DJ and dancing, as well as pool, darts, and a game room. The bar attracts a young crowd with its three floors of action. ⌧ 6 Circuit Ave. ☎ 508/696–9352 ⊙ Closed Dec.–Mar.

Loft

BARS/PUBS | This adults-only venue makes its home in the vast space above the MV Chowder Co. and has long historic roots. Today it's home to an over-21 "playground" consisting of numerous pool tables, Ping-Pong, darts, shuffleboard, foosball, video games, a full bar, and frequent live music and DJ-led dance parties. A full menu is available in the restaurant below. ⊠ *9 Oak Bluffs Ave.* ☎ *508/696–3000* ⊕ *www.loftob.com.*

 Activities

FISHING

Dick's Bait & Tackle

FISHING | You can buy fishing accessories and bait, and check out a current copy of the fishing regulations here. ⊠ *108 New York Ave.* ☎ *508/693–7669.*

Edgartown

6 miles southeast of Oak Bluffs.

★ Once a well-to-do whaling center, Edgartown remains the Vineyard's toniest town and has preserved parts of its elegant past. Sea captains' houses from the 18th and 19th centuries, with well-manicured gardens and lawns, line the streets.

A sparsely populated area with many nature preserves, where you can fish, Chappaquiddick Island, 1 mile southeast of Edgartown, makes for a pleasant day trip or bike ride on a sunny day. The "island" is actually connected to the Vineyard by a long sand spit that begins in South Beach in Katama. It's a spectacular 2¾-mile walk, or you can take the ferry, which departs about every five minutes.

GETTING HERE AND AROUND

Once you've reached Edgartown, a car isn't necessary. It's actually a hindrance, as parking can be very tight in summer. The Martha's Vineyard Transit Authority operates a fleet of buses that can get you almost anywhere you want to go.

The town runs a helpful visitor center on Church Street.

The best way to get around Chappaquiddick Island is by bike; bring one over on the ferry ($6 round-trip for bike and rider) and ride the few miles to Cape Pogue Wildlife Refuge. Sign up for a tour with the Trustees of Reservations for an indepth look at the island's wonders.

 Sights

Cape Poge Wildlife Refuge

BEACH—SIGHT | **FAMILY** | A conglomeration of habitats where you can swim, walk, fish, or just sit and enjoy the surroundings, the Cape Poge Wildlife Refuge, on the easternmost shore of Chappaquiddick Island, encompasses more than 6 square miles of wilderness. Its dunes, woods, cedar thickets, moors, salt marshes, ponds, tidal flats, and barrier beach serve as an important migration stopover and nesting area for numerous sea- and shorebirds. The best way to get to the refuge is as part of a naturalist-led jeep drive. Other tours are also provided by the Trustees of Reservations. ⊠ *East end of Dike Rd., Chappaquiddick Island* ☎ *508/627–3599* ⊕ *www.thetrustees.org/places-to-visit/cape-cod-islands/cape-pogue.html.*

Edgartown Lighthouse

LIGHTHOUSE | **FAMILY** | Surrounded by a public beach, this cast-iron tower was floated by barge from Ipswich, Massachusetts, in 1938. It is still an active navigational aid. ⊠ *121 N. Water St.* ⊕ *www.mvmuseum.org* ⊠ *$5* ⊗ *Closed Labor Day–May.*

Felix Neck Wildlife Sanctuary

NATURE PRESERVE | **FAMILY** | The nearly 200-acre Massachusetts Audubon Society preserve, 3 miles outside Edgartown toward Oak Bluffs and Vineyard Haven, has 4 miles of hiking trails traversing marshland, fields, woods, seashore, and waterfowl and reptile ponds. Naturalist-led events include sunset hikes, stargazing, snake or bird walks, and kayaking tours. ⊠ *100 Felix Neck Rd., off Edgartown–Vineyard Haven Rd.* ☎ *508/627–4850* ⊕ *www.massaudubon.org* ⊠ *$4.*

★ Mytoi

GARDEN | The Trustees of Reservations' 14-acre preserve is a serene, beautifully tended, Japanese-inspired garden with a creek-fed pool spanned by a bridge and rimmed with Japanese maples, azaleas, bamboo, and irises. A boardwalk runs through part of the grounds, where you're apt to see box turtles and hear the sounds of songbirds. There are few more enchanting spots on the island. Restrooms and fresh water are available. ⊠ *56 Dike Bridge Rd., 2 miles from Chappaquiddick Rd., Chappaquiddick Island* ☎ *508/627–7689* ⊕ *www.thetrustees.org/places-to-visit/cape-cod-islands/mytoi.html* ⊠ *Free.*

Beaches

South Beach Katama Beach

BEACH—SIGHT | This very popular and accessible 3-4 mile stretch of Atlantic-facing beach is backed by high dunes. The protected cove is good for families, and buses leave about every 30 minutes from town ($1.25 each way). **Amenities:** toilets; lifeguards; parking (no fee). **Best for:** surfing; sunrise; walking. ⊠ *Katama Rd., Chappaquiddick Island* ✛ *4 miles south of Edgartown* ⊕ *www.mvy.com.*

Restaurants

Alchemy Bistro and Bar

$$$$ | EUROPEAN | Alchemy aims for a European-chic bistro-style scene and menu, missing only the patina of age—and French working-folks' prices—but you can expect quality and imagination. On balmy evenings, the half-dozen outdoor tables on the candlelit brick patio are highly coveted. **Known for:** specialty cocktails; swanky candle-lit ambience; impressive wine list. ⑤ *Average main: $38* ⊠ *71 Main St.* ☎ *508/627–9999* ⊕ *www.alchemyedgartown.com* ⊗ *No lunch.*

★ Détente

$$$$ | AMERICAN | A dark, intimate wine bar and restaurant with hardwood floors and richly colored banquette seating, Détente serves more than a dozen wines by the glass as well as numerous half bottles. Even if you're not much of an oenophile, it's worth a trip just for the innovative food, much of it from local farms and seafood purveyors. **Known for:** hip, sophisticated atmosphere; five-course tasting menu; exquisite food preparations. ⑤ *Average main: $38* ⊠ *15 Winter St.* ☎ *508/627–8810* ⊕ *www.detentemv.com* ⊗ *Closed Tues. and Nov.–late Apr. No lunch.*

The Dunes

$$$$ | SEAFOOD | FAMILY | The airy restaurant at Winnetu Oceanside Resort draws plenty of discerning diners to sample some of the island's most exquisite and creatively prepared seafood. It's the only dining room with a south-facing water view, and a stunning one at that—especially if you're lucky enough to sit outside on the large dining and drinking area. **Known for:** supervised separate dining area for families with children; water taxi from Edgartown; exceptional service. ⑤ *Average main: $37* ⊠ *Winnetu Oceanside Resort, 31 Dunes Rd.* ☎ *508/627–3663* ⊕ *www.winnetu.com* ⊗ *Closed mid-Oct.–mid-Apr. No lunch.*

l'étoile

$$$$ | FRENCH | Michael Brisson has been at the helm of this creative French kitchen since the mid-1980s, yet his dedication to fresh, exquisitely prepared local food remains as fervent as ever. Changing with what's seasonally available, his menu many include sautéed Menemsha fluke or perhaps roasted Long Island duck breast; for lighter fare or to indulge in a fancy martini, head to the stunning copper bar with its sleek leather-backed chairs or the lovely terrace for alfresco dining. **Known for:** elegant surroundings; foie gras; succulent tasting menu. ⑤ *Average main: $45* ⊠ *The*

Sydney Martha's Vineyard, 22 N. Water St. ☎ 508/627–5187 ⊕ www.letoile.net ⊘ Closed Dec.–late Apr.

Hotels

Charlotte Inn
$$$$ | B&B/INN | From the moment you walk up to the dark-wood Scottish barrister's desk to check in at this regal 1864 inn, you'll be surrounded by the trappings and customs of a bygone era—beautiful antique furnishings, objets d'art, and paintings fill the property. **Pros:** over-the-top lavish; quiet yet convenient location; beautifully landscaped. **Cons:** can feel overly formal; intimidating if you don't adore museum-quality antiques; not for those with children. ⑤ *Rooms from: $800* ✉ *27 S. Summer St.* ☎ *508/627–4751, 800/735–2478* ⊕ *www.thecharlotteinn. com* ⋑ *19 rooms* ⦿❙ *No meals.*

Edgartown Inn
$$ | B&B/INN | The inside of the former home of whaling captain Thomas Worth still evokes its late-18th-century origins—its cozy parlor and antiques-filled rooms look as if the captain still lives here. **Pros:** great value; rich in history—Nathaniel Hawthorne wrote much of his Twice-Told Tales here; close to shopping and dining. **Cons:** no credit cards; not for those with small children. ⑤ *Rooms from: $250* ✉ *56 N. Water St.* ☎ *508/627–4794* ⊕ *www.edgartowninn.com* ⊟ *No credit cards* ⊘ *Closed Nov.–early Apr.* ⋑ *14 rooms* ⦿❙ *Free breakfast.*

★ Hob Knob
$$$$ | B&B/INN | This 19th-century Gothic Revival boutique hotel blends the amenities and service of a luxury property with the ambience and charm of a small B&B with art and antiques that help capture the island's rural, seaside charm. **Pros:** full breakfast—organic and locally gathered—and lavish afternoon tea are included; on-site spa; a short walk from the harbor, it's on the main road into town—but far enough out to avoid crowds. **Cons:** steep rates; not overlooking harbor; not

for those with small children. ⑤ *Rooms from: $495* ✉ *128 Main St.* ☎ *508/627–9510, 800/696–2723* ⊕ *www.hobknob. com* ⋑ *17 rooms* ⦿❙ *Free breakfast.*

★ Winnetu Oceanside Resort
$$$$ | RESORT | FAMILY | A departure from most properties on the island, the contemporary Winnetu—styled after the grand multistory resorts of the Gilded Age—has successfully struck a fine balance in that it both encourages families and provides a contemporary seaside-resort experience for couples. **Pros:** a full slate of excellent children's programs offered late June–early September; resort arranges bicycling and kayaking trips, lighthouse tours, boat excursions to Nantucket Island, and other island activities; fantastic restaurant. **Cons:** not an in-town location; lots of kids in summer. ⑤ *Rooms from: $495* ✉ *31 Dunes Rd.* ☎ *866/335–1133, 508/310–1733* ⊕ *www.winnetu.com* ⊘ *Closed late Oct.–mid-Apr.* ⋑ *58 suites, 80 homes* ⦿❙ *No meals.*

Shopping

Edgartown Books
BOOKS/STATIONERY | This longtime island favorite carries a large selection of island-related titles and periodicals, and the staff will be happy to make a summer reading recommendation. New for 2018 is a wonderful little café behind the bookshop, serving fine coffee, breakfast, lunch, and dinner. ✉ *44 Main St.* ☎ *508/627–8463* ⊕ *www.edgartownbooks.com/.*

West Tisbury

8 miles west of Edgartown, 6½ miles south of Vineyard Haven.

West Tisbury retains its rural appeal and maintains its agricultural tradition at several active horse and produce farms. The town center looks very much like a small New England village, complete with a white-steepled church.

Sights

Polly Hill Arboretum
GARDEN | FAMILY | The late horticulturist and part-time Vineyard resident Polly Hill tended some 2,000 species of plant and developed nearly 100 species herself on her old sheep farm in West Tisbury. On-site are azaleas, tree peonies, dogwoods, hollies, lilacs, magnolias, and more. Hill raised them from seeds without the use of a greenhouse, and her patience is the inspiration of the arboretum. Run as a nonprofit center, the arboretum also runs guided tours, a lecture series, and a visitor center and gift shop. It's a beautiful spot for a picnic. ✉ *809 State Rd.* ☎ *508/693–9426* ⊕ *www.pollyhillarboretum.org* 💲 *$5.*

Sepiessa Point Reservation
NATURE PRESERVE | A paradise for bird-watchers, Sepiessa Point Reservation consists of 164 acres on splendid Tisbury Great Pond. There are expansive pond and ocean views, walking trails around coves and saltwater marshes, horse trails, swimming areas, and a boat launch. ✉ *Tiah's Cove Rd.* ☎ *508/627–7141* ⊕ *www.mvlandbank. com* 💲 *Free.*

Restaurants

★ State Road Restaurant
$$$ | AMERICAN | FAMILY | High ceilings, exposed beams, and a beautiful stone fireplace make for a warm and light-filled meal. The menu takes advantage of local and organic products, creating memorable dishes. **Known for:** creative and large selection of plates ample for sharing and sampling; wonderful ambience; Sunday brunch (no reservations accepted). 💲 *Average main: $35* ✉ *688 State Rd.* ☎ *508/693–8582* ⊕ *www.stateroadrestaurant.com.*

🛏 Hotels

★ Lambert's Cove Inn, Farm & Restaurant
$$ | B&B/INN | A narrow road winds through pine woods and beside creeper-covered stone walls to this posh, handsomely designed farmhouse inn (1790) surrounded by extraordinary gardens and old stone walls. **Pros:** guests receive free passes (and transport) to beautiful and private Lambert's Cove beach (there's also a pool); fantastic restaurant; serene grounds. **Cons:** need a car to explore island; far from the action. 💲 *Rooms from: $275* ✉ *90 Manaquayak Rd., off Lambert's Cove Rd.* ☎ *508/693–2298* ⊕ *www.lambertscoveinn.com* 🛏 *15 rooms* 🍴 *Free breakfast.*

🛍 Shopping

Alley's General Store
CONVENIENCE/GENERAL STORES | FAMILY | Step back in time with a visit to Alley's General Store, a local landmark since 1858. Alley's sells a truly general variety of goods: everything from hammers to housewares and dill pickles to sweet muffins as well as great things you find only in a country store. There's even a post office inside. ✉ *299 State Rd.* ☎ *508/693–0088.*

Menemsha

1½ miles southwest of West Tisbury.

Unspoiled by the "progress" of the past few decades, this working port is a jumble of weathered fishing shacks, fishing and pleasure boats, drying nets, and lobster pots. The village is popular with cyclists who like to stop for ice cream or chowder. Menemsha is often busy with folks eager to see the sunset.

GETTING HERE AND AROUND
You can take a Martha's Vineyard Transit Authority bus here; there's frequent service in summer and more limited service the rest of the year. If you're

exploring the area by bike, you can get between Menemsha and the Aquinnah Cliffs via the Menemsha Bike Ferry. It's a quick trip across the water ($8 round-trip), but it saves a lot of riding on the busy State Road.

Sights

Menemsha Harbor

BEACH—SIGHT | Where Menemsha Pond meets Vineyard Sound, this tiny seaside outpost has been an active fishing center for centuries. Well-weathered fishing boats, including some that have been in the same family for generations, tie up at the docks when not out to sea. Spectacular sunsets make this a very popular evening spot. Several fish markets offer the freshest catch of the day. There's also a beach here, with gentle waters that are welcoming to families. If the harbor looks familiar, it might be because several scenes from the movie *Jaws* were filmed here. ✉ *Basin Rd.*

Aquinnah

6½ miles west of Menemsha, 10 miles southwest of West Tisbury, 17 miles southwest of Vineyard Haven.

Aquinnah, called Gay Head until the town voted to change its name in 1997, is an official Native American township. The Wampanoag tribe is the guardian of the 420 acres that constitute the Aquinnah Native American Reservation. Aquinnah (pronounced a-*kwih*-nah) is Wampanoag for "land under the hill." You can get a good view of Menemsha and Nashaquitsa ponds, the woods, and the ocean beyond from Quitsa Pond Lookout on State Road. The town is best known for the red-hued Aquinnah Cliffs. This is the end of the world, or so it seems when you're standing on the edge of the cliff looking out over the ocean.

GETTING HERE AND AROUND

Aquinnah, 6½ miles west of Menemsha and 10 miles southwest of West Tisbury, gets lots of traffic, for good reason. You can drive here (and pray for a parking space) or ride the Martha's Vineyard Transit Authority buses, which have frequent service in summer.

Sights

★ Aquinnah Cliffs

NATURE SITE | A National Historic Landmark, the spectacular Aquinnah Cliffs are part of the Wampanoag Reservation land. These dramatically striated walls of red clay are the island's major attraction, as evinced by the tour bus–filled parking lot. Native American crafts and food shops line the short approach to the overlook, from which you can see the Elizabeth Islands to the northeast across Vineyard Sound and Nomans Land Island, a wildlife preserve, 3 miles off the Vineyard's southern coast. ✉ *State Rd.*

Gay Head Lighthouse

LIGHTHOUSE | This brick lighthouse (also called the Aquinnah Lighthouse) was successfully moved back from its precarious perch atop the rapidly eroding cliffs in spring 2015. Bad weather may affect its hours. Parking can be limited here. ✉ *9 Aquinnah Circle* ☎ *508/627–4441* ⊕ *www.aquinnah-ma.gov/* ✉ *$5.*

Hotels

Outermost Inn

$$$ | B&B/INN | This rambling, sun-filled inn by the Aquinnah Cliffs stands alone on acres of moorland, a 10-minute walk from the beach. **Pros:** spectacular setting; extremely popular restaurant, open to the public, serves a nightly prix-fixe dinner in summer; service. **Cons:** far from bigger towns on island; steep rates; not suitable for young kids. ⑤ *Rooms from: $360* ✉ *81 Lighthouse Rd.* ☎ *508/645–3511* ⊕ *www.outermostinn.com* ☉ *Closed mid-Oct.–mid-May* ⤴ *7 rooms* ⦿ *Free breakfast.*

Nantucket

At the height of its prosperity in the early 19th century, the little island of Nantucket was the foremost whaling port in the world. Its harbor bustled with whaling ships and merchant vessels; chandleries, cooperages, and other shops crowded the wharves. Burly ship hands loaded barrels of whale oil onto wagons, which they wheeled along cobblestone streets to refineries and candle factories. Sea breezes carried the smoke and smells of booming industry through town as its inhabitants eagerly took care of business. Shipowners and sea captains built elegant mansions, which today remain remarkably unchanged, thanks to a very strict building code initiated in the 1950s. The entire town of Nantucket is now an official National Historic District encompassing more than 800 pre-1850 structures within 1 square mile.

Day-trippers usually take in the architecture and historical sites, dine at one of the many delightful restaurants, and browse in the pricey boutiques, most of which stay open mid-April–December. Signature items include Nantucket lightship baskets, originally crafted by sailors whiling away a long watch; artisans who continue the tradition now command prices of $700 and up, and antiques are exponentially more expensive.

GETTING ORIENTED

Nantucket is a boomerang-shape island 26 miles southeast of Hyannis on Cape Cod, and 107 miles southeast of Boston. Its nearest neighbor to the west is the somewhat larger island of Martha's Vineyard; eastward, the nearest landfall would be the Azores off Portugal. The island has only one town, which also goes by the name of Nantucket. The only other community of note is tiny Siasconset, a cluster of shingled seaside manses and lovingly restored fishing shacks 8 miles west of town. A 3-mile main road directly south of town leads to Surfside

Beach, among the island's most popular. Nantucket's small but busy airport is located east of Surfside.

Nantucket Town. As the ferry terminal—from Hyannis and, seasonally, Martha's Vineyard—Nantucket Town is the hub of all activity and the starting point for most visits. At the height of summer, its narrow cobblestone streets are in a constant state of near-gridlock. The town itself is easily walkable, and bikes are available for exploring.

Siasconset and Wauwinet. An allee of green lawns leads to the exclusive summer community of Siasconset (or 'Sconset, as locals say). Tucked away on either side of the village center are warrens of tiny, rose-covered cottages, some of them centuries old. About 5 miles northwest is the even tinier community of Wauwinet, which boasts the country's second-oldest yacht club.

GETTING HERE AND AROUND

Year-round flight service to Nantucket from Boston and Hyannis is provided by Cape Air and Nantucket Airlines. American Airlines offers seasonal service to the island from Washington, D.C., Philadelphia, and New York's LaGuardia; from Newark Airport, American Airlines also provides seasonal service.

Arriving by ferry puts you in the center of town, and several ferry companies offer service to Nantucket from two different ports, either year-round or seasonally. You can board in Hyannis (Hy-Line, Steamship Authority) or Harwich Port (Freedom Cruise Line). The only company that carries cars is Steamship Authority; car service is very expensive, and reservations must be made far in advance.

There is little need for a car here to explore; ample public transportation and smoothly paved bike paths can take you to the further reaches with ease. The Nantucket Regional Transit Authority (NRTA) runs shuttle buses from in town to most areas of the island. Service is

Nantucket

Nantucket Sound

Great Point Light

Coskata

TO MARTHA'S VINEYARD (SUMMER ONLY)

TO HYANNIS

Nantucket Harbor

Coatue

Wauwinet

Wauwinet Rd.

Jetties Beach

First Congregational Church

Quidnet Rd.

Quidnet

Polpis

Sesachacha Pond

Eel Point

Dionis Beach

Brant Point Lighthouse

Eel Point Rd.

Cliff Rd.

Children's Beach

Altar Rock

Polpis Rd.

Madaket Rd.

Whaling Museum

Nantucket Town

Siasconset ('Sconset) Beach

Madaket

Long Pond

Polpis Rd.

Milestone Rd.

Old South Rd.

Surfside Rd.

Siasconset

Madaket Beach

Hummock Pond Rd.

Bartlett Farm Rd.

Miacomet Pond

New South Rd.

Tom Nevers Rd.

Cisco Beach

Miacomet Beach

Nantucket Memorial Airport

Surfside Beach

ATLANTIC OCEAN

0 ————— 4 miles
0 ————— 6 km

---

generally available late May–mid-October. If you're still determined to rent a car while on Nantucket, book early—and expect to spend at least $95 a day during high season. If your car is low-slung, don't attempt the dirt roads. Some are deeply pocked with puddles, and some are virtual sandpits, challenging even to four-wheel-drive vehicles.

VISITOR INFORMATION
CONTACTS Nantucket Chamber of Commerce ☎ 508/228–1700 ⊕ www.nantucketchamber.org. **Nantucket Visitor Services and Information Bureau** ☎ 508/228–0925 ⊕ www.nantucket-ma.gov.

Nantucket Town

30 miles southeast of Hyannis, 107 miles southeast of Boston.

★ After the Great Fire of 1846 leveled all its wooden buildings, Main Street was widened to prevent future flames from hopping across the street. The cobblestone thoroughfare has a harmonious symmetry: the Pacific Club anchors its foot, and the Pacific National Bank, another redbrick building, squares off the head. The cobblestones were brought to the island as ballast in returning ships and laid to prevent the wheels of carts heavily laden with whale oil from sinking into the dirt. At the center of Lower Main is an old horse trough, today overflowing with flowers. From here the street gently rises; at the bank it narrows to its prefire width and leaves the commercial district for an area of mansions that escaped the blaze.

TOURS

⭐ **Nantucket Historical Association** (*NHA*)

BUILDING | This association maintains an assortment of venerable properties in town. A $20 pass gets you into all of the association's sites, including the glorious Whaling Museum. A cheaper $6 pass excludes the Whaling Museum but includes the Oldest House, Old Mill, Old Gaol, Greater Light, and the Fire Hose Cart House. Reserve in advance for two very popular walking tours, which depart daily late May–early November: a 60-minute downtown tour and an 80-minute historic house tour. Both cost $10. ⊠ *13 Broad St., Nantucket* ☎ *508/228–1894* ⊕ *www.nha.org.*

Sights

African Meeting House

HISTORIC SITE | When the island abolished slavery in 1773, Nantucket became a destination for free blacks and escaping slaves. The African Meeting House was built in the 1820s as a schoolhouse, and it functioned as such until 1846, when the island's schools were integrated. A complete restoration has returned the site to its authentic 19th-century appearance. Next door is the late-18th-century Florence Higginbotham house, originally purchased by Seneca Boston, a former slave and weaver. ⊠ *29 York St., Nantucket* ☎ *508/228–9833* ⊕ *maah. org* ⊠ *$10.*

Brant Point Light

LIGHTHOUSE | The promontory where this 26-foot-tall, white-painted beauty stands offers views of the harbor and town. The point was once the site of the second-oldest lighthouse in the country (1746); the present, much-photographed light was built in 1901. There are no tours inside the lighthouse, but the grounds are open to the public. ⊠ *End of Easton St., across footbridge, Nantucket.*

First Congregational Church

RELIGIOUS SITE | The tower of this church provides the best view of Nantucket—for those willing to climb its 94 steps. Rising 120 feet, the tower is capped by a weather vane depicting a whale catch. Peek in at the church's 1852 trompe-l'oeil ceiling. ⊠ *62 Centre St., Nantucket* ☎ *508/228–0950* ⊕ *www.nantucketfcc. org* ⊠ *Tower tour $5.*

⭐ Whaling Museum

HISTORIC SITE | **FAMILY** | With exhibits that include a fully rigged whaleboat and a skeleton of a 46-foot sperm whale, this must-see museum—a complex that includes a restored 1846 spermaceti candle factory—offers a crash course in the island's colorful history. Items on display include harpoons and other whale-hunting implements; portraits of whaling captains and their wives (a few of whom went whaling as well); the South Seas curiosities they brought home; a large collection of sailors' crafts; a full-size tryworks once used to process whale oil; and the original 16-foot-high 1850 lens from Sankaty Head Lighthouse. The Children's Discovery Room provides interactive-learning opportunities. Be sure to climb—or take the elevator—up to the observation deck for a view of the harbor. ⊠ *13–15 Broad St., Nantucket* ☎ *508/228–1894* ⊕ *www. nha.org* ⊠ *$20, includes other historic sites* ☉ *Closed Jan.–Mar.*

Beaches

Jetties Beach

BEACH—SIGHT | **FAMILY** | A short bike or shuttle-bus ride from town, Jetties Beach is popular with families because of its calm surf. It's also a good place to try out kayaks and sailboards. The shore is a lively scene, with a playground and volleyball nets on the beach and adjacent public tennis courts. There is a boardwalk to the beach (special wheelchairs are available). You'll have a good view of passing ferries—and an even better one if you

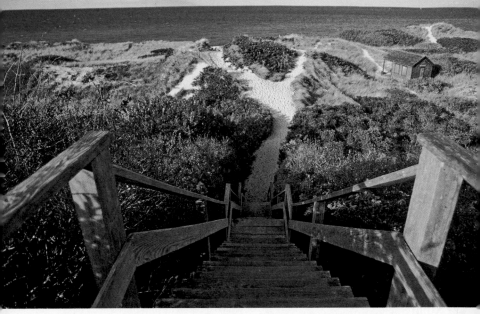

Each beach on Nantucket has a unique approach—sometimes getting there is half the fun.

clamber out on the jetty itself. (Careful, it's slippery.) **Amenities**: food and drink; lifeguards; parking (fee); showers; toilets; water sports. **Best for**: swimming; windsurfing. ⊠ *Bathing Beach Rd., 1½ miles northwest of Straight Wharf, Nantucket.*

★ Surfside Beach

BEACH—SIGHT | Surfside Beach, accessible via the Surfside Bike Path (3 miles) or by shuttle bus, is the island's most popular surf beach. This wide strand of sand comes fully equipped with conveniences. It draws teens and young adults as well as families and is great for kite flying and, after 5 pm, surf casting. **Amenities**: food and drink; lifeguards; parking (fee); showers; toilets. **Best for**: surfing; swimming; walking. ⊠ *Surfside Rd., South Shore.*

🍴 Restaurants

Brotherhood of Thieves

$$$ | AMERICAN | FAMILY | No, it's not really an 1840s whaling bar—though the atmospheric basement, which dates all the way back to 1972, presents a more convincing front than the newer, spiffier upper floors, which attract families and friendly singles alike. A swanky lounge offers a tapas menu, along with a large and varied wine and craft beer selection; outside seating is a delight under the canopy of trailing vines and foliage. **Known for:** juicy burgers and signature curly fries; reasonably priced meals; appealing shared plates menu. ⑤ *Average main: $26* ⊠ *23 Broad St., Nantucket* ☎ *508/228–2551* ⊕ *www.brotherhoodofthieves.com.*

Fog Island Café

$ | AMERICAN | FAMILY | Cherished year-round for its exceptional breakfasts, Fog Island is just as fine a spot for lunch. The storefront space is cheerily decked out in a fresh country style, and chef-owners Mark and Anne Dawson—both Culinary Institute of America grads—seem determined to provide the best possible service to visitors and locals alike. **Known for:** exceptional breakfasts like huevos rancheros; ample portions; reasonable prices. ⑤ *Average main: $14* ⊠ *7 S. Water St., Nantucket* ☎ *508/228–1818* ⊕ *www.fogisland.com* ⊘ *No dinner. No lunch Sun.*

Lola 41 degrees

$$$$ | **ECLECTIC** | The menu at Lola features items from countries on the 41st parallel like Japan and Italy—believe us when we say everywhere this restaurant ventures is good. The place started out as (and remains) a superpopular watering hole for the chic set. **Known for:** sushi and sake; specialty cocktails; hopping scene for young sophisticates. $ *Average main: $38* ⊠ *15 S. Beach St., Nantucket* 📞 *508/325–4001* ⊕ *www.lola41.com* ⊗ *No lunch mid-Apr.–mid-Oct.*

The Pearl

$$$$ | **ASIAN** | With its white onyx bar illuminated a Curaçao blue and its walls awash in flowing voile, this ultracool space would seem right at home in South Beach. Asian-themed selections focus on local shellfish and seafood with some very rewarding results. **Known for:** wok-fried lobster; specialty cocktails; sophisticated scene. $ *Average main: $39* ⊠ *12 Federal St., Nantucket* 📞 *508/228–9701* ⊕ *www.thepearlnantucket.com* ⊗ *Closed Jan.–Apr. No lunch.*

★ Straight Wharf

$$$$ | **MODERN AMERICAN** | This loftlike restaurant with a harborside deck has enjoyed legendary status since the mid-1970s; the couple now in command—Gabriel Frasca and Amanda Lydon—have lent this venerable institution a more barefoot air, appropriate to the place and season, and are intense champions of local crops and catches. Hurricane lamps lend a soft glow to well-spaced tables lined with butcher paper, and dish towels serve as napkins. **Known for:** menu changes daily; locally sourced ingredients; outdoor seating with water view. $ *Average main: $42* ⊠ *6 Harbor Sq., Nantucket* 📞 *508/228–4499* ⊕ *www.straightwharfrestaurant.com* ⊗ *Closed mid-Oct.–mid-May.*

Hotels

Jared Coffin House

$$$ | **B&B/INN** | The largest house in town when it was built in 1845, this three-story brick manse is still plenty impressive. **Pros:** knowledgeable concierge; in-town location; historical setting. **Cons:** some tiny rooms; street noise in front. $ *Rooms from: $345* ⊠ *29 Broad St., Nantucket* 📞 *508/228–2400* ⊕ *www.jaredcoffinhouse.com* ⊐ *54 rooms* ⏹ *Free breakfast.*

★ The Nantucket Hotel and Resort

$$$$ | **RESORT** | **FAMILY** | The original impressive 19th-century shell remains, though its interior is sleek, gleaming, and crisp, with a blend of calming neutrals and navy. **Pros:** immaculate and large rooms, many with kitchens; ideal for families; full-service restaurant. **Cons:** can be noisy in summer; five-minute walk to town; many children in summer. $ *Rooms from: $575* ⊠ *77 Easton St., Nantucket* 📞 *508/228–4747, 866/807–6011* ⊕ *www.thenantuckethotel.com* ⊗ *Closed Feb.* ⊐ *42 rooms, 2 cottages* ⏹ *Free breakfast.*

Ships Inn

$$ | **B&B/INN** | This 1831 home exudes history: it was built for whaling captain Obed Starbuck on the site of the birthplace of abolitionist Lucretia Mott. **Pros:** large rooms; handsome decor; ideal in-town location. **Cons:** on busy street; not for those traveling with small children (under nine). $ *Rooms from: $250* ⊠ *13 Fair St., Nantucket* 📞 *508/228–0040* ⊕ *www.shipsinnnantucket.com* ⊗ *Closed late Oct.–late May* ⊐ *10 rooms* ⏹ *Free breakfast.*

★ Union Street Inn

$$$$ | **B&B/INN** | Ken Withrow worked in the hotel business, Deborah Withrow in high-end retail display, and guests get the best of both worlds in this 1770 house, a stone's throw from the bustle of Main Street. **Pros:** pampering by pros; several rooms have a wood-burning fireplace;

Cranberry harvest season begins around Labor Day and usually runs into November.

impeccable design. **Cons:** bustle of town; some small rooms; not for those with children. ⑤ *Rooms from: $589* ✉ *7 Union St., Nantucket* ☎ *888/517–0707* ⊕ *www.unioninn.com* ⊘ *Closed Nov.–late Apr., except for Christmas stroll weekend in early Dec.* ⇨ *12 rooms* ❍ *Free breakfast.*

Ⓨ Nightlife

Chicken Box (*The Box*)
MUSIC CLUBS | Live music—including some big-name bands—plays six nights a week in season, and weekends year-round. ✉ *16 Dave St., Nantucket* ☎ *508/228–9717* ⊕ *www.thechickenbox.com.*

Muse
BARS/PUBS | This is a year-round venue hosting live bands, including the occasional big-name act. The crowd—the barnlike space can accommodate nearly 400—can get pretty wild. There's also an eatery serving great pizza, burgers, and other bar-type snacks. ✉ *44 Surfside Rd., Nantucket* ☎ *508/228–6873* ⊕ *www.themusenantucket.com.*

🎭 Performing Arts

Dreamland
CULTURAL FESTIVALS | Originally built in 1832 as a Quaker meetinghouse, this gem has been fully restored and is now home to year-round entertainment and enrichment. Current movies are shown here, as well as live theater, comedy, and other performing arts. Theater workshops are available for all ages. ✉ *17 S. Water St., Nantucket* ☎ *508/228–1784, 508/332–4822* ⊕ *www.nantucketdreamland.org.*

🏃 Activities

BICYCLING
The best way to tour Nantucket is by bicycle. Nearly 30 miles of paved bike paths wind through all types of terrain from one end of the island to the other: for details, consult the maps posted by Wheels, Heels, and Pedals (⊕ *www.wheelsheelsandpedals.com*), which supports alternative modes of transportation. It is possible to bike around the

entire island in a day; should you tire, however, you and your bike are welcome aboard the in-season Nantucket Regional Transit Authority (NRTA) buses. The main bike routes start within ½ mile of town. ⚠ **That first stretch can be dauntingly congested.** All routes are well marked and lead—eventually—to popular beaches. The paths are also perfect for runners and bladers—but not mopeds, which must remain on the road (to the frustration of impatient drivers). Note that Nantucket requires bike riders 12 and under to wear a helmet. Several shorter spurs connecting popular routes have been continuously added in the island's quest to make Nantucket even more bike-friendly. ■ **TIP→ There are multiple bike rental outfits downtown, very close to the ferry terminal; most offer delivery to lodging per request.**

The easy 2.2-mile **Surfside Bike Path** leads to Surfside, the island's premier ocean beach. A drinking fountain and rest stop are placed at about the halfway point. The **Milestone Bike Path,** a straight shot linking Nantucket Town and 'Sconset, is probably the most monotonous of the paths but can still be quite pleasant. (It's about 6 miles; paired with the scenic Polpis Road Path, it becomes a 16-mile island loop.) The **Old South Road Bike Path** spurs off from the Milestone Rotary and ends about 1½ miles later close to the airport. At 1.2 miles, the **Cliff Road Path,** on the north shore, is one of the easiest bike paths, but it's still quite scenic, with gentle hills. It intersects with the Eel Point and Madaket paths.

The **Eel Point/Dionis Beach Path** starts at the junction of Eel Point Road and Madaket Road and links the Cliff Road and Madaket bike paths to Dionis Beach; it's less than a mile long. The 9-mile **Polpis Road Path** skirts scenic bays and bogs as it wends its way toward 'Sconset; it intersects with Milestone Path east of the rotary. The **Madaket Path** starts at the intersection of Quaker and Upper Main Streets and follows Madaket Road out to

Madaket Beach on the island's west end, about 6 miles from the edge of Nantucket Town. About a third of the way along, you could turn off onto Cliff Road Path or the Eel Point/Dionis Beach Path.

BOATING
Nantucket Community Sailing

BOATING | FAMILY | Renting sailboats, sailboards, and kayaks at Jetties Beach, NCS also offers youth and adult sailing classes and water-sport clinics for disabled athletes. Its Outrigger Canoe Club—a Polynesian tradition—heads out several evenings a week in season. ⊠ *Jetties Beach, Bathing Beach Rd., Nantucket* ☎ *508/228–6600 ⊕ www.nantucketcommunitysailing.org.*

Shopping

Much of the appeal of Nantucket is its concentrated downtown area, all of it easily walkable—just watch your step along the lumpy historic cobblestones. Shoppers will find many high-end stores here, offering up elegant housewares, art, jewelry, upscale women and men's clothing, and many things that Nantucket holds dear: whale belts, "Nantucket Reds," Nantucket baskets, and all things maritime and nautical. The annual Christmas Stroll (⊕ *christmasstroll.com*) during the first weekend in December is still a popular time, when shops stay open late and offer refreshments, but it's more than just a holiday shopping event now.

LIQUOR
Cisco Brewers

WINE/SPIRITS | The microconglomerate of Cisco Brewers, Nantucket Vineyard, and Triple Eight Distillery makes boutique beers, wine, and vodka on-site. Tours and tastings are available (fee) and there is regular live music starting in the late afternoon. There is no food here; you are encouraged to bring a picnic or some snacks to go with the libations. ⊠ *5 Bartlett Farm Rd., Nantucket* ☎ *508/325–5929 ⊕ www.ciscobrewers.com.*

MARKETS
★ Bartlett's Farm
OUTDOOR/FLEA/GREEN MARKETS | Bartlett's Farm encompasses 100 acres overseen by eighth-generation Bartletts. Healthy, tasty prepared foods—within a minisupermarket—are added incentive to make the trek out. If you're not up it, however, a produce truck is parked on Main Street through the summer. ⊠ *33 Bartlett Farm Rd., Nantucket* ☎ *508/228–9403* ⊕ *www. bartlettsfarm.com.*

Siasconset

7 miles east of Nantucket Town.

First a fishing outpost and then an artists' colony—Broadway actors favored it in the late 19th century—Siasconset (or 'Sconset, in local vernacular) is a charming cluster of rose-covered cottages linked by driveways of crushed clamshells; at the edges of town, the former fishing shacks give way to magnificent sea-view mansions. The small town center consists of a market, post office, café, lunchroom, and a combination liquor store–lending library.

Sights

Altar Rock
VIEWPOINT | A dirt track leads to the island's highest point, Altar Rock (101 feet), and the view is spectacular. The hill overlooks approximately 4,000 acres of rare coastal heathland laced with paths leading in every direction. ⊠ *Altar Rock Rd., 3 miles west of Milestone Rd. rotary on Polpis Rd., Siasconset.*

Restaurants

Topper's
$$$$ | **MODERN AMERICAN** | The Wauwinet, a lavishly restored 19th-century inn on Nantucket's northeastern shore, is where islanders and visitors alike go to experience utmost luxury—and that includes the food. In the creamy-white dining room, awash in lush linens and glorious flowers, you can choose from a three-course prix-fixe menu ($95) or order à la carte, and more casual fare is on offer out on the deck. **Known for:** vast wine list; atmospheric experience; boat taxi from town to restaurant and back. $ *Average main: $48* ⊠ *The Wauwinet, 120 Wauwinet Rd., Wauwinet* ☎ *508/228–8768* ⊕ *www.wauwinet.com* ⊙ *Closed Nov.– Apr. No dinner Sun.*

Hotels

★ The Wauwinet
$$$$ | **RESORT** | This resplendently updated 1850 resort straddles a "haulover" poised between ocean and bay (think beaches on both sides); it features cushy country-chic guest rooms (lavish with Pratesi linens) and a splendid restaurant, Topper's. **Pros:** the staff-to-guest ratio exceeds one-to-one; dual beaches; peaceful setting. **Cons:** not for those with small children; distance from town; overly chichi. $ *Rooms from: $925* ⊠ *120 Wauwinet Rd., Wauwinet* ☎ *508/228– 0145* ⊕ *www.wauwinet.com* ⊙ *Closed Nov.–Apr.* ⌑ *32 rooms, 4 cottages* ○ *Free breakfast.*

Activities

BIKING
'Sconset Bike Path
BICYCLING | This 6½-mile bike path starts at the rotary east of Nantucket Town and parallels Milestone Road, ending in 'Sconset. It is mostly level, with some gentle hills. Slightly longer (and dippier), the 9-mile **Polpis Road Path,** veering off to the northeast, is far more scenic and leads to the turnoff to Wauwinet. ⊠ *Off Milestone Rd., Siasconset.*

Chapter 6

THE BERKSHIRES AND WESTERN MASSACHUSETTS

6

Updated by
Seth Brown

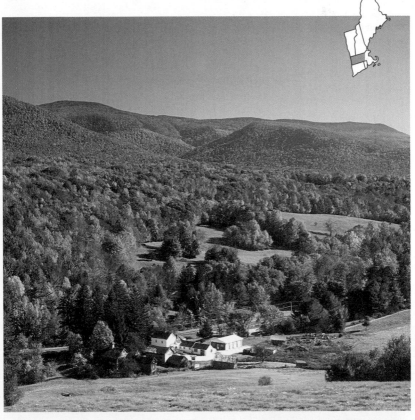

👁 **Sights**
★★★★☆

🍴 **Restaurants**
★★★★☆

🛏 **Hotels**
★★★★☆

🛍 **Shopping**
★★★★☆

🍸 **Nightlife**
★★☆☆☆

WELCOME TO THE BERKSHIRES AND WESTERN MASSACHUSETTS

TOP REASONS TO GO

★ **The Countryside:** Rolling hills, dense stands of forest, open pastures, and scenic valleys greet your eye at every turn.

★ **Early American History:** Visit preserved villages, homes, and inns, where memories of Colonial history and personalities are kept alive.

★ **Summer Festivals:** Watch renowned dance companies perform against a Berkshire backdrop at Jacob's Pillow, or listen to the Boston Symphony Orchestra at Tanglewood in Lenox.

★ **Under-the-Radar Museums:** Western Massachusetts has an eclectic assortment of institutions, from the Eric Carle Museum of Picture Book Art to the Basketball Hall of Fame.

★ **Pioneer Valley College Towns:** Three academic centers—Amherst (University of Massachusetts, Amherst College, and Hampshire College), Northampton (Smith College), and South Hadley (Mount Holyoke College)—pulse with cultural activity and youthful energy.

1 North Adams. The ideal Berkshires getaway location is home to the Massachusetts Museum of Contemporary Arts.

2 Williamstown. Built around the prestigious Williams College, this town has two noteworthy art museums and the renowned Williamstown Theatre Festival.

3 Hancock. A great location for year-round outdoor enthusiasts, it's also the closest town to the ski and snowboard resort, Jiminy Peak.

4 Pittsfield. This busy little city is home to the Hancock Shaker Village, a living history museum with restored buildings, crafts, and activities.

5 Lenox. The famed Tanglewood music festival takes up residence every summer.

6 Stockbridge. A quintessential New England town that even Norman Rockwell called home.

7 Great Barrington. A great place for delicious food and antique hunting.

8 Springfield. The city's home to the Naismith Memorial Basketball Hall of Fame and the Springfield Museums, which includes the Amazing World of Dr. Seuss.

9 Sturbridge. A re-created early-19th-century village, Old Sturbridge Village is the area's premier attraction.

10 South Hadley. A quiet college town home to Mount Holyoke College.

11 Northampton. The cultural hub of Western Massachusetts is also home to Smith College.

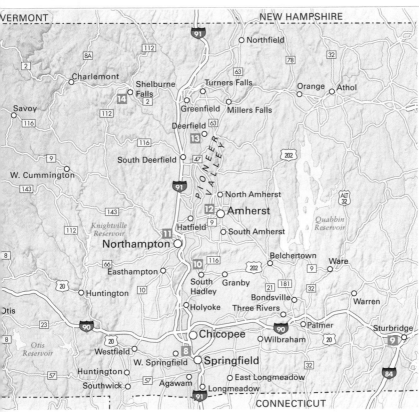

12 Amherst. A mecca for world-renowned authors, poets, and artists, Amherst is also known for its trio of colleges: Amherst, Hampshire, and the University of Massachusetts.

13 Deerfield. The perfect New England village complete with a white-steepled church and perfectly maintained 18th-century homes.

14 Shelburne Falls. The community is filled with art galleries, shops, and farm stands.

The Bay State's most westerly portion consists of the Berkshires, a bucolic highland region filled with winding mountain roads, and the Pioneer Valley, home to the elite "Five College Consortium": Amherst, Hampshire, Mount Holyoke, Smith, and UMass Amherst. In addition to their natural advantages, the area supports dynamic cultural venues and risk-taking restaurants.

The burgeoning Berkshires arts community arose from the ruins of a manufacturing economy—aging mills having been converted into artist lofts and a former electric plant morphing into a contemporary art museum. Smaller museums can be found throughout the region, and you can view the creations of its myriad artists and craftspeople at their studios or in local galleries. Hikers, from the casual wanderer to the intrepid trailblazer, also have plenty to experience. In autumn, leaf peepers descend to explore this area renowned for fall foliage whose vibrant oranges, yellows, and reds typify the harvest season.

Though it might be presumptuous to proclaim a "renaissance," it can't be denied that the concentration of arts and culture in the Berkshires has reinvigorated the whole region. Following the artistic explosion, boutique shopping and international cuisine have transformed a formerly depressed postindustrial area into a hot spot for festivals celebrating everything from ice sculptures to the spoken word. The trend continues in the Pioneer Valley, especially in college towns like Northampton, propelled forward by the youthful energy of a large student population.

MAJOR REGIONS

Occupying the far western end of the state, **the Berkshires** are only about three hours by car from Boston or New York City, yet the region lives up to the storybook picture of rural New England: wooded hills, narrow winding roads, fall foliage, and quaint downtowns. Skiing is popular in winter—**Hancock** is the closest village to Jiminy Peak—and sugar-maple sap runs in the spring. Summer brings cultural events, like the renowned Tanglewood classical music festival in **Lenox,** the theater festival in **Williamstown,** and the Jacob's Pillow Dance Festival in Becket. Norman Rockwell called **Stockbridge** home, the Hancock Shaker Village is in **Pittsfield,** and **North Adams** has the Massachusetts Museum of Contemporary Arts. **Great Barrington** has great food and antique shops.

Overshadowed somewhat by Boston to the east and the Berkshires to the west, **the Pioneer Valley** is home to historic settlements, unique museums, college towns, and natural treasures. **Sturbridge's** Old Sturbridge Village—a re-created early-19th-century village with restored buildings, reenactments, and activities—is the premier attraction here. The principal city here is **Springfield,** home to the Naismith Memorial Basketball Hall of Fame and the family-friendly Springfield Museums, but most of the area is quite rural—this is where the idyllic New England countryside of the imagination comes to life. College towns like **South Hadley, Northampton,** and **Amherst** serve as cultural hubs that have attracted former city dwellers who relish the ample natural scenery, sophisticated cultural venues, and lively dining and shopping. The picturesque towns of **Deerfield** and **Shelburne Falls** draw visitors for foliage and history tours.

Planning

WHEN TO GO

The dazzling foliage and cool temperatures make fall the best time to visit Western Massachusetts, but the Berkshires and the Pioneer Valley are evolving into a year-round destination. Visit in spring, and witness the burst of color that signals winter's end. Summer is a time of festivals, adventure sports, and outdoor concerts. Many towns save their best for winter, when inns open their doors to carolers and shops serve eggnog. Though usually considered the off-season, it's the perfect time to try cross-country skiing or to spend a night by the fireplace, tucked under a quilt while catching up on books by Nathaniel Hawthorne or Henry David Thoreau.

GETTING HERE AND AROUND
AIR TRAVEL

Most travelers arrive at Boston's Logan International Airport, the state's major airline hub. From Boston you can reach most parts of the Pioneer Valley in less than two hours by car, the Berkshires in about three.

Bradley International Airport in Windsor Locks, Connecticut, 18 miles south of Springfield, Massachusetts, on Interstate 91, serves the Pioneer Valley and the Berkshires. Another alternative—and actually closer to the area than Logan—is T.F. Green International Airport in Providence, Rhode Island.

CAR TRAVEL

Public transportation can be spotty in this region, with buses that don't run on Sunday or in the evening, so you'll almost certainly need a car. But you'll want one anyway so you can take leisurely drives to see the fall foliage. Be warned, though, that the winding mountain roads here are not for the fainthearted.

TRAIN TRAVEL

The Northeast Corridor and high-speed Acela services of Amtrak link Boston with the principal cities between it and Washington, D.C. Amtrak's *Lake Shore Limited,* which stops at Springfield and Pittsfield in the Berkshires, carries passengers from Chicago to Boston. For destinations north and west of Boston, trains depart from Boston's North Station.

RESTAURANTS

At country inns in the Southern Berkshires and the Pioneer Valley, you can find dishes strongly reminiscent of old England—double-cut pork chops, rack of lamb, and game—as well as traditional New England fare like Boston baked beans, Indian pudding, and the dubiously glorified "New England boiled dinner" (slow-boiled meat and vegetables). For those who come to the Berkshires for a taste of history, you'll find plenty of it on the menu.

If you prefer more creative contemporary fare, though, you will not be disappointed. Modern cafés and trendy restaurants serving everything from fusion cuisine to pizza with inspired toppings also do business here.

HOTELS

The signature accommodation outside Boston is the country inn; in the Berkshires, where magnificent mansions have been converted into luxury lodgings, these inns have reached a very grand scale indeed. Less extravagant and less expensive are bed-and-breakfast establishments, many in private homes. Make reservations for inns well ahead during peak periods (summer through winter in the Berkshires). Smoking is banned in all Massachusetts hotels.

Campers can pitch their tents amid acres of pine forest dotted with rivers and lakes or in the shadows of the rolling Berkshire Hills. The camping season in Massachusetts generally runs late May–mid-October. For more about camping, contact the Massachusetts Department of Conservation and Recreation (☎ 617/626–1250 ⊕ www.mass.gov/portal/transportation-recreation/camping/). *Hotel reviews have been shortened. For full information, visit Fodors.com.*

What It Costs

	$	$$	$$$	$$$$
RESTAURANTS				
	under $18	$18–$24	$25–$35	over $35
HOTELS				
	under $200	$200– $299	$300– $399	over $399

ESSENTIALS

TRANSIT INFORMATION Amtrak
☎ 800/872–7245 ⊕ www.amtrak. com. **Berkshire Regional Transit Authority** ☎ 800/292–2782, 413/499–2782 ⊕ www. berkshirerta.com.

VISITOR INFORMATION Massachusetts Department of Fish and Game ☎ 617/626–1500 ⊕ www.mass.gov/eea/agencies/dfg. **Massachusetts Office of Travel & Tourism** ☎ 617/973–8500 ⊕ www.massvacation.com. **1Berkshire** ☎ 413/499–1600, 413/743–4500 ⊕ www.berkshires.org.

North Adams

130 miles northwest of Boston; 73 miles northwest of Springfield; 20 miles south of Bennington, Vermont.

If you're looking for a Berkshires getaway that combines culture with outdoor fun and a cool place to stay, put North Adams on your short list. In addition to the Massachusetts Museum of Contemporary Arts (Mass MoCA), North Adams has a number of smaller art galleries, as well as a few mills and factory buildings that have been converted into artist studios. The Porches Inn, a row of eye-catching multihue Victorians, has added "hip" to downtown. The 11-mile Ashuwillticook Rail Trail is accessible in nearby Adams, as is Mt. Greylock State Reservation, if you venture there on foot via one of the local trailheads.

GETTING HERE AND AROUND

Arrive North Adams from Pittsfield in the south via Route 8, or from Williamstown in the west via Route 2. Once in town you can see everything on foot in good weather, with most of the action within a few blocks of Main Street. Natural Bridge State Park is the exception, but it's still a reasonable walk.

Sights

Down Street Art

ARTS VENUE | FAMILY | This public-arts project includes 31 galleries in downtown North Adams. From late June through September, DSA presents visual and performing arts events including exhibitions, video screenings, site-specific installations, and, on the last Thursday of the month, opening galas and performances. ✉ 51 Main St. ☎ 413/663–5253 ⊕ www. downstreetart.org.

★ Massachusetts Museum of Contemporary Arts (*Mass MoCA*)

ARTS VENUE | FAMILY | Formerly the home of the Sprague Electrical Company, the nation's largest center for contemporary visual and performing arts is one of the finest such facilities in the world, a major draw for its art shows, music and dance presentations, and film screenings. Expansion in 2017 nearly doubled the amount of gallery space, bringing the total to a quarter million square feet, which includes the wall drawings of Sol LeWitt, an immersive light-based exhibit by James Turrell, sculptures from Louise Bourgeois, and a large room in the main gallery that allows for massive exhibits that wouldn't fit anywhere else. A Kidspace, studios, cafés, shops, and festivals and other special events round out the offerings. ⊠ *87 Marshall St.* 🕾 *413/662–2111* ⊕ *www. massmoca.org* 🖾 *$20 (2-day ticket).*

Natural Bridge State Park

NATIONAL/STATE PARK | The 30-foot span that gives this 48-acre park its name crosses Hudson Brook, yielding appealing views of rocky chasms. The marble arch at the park's center rises in what functioned as a marble quarry from the early 1880s to the mid-1900s. Natural Bridge has picnic sites, hiking trails, and well-maintained restrooms. In winter the area is popular for cross-country skiing. ⊠ *McCauley Rd., off Rte. 8* 🕾 *413/663– 6392* ⊕ *www.mass.gov/locations/ natural-bridge-state-park.*

Susan B. Anthony Birthplace Museum

MUSEUM | This museum celebrates the extraordinary life and legacy of Susan B. Anthony, who played a pivotal role in winning women the right to vote. In addition to viewing suffrage mementos, you can learn about the abolition and temperance movements, in which she also participated. Definitely worth a look is the collection of 19th-century postcards supporting these three campaigns. ⊠ *67 East Rd., Adams* 🕾 *413/743–7121* ⊕ *www.susanbanthonybirthplace.com* 🖾 *$6* ⊘ *Closed Tues. and Wed.; also closed Thurs. Oct.–May.*

Western Gateway Heritage State Park

LOCAL INTEREST | **FAMILY** | The old Boston & Maine Railroad yard is the site of this park whose free museum has exhibits

that trace the construction of the Hoosac Tunnel and the impact of train travel on the region. A scale model of North Adams in the 1950s is on display, and there's a short film that documents the intense labor required to construct the nearby Hoosac Tunnel; the tunnel is best viewed from a pedestrian bridge one block from the park where you can see the tracks as they disappear into the tunnel. ⊠ *115 State St.* 🕾 *413/663–6312* ⊕ *www.mass.gov/locations/west- ern-gateway-heritage-state-park* 🖾 *Free* ⊘ *Museum closed Tues. and Wed. Nov.–Apr.*

Restaurants

Brewhaha

$ | **CAFÉ** | After moving to the historic West End Market in 2018, Brewhaha is no longer as convenient to Main Street but remains an excellent option for brunch or breakfast at any hour. The spacious interior with its open kitchen welcomes guests with ubiquitous world music and shelves of books that keep children (and adults) entertained while enjoying a coffee or grilled panini sandwich. **Known for:** variety of grilled muffins; cider chai; lack of parking. 🖇 *Average main: $9* ⊠ *437 W. Main St.* 🕾 *413/664–2020* ⊕ *www.cafebrewhaha. com* ⊘ *Closed Wed. No dinner.*

Gramercy Bistro

$$ | **FRENCH FUSION** | Within the Mass MoCA complex, the Edison bulbs and large windows that overlook the patio lend a comfortable atmosphere to this upscale-casual eatery that serves everything from chicken-liver mousse to seafood paella. Chef-owner Alexander Smith relies on organic meats and locally grown produce when possible, adding serious zip with sauces made from wasabi and saffron. **Known for:** Sunday brunch; sweet breads; chocolate desserts. 🖇 *Average main: $24* ⊠ *87 Marshall St.* 🕾 *413/663–5300* ⊕ *www.gramercybistro. com* ⊘ *Closed Tues. No lunch Mon.*

Jack's Hot Dog Stand

$ | **HOT DOG** | Not much has changed at this hole-in-the-wall including its single lunch counter lined with a small row of stools and its cash-only policy. Locals head here for inexpensive wieners and hamburgers, plain or topped with chili, cheese, or both, but don't expect to find a seat during lunch hour. **Known for:** a family-owned institution since 1917; onion rings and fries; hot-dog-eating contests. ⑤ *Average main: $3* ⊠ *12 Eagle St.* ☎ *413/664–9006* ⊕ *www.jackshotdogstand.com* ▭ *No credit cards* ◷ *Closed Sun.*

Meng's Pan-Asian

$ | **ASIAN** | Formerly known as Sushi House, this pan-Asian restaurant on the main drag offers up Chinese, Thai, Korean, and Japanese classics in a comfortable atmosphere. From curries and *bibim bap* to sushi and bento boxes, Meng's extensive menu has something for everyone, at an affordable price. **Known for:** pad see you; cheap lunch specials; half-price-sushi Tuesdays. ⑤ *Average main: $13* ⊠ *45 Main St.* ☎ *413/664–9388.*

 Hotels

★ Porches Inn

$$ | **B&B/INN** | Around the corner from Mass MoCA and Main Street, these Victorian mill-workers' houses dating to the 1890s have been restored and are connected with one long porch and some interior hallways walled with exteriors of the old houses to become one of New England's quirkiest hotels. **Pros:** outdoor heated pool and hot tub; large guest rooms; pet-friendly building available. **Cons:** small breakfast room; no indoor pool; not much indoor public space. ⑤ *Rooms from: $289* ⊠ *231 River St.* ☎ *413/664–0400* ⊕ *www.porches.com* ⌕ *47 rooms* ¡○¡ *Free breakfast.*

Topia Inn

$$ | **B&B/INN** | Innkeepers Nana Simopoulos and Caryn Heilman have transformed a derelict downtown building into an eco-friendly marvel, with solar panels and natural clay walls. **Pros:** artsy rooms; organic breakfasts; workshops on green cooking and cleaning. **Cons:** short on parking; next door to a bar; you can't bring your own nonorganic shampoos—it's a hotel rule. ⑤ *Rooms from: $275* ⊠ *10 Pleasant St., Adams* ☎ *413/743–9600* ⊕ *www.topiainn.com* ⌕ *8 rooms* ¡○¡ *Free breakfast.*

★ TOURISTS

$$ | **HOTEL** | This minimalist hotel has many oak-covered surfaces, a large fireplace in the rustic lobby, amazing views of Mt. Greylock from the patio deck and courtyard, and walking trails that lead guests to a suspension bridge, sound sculpture, and a restaurant. **Pros:** outdoor showers in every room; lanterns available for night hikes; some rooms have private balconies. **Cons:** no tubs in bathrooms; no phone in room; location is traffic heavy. ⑤ *Rooms from: $290* ⊠ *915 State Rd.* ☎ *413/346–4933* ⊕ *www.touristswelcome.com* ⌕ *48 rooms* ¡○¡ *No meals.*

 Activities

KAYAKING

Berkshire Outfitters

KAYAKING | If you're itching to explore the Cheshire lakes by kayak, the Ashuwillticook Rail Trail by bike, or Mt. Greylock's summit on snowshoes, visit Berkshire Outfitters. Just 300 yards from the trail, this shop rents bicycles, kayaks, canoes, paddleboards, snowshoes, and cross-country skis. The knowledgeable staff are happy to dispense free trail maps and advice. ⊠ *169 Grove St., Adams* ☎ *413/743–5900* ⊕ *www.berkshireoutfitters.com.*

Williamstown

5 miles west of North Adams.

Williamstown is largely built around the prestigious Williams College, a smallish but verdant campus bisected by Route 2. Williams is one of the "Little Ivies," and indeed there are ivy-covered buildings, a Gothic-style chapel, marble columns, and various other architectural features. Although "downtown" consists of just a few streets, two noteworthy art museums can be found near the town center, and there are enough upscale shops and restaurants offering international cuisine. In summertime, theatergoers replace college students for the **Williamstown Theatre Festival**; if you're lucky, you may catch a famous actor at a local bar.

GETTING HERE AND AROUND

Williamstown encompasses the surrounding farms and rolling hills, but the town proper straddles Route 2. On the Williams College campus you can walk to Spring Street and Water Street, and anything else you want to see is probably just a short drive off Route 2 (or you can a hop onto the BRTA bus).

Sights

★ Clark Art Institute

MUSEUM | One of the nation's notable small art museums, the Clark has won numerous architectural awards for its 2014 redesign by Reed Hilderbrand and for the new Clark Center by Pritzker Prize–winning architect Tadao Ando. The polished concrete of the latter visually connects it to the landscape through glass windows and open spaces. The museum has a large collection of Impressionist works, in particular many significant Renoir paintings. Other strengths include English silver, European and American photography 1840–1920, and 17th- and 18th-century Flemish and Dutch masterworks. ⊠ *225*

South St. ☎ *413/458–2303* ⊕ *www. clarkart.edu* ✉ *$20 (2-day ticket)* ◷ *Closed Mon. Sept.–June.*

★ Williams College Museum of Art

MUSEUM | FAMILY | The collection at this fine museum spans a range of eras and cultures, with American and 20th-century art two major focuses. The original octagonal structure facing Main Street was built as a library in 1846, and the painted wall above the stairs is by Sol LeWitt—actually the third mural to occupy the wall. Special events take place on the outdoor patio on Thursday night in summer. ⊠ *15 Lawrence Hall Dr.* ☎ *413/597–2376* ⊕ *wcma.williams. edu* ✉ *Free.*

Restaurants

A-Frame Bakery

$ | **BAKERY** | The tiny A-frame at the intersection of U.S. 7 and Route 2 isn't much to look at, but the bakery within sells delectable goods that inspire loyalty in locals and visitors alike. The babka—especially the chocolate, though there's also a cinnamon edition—is second to none and must be ordered a day ahead. **Known for:** crumb cakes; many items need to be ordered a day in advance; buttercream frosting. ⑤ *Average main: $3* ⊠ *1194 Cold Spring Rd.* ☎ *413/458–3600* ◷ *Closed Mon. and Tues.* ▭ *No credit cards.*

★ Coyote Flaco

$ | **MEXICAN** | The best Mexican food in the Berkshires can be found at this unassuming spot where traditional cuisine meets local ingredients. The menu is small but every item is done well, and often served with side dishes in cute little tortilla cups. **Known for:** Enchilada Oaxaca with mole sauce; delicious margaritas; nightly specials. ⑤ *Average main: $16* ⊠ *505 Cold Spring Rd.* ☎ *413/458–4240* ⊕ *www.coyoteflacomass.com* ◷ *Closed Mon.*

Winslow Homer's *West Point, Prout's Neck* is among the notable paintings at Williamstown's Clark Art Institute.

Mezze Bistro & Bar

$$$ | ECLECTIC | With a beautiful hilltop location and charming grounds, the bistro can get crowded in summer, when everyone wants to rub elbows with stars from the Williamstown Theatre Festival. With an emphasis on local and seasonal ingredients, the menu is always in a state of flux, but it's bound to contain steak, duck, and the like. **Known for:** hen-of-the-woods mushrooms; Garganelli pasta with beef ragu; smallish portions. ⑤ *Average main: $27* ✉ *777 Cold Spring Rd.* ☎ *413/458–0123* ⊕ *www.mezzeres-taurant.com* ⊙ *No lunch.*

'6 House Pub

$$ | AMERICAN | Set in an old cow barn, this rustic, wood-paneled pub has buckets of character and an interesting array of antiques and upholstered furniture— you can nestle into an old wing chair to dine if you like. The extensive menu runs the gamut from traditional pub food to upscale vegetarian fare, so whether you want burrata ravioli or just a burger, there are plenty of options, including daily specials. **Known for:** lobster mac and cheese; Sunday brunch; fire pit on patio on summer nights. ⑤ *Average main: $19* ✉ *1896 House Inn, 910 Cold Spring Rd.* ☎ *413/458–1896, 888/999–1896* ⊕ *www.6housepub.com* ⊙ *No lunch Mon.–Thurs. Oct.–Apr.*

Hotels

Guest House at Field Farm

$ | B&B/INN | Built in 1948, this guest-house contains a fine collection of art on loan from Williams College and the Whitney Museum, as well as lobby that wouldn't be out of place on a 1960s movie set. **Pros:** wonderful art collection; luxurious robes and towels; seasonal swimming pool. **Cons:** no TV in rooms; children under 12 not permitted; off the beaten path. ⑤ *Rooms from: $195* ✉ *554 Sloan Rd.* ☎ *413/458–3135* ⊕ *www. guesthouseatfieldfarm.org* ⊙ *Closed Jan.–Mar.* ⇝ *6 rooms* ⚬ *Free breakfast.*

Orchards Hotel

$$ | HOTEL | Although it's near Route 2 and surrounded by parking lots, this thoroughly proper hostelry compensates with a courtyard filled with fruit trees and a pond stocked with koi, which the inner guest rooms look out onto; outer rooms with fireplaces are more appealing in winter. **Pros:** elegant rooms; flat-screen TVs; chocolate chip cookies at turndown. **Cons:** no in-room coffeemakers; some service lapses; minor wear and tear visible. ⑤ *Rooms from: $279* ✉ *222 Adams Rd.* ☎ *413/458–9611, 800/225–1517* ⊕ *www.orchardshotel.com* ⇨ *49 rooms* ⑩ *No meals.*

★ River Bend Farm
$ | B&B/INN | Listed on the National Register of Historic Places, this 1770 Georgian Colonial is a rustic place to discover simpler times. **Pros:** free Wi-Fi; good breakfast; friendly innkeepers. **Cons:** uneven floors; shared bathrooms; no TVs; credit cards not accepted. ⑤ *Rooms from: $120* ✉ *643 Simonds Rd.* ☎ *413/458–3121* ⊕ *www.riverbendfarmbb.com* ▭ *No credit cards* ⊗ *Closed Nov.–Mar.* ⇨ *4 rooms* ⑩ *Free breakfast.*

🎭 Performing Arts

Images Cinema
FILM | The Berkshires' premier (and, admittedly, only) year-round nonprofit independent film house showcases art-house films, documentaries, and the latest from Sundance on two screens. There are outdoor shows during the summer. ✉ *50 Spring St.* ☎ *413/458–5612* ⊕ *www.imagescinema.org.*

★ Williamstown Theatre Festival
ARTS FESTIVALS | The festival, a past Tony Award winner for outstanding regional theater, is Williamstown's hottest summer ticket. From June through August, the long-running event presents well-known theatrical works featuring famous performers on the Main Stage and contemporary works on the Nikos Stage. ✉ *Williams College, '62 Center for Theatre and Dance, 1000 Main St.* ☎ *413/597–3400, 413/458–3200 (off-season)* ⊕ *www.wtfestival.org.*

🏃 Activities

Mt. Greylock State Reservation
HIKING/WALKING | The centerpiece of this 10,327-acre reservation south of Williamstown is Mt. Greylock, the highest point in Massachusetts at 3,491 feet, and the fictional location of Pottermore's North American school of magic, Ilvermorny School of Witchcraft and Wizardry. The reservation has facilities for cycling, fishing, horseback riding, camping, and snowmobiling. Many treks—including a portion of the Appalachian Trail—start from the parking lot at the summit in Adams, an 8-mile drive from the mountain's base. ✉ *Visitor center, 30 Rockwell Rd., Lanesborough* ☎ *413/499–4262* ⊕ *www.mass.gov/locations/mount-greylock-state-reservation.*

🛍 Shopping

The Store at 5 Corners
FOOD/CANDY | This store's 239-year streak of continual operation ended in 2011, when it closed for the first time since the 1770s. In addition to being a gift shop and small market for fresh fruits and cheeses, its reincarnation doubles as a café, with a large wooden table and benches where you can have breakfast, fancy baked goods, or just coffee. ✉ *6 New Ashford Rd., U.S. 7 at Rte. 43* ☎ *413/458–6105* ⊕ *www.thestoreatfive-corners.com.*

★ Where'd You Get That?
TOYS | FAMILY | Jam-packed with toys, games, and more bizarre novelty items than you could possibly imagine, this store benefits from the enthusiasm of owners Ken and Michele Gietz. Grab an offbeat gift for a friend (and some of the interesting candies for yourself). ✉ *100 Spring St.* ☎ *413/458–2206* ⊕ *www.wygt.com.*

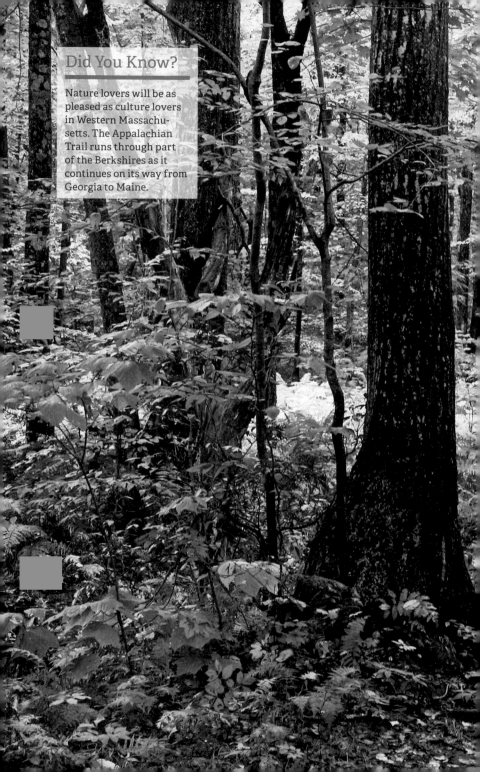

Did You Know?

Nature lovers will be as pleased as culture lovers in Western Massachu-setts. The Appalachian Trail runs through part of the Berkshires as it continues on its way from Georgia to Maine.

Hancock

15 miles south of Williamstown.

Tiny Hancock, the village closest to the Jiminy Peak ski resort, really comes into its own in winter, though it's also a great base for outdoors enthusiasts year-round, with biking, hiking, and other options in summer.

GETTING HERE AND AROUND

You can take Route 43 from Williamstown, U.S. 7 north from Pittsfield to Bailey Road west in Lanesborough, or the BRTA bus from Lanesborough, with plenty of mountain views and trees along the way.

Sights

Ioka Valley Farm

FARM/RANCH | FAMILY | Bring the kids to this 600-acre farm whose family-friendly activities include games and tractor rides. Seasonal offerings range from pick-your-own pumpkins (mid-September–October) to cut-your-own Christmas trees (late November–late December) and a petting farm from late June through August. For a real treat, catch a weekend brunch (late February–early April) with homemade maple syrup atop pancakes, waffles, and French toast. ✉ *3475 Rte. 43* ☎ *413/738-5915* ⊕ *www.iokavalleyfarm.com.*

Hotels

Country Inn at Jiminy Peak

$ | RESORT | FAMILY | Massive stone fireplaces in the lobby and lounge lend this hotel a ski-lodge atmosphere—suites in the building's rear overlook the slopes—and the condo-style suites (privately owned but put into a rental pool) can accommodate up to four people. **Pros:** lodging-and-skiing package deals; nice bathrooms; eat-in kitchenettes. **Cons:** remote location; outdoor pool is small; rooms have no character. ⑤ *Rooms from:*

$135 ✉ *37 Corey Rd.* ☎ *413/738-5500, 800/882-8859* ⊕ *www.jiminypeak.com* ⤳ *103 suites* ⑩ *No meals.*

Activities

SKIING

Jiminy Peak

SKIING/SNOWBOARDING | The only full-service ski and snowboard resort in the Berkshires, Jiminy Peak is also the largest in southern New England. This is mostly a cruising mountain. Trails are groomed daily, though some small moguls are left to build up along the slope sides. The steepest black-diamond runs are on the upper head walls; longer, outer runs make for good intermediate terrain. There's night skiing daily, and snowmaking capacity can cover 93% of skiable terrain. Jiminy has three terrain parks, as well as a weekends-only mountain coaster: a two-person cart that shoots down the mountain at speeds of up to 25 mph. During the summer, the resort transforms into an adventure park. **Facilities:** 45 trails; 170 acres; 1,150-foot vertical drop; 9 lifts. ✉ *37 Corey Rd.* ☎ *413/738-5500, 888/454-6469* ⊕ *www. jiminypeak.com* ✉ *Lift ticket: $76.*

Pittsfield

21 miles south of Williamstown, 11 miles southeast of Hancock.

Pittsfield is a workaday city without the quaint, rural demeanor of the comparatively small Colonial towns that surround it. There's a positive buzz in Pittsfield these days, though, thanks to a resurgence of sorts: the beautifully restored Colonial Theatre hosts 250 performances every year, and a number of new shops and restaurants have appeared along North Street. City-sponsored art walks and a major renovation of the Berkshire Museum are additional evidence of Pittsfield's comeback.

Many of New England's back roads are lined with historic split-rail fences or stone walls.

GETTING HERE AND AROUND

U.S. 7 (1st Street, in town), U.S. 20 (South Street), and Route 9 (East Street) all converge on Pittsfield. Trains and buses stop at the Intermodal Transportation Center, one block from North Street, along which you can walk to museums, interesting stores, and all sorts of restaurants. Buses service the mall and Allendale, but to get elsewhere you'll need to drive.

 ## Sights

Arrowhead

HISTORIC SITE | Literary fans (and those particularly fond of *Moby-Dick*) will want to visit this historical 18th-century house where Herman Melville lived and wrote his most famous works. After viewing all the exhibits, take a walk around the gardens, hike a trail, or just enjoy the majestic view of Mt. Greylock, the inspiration for Melville's white whale. ■ **TIP→ Tours are on the hour.** ⊠ *780 Holmes Rd.* ☎ *413/442–1793* ⊕ *www.mobydick.org* ✉ *$15 (guided tours included)* ⊘ *Closed Nov.–May.*

★ Berkshire Museum

MUSEUM | FAMILY | Opened in 1903, this "universal" museum has a little bit of everything: paintings from the Hudson River School, Alexander Calder mobiles, local artifacts, and natural history specimens both animal and mineral. The Hall of Innovation showcases Berkshires innovators whose creations range from special effects for *Star Wars* to the paper used for U.S. currency. The 10-foot-high stegosaurus outside the museum advertises the dinosaur gallery, where families can sift through the dig pit for bones, but don't miss the Egyptian mummy, or the aquarium with a touch tank in the basement. The museum's cinema screens American independent and foreign films. ⊠ *39 South St.* ☎ *413/443–7171* ⊕ *www. berkshiremuseum.org* ✉ *$13.*

★ Hancock Shaker Village

HISTORIC SITE | America's third Shaker community, Hancock was founded in the 1790s. At its peak in the 1840s, the village had almost 300 inhabitants who made their living farming, selling seeds and herbs, making medicines, and producing crafts. The religious community officially closed in 1960, but visitors today can still see demonstrations of blacksmithing, woodworking, and more. Many examples of Shaker ingenuity are on display: the Round Stone Barn and the Laundry and Machine Shop are two of the most interesting buildings. The Shaker focus on sustainability has been maintained in the form of water turbines, sustainable gardens, and a solar array. There's also a farm (with a wonderful barn), some period gardens, a museum shop with reproduction Shaker furniture, a picnic area, and a café. Visit in April to catch the baby animals at the farm, or in September for the country fair. Reserve early if you want a spot at the Shaker-inspired suppers in October. ⊠ *34 Lebanon Mountain Rd., off U.S. 20 at Rte. 41, Hancock* ☎ *413/443–0188, 800/817–1137* ⊕ *www.hancockshakervillage.org* ⊠ *$20.*

🍴 Restaurants

Dottie's Coffee Lounge
$ | AMERICAN | The raised seating area by the windows somehow adds a touch of class to this quintessential coffee shop where the art crowd hangs out. In addition to fine coffee, friendly baristas serve soups and sandwiches, as well as pre-wrapped meals that are perfect if you're late to a show. **Known for:** tasty baked goods; local and organic ingredients; artsy events. $ *Average main: $8* ⊠ *444 North St.* ☎ *413/443–1792* ⊕ *www.dottiescoffeelounge.com* ☾ *No food Sat.*

★ Elizabeth's
$$ | ITALIAN | You'd never guess this little white house was a restaurant, let alone one serving such superb Italian fare that emphasizes high-quality ingredients. Between the large portions of rich entrées and tableside visits from the owner-chef, an evening at Elizabeth's can feel like dinner at a dear friend's house. **Known for:** accepting personal checks or even IOUs; giant salads of local ingredients; bagna cauda (hot anchovy dipping

sauce). $ *Average main: $23* ⊠ *1264 East St., off Rte. 9* ☎ *413/448–8244* ▤ *No credit cards* ☾ *No lunch. Closed Sun.–Tues.*

★ Enso Asian Bistro
$$ | ASIAN | Don't be fooled by the giant log-cabin exterior: an Asian bistro with a full hibachi grill and sushi bar lies within, its spacious interior accented with lantern lights and a colorful bar. The menu includes typical favorites alongside innovative concoctions. **Known for:** broad sake selection; Treasure Island appetizer; half-price menu 3–6 pm. $ *Average main: $21* ⊠ *1035 South St.* ☎ *413/499–7900* ⊕ *www.ensoasianbistro.com.*

La Fogata
$ | SOUTH AMERICAN | The open kitchen looks almost like a lunch counter at this no-frills corner restaurant known for good, honest Colombian food, where it's hard to go wrong unless you're a vegetarian. Served with chimichurri and plantains, all the meats are delicious, from the thin, perfectly seasoned chicken to the pork rind that bacon aspires to be. **Known for:** Latin American soft drinks; South American food market in corner; "Picada La Fogata" giant meat platter. $ *Average main: $15* ⊠ *770 Tyler St.* ☎ *413/443–6969* ☾ *Closed Mon.*

Mission Bar and Tapas
$$ | MODERN AMERICAN | The slightly rustic high wooden tables combine with the art triptychs on the wall to create a very upscale casual atmosphere, which is reflected in the food as well. Standard favorites like meatballs and tacos are spruced up with interesting twists (think peppercorn cream sauce or blue cheese mousse) and locally sourced ingredients. **Known for:** truffle fries; bacon-wrapped dates; occasional live music. $ *Average main: $19* ⊠ *438 North St.* ☎ *413/499–1736* ⊕ *www.missionbarandtapas.com* ☾ *Closed Sun. No lunch.*

Hotels

★ Hotel on North

$ | **HOTEL** | This restored building in the center of town mixes original brickwork and hardwood with tasteful modern decor to provide spacious accommodations and common spaces, including a large horseshoe bar. **Pros:** on-site restaurant with oyster bar; spacious bathrooms; flat-screen TVs and Wi-Fi in rooms. **Cons:** creaky floors; exposed brick may not appeal to everyone; Central Pittsfield location is not picturesque. $ *Rooms from: $199* ✉ *297 North St.* ☎ *413/358–4741* ⊕ *hotelonnorth.com* ⬏ *45 rooms* ❖ *No meals.*

Performing Arts

Colonial Theatre

THEATER | Back in the day, stars such as Helen Hayes and Al Jolson appeared at this 780-seat 1903 theater; now restored, it hosts the likes of Audra McDonald and James Taylor. A second stage, the Garage, hosts comedy acts and programs for children. ✉ *111 South St.* ☎ *413/997–4444* ⊕ *www.berkshiretheatregroup.org.*

South Mountain Concerts

CONCERTS | One of the country's most distinguished chamber music series presents concerts every Sunday in September at 3 pm on South Mountain's wooded slope. ✉ *New S. Mountain Rd., 720 South St., off U.S. 20, 2 miles south of town* ☎ *413/442–2106* ⊕ *www.southmountainconcerts.org.*

Activities

HIKING

Ashuwillticook Rail Trail

TRAIL | Passing through the Hoosac River Valley, the paved 11-mile Ashuwillticook (pronounced *Ash*-oo-will-ti-cook) trail links Adams with Lanesborough. The trail follows an old railroad, passing through rugged woodland and alongside Cheshire Lake. Walkers, joggers, cyclists, in-line skaters, and cross-country skiers all enjoy this route. ✉ *3 Hoosac St., Adams* ☎ *413/442–8928* ⊕ *www.mass.gov/eea/agencies/dcr/massparks/region-west/ashuwillticook-rail-trail.html.*

SKIING

Bousquet Ski Area

SKIING/SNOWBOARDING | **FAMILY** | On the tamer side of Berkshire ski options, Bousquet has 23 trails if you count merging slopes separately. Experts will probably wish to go elsewhere: Bousquet has a few steeper pitches, but it's focused mainly on good beginner and intermediate runs. There are three double chairlifts, two carpet lifts, and a small terrain park. In summer, Bousquet offers waterslides, a large activity pool, a miniature golf course, a climbing wall, an adventure park, a bouncy castle, go-karts, and a zipline. **Facilities:** 23 trails; 200 acres; 750-foot vertical drop; 5 lifts. ✉ *101 Dan Fox Dr., off U.S. 7* ☎ *413/442–8316, 413/442–2436 for snow conditions* ⊕ *www.bousquets.com* ⬚ *Lift ticket: $45.*

ZIPLINING

Ramblewild

ZIP LINING | **FAMILY** | One of the Northeast's largest tree-to-tree adventure parks, Ramblewood has eight trails with over a hundred physical challenges that range in difficulty—including climbing, swinging, leaping, ziplining, and even a "skayak"—throughout 11 acres of forest. Privately guided hikes and climbing tours are also available on the 1,400-acre property. ✉ *110 Brodie Mountain Rd., Lanesborough* ☎ *413/499–9914* ⊕ *www.ramblewild.com* ⬚ *$69.*

⬤ Shopping

Bartlett's Orchard

FOOD/CANDY | The smell of freshly baked cider doughnuts greets you upon entering this orchard's market, which also sells cider and maple syrup. Seasonally you'll find many apple varieties bagged for purchase, but it's more fun to head into the orchard and pick your own. ⊠ *575 Swamp Rd., Richmond* ☎ *413/698–2559* ⊕ *www.berkshires.org/member/ bartletts-orchard.*

Whitney's Farm

FARM/RANCH | In addition to offering pick-your-own blueberries, tomatoes, and pumpkins on a seasonal basis, Whitney's sells fresh produce, herbs, and dairy products. A deli and a bakery are also on-site, as well as an outdoor playground and greenhouse. ⊠ *1775 S. State Rd., Cheshire* ☎ *413/442–4749* ⊕ *www.whit-neysfarm.com.*

Lenox

10 miles south of Pittsfield, 130 miles west of Boston.

The famed Tanglewood music festival has been a fixture in upscale Lenox for decades, and it's one of the reasons the town remains fiercely popular in summer. Booking a room here or in any of the nearby communities can set you back dearly during musical or theatrical events. Many of the town's most impressive homes are downtown; others you can only see by setting off on the curving back roads that thread the region. In the center of the village, a few blocks of shabby-chic Colonial buildings contain shops and eateries. Five miles south of Lenox is **Lee,** famous for its hard-er-than-average marble, quarried in 19th century for use in the cottages of the Vanderbilts and their ilk. Today the bus-tling downtown area has a mix of touristy and workaday shops and restaurants.

GETTING HERE AND AROUND
Just off Interstate 90, Lenox is south of Pittsfield. During the summer Tangle-wood season, traffic in Lenox and envi-rons often moves at a slow pace.

ESSENTIALS
VISITOR INFORMATION Lenox Chamber of Commerce ☎ *413/637–3646* ⊕ *www. lenox.org.*

 Sights

Berkshire Scenic Railway Museum
MUSEUM | FAMILY | In a restored 1903 railroad station, the museum's collection includes antique rail equipment, vintage items, a children's area, and a large work-ing model railway. Short rides aboard the Lennox Jitney train from one end of the grounds to the other are available, but if you want a longer ride, try the sister site, Hoosac Valley Service, in North Adams, where themed (fall foliage, Christmas) hour-long train rides make the 10-mile journey between Adams and North Adams in restored historic cars. ⊠ *10 Wil-low Creek Rd.* ☎ *413/637–2210* ⊕ *www. berkshirescenicrailroad.org* ☑ *Museum free* ⊙ *Museum closed Sun.–Fri. and Sept.–May; trains closed weekdays and Jan.–Apr.*

Frelinghuysen Morris House & Studio
HOUSE | This modernist property on a 46-acre site exhibits the works of Amer-ican abstract artists Suzy Frelinghuysen and George L.K. Morris, as well as those of their contemporaries, including Pablo Picasso, Georges Braque, and Juan Gris. In addition to the paintings, frescoes, and sculptures on display, a 57-minute documentary on Frelinghuysen and Mor-ris plays on a continuous loop. Tours are offered on the hour—just be aware that it's a long walk to the house. Painting demonstrations and workshops occa-sionally take place. ⊠ *92 Hawthorne St.* ☎ *413/637–0166* ⊕ *www.frelinghuysen. org* ☑ *$16.*

★ The Mount
HOUSE | This 1902 mansion with myriad classical influences was the summer home of novelist Edith Wharton. The 42-room house and 3 acres of formal gardens were designed by Wharton, who is considered by many to have set the standard for 20th-century interior decoration. In designing the Mount, she followed the principles set forth in her book *The Decoration of Houses* (1897), creating a calm and well-ordered home.

To date, nearly $15 million has been spent on an ongoing restoration project. Summer is a fine time to enjoy the informal café and occasional free concerts on the terrace. Guided tours take place during regular hours, the private "ghost tour" after hours. ⊠ *2 Plunkett St.* ☎ *413/551–5111, 888/637–1902* ⊕ *www. edithwharton.org* ⊠ *$20.*

★ Schantz Galleries

MUSEUM | Jim Schantz's gallery is small and tucked behind a bank, but it displays some of the finest glasswork in the world. With items from nearly five dozen contemporary artists—including Dale Chihuly and Lino Tagliapietra—the museum-quality collection is truly stunning. ⊠ *3 Elm St., Stockbridge* ☎ *413/298–3044* ⊕ *www.schantzgalleries.com.*

★ The Wit Gallery

MUSEUM | If you walked past this gallery, you'd inevitably end up ducking in for a closer inspection of the stunning glassworks in the windows. The expertly curated selection inside has more to offer, however, including everything from wooden sculptures to cold-cast metal faces, almost every piece demanding attention. ⊠ *27 Church St.* ☎ *413/637–8808* ⊕ *www.thewitgallery.com* ⊠ *Free.*

 Restaurants

★ Alpamayo

$$ | PERUVIAN | Don't let the no-frills decor fool you; what this family-owned restaurant lacks in style it more than makes up for in bold flavors, especially at dinner. Enjoy a menu of fresh and flavorful Peruvian favorites ranging from ceviche to plantains, and don't forget to grab a caramel custard for dessert. **Known for:** chicha morada (incredible purple corn drink); lomo saltado (steak strips sauteed with tomatoes, onions, and fries); Peruvian corn on the cob. ⑤ *Average main: $19* ⊠ *60 Main St., Lee* ☎ *413/243–6000* ⊕ *www.alpamayorestaurant.com* ⊗ *Closed Mon.*

Bistro Zinc

$$$ | FRENCH | Pastel-yellow walls, tall windows, a pressed-metal ceiling, and small-tile floors set an inviting tone at this stylishly modern French bistro with a long zinc-top bar from which it gets its name. The kitchen turns out expertly prepared and refreshingly simple classics, from steak frites to coq au vin. **Known for:** attentive service; duck confit rolls; trendy nightlife at the bar. ⑤ *Average main: $26* ⊠ *56 Church St.* ☎ *413/637–8800* ⊕ *www.bistrozinc.com.*

Café Lucia

$$$ | ITALIAN | The menus change with the seasons at this northern Italian restaurant, so you might find anything from veal piccata with anchovies, lemons, and capers in summer to osso buco in winter. The spacious porch is one of the best places to take everything in during the summer; otherwise, you can enjoy the intimate elegance of the bar and tables inside this converted farmhouse. **Known for:** wild mushroom ravioli; linguine Bolognese; busy on weekends. ⑤ *Average main: $29* ⊠ *80 Church St.* ☎ *413/637–2640* ⊕ *www.cafelucialenox. com* ⊗ *Closed Sun. and Mon. No lunch.*

★ Chocolate Springs Cafe

$ | BAKERY | Escape into chocolate bliss here, where even the aromas are intoxicating. This award-winning chocolatier offers wedges of decadent cakes, ice creams, and sorbets, and dazzling chocolates all made on-site. ⑤ *Average main: $6* ⊠ *Lenox Commons, 55 Pittsfield/ Lenox Rd.* ☎ *413/637–9820* ⊕ *www. chocolatesprings.com.*

Firefly Gastropub and Catering Co.

$$$ | MODERN AMERICAN | This upscale pub with a few modern dining rooms and porch seating is the perfect place to grab dinner if you're looking for something casual. The menu isn't large, but offers reliably good pub standards. **Known for:** Pig on a Stick (pork belly); nightly discount specials; live music Friday and Saturday. ⑤ *Average main:*

$25 ✉ 71 Church St. ☎ 413/637–2700 ⊕ www.fireflylenox.com ☽ Closed Mon. and Tues. Sept.–June. No lunch.

Hotels

Applegate Inn

$$ | B&B/INN | Just across from a golf course, this 1925 Georgian Revival mansion sits at the end of a regal circular drive, overlooking 6 acres of lush lawns and apple trees. **Pros:** charming dining room; complimentary snacks always available; heated pool. **Cons:** some traffic noise; archaic bathrooms; could use some renovation. ⑤ *Rooms from: $210 ✉ 279 W. Park St. ☎ 413/243–4451 ⊕ www.applegateinn.com ⇨ 11 rooms ⧀ Free breakfast.*

Blantyre

$$$$ | B&B/INN | Modeled after a castle in Scotland, this supremely elegant 1902 manor house sits amid nearly 117 acres of manicured lawns and woodlands where guests can enjoy the impressive surroundings and exceedingly attentive service. **Pros:** impressive lobby; high-end toiletries; exquisitely maintained property; sophisticated restaurant. **Cons:** some rooms have quirky configurations; very pricey; cottage rooms don't feel supremely elegant. ⑤ *Rooms from: $795 ✉ 16 Blantyre Rd., off U.S. 20 ☎ 413/637–3556 ⊕ www.blantyre.com ⇨ 32 rooms, 4 cottages ⧀ No meals.*

Brook Farm Inn

$$ | B&B/INN | Tucked away in a wooded glen a short distance from Tanglewood, this cozy 1880s inn often has classical music playing in the fireplace-lighted library; the breakfast room, overlooking the glen, serves afternoon tea with homemade scones on weekends. **Pros:** massage room; delicious breakfasts; close proximity to Tanglewood. **Cons:** books up fast; feels old-fashioned; surrounding area busy during Tanglewood season. ⑤ *Rooms from: $200 ✉ 15 Hawthorne St. ☎ 413/637–3013,*

800/285–7638 ⊕ www.brookfarm.com ⇨ 15 rooms ⧀ Free breakfast.

Chambery Inn

$ | B&B/INN | A converted 19th-century country schoolhouse houses these unique accommodations in downtown Lee where the cavernous guest rooms—some big enough for two queen beds—maintain their schoolhouse roots with blackboards still hanging on their walls. **Pros:** good value; spacious suites; restaurants within walking distance. **Cons:** limited choices for breakfast; walls are a bit thin; no common space. ⑤ *Rooms from: $189 ✉ 199 Main St. ☎ 413/243–2221, 800/537–4321 ⊕ www.chamberyinn.com ⇨ 9 rooms ⧀ Free breakfast.*

Cranwell Resort, Spa, and Golf Club

$$ | RESORT | FAMILY | This 380-acre resort is tastefully upscale, as you'll see from the spacious lobby with leather couches and the guest rooms in the Mansion, all furnished with ornate antiques, marble bathrooms, refrigerators, and flat-screen TVs. **Pros:** golfing with a view; many activities good for families; weekend breakfast buffets. **Cons:** extra cost for some amenities; some complaints of housekeeping issues; rooms lack character. ⑤ *Rooms from: $219 ✉ 55 Lee Rd., Rte. 20 ☎ 413/637–1364, 800/272–6935 ⊕ www.cranwell.com ⇨ 104 rooms ⧀ No meals.*

★ Devonfield Inn

$$ | B&B/INN | Occupying a grand Federal house from 1800, the Devonfield sits atop a birch-shaded hillside overlooking 32 acres of rolling meadows, and offers elegant but not ostentatious guest rooms that deftly blend Colonial style (four-poster beds, working fireplaces, some Oriental rugs) and modern convenience (Wi-Fi, flat-screen TVs, and in some cases whirlpool tubs). **Pros:** heated pool; separate cottage available; beautiful lawns and tennis court. **Cons:** not ideal for children; only 11 rooms; breakfast menu is not very large. ⑤ *Rooms from: $265 ✉ 85 Stockbridge Rd., Lee ☎ 413/243–3298,*

800/664–0880 ⊕ www.devonfield.com
↪ 11 rooms ⏋◎⏋ Free breakfast.

★ Gateways Inn and Restaurant

$$$ | **B&B/INN** | Once the 1912 summer cottage of Harley Procter (as in, Procter & Gamble), this beautifully updated country inn has guest rooms and suites in various configurations and styles; most have working fireplaces, detailed moldings, and plush carpeting. **Pros:** well-appointed rooms; great location in the heart of Lenox; late-night nibbles in the piano bar. **Cons:** lots of stairs; weddings sometimes take over the lobby; in-house dining options lacking. ⑤ *Rooms from: $300* ✉ *51 Walker St.* ☎ *413/637–2532* ⊕ *www.gatewaysinn.com* ↪ *11 rooms* ⏋◎⏋ *Free breakfast.*

Performing Arts

★ Jacob's Pillow Dance Festival

FESTIVAL | For 10 weeks every summer, the tiny town of Becket, 14 miles southeast of Lenox, becomes a hub of the dance world. The Jacob's Pillow Dance Festival showcases world-renowned performers of ballet, modern, and international dance. Before the main events, works in progress and even some of the final productions are staged outdoors, often free of charge. ✉ *358 George Carter Rd., at U.S. 20, Becket* ☎ *413/243–0745* ⊕ *www.jacobspillow.org.*

Shakespeare and Company

THEATER | The works of William Shakespeare and other writers are performed between four theaters. The Tina Packer Playhouse and Elayne P. Bernstein Theatre are both indoors, so you can enjoy productions throughout much of the year. Outdoor theaters include the Roman Garden Theatre and the Rose Footprint Theatre, the latter of which reflects the dimensions of the Rose, Shakespeare's first performance space in London. ✉ *70 Kemble St.* ☎ *413/637–3353* ⊕ *www.shakespeare.org.*

★ Tanglewood

CONCERTS | **FAMILY** | The 200-acre summer home of the Boston Symphony Orchestra, Tanglewood attracts thousands every summer to concerts by world-famous musicians. The 5,000-seat main shed hosts larger concerts; the more intimate Seiji Ozawa Hall seats around 1,200 and is used for chamber music and solo performances. The hall is named for the renowned conductor, for years the BSO's music director, a job now held by the Latvian-born Andris Nelsons. Among the most rewarding ways to experience Tanglewood is to purchase lawn tickets, arrive early with blankets or lawn chairs, and enjoy a picnic under the stars. Except for the occasional big-name concert, lawn tickets cost only $21–$23. Inside the shed, tickets vary in price, with most of the good seats costing $50–$120. You can hear the same music for much less by attending an open rehearsal. ✉ *297 West St., off Rte. 183* ☎ *617/266–1492, 888/266–1492* ⊕ *www.tanglewood.org.*

Activities

HIKING

Pleasant Valley Wildlife Sanctuary

HIKING/WALKING | **FAMILY** | Beaver ponds, hardwood forests, and sun-dappled meadows abound at this preserve run by the Massachusetts Audubon Society. Recent wildlife sightings are noted on whiteboards at the entrance and the visitor center, so you'll know what to watch for on the 7 miles of trails. These include loops that range in difficulty from a half-hour stroll around a pond to a three-hour mountain hike. Trails are also open in winter for snowshoeing. At the visitor center there's a nature play area for children. ✉ *472 W. Mountain Rd.* ☎ *413/637–0320* ⊕ *www.massaudubon.org* ▧ *$5.*

🖥 Shopping

Canyon Ranch

SPA/BEAUTY | Set in Bellefontaine Mansion, an 1897 replica of Le Petit Trianon in Versailles, the Berkshires' outpost of the Arizona resort couldn't be more elegantly old-fashioned. Looks can be deceiving, though: housed within is a state-of-the-art fitness center with the latest classes and the best equipment, a staff of chefs cooking up healthful cuisine, and of course, a holistic spa. Treatments range from Eastern-inspired therapies like ayurvedic treatments to the Canyon Ranch's signature full-body massages—hot stones optional. If you're looking to get away from it all, this is the place to enjoy a spa day in between hiking and paddling through the Berkshire countryside. ⊠ *165 Kemble St.* ☎ *800/742–9000, 413/637–4400* ⊕ *www.canyonranch.com.*

Hoadley Gallery

ART GALLERIES | One of New England's foremost crafts centers, the gallery shows and sells American arts and crafts, with a strong focus on pottery, jewelry, and textiles. ⊠ *21 Church St.* ☎ *413/637–2814* ⊕ *www.hoadleygallery.com.*

Stockbridge

20 miles northwest of Otis, 7 miles south of Lenox.

The quintessence of small-town New England charm, Stockbridge is untainted by large-scale development. It is also the blueprint for small-town America as represented on the covers of the *Saturday Evening Post* by painter Norman Rockwell, the official state artist of Massachusetts. From 1953 until his death in 1978, Rockwell lived in Stockbridge and painted the simple charm of its buildings and residents. James Taylor sang about the town in his hit "Sweet Baby James," as did balladeer Arlo Guthrie in his famous Thanksgiving anthem "Alice's

Restaurant," in which he tells what ensued when he tossed some garbage out the back of his Volkswagen bus down a Stockbridge hillside.

GETTING HERE AND AROUND

Stockbridge is accessible from West Stockbridge or Lee, both of which are exits off the Massachusetts Turnpike (Interstate 90). Once here, you can easily walk around the village and drive around the larger area.

ESSENTIALS

VISITOR INFORMATION Stockbridge Chamber of Commerce ☎ *413/298–5200, 413/298–5200* ⊕ *www.stockbridgechamber.org.*

👁 Sights

Berkshire Botanical Gardens

GARDEN | The gardens' 15 acres contain extensive plantings of exotic and native flora—some 2,500 varieties in all—plus greenhouses, ponds, nature trails, and a small gallery. A guided tour, included with admission, leaves daily at 11 am, or grab a self-guided tour at your leisure. October's Harvest Festival is by far the biggest of the facility's annual events. ⊠ *5 W. Stockbridge Rd.* ☎ *413/298–3926* ⊕ *www.berkshirebotanical.org* 🎟 *$15.*

★ Chesterwood

HISTORIC SITE | For 33 years, this was the summer home of the sculptor Daniel Chester French (1850–1931), who created *The Minute Man* in Concord and the Lincoln Memorial's famous seated statue of the president in Washington, D.C. Occasional tours are given of the house, which is maintained in the style of the 1920s, but the real prize is the studio, where you can view the casts and models French used to create the Lincoln Memorial. The beautifully landscaped 122-acre grounds make for an enchanting stroll or bucolic picnic. ⊠ *4 Williamsville Rd., off Rte. 183* ☎ *413/298–3579* ⊕ *www.chesterwood.org* 🎟 *From $10* ☽ *Closed Oct.–May.*

Norman Rockwell: Illustrating America

I was showing the America I knew and observed to others who might not have noticed. My fundamental purpose is to interpret the typical American. I am a storyteller.

—Norman Rockwell

If you've ever seen old copies of the *Saturday Evening Post*, no doubt you're familiar with American artist Norman Rockwell. He created 321 covers for the well-regarded magazine, and the *Post* always sold more copies when one of Rockwell's drawings was on the front page. The accomplished artist also illustrated Boy Scouts of America calendars, Christmas cards, children's books, and even a few stamps for the U.S. Postal Service—in 1994 a stamp bearing his image came out in his honor. His illustrations tended to fit the theme of Americana, family, or patriotism.

Born in New York City in 1894, the talented designer had a knack for art early on but strengthened his talent with instruction at the National Academy of Design and the Art Students League. He was only 22 when he sold his first cover to the *Post*. He married three times and had three sons by his second wife. He died in 1978 in Stockbridge, Massachusetts, where he had lived since 1953.

Famous Rockwell works include his *Triple Self-Portrait* and the *Four Freedoms*, illustrations done during World War II. The latter series of oil paintings represents freedom of speech, freedom of worship, freedom from want, and freedom from fear. In a poetic turn, in 1977, President Gerald R. Ford bestowed on Rockwell the Presidential Medal of Freedom, the highest civilian honor a U.S. citizen can be given. Ford praised Rockwell for his "vivid and affectionate portraits of our country."

Naumkeag

HOUSE | The Berkshire cottage of Joseph Choate (1832–1917), an influential New York City lawyer and the ambassador to Great Britain during President William McKinley's administration, provides a glimpse into the Gilded Age lifestyle. The 44-room gabled mansion, designed by Stanford White and completed in 1887, sits atop Prospect Hill. Its many original furnishings and artworks span three centuries; the collection of Chinese porcelain is particularly noteworthy. The meticulously kept 8 acres of formal gardens, a three-decade project of Choate's daughter, Mabel, and landscape designer Fletcher Steele, alone make this site worth a visit. ⊠ *5 Prospect Hill Rd.* ☎ *413/298–8138* ⊕ *www.thetrustees.org/places-to-visit/berkshires/naumkeag.html* 🎟 *$20* ⊙ *Closed Oct.–May.*

Norman Rockwell Museum

MUSEUM | FAMILY | This charming museum traces the career of one of America's most beloved illustrators, beginning with his first *Saturday Evening Post* cover in 1916. The crown jewel of the 570 Rockwell illustrations is the famed Four Freedoms gallery (on loan until 2020), although various works—including his *Post* covers and self-portraits—are equally charming. The museum also mounts exhibits of work by other artists. Rockwell's studio was moved to the museum grounds and is complete in every detail. Stroll the 36-acre site, picnic on the grounds, or relax at the outdoor café (late May–mid-October). There's a children's version of the audio tour and a scavenger hunt. ⊠ *9 Rte. 183* ☎ *413/298–4100* ⊕ *www.nrm.org* 🎟 *$20.*

Restaurants

Once Upon a Table

$$$ | ECLECTIC | They picked a cute little name for a cute little restaurant in the mews off Stockbridge's Main Street. And the owners of this upscale eatery picked a menu to match: a small but appealing selection of Continental and contemporary American cuisine ranging from raspberry-sauced duck to rack of lamb. **Known for:** escargot potpie; seared crab cakes with capers; garlic mashed potatoes. ⑤ *Average main: $25 ⊠ 36 Main St.* ☎ *413/298–3870* ⊕ *www.onceuponatablebistro.com.*

Rouge Restaurant and Bistro

$$$ | FRENCH | In West Stockbridge (5 miles northwest), this intimate French restaurant has been such a success that it has expanded to include a bar and a larger dining area. Chef William Merelle is from Provence, and his American wife and co-owner, Maggie, was formerly a wine merchant; together they provide a mix of French and new American cuisine, backed by a solid wine list. **Known for:** braised duck with shredded potato cake; upscale desserts; cooking classes. ⑤ *Average main: $30 ⊠ 3 Center St., West Stockbridge* ☎ *413/232–4111* ⊕ *www.rougerestaurant.com* ☯ *Closed Mon. and Tues. No lunch.*

Truc Orient Express

$$ | VIETNAMESE | Mixed in among shops filled with arts and crafts, this family-owned business has been serving up authentic Vietnamese food for more than 30 years. *Bánh xèo* (rice pancakes) figure prominently on the menu, among other classics, but there's some adventurous fare, too. **Known for:** ca chien (whole fried flounder in a pungent fish sauce); bánh xèo; Vietnamese crafts store in entryway. ⑤ *Average main: $21 ⊠ 3 Harris St.* ☎ *413/232–4204* ☯ *Closed Mon.–Thurs. No lunch.*

Hotels

★ The Inn at Stockbridge

$$$ | B&B/INN | Antique furnishings accent the guest rooms of this comfortable 1906 Georgian Revival inn, where each of the spacious and airy rooms has a decorative theme, such as Kashmir, Provence, or the Berkshires. **Pros:** heated pool; some rooms have gas fireplaces or whirlpool tubs; lovely furniture. **Cons:** noise from highway (most noticeable in suites); not within walking distance of town; pool is outdoors. ⑤ *Rooms from: $320 ⊠ 30 East St.* ☎ *413/298–3337, 888/466–7865* ⊕ *www.stockbridgeinn.com* ⇥ *16 rooms* ⑩ *Free breakfast.*

The Red Lion Inn

$$$ | B&B/INN | An inn since 1773, the Red Lion has hosted presidents, senators, and other celebrities, in the large and historic main building filled with antiques and small guest rooms. **Pros:** inviting lobby with fireplace; rocking chairs on porch; quaintly romantic. **Cons:** overpriced dining; minuscule fitness center; no mobile reception. ⑤ *Rooms from: $300 ⊠ 30 Main St.* ☎ *413/298–5545, 413/298–1690* ⊕ *www.redlioninn.com* ⇥ *150 rooms* ⑩ *No meals.*

Performing Arts

Berkshire Theatre Festival

THEATER | This summerlong festival has presented plays since 1929. Those on the Main Stage tend to be better-known works with established actors. A smaller theater mounts more experimental works, and some festival productions also take place at the Colonial Theatre in Pittsfield. ⊠ *6 Main St.* ☎ *413/298–5576* ⊕ *www.berkshiretheatregroup.org.*

Shopping

Kripalu Center

SPA/BEAUTY | You'll see many people sitting peacefully on the grounds as you approach this health and yoga retreat proficient at helping patrons achieve a heightened state of grace. Meals always include gluten-free items in addition to more standard fare. ⊠ *57 Interlaken Rd.* 🕾 *866/200–5203, 800/741–7353* ⊕ *www. kripalu.org.*

Williams and Sons Country Store
CONVENIENCE/GENERAL STORES | FAMILY | Well-worn wooden floors and old-time music provide an authentic feel that pairs well with the country-store staples for sale here: toys, maple goodies, jams, and an abundance of candy. ■ TIP→ Don't confuse Williams and Sons with the sparse "general store" down the street. ⊠ *38 Main St.* 🕾 *413/298–3016.*

Great Barrington

7 miles southwest of Stockbridge; 13 miles north of Canaan, Connecticut.

The largest town in South County became, in 1781, the first place in the United States to free a slave under due process of law and was also the birthplace, in 1868, of W.E.B. DuBois, the civil rights leader, author, and educator. The many ex–New Yorkers who live in Great Barrington expect great food and service, and the restaurants here accordingly deliver complex, delicious fare. The town is also a favorite of antiques hunters, as are the nearby villages of South Egremont and Sheffield. On U.S. 7 alone, dozens of antiques shops await your discerning eye.

GETTING HERE AND AROUND
The nearest international airports are Bradley International Airport in Windsor Locks, Connecticut, and Albany International Airport in Albany, New York, but you are better off driving in on U.S. 7 from either Stockbridge or Canaan, Connecticut. Great Barrington is also on the BRTA bus line from Stockbridge. There's plenty of parking in town, most of which is walkable as well.

ESSENTIALS
VISITOR INFORMATION Southern Berkshire Chamber of Commerce 🕾 *413/528–1510, 800/269–4825* ⊕ *southernberkshirechamber.com.*

Sights

★ Berkshire Mountain Distillers
WINERY/DISTILLERY | The sweet scent of the country's premier craft gin permeates the Berkshires' first legal distillery since Prohibition. The retail store, open every afternoon, sells Greylock Gin, a multiple gold-medal winner, and Ethereal Gin, whose ingredients are reimagined every season, among other spirits. Hour-long distillery tours take place on Friday and Saturday. The head distiller, Jon, is friendly, knowledgeable, and happy to pour a taste of a gin, whiskey, or even maple syrup aged in a bourbon cask. ⊠ *356 S. Main St., Sheffield* 🕾 *413/229–0219* ⊕ *www.berkshiremountaindistillers.com* 🎫 *Tour $10.*

Vault Gallery
BANK | Housed inside a former bank, this small art gallery based on French salon galleries includes the vault room with the original safe door intact. While the building itself is impressive, the gallery also features artwork by owner Marilyn Kalish in a variety of media, as well as some work by other artists and a small collection of antiques. ⊠ *322 Main St.* 🕾 *413/854–7744* ⊕ *vaultgallery.net.*

🍴 Restaurants

Aroma Bar and Grill
$ | INDIAN | Popular with college students for its reasonable prices, this restaurant serves up delicious food all day with especially good deals at lunch and the Sunday brunch buffets. The cooks do well with everything from tandoori chicken and other standards to the full Raja Thali dinner special, all served with a trio of flavorful chutneys. **Known for:** stuffed naan; moist minced-lamb seekh kebab;

takeout available on Monday. $ *Average main: $16* ✉ *485 Main St.* ☎ *413/528-3116* ⊕ *www.aromabarandgrill.com* ⊘ *Closed Mon.*

Baba Louie's Sourdough Pizza Co

$ | PIZZA | Specialty pizzas at this trattoria go far beyond the usual toppings, from roasted sweet potatoes and fennel to pineapple and coconut: combinations are weird, but tasty. Baba Louie's fires up sourdough ground wheat, spelt-berry, and even gluten-free crusts in their often crowded, rustic interior. **Known for:** excellent thin-crust pizza; Hannah Jo special (mozz, ricotta, shrimp, pineapple, green chili sauce); smallish dining area and portions. $ *Average main: $14* ✉ *286 Main St.* ☎ *413/528-8100* ⊕ *www.babalouiespizza.com.*

Bizen

$$ | JAPANESE | Expect crowds—and, on busy nights, a wait—at this Railroad Street mainstay where dining room tables wrap around three sides of the large central sushi bar that offers an extensive menu of very fresh fish. Besides the sushi menu, dishes range from *robata* (charcoal grill) to katsu and tempura. **Known for:** harumaki (deep-fried lobster and fish in rice paper); una jyu (grilled river eel in a sweet sauce); tea ceremonies and 10-course tasting menus by reservation. $ *Average main: $22* ✉ *17 Railroad St.* ☎ *413/528-4343.*

 ## Hotels

The Barrington

$$ | B&B/INN | As a third-floor bed-and-breakfast above retail frontage, the Barrington may lack the exterior aesthetic appeal of its Berkshire peers, but it more than compensates for this by its central Main Street location and spacious, eclectically furnished guest rooms. **Pros:** flat-screens and Wi-Fi; conscientious innkeepers; handicapped-accessible suite with piano. **Cons:** no guest lobby; dismal exterior and hallway; pricey for the setting. $ *Rooms from:*

$275 ✉ *281 Main St., 3rd fl.* ☎ *413/528-6159* ⊕ *www.thebarringtongb.com* ⇄ *6 rooms* ⫮◎⫯ *Free breakfast.*

 ## Performing Arts

Mahaiwe Performing Arts Center

ARTS CENTERS | Catch a performance by Arlo Guthrie or the Paul Taylor Dance Company at the center's stunning 1905 theater. The year-round schedule includes theater, music, dance, comedy, and film. ✉ *14 Castle St.* ☎ *413/528-0100* ⊕ *www.mahaiwe.org.*

 ## Activities

HIKING

A 90-mile swath of the Appalachian Trail cuts through the Berkshires. You'll also find hundreds of miles of trails elsewhere throughout the area's forests and parks.

Appalachian Trail

HIKING/WALKING | You can walk part of the Appalachian Trail on a moderately strenuous stretch that leads to Ice Gulch, a gorge so deep and cold that there is often ice in it, even in summer. Follow the Ice Gulch ridge to the shelter and a large, flat rock from which you can enjoy a panoramic view of the valley. The hike takes about 45 minutes one way. ✉ *Trailhead on Lake Buel Rd., about 100 feet northwest of Deerwood Park Dr.* ⊕ *www.appalachiantrail.org.*

Bartholomew's Cobble

HIKING/WALKING | This rock garden beside the Housatonic River (the Native American name means "river beyond the mountains") is a National Natural Landmark, with 5 miles of hiking trails passing through fields of wildflowers. The 277-acre site has a visitor center and a museum, as well as the state's largest cottonwood trees. ✉ *105 Weatogue Rd., Sheffield* ☎ *413/229-8600* ⊕ *www.thetrustees.org/places-to-visit/berkshires/bartholomews-cobble.html* ⫯ *$5.*

Monument Mountain

HIKING/WALKING | For great views with minimal effort, hike Monument Mountain, famous as a spot for literary inspiration. Nathaniel Hawthorne and Herman Melville trekked it on August 5, 1850, seeking shelter in a cave during a thunderstorm. There they discussed ideas that would become part of a novel called *Moby-Dick*. While poet William Cullen Bryant stayed in the area, he penned a lyrical poem, "Monument Mountain," about a lovesick Mohican maiden who jumped to her death from the cliffs. Most hikers find the 2½-mile loop an easy stroll. ⊠ *Trailhead at parking lot on west side of U.S. 7, 3 miles north of Rte. 183* ☎ *413/298–3239* ⊕ *www.thetrustees.org/places-to-visit/berkshires/monument-mountain.html.*

SKI AREAS

Catamount Ski Area

SKIING/SNOWBOARDING | Skiers seeking a family experience often end up here. Although it's not the biggest mountain in the area, Catamount can be less crowded than other options when it's not a holiday weekend, and the terrain is varied. The Sidewinder, an intermediate cruising trail, is more than 1 mile from top to bottom. Just watch out for ice on the tougher trails. There's also night skiing and snowboarding, plus three terrain parks for snowboarders and others. During the summer, the aerial adventure park has guests traveling between treetops. **Facilities:** 36 trails; 130 acres; 1,000-foot vertical drop; 7 lifts. ⊠ *3290 Rte. 23, South Egremont* ☎ *413/528–1262, 413/528–1262 for snow conditions* ⊕ *www.catamount-ski.com* ⫶ *Lift ticket: $68.*

Ski Butternut

SKIING/SNOWBOARDING | With a variety of trails and slopes, including a 1½-mile run, Ski Butternut is good for skiers of all ability levels. There are a few beginner and advanced trails, and more than half the mountain is mellow intermediate terrain. For snowboarders there are top-to-bottom terrain parks and a beginner park, and

eight lanes are available for snow tubing. Eleven lifts, including four carpet lifts and the longest quad in the Berkshires, keep traffic spread out. **Facilities:** 22 trails; 110 acres; 1,000-foot vertical drop; 11 lifts. ⊠ *380 State Rd.* ☎ *413/528–2000, 413/528–4433 for ski school, 800/438–7669 for snow conditions* ⊕ *www.skibutternut.com* ⫶ *Lift ticket: $60.*

Shopping

ANTIQUES

The Great Barrington area, including the small towns of Sheffield and South Egremont, has the Berkshires' greatest concentration of antiques stores. Some shops are open sporadically, and many are closed on Tuesday.

Elise Abrams Antiques

ANTIQUES/COLLECTIBLES | The owner of this store selling dining-related antique porcelain, glassware, and tabletop accessories is an expert in the field. The prices match the high quality of her selections. ⊠ *11 Stockbridge Rd., near Rte. 183* ☎ *413/528–3201* ⊕ *www.eliseabramsantiques.com.*

Great Barrington Antiques Center

ANTIQUES/COLLECTIBLES | The feeling is "indoor flea market" in this space, where 30-plus dealers sell Oriental rugs, vintage furniture, and smaller decorative pieces. ⊠ *964 S. Main St.* ☎ *413/644–8848* ⊕ *www.greatbarringtonantiquescenter.com.*

CRAFTS

Sheffield Pottery

CERAMICS/GLASSWARE | Many of the roughly 100 local potters whose creative output can be found here use native Sheffield clay to fashion their vases, birdbaths, colorful dinner platters, and other ceramics. The resident shop cat adds to the down-home ambience. In addition to the diverse pottery, ceramics supplies are available for purchase. ⊠ *995 N. Main St., Sheffield* ☎ *888/774–2529* ⊕ *www.americanmadepottery.com.*

FOOD

Bizalion's Fine Food

FOOD/CANDY | This French specialty-food shop carries imported cheeses, cured meats, and the finest olive oils from carefully sourced producers, who also sell their wares to fancy restaurants in New York City and Martha's Vineyard. Bizalion doubles as an informal eatery; on the small menu are some appealing sandwiches, including one with arugula, pine nuts, prosciutto, goat cheese, and olive oil on toasted bread. ⊠ *684 Main St.* ☎ *413/644–9988* ⊕ *www.bizalions.com.*

Blueberry Hill Farm

FOOD/CANDY | Organic blueberries are ripe for the picking here on midsummer weekends starting in late July. Bring your own container; payment is by cash or check only. ⊠ *100 East St., Mount Washington* ✛ *About 10 miles southwest of Great Barrington* ☎ *413/528–1479* ⊕ *www.austinfarm.com* ⧠ *Free.*

Boardman's Farm Stand

FOOD/CANDY | Known for its sweet corn, Boardman's makes a fine quick stop to pick up fresh fruits and vegetables, from pumpkins and peppers to peaches and nectarines. ⊠ *64 Hewins St., off Maple Ave., southeast from U.S. 7, Sheffield* ☎ *413/229–8554.*

Howden Farm

FOOD/CANDY | About 4 miles south of the town center, you can pick raspberries from Labor Day to mid-October and pumpkins late September–October. Locals have snatched up the farm's famous sweet corn for decades. ⊠ *303 Rannapo Rd., off Rte. 7A, Sheffield* ☎ *413/229–8481* ⊕ *www.howdenfarm.com.*

Taft Farms

FOOD/CANDY | **FAMILY** | Raspberries ripen here early July–August, and you can pick your own pumpkin September–October. Grab a roast turkey (or other) sandwich, served on freshly baked bread, for a fine homemade lunch. If you have time to linger, check out the small turtle pond in the plant nursery, and see the animal area replete with goats, chickens, llamas, and more. ⊠ *119 Park St. N* ☎ *413/528–1515* ⊕ *www.taftfarms.com.*

HOME DECOR

★ Asia Barong

ANTIQUES/COLLECTIBLES | The eye-catching sculptures visible from the roadside only hint at the vast spectacle inside what bills itself as America's largest Asian art store—customers include the Smithsonian and the Hell's Angels Clubhouse. Carvings of every conceivable material (from wood to whalebone), size (from half an inch to 8 feet tall), and subject matter (albeit heavy on the gods and dragons) can be found here (or made to order and shipped). The sheer volume of art outstrips many museums, but you can still buy a traditional sarong or a gift from the $5 shelves. Humorous signs throughout the store add a touch of character. ⊠ *199 Stockbridge Rd.* ☎ *413/528–5091* ⊕ *www.asiabarong.com.*

Springfield

90 miles west of Boston; 30 miles north of Hartford, Connecticut.

Springfield is the busy hub of the Pioneer Valley. Known as the birthplace of basketball—the game was devised here in 1891 as a gym instructor's last-ditch attempt to keep a group of unruly teenagers occupied in winter—the city also has a cluster of fine museums and family attractions.

GETTING HERE AND AROUND

Springfield is roughly the center of Massachusetts, accessible by bus, train, and Interstates 90 and 91. Parts of Springfield are walkable, but you're better off driving or using the local PVTA buses.

ESSENTIALS

VISITOR INFORMATION Greater Springfield Convention & Visitors Bureau ☎ *413/787–1548, 800/723–1548* ⊕ *explorewesternmass.com.*

Sturbridge and the Pioneer Valley

VERMONT

Winchendon

Northfield

Baldwinville

Shelburne Falls

Turners Falls
Orange
Athol

Greenfield
Millers Falls

Deerfield
The Montague Bookmill
Montague
Locks Village
New Salem

Magic Wings Butterfly
Conservatory and Gardens

South Deerfield
Sunderland
Shutesbury

Whately

North Amherst
Barre

North Hatfield

Amherst

Hatfield
South Amherst
Quabbin
Reservoir

Northampton

Smith College

Belchertown

Easthampton
Ware
Lake
Lashaway

South Hadley
East Brookfield

Mount Holyoke College
Granby

Warren

Southampton
Westover
Air Force Base
Quaboag
Pond

Holyoke
Bondsville
Three Rivers

Chicopee
Palmer

Wilbraham
Fiskdale

W. Springfield
Sturbridge

Springfield
Old Sturbridge
Village

Holland

Agawam
East Longmeadow
Hamilton
Reservoir

Longmeadow
Mashapaug
Pond

Congamond
Lakes

Sherwood Manor

CONNECTICUT

THE PIONEER VALLEY

Stafford Springs

0   5 mi

0   5 km

Sights

★ Naismith Memorial Basketball Hall of Fame

MUSEUM | FAMILY | This 80,000-square-foot facility—named for Canadian phys-ed instructor Dr. James Naismith, who invented the game of basketball in 1891 during his five years at Springfield's YMCA Training Center—showcases plenty of jerseys, memorabilia, and video highlights. High-profile players such as Michael Jordan and Kareem Abdul-Jabbar of the NBA and Nancy Lieberman of the WNBA are among the nearly 300 enshrinees, but the hall celebrates the accomplishments of players, coaches, and others at all levels of the sport. In addition to displays chronicling basketball history, the hall has a soaring domed arena where you can practice jumpers, walls of inspirational quotes you can view, dozens of interactive exhibits, and video footage and interviews with former players. The hall is easy to find: look for the 15-story spire with an illuminated basketball on top. ⊠ *1000 W. Columbus Ave.* ☏ *413/781–6500, 877/446–6752* ⊕ *www.hoophall. com* 🖭 *$24.*

Six Flags New England

AMUSEMENT PARK/WATER PARK | FAMILY | With more than 160 rides and shows, this massive attraction is the region's largest theme and water park. You can visit Looney Tunes town and climb aboard DC Superhero rides such as Batman: The Dark Knight and Superman: The Ride, which is more than 20 stories tall and has a top speed of 77 mph. New rides are added frequently, like the Wicked Cyclone, a hybrid wooden structure with a steel track, and the Fireball, a seven-story loop coaster. Visit in autumn to catch Fright Fest haunted events and attractions. ⊠ *1623 Main St., Agawam* ☏ *413/786–9300* ⊕ *www.sixflags.com/ newengland* 🖭 *$70.*

Springfield Museums

MUSEUM | FAMILY | This complex of museums in the Quadrangle includes five impressive facilities (single admission), plus a free sculpture garden. The **George Walter Vincent Smith Art Museum** houses a fascinating private art collection that includes a salon gallery with 19th-century American paintings by Frederic Church and Albert Bierstadt, as well as a Japanese antiquities room filled with armor, textiles, porcelain, and carved jade. The **Museum of Fine Arts** has paintings by Paul Gauguin, Claude Monet, Pierre-Auguste Renoir, Edgar Degas, Winslow Homer, and Georgia O'Keeffe. The **Springfield Science Museum** has an Exploration Center of touchable displays, the oldest operating planetarium in the United States, dinosaur exhibits, an extensive collection of stuffed and mounted animals, and an African Hall through which you can take an interactive tour of that continent's flora and fauna. The **Museum of Springfield History** tells the story of the town's manufacturing heritage, including bikes and memorabilia from the former Indian Motorcycle Company, which was headquartered in Springfield. **The Amazing World of Dr. Seuss Museum,** opened in 2017, offers a look into the Springfield childhood of Theodor Geisel (aka Dr. Seuss) and a wide range of interactive exhibits and wall drawings, all among rooms so colorful that the museum is like walking into a Dr. Seuss book.

Also amid the Quadrangle is the free **Dr. Seuss National Memorial Sculpture Garden,** an installation of bronze statues depicting scenes from Geisel's famously whimsical children's books. Born in Springfield in 1904, Geisel was inspired by the animals at the Zoo in Forest Park, where his father served as director. ⊠ *220 State St.* ☏ *413/263–6800* ⊕ *www.springfieldmuseums.org* 🖭 *$25.*

Zoo in Forest Park and Education Center

CITY PARK | FAMILY | At this leafy, 735-acre retreat, hiking paths wind through the trees, paddleboats navigate Porter Lake, and hungry ducks float on a small pond. The zoo, where Theodor Geisel—better known as Dr. Seuss—found inspiration for his children's books, is home to nearly 200 animals, from camels and bobcats to lemurs and wallabies. It's manageable in size, and spotting animals in the exhibits is fairly easy, which makes this an especially good stop for families with small children. Another plus: you can purchase small cones of food from the gift shop to feed many of the animals. Leave time to explore the park after you finish the zoo. ✉ *293 Sumner Ave.* ☎ *413/733–2251* ⊕ *www.forestparkzoo.org* 🎫 *$10.*

 Restaurants

★ **Chef Wayne's Big Mamou**

$ | CAJUN | This casual single-room joint serves up some seriously good Louisiana grub, which is why it gets so crowded that you may find yourself chatting with the next table over, likely about how good the food is. Owner-chef Wayne Booker's hometown recipes run the gamut of creole and Cajun classics, from blackened catfish to jambalaya to sweet potato pie. **Known for:** the eponymous "Big Mamou" dish; anything with crawfish; BYOB. ⑤ *Average main: $16* ✉ *63 Liberty St.* ☎ *413/732–1011* ⊕ *www.chefwaynes-big-mamou.com* ◔ *No dinner Sun. No lunch Sun. June–Sept.*

La Fiorentina Pastry Shop

$ | BAKERY | Springfield's South End is home to a lively Little Italy, including this full bakery that has doled out a wide variety of heavenly pastries (and coffee) since the 1940s. **Known for:** chocolate-covered cannoli; breakfast menu; attached deli. ⑤ *Average main: $3* ✉ *883 Main St.* ☎ *413/732–3151* ⊕ *www.lafiorentinapastry.com.*

Pho Saigon

$ | VIETNAMESE | A little out of the way, this understated eatery serves authentic Vietnamese cuisine at wallet-pleasing prices. Whether you enjoy the eponymous made-from-scratch soups, fried dishes with meat, or plentiful vegetarian options, the menu has you covered. **Known for:** variety of authentic homemade pho; bánh xèo; getting your car towed if you park in the lot across the street. ⑤ *Average main: $10* ✉ *400 Dickinson St.* ☎ *413/781–4488* ⊕ *www.phosaigonspringfield.com* ◔ *Closed Wed.*

Red Rose

$$ | ITALIAN | FAMILY | Featuring massive chandeliers, an open kitchen, and a large dining area, this half-century-old family restaurant is a big, brassy eatery where everyone from canoodling couples to huge parties can feel right at home. The menu features the usual gamut of Italian favorites such as the exquisite eggplant dishes, as well as a variety of pizzas made from a half-century-old recipe. **Known for:** eggplant Parmigiana; primavera pizza; heaping platters of pasta. ⑤ *Average main: $19* ✉ *1060 Main St.* ☎ *413/739–8510* ⊕ *www.redrosepizzeria.com* ◔ *Closed Mon.*

★ **Student Prince**

$$ | GERMAN | Impressive beer-stein and corkscrew collections at the bar and darkwood paneling lend this restaurant inside an old fort the feel of a convivial hunting lodge, which the antlers and stained-glass windows in the side dining room accentuate. The menu is decidedly meat-centric— beef, chicken, veal, lamb, pork, and delectable homemade sausages— focused on German dishes with some must-have sauerkraut. **Known for:** incredible homemade sauerkraut; various German sausages; impressive decor. ⑤ *Average main: $21* ✉ *8 Fort St.* ☎ *413/734–7475* ⊕ *www.studentprince.com.*

Hotels

★ **Naomi's Inn**

$ | B&B/INN | This elegantly restored house in a residential neighborhood is long on charm, due in no small part to the comfortable and character-filled suites, which are individually decorated—the Louis XIV suite has 19th-century armoires and a down-filled sofa, while the Global Fusion suite has a four-poster bed and a loveseat; a family suite offers a custom-made king-size bed and adjoining room with bunk beds. **Pros:** Bluetooth, bidets, and big-screen TVs with Netflix in rooms; luxe linens and other fabrics; warm and knowledgeable hosts. **Cons:** near a hospital, so you may hear sirens; smallish kitchen; no pool. ⑤ *Rooms from: $125* ✉ *20 Springfield St.* ☎ *413/433–6019, 888/762–6647* ⊕ *www.naomisinn. net* ⇗ *8 suites* ❏ *Free breakfast.*

Sturbridge

35 miles east of Springfield.

Sturbridge is a bit farther toward the coast than the rest of the Pioneer Valley, and off the beaten path lies a rural area that exemplifies old New England. Nowhere is this more true than in Old Sturbridge Village, a re-created early-19th-century village with restored buildings and reenactments, which serves as the central attraction of the town. This is a large enough draw that many inns and hotels are available within walking distance of Old Sturbridge Village, but most of the more appealing dining options, such as The Duck, will require a drive.

GETTING HERE AND AROUND
From Springfield, take Interstate 90 East (or the slower Route 20 East if you're allergic to toll roads). Old Sturbridge Village is centrally located just off Route 20, as are most places you'll want to eat or stay (if they're not right on Route 20, known as Sturbridge's Main Street).

ESSENTIALS
VISITOR INFORMATION Sturbridge Area Tourist Association ☎ *800/628–8379, 508/347–2761* ⊕ *www.sturbridgetownships.com.*

 Sights

★ **Old Sturbridge Village**

MUSEUM VILLAGE | A re-creation of a New England village circa 1790–1840, this site contains more than 40 historic buildings moved here from other towns. There are several industrial buildings, including a working sawmill, and guides in period costumes demonstrate home-based crafts like spinning, weaving, and shoemaking. In season, take an informative stagecoach ride, or cruise the Quinebaug River while learning about river life in 19th-century New England and catching glimpses of ducks, geese, turtles, and other local wildlife. Other popular seasonal events include Christmas by Candlelight weekends in December, and the Redcoats and Rebels reenactment brigade during the first week of August. An associated inn is available for those looking to spend multiple days immersed. ✉ *1 Old Sturbridge Village Rd., Sturbridge* ☎ *508/347–3362, 800/733–1830* ⊕ *www.osv.org* ⊠ *$28* ⊘ *Closed Mon. and Tues.*

 Restaurants

B.T.'s Smokehouse

$ | BARBECUE | Walk up to the counter and order perfectly cooked barbecued meat by the pint or tray at this no-frills barbecue joint. There aren't many tables: grab one while someone else in your group orders. **Known for:** friendly staff; pulled pork and beef brisket; constantly busy. ⑤ *Average main: $11* ✉ *392 Main St., Sturbridge* ☎ *508/347–3188* ⊕ *btsmokehouse.com* ⊘ *Closed Mon.*

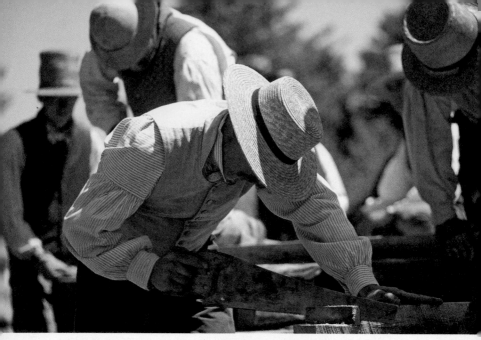

Costumed historians are part of the 19th-century Old Sturbridge Village.

The Duck

$$ | **MODERN AMERICAN** | In a Greek Revival-style building known as the Whistling Swan lie two restaurants; the more notable one is on the second floor in an unpretentious space resembling a barn hayloft. The Duck offers up generous portions of everything from salad to braised lamb as well as various dishes, which, naturally, incorporate duck.
Known for: duck confit poutine; lobster deviled duck eggs; bar and sister Italian restaurant (Avellino) downstairs. ⑤ *Average main: $24* ✉ *502 Main St., 2nd fl., Sturbridge* ☎ *508/347-2321* ⊕ *www.theducksturbridge.com* ⊗ *Closed Mon.*

 Hotels

The Publick House

$ | **B&B/INN** | Step back in time at this rambling 1771 inn, whose 60-acre property sits on the town green encompassing five buildings including the neighboring Chamberlain House and the Country Motor Lodge. **Pros:** Colonial ambience and architecture; historical significance; flat-screen TVs. **Cons:** slanted hallway floor; thin walls, loud pipes; rooms outside main inn less appealing. ⑤ *Rooms from: $189* ✉ *277 Main St., Sturbridge* ☎ *508/347-3313, 800/782-5425* ⊕ *www.publickhouse.com* ⤵ *100 rooms* ⍐ *No meals.*

Sturbridge Host

$ | **HOTEL** | Across the street from Old Sturbridge Village and beside a pleasant lake that some room balconies overlook, this hotel has luxuriously appointed bedrooms in Colonial style, reproduction furnishings, and updated baths with granite tops. **Pros:** lakefront property with picnic tables and paddleboat rentals; quiet setting; indoor courtyard with pool and restaurants. **Cons:** often hosts conferences; smell of the pool's chlorine through whole building; inner courtyard can be noisy. ⑤ *Rooms from: $145* ✉ *366 Main St., Sturbridge* ☎ *508/347-7393, 800/582-3232* ⊕ *www.sturbridgehosthotel.com* ⤵ *233 rooms* ⍐ *No meals.*

South Hadley

12 miles north of Springfield.

A quiet college town with a cluster of Main Street cafés and stores, South Hadley is surrounded by rolling hills and farmland. It's best known for the Mount Holyoke College Art Museum, one of the region's finest cultural facilities.

GETTING HERE AND AROUND

With Bradley International Airport and the Springfield Amtrak station to the south, South Hadley is easy to access. By car, it's east of Interstate 91 and north of U.S. 202 at the intersection of Route 47 and Route 116. You can walk around the Mount Holyoke campus, but you'll need to drive to get most anywhere else.

Sights

Mount Holyoke College

COLLEGE | Founded in 1837, Mount Holyoke was the first women's college in the United States. Among its alumnae are poet Emily Dickinson and playwright Wendy Wasserstein. The handsome wooded campus, encompassing two lakes and lovely walking or riding trails, was landscaped by Frederick Law Olmsted, the co-designer of Manhattan's Central Park. ⊠ *50 College St.* ☎ *413/538–2000* ⊕ *www.mtholyoke.edu.*

Mount Holyoke College Art Museum

MUSEUM | The 24,000 works in the college's collection include Asian, European, and American paintings, as well as sculpture and contemporary art from around the world. The coins and numismatics exhibit is definitely worth a look. On summer Wednesdays and Sundays, the Skinner Museum, a church packed full of the eclectic collection of a wealthy mill owner, is open. ⊠ *Lower Lake Rd.* ⊕ *3 blocks north of Morgan St.* ☎ *413/538–2245* ⊕ *www.mtholyoke.edu/artmuseum* ☜ *Free* ⊗ *Closed Mon.*

Restaurants

Flavyors of Cook Farm

$ | **AMERICAN** | **FAMILY** | The main advantage of stopping for the delicious homemade ice cream at this family farm is that you can see the dairy cows from the dining tables—and even pet them, if you're brave. Sandwiches and mac and cheese are available as well, if for some reason, you're not in the mood for ice cream. **Known for:** very locally sourced dairy; proximity to cows; asparagus ice cream. ⑤ *Average main: $5* ⊠ *Cook Farm, 129 S. Maple St., Hadley* ☎ *413/584–2224* ⊕ *www.flayvors.com.*

Food 101 Bar & Bistro

$$$ | **ECLECTIC** | There's nothing basic about this popular restaurant across from the Mount Holyoke campus, and the atmosphere—from the fancy plating to the nice lighting—almost justifies the high prices, which is why this little spot is a magnet for foodies, yuppies, and college students on their parents' tabs. Dishes—everything from seafood to steak—are complicated but mostly successful. **Known for:** bread sticks with various dips; French fries with wasabi mayo; mushroom ravioli in veal shallot reduction. ⑤ *Average main: $26* ⊠ *19 College St.* ☎ *413/535–3101* ⊕ *www.food101bistro.com* ⊗ *Closed Mon. No lunch.*

IYA Sushi and Noodle Kitchen

$ | **JAPANESE** | With puns on the menu and the staff's shirts, this sushi and noodle bar serves up fun in addition to ramen, bao, and a wide variety of sushi. The atmosphere is upscale casual and would be even more pleasant if it weren't always busy, but that's the price you pay for good food. **Known for:** amusing food puns located everywhere; big bowls of rich-brothed ramen; poke bowls. ⑤ *Average main: $13* ⊠ *Village Commons, 15 College St.* ☎ *413/532–8000* ⊕ *iyasushi.com.*

🛍 Shopping

The Odyssey Bookshop

BOOKS/STATIONERY | In addition to stocking 50,000 new and used titles, Odyssey has readings and book signings by locally (and sometimes nationally) known authors. There's a special event more nights than not. ⊠ *9 College St.* ☎ *413/534–7307* ⊕ *www.odysseybks.com.*

Northampton

10 miles northeast of South Hadley.

The cultural center of Western Massachusetts is without a doubt the city of Northampton (nicknamed "Noho"), whose vibrant downtown is packed with interesting restaurants, lively clubs, and offbeat boutiques. The city attracts artsy types, academics, activists, lesbians and gays, and just about anyone else seeking the culture and sophistication of a big metropolis but the conviviality and easy pace of a small town.

GETTING HERE AND AROUND

Amtrak's *Vermonter* train, which travels between Washington, D.C., and St. Albans, Vermont, stops in Northampton. The city is also served by buses from nearby Springfield's train station, although most people arrive by car on Interstate 91. Downtown is crossed by Routes 5, 9, and 10, and walking to most downtown locations is not only possible, but an excellent way to spend an afternoon. Local PVTA buses are also available. If you're arriving by car, your best bet is to park in the garage attached to Thorne's Marketplace, which is the center of this mostly walkable city.

ESSENTIALS

VISITOR INFORMATION **Greater Northampton Chamber of Commerce** ☎ *413/584–1900* ⊕ *www.explorenorthampton.com.*

◉ Sights

★ R. Michelson Galleries

MUSEUM | FAMILY | In an unassuming former bank lies a large multifloor gallery filled with the works of many artists, but the collection's crown jewel is the room filled with the work from dozens of children's book illustrators. Originals by everyone from Maurice Sendak to Mo Willems are featured, as well as a Dr. Seuss area that includes a few sculptures along with his illustrations. ⊠ *132 Main St.* ☎ *413/586–3964* ⊕ *www. rmichelson.com.*

Smith College

COLLEGE | The nation's largest liberal arts college for women opened its doors in 1875, funded by a bequest from Sophia Smith, a local heiress. Renowned for its School of Social Work, Smith has a long list of distinguished alumnae, among them activist Gloria Steinem, chef Julia Child, and writer Margaret Mitchell. One of New England's most serene campuses, Smith is a leading center of political and cultural activity. The on-campus **Lyman Plant House** is worth a visit. The flourishing **Botanic Garden of Smith College** covers the entire 150-acre campus. ⊠ *College La.* ☎ *413/584–2700* ⊕ *www.smith.edu.*

Smith College Museum of Art

MUSEUM | A floor of galleries with natural light, an enclosed courtyard, and artist-designed restrooms and benches make up this museum, whose permanent collection's highlights include pivotal paintings by Mary Cassatt, Paul Cézanne, Edgar Degas, Georgia O'Keeffe, Auguste Rodin, and Georges Seurat. More recent acquisitions include African, Asian, and Islamic art. ⊠ *Brown Fine Arts Center, 22 Elm St., at Bedford Terr.* ☎ *413/585–2760* ⊕ *www.smith. edu/artmuseum* 🎟 *$5 (free 2nd Fri. of month 4–8)* ⊘ *Closed Mon.*

🍴 Restaurants

Bombay Royale

$ | **INDIAN** | The deep-blue walls and spacious interior lend a calming vibe to this Indian restaurant, whose extensive menu ranges from South Indian to Indo-Chinese dishes. Whether you're in the mood for chicken, lamb, or something vegan, you'll have a dozen good options in your chosen category. **Known for:** lunch buffets; giant masala dosa; spotty service. $ *Average main: $16* ✉ *1 Roundhouse Plaza, Suite 4* ☎ *413/341–3537* ⊘ *Closed Mon.*

Caminito Steakhouse

$$$ | **ARGENTINE** | Caminito's red-and-black interior offers casual elegance in spades. The menu is small, but the flavor is not, so you can count on excellent results whether you order your steak raw as tartare, baked into empanadas, or simply as a large individual cut. **Known for:** filet mignon; empanadas with rotating fillings; live Spanish guitar music at a reasonable volume. $ *Average main: $26* ✉ *7 Old South St.* ☎ *413/387–6387* ⊕ *caminitosteakhouse.com* ⊘ *Closed Mon. No lunch.*

★ Herrell's Ice Cream

$ | **CAFÉ** | On the lower level of Thornes Marketplace, Herrell's is known for not only having some of the state's best ice cream, but also for being the first ice-cream shop to mix in brand-name candies with its ice cream. Flavors often rotate, but an up-to-the-minute list is available online. **Known for:** homemade small-batch hot fudge; malted vanilla and chocolate pudding flavors; dairy-free and sugar-free flavors. $ *Average main: $5* ✉ *8 Old South St.* ☎ *413/586–9700* ⊕ *www.herrells.com* ▤ *No credit cards.*

Northampton Brewery

$$ | **AMERICAN** | In a rambling building in Brewster Court, this noisy and often-packed pub has extensive outdoor seating on a deck. The kitchen turns out sandwiches and comfort food, including stuffed peppers and burgers with blue cheese and caramelized onions. **Known for:** flaky-light catfish bites; humanely sourced meat; beer-battered appetizers. $ *Average main: $18* ✉ *11 Brewster Ct., near Hampton Ave.* ☎ *413/584–9903* ⊕ *www.northamptonbrewery.com.*

Osaka

$$ | **JAPANESE** | The hillside enclosed porch overlooking the center of town makes Osaka the most recognizable restaurant in Northampton, as well as one of the best dining spots. Whether you're in the mood for sushi, a bento box lunch, or a full hibachi dinner, Osaka serves up traditional Japanese favorites in a welcoming atmosphere. **Known for:** kobe beef sushi; entertaining hibachi chefs; bento box lunches. $ *Average main: $20* ✉ *7 Old South St.* ☎ *413/587–9548* ⊕ *www.osakarestaurantgroup.com.*

Nightlife

Fitzwilly's

BARS/PUBS | A reliable bar for a night out, Fitzwilly's draws a friendly mix of locals and tourists for drinks and tasty pub fare. (Try the Gorgonzola garlic bread.) ✉ *23 Main St.* ☎ *413/584–8666* ⊕ *www.fitzwillys.com.*

Hugo's

BARS/PUBS | A bit of a dive, the dimly lighted Hugo's has cheap beer, affordable pool, a rocking jukebox, and all the local color you could want. ✉ *315 Pleasant St.* ☎ *413/387–6023.*

Activities

Norwottuck Rail Trail

BICYCLING | FAMILY | Part of the Connecticut River Greenway State Park, this paved 10-mile path links Northampton with Belchertown by way of Amherst. Great for biking, rollerblading, jogging, and cross-country skiing, it runs along the old Boston & Maine Railroad route. Free trail maps are available on the Mass. gov website. ✉ *446 Damon Rd., at Rte. 9* ☎ *413/586–8706* ⊕ *www.mass.gov.*

🛍 Shopping

★ Thornes Marketplace

SHOPPING CENTERS/MALLS | A quintessential stop on any Northampton visit—and not just because the market's centrally located garage is your best bet for convenient parking—Thornes contains an eclectic lineup of shops ranging from **Glimpse of Tibet** for Tibetan handicrafts to **Herrell's Ice Cream** and **Captain Candy** for sweets and desserts. Also here are **Booklink Booksellers, Cedar Chest,** a yoga studio, a chair-massage parlor, and clothing and jewelry stores. ⊠ *150 Main St.* ☎ *413/584–5582* ⊕ *www.thornes-marketplace.com.*

Williamsburg General Store

CONVENIENCE/GENERAL STORES | This Pioneer Valley landmark has an in-store bakery in addition to the usual candy, spices, jams, maple confections, kitchen items, and other gifts you might expect. Try a "Wrapple": a hand pie made with apples from local orchards. ⊠ *12 Main St.* ☎ *413/268–3036* ⊕ *www.wgstore.com.*

Amherst

8 miles northeast of Northampton.

★ One of New England's most visited spots, Amherst is known for its scores of world-renowned authors, poets, and artists. The above-average intelligence quotient of its population is no accident, as Amherst is home to a trio of colleges: Amherst, Hampshire, and the University of Massachusetts. Art galleries, book and music stores, and several downtown cultural venues tickle the intellectual fancy of the college-age crowd, the locals, and the profs.

GETTING HERE AND AROUND

The closest airport is Bradley International in Connecticut. Amtrak's *Vermonter* train stops in nearby Northampton. From there you can take a PVTA bus into town, where the buses are also a good way to get around. If driving, reduce hassle by bringing change for the parking kiosks.

ESSENTIALS

VISITOR INFORMATION Amherst Area Chamber of Commerce ☎ *413/253–0700* ⊕ *www.amherstarea.com.*

👁 Sights

Emily Dickinson Museum

HOUSE | The famed Amherst poet lived and wrote in this brick Federal-style home. Admission is by guided tour only, and to say that the tour guides are knowledgeable would be a massive understatement; the highlight of the tour is the sunlit bedroom where the poet wrote many of her works. Next door is **The Evergreens,** the imposing Italianate Victorian mansion in which Emily's brother Austin and his family resided for more than 50 years. ⊠ *280 Main St.* ☎ *413/542–8161* ⊕ *www.emily-dickinsonmuseum.org* ✎ *$15* ⊘ *Closed Mon. and Tues. and Jan. and Feb.*

★ Eric Carle Museum of Picture Book Art

ARTS VENUE | **FAMILY** | If you have kids in tow—or if you just love children's book illustrations—"the Carle" is a must-see. This light-filled museum celebrates and preserves not only the works of renowned children's book author Eric Carle, who penned *The Very Hungry Caterpillar,* but also original picture-book art by Maurice Sendak, William Steig, Chris Van Allsburg, and many others. Puppet shows and storytelling events are among the museum's ongoing programs. Children are invited to create their own works of art in the studio or read classics or discover new authors in the library. ⊠ *125 W. Bay Rd.* ☎ *413/559–6300* ⊕ *www.picturebookart.org* ✎ *$9* ⊘ *Closed Mon. Sept.–June.*

Yiddish Book Center

LIBRARY | Founded in 1980, this nonprofit organization received a National Medal for Museum and Library Service for its role in preserving the Yiddish language and Jewish culture. The award recognized the center's rescue of more than a million Yiddish books that might otherwise have been lost. Housed in a cool, contemporary structure that mimics a traditional Eastern European shtetl, or village, the collection comprises more than 100,000 volumes. Special programs take place throughout the year. The biggest is Yidstock, a mid-July festival celebrating klezmer and other Jewish music. ⊠ *Hampshire College, 1021 West St.* ☎ *413/256–4900* ⊕ *www.yiddishbookcenter.org* ⌁ *$8* ⊗ *Closed Sat.*

Restaurants

Bub's Bar-B-Q

$ | **BARBECUE** | You can smell the sweet and tangy homemade barbecue sauce even before you enter this down-home rib joint where awards and positive newspaper reviews line the walls and a stuffed pig carries your order to the kitchen. Everything from fried gator to pulled pork is expertly done, and the dinners all come with a large and sumptuous buffet of sides. **Known for:** free jukebox; hot bar and cold bar; copious outdoor seating. ⑤ *Average main: $14* ⊠ *676 Amherst Rd., Sunderland* ☎ *413/548–9630* ⊕ *www.bubsbbq.com* ⊗ *Closed Mon. No lunch Tues.–Fri.*

★ Judie's

$$ | **AMERICAN** | Since 1977, academic types have crowded around small tables on Judie's glassed-in porch. The menu offers various traditional dishes, but your best bet is ordering one of the creative popover specials in flavors such as gumbo and shrimp scampi. **Known for:** French onion soup; haunt for academics; tabletops covered in paintings. ⑤ *Average main: $22* ⊠ *51 N. Pleasant St.* ☎ *413/253–3491* ⊕ *www.judiesrestaurant.com.*

Mission Cantina

$ | **MEXICAN** | Diners pack this loud and colorful cantina daily to enjoy Mexican food at reasonable prices. What the small menu lacks in variety, it makes up for in reliability; everything from the crispy fish tacos to the carnitas enchiladas is worth trying. **Known for:** long waits during prime dinner hours; delicious (but not free) chips and salsa; offbeat margaritas with interesting fruits and flavors. ⑤ *Average main: $13* ⊠ *485 West St.* ☎ *413/230–3580* ⊕ *www.themissioncantinaamherst.com* ⊗ *No lunch weekdays.*

Hotels

Allen House Inn

$ | **B&B/INN** | Meticulous attention to detail distinguishes this late-19th-century inn, which has been gloriously restored to reflect Victorian aesthetics—colorful wall coverings, plentiful antiques, lace curtains, and hand-stenciled details—though the guest-room beds topped with goose-down comforters are the finest that modernity has to offer. **Pros:** charm and elegance; great linens; free parking. **Cons:** dark and cluttered with ornate furnishings; tiny baths; easy to drive past. ⑤ *Rooms from: $175* ⊠ *599 Main St.* ☎ *413/253–5000* ⊕ *www.allenhouse.com* ⊿ *14 rooms* ⦿ *Free breakfast.*

The Lord Jeffery Inn at Amherst College

$$ | **B&B/INN** | On the town common of downtown Amherst, this rambling 1926 inn owned by Amherst College is a favorite among visiting parents and professors for its variety of rooms, from smallish doubles to larger suites. **Pros:** great location on the town common; various weekend packages including a farmers' market special; spacious lobby and rooms. **Cons:** some baths are closet-size; many wedding, school, and graduation celebrations are held here. ⑤ *Rooms from: $285* ⊠ *30 Boltwood Ave.* ☎ *413/253–2576* ⊕ *www.lordjefferyinn.com* ⊿ *49 rooms* ⦿ *No meals.*

Shopping

Atkins Farms Country Market

OUTDOOR/FLEA/GREEN MARKETS | An institution in the Pioneer Valley, this market sells produce, baked goods, and specialty foods—try a cider doughnut to sample the best of all three. ⊠ *1150 West St.* ☎ *413/253–9528* ⊕ *www. atkinsfarms.com.*

Deerfield

10 miles northwest of Amherst.

In Deerfield a horse pulling a carriage clip-clops past perfectly maintained 18th-century homes, neighbors tip their hats to strangers, kids play ball in fields by the river, and the bell of the impossibly beautiful brick church peals from a white steeple. This is the perfect New England village, though not without a past darkened by tragedy. Its original Native American inhabitants, the Pocumtucks, were all but wiped out by deadly epidemics and a war with the Mohawks. English pioneers eagerly settled into this frontier outpost in the 1660s and '70s, but two bloody massacres at the hands of Native Americans and the French prompted them to abandon it until 1707, when construction began on the buildings that remain today.

GETTING HERE AND AROUND
You can take the train to Springfield, but the most direct public transportation to Deerfield is a Peter Pan bus. If you're driving, take Route 10 from the south or Route 2 from the west. Aside from walking around Historic Deerfield, however, you won't get far without a car.

Sights

★ Historic Deerfield
HISTORIC SITE | With 52 buildings on 93 acres, Historic Deerfield provides a vivid glimpse into 18th- and 19th-century America. Along the tree-lined main street are 12 museum houses, built between 1720 and 1850, some with original doorways. Four are open to the public on self-guided tours, and the remainder can be seen on guided tours that begin on the hour. The **Frary House** displays arts and crafts from the 1900s; the attached Barnard Tavern was the main meeting place for Deerfield's villagers. Other houses depict 18th-century life, including everything from kitchens to adult cradles for those who had fallen victim to tuberculosis. Also of note is a one-room schoolhouse, an old burial ground, and the **Flynt Center of Early New England Life,** which contains needlework, textiles, and clothing dating back to the 1600s. The visitor center is located at Hall Tavern, 80 Old Main Street. Plan to spend at least one full day at Historic Deerfield. ⊠ *Old Main St.* ☎ *413/775–7214* ⊕ *www.historic-deerfield.org* ⊠ *$18.*

Magic Wings Butterfly Conservatory and Gardens
GARDEN | FAMILY | This glass conservatory glitters with more than 4,000 butterflies. Kids love the butterfly nursery, where newborns first take flight. Outside is a three-season garden filled with plants that attract local species. There's also a snack bar and gift shop. ⊠ *281 Greenfield Rd., South Deerfield* ☎ *413/665–2805* ⊕ *www.magicwings.com* ⊠ *$16.*

The Montague Bookmill
STORE/SHOP/MALL | This old mill complex along the Saw Mill River—since converted into a quintet of businesses—exudes old New England. **The Bookmill** is a quirky secondhand bookshop whose comfortable chairs make it easy to curl up with a book. The good-humored staffers at the adjoining **Lady Killigrew** café serve beer, coffee, and bagels; there's free Wi-Fi, too. The fantastic waterfall views from the deck of **Alvah Stone,** which serves lunch and dinner, justify its slightly elevated prices. From Friday to Sunday, you can visit **Turn It Up** for music and movies, and Wednesday through

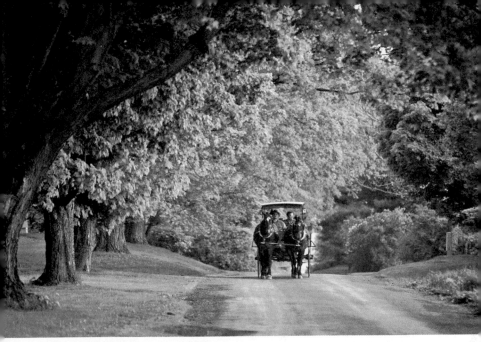

Historic Deerfield is one of many places in the region to experience America's past through living history.

Monday the **Sawmill River Arts** crafts gallery offers items by local artists. The complex is incredibly picturesque, if not entirely wheelchair accessible. ✉ *440 Greenfield Rd., Montague ✛ ¼ mile past village green over small bridge* ☎ *413/367–9206* ⊕ *www.montaguebookmill.com.*

Restaurants

Richardson's Candy Kitchen

$ | CAFÉ | The name is no joke: the back half of this store is a kitchen where you can see delectable chocolates being made. A short drive from Historic Deerfield, Richardson's sells luscious cream-filled chocolates, truffles, and other handmade confections, not to mention ice cream. **Known for:** melt-in-your-mouth Almond Acorns; selection of sugar-free chocolates; chocolate-covered strawberries. ⑤ *Average main: $5* ✉ *500 Greenfield Rd.* ☎ *413/772–0443* ⊕ *www.richardsonscandy.com* ▭ *No credit cards.*

Shelburne Falls

18 miles northwest of Deerfield.

A tour of New England's fall foliage wouldn't be complete without a trek across the famed Mohawk Trail, a 63-mile section of Route 2 that runs past Shelburne Falls. The community, separated from neighboring Buckland by the Deerfield River, is filled with little art galleries and interesting shops on Bridge Street. The surrounding area is filled with orchards, farm stands, and sugar houses.

GETTING HERE AND AROUND

Shelburne Falls lies on Route 2, otherwise known as the Mohawk Trail, useful not only for driving through town, but for setting off to the Berkshires as well.

◉ Sights

Bridge of Flowers

GARDEN | From April to October, an arched, 400-foot trolley bridge is transformed into this promenade bursting with color and a wide variety of flowers. ✉ *Water St.* ☎ *413/625–2544* ⊕ *www. bridgeofflowersmass.org.*

Shelburne Falls Trolley Museum

MUSEUM | Take a ride on an old-fashioned trolley from 1896 at this tribute to the old Colrain Street Railway Combine No. 10, which was the first car on the Shelburne line in the early 20th century. A car barn and rails host other trolleys being restored, including a PCC, the last trolley built in Massachusetts. ✉ *14 Depot St.* ☎ *413/625–9443* ⊕ *www.sftm.org* ⊟ *All-day trolley pass $4.*

Restaurants

Hearty Eats

$ | **VEGETARIAN** | You don't have to be vegetarian to appreciate the fresh, local, organic offerings at this tiny commu-nity-focused café. Sharing an entrance with an arts co-op, the café itself lacks ambience, but does offer up a tasty variety of healthy options that exclude any meat except fish. **Known for:** wide vegetarian selection; falafel and fried-fish bites; fresh juices. $ *Average main: $10* ✉ *24 Bridge St.* ☎ *413/625–6460* ⊕ *heartyeats.org.*

West End Pub

$$ | **AMERICAN** | Overlooking the Bridge of Flowers and Deerfield River, this quaint upscale pub filled with plants and local artwork is a charming place to catch lunch. Tables on the enclosed porch offer a nice view while you enjoy a hearty burger or fancy salad. **Known for:** grass-fed Black Angus beef burgers from local farms; gluten-free rolls and pasta; tough to access bathroom. $ *Average main: $18* ✉ *16 State St.* ☎ *413/625–6216* ⊕ *westendpubinfo.com* ⊗ *Closed Mon.*

Activities

RAFTING

Zoar Outdoor

WHITE-WATER RAFTING | White-water rafting, canoeing, and kayaking in the Class II–III rapids of the Deerfield River are popular summer activities. From April to October, Zoar Outdoor conducts kid-friendly rafting trips along 10 miles of challenging rapids, as well as floats along gentler sections of the river. Zipline tours and rock climbing are also offered in season. ✉ *7 Main St., off Rte. 2, Charlemont* ☎ *800/532–7483* ⊕ *www. zaroutdoor.com.*

Shopping

Salmon Falls Artisans Showroom

CERAMICS/GLASSWARE | The showroom features sculpture, pottery, and glass by more than 100 artisans, including hand-blown pieces by Josh Simpson. ✉ *1 Ashfield St., Suite 9* ☎ *413/625–9833* ⊕ *www.salmonfallsgallery.com* ⊗ *Closed Tues.–Thurs. Jan.–Apr.*

Sidehill Farm

FOOD/CANDY | This farm sells yogurt, raw milk, and cheese, as well as beef, from grass-fed cows. Vegetables and fruits are generally available throughout the year. ✉ *58 Forget Rd., Hawley* ☎ *413/339–0033* ⊕ *www.sidehillfarm.net.*

Chapter 7

CONNECTICUT

Updated by
Jane E. Zarem

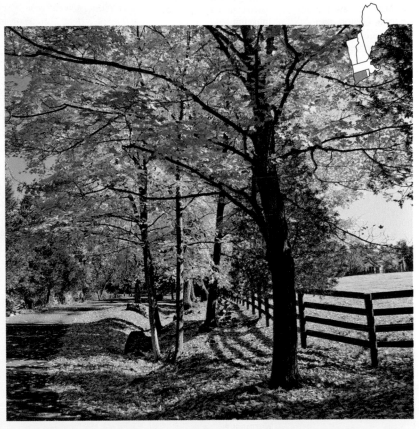

⊙ Sights	🍴 Restaurants	🛏 Hotels	🛍 Shopping	🍸 Nightlife
★★★★★	★★★★☆	★★★☆☆	★★★☆☆	★★☆☆☆

272

WELCOME TO CONNECTICUT

TOP REASONS TO GO

★ **Country Driving:** Meander along the winding roads of Litchfield County through charming towns and villages like Kent, Salisbury, Washington, and Litchfield.

★ **Maritime History:** New London, Groton, and Mystic are all packed with interesting nautical attractions related to Connecticut's rich seafaring history.

★ **Urban Exploring:** Anchored by Yale University, downtown New Haven buzzes with hip restaurants, smart boutiques, and acclaimed theaters.

★ **Literary Giants:** In one historic Hartford neighborhood, you can explore the homes—and legacies—of Mark Twain and Harriet Beecher Stowe; in New London, visit Eugene O'Neill's summer cottage.

★ **Antiques Hunting:** You'll find fine antiques shops, galleries, and auction houses in cities and towns all around the state, but Woodbury and Putnam are two towns that particularly stand out.

1 Greenwich. Beaches, forests, and picture-perfect downtown.

2 Stamford. Great restaurants, nightclubs, and shopping.

3 Norwalk. A center for shopping, dining, and culture.

4 Ridgefield. Inviting town center and great art museum.

5 Westport. An art and culture spot since the turn of the 20th century.

6 Bridgeport. A handful of family-friendly attractions.

7 Essex. Home to the Essex Steam Train.

8 East Haddam. Old-fashioned charm and a historic downtown.

9 Middletown. Home to Wesleyan University and Dinosaur State Park.

10 Wethersfield. A Hartford suburb with a great historic district.

11 Hartford. Capital city with arts and culture.

12 Farmington. A classic river town with a preserved main street.

13 New Milford. Shops, galleries, and dining around the town green.

14 New Preston. Quaint town center near Lake Waramaug.

15 Kent. Numerous art galleries and Kent Falls State Park.

16 Cornwall. Great vistas and a covered bridge.

17 Norfolk. One of the Northeast's best-preserved villages.

18 Litchfield. A walkable downtown with shops and restaurants.

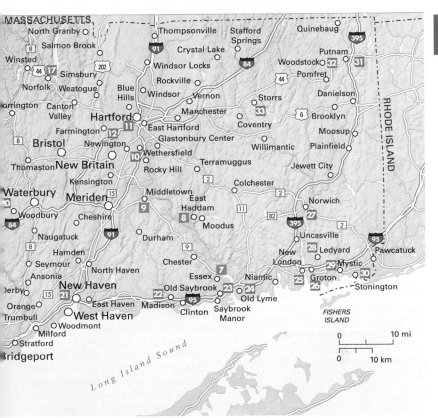

19 Washington. One of Connecticut's best-preserved Colonial towns.

20 Woodbury. Town has numerous antiques shops.

21 New Haven. Yale, the Peabody Museum, and New Haven pizza.

22 Madison. Ice-cream shops, boutiques, and Hammonasset Beach State Park.

23 Old Saybrook. A picturesque small town.

24 Old Lyme. Lovely countryside and shoreline.

25 New London. Home to the U.S. Coast Guard.

26 Groton. Location of the Naval Submarine Base.

27 Norwich. Mill town with beautiful homes.

28 Ledyard. Foxwoods and Mohegan Sun.

29 Mystic. Mystic Seaport and Mystic Aquarium.

30 Stonington. A pretty fishing village.

31 Putnam. Hub of the Quiet Corner's antiques trade.

32 Woodstock. A picturesque town.

33 Storrs. Home to the UCONN's main campus.

You can travel from just about any point in Connecticut to any other in less than two hours; this small state is fewer than 60 miles top to bottom and only about 100 miles across. Yet, it would take weeks to ramble all of Connecticut's "back roads," visit all of its small towns and quaint villages, and enjoy all of its unique attractions.

Along Connecticut's 253 miles of shoreline, salty sea air wafts across beach communities like Madison, Old Lyme, and Stonington, while a patchwork of forested hills and tiny towns fill the state's northwestern corner—and once-upon-a-time mill towns line rivers such as the Housatonic, Moodus, and Quinebaug. Connecticut has seemingly endless farmland in the northeast, where cows might just outnumber people; directly opposite, in the upscale communities of Fairfield County, boutique shopping bags probably outnumber the people.

Just as diverse as the landscape are the state's residents, who number more than 3½ million. Many "Connecticut Yankees" can trace their roots to the 1600s, when Connecticut was settled as one of the 13 original colonies; but the state motto is "He who transplanted still sustains." And so the face of the Nutmegger today is both the family from Naples making pizza in New Haven and the farmer in Norfolk whose land dates back five generations, the grandmother in New Britain who makes the state's best pierogi and the ladies who lunch in Westport, the celebrity nestled in the Litchfield Hills and the

Bridgeport entrepreneur trying to close the gap between Connecticut's struggling cities and its affluent suburbs.

Qualities that all Connecticut Yankees seem to have in common, historically, is inventiveness, intellect, and the desire to have a little fun. For example: the nation's first public library opened in New Haven in 1656; its first state house, in Hartford in 1776. Tapping Reeve developed America's first law school in Litchfield in 1784, West Hartford's Noah Webster published the first dictionary in 1806, and New Haven's Eli Whitney invented the cotton gin. On the fun side, Lake Compounce in Bristol was the country's first amusement park; Bethel's P. T. Barnum staged the first three-ring circus; and the hamburger, the lollipop, the can opener, the Frisbee, the whiffle ball, FM radio, the portable typewriter, the Colt.45 revolver, even the lobster roll—and, of course, the nuclear submarine—were all invented in Connecticut.

Today, due to the state's rich history, cultural environment, and abundant natural beauty (including 92 state parks and 30 state forests), tourism has become one of Connecticut's leading industries.

MAJOR REGIONS

Southwestern Connecticut, otherwise known as Fairfield County, is a rich swirl of vintage New England and suburban New York—a region that consistently reports one of the highest costs of living and most expensive homes of any area in the country. Its commuter towns are home primarily to white-collar executives. Venture beyond the wealthy bedroom communities of **Greenwich** and **Westport,** and you'll discover cities struggling through various stages of urban renewal: **Stamford, Norwalk, Bridgeport,** and Danbury. These four have some of the region's best cultural and shopping opportunities, but the economic disparity between Connecticut's large cities and its upscale towns is perhaps most visible in Fairfield County.

Less touristy than the coast, the **Connecticut River Valley** is a swath of small towns and uncrowded state parks punctuated by a few small cities and one large one: the capital city of **Hartford.** South of Hartford, with the exception of industrial **Middletown,** genuinely quaint hamlets with names like **Essex, East Haddam, Wethersfield,** and **Farmington** vie for attention with their antiques shops, scenic drives, and romantic restaurants and country inns.

The Litchfield Hills present some of the most enchanting scenery in Connecticut. Two highways, Interstate 84 and Route 8, form the southern and eastern boundaries of the region; New York, to the west, and Massachusetts, to the north, complete the rectangle. Rolling farmlands abut thick forests, and trails—including a section of the Appalachian Trail—traverse state parks and forests. Two rivers, the Housatonic and the Farmington, and two large lakes, Bantam and Waramaug, attract anglers, canoers, hikers, and campers. Sweeping town greens and stately homes anchor **Litchfield** and **New Milford; Kent, New Preston,** and **Woodbury** draw avid antiquers; **Washington** and **Norfolk** provide a

glimpse of New England village life as it might have been two centuries ago; and **Cornwall** is known for its fantastic vistas and covered bridge.

New Haven, Mystic, and the **Coast.** Wander through Yale's campus or visit the dinosaurs at the Peabody Museum of Natural History before dining at a classic New Haven pizzeria. Head east along the coastline through one unspoiled seaside town after the next, spend a day at Mystic Seaport, or head inland and roll the dice at a casino—either Foxwoods or Mohegan Sun.

As you drive northeast along Interstate 95, culturally rich **New Haven** is the final urban obstacle between southwestern Connecticut's overdeveloped coast and it's quiet **Southeastern Coast.** This remaining jagged coast, which stretches to Rhode Island, consists of small fishing villages, quiet hamlets, and relatively undisturbed beaches found in **Madison.** The only interruptions along this seashore are the industry and piers of **New London and Groton. Mystic, Stonington, Old Saybrook,** Clinton, and Guilford are havens for fans of antiques and boutiques. The Mashantucket Pequot Reservation owns and operates the Foxwoods Casino and the Mashantucket Pequot Museum & Research Center, near the towns of **Ledyard** and North Stonington, and the Mohegan Tribe runs the Mohegan Sun casino in Uncasville, north of New London. Along with gaming, these two properties have noteworthy hotels and marquee restaurants.

Few visitors to Connecticut experience the old-fashioned ways of the **The Quiet Corner,** a vast patch of sparsely populated, mostly rural towns that seem a world away from the rest of the state. There's actually a reclusive allure here. The cultural capital of the Quiet Corner is **Putnam,** a small mill town on the Quinebaug River whose formerly industrial town center has been transformed into a year-round antiques mart. In **Woodstock,** authentic

7

Connecticut

Colonial homesteads still abound. The scenic drive along 169 toward Woodstock has been named a National Scenic Byway. University of Connecticut's main campus occupies the majority of the tiny village of **Storrs**.

Planning

WHEN TO GO

Connecticut is lovely year-round, but fall and spring are particularly appealing times to visit. A fall drive along the state's back roads or the Merritt Parkway, a National Scenic Byway, is a memorable experience when spots of yellow, orange, and red dot the fall landscape. The state blooms in springtime, too, when town greens are filled with daffodils and tulips and dogwoods and flowering fruit trees punctuate the rich green countryside. The prime time for attractions, however, is summer, when travelers have the most options but also plenty of company—especially at beaches along the shore.

PLANNING YOUR TIME

The Nutmeg State is a confluence of different worlds—where farm country meets country homes, and fans of the New York Yankees and Boston Red Sox can (quasi-) peacefully coexist. To get a true sense of Connecticut's variety, start in the scenic Litchfield Hills, where you can relax on historic town greens and at trendy cafés. Head south, if you have a bit more time, to explore the wealthy southwestern corner of the state and then over to New Haven, with its cultural pleasures. If you have five days or a week, take in the capital city of Hartford, the villages of the Connecticut River Valley, and the southeastern shoreline.

GETTING HERE AND AROUND
AIR TRAVEL

People visiting Connecticut from afar can fly into New York City, Boston, or Providence—or directly into Hartford or smaller regional airports in New Haven or Westchester County (NY).

AIRPORT CONTACTS Bradley International Airport ⊠ *11 Schoephoester Rd., Windsor Locks* ☎ *860/292-2000* ⊕ *www.bradleyairport.com*. **Tweed New Haven Airport** ⊠ *155 Burr St., New Haven* ☎ *203/466-8833* ⊕ *www.flytweed.com*.

CAR TRAVEL

Interstates are the quickest routes between many points in Connecticut, but they can be quite congested. From New York City, head north on Interstate 95, which hugs the Connecticut shoreline into Rhode Island, or, for Hartford and the Litchfield Hills, head north on Interstate 684, then east on Interstate 84. From central New England, go south on Interstate 91, which intersects Interstate 84 in Hartford and Interstate 95 in New Haven. From Boston, take Interstate 95 south through Providence or take the Massachusetts Turnpike west to Interstate 84. Interstate 395 runs north–south from southeastern Connecticut to Massachusetts.

Often more pleasant because of no truck traffic, the historic Merritt Parkway (Route 15) winds its way between Greenwich and Stratford, then becomes the Wilbur Cross Parkway and continues on to Middletown; U.S. 7 and Route 8 extend between Interstate 95 and the Litchfield Hills; Route 9 heads south from Hartford through the Connecticut River Valley to Essex and Old Saybrook; and scenic Route 169 meanders through the Quiet Corner.

FERRY TRAVEL

Seasonal ferry service is available to passengers (and bicycles) between New London and Rhode Island's Block Island, while year-round ferries carry passengers and vehicles between New London and Orient Point, at the tip of New York's Long Island. Year-round ferries also transport passengers and vehicles between Bridgeport and Port Jefferson, Long Island.

FERRY CONTACTS Block Island Express ✉ *2 Ferry St., New London* ☎ *860/444–4624* ⊕ *www.goblockisland.com.* **Bridgeport & Port Jefferson Steamboat Co.** ✉ *1 Ferry Access Rd., Bridgeport* ☎ *888/443–3779* ⊕ *www.88844ferry.com.* **Chester–Hadlyme Ferry** ✉ *Ferry Rd., Rte. 148, Chester* ☎ *860/526–2743* ⊕ *www.ct.gov/dot/cwp/view.asp?a=1390&Q=499780.* **Cross Sound Ferry** ✉ *2 Ferry St., New London* ☎ *860/443–5281* ⊕ *www.longislandferry.com.*

TRAIN TRAVEL

Amtrak runs from New York to Boston, stopping in Stamford, Bridgeport, and New Haven, before heading either north through Hartford or east through New London. Metro-North runs along the coastline between New York and New Haven, stopping in several towns in Fairfield County (including Greenwich, Stamford, Darien, South Norwalk, Westport, and Fairfield). Shore Line East is a commuter line that runs between New Haven and New London, stopping at towns in between.

TRAIN CONTACTS Amtrak ☎ *800/872–7245* ⊕ *www.amtrak.com.* **Metro-North Railroad** ☎ *877/690–5116* ⊕ *www.mta.info.* **Shore Line East** ☎ *877/287–4337* ⊕ *www.shorelineeast.com.*

RESTAURANTS

Southern New England is enjoying a gastronomic revolution. Preparation and ingredients reflect the culinary trends of nearby Manhattan and Boston; indeed, the quality and diversity of many Connecticut restaurants rival those of sophisticated metropolitan areas. Although traditional favorites remain—New England clam chowder, buttery lobster rolls, and fish 'n' chips—you may also find that sliced duck is wrapped in phyllo, served with a ginger-plum sauce (the orange glaze decidedly absent) and that everything from lavender to fresh figs is used to season and complement dishes.

Dining is also increasingly international: you'll find Indian, Vietnamese, Thai, Malaysian, South American, and Japanese restaurants—even Spanish tapas bars—in both cities and suburbs. The farm-to-table movement influences what appears on your plate in many establishments, with conscientious chefs partnering up with local producers to provide the best seasonal ingredients. The one drawback of this turn toward sophistication is that finding a dinner entrée for less than $10 is difficult. *Restaurant reviews have been shortened. For full information, visit Fodors.com.*

HOTELS

Connecticut has plenty of the usual chain hotels and low-budget motels, along with the more unusual and atmospheric inns, resorts, bed-and-breakfasts, and country hotels that are typical of New England. You'll pay dearly for rooms on the coast in summer, when the beaches beckon, and in the hills in autumn, when the changing leaves attract thousands of visitors. Rates are lowest in winter, but so are the temperatures; spring is lovely and also a good season for bargain seekers. *Hotel reviews have been shortened. For full information, visit Fodors.com.*

What It Costs			
$	$$	$$$	$$$$
RESTAURANTS			
under $18	$18–$24	$25–$35	over $35
HOTELS			
under $200	$200–$299	$300–$399	over $399

TOURS

Connecticut Freedom Trail

DRIVING TOURS | FAMILY | The state's African American heritage is documented and celebrated on the trail, which includes more than 130 historic sights across 50 towns. ☎ *860/256–2800* ⊕ *www.ctfreedomtrail.org.*

7

Connecticut PLANNING

Taste of New Haven

GUIDED TOURS | Colin Caplan and his guides take you on foodie adventures—walking, bike, and party bike tours—in and around New Haven, which boasts a burgeoning restaurant scene and, of course, the famous New Haven pizza! ☎ *888/975–8664* ⊕ *tasteofnewhaven.com.*

VISITOR INFORMATION

VISITOR CONTACTS Central Regional Tourism District ☎ *860/787–9640, 888/288–4748* ⊕ *www.ctvisit.com/centerofct* **Connecticut Office of Tourism** ☎ *888/288–4748* ⊕ *www.ctvisit.com* **Western CT Convention & Visitors Bureau** ☎ *800/663–1273* ⊕ *www.visitfairfieldcountyct.com.*

Greenwich

35 miles northeast of New York City, 82 miles southwest of Hartford.

Leafy woodlands, rolling hills, sandy beaches overlooking sparkling Long Island Sound, and a picture-perfect downtown area filled with chic boutiques and trendsetting restaurants: welcome to Greenwich. It's easy to see why this ritzy enclave has become a haven for Fairfield County's rich and famous. Soak up some history and culture at the Bruce Museum, then head to Greenwich Avenue for excellent (expensive) shopping and dining.

GETTING HERE AND AROUND

If you're traveling north from New York City, Greenwich will be the first town in Connecticut once you cross the state border. It's easily accessible from either Interstate 95 or the Merritt Parkway if you're coming by car; Metro-North commuter trains also service Greenwich.

 Sights

Audubon Greenwich

NATURE PRESERVE | **FAMILY** | Opened in 1943 as the National Audubon Society's first educational nature center, the sanctuaries and trails are the best location in the area for bird-watching. During the Fall Festival and Hawk Watch each September, you can spot large numbers of hawks and other migrating raptors. Other events include early morning bird walks, summer and winter bird counts, birding classes, and field trips. The center is filled with interactive exhibits, galleries, classrooms, a wildlife observation room, and a deck with sweeping views of wildlife activity. Outside are 7 miles of hiking trails passing through 285 acres of woodland, wetland, and meadow. ☒ *613 Riversville Rd.* ☎ *203/869–5272* ⊕ *greenwich.audubon.org* ⬢ *$6.*

★ Bruce Museum of Arts and Science

MUSEUM | **FAMILY** | The owner of this 19th-century home, wealthy textile merchant Robert Moffat Bruce, bequeathed it to the town of Greenwich in 1908 with the stipulation that it be used "as a natural history, historical, and art museum." Today this diversity remains, reflected in the museum's changing exhibitions—more than a dozen new ones each year—highlighting fine and decorative arts, natural history, and anthropology. On permanent display is a spectacular mineral collection. Kids especially enjoy the touchable meteorite and glow-in-the-dark minerals, as well as the fossilized dinosaur tracks. ☒ *1 Museum Dr.* ⊕ *Off I–95, Exit 3* ☎ *203/869–0376* ⊕ *www.brucemuseum.org* ⬢ *$10 (free Tues.).*

Bush-Holley Historic Site

HISTORIC SITE | In the 1890s, visitors from New York's Art Students League journeyed to the Cos Cob section of Greenwich to take classes taught by American Impressionist John Henry Twachtman at a boarding house for artists and writers run by Josephine and Constant Holley. Thus, the Cos Cob Art Colony was born and flourished until 1920. Today, the circa-1730 house is the Bush-Holley Historic Site, which displays a wonderful collection of 19th- and 20th-century art by sculptor John Rogers, potter Leon Volkmar, and painters that include Childe Hassam, Elmer Livingston MacRae, and, of course, Twachtman. The collection also includes personal papers, photographs, and records that reflect the long history of Greenwich and its inhabitants, from farmers to Gilded Age barons, politicians, artists and writers, shopkeepers, and more. ⊠ *39 Strickland Rd.* ☎ *203/869–6899* ⊕ *www.hstg.org* ⊴ *$10* ☉ *Closed weekdays Jan. and Feb.; Mon. and Tues. Mar.–Dec.*

 ## Restaurants

Boxcar Cantina
$$ | SOUTHWESTERN | FAMILY | If it's Southwestern food you're craving, Boxcar Cantina delivers the freshest and most authentic Tex-Mex dishes in the area. Diners rave about the margaritas, pairing them happily with fish tacos, quesadillas, enchiladas, and burritos. **Known for:** chefs take special care to source local organic ingredients; the restaurant has a stand at the nearby Westport Farmers' Market on Thursday; takeout is available. Ⓢ *Average main: $19* ⊠ *44 Old Field Point Rd.* ☎ *203/661–4774* ⊕ *www.boxcarcantina. com* ☉ *No lunch weekends.*

Elm Street Oyster House
$$$ | SEAFOOD | Locals come here for outstanding oysters and the freshest fish in town; expect an especially lively crowd on weekends. Menu standouts include the varied selection of fresh oysters from all over the country, classic lobster rolls, and outstanding seafood chili. **Known for:** seafood, seafood, seafood—and a cheeseburger, steak, penne, or grilled cheese for landlubbers; colorful artwork adds cheer to the rather cramped dining room; friendly, efficient service—but you're never rushed. Ⓢ *Average main: $34* ⊠ *11 W. Elm St.* ☎ *203/629–5795* ⊕ *www.elmstreetoysterhouse.com.*

The Ginger Man
$$$ | AMERICAN | FAMILY | Come for lunch when shopping along Greenwich Avenue, brunch on Sunday, dinner anytime, or just liquid refreshment, as The Ginger

Man has a long, friendly bar and casual seating up front, a cozy dining room with a fireplace in back, and formal dining upstairs via a grand curved staircase. Whether you order a burger and fries or a NY strip with roasted fingerlings, you won't leave hungry—or thirsty. **Known for:** burgers famously served on an English muffin; relaxing, local atmosphere; more than 50 beers, half on tap. Ⓢ *Average main: $27* ⊠ *64 Greenwich Ave.* ☎ *203/861–6400* ⊕ *gingermanct.com.*

 ## Hotels

★ Delamar Greenwich Harbor Hotel
$$$ | HOTEL | This luxury waterfront hotel just blocks from downtown Greenwich resembles a villa on the Italian Riviera. **Pros:** the champagne welcome sets a luxe tone; easy walk (or free Tesla shuttle) to downtown restaurants, shopping, and train; complimentary kayaks, bicycles, and (seasonal) harbor cruises. **Cons:** very pricey; "nontipping" hotel adds a fee to your bill to cover tips; dogs are welcome in first floor rooms—just so you know. Ⓢ *Rooms from: $379* ⊠ *500 Steamboat Rd.* ☎ *203/661–9800, 866/335–2627* ⊕ *www.delamar. com/greenwich* ⊅ *82 rooms* ⦿ *Free breakfast.*

Hyatt Regency Greenwich
$ | HOTEL | In a grand turreted building that once housed the Condé Nast publishing offices, the Hyatt greets guests in its vast but comfortable atrium containing a flourishing lawn and abundant flora. **Pros:** courtesy shuttle to downtown and the train; the heated indoor pool; buffet breakfast in the atrium. **Cons:** frequent wedding, meeting, and event venue; pay to park; noise from halls or neighboring rooms. Ⓢ *Rooms from: $149* ⊠ *1800 E. Putnam Ave.* ☎ *203/637–1234* ⊕ *greenwich.hyatt.com* ⊅ *373 rooms* ⦿ *No meals.*

Stamford

6 miles northeast of Greenwich, 40 miles southwest of New Haven.

While business is often what brings people to Stamford, what keeps them here are the quality restaurants, nightclubs, and shops along Atlantic and lower Summer Streets. Weekenders have plenty of options beyond the downtown canyons: beaches, boating on the sound, and hiking are only minutes away.

GETTING HERE AND AROUND

Stamford is easily accessible from Interstate 95 and the Merritt Parkway. It is also a major rail hub for Metro-North commuter trains and Amtrak; the high-speed Acela makes a stop here en route between Boston and Washington, D.C.

Sights

Bartlett Arboretum & Gardens

GARDEN | FAMILY | This 93-acre arboretum is home to more than 2,000 varieties of annuals, perennials, wildflowers, and woody plants. There's also a greenhouse, marked ecology trails (dogs are welcome), a pretty pond, and a boardwalk through a red maple swamp. Brilliant, bold colors make the wildflower garden stunning in spring. Sunday afternoon is the time to visit for a guided walk. ⊠ *151 Brookdale Rd., off High Ridge Rd.* ☎ *203/322–6971* ⊕ *www.bartlettarboretum.org* ⌁ *Free.*

Stamford Museum & Nature Center

MUSEUM VILLAGE | FAMILY | Oxen, sheep, pigs, and other animals roam this 118-acre New England farmstead. Once the estate of Henri Bendel, the property includes a Tudor Revival stone mansion housing exhibits on natural history, art, and Americana. An observatory, open to the public on Friday evenings (except January and February), has a 22-inch research telescope—perfect for stargazing—and nature trails wind through 80 acres of woods. Maple sugaring is a special February experience, and there's cidering on fall weekends. ⊠ *39 Scofieldtown Rd.* ☎ *203/322–1646* ⊕ *www.stamfordmuseum.org* ⌁ *Grounds $10, observatory $5* ⊙ *Observatory closed Jan. and Feb.*

Restaurants

The Capital Grille

$$$$ | STEAKHOUSE | This swanky and splurge-worthy steak house serves up impeccable steaks and chops, along with a host of other well-crafted entrées, in the dimly lit dining room with an old-school gentleman's club feel. Though dry-aged steaks are the specialty, Capital Grille also excels at seafood: pan-seared scallops, Maine lobster, and sushi-grade seared sesame tuna are equally delicious choices. **Known for:** the steaks, of course, prepared exactly as you like; creamed spinach, truffle fries, lobster mac 'n' cheese—lots of sides to share; perfect for a special occasion (or when you're really hungry). ⑤ *Average main: $48* ⊠ *Stamford Town Center, 230 Tressor Blvd.* ☎ *203/967–0000* ⊕ *www.thecapitalgrille.com* ⊙ *No lunch weekends.*

Harlan Social

$$$ | AMERICAN | In the industrial-chic dining room of this lively gastropub, you can sample small plates—short-rib empanadas, steamed P.E.I. mussels, and poached lobster and avocado salad are all on offer—or choose some charcuterie or a selection from the mozzarella bar. Main courses range from burgers and homemade gnocchi to pan-seared salmon; chances are there's something for everyone here. **Known for:** menus follow the season; excellent wine and craft beer offerings; desserts here are worth every calorie. ⑤ *Average main: $30* ⊠ *The Lockworks, 121 Towne St.* ☎ *203/883–8000* ⊕ *harlansocial.com.*

The Stamford Diner

$$ | AMERICAN | FAMILY | The menu at this Art Deco–style diner, alive with bright colors and shiny chrome, runs the gamut from griddle cakes to smoked salmon Benedict at breakfast, classic sandwiches to Greek specialties at lunch, chicken in a basket to rib-eye steak at dinner—or anything you'd like at any time of day or night. If that's not enough, the diner hosts frequent musical, comedy, and kids' events. **Known for:** classic diner menu—v-e-r-y long and varied; early-morning breakfast and late-night dinner—every day; family-friendly atmosphere. ⑤ *Average main: $20* ⊠ *135 Harvard Ave.* ☎ *203/348–7000* ⊕ *www.thestamford-diner.com.*

Hotels

Hotel Zero Degrees
$ | HOTEL | FAMILY | Business travelers, couples, and families all find the design and style of this contemporary hotel—the spacious rooms, modern furnishings, and touches of whimsy—quite appealing. **Pros:** discounted meals at several nearby restaurants and bars; complimentary breakfast buffet is fresh, extensive, and delicious; free access to the YMCA fitness center and pool, next door. **Cons:** no on-site restaurant or bar; busy street out front can be noisy, especially from lower floors; free parking is limited but there's a garage nearby. ⑤ *Rooms from: $139* ⊠ *909 Washington St.* ☎ *203/363–7900* ⊕ *www.hotelzerodegrees.com* ⮑ *97 rooms* ⦿ *Free breakfast.*

Stamford Marriott Hotel & Spa
$ | HOTEL | FAMILY | Business travelers in particular appreciate the 16-floor hotel's up-to-date facilities and convenience to trains and airport shuttles. **Pros:** an easy walk to downtown restaurants and Stamford Mall; views of Long Island Sound from upper floors; weekend travelers enjoy lower prices. **Cons:** rooms are ready for updating; it's big and feels rather anonymous; parking garage is expensive. ⑤ *Rooms from: $152* ⊠ *243 Tresser Blvd.* ☎ *203/357–9555, 800/732–9689* ⊕ *www.marriott.com* ⮑ *506 rooms* ⦿ *No meals.*

Nightlife

BARS
Tigín Irish Pub
BARS/PUBS | Stop in for the perfect pint at this Irish pub with an authentic atmosphere. ⊠ *175 Bedford St.* ☎ *203/353–8444* ⊕ *www.tiginirishpub.com.*

Performing Arts

MUSIC
★ **Stamford Symphony**
MUSIC | Performing at the Palace Theatre October–April, this orchestra always includes a popular holiday concert performed at a local church—and kids' tickets are free. ⊠ *263 Tresser Blvd.* ☎ *203/325–1407, 203/325–4466 for tickets* ⊕ *www.stamfordsymphony.org.*

THEATER
The Palace Theatre
THEATER | FAMILY | Plays, comedy shows, musicals, and film festivals are presented at the 1,500-seat Palace, originally a vaudeville house, which is now owned and operated by the Stamford Center for the Arts. ⊠ *61 Atlantic St.* ☎ *203/325–4466* ⊕ *www.palacestamford.org.*

Norwalk

10 miles northeast of Stamford, 45 miles northeast of New York City.

In the 19th century, Norwalk was a major New England port and manufacturing center that produced hats, pottery, clocks, watches, shingle nails, and paper. It later fell into neglect, in which it remained for much of the 20th century. In the early 1990s, however, Norwalk's coastal business district was the focus of major redevelopment. Much of South Norwalk has since turned it into a hot spot for trendy shopping, culture, and dining—much of it along Washington Street. Known as SoNo, it's *the* place to be if you're young, single, and living it up in Fairfield County.

GETTING HERE AND AROUND

If you are traveling by car, Norwalk is most easily reached by Interstate 95 or the Merritt Parkway. Metro-North commuter trains also stop here. Exit at the South Norwalk stop to put yourself within walking distance of SoNo shops, restaurants, and bars.

 Sights

The Lockwood-Mathews Mansion Museum

HOUSE | This ornate tribute to Victorian decorating, built in 1864 as the summer home of LeGrand Lockwood, remains one the oldest (and finest) surviving Second Empire–style country homes in the United States. It's hard not to be impressed by its octagonal skylighted rotunda and more than 50 rooms of gilt, frescoes, marble, intricate woodwork, and etched glass. Movie buffs will be interested in knowing that the mansion was used as the location of the Stepford Men's Association in *The Stepford Wives*—the original (1975) film. ⊠ *295 West Ave.* ☎ *203/838–9799* ⊕ *www.lockwoodmathewsmansion.com* ⊠ *From $10* ⊙ *Closed Mon., Tues., Feb., and Mar.*

★ Maritime Aquarium at Norwalk

ZOO | FAMILY | This 5-acre waterfront center, the cornerstone of the city's SoNo district, explores the marine life and maritime culture of Long Island Sound. The aquarium's more than 20 habitats include some 1,000 creatures indigenous to the sound, including sting rays, sea turtles, harbor seals, river otters, and dozens of jellyfish. You can see toothy bluefish and sand tiger sharks in the 110,000-gallon Ocean Beyond the Sound aquarium. The aquarium also operates an Environmental Education Center, leads marine-mammal cruises aboard *R/V Spirit of the Sound*, and has the state's largest IMAX theater. ⊠ *10 N. Water St.* ☎ *203/852–0700* ⊕ *www.maritimeaquarium.org* ⊠ *$25.*

Sheffield Island and Lighthouse

LIGHTHOUSE | FAMILY | This 3-acre island, part of the Stewart B. McKinney National Wildlife Refuge, is a prime spot for a picnic and some bird-watching. The 1868 lighthouse has 10 rooms to explore between four levels. Clambakes are held Thursday evenings June–September. To get here, take a ferry from the Sheffield Island Dock. ⊠ *Sheffield Island Dock, 4 N. Water St. at Washington St.* ☎ *800/838–3006, 203/838–9444* ⊕ *www.seaport.org* ⊠ *$25, includes ferry* ⊙ *Closed Oct.–Apr.*

Stepping Stones Museum for Children

MUSEUM | FAMILY | The ColorCoaster, a 27-foot-high kinetic structure in constant motion, is the centerpiece of this hands-on museum. Visit the Energy Lab, where youngsters learn about wind, water, and solar power while splashing around the extensive water play area. The Light Gallery has colorful LED displays, and for babies and toddlers, there's Tot Town, a safe place where they can play with toys and puzzles, "cook" in a play kitchen, and learn about animals on Old MacDonald's Farm. ⊠ *Mathews Park, 303 West Ave.* ☎ *203/899–0606* ⊕ *www.steppingstonesmuseum.org* ⊠ *$15* ⊙ *Closed Mon. Labor Day–Memorial Day.*

Restaurants

★ Match

$$$ | MODERN AMERICAN | A SoNo fixture since 1999, Match's high ceilings, exposed brick, and industrial fixtures provide a sleek, urban look. Indulge in one of the signature wood-fired pizzas straight out of the oven or savor the light-as-air gnocchi in Bolognese ragù, blackened swordfish, or steak frites. **Known for:** something delicious at every price point; creative wood-oven pizzettes, including bacon-potato-egg and shrimp fra diablo; "New School" raw bar, featuring Norwalk oysters. ⑤ *Average main: $30* ⊠ *98 Washington St.* ☎ *203/852–1088* ⊕ *www.matchsono.com.*

Norwalk's Maritime Aquarium is a great way to come eye-to-eye with animals endemic to Long Island Sound, like green sea turtles.

Hotels

Hotel Zero Degrees Norwalk

$ | HOTEL | FAMILY | This ultramodern boutique lodging is a great addition to a region choked with lackluster chain hotels. **Pros:** large bathrooms with a huge walk-in shower; tasty food at Mediter- raneo, the in-house restaurant; free shuttle service. **Cons:** noise from the nearby train tracks; not walking distance to downtown; complimentary breakfast is less than dazzling. ⑤ *Rooms from: $189* ⊠ *353 Main Ave.* ☎ *203/750–9800* ⊕ *www.hotelzerodegrees.com/hotels/ norwalk* ⌸ *96 rooms* ⦿ *Free breakfast.*

Nightlife

★ Barcelona Wine Bar

WINE BARS—NIGHTLIFE | Savor wines primarily from Spain—tinto, rosado, or blanco, with more than 40 available by the glass—while nibbling on charcuterie, cheese, or a selection of tapas. ⊠ *515 West Ave.* ☎ *203/854–5600* ⊕ *www. barcelonawinebar.com.*

Local Kitchen and Beer Bar

BARS/PUBS | Exposed brick, rustic wooden booths, and metal accents give this pub in the heart of bustling SoNo an industrial feel. Pair one of the 30-plus craft beers on tap with the to-die-for burger. ⊠ *68 Washington St.* ☎ *203/957–3352* ⊕ *www. sonolocal.com.*

Ridgefield

15 miles north of Norwalk, 43 miles west of New Haven.

In Ridgefield, you'll find an outstanding contemporary art museum nestled in a classic New England town within an hour of Manhattan. Main Street, a large leafy boulevard, has a number of small businesses; otherwise, "downtown" is largely a residential sweep of lawns and majestic homes. Ridgefield is snug against the Connecticut/New York border; to reach the state line, you drive along Peaceable Street—which pretty much sums up Ridgefield.

GETTING HERE AND AROUND

From Interstate 95 or the Merritt Parkway, head north on U.S. 7 to Route 33 to reach Ridgefield, or take Metro-North to the Branchville station.

Sights

★ The Aldrich Contemporary Art Museum

MUSEUM | Cutting-edge art is not necessarily what you'd expect to find in a stately 18th-century structure that, by turns, served as a general store, a post office, and, for 35 years, a church. Nicknamed "Old Hundred," this historic building is just part of the vast facility, which includes a 17,000-square-foot exhibition space that puts its own twist on traditional New England architecture. The white-clapboard-and-granite structure houses 12 galleries, a screening room, a sound gallery, a 22-foot-high project space for large installations, a 100-seat performance space, and an education center. Outside is a 2-acre sculpture garden. ■ TIP→ **Every third Saturday, admission is free.** ⊠ 258 Main St. ☎ 203/438–4519 ⊕ www.aldrichart. org ⊠ $10 ⊗ Closed Tues.

🍴 Restaurants

Luc's Café

$$ | FRENCH | A cozy bistro set inside a stone building with low ceilings and closely spaced tables, Luc's takes full advantage of its handy location in Ridgefield's iconic downtown. The place charms patrons with carefully prepared food and low-key, friendly service. **Known for:** nonstop service from 11 am until closing; special plat du jour offered daily; all dishes prepared à la minute. ⑤ Average main: $22 ⊠ 3 Big Shop La. ☎ 203/894–8522 ⊕ www.lucscafe.com ⊗ Closed Sun.

Performing Arts

★ The Ridgefield Playhouse

FILM | FAMILY | This historic, fully renovated, country playhouse presents national and local musicians, comedians, magicians, theatrical performances, classic and new films, and insightful lectures. Stars ranging from Stevie Wonder to Marcel Marceau, Dana Carvey to Stephen Sondheim, Kathy Griffin to Trace Adkins have been headliners over the years. ⊠ 80 East Ridge ☎ 203/438–5795 ⊕ ridgefieldplayhouse.org.

Westport

47 miles northeast of New York City.

Westport, an artists' community since the turn of the 20th century, continues to attract creative types despite an influx of commuters and corporations over the years.

GETTING HERE AND AROUND

You can reach Westport by car via Interstate 95 (Exit 17 will take you closer to the center of town and main shopping areas) or the Merritt Parkway. Metro-North also has two stops here: Westport (closer to town) and Greens Farms (farther east).

👁 Sights

★ Sherwood Island State Park

BEACH—SIGHT | FAMILY | Summer visitors congregate at this state park, which has a 1½-mile sweep of sandy beach, two picnic areas at the water's edge, sports fields, and several food stands (open seasonally). The on-site nature center offers various programs from bird-watching to nature walks. Note that there's a parking fee for non-Connecticut residents Memorial Day–Labor Day. ⊠ Sherwood Island Connector ✛ Off I–95, Exit 18 ☎ 203/226–6983 ⊕ www.ct.gov/deep/sherwoodisland ⊠ Free.

🍴 Restaurants

Spotted Horse Tavern

$$ | MODERN AMERICAN | The theme in this neighborhood favorite is horse, of course; the atmosphere reflects the historic building (circa 1808), and the menu offers old-fashioned comfort foods with modern flourishes. The grilled pork chop has a whole-grain mustard glaze, chicken Milanese includes a side of lemon yogurt sauce, steak frites has Parmesan fries—and items on the Pony Menu will delight the kids. **Known for:** street-side alfresco dining in warm months; busy bar; convenient downtown location. ⑤ *Average main: $22* ✉ *26 Church La.* ☎ *203/557–9393* ⊕ *spottedhorsect.com.*

★ Tavern on Main

$$$ | MODERN AMERICAN | For decades at this downtown mainstay, the three cozy fireplaces in the dining room have attracted hungry Westporters on cold winter evenings, and the patio invites alfresco dining in the warmer months. There's a full menu of appetizers, small plates, an artisanal cheese board, entrées, pasta, burgers, and sandwiches, but you won't find a more succulent NY strip steak anywhere in town. **Known for:** convivial taproom; delicious, well-prepared food; substantial portions. ⑤ *Average main: $25* ✉ *150 Main St.* ☎ *203/221–7222* ⊕ *www.tavernonmain.com.*

Terrain Garden Café

$$$ | AMERICAN | Within the Terrain garden store, you'll find a bright, cheery café that offers exquisitely prepared dishes using locally sourced organic produce so fresh you'll want to become a gardener yourself. Entrées like line-caught Atlantic cod with squash risotto or the braised beef short ribs are served with a delicious (and frankly adorable) terra-cotta pot of baked bread. **Known for:** creatively presented dishes; artisanal cuisine (like the grilled avocado snack); browse the store and its eclectic home accessories, plants, and garden supplies while awaiting your table. ⑤ *Average main:*

$26 ✉ *561 Post Rd. E* ☎ *203/226–2750* ⊕ *www.shopterrain.com/westport-restaurant* ⊙ *No dinner Mon. and Tues.*

The Whelk

$$$ | SEAFOOD | This upscale seafood restaurant serves straight-from-the-sea clams, oysters, and fish inventively prepared and exquisitely presented. The clean lines of the dining room give the nearly always crowded restaurant a maritime feel that perfectly complements the food. **Known for:** extensive raw bar; seafood, of course, but also roast chicken or a burger; outdoor seating in nice weather. ⑤ *Average main: $35* ✉ *575 Riverside Ave.* ☎ *203/557–0902* ⊕ *www.thewhelkwestport.com* ⊙ *Closed Sun. and Mon. No lunch Tues.–Thurs.*

🎭 Performing Arts

The Levitt Pavilion for the Performing Arts

CONCERTS | FAMILY | Enjoy an excellent series of free outdoor summer concerts here that range from jazz to classical, folk to blues, and one night each week focused especially on children. Bring a blanket or beach chair—and a picnic, if you like. ✉ *40 Jesup Rd.* ☎ *203/221–2153* ⊕ *www.levittpavilion.com* ⊠ *Free.*

Westport Country Playhouse

THEATER | Long associated with benefactors Joanne Woodward and Paul Newman, the venerable and intimate Westport Country Playhouse presents high-quality plays from April through November and special family programs from December through March. ✉ *25 Powers Ct.* ☎ *203/227–4177* ⊕ *www.westportplayhouse.org.*

Bridgeport

12 miles east of Westport, 22 miles west of New Haven.

Bridgeport, Connecticut's most populous city, is working hard to revitalize itself with improvements such as Webster

Arena at Harbor Yard, a 10,000-seat indoor sports and entertainment space, and Harbor Yard Amphitheater, a 5,500-seat outdoor entertainment venue hosting concerts from spring through fall. A handful of family-friendly attractions make Bridgeport a worthwhile stop for families with young kids.

Sights

Barnum Museum

MUSEUM | FAMILY | This Romanesque red sandstone-and-brick building stands out in downtown Bridgeport, much like P.T. Barnum, the "Greatest Showman on Earth" and former mayor of Bridgeport, did in his day. The museum exhibits depict the life and times of Barnum, who founded his circus in 1871 and presented performers such as General Tom Thumb and Jenny Lind, the Swedish Nightingale. Among the exhibits is a scale model of Barnum's legendary five-ring circus, containing more than 3,000 pieces. During renovations to the historic museum building—and in the spirit of "the show must go on," the exhibits have been installed in the adjacent People's United Bank Gallery. ⊠ *820 Main St.* ☎ *203/331–1104* ⊕ *www. barnum-museum.org* ⊠ *Free* ⊙ *Closed Sun.–Wed.; also closed Sat. Sept.–May.*

★ Connecticut's Beardsley Zoo

ZOO | FAMILY | The indoor, walk-through South American rain forest alone justifies a visit to this zoo. It comes alive with dozens of species, some rare and endangered, such as keel-billed toucans, broad-snouted caimans, and black-and-gold howler monkeys living in a lush environment of waterfalls, ponds, greenery, and bamboo. The zoo itself has 36 acres of exhibits featuring more than 300 animals: bison, tigers, timber wolves, sloths, a red panda, bald eagles—and proud peacocks that freely roam the property right along with you. There's also a colorful carousel and a New England farmyard. ⊠ *1875 Noble Ave.* ☎ *203/394–6565* ⊕ *www. beardsleyzoo.org* ⊠ *$15.*

Discovery Museum and Planetarium

MUSEUM | FAMILY | Visitors young and old learn about science and technology through hands-on STEM learning experiences and demonstrations that explore electricity, computers, sound, light, magnetism, and energy. Particular draws include the Space Galleries, where you can touch a real meteorite and Skylab artifacts, and the toddler-friendly Preschool Power, where little ones can explore soft, brightly colored structures while developing balance and motor skills. Don't miss the planetarium shows—some geared to young children and others to all age groups. ■**TIP**➔ **Bring a picnic to enjoy in the adjacent park.** ⊠ *4450 Park Ave.* ☎ *203/372–3521* ⊕ *www.discoverymuseum.org* ⊠ *$11* ⊙ *Museum closed Mon.*

Essex

29 miles east of New Haven.

Essex, consistently named one of the best small towns in the United States, looks much like it did at the height of its shipbuilding prosperity in the mid-19th century. Essex's boat manufacturing was so important to the early United States that the British burned 28 ships here during the War of 1812. Gone are the days of steady trade with the West Indies, when the aroma of imported rum, molasses, and spices hung in the air. Whitewashed houses—many the former roosts of sea captains—line Main Street, which has shops that sell clothing, antiques, paintings and prints, and sweets.

GETTING HERE AND AROUND

The best way to reach Essex is by car; take Interstate 95 to Route 9 north.

Sights

★ Connecticut River Museum

MUSEUM | FAMILY | Housed in an 1878 steamboat warehouse, this museum tells the story of the Connecticut River

7

Connecticut ESSEX

Hartford and the Connecticut River Valley

through maritime artifacts, interactive displays, and ship models. The riverfront museum even has a full-size working reproduction of the world's first submarine, the *American Turtle* (named for its appearance); the original was built by David Bushnell in 1775 as a "secret weapon" to win the Revolutionary War. ✉ *Steamboat Dock, 67 Main St.* ☎ *860/767–8269* ⊕ *www.ctrivermuseum. org* ⊡ *$10* ⊗ *Closed Mon. Columbus Day–Memorial Day.*

★ Essex Steam Train & Riverboat
TRANSPORTATION SITE (AIRPORT/BUS/FERRY/ TRAIN) | **FAMILY** | This excursion offers some of the best views of the Connecticut River Valley from 1920s-era coaches pulled by a vintage steam locomotive and an old-fashioned riverboat. The train, traveling along the Connecticut River through the lower valley, makes a 12-mile round-trip from Essex to Deep River Landing. Before returning by train to Essex, you have the option of boarding the *Becky Thatcher* riverboat and cruising along the river past Gillette Castle, Goodspeed Opera House, and fascinating deep-water coves and inlets. (The open promenade deck on the boat's third level offers the best views.) The train also hosts themed excursions such as Tha'r Be Pirates on the Connecticut River, the seasonal North Pole Express (a nighttime trip to pick up Santa), Day Out With Thomas—(perfect for little ones who love the *Thomas & Friends* television show), and many more. ✉ *Valley Railroad Company, 1 Railroad Ave.* ☎ *860/767–0103, 800/377–3987* ⊕ *www.essex-steamtrain.com* ⊡ *From $20* ⊗ *Closed mid-Oct.–mid-May.*

Restaurants

The Oak Room
$$$ | **MODERN AMERICAN** | Crystal sparkles, silver shines, and candles glow in Copper Beach Inn's main dining room—or you can dine more casually at the bar. Notable dishes have included a starter of jumbo lump crab cakes with shaved fennel and orange salad and entrées such as honey-roasted half duckling with sweet potato au gratin or pan-seared diver scallops with lobster-corn risotto. **Known for:** venerable country inn environment; menu follows the seasons; locally sourced ingredients whenever possible. ⑤ *Average main: $25* ✉ *46 Main St., Ivoryton* ✚ *4 miles west of Essex* ☎ *860/767–0330* ⊕ *www.copper-beechinn.com* ⊗ *Closed Mon. No lunch.*

Hotels

Copper Beech Inn
$ | **B&B/INN** | A magnificent copper beech tree shades this 1890 inn, set on 7 acres of the Connecticut River Valley woodlands. **Pros:** perfect for a romantic weekend; excellent on-site dining in the Oak Room; Carriage House rooms are a good deal. **Cons:** some rooms and baths are ready for a face-lift; short drive from downtown Essex; rooms too near the bar-restaurant can be noisy. ⑤ *Rooms from: $179* ✉ *46 Main St., Ivoryton* ✚ *4 miles west of Essex* ☎ *860/767–0330* ⊕ *www.copperbeechinn.com* ⊐ *22 rooms* ⦿ *No meals.*

The Griswold Inn
$ | **B&B/INN** | Two-plus centuries of catering to changing tastes at what's billed as one of America's oldest continuously operating inns has resulted in a kaleidoscope of decor—some Colonial, a bit of Federal, a little Victorian—with just as many modern touches as necessary to meet present-day expectations. **Pros:** in the heart of historic downtown Essex; rich history—since opening in 1776; fun pub with live music every night. **Cons:** dated furnishings, but that's being addressed; no room TVs—head for the common room if you must; some rooms are quite small. ⑤ *Rooms from: $160* ✉ *36 Main St.* ☎ *860/767–1776* ⊕ *www.griswoldinn.com* ⊐ *34 rooms* ⦿ *Free breakfast.*

Ride through the Connecticut River Valley on a vintage Essex Steam Train.

East Haddam

15 miles north of Essex, 28 miles southeast of Hartford.

Farms, tanneries, and blacksmiths were the chief enterprises of 17th-century East Haddam, on the east bank of the Connecticut River. By the 20th century, residents (including actor William Gillette) were drawn to the area for its rural nature and riverside location. This lovely community still retains much of its old-fashioned charm, most of it centered around its historic downtown.

GETTING HERE AND AROUND

The best way to reach East Haddam is by car. From Interstate 95, take Route 156 north in Old Lyme to Route 82 west.

Sights

★ Gillette Castle State Park

CASTLE/PALACE | FAMILY | The outrageous, 24-room, oak-and-fieldstone hilltop castle—modeled after medieval castles of the Rhineland and built between 1914 and 1919 by the eccentric actor and playwright William Gillette—is the park's main attraction. You can tour the castle and hike trails near the remains of a 3-mile private railroad, which chugged about the property until the owner's death in 1937. Gillette, who was born in Hartford, wrote two famous plays about the Civil War and was especially beloved for his play *Sherlock Holmes* (in which he performed the title role). In his will, he demanded that the castle not fall into the hands of "some blithering saphead who has no conception of where he is or with what surrounded." ⊠ *67 River Rd., off Rte. 82* ☎ *860/526–2336* ⊕ *www.ct.gov/deep/gillettecastle* ⊠ *Park free, castle $6.*

★ Goodspeed Opera House

ARTS VENUE | This magnificent 1876 Victorian-gingerbread "wedding cake" theater on the Connecticut River—so called for its turrets, mansard roof, and grand filigree—is widely recognized for its role in the preservation and development of American musical theater. Well over a dozen Goodspeed productions have gone on to Broadway, including *Annie* and *Man of La Mancha*. Performances take place from May through early December; one-hour tours are offered on Saturdays from June through October. ⊠ *6 Main St.* 📞 *860/873–8668* 🌐 *www.goodspeed.org* 🎫 *Tour $5.*

Middletown

16 miles south of Hartford, 27 miles northeast of New Haven.

With its Connecticut River setting, easy access to major highways, and historic architecture, Middletown is perhaps best known as the location of Wesleyan University. The town's High Street is an architecturally eclectic thoroughfare—Charles Dickens once called it "the most beautiful street I have seen in America." Wesleyan students add a youthful vigor to the town when school is in session.

GETTING HERE AND AROUND
Middletown is best reached by car. From Hartford, follow Interstate 91 south to Route 9 south. From the coast, take Interstate 95 to Route 9 north.

Sights

Dinosaur State Park
ARCHAEOLOGICAL SITE | FAMILY | In this park, see 500 tracks left by the dinosaurs that roamed the area around Rocky Hill, a few miles south of Hartford, some 200 million years ago. The tracks are preserved under a giant geodesic dome and 1,500 more are buried for preservation, making it one of the largest dinosaur-track sites in North America. You can even make plaster casts of tracks on a special area of the property; call ahead to learn what materials you need to bring. ⊠ *400 West St., east of I–91, Rocky Hill* 📞 *860/529–8423* 🌐 *www.dinosaurstatepark.org* 🎫 *$6* 🕐 *Closed Mon.*

★ Lyman Orchards
FARM/RANCH | FAMILY | Looking for a quintessential New England outing? These orchards just south of Middletown are not to be missed. Get lost in the sunflower maze, then pick your own seasonal fruits—berries, peaches, pears, apples, and even pumpkins—from June to October. Or stop by the Apple Barrel Market, open all year long, to shop for farm-fresh pies, fruit baskets, jams and preserves, and gifts. ⊠ *150 South St., Junction of Rtes. 147 and 157, Middlefield* 📞 *860/756–5377* 🌐 *www.lymanorchards.com.*

Wesleyan University
COLLEGE | Founded in 1831, Wesleyan University is one of the oldest Methodist institutions of higher education in the country. There are roughly 2,800 undergraduates, which gives Middletown a contemporary, college-town feel. Note the massive, fluted Corinthian columns of the 1828 Greek Revival Russell House at the corner of Washington Street, across from the pink Mediterranean-style Davison Art Center, built 15 years later. Farther along you'll find gingerbreads, towering brownstones, Tudors, and Queen Annes. A few hundred yards up on Church Street, which intersects High Street, is the Olin Library. This 1928 structure was designed by Henry Bacon, architect of the Lincoln Memorial. ⊠ *45 Wyllys Ave., off High St.* 📞 *860/685–2000* 🌐 *www.wesleyan.edu.*

Restaurants

O'Rourke's Diner
$ | AMERICAN | FAMILY | This glass-and-steel classic is the place to go for top-notch diner fare, including creative specialties like the omelet stuffed with roasted portobello mushrooms, Brie, and asparagus. Arrive early for lunch, as the lines often file out the door. **Known for:** steamed cheeseburgers—a favorite since 1941; Irish dishes, like bangers, colcannon, and Irish stew; breakfast

Connecticut's Historic Gardens

These extraordinary Connecticut gardens form Connecticut's Historic Gardens, a "trail" of natural beauties across the state. For more information on each of the gardens, visit ⊕ *www.cthistoricgardens.org.*

Bellamy-Ferriday House & Garden, Bethlehem. Highlights of this garden include an apple orchard and a circa-1915 formal parterre garden that blossoms with peonies, roses, and lilacs.

Butler-McCook House & Garden, Hartford. Landscape architect Jacob Weidenmann created a Victorian garden full of peonies, roses, and iris that serves as an amazing respite from downtown city life.

Florence Griswold Museum, Old Lyme. The gardens at the historic Florence Griswold Museum, once the home of a prominent Old Lyme family and later a haven for artists, have been restored to their 1910 appearance and feature masses of hollyhocks, iris, foxglove, day lilies, and heliotrope.

Glebe House Museum, Woodbury. Legendary British garden writer and designer Gertrude Jekyll designed only three gardens in the United States, and the one at the Glebe House Museum is the only one still in existence. It is a classic example of Jekyll's ideas about color harmony and plant combinations; a hedge of mixed shrubs encloses a mix of perennials.

Harriet Beecher Stowe Center, Hartford. The grounds at the Harriet Beecher Stowe Center feature Connecticut's largest magnolia tree, a pink dogwood that's more than 100 years old, and eight distinct gardens: an antique rose garden; a woodland garden; a wildflower meadow; a high-Victorian texture garden; a blue cottage garden; and formal color-coordinated gardens.

Hill-Stead Museum, Farmington. The centerpiece of the Hill-Stead Museum is a circa-1920 sunken garden enclosed in a yew hedge and surrounded by a wall of rough stone. At the center of the octagonal design is a summerhouse with 36 flower-beds and brick walkways radiating outward.

Promisek at Three Rivers Farm, Bridgewater. The prolific Beatrix Farrand designed the original garden at Promisek; restored in recent years, it now overflows with beds of annuals and perennials that include hollyhocks, peonies, and always-dashing delphiniums.

Roseland Cottage, Woodstock. At Roseland Cottage, the boxwood parterre garden includes 21 flower-beds surrounded by boxwood hedges.

Thankful Arnold House Museum, Haddam. Gravel paths divide granite-edged Colonial Revival-style gardens filled with more than 50 varieties of herbs that Thankful Arnold likely used in the early 1800s for cooking, medicine, dyeing, fragrance, and other household uses.

Webb-Deane-Stevens Museum, Wethersfield. This Colonial Revival garden is filled with fragrant, old-fashioned flowers such as peonies, pinks, phlox, hollyhocks, and larkspur, as well as a profusion of roses.

served 6 am–3 pm. ⑤ *Average main:*
$13 ✉ *728 Main St.* ☎ *860/346–6101*
⊕ *www.orourkesmiddletown.com* ⊙ *No*
dinner. No lunch weekends.

Hotels

Inn at Middletown

$ | **HOTEL** | The Inn is centrally located
in an 1800s-era National Guard Armory
in the heart of downtown Middletown.
Pros: two blocks from Wesleyan campus;
steps from downtown shopping; accessible rooms available with ADA-compli-
ant amenities. **Cons:** no real grounds;
rates rise when Wesleyan is in session;
spotty Wi-Fi service. ⑤ *Rooms from:*
$199 ✉ *70 Main St.* ☎ *860/854–6300*
⊕ *www.innatmiddletown.com* ⤵ *88*
rooms, 12 suites ⑪ *No meals.*

Nightlife

BARS

Eli Cannon's Tap Room

BREWPUBS/BEER GARDENS | At last count,
the cozy Eli Cannon's had more than
35 microbrew beers on tap, as well
as a selection of bottled beers and a
dinner-and-snack menu. ✉ *695 Main*
St. ☎ *860/347–3547* ⊕ *www.elican-*
nons.com.

Performing Arts

THEATER

Wesleyan University Center for the Arts

ARTS CENTERS | See modern dance or a
provocative new play, hear top play-
wrights and actors discuss their craft,
or take in an art exhibit or concert at
this college arts center. ✉ *283 Wash-*
ington Terr. ☎ *860/685–3355* ⊕ *www.*
wesleyan.edu/cfa.

Wethersfield

6 miles south of Hartford, 34 miles north-
east of New Haven.

Wethersfield, a vast Hartford suburb,
dates to 1634 and has the state's largest—and, some say, the most picturesque—historic district, with more than
100 pre-1849 buildings. Old Wethersfield
has the oldest firehouse in the state, the
oldest historic district in the state, and
the oldest continuously operating seed
company. Today, this "dated" community
has new parks and new shops; but history is still its main draw.

GETTING HERE AND AROUND

Wethersfield is only a few miles south of
Hartford, and most easily reached by car.
From Hartford, take Interstate 91 south
to Route 3 south.

Sights

★ New Britain Museum of American Art

MUSEUM | An important stop for art lovers,
this 100-year-old museum's collection of
more than 10,000 works from 1740 to
the present focuses solely on American
art. Among its treasures number paintings by John Singer Sargent, Winslow
Homer, and Georgia O'Keeffe, as well as
sculpture by Isamu Noguchi. Of particular
note is the selection of Impressionist
artists, including Mary Cassatt, William
Merritt Chase, Childe Hassam, and John
Henry Twachtman, as well as Thomas
Hart Benton's five-panel mural *The Arts*
of Life in America. The museum also has
a café, a large shop, and a library of art
books. ✉ *56 Lexington St., New Britain*
⊹ *About 10 miles west of Wethersfield*
☎ *860/229–0257* ⊕ *www.nbmaa.org*
▣ *$15 (free Sat. 10–noon).*

Webb-Deane-Stevens Museum

MUSEUM | For a true sample of Wethers-
field's historic past, stop by the Joseph
Webb House, the Silas Deane House,
and the Isaac Stevens House—all
adjacent to each other along Main Street

Connecticut's Unusual Museums

American Clock & Watch Museum in Bristol is devoted entirely to clocks and watches—more than 5,500 timepieces are on display, including clocks dating back to 1680 and watches dating back to 1595. The best time to come? Noon, of course.

Also in Bristol, the **New England Carousel Museum** has one of the largest antique carousel collections in the country, both full-size pieces and miniatures. Oddly enough, it's also home to the **Museum of Fire History,** which displays antique equipment and memorabilia.

The Company of Fifers & Drummers in Ivoryton, whose mission is to perpetuate America's heritage in fife and drum music, maintains **The Museum of Fife & Drum,** which has artifacts dating back to the 1700s. It's open on some weekends in summer.

At Windsor's **Vintage Radio & Communications Museum of Connecticut** exhibits explain how communications have changed over the years—from Morse code to satellites and everything in between. An offshoot of the museum, **Vintage Hi-Fi Museum** in West Hartford, displays mid-20th-century TVs, stereo sets, and other baby boomer artifacts.

If you're fascinated by locks, the **Lock Museum of America** in Terryville is for you. The collection includes thousands of antique door locks, padlocks, safe locks, handcuffs, keys, escutcheon plates, and more—including a 4,000-year-old lock from Egypt and a treasure chest from the Spanish Armada.

Many of the buttons for soldier uniforms in the Revolutionary War,

the War of 1812, both sides of the Civil War, and even recent wars were made in Connecticut. The **Waterbury Button Museum** has examples of military buttons and thousands of others on display.

At New Haven's **Eli Whitney Museum**, there are exhibits on the man, his cotton gin, and the dam built to power the historic building—plus exhibits on A. C. Gilbert, the inventor of the erector set.

The buildings and grounds at the **Connecticut Antique Machinery Association Museum** in Kent display old-fashioned steam engines, agricultural equipment, combustion engines, steam shovels, a narrow-gauge railroad with a steam locomotive, and mining artifacts. The Hall of Geology and Paleontology adds dinosaur tracks and fossils.

The whole family will get a chuckle out of the **Barker Character Comic & Cartoon Museum** in Cheshire, which has 80,000 toys and collectibles on display—from Betty Boop to Popeye, Shirley Temple dolls to Howdy Doody, Gumby to the Simpsons, Halloween costumes, lunch boxes, and so much more.

The Glass House in New Canaan, built between 1949 and 1995 by architect Philip Johnson and now a National Trust Historic Site, has a permanent collection of 20th-century paintings and sculpture.

And for all things PEZ, head for the **PEZ Visitor Center** in Orange, which has the largest collection of PEZ memorabilia in the world, the world's largest PEZ dispenser, interactive trivia games—and, of course, a retail shop.

and all built in the mid- to late 1700s. These well-preserved examples of Georgian architecture reflect their owners' lifestyles as, respectively, a merchant, a diplomat, and a tradesman. The Webb House, a registered National Historic Landmark, was the site of the strategy conference between George Washington and the French general Jean-Baptiste Rochambeau that led to the British defeat at Yorktown. ⊠ *211 Main St., off I-91* ☎ *860/529–0612* ⊕ *webb-deane-stevens.org* ⊠ *$12* ⊘ *Closed Jan.–Mar.*

Hartford

39 miles north of New Haven, 52 miles northwest of New London, 78 miles northeast of Stamford.

Midway on the inland route between New York City and Boston, Hartford is Connecticut's capital city and the former insurance capital of the United States. Founded in 1635 on the banks of the Connecticut River, Hartford was at various times home to authors Mark Twain and Harriet Beecher Stowe, inventors Samuel and Elizabeth Colt, landscape architect Frederick Law Olmsted, and Ella Grasso, the first woman to be elected a state governor. Today Hartford boasts a revitalized downtown core featuring a bustling convention center and a top-notch science museum, the Connecticut Science Center. The city is once again on the verge of discovery.

GETTING HERE AND AROUND

Hartford is located in the middle of the state, at the intersection of two main highways: Interstate 91, which runs north from New Haven, across central Massachusetts and along the entire length of Vermont to the Canadian border, and Interstate 84, which runs generally east–west from the small town of Union at Connecticut's northeast border with Massachusetts, through Hartford and Danbury to the New York border. Amtrak serves Hartford on the Northeast

Regional line. Bradley International Airport in Windsor Locks, 15 minutes north of Hartford, offers flights to more than 30 destinations in the United States, Canada, and the Caribbean.

 ## Sights

Bushnell Park

CITY PARK | FAMILY | Fanning out from the State Capitol building, this city park, created in 1850, was the first public space in the country with natural landscaping. The original designer, a Swiss-born landscape architect and botanist named Jacob Weidenmann, planted 157 varieties of trees and shrubs to create an urban arboretum. Kids love the Bushnell Park Carousel (open April–September), with its intricately hand-carved horses and booming Wurlitzer band organ, built in 1914 by the Artistic Carousel Company of Brooklyn, New York. A welcome oasis of green in a busy city, the park has a pond and about 750 trees, including a first-generation offspring of the state's historic Charter Oak (the state tree) and four enormous state champion trees. ⊠ *Asylum and Trinity Sts.* ☎ *860/232–6710* ⊕ *www.bushnell-park.org* ⊠ *Free.*

Butler-McCook Homestead

GARDEN | Built in 1782, this was home to four generations of Butlers and McCooks until it became a museum in 1971. Today, it houses Hartford's oldest intact collection of art and antiques, including furnishings, family possessions, and Victorian-era toys that show the evolution of American tastes over nearly 200 years. The beautifully restored Victorian garden was originally designed by Jacob Weidenmann. ⊠ *396 Main St.* ☎ *860/522–1806* ⊕ *www.ctlandmarks.org* ⊠ *$12* ⊘ *Closed Jan.–Apr. and Mon.–Thurs.; also closed Fri. in Oct.–Dec.*

The Children's Museum

MUSEUM | FAMILY | A life-size walk-through replica of a 60-foot sperm whale greets patrons at this museum. Located in West Hartford, the museum also has a

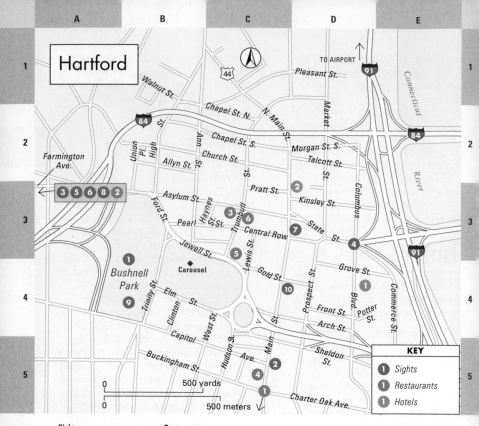

Hartford

TO AIRPORT

Sights ▼

1 Bushnell Park **B4**
2 Butler-McCook Homestead **C5**
3 The Children's Museum **A3**
4 Connecticut Science Center **D3**
5 Harriet Beecher Stowe Center............ **A3**
6 Mark Twain House & Museum **A3**
7 Old State House......... **D3**
8 Noah Webster House **A3**
9 State Capitol............. **B4**
10 Wadsworth Atheneum Museum of Art........... **C4**

Restaurants ▼

1 First and Last Tavern **C5**
2 Grant's Restaurant and Bar **A3**
3 Max Downtown.......... **C3**
4 Peppercorn's Grill........ **C5**
5 Salute **C3**
6 Trumbull Kitchen......... **C3**

Hotels ▼

1 Hartford Marriott Downtown............... **D4**
2 Residence Inn Hartford Downtown **D3**

KEY

1 Sights
1 Restaurants
1 Hotels

wildlife sanctuary and a planetarium with real-life images of outer space beamed in from NASA, as well as a hands-on puzzle exhibit that introduces kids to various scientific and mathematical concepts and optical illusions. ⊠ *950 Trout Brook Dr., 5 miles west of downtown, West Hartford* ☎ *860/231–2824* ⊕ *www.thechildrens-museumct.org* ✉ *$15* ⊙ *Closed Mon. Sept.–June.*

★ Connecticut Science Center

MUSEUM | FAMILY | This strikingly modern building, designed by world-renowned architect César Pelli, houses 40,000 square feet of exhibit space under a wavelike roof that appears to float over the structure. Among the more than 165 hands-on exhibits, youngsters, teens, and adults alike can dive into a black hole and examine the moon's craters in the Exploring Space exhibit, race mini-sailboats and magnetic trains at Forces in Motion, and discover hidden athletic talents in the Sports Lab. Kid Space is perfect for ages three–six, and everyone enjoys mingling with free-flying butterflies in the Butterfly Encounter. Complete your visit by taking in a movie in the 3-D digital theater. ⊠ *250 Columbus Blvd.* ☎ *860/724–3623* ⊕ *www.ctsciencecenter.org* ✉ *From $24* ⊙ *Closed Mon. Labor Day–Memorial Day.*

Harriet Beecher Stowe Center

HOUSE | Abolitionist and author Harriet Beecher Stowe (1811–96) spent her final years at this 1871 Victorian Gothic cottage, now a popular stop on the Connecticut Freedom Trail. The center was built around the cottage in tribute to the author of the antislavery novel, *Uncle Tom's Cabin*. Stowe's personal writing table and effects are housed inside. ⊠ *77 Forest St.* ☎ *860/522–9258* ⊕ *www. harrietbeecherstowecenter.org* ✉ *$16* ⊙ *Closed Tues. Jan.–Mar.*

★ Mark Twain House & Museum

HOUSE | Built in 1874, this building was the home of Samuel Langhorne Clemens (better known as Mark Twain) until 1891. In the time he and his family lived in this 25-room Victorian mansion, Twain published seven major novels, including *The Adventures of Tom Sawyer, The Adventures of Huckleberry Finn,* and *The Prince and the Pauper.* The home has one of only two Louis Comfort Tiffany–designed domestic interiors open to the public. A contemporary museum on the grounds presents an up-close look at the author and screens an outstanding documentary on his life introduced by Ken Burns. ⊠ *351 Farmington Ave., at Woodland St.* ☎ *860/247–0998* ⊕ *www. marktwainhouse.org* ✉ *$20* ⊙ *Closed Tues. Jan. and Feb.*

Noah Webster House

HOUSE | This 18th-century farmhouse is the birthplace and childhood home of Noah Webster (1758–1843), the famed teacher, lawyer, early abolitionist, and author of the first American dictionary. Inside you'll find Webster memorabilia and period furnishings and a one-room schoolhouse theater. ⊠ *227 S. Main St., West Hartford* ☎ *860/521–5362* ⊕ *www.noahwebster-house.org* ✉ *$8* ⊙ *Closed mornings.*

Old State House

HISTORIC SITE | This Federal-style house with an elaborate cupola and roof balustrade was designed in the early 1700s by Charles Bulfinch, architect of the U.S. Capitol. It served as Connecticut's state capitol until a new building opened in 1879, when it became Hartford's city hall until 1915. In the 1820 Senate Chamber, where everyone from John Adams and Abraham Lincoln to Jimmy Carter and George H. W. Bush has spoken, you can view a portrait of George Washington by Gilbert Stuart; and in the Courtroom, you can find out about the trial of the *Amistad* Africans in the very place it began. In summer, enjoy concerts and a farmers' market (which dates back to the 1600s); don't forget to stop by the Museum of Natural and Other Curiosities. ⊠ *800 Main St.* ☎ *860/522–6766* ⊕ *www.cga. ct.gov/osh* ✉ *$6* ⊙ *Closed Sun. Also closed Mon. early July–early Oct., Sat. early Oct.–early July.*

7

Connecticut HARTFORD

Connecticut's Victorian Gothic state capitol rises from Hartford's Bushnell Park.

★ State Capitol

GOVERNMENT BUILDING | FAMILY | The gold-domed State Capitol building, built in 1878 overlooking Bushnell Park, houses the state's executive offices and legislative chamber, as well as historical memorabilia. On a tour, you walk past a statue Nathan Hale, the official state hero, to the Hall of Flags, which displays a number of historic battle flags carried by Connecticut troops in wars from the Civil War through the Korean Conflict, along with a camp bed used by Marquis de Lafayette when he came to Hartford to meet with George Washington during the Revolutionary War. When the General Assembly is in session (January–early June in odd-numbered years; February–early May in even-numbered years), visitors can observe the proceedings from the public galleries. ✉ *210 Capitol Ave.* ☎ *860/240–0222* ⊕ *www.cga.ct.gov/ capitoltours* 🎫 *Free* ☾ *Closed weekends.*

★ Wadsworth Atheneum Museum of Art

MUSEUM | The nation's oldest public art museum—and the first American museum to acquire works by Salvador Dalí and Italian Renaissance artist Caravaggio—houses more than 50,000 artworks and artifacts spanning 5,000 years, along with 7,000 items documenting African American history and culture in partnership with the Amistad Foundation. Particularly impressive are the museum's Baroque, Impressionist, and Hudson River School collections. ✉ *600 Main St.* ☎ *860/278–2670* ⊕ *www.thewadsworth.org* 🎫 *$15* ☾ *Closed Mon. and Tues.*

🍴 Restaurants

First and Last Tavern

$$ | ITALIAN | What looks to be a simple neighborhood spot south of downtown is actually one of the state's most hallowed Italian restaurants and pizza parlors, serving superb thin-crust pies and much more since 1936. The old-fashioned wooden bar is jammed most evenings with suburbia-bound daily-grinders; the main dining room, which is just as noisy, has a brick wall covered with celebrity photos. **Known for:** brick-oven pizzas and great bread; sauce like

Mom used to make (if she's Italian!); lively atmosphere. $ *Average main: $18* ✉ *939 Maple Ave.* ☎ *860/956–6000* ⊕ *www.firstandlasttavern.com.*

Grants Restaurant and Bar

$$$ | AMERICAN | Whether you're in jeans and looking for a light lunch or dressed to the nines in search of finer fare, this long, narrow space with leather-and-suede banquettes, distressed wood floors, and smoked-glass mirrors suits the occasion. The classic American menu features selections from the raw bar, rack of lamb, and blue plate specials like chicken potpie or Mom's meat loaf, and, of course, tavern burgers. **Known for:** "scratch" cooking; consistently good food; tavern menu at the bar. $ *Average main: $25* ✉ *977 Farmington Ave., West Hartford* ☎ *860/236–1930* ⊕ *www. billygrant.com/grants.*

★ Max Downtown

$$$$ | AMERICAN | With its contemporary design, extensive martini list, and sophisticated cuisine, Max Downtown is a favorite among the city's well-heeled, as well as a popular after-work spot. Creative entrées include spiced tuna with Korean bacon, aged shoyu, and puffed rice; seared sea scallops with heirloom grains and black trumpet mushrooms; and a wide range of perfectly prepared steaks with sauces like red wine rosemary jus or cognac peppercorn cream. **Known for:** shellfish plateau—a heap of deliciousness; simply but exquisitely prepared fish; chef's tasting menu as a tasty option. $ *Average main: $40* ✉ *185 Asylum St.* ☎ *860/522–2530* ⊕ *www. maxrestaurantgroup.com/downtown* ⊗ *No lunch weekends.*

Peppercorn's Grill

$$$ | ITALIAN | This mainstay of Hartford's restaurant scene presents contemporary Italian cuisine in a lively but cozy setting. Enjoy homemade potato gnocchi, slow-roasted osso buco, or a simply grilled veal chop—but save room for the warm chocolate bread pudding or

warm Valrhona chocolate cake. **Known for:** homemade gelato and sorbet; mozzarella bar with your choice of toppings; first Thursday of the month happy hour with live music. $ *Average main: $25* ✉ *357 Main St.* ☎ *860/547–1714* ⊕ *www. peppercornsgrill.com* ⊗ *Closed Sun. No lunch Sat.*

Salute

$$ | ITALIAN | Packed every night, Salute is *the* downtown spot for consistently delicious Italian fare and pleasant service. The kitchen serves up a lengthy list of pasta dishes—try the chicken gnocchi with pesto cream or the perfectly executed fettuccine with clams—and traditional Italian desserts like tiramisu and gelato. **Known for:** warm, comfortable, welcoming spot to enjoy good food; excellent selection of wine and draft beer; half-price garage parking next door—important in the city. $ *Average main: $24* ✉ *100 Trumbull St.* ☎ *860/899–1350* ⊕ *www.salutect.com* ⊗ *No lunch Sun.*

Trumbull Kitchen

$$$ | ECLECTIC | FAMILY | Upbeat, hip, and casual, Trumbull Kitchen is the place to see and be seen. A loft-style dining area with leather-clad walls overlooks the action below where an eclectic, global-themed menu features selections like Asian lettuce cups, Szechuan pork dumplings, seafood pad Thai, and prosciutto-crusted Atlantic haddock or a "stone pie" (pizza). **Known for:** the place to see and be seen; something for everyone, even the kids; convenient to the XL Center and nearby theaters. $ *Average main: $27* ✉ *150 Trumbull St.* ☎ *860/493–7412* ⊕ *www.maxrestaurantgroup.com/trumbull* ⊗ *No lunch Sun.*

 Hotels

Hartford Marriott Downtown

$$$ | HOTEL | FAMILY | This convenient, upscale hotel is connected to the Connecticut Convention Center and within walking distance of the Connecticut Science Center, the Wadsworth Atheneum, the Old State House, and other attractions. **Pros:** close to major attractions; in the heart of downtown; accessible rooms available. **Cons:** convenient location comes at a price; pay for parking (nearby or valet); room service items are prepackaged and ready-to-eat—not cooked to order. $ *Rooms from: $303* ✉ *200 Columbus Blvd.* ☎ *860/249–8000* ⊕ *www.marriott.com* ⇴ *409 rooms* ○ *No meals.*

Residence Inn Hartford Downtown

$ | HOTEL | FAMILY | The all-suites Residence Inn, in the historic Richardson Building, is convenient to the XL Center, theaters, and the Old State House. **Pros:** spacious suites are perfect for families or extended stays; walk to nearby attractions; free shuttle service within 5 miles. **Cons:** rather dull room furnishings; walking around area at night isn't recommended; street noise can be an issue in some rooms. $ *Rooms from: $174* ✉ *942 Main St.* ☎ *860/524–5550* ⊕ *www.marriott.com* ⇴ *120 suites* ○ *Free breakfast.*

 Nightlife

BARS

Arch Street Tavern

BARS/PUBS | This bar—in a former carriage factory, firehouse, and body shop—hosts local rock bands. You can get a bite to eat, too. ✉ *85 Arch St.* ☎ *860/246–7610* ⊕ *www.archstreettavern.com.*

Black-Eyed Sally's Southern Kitchen & Bar

BARS/PUBS | For barbecue and live blues, jazz, rock, and roots music, head to laid-back Black-Eyed Sally's. ✉ *350 Asylum St.* ☎ *860/278–7427* ⊕ *www.blackeyedsallys.com.*

 Performing Arts

MUSIC

Infinity Music Hall & Bistro

CABARET | This intimate, acoustically excellent, 500-seat music hall—a sister venue to Infinity Hall in Norfolk, Connecticut—presents live music (folk, jazz, rock, alternative) and comedy shows throughout the year. The mezzanine level features cabaret-style dining and beverage service, or you can enjoy drinks or a meal at the bistro before the performance. ✉ *32 Front St.* ☎ *860/560–7757* ⊕ *www.infinityhall.com.*

THEATER

The Bushnell

CONCERTS | In addition to national tours of major Broadway shows, concerts, comedy acts, and family theater, The Bushnell is home to the Hartford Symphony Orchestra. ✉ *166 Capitol Ave.* ☎ *860/987–5900, 888/824–2874* ⊕ *www.bushnell.org.*

Hartford Stage Company

THEATER | The Hartford Stage Company presents new and classic plays from around the world in an intimate (489-seat) setting. ✉ *50 Church St.* ☎ *860/527–5151* ⊕ *www.hartfordstage.org.*

TheatreWorks

THEATER | This is the Hartford equivalent of Off-Broadway, where new and experimental dramas are presented. ✉ *233 Pearl St.* ☎ *860/527–7838* ⊕ *www.theaterworkshartford.org.*

Farmington

10 miles southwest of Hartford.

Farmington, incorporated in 1645, is a classic river town with a perfectly preserved main street. This bucolic and affluent suburb of Hartford oozes historical charm. Antiques shops are near the intersection of Routes 4 and 10, along with some fascinating historic homes that are now museums.

GETTING HERE AND AROUND
Farmington is most easily reachable by car. From Hartford, take Interstate 84 west to Route 4 west.

👁 Sights

Hill-Stead Museum

HISTORIC SITE | Converted from a private home into a museum by its talented owner, turn-of-the-20th-century female architect (unusual at the time) Theodate Pope, the house has a superb collection of French Impressionist art displayed in situ, including Claude Monet's *Grainstacks* and Edouard Manet's *The Guitar Player* hanging in the drawing room. Poetry readings take place in the elaborate Beatrix Farrand–designed sunken garden every other week in summer. ⊠ *35 Mountain Rd.* ☎ *860/677–4787* ⊕ *www.hillstead.org* ⊠ *$16* ⊙ *Closed Mon.*

Lake Compounce

AMUSEMENT PARK/WATER PARK | **FAMILY** | Opened in 1846, the country's oldest amusement park is known to locals simply as "the Lake." Today's attractions include a lakefront beach, a water park, and a clipper ship with a 300-gallon bucket of water that gives unsuspecting guests a good dousing. There are also such hair-raising rides as the Sky Coaster, the Boulder Dash, and the Zoomerang. ⊠ *822 Lake Ave., off I–84, Bristol* ☎ *860/583–3300* ⊕ *www.lakecompounce.com* ⊠ *$42* ⊙ *Closed Labor Day–Memorial Day.*

★ New England Air Museum

MUSEUM | **FAMILY** | The more than 100 aircraft at this museum include gliders and helicopters, a World War II–era P-47 Thunderbolt, and a B-29 Superfortress, along with other vintage fighters and bombers—and an extensive collection of engines, instruments, parts, uniforms, and personal memorabilia. There's even a fighter-jet simulator. Next to Bradley International Airport, the museum also frequently holds open-cockpit days, allowing both young and old to play pilot. ⊠ *36 Perimeter Rd., off Rte. 75, Windsor Locks* ☎ *860/623–3305* ⊕ *www.neam.org* ⊠ *$15* ⊙ *Closed Mon. Labor Day–Memorial Day.*

🍴 Restaurants

Mama Luke's

$$ | **ITALIAN** | Come to this Italian-American eatery for huge portions of classic dishes and a family-friendly atmosphere. Patrons rave about the eggplant fries and the meatball salad, specialty pizzas, overstuffed calzones, and grinders. **Known for:** New Haven-style brick-oven pizza; Italian-American favorites made from scratch; huge portions—you'll need a doggie bag. ⑤ *Average main: $19* ⊠ *372 Scott Swamp Rd., Rte. 6* ☎ *860/678–7231* ⊕ *mamalukesct.com.*

🏨 Hotels

Avon Old Farms Hotel

$ | **HOTEL** | A country hotel at the base of Avon Mountain, this 20-acre compound of Colonial-style buildings with manicured grounds sits midway between Farmington and Simsbury. **Pros:** outdoor pool; central location in an attractive town; pet-friendly accommodations are available; Seasons restaurant serves a particularly good Sunday brunch. **Cons:** furniture somewhat dated; rooms in the annex are motel style; asthmatics beware—feather-bed toppers and feather pillows. ⑤ *Rooms from: $159* ⊠ *279 Avon Mountain Rd., Avon* ☎ *860/677–1651, 800/836–4000* ⊕ *www.avonoldfarmshotel.com* ⇌ *158 rooms* ⑩ *Free breakfast.*

Farmington Inn

$ | **B&B/INN** | In the center of Farmington's historic district, this European-style hotel has large guest rooms with four-poster canopied beds and European linens, antiques, and reproductions. **Pros:** within walking distance to downtown shopping and dining; fluffy linens and feather beds; good value. **Cons:** continental breakfast is unremarkable; lacks a pool or other recreational facilities; no elevator makes it difficult for those with physical issues. ⑤ *Rooms from: $139* ⊠ *827 Farmington Ave.* ☎ *860/677–2821, 800/648–9804* ⊕ *www.farmingtoninn.com* ⇌ *72 rooms* ⑩ *Free breakfast.*

New Milford

56 miles west of Hartford, 37 miles north of Norwalk.

If you're approaching the Litchfield Hills from the south, New Milford is a practical starting point to begin a visit. It was also a starting point for a young cobbler (and later a lawyer) named Roger Sherman, who opened the town's first shop in 1743 at the corner of Main and Church Streets. A Declaration of Independence signatory, Sherman also helped draft the Articles of Confederation and the Constitution. You'll find shops, galleries, and eateries all within a short stroll of the New Milford town green.

GETTING HERE AND AROUND
New Milford is best visited by car. From Danbury and points south, take U.S. 7 to U.S. 202 to reach the town.

Sights

★ Elephant's Trunk Flea Market
MARKET | FAMILY | In the same spot since 1976, this outdoor flea market has grown from a dozen or so vendors to more than 500 on a typical Sunday, along with food trucks offering everything from a snack to full meals. You'll never know what usual and unusual treasures you'll find spread out on the field, as every Sunday brings out a different collection of vendors selling all manner of antiques, collectibles, housewares, and merchandise, along with, simply, "things." ⊠ *490 Danbury Rd., U.S. 7 at U.S. 202* ☎ *203/355–1448* ⊕ *www.etflea.com* ⊗ *Closed Mon.–Sat. and mid-Dec.–late Mar.*

Restaurants

The Cookhouse
$$ | BARBECUE | Stop here for some of the best "slow-smoked" barbecue in Connecticut or one of the comfort-food staples on the extensive menu. Try the chicken-fried steak, cookhouse meat loaf, or anything barbecued. **Known for:** barbecue baby back ribs and pulled pork; Thursday night's all-you-can-eat–and a free beer—for $21; good selection of draft beers. ⑤ *Average main: $20* ⊠ *31 Danbury Rd.* ☎ *860/355–4111* ⊕ *thecookhouse.com.*

Hotels

★ The Homestead Inn
$ | B&B/INN | FAMILY | High on a hill overlooking New Milford's town green, this Victorian masterpiece opened as an inn in 1928. **Pros:** reasonably priced; close to shops and restaurants; substantial, delicious, homemade breakfasts. **Cons:** on a busy street; free breakfast only for main house guests; some bathrooms are tiny, with sinks in the bedroom. ⑤ *Rooms from: $170* ⊠ *5 Elm St.* ☎ *860/354–4080* ⊕ *www.homesteadct.com* ⌁ *15 rooms* ⑩ *Free breakfast.*

New Preston

8 miles north of New Milford.

The crossroads village of New Preston, perched above a 40-foot waterfall on the Aspetuck River, has a little town center that's packed with antiques shops specializing in everything from 18th-century furnishings to contemporary art.

Lake Waramaug, north of New Preston on Route 45, is named for Chief Waramaug, one of the most revered figures in Connecticut's Native American history. You can drive around the 8-mile perimeter of the lake, but you'll definitely want to stop and enjoy the view—especially in autumn.

Sights

Hopkins Vineyard
WINERY/DISTILLERY | This 35-acre vineyard overlooking Lake Waramaug produces more than 13 varieties of wine—from sparkling to dessert. Guided tours take in the winery and cellar, where the

wine-making process is explained, but you can also walk through the vineyards. A weathered red barn houses a gift shop and a tasting room, and there's also a picnic area. A wine bar in the Hayloft, with views of the lake, serves a fine cheese and pâté board. ⊠ *25 Hopkins Rd.* ☎ *860/868–7954* ⊕ *www.hopkins-vineyard.com* ✉ *Tour and tasting $20* ☼ *Closed Mon.–Thurs. Jan.–Mar.; Mon. and Tues. Apr.*

Lake Waramaug State Park

NATIONAL/STATE PARK | **FAMILY** | The 95-acre parkland surrounding idyllic Lake Waramaug, one of Connecticut's largest natural lakes, is a great place for swimming, boating, fishing, and picnicking. The park has 76 campsites in wooded and open settings (with bathrooms and showers available). From Memorial Day through Labor Day, canoes and kayaks can be rented on-site. ⊠ *30 Lake Waramaug Rd.* ☎ *860/868–0220* ⊕ *www.ct.gov/deep/lakewaramaug* ✉ *$15 parking fee for non-residents; free for Connecticut residents.*

🍴 Restaurants

The Hopkins Inn Restaurant

$$ | **ECLECTIC** | **FAMILY** | This lakeside 19th-century country inn is a lovely place for breakfast, alfresco lunch, midafternoon tea or, of course, dinner. The menu includes American favorites like broiled Atlantic salmon, but also features French escargot, Austrian Wiener schnitzel, Swiss *rösti* potatoes, and Italian veal piccata. **Known for:** beautiful setting overlooking Lake Waramaug; gluten-free and children's menus, too. ⑤ *Average main: $20* ⊠ *22 Hopkins Rd.* ☎ *860/868–7295* ⊕ *www.thehopkinsinn.com* ☼ *Closed Mon.*

★ The White Horse

$$ | **AMERICAN** | **FAMILY** | Locals, leaf peepers, and folks just passing through stop at the White Horse, a country pub and restaurant that draws its varied menu from British pub, American comfort, and French bistro favorites. Dine on the deck, on the patio, or along the river in the warm months, or inside in front of the fire during the winter chill. **Known for:** historical artifacts throughout and a London-style taxi named Audrey; produce grown on its own farm, "The Back Forty"; vegan, gluten-free, and vegetarian menus, too. ⑤ *Average main: $20* ⊠ *258 New Milford Tpke. (Rte. 202)* ☎ *860/868–1496* ⊕ *www.whitehorsecountrypub.com.*

🛏 Hotels

Hopkins Inn

$ | **B&B/INN** | A grand 1847 Victorian atop a hill overlooking Lake Waramaug, the Hopkins Inn may be one of the best bargains in the area. **Pros:** quintessential New England inn; magnificent views; good restaurant. **Cons:** shared bathrooms for some rooms; service can be a little uneven; complimentary breakfast only January–March. ⑤ *Rooms from: $135* ⊠ *22 Hopkins Rd.* ✚ *1 mile off Rte. 45* ☎ *860/868–7295* ⊕ *www.thehopkinsinn.com* ↝ *14 rooms* ◎ *No meals.*

Kent

14 miles northwest of New Milford.

Kent once had many ironworks; today, it boasts the area's greatest concentration of art galleries—some nationally renowned—as well as a eponymous prep school, and the Schaghticoke Indian Reservation. During the Revolutionary War, 100 Schaghticokes helped defend the colonies by transmitting army intelligence from the hilltops of Litchfield Hills to Long Island Sound by way of shouts and drumbeats.

GETTING HERE AND AROUND

To reach Kent by car, travel north from New Milford on U.S. 7.

⊙ Sights

Eric Sloane Museum & Kent Iron Furnace

MUSEUM | Hardware-store buffs and vintage-tool aficionados will feel right at home at this museum. Artist and author Eric Sloane (1905–85) was fascinated by Early American woodworking tools, and his collection showcases examples of American craftsmanship from the 17th to the 19th century. The museum contains a re-creation of Sloane's last studio and also encompasses the ruins of a 19th-century iron furnace. Sloane's books and prints, which celebrate vanishing aspects of Americana such as barns and covered bridges, are available for sale here. ⊠ 31 Kent–Cornwall Rd. (U.S. 7) ☎ 860/927–3849 ⊕ www.ericsloane.com/museum.htm ⊠ $8 ⊙ Closed Labor Day–Memorial Day.

Kent Falls State Park

NATIONAL/STATE PARK | Heading north from Kent toward Cornwall, you'll pass the entrance to 295-acre Kent Falls State Park, where you can hike a short way to one of the most impressive series of waterfalls in the state and picnic in the green meadows at the base of the falls. ⊠ 462 Kent Cornwall Rd. (U.S. 7) ☎ 860/927–3238 ⊕ www.ct.gov/deep/kentfalls ⊠ Parking for nonresidents Memorial Day–Oct. weekends $15, free for Connecticut residents.

Macedonia Brook State Park

NATIONAL/STATE PARK | Early-season trout fishing (license required) is superb at 2,300-acre Macedonia Brook State Park, where you can also hike and cross-country ski. The Blue Trail crosses several peaks, and you can see as far away as New York's Catskills and Taconics. The leaves are magnificent in the fall. ⊠ 159 Macedonia Brook Rd., off Rte. 341 ☎ 860/927–3238 ⊕ www.ct.gov/deep/macedoniabrook ⊠ Free.

🛏 Hotels

Fife 'n Drum Inn

$ | B&B/INN | If you like to shop, eat, and rest your head in a cozy, simple place, you can do all three at this family-owned inn. **Pros:** convenient downtown location; pretty building; adjacent to popular restaurant. **Cons:** if you aren't into flowery decor, this place isn't for you; book early for fall foliage season; two-night minimum May–October weekends. $ Rooms from: $180 ⊠ 53 N. Main St. ☎ 860/927–3509 ⊕ www.fifendrum.com ⊙ Restaurant closed Tues. ⇆ 14 rooms ⊗ No meals.

★ The Inn at Kent Falls

$$ | B&B/INN | This 18th-century Colonial carefully preserves the charm of the past while providing the convenience that today's travelers expect with exposed beams, claw-foot tubs, a perfectly curated mix of modern and antique furnishings, bucolic walking paths, and an inviting pool surrounded by casual English gardens. **Pros:** stylishly decorated rooms; country setting; swimming pool. **Cons:** rooms are on the small side; street noise starts early in front rooms; breakfast just okay. $ Rooms from: $245 ⊠ 107 Kent Cornwall Rd. ☎ 860/927–3197 ⊕ www.theinnatkentfalls.com ⇆ 6 rooms ⊗ Free breakfast.

🏃 Activities

Appalachian Trail

HIKING/WALKING | The 2,190-mile Appalachian Trail, which stretches through 14 states from Georgia to Maine, is the longest hiking-only footpath in the world. About 51 miles of the trail pass through the northwestern tip of Connecticut, and just off Route 341, the nearly 5-mile-long, well-maintained River Walk from Kent to Cornwall Bridge meanders along the Housatonic River—one of the longest sections of the trail that, mile after mile, follows a river. ⊠ Kent ⊕ www.appalachiantrail.org.

Cornwall

12 miles northeast of Kent.

Connecticut's Cornwalls can get confusing: there's Cornwall, Cornwall Bridge, West Cornwall, Cornwall Hollow, East Cornwall, and North Cornwall. This quiet part of the Litchfield Hills is known for its fantastic vistas of woods and mountains and for its covered bridge, which spans the Housatonic.

GETTING HERE AND AROUND
Head north from Kent on U.S. 7 to reach Cornwall.

Sights

Cornwall Bridge Pottery
FACTORY | Visitors are welcome to watch potters as they work, producing a variety of items that are fired in an on-site, 35-foot-long, wood-fired tube kiln. A selection of items are available for purchase—including seconds. ⊠ *69 Kent Rd. S (U.S. 7), Cornwall Bridge* ☎ *860/946–9679* ⊕ *cbpots.com.*

Housatonic Meadows State Park
NATIONAL/STATE PARK | The park is marked by its tall pine trees near the Housatonic River and has terrific riverside campsites. Fly-fishers consider this 2-mile stretch of the river among the best places in New England to test their skills against trout and bass (license required). ⊠ *U.S. 7, Sharon* ☎ *860/927–3238* ⊕ *www.ct.gov/deep/housatonicmeadows* ☜ *Free.*

Sharon Audubon Center
NATURE PRESERVE | FAMILY | With 11 miles of hiking trails, this 1,147-acre property—a mixture of forests, meadows, wetlands, ponds, and streams—provides myriad hiking opportunities. The visitor center shares its space with small hawks, an owl, and other animals in the live-animal display in the Natural History Exhibit Room; in the Children's Adventure Center, kids learn about the importance of water quality and watersheds, crawl through a tunnel to a beaver lodge, and look for various fish and other sea life in the large aquarium. ⊠ *325 Cornwall Bridge Rd., Sharon* ☎ *860/364–0520* ⊕ *www.sharon.audubon.org* ☜ *Visitor center free, aviaries and trails $3* ☽ *Visitor center closed Mon.*

West Cornwall Covered Bridge
BRIDGE/TUNNEL | A romantic reminder of the past, this single-lane bridge over the Housatonic River is on Route 128, just east of U.S. 7, in West Cornwall. The 172-feet-long and 15-feet-wide bridge was built in 1841 and still carries vehicular traffic. The design incorporates strut techniques that were later copied by bridge builders around the country. ⊠ *Junction of Rtes. 7 and 128, West Cornwall.*

Hotels

Cornwall Inn
$ | B&B/INN | FAMILY | This 19th-century inn, with four bedrooms and a two-bedroom suite, combines country charm with contemporary elegance; eight rustic guest rooms in the adjacent lodge are slightly more private and have cedar-post beds. **Pros:** tranquil setting and lovely grounds; swimming pool and year-round hot tub; welcoming to kids and pets. **Cons:** a bit far from neighboring towns; allergy alert: pets are allowed in lodge rooms but not in the main inn; rooms are fairly small and bathrooms are quite small. ⑤ *Rooms from: $169* ⊠ *270 Kent Rd. S* ☎ *860/672–6884* ⊕ *www.cornwallinn.com* ⤴ *13 rooms* ⦿ *Free breakfast.*

Activities

CANOEING AND KAYAKING
Clarke Outdoors
CANOEING/ROWING/SKULLING | FAMILY | This outfitter rents canoes, kayaks, and rafts—and operates 10-mile canoe or raft trips downstream from Falls Village to Housatonic Meadows State Park. The water is a mix of flat water and easy white water, suitable for novices. ⊠ *163*

U.S. 7, West Cornwall ⊹ 1 mile south
of covered bridge ☏ 860/672–6365
⊕ www.clarkeoutdoors.com.

FISHING
Housatonic Anglers

FISHING | Enjoy a half- or full-day guided
fishing trip on the Housatonic River and
its tributaries with this company. You can
also take fly-fishing lessons. ⊠ 26 Bolton
Hill Rd. ☏ 860/672–4457 ⊕ www.housa-
tonicanglers.com.

Housatonic River Outfitters

FISHING | This outfitter operates a full-
service fly shop, leads guided trips of the
region, conducts classes in fly-fishing,
and stocks a good selection of vintage
and antique gear. ⊠ 24 Kent Rd., Cornwall Bridge ☏ 860/672–1010 ⊕ www.
dryflies.com.

SKIING
Mohawk Mountain

SKIING/SNOWBOARDING | **FAMILY** | The trails
at Mohawk Mountain include plenty
of intermediate terrain, a few trails for
beginners, and a few steeper sections
for more advanced skiers. A small area is
devoted to snowboarders. Trails are ser-
viced by five triple lifts and three magic
carpets; 12 trails are lighted for night skiing. The base lodge has munchies and a
retail shop, and halfway up the slope the
Pine Lodge Restaurant has an outdoor
patio. **Facilities**: 25 trails; 112 acres; 650-
foot vertical drop; 8 lifts; snowmaking
on 99% of all terrain. ⊠ 46 Great Hollow
Rd., off Rte. 4 ☏ 860/672–6100 ⊕ www.
mohawkmtn.com ▱ Lift ticket $30 mid-
week, $64 weekend/holiday.

Norfolk

23 miles northeast of Cornwall, 41
miles west of Hartford, 60 miles north
of New Haven.

Thanks to having the coolest temperatures in Connecticut and a rather
rocky terrain, Norfolk has resisted
development and stands as one of the
best-preserved villages in the Northeast. Notable industrialists have been
summering here for two centuries, and
many enormous homesteads still exist.
The striking town green, at the junction
of Route 272 and U.S. 44, has a fountain
designed by Augustus Saint-Gaudens
(executed in 1889 by Stanford White)
at its southern corner. The fountain is a
memorial to Joseph Battell, who turned
Norfolk into a major trading center in the
mid-19th century.

GETTING HERE AND AROUND
To reach Norfolk by car, use U.S. 7 or
U.S. 8 and U.S. 44.

⊙ Sights
Dennis Hill State Park

NATIONAL/STATE PARK | **FAMILY** | Dr. Freder-
ick Shepard Dennis, the former owner of
these 240 acres, lavishly entertained his
guests—among them President William
Howard Taft and several Connecticut
governors—in the stone pavilion at the
summit of the estate. From its 1,627-
foot height, you have a panoramic view
of Haystack Mountain and parts of New
Hampshire to the north and, on a clear
day, the New Haven harbor—about 60
miles south. Picnic on the park's grounds
or hike one of its many trails. ⊠ Rte. 272
☏ 860/482–1817 ⊕ www.ct.gov/deep/
dennishill ▱ Free.

Haystack Mountain State Park

NATIONAL/STATE PARK | **FAMILY** | One of
the most spectacular views in the state
can be seen from the 34-foot high stone
tower atop Haystack Mountain (1,716
feet). You can see the Berkshires in
Connecticut and Massachusetts, as well
as peaks in New York and the Green
Mountains of Vermont. A winding road
will get you halfway there; then you hike
a rugged half-mile trail to the top. ⊠ Rte.
272 ☏ 860/482–1817 ⊕ www.ct.gov/
deep/HaystackMountain.

Hotels

Blackberry River Inn

$ | B&B/INN | Set upon 27 acres in Connecticut's Berkshire Mountains, this historic (1763) home-turned inn has two rooms and two suites in the Main House and a dozen simpler—but still lovely—rooms in the adjacent Carriage House, plus a full home-cooked breakfast is served in a sunny breakfast room every morning. **Pros:** swimming pool open in summer; wood-burning fireplaces in most Main House rooms; raised waffles (made with yeast) and real maple syrup at breakfast. **Cons:** two-night minimum on weekends; no room TV in Main House rooms; beware of wildlife (an occasional bear). ⑤ *Rooms from: $129* ⊠ *538 Greenwoods Rd. W (Rte. 44 W)* ☎ *860/542–5100* ⊕ *www.blackberryriverinn.com* ⬡ *17 rooms* ⦾*⧉ Free breakfast.*

Manor House Inn

$$ | B&B/INN | Among the remarkable appointments in this 1898 Bavarian Tudor-style building are its wood-beam ceilings, graceful arches, and antique beds—along with 20 stained-glass windows designed by Louis Comfort Tiffany. **Pros:** interesting building with lots of nooks and crannies and sumptuous decor; lavish breakfasts; peaceful atmosphere with lots to do nearby. **Cons:** no phone or TV in guest rooms (and mobile reception is iffy in these parts); rooms and bathrooms need updating; third-floor rooms are the least comfortable. ⑤ *Rooms from: $219* ⊠ *69 Maple Ave.* ☎ *860/542–5690* ⊕ *www.manorhouse-norfolk.com* ⬡ *9 rooms* ⦾*⧉ Free breakfast.*

✪ Performing Arts

★ Infinity Music Hall & Bistro

CONCERTS | Built in 1883, this modernized 300-seat music hall hosts more than 200 shows a year by local performers as well as nationally known folk, soft rock, and jazz groups. The intimate setting puts you close to the stage. Have drinks, snacks, or a meal in the Bistro before the performance. ⊠ *20 Greenwoods Rd. W* ☎ *860/542–5531* ⊕ *www.infinityhall.com.*

Norfolk Chamber Music Festival

FESTIVALS | Held at the Music Shed on the 70-acre Ellen Battell Stoeckel Estate, the Norfolk Chamber Music Festival presents world-renowned artists and ensembles on Friday and Saturday evenings in summer. Students from the Yale School of Music perform on Thursday evening and Saturday morning. Stroll the 70-acre grounds or visit the art gallery. ⊠ *Ellen Battell Stoeckel Estate, 20 Litchfield Rd.* ☎ *860/542–3000* ⊕ *norfolk.yale.edu.*

Litchfield

60 miles northeast of Norwalk, 34 miles west of Hartford, 40 miles northwest of New Haven.

Everything in Litchfield, the most noteworthy town in the Litchfield Hills, seems to exist on a larger scale than in neighboring villages, especially the impressive Litchfield Green and the white Colonial and Greek Revival homes that line the broad, tree-lined streets. Harriet Beecher Stowe, author of *Uncle Tom's Cabin,* and her brother, abolitionist preacher Henry Ward Beecher, were born and raised in Litchfield, and many famous Americans earned their law degrees at the Litchfield Law School. Today, lovely but expensive boutiques and restaurants line the downtown area.

GETTING HERE AND AROUND

To reach Litchfield by car from points north or south, take Route 8 to Route 118 west.

Sights

Haight-Brown Vineyard

WINERY/DISTILLERY | A founding member of the Connecticut Wine Trail, the state's oldest winery opened its doors in 1975. You can stop in for tastings and winery tours. Seasonal events include barrel tastings in April and a harvest festival in September. ⊠ *29 Chestnut Hill Rd., off Rte. 118* 🖬 *860/567–4045* ⊕ *www.haight-vineyards.com* 🖫 *Tasting $12* ⊙ *Closed Mon.–Thurs. Nov.–Apr.*

Litchfield History Museum

MUSEUM | In this well-regarded museum, seven neatly organized galleries highlight family life and work during the 50 years following the American Revolution. The extensive reference library has informa-tion about the town's historic buildings, including the Sheldon Tavern where George Washington slept on several occasions, and the Litchfield Female Academy where, in the late 1700s, Sarah Pierce taught girls not only sewing and deportment but also mathematics and history. ⊠ *7 South St., at Rtes. 63, 118, and 202* 🖬 *860/567–4501* ⊕ *www.litchfieldhistoricalsociety.org* 🖫 *Free* ⊙ *Closed Mon. and Dec.–mid-Apr.*

Tapping Reeve House and Litchfield Law School

HISTORIC SITE | In 1773, Judge Tapping Reeve enrolled his first student, Aaron Burr, in what became the first law school in the country. (Before Judge Reeve, students studied the law as apprentices, not in formal classes.) This school is dedi-cated to Reeve's achievement and to the notable students who passed through its halls, including three U.S. Supreme Court justices. There are multimedia exhibits, an excellent introductory film, and restored facilities. ⊠ *82 South St.* 🖬 *860/567–4501* ⊕ *www.litchfieldhistoricalsociety.org* 🖫 *Free* ⊙ *Closed Mon. and Dec.–mid-Apr.*

White Flower Farm

GARDEN | A stroll through these land-scaped grounds is always a pleasure and will provide gardeners with myriad ideas. The nursery and garden center ships annuals, perennials, shrubs, vines, bulbs, and houseplants to gardeners throughout the United States. Visitors are welcome to stroll through and around the acres of trial and display gardens. There is also a retail store on-site. ⊠ *167 Litchfield Rd.,* *Morris* 🖬 *860/567–8789* ⊕ *www.white-flowerfarm.com* ⊙ *Closed Nov.–Mar.*

★ White Memorial Conservation Center

MUSEUM | **FAMILY** | This 4,000-acre nature preserve houses top-notch natural-history exhibits. There are 30 bird-watching platforms, two self-guided nature trails, several boardwalks, boating facilities, and 35 miles of hiking, cross-country-skiing, and horseback-riding trails. The Nature Museum has displays depicting the natural diversity found throughout the preserve, dioramas, live animals, a beehive, a digital microscope, and other unique exhibits of interest to kids of all ages (especially the scavenger hunt). ⊠ *80 Whitehall Rd., off U.S. 202* 🖬 *860/567–0857* ⊕ *www.whitememori-alcc.org* 🖫 *Grounds free, museum $6.*

🍴 Restaurants

The Village Restaurant

$$ | **AMERICAN** | Beloved among visitors and locals alike, this storefront eatery in a redbrick town house serves tasty, unfussy food—inexpensive pub grub in one room, updated contemporary American cuisine in the other. Whether you order a burger or horseradish-and-Parmesan-crusted salm-on, you're bound to be pleased. **Known for:** really good food at reasonable prices; Mexican Monday and Italian Wednesday; weekday happy hours. ⑤ *Average main: $23* ⊠ *25 West St.* 🖬 *860/567–8307* ⊕ *www.village-litchfield.com.*

West Street Grill

$$$ | **MODERN AMERICAN** | This sophisticated dining room on the town green is *the* place to see and be seen. Dinner selec-tions might include free-range chicken with potato puree and mushrooms, braised short ribs over a Gorgonzola-polenta cake, or organic Irish salmon with fingerling potatoes. **Known for:** alfresco tables overlooking the town green; perfect for a casual lunch or formal dinner; house-made ice creams and sorbets. ⑤ *Average main: $34* ⊠ *43 West St.* 🖬 *860/567–3885* ⊕ *www.weststreetgrill.com.*

Hotels

The Litchfield Inn

$ | **B&B/INN** | This Colonial-style inn offers 12 themed rooms, each uniquely decorated, as well as more standard-style guest rooms with modern decor. **Pros:** on-site restaurant and lounge; complimentary bikes; comfy beds. **Cons:** not within walking distance of attractions and restaurants; uneven service; more like a small hotel than a country inn. $ *Rooms from: $179 ⊠ 432 Bantam Rd.* ☎ *860/567–4503* ⊕ *www.litchfieldinnct.com* ⬥ *32 rooms* ⎮◎⎮ *No meals.*

★ Winvian

$$$$ | **RESORT** | This private, 113-acre hideaway a few miles south of Litchfield consists of 18 of the most imaginative and luxuriously outfitted cottages you'll ever lay eyes on, each with a distinctive, often amusing, theme—like the Helicopter Cottage, with a genuine, 17,000-pound U.S. Coast Guard helicopter (the fuselage has been fitted with a wet bar) in it. **Pros:** whimsical and superplush accommodations; outstanding cuisine; stunning setting. **Cons:** superpricey; size and amenities differ in each cottage; unique cottages but no overall "awe" factor. $ *Rooms from: $695 ⊠ 155 Alain White Rd., Morris* ☎ *860/567–9600* ⊕ *www.winvian.com* ⬥ *19 suites* ◎⎮ *Free breakfast.*

Activities

HIKING

Mt. Tom State Park

HIKING/WALKING | Hike the mile-long trail to the stone lookout tower atop Mt. Tom and enjoy expansive views—or take a swim in the pond below and picnic on the beach. ⊠ *U.S. 202* ✛ *7 miles southwest of Litchfield* ☎ *860/868–2592 (Labor Day–Memorial Day), 860/567–8870 (Memorial Day–Labor Day)* ⊕ *www.ct.gov/deep/mounttom* ⬥ *Parking free for residents, $15 on weekends for nonresidents.*

HORSEBACK RIDING

Lee's Riding Stable

HORSEBACK RIDING | **FAMILY** | Ride a well-behaved steed through Litchfield's rolling hills and countryside. Adults and kids age seven and up are welcome to join a guided, hour-long trail ride. Youngsters enjoy a pony ride around the ring. Private or semiprivate lessons are also available. ⊠ *57 E. Litchfield Rd.* ☎ *860/567–0785* ⊕ *www.windfieldmorganfarm.com* ⬥ *From $20.*

Washington

14 miles southwest of Litchfield.

The beautiful buildings of the Gunnery prep school mingle with stately Colonials and churches in Washington, one of the best-preserved Colonial towns in Connecticut. The Mayflower Inn, south of The Gunnery, a private prep school on Route 47, attracts an exclusive clientele. In 1779 Washington, which was settled in 1734, became the first town in the United States to be named for the first president.

GETTING HERE AND AROUND

Washington is accessible only by car. Route 47 runs through rural town, connecting it with New Preston to the north and Woodbury to the south.

Sights

The Institute for American Indian Studies

MUSEUM | **FAMILY** | The exhibits in this small but excellent and thoughtfully arranged collection detail the history and continuing presence of 10,000 years of Native American life in New England. Highlights include nature trails, a simulated archaeological site, and an authentically constructed Algonquian Village with wigwams, a longhouse, a rock shelter, and more. A gift shop presents the work of some of the country's best Native American artists. ⊠ *38 Curtis Rd., off Rte. 199* ☎ *860/868–0518* ⊕ *www.iaismuseum.org* ⬥ *$10* ⊙ *Closed Mon. and Tues.*

Continued on page 318

ANTIQUES AND CRAFTS SHOPPING
SOMETHING OLD, SOMETHING NEW

By Christina Valhouli

Forget the mall. In New England, shoppers can pick up serious antiques or quirky bric-a-brac in old mills and converted barns. Or hit funky galleries or annual craft fairs to meet artisans and buy one-of-a-kind products. Your shopping experience will be as memorable as your souvenirs.

Alongside New England's wealth of early American history is some of the best antique and craft shopping in the country—and often in beautiful settings perfect for browsing. You can explore galleries in converted farmhouses, craft shops clustered around the village green, or quaint antique shops on a picturesque Main Street (Woodstock, Vermont, or Camden, Maine, are good bets). Drive through historic coastal towns, like Essex, Massachusetts, where finds such as sun-bleached, centuries-old wooden tables or antique compasses evoke the area's maritime heritage. Picture-perfect towns like Blue Hill, Maine, and Chester, Connecticut, are home to plenty of contemporary artists' galleries and cooperatives; the Connecticut River Artisans in Essex, CT, showcases handmade quilts, jewelry, and ceramics; or try your luck at the Frog Hollow Vermont State Craft Center in Burlington.

Top Left, Hand-blown glass. Top right, Brimfield Antique Show. Bottom, antique pocket watch.

GREAT FINDS: CRAFTS

When most people think of a typical New England look, the austere lines of a Shaker table or the colorful patterns in a quilt come to mind. Artisans here still make crafts the old-fashioned way, but a new generation of glassblowers, potters, and weavers is creating products that will appeal to modernistas.

QUILTS. Today's quilters continue to produce traditional quilts, but there are plenty of contemporary styles available. Instead of star patterns, go for bold stripes or blocky squares made from funky fabrics. Buy one for your bed or to hang; baby quilts start around $50.

SHAKER-STYLE FURNITURE. The Shakers believed that form must follow function, and a typical Shaker design is clean, straight-lined, and devoid of decoration. Carpenters still make Shaker-inspired furniture, including ladderback chairs, tables, and bookcases. Chairs start around $350.

FELT. Humble felt is simply unspun wool that has been rolled and beaten into a solid form, but it's one of the most versatile (and eco-friendly) products around. Contemporary artists fashion felt into handbags, rugs, and even lightweight sculptures. Handbags start at $60.

CERAMICS. Visit a pottery studio or an art gallery and choose from ceramic plates and mugs or sturdier stoneware products that can survive the dishwasher. Small ceramic pieces start at $25.

WOOD BOWLS. Hand turned bowls are individually shaped on a lathe from solid blocks of wood. Each piece has a unique size, shape, grain pattern, and color. Burl and spalted bowls are highly valued for their patterns and rich contrasts. Small bowls start around $50.

BLOWN GLASS. It's worth a trip to a glassblowing studio just to see the artisans blow a gob of molten glass into a beautiful object. Best bets include colorful vases, bowls, and sculptures; handblown glass items run about $25 and up—way up!

GREAT FINDS: ANTIQUES

Antiques can run the gamut from auction-worthy pieces to decorative trinkets and vintage items from the '40s, '50s, and '60s. Antique trends come and go, but popular New England buys include items like old prints and glass bottles. Don't be put off if you don't know a lot about antiques but keep in mind that a true antique must be at least 100 years old.

KITCHEN TOOLS. Although you won't be tempted to cook with an old iron cauldron, items like engraved stove plates, mortar and pestles, and spoon racks look great on display for about $40–$180.

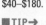

■TIP→
Start a collection easily with two or more of the same item (salt and pepper shakers) or style (speckled graniteware).

PENS. Hardly anyone writes letters anymore, which makes collecting old pens even more special. Parker pens from the 1970s are mostly ballpoint, while antique fountain pens sheathed in beautiful wood or mother of pearl are a joy to use. Prices are $100 up to thousands.

MIRRORS. If your taste runs toward the ornate, browse for 19th-century Federal and Queen Anne–style gilt mirrors. For something smaller and more understated, try a concave or vintage sunburst mirror. Prices range from $200–$2,000.

JEWELRY. Cuff links, earrings, and brooches make great gifts and will take up little room in your luggage. Antique jewelry runs the gamut from fun beaded necklaces to delicate Art Deco pieces. Prices start at $20.

MAPS. Frame an old nautical chart or map of a town you vacationed in for a stylish memento. Reproductions are easier on the wallet but still look good. Prices start at $40 for prints and run up to the thousands for antiques.

AMERICANA. This can be anything from painted signs to photographs of historic villages or kitschy porcelain figurines that evoke what it means to be American. Items inspired by the Stars and Stripes make colorful decorative accents for a country home feel. Vintage postcards and other small items start at $5.

TOP SHOPPING ROUTES & SIGHTS

Green Mountains, Waitsfield, East Warren Road

One of the most effective and fun ways to shop is to hop in the car and drive through sleepy, scenic towns. On several key shopping routes in New England, stretches of road are absolutely packed with shops. Charles Street in Boston and downtown Providence and Portland are ideal, compact urban shopping areas for walking. If you do have wheels, try these routes.

❶ Route 100. One of the most picturesque drives in the Green Mountain State, this winding road goes from Wilmington all the way north to Stowe. You'll pass craft studios, general stores like the Vermont Country Store in Weston, and plenty of red barns and covered bridges.

❷ Route 7, Berkshire County. Practically the entire route is chock-a-block with antiques stores. The Berkshire County Antiques and Art Dealers Association (⊕ *bcaada.com*) publishes a handy guide to the various shops. Key Western Massachusetts shopping towns include Great Barrington, Sheffield, and Lenox.

❸ Main Street, Putnam. Most of the town has a stuck-in-time quality, so it's a great place to spend the day in Connecticut's "Quite Corner." The majority of antique stores are clustered around Main Street and its offshoots. Start your hunt at the massive Antiques Marketplace.

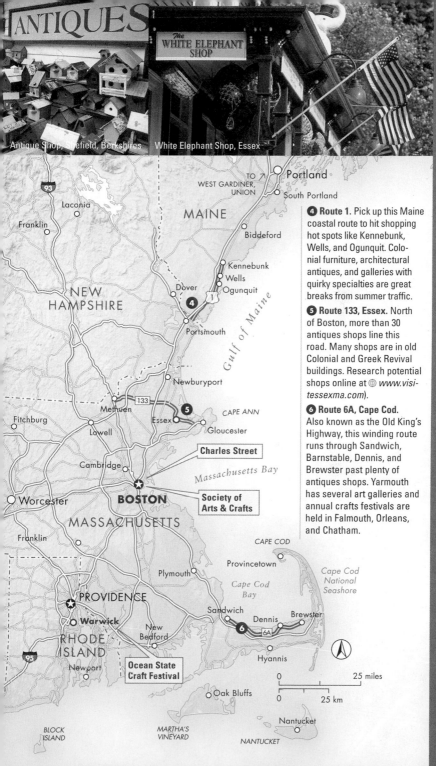

ANTIQUES

The WHITE ELEPHANT SHOP

Antique Shop, Sheffield, Berkshires   White Elephant Shop, Essex

④ Route 1. Pick up this Maine coastal route to hit shopping hot spots like Kennebunk, Wells, and Ogunquit. Colonial furniture, architectural antiques, and galleries with quirky specialties are great breaks from summer traffic.

⑤ Route 133, Essex. North of Boston, more than 30 antiques shops line this road. Many shops are in old Colonial and Greek Revival buildings. Research potential shops online at ⊕ *www.visitessexma.com*).

⑥ Route 6A, Cape Cod. Also known as the Old King's Highway, this winding route runs through Sandwich, Barnstable, Dennis, and Brewster past plenty of antiques shops. Yarmouth has several art galleries and annual crafts festivals are held in Falmouth, Orleans, and Chatham.

Map labels

TO 7
WEST GARDINER,
UNION

Portland
South Portland

MAINE

Laconia

Franklin

Biddeford

Kennebunk
Wells
Ogunquit

NEW HAMPSHIRE

Dover

④ 1

Portsmouth

Gulf of Maine

Newburyport

133

Methuen

Fitchburg

⑤ Essex

CAPE ANN

Lowell

Gloucester

Cambridge

Charles Street

Massachusetts Bay

Worcester

BOSTON

Society of Arts & Crafts

MASSACHUSETTS

Franklin

CAPE COD

Plymouth

Provincetown

Cape Cod Bay

Cape Cod National Seashore

PROVIDENCE

Sandwich

Dennis   Brewster

⑥ 6A

Warwick

New Bedford

Hyannis

RHODE ISLAND

95

Newport

Ocean State Craft Festival

Oak Bluffs

0   25 miles
0   25 km

Nantucket

BLOCK ISLAND

MARTHA'S VINEYARD

NANTUCKET

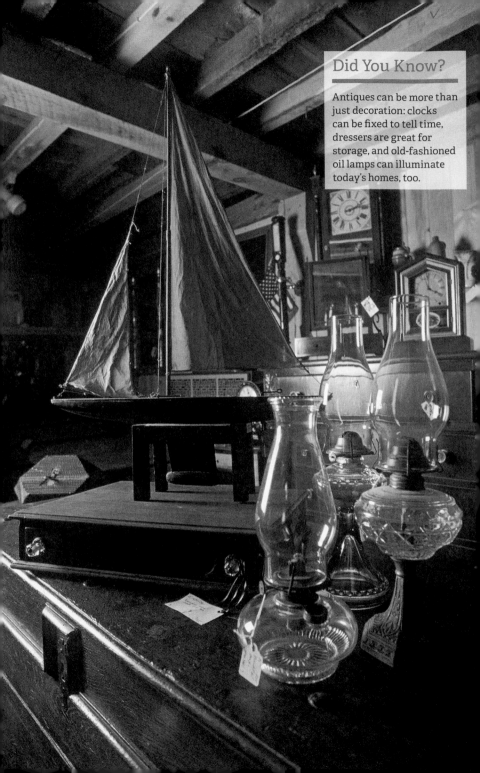

WHERE TO GET THE GOODS

Depending on your budget, there are plenty of places to shop. Take your pick from artisan studios, art galleries, auction houses, and multi-dealer antique centers. Some antiques shops are one step above flea markets, so prices can vary widely. Antiques shows and craft fairs also offer excellent one-stop shopping opportunities.

TOP ANTIQUES SHOWS

★ **Brimfield Antique and Collectible Shows,** Brimfield, Massachusetts. May, July and September (⊕ www.brimfieldshow.com).

Connecticut Spring Antiques Show, Hartford, Connecticut. March (⊕ www.ctspringantiquesshow.com).

Elephant's Trunk Country Flea Market, New Milford, Connecticut. Sundays except mid-December through mid-March (⊕ www.etflea.com).

Maine Antiques Festival, Union, Maine. August (⊕ maineantiquesfestival.com).

TOP CRAFT FAIRS AND CENTERS

Center for Maine Crafts, West Gardiner, Maine (⊕ mainecrafts.org).

★ **League of New Hampshire Craftsmen's Fair,** Newbury, New Hampshire. August (⊕ www.nhcrafts.org).

Ocean State Artisans Holiday Craft Festival, Warwick, Rhode Island. November (⊕ www.oceanstateartisans.com).

Petersham Craft Center, Petersham, Massachusetts (⊕ www.petershamcommon.com).

Society of Arts and Crafts, Boston, Massachusetts (⊕ www.societyofcrafts.org).

Stonehouse Antique Center, Chester, Vermont (☎ 800/875-4477).

Top, Ceramics sold along Route 100, Vermont.

Right, antique rocking horse.

SHOPPING KNOW-HOW

Many shops are often closed on Sundays and Mondays. Call ahead to confirm. Before you whip out the credit card (or a wad of cash), there are a few other things to remember.

■ Unless you're an expert, it can be difficult to tell if an item is a reproduction or a genuine antique. Buy a price guide or a reference book like Miller's *Antiques & Collectibles* or *Kovel's* to have an idea of a fair value.

■ To ensure you are buying from a legitimate source, make sure the dealer belongs to a professional organization.

■ Think carefully about shipping costs for bulky items. It's also a good idea to carry with you some key measurements from your house.

■ If you find a piece that you love, check it carefully for any flaws. Point out any dings or scratches and use those as a bargaining chip when negotiating a price.

■ Always remember this golden rule: Buy what you love at a price you can afford.

🍽 Restaurants

★ The Mayflower Dining Room

$$$$ | AMERICAN | At the refined and romantic restaurant of the Grace Mayflower Inn & Spa, gaze through the dining room's large windows—or from your seat on the terrace in warm weather—toward the formal English gardens while enjoying deftly prepared regional American cuisine. After dinner, stop by the wood-paneled library for a glass of cognac. **Known for:** classic, seasonal dishes beautifully presented; herbs and vegetables grown in the inn's own kitchen garden; outstanding service. ⑤ *Average main: $42* ✉ *118 Woodbury Rd.* ☎ *860/868–9466* ⊕ *www.gracehotels.com/mayflower.*

🛏 Hotels

★ Grace Mayflower Inn & Spa

$$$$ | RESORT | Running streams, rambling stone walls, and rare-specimen trees fill the country manor–style inn's 28 manicured acres. **Pros:** beautifully landscaped grounds; solicitous but relaxed service; hiking, biking, and nature walks at the back door. **Cons:** very pricey; $40 per day resort fee added to all rates. ⑤ *Rooms from: $740* ✉ *118 Woodbury Rd.* ☎ *860/868–9466* ⊕ *www.gracehotels.com/mayflower/* 🛏 *30 rooms* ⊘ *No meals.*

Woodbury

10 miles southeast of Washington.

There may be more antiques shops in Woodbury than in all other towns in the Litchfield Hills combined. Some of the best-preserved examples of Colonial architecture in New England can be found here, including five magnificent churches and the Greek Revival King Solomon's Lodge No. 7 Masonic Temple (1838).

GETTING HERE AND AROUND

To reach Woodbury by car from Washington, take Route 47 south; from elsewhere, take Interstate 84 to U.S. 6 north.

◉ Sights

Glebe House Museum and The Gertrude Jekyll Garden

GARDEN | This property in the center of town consists of the large, antiques-filled, gambrel-roof Georgian Colonial home of Dr. Samuel Seabury—who, in 1783, was elected the first Episcopal bishop in the United States. The house, built in 1740, and its outstanding furniture collection, is one of the earliest and most authentic house museums in the region. The garden was designed in the 1920s by renowned British horticulturist Gertrude Jekyll. Though small, it's a classic, old-fashioned, English-style garden and the only one of the three Jekyll-designed gardens in the United States that are still in existence. ✉ *49 Hollow Rd.* ☎ *203/263–2855* ⊕ *www.glebehousemuseum.org* 💲 *$7* ⊘ *Closed Mon. and Tues. and mid-Oct.–Apr.*

Quassy Amusement Park & Water Park

AMUSEMENT PARK/WATER PARK | FAMILY | Families have been enjoying the rides here for more than a century. There are kiddie rides, family rides that Mom & Dad even enjoy, and thrill rides—more than two dozen rides altogether—plus Splash Away Bay Water Park. The custom-designed Wooden Warrior roller coaster is rated one of the top 25 in the world. ✉ *2132 Middlebury Rd.* ✛ *4 miles southeast of Woodbury via U.S. 6 and Rte. 64* ☎ *203/758–2913* ⊕ *www.quassy.com* 💲 *$29* ⊘ *Closed Oct.–Apr.*

🍽 Restaurants

★ Good News Restaurant & Bar

$$ | AMERICAN | Since Carole Peck—a well-known name throughout New England (and beyond)—opened here in 1992, foodies have been flocking to Woodbury to sample her superb cuisine. The emphasis is on healthy, innovative, and surprisingly well-priced fare like wok-seared Gulf shrimp with new potatoes, grilled green beans, and a

garlic aioli. **Known for:** "star" chef cooks up creative cuisine; farm-to-table dishes feature local, seasonal ingredients; decor includes original artwork by local artists. $ *Average main: $24* ⊠ *Sherman Village Plaza, 694 Main St.* S ☎ *203/266–4663* ⊕ *www.goodnewsrestaurantandbar.com* ☽ *Closed Tues.*

Hotels

The Evergreen Inn

$ | **B&B/INN** | A short drive from Woodbury's antiques shops and restaurants, this Federal Colonial house (circa 1818) offers a bounty of pleasing comforts—from high-quality antique furnishings and soft bedding with lots of pillows to floral gardens and a stone-and-granite pool surrounded by a private hedge. **Pros:** delicious, made-from-scratch full breakfast; beautifully kept grounds and garden; 24-hour self-serve snack bar with coffee/wine/beer. **Cons:** only five rooms so reserve in advance; on a fairly busy road; you won't want to leave. $ *Rooms from: $149* ⊠ *782 Main St. N, Southbury* ☎ *203/586–1876* ⊕ *www. evergreeninnsouthbury.com* ↝ *5 rooms* ⬚| *Free breakfast.*

Shopping

Mill House Antiques

ANTIQUES/COLLECTIBLES | The Mill House carries formal and country English and French furniture and decor. ⊠ *1068 Main St. N* ☎ *203/263–3446* ⊕ *www.millhouseantiquesandgardens.com.*

Monique Shay Antiques & Designs

ANTIQUES/COLLECTIBLES | The six barns that make up Monique Shay's store are packed with French Canadian country antiques. ⊠ *920 Main St.* S ☎ *203/263–3186* ⊕ *www.moniqueshay.com.*

New Haven

46 miles northeast of Greenwich.

Though the city is best known as the home of Yale University, New Haven's historic district dates back to the 17th century—and the city's distinctive shops, prestigious museums, and highly respected theaters are major draws. In recent years, the restaurant scene has also garnered considerable acclaim, particularly the city's unique "apizza" legacy.

GETTING HERE AND AROUND

By car, New Haven is accessible from both Interstate 95 and Interstate 91. By rail, Amtrak's Northeast Regional and high-speed Acela trains stop here; New Haven is also the end of the Metro-North commuter line from New York City. Shore Line East train service connects New Haven with Old Saybrook, Madison, and New London.

ESSENTIALS

VISITOR INFORMATION Visit New Haven
☎ *203/777–8550, 800/332–7829* ⊕ *www.visitnewhaven.com.*

Sights

Beinecke Rare Book and Manuscript Library

LIBRARY | The library's collection of literary papers, early manuscripts, and rare books include a Gutenberg Bible and original Audubon bird prints; the exhibition spaces on the ground floor and mezzanine are open to the public. The building that houses them is an attraction in its own right: the walls are made of marble cut so thin that the light shines through, making the interior a breathtaking sight on sunny days. Introductory tours for individuals are offered on Saturday afternoons; group tours are Yale-led and require advance registration at the Yale Visitor Information Center ⊠ *121 Wall St.* ☎ *203/432–2977* ⊕ *beinecke.library. yale.edu* ⬚ *Free.*

New Haven, Mystic, and the Coast

KEY
Ferry Lines

Connecticut Lobster Rolls

Behold the lobster roll: sweet, succulent, and sinfully rich, it's the ultimate buttery icon of a Connecticut summer. Many New Englanders prefer to chill out with a cold lobster salad in their bun, but Nutmeggers generally like their lobster rolls served hot, hot, hot.

The traditional Connecticut lobster roll, said to have been invented in the early 1930s at Perry's, a now-defunct seafood shack on the Boston Post Road in Milford, consists of nothing more than plump chunks of hot lobster meat and melted butter served on a butter-toasted roll; in other words: heaven on a bun. From seafood shanties along the shore to gourmet getaways farther inland, Connecticut is fairly swimming in eateries that offer these revered rolls. Here are three favorites:

Abbott's Lobster in the Rough, Noank. A lobster roll at Abbott's Lobster in the Rough is best enjoyed from a picnic table at the edge of Noank Harbor, watching the boats bob by.

Captain Scott's Lobster Dock, New London. Whether hot and buttery or cold and creamy, the lobster rolls at Captain Scott's Lobster Dock, on a spit of land overlooking Shaw's Cove, come on grilled-in-butter buns—either regular size or "foot-long."

Lenny and Joe's Fish Tale, Madison. At Lenny and Joe's Fish Tale, kids of all ages love to eat their lobster rolls or fried seafood outdoors by a hand-carved Dentzel carousel with flying horses (and a whale, frog, lion, seal, and more), which the restaurant runs early May–early October.

7

Connecticut   NEW HAVEN

★ IT Adventure Indoor Ropes Course
AMUSEMENT PARK/WATER PARK | FAMILY | Oddly enough, you'll find the world's largest indoor adventure ropes course within Jordan's Furniture Store. The 60-foot-high courses have more than 100 activities like walking across zigzag swinging beams, climbing walls, rope ladders, bridges, moving planks, a 50-foot free-fall jump, four 200-foot-long ziplines, and more. At Little IT, toddlers and little kids can zip along, too. ⊠ *Jordan's Furniture Store, 41 Sargent Dr., adjacent to I-95* ☎ *203/812–9981* ⊕ *www.jordans.com/attractions/it* ⊠ *$25.*

New Haven Green
HISTORIC SITE | FAMILY | Bordered on its west side by the Yale campus, the New Haven Green is a fine example of early urban planning. Village elders set aside the 16-acre plot as a town common as early as 1638. Three early-19th-century churches—the Gothic Revival-style

Trinity Episcopal Church, the Federal-style **Center Congregational Church,** and **United Church**—have contributed to its present appeal. For a year, from September 1839 to August 1840, survivors of the slave ship *Amistad* were incarcerated in a jail on the east side of the green and were brought out of jail to exercise there. An *Amistad* memorial now resides at the site of the former jail. ⊠ *250 Temple St., between Church, College, Elm, and Chapel Sts.*

★ Peabody Museum of Natural History
MUSEUM | FAMILY | First opened to the public in 1876, the Peabody Museum houses more than 13 million specimens, making it one of the largest natural history museums in the nation. In addition to exhibits on Andean, Mesoamerican, and Pacific cultures, the venerable museum has an excellent ornithology collection, including a stuffed dodo and passenger pigeon. The main attractions for both

New Haven

Grove St. Cemetery

THE GREEN

◆ Amistad Memorial

KEY
- 1 Sights
- 1 Restaurants
- 1 Hotels

0 ——— 300 yds
0 ——— 300 meters

children and amateur paleontologists are some of the world's earliest reconstructions of dinosaur skeletons—including the huge brontosaurus that overwhelms the Great Hall. ⊠ *170 Whitney Ave.* 🕾 *203/432–8987* ⊕ *peabody.yale.edu* 🎟 *$13* 🕙 *Closed Mon.*

★ Yale Center for British Art

MUSEUM | Featuring the largest collection of British art outside Britain, the center surveys the development of English art, life, and thought from the Elizabethan period to the present. The skylighted galleries, one of architect Louis I. Kahn's final works, contain artwork by John Constable, William Hogarth, Thomas Gainsborough, Joshua Reynolds, and J.M.W. Turner, to name but a few. You'll also find rare books and paintings documenting English history. ⊠ *1080 Chapel St.* 🕾 *203/432–2800, 877/274–8278* ⊕ *britishart.yale.edu* 🎟 *Free* 🕙 *Closed Mon.*

★ Yale University

COLLEGE | **FAMILY** | New Haven's manufacturing history dates to the 19th century, but the city owes its fame to merchant Elihu Yale. In 1718 his contributions enabled the Collegiate School, founded in 1701 at Saybrook, to settle in New Haven and change its name to Yale College. In 1887, all its schools were consolidated into Yale University. This is one of the nation's great institutions of higher learning, and its campus holds some handsome neo-Gothic buildings and noteworthy museums. Student guides conduct hour-long walking tours that include Connecticut Hall in the Old Campus, one of the oldest buildings in the state, which housed a number of illustrious students—including Nathan Hale, Noah Webster, and Eli Whitney. Tours start from the visitor center. ⊠ *Yale Visitor Center, 149 Elm St.* 🕾 *203/432–2300* ⊕ *visitorcenter.yale.edu* 🎟 *Free.*

★ Yale University Art Gallery

MUSEUM | Since its founding in 1832, this art gallery has amassed more than 200,000 works from around the world,

dating from ancient Egypt to the present day. Highlights include works by Vincent van Gogh, Edouard Manet, Claude Monet, Pablo Picasso, Winslow Homer, and Thomas Eakins, as well as Etruscan and Greek vases, Chinese ceramics and bronzes, early Italian paintings, and a collection of American decorative arts that is considered one of the world's finest. The gallery's landmark main building is also of note: opened in 1953, it was renowned architect Louis I. Kahn's first major commission and the first modernist building on the neo-Gothic Yale campus. ⊠ *1111 Chapel St.* 🕾 *203/432–0600* ⊕ *artgallery.yale.edu* 🎟 *Free* 🕙 *Closed Mon.*

🍴 Restaurants

Atticus Bookstore Café

$ | **CAFÉ** | Come to this independent bookstore, café, and bakery to buy a book, have lunch (or breakfast), or have breakfast (or lunch) *and* buy a book. "Nourishment for mind and body" is the approach here—in the style of a European neighborhood café. **Known for:** sandwiches, salads, soups, and a few "plates & bowls"; delicious homemade breads and pastries; congenial atmosphere all day long. ⑤ *Average main: $10* ⊠ *1082 Chapel St.* 🕾 *203/776–4040* ⊕ *www.atticusbookstorecafe.com.*

Barcelona

$$ | **SPANISH** | There's no need to take a transatlantic flight to Spain when you can feast on authentic Spanish cuisine right here in New Haven. There are entrées and salads on the menu, but the tapas are the best bet—rich, tasty, and full of flavor. **Known for:** more than a dozen tapas on the menu; charcuterie and cheese menu; 2,000-bottle wine cellar. ⑤ *Average main: $22* ⊠ *Omni New Haven Hotel, 155 Temple St.* 🕾 *203/848–3000* ⊕ *www.barcelonawinebar.com* 🕙 *No lunch Mon.–Sat.*

New Haven Pizza 101

New Haven has been on pizza lovers' radars for decades. The "apizza" (pronounced "ah-beetz" by locals) style, defined by its thin, chewy crust, is baked in a coal-fired brick oven, which makes for a unique—and, some would argue, superior—pizza experience. For everything from the original tomato pie to white clam and other specialty pies, check out these three authentic New Haven pizzerias *(see Restaurants for more details).*

Frank Pepe Pizzeria Napoletana— known simply as Pepe's Pizza—is where it all began: in 1925, Frank Pepe opened his eponymous pizzeria and created what would become the iconic New Haven–style pizza. Eager customers line up for hours to get a taste of the famous thin-crust pies, in particular Frank Pepe's pièce de résistance—the white clam pizza. This masterful creation consists of olive oil, garlic, oregano, grated Parmesan cheese, and littleneck clams atop a thin crust.

Just two blocks from Pepe's on Wooster Street (New Haven's Little Italy), **Sally's Apizza** has been a rival of Frank Pepe's since 1938, when Pepe's nephew opened his own place. Now visitors to New Haven must pledge their allegiance to just one of these famed Wooster Street pizzerias, although no one will blame you if you decide to be a double agent.

If you don't want to get involved with that feud, there's always **Modern Apizza**, which differentiates itself by *not* being on Wooster Street. Serving its signature plain pies (with a layer of tomato sauce and a sprinkling of Parmesan cheese) since 1934, you can add mozzarella and other toppings if you want, including clams, bacon, hot cherry peppers, salami, and more.

Claire's Corner Copia
$ | VEGETARIAN | Claire's has been a New Haven institution since 1975, and it remains a popular destination for vegetarians and vegans. The large menu offers quesadillas, burritos, vegan dishes, salads of every sort, and breakfast items served all day. **Known for:** organic, sustainable ingredients; gluten-free and kosher food, too; try the signature Lithuanian coffee cake. $ *Average main: $12* ✉ *1000 Chapel St.* ☎ *203/562–3888* ⊕ *www.clairescornercopia.com.*

★ Frank Pepe's Pizzeria Napoletana
$$ | PIZZA | FAMILY | This place may serve the best pizza in the world, as so many people claim. Try the justifiably famous white-clam pie (especially good topped with bacon), but just thinking about the original tomato pie (with mozzarella), makes your mouth water. **Known for:** long line for a table—often an hour or more; thin-crust pizza baked in a coal-fired brick oven; pies cut in odd-shaped pieces—great for kids. $ *Average main: $24* ✉ *157 Wooster St.* ☎ *203/865–5762* ⊕ *www.pepespizzeria.com* ▭ *No credit cards.*

Heirloom
$$$ | AMERICAN | FAMILY | This isn't your typical hotel restaurant: occupying half of the lobby of the Study at Yale, this contemporary American eatery has a casually refined decor. The chalkboard, seasonal menu emphasizes the freshest locally sourced ingredients, with highlights like baked Connecticut clams with rosemary and pancetta or an elevated version of chicken and dumplings: local ricotta gnocchi with vegetables in a chicken *brodetto*. **Known for:** fresh, bright, and contemporary; innovative farm-to-table cuisine; enjoy a pre- or

postdinner cocktail at the bar. $ *Average main: $25 ⊠ The Study at Yale, 1157 Chapel St. ☎ 203/503–3919 ⊕ www. heirloomnewhaven.com.*

Louis' Lunch

$ | AMERICAN | This all-American luncheonette, opened since 1895 and now on the National Register of Historic Places, is also recognized as the birthplace of the "hamburger sandwich." Its first-rate burgers are cooked in an old-fashioned upright broiler and served with a slice of tomato, onion, and cheese on two pieces of white toast. **Known for:** no ketchup allowed; fourth-generation family-run restaurant; open until 2 am Thursday–Saturday. $ *Average main: $10 ⊠ 261 Crown St. ☎ 203/562–5507 ⊕ www.louislunch. com* ▭ *No credit cards* ☽ *Closed Sun. and Mon. No dinner Tues. and Wed.*

Modern Apizza

$$ | PIZZA | FAMILY | It's not what Modern Apizza has that sets it apart from the rest but what it doesn't have: toppings. The pizzeria's signature "plain" pie is a thin crust with a layer of tomato sauce and just a sprinkling of Parmesan cheese. $ *Average main: $19 ⊠ 874 State St. ☎ 203/776–5306 ⊕ modernapizza.com.*

Sally's Apizza

$$ | PIZZA | FAMILY | This place has been a rival of Frank Pepe's since 1938, when Salvatore Consiglio, Pepe's nephew, decided to break away from his relatives and open his own place. The result of this family feud is two competing pizzerias and a divided city: those who believe Frank Pepe's serves the best pizza and those who are devoted to Sally's. **Known for:** plan to wait—for a table and then for your pizza; hand-tossed pies baked in a coal-fired brick oven; Sal's family sold out in 2017, but new owners vow to continue the tradition. $ *Average main: $18 ⊠ 237 Wooster St. ☎ 203/624–5271 ⊕ www. sallysapizza.com* ☽ *No lunch. Closed Mon. and Tues.*

Sugar Bakery and Sweet Shop

$ | BAKERY | Stop in to try one of 25 different kinds of cupcake rotated daily or one of the 16 special flavors each month—or you may see one of its "cupcake trucks" parked around town. With flavors like cannoli, cookie dough, and the Elvis (banana cupcake with peanut-butter-and-jelly buttercream frosting), you're bound to find one (or more) to fuel your perfect sugar high. **Known for:** past winner of Food Network's Cupcake Wars; full-size cakes, too; plus vegan and gluten-free cupcakes. $ *Average main: $3 ⊠ 424 Main St., East Haven ☎ 203/469–0815 ⊕ www.thesugarbakery.com* ☽ *Closed Sun.*

★ Union League Cafe

$$$$ | FRENCH | In a gorgeous Beaux Arts dining room, this lively brasserie wins high marks for its updated French cuisine. The knowledgeable staff are happy to recommend wine pairings to complement whatever dishes you select—perhaps walnut-crusted Arctic char with lemon and parsley, slow-roasted veal chop with creamy morel sauce, or entrecôte au poivre with cippolini onions. **Known for:** prices are steep but worth the splurge; elegant atmosphere and impeccable service; quite reasonable midafternoon Club Room menu. $ *Average main: $36 ⊠ 1032 Chapel St. ☎ 203/562–4299 ⊕ www.unionleaguecafe.com* ☽ *Closed Sun. No lunch Sat.*

ZINC New Haven

$$$ | MODERN AMERICAN | In a sexy, dimly lighted storefront space looking toward the glorious New Haven green, ZINC turns heads with its artfully prepared and globally inspired farm-to-table cooking. Menu items include typical American standbys (rib-eye steak, duck breast, cod, chicken) modernized by adding an Asian influence (in dishes like curry-scented bamboo rice, spring rolls, and red dal with cardamom). **Known for:** regionally farmed produce, sustainably raised meat, and line-caught fish; outstanding wine list complements the food; happy hour at

Yale's leafy campus is home to many neo-Gothic buildings.

the bar (all night long) Monday–Thursday. **$** *Average main: $29* ✉ *964 Chapel St.* ☎ *203/624–0507* ⊕ *www.zincfood.com* ⊘ *Closed Sun. No lunch Sat.*

Hotels

Omni Hotels & Resorts
$$ | HOTEL | FAMILY | This comfortable hotel is near the heart of New Haven and outfitted with all the modern amenities; some upper-floor guest rooms enjoy the same great views. **Pros:** inviting lobby with complimentary fruit-infused ice water or hot chocolate; nice gym and spa; walking distance from many shops and restaurants. **Cons:** no pool; rooms could use upgrading; views from most rooms is of rooftops. **$** *Rooms from: $235* ✉ *155 Temple St.* ☎ *203/772–6664* ⊕ *www.omnihotels.com/hotels/new-haven-yale* ⥵ *306 rooms* ⦿ *No meals.*

The Study at Yale
$$ | HOTEL | With a pair of spectacles emblazoned on all hotel signature items and overflowing bookshelves in the hotel's lobby, the Study is chic lodging for the scholarly set. **Pros:** valet parking; excellent restaurant; great location in the middle of everything. **Cons:** tiny bathrooms; room refrigerator available only upon request; street noise can be an issue in front-facing rooms. **$** *Rooms from: $253* ✉ *1157 Chapel St.* ☎ *203/503–3900* ⊕ *www.thestudyatyale.com* ⥵ *124 rooms* ⦿ *No meals.*

Nightlife

BARS
★ BAR
BREWPUBS/BEER GARDENS | This spot is a cross between a dance club, a brick-oven pizzeria, and a brewpub. Come for dancing and drinks Thursday–Saturday; pizza, anytime. ✉ *254 Crown St.* ☎ *203/495–8924* ⊕ *www.barnightclub.com.*

Toad's Place of New Haven
MUSIC CLUBS | Alternative and traditional rock bands play at Toad's Place. ✉ *300 York St.* ☎ *203/624–8623* ⊕ *www.toadsplace.com.*

Performing Arts

THEATER

★ Long Wharf Theatre

THEATER | The well-regarded Long Wharf Theatre presents works by contemporary writers and revivals of neglected classics. The season runs October through May. ✉ *222 Sargent Dr.* ☎ *203/787–4282* ⊕ *www.longwharf.org.*

Shubert Theatre

ARTS CENTERS | Broadway musicals, dance performances, comedy, music concerts, and more are on the bill at the Shubert, a 1,600-seat theater that originally opened in 1914. ✉ *247 College St.* ☎ *203/624– 1825* ⊕ *www.shubert.com.*

Woolsey Hall

MUSIC | Built in 1901 to commemorate Yale's bicentennial, Woolsey Hall hosts performances by the New Haven Symphony Orchestra and the Philharmonia Orchestra of Yale, as well as recitals on the Newberry Memorial Organ. ✉ *500 College St., at Grove St.* ⊕ *woolsey.yale.edu.*

Yale Repertory Theatre

THEATER | This theater stages both premieres and fresh interpretations of classics from October through May. ✉ *1120 Chapel St.* ☎ *203/432–1234* ⊕ *www. yalerep.org.*

Yale School of Music

MUSIC | Most of the 200-plus performances in the impressive roster of concerts by the Yale School of Music take place in Sprague Memorial Hall. ✉ *470 College St.* ☎ *203/432–4158* ⊕ *music.yale.edu.*

Madison

21 miles east of New Haven, 65 miles northeast of Greenwich.

Coastal Madison has an understated charm. Ice-cream parlors and dozens of locally owned boutiques prosper along U.S. 1, the town's main street. Stately Colonial homes line the town green, site of summer concerts and a farmers' market, while iconic cedar-shingled beach homes line the waterfront. The Madison shoreline, particularly the long stretch of soft white sand at Hammonasset Beach State Park, draws visitors year-round, although they have to bundle up in the dead of winter.

GETTING HERE AND AROUND

Madison is accessible by car and train. Drive north on Interstate 95 from New Haven or take the Shore Line East train to the Madison stop.

Beaches

★ Hammonasset Beach State Park

PARK—SPORTS-OUTDOORS | FAMILY | The largest of the state's public beach parks, Hammonasset Beach State Park has 2 miles of white-sand beach, a top-notch nature center, excellent birding, and a hugely popular campground with more than 550 open sites. **Amenities:** food and drink; lifeguards; parking (fee); showers; toilets. **Best for:** swimming; walking. ✉ *1288 Boston Post Rd. (Rte. 1), off I–95* ☎ *203/245–2785 for park, 203/245–1817 for campground* ⊕ *www.ct.gov/deep/ hammonasset* 💲 *CT residents free; nonresidents parking fee $22 weekend, $15 weekday.*

Restaurants

Lenny and Joe's Fish Tale

$$ | SEAFOOD | FAMILY | At Lenny and Joe's Fish Tale, kids of all ages love to eat their lobster rolls or fried seafood outdoors by a hand-carved Dentzel carousel with flying horses (and a whale, frog, lion, seal, and more), which the restaurant runs from early May through early October. Most of the menu involves fish of one kind or another, but Lenny and Joe's also serves burgers, franks, and chicken sandwiches or dinners. 💲 *Average main: $19* ✉ *1301 Boston Post Rd. (Rte. 1)* ☎ *203/245–7289* ⊕ *www.ljfishtale.com.*

Hotels

Scranton Seahorse Inn

$ | **B&B/INN** | In the heart of Madison, this historic (1833) inn run by pastry chef Michael Hafford offers a restful retreat within walking distance of the beach and shops. **Pros:** central location; gracious innkeeper; meticulous attention to detail; pets are allowed in some rooms, but you must make advance arrangements. **Cons:** books up quickly; rooms need a little attention; rooms are small, but this is a historic home after all. $ Rooms from: $160 ⊠ 818 Boston Post Rd. ☎ 203/245–0550 ⊕ www.scrantonseahorseinn.com ⤳ 7 rooms ⦿| Free breakfast.

Old Saybrook

19 miles west of New London, 32 miles east of New Haven.

Old Saybrook, at the mouth of the Connecticut River, was one of the three original settlements of the Connecticut Colony (called Saybrook at the time) and an important 17th-century trading port. Today, Old Saybrook is a picturesque small town with more than 100 historic homes, a downtown that's an especially pleasing place for a stroll, and a shoreline that attracts boaters and others lured by the salt air of summer.

GETTING HERE AND AROUND

Drive north on Interstate 95 to Route 154 south to reach Old Saybrook. The town is also served by Amtrak's Northeast Regional line, and the Shore Line East commuter trains between New Haven and New London.

⊙ Sights

Katharine Hepburn Cultural Arts Center

ARTS VENUE | The Kate, as the Center is generally known, is an intimate, 250-seat theater in the historic Old Saybrook Town Hall building. The Center presents a full calendar of concerts, dance, drama, opera, comedy, films (including some classic Hepburn films), and children's theater. In addition to the performances and presentations, a small museum displays memorabilia and reminiscences about Katharine Hepburn's life and career. She was a resident of Old Saybrook from 1912 (age five) until her death in 2003. ⊠ 300 Main St. ☎ 860/510–0453 ⊕ www.katharinehepburntheater.org ⤳ Museum free ⊙ Museum closed Sat.–Mon.

🍴 Restaurants

The Back Porch Restaurant

$$ | **AMERICAN | FAMILY** | If you're going to be on the coast, you'll want to dine in an open-air restaurant on the waterfront—and the Back Porch is just that. Gaze at the river, watch the boats come and go, and dine on New England classics like fried clams, fish-and-chips, crumb-crusted scrod, sandwiches, burgers, salads, and plenty more. **Known for:** indoor and outdoor seating; kids' menu; live entertainment on summer weekends. $ Average main: $24 ⊠ 142 Ferry Rd. ☎ 860/510–0282 ⊕ www.backporcholdsaybrook.com ⊙ Closed Mon. and Tues. Oct.–May.

Café Routier

$$$ | **FRENCH** | Grilled hanger steak with cauliflower gratin and seared scallops with pancetta and butternut squash puree are among the favorites at this bistro, which specializes in regional favorites and seasonal dishes. Check out the Mood Lounge for excellent cocktails and smaller plates meant for sharing. $ Average main: $26 ⊠ 1353 Boston Post Rd., 5 miles west of Old Saybrook, Westbrook ☎ 860/399–8700 ⊕ www.caferoutier.com ⊙ No lunch.

🛏 Hotels

Saybrook Point Inn & Spa

$$$$ | **HOTEL** | Guest rooms at the cushy Saybrook Point Inn are done up in 18th-century style, with reproductions of British furnishings and Impressionist art; many have fireplaces, making them

especially cozy on cool evenings. **Pros:** tasteful decor; great spa; marina provides a picturesque setting. **Cons:** pricey; you'll need a car to get downtown; the water view from "water view" rooms varies considerably. ⑤ *Rooms from: $489* ✉ *2 Bridge St.* ☎ *860/395–2000* ⊕ *www.saybrook.com* ⊃ *82 rooms* ⦿ *No meals.*

Old Lyme

34 miles east of New Haven, 15 miles west of New London.

Old Lyme, on the eastern shore at the mouth of the Connecticut River (opposite Old Saybrook), is renowned among art lovers for its past as the home of the Lyme Art Colony—the most famous gathering of Impressionist painters in the United States. Artists (and others) continue to be attracted to the area for its lovely countryside and shoreline, especially in the summer.

GETTING HERE AND AROUND

Old Lyme is best reached by car. Drive north on Interstate 95 and over the bridge from Old Saybrook.

Sights

★ Florence Griswold Museum

MUSEUM | FAMILY | Central to Old Lyme's artistic reputation is this grand late-Georgian-style mansion, which served as a boardinghouse for members of the Lyme Art Colony in the first decades of the 20th century. When artists such as Willard Metcalf, Clark Voorhees, Childe Hassam, and Henry Ward Ranger flocked to the area to paint its varied landscape, Miss Florence Griswold offered housing as well as artistic encouragement. The house has been restored to its 1910 appearance, when the colony was in full flower (clues to the house's layout and decor were gleaned from members' paintings). The museum's 10,000-square-foot Krieble Gallery, on the riverfront, hosts changing exhibitions of American

art. ✉ *96 Lyme St.* ☎ *860/434–5542* ⊕ *www.florencegriswoldmuseum.org* 🎫 *$10* ⊙ *Closed Mon.*

Hotels

★ Bee and Thistle Inn

$$ | B&B/INN | Behind a weathered stone wall in the historic district sits this three-story 1756 Colonial house with 5½ acres of broad lawns, formal gardens, and herbaceous borders. **Pros:** a short walk from Griswold Museum; lovely old home; the on-site Chestnut Grille exudes romance, with fireplaces and candlelight, and innovative American cuisine. **Cons:** may hear traffic noise from Interstate 95; lacks some modern amenities. ⑤ *Rooms from: $229* ✉ *100 Lyme St.* ☎ *860/434–1667* ⊕ *www.beeandthistleinn.com* ⊃ *11 rooms* ⦿ *Free breakfast.*

New London

46 miles east of New Haven, 52 miles southeast of Hartford.

New London, on the western bank of the Thames River (pronounced *thaymes*, not *tems*), was founded in 1646. In the mid-1800s, it was the second-largest whaling port in the world. Today the U.S. Coast Guard Academy uses its campus on the Thames to educate and train its cadets. The prestigious Connecticut College is across the avenue from the Academy, and Ocean Beach Park, an old-fashioned playland with a broad sandy beach and long wooden boardwalk, is a perfect place for the whole family to spend a hot summer day.

GETTING HERE AND AROUND

New London is accessible by car off Interstate 95 and can also be reached via Amtrak's high-speed Acela and Northeast Regional trains, as well as Shore Line East commuter trains from New Haven and towns in between.

Sights

Lyman Allyn Art Museum

MUSEUM | Housed in a neoclassical granite building that overlooks the U.S. Coast Guard Academy and the Long Island Sound, this museum was founded in 1932 with funds bequeathed by Harriet Upson Allyn in memory of her whaling merchant father, Captain Lyman Allyn (1797–1874). Inside is an impressive collection of more than 15,000 objects covering a span of 5,000 years. Works include contemporary, modern, and Early American fine arts; American Impressionist paintings; Connecticut decorative arts; and European works from the 16th through 19th centuries. ⊠ 625 Williams St. 🕾 860/443–2545 ⊕ www.lymanallyn. org 🕾 $10 ⊙ Closed Mon.

U.S. Coast Guard Academy

COLLEGE | The 100-acre cluster of redbrick buildings you see overlooking the Thames River makes up one of the four U.S. military academies. Visitors are welcome, and security is obviously tight, but being there when the Coast Guard training ship, the barque *Eagle,* is in port is a special treat. A small museum on the property explores the Coast Guard's 200 years of maritime service and includes some 200 ship models, as well as figureheads, paintings, uniforms, life-saving equipment, and cannon. ⊠ 31 Mohegan Ave. 🕾 860/444–8270 for public affairs ⊕ www.uscga.edu 🕾 Free.

 Restaurants

Captain Scott's Lobster Dock

$$ | SEAFOOD | FAMILY | Don't be put off by the long line waiting to order classic fare like lobster rolls (small or large), steamers, fried clams, homemade clam fritters, and "chowda." This outdoor restaurant on Shaw's Cove—where you eat at picnic tables (BYOB) alongside the marina—is a great place to eat and a great place to spend time on a hot summer day. **Known for:** lobster rolls—hot or cold, large or

small; everything made on-site and to order; Ed's hot fudge sundae. 🕏 Average main: $18 ⊠ 80 Hamilton St., off Howard St. 🕾 860/439–1741 ⊙ Closed mid-Oct.–mid-Apr.

 Activities

Fort Trumbull State Park

PARK—SPORTS-OUTDOORS | FAMILY | Here you'll find a 19th-century stonework-and-masonry fort, an extensive visitor center focusing on military history, a top-rate fishing pier, a waterfront boardwalk with fantastic views, and a picnic area when you want to relax. ⊠ 90 Walbach St. 🕾 860/444–7591 ⊕ www.ct.gov/deep/ FortTrumbull 🕾 Grounds and parking free, visitor center $6.

★ Ocean Beach Park

PARK—SPORTS-OUTDOORS | FAMILY | Possibly the state's finest beach, the 50-acre park has a broad white-sand beach, an Olympic-size outdoor pool with a triple waterslide, an 18-hole miniature-golf course, an arcade, a ½-mile-long boardwalk, kiddie rides, food concessions, a nature trail, and a picnic area. **Amenities:** food and drink; lifeguards; parking (fee); showers; toilets. **Best for:** partiers; swimming; walking. ⊠ 98 Neptune Ave., at foot of Ocean Ave. 🕾 860/447–3031 ⊕ www. ocean-beach-park.com 🕾 From $7.

Groton

10 miles south of Ledyard.

Across the river from New London, Groton is the location of Naval Submarine Base New London and of the Electric Boat Division of General Dynamics, designer and manufacturer of nuclear submarines. Often referred to as the "Submarine Capital of the World," Groton is the birthplace of Nautilus, the nation's first nuclear submarine and a National Historic Landmark, which is now permanently berthed at the Submarine Force Museum.

Sights

Fort Griswold Battlefield State Park

MEMORIAL | FAMILY | It was here (legend has it), on the Groton side of the Thames River, that the infamous traitor Benedict Arnold stood watching the important port of New London burn in 1781 during the Revolutionary War. Whether Arnold actually stood there is open to question; but the American defenders of Ft. Griswold were massacred by Arnold's British troops—and New London did burn according to his orders. The 134-foot-high Groton Monument, which you can climb for a sweeping view of the river and New London, is a memorial to the fallen. The adjacent Monument House Museum has historic displays. ⊠ *Park Ave. at Monument St.* ☎ *860/449–6877 seasonal, 860/444–7591 c/o Fort Trumbull State Park* ⊠ *Free.*

★ Submarine Force Museum

MILITARY SITE | FAMILY | The world's first nuclear-powered submarine, USS *Nautilus (SSN-571)*—and the first submarine to complete a submerged transit of the North Pole (in 1958)—was launched and commissioned in Groton in 1954. The *Nautilus* spent 25 active years as a showpiece of U.S. technological know-how and is now permanently docked at the Submarine Force Museum, a couple of miles upriver from where it was built, and visitors are welcome to climb aboard and explore. The museum, just outside the entrance to the U.S. Naval Submarine Base New London, is a repository of artifacts, documents, and photographs detailing the history of the U.S. Submarine Force component of the U.S. Navy, along with educational and interactive exhibits. ⊠ *1 Crystal Lake Rd.* ☎ *860/694–3174* ⊕ *www.ussnautilus.org* ⊠ *Free* ⊗ *Closed Tues.*

Norwich

15 miles north of New London, 40 miles southeast of Hartford.

Handsome restored Georgian and Victorian houses surround the historic Norwich town green in the city of Norwich, and more can be found downtown by the Thames River. The former mill town is hard at work on restoration and rehabilitation efforts. So eye-catching are these brightly colored homes that the Paint Quality Institute named two of them among 27 winners of its initial "Prettiest Painted Places in America" contest back in the 1990s.

GETTING HERE AND AROUND

To reach Norwich from the coast by car, take Interstate 95 to Interstate 395 north to Route 82 east.

Sights

Leffingwell House Museum

HISTORIC SITE | What began as a two-room home around 1675 evolved into a pre-Revolutionary War tavern, and, by 1776, was the elegant home of a local patriot that has since been lovingly restored by the Society of the Founders of Norwich. The house is furnished with Early American artifacts, and interpreters explain the architecture of the house and the lifestyle of those who lived or frequented the home so many centuries ago. ⊠ *348 Washington St.* ☎ *860/889–9440* ⊕ *www.leffingwellhousemuseum.org* ⊠ *$5* ⊗ *Closed Sun.–Fri. and Nov.–Mar.*

Slater Memorial Museum & Converse Art Gallery

MUSEUM | On the Norwich Free Academy campus, this museum's permanent collection features 150 plaster casts of some of the world's greatest Egyptian, Greek, Roman, and Italian Renaissance sculptures, including Winged Victory (the Nike of Samothrace), Venus de Milo (Aphrodite of Milos), and Michelangelo's *Pietà*. The Converse Art Gallery, adjacent to the museum, hosts six to eight shows a year, many of which showcase Connecticut artists and craftsmen, as well as student work. ✉ *108 Crescent St.* ☎ *860/887–2506* ⊕ *www.slatermuseum.org* 🎟 *$3* 🕑 *Closed Mon.*

The Spa at Norwich Inn

$$$$ | **HOTEL** | On 42 rolling acres right by the Thames River and a stone's throw from Mohegan Sun, this Georgian-style inn is best known for its spa, which offers the full range of skin-care regimens, body treatments, and fitness classes. **Pros:** excellent spa treatments; expansive grounds; Kensington's serves tasty, Connecticut-sourced, health-conscious fare (it has a chocolate truffle menu, too). **Cons:** focused mainly on spa guests (who are often wandering around in their robes); tired room decor in need of an upgrade; small pool. $ *Rooms from: $450* ✉ *607 W. Thames St. (Rte. 32)* ☎ *860/425–3500, 800/275–4772* ⊕ *www.thespaatnorwichinn.com* 🛏 *90 rooms* 🍽 *No meals.*

Ledyard

10 miles south of Norwich, 37 miles southeast of Hartford.

In the woods of southeastern Connecticut between Norwich and the coastline, Ledyard is known first and foremost for the vast Mashantucket Pequot Tribal Nation's Foxwoods Resort Casino. With the opening of the excellent Mashantucket Pequot Museum & Research Center, however, the tribe has moved beyond gaming to educating the public about its history, as well as that of other Northeast Woodland tribes.

15 minutes west of Foxwoods, in Unacasville is Connecticut's other major casino, Mohegan Sun.

GETTING HERE AND AROUND

Driving is probably the best way to get to Ledyard: take Interstate 95 to Route 2 west. If you are only planning to visit Foxwoods, many bus companies run charter trips directly there.

Sights

Foxwoods Resort Casino

CASINO—SIGHT | Owned and operated by the Mashantucket Pequot Tribal Nation on reservation lands near Ledyard, Foxwoods is the second-largest resort casino in North America. The enormous compound, which opened in 1992, draws 40,000-plus visitors daily to its seven casinos with more than 4,800 slot machines, 250 gaming tables, and a 3,600-seat bingo parlor. This 9-million-square-foot complex includes four luxury hotels, a 5,500-square-foot pool "sanctuary," two full-service spas, a retail concourse, numerous dining options, several theaters and other venues that attract national performers, a video arcade, extreme sports facilities, a bowling alley, an 18-hole championship golf course, and—as counterpoint to all that action—marked trails through the surrounding woods. ✉ *350 Trolley Line Blvd., Mashantucket* ☎ *800/369–9663* ⊕ *www.foxwoods.com.*

★ Mashantucket Pequot Museum & Research Center

MUSEUM | **FAMILY** | Housed in a large complex 1 mile from Foxwoods, this museum brings to life the history and culture of the Northeastern Woodland tribes in general and the Mashantucket Pequots in particular with exquisite detail. Highlights include views of an 18,000-year-old glacial crevasse, a caribou hunt from 11,000 years ago, and a 17th-century fort. Perhaps most remarkable is a sprawling "immersion environment": a 16th-century village with more than 50 life-size figures and real smells and sounds. Audio devices provide detailed information about the sights. A full-service restaurant offers both Native and traditional American cuisine. ✉ *110 Pequot Tr., Mashantucket* ☎ *800/411–9671* ⊕ *www.pequotmuseum.org* 🎟 *$20* 🕑 *Closed Jan.–Mar. and Mon. and Tues. Apr.–Dec.*

Mohegan Sun

CASINO—SIGHT | The Mohegan Tribe, known as the Wolf People, operate this casino west of Ledyard and just south of Norwich, which has more than 300,000 square feet of gaming space, including 6,000 slot machines and more than 250 gaming tables. Also part of the complex: the Kids Quest family-entertainment center, a 130,000-square-foot shopping mall, more than 40 restaurants and food-and-beverage suppliers, and a 34-story, 1,200-room luxury hotel with a full-service spa. A 10,000-seat arena, home to the WNBA's Connecticut Sun, draws major national acts, while a swanky 300-seat cabaret hosts intimate shows and comedy acts. There are numerous bars and nightclubs as well. ⊠ *1 Mohegan Sun Blvd., off I-395, Uncasville* ☎ *888/226-7711* ⊕ *www.mohegansun.com.*

Hotels

Mohegan Sun

$$ | HOTEL | Two luxury high-rise hotels—the huge, 34-story Sky Tower and the newer, more contemporary 13-story Earth Tower—are Mohegan Sun's on-site lodging choices. **Pros:** numerous restaurants just steps from the lobby; beautiful views from upper floors; excellent spas. **Cons:** casinos are the primary focus; kids are welcome but it is a casino environment; 4 pm check-in (5 pm on Sunday). $ *Rooms from: $299* ⊠ *1 Mohegan Sun Blvd., off I-395, Uncasville* ☎ *888/777-7922* ⊕ *mohegansun.com* ⤣ *1563 rooms* ⦿ *No meals.*

Mystic

10 miles east of New London, 8 miles south of Ledyard.

Mystic, a village that lies half in the town of Groton and half in the town of Stonington, has devoted itself to recapturing the seafaring spirit of the 18th and 19th centuries. Some of the nation's fastest clipper ships were built here in the mid-19th century; today, the 37-acre Mystic Seaport is the state's most popular attraction. Downtown Mystic has an interesting collection of boutiques and galleries.

GETTING HERE AND AROUND
By car, take Interstate 95 to Route 27 south to reach Mystic. Amtrak's Northeast Regional train service also stops here.

ESSENTIALS
VISITOR INFORMATION Eastern Regional Tourism District/Mystic Country ☎ *860/536-8822* ⊕ *www.ctvisit.com/mystic.*

Sights

★ Mystic Aquarium

ZOO | FAMILY | The famous Arctic Coast exhibit—which holds 750,000 gallons of water, measures 165 feet at its longest point by 85 feet at its widest point, and ranges from just inches to 16½ feet deep—is just a small part of this revered establishment and home to several graceful beluga whales and a pair of rescued harbor seals. You can also see African penguins, fascinating sea horses, Pacific octopuses, and sand tiger sharks. Don't miss feeding time at the Ray Touch Pool, where rays suction sand eels right out of your hand. The animals here go through 1,000 pounds of herring, capelin, and squid each day—Juno, a male beluga whale, is responsible for consuming 85 pounds of that himself. ■**TIP→ For an up-close-and-personal experience with a beluga whale, take part in the Trainer for a Day ($389) or Beluga Encounter ($179) program. Both allow you to touch and interact with these magnificent animals.** ⊠ *55 Coogan Blvd.* ☎ *860/572-5955* ⊕ *www.mysticaquarium.org* ⤣ *$35.*

★ Mystic Seaport Museum

MUSEUM VILLAGE | FAMILY | The nation's leading maritime museum, Mystic Seaport encompasses 19 acres stretched along the Mystic River. The indoor and outdoor exhibits include a re-created

Mystic Seaport exhibits a number of vessels that you can board and tour, including the *Charles W. Morgan*.

New England coastal village, a working shipyard, and formal museum buildings with more than 1 million artifacts including figureheads, paintings, models, tools, ship plans, scrimshaw, paintings, photos, and recordings. Along the narrow village streets and in some of the historic buildings, craftspeople demonstrate skills such as open-hearth cooking and weaving, interpreters bring the past to life, musicians sing sea chanteys, and special squads with maritime skills show how to properly set sails on a square-rigged ship. The museum's more than 500 vessels include the *Charles W. Morgan*, the last remaining wooden whaling ship afloat, and the 1882 training ship *Joseph Conrad*; you can climb aboard both for a look around, or for sail-setting demonstrations and reenactments of whale hunts. ■TIP→ **Children under three are admitted free.** ⊠ *75 Greenmanville Ave. (Rte. 27)* ✚ *1 mile south of I–95* ☎ *860/572–0711* ⊕ *www.mysticseaport.org* 🎫 *$25.*

🍴 Restaurants

★ Abbott's Lobster in the Rough

$$ | **SEAFOOD** | **FAMILY** | If you want some of the freshest lobsters, mussels, crabs, or clams on the half shell (there are non-seafood options), head down to this unassuming seaside lobster shack in sleepy Noank, a few miles southwest of Mystic. Most seating is outdoors or on the dock, where the views of Noank Harbor are magnificent. **Known for:** fresh seafood by the seaside in the fresh air; lobster dinner, lobster roll, lobster bisque—all delish; perfect coastal atmosphere. $ *Average main: $22* ⊠ *117 Pearl St., Noank* ☎ *860/536–7719* ⊕ *abbottslobster.com* ⊗ *Closed Columbus Day–Apr. and Mon.–Thurs. early May and Sept.*

Oyster Club

$$$ | **MODERN AMERICAN** | In the Oyster Club's rustic, barnlike dining room, start your meal with a selection of oysters and clams from the raw bar or a cup of the raved-about quahog clam chowder—New England (creamy) or Rhode Island (clear) style—before moving along to either fresh-from-the-sea surf or prime turf for your entrée. In summer, the open-air Treehouse offers another lively spot to enjoy a casual meal or a drink—weather permitting. **Known for:** menu changes daily; ingredients sourced from local farms and waters; happy hour at the Treehouse every summer afternoon. ⑤ *Average main: $35* ⊠ *13 Water St.* ☎ *860/415–9266* ⊕ *www.oysterclubct. com* ☉ *No lunch weekdays.*

Hotels

Mystic Marriott Hotel and Spa
$$ | HOTEL | This six-story, Georgian-style hotel has modern rooms accented with old-world touches, such as rich fabrics, gleaming wood furnishings, and elegant detailing. **Pros:** convenient to Mystic attractions; Starbucks coffee bar in the lobby; swim winter or summer in the indoor pool. **Cons:** on a busy road; often busy with conference or wedding guests; you might prefer an outdoor pool. ⑤ *Rooms from: $269* ⊠ *625 North Rd. (Rte. 117), Groton* ☎ *860/446–2600, 860/446–2600* ⊕ *www.marriott.com* ⤵ *285 rooms* ❖❖ *No meals.*

Old Mystic Inn
$ | B&B/INN | This 1784 inn was once a well-regarded bookstore, so it's no surprise that all of the guest rooms in the cozy main house and carriage house are named for New England authors. **Pros:** beautifully kept historic house; delicious breakfasts; friendly host. **Cons:** you'll need a car to get to town or local attractions; busy road out front; might be too quiet for some. ⑤ *Rooms from: $185* ⊠ *52 Main St.* ☎ *860/572–9422* ⊕ *www.oldmysticinn.com* ⤵ *8 rooms* ❖❖ *Free breakfast.*

The Whaler's Inn
$$ | HOTEL | A perfect compromise between a chain motel and a country inn, this five-building complex with public rooms furnished with lovely antiques is one block from the Mystic River and downtown area. **Pros:** within walking distance of downtown shopping; on-site restaurant, Bravo Bravo, serves well-executed Italian dishes; lots of amenities. **Cons:** rooms in some buildings have less character; on the busy main street; pleasant enough hotel but not luxurious. ⑤ *Rooms from: $200* ⊠ *20 E. Main St.* ☎ *860/536–1506* ⊕ *www.whalersinnmystic.com* ⤵ *49 rooms* ❖❖ *Free breakfast.*

Setting Sail at Mystic Seaport

Kids can learn the ropes—literally—of what it takes to be a sailor during one of Mystic Seaport's many sailing classes and camps. Younger children and those who wish to stay ashore can sign up for courses on building boats (from construction to varnish), blacksmithing, wood carving, and open-hearth cooking. The Seaport's planetarium also offers instruction on navigating a ship by the stars. Prices for classes vary. Call Mystic Seaport (☎ *860/572–5322*) or visit its website (⊕ *www.mysticseaport.org*) for details.

Stonington

7 miles southeast of Mystic, 57 miles east of New Haven.

Pretty Stonington Borough, the seaside "downtown" of the town of Stonington, pokes into Fishers Island Sound. A quiet fishing community clustered around white-spired churches, "the Borough," as it's called, is far less commercial than downtown Mystic. In the 19th century, though, it was a busy whaling, sealing, and transportation center. Historic buildings line the town green and border both sides of Water Street up to the imposing Old Lighthouse Museum.

GETTING HERE AND AROUND

From Mystic by car, take Route 1 north (you'll actually be heading due east, but don't be concerned) to Route 1A.

 Sights

Old Lighthouse Museum

HISTORIC SITE | FAMILY | This museum occupies a stone citadel with an attached lighthouse tower originally built in 1823 and moved to higher ground 17 years later. Climb to the top of the tower for a spectacular view of Long Island Sound and three states. Six rooms of exhibits depict the varied history of the small coastal town. ⊠ *7 Water St.* ☎ *860/535–1440* ⊕ *www.stonington-history.org* ⊠ *$9* ⊗ *Closed Wed. and Nov.–Mar.*

Stonington Vineyards

WINERY/DISTILLERY | At this small coastal winery, you can browse the works of local artists in the gallery or enjoy a picnic lunch on the grounds. Whichever you choose, the vineyard's Seaport White, a Vidal-Chardonnay blend, is a nice accompaniment. ⊠ *523 Taugwonk Rd.* ☎ *860/535–1222* ⊕ *www.stoningtonvineyards.com* ⊠ *Tasting $12, tour free.*

 Hotels

★ The Inn at Stonington

$$ | B&B/INN | The views of Stonington Harbor and Fishers Island Sound are spectacular from this waterfront inn in the heart of Stonington Village. **Pros:** smartly furnished rooms; walking distance from village shops and dining; intimate adult (and kids 14-plus) atmosphere. **Cons:** no on-site restaurant (but several nearby); minimum stay on summer weekend and holidays; strict seven-day notice for cancellations, no exceptions. ⑤ *Rooms from: $270* ⊠ *60 Water St.* ☎ *860/535–2000* ⊕ *www.innatstonington.com* ⇌ *18 rooms* ⑩⊙ *Free breakfast.*

Putnam

50 miles east of Hartford, 34 miles north of Norwich.

Ambitious antiques dealers have reinvented Putnam, a mill town 30 miles west of Providence, Rhode Island, that was neglected after the Depression. Putnam's downtown Antiques Marketplace, a four-level emporium with space for 350 antiques and collectibles dealers, is the heart of the Quiet Corner's antiques trade.

GETTING HERE AND AROUND

By car from Hartford, take Interstate 384 and U.S. 44 east; from Norwich, follow Interstate 395 north to Route 12 north.

 Restaurants

85 Main

$$$ | MODERN AMERICAN | FAMILY | This stylish bistro is *the* place to go for a break from antiquing. Typical lunchtime offerings include roasted corn and clam chowder, pesto chicken salad, and burgers with fries; dinner could be maple-glazed sea scallops or veal Bolognese. **Known for:** seafood and steaks worthy of a big city; raw bar and full sushi menu; outdoor patio for warm-weather dining. ⑤ *Average main: $27* ⊠ *85 Main St.* ☎ *860/928–1660* ⊕ *www.85main.com.*

⬤ Shopping

Antiques Marketplace

ANTIQUES/COLLECTIBLES | This four-level emporium features more than 350 dealers selling everything from fine furniture to tchotchkes. ⊠ *109 Main St.* ☎ *860/928–0442* ⊕ *antiquesmarketplace.tumblr.com.*

Woodstock

40 miles north of Norwich, 46 miles northeast of Hartford.

The landscape of this enchanting town that cozies up to the Massachusetts border is splendid in every season: the rolling hills seem to stretch for miles. Scenic roads lead past antiques shops, a country inn in the grand tradition, orchards, livestock grazing in grassy fields, and the fairgrounds of one of the state's oldest agricultural fairs, held each Labor Day weekend.

GETTING HERE AND AROUND

By car from Hartford, follow Interstate 384 east to U.S. 44 east and Route 169 north; from Norwich, follow Interstate 395 north to U.S. 44 west and Route 169 north.

Sights

Roseland Cottage

HOUSE | This pink board-and-batten Gothic Revival-style house was built in 1846 as a summer home for New York silk merchant, publisher, and abolitionist Henry C. Bowen. The house and outbuildings (including a carriage house with private bowling alley) hold a prominent place in history, having hosted four U.S. presidents: Ulysses S. Grant, Rutherford B. Hayes, William Henry Harrison, and William McKinley. The parterre garden features 21 flower beds surrounded by 600 yards of boxwood hedge. ⊠ *556 Rte. 169* ☎ *860/928–4074* ⊕ *www.historicnewengland.org/historic-properties/homes/roseland-cottage* ✉ *$10* ⊙ *Closed Mon. and Tues. and Oct.–May.*

Hotels

The Inn at Woodstock Hill

$$ | B&B/INN | Filled with antiques, this massive inn overlooking the countryside has guest rooms with four-poster beds, handsome fireplaces, pitched ceilings, and timber beams. **Pros:** beautiful grounds and gardens; pretty rooms; several pleasant sitting areas for afternoon tea. **Cons:** old-fashioned decor; quite a hike up to third-floor rooms; expensive restaurant. ⑤ *Rooms from: $200* ⊠ *94 Plaine Hill Rd.* ☎ *860/928–0528* ⊕ *www.woodstockhill.com* ⤴ *21 rooms* �◎ *Free breakfast.*

Storrs

25 miles southwest of Woodstock.

Storrs, an otherwise rural village in the town of Mansfield, is primarily occupied by the 4,100 acres (and some 19,000 students) of the main campus of the University of Connecticut. Many cultural programs, sporting events, and other happenings take place here.

Sights

Mansfield Drive-In

FILM | FAMILY | Spring through fall, one of the state's few remaining drive-in theaters shows films on its three big screens, and there's a huge flea market held on the grounds each Sunday. ⊠ *228 Stafford Rd., Mansfield* ☎ *860/423–4441* ⊕ *mansfielddrivein. com* ✉ *$11.*

UConn Dairy Bar

COLLEGE | FAMILY | Stop by the UConn Dairy Bar in the UConn Department of Animal Science Creamery for the most delicious ice cream you've ever tasted. Students produce the 24 regular, two seasonal, and occasional limited-edition flavors. To see the ice-cream-making process from start to finish, begin at the barn at the Kellogg Dairy Center on Horsebarn Hill: mingle with the cows and watch them being milked (12:30–3 pm), then walk to the manufacturing plant where more than 50,000 gallons of ice cream are produced each year. You don't have to start at the barn, though; there's an observation window in the Dairy Bar where you can see the delicious treat being made. ⊠ *George White Bldg., 3636 Horsebarn Hill Rd. Ext.* ☎ *860/486–1021* ⊕ *dining.uconn. edu/uconn-dairy-bar.*

University of Connecticut

COLLEGE | FAMILY | UConn's large, sprawling main campus offers lots for visitors to see and do. The William Benton Museum of Art's permanent collection includes centuries-old European and American paintings, drawings, prints, photographs, and sculptures, and the Jorgensen Center for the Performing Arts presents a series of 25–30 music, dance, and theater programs during the academic year. The Ballard Institute & Puppetry Museum has more than 2,500 puppets on display (UConn is one of two colleges in the country that offers a puppetry degree) and, depending on the season, you might catch a Connecticut Huskies football game or watch the amazing women's basketball team play at home. ⊠ *99 Rte. 430, Mansfield* ☎ *860/486–2000* ⊕ *uconn.edu.*

Chapter 8

RHODE ISLAND

Updated by
Jane E. Zarem

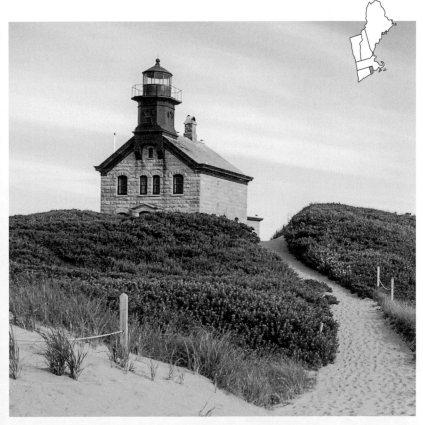

⊙ Sights   🍴 Restaurants   🛏 Hotels   🛍 Shopping   🍸 Nightlife
★★★★★   ★★★★★   ★★★☆☆   ★★★★☆   ★★☆☆☆

WELCOME TO RHODE ISLAND

TOP REASONS TO GO

★ **Mansions:** See how the social elite lived during Newport's Gilded Age on a tour of The Breakers, Cornelius Vanderbilt's opulent, 70-room "summer cottage."

★ **Historic Street:** For a mile-long walk through history, follow Benefit Street on Providence's East Side and see ornate homes built by leading Colonial merchants.

★ **Nature:** Block Island is one of the most serene spots on the Eastern Seaboard—especially at Rodman's Hollow, where winding paths lead to the sea.

★ **Sand:** Take your pick of South County's numerous white-sand beaches—perhaps East Matunuck State Beach in South Kingstown.

★ **Food Enclave:** From food trucks to upscale dining, Providence has an exciting culinary scene fueled in large part by young chefs trained at Johnson & Wales University.

1 Providence. The capital of Rhode Island is also a vibrant college town with great food and a thriving arts community.

2 Pawtucket. This former mill town has found new life as a hub for arts and culture.

3 Woonsocket. South of Providence, this tiny mill town is home to the fabulous Museum of Work and Culture.

4 Westerly. Galleries, shops, restaurants, and more than 55 buildings on the National Historic Register provide this seaside town with tons of charm.

5 Watch Hill. With 2 miles of perfect beaches, this seaside village is the ideal spot for a low-key vacation.

6 Misquamicut. This family-friendly destination has several amusement parks, movies on the beach, and evening concerts.

7 Charlestown. A sheltered coastline makes it a great spot for swimming, sailing, bird-watching, and beachcombing.

8 South Kingstown. Home to the 1,200 acre main campus of the University of Rhode Island.

9 Narragansett. Beautiful beaches and the Point Judith Lighthouse are highlights of this quiet beach town.

10 Jamestown. Also known as Conanicut Island, Jamestown has beautiful parks and a quaint downtown.

11 Newport. One of the world's great sailing cities also hosts world-class music festivals, Gilded Age mansions, and the International Tennis Hall of Fame.

12 Portsmouth. Part of Aquidneck Island, the community has polo matches and the Greenvale Vineyards.

13 Bristol. Once a center for boatbuilding, Bristol is now known for its long running July 4 celebration.

14 Tiverton and Little Compton. South of Bristol, this bucolic corner of the state is home to artists and farmers.

15 Block Island. This laid-back island community is about an hour's ferry ride from Newport.

Consider the Ocean State's small size its biggest asset. You can drive across it in less than an hour—but take your time: Rhode Island has nearly 400 miles of shoreline to explore, more than 100 beaches, acres of open space with hiking and biking paths, and dozens of historic landmarks.

Rhode Island and Providence Plantations, the state's official name, has a long history of forward thinking and a spirit of determination and innovation embodied in the bronze, 11-foot-tall Independent Man atop the marble-domed State House. The first of the 13 colonies to declare independence from Britain can also claim the first successful textile mill (Slater Mill in Pawtucket), America's oldest synagogue (Touro in Newport), and the first lunch wagon (by Walter Scott in Providence). A state founded on the principle of religious liberty drew Baptists, Jews, Quakers, and others throughout the 17th and 18th centuries, then flourished in the 19th and 20th centuries with the factories, silver foundries, and jewelry companies that brought workers from French Canada, Italy, Ireland, England, Portugal, and Eastern Europe.

Rhode Island remains an attractive, spirited place to live or visit. A public works project in the mid-1980s opened up the rivers in Downtown Providence; infrastructural improvements at Ft. Adams State Park in Newport allow it to host the famed music festivals; extended commuter rail service makes it easy to travel between Providence and T.F. Green Airport; and bike-path expansions allow cyclists to traverse South County, East

Bay, and Blackstone Valley. Rhode Island's 39 cities and towns—none more than 50 miles apart—offer natural beauty, inspired culinary artistry, and many opportunities to relax and enjoy its scenic vistas.

MAJOR REGIONS

Visit **Providence** on an empty stomach, so you can fully enjoy its exciting culinary scene. Prestigious colleges and universities give Providence intellectual and cultural vitality, while restored Colonial houses on the East Side preserve its history.

The Blackstone Valley powered the factories that led America's Industrial Revolution in the 19th century. Both **Pawtucket** and **Woonsocket** have fascinating museums that honor the laborers and labor movement. There's also nearly 16 miles of paved bike path follow the river's edge.

Officially called Washington County, **South County** is home to beautiful beaches and charming towns like **Westerly, Watch Hill, Misquamicut, Charlestown, Narragansett, Wickford,** and **South Kingstown.**

Newport County, a longtime yachting enclave, consists of **Newport, Jamestown, Portsmouth,** and **Tiverton and Little Compton.** Between Newport and Providence, **East**

Bay's Bristol host's one of the country's oldest July 4 festivals.

Block Island has 17 miles of beaches—including Crescent Beach, one of New England's best—offering a classic seaside escape in summer, even when the population swells from the regular 950 to nearly 15,000. Relax at one of the Victorian inns or bed-and-breakfasts, peruse the galleries and shops, and have a comfort-food lunch or haute-cuisine dinner.

Planning

WHEN TO GO

With its arts and music festivals and gorgeous beach days, summer is high season in Rhode Island and a great time to visit, but there are fun and exciting things to do here year-round. Newport's Jazz and Folk festivals heat up the town in late July and early August, just after the Newport Music Festival for classical music fans in July. This is also the time to take the ferry to low-key, beach-ringed Block Island for a day trip or overnight stay.

The shoulder seasons (April and May and September and October) bring pleasant weather and more affordable accommodations. In early fall, the return of student life to Providence colleges and universities gives the capital city energy and a youthful vibe. October is a good time to catch fall foliage in the Blackstone Valley, around the University of Rhode Island in Kingston, or in picturesque Tiverton and Little Compton.

Late fall, winter, and early spring each have their own charms—such as restaurant week in Providence, Newport, and Narragansett, when eateries join together to promote special three-course prix-fixe menus.

PLANNING YOUR TIME

By car, it's an hour or less from any one place in Rhode Island to another. Although distances are short, Rhode Island is the second-most-densely populated state (after New Jersey), so allow extra time for traffic congestion in and around Providence.

Most sights in Providence can be seen in a day or two. The Blackstone Valley and Tiverton/Little Compton make good half-day side trips from Providence. Newport, though not even 12 square miles, offers enough to fill two days—and the same can be said for South County, with its superb beaches. If you have a full week, you can visit all four regions of the state, as well as Block Island.

GETTING HERE AND AROUND
AIR TRAVEL

Rhode Island's main airport is T.F. Green International Airport (PVD) in Warwick, just south of Providence, and served by most domestic air carriers. Smaller commercial airports, with limited carriers, are in Westerly and on Block Island, and Newport has a general aviation airport. Boston's Logan Airport is an hour's drive from Providence.

AIR CONTACT T. F. Green Airport ✉ *2000 Post Rd., off I–95, Warwick* ☎ *401/691–2471* ⊕ *www.pvdairport.com.*

BUS TRAVEL

Rhode Island Public Transit (RIPTA) offers low-cost bus service throughout the entire state—just $2 per ride or $6 per day within the city, to another town, or to the beach.

BUS CONTACT Rhode Island Public Transit Authority (RIPTA) ✉ *Kennedy Plaza Passenger Terminal, 1 Kennedy Plaza, Providence* ☎ *401/781–9400* ⊕ *www.ripta.com.*

CAR TRAVEL

New England's main highway, Interstate 95, cuts diagonally through Rhode Island, spanning 43 miles from Connecticut to Massachusetts.

Interstate 195 southeast from Providence leads to New Bedford, Massachusetts, and Cape Cod. Route 146 northwest from Providence passes through the Blackstone Valley en route to Worcester,

Massachusetts, and Interstate 90 (Massachusetts Turnpike). U.S. 1 follows much of the Rhode Island coast heading east from Connecticut before turning north to Providence. Route 138 heads east from Interstate 95 or U.S. 1 to Jamestown, Newport, and Portsmouth in easternmost Rhode Island. Route 114 leads south from East Providence down through the East Bay community of Bristol and then to Newport.

Once you're here, a car is your best way to get around the state. Parking is easy to find outside cities, though challenging and sometimes expensive in Downtown Providence and Newport. Parts of Providence and Newport are easily walkable.

RESTAURANTS

The creative passion of award-winning chefs, many in their twenties and early thirties, fuels Rhode Island's vibrant restaurant scene. Abundant fresh seafood makes for outstanding variations on New England staples like fish 'n' chips, clam chowder, and stuffed quahogs (hard clams)—all best savored at a beachside clam shack. Fresh-caught Block Island swordfish can't be beat. Then there's uniquely Rhode Island fare, such as the johnnycake (a thin corn pancake cooked on a griddle), coffee milk, Del's frozen lemonade, and Gray's Ice Cream. Authentic Italian-American restaurants can be found in Providence's Federal Hill neighborhood.

HOTELS

Major chain hotels are certainly represented in Rhode Island, but boutique hotels, small bed-and-breakfasts, and historic inns provide a more intimate experience. Rates vary seasonally. In Newport, for example, a winter stay often costs half the summer price. Many inns in coastal towns are closed in winter. *Reviews have been shortened. For full information, visit Fodors.com.*

What It Costs

	$	$$	$$$	$$$$
RESTAURANTS				
	under $18	$18–$24	$25–$35	over $35
HOTELS				
	under $200	$200–$299	$300–$399	over $399

OUTDOOR SPORTS

Department of Environmental Management's Division of Licensing

Contact the department for boating and fishing information, regulations, and licenses. A three-day nonresident freshwater fishing license costs $16; a nonresident saltwater fishing license costs $10 and is good for a year. Licenses may be purchased online. ⊠ *235 Promenade St., Providence* ☎ *401/222–6647 boating, 401/222–3576 licenses* ⊕ *www.dem. ri.gov/programs/managementservices/ licenses.*

HIKING

Audubon Society of Rhode Island

The society manages nearly 9,500 acres in more than a dozen wildlife refuges across the state. Most are open to the public, and visitors are welcome to use the hiking trails from sunrise to sunset (unless posted otherwise). ⊠ *12 Sanderson Rd., Smithfield* ☎ *401/949–5454* ⊕ *www.asri.org.*

TOURS

Blackstone Valley Explorer

TOUR—SIGHT | FAMILY | Narrated 50-minute Blackstone River tours aboard the 40-passenger riverboat *Blackstone Valley Explorer* take place on Sunday afternoon and depart from different locations as the warm weather progresses: Central Falls, East Providence, Pawtucket, and Woonsocket. Topics covered on this pretty ride include area ecology and industrial history. ⊠ *Blackstone Valley Visitor Center, 175 Main St., Pawtucket* ☎ *401/724–2200* ⊕ *www.rivertourblackstone.com* ✉ *$12* ⊙ *Closed late Oct.–late May.*

VISITOR INFORMATION
CONTACTS Blackstone Valley Visitor Center ☎ *401/724–2200* ⊕ *www.tourblackstone.com* **South County Tourism Council** ☎ *401/789–4422, 800/548–4662* ⊕ *www.southcountyri.com* **Visit Rhode Island** ☎ *800/556–2484* ⊕ *www.visitrhodeisland.com.*

Providence

Big-city sophistication with small-city charm: Providence has the best of both worlds. A thriving arts community, prestigious Brown University and Rhode Island School of Design (RISD), an impressive restaurant scene bolstered by local Johnson & Wales University, countless festivals and events, a revitalized Downtown, and countless festivals and events all help the city live up to its nickname: the Creative Capital. Providence is a worthy stop on any New England tour.

The Moshassuck and Woonasquatucket rivers merge just southeast of the Rhode Island State House to form the Providence River. Scenic Waterplace Park hosts WaterFire, a series of crowd-pleasing summer-evening bonfires on the Woonasquatucket just west of the confluence. This relatively recent tradition beloved by locals and visitors alike began in the 1990s, but Providence gives equal weight to its long history, celebrating everything from its wealth of Colonial architecture to its literary tradition. After all, H.P. Lovecraft, author of fantasy and horror fiction, was a son of Providence; and Edgar Allan Poe courted poet Sarah Helen Whitman here.

GETTING ORIENTED

The narrow Providence River acts as a natural boundary between two major neighborhoods in the heart of the city. Downtown, the business district, lies west of the river; the East Side, on the opposite shore, is where the city's history began, (Don't confuse Providence's East Side with East Providence,

a separate city.) Federal Hill, historically an Italian neighborhood, pushes west of Downtown along Atwells Avenue, Broadway, and Westminster Street. The white-marble dome of the Rhode Island State House is visible just north of Downtown. On the East Side, South Main and Benefit Streets run parallel to the Providence River. The Brown University campus is in the East Side neighborhood called College Hill, at the top of which Thayer Street runs north–south. Farther north and east are mainly residential neighborhoods.

GETTING HERE AND AROUND
AIR TRAVEL
T. F. Green International Airport, 10 miles south of Providence in Warwick, is served by Air Canada, Allegiant, American, Azores, Delta, Frontier, JetBlue, Norwegian, Southwest, and United. By taxi, the ride between the airport and Downtown hotels takes about 20 minutes and costs around $40. An Uber ride will cost $20–$25, depending on your destination. The Massachusetts Bay Transportation Authority (MBTA) commuter rail service connects the airport and Downtown on weekdays for $3.25.

BUS TRAVEL
At Kennedy Plaza, Downtown, you can board the local Rhode Island Public Transit Authority (RIPTA) buses. The Route 92 bus links Federal Hill to the East Side, and the Route 6 bus links Downtown to the Roger Williams Park and Zoo. RIPTA fares are $2 per ride; an all-day pass is $6. Exact change is needed when boarding buses, or you'll get your change back in the form of a fare card. RIPTA buses also service T.F. Green International Airport from Providence via Routes 14 and 20.

CAR TRAVEL
Overnight parking is not generally allowed on Providence streets. During the day it can be difficult to find curbside parking, especially Downtown and on Federal Hill and College Hill. There is a large parking garage at Providence Place mall.

TAXI TRAVEL

The basic taxi rate in Providence is $3 for the first mile, and $3.50 for each succeeding mile.

TRAIN TRAVEL

Amtrak trains between New York and Boston stop at Westerly, Kingston, and Providence. From Boston, you can also take an MBTA commuter train to Providence.

NIGHTLIFE

For events listings, consult the daily *Providence Journal* or the website ⊕ *www. golocalprov.com*. The weekly *Motif* or *Providence Monthly* are both available (free) in restaurants and shops.

RESTAURANTS

The hard part about dining in Providence is choosing among its many superb restaurants. If you're in the mood for Italian, take a stroll along Atwells Avenue in Federal Hill; Downtown is home to excellent fine-dining establishments; and the East Side has great neighborhood and upscale-casual restaurants, as well as an assortment of spots with a hip ambience and an international menu.

SHOPPING

Providence has a handful of small but engaging shopping areas. In Fox Point, Wickenden Street has many antiques stores and several art galleries. Near Brown University, Thayer Street has a number of boutiques, though there has been an influx of chain stores. With its eclectic collection of specialty stores, Hope Street has branded itself as the East Side's "Main Street." Downtown's Westminster Street has morphed into a strip of independently owned fashion boutiques, galleries, and design stores.

TOURS

Providence Preservation Society

SELF-GUIDED | The society publishes booklets with self-guided walking tours of the city's Benefit Street and Elmwood neighborhoods. The booklets are available at the Society's headquarters or at the John Brown House Museum (52 Power Street). ⊠ *24 Meeting St., at Benefit St.* ☎ *401/831–7440* ⊕ *www.ppsri.org/ resources* 💲 *$3*.

Rhode Island Red Food Tours

SPECIAL-INTEREST | This Newport-based tour company offers food journeys (3–3½ hours) through Providence's Downtown Arts District, tasting and sipping your way into and through at least six eateries—from casual comfort food to fine-dining restaurants. Along the way you'll learn about the district's architecture and history. The tours are offered on Friday and Saturday, April through November, starting at noon. It's a walking tour, so wear comfortable shoes. ⊠ *270 Bellevue Ave., Newport* ☎ *866/736–6343* ⊕ *www.rhodeisland- redfoodtours.com* 💲 *From $69*.

ESSENTIALS

TRANSPORTATION CONTACTS Amtrak

☎ *800/872–7245* ⊕ *www.amtrak.com*. **Massachusetts Bay Transportation Authority** (*MBTA*) ☎ *617/222–3200, 800/392–6100* ⊕ *www.mbta.com*. **Rhode Island Public Transit Authority** (*RIPTA*) ⊠ *Kennedy Plaza Passenger Terminal, 1 Kennedy Plaza, Downtown* ☎ *401/781–9400* ⊕ *www. ripta.com*.

VISITOR INFORMATION

Providence Warwick Convention & Visitors Bureau ☎ *401/456–0200* ⊕ *www.goprovi- dence.com*.

Downtown

Providence has 25 official neighborhoods and a handful of unofficial ones, each with its own identity. The Downtown neighborhood, sometimes referred to as Downcity, is the city's thriving artistic, financial, mercantile, transportation, and political core. Downtown comprises a very walkable area (it's flat!) roughly bordered by the Providence River on the east, Interstate 95 on the west, the Rhode Island State House to the north, and the Point St. Bridge in the south. You'll find theaters, hotels, shops, restaurants, and college buildings on Downtown's maze of streets, as well as the often-bustling Waterplace Park—a perfect place to watch the summer WaterFire displays.

Sights

★ Alex and Ani City Center

LOCAL INTEREST | **FAMILY** | The 14,000-square-foot outdoor ice rink, right in the heart of downtown Providence, is twice the size of the one at New York City's Rockefeller Plaza. The facility is open for skating daily, late November–mid-March, and skate and helmet rentals are available. In summer, kids love driving the bumper cars, playing foot darts (kicking Velcro soccer balls onto a target), and human bowling (rolling along a course inside a bubble ball). The center also hosts summer concerts, festivals, and other events. ⊠ *2 Kennedy Plaza, Downtown* ☎ *401/331–5544* ⊕ *www. theprovidencerink.com* ⊠ *From $7.*

Market House

BUILDING | Built in 1775 and designed by Joseph Brown, this Georgian-style brick building on South Main Street originally had a vendor arcade on the ground floor and government offices on the upper floor. A third-floor Masonic Hall was added later. The building now belongs to the Rhode Island School of Design and is not open to the public, but it's beautiful to look at and historically significant. Tea was burned here in March 1775, and the upper floors were used as barracks for French soldiers during the Revolutionary War; from 1832 to 1878, Market House served as the seat of city government. A plaque shows the height reached by raging floodwaters during the Great Hurricane of 1938; because the water was able to flow through the arcade windows on the ground floor, the building itself was saved from destruction. ⊠ *8 N. Main St., Downtown.*

★ Providence Children's Museum

MUSEUM | **FAMILY** | The vibrant, interactive, hands-on learning environments here are geared to children ages 1 to 11 and their families. Favorite exhibits and activities include Water Ways, ThinkSpace, Discovery Studio, Iway bridge-building, puppetry, and an engaging playground full of pumps, mazes, dams, and fountains. Littlewoods, for toddlers, has a tree house, bear cave, and a slide. Kids can also explore an outdoor climbing structure. ⊠ *100 South St., Downtown* ☎ *401/273–5437* ⊕ *www.childrenmuseum.org* ⊠ *$12.*

Rhode Island State House

GOVERNMENT BUILDING | **FAMILY** | Designed by the noted architecture firm McKim, Mead & White and opened in 1904, Rhode Island's beautiful capitol building boasts the world's fourth-largest self-supporting marble dome. The gilded Independent Man statue that tops the dome was struck by lightning 27 times before lightning rods were installed in 1975. The State Library, on the north side of the second floor, contains the military accoutrements of Nathanael Greene, a Quaker who served as George Washington's second-in-command during the Revolutionary War, as well as the state flag carried on board Apollo 11's first lunar landing mission in 1969. In the State Room is a full-length portrait of Washington by Rhode Islander Gilbert Stuart, who also painted the portrait of Washington that appears on the $1 bill. The museum's centerpiece is Rhode Island's original 1663 Colonial Charter granted by King Charles II—the first charter signed by a monarch that guaranteed religious liberty. Look for the brooding, dark portrait of former governor Lincoln Chafee, who also served as U.S. senator. Guided tours lasting 50 minutes are offered on weekdays. You can also follow a self-guided tour. ⊠ *82 Smith St., Downtown* ☎ *401/222–3983* ⊕ *sos.ri.gov/ divisions/Civics-And-Education/State-House-Tour* ⊠ *Free* ⊙ *Closed weekends.*

Providence

KEY

- **1** Sights
- **1** Restaurants
- **1** Hotels

★ Roger Williams Park Zoo & Carousel Village

NATIONAL/STATE PARK | FAMILY | Plan a full day to take in this regal 435-acre Victorian park where you can picnic, feed ducks in the lakes, rent a swan-shape paddleboat, and ride a Victorian-style carousel. The 40-acre zoo—one of the nation's oldest—has African elephants, Masai giraffes, zebras, red pandas, snow leopards, moon bears, gibbons, giraffes, and river otters in natural settings. Howler monkeys, Chilean flamingos, giant river otters, a giant anteater, toucans, and more inhabit the Rainforest exhibit, opened in summer 2018. In October, more than 5,000 carved pumpkins line the ¾-mile Wetlands Trail for the well-attended Jack-O-Lantern Spectacular. In Carousel Village, a short walk from the zoo, kids love to ride the classic horses and other creatures on the carousel ($2), jump in the bounce house ($3), ride a pony ($5), and take a train ride ($3). ⊠ *1000 Elmwood Ave., Elmwood* ☎ *401/785–9450 for museum, 401/785–3510 for zoo* ⊕ *www.rwpzoo. org* 🖵 *Zoo $18.*

Roger Williams National Memorial

MEMORIAL | FAMILY | This 4½-acre park dedicated to Rhode Island's founder has a symbolic well to mark the site of the spring around which Roger Williams built Providence's original settlement in 1636. A visitor center has a five-minute film about the park's namesake. A demonstration garden shows how Native Americans cultivated corn, beans, and squash, and how English colonists grew herbs. The park has several picnic tables and 20 free parking spaces (a two-hour parking limit is strictly enforced). ⊠ *282 N. Main St., Downtown* ☎ *401/521–7266* ⊕ *www. nps.gov/rowi* 🖵 *Free.*

Waterplace Park

ARTS VENUE | FAMILY | Venetian-style footbridges, cobblestone walkways, and an amphitheater encircling a tidal basin set the tone at this 4-acre tract along the Woonasquatucket River near where it joins the Moshassuck to form the Providence River. In summer, the park is a gathering place for free concerts. It's also the site of **WaterFire,** a multimedia installation featuring music and nearly 100 wood-fired braziers permanently placed in the middle of the river and set afire between dusk and midnight on some nights spring–fall. WaterFire attracts nearly 1 million visitors annually. ⊠ *1 Finance Way, overlooking Woonasquatucket River, Downtown* ☎ *401/273–1155 for WaterFire information.*

Restaurants

Birch

$$$$ | AMERICAN | Benjamin Sukle, a nominee for the James Beard Foundation's best chef of the Northeast, serves creative, modern, four-course prix-fixe meals at his 18-seat restaurant. Seating in the minimalist, exposed-redbrick space is around a U-shape bar. **Known for:** beverage pairing for an additional $40; unusual and beautifully composed food combinations; courses are small but rich and delicious. ⑤ *Average main: $60* ⊠ *200 Washington St., Downtown* ☎ *401/272–3105* ⊕ *www.birchrestaurant. com* ⊗ *Closed Tues. and Wed. No lunch* ▤ *No credit cards.*

CAV

$$$ | ECLECTIC | Chandeliers hang from the ceiling, and African and Asian artwork adorns the walls (everything is for sale) at this restaurant-antiques store. The menu is extensive, the food is rich in flavor, and the ambience is full of personality. **Known for:** imaginative presentation of menu favorites; bistro menu Monday–Wednesday; sit at a table or the 18th-century bar. ⑤ *Average main: $27* ⊠ *14 Imperial Pl., Downtown* ☎ *401/751–9164* ⊕ *www. cavrestaurant.com.*

The Dorrance Kitchen & Cocktails

$$$ | MODERN AMERICAN | The opulent first floor of the former Union Trust Building is home to one of Providence's best known purveyors of farm-to-table food. Siena marble, ornate plaster detailing, and

Providence's annual Waterfire festival has more than eighty bonfires set upon the river.

stained-glass windows lend the place a Newport-mansion vibe. **Known for:** creative cocktails at the long and luxurious bar; contemporary New England cuisine in a spectacular dining room; "Rhody Style" (coffee milk sorbet) baked Alaska dessert. $ *Average main: $28* ⊠ *60 Dorrance St., Downtown* ☎ *401/521–6000* ⊕ *www.thedorrance.com* ⊗ *Closed Sun. and Mon. No lunch.*

★ Gracie's

$$$ | **MODERN AMERICAN** | The city's best spot for a romantic meal is Table 21 in a private alcove at Gracie's, across the street from the Trinity Rep theater. Owner Ellen Slattery mixes sophistication with whimsy in the main dining room, and executive chef Matthew Varga harvests many of his ingredients from the restaurant's rooftop garden. **Known for:** seasonally inspired menu; three-course prix-fixe and five-, seven-, or nine-course chef's tasting menus; personalized service. $ *Average main: $28* ⊠ *194 Washington St., Downtown* ☎ *401/272–7811* ⊕ *www.graciesprov.com* ⊗ *Closed Sun. and Mon. No lunch.*

North

$$$ | **FUSION** | This nontraditional restaurant adjacent to the Dean Hotel serves a creative menu of small plates and larger dishes to share. Most menu items have an Asian flare—or try grilled bluefish, whole fried flounder, or almost boneless brick chicken. **Known for:** tiny country ham biscuits with mustard appetizer; lively, noisy, and delicious; no phone, no reservations. $ *Average main: $30* ⊠ *Dean Hotel, 122 Fountain St., Downtown* ⊕ *www.foodbynorth.com* ⊗ *No lunch* ⊟ *No credit cards.*

Red Fin Crudo + Kitchen

$$$ | **TAPAS** | Television celebrity chefs Julio Lazzarini and Jenny Behm-Lazzarini—he's been on *Chopped,* and she's been on *Cutthroat Kitchen*—serve up the tastes of New England, northern Spain, the Mediterranean, and the Caribbean at their amazing tapas and cocktails restaurant. **Known for:** if you like ceviche, you'll love theirs; eat at the bar or at a cozy table; menu combines locally sourced ingredients and imported specialty items. $ *Average main: $25* ⊠ *71 Washington*

St., Downtown ☎ 401/454–1335 ⊕ www. redfincrudo.com ⊗ Closed Sun. and Mon. No lunch Tues.–Fri. ⊟ No credit cards.

★ Rosalina

$$$ | ITALIAN | You'll find some of the best southern Italian food you've ever tasted at this cozy, family-run Italian restaurant, although the chef also serves up delicious grilled swordfish, whole grilled branzino, NY strip steak, and more. Be sure to have the antipasto, fried dough with pomodoro sauce, or eggplant parm appetizers—all great for sharing. **Known for:** focus on locally sourced foods; imported olive oil from family-owned groves in Kalamata, Greece; portions are generous so prepare to share. **$** Average main: $21 ✉ 50 Aborn St., Downtown ☎ 401/270–7330 ⊕ www.rosalina-ri.com ⊗ No lunch.

 ## Hotels

Christopher Dodge House

$ | B&B/INN | Rooms on the east side of this three-story 1858 Italianate brick town house have direct views of the State House, though Interstate 95 lies between. **Pros:** huge windows in most rooms; free passes to a nearby health club and free parking; 24-hour honor system for drinks and snacks. **Cons:** I–95 may be too close for light sleepers; steep stairs to third-floor rooms; 30-minute walk to Federal Hill restaurants. **$** Rooms from: $149 ✉ 11 W. Park St., Downtown ☎ 401/351–6111 ⊕ www.providence-hotel.com ⊃ 14 rooms ⦿ Free breakfast.

Courtyard by Marriott Providence Downtown

$ | HOTEL | FAMILY | Located across from Rhode Island Convention Center and Providence Place Mall and near Water-Place Park and the State House, this is one of New England's larger links in the Courtyard by Marriott chain. **Pros:** central location; reasonable price; microwaves in some rooms. **Cons:** limited baggage service; self-parking only; limited dining in The Bistro. **$** Rooms from: $169 ✉ 32

Exchange Terr., at Memorial Blvd., Downtown ☎ 401/272–1191, 888/887–7955 ⊕ www.marriott.com/hotels/hotel-rooms/pvddt-courtyard-providence-downtown/ ⊃ 219 rooms ⦿ No meals.

The Dean

$ | HOTEL | A building that once housed a strip club is now a trendy boutique hotel with a minimalist, masculine vibe and a sexy cocktail den. **Pros:** central location; setting looks adult, but the property welcomes guests with children and pets; coffee shop, trendy restaurant, and karaoke bar on-site. **Cons:** central location can be noisy; masculine vibe may not appeal to everyone; European-size (smallish) rooms. **$** Rooms from: $99 ✉ 122 Fountain St., Downtown ☎ 401/455–3326 ⊕ www.thedeanhotel.com ⊃ 52 rooms ⦿ No meals.

Hotel Providence

$ | HOTEL | In the heart of the city's Arts and Entertainment District, this intimate boutique hotel sets the standard for elegant decor and attentive service. **Pros:** convenient location; handicapped accessible rooms available; pet-friendly; restaurant, Backstage Kitchen + Bar, serves creative, well-prepared small plates, light meals, and full entrées. **Cons:** late risers may not appreciate the 8 am pealing of Grace Church's 16 bells; street noise also an issue; could benefit from more staff. **$** Rooms from: $189 ✉ 139 Mathewson St., Downtown ☎ 401/861–8000, 800/861–8990 ⊕ www.hotelprovidence.com ⊃ 80 rooms ⦿ No meals.

★ Omni Providence

$ | HOTEL | FAMILY | Towering over Downtown, the huge, modern Omni is steps from restaurants, the Rhode Island Convention Center, the Dunkin Donuts Center, and Waterplace Park, home of the WaterFire event. **Pros:** indoor pool; beautiful views of the city from upper floors; child and pet friendly. **Cons:** rooms are rather ordinary; Wi-Fi costs extra; breakfast is pricey. **$** Rooms from: $169 ✉ 1 W. Exchange St., Downtown

The Independent Man sculpture atop the State House symbolizes Rhode Island's free-thinking spirit.

☎ 401/598–8000, 888/444–6664 ⊕ www.omnihotels.com/hotels/providence ⇨ 564 rooms ⧉ No meals.

Providence Biltmore

$ | HOTEL | FAMILY | The city's beloved landmark since 1922, the hotel revels in nostalgia for its flapper heyday, but it remains a draw for tourists because of its attention to service and detail. **Pros:** spacious, traditionally decorated suites; great Downtown location; attention to service and detail; McCormick & Schmick's Seafood Restaurant, a Starbucks, and a spa are off the lobby. **Cons:** some bathrooms are cramped; street noise, especially in lower-floor rooms; somewhat tired "grand old lady". ⑤ Rooms from: $160 ⊠ 11 Dorrance St., Downtown ☎ 401/421–0700 ⊕ www.providencebiltmore.com ⇨ 294 rooms ⧉ No meals.

Renaissance Providence Downtown Hotel

$$ | HOTEL | This luxury hotel occupies one of Providence's most mysterious addresses, a stately nine-story Neoclassical Revival building constructed as a Masonic temple between 1926 and 1928 but unoccupied for an inconceivable 75 years. **Pros:** convenient location next to Providence Place Mall; supercomfortable linens and bedding; beautiful views of the Capitol. **Cons:** some rooms have small windows or no view; rooms on I–95 side can be noisy; service needs a boost. ⑤ Rooms from: $239 ⊠ 5 Ave. of the Arts, Downtown ☎ 401/919–5000, 800/468–3571 ⇨ 272 rooms ⧉ No meals.

Nightlife

BARS

Eddy

BARS/PUBS | Eddy specializes in classic cocktails like a manhattan, gin and tonic, or Americano; creative concoctions like the bourbon-based "down and derby" or rum-based "orange julius caesar"; draft and bottled beers; and a few interesting wines. Add charcuterie, cheese, seafood, good bread—topped off with sorbet or gelato—and you have a great night out. ⊠ 95 Eddy St., Downtown ☎ 401/831–3339 ⊕ eddybar.com.

★ The Magdalenae Room

BARS/PUBS | Dimly lit and oozing sex appeal, this intimate speakeasy has first-rate bartenders who can make all the classics or craft a trendy cocktail, whatever your whim. ⊠ *The Dean, 122 Fountain St., Downtown* ☎ *401/861–0040* ⊕ *www.thedeanhotel.com/eat-and-drink.*

Rooftop at the Providence G

BARS/PUBS | On the rooftop of the Providence G hotel, the lively bar is open evenings year-round (it has a retractable glass rooftop and fire pits) for drinks, snacks, dinner, music, and general conviviality. Valet parking is complimentary. ⊠ *Providence G Hotel, 100 Dorrance St., Downtown* ☎ *401/632–4904* ⊕ *www. rooftopattheg.com.*

MUSIC CLUBS
The Boombox Karaoke

MUSIC CLUBS | At the city's first and only karaoke lounge, have a drink, belt out a tune from its library of more than 30,000 songs (updated each month), or book a private room for yourself and your friends. ⊠ *The Dean, 122 Fountain St., Downtown* ☎ *401/861–0040* ⊕ *sing-boombox.com.*

Point Street Dueling Pianos

PIANO BARS/LOUNGES | Two pianists play whatever the audience wants to hear— from "Happy Birthday" to "Piano Man" to an assortment of rock 'n' roll, heavy metal, and pop. If you're in the mood to sing, you may find yourself invited on stage. Reservations are taken for groups of three or more (four on Saturday). ⊠ *3 Davol Sq., Downtown* ☎ *401/270–7828* ⊕ *www.pointstreetpianos.com* ⌨ *$10 Fri. and Sat.*

The Strand Ballroom & Theatre

MUSIC CLUBS | This 100-year-old, five-story theater (operated as Lupo's Heartbreak Hotel until the venue resumed its original name in late 2017), hosts nationally known musical acts: rock, blues, hip-hop, Americana, country, Latin, metal, funk—plus live comedy. ⊠ *79 Washington St., Downtown* ☎ *401/331–5876* ⊕ *thestrandri.com.*

Performing Arts

GALLERY TOURS
Gallery Night Providence

ART GALLERIES—ARTS | During Gallery Night, held on the third Thursday of the month March–November, many galleries and museums hold open houses and mount special exhibitions. Two-hour Art Bus Tours visit four or five galleries; buses depart every 20 minutes, 5:30 pm–7 pm, from 1 Regency Plaza. ⊠ *Information Center, 1 Regency Plaza, Downtown* ☎ *401/400–3397* ⊕ *www.gallerynight.org.*

THEATERS
Providence Performing Arts Center

ARTS CENTERS | The 3,100-seat center, which opened in 1928 as a Loew's Movie Palace, hosts concerts, national tours of hit Broadway shows, and other large-scale performances and events. Major renovations to this building, which is listed on the National Register of Historic Places, restored the stage, lobby, and arcade to their original splendor. The Mighty Wurlitzer organ is a particular source of pride. ⊠ *220 Weybosset St., Downtown* ☎ *401/421–2787* ⊕ *www. ppacri.org.*

Trinity Repertory Company

THEATER | A past Tony Award winner for best regional theater, this troupe presents classic plays, intimate musicals, and new works by young playwrights, as well as an annual version of *A Christmas Carol*—all in a renovated former vaudeville house. ⊠ *201 Washington St., Downtown* ☎ *401/351–4242* ⊕ *www. trinityrep.com.*

The Vets

CONCERTS | This 1,900-seat auditorium has a proscenium stage and an exquisite interior; it hosts concerts, operas, and spoken word and dance performances. From September to May, the Vets is the home of the Rhode Island Philharmonic Orchestra. ⊠ *1 Ave. of the Arts, Downtown* ☎ *401/421–2787* ⊕ *www. vmari.com.*

Roger Williams

It was an unthinkable idea: total separation of church and state. Break the tie between them, and where would the government get its authority? The answer threatened the Puritan way of life. And that's why in the winter of 1636 the Massachusetts Bay Colony banished a certain preacher with radical opinions named Roger Williams. He fled south into the wilderness, with the goal of establishing a new colony founded on religious tolerance and fair dealings with native tribes, and arranged to buy land from the Narragansett sachems Canonicus and Miantonomoh at the confluence of the Woonasquatucket and Moshassuck rivers. Word spread that this new settlement, which Williams named Providence, was a place where civil power rested in the hands of the people. Those persecuted for their beliefs flocked there, and it thereafter grew into a prosperous Colonial shipping port. What started out as a radical experiment became the basis of American democracy.

🛍 Shopping

ANTIQUES AND HOME FURNISHINGS
Craftland
CRAFTS | Etsy fans will be delighted by the arts and crafts at this colorful shop and gallery: jewelry, notecards, prints, silk-screened T-shirts, fashion accessories, bags, and other sparkly handmade objects by local artists are all for sale. ⊠ *212 Westminster St., Downtown* ☎ *401/272–4285* ⊕ *www.craftlandshop. com* ☞ *Validated parking in Grant's Block Lot.*

HomeStyle
ANTIQUES/COLLECTIBLES | Drop by HomeStyle along increasingly gentrified Westminster Street for eye-catching objets d'art, stylish housewares, and other innovative, extraordinary, or whimsical decorative items. ⊠ *229 Westminster St., Downtown* ☎ *401/277–1159* ⊕ *www. homestyleri.com* ☞ *Validated parking at InTown Parking Lot on Weybosset St.*

FOOD
★ **Yoleni's**
FOOD/CANDY | There's a deli to the left and café seating to the right, but straight back in this bright corner shop you'll find all kinds of amazing Greek specialty products all packaged up and ready to go: olives, olive oil, honey, nuts, sauces, spreads and dips, pastas, legumes, herbs and spices, cookies and candy. Buy some for yourself, pick out a ready-made gift basket, or both. ⊠ *292 Westminster St., Downtown* ☎ *401/500–1127* ⊕ *www.yolenis.com.*

JEWELRY
Copacetic Rudely Elegant Jewelry
SPECIALTY STORES | Expect the unusual at this 30-year-old shop, which sells handmade jewelry, gadgets, and clocks created by more than 100 artists. ⊠ *17 Peck St., Downtown* ☎ *401/273–0470* ⊕ *www.copaceticjewelry.com.*

MALLS
The Arcade Providence
SHOPPING CENTERS/MALLS | Built in 1828, the Arcade has shops and restaurants on its first floor, including **Camen & Ginger** for vintage and antique items and the **Lovecraft Arts & Sciences Council** for books on the supernatural by H.P. Lovecraft and other authors. The Greek Revival building has entrances on both Westminster and Weybosset Streets. ⊠ *65 Weybosset St., Downtown* ☎ *401/454–4568* ⊕ *www. arcadeprovidence.com.*

Providence Place

SHOPPING CENTERS/MALLS | Nordstrom, Macy's, and an Apple Store are among the anchor tenants at this large mall whose restaurants include the Cheesecake Factory and P. F. Chang's. Also here are Dave & Buster's, and a 16-screen cinema and IMAX theater. Parking in the garage is free for the first two hours. ⊠ *1 Providence Pl., at Francis and Hayes Sts., Downtown* ☎ *401/270–1000* ⊕ *www. providenceplace.com.*

East Side

Home to Brown University and the Rhode Island School of Design (RISD), the East Side is Providence's intellectual center and a beautiful residential neighborhood. The East Side neighborhood highlights include Benefit Street, dubbed the "mile of history" for its high concentration of Colonial architecture; RISD's top-quality art museum; and Thayer Street, a gentrified mix of shops, restaurants, and an art-house cinema.

Sights

★ Benefit Street

HISTORIC SITE | **FAMILY** | The city's wealthiest families lived along this Colonial thoroughfare, dubbed "the mile of history," during the 18th and early 19th centuries—and most of the original wood-frame structures have been beautifully restored as homes for today's families. Benefit Street passes through the campuses of Brown University and the Rhode Island School of Design. From mid-June through October, the Rhode Island Historical Society conducts 90-minute street tours ($15) that depart from the John Brown House Museum (92 Power St.) daily (except Wednesday and Sunday) at 10 am. ⊠ *Benefit St., Downtown* ☎ *401/273–7507 for tour information* ⊕ *www.rihs.org.*

Brown University

COLLEGE | Founded in 1764, this Ivy League institution is the nation's seventh-oldest college and offers degrees in 81 undergraduate concentrations, 32 master's programs, and 51 doctoral programs. On a stroll through the College Hill campus, you'll encounter Gothic and Beaux Arts structures, as well as the imposing Van Wickle Gate, which opens twice a year—in fall to welcome the students and spring to bid them farewell. On the ground floor of Manning Hall, the Haffenreffer Museum of Anthropology exhibits artifacts from around the world. The David Winton Bell Gallery in the List Art Building hosts several major art exhibitions a year. The Humanity-Centered Robotics Initiative's Robot Block Party, held in April, celebrates robots and how they are being used to solve the world's problems. ⊠ *Stephen Robert '62 Campus Center, 75 Waterman St., East Side* ☎ *401/863–2378* ⊕ *www.brown.edu.*

First Baptist Church in America

HISTORIC SITE | This historic house of worship was built in 1775 for a congregation originally established in 1638 by Roger Williams and his fellow Puritan dissenters. The writer H.P. Lovecraft attended Sunday school here briefly as a child, and the church now hosts the kickoff of NecronomiCon Providence, an international festival celebrating Lovecraft and other creators of "weird fiction, art, and academia." Architecture and design buffs will appreciate the 185-foot, glistening white steeple, erected in just 3½ days, as well as the auditorium's large crystal chandelier from Ireland, installed in 1792. Guided tours of the Meeting House are available weekdays from Memorial Day through Columbus Day. Self-guided tours are available during the rest of the year, and booklets are available in multiple languages. ⊠ *75 N. Main St., East Side* ☎ *401/454–3418* ⊕ *www.fbcia.org* 🎫 *Guided tour $2, self-guided tour free.*

John Brown House Museum

HISTORIC SITE | Rhode Island's most famous 18th-century home was the stately residence of John Brown, a wealthy businessman, slave trader, politician, and China trade merchant. John Quincy Adams called the home, designed in late-Georgian, early-Federal style and the first mansion built in Providence, "the most magnificent and elegant private mansion that I have ever seen on this continent." An ardent patriot, Brown was a noteworthy participant in the defiant burning of the British customs ship *Gaspee* in 1772—which, Rhode Islanders will remind you, took place 18 months before the Boston Tea Party. A variety of musical concerts are held on the lawn in summer. ⊠ *52 Power St., East Side* ☎ *401/273–7507* ⊕ *www. rihs.org/museums/john-brown-house* ⌨ *$10* ⊙ *Closed Sun. and Mon.; also closed Tues.–Fri. Dec.–Mar.*

John Hay Library

LIBRARY | Built in 1910 and named for Abraham Lincoln's secretary, "the Hay" houses Brown University Library's collections of rare books and manuscripts. World-class collections of Lincoln-related items, H. P. Lovecraft letters, Napoléon's death mask, Walt Whitman's personal copy of *Leaves of Grass,* and 6,000 toy soldiers are of particular interest. The library is open to the public, but you need a photo ID to enter. ⊠ *20 Prospect St., East Side* ☎ *401/863– 2146* ⊕ *library.brown.edu/hay* ⌨ *Free* ⊙ *Closed weekends.*

★ Museum of Art, Rhode Island School of Design

MUSEUM | This museum houses about 100,000 objects ranging from ancient art to work by contemporary artists and designers from around the world. Highlights include Impressionist paintings, costumes, textiles, decorative arts, Gorham silver, Newport furniture, an ancient Egyptian mummy, and a 12th-century Buddha—the largest historic Japanese wooden sculpture in the United States.

Artists represented include major figures in the history of visual art and culture, including Cézanne, Chanel, Copley, Degas, Hirst, Homer, LeWitt, Matisse, Manet, Picasso, Rothko, Sargent, Turner, Twombly, van Gogh, and Warhol—to name a few. Particularly significant are the displays of current and past RISD faculty and students. Stop by the museum's Café Pearl for a bite to eat. ⊠ *20 N. Main St., East Side* ⊹ *Additional entrance at 224 Benefit St.* ☎ *401/454–6500* ⊕ *www.risdmuseum. org* ⌨ *$15, free Sun.*

Prospect Terrace

NEIGHBORHOOD | **FAMILY** | This pocket park in College Hill offers one of the most scenic views of Downtown, particularly in the fall when the surrounding foliage plays spectacularly off the urban backdrop. Prospect Terrace's centerpiece is a statue of Roger Williams, Rhode Island's forward-thinking founder—who here seems to be groovin' to the 1980s song "Walk Like an Egyptian." ⊠ *Between Congdon and Pratt Sts., at Cushing St., East Side.*

Providence Athenaeum

LIBRARY | Philadelphia architect William Strickland designed this 1838 Greek Revival library building in which Edgar Allan Poe courted the poet (and avid reader) Sarah Helen Whitman; the collection here includes a Poe-signed periodical containing "Ulalume," a poem he published anonymously. An 1870s Manet print that illustrated Poe's "The Raven" hangs in the rare book room, which also contains two medieval illuminated manuscripts. Raven signs are posted at eight points of interest on a self-guided library tour. Among them is a special cabinet modeled after an Egyptian temple, which houses the library's multivolume imperial edition of *Description de l'Egypte* (1809–22), commissioned by Napoléon. ⊠ *251 Benefit St., East Side* ☎ *401/421–6970* ⊕ *www. providenceathenaeum.org* ⌨ *Free.*

Thayer Street

NEIGHBORHOOD | Bustling Thayer Street bears a proud old New England name and is very much a part of campus life at Brown, RISD, and other local colleges. Gentrification has resulted in an influx of chain stores. In the blocks between Waterman and Bowen Streets, though you'll still find fashion boutiques, shops selling funky gifts, the Art Deco-style Avon Cinema, and restaurants serving every kind of cuisine from Greek to Korean. ⊠ *Thayer St., between Waterman and Bowen Sts., East Side* ⊕ *www. thayerstreetdistrict.com.*

Wickenden Street

NEIGHBORHOOD | Named for a Baptist minister who was one of Providence's first settlers, this main artery in the Fox Point district is home to antiques stores, art galleries, a farmers' market, and trendy cafés. It also hosts the Coffee Exchange, one of the area's most popular gathering spots. Sidewalk sales are held in the spring and fall. Once home to mainly working-class Portuguese-Americans, the Wickenden Street area has seen waves of gentrification over the years; Our Lady of the Rosary Church on adjacent Traverse Street still conducts weekend Masses in Portuguese. ⊠ *Wickenden St., East Side.*

🍴 Restaurants

★ Al Forno

$$$ | **ITALIAN** | When it opened in 1980, Al Forno put Providence on the national dining map. Still consistently good, the restaurant retains a loyal following for its thin-crust pizzas, handmade pasta, and wood-grilled or roasted entrées. **Known for:** short rib ravioli; fabulous desserts; upstairs tables, where the city's movers and shakers congregate. ⑤ *Average main: $28* ⊠ *577 S. Water St., East Side* ☎ *401/273–9760* ⊕ *www.alforno.com* ⊘ *Closed Sun. and Mon. No lunch.*

Bácaro

$$$ | **ITALIAN** | The informal first floor of this two-level Italian restaurant has a deli case stocked with cured meats, cheeses, olives, and traditional Italian-style small plates; upstairs is a more traditional dining room with impressive views of the Providence River. Every table receives a separate checklist of the cured meats and other items the deli sells, and selections come on a beautifully arranged board. **Known for:** seasonal menu with farm-to-table focus; garden patio for alfresco dining; homemade ice cream. ⑤ *Average main: $35* ⊠ *262 S. Water St., East Side* ☎ *401/751–3700* ⊕ *www.bacarorestaurant. net* ⊘ *Closed Sun. and Mon. No lunch.*

Chez Pascal

$$$ | **FRENCH** | You can tell that this French bistro will be welcoming and unpretentious from its logo: a trio of pigs in striped shirts and berets. In a quiet residential neighborhood, Chez Pascal's menu follows the French tradition but also includes homemade sausages and "pork of the day." **Known for:** house-butchered pork; escargot a la bourguignonne, of course; homemade sausages in the Wurst Kitchen (in the main dining room) or takeout. ⑤ *Average main: $28* ⊠ *960 Hope St., East Side* ☎ *401/421–4422* ⊕ *chez-pascal.com* ⊘ *Closed Sun. No lunch Mon.*

★ The Duck & Bunny

$ | **CAFÉ** | This creperie and café is a cool spot for brunch, afternoon tea and sandwiches, dessert, or a late-night snack. At brunch, light-as-air crepes filled with all manner of deliciousness and the "crèpioli" and "crèpizza" (the restaurant's variation of those Italian favorites) are popular, but the dessert crepes and cupcakes are standouts at any time of day or night. **Known for:** long list of coffees and teas plus cider, wine, beer, and cocktails; cakes, cupcakes, and pies to go; gluten-free and vegan treats, too. ⑤ *Average main: $10* ⊠ *312 Wickenden St., Fox Point* ☎ *401/270–3300* ⊕ *www. theduckandbunny.com* ⊘ *Closed Mon.* ⊟ *No credit cards.*

Hemenway's Seafood Grill & Oyster Bar

$$$ | SEAFOOD | In a city where culinary newcomers tend to garner all the attention, Hemenway's continues to be one of the best seafood restaurants. The high-ceiling dining room's huge windows look out on Providence's World War II Memorial; in warm weather, dine outside on the front patio. **Known for:** New England or Rhode Island clam "chowdah," live "lobstah," and other seafood specialties; two-course power lunch; extensive wine cellar and craft-beer list. $ *Average main: $30* ⊠ *121 S. Main St., East Side* ☎ *401/351–8570* ⊕ *www.hemenwaysrestaurant.com.*

Mill's Tavern

$$$ | MODERN AMERICAN | Handsome brick walls and vaulted casement ceilings lend a cozy New England vibe to this contemporary, French-influenced American restaurant. The menu includes selections from both a raw bar and a wood-burning oven and rotisserie. **Known for:** seasonal menu changes quarterly; steaks, chops, and seafood always a good choice; three-course prix-fixe menu offered nightly (except Saturday). $ *Average main: $28* ⊠ *101 N. Main St., East Side* ☎ *401/272–3331* ⊕ *www.millstavernrestaurant.com* ⊙ *No lunch.*

Red Stripe

$$ | ECLECTIC | A giant fork hangs outside this neighborhood brasserie in Wayland Square, and the chefs do things big here—from the 10-ounce Red Stripe burger to the everything-but-the-kitchen-sink chopped salad. The menu is eclectic, but you'll find plenty of French-inspired bistro items, including duck confit, French onion soup, steak frites, and mussels prepared 10 ways. **Known for:** large, varied menu with something to appeal to everyone; homemade bread is fabulous; lively atmosphere (i.e., noisy). $ *Average main: $18* ⊠ *465 Angell St., East Side* ☎ *401/437–6950* ⊕ *www.redstriperestaurants.com.*

The Salted Slate

$$$ | AMERICAN | Ben Lloyd, the chef-owner of this "agri-driven" American restaurant, is committed to honoring the origins of the food he prepares. He purchases humanely raised and harvested meat, poultry, and fish whole from local vendors, butchers them in-house, and uses every part from nose to tail—combined with eggs at breakfast, cheese and fries at lunch, and fresh vegetables at dinner. **Known for:** small-batch artisanal cheeses and house-cured charcuterie; innovative menus change frequently; best bacon you'll ever eat. $ *Average main: $27* ⊠ *Wayland Sq., 186 Wayland Ave., East Side* ☎ *401/270–3737* ⊕ *www.saltedslate.com* ⊙ *Closed Mon.*

 ## Hotels

The Old Court Bed and Breakfast

$ | B&B/INN | You'll understand why parents of Brown and RISD students book their stays in this three-story Italianate inn on historic Benefit Street a few years before graduation, once you see the lovely antiques, richly colored wallpaper, and authentic period light fixtures. **Pros:** on a historic residential street; period decor and modern-day conveniences; free parking. **Cons:** small bathrooms; third-floor rooms require a trek upstairs; street traffic can be noisy at times. $ *Rooms from: $145* ⊠ *144 Benefit St., East Side* ☎ *401/751–2002* ⊕ *www.oldcourt.com* ⇄ *10 rooms* ⊙| *Free breakfast.*

 ## Nightlife

BARS
Hot Club

BARS/PUBS | You may recognize the Hot Club from the opening scenes of the movie *Something About Mary*. For more than 30 years, this place has been a favorite hangout for young professionals, university professors, and politicians. On summer afternoons until the wee hours of the morning, you'll find a crowd on the outdoor deck overlooking the Providence

River. For cheap eats, try local favorites like the saugy dog (hot dog) or the stuffed quahog (a Rhode Island staple). ⊠ *25 Bridge St., East Side* ☎ *401/861–9007* ⊕ *www.hotclubprov.com.*

Performing Arts

FILM
Avon Cinema
ART GALLERIES—ARTS | This independent movie theater on College Hill, near Brown University, screens primarily art-house, independent, and foreign films. The theater's Art Deco styling dates back to its opening in 1938. ⊠ *260 Thayer St., East Side* ☎ *401/421–0020* ⊕ *www.avoncinema.com.*

Activities

BIKING
East Bay Bicycle Path
BICYCLING | **FAMILY** | This mostly flat, 14½-mile bike path connects Providence's India Point Park with Independence Park in Bristol. Along the way, you pass eight parks and two wooden-deck bridges with views of coves and saltwater marshes. The route can be congested on fine-weather weekends. ■**TIP**➔ **Check out the George Redman Linear Park on the Washington Bridge over the Seekonk River. It's accessible from India Point Park.** ⊠ *India Point Park, India St., Fox Point* ☎ *401/667–6200* ⊕ *www.dot.ri.gov/community/bikeri/eastbay.php.*

● Shopping

ANTIQUES
The Stanley Weiss Collection
ANTIQUES/COLLECTIBLES | The country's largest collection of fine classical and Colonial furniture and antiques is available for viewing (and for sale) Saturday 11–5, or by appointment. ⊠ *212 4th St., East Side* ☎ *401/272–3200* ⊕ *www.stanleyweiss.com.*

ART GALLERIES
Bert Gallery
ART GALLERIES | This gallery showcases late 19th- and early-20th-century paintings by regional artists, by appointment only. ⊠ *24 Bridge St., East Side* ☎ *401/751–2628* ⊕ *www.bertgallery.com.*

The Peaceable Kingdom
ART GALLERIES | This gallery stocks folk art from around the world, including nativities, weavings and rugs, clothing, jewelry, masks, and musical instruments. In October, hundreds of colorful skeletons are on display leading up to the Mexican Day of the Dead. ⊠ *116 Ives St., East Side* ☎ *401/351–3472* ⊕ *www.pkgifts.com.*

HANDICRAFTS AND HOME FURNISHINGS
Frog + Toad
CLOTHING | Clothing, housewares, fair trade handicrafts, and locally designed goods can all be found at this small curiosity shop and gift boutique. ⊠ *795 Hope St., East Side* ☎ *401/831–3434* ⊕ *www.frogandtoadstore.com.*

RISD WORKS Museum Store
ART GALLERIES | This shop on the ground floor of RISD's Art Museum has a selection of quirky kitchen gadgets, toys, totes, hand-blown glass, jewelry, and prints by Rhode Island School of Design faculty and alumni, including *Family Guy* creator Seth MacFarlane's custom RISD T-shirt. ⊠ *20 N. Main St., East Side* ☎ *401/277–4949* ⊕ *www.risdworks.com.*

Stock Culinary Goods
CERAMICS/GLASSWARE | Useful, whimsical, and always well-designed utensils, stemware, dishes, and culinary gifts are the specialty of this foodie paradise with an industrial kitchen vibe. ⊠ *756 Hope St., East Side* ☎ *401/521–0101* ⊕ *www.stockculinarygoods.com.*

Federal Hill

Federal Hill has been home to generations of Italian-American families. While the neighborhood may no longer be predominantly Italian-American, it remains infused with Italian charm and hospitality. The stripe down Atwells Avenue, the main thoroughfare, is painted in red, white, and green; and a huge *pignoli* (pine nut), an Italian symbol of abundance and quality, hangs on an arch soaring over the street. Grocers sell pasta, pastries, and hard-to-find Italian groceries. To get the full experience, have a seat near the fountain in DePasquale Square, especially during the Feast of St. Joseph in March, the Federal Hill Stroll in early in June, the Federal Hill Summer Festival in late June, or the three-day Columbus Day Weekend Festival and parade in October. Federal Hill lies to the west of Downtown, separated by Interstate 95, and is bounded by Westminster Street to the south and Route 6 to the west and north. For a look at what's on, check out ⊕ *www.federalhillprov.com.*

Restaurants

Angelo's Civita Farnese

$ | ITALIAN | FAMILY | Locals come to this third-generation, family-owned restaurant in the heart of Federal Hill for the chicken or eggplant Parmesan, veal with peppers, and braciola like (your Italian) grandma used to make. The prices are reasonable; the atmosphere, warm and casual. **Known for:** family-friendly; communal dining tables; familiar southern Italian menu. ⑤ *Average main: $15* ⊠ *141 Atwells Ave., Federal Hill* ☎ *401/621–8171* ⊕ *www. angelosonthehill.com.*

Broadway Bistro

$ | AMERICAN | Another neat addition to the city's increasingly gentrified West Side (which fringes Federal Hill), this convivial bar and restaurant occupies a single-story redbrick storefront with a handful of sidewalk tables. A mix of students, artists, and neighborhood locals congregates here nightly for fair-priced, deftly prepared, globally influenced bistro chow. **Known for:** foodies love this cozy bistro; reservations only for six or more people; good wine and beer selection. ⑤ *Average main: $16* ⊠ *205 Broadway, Federal Hill* ☎ *401/331–2450* ⊕ *www. broadwaybistrori.com* ⊗ *No lunch.*

Kitchen

$ | AMERICAN | The lone chef and solitary waiter at this five-table restaurant produce what some patrons describe as "breakfast nirvana." People wait in line for thick-cut bacon, Portuguese sweetbread toast, and grilled blueberry corn muffins. **Known for:** limited seating—plan to wait in line; order extra muffins to take home; cash only—no credit cards. ⑤ *Average main: $8* ⊠ *94 Carpenter St., Federal Hill* ☎ *401/272–1117* ⊗ *Closed Mon. and Tues.* ▬ *No credit cards.*

★ Nick's on Broadway

$$ | MODERN AMERICAN | Expect a wait for brunch at this trendy West End restaurant, where chef Derek Wagner entices his morning crowd with blueberry pancakes, poached eggs on a buttermilk biscuit with hollandaise and basil, and other well-prepared brunch fare. The restaurant also serves dinner, at which the chef's passionate embrace of farm-to-table precepts—not to mention his attention to detail—are even more in evidence. **Known for:** buttery grilled breakfast toast; four- or seven-course chef's tasting menu; opt for counter seating for a front-row view of the open kitchen. ⑤ *Average main: $24* ⊠ *500 Broadway, Federal Hill* ☎ *401/421–0286* ⊕ *www. nicksonbroadway.com* ⊗ *Closed Mon. and Tues. No dinner Sun.*

Ogie's Trailer Park

$ | AMERICAN | Fun and kitschy Ogie's bar and restaurant fuses trailer-park chic and colorful (maybe even garish) 1950s-style decor. The menu emphasizes "gourmet comfort food," which translates into the likes of tater tots in béchamel sauce, grilled peanut butter and jelly, and mac 'n' cheese croquettes. **Known for:** Rhody fried chicken, encrusted with Doritos!; patio dining outside around the fire pit—year-round, if you're brave; drinks at the outdoor tiki bar in warm weather. Ⓢ *Average main: $8* ✉ *1155 Westminster St., Federal Hill* ☎ *401/383-8200* ⊕ *www.ogiestrailerpark.com* ◷ *No lunch Mon.–Sat.*

Pane e Vino

$$$ | **ITALIAN** | Portions are big in the Rhode Island comfort-food tradition at this southern Italian *ristorante* on Federal Hill; count on fresh ingredients served in a simple, straightforward way. Share a pasta if you dare, but keep in mind that the veal chop could probably topple Fred Flintstone's footmobile; gluten-free dishes are also available. **Known for:** all your favorites, Italian style; more than 120 regional Italian wines; $24 prix-fixe menu at dinner (except Friday and Saturday). Ⓢ *Average main: $25* ✉ *365 Atwells Ave., Federal Hill* ☎ *401/223-2230* ⊕ *www. panevino.net* ◷ *No lunch.*

Providence Oyster Bar

$$$ | **SEAFOOD** | In a neighborhood where Italian food dominates, this spirited seafood restaurant offers a refreshing alternative. Oysters—and clams, lobster, and shrimp—are the main attraction, of course, but landlubbers will enjoy a steak or grilled chicken breast. **Known for:** oysters—more than a dozen varieties on the raw bar; paella for two; raw-bar "appy hour" with $1 each shellfish and $6 appetizers. Ⓢ *Average main: $27* ✉ *283 Atwells Ave., Federal Hill* ☎ *401/272-8866* ⊕ *www.providenceoysterbar.com.*

Siena

$$ | **NORTHERN ITALIAN** | This place generates well-deserved buzz for its branzino (sea bass) with scallops in a creamy scallion sauce and for its pasta with a rich Bolognese—both of which are legendary. It's best to split an appetizer, as portions here are huge. **Known for:** Tuscan-style cuisine; excellent wine list; signature "tasting board" antipasti. Ⓢ *Average*

main: $23 ✉ *238 Atwells Ave., Federal Hill* ☎ *401/521-3311* ⊕ *www.sienari.com* ◷ *No lunch.*

Nightlife

BARS

Lili Marlene's

BARS/PUBS | Nondescript and easygoing, this understated watering hole with cozy booths has a loyal following among in-the-know locals who like a good burger and free pool with their martinis and beer. ✉ *422 Atwells Ave., Federal Hill* ☎ *401/751-4996.*

Shopping

FOOD

★ Costantino's Venda Ravioli

FOOD/CANDY | **FAMILY** | The sights, scents, and flavors of Italy surround you at Costantino's as you peruse the amazing selection of imported foods. The convivial banter between customers and employees adds to the atmosphere. Stop here for lunch, or grab an espresso or gelato at the bar; in the summer, enjoy the gelato at neighboring DePasquale Square's fountain. ✉ *265 Atwells Ave., Federal Hill* ☎ *401/421-9105* ⊕ *www.vendaravioli.com.*

Scialo Bros. Bakery

FOOD/CANDY | Get your Italian cookie or cannoli fix at this family-owned bakery in business since 1916. ✉ *257 Atwells Ave., Federal Hill* ☎ *401/421-0986, 877/421-0986* ⊕ *scialobakery.com.*

Tony's Colonial Food

FOOD/CANDY | This superb grocery offers a family-friendly atmosphere in which to peruse the finest of Italian meats and cheeses; imported vinegars and olive oils; and candies and confections—all at reasonable prices. In addition, Tony's deli stocks freshly prepared foods to eat on the premises or take with you; try the Italian grinder, a Rhode Island lunchtime staple. ✉ *311 Atwells Ave., Federal Hill* ☎ *401/621-8675* ⊕ *tonyscolonial.mybig-commerce.com.*

Pawtucket

5 miles north of Providence.

Once a thriving mill town, Pawtucket went through tough times before artists discovered its old mills and low rents. The city remains the world headquarters of the toy manufacturer Hasbro, creator of Mr. Potato Head, and has a thriving arts and cultural scene. A visit to the engaging Slater Mill Museum, America's first successful water-powered factory, provides a sense of Pawtucket's pivotal role in the American Industrial Revolution. Inside a converted mill, the Hope Artiste Village hints at the future with its mix of art studios, lofts, retail shops, light-industrial workshops, and the Met music venue.

◉ Sights

Hope Artiste Village

LOCAL SPECIALTIES | The surviving redbrick buildings of the former Hope Webbing Company's textile mill now hold artists' studios, galleries (including the always-interesting Candita Clayton Gallery), cafés, shops, the Met music venue, the marvelously retro BreakTime Bowl and Bar duckpin bowling alley, and a well-attended winter farmers' market on Saturday mornings, November–May. ⊠ *999–1005 Main St.* ☎ *401/321–3850* ⊕ *www.hopeartistevillage.com.*

Slater Memorial Park

CAROUSEL | **FAMILY** | Within the stately grounds of this park along Ten Mile River are picnic tables, tennis courts, a playground, a dog park, and a river walk. The park's **Looff Carousel,** built by Charles I. D. Looff in 1894, has 39 horses, three dogs, a lion, a camel, a giraffe, and two chariots that are the earliest examples of the Danish immigrant's work—rides operate July 4–Labor Day and cost 50¢. The Pawtucket chapter of the Daughters of the American Revolution gives tours (by appointment) of the park's **Daggett House,** which dates to 1685. ⊠ *825 Armistice Blvd.* ☎ *401/728–0500 park information* ⊕ *pawtucketri.com* ⊠ *Free.*

★ Slater Mill Museum

HISTORIC SITE | **FAMILY** | Concord and Lexington may legitimately lay claim to what Ralph Waldo Emerson called "the shot heard round the world" in 1776, but Pawtucket's Slater Mill provided the necessary economic shot in the arm in 1793. This National Historic Landmark, the first successful water-powered spinning mill in America, touched off an industrial revolution that helped secure America's sovereign independence in the early days of the republic. The museum complex explores this era with expert interpretive guides dressed in period clothing, who demonstrate fiber-to-yarn and yarn-to-fabric processes and discuss how industrialization forever changed this nation. On-site are collections of hand-operated and-powered machinery, a 120-seat theater, two gift shops, a gallery, and a recreational park. ⊠ *67 Roosevelt Ave.* ☎ *401/725–8638* ⊕ *www.slatermill.org* ⊠ *$12* ⊙ *Closed Tues. year-round, closed Mon. July 4–Labor Day.*

🍴 Restaurants

Modern Diner

$ | **DINER** | **FAMILY** | On weekends, the line often trails out the door for a seat in this 1941 Sterling Streamliner diner that's a beauty to behold. In addition to the extensive breakfast and lunch menu, you'll often find 30 or more specials posted on the wall. **Known for:** breakfast served all day until closing at 2 pm; modern addition with retro counter seating; first diner to appear on National Register of Historic Places. ⑤ *Average main: $8* ⊠ *364 East Ave.* ☎ *401/726–8390* ⊕ *www.moderndinerri.com* ⊟ *No credit cards* ⊙ *No dinner.*

Rasoi

$ | **INDIAN** | Taking its name from the Hindi word for kitchen, this restaurant near the Providence city line serves cuisine from a staggering 27 regions of India. The menu

Slater Mill in Pawtucket is regarded as the country's first successful water-powered spinning mill.

includes numerous spicy, gluten-free, and vegan selections. **Known for:** small plates and full entrées; lunch buffets on Saturday (vegan) and Sunday (regional); colorful dining room with orange walls and blue floors. ⑤ *Average main: $15* ✉ *727 East Ave.* ☎ *401/728–5500* ⊕ *www.rasoirestaurant.com.*

Performing Arts

The Gamm Theatre

THEATER | Known for its Shakespearean performances, the theater also presents edgy productions of classic and contemporary works in an intimate 137-seat setting. The season runs September–May. ✉ *172 Exchange St.* ☎ *401/723–4266* ⊕ *www.gammtheatre.org.*

Activities

Pawtucket Red Sox

BASEBALL/SOFTBALL | FAMILY | The longtime minor-league affiliate of baseball's Boston Red Sox has been toying with the idea of moving to Worcester (or Newport or Providence), but for now the Pawsox continue to play home games at the 10,000-seat McCoy Stadium in Pawtucket. The season runs April–early September. ✉ *1 Columbus Ave.* ☎ *401/724–7300* ⊕ *www.pawsox.com* ✈ *From $9.*

Woonsocket

10 miles north of Pawtucket, 15 miles north of Providence.

A former mill town struggling to gentrify, Woonsocket has a very fine museum about immigrant factory life and textile milling, as well as a jazz and blues club and a fish 'n' chips restaurant worthy of a special trip.

◉ Sights

★ Museum of Work and Culture

MUSEUM | FAMILY | In a former textile mill, this interactive museum examines the lives of American factory workers and owners during the Industrial Revolution. Focusing on French Canadian immigrants who came to work in Woonsocket's mills, the museum's cleverly laid out, walk-through exhibits begin with a 19th-century Québécois farmhouse, then continue with displays of life in a 20th-century tenement, a Catholic school, a church, and the shop floor. The genesis of the textile workers' union is described, as are the events that led to the National Textile Strike of 1934. There's also a fascinating presentation about child labor. ⊠ *42 S. Main St.* ☎ *401/769–9675* ⊕ *www.rihs. org* ☞ *$8* ⊗ *Closed Mon.*

Restaurants

Ye Olde English Fish & Chips
$ | SEAFOOD | Folks come from all over to savor the affordable, fresh, lightly battered, gently fried fish and hand-cut, English-style "chips" at this local institution in Market Square. The family-owned restaurant, which celebrated its 95th anniversary in 2017, serves up a casual and relaxed feast in a wood-paneled dining room. **Known for:** batter recipe brought from Yorkshire, England, and unchanged since 1922; clam chowder and clam cakes are also delish; easy walk to/from Museum of Work and Culture. ⑤ *Average main: $12* ⊠ *25 S. Main St.* ☎ *401/762–3637* ⊕ *www.yeol-deeenglishfishandchips.com* ⊗ *Closed Sun. and Mon.*

Hotels

Pillsbury House Bed & Breakfast
$ | B&B/INN | Tucked away on a historic street a half mile from the Blackstone River, this inn occupying an 1875 Victorian offers peace, quiet, and a splendid breakfast. **Pros:** attractive architecture; reasonable room rate; free off-street parking. **Cons:** old-fashioned decor isn't for everyone; third-floor bathroom is private but outside the guest room; no room TV. ⑤ *Rooms from: $125* ⊠ *341 Prospect St.* ☎ *401/766–7983, 800/205–4112* ⊕ *www.pillsburyhouse.com* ⟿ *4 rooms* ⦿ *Free breakfast.*

Nightlife

Chan's Fine Oriental Dining
MUSIC CLUBS | Renowned blues and jazz performers are on the menu, along with folk, cabaret, and comedy acts. (Chan's also serves Chinese cuisine, but you're here for the music.) Reservations are recommended. ⊠ *267 Main St.* ☎ *401/765–1900* ⊕ *www.chanseggroll-sandjazz.com* ☞ *From $10.*

Westerly

45 miles southwest of Providence, 115 miles southwest of Boston, 140 miles northeast of New York City.

The picturesque and thriving business district in this town of 18,000 people bordering Pawcatuck, Connecticut, has a lot going for it: galleries and artist studios, shops and restaurants, a Victorian strolling park, and more than 55 structures on the National Register of Historic Places. Once a busy little railroad town in the late 19th century, Westerly is now a stop on the New York–Boston Amtrak corridor. The town was known in the past for its red granite, which was used in monuments around the country. It has since sprawled out along U.S. 1 and grown to encompass seven villages in a 33-square-mile area: Westerly itself (also called downtown Westerly), along with Watch Hill, Dunn's Corners, Misquamicut, Bradford, Shelter Harbor, and Weekapaug.

GETTING HERE AND AROUND
When traveling between New York City and Boston, Amtrak makes stops at Westerly, Kingston, and Providence.

Sights

Westerly Library and Wilcox Park
HISTORIC SITE | FAMILY | The library, in the heart of downtown Westerly, also serves neighboring Pawcatuck, Connecticut. The library's Hoxie Gallery holds monthly

art exhibitions. Adjacent to the library, Wilcox Park, a 14½-acre Victorian strolling park designed in 1898 by Warren Manning—an associate of Frederick Law Olmsted, co-creator of New York's Central Park—has a pond, a meadow, an arboretum, a perennials garden, sculptures, fountains, and monuments. *The Runaway Bunny,* a sculpture inspired by the children's book of the same name, is popular with the little ones. A garden market, arts festivals, concerts, and Shakespeare-in-the-park productions are held periodically. ⊠ *44 Broad St.* ☎ *401/596–2877* ⊕ *www.westerlylibrary. org* ⊠ *Free.*

Restaurants

B&B Dockside

$ | **AMERICAN** | It's all about breakfast and burgers at this café overlooking the Pawcatuck River. Burgers rule the lunch menu, including the deliciously decadent Fat Elvis—with peanut butter, bacon, cheese, and caramelized bananas, it'll leave you saying, "Thank you, thankyouverymuch." **Known for:** great waterfront view; mouthwatering roast beef hash—for breakfast; friendly service, even when crowded. ⑤ *Average main: $12* ⊠ *19 Margin St.* ☎ *401/315–2520* ⊕ *www.bnbdockside. com* ⊗ *Closed Tues.*

Bridge

$$ | **AMERICAN** | On the banks of the Pawcatuck River, this restaurant serves affordable American regional cuisine with an emphasis on local ingredients. The riverside bar and outdoor patio are great for taking in summer concerts in the park across the river. **Known for:** raw bar; gluten-free and vegan items available; "gathering menu" of small plates weekday afternoons. ⑤ *Average main: $18* ⊠ *37 Main St.* ☎ *401/348–9700* ⊕ *www. bridgeri.com.*

Nightlife

The Knickerbocker Music Center

MUSIC CLUBS | The band Roomful of Blues was born at "The Knick," and they still gig at this club near the Westerly train station. The venue hosts R&B, jazz, blues, and alt-country touring acts; local bands also perform, and there are open-mike nights. ⊠ *35 Railroad Ave.* ☎ *401/315–5070* ⊕ *www.knickmusic.org.*

Watch Hill

6 miles south of downtown Westerly.

For generations, this seaside village has attracted movers and shakers looking for a low-key getaway. Watch Hill has nearly 2 miles of gorgeous beaches, including Napatree Point Conservation Area, a great spot to see shorebirds and raptors and take in the sunset. Stargazers might catch a glimpse of Taylor Swift or Conan O'Brien, both of whom have homes here. The heart of the town is Bay Street, a seasonal business district with boutiques selling upscale beachwear, fashions, home goods, T-shirts, and souvenirs. There are also cafés and a historic carousel.

Sights

Flying Horse Carousel

CAROUSEL | **FAMILY** | At the beach end of Bay Street twirls one of the oldest carousels in America, built by the Charles W. F. Dare Company of New York City and part of a traveling carnival that came to Watch Hill before 1883. The carved wooden horses with real horsehair manes and leather saddles are suspended from chains attached to the ceiling, creating the impression the horses are flying. Riders must be under 12. Grab the brass ring for a free ride. ⊠ *151 Bay St.* ☎ *401/348–6007* ⊕ *watchhillbeachandcarousel.com/* ⊠ *$2.*

South County and Newport County

MASSACHUSETTS

CONNECTICUT

KEY
Ferry Lines

Rhode Island Sound

Block Island Sound

Narragansett Bay

Sakonnet River

Goosewing Beach
South Shore Beach
Sakonnet Point
Sakonnet
Third Beach
Second Beach
Easton's Beach
Sandy Point
Greenvale Vineyards
Little Compton
Adamsville
Tiverton Four Corners
Tiverton
Bristol
Warren
Woonsocket
Pawtucket
Blithewold Mansion, Gardens, and Arboretum
Homestead
Green Animals Topiary Garden
Portsmouth
South Portsmouth
Prudence Island
Conanicut Island
Middletown
Newport Bridge
Newport see detail map
Watson Farm
Jamestown
Jamestown Bridge
Casey Farm
Saunderstown
Gilbert Stuart Birthplace and Museum
Allenton
Hamilton
Wickford
Smith's Castle
Quonset Point
Adventureland of Narragansett
Narragansett
Narragansett Pier
Narragansett Town Beach
Scarborough State Beach
FISHERMEN'S MEMORIAL STATE PARK
Point Judith Lighthouse
Roger W. Wheeler State Beach
Point Judith
Galilee
Jerusalem
East Matunuck State Beach
Point Judith Pond
Snug Harbor
South Kingstown
Wakefield
Peace Dale
Kingston
West Kingston
Worden Pond
GREAT SWAMP MANAGEMENT AREA
Exeter
Nooseneck
Coventry
Green Hill
Matunuck
South Kingstown Town Beach
Charlestown
Charlestown Town Beach
Charlestown Breachway
East Beach
Ninigret Park/ Frosty Drew Observatory and Sky Theatre
Ninigret National Wildlife Refuge
Shelter Harbor
Watchaug Pond
Shelter Pond
Dunn's Corner
Weekapaug
Misquamicut State Beach
Misquamicut
Watch Hill
Westerly
BURLINGAME STATE PARK
Ashaway
Bradford
Hope Valley
ARCADIA MANAGEMENT AREA

TO BLOCK ISLAND

10 miles
15 km

95
24
77
81
114
138
1
4
2
102
3
112
91
165
138
1A
108

Watch Hill Lighthouse

MUSEUM | A tiny museum at this 1808 lighthouse contains the original Fresnel light, letters and journals from lighthouse keepers, documentation of famous local shipwrecks, and photographs of the hurricane of 1938 and 19th- and early-20th-century sailing vessels off Watch Hill. Parking is for the handicapped and senior citizens only; everyone else must walk down the peninsula along a private road off Larkin Road. ⊠ *Lighthouse Rd.* ☏ *401/596–7761* ⊕ *www.watchhilllighthousekeepers.org* ⌦ *Free* ⊗ *Museum closed Labor Day–June and Fri.–Mon.*

Restaurants

★ Olympia Tea Room

$$ | **AMERICAN** | Overlooking the water since it first opened as an ice cream parlor in 1916, the Olympia's varnished wood booths and a long marble counter echo the restaurant's rich history. The kitchen focuses on local and artisanal ingredients served with simple elegance, including whole roasted flounder and braised lamb shanks. **Known for:** bistro-style menu; sidewalk tables outside and antique booths inside; extensive wine list, including scores available by the glass. ⑤ *Average main: $24* ⊠ *74 Bay St.* ☏ *401/348–8211* ⊕ *www.olympiatearoom.com* ⊗ *Closed late Nov.–Apr., and Tues. in Sept. and Oct.*

Hotels

★ Ocean House

$$$$ | **RESORT** | High on bluffs overlooking Block Island Sound stands this extraordinary replica of the Victorian grande dame of the same name built here in 1868. **Pros:** exceptional service; beach with private cabanas; championship croquet lawn; spa with 25-meter lap pool. **Cons:** expensive during high season (and the low season); three-night minimum on weekends; less than impressive dining. ⑤ *Rooms from: $1025* ⊠ *1 Bluff Ave.* ☏ *401/584–7000, 855/678–0364* ⊕ *www.oceanhouseri.com* ⌦ *67 rooms* ⦿ *No meals.*

★ Weekapaug Inn

$$$$ | **RESORT** | Guest rooms at this lovingly restored inn on Quonochontaug (Quonnie) Pond are furnished with luxury linens and the work of area artists. **Pros:** low-key luxury; guest pantry stocked with tasty treats; charming, attentive service; breakfast made with locally sourced food. **Cons:** expensive; slow service in the restaurant; few off-season activities (after Labor Day). ⑤ *Rooms from: $690* ⊠ *25 Spray Rock Rd., Westerly* ☏ *401/637–7600, 855/679–2995* ⊕ *www.weekapauginn.com* ⌦ *31 rooms* ⦿ *Free breakfast.*

Misquamicut

2½ miles northeast of Watch Hill.

This family-oriented summer destination, stretching 7 miles from Watch Hill to Weekapaug, has an ocean-facing sandy beach the color of brown sugar. From waterslides to kiddie rides, the town's several amusement parks provide countless diversions. You can also hop on a Jet Ski, paddle a kayak, or find a spot for sunbathing. Evenings bring concerts and movies on the beach, and there are shoreside festivals in the spring and fall.

The Native American name for this sandy strip of beachfront means "Red Fish," referring to the Atlantic salmon common to the Pawcatuck River; the entire Westerly area, settled in 1661, once bore this name.

Sights

Atlantic Beach Park

AMUSEMENT PARK/WATER PARK | **FAMILY** | The largest and busiest of the several kid-oriented amusements along Misquamicut Beach, this facility offers old-fashioned fun for the entire family, including an antique (1915) carousel, bumper cars, a minigolf course, waterslides, batting cages, a roller coaster, a hurricane simulator, and a large arcade with more than 75 games. ✉ *321 Atlantic Ave.* ☎ *401/322–0504* ⊕ *www.atlanticbeachpark.com* ✍ *Free entry, $2 per ride; parking from $15* ⊘ *Closed mid-Oct.–Apr.*

Beaches

Misquamicut State Beach

BEACH—SIGHT | FAMILY | Part of the several-mile-long stretch of sandy beach that makes up Misquamicut, this ½-mile state-run portion is Rhode Island's longest beach. Expect the 2,100-space parking lot to fill up on sunny summer holiday weekends. Bring your own chairs or blankets. **Amenities:** food and drink; lifeguards; parking (fee); showers; toilets. **Best for:** sunset; swimming; walking. ✉ *257 Atlantic Ave.* ☎ *401/322–8910* ⊕ *www.riparks.com/locations/location-misquamicut.html* ✍ *Parking: from $6.*

Restaurants

Maria's Seaside Cafe

$$ | MEDITERRANEAN | This family-owned restaurant serves Italian cuisine at lunch and dinner. It's right across the street from the beach and a standout on a strip of ice-cream stands, take-out shacks, and motels that have seen better days. **Known for:** raw bar with oysters, littlenecks, and shrimp; homemade pasta; happy hour at the bar with half-price appetizers. ⑤ *Average main: $23* ✉ *132 Atlantic Ave.* ☎ *401/596–6886* ⊕ *www.mariasseasidecafe.com* ⊘ *Closed early-Oct.–May. No dinner after Labor Day.*

Hotels

Breezeway Resort

$$ | HOTEL | A great choice for families, this well-maintained boutique motel is less than a quarter-mile from the ocean. **Pros:** nice range of room configurations; beach towels provided; on-site laundry; complimentary bicycles for adults. **Cons:** a bit noisy with so many kids; Wi-Fi in main lodge only; hotel prices, motel accommodations. ⑤ *Rooms from: $275* ✉ *70 Winnapaug Rd.* ☎ *401/348–8953* ⊕ *www.breezewayresort.com* ⊘ *Closed late Oct.– early May* ↩ *50 rooms* ¶ *Free breakfast.*

Charlestown

12 miles northeast of Misquamicut.

Charlestown's secluded coastline makes it a great spot for swimming, sailing, surfing, beachcombing, bird-watching, and boating. Approximately 20% of Charlestown is conservation and recreation land, including Burlingame State Park, Ninigret Wildlife Refuge, Ninigret Park, and East Beach. The city regulates outdoor lighting to keep the night sky dark, so it's a fantastic place for sky watchers of all ages. Charlestown is also home to the Narragansett Indian Tribe Reservation, which every August holds the oldest recorded annual powwow in North America.

Sights

★ Frosty Drew Observatory and Sky Theatre

OBSERVATORY | FAMILY | In Ninigret Park but independently owned and managed, the observatory offers the state's best views of the night sky. Frosty Drew opens every Friday at sunset for stargazing and stays open until early Saturday morning if the skies are clear. It's also open on nights when meteor showers and other astronomical events are forecast. On cloudy nights, astronomers give presentations and offer tours. The place isn't heated, so dress for the season. ✉ *Ninigret Park, 61 Park La., off Old Post Rd.* ☎ *401/859–1450* ⊕ *www.frostydrew.org/observatory* ✍ *Free.*

Ninigret National Wildlife Refuge

BODY OF WATER | FAMILY | Spring brings opportunities to view the male American woodcock's mating ritual at this 858-acre refuge, but bird-watchers flock here year-round to commune with nature among 9 miles of trails and diverse upland and wetland habitats, including grasslands, shrublands, wooded swamps, and freshwater ponds. There's an abandoned naval air station on Ninigret Pond, the state's largest coastal salt pond, and a fine place to watch the sunset. Hiking trails are closed December and January, when bow hunters are allowed to cull white-tailed deer. Explore an impressive collection of wildlife and natural history displays at the Kettle Pond Visitor Center on the southbound side of U.S. 1 at 50 Bend Road. ⊠ *Ninigret Entrance Rd., off U.S. 1* ☎ *401/364–9124* ⊕ *www.fws.gov/ refuge/ninigret/* 🎫 *Free.*

Ninigret Park

CITY PARK | FAMILY | This 227-acre park off Old Post Road, formerly a World War II–era naval air training base, now features picnic grounds, ball fields, a playground, a bike path, tennis and basketball courts, a criterium bicycle course, nature trails, a disc-golf course, a nature center, and a 3-acre spring-fed swimming pond. The Charlestown Seafood Festival is held here in August. ⊠ *5 Park La., off U.S. 1* ☎ *401/364–1222* ⊕ *www.charlestownri. org* 🎫 *Free.*

Beaches

Blue Shutters Town Beach

BEACH—SIGHT | FAMILY | Just west of the Ninigret Conservation Area with wonderful views of Block Island Sound, Blue Shutters is a popular escape for families, who enjoy building sandcastles, beachcombing, and bodysurfing the gentle waves. Beachgoers can see Block Island and Long Island from the shaded deck of the pavilion. Beach-accessible wheelchairs are available at no cost. **Amenities:** lifeguards; showers; toilets; parking (fee); food and drink. **Best for:** walking; sunsets; swimming. ⊠ *469 East Beach Rd.* ☎ *401/364–1222* 🎫 *Parking $20.*

East Beach

BEACH—SIGHT | FAMILY | This tranquil and unspoiled barrier beach spans 3 narrow miles of shoreline that fronts and separates Ninigret Pond from the ocean. East Beach stands in stark contrast to Narragansett's bustling Scarborough Beach. Parking is limited, and the lot fills up quickly. Be careful when swimming: the ocean side is known for riptides. **Amenities:** lifeguards; parking (fee); toilets. **Best for:** solitude; swimming; walking. ⊠ *E. Beach Rd., off U.S. 1* ☎ *401/322–8910.*

Restaurants

The Charlestown Rathskeller

$$ | AMERICAN | The hand-cut fries at this former speakeasy hidden in the woods are revered across southern New England, and steaks and burgers are big and cooked to perfection. For a lighter bite, try the locally sourced seafood and raw-bar options. **Known for:** fries served a half-dozen delicious ways; schnitzels, sausages, and pretzels; full menu of standard dishes, too. ⑤ *Average main: $23* ⊠ *489A Old Coach Rd.* ☎ *401/792–1000* ⊕ *www.thecharlestownrathskeller.com.*

Activities

BOATING
Ocean House Marina

BOATING | This full-service marina on scenic Ninigret Pond offers boat rentals, fishing supplies, fuel, and maintenance service. ⊠ *60 Town Dock Rd., off U.S. 1* ☎ *401/364–6040* ⊕ *oceanhousemarina.com.*

PARKS
Burlingame State Campground

CAMPING—SPORTS-OUTDOORS | The 3,100-acre Burlingame State Park attracts many campers to its 700 rustic campsites, nature trails, picnic and swimming areas, and boating and fishing opportunities on crystal clear Watchaug Pond. ⊠ *1 Burlingame State Park Rd.* ☎ *401/322–8910* ⊕ *www.riparks.com/Locations/Location-BurlingameCampground.html* 🎫 *Free.*

Rhode Island Treats

Clam Cakes. It's not summer for locals without a pilgrimage to a clam shack for these hunks of fried dough with briny, meaty clams inside. Pair them with the chowder of your choice.

Coffee Milk. The official state drink, coffee milk is like chocolate milk but made instead with coffee-flavored syrup, preferably Autocrat Coffee Syrup.

Del's Frozen Lemonade. You can get one of these refreshingly cold drinks from one of many Del's trucks making the rounds in the summer or at a Del's storefront.

NY System Wieners. Try a hot dog "done all the way": topped with meat sauce, mustard, onions, and celery salt. (They're said to be a great hangover cure.)

Rhode Island Jonnycakes. Essentially unleavened cornmeal pancakes typically served for breakfast in diners—or anywhere in South County—jonnycakes can be thick or thin and served with maple syrup, honey, fruit, or powdered sugar.

Rhode Island Style Calamari. This dish of lightly fried squid with hot cherry peppers and garlic is the official state appetizer for a good reason: the Port of Galilee in Narragansett processes millions of pounds of squid annually.

🛍 Shopping

Fantastic Umbrella Factory

GIFTS/SOUVENIRS | FAMILY | With a hippie vibe, the kid- and first date–friendly Fantastic Umbrella Factory contains a handful of rustic shops built around a wild garden and bamboo forest. Hardy, unusual daylilies and other plants are for sale, along with interesting clothing and jewelry, vintage eyewear, soy candles, creative pottery, blown glass, penny candy, and incense. In the South County Artisans Loft, a renovated second-floor barn space, you can meet local fine and craft artists and peruse their wares. For 50¢ you can scoop a cone full of seeds to feed the fenced-in emus, guinea hens, and ducks. The Small Axe Cafe (BYOB) serves an organic menu. ⊠ *4820 Old Post Rd., off U.S. 1* ☎ *401/364–1060* ⊕ *www. fantasticumbrellafactory.com.*

South Kingstown

10 miles northeast of Charlestown.

People often discover South Kingstown through the University of Rhode Island but return for its historic charm, arts-oriented community, great surfing beaches, and outdoors lifestyle. Almost a third of South Kingstown's 57 square miles is protected open space, allowing the town to maintain a rural character even as the population has doubled. There are two beaches, three rivers, several salt ponds, an 8-mile bike path, and numerous hiking trails, making it a great place for outdoors enthusiasts. ■ **TIP→ Locals don't refer to it as South Kingstown. They use the names of its 14 distinct villages, including Wakefield, Peace Dale, Matunuck, Snug Harbor, West Kingston, and Kingston, home of the University of Rhode Island's main campus. Note that Kingston and West Kingston omit South Kingstown's "w."**

Beaches

★ East Matunuck State Beach
BEACH—SIGHT | FAMILY | Its vigorous waves, white sands, and picnic areas account for the popularity of this 144-acre beach. Crabs, mussels, and starfish populate the rock reef that extends to the right of the strand, inspiring visitors to channel their inner marine biologist. A wind turbine provides power for the Daniel L. O'Brien Pavilion, named for a police officer killed in the line of duty while rescuing people stranded in this area during Hurricane Carol in 1954. ⚠ **Currents can be strong, so keep an eye on kids. Amenities:** food and drink; lifeguards; parking (fee); showers; toilets. **Best for:** surfing; swimming; walking; windsurfing. ✉ *950 Succotash Rd.* ☎ *401/789–8374* ⊕ *www.riparks.com/locations/locationeastmatunuck.html* ⛁ *Parking: from $6.*

South Kingstown Town Beach
BEACH—SIGHT | FAMILY | The ⅓-mile-long town beach—with a playground, a boardwalk, a volleyball court, and picnic tables—cannot be seen from the road and doesn't fill as quickly as the nearby state beaches. Surfers like this beach's waves; you can take lessons here in the summer. **Amenities:** lifeguards; parking (fee); toilets. **Best for:** sunset; surfing; swimming; walking. ✉ *719 Matunuck Beach Rd.* ☎ *401/789–9331* ⊕ *southkingstownri.com/Facilities/Facility/Details/Town-Beach-8* ☽ *Closed Labor Day–Memorial Day.*

🍴 Restaurants

★ Matunuck Oyster Bar
$$ | SEAFOOD | Shuckers are hard at work at the raw bar in this awesome waterside restaurant, an offshoot of the nearby Matunuck Oyster Farm. This year-round business committed to serving fresh, local produce, along with farm-raised and wild-caught seafood, draws a crowd—snag an outside table if you can. **Known for:** simple food, fairly priced; alfresco dining at sunset; mainly seafood menu but lots of other choices. ⑤ *Average main: $22* ✉ *629 Succotash Rd., Matunuck* ☎ *401/783–4202* ⊕ *www.rhodyoysters.com.*

Mews Tavern
$ | AMERICAN | This cheery tavern always has three bars and several dozen beers on tap, but hungry folks flock here for burgers and tasty pizzas—like the Salt Pond Oyster, which is topped with fried local oysters in a cornmeal crust. Also on the menu are Mexican dishes, chicken wings, and other comfort foods. **Known for:** going strong since 1947; appetizers, snacks, full entrées, and more; "rack of draughts" beer-tasting menu. ⑤ *Average main: $13* ✉ *456 Main St., Wakefield* ☎ *401/783–9370* ⊕ *www.mewstavern.com.*

🍸 Nightlife

For an extensive calendar of South County events pick up the free *South County Life* magazine or the weekly *Independent* newspaper.

Ocean Mist
BARS/PUBS | The Ocean Mist has a beachfront deck where you can watch surfers on the point and catch some rays while enjoying a beer, a burger, or breakfast. Bands, including rock and reggae acts, perform nightly in summer and on weekends the rest of the year. Considered one of Rhode Island's best hangouts, "the Mist," as it's called by locals, is that cool beach bar that every coastal area has—or wishes it had. ✉ *895 Matunuck Beach Rd., Matunuck* ☎ *401/782–3740* ⊕ *www.oceanmist.net.*

🎭 Performing Arts

★ Theatre By The Sea
THEATER | FAMILY | Directors, choreographers, and performers come from New York City to present a season of summer musicals, concerts, and events (including a children's festival) in an old 500-seat barn theater a quarter mile from the

ocean. This is high-quality summer stock. Arrive early for dinner at the bistro on the property and to enjoy the stunning gardens. ⊠ *364 Cards Pond Rd., Wakefield* ☎ *401/782–8587* ⊕ *www.theatrebythesea.com* 🖃 *Varied* ⊘ *Closed early Sept.–late May.*

Activities

BIKING
William C. O'Neill Bike Path
BICYCLING | FAMILY | This scenic 8-mile paved path begins at Kingston Trail Station in West Kingston and travels through farmlands, the Great Swamp, and downtown Peace Dale and Wakefield, ending at Narragansett Town Beach. Public art, including a sanctioned graffiti tunnel, decorates the path. Where it crosses Main Street in Wakefield, a comfort station with restrooms is open during daylight hours. ⊠ *1 Railroad Ave.* ☎ *401/783–8886* ⊕ *www.southcountybikepath.org.*

BOATING AND FISHING
Snug Harbor Marina
BOATING | On the docks at Snug Harbor, an annual shark tournament takes place on the weekend after July 4. You'll see mako, blue, and the occasional tiger shark being weighed in. The harbor is a fine spot for kayaking, and the marina has a fish market, arranges fishing charters, and sells bait. ⊠ *410 Gooseberry Rd., Wakefield* ☎ *401/783–7766* ⊕ *www. snugharbormarina.com.*

Narragansett

6 miles east of South Kingstown, 30 miles south of Providence.

A summer resort destination during the Victorian era, Narragansett still has as its main landmark The Towers, the last remaining section of the 1886 Narragansett Pier Casino designed by McKim, Mead & White. The town is much quieter now, but it has beautiful beaches and remains home to a large commercial fishing fleet. Take a scenic drive down Route 1A to see the ocean and grand old shingle-style homes. You'll eventually wind up at Point Judith Lighthouse, which has been in continuous operation since the 19th century.

◉ Sights

Adventureland of Narragansett
AMUSEMENT PARK/WATER PARK | FAMILY | Kids love the bumper boats, miniature golf, batting cages, a carousel, and a go-cart track, which all add up to great fun. ⊠ *112 Point Judith Rd. (Rte. 108)* ☎ *401/789–0030* ⊕ *www.adventurelandri.com* 🖃 *From $2* ⊘ *Closed mid-Oct.–mid-Apr.*

Point Judith Lighthouse
LIGHTHOUSE | From the Port of Galilee, it's a short drive to this 1857 lighthouse and a beautiful ocean view. Because the lighthouse is an active Coast Guard Station, only the grounds are open to the public. ⊠ *1470 Ocean Rd.* ☎ *401/789–0444* 🖃 *Free.*

Port of Galilee
COMMERCIAL CENTER | FAMILY | This little corner of Narragansett is a working fishing village, where you can eat at a fish shack, go for a swim at one of two state beaches, or just watch fishermen unload their catch. This is also the location of the mainland terminal for the ferry service to Block Island. ⊠ *Great Island Rd., off Galilee Escape Rd., west from Rte. 108* ☎ *401/789–1044* ⊕ *www.narragansettri. gov/383/port-of-galilee.*

South County Museum
MUSEUM | FAMILY | On part of Rhode Island's Civil War-era governor William Sprague's 19th-century estate, now a town park, this museum founded in 1933 holds 25,000 artifacts dating from pre-European settlement to the mid-20th century. Six exhibit buildings include a print shop, a smithy, a carpentry shop, and a textile arts center. A living-history farm has Romney sheep, Nubian goats,

Point Judith Lighthouse is just one of 21 such beacons in the Ocean State.

and a flock of Rhode Island Red chickens, the state bird. ■TIP→ **Attending the annual chick hatching is an Independence Day tradition for local families.** ⊠ *115 Strathmore St., off Rte. 1A* ☎ *401/783–5400* ⊕ *www.southcountymuseum.org* 🖃 *$12* ⊙ *Closed Oct.–Apr., Sun., and Mon. Also closed Tues.–Thurs. in May, June, and Sept.*

Beaches

Narragansett Town Beach

BEACH—SIGHT | This crowded and lively beach is perfect for bodysurfing, sunbathing, people-watching, sandcastle making, crab hunting, and strolling its half-mile length. A sea wall (with free on-street parking) stretches along Ocean Road and attracts an eclectic crowd, including guitarists and motorcyclists. Covering approximately 19 acres, Narragansett Town Beach has a beautiful sandy beachfront, but is the only beach in the state that charges fees for both admission and parking. **Amenities:** food and drink; lifeguards; parking (fee); showers; toilets.

Best for: surfing; swimming; walking. ■TIP→ **The beach has seven ADA surf chairs, offered on a first-come, first-served basis.** ⊠ *39 Boston Neck Rd.* ☎ *401/783–6430* ⊕ *www.narragansettri.gov* 🖃 *Beach $10; parking from $10.*

Roger W. Wheeler State Beach

BEACH—SIGHT | **FAMILY** | This beach—which some locals still call Sand Hill Cove, even though the name changed decades ago—has fine white sand, calm water, and a slight drop-off. It's a perennial favorite for parents with young children. **Amenities:** food and drink; lifeguards; parking (fee); showers; toilets. **Best for:** sunrise; sunset; swimming; walking. ⊠ *100 Sand Hill Cove Rd.* ☎ *401/789–3563* ⊕ *www.riparks.com/locations/locationrogerwheeler.html* 🖃 *Parking: from $6.*

Salty Brine State Beach

BEACH—SIGHT | **FAMILY** | Formerly known as Galilee State Beach, Salty Brine was renamed in 1990 for a Rhode Island radio legend. It's a small but popular destination, especially for families with young children. Located near the state's largest commercial fishing port of Galilee, Salty Brine is permeated with the sights, sounds, and scents of Rhode Island's daily fishing culture. The beach, near bustling seafood restaurants, provides the best seat in the state for viewing the steady parade of ferries, fishing boats, and charters moving in and out of the channel. People flock to the beach for the annual Blessing of the Fleet parade of vessels on the last weekend in July. **Amenities:** food and drink; lifeguards; parking (fee); showers; toilets. **Best for:** sunrise; sunset; swimming; walking. ⊠ *254 Great Rd.* ☎ *401/789–3563* ⊕ *www.riparks. com/Locations/LocationSaltyBrine.html* ⊠ *Parking: from $6.*

🍴 Restaurants

★ Aunt Carrie's
$$ | **SEAFOOD** | **FAMILY** | Family owned and operated for four generations, this iconic Point Judith dining hall has been a must for Rhode Islanders every summer since it opened in 1920. Its peerless location and unpretentious atmosphere are the main draws, along with comfortable favorites like clam cakes, steamers, and fish 'n' chips. **Known for:** shore dinners; delicious pies based on namesake Carrie Cooper's recipes; picnic tables and an ice-cream stand across the street. ⓢ *Average main: $19* ⊠ *1240 Ocean Rd., Point Judith* ☎ *401/783–7930* ⊕ *www. auntcarriesri.com* ☉ *Closed Oct.–Mar.*

★ Coast Guard House
$$ | **SEAFOOD** | Built in 1888 as a U.S. Life Saving Service Station, this restaurant has been nearly destroyed twice by storms—by Hurricane Bob in 1991 and Superstorm Sandy in 2012. **Known for:** raw bar and local seafood; alfresco dining on the deck; stunning view of Narragansett Bay. ⓢ *Average main: $24* ⊠ *40 Ocean Rd.* ☎ *401/789–0700* ⊕ *www. thecoastguardhouse.com.*

Crazy Burger Cafe & Juice Bar
$ | **ECLECTIC** | Vegetarians, vegans, and omnivores flock to this funky BYOB café not far from Narragansett Town Beach for smoothies, creative juice blends, and breakfast served until 4 pm daily. White Christmas lights and colorful cloth napkins are part of the decor, as is a red phone booth behind the counter that houses condiments (like the house-made ketchup). **Known for:** extensive menu; often a wait to get seated; friendly waitstaff. ⓢ *Average main: $12* ⊠ *144 Boon St.* ☎ *401/783–1810* ⊕ *www.crazyburger.com.*

★ George's of Galilee
$$ | **SEAFOOD** | Owned by the same family since 1948, this local landmark near Salty Brine State Beach serves traditional Rhode Island favorites, including clambakes and "stuffies" (stuffed quahogs), and has a raw bar. Get your fried or broiled seafood here at reasonable prices: George's buys seafood directly from fishermen in Galilee. **Known for:** alfresco dining with spectacular waterfront views; summertime takeout clam shack with beach service; live music on the deck on weekends. ⓢ *Average main: $23* ⊠ *250 Sand Hill Cove Rd., Port of Galilee* ☎ *401/783–2306* ⊕ *www.georgesofgalilee.com* ☉ *Closed Jan.–mid-Feb.*

Spain of Narragansett
$$$ | **SPANISH** | This Spanish restaurant earns high marks for superbly prepared food and deft service. Arched entryways and tall plants help create a Mediterranean mood, and in summer you can dine on a patio anchored by a three-tier fountain. **Known for:** traditional seafood paella (for two); impressive wine list—plus sangria; well-run restaurant with excellent service. ⓢ *Average main:* ⊠ *1144 Ocean Rd.* ☎ *401/783–9770* ⊕ *www.spainri.com* ☉ *Closed Mon. No lunch.*

Trio
$$ | **SEAFOOD** | Close to Narragansett's best beaches, this welcoming place emphasizes seafood and classic comfort

food favorites but also offers vegetarian and gluten-free dishes—and artisanal pizzas. Vintage photos of turn-of-the-20th-century beachgoers decorate the walls of the cool-hued dining room and expansive bar area. **Known for:** house-made pasta; patio dining in summer; special "Fast Friday" lunch menu. ⑤ *Average main: $22* ✉ *15 Kingstown Rd.* ☎ *401/792–4333* ⊕ *www.trio-ri.com* ⊙ *No lunch weekdays.*

 Hotels

★ The Break

$$ | HOTEL | Narragansett's first upscale boutique hotel has a laid-back boho surfer vibe—minus the feel of the cramped VW Vanagon—and on a clear day, you can see the Newport Bridge and Block Island from the rooftop bar. **Pros:** complimentary gourmet small-plates breakfast; Chair Five, the restaurant named after a gathering spot at the town beach, serves locally sourced seasonal cuisine; spa services available. **Cons:** a hike to the beach; small signs, you might miss it the first drive by; two-night minimum on summer weekends. ⑤ *Rooms from: $279* ✉ *1208 Ocean Rd.* ☎ *401/363–9800* ⊕ *www.thebreakhotel. com* ⇋ *16 rooms* ⫶◎⫶ *Free breakfast.*

The Richards Bed and Breakfast

$ | B&B/INN | Accomplished gardener Nancy Richards, who owns and operates this circa-1884 English-style stone mansion as a bed-and-breakfast with her husband, Steven, has created a lovely sanctuary for rest and relaxation—the lush grounds are alive with blooming color most of the year, and a koi pond and walking path to the shore add to the tranquillity. **Pros:** lots of quiet; walking path leads to rocky coast; great breakfast; only a mile from Narragansett Town Beach. **Cons:** a bit of a walk from the sandy beach; two-night minimum (four nights in August); credit cards not accepted. ⑤ *Rooms from: $180* ✉ *144 Gibson Ave.* ☎ *401/789–7746* ⊕ *www.therichardsbnb.com* ▤ *No credit cards* ⇋ *4 rooms* ⫶◎⫶ *Free breakfast.*

 Activities

FISHING

Seven B's V

FISHING | The 80-foot *Seven B's V* holds up to 113 passengers and offers daily fishing trips. ✉ *Port of Galilee Dock RR, 30 State St.* ☎ *401/789–9250, 800/371–3474* ⊕ *www.sevenbs.com.*

SURFING

Narragansett Surf and Skate Shop

SURFING | This shop rents surfboards, bodyboards, and wet suits and offers individual and group surfing or standup paddleboard lessons. ✉ *74 Narragansett Ave.* ☎ *401/789–7890* ⊕ *www.narragansettsurfandskate.com.*

WHALE-WATCHING

Lady Frances

WHALE-WATCHING | FAMILY | In July and August, whale-watching excursions aboard the 105-foot *Lady Frances* party boat take you through warm waters where you'll get a chance to spot finback whales and other species. The company also conducts fishing trips. ■TIP➜ **The family specials on Tuesday and Friday are a good deal.** ✉ *Frances Fleet, 33 State St., Point Judith* ☎ *401/783–4988* ⊕ *www. francesfleet.com* ✉ *$50.*

Jamestown

32 miles south of Providence, 5 miles west of Newport.

Surrounded by Narragansett Bay's East and West passages, Conanicut Island comprises the town of Jamestown. About 9 miles long and 1 mile wide, the island is home to beautiful state parks, historic Beavertail Lighthouse, farmland, and a downtown village with a quaint mix of shops and restaurants.

👁 Sights

Jamestown Fire Department Memorial Museum

MUSEUM | FAMILY | A working 1859 hand tub and an 1894 horse-drawn steam pump are among the antique equipment at this informal firefighting equipment display in a garage that once housed the fire company. Inquire at the fire station next door if the place is locked. ✉ *50 Narragansett Ave.* ☎ *401/423–0062* ⊕ *www.jamestownfd.com/museum.html* ⌦ *Free.*

Jamestown Windmill

WINDMILL | This English-designed smock windmill built in 1787 ground corn for more than 100 years. One of the most photographed sights on the island, the structure, named for its resemblance to farmers' smocks of yore, still works. In summer and early fall, you can enter the three-story, octagonal structure and see the 18th-century technology. ✉ *North Rd., north of Weeden La.* ☎ *401/423–0784* ⊕ *www.jamestownhistoricalsociety.org* ⊗ *Closed mid-Oct.–mid-June and weekdays.*

Watson Farm

FARM/RANCH | FAMILY | This historic New England farm, in operation since 1789, is still a working family farm. The farmers use sustainable practices to raise grass-fed beef and lamb, and to produce wool blankets for local markets. They also host educational programs; for example, during the annual Sheep Shearing Day (the second Saturday in May) you can visit the baby lambs, see the flock being shorn by local shearers, and watch spinning and weaving demonstrations. You can also stroll 2 miles of trails and view seasonal farm activities. ✉ *455 North Rd.* ☎ *401/423–0005* ⊕ *www.historicnewengland.org/property/watson-farm* ⌦ *$6* ⊗ *Closed mid-Oct.–May and Mon., Wed. Fri., Sat.*

🍴 Restaurants

Chopmist Charlie's

$$ | SEAFOOD | FAMILY | An old-school seafood house in the center of Jamestown's small commercial strip, this reliable spot serves all the regional Rhode Island favorites: stuffies, clear-broth chowder, clam cakes, steamers, and broiled or fried fish. Service is cheery and brisk. **Known for:** classic New England seafood; short walk to the marina; "Little Sailor's" menu for kids. ⑤ *Average main: $23* ✉ *40 Narragansett Ave.* ☎ *401/423–1020* ⊕ *www.chopmistcharlie.com.*

Jamestown FiSH

$$$ | SEAFOOD | This upscale Jamestown restaurant with a noteworthy wine list showcases the ocean bounty, including swordfish, striped bass, lobster, scallops, and clams. The adventurous menu changes often to reflect available fresh seafood and produce. **Known for:** steak and Wagyu burger on the menu, too; five-course tasting menu with wine pairings; no reservations for patio seating. ⑤ *Average main: $28* ✉ *14 Narragansett Ave.* ☎ *401/423–3474* ⊕ *www.jamestownfishri.com* ⊗ *Closed Tues. No lunch weekdays.*

★ Simpatico Jamestown

$$$ | AMERICAN | With nine dining rooms and a menu of seasonal classic American cuisine prepared with flair, it's tough to have a bad evening at this casually elegant restaurant. Couples looking for romance should seek out the Beech Tree room, a high-end adults-only tree fort, where seating is limited to parties of two; later, it becomes a hopping bar scene, with an incredible light show as the moon and stars sparkle through the tree leaves. **Known for:** interesting appetizers; expect to wait for a table; no reservations. ⑤ *Average main: $25* ✉ *13 Narragansett Ave.* ☎ *401/423–2000* ⊕ *www.simpaticojamestown.com* ⊗ *Closed Mon.–Tues. mid-Oct.–mid-May. No lunch.*

Hotels

East Bay Bed & Breakfast

$ | B&B/INN | This 1892 Victorian is peaceful day and night, even though it's only a block from Jamestown's two main streets and ferry wharf. **Pros:** quick, easy access to Newport; large rooms; fireplace in common area. **Cons:** small showers; only three parking spaces; no kids under 12. ⑤ *Rooms from: $185* ⊠ *14 Union St.* ☎ *401/423–0330, 800/243–1107* ⊕ *www.eastbaybnb.com* ⮡ *6 rooms* ⏸ *Free Breakfast.*

 Activities

PARKS

Beavertail State Park

PARK—SPORTS-OUTDOORS | FAMILY | Water conditions range from tranquil to harrowing at this park straddling the southern tip of Conanicut Island. On a clear, calm day, however, the park's craggy shoreline seems intended for sunning, hiking, and climbing. There are restrooms with composting toilets open daily, year-round. On several dates (May–October), the Beavertail Lighthouse Museum Association opens the 1856 **Beavertail Lighthouse,** the nation's third-oldest lighthouse, letting you climb the tower's 49 steps (and then a 7-foot ladder) to enjoy the magnificent panorama from the observation catwalk. A museum occupies the lighthouse keeper's former quarters; the lighthouse's last "beehive" Fresnel lens is on display, The old steam-engine room has a saltwater aquarium with local species of fish. Both are open seasonally. ⊠ *800 Beavertail Rd.* ☎ *401/423–3270* ⊕ *www. riparks.com/Locations/LocationBeavertail.html* ▨ *Free.*

Newport

34 miles south of Providence, 85 miles south of Boston.

The Gilded Age mansions on Bellevue Avenue are the go-to attraction for many Newport visitors. These ornate, late-19th-century "cottages," designed for very wealthy New Yorkers, are almost obscenely grand. Their owners—Vanderbilts, Astors, Belmonts, and other budding aristocrats who made Newport their summer playground for a mere six–eight weeks each year—helped establish the best young American architects and precipitated the arrival of the New York Yacht Club, which turned Newport into the sailing capital of the world.

Newport's music festivals are another draw: Bob Dylan famously went electric at the Newport Folk Festival; in recent years, the outdoor festival has featured up-and-coming and internationally known indie and folk bands. In its earlier days, the Newport Jazz Festival hosted the likes of Miles Davis and Frank Sinatra; today it remains a showcase of traditional and avant-garde jazz. The Newport Music Festival brings classical music to the mansions, many of the artists and ensembles making their American debuts.

History buffs are enthralled by the large collection of Colonial-era architecture—Trinity Episcopal Church, Touro Synagogue, and the Colony House among them—reveling in these monuments to Newport's past as a haven for believers in religious freedom.

Pedestrian-friendly Newport has so much else to offer in such a relatively small geographical area—beaches, seafood restaurants, galleries, shopping, and cultural life. Summer can be extremely busy, but fall and spring are almost as nice and far less crowded.

GETTING HERE AND AROUND

You'll need to cross at least one of four major bridges to reach Newport. The largest is the Newport Pell Bridge, spanning Narragansett Bay's East Passage via Route 138 and linking the island community of Jamestown with Newport. The toll is $4 for motorists without an EZ-Pass transponder. Newport anchors Aquidneck Island, also home to the towns of Middletown and Portsmouth. From the north end of Portsmouth, Route 24 takes you across the Sakonnet River Bridge to Tiverton. Follow Route 77 south through Tiverton to reach quiet Little Compton. From the northwestern end of Portsmouth, you cross the Mt. Hope Bridge to reach the charming town of Bristol in Bristol County, home to the oldest continuously held Independence Day parade in the country. The Jamestown Verrazzano Bridge connects Jamestown to North Kingstown over Narragansett Bay's West Passage.

FERRY TRAVEL

Visitors headed to Newport from the west can save themselves the hassle of parking in Newport, as well as the Newport Pell Bridge toll, by parking their cars for free in Jamestown and boarding the Jamestown Newport Ferry. Conanicut Marine operates the 40-foot passenger ferry from 1 East Ferry Wharf in Jamestown and offers a free shuttle service to a large parking area at nearby Taylor Point. The ferry runs daily, mid-June–early September, and on weekends, late May–mid-June and late September–mid-October. The ferry links the village of Jamestown to Rose Island, Ft. Adams State Park, Perrotti Park, and Ann Street Pier. A $23 round-trip rate is good for all day, but one-way passage rates and bicycle rates are available. Ferry service starts at 9:15 am in Jamestown, and the last run leaves Newport around 7:20 pm on weekdays and around 11 on weekends.

Oldport Marine Services operates a harbor shuttle service Monday–Thursday noon–6 and on Friday and weekends 11–7 ($12 hop on/off all day). The shuttle lands at Perrotti Park, Bowen's Wharf, Ann Street Pier, the Sail Newport dock, Ft. Adams, and Goat Island.

Seastreak Ferry Service operates seasonal ferry service (Memorial Day–Columbus Day) between Providence (India Point) and Newport (Perrotti Park). The fare is $10 each way, and parking is free at the Providence Ferry Terminal; a complimentary shuttle bus makes several trips between the ferry terminal and the train station, convention center, and downtown.

TAXI TRAVEL

Orange Cab of Newport runs a shuttle service ($25 each way) between T.F. Green Airport in Warwick and the Newport Visitors' Information Center, as well as major hotels.

PARKING

In Newport several lots around town offer pay parking. The largest and most economical is the garage behind the Newport Visitors' Information Center. Street parking can be difficult to find in summer.

FESTIVALS

★ **Newport Folk Festival**

CONCERTS | The Newport Folk Festival has been going strong since 1959, when it introduced musicians such as Joan Baez and the Kingston Trio. Held the last weekend in July, the festival's acts now span folk, blues, country, bluegrass, folk rock, alt-country, indie folk, folk punk, even reggae. Lineups mix veteran performers like Jackson Browne, Patty Griffin, and Arlo Guthrie with younger stars like Conor Oberst, Brandi Carlile, and Nathaniel Rateliff & the Night Sweats. The festival is held rain or shine, and seating is general admission on a large, uncovered lawn. Purchase tickets early: the last few festivals have sold out months in advance. ⊠ *Fort Adams State Park, 90 Fort Adams Dr.* ☎ *401/848–5055* ⊕ *www.newportfolk.org* ✉ *From $85, parking from $15.*

Newport Jazz Festival

MUSIC | The grandfather of all jazz festivals, founded in 1954, takes place on the first weekend in August. The festival showcases both jazz veterans and up-and-coming artists, playing traditional and avant-garde styles. Performers in recent years have included Esperanza Spalding, Wynton Marsalis, Dianne Reeves, Dr. John, the Maria Schneider Orchestra, and the Bad Plus with Bill Frisell. The festival is held rain or shine, with open-air lawn seating. ⊠ *Fort Adams State Park, 90 Fort Adams Dr.* 🕾 *401/848–5055, 800/745–3000* ⊕ *www. newportjazz.org* 🖅 *From $65, parking from $15.*

★ Newport Music Festival

CONCERTS | A great way to experience one of the Newport mansions is at one of the 40 or so classical music concerts presented every July during the Newport Music Festival. Morning, afternoon, evening—even midnight—performances by world-class artists are scheduled at the Elms, the Breakers, and other venues. Selected works are chosen from 19th-century chamber music, vocal repertoire, and Romantic-era piano literature. Every year features at least one American debut and a tribute to a composer—and a free family concert. ⊠ *Newport* 🕾 *401/849–0700* ⊕ *www. newportmusic.org* 🖅 *From $45.*

TOURS

More than a dozen yacht companies run tours of Newport Harbor and Narragansett Bay. Outings usually run two hours and cost about $25–$35 per person.

★ Classic Cruises of Newport

BOAT TOURS | **FAMILY** | You have your choice of two vessels at Classic Cruises of Newport: the 19th-century *Madeleine* is a 72-foot schooner that cruises around the harbor; the 1929 yacht *RumRunner II,* built for two New Jersey mobsters to carry "hooch," evokes the days of smuggling along the coast. Choose from a variety of tours, including

gorgeous sunset sails. ⊠ *24 Bannister's Wharf* 🕾 *401/847–0298* ⊕ *www.cruise-newport.com* 🖅 *From $28.*

Newport Historical Society

WALKING TOURS | Various guided walking tours focus on Newport's five centuries of American history. The 75-minute tours are available April–December, weather permitting, as well as during Winter Festival in February. ⊠ *127 Thames St.* 🕾 *401/841–8770* ⊕ *www.newporthistorytours.org* 🖅 *From $15.*

Sightsailing of Newport

BOAT TOURS | From May through mid-October, the 80-foot schooner *Aquidneck*, 40-foot sailboat *Sightsailer*, and 34-foot sailboat *Starlight* depart Bowen's Wharf on up to two-hour tours of Newport Harbor and Narragansett Bay. ⊠ *32 Bowen's Wharf* 🕾 *401/849–3333* ⊕ *www.sightsailing.com* 🖅 *From $33.*

★ Viking Tours of Newport

BUS TOURS | Viking offers 90-minute narrated trolley tours of Newport daily, April–October, and on Tuesday, Friday, and Saturday, November–March. ⊠ *44 Long Wharf Mall* 🕾 *401/847–6921* ⊕ *www. vikingtoursnewport.com* 🖅 *$39.*

ESSENTIALS

TRANSPORTATION CONTACTS Jamestown Newport Ferry ⊠ *1 E. Ferry Wharf, Jamestown* 🕾 *401/423–9900* ⊕ *www. jamestownnewportferry.com.* **Oldport Marine Services** ⊠ *1 Sayer's Wharf* 🕾 *401/847–9109* ⊕ *www.oldportmarine. com.* **Orange Cab of Newport** ⊠ *312 Connell Hwy.* 🕾 *401/841–0030* ⊕ *www.newportshuttle.com.* **Seastreak New England** ⊠ *25 India St., Providence* 🕾 *800/262–8743* ⊕ *seastreak.com.*

VISITOR INFORMATION Discover Newport 🕾 *401/849–8048, 800/326–6030* ⊕ *www. gonewport.com.*

Sights

DOWNTOWN NEWPORT AND HISTORIC HILL

Downtown Newport and, just beyond, the city's Historic Hill neighborhood are the city's Colonial heart. More than 200 pre-Revolutionary buildings, mostly private residences, remain on the streets running uphill from Newport Harbor; but you'll also encounter landmarks such as St. Mary's Church, at the corner of Spring Street and Memorial Boulevard West, where John Fitzgerald Kennedy and Jacqueline Bouvier were married on September 12, 1953. The waterfront is beautiful, and there are many boutiques and restaurants on the very active wharfs that jut into the harbor. In summer, traffic is thick and narrow one-way streets can be frustrating to navigate; consider parking in a pay lot and exploring the area on foot.

Colony House

HISTORIC SITE | Completed in 1739, this National Historic Landmark on Washington Square was the center of political activity in Colonial Newport. The Declaration of Independence was read from its steps on July 20, 1776, and British troops later used this structure as a barracks during their occupation of Newport. In 1781, George Washington met here with the French general Rochambeau, cementing an alliance that led to the American victory at Yorktown. Colony House served as Rhode Island's primary statehouse until 1901, when the new statehouse opened in Providence. The Newport Historical Society manages the Colony House and offers guided tours. ⊠ *Washington Sq.* ☎ *401/846–2980* ⊕ *newporthistory.org* 🖼 *Walking tour $15.*

Great Friends Meeting House

BUILDING | The oldest surviving house of worship in Rhode Island reflects the quiet reserve and steadfast faith of Colonial Quakers, who gathered here to discuss theology, peaceful alternatives to war, and the abolition of slavery. Built in 1699, the two-story shingle structure has wide-plank floors, simple benches, a balcony, and a wood-beam ceiling. ⊠ *21 Farewell St.* ☎ *401/846–0813* ⊕ *newporthistory.org* 🖼 *Tour $8.*

Hunter House

HOUSE | The oldest house owned and maintained by the Preservation Society of Newport County, constructed between 1748 and 1759, Hunter House served as the Revolutionary War headquarters of French admiral Charles Louis d'Arsac de Ternay after the home's Loyalist owner fled the city. Featuring a balustraded gambrel roof and heavy stud construction, it is an excellent example of early Georgian Colonial architecture. The carved pineapple over the doorway was a symbol of welcome throughout Colonial America. A collection of Colonial furniture includes pieces crafted by Newport's famed 18th-century Townsend-Goddard family of cabinetmakers and paintings by Cosmo Alexander, Gilbert Stuart, and Samuel King. The house is named for Ambassador William Hunter, President Andrew Jackson's chargé d'affaires in Brazil. ⊠ *54 Washington St.* ☎ *401/847–1000* ⊕ *www.newportmansions.org* 🖼 *$30* ⊗ *Closed mid-Oct.–mid-May.*

Museum of Newport History at Brick Market

MUSEUM | FAMILY | The restored 1762 Brick Market building on Washington Square houses the Museum of Newport History that explores the city's social and economic influences. Antiques such as the printing press of James Franklin (Ben's brother) inspire the imagination. Designed by Peter Harrison, who was responsible as well for the Touro Synagogue and the Redwood Library, the building also served as a theater and a town hall. Today, besides the museum exhibits, there's a very nice gift shop and the Newport Visitors' Information Center, which is a departure points for guided walking tours of Newport. ⊠ *127 Thames St.* ☎ *401/841–8770* ⊕ *www.newporthistorical.org* 🖼 *$4 donation.*

Newport Art Museum

MUSEUM | Founded in 1912, the museum today spans three buildings: the Cushing Gallery, the Coleman Center for Creative Studies, and the 1864 Griswold House, a National Historic Landmark designed by Richard Morris Hunt. In the museum's permanent collection are works by Fitz Henry Lane, George Inness, William Trost Richards, John La Farge, Nancy Elizabeth Prophet, Gilbert Stuart, and Helena Sturtevant, as well as contemporary artists like Dale Chihuly, Howard Ben Tré, and Joseph Norman. ⊠ *76 Bellevue Ave.* ☎ *401/848–8200* ⊕ *www.newportartmuseum.org* ⌚ *$15* ⊙ *Closed Mon.*

Redwood Library & Athenaeum

HISTORIC SITE | In 1747, Abraham Redwood gave 500 pounds sterling to found a library of arts and sciences; three years later, this Georgian Palladian–style building opened with 751 titles. More than half of the original collection vanished during the British occupation of Newport, though most of it has been recovered or replaced. Paintings on display include five portraits by Gilbert Stuart. Look for the portrait of the Colonial governor's wife, whose low neckline later led to the commissioning of Stuart's daughter, Jane, to paint a bouquet over her cleavage. A 35-minute guided tour, included with admission, is offered daily at 10:30 am. The library presents talks by authors, musicians, and historians. ⊠ *50 Bellevue Ave.* ☎ *401/847–0292* ⊕ *www.redwoodlibrary.org* ⌚ *$10.*

★ Touro Synagogue

HISTORIC SITE | In 1658, more than a dozen Jewish families whose ancestors had fled Spain and Portugal during the Inquisition founded a congregation in Newport. A century later, Peter Harrison designed this two-story Palladian house of worship for them. George Washington wrote a famous letter to the group in which he pledged the new American nation "would give to bigotry no sanction, to persecution no assistance." The oldest surviving synagogue in the country, Touro was dedicated in 1763 and its simple exterior and elegant interior remain virtually unchanged. A small trapdoor in the platform upon which the Torah is read symbolizes the days of persecution when Jews were forced to worship in secret. The John L. Loeb Visitors Center has two floors of state-of-the-art exhibits on early American Jewish life and Newport's Colonial history. ■**TIP→ Tickets, available at the Loeb Visitors Center, are required for entry into the synagogue.** ⊠ *Loeb Visitors Center, 52 Spring St.* ☎ *401/847–4794* ⊕ *www.tourosynagogue.org* ⌚ *$12* ⌖ *No tours on Jewish holidays.*

Trinity Episcopal Church

CEMETERY | George Washington once sat in the distinguished visitor pew close to this church's distinctive three-tier wineglass pulpit. Completed in 1726, this structure is similar to Boston's Old North Church; both were inspired by the designs of Sir Christopher Wren. Trinity's 1733 London-made organ is believed to be the first big pipe organ in the 13 colonies. Among those buried in the churchyard's historic cemetery is French admiral d'Arsac de Ternay, commander of the allied French Navy in Newport, who was buried with special permission in 1780 as there were then no Roman Catholic cemeteries in New England. ⊠ *Queen Anne Sq., 141 Spring St.* ☎ *401/846–0660* ⊕ *www.trinitynewport.org* ⌚ *$5 donation* ⊙ *No tours during parish events and Mon.–Sat. in Nov.–late May.*

Wanton-Lyman-Hazard House

HISTORIC SITE | As Newport's oldest surviving house, built circa 1697, this residence provides a glimpse of the city's Colonial and Revolutionary history. The dark-red building was the site of the city's Stamp Act riot of 1765. After the British Parliament levied a tax on most printed material, the Sons of Liberty stormed the house, which was then occupied by a prominent Loyalist. ⊠ *17 Broadway* ☎ *401/846–3622* ⊕ *newporthistory.org* ⌚ *Walking tour $15.*

Easton Pond

Green End Pond

Easton Bay

Cliff Walk (Begins)

| 0 | 250 yards |
| 0 | 250 meters |

Colonial Newport

Established in 1639 by a small band of religious dissenters led by William Coddington and Nicholas Easton, Newport became a haven for those who believed in religious freedom. The deepwater harbor at the mouth of Narragansett Bay ensured Newport's success as a major Colonial port, and a building boom produced hundreds of houses and many landmarks that still survive. These include the Wanton-Lyman-Hazard House and the White Horse Tavern, both built during the 17th century, plus Trinity Episcopal Church, Touro Synagogue, Colony House, and the Redwood Library, all built in the 18th century.

War and Peace

British troops occupied Newport from 1776 to 1779, causing half the city's population to flee and the end of a golden age of prosperity. The economic downturn that followed peace may not have been so great for Newport's citizens, but it certainly played a part in preserving Newport's architectural heritage; few owners had the capital to raze buildings and replace them with bigger and better ones.

BELLEVUE AVENUE AND BEYOND

South of Newport Harbor and the historic part of town, you begin to discover stunning, opulent mansions along Bellevue Avenue and its ocean-facing side streets. These "summer cottages" were built by wealthy families in the late 1800s and early 1900s as seasonal residences.

Audrain Automobile Museum

MUSEUM | The museum's collection includes more than 160 rare, fully restored automobiles dating from 1899 to the present day. The selection of vehicles on display varies—hot rods, super cars, and pre-World War II specimens are among past exhibition topics. ✉ *222 Bellevue Ave.* ☎ *401/856–4420* ⊕ *www.audrainautomuseum.org* 💲 *$12.*

Belcourt Castle

HOUSE | Richard Morris Hunt based his design for this 60-room mansion, built in 1894 for wealthy bachelor Oliver H.P. Belmont, on the hunting lodge of Louis XIII. Billionaire founder and CEO of Alex & Ani, Carolyn Rafaelian, a native Rhode Islander, purchased Belcourt in 2012 and has been working to restore the home to its former glory in an eco-conscious way, employing solar panels and thermal-heating-and-cooling systems. On a restoration tour, which takes about 45 minutes followed by a 15-minute Q&A session, you can admire the stained glass, carved wood, and chandeliers—one of which has 20,000 pieces and another that weighs 460 pounds and was originally held up by a single nail. ✉ *657 Bellevue Ave.* 💲 *$18* 🕐 *Closed Mon. and Tues.*

★ The Breakers

HOUSE | The 70-room summer estate of Cornelius Vanderbilt II, chairman and president of the New York Central Railroad, was built in 1895. Architect Richard Morris Hunt modeled the four-story residence after 16th-century Italian Renaissance palaces. This mansion is not only big, but grand—be sure to look for the sculpted figures tucked above the pillars. The interior includes rare marble, alabaster, and gilded rooms with open-air terraces that reveal magnificent ocean views. Noteworthy are a blue marble fireplace, rose alabaster pillars in the dining room, and a porch with a mosaic ceiling that took six months for Italian artisans, lying on their backs, to install. ✉ *44 Ochre Point Ave.* ☎ *401/847–1000* ⊕ *www.newportmansions.org* 💲 *$24.*

★ Chateau-sur-Mer

HOUSE | Built in 1852 for William Shepard Wetmore, a merchant in the China Trade, the palatial Chateau-sur-Mer, a landmark of High Victorian architecture, was Newport's first grand residence. In 1857, Wetmore threw an extravagant, unprecedented "country picnic" for more than 2,000 people, ushering in the Gilded Age in Newport. The house is a treasure trove of Victorian architecture, furniture, wallpapers, ceramics, and stenciling; see hand-carved Italian woodwork, Chinese porcelains, and Japanese and Egyptian Revival wallpapers. The grounds contain rare trees imported from Mongolia. ⊠ *474 Bellevue Ave.* ☎ *401/847–1000* ⊕ *www. newportmansions.org* ⊠ *$18* ⊙ *Closed mid-Nov.–mid-Mar.*

Chepstow

HOUSE | Though only slightly less grand than some of the other Newport mansions, this Italianate-style villa with a mansard roof houses a remarkable collection of art and furniture gathered by the Morris family of New York City. Its significant 19th-century American paintings include Hudson River landscapes. Built in 1861, the home was designed by George Champlin Mason, a Newport architect for Edmund Schermerhorn, a descendent of one of the first settlers of New Netherland and first cousin of Mrs. William Astor. ⊠ *120 Narragansett Ave.* ☎ *401/847–1000* ⊕ *www.newportmansions.org* ⊠ *$18* ⊙ *Closed mid-Oct.–Apr. and weekdays May, June, Sept.*

★ Cliff Walk

TRAIL | See the "backyards" of Newport's famous Gilded Age mansions while strolling along this 3½-mile public walkway atop an oceanfront cliff. The designated National Recreation Trail stretches from Memorial Boulevard at the western end of Easton's Beach (also called First Beach) south to the eastern end of Bailey's Beach. Along the way you'll pass Salve Regina University's Ochre Court, the Breakers, Forty Steps

at Narragansett Avenue, Rosecliff, and Marble House and its Chinese Tea House. Park on either Memorial Boulevard or Narragansett Avenue. The trail is relatively flat and easily walkable, although some parts are unpaved and rocky. ∎ **TIP➜ Apply sunscreen, wear comfortable rubber-soled shoes, and bring your own water.** ⊠ *Memorial Blvd.* ☎ *401/845–5300* ⊕ *www.cliffwalk.com* ⊠ *Free.*

★ The Elms

HOUSE | Architect Horace Trumbauer modeled this imposing 48-room French neoclassical home and its grounds after the Château d'Asnières near Paris. The Elms was built in 1901 for Edward Julius Berwind, a coal baron from Philadelphia and New York. It was one of the first Newport mansions to be fully electrified. At the foot of the 10-acre estate is a spectacular sunken garden, marble pavilions, and fountains. The Behind the Scenes tour, which offers a glimpse into the lives of the Elms' staff members and the operation of facilities like the boiler room and kitchen, is one of the best of any of the mansion tours. ⊠ *367 Bellevue Ave.* ☎ *401/847–1000* ⊕ *www. newportmansions.org* ⊠ *$18* ⊙ *Closed Jan.–mid-Feb.*

Fort Adams State Park

BEACH—SIGHT | FAMILY | The largest coastal fortress in the United States can be found at this park, which hosts Newport's annual folk and jazz festivals and sailing events like the Volvo Ocean Race. From mid-May through mid-October, the nonprofit Ft. Adams Trust offers daily guided tours of the fort, where soldiers lived from 1824 to 1950. Tours take in the fort's overlooks and underground tunnels, as well as its impressive walls. The views of Newport Harbor and Narragansett Bay are exquisite. ⊠ *90 Fort Adams Dr.* ☎ *401/841–0707* ⊕ *www.fortadams.org* ⊠ *Park free, tour $12.*

Continued on page 392

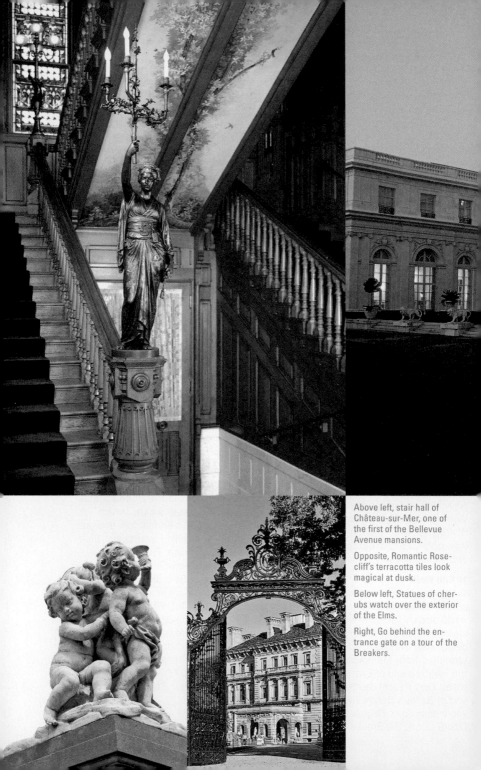

Above left, stair hall of Château-sur-Mer, one of the first of the Bellevue Avenue mansions.

Opposite, Romantic Rosecliff's terracotta tiles look magical at dusk.

Below left, Statues of cherubs watch over the exterior of the Elms.

Right, Go behind the entrance gate on a tour of the Breakers.

The Mansions of Newport

GILDED AGE GEMS

By Andrew Collins, Debbie Harmsen, and Janine Weisman

Would you call a home with 70 rooms a cottage? If not, you're obviously not Cornelius Vanderbilt II. The Breakers, the "summer cottage" of the 19th-century multimillionaire, is one of the elaborate mansions in Newport that are now among the city's top attractions. Many of the homes are open to the public for tours, giving you a peek into the lives of the privileged.

THE SOCIAL SCENE

The Breakers dining room, just one of the opulent mansion's 70 rooms.

To truly appreciate a visit to Newport's mansions, you need to understand the times and the players—those who built these opulent homes and summered here for six weeks a year.

Newport at the turn of the 20th century was where the socialites of Boston, New York, and Philadelphia came for the summer. They were among the richest people in America at the time—from railroad tycoons and coal barons to plantation owners.

The era during which they lived here, the late 1800s through the 1920s, is often referred to as the Gilded Age, a term coined by Mark Twain and co-author Charles Dudley Warner in a book by the same name. It was a time when who you knew was everything. Caroline Schermerhorn Astor was the queen of New York and Newport society; her list of the "Four Hundred" was the first social register. Three übersocialites were Alva Vanderbilt Belmont, Mary Ann (Mamie) Fish, and Tessie Oelrichs. These ladies who seriously lunched threw most of *the* parties in Newport.

While the women gossiped, planned soirées, and dressed and redressed throughout the summer days, the men were usually off yachting.

In terms of the deepest pockets, the two heavyweight families during Newport's Gilded Age were the Vanderbilts and the Astors.

Madeleine Force was only 18 when she married John Jacob Astor IV at the Beechwood mansion in 1911; he was 47. Just seven months later, he perished aboard the Titanic; she survived.

LEADING FAMILIES

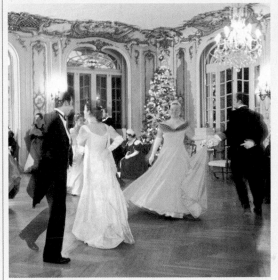

Beechwood will soon be reinvented as an art museum.

Alva Vanderbilt Belmont

Cornelius Vanderbilt

John Jacob Astor IV

John Jacob Astor

THE VANDERBILTS Cornelius Vanderbilt I, known as Commodore Vanderbilt, built his empire on steamships and railroads. He had amassed more than $100 million before he died in 1877. He bequeathed most of it to his son William Henry, who, also shrewd in the railroading business, nearly doubled the family fortune over the next decade. William Henry Vanderbilt willed $70 million to his son, Cornelius Vanderbilt II, who became the chairman and president of New York Central Railroad; and $55 million to son William K. Vanderbilt, who also managed railroads for a while and saw his yacht, *The Defender*, win the America's Cup in 1895. One of Cornelius Vanderbilt II's sons, Alfred Gwynne Vanderbilt, died on the *Lusitania*, which sank three years after his great-grandfather perished on the *Titanic*. **Visit:** The Breakers, Marble House.

THE ASTORS Meanwhile, in the Astor camp, John Jacob Astor IV, who also perished on the *Titanic*, had the riches his great-granddad had made in the fur trade as well as his own millions earned from successful real estate ventures, including New York City hotels such as the St. Regis and the Astoria (later the Waldorf–Astoria). His mother was Caroline Astor. Her mansion, Beechwood, is now owned by Oracle CEO Larry Ellison.

WHICH MANSION SHOULD I VISIT?

Even though the Newport "summer cottages" were inhabited for only six weeks each year, it would take you almost that long to explore all the grand rooms and manicured grounds. Each mansion has its own style and unique features. Here are the characteristics of each to help you choose those you'd like to visit:

★ **The Breakers:** The most opulent; enormous Italian Renaissance mansion built by Cornelius Vanderbilt II; tours are often big and very crowded; open all year.

Château-sur-Mer: The prettiest gardens and grounds; High Victorian–style mansion built in 1852; remodeled and redecorated in 1870s by architect Richard Morris Hunt; open most of the year.

Chepstow: Italianate villa built in 1860, with a fine collection of art; a bit less wow factor; open May–October.

★ **The Elms:** A French chateau-style home with 10 acres of stunningly restored gardens; new guided servant quarters tour takes you into a hidden dormitory, roof, and basement; open most of the year.

Hunter House: Georgian-style home with Colonial furnishings; waterfront location, not on Bellevue Avenue; pricey admission; open May–October.

Isaac Bell House: Magnificent American Shingle, Queen Anne-style, mansion; period-appropriate furnishings display in an unusual mix of influences; less visited; open May–October.

Kingscote: Gothic Revival–style home includes an early Tiffany glass-brick wall; the first of the summer cottages built in 1839; open May–October.

★ **Marble House:** Outrageously opulent and sometimes crowded; the other Vanderbilt home inspired by Petit Trianon in Versailles; tour at your own pace with a digital audio tour; open most of the year.

Rosecliff: Romantic 1902 mansion; modeled after Grand Trianon in Versailles; somewhat crowded tours; open most of the year.

MANSION TOURS

Preservation Society of Newport County. The Preservation Society maintains 11 historic properties and the Newport Mansions Store on Bannister's Wharf. Both guided tours and audio tours are available; you can purchase a combination ticket to see multiple properties for a substantial discount. The hours and days the houses are open in fall and winter vary. ☎ 401/847–1000 ⊕ www.newportmansions.org. ✉ The Newport Mansions Experience (admission to any 5 properties excluding Hunter House) $35.

Rough Point: 1889 English manor–style mansion built by Frederick Vanderbilt, later owned and furnished by Doris Duke; small-group or self-guided tours; open April–November.

Portrait of Mrs. Cornelius Vanderbilt II circa 1880, The Breakers.

Consider viewing mansions from the Cliff Walk for a different perspective.

Marble House at night.

TOP EXPERIENCE

★ **Cliff Walk.** See the backyards of Newport's famous oceanfront Gilded Age mansions while strolling along this 3½-mile public access walkway. The designated National Recreation Trail stretches from Memorial Boulevard at the west end of Easton's Beach (also called First Beach) southerly to the east end of Bailey's Beach. Along the way you'll pass the Breakers, Rosecliff, and Marble House and its Chinese Tea House. The north half of the walk is paved but the trail turns to large flat boulders south of Ruggles Avenue. Be prepared for increasingly rough terrain not suitable for small children, strollers, or people with mobility problems. Park on either Memorial Boulevard or Narragansett Avenue.

★ International Tennis Hall of Fame

MUSEUM | FAMILY | Tennis fans and lovers of history, art, and architecture will enjoy visiting the birthplace of American lawn tennis. The museum contains interactive exhibits, a holographic theater that simulates being in a room with Roger Federer, displays of clothing worn by the sport's biggest stars, video highlights of great matches, and memorabilia that includes the 1874 patent from England's Queen Victoria for the game of lawn tennis. The 6-acre site is home to the Bill Talbert Stadium with its manicured grass courts, the historic shingle-style Newport Casino—which opened in 1880 and was designed by architects McKim, Mead & White—and the recently restored Casino Theatre. The 13 grass tennis courts, one clay court, and an indoor tennis facility are open to the public for play. ⊠ *194 Bellevue Ave.* ☎ *401/849–3990* ⊕ *www. tennisfame.com* ✉ *$15* ⊙ *Closed Tues. in Jan.–Mar.*

Isaac Bell House

HOUSE | Revolutionary in design when it was completed in 1883, the shingle-style Isaac Bell House combines Old English and European architecture with Colonial American and exotic details, such as a sweeping open floor plan and bamboo-style porch columns. McKim, Mead & White of New York City designed the home for Isaac Bell, a wealthy cotton broker. ⊠ *70 Perry St., at Bellevue Ave.* ☎ *401/847–1000* ⊕ *www. newportmansions.org* ✉ *$18* ⊙ *Closed mid-Oct.–mid-May.*

Kingscote

HOUSE | Among Newport's first summer cottages, this 1841 Gothic Revival mansion designed by Richard Upjohn was built for George Noble Jones, a Georgia plantation owner. The house is named for its second owners, the King family, one of whose members hired McKim, Mead & White to expand and redesign it. The dining room, one of the 1881 additions, contains a cork ceiling and one of the first installations of Tiffany glass

Scenic Drive

Ocean Drive. Also called Ten-Mile Drive, this is a stunningly scenic route from Bellevue Avenue at Memorial Boulevard south to Ocean Avenue and out to Castle Hill Avenue, Ridge Road, and Harrison Avenue. You'll pass by Ft. Adams State Park and President Eisenhower's "summer White House"; Hammersmith Farm, Jacqueline Bouvier Kennedy Onassis' family home and the site of her wedding reception when she married John F. Kennedy in 1953; and, about halfway along, the 89-acre Brenton Point State Park.

windows. Furnishings reflect the King family's involvement in the China Trade. ⊠ *253 Bellevue Ave.* ☎ *401/847–1000* ⊕ *www.newportmansions.org* ✉ *$18* ⊙ *Closed mid-Oct.–mid-May.*

★ Marble House

HOUSE | One of the most opulent of the Newport mansions, Marble House contains 500,000 cubic feet of marble (valued at $7 million when the house was built from 1888 to 1892). William Vanderbilt, grandson of Commodore Cornelius Vanderbilt, gave Marble House to his wife, Alva, as a gift for her 39th birthday. The house was designed by the architect Richard Morris Hunt, who took inspiration from the Petit Trianon at Versailles. The Vanderbilts divorced three years later, in 1895. Alva married Oliver H.P. Belmont and moved down the street to Belcourt Castle. After his death, she reopened Marble House and had the Chinese Tea House built on the back lawn, where she hosted "Votes for Women" rallies. ⊠ *596 Bellevue Ave.* ☎ *401/847–1000* ⊕ *www. newportmansions.org* ✉ *$18.*

National Museum of American Illustration

MUSEUM | This museum exhibits original work by Norman Rockwell, J.C.

Leyendecker, Maxfield Parrish, N.C. Wyeth, and 150 others spanning the "Golden Age of American Illustration" (1895–1945). All 323 printed *Saturday Evening Post* covers are on display. The 1898 Beaux Arts-style building, an adaptation of an 18th-century French château, was designed by the same architects responsible for the New York Public Library and other landmarks; Frederick Law Olmsted designed the adjacent grounds. ✉ *492 Bellevue Ave.* ☎ *401/851–8949* ⊕ *www.americanillustration.org* 🎫 *$18.*

Norman Bird Sanctuary

NATURE PRESERVE | FAMILY | Stroll through the woods or hike to the top of Hanging Rock for a spectacular view at this 325-acre sanctuary for more than 300 species of birds, plus deer, foxes, mink, turtles, and rabbits. The sanctuary has about 7 miles of trails. A 19th-century barn holds the visitor center, whose wildlife and ecosystem exhibits document Rhode Island's natural history. ■**TIP**➔ **The raucous dawn chorus of birdsong in the spring is one of the great wildlife experiences in Rhode Island.** ✉ *583 3rd Beach Rd., Middletown* ☎ *401/846–2577* ⊕ *www.normanbirdsanctuary.org* 🎫 *$7.*

Rosecliff

HOUSE | Newport's most romantic mansion was commissioned by Tessie Hermann Oelrichs, who inherited a Nevada silver fortune from her father. Stanford White modeled the 1902 palace after the Grand Trianon at Versailles. Rosecliff has a heart-shaped staircase and Newport's largest private ballroom. Rosecliff stayed in the Oelrichs family until 1941, went through several ownership changes, and then was purchased by Mr. and Mrs. J. Edgar Monroe of New Orleans in 1947. The Monroes were known for throwing big parties. Scenes from the films *The Great Gatsby* (1974), *True Lies* (1994), and *Amistad* (1997) were shot here. ✉ *548 Bellevue Ave.* ☎ *401/847–1000* ⊕ *www.newportmansions.org* 🎫 *$18* ☾ *Closed Nov.*

★ Rough Point Museum

HOUSE | Tobacco heiress, philanthropist, and preservationist Doris Duke furnished her 39,000-square-foot English manorial–style house at the southern end of Bellevue Avenue with family treasures and fine art and antiques purchased on her world travels. Highlights include paintings by Renoir, Van Dyck, and Gainsborough, numerous Chinese porcelains, Turkish carpets and Belgian tapestries, and a suite of Louis XVI chairs. Duke's two camels, Baby and Princess (who came with an airplane she had purchased from a Middle Eastern businessman), once summered here on the expansive grounds designed by landscape architect Frederick Law Olmsted. Duke bequeathed the oceanfront house with all of its contents to the Newport Restoration Foundation to operate as a museum after her death. Each year, the foundation assembles an exhibit devoted to Duke's lifestyle and interests, which is included with a guided tour. ✉ *680 Bellevue Ave.* ☎ *401/847–8344* ⊕ *www. newportrestoration.org* 🎫 *$25.*

Beaches

Easton's Beach (*First Beach*)

BEACH—SIGHT | A ¾-mile-long surfing beach, Easton's has a boardwalk, vintage carousel, aquarium, and playground. Public facilities include restrooms, indoor and outdoor showers, a skate park, an elevator, and beach wheelchairs for people with disabilities. The snack bar's twin lobster rolls are very popular (and a great deal). **Amenities:** food and drink; lifeguards; parking (fee); showers; toilets. **Best for:** sunrise; sunset; swimming; walking. ✉ *175 Memorial Blvd.* ☎ *401/845–5810* ⊕ *www.cityofnewport. com/departments/easton-s-beach.*

Sachuest Beach (*Second Beach*)

BEACH—SIGHT | The western end of this 1¼-mile-long sandy beach attracts many surfers. Surfboard and standup paddleboard rentals are available.

Amenities: food and drink; lifeguards; parking (fee); showers; toilets. **Best for:** surfing; swimming; walking; windsurfing. ⊠ *474 Sachuest Point Rd., Middletown* ☎ *401/849–2822* ⊕ *beach. middletownri.com/.*

Third Beach

BEACH—SIGHT | Located at the mouth of the Sakonnet River, Third Beach is more peaceful than the nearby ocean beaches and a great spot for families. It has grills, picnic tables, and a shade structure near the boat ramp. Third Beach is a favorite of windsurfers. You'll find a mobile concession stand on weekends. **Amenities:** parking (fee); lifeguards. **Best for:** swimming; walking; windsurfing. ⊠ *3rd Beach Rd., Middletown* ☎ *401/849–2822* ⊕ *beach. middletownri.com/.*

 Restaurants

DOWNTOWN NEWPORT AND HISTORIC HILL

The Black Pearl

$$$ | SEAFOOD | Choose your ambience at this mainstay on the Newport waterfront: the posh, forest-green Commodore Room (jacket required and reservations essential) features country pâté, escargots, rack of lamb, roast duck with Modena sauce, and other classic offerings; for a more casual experience, with standard American fare like salads, burgers, and grilled meat or fish, visit Tavern (no reservations accepted), where old nautical maps hang on the walls. **Known for:** popular dining spot for nearly a half century; raw bar and clam chowder at the very casual outdoor patio; chowder to go—by the quart or half gallon. ⑤ *Average main: $32* ⊠ *Bannister's Wharf* ☎ *401/846–5264* ⊕ *www.blackpearl-newport.com* ۞ *Closed Jan.–mid-Mar.* ⋒ *Jacket required.*

★ Clarke Cooke House

$$$$ | AMERICAN | Drinks at a bar favored by the sailing crowd, intimate dinners by the fire, and relaxing lunches overlooking Newport Harbor are a few of the experiences possible at this multilevel complex. The first-floor Candy Store serves casual fare and has a sushi bar; the second floor offers casual dining in the Bistro and cocktails on the Midway; and the Porch and Club Room on the third floor have elegant fine dining requiring proper dress. **Known for:** clam chowder—"best in the city"; "Snowball in Hell" ice cream dessert; busy, busy, busy place. ⑤ *Average main: $48* ⊠ *26 Bannister's Wharf* ☎ *401/849–2900* ⊕ *www.clarkecooke.com.*

Fluke Newport

$$$ | SEAFOOD | Handcrafted cocktails made with freshly pressed juices, along with one or more appetizers, are the best way to start your meal at this hot spot. Entrées focus on local seafood—maybe roasted monkfish, crispy striped bass, pan-seared skate, and (of course) fluke. **Known for:** menu changes frequently to reflect local markets; steak, chicken, and seared duck breast for landlubbers; extensive wine list. ⑤ *Average main: $32* ⊠ *33 Bannister's Wharf* ☎ *401/849–7778* ⊕ *www.fluke-newport.com* ۞ *Closed Jan.–mid-Feb. and Sun.–Wed. mid-Nov.–Apr. No lunch.*

Franklin Spa

$ | AMERICAN | A local landmark where the line trails out the door on summer weekend mornings, this no-frills diner serves satisfying breakfasts (and lunches, too) worth the wait. The Portuguese Sailor (grilled chouriço and egg with melted cheese on sweet Portuguese bread) is a house specialty. **Known for:** fresh-squeezed orange juice; fruit smoothies; friendly service. ⑤ *Average main: $8* ⊠ *229 Spring St.* ☎ *401/847–3540* ▭ *No credit cards.*

Mission

$ | AMERICAN | Head to this small, unpretentious restaurant for the best burgers in town. Made from beef ground in-house, they come with lettuce, raw onion, and aioli ketchup—but you can add bacon, cheese, caramelized-onion sauerkraut, slaw, grilled jalapeños, and other toppings. **Known for:** limited menu;

hand-cut fries; house-made hot dogs and popsicles, too. $ *Average main: $10* ✉ *29 Marlborough St.* ☎ *401/619–5560* ⊕ *www.missionnpt.com* ☺ *Closed Mon.* ▤ *No credit cards.*

Restaurant Bouchard

$$$ | FRENCH | Regional variations on French cuisine are the focus at this upscale yet laid-back establishment inside a gambrel-roof 1785 Colonial. Nightly specials are based on the fresh catch from Rhode Island waters, which may include scallops, swordfish, and clams. **Known for:** excellent dining, excellent service; extensive wine list; no children under age seven. $ *Average main: $35* ✉ *505 Thames St.* ☎ *401/846–0123* ⊕ *www.bouchardnewport.com* ☺ *Closed Tues. No lunch.*

Salvation Café

$$ | CAFÉ | Vegetarians and red-meat fanatics alike can easily find a dish to love at this funky lounge and eatery adored by local hipsters for its lighthearted vibe. You could build a meal around starters such as the roasted beet salad or shrimp and grits with applewood bacon, while the vegetarian pad Thai, bistro fillet, and teriyaki salmon are solid entrées. **Known for:** "craft-on-draft" beers; lavish desserts; alfresco seating at the mojito bar. $ *Average main: $22* ✉ *140 Broadway* ☎ *401/847–2620* ⊕ *www.salvationcafe.com* ☺ *No lunch.*

★ 22 Bowen's Wine Bar & Grille

$$$$ | STEAKHOUSE | Excellent service, world-class steaks, and an extensive, award-winning wine list make dinner here a memorable experience. Although the restaurant is known for its steaks—and it's impossible to go wrong ordering one—you'll find plenty of choices if you're in the mood for something from the sea. **Known for:** steaks, chops, and fresh local seafood; choose one of 11 sauces/butters to accompany your steak; gluten-free menus. $ *Average main: $38* ✉ *22 Bowen's Wharf* ☎ *401/841–8884* ⊕ *www.22bowens.com.*

The White Horse Tavern

$$$ | AMERICAN | The first tavern opened here in 1673—and ever since, the premises have served, in turn, as a tavern, boardinghouse, restaurant, and even a meetinghouse for Colonial Rhode Island's General Assembly. Today, the tavern provides an intimate fine-dining experience, the mood set by the low dark-beam ceilings, cavernous fireplace, and uneven plank floors. **Known for:** beef Wellington, fresh seafood, just-picked produce; extensive wine list; "business casual" dress required at dinner. $ *Average main: $32* ✉ *26 Marlborough St.* ☎ *401/849–3600* ⊕ *www.whitehorsenewport.com.*

BELLEVUE AVENUE AND BEYOND
★ Castle Hill Inn

$$$$ | AMERICAN | No other restaurant in Newport can compete with the spectacular water views from the Sunset Room, one of four dining rooms inside the historic main inn. A perfect spot for a romantic dinner, Castle Hill also serves lunch, allowing you to savor ethereal cuisine while watching sunlit clouds drift by. **Known for:** New England food done well; three-, four-, or six-course prix-fixe dinner menu; Sunday brunch. $ *Average main: $82* ✉ *590 Ocean Dr.* ☎ *888/466–1355, 401/849–3800* ⊕ *www.castlehillinn.com.*

Flo's Clam Shack

$$ | SEAFOOD | FAMILY | With an old boat in front, peeling paint, and a bamboo-lined walkway leading to the order windows, this local institution across from Easton's Beach is as casual as they come. Lobster rolls, fried seafood, steamed clams, clam cakes, cold beer, and a great raw bar make for long lines in summer. **Known for:** the best fried clams—ever; seafood, chilled lobster, and other dishes served at the upstairs bar; outdoor seating is available. $ *Average main: $18* ✉ *4 Wave Ave., Middletown* ☎ *401/847–8141* ⊕ *www.flosclamshacks.com* ▤ *No credit cards* ☺ *Closed Mon., Tues., and Nov.– early Mar.*

Hotels

DOWNTOWN NEWPORT AND HISTORIC HILL

Admiral Fitzroy Inn

$$ | B&B/INN | The restful retreat in the heart of Newport's bustling waterfront district was once a convent in a different location—the tidy 1854 Victorian building was dismantled in 1986 and rebuilt to its original size and style in its current location. **Pros:** elevator service to first three floors; close to shops, restaurants, and bars; complimentary parking; continental breakfast includes fresh fruit, cheeses, yogurt, the house granola, scones and croissants (including ham and cheese), muffins, sweet breads, and cereals. **Cons:** some noise from Thames Street in summer; walk up from third floor to rooftop rooms and deck; rooms are fairly small but it is a historic property. ⑤ *Rooms from: $209* ⊠ *398 Thames St.* ☎ *401/848–8000, 866/848–8780* ⊕ *www.admiralfitzroy.com* ↶ *18 rooms* ⑩ *Free breakfast.*

The Francis Malbone House

$$ | B&B/INN | The painted-brick main house overlooks a private courtyard with a fountain and, across the street, to the harbor. **Pros:** steps from many restaurants and shops; highly professional service; complimentary off-street parking; a sumptuous breakfast is served in a dome-ceiling dining room, and tea is served daily 3–6. **Cons:** Thames Street abounds with tourists in summer; two-night stay required on weekends; three-night stay required on weekends Memorial Day–Columbus Day. ⑤ *Rooms from: $255* ⊠ *392 Thames St.* ☎ *401/846–0392, 800/846–0392* ⊕ *www.malbone.com* ↶ *20 rooms* ⑩ *Free breakfast.*

★ Grace Vanderbilt

$$$$ | HOTEL | Built in 1909 by Alfred Gwynne Vanderbilt for his mistress, Agnes O'Brien Ruiz, this Grace Hotels property aims to impress—and does, with more than 70 early-20th-century paintings, including magazine cover illustrations for *Vogue* and *The New Yorker,* that hang in common areas on permanent loan from the hotel's prior owner. **Pros:** full-service spa; indoor and outdoor pools; stylish snooker room. **Cons:** on a narrow street that's busy in summer; municipal parking lot next door; two-night minimum in high season. ⑤ *Rooms from: $450* ⊠ *41 Mary St.* ☎ *401/846–6200, 888/826–4255* ⊕ *www.gracehotels.com/vanderbilt* ↶ *62 rooms* ⑩ *No meals.*

★ Gurney's Newport Resort & Marina

$$$$ | RESORT | FAMILY | A former Navy base that's now connected by causeway to the downtown area, this resort and marina on Goat Island includes a walking path around the island, a marina full of yachts, Seawater Spa, a fitness center, and a picturesque lighthouse. **Pros:** indoor and outdoor swimming pools; kids' club (seasonal); ADA "accessible" rooms available; numerous dining options. **Cons:** 10-minute walk or taxi ride (complimentary) to downtown activities; parking, even self-parking, is an extra; service could use "a smile". ⑤ *Rooms from: $400* ⊠ *1 Goat Island* ☎ *401/849–2600* ⊕ *www.gurneysresorts.com/newport* ↶ *257 rooms* ⑩ *No meals.*

Hotel Viking

$$$$ | HOTEL | At the north end of Bellevue Avenue, this elegant redbrick hotel dates back to 1926. **Pros:** great Historic Hill location; beautiful woodwork and chandeliers; outstanding SpaFjör; One Bellevue restaurant serves fresh seafood and afternoon tea. **Cons:** comparatively expensive; relatively small rooms and tiny bathrooms; valet parking is available but expensive. ⑤ *Rooms from: $500* ⊠ *1 Bellevue Ave.* ☎ *401/847–3300* ⊕ *www.hotelviking.com* ↶ *230 rooms* ⑩ *No meals.*

Hydrangea House Inn

$$ | B&B/INN | This mid-19th-century inn, with decadent suites and guest rooms, exudes romance. **Pros:** convenient central location; huge rooms and great bathrooms; highly personal service. **Cons:** slightly over-the-top decor; street-level rooms can be noisy at night; no kids 12 and under. $ *Rooms from: $258* ✉ *16 Bellevue Ave.* ☎ *401/846–4435, 800/945–4667* ⊕ *www.hydrangeahouse. com* ⇆ *10 rooms* ⏐○⏐ *Free breakfast.*

Newport Marriott

$$$$ | HOTEL | A light-filled atrium lobby with marble floors and a front desk that looks like a boat unfolds as you enter this luxury hotel on the harbor at Long Wharf. **Pros:** convenient location; harbor views from many rooms; swimming pool. **Cons:** no local color; pricey for a Marriott; rather typical hotel guest rooms. $ *Rooms from: $469* ✉ *25 America's Cup Ave.* ☎ *401/849–1000, 888/236–2427* ⊕ *www. newportmarriott.com* ⇆ *319 rooms* ⏐○⏐ *No meals.*

BELLEVUE AVENUE AND BEYOND

★ Castle Hill Inn

$$$$ | HOTEL | Built as a summer house in 1874 for Alexander Agassiz, a scientist and explorer, this luxurious and romantic getaway on a 40-acre peninsula has its own private beach, clambake pit, and trails to the Castle Hill, as well as Adirondack chairs on the lawn that beckon you to relax and watch the passing boats. **Pros:** stunning views; excellent restaurant with an elaborate Sunday brunch with live jazz music; variety of rooms; home to the Retreat at Castle Hill, a "wellness sanctuary". **Cons:** 3 miles from downtown Newport; very expensive; no children under 12 in mansion rooms. $ *Rooms from: $835* ✉ *590 Ocean Dr.* ☎ *401/849–3800, 888/466–1355* ⊕ *www.castlehillinn.com* ⇆ *33 rooms* ⏐○⏐ *Free breakfast.*

★ The Chanler at Cliff Walk

$$$$ | HOTEL | The custom-designed rooms at this 19th-century mansion on the Cliff Walk, now a landmark boutique hotel, represent the most unique and luxurious accommodations in Newport. **Pros:** panoramic water views from many rooms; complimentary car service;

excellent fine-dining restaurant. **Cons:** no elevator; some rooms have steps to access bathroom; traffic can be noisy. $ *Rooms from: $780* ✉ *117 Memorial Blvd.* ☎ *401/847–1300, 866/793–5664* ⊕ *www.thechanler.com* ⇆ *20 rooms* ⏐○⏐ *No meals.*

Nightlife

To sample Newport's lively nightlife, you need only stroll down Thames Street or the southern end of Broadway after dark.

BARS AND CLUBS

Fastnet Pub

BARS/PUBS | Named for the Fastnet Lighthouse off the coast of Cork, Ireland, this pub hosts Irish jam sessions on Sunday evening, when guest musicians, singers, and dancers familiar with traditional Irish repertoire are invited to participate. ✉ *1 Broadway* ☎ *401/845–9311*⊕ *www. thefastnetpub.com.*

The Fifth Element

BARS/PUBS | This chic lounge offers specialty martinis and gourmet pizza. Monday is jazz night with a live band. This is also a good Sunday brunch spot. ✉ *111 Broadway* ☎ *401/019–2552*⊕ *www. thefifthri.com.*

Newport Blues Café

MUSIC CLUBS | Housed in a former bank building built in 1892, this café hosts live music, including touring blues acts and tribute bands that perform the music of AC/DC, Journey, Sublime, and other groups. ✉ *286 Thames St.* ☎ *401/841–5510*⊕ *www.newportblues.com.*

One Pelham East

MUSIC CLUBS | A young crowd heads here for DJ music, dueling pianos, and live rock cover bands. ✉ *270 Thames St.* ☎ *401/847–9460*⊕ *www.thepelham.com.*

Newport Off Season

Summer in Newport can be busy and noisy, but the off-season takes on a serene, romantic character. No crowds, lower lodging rates, easy and free parking, and midweek specials at restaurants all make the city an appealing destination. The twice-a-year Newport Restaurant Week, held in early November and late March–April, offers three-course $16 lunches and $35 dinners at 50 or more participating restaurants.

Fall visitors will enjoy end-of-season sales up and down Thames Street. Although there may be no need to pack a bikini, brisk walks on the beach and Cliff Walk get the blood flowing. In the wintertime, holiday lights glimmer in the early dusk, and bundled-up folks duck into restaurants to warm themselves by the fire and enjoy a drink and a bite to eat.

Newport's holiday season is lovely. A light snowfall can peel back the years, and it isn't difficult to imagine the city 200 years ago. Bowen's Wharf, decked out in white lights, provides Newport with its version of the Rockefeller Center tree. "Christmas in Newport," a program that began in 1971, hosts a number of activities—tree lightings, Nativity scenes, a lighted boat parade, dances, concerts, and visits by Santa—for nearly every day of the December calendar. The Breakers, the Elms, and Marble House are dressed up in full holiday regalia beginning in mid-November. Mansions, filled with evergreens and thousands of poinsettias, open their doors for live holiday music on Saturday evening and Sunday afternoon.

Fun options with the kids are the Newport Skating Center and, during February school break, the annual Newport Winter Festival, with live shows, an ice-carving competition, beach sand/snow sculptures, a citywide scavenger hunt, and a chili cook-off.

🎭 Performing Arts

Pick up the free *Newport Mercury* or *Newport This Week*, or visit ⊕ *www. newportri.com* for entertainment listings and news about featured events.

FILM
newportFILM

FILM | FAMILY | Enjoy sneak peeks of documentary films curated from film festivals around the world thanks to this nonprofit group that hosts outdoor screenings and minifestivals in various outdoor spaces around Newport, with programming for both adults and kids throughout the year. ⊠ *174 Bellevue Ave., Suite 314* ☎ *401/649-2784* ⊕ *www.newportfilm.com*.

THEATER
Firehouse Theater

THEATER | FAMILY | It's all about comedy here—local comics, improv, audience participation, even some geared to children. Management tries to keep all shows PG-13, but there's no guarantee. It's BYOB; you can buy water and soda. ⊠ *4 Equality Park Pl.* ☎ *401/849-3473* ⊕ *www.firehousetheater.org*.

The Newport Playhouse and Cabaret Restaurant

THEATER | The playhouse offers a varied schedule of comedies and musical shows. Dinner packages are available. ⊠ *102 Connell Hwy.* ☎ *401/848-7529* ⊕ *www.newportplayhouse.com*.

Newport's naturally protected harbor has made the city a sailing capital.

Activities

BASEBALL

Cardines Field

BASEBALL/SOFTBALL | **FAMILY** | One of America's oldest ballparks, with a circa-1908 original backdrop, is home to the Newport Gulls of the New England Collegiate Baseball League. Home games, June–early August, draw a family-friendly crowd. The field hosted barnstorming all-stars in the early 20th century, including the players of Negro League clubs. ⊠ *20 America's Cup Ave.* ⊕ *www.newport-gulls.com* ⊠ *$5.*

BIKING

The 10-mile swing down Bellevue Avenue to Ocean Drive and back offers amazing coastal views.

Ten Speed Spokes

BICYCLING | **FAMILY** | This shop rents hybrid bikes for $35 per day, road bikes for $45, and "fat" bikes for $50. You can also rent by the week. ⊠ *18 Elm St.* ☎ *401/847-5609* ⊕ *www.tenspeedspokes.com.*

BOATING

Sail Newport

BOATING | Take a private two-hour sailing lesson or rent a 19- or 22-foot sailboat or a kayak at Sail Newport, New England's largest public sailing center. ⊠ *Ft. Adams State Park, 72 Ft. Adams Dr.* ☎ *401/846-1983* ⊕ *www.sailnewport.org.*

FISHING

Sara Star Charters

FISHING | Capt. Joe Aiello and his first mate, daughter Coral Rose, will take you on a half- or full-day inshore or offshore fishing trip where you can try to catch your dinner and have a good time. All gear is provided—you just relax and reel. ⊠ *142 Long Wharf* ☎ *401/623-1121* ⊕ *www.sarastarcharters.com.*

Shopping

Many of Newport's shops and art and crafts galleries are on Thames Street, Spring Street, and at Bowen's and Bannister's wharves. The Brick Market area—between Thames Street and America's Cup Avenue—has more than

40 shops. Bellevue Avenue, just south of Memorial Boulevard near the International Tennis Hall of Fame, contains a strip of high-end fashion and home decor boutiques and gift shops.

ANTIQUES

Armory Antiques

ANTIQUES/COLLECTIBLES | The several dozen vendors in the vast Newport Armory, which dates to 1894, carry antiques, china, vintage clothing, nautical items, militaria, sports memorabilia, estate jewelry, and more. ⊠ *365 Thames St.* ☎ *401/848–2398* ⊕ *www.armoryantiquesnewport.com.*

ART AND CRAFTS GALLERIES

Spring Bull Gallery

ART GALLERIES | This Rhode Island artists' cooperative, a working studio gallery, changes its shows monthly. One wall is dedicated to its members, who exhibit paintings, sculpture, and glasswork. ⊠ *55 Bellevue Ave.* ☎ *401/849–9166* ⊕ *www.springbullgallery.com.*

★ Thames Glass

ART GALLERIES | Through a window in the gallery at Thames Glass, you can watch Matthew Buechner and his team making blown-glass gifts. Sign up for a lesson to make an ornament, paperweight, or vase out of molten glass. ⊠ *688 Thames St.* ☎ *401/846–0576* ⊕ *www.thamesglass.com.*

SPAS

The Retreat at Castle Hill by Farmaesthetics

SPA—SIGHT | Located at Castle Hill Inn, this "wellness sanctuary" operates in collaboration with Farmaesthetics, a Rhode Island-based line of 100% natural herbal skin-care products. Many of the ingredients are harvested from local seaside farms. Spa services include facials, therapeutic and acupressure massage, and pre- and posttreatment saltwater soaks. ⊠ *Castle Hill Inn, 590 Ocean Dr.* ☎ *401/849–3800* ⊕ *www.castlehillinn/wellness.*

SpaFjör

SPA—SIGHT | The outstanding SpaFjör, located in Hotel Viking, offers custom-designed Balinese spa experiences and Thai body rituals—massages, facials, and body treatments—that promote health and well-being but also provide a sense of complete relaxation. For a truly luxurious escape, pick a package: the 3-hour Day of Bliss (massage, body wrap, and facial) or the 4½-hour Sacred Journey (stone massage, facial, back treatment, foot rub, manicure, and pedicure). ⊠ *Hotel Viking, 1 Bellevue Ave.* ☎ *401/848–4848* ⊕ *www.hotelviking.com/spa.*

Portsmouth

10 miles north of Newport.

Largely a bedroom community for Newport, Portsmouth attracts visitors for polo matches, its fanciful topiary garden, and the Greenvale winery. The town also has an interesting history. A religious dissident named Anne Hutchinson (for whom New York's Hutchinson River Parkway is named) led a group of settlers to the Portsmouth area in 1638 after being banished from the Massachusetts Bay Colony. The town was also the site of the Battle of Rhode Island on August 29, 1778, when American troops—including a locally recruited African American regiment—withdrew, leaving Aquidneck Island under British control.

Sights

Green Animals Topiary Garden

GARDEN | FAMILY | Fanciful animals, a sailing ship, and geometric shapes populate this large topiary garden on a Victorian estate that served as the summer residence of a Fall River, Massachusetts, textile mill owner. In addition to the formal topiaries, there are flower and herb gardens, orchards, winding pathways, and an 1872 white clapboard house with original family furnishings and an antique

Spend an afternoon wandering among living sculptures at the Green Animals Topiary Garden in Portsmouth.

toy collection. ✉ *380 Cory's La., off Rte. 114* ☎ *401/683–1267* ⊕ *www.newport-mansions.org* 🎟 *$18.*

Greenvale Vineyards

WINERY/DISTILLERY | A restored stable on a farm owned by the same family for four generations houses the tasting room of this small producer. Two unusual wines, both whites, are Skipping Stone, made mostly with the Cayuga grape, and Greenvale Vidal Blanc. Reds include the Merlot-dominant Elms Meritage blend. Tastings and a tour take place daily at 2 pm. On Saturdays, May–early December, the winery hosts live jazz concerts. ✉ *582 Wapping Rd.* ☎ *401/847–3777* ⊕ *www.greenvale.com* 🎟 *Tasting and tour $15 (7–8 wines plus a glass to take home), $20 including jazz.*

 Beaches

Sandy Point Beach

BEACH—SIGHT | **FAMILY** | This Sakonnet River beach is a choice spot for families and beginning windsurfers due to its calm surf. Lifeguards are on duty on weekends, late May–mid-June, and daily mid-June–early September. **Amenities:** food and drink; lifeguards; parking (fee); showers; toilets. **Best for:** solitude; swimming; walking; windsurfing. ✉ *Sandy Point Ave.* ☎ *401/297–1263* ⊕ *www.portsmouthri.com/168/Beaches* 🎟 *$10 weekdays, $15 weekends (free for residents).*

 Activities

POLO

Newport International Polo Series

PARK—SPORTS-OUTDOORS | **FAMILY** | Teams from across the nation and around the world compete in Saturday matches during the Newport International Polo Series, June to November, in Portsmouth. Spectators are invited to stomp divots at the half and mingle with players and pet the horses after the match. Arrive early with your picnic lunch to get a choice tailgating spot. The concession stand has a bar and sells grilled fare. ✉ *Glen Farm, 250 Linden La.* ☎ *401/846–0200* ⊕ *www.nptpolo.com* 🎟 *$15–$65.*

Bristol

15 miles north of Newport, 18 miles southeast of Providence.

The home of the longest-running Fourth of July celebration—it began in 1785—Bristol shows off its patriotism with a red-white-and-blue center stripe down Hope Street, its charming business district, and flags flying from many homes and businesses. Midway between Newport and Providence—each a 30-minute drive away—Bristol sits on a 10-square-mile peninsula between Narragansett Bay to the west and Mt. Hope Bay to the east. Bristol was once a boatbuilding center; the Herreshoff Manufacturing Company built five consecutive America's Cup defenders between 1893 and 1920. Independence Park marks the southern end of the 14½-mile East Bay Bike Path, which crosses the access road for Colt State Park, a great spot for picnicking and kite flying.

Sights

Blithewold Mansion, Gardens, and Arboretum

GARDEN | FAMILY | Starting with a sea of daffodils in April, this 33-acre estate on Bristol Harbor blooms all the way to fall. Highlights include fragrant pink chestnut roses and one of the largest giant sequoia trees on the East Coast. The gardens are open year-round. The 45-room English-style manor house, opened seasonally, is filled with original antiques and artworks. ⊠ *101 Ferry Rd. (Rte. 114)* ☏ *401/253–2707* ⊕ *www.blithewold.org* ⊒ *$15* ⊗ *Mansion closed Mon. and mid-Oct.–early Apr.*

Herreshoff Marine Museum/America's Cup Hall Of Fame

MUSEUM | This maritime museum, devoted to the sport of yachting, honors the Herreshoff Manufacturing Company, maker of yachts for eight consecutive America's Cup defenses. The museum's several dozen boats range from an 8½-foot dinghy to the *Defiant,* a 75-foot successful America's Cup defender. Halsey Herreshoff, a four-time cup defender and the grandson of yacht designer and company founder Nathanael Greene Herreshoff, established the hall of fame in 1992 as an arm of the museum, which hosts talks on yacht design and restoration and operates a sailing school for both kids and adults. ⊠ *1 Burnside St.* ☏ *401/253–5000* ⊕ *www.herreshoff.org* ⊒ *$15.*

Warren

TOWN | North of Bristol, Warren has the distinction of being the smallest town in the smallest county in the smallest state in the United States. The East Bay Bike Path travels through Warren's commercial district, so stop for a Del's frozen lemonade. ⊠ *Warren* ⊕ *www.discoverwarren.com.*

Restaurants

Beehive Café

$ | AMERICAN | This aptly named two-story café is abuzz with college students and foodies who appreciate the freshly baked bread, especially when it's used to make inventive sandwiches like roasted butternut squash with caramelized onions, Vermont cheddar, and tangy-sweet pesto. The extensive breakfast menu (served daily until 3:30) includes thick-cut French toast, cornbread and granola made on-site, and a tasty side of fried chickpeas. **Known for:** downtown location; cozy seating; patio and balcony dining in warm weather. ⑤ *Average main: $14* ⊠ *10 Franklin St.* ☏ *401/396–9994* ⊕ *www.thebeehivecafe.com* ⊗ *No dinner Sun.–Wed.*

DeWolf Tavern

$$$ | ECLECTIC | An 1818 rum distillery houses this distinctive restaurant—look for the timber ceilings, African granite from slave ship ballast in the walls, and framed sections of early-19th-century graffiti-covered plaster. Chef

Sai Viswanath reinvents traditional New England fare by combining it with Indian preparations to create dishes like lobster roasted in a 900°F tandoor oven and seafood stew simmered in a coconut, coriander, star anise, and mustard-seed broth. **Known for:** homemade ice cream; alfresco dining on the back deck in summer; cozy dining upstairs by the fireplace in winter. ⑤ *Average main: $28* ⊠ *259 Thames St.* ☎ *401/254–2005* ⊕ *www.dewolftavern. com* ⊘ *No breakfast weekdays.*

The Lobster Pot

$$$ | **SEAFOOD** | Folks have been coming here since 1929 for lobster: salad, roll, or whole—but wait, there's also grilled swordfish, seared tuna, roasted cod, broiled scallops, bouillabaise, and steak or chicken, too. At lunch or dinner, start with a microbrew or cocktail, then build your own plate from the raw bar: jumbo shrimp, oysters, littleneck and cherrystone clams, or half a cold lobster. **Known for:** classic New England seafood; harborside location; patio dining in summer, cozy fireplace in winter. ⑤ *Average main: $30* ⊠ *119 Hope St.* ☎ *401/253–9100* ⊕ *www.lobsterpotri.com* ⊘ *Closed Mon. mid-Oct.–mid-May.*

Roberto's

$$ | **ITALIAN** | The East Bay's best Italian restaurant can compete with any establishment on Federal Hill with its delicious braciole, 10 classic veal and chicken preparations, and owner Robert Vanderhoof's thoughtful wine list. One wall of the elegant dining room has a lovely mural of Tuscany painted by renowned local artist Kendra Ferreira. **Known for:** be prepared to wait; reservations essential on summer weekends; alfresco dining in summer. ⑤ *Average main: $24* ⊠ *450 Hope St.* ☎ *401/254–9732* ⊕ *www.robertosbristol.com* ⊘ *No lunch.*

Hotels

Bristol Harbor Inn

$ | **HOTEL** | This waterfront hotel was constructed with timber and architectural detailing from the 1818 rum distillery and warehouse that once occupied this site. **Pros:** reasonably priced for a waterfront hotel; some rooms have full kitchens and washer/dryer; convenient location; Thames Landing has a marina and bike-rental shop. **Cons:** other than shops and marina, there are no exterior grounds; some rooms are rather small; no room service. ⑤ *Rooms from: $169* ⊠ *Thames Landing, 259 Thames St.* ☎ *401/254–1444, 866/254–1444* ⊕ *www.bristolharborinn.com* ⇆ *44 rooms* ⌾⏐ *No meals.*

Point Pleasant Inn

$$$ | **B&B/INN** | A regal East Bay estate set on a peninsula near Colt State Park, this rambling 1940 mansion anchors a gloriously situated 33-acre compound of well-tended lawns, manicured gardens, tennis and bocce courts, and a pool with a slate lanai. **Pros:** magnificent waterfront setting; huge, beautifully decorated rooms; gracious staff; full breakfast buffet includes Scotch eggs and blueberry pancakes, along with other treats; cocktail hour features an open bar and hors d'oeuvres. **Cons:** pricey; not within walking distance of shopping and dining; site of many weddings and functions. ⑤ *Rooms from: $350* ⊠ *333 Poppasquash Rd.* ☎ *401/253–0627* ⊕ *www.pointpleasantinn.com* ⊘ *Closed Nov.–Apr.* ⇆ *7 rooms* ⌾⏐ *Free breakfast.*

Activities

BIKING

East Bay Bike Path

BICYCLING | **FAMILY** | Affording majestic views of Narragansett Bay, the flat, paved, 14½-mile East Bay Bike Path connects Providence and Bristol's historic downtown. ⊠ *Thames St.* ☎ *401/253–7482* ⊕ *www.riparks.com/Locations/LocationEastBay.html.*

Fishing boats off the coast of Rhode Island

Tiverton and Little Compton

Tiverton, 9 miles south of Bristol; Little Compton, 11 miles south of Tiverton.

This southernmost corner of Rhode Island, home to artists and working farms, is a pleasant afternoon drive from Newport or Bristol. Consider a hike in Tiverton's Weetamoo Woods or Little Compton's Wilbour Woods—or wander Tiverton Four Corners and check out the village's artist studios and arts center.

GETTING HERE AND AROUND

From Route 24 at the Sakonnet River Bridge, take Route 77 south for about 5¾ miles to reach historic Tiverton Four Corners. Continuing south to Little Compton you'll pass rolling estates, lovely homes, farmland, woods, and a gentle shoreline.

Sights

Carolyn's Sakonnet Vineyard
WINERY/DISTILLERY | White, rosé, red, and dessert wines are all in the portfolio of this winery founded in 1975. If you've ever wondered what a Rhode Island Red (not the chicken!) might taste like, here's your chance to find out. Several of the wines are award winners. In the winery's tasting room you can sample seven of them and keep the glass. ⊠ *162 W. Main Rd., Little Compton* ☎ *401/635–8486* ⊕ *www.sakonnetwine.com* ✉ *Tasting $14* ⊗ *Closed Tues. and Wed. from Columbus Day–Memorial Day.*

Little Compton Commons
PLAZA | This archetypal rural New England town square is actually Rhode Island's only town common. More of a long triangle than a square, the common is anchored by the Georgian-style United Congregational Church. Among the headstones in the nearby cemetery, you'll find one for Elizabeth Pabodie, the eldest daughter of John and Priscilla Alden and said to be the first white

woman born in New England. Surrounding the green are a rock wall and all the elements of a small community: town hall, community center, police station, school, library, general store, and restaurant. ⊠ *1 Commons, Little Compton* ⊕ *www.little-compton.com.*

Sakonnet Point

NATURE SITE | A scenic drive down Route 77 ends at this quiet southeastern tip of Rhode Island. People like to fish off the Army Corps of Engineers breakwater, or walk along it to enjoy views of the harbor. The 1884 Sakonnet Lighthouse on Little Cormorant Rock is picturesque, offshore, and not open to the public. Parking is limited in the area. ⊠ *Sakonnet Point, 19 Bluff Head Ave., Little Compton.*

Tiverton Four Corners

ARTS VENUE | Historic Tiverton Four Corners, a part of Tiverton's history that dates back to 1629 when Governor Bradford of the Plymouth Colony purchased the area (then called Pocasset) from the native inhabitants. The "four corners" intersection follows the original trails. Today, the Four Corners Arts Center, in the historic Soule-Seabury House, hosts an annual antiques show, as well as art festivals and exhibits, concerts and dances, and other special events. ⊠ *8 Puncatest Neck Rd. (Rte. 179), at Rte. 77, Tiverton* ⊕ *www.tivertonfourcorners.com.*

Restaurants

★ **Gray's Ice Cream**

$ | AMERICAN | A summertime pilgrimage destination for people from every corner of the state, this ice cream stop that's been around since 1923 sells more than 40 flavors of ice cream, all made on the premises. Coffee is the go-to flavor for most Rhode Islanders, but specialties such as Indian pudding and apple caramel spice have their adherents. **Known for:** cones, cups, cabinets (milk shakes without ice cream), and frappes (milk shakes with ice cream), frozen yogurt,

sherbet, and sugar-free flavors, too; open year-round. $ *Average main:* ⊠ *16 East Rd., Tiverton* ☎ *401/624–4500* ⊕ *www.graysicecream.com.*

★ **Provender**

$ | DELI | Provender has fantastic sandwiches with cheeky names like the Scarlet Letter (turkey and cranberry with tarragon mayo) and the Trekkie, a medley of edamame hummus, minted goat-cheese spread, roasted peppers, and veggies. The gourmet food store, coffee shop, and bakery are in a Victorian building that once housed a general store. **Known for:** chewy brownies, giant cookies, and other delicious treats; wraparound porch or back lawn seating; so many great sandwiches it's hard to choose. $ *Average main:* ⊠ *Tiverton Four Corners, 883 Main Rd., Tiverton* ☎ *401/624–8084* ⊕ *www.provenderfinefoods.com* ⊘ *Closed Mon.*

Activities

HIKING

Weetamoo Woods

HIKING/WALKING | **FAMILY** | Weetamoo Woods takes its name from the last sachem of the Pocasset Tribe of Wampanoag Indians. There are more than 10 miles of walking trails in this 850-acre nature preserve, which encompasses a coastal oak-holly forest, an Atlantic white cedar swamp, two grassland meadows, early-American cellar holes, and the remains of a mid-19th-century village sawmill. The main entrance to Weetamoo Woods, ¼-mile east of Tiverton Four Corners, has a parking area and a kiosk with maps. ⊠ *721 Lafayette Rd., at Rte. 77, Tiverton* ☎ *401/625–1300* ⊕ *www.tivertonlandtrust.org.*

Wilbour Woods

HIKING/WALKING | **FAMILY** | This 30-acre hollow with picnic tables and a waterfall is a good place for a casual hike along a marked 1.2-mile loop trail that winds along and over Dundery Brook. The trail passes a boulder dedicated to

Queen Awashonks, who ruled the local Saugkonnates tribe during the early Colonial period. ⊠ *123 Swamp Rd., Little Compton.*

Block Island

Block Island, with its 1,050 year-round residents, is a laid-back community about 12 miles off Rhode Island's southern coast. The island has 17 miles of beaches that are all open to everyone. Despite the influx of summer visitors and thanks to the efforts of local conservationists, Block Island's beauty remains intact. More than 43% of the land is preserved, and the relatively small island's 365 freshwater ponds support thousands of bird species that migrate seasonally along the Atlantic Flyway.

Block Island is not all beaches and birds. Nightlife abounds in the summer at bars and restaurants, and it's casual—you can go anywhere in shorts and a T-shirt. The busiest season, when the population explodes to 15,000 to 20,000 per day, is May–mid-October. If you plan to stay overnight in the summer, make reservations well in advance: for weekends in July and August, calling in March is not too early. In the off-season, most restaurants, inns, stores, and visitor services close down, though some visitors brave the elements on Groundhog Day to watch island residents gather at a local pub for an informal census.

Cell service and Internet can be spotty here, especially when it is raining and the entire island seems to be trying to stream content simultaneously. GPS isn't terribly useful, because street addresses aren't commonly used.

GETTING HERE AND AROUND
AIR TRAVEL
New England Airlines operates frequent scheduled flights year-round between Westerly and Block Island State Airport.

FERRY TRAVEL
There's year-round car-and-passenger ferry service to Block Island from the Port of Galilee, in the town of Narragansett in Rhode Island's South County. Seasonal passenger-only ferry service is available from Newport; New London, Connecticut; and Montauk, New York. Most ferry companies permit bicycles; the charge for bicycles runs $3–$10 each way.

The most heavily trafficked route is Block Island Ferry's car-passenger service and high-speed passenger service between Point Judith Terminal in Galilee, on the mainland, and Block Island's Old Harbor. By traditional ferry, the 55-minute trip costs about $13 one-way for passengers (rates fluctuate with oil prices) and $40 one-way for automobiles. Ferries run from one or two times per day in winter to nine times per day in summer. Make car reservations well ahead by telephone. Arrive 45 minutes ahead in high season to allow time to find parking in the pay lots ($10–$15 per day) that surround the docks. From early June to mid-October (and Thanksgiving week in November), the high-speed service makes four to six 30-minute trips each day ($20 one-way) along the same route. There is no auto service on the high-speed ferry, but you can bring a bicycle ($4); passenger reservations are recommended.

Block Island Ferry also operates seasonal high-speed service from Newport's Perrotti Park to Old Harbor. The passengers-only ferry makes two trips a day, each way, from late June through Labor Day. One-way rates are about $25.50; online reservations are recommended. Approximate sailing time is 60 minutes.

From late May through September, passenger-only ferries operated by Block Island Express run between New London, Connecticut, and Old Harbor. The ferries depart from New London several times a day and take 80–90 minutes, depending on the boat. Tickets are about $26 one-way; bikes cost $10. Reservations are recommended.

Viking Fleet runs high-speed passenger service from Montauk, Long Island, to New Harbor on Block Island from Memorial Day through Columbus Day. The boat departs from Montauk at 10 am and leaves Block Island at 5 pm, plus an additional trip on Sundays in July and August that departs from Block Island at noon and Montauk at 5 pm. The fare is $40 one-way; bicycles are allowed. Travel time is one hour.

GETTING AROUND

Block Island has two harbors, Old Harbor and New Harbor. Approaching the island by sea from New London, Newport, or Point Judith, you'll see Old Harbor, the island's only village, and its group of Victorian hotels. Most of the smaller inns, shops, and restaurants are also here. It's a short walk from the ferry landing to most of the interesting sights and many accommodations.

A car isn't necessary but can be helpful if you're staying far from Old Harbor or visiting for a long time. You can rent one at Block Island Bike and Car Rental.

ESSENTIALS

AIR TRAVEL CONTACTS Block Island State Airport ⊠ *4 Center Rd., New Shoreham* ☎ *401/466–5511* ⊕ *blockisland. stateairportri.com.* **New England Airlines** ⊠ *Westerly State Airport, 56 Airport Rd., Westerly* ☎ *401/596–2460, 800/243–2460* ⊕ *www.blockislandairline.com.* **Westerly State Airport** ⊠ *56 Airport Rd., Westerly* ☎ *401/596–2357* ⊕ *westerly. stateairportri.com.*

BIKE AND CAR RENTAL CONTACT Block Island Bike and Car Rental ⊠ *834 Ocean Ave., New Shoreham* ☎ *401/466–2297* ⊕ *www.blockislandbikeandcarrental.com.*

BOAT AND FERRY CONTACTS Block Island Express ⊠ *2 Ferry St., New London* ☎ *401/466–2212, 860/444–4624* ⊕ *www. goblockisland.com.* **Block Island Ferry** ⊠ *304 Great Island Rd., Narragansett* ☎ *401/783–7996, 866/783–7996* ⊕ *www. blockislandferry.com.* **Viking Fleet** ⊠ *462*

West Lake Dr., Montauk ☎ *631/668–5700* ⊕ *www.vikingfleet.com.*

VISITOR INFORMATION Block Island Chamber of Commerce ☎ *401/466–2474, 401/466–2982* ⊕ *www.blockislandchamber.com.* **Block Island Tourism Council** ☎ *800/383–2474* ⊕ *www.blockislandinfo.com.*

Sights

★ Mohegan Bluffs

BEACH—SIGHT | FAMILY | The dramatic 200-foot cliffs along Mohegan Trail, one of the island's top sights, offer a craggy beauty not found anywhere else in New England. On a clear day you can see all the way to Montauk Point on Long Island. The bluffs can be enjoyed from street level, but to access the beach below requires descending a steep set of more than 100 stairs that lead almost to the bottom. Because of erosion, you have to scramble down the rock-strewn final yards to reach the beach. It is pebbly at the base of the stairs but sandy in the cove to the west, with wave action that attracts surfers. ■**TIP→ Wear walking shoes, and don't attempt the descent unless you're in reasonably good shape.** Remember, you'll have to climb back up! ⊠ *Mohegan Bluffs Trailhead, 289 Spring St., New Shoreham.*

New Harbor

COMMERCIAL CENTER | The Great Salt Pond has a culture all its own, centered on the three marinas, two hotels, and five restaurants clustered along its southern shore that make up this commercial area about a 20-minute walk from Old Harbor. Up to 2,000 boats create a forest of masts on summer weekends, drawn by sail races and fishing tournaments. Over on the quiet north and east shores, clammers and windsurfers claim the tidal flats. The Montauk ferry docks at Champlin's, the largest of the marinas. ⊠ *Great Salt Pond, New Shoreham.*

Block Island

To New London, CT
To Point Judith
To Newport
To Montauk

Sandy Point
North Light
BLOCK ISLAND NATIONAL WILDLIFE REFUGE
Settler's Rock
Sachem Pond
Block Island Sound
Middle Pond
Rhode Island Sound
Logwood Cove
Clay Head Nature Trail
Mansion Beach Rd.
Jerry's Point
Beane Point
Mansion Beach
Great Salt Pond
Corn Neck Rd.
Crescent Beach
Scotch Beach
Grace Cove
Champlins Rd.
Frederick J. Benson Town Beach
Grace Cove Rd.
New Harbor
Side Rd.
Beach Ave.
Ocean Ave.
Water St.
West Rd.
Dorie's Cove Rd.
Center Rd.
Old Town Rd.
High St.
Spring St.
Old Harbor
Block Island State Airport
1661 Farm and Gardens
Lakeside Dr.
Fresh Pond
Rodman's Hollow
Pilot Hill Rd.
Southeast Rd.
Mohegan Trail
Mohegan Bluffs
Southeast Lighthouse Museum
Black Rock Point

ATLANTIC OCEAN

0   1/2 mile
0   1 km

KEY
Ferry Lines

North Light

HISTORIC SITE | FAMILY | An 1867 granite lighthouse on the northern tip of the Block Island National Wildlife Refuge (the fourth lighthouse on this site), North Light also serves as a maritime museum. The refuge is home to American oyster-catchers, piping plovers, and other rare migrating birds. From a parking lot at the end of Corn Neck Road, it's a ¾-mile hike over sand to the lighthouse. Seals sun themselves on nearby Sandy Point in winter. ⊠ *Block Island National Wildlife Refuge, Corn Neck Rd., New Shoreham* ☎ *401/364–9124* ⊕ *www.fws.gov/refuge/ block_island* ⊠ *Suggested donation.*

★ Rodman's Hollow

NATURE PRESERVE | FAMILY | This easy-to-find nature preserve is many people's first point of contact with the island's Greenway Trail system. The main trail runs south about 1 mile to clay bluffs with great ocean views, from which a winding path descends to the rocky beach below. Side trails cross the 50-acre hollow, offering longer hikes and the allure of getting mildly lost. The striking, if muted, natural beauty makes it easy to understand why, 40 years ago, this was the property that first awoke the local land conservation movement, now close to achieving its goal of preserving half the island. Geology buffs will appreciate this fine example of a glacial outwash basin. Nature lovers may enjoy looking for the Block Island meadow vole (field mouse), the northern harrier (an endangered raptor species), and the American burying beetle (the equally imperiled state insect). A small parking lot sits just south of Cooneymus Road near a stone marker. ⊠ *Cooneymus Rd., New Shoreham* ⊕ *www.nature.org.*

Settler's Rock

MEMORIAL | On the spit of land between Sachem Pond and Cow Cove, this monument lists the names of the original settlers and marks the spot where they landed in 1661 (swimming to shore with their cows). A ¾-mile hike from here over sandy terrain will get you to the North Light. ⊠ *Corn Neck Rd., New Shoreham.*

1661 Farm and Gardens

FARM/RANCH | FAMILY | Animals you never knew existed—like the zedonk, a cross between a zebra and a donkey—are on display at this farm, as well as some you did. Camels, llamas, emus, kangaroos, and even fainting goats (whose legs stiffen when they get excited, causing them to keel over) will all gladly munch pellets out of your hand. Black swans stroll about, and lemurs leap around their own enclosure. A herd of gentle alpacas helps provide fibers for the adjacent North Light Fibers textile mill. ⊠ *Off Spring St., New Shoreham* ☎ *401/466–2421* ⊕ *www.blockislandresorts.com* ⊠ *Free.*

Southeast Lighthouse Museum

MUSEUM | The small museum is housed inside an 1875 redbrick lighthouse with gingerbread detail. The lighthouse, which was moved back 360 feet from the eroded clay cliffs, is a National Historic Landmark. Tours are offered during the summer. ⊠ *122 Mohegan Tr., New Shoreham* ☎ *401/466–5009* ⊠ *Tours $10* ⊗ *Closed Jan.–Memorial Day.*

⊕ Beaches

Block Island is ringed by 17 ocean beaches, all open to the public. Beaches on the eastern side of the island, in particular, have calm, warm waters that are ideal for swimming June–September.

★ Crescent Beach

BEACH—SIGHT | This 3-mile beach runs north from Old Harbor, and its white sands become wider and the crowds thinner the farther away from town you go. It is divided into smaller beaches with access points off Corn Neck Road. Farthest north is Mansion Beach: look for the sign, then follow the dirt road to the right. From the parking area, it's a short hike to reach what is easily one of New England's most beautiful beaches. In the morning, you might spot deer on the dunes; to the north, surfers can often be seen dotting Jerry's Point. Closer to Old Harbor, Scotch Beach, with its small parking lot directly off Corn Neck Road, attracts a lively crowd of young adults. **Amenities:** food and drink; lifeguards; parking (no fee); showers; toilets. **Best for:** sunrise; sunset; swimming; walking. ✉ *Corn Neck Rd., New Shoreham.*

🍽 Restaurants

The Beachead

$$ | **SEAFOOD** | **FAMILY** | The food—especially the Rhode Island clam chowder—is consistently great, the price is right, and you won't feel like a tourist at this local favorite. Catch ocean breezes on the patio, or in stormy weather sit at the bar and watch breakers roll in 30 feet away. **Known for:** raw bar and daily seafood specials; children's menu; alfresco dining on the patio or porch. ⑤ *Average main: $24* ✉ *598 Corn Neck Rd., New Harbor, New Shoreham* ☏ *401/466–2249* ⊕ *beacheadbi.com* ⊘ *Closed Dec.–Apr.*

Eli's

$$$ | **AMERICAN** | Creative cuisine emerges from the kitchen of this intimate bistro. The fare changes seasonally but may include pan-seared sea scallops, Cornish game hen, and the mouthwatering Eli's burger with sweet potato fries. **Known for:** vegetarian menu; popular bar; long wait times in summer. ⑤ *Average main: $26* ✉ *456 Chapel St., Old Harbor, New Shoreham* ☏ *401/466–5230* ⊕ *www.elisblockisland.com* ⊘ *Closed Nov.–Mar. No lunch.*

Finn's

$$$ | **SEAFOOD** | A Block Island institution, Finn's serves fresh, reliable fried and broiled seafood, and a wonderful smoked bluefish pâté. The island's best bet for simple steamed lobster, this is also the spot for an unfussy lunch like the Workman's Special, which includes a burger, coleslaw, and fries. **Known for:** deck seating; takeout window and raw bar; on-site fish market. ⑤ *Average main:*

$26 ✉ *212 Water St., at ferry landing, Old Harbor, New Shoreham* ☏ *401/466–2473* ⊕ *www.finnsseafood.com* ⊘ *Closed mid-Oct.–May.*

Froozies Juice Bar & Café

$ | **VEGETARIAN** | What began as a smoothie bar on the back porch of the National Hotel has evolved into a standout café with hearty but healthy options, a varied vegetarian menu, and good people-watching. Active types stop by early for a black bean–and-avocado breakfast burrito and fair-trade coffee. **Known for:** fresh-fruit smoothies; organic produce; delicious sandwiches. ⑤ *Average main: $8* ✉ *26 Dodge St., Old Harbor, New Shoreham* ☏ *401/466–2230* ⊕ *www.frooziesblockisland.com* ⊘ *Closed Oct.–Apr.*

★ Manisses Restaurant

$$$ | **AMERICAN** | The chef at the island's premier restaurant for elegant American cuisine relies heavily on locally caught seafood and herbs and vegetables from local farms. The many small plates make this a place to splurge without breaking the bank, and the garden seating around a fountain is tranquil. **Known for:** tasty "glambake" prix-fixe menu; weekend brunch; garden dining. ⑤ *Average main: $30* ✉ *Hotel Manisses, 251 Spring St., Old Harbor, New Shoreham* ☏ *401/466–9898, 800/626–4773* ⊕ *hotelmanisses.com* ⊘ *Closed late Oct.–Apr.*

Restaurant 1879

$$$ | **AMERICAN** | Because it shares an executive chef with popular Eli's, expectations are high for the Atlantic Inn's restaurant, and it doesn't disappoint. The menu, which evolves daily, includes both small and large plates served à la carte or as part of the chef's four-course tasting menu. **Known for:** extensive tapas menu; house-made charcuterie platter; impressive wine list. ⑤ *Average main: $30* ✉ *The Atlantic Inn, 359 High St., Old Harbor, New Shoreham* ☏ *401/466–5883* ⊕ *www.atlanticinn.com.*

Hotels

It's advisable to book accommodations well in advance, especially for weekends in July and August when many hotels require a two-night minimum. The Block Island Chamber of Commerce runs a room reservation service that's handy for last-minute trips. Many visitors rent homes for stays of a week or more.

★ The Atlantic Inn

$$ | **HOTEL** | Perched on a hill amid floral gardens and undulating lawns, away from the hubbub of the Old Harbor area, this classic Victorian (1879) seaside resort dazzles guests with its big windows, high ceilings, sweeping staircase, and mesmerizing views. **Pros:** spectacular hilltop location; beautiful veranda for whiling away the afternoon; grand decor; excellent Restaurant 1879 serves small and large plates, à la carte or prix fixe. **Cons:** no TVs or high-speed Internet in rooms; no handicap-accessible rooms; minimum stay requirements. ⑤ *Rooms from: $225 ✉ 359 High St., Old Harbor, New Shoreham* ☎ *401/466–5883, 800/224–7422* ⊕ *www.atlanticinn.com* ۞ *Closed late Oct.–early May* ⊊ *21 rooms* ⭕ *Free breakfast.*

The Barrington

$$ | **B&B/INN** | **FAMILY** | This 19th-century Victorian farmhouse, high on a hill overlooking Great Salt Pond, is now a quiet and bright B&B inn. **Pros:** commanding views; reasonably priced; close to beaches. **Cons:** furnishings are quite simple; additional fee for a cot; breakfast not included for weekly guests. ⑤ *Rooms from: $285 ✉ 584 Beach Ave., New Harbor, New Shoreham* ☎ *401/466–5524, 877/324–4667* ⊕ *www.theinnatblockisland.com* ۞ *Closed Nov.–Apr.* ⊊ *8 rooms* ⭕ *Free breakfast.*

Blue Dory Inn

$$ | **B&B/INN** | This Old Harbor district inn, with a main lodging and three small shingle-and-clapboard outbuildings, has been a guesthouse since its construction in 1898. **Pros:** great in-town location—walk to the ferry; adjacent to Crescent Beach; pets allowed in some rooms with notice. **Cons:** some units are small; bed linens replaced only between guests (not daily); extra charge for pets. ⑤ *Rooms from: $245 ✉ 61 Dodge St., Old Harbor, New Shoreham* ☎ *401/466–5891, 800/992–7290* ⊕ *www.blockislandinns.com/blue-dory* ⊊ *11 rooms* ⭕ *Free breakfast.*

★ Payne's Harbor View Inn

$$ | **B&B/INN** | This 2002 inn, designed to blend with the island's historic architecture, occupies a breezy hillside overlooking the Great Salt Pond and is just minutes from Crescent Beach. **Pros:** free parking; kayak and paddleboard rentals; handicap ramp and accessible shower in Room 1. **Cons:** books up fast; no children under 12; about a mile from "town." ⑤ *Rooms from: $295 ✉ 111 Beach Ave., corner of Ocean Ave., New Shoreham* ✛ *New Harbor* ☎ *401/466–5758* ⊕ *www.paynesharborviewinn.com* ⊊ *10 rooms* ⭕ *Free breakfast.*

The Rose Farm Inn

$$ | **B&B/INN** | With simple accommodations in a late-19th-century farmhouse and more luxurious units in a more modern structure across a country lane, this property is set on a 20-acre pastoral farmstead. **Pros:** choose an ocean or countryside view; informal hospitality; quiet setting yet easy walk to Old Harbor. **Cons:** 2 Farm House share a bath; no kids under age 12; "light" continental breakfast. ⑤ *Rooms from: $229 ✉ 1005 High St., Old Harbor, New Shoreham* ☎ *401/466–2034* ⊕ *www.rosefarminn.com* ۞ *Closed mid-Oct.–early May* ⊊ *19 rooms* ⭕ *Free breakfast.*

★ Spring House Hotel

$$$ | **HOTEL** | **FAMILY** | Most rooms in this charming old (1852) seaside inn—the island's oldest and largest hotel—have been renovated to suit today's expectations. **Pros:** welcoming atmosphere; stunning views from the breezy front porch; happily accommodates infants and children; within walking distance (about

15 minutes) of the activity at Old Harbor. **Cons:** choose a renovated room; Thursday "Martini Night" music can get loud; room refrigerator only upon request for $10 per day. ⑤ *Rooms from: $345* ✉ *52 Spring St., Old Harbor, New Shoreham* ☎ *401/466–5844* ⊕ *www.springhouse-blockisland.com* ⊗ *Closed mid-Oct.–May* ⇨ *33 rooms* ⦿ *No meals.*

Nightlife

Nightlife, at least in season, is one of Block Island's highlights—and you have your pick of some two dozen places to grab a drink. Check the *Block Island Times* for band listings.

Ballard's Inn and Beach Club

BARS/PUBS | On its own private beach, Ballard's has oceanfront tiki bars, sandside cocktail service, and a barnlike restaurant with a dance floor and live music. It's party time all the time here. ✉ *42 Water St., Old Harbor, New Shoreham* ☎ *401/466–2231, 844/405–3275* ⊕ *www.ballardsbi.com.*

Captain Nick's Rock n' Roll Bar

BARS/PUBS | This place sets itself apart from the others by hosting June's Block Island Music Festival, a free roundup of soon-to-be-discovered bands from around the country. It has a bi-level bar, live music inside and out, and a suntanned crowd. Disco Monday has been an island tradition for more than two decades. The owner, a gifted pianist and singer, performs on Tuesday and Wednesday. Sushi is served Thursday–Sunday. ✉ *34 Ocean Ave., New Shoreham* ☎ *401/466–5670* ⊕ *www.captainnicksbi.com.*

Club Soda

BARS/PUBS | One of the few spots open year-round, Club Soda is a lively hangout with a wraparound mural depicting Block Island in the 1940s. Shoot pool or tuck into some tasty pub grub. Live music alternates with open-mike and karaoke nights during the summer. ✉ *35 Connecticut Ave., New Shoreham* ☎ *401/466–5397.*

Mahogany Shoals

BARS/PUBS | A tiny shack built over the water at Payne's Dock, Mahogany Shoals is where Irish sea chanteys are likely to be the evening entertainment. The place has expanded, gracefully, with an outdoor bar and an upper-level deck. It remains the best spot on the island to enjoy a quiet drink, peer at beautiful yachts, and catch a breeze on even the hottest of nights. ✉ *Payne's Dock, 133 Ocean Ave., New Harbor, New Shoreham* ☎ *401/865–3832* ⊕ *paynesdock.com.*

Yellow Kittens Tavern

BARS/PUBS | Patrons here amuse themselves with darts, pinball, table tennis, and pool, to the sound of live bands or DJs on many summer nights. A big deck overlooks the dunes at the southern end of Crescent Beach. ✉ *214 Corn Neck Rd., New Harbor, New Shoreham* ☎ *401/466–5855* ⊕ *www.yellowkittens.com.*

Activities

BIKING

The best way to explore Block Island is by bicycle ($25 a day to rent) or moped ($40 per hour, $105 per day). Most rental places are open spring–fall and offer baby seats and tag-alongs for bikes and free helmets. All rent bicycles in various styles and sizes, including mountain bikes, hybrids, tandems, and children's bikes.

Island Moped and Bike Rentals

BICYCLING | **FAMILY** | This shop has bikes of all kinds and scooters for hourly, daily, multiday, and weekly rentals. Pickup is free from anywhere on the island; discounts are available for groups of three or more. ✉ *41 Water St., Old Harbor* ☎ *401/466–2700* ⊕ *www.bimopeds.com.*

Old Harbor Bike Shop

BICYCLING | Descend from the Block Island Ferry and hop right on a bike at this shop, which rents cruisers, tandems, and baby seats, tag-alongs, and trailers, as well as mopeds. ✉ *1 Water St., south*

Digging for clams is a fun pastime on Block Island's beaches.

of ferry dock, New Shoreham ☎ 401/466–2029 ⊕ blockislandmoped.com.

BOATING

Fort Island Kayaks & SUPs

KAYAKING | FAMILY | Kayaks and standup paddleboards (including pedalboards) are available for all ages and abilities and may be rented by the hour, half- or full-day, or week. Lessons are available, too. ⊠ Block Island Fishworks, 40 Ocean Ave., New Harbor, New Shoreham ☎ 401/466–5392⊕ www.sandypointco.com.

★ Pond and Beyond

BOATING | FAMILY | Guided wildlife kayak trips around the Great Salt Pond are a specialty here. Children ages 12 and older can join tours suited to their skill level, and younger kids can hang out at the sea-life touch tanks run nearby by the Block Island Maritime Institute. ⊠ 216 Ocean Ave., corner West Side Rd., New Harbor, New Shoreham ☎ 401/578–2773 ⊕ www.pondandbeyondkayak.com ⊙ Closed mid-Oct.–late May.

FISHING

Most of Rhode Island's record-setting fish have been caught on Block Island—in fact, it's held the striped bass record (currently a 77.4-pound whopper caught in 2011) since 1984. From almost any beach, skilled anglers can land tautog and bass. The New Harbor channel is a good spot to hook bonito and fluke. Shellfishing licenses ($20 per week) may be obtained at the harbormaster's building at the Boat Basin in New Harbor.

Block Island Fishworks

DIVING/SNORKELING | A tiny shop in New Harbor, Block Island Fishworks sells bait and tackle. It also offers guide services, spearfishing lessons, and charter fishing trips targeting stripers, blues, sea bass, bonito, fluke, and the occasional tuna. ⊠ 40 Ocean Ave., New Shoreham ☎ 401/742–3992 ⊕ www.bifishworks.com.

Twin Maples

FISHING | For more than 60 years this family-run shop has sold bait, handmade lures, sophisticated fishing tackle, and coveted "Eat Fish" T-shirts from its Great

Salt Pond location. ⊠ *63 Beach Ave., New Harbor, New Shoreham* ☎ *401/466–5547* ⊕ *jswienton.squarespace.com.*

HIKING

★ Clay Head Nature Trail

HIKING/WALKING | FAMILY | The outstanding Clay Head Nature Trail meanders past Clay Head Swamp and along 150-foot clay bluffs. Songbirds chirp and flowers bloom along the paths; stick close to the ocean for a stunning hike that ends at Sachem Pond or venture into the interior's intertwining paths for hours of wandering and blackberrying in an area called The Maze. The trailhead is recognizable by a simple white post marker on the east side of Corn Neck Road, about 2 miles north of Old Harbor. ⊠ *Clay Head Trail Rd., New Shoreham.*

WATER SPORTS

Block Island Parasail and Watersports

WATER SPORTS | This outfitter will take you parasailing. It also rents five-person jet boats and 10-person banana boats. ⊠ *Old Harbor Dock, Water St., New Shoreham* ☎ *401/864–2474* ⊕ *www.blockislandparasail.com* ◷ *Closed Nov.–May.*

Diamondblue Surf Shop

WATER SPORTS | This shop stocks surf gear and offers wet suit, boogie board, surfboard, and standup paddleboard rentals. ⊠ *442 Dodge St., corner Corn Neck Rd., New Harbor, New Shoreham* ☎ *401/466–3145* ⊕ *www.diamondbluebi.com.*

🛍 Shopping

ART GALLERIES

Jessie Edwards Studio

ART GALLERIES | This gallery specializes in the work of local and regional artists: photographs, sculptures, and contemporary American paintings, often with nautical themes. ⊠ *Post Office Bldg., 30 Water St., 2nd fl., New Shoreham* ✛ *Old Harbor* ☎ *401/466–5314* ⊕ *www.jessieedwardsgallery.com.*

Malcolm Greenaway Gallery

ART GALLERIES | Malcolm Greenaway has taken magnificent photographs of Block Island places and scenes since moving here in 1974. In his Water Street gallery, he sells prints in various sizes—print only, matted, or matted and framed. ⊠ *Water St., Old Harbor, New Shoreham* ☎ *800/840–5331* ⊕ *www.malcolmgreenaway.com.*

Spring Street Gallery

ART GALLERIES | The gallery, located in an old (renovated) horse barn for more than 30 years, exhibits paintings, photographs, stained glass, and serigraphs by island artists and artisans. ⊠ *105 Spring St., Old Harbor, New Shoreham* ☎ *401/466–5374* ⊕ *www.springstreetgallery.org.*

TEXTILES

★ North Light Fibers

CLOTHING | The adjoining Abrams Animal Farm supplies wool from its alpacas, llamas, yaks, and sheep to make beautiful yarns, clothing, and blankets. Classes are offered in knitting, weaving, and felting—and you can tour the Micro Yarn Mill where the yarns are made. ⊠ *1661 Farm, 10 Spring St., Old Harbor, New Shoreham* ☎ *401/466–2050* ⊕ *www.northlightfibers.com.*

Chapter 9

VERMONT

Updated by
Mike Dunphy

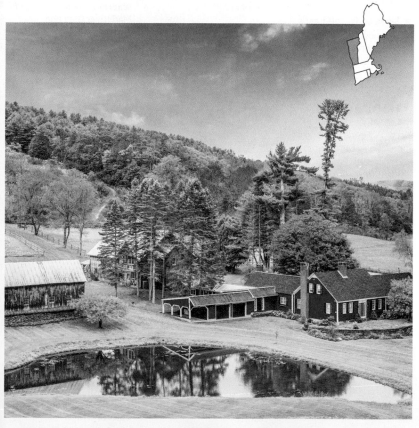

⊙ Sights	🍴 Restaurants	🛏 Hotels	🛍 Shopping	🍸 Nightlife
★★★★★	★★★★☆	★★★★☆	★★★☆☆	★★☆☆☆

WELCOME TO VERMONT

TOP REASONS TO GO

★ **Small-Town Charm:** Vermont rolls out a seemingly never-ending supply of tiny towns replete with white-steepled churches, town greens, red barns, general stores, and bed-and-breakfasts.

★ **Ski Resorts:** The East's best skiing can be found in well-managed, modern facilities with great views and lots and lots of powdery, fresh snow.

★ **Fall Foliage:** Perhaps the most vivid colors in North America wave from the trees in September and October, when the whole state is ablaze.

★ **Gorgeous Landscapes:** This sparsely populated, heavily forested state is an ideal place to find peace and quiet amid the mountains, valleys, and lakes.

★ **Tasty and Healthy Eats:** The rich soil and emphasis on local ingredients has led to great dairies, orchards, vineyards, specialty stores, and farm-to-table restaurants.

1 Brattleboro. A hippie enclave with an artistic and activist disposition.

2 Wilmington. The hub of Mt. Snow Valley.

3 Bennington. The economic center of southwest Vermont.

4 Arlington. Once the home of painter Norman Rockwell.

5 Manchester. Sophisticated with upscale shopping.

6 Dorset. Home to two of the state's best and oldest general stores.

7 Stratton. It's all about Stratton Mountain Resort.

8 Weston. Home to the Vermont Country Store.

9 Ludlow. Okemo Mountain Resort's home.

10 Grafton. Both a town and a museum.

11 Townshend. Lush town green and towering church spire.

12 Norwich. One of the state's most picture-perfect towns.

13 Quechee. Restaurants and shops in old mills.

14 Woodstock. Upscale shops and the venerable Woodstock Inn.

15 Killington. East Coast's largest downhill ski resort.

16 Rutland. Slowly gaining traction as a foodie town.

17 Brandon. Artists Guild and the Basin Bluegrass Festival.

18 Middlebury. Restaurants, shops, and Middlebury College.

19 Waitsfield and Warren. The ski meccas of Mad River Glen and Sugarbush.

20 Montpelier. The state's capital.

21 Stowe. Quintessential eastern ski town.

22 Jeffersonville. The four-season Smugglers' Notch Resort.

23 Burlington. Vermont's most populous city with a sophisticated food scene.

24 Shelburne. Shelburne Farms and Shelburne Museum.

25 Vergennes. Vermont's oldest city.

26 Lake Champlain Islands. Numerous islands including Isle La Motte, North Hero, Grand Isle, and South Hero.

27 Montgomery and Jay. Small village near the Jay Peak ski resort and the Canadian border.

28 St. Johnsbury. Adventure sports and arts-and-culture center.

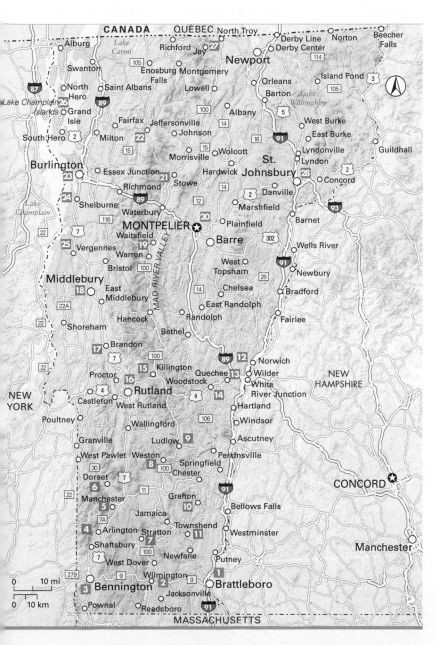

Vermont's a land of hidden treasures and unspoiled scenery. Wander anywhere in the state—nearly 80% is forest—and you'll find pristine countryside dotted with farms and framed by mountains. Tiny towns with picturesque church steeples, village greens, and clapboard Colonial-era houses are perfect for exploring.

Sprawl has no place here. Highways are devoid of billboards by law, and on some roads cows still stop traffic twice a day en route to and from pasture. In spring, sap boils in sugarhouses, some built generations ago, while up the road a chef trained at the New England Culinary Institute in Montpelier might use the syrup to glaze a pork tenderloin.

It's the landscape, for the most part, that attracts people to Vermont. Rolling hills belie rugged terrain underneath the green canopy of forest growth. In summer, clear lakes and streams provide ample opportunities for swimming, boating, and fishing; hills attract hikers and mountain bikers. The more than 14,000 miles of roads, many of them only intermittently traveled by cars, are great for biking. In fall the leaves have their last hurrah, painting the mountainsides in vibrant yellow, gold, red, and orange. Vermont has the best ski resorts in the eastern United States, centered along the spine of the Green Mountains running north to south; and the traditional heart of skiing here is the town of Stowe. Almost anywhere you go, no matter what time of year, the Vermont countryside will make you reach for your camera.

Although Vermont may seem locked in time, technological sophistication appears where you least expect it: wireless Internet access in a 19th-century farmhouse-turned-inn and cell phone coverage from the state's highest peaks. Like an old farmhouse under renovation, though, the state's historic exterior is still the main attraction.

MAJOR REGIONS
Vermont can be divided into three regions: **Southern Vermont, Central Vermont,** and **Northern Vermont.**

Most people's introduction to the state is **Southern Vermont,** a relatively short drive from New York and Boston. As elsewhere across the state, you'll find unspoiled towns, romantic bed-and-breakfasts, lush farms, and pristine forests. The area is flanked by **Bennington** on the west and **Brattleboro** on the east. There are charming towns like **Wilmington, Arlington, Manchester, Dorset, Weston, Grafton,** and **Townshend,** as well as ski destinations like **Stratton** and **Ludlow** (home to Okemo Resort).

Central Vermont is characterized by the rugged Green Mountains, which run north–south through the center of the state, and the gently rolling dairy lands east of Lake Champlain. It's home to the state's capital, **Montpelier,** the former mill towns of **Quechee** and **Middlebury,** artist enclaves like **Brandon,** beautiful towns like **Norwich** and **Woodstock,** and plucky **Rutland.** Ski buffs flock to **Killington** and **Waitsfield** and **Warren** (for Mad River Glen and Sugarbush).

Northern Vermont is a place of contrasts. It's where you'll find the area known as the Northeast Kingdom, a refuge for nature lovers and those who love getting away from it all, as well as the state's largest city, **Burlington,** which has dramatic views of Lake Champlain and the Adirondacks. There's plenty of skiing in **Stowe, Jeffersonville** (Smugglers' Notch Resort), and **Jay** (Jay Peak) as well as outdoor adventures in **Lake Willoughby, East Burke,** and **St. Johnsbury.** And postcard perfect scenery oozes in **Shelburne, Vergennes, Montgomery,** and the **Lake Champlain Islands.**

Planning

WHEN TO GO
In summer Vermont is lush and green, and in winter the hills and towns are blanketed white with snow, inspiring skiers to challenge the peaks at Stowe and elsewhere. Fall, however, is always the most amazing time to come. If you have never seen the state's kaleidoscope of autumn colors, it's well worth braving the slow-moving traffic and shelling out a few extra bucks for lodging. The only time things really slow down is during "stick season" in November, when the leaves have fallen but there's no snow yet, and "mud season" in late spring, when even innkeepers counsel guests to come another time. Activities in the Champlain Islands essentially come to a halt in the winter, except for ice fishing and snowmobiling, and two of the biggest attractions, Shelburne Farms and the Shelburne Museum, are closed

mid-October–April. Otherwise, Vermont is open for business year-round.

PLANNING YOUR TIME
There are many ways to take advantage of Vermont's beauty: skiing or hiking its mountains, biking or driving its back roads, fishing or sailing its waters, shopping for local products, visiting museums and sights, or simply finding the perfect inn and never leaving the front porch.

Distances are relatively short, yet the mountains and back roads will slow a traveler's pace. You can see a representative north–south cross section of Vermont in a few days; if you have up to a week, you can really hit the highlights.

AIR TRAVEL
American, Delta, JetBlue, Porter, and United fly into Burlington International Airport. Rutland State Airport has daily service to and from Boston on Cape Air.

BOAT TRAVEL
Lake Champlain Ferries
This company operates ferries on three routes between Vermont and New York: from Grand Isle to Plattsburgh, New York; Burlington to Port Kent; and Charlotte to Essex. ☎ 802/864–9804 ⊕ www.ferries. com ⊗ No Burlington–Port Kent service late Sept.–mid-June.

CAR TRAVEL
Vermont is divided by a mountainous north–south middle, with a main highway on either side: scenic U.S. 7 on the western side and Interstate 91 (which begins in New Haven, Connecticut, and runs through Hartford, central Massachusetts, and along the Connecticut River in Vermont to the Canadian border) on the east. Interstate 89 runs from New Hampshire across central Vermont from White River Junction to Burlington and up to the Canadian border. For current road conditions, check ⊕ www.511vt.com or call ☎ 511 in Vermont and ☎ 800/429–7623 from other states.

TRAIN TRAVEL
Amtrak
Amtrak has daytime service on the *Vermonter*, linking Washington, D.C., and New York City with Brattleboro, Bellows Falls, Windsor, White River Junction, Randolph, Montpelier, Waterbury, Essex Junction, and St. Albans. Amtrak's *Ethan Allen Express* connects New York City with Castleton and Rutland. ☎ *800/872–7245* ⊕ *www.amtrak.com*.

RESTAURANTS
Everything that makes Vermont good and wholesome is distilled in its restaurants. Many of them belong to the **Vermont Fresh Network** (⊕ *www.vermontfresh.net*), a partnership that encourages chefs to create menus emphasizing Vermont's wonderful bounty; especially in summer and early fall, the produce and meats are impeccable.

Great chefs come to Vermont for the quality of life, and the Montpelier-based New England Culinary Institute is a recruiting ground for new talent. Seasonal menus use local fresh herbs and vegetables along with native game. Look for imaginative approaches to native New England foods like maple syrup (Vermont is the largest U.S. producer); dairy products (cheese in particular); native fruits and berries; "new Vermont" products such as salsa and salad dressings; and venison, quail, pheasant, and other game. Beer has become yet another claim to fame in Vermont, thanks to more breweries per capita than any other state and recognition far and wide. Indeed, craft brewers as far away as Poland are now producing "Vermont-style" IPAs, and Hill Farmstead in Greensboro has been dubbed the best brewery in the world four years in a row by RateBeer, a brew-review website, as of 2018.

Your chances of finding a table for dinner vary with the season: lengthy waits are common in tourist centers at peak times—a reservation is always advisable. Some of the best dining is at country inns.

HOTELS
Vermont's only large chain hotels are in Burlington, Manchester, and Rutland; elsewhere it's just inns, bed-and-breakfasts, and small motels. The inns and B&Bs, some of them quite luxurious, provide what many visitors consider the quintessential Vermont lodging experience. Most areas have traditional ski-base condos; at these you sacrifice charm for ski-and-stay deals and proximity to the lifts. Lodging rates are highest during foliage season, late September–mid-October, and lowest in late spring and November, although many properties close during these times. Winter is high season at ski resorts. *Hotel reviews have been shortened. For full reviews visit Fodors.com.*

What It Costs			
$	$$	$$$	$$$$
RESTAURANTS			
under $18	$18–$24	$25–$35	over $35
HOTELS			
under $200	$200–$299	$300–$399	over $399

TOURS
Inn to Inn
TOUR—SPORTS | This company arranges guided and self-guided hiking, skiing, snowshoeing, and biking trips from inn to inn in Vermont. ✉ *52 Park St., Brandon* ☎ *802/247–3300, 800/838–3301* ⊕ *www.inntoinn.com* ⊠ *From $645.*

P.O.M.G. Bike Tours of Vermont
TOUR—SPORTS | The initials in this outfitter's name are short for "Peace Of Mind Guaranteed." The company leads weekend and multiday bike tours around the state. ☎ *802/434–2270, 888/635–2453* ⊕ *www.pomgbike.com* ⊠ *From $1795.*

VBT Bicycling and Walking Vacations
TOUR—SPORTS | This guide company leads bike tours across the state.

☎ 802/951–6100, 800/245–3868 ⊕ www. vbt.com ✉ From $1945.

VISITOR INFORMATION

CONTACTS Ski Vermont/Vermont Ski Areas Association ☎ 802/223–2439 ⊕ www. skivermont.com **Vermont Department of Tourism and Marketing** ☎ 802/828–3237, 800/837–6668 ⊕ www.vermontvacation. com **Vermont Foliage Hotline** ☎ 802/828–3239 for foliage information. **Vermont's Northeast Kingdom** ☎ 802/626–8511 ⊕ www.northeastkingdom.com.

Brattleboro

60 miles south of White River Junction.

Brattleboro has drawn political activists and earnest counterculturists since the 1960s. The arts-oriented town and environs (population 12,000) remains politically and culturally active; after Burlington, this is Vermont's most offbeat locale.

GETTING HERE AND AROUND

Brattleboro is near the intersection of Route 9, the principal east–west highway also known as the Molly Stark Byway, and Interstate 91. For downtown, take Exit 2 from Interstate 91.

ESSENTIALS

VISITOR INFORMATION Brattleboro Area Chamber of Commerce ☎ 802/254–4565, 877/254–4565 ⊕ www.brattleborochamber.org.

Sights

Brattleboro Museum and Art Center

MUSEUM | Downtown is the hub of Brattleboro's art scene, at the forefront of which is this museum in historic

Union Station. It presents changing exhibitions of works by local, national, and international artists, and hosts lectures, readings, and musical performances. ⊠ *10 Vernon St.* ☎ *802/257–0124* ⊕ *www.brattleboromuseum.org* ✉ *$8* ⊘ *Closed Tues.*

Putney

TOWN | Nine miles upriver, this town of fewer than 3,000 residents—the country cousin of bustling Brattleboro—is a haven for writers and fine-craft artists. There are many pottery studios to visit, the requisite general store, and a few orchards. Each November during the Putney Craft Tour, dozens of artisans open their studios and homes for live demonstrations and plenty of fun. ⊠ *Putney* ⊕ *www.discoverputney.com.*

🍴 Restaurants

Duo

$$ | **MODERN AMERICAN** | A corner location in the historic Brooks House and huge, inviting windows make this stylish farm-to-table restaurant impossible to miss. The locally sourced fare changes with the season, but the menu always includes an innovative takes on American comfort classics. **Known for:** cider pork Benedict; "Main St. beet down" cocktail; inventive interior design. ⑤ *Average main: $23* ⊠ *136 Main St.* ☎ *802/254–4141* ⊕ *www.duorestaurants.com* ⊘ *No lunch weekdays.*

Mocha Joe's Cafe

$ | **CAFÉ** | The team at this spot for coffee and conversation takes great pride in sourcing direct-trade beans from places like Kenya, Ethiopia, and Guatemala, and pairs them with an assortment of cookies, cakes, and muffins. This is ground zero for Brattleboro's bohemian contingent and fellow travelers. **Known for:** socially conscious coffee; maple latte; trendy clientele. ⑤ *Average main: $5* ⊠ *82 Main St., at Elliot St.* ☎ *802/257–7794* ⊕ *www.mochajoes.com.*

★ Peter Havens

$$$ | **AMERICAN** | A longtime Brattleboro favorite helmed since 2012 by chef Zachary Corbin, this chic little bistro is known for impeccably presented cuisine that draws heavily on local sources. One room is painted a warm red, another in sage, and a changing lineup of contemporary paintings adorns the walls of both rooms. **Known for:** pan-roasted duck breast; cocktail and wine list; vanilla bean crème brûlée. ⑤ *Average main: $30* ⊠ *32 Elliot St.* ☎ *802/257–3333* ⊕ *www.peterhavens.com* ⊘ *Closed Mon. and Tues. No lunch Sun., Wed., and Thurs. Nov.–May.*

★ T.J. Buckley's

$$$$ | **AMERICAN** | This converted 1925 lunch car (diner) is one of Vermont's most romantic restaurants. The sleek red and black space amounts to an intimate, candlelit theater, thanks to an open kitchen whose flames flare in production of French-influenced, new American cuisine, drawn heavily from local ingredients. **Known for:** vintage decor; romantic occasions; verbal menu only. ⑤ *Average main: $40* ⊠ *132 Elliot St.* ☎ *802/257–4922* ⊕ *www.tjbuckleysuptowndining.com* ⊘ *Closed Mon., Tues., and most Wed. No lunch.*

Top of the Hill Grill

$ | **BARBECUE** | **FAMILY** | Don't let the diminutive size of this roadside smokehouse deceive you. The place produces big flavors locals line up for: hickory-smoked ribs, apple-smoked turkey, beef brisket, and pulled pork, to name a few. **Known for:** "burnt ends" (brisket burnt ends); excellent view of West River; outdoor deck. ⑤ *Average main: $15* ⊠ *632 Putney Rd.* ☎ *802/258–9178* ⊕ *www.topofthehillgrill.com* ⊘ *Closed Nov.–Mar.*

Whetstone Station Restaurant and Brewery

$ | **INTERNATIONAL** | One of Brattleboro's most happening hangouts is this nano-brewery and restaurant perched over the Connecticut River. The beer and classic American comfort food are good, but it's the view of the river and

The rolling green hills of Putney are home to many organic farm operations.

its forested banks that drops jaws. **Known for:** rooftop beer garden; "Big 'Stoner" imperial IPA; poutine and steak tips. $ *Average main: $16* ⊠ *36 Bridge St.* ☎ *802/490–2354* ⊕ *www.whetstonestation.com.*

The Works Bakery Cafe

$ | **CAFÉ** | Natural light fills this spot in the center of town, whose patrons work on laptops at long wooden tables or sit with a book and some coffee in one of the comfortable armchairs. Fresh-fruit smoothies, panini, wraps, and salads are among the menu highlights. **Known for:** local hangout; breakfast all day; New York-style bagels. $ *Average main: $7* ⊠ *118 Main St.* ☎ *802/579–1851* ⊕ *www. worksbakerycafe.com.*

 ## Hotels

Hickory Ridge House

$$ | **B&B/INN** | The historic redbrick 1808 Federal-style mansion strikes a sturdy pose on a wide meadow of a former sheep farmhouse. **Pros:** surrounded by hundreds of acres of preserved land; historic property; great for hiking and cross-country skiing. **Cons:** not within walking distance of town; lots of flowered upholstery, rugs, and curtains; two-night minimum during peak periods. $ *Rooms from: $255* ⊠ *53 Hickory Ridge Rd., Putney* ✛ *11 miles north of Brattleboro* ☎ *802/387–5709, 800/380–9218* ⊕ *www.hickoryridgehouse.com* ⇌ *8 rooms* ⃝ *Free breakfast.*

★ The Inn on Putney Road

$$ | **B&B/INN** | Thoughtful and comforting details abound in this 1931 French-style manse such as the mini-refrigerator and basket stocked with complimentary soda, water, granola bars, and snacks, as well as gas fireplaces in several guest rooms. **Pros:** lovely breakfast room; nice blend of traditional and modern design; pottery by artist Steven Procter scattered throughout. **Cons:** tight parking; outside downtown; rooms in front sometimes suffer traffic noise. $ *Rooms from: $239* ⊠ *192 Putney Rd.* ☎ *802/536–4780* ⊕ *www.vermontbandbinn.com* ⇌ *6 rooms* ⃝ *Free breakfast.*

Latchis Hotel

$ | HOTEL | Though not lavish, the guest rooms in this 1938 Art Deco building have the original sinks and tiling in the bathrooms, and many overlook Main Street, with New Hampshire's mountains in the background. **Pros:** heart-of-town location; lots of personality; reasonable rates. **Cons:** limited breakfast; sound-masking machines sometimes required; few parking spots. $ *Rooms from: $130* ⊠ *50 Main St.* ☎ *802/254–6300, 800/798–6301* ⊕ *www.latchishotel.com* ⊃ *33 rooms* ⦿ *Free breakfast.*

Performing Arts

Latchis Theatre

THEMED ENTERTAINMENT | This movie theater's architecture represents a singular blending of art deco and Greek Revival style, complete with statues, columns, and 1938 murals by Louis Jambor (1884–1955), a noted artist and children's book illustrator. The Latchis hosts art exhibits, streams live events, and has four screening rooms. For a sense of the theater's original grandeur, buy a ticket for whatever is showing on the big screen. Though the space may not be a state-of-the-art cinema, watching a film here is far more memorable than at any multiplex. ⊠ *50 Main St.* ☎ *802/254–6300, 800/798–6301* ⊕ *www.latchis.com.*

Activities

BICYCLING

Brattleboro Bicycle Shop

BICYCLING | This shop rents hybrid bikes (call ahead to reserve one), does repair work, and sells maps and equipment. ⊠ *165 Main St.* ☎ *802/254–8644, 800/272–8245* ⊕ *www.bratbike.com.*

CANOEING

Vermont Canoe Touring Center

CANOEING/ROWING/SKULLING | Canoes and kayaks are available for rent here. Payment is by cash or check only. ⊠ *451*

Putney Rd. ☎ *802/257–5008* ⊕ *www. vermontcanoetouringcenter.com.*

HIKING

Fort Dummer State Park

PARK—SPORTS-OUTDOORS | You can hike and camp within the 217 acres of forest at this state park, the location of the first permanent European settlement in Vermont. That site is now submerged beneath the Connecticut River, but it is viewable from the northernmost scenic vista on Sunrise Trail. ⊠ *517 Old Guilford Rd.* ☎ *802/254–2610* ⊕ *www. vtstateparks.com/fortdummer.html* ⊠ *$4* ⊙ *Facilities closed early Sept.–late May.*

MULTISPORT OUTFITTERS

Burrows Specialized Sports

BICYCLING | This full-service sporting goods store rents and sells bicycles, snowboards, skis, and snowshoes, and has a repair shop. ⊠ *105 Main St.* ☎ *802/254–9430* ⊕ *www.burrowssports.com.*

Sam's Outdoor Outfitters

LOCAL SPORTS | At this labyrinthine two-story sports emporium you can find outerwear, shoes, and gear for all seasons and activities. Grab a bag of free popcorn while you're shopping. ⊠ *74 Main St.* ☎ *802/254–2933* ⊕ *www.samsoutfitters. com.*

Shopping

ART GALLERIES

Gallery Art Walk

ART GALLERIES | On this walk, you'll pass more than 30 galleries and other venues downtown and nearby that exhibit art; it takes place 5:30–8:30 pm on the first Friday evening of the month. ☎ *802/257–2616* ⊕ *www.gallerywalk.org.*

Gallery in the Woods

ART GALLERIES | This funky trilevel store sells art, jewelry, and light fixtures from around the world. Rotating shows take place in the upstairs and downstairs galleries. ⊠ *145 Main St.* ☎ *802/257–4777* ⊕ *www.galleryinthewoods.com.*

Vermont Artisan Designs
ART GALLERIES | Artworks and functional items in ceramic, glass, wood, fiber, and other media created by more than 300 artists are on display at this gallery. ⊠ *106 Main St.* ☎ *802/257–7044* ⊕ *www.vtart.com.*

Vermont Center for Photography
ART GALLERIES | The center exhibits works by American photographers. Opening receptions are held on the first Friday evening of the month. ⊠ *49 Flat St.* ☎ *802/251–6051* ⊕ *www.vcphoto.org.*

BOOKS

Brattleboro Books
BOOKS/STATIONERY | Bibliophiles will love hunting for buried treasure in this mini labyrinth of used books. ⊠ *36 Elliot St.* ☎ *802/257–7777* ⊕ *www.brattleborobooks.com.*

Wilmington

18 miles west of Brattleboro.

The village of Wilmington, with its classic Main Street lined with 18th- and 19th-century buildings, anchors the Mount Snow Valley. Most of the valley's lodging and dining establishments, however, can be found along Route 100, which travels 5 miles north to West Dover and Mount Snow, where skiers flock on winter weekends. The area abounds with cultural activity from concerts to art exhibits year-round.

GETTING HERE AND AROUND
Wilmington is at the junction of Route 9 and Route 100. West Dover and Mount Snow are a few miles to the north along Route 100.

ESSENTIALS
VISITOR INFORMATION Southern Vermont Deerfield Valley Chamber of Commerce
☎ *802/464–8092, 877/887–6884* ⊕ *www.visitvermont.com.*

 Sights

Adams Family Farm
FARM/RANCH | FAMILY | At this working farm you can collect fresh eggs from the chicken coop, feed a rabbit, milk a goat, ride a tractor or a pony, catch a fish in the pond, or take a sleigh ride in winter. A livestock barn is open November–mid-June; the animals roam free the rest of the year. ⊠ *15 Higley Hill Rd., off Rte. 100* ☎ *802/464–3762* ⊕ *www.adamsfamilyfarm.com* ☜ *$8.*

Southern Vermont Natural History Museum
MUSEUM | FAMILY | This museum 5 miles east of Wilmington houses one of New England's largest collections of mounted birds, including three extinct species and a complete collection of mammals native to the Northeast. The museum also has exhibits with live hawks, owls, and reptiles, and there's an adjacent 600-acre nature preserve. ⊠ *7599 Rte. 9* ☎ *802/464–0048* ⊕ *www.vermontmuseum.org* ☜ *$5.*

 Restaurants

Dot's Restaurant
$ | DINER | FAMILY | Under the classic red neon sign at the main corner in downtown Wilmington, Dot's remains a local landmark and a reminder of diners of yore. Friendly locals and skiers pack the tables and counter for American comfort food classics, starting at 5:30 am with the Berry-Berry pancake breakfast, with four kinds of berries. **Known for:** convivial community hangout; river-view seating; Dot's "jailhouse" chili. ⑤ *Average main: $10* ⊠ *3 W. Main St.* ☎ *802/464–7284* ⊕ *www.dotsofvermont.com.*

The Village Roost
$ | INTERNATIONAL | This bigger-on-the-inside café and lunch joint comes with ample space, especially in the barn-chic back room that serves resting travelers, gaming locals, and conferring coworkers. Keeping them oiled is a menu of organic, non-GMO, locally sourced

sandwiches, burgers, soups, and salads. **Known for:** large stone fireplace in the back; quality coffee and tea; hangout space. ⑤ *Average main: $11* ⊠ *20 W. Main St.* ☎ *802/464–3344* ⊕ *www.villageroost.com.*

Hotels

Deerhill Inn

$ | **B&B/INN** | The restaurant at this quintessential New England inn is among the best in town. **Pros:** complimentary house-baked cookies; some rooms have whirlpool tubs; toiletries by L'Occitane. **Cons:** must drive to Mount Snow and town; traditional flowered wallpaper and upholstery in spots; two-night minimum required for weekends. ⑤ *Rooms from: $165* ⊠ *14 Valley View Rd., West Dover* ☎ *802/464–3100, 800/993–3379* ⊕ *www.deerhill.com* ➭ *13 rooms* ⑩ *Free breakfast.*

Grand Summit Hotel

$$$ | **RESORT** | **FAMILY** | Mount Snow's comfortable main hotel is an easy choice for skiers whose main priority is getting on the slopes as quickly as possible. **Pros:** easy ski access; lots of children's activities; fitness center. **Cons:** somewhat bland decor; can be busy and crowded; resort fee. ⑤ *Rooms from: $380* ⊠ *39 Mount Snow Rd., West Dover* ☎ *800/451–4211* ⊕ *www.mountsnow. com* ➭ *196 rooms* ⑩ *No meals.*

Activities

FISHING
Lake Whitingham

FISHING | Eight-mile-long Lake Whitingham is the largest body of water completely contained within the state's boundaries. Also known as Harriman Reservoir, it has good fishing and 28 miles of undeveloped shoreline. There are boat launches at Wards Cove, Whitingham, Castle Hill, and Mountain Mills. ⊠ *Wilmington.*

Billboardless Vermont

Did you know that there are no billboards in Vermont? The state banned them in 1967 (similar laws exist in Maine, Alaska, and Hawaii), and the last one came down in 1975, so when you look out your window, you see trees and other scenery—not advertisements.

SKI AREAS
Mount Snow

SKIING/SNOWBOARDING | The closest major ski area to all of the Northeast's big cities, Mount Snow prides itself on its hundreds of snowmaking fan guns—more than any other resort in North America. There are four major downhill areas. The main mountain comprises mostly intermediate runs, while the north face has the majority of expert runs. The south face, Sunbrook, has wide, sunny trails. It connects to Carinthia, which is dedicated to terrain parks and glade skiing. In summer, the 600-acre resort has an 18-hole golf course, 11.3 miles of lift-serviced mountain-bike trails, and an extensive network of hiking trails. In 2018, the resort debuted a brand-new, $22 million, 42,000-square-foot Carinthia Base Lodge, five times the size of the previous lodge. **Facilities:** 86 trails; 600 acres; 1,700-foot vertical drop; 20 lifts. ⊠ *39 Mount Snow Rd., West Dover* ☎ *802/464–3333, 802/464–2151 for snow conditions, 800/245–7669* ⊕ *www.mountsnow.com* ▨ *Lift ticket: $110.*

Timber Creek

SKIING/SNOWBOARDING | North of Mount Snow, this appealingly small cross-country skiing and snowshoeing center has 4½ miles of groomed loops. You can rent equipment and take lessons here. ⊠ *13 Tanglewood Rd., at Rte. 100,*

*West Dover ☎ 802/464–0999 ⊕ www.
timbercreekxc.com ☜ $20.*

SNOWSHOE TRAIL
Molly Stark State Park

SNOW SPORTS | FAMILY | This park is home
to some of the state's most popular
snowshoe trails. Mount Olga Trail is a
relatively easy 1.7-mile loop culminat-
ing in a 360-degree view of southern
Vermont and northern Massachusetts.
⊠ *705 Rte. 9 E ☎ 802/464–5460 ⊕ www.
vtstateparks.com/mollystark.html.*

Shopping

Quaigh Design Centre

ART GALLERIES | For half a century, this
store has sold great pottery and artworks
from Britain and New England, including
woodcuts by Mary Azarian, a Vermont-
based artist. Scottish woolens are also on
offer. ⊠ *11 W. Main St. ☎ 802/464–2780.*

Bennington

21 miles west of Wilmington.

Bennington is the commercial focus of
Vermont's southwest corner and home
to Bennington College. It's really three
towns in one: Downtown Bennington,
Old Bennington, and North Bennington.
Downtown has retained much of the
industrial character it developed in the
19th century, when paper mills, grist-
mills, and potteries formed the city's
economic base. The outskirts of town
are commercial and not worth a stop, so
make your way right into Downtown and
Old Bennington to appreciate the area's
true charm.

GETTING HERE AND AROUND

The heart of modern Bennington is the
intersection of U.S. 7 and Route 9. Old
Bennington is a couple of miles west on
Route 9, at Monument Avenue. North
Bennington is a few miles north on
Route 67A.

ESSENTIALS
VISITOR INFORMATION Bennington Area
Chamber of Commerce ☎ 802/447–3311
⊕ www.bennington.com.

Sights

Bennington Battle Monument

MEMORIAL | FAMILY | This 306-foot stone
obelisk with an elevator to the top commemorates General John Stark's Revolutionary War victory over the British, who
attempted to capture Bennington's stock-
pile of supplies. Inside the monument
you can learn all about the battle, which
took place near Walloomsac Heights
in New York State on August 16, 1777,
and helped bring about the surrender of
British commander "Gentleman Johnny"
Burgoyne two months later. The top of
the tower affords commanding views of
the Massachusetts Berkshires, the New
York Adirondacks, and the Vermont Green
Mountains. ⊠ *15 Monument Circle, Old
Bennington ☎ 802/447–0550 ⊕ www.
benningtonbattlemonument.com ☜ $5
⊙ Closed Nov.–Apr.*

Bennington College

COLLEGE | Contemporary stone sculpture
and white-frame neo-Colonial dorms surrounded by acres of cornfields punctuate
the green meadows of the placid campus
of Bennington College. ⊠ *1 College Dr.,
off U.S. 7, North Bennington ☎ 802/442–
5401 ⊕ www.bennington.edu.*

★ Bennington Museum

MUSEUM | The rich collections here feature
military artifacts, early tools, dolls, and
the Bennington Flag, one of the oldest of
the Stars and Stripes in existence. Other
areas of interest include early Bennington pottery, the Gilded Age in Vermont,
mid-20th-century modernist painters
who worked in or near Bennington, glass
and metalwork by Lewis Comfort Tiffany,
and photography, watercolors, and other
works on paper. The highlight for many
visitors, though, is the largest public
collection of works by Grandma Moses
(1860–1961), the popular self-taught

The poet Robert Frost is buried in Bennington at the Old First Church.

artist who lived and painted in the area. ✉ *75 Main St., Old Bennington* 🕾 *802/447–1571* ⊕ *www.benningtonmuseum.com* 🎫 *$10* 🕐 *Closed Jan.; Wed. Feb.–May.*

The Laumeister Art Center

MUSEUM | The center mounts exhibitions by local and national artists in its galleries, and sculptures often dot the lawns. Permanent-collection highlights include wildlife paintings and Native American art and artifacts. ✉ *44 Gypsy La.* 🕾 *802/442–7158* ⊕ *www.artcenter.svc.edu* 🎫 *$10.*

Old Bennington

HISTORIC SITE | West of downtown, this National Register Historic District is well endowed with stately Colonial and Victorian mansions. The site of the Catamount Tavern, where Ethan Allen organized the Green Mountain Boys to capture Ft. Ticonderoga in 1775, is marked by a bronze statue of Vermont's indigenous mountain lion, now extinct. ✉ *Monument Ave., Old Bennington.*

The Old First Church

CEMETERY | In the graveyard of this church, the tombstone of the poet Robert Frost proclaims, "I had a lover's quarrel with the world." ✉ *1 Monument Circle, at Monument Ave., Old Bennington* 🕾 *802/447–1223* ⊕ *www.oldfirstchurchbenn.org* 🎫 *Free.*

Park-McCullough House

HOUSE | The architecturally significant Park-McCullough House is a 35-room classic French Empire–style mansion, built in 1865 and furnished with period pieces. Several restored flower gardens grace the landscaped grounds, and a barn holds some antique carriages. Guided tours happen on the hour while the house is open. The grounds are open daily year-round. ✉ *1 Park St., at West St., North Bennington* 🕾 *802/442–5441* ⊕ *www.parkmccullough.org* 🎫 *$15* 🕐 *Closed Oct.–May; Mon.–Thurs. June–Sept.*

Robert Frost Stone House Museum

HOUSE | Robert Frost came to Shaftsbury in 1920, he wrote, "to plant a new Garden of Eden with a thousand apple trees of some unforbidden variety." The museum, now part of Bennington College, tells the story of the poet's life and highlights the nine years (1920–29) he spent living in the house with his wife and four children. It was here that he penned "Stopping by Woods on a Snowy Evening" and published two books of poetry. You can wander 7 of the Frost family's original 80 acres. Among the apple boughs you just might find inspiration of your own. ⊠ *121 Historic Rte. 7A, Shaftsbury* ☎ *802/447–6200* ⊕ *www. bennington.edu* ✉ *$10* ⊙ *Closed Mon., Tues., and Nov.–Apr. also Sun. in May.*

Restaurants

Bakkerij Krijnen

$ | DUTCH | Some of the flakiest and most delectable pastries in Vermont can be ordered at this Dutch bakery helmed by husband-and-wife team Hans and Jennifer Krijne. Everything is made from scratch and uses local, organic, and all-natural ingredients—and tastes that way. **Known for:** artisanal breads; Douwe Egberts Dutch coffee; homemade stroopwafels. ⑤ *Average main: $10* ⊠ *1001 Main St.* ☎ *802/ 442–1001.*

Blue Benn Diner

$ | DINER | Classic American breakfast and lunch is served all day in this authentic, greasy-spoon diner, fashioned from a circa-1945 railcar. The line may be long, especially on weekends: locals and tourists can't stay away. **Known for:** local hangout; large menu beyond classic diner food; breakfast all day. ⑤ *Average main: $10* ⊠ *314 North St.* ☎ *802/442–5140* ▱ *No credit cards.*

Pangaea/Lounge

$$$ | AMERICAN | This rustic-chic restaurant comes with two faces: the classy, casual "Lounge" on one side that turns out tuned-up, locally sourced versions of bistro classics; and a full-blown, fine-dining experience on the "Pangaea" side. The latter is the more memorable, with gussied-up and coiffed waiters guiding you

through a three-course meal of French-influenced American cuisine. **Known for:** extensive wine list; roasted Long Island duck; Vermont boar and Brie Wellington. ⑤ *Average main: $31* ⊠ *1 Prospect St., 3 miles north of Bennington, North Bennington* ☎ *802/442–7171* ⊕ *www.vermontfinedining.com* ⊙ *No lunch.*

The Publyk House

$$ | AMERICAN | FAMILY | This antique three-story horse barn north of downtown now hosts an exceptionally spacious bistro serving American comfort food. The woody interior charms on its own, but it's the impressive views of Mt. Anthony and surrounding forests, particularly from the outdoor seating area, that wins lifetime fans. **Known for:** generous portions; bountiful, "endless" salad bar; can handle large groups. ⑤ *Average main: $20* ⊠ *782 Harwood Hill Rd.* ☎ *802/442–7500* ⊕ *www.thepublykhouse.com* ⊙ *No lunch weekdays.*

Hotels

The Eddington House Inn

$ | B&B/INN | In the heart of North Bennington, just around the corner from three covered bridges and Bennington College, this impeccably maintained, 18th-century three-bedroom house is a great value. **Pros:** budget prices for a great bed-and-breakfast; "endless desserts" in dining room 24 hours a day; summer guest passes to Lake Paran. **Cons:** slightly off usual tourist track; only three rooms so it fills up fast; no front desk or after-hours reception. ⑤ *Rooms from: $159* ⊠ *21 Main St., North Bennington* ☎ *802/442–1511* ⊕ *www.eddingtonhouseinn.com* ⇄ *3 suites* ❢❂❢ *Free breakfast.*

★ Four Chimneys Inn

$ | B&B/INN | This exquisite, three-story, neo-Georgian (circa 1915) looks out over a substantial lawn and a wonderful old stone wall. **Pros:** walking distance to several Bennington sights; a complimentary full country breakfast; extremely well kept. **Cons:** dinner only offered for special events; no coffee or tea in rooms; a bit stuffy. $ *Rooms from: $189* ✉ *21 West Rd., Old Bennington* ☎ *802/447–3500* ⊕ *www.fourchimneys.com* ⤴ *11 rooms* ⦿ *Free breakfast.*

The Hardwood Hill

$ | HOTEL | Built in 1937, this fully renovated roadside motel has been given a distinct artsy, boutique upgrade by a foursome of new owners, three of whom are working artists, which translates into a sculpture garden out front, regular workshops by a resident artist, and performances on the red stage on the vast, hammock-dappled back lawn. **Pros:** excellent restaurant right next door; good value for cost; "arts package" includes tickets and discounts at local sights. **Cons:** must drive to town; rooms somewhat small; no restaurant or dining area. $ *Rooms from: $99* ✉ *864 Harwood Hill Rd.* ☎ *802/442–6278* ⊕ *www.harwoodhillmotel.com* ⤴ *17 rooms* ⦿ *Free breakfast.*

 Performing Arts

Basement Music Series

MUSIC | The Vermont Arts Exchange sponsors this fun and funky contemporary music series at the downtown Masonic Lodge. Some performances sell out, so it's wise to purchase tickets in advance. ✉ *504 Main St.* ☎ *800/838–3006 for ticket hotline* ⊕ *www.vtartxchange.org/music.*

Oldcastle Theatre Company

MUSIC | This fine regional theater company focuses on American classics and crowd-pleasing musicals. The group's venue also hosts occasional concerts. ✉ *331 Main St.* ☎ *802/447–0564* ⊕ *www.oldcastletheatre.org* ⊙ *Closed Dec.–Mar.*

 Activities

Lake Shaftsbury State Park

PARK—SPORTS-OUTDOORS | FAMILY | You'll find a swimming beach, nature trails, boat and canoe rentals, and a snack bar

at this pretty park. ✉ *262 Shaftsbury State Park Rd., 10½ miles north of Bennington* ☎ *802/375–9978* ⊕ *www.vtstateparks.com/shaftsbury.html* ⊙ *Facilities closed early Sept.–mid-May.*

Woodford State Park

PARK—SPORTS-OUTDOORS | FAMILY | At 2,400 feet, this has the highest state campground in Vermont. Adams Reservoir is the dominant feature and focus of activities, with swimming, fishing, and boating, including canoes, kayaks, and paddleboards for rent. A nature trail also circles the reservoir. ✉ *142 State Park Rd.* *10 miles east of Bennington* ☎ *802/447–7169* ⊕ *www.vtstateparks.com/woodford.html* ⊙ *Facilities closed mid-Oct.–mid-May.*

🛍 Shopping

The Apple Barn & Country Bake Shop

FOOD/CANDY | FAMILY | Homemade baked goods, fresh cider, Vermont cheeses, maple syrup, and around a dozen varieties of apples are among the treats for sale here. There's berry picking in season, for a fun family stop, and on weekends you can watch the bakers make cider doughnuts. ✉ *604 Rte. 7S, 1½ miles south of downtown Bennington* ☎ *802/447–7780* ⊕ *www.theapplebarn.com.*

The Bennington Bookshop

BOOKS/STATIONERY | The state's oldest independent bookstore sells the latest new releases and hosts weekly readings, signings, and lectures. ✉ *467 Main St.* ☎ *802/442–5059* ⊕ *www.benningtonbookshop.com.*

Bennington Potters Yard

CERAMICS/GLASSWARE | The yard's showroom stocks goods from the famed Bennington Potters. On a self-guided tour you can see the potters at work (except Sunday). ✉ *324 County St.* ☎ *802/447–7531, 800/205–8033* ⊕ *www.benningtonpotters.com.*

Vermont Maple Syrup

Vermont is the country's largest producer of maple syrup. A visit to a maple farm is a great way to learn all about sugaring, the process of extracting maple tree sap and making syrup. Sap is stored in a sugar maple tree's roots in the winter, and in the spring when conditions are just right, the sap runs up and can be tapped. Sugaring season runs March to April, which is when all maple syrup in the state is produced.

One of the best parts of visiting a maple farm is getting to taste and compare the four grades of syrup. As the sugaring season goes on and days become warmer, the sap becomes progressively darker and stronger in flavor. Grades are defined by color, clarity, density, and flavor. Is one grade better than another? Nope, it's just a question of taste. Sap drawn early in the season produces the lightest color, and has the most delicate flavor: this is called golden. Amber has a mellow flavor. Dark is much more robust, and Very Dark is the most flavorful, making it often the favorite of first-time tasters.

When visiting a maple farm, make sure they make their own syrup, as opposed to just bottling or selling someone else's. You'll learn more about the entire process that way. **Vermont Maple Syrup** (☎ *802/858–9444* ⊕ *www.vermontmaple.org*), a great resource, has a map of maple farms that host tours, a directory of producers open year-round, and a list of places from which you can order maple syrup by mail. You can also get the lowdown on events such as the annual Maple Open House Weekend, when sugarhouses throughout the state open their doors to visitors.

Now And Then Books

BOOKS/STATIONERY | This labyrinthine second-story bookstore stocks nearly 45,000 secondhand volumes. ⊠ *439 Main St.* ☎ *802/442–5566* ⊕ *www.nowandthenbooksvt.com.*

Arlington

15 miles north of Bennington.

Smaller than Bennington and more down-to-earth than upper-crust Manchester to the north, Arlington exudes a certain Rockwellian folksiness, and it should: the illustrator Norman Rockwell lived here from 1939 to 1953, and many neighbors served as models for his portraits of small-town life.

GETTING HERE AND AROUND

Arlington is at the intersection of Route 313 and Route 7A. Take Route 313 West to reach West Arlington.

Sights

West Arlington

TOWN | Norman Rockwell once lived in this place with a quaint town green. If you follow Route 313 west from Arlington, you'll pass by the Wayside Country Store, a slightly rickety charmer where you can pick up sandwiches and chat with locals. The store carries everything from ammo and sporting goods to toys, teas, and maple syrup. Continue on, and cross West Arlington's red covered bridge, which leads to the town green. To loop back to Route 7A, take River Road along the south side of the Battenkill River, a scenic drive. ⊠ *West Arlington.*

Hotels

The Arlington Inn

$ | B&B/INN | The Greek Revival columns of this 1847 home lend it an imposing presence in the middle of town, but the atmosphere within is friendly and old-fashioned. **Pros:** heart-of-town location; friendly atmosphere; rigorously eco-friendly. **Cons:** expensive dining; elegant but old-fashioned decor; no tea or coffee in rooms. ⑤ *Rooms from: $199* ✉ *3904 Rte. 7A* ☎ *802/375–6532* ⊕ *www.arlingtoninn.com* ⮏ *17 rooms* ⑩ *Free breakfast.*

★ Hill Farm Inn

$$ | B&B/INN | FAMILY | Few hotels or inns in Vermont can match the sumptuous views of Mt. Equinox and surrounding hillscape of this former dairy farm built in 1830, whether seen from the large wrap-around porch, the fire pit (where you can roast s'mores), or the outdoor hot tub. **Pros:** outdoor pool and hot tub; perfect Vermont wedding setting; Vermont Castings stoves in many rooms. **Cons:** books up on weekends with weddings; bringing alcohol not allowed; can be buggy in summer, like all Vermont. ⑤ *Rooms from: $235* ✉ *458 Hill Farm Rd., off Rte. 7A, Sunderland* ☎ *802/375–2269* ⊕ *www.hillfarminn.com* ⮏ *12 rooms* ⑩ *Free breakfast.*

West Mountain Inn

$$ | B&B/INN | FAMILY | This 1810 farmhouse sits on 150 mountainside acres with hiking trails and easy access to the Battenkill River, where you can canoe or go tubing; in winter, guests can sled down a former ski slope or borrow snowshoes or cross-country skis. **Pros:** atmospheric Colonial dining room; lots of activities; wood-panel dining room with fireplace. **Cons:** dining room not ideal for kids; dirt road to property uneven and pitted; tiny bathrooms in some rooms. ⑤ *Rooms from: $205* ✉ *144 W. Mountain Inn Rd., at Rte. 313* ☎ *802/375–6516* ⊕ *www.westmountaininn.com* ⮏ *20 rooms* ⑩ *Free breakfast.*

Shopping

GIFTS

Village Peddler

GIFTS/SOUVENIRS | FAMILY | This shop has a "chocolatorium," where you can learn all about cocoa. It sells fudge and other candies and stocks a large collection of teddy bears, one of whom is giant and made of chocolate. ✉ *261 Old Mill Rd., East Arlington* ☎ *802/375–6037* ⊕ *www.villagepeddlervt.com.*

Manchester

9 miles northeast of Arlington.

Well-to-do Manchester has been a popular summer retreat since the mid-19th century, when city dwellers traveled north to take in the cool, clean air at the base of 3,840-foot Mt. Equinox. Manchester Village's tree-shaded marble sidewalks and stately old homes—Main Street here could hardly be more picture-perfect—reflect the luxurious resort lifestyle of more than a century ago. A mile north on Route 7A, Manchester Center is the commercial twin to Colonial Manchester Village; it's also where you'll find the town's famed upscale factory outlets doing business in attractive faux-Colonial shops.

Manchester Village houses the world headquarters of Orvis, the outdoor-goods brand that was founded here in the 19th century and has greatly influenced the town ever since. The complex includes a fly-fishing school featuring lessons given in its casting ponds and the Battenkill River.

GETTING HERE AND AROUND

Manchester is the main town for the ski resorts of Stratton (a half-hour drive on Route 30) and Bromley (15 minutes to the northeast on Route 11). It's 15 minutes north of Arlington along scenic Route 7A.

ESSENTIALS

VISITOR INFORMATION Green Mountain National Forest Visitor Center ☎ *802/362–2307* ⊕ *www.fs.usda.gov/main/gmfl.* **Manchester Visitors Center** ⊕ *www.visit-manchestervt.com.*

Sights

American Museum of Fly Fishing

MUSEUM | This museum houses the world's largest collection of angling art and angling-related objects—more than 1,500 rods, 800 reels, 30,000 flies, including the tackle of Winslow Homer, Babe Ruth, Jimmy Carter, and other notables. Every August, vendors sell antique equipment at the museum's fly-fishing festival. You can also practice your casting out back. ⊠ *4070 Main St.* ☎ *802/362–3300* ⊕ *www.amff.org* 🎫 *$5* ⊗ *Closed Mon.; also Sun. Nov.–May.*

★ Hildene

GARDEN | **FAMILY** | A twofold treat, the summer home of Abraham Lincoln's son Robert provides insight into the lives of the Lincoln family, as well as an introduction to the lavish Manchester life of the early 1900s. In 1905, Robert built a 24-room Georgian Revival mansion where he and his descendants lived until 1975. It's the centerpiece of a beautifully preserved 412-acre estate and holds many of the family's prized possessions, including one of three surviving stovepipe hats owned by Abraham and a Lincoln Bible. When the 1,000-pipe Aeolian organ is played, the music reverberates as though from the mansion's very bones.

Rising from a 10-acre meadow, Hildene Farm is magnificent. The agriculture center is built in a traditional style—post-and-beam construction of timber felled and milled on the estate, and you can watch goat cheese being made.

The highlight, though, may be the elaborate formal gardens, where a thousand peonies bloom every June. There is also a teaching greenhouse, restored 1903

Pullman car, a 600-foot floating boardwalk across the Battenkill wetlands, and more than 12 miles of walking trails. When conditions permit, you can cross-country ski and snowshoe on the property. ⊠ *1005 Hildene Rd., at Rte. 7A* ☎ *802/362–1788, 800/578–1788* ⊕ *www.hildene.org* 🎫 *$23.*

★ Southern Vermont Arts Center

ARTS VENUE | At the end of a long, winding driveway, this center has a permanent collection of more than 800 19th- and 20th-century American artworks and presents temporary exhibitions. The original building, a Georgian mansion set on 100 acres, contains 12 galleries with works by more than 600 artists, many from Vermont. The center also hosts concerts, performances, and film screenings. In summer and fall, the views from the café at lunchtime are magnificent. ⊠ *930 SVAC Dr., West Rd.* ☎ *802/362–1405* ⊕ *www.svac.org* 🎫 *Free* ⊗ *Closed Mon. Nov.–May.*

Restaurants

Bistro Henry

$$$ | **FRENCH** | The presence of chef-owner Henry Bronson accounts for the popularity of this friendly bistro, serving classics like steak au poivre and medium-rare duck breast. Bronson mixes things up, though, with dishes like tuna wasabi with spicy pad Thai, while Dina (Henry's wife) complements with a well-curated wine list and homemade desserts. **Known for:** the perfect date-night spot; Grand Marnier crème brûlée; 100% solar powered. ⑤ *Average main: $30* ⊠ *1942 Depot St.* ✢ *3 miles east of Manchester Center* ☎ *802/362–4982* ⊕ *www.bistrohenry.com* ⊗ *Closed Mon. No lunch.*

Chantecleer

$$$$ | **EUROPEAN** | There is something wonderful about eating by candlelight in an old barn; and with the rooster art above their rough-hewn wooden beams, Chantecleer's dining rooms are especially romantic. The international menu runs

The formal gardens and mansion at Robert Todd Lincoln's Hildene are a far cry from his father's log cabin.

the gamut from veal schnitzel to New York strip to Dover sole. **Known for:** great fieldstone fireplace; duck Grand Marnier; Thursday burger night at the bar. ⑤ *Average main: $38* ✉ *8 Reed Farm La., 3½ miles north of Manchester, East Dorset* ☎ *802/362–1616* ⊕ *www.chantecleerrestaurant.com* ⊗ *Closed Mon., Tues., mid-Nov., and mid-Apr. No lunch.*

Chop House

$$$$ | **STEAKHOUSE** | Walk to the very back room of the Equinox's Marsh Tavern to enter this special, very expensive, and very delicious steak house, with aged corn- or grass-fed beef broiled at 1,400°F and finished with marrow butter. The marble above the fireplace is chiseled "L.L. ORVIS 1832," and way before he claimed the spot, the Green Mountain Boys gathered here to plan their Revolutionary War-era resistance. **Known for:** New York strip; craft cocktails; tuna tartare. ⑤ *Average main: $47* ✉ *3567 Main St.* ☎ *802/362–4700* ⊕ *www.equinoxresort.com* ⊗ *No lunch.*

Mistral's at Toll Gate

$$$$ | **FRENCH** | This classic French restaurant is tucked in a grotto on the climb to Bromley Mountain. The two dining rooms are perched over the Bromley Brook, and at night a small waterfall is magically illuminated—ask for a window table. **Known for:** chateaubriand béarnaise; crispy sweetbreads Dijonnaise; wine list. ⑤ *Average main: $36* ✉ *10 Toll Gate Rd., off Rte. 11/30* ☎ *802/362–1779* ⊕ *www.mistralsattollgate.com* ⊗ *Closed Tues. and Wed. No lunch.*

★ Mystic Cafe & Wine Bar

$$ | **ECLECTIC** | This spacious, brand-new, Euro-chic restaurant is earning plenty of local praise for its gussied-up takes on international cuisines with a Vermont-farmhouse accent. That means plenty of kale, butternut squash, sweet potato, and cheddar in the salads, sandwiches, and tapas-style shared plates. **Known for:** paella with Israeli couscous; French toast; wine list. ⑤ *Average main: $20* ✉ *4928 Main St., Manchester Center* ☎ *802/768–8086* ⊕ *www.mysticcafeandwinebar.com* ⊗ *Closed Mon.*

Perfect Wife

$$ | **ECLECTIC** | Owner-chef Amy Chamberlain, a Manchester native, creates a fun, free-form atmosphere at this restaurant and tavern, livened up by live funk, blues, and jazz on summer weekends. The menu covers the classics of the region, with a few international forays, but with smart and pleasing culinary twists. **Known for:** Monday burger nights; turkey schnitzel; craft cocktails with Vermont-made spirits. $ *Average main: $21 ⊠ 2594 Depot St. ✛ 2½ miles east of Manchester Center ☎ 802/362–2817 ⊕ www.perfectwife.com ☉ Closed Sun. No lunch.*

Ponce Bistro

$$$ | **INTERNATIONAL** | The Spanish influence adds much to the charm of this small, atmospheric restaurant, as does a fireplace in the front room. No alcohol is served, but glasses are happily provided for any who bring their own beer and wine, and no corkage fee, to boot. **Known for:** Spanish meat loaf; beef stroganoff; homemade salad dressings. $ *Average main: $28 ⊠ 4659 Main St., Mendon ☎ 802/768–8095 ⊕ www.poncebistro.com ☉ Closed Sun. No dinner Mon. and Tues.*

The Reluctant Panther Inn & Restaurant

$$$$ | **AMERICAN** | The dining room at this luxurious inn is a large, modern space where rich woods and high ceilings meld into a kind of "nouveau Vermont" aesthetic. The contemporary American cuisine emphasizes farm-to-table ingredients and has earned the restaurant "Gold Barn" honors from the Vermont Fresh Network. **Known for:** wine list; chef of the year award by the Vermont Chamber of Commerce; lobster-and-Brie fondue. $ *Average main: $37 ⊠ 39 West Rd. ☎ 800/822–2331, 802/362–2568 ⊕ www.reluctantpanther. com ☉ Closed Sun. No lunch.*

★ The Silver Fork

$$$ | **ECLECTIC** | This intimate, elegant bistro is owned by husband-and-wife team Mark and Melody French, who spent years in Puerto Rico absorbing the flavors of the island that are reflected in the eclectic international menu. Reserve one of the six tables ahead of time, or sit at the wine bar for a casual and romantic dinner with a maple martini or a bottle from the impressive wine list. **Known for:** shrimp mofongo (with mashed plantains); wine and cocktail list; special occasions. $ *Average main: $30 ⊠ 4201 Main St., across from Orvis Flagship Store ☎ 802/768–8444 ⊕ www.thesilverforkvt. com ☉ Closed Sun. No lunch.*

Ye Olde Tavern

$$$ | **AMERICAN** | This circa-1790 Colonial inn dishes up Yankee favorites along with plenty of New England charm, made all the more intimate by the candlelight. To learn more about the colorful history of the building, simply ask the manager, who makes a regular appearance at tables. **Known for:** cheddar-and-ale onion soup; traditional pot roast; 1790 Taproom Ale (custom brew by Long Trail). $ *Average main: $26 ⊠ 5183 Main St. ☎ 802/362–0611 ⊕ www.yeoldetavern.net.*

 Hotels

Equinox

$$$ | **RESORT** | In Manchester Village, nearly all life revolves around the historic Equinox Inn, whose fame and service have carved it into the Mount Rushmore of accommodation in Vermont. **Pros:** fitness center and pool; excellent steak house on-site; extensive network of walking trails. **Cons:** somewhat corporate feel; lines at reception can make checking in and out take long; lots of weddings can sometimes overcrowd. $ *Rooms from: $391 ⊠ 3567 Main St. ☎ 802/362–4700, 866/837–4219 ⊕ www.equinoxresort. com ⇨ 147 rooms* ❍| *No meals.*

Taconic Hotel

$$$ | **HOTEL** | Vermont's only Kimpton, which opened in 2015, attempts to walk the fine line between its corporate boutique design and a Vermont flavor. **Pros:** locally handmade walking sticks from Manchester Woodcraft in rooms;

no additional fee for pets; the house restaurant, the Copper Grouse, does a pretty good turn on American bistro cuisine. **Cons:** not very Vermonty experience; only chain's rewards members get free high-speed Internet/Wi-Fi; tiny pool. $ *Rooms from: $339* ✉ *3835 Main St.* ☎ *802/362–0147* ⊕ *www.taconichotel. com* 🛏 *87 rooms* ⦿❘ *No meals.*

★ **Wilburton Inn**

$$ | **B&B/INN** | Stepping into this hilltop 1902 Tudor-style mansion, you might think you've stumbled on a lavish film set: there's a palpably cinematic quality to the richly paneled guest rooms and the common rooms, which make an ideal setting for "murder-mystery weekends," "Innkeeper's Daughter Cabaret," and more quirky events. **Pros:** unique activities and adornments; easy access to Manchester; views of surrounding landscape. **Cons:** limited indoor facilities; lots of floral wallpaper and traditional frills; two-night minimum stay is required on most weekends. $ *Rooms from: $205* ✉ *257 Wilburton Dr.* ☎ *802/362–2500* ⊕ *www.wilburton.com* 🛏 *40 rooms* ⦿❘ *Free breakfast.*

 Nightlife

Falcon Bar

MUSIC CLUBS | This sophisticated bar has live music on weekends. In summer, don't miss the wonderful outdoor deck. In winter, the place to be is around the giant Vermont slate fire pit. ✉ *Equinox Resort, 3567 Main St.* ☎ *800/362–4747* ⊕ *www.equinoxresort.com.*

Union Underground

BARS/PUBS | One of Manchester's newest hot spots, this part underground, part aboveground pub and restaurant offers lots of space, a sleek green-marble bar, craft beer, a pool table, and tasty classics with all the fixings. ✉ *4928 Main St., Manchester Center* ☎ *802/367–3951* ⊕ *www.unionundergroundvt.com.*

 Activities

BIKING
Battenkill Bicycles

BICYCLING | This shop rents, sells, and repairs bikes and provides maps and route suggestions. ✉ *99 Bonnet St.* ☎ *802/362–2734* ⊕ *www.battenkill-sports.com.*

FISHING
Battenkill Anglers

FISHING | Teaching the art and science of fly-fishing, Battenkill Anglers offers both private and group lessons. ✉ *6204 Main St.* ☎ *802/379–1444* ⊕ *www.battenkillangler.com.*

HIKING
There are bountiful hiking trails in the Green Mountain National Forest. Shorter hikes begin at the Equinox Resort, which owns about 1,000 acres of forest and has a great trail system open to the public.

Equinox Preserve

HIKING/WALKING | A multitude of well-groomed walking trails for all abilities thread the 914 acres on the slopes of Mt. Equinox, including a trail to the summit. ✉ *Multiple trailheads, End of West Union St.* ☎ *802/366–1400 Equinox Preservation Trust* ⊕ *www.equinoxpreservationtrust.org.*

Long Trail

HIKING/WALKING | One of the most popular segments of Vermont's Long Trail leads to the top of Bromley Mountain. The strenuous 5.4-mile round-trip takes about four hours. ✉ *Rte. 11/30* ⊕ *www.greenmountainclub.org.*

Lye Brook Falls

HIKING/WALKING | This 4.6-mile hike starts off Glen Road and ends at Vermont's most impressive cataract, Lye Brook Falls. The moderately strenuous journey takes four hours. ✉ *Off Glen Rd., south from E. Manchester Rd. just east of U.S. 7* ⊕ *www.greenmountainclub.org.*

Mountain Goat

HIKING/WALKING | Stop here for hiking, cross-country-skiing, and snowshoeing equipment (some of which is available to rent), as well as a good selection of warm clothing. ⊠ *4886 Main St.* ☎ *802/362–5159* ⊕ *www.mountaingoat.com.*

ICE-SKATING
Riley Rink at Hunter Park

ICE SKATING | **FAMILY** | This Olympic-size indoor ice rink has skate rentals and a concession stand. ⊠ *410 Hunter Park Rd.* ☎ *802/362–0150* ⊕ *www.rileyrink.com.*

 Shopping

ART AND ANTIQUES
Long Ago & Far Away

ANTIQUES/COLLECTIBLES | This store specializes in fine indigenous artwork, including Inuit stone sculpture. ⊠ *Green Mountain Village Shops, 4963 Main St.* ☎ *802/362–3435* ⊕ *www.longagoandfaraway.com.*

Manchester Woodcraft

CRAFTS | The millions of trees in the Green Mountains make Vermont a wood-carver's dreamscape. The saws, planes, and scrapers of the woodshop here turn out a range of handsome household goods, plus a wide selection of pieces and parts for DIY fans. ⊠ *175 Depot St., Manchester Center* ☎ *802/362–5770* ⊕ *www. manchesterwoodcraft.com.*

Tilting at Windmills Gallery

ANTIQUES/COLLECTIBLES | This large gallery displays the paintings and sculptures of nationally known artists. ⊠ *24 Highland Ave., Manchester Center* ☎ *802/362–3022* ⊕ *www.tilting.com.*

BOOKS
Northshire Bookstore

BOOKS/STATIONERY | **FAMILY** | The heart of Manchester Center, this bookstore is adored by visitors and residents alike for its ambience, selection, and service. Up the iron staircase is a second floor dedicated to children's books, toys, and clothes. Connected to the store is the Spiral Press Café, where you can sit down to a grilled pesto-chicken sandwich or a latte and scone. ⊠ *4869 Main St.* ☎ *802/362–2200, 800/437–3700* ⊕ *www. northshire.com.*

CLOTHING
Manchester Designer Outlets

CLOTHING | This is the most upscale collection of stores in northern New England—and every store is a discount outlet. The architecture reflects the surrounding homes, so the place looks a bit like a Colonial village. The long list of famous-brand clothiers here includes Kate Spade, Yves Delorme, Michael Kors, Ann Taylor, Tumi, BCBG, Armani, Coach, Polo Ralph Lauren, Brooks Brothers, and Theory. ⊠ *97 Depot St.* ☎ *802/362–3736, 800/955–7467* ⊕ *www.manchesterdesigneroutlets.com.*

Orvis Flagship Store

CLOTHING | The lodgelike Orvis store carries the company's latest clothing, fly-fishing gear, and pet supplies—there's even a trout pond. At this required shopping destination for many visitors—the Orvis name is pure Manchester—there are demonstrations of how fly rods are constructed and tested. You can attend fly-fishing school across the street. ⊠ *4180 Main St.* ☎ *802/362–3750* ⊕ *www.orvis.com.*

SPAS
★ Spa at Equinox

SPA/BEAUTY | Some of Vermont's best spa treatments are found behind the mahogany doors and beadboard wainscoting of the Equinox Spa and are well worth the splurge. At one end are an indoor pool and outdoor hot tub; at the other end are the treatment rooms. The signature 100-minute Spirit of Vermont combines Reiki, reflexology, and massage, and will leave you feeling like a whole, complete person. The locker rooms feature steam rooms and saunas. Day passes are available for all ages. ⊠ *Equinox Resort, 3567 Rte. 7A* ☎ *802/362–4700, 800/362–4747* ⊕ *www.equinoxresort.com.*

Dorset

7 miles north of Manchester.

Lying at the foot of many mountains and with a village green surrounded by white clapboard homes and inns, Dorset has a solid claim to the title of Vermont's most picture-perfect town. Dorset has just 2,000 residents, but two of the state's best and oldest general stores.

The country's first commercial marble quarry opened here in 1785. Dozens more opened, providing the marble for the main research branch of the New York Public Library and many 5th Avenue mansions, among other notable landmarks, as well as the sidewalks here and in Manchester. A remarkable private home made entirely of marble can be seen on Dorset West Road, a beautiful residential road west of the town green. The marble Dorset Church on the green has two Tiffany stained-glass windows.

◉ Sights

★ Dorset Quarry

BODY OF WATER | FAMILY | On hot summer days the sight of dozens of families jumping, swimming, and basking in the sun around this massive 60-foot-deep swimming hole makes it one of the most wholesome and picturesque recreational spots in the region. First mined in 1785, the stone from the country's oldest commercial marble quarry was used to build the main branch of the New York Public Library and the Montreal Museum of Fine Arts. ⊠ *Rte. 30* 🆓 *Free.*

Merck Forest & Farmland Center

FARM/RANCH | FAMILY | This 3,162-acre educational center has 30 miles of nature trails for hiking, cross-country skiing, snowshoeing, horseback riding, and rustic camping. You can visit the 62-acre farm, which grows organic fruit and vegetables (sold at the visitor center), and check out the horses, sheep, pigs, and chickens while you're there—you're even welcome to help out with the chores. ⊠ *3270 Rte. 315, Rupert* ☎ *802/394–7836* ⊕ *www.merckforest.org* 🆓 *Free.*

Restaurants

The Dorset Inn

$$$ | AMERICAN | Built in 1796, this inn has been continuously operating ever since, and the comfortable tavern and formal dining room serve a Colonial-influenced bistro menu. A member of the Vermont Fresh Network, the restaurant benefits greatly from its strong connections with local farmers. **Known for:** wine list; brunch in sunny garden room; whiskey and bourbon menu. ⑤ *Average main: $27* ⊠ *Dorset Green, 8 Church St.* ☎ *802/867–5500* ⊕ *www.dorsetinn.com* ⊗ *No lunch.*

Inn at West View Farm

$$$ | ECLECTIC | Chef-owner Raymond Chen was the lead line cook at New York City's Mercer Kitchen before opening this restaurant inside a traditional inn. Chen skillfully applies French techniques to Asian dishes crafted from fresh Vermont ingredients for a nice break from the usual regional cuisine. **Known for:** big picture windows with view; dim sum; roasted and confit duck. ⑤ *Average main: $30* ⊠ *2928 Rte. 30* ☎ *802/867–5715, 800/769–4903* ⊕ *www.innatwestviewfarm.com* ⊗ *Closed Tues. and Wed. No lunch.*

Hotels

Barrows House

$$ | HOTEL | This renovated 19th-century manse, once the residence of the town's pastor, incorporates a modern boutique aesthetic into the traditional-style inn, especially in the attached gastropub, which features a long, polished metal bar and backlighted marble. **Pros:** good bar and restaurant; chintz-free decor; large gardens. **Cons:** rooms can become drafty in cold weather; robes only in luxury suites; no coffee or tea in rooms. ⑤ *Rooms from: $275* ⊠ *3156*

Rte. 30 ☎ *802/867–4455* ⊕ *www.barrowshouse.com* ⤴ *27 rooms* ⦅⦆ *Free breakfast.*

Squire House Bed & Breakfast

$$ | **B&B/INN** | On a wonderfully quiet road, this inn, built in 1918, has guest rooms that combine modern comforts and antique fixtures. **Pros:** big estate feels like your own; wood-burning fireplace in two rooms; crème brûlée French toast at breakfast. **Cons:** basic bathrooms; two-night minimum required for peak periods; one-night reservation costs additional $60 fee in some periods. ⑤ *Rooms from: $210* ⊠ *3395 Dorset West Rd.* ☎ *802/867–0281* ⊕ *www.squirehouse. com* ⤴ *4 rooms* ⦅⦆ *Free breakfast.*

🎭 Performing Arts

Dorset Players

THEATER | The prestigious summer theater troupe presents the annual Dorset Theater Festival. Plays are staged in a wonderful converted pre-Revolutionary War barn. ⊠ *Dorset Playhouse, 104 Cheney Rd.* ☎ *802/867–5570* ⊕ *www. dorsetplayers.org.*

Activities

Emerald Lake State Park

PARK—SPORTS-OUTDOORS | This park has a well-marked nature trail, a small beach, boat rentals, and a snack bar. ⊠ *65 Emerald Lake La., East Dorset* ☎ *802/362–1655* ⊕ *www.vtstateparks. com/emerald.html* 🅿 *$4* ⦿ *Facilities closed mid-Oct.–mid-May.*

Shopping

Dorset Union Store

CONVENIENCE/GENERAL STORES | Dating to 1816, this general store has good prepared dinners and a big wine selection. It also sells interesting gifts. ⊠ *Dorset Green, 31 Church St.* ☎ *802/867–4400* ⊕ *www.dorsetunionstore.com.*

H. N. Williams General Store

CONVENIENCE/GENERAL STORES | Started in 1840 by William Williams, this trilevel country store has been run by the same family for six generations. This is one of those places where you can buy maple syrup and ammo, while catching up on posted town announcements. There's a deli on-site for sandwiches; a farmers' market is held outside on Sunday in summer. ⊠ *2732 Rte. 30* ☎ *802/867–5353* ⊕ *www.hnwilliams.com.*

Stratton

26 miles southeast of Dorset.

Stratton is really Stratton Mountain Resort, a mountaintop ski resort with a self-contained "town center" of shops, restaurants, and lodgings clustered at the base of the slopes. When the snow melts, golf, tennis, and a host of other summer activities are big attractions, but the ski village remains quiet.

GETTING HERE AND AROUND

From Manchester or U.S. 7, follow Route 11/30 east until they split. Route 11 continues past Bromley ski mountain, and Route 30 turns south 10 minutes toward Bondville, the town at the base of the mountain. At the junction of Routes 30 and 100 is the village of Jamaica, with its own cluster of inns and restaurants on the eastern side of the mountain.

Restaurants

J.J. Hapgood General Store and Eatery

$ | **AMERICAN** | **FAMILY** | You won't find a better meal at any other general store in the state. This is really more of a classic American restaurant, serving farm-to-table breakfast, lunch, and dinner, than a place to pick up the essentials, but like any good general store, it's a friendly and relaxed gathering spot for locals. **Known for:** buttermilk biscuits; outdoor patio; wood-fired pizzas. ⑤ *Average main: $12* ⊠ *305 Main St., Peru* ☎ *802/824–4800* ⊕ *www.jjhapgood. com* ⦿ *No dinner Mon. and Tues.*

The Red Fox Inn

$$$ | **AMERICAN** | This converted bi-level barn has the best nightlife in town, including Grammy-award-winning acts, and a fun dining room. The restaurant, serving elk chops, shepherd's pie, coq au vin, and the like is on the upper level, where you'll see wagon wheels and a carriage suspended from the A-frame ceiling. **Known for:** apple pie was served at the inauguration of President Obama; huge fireplace; Irish music with half-price Guinness, and fish 'n' chips on Wednesday. $ *Average main: $26* ⊠ *103 Winhall Hollow Rd., Bondville* ☎ *802/297–2488* ⊕ *www.redfox-inn.com* ⊙ *Closed mid-Apr.–mid-May; Sun. and Mon. late May–July. No lunch.*

Hotels

Long Trail House

$$ | **RENTAL** | Directly across the street from the ski village, this condo complex is one of the closest to the slopes. **Pros:** across the street from ski lift; views of the mountain; outdoor heated pool and hot tub. **Cons:** 4:30 check-in later than most in Vermont; two-night stay required on weekends; busy tourist center in season. $ *Rooms from: $230* ⊠ *759–787 Stratton Mountain Access Rd.* ☎ *802/297–4000, 800/787–2886* ⊕ *www.stratton.com* ⇆ *145 rooms* ❑ *No meals.*

★ Three Mountain Inn

$$ | **B&B/INN** | A 1780s tavern, this romantic inn in downtown Jamaica feels authentically Colonial, from the wide-plank paneling to the low ceilings. **Pros:** romantic setting; well-kept rooms; enchanting dinners alongside wood-burning fireplaces. **Cons:** 15-minute drive to skiing; two-night reservations requested for weekends and peak foliage; deposit equal to 50% of the reserved stay required. $ *Rooms from: $234* ⊠ *30 Depot St., Jamaica* ✛ *10 miles northeast of Stratton* ☎ *802/874–4140* ⊕ *www.threemountaininn.com* ⇆ *10 rooms* ❑ *Free breakfast.*

Nightlife

Mulligans

BARS/PUBS | Popular Mulligans hosts bands and DJs in the downstairs Green Door Pub on weekends. ⊠ *Village Sq., Stratton Mountain* ☎ *802/297–9293* ⊕ *www.green-door-pub.com.*

Activities

SKI AREAS
Bromley Mountain Resort

SKIING/SNOWBOARDING | **FAMILY** | About 20 minutes from Stratton, Bromley is a favorite with families thanks to a child-care center for kids ages six weeks–six years and programs for ages 2½–17. The trails are evenly split among beginner, intermediate, and advanced, with nothing too challenging. Beginning skiers and snowboarders have expanded access to terrain-based training in the dedicated Learning Zone, and everyone can unwind in the base lodge and "village." An added bonus: trails face south, making for glorious spring skiing and warm winter days. **Facilities:** 47 trails; 300 acres; 1,334-foot vertical drop; 9 lifts. ⊠ *3984 Rte. 11, Peru* ☎ *802/824–5522, 866/856–2201 for snow conditions* ⊕ *www.bromley.com* ⇆ *Lift ticket: $80.*

Stratton Mountain

SKIING/SNOWBOARDING | About 25 minutes from Manchester, and featuring an entire faux Swiss village at its base, Stratton Mountain draws families and young professionals. Beginners will find more than 40% of the mountain accessible to them, but that doesn't mean there aren't some great steeps for the experts. The resort prides itself on its immaculate grooming and excellent cruising on all trails. An on-site day-care center takes children ages six weeks–five years for indoor activities and outdoor excursions. Children also love careening down one of four groomed lift-serviced lanes at the resort's Coca Cola Tube Park. Stratton has 11 miles of cross-country skiing, and in summer there are 15 outdoor clay tennis courts, 27 holes of golf, and hiking trails accessed by a gondola. The sports complex (open year-round) has a 75-foot indoor saltwater pool, sauna, indoor tennis courts, and a fitness center. **Facilities:** 97 trails; 670 acres; 2,003-foot vertical drop; 11 lifts. ⊠ *5 Village Lodge Rd., Bondville* ☎ *802/297–4211 for snow conditions, 800/787–2886* ⊕ *www.stratton.com* 🎫 *Lift ticket: $115.*

Weston

17 miles north of Stratton.

Best known as the home of the Vermont Country Store, Weston was one of the first Vermont towns to discover its own intrinsic loveliness—and marketability. With its summer theater, classic town green with Victorian bandstand, and an assortment of shops, the little village really lives up to its vaunted image.

Hotels

The Inn at Weston
$$ | **B&B/INN** | A short walk from the town green and a stone's throw from four ski areas, this 1848 inn is run by Bob and Linda Aldrich, whose love of plants is evident from their immaculate gardens. **Pros:** afternoon refreshments in library; terrific town location; outdoor and gazebo dining. **Cons:** high-end rooms are expensive; lots of flower wallpaper, upholstery, and bedding; on busy main road. $ *Rooms from: $239* ⊠ *630 Main St.* ☎ *802/824–6789* ⊕ *www.innweston.com* ➥ *13 rooms* ⏹️ *Free breakfast.*

Performing Arts

Weston Playhouse
THEATER | The oldest professional theater in Vermont produces plays, musicals, and other works. The season runs mid-June–late October. ⊠ *703 Main St., off Rte. 100* ☎ *802/824–5288* ⊕ *www.westonplayhouse.org.*

Shopping

The Vermont Country Store
CONVENIENCE/GENERAL STORES | This store opened in 1946 and is still run by the Orton family, though it has become something of an empire, with a large catalog and online business. One room is set aside for Vermont Common Crackers and bins of fudge and copious candy. In others you'll find nearly forgotten items such as Lilac Vegetol aftershave, as well as practical items like sturdy outdoor clothing. Nostalgia-evoking implements dangle from the rafters. The associated Bryant House restaurant next door serves three country meals a day and, if you can't get enough, there's a second store on Route 103 in Rockingham. ⊠ *657 Main St.* ☎ *802/824–3184* ⊕ *www.vermontcountrystore.com.*

Ludlow

9 miles northeast of Weston.

Ludlow is a largely nondescript industrial town whose major draw is Okemo, one of Vermont's largest and most popular ski resorts.

GETTING HERE AND AROUND
Routes 100 and 103 join in northern Ludlow, separating about 2 miles south in the small downtown, where Route 103 becomes Main Street.

Restaurants

Coleman Brook Tavern
$$$ | **AMERICAN** | Slope-side at the Jackson Gore Inn, Coleman Brook is the fanciest and most expensive of Okemo's dozen or so places to eat, but it's not formal—you'll find diners in the large wing chairs and big banquettes along the window bays wearing ski boots at lunch while dining on tuned-up bar classics like maple bourbon hot wings, Wagyu burger, and curried mussels. Ask to sit in the Wine Room, a separate

section where tables are surrounded by a noteworthy collection of bottles. **Known for:** s'mores dessert cooked over a tabletop "campfire"; wine list; full brunch menu. ⑤ *Average main: $26* ✉ *Jackson Gore Inn, Okemo, 111 Jackson Gore Rd.* ☎ *802/228–1435* ⊕ *www.okemo.com/ dining/coleman-brook-tavern.*

Goodman's American Pie

$ | PIZZA | FAMILY | This place has the best wood-fired pizza in town. It also has character to spare: sit in chairs from old ski lifts and step up to the counter fashioned from a vintage VW bus to design your pie from 29 ingredients. **Known for:** arcade games and pool table in the back; pizza by the slice; outdoor deck. ⑤ *Average main: $17* ✉ *5 Lamere Sq.* ☎ *802/228–4271* ⊕ *www.goodmansamericanpie.com.*

★ The Hidden Kitchen at The Inn at Weathersfield

$$$ | FRENCH FUSION | So many Vermont restaurants claim the farm-to-table, local-sourcing, organic approach to cooking, but the chef at the Inn at Weathersfield is more passionate and rigorous than most, with more than 75% of ingredients coming from within a 25-mile radius in season. Enjoy the exquisite French-influenced regional dishes inside the inn itself, on its back patio, or in the separate "Hidden Kitchen" at the back of the property, where monthly cooking workshops and tastings take place. **Known for:** wine list; charcuterie and cheese boards; atmospheric inside and out. ⑤ *Average main: $28* ✉ *1342 Rte. 106, Perkinsville* ✛ *15 miles east of Ludlow* ☎ *802/263–9217* ⊕ *www.weathersfieldinn.com* ☾ *Closed Mon., Tues., and mid-Apr. and early Nov. No lunch.*

🛏 Hotels

Inn at Water's Edge

$ | B&B/INN | Former Long Islanders Bruce and Tina Verdrager converted their old ski house and barns into this comfortably refined haven, perfect for those who want to ski but not stay in town. **Pros:** bucolic setting on a lakefront, with swimming access; two canoes for guest use; golf and spa packages are available. **Cons:** ordinary rooms; lots of flowered wallpaper and upholstery; no sights within walking distance. ⑤ *Rooms from: $175* ✉ *45 Kingdom Rd.* ✛ *5 miles north of Ludlow* ☎ *802/228–8143, 888/706–9736* ⊕ *www.innatwatersedge.com* ⇨ *11 rooms* ⦿ *Free breakfast.*

★ Inn at Weathersfield

$$ | B&B/INN | Set far back from the road, this 1792 home built by a Revolutionary War veteran is a world unto itself, and an Eden-esque one at that, with flowering gardens, croaking frog pond, and extensive forest on its 21 acres. **Pros:** dynamite restaurant and tavern; ideal for weddings; monthly cooking classes. **Cons:** 15-mile drive from the Okemo slopes; no sights within walking distance; no coffee or tea in rooms. ⑤ *Rooms from: $219* ✉ *1342 Rte. 106, Perkinsville* ☎ *802/263–9217* ⊕ *www. weathersfieldinn.com* ☾ *Closed 1st 2 wks in Nov.* ⇨ *12 rooms* ⦿ *Free breakfast.*

Jackson Gore Village

$$$ | HOTEL | FAMILY | This slope-side base lodge is the place to stay if your aim is Okemo skiing, as most units have full kitchen facilities stocked with cooking supplies; the Adams House and Bixby House offer slightly more contemporary furnishings and whirlpool tubs. **Pros:** ski-in, ski-out access to mountain; good for families; wide range of activities for all ages. **Cons:** chaotic and noisy on weekends; expensive all around; two-night minimums may be required on prime weekends. ⑤ *Rooms from: $355* ✉ *111 Jackson Gore Rd., off Rte. 103* ☎ *802/228–1400, 866/786–5366* ⊕ *www.okemo.com* ⇨ *263 rooms* ⦿ *No meals.*

Vermont Artisanal Cheese

Vermont is the artisanal cheese capital of the country, with several dozen creameries open to the public churning out hundreds of different cheeses. Many creameries are "farmstead" operations, meaning that the animals whose milk is made into cheese are kept on-site. If you eat enough cheese during your time in the state, you may be able to differentiate between the many types of milk (cow, goat, sheep, or even water buffalo) and make associations between the geography and climate of where you are and the taste of the local cheeses.

This is one of the reasons that taking a walk around a dairy is a great idea: you can see the process in action, from grazing to aging to eating. The **Vermont Cheese Trail map,** which you can view or download on the website of the Vermont Cheese Council (☎ 866/261–8595 ⊕ www. vtcheese.com), has a comprehensive list of dairies, many of which you can visit. Though hours are given for some, it's generally recommended that you still call ahead.

At the **Vermont Cheesemakers Festival** (☎ 802/261–8595 ⊕ www.vtcheese-fest.com), which takes place in July or August in Shelburne, cheese makers gather to sell their various cheeses. Beer and wine are served to wash it all down.

 Activities

SKI AREAS
Okemo Mountain Resort
SKIING/SNOWBOARDING | FAMILY | Family fun is the focus of southern Vermont's highest vertical ski resort, which has dozens of beginner trails, some wide intermediate runs, terrain parks throughout, a tubing facility, a nursery, an ice rink, indoor basketball and tennis courts, and a children's pool with slides. There's even a Kids' Night Out child-care program on Saturday evening during the regular season, so parents can have date nights. The Okemo Valley Nordic Center has miles of cross-country and snowshoeing trails. Summer diversions include golfing, mountain biking, and activities and rides in the Adventure Zone. The newer Jackson Gore base features the latest (and fanciest) venues the resort has to offer. **Facilities:** 121 trails; 667 acres; 2,200-foot vertical drop; 20 lifts. ✉ 77 Okemo Ridge Rd. ☎ 802/228–1600 resort services, 802/228–5222 for snow conditions, 800/786–5366 ⊕ www.okemo. com ⌨ Lift ticket: $92.

Grafton

20 miles south of Ludlow.

Out-of-the-way Grafton is as much a historical museum as a town. During its heyday, citizens grazed 10,000 sheep and spun their wool into sturdy yarn for locally woven fabric. As the wool market declined, so did Grafton. In 1963 the Windham Foundation—Vermont's second-largest private foundation—commenced the town's rehabilitation. The Old Tavern (now called the Grafton Inn) was preserved, along with many other commercial and residential structures.

GETTING HERE AND AROUND
Routes 11, 35, and 103 intersect in Grafton.

 Sights

Historical Society Museum
MUSEUM | This endearingly cluttered museum documents the town's history with photographs, soapstone displays,

quilts, musical instruments, furniture, tools, and other artifacts. ⊠ *147 Main St.* ☎ *802/843–2584* ⊕ *www.graftonhis-toricalsociety.com* ⊠ *$5* ⊘ *Closed Tues. and Wed. Memorial Day–Columbus Day, and Tues. and Wed. and weekends Columbus Day–Memorial Day.*

Hotels

The Grafton Inn
$ | B&B/INN | This 1801 classic encourages you to linger on its wraparound porches, in its authentically Colonial common rooms, or with a book by the fire in its old-fashioned library, but those who want to get outside can access the nearby Grafton Ponds Outdoor Center and its 2,000 acres of trails, forests, and fields. **Pros:** handsome historic building; seasonal swim pond; game room with pool table and Ping-Pong; two dining options—the Old Tavern and Phelps Barn Pub—serve American fare. **Cons:** lots of flowered upholstery and wallpaper; resort fee; no tea or coffee in rooms. ⑤ *Rooms from: $189* ⊠ *92 Main St.* ☎ *802/234–8718, 800/843–1801* ⊕ *www.graftoninnvermont.com* ⇆ *45 rooms* ⦿⊢ *Free breakfast.*

Shopping

Gallery North Star
ART GALLERIES | Inside this restored 1877 home, original oil paintings, watercolors, lithographs, and sculptures by more than 30 New England artists are on display. ⊠ *151 Townshend Rd.* ☎ *802/843–2465* ⊕ *www.gnsgrafton.com.*

Townshend

9 miles south of Grafton.

One of a string of attractive villages along the banks of the West River, Townshend embodies the Vermont ideal of a lush town green presided over by a gracefully proportioned church spire.

The spire belongs to the 1790 Congregational Meeting House, one of the state's oldest houses of worship. North on Route 30 is the Scott Bridge, the state's longest single-span covered bridge. It makes for a pretty photo and is once again open to foot traffic after a $2.35 million renovation.

GETTING HERE AND AROUND
Route 35 heading south from Grafton dead-ends into Route 30 at Townshend Common. Route 30 is the town's main drag.

Sights

Newfane
TOWN | With a village green surrounded by pristine white buildings, Newfane, 6 miles southeast of Townshend, is sometimes described as the quintessential New England small town. The 1839 First Congregational Church and the Windham County Courthouse, with green-shuttered windows and a rounded cupola, are often open. The building with the four-pointed spire is Union Hall, built in 1832. ⊠ *Newfane* ⊕ *www.newfanevt.com.*

Restaurants

Townshend Dam Diner
$ | DINER | Folks come from miles around to enjoy traditional diner fare, a few miles northwest of the village. You can sit at any of the 1930s enamel-top tables or in the big swivel chairs at the U-shaped counter. **Known for:** raspberry-chocolate chip-walnut pancakes; local hangout; house-roasted turkey and meat loaf. ⑤ *Average main: $10* ⊠ *5929 Rte. 30, West Townshend* ☎ *802/874–4107* ⊘ *Closed Tues.*

Hotels

Four Columns Inn
$ | B&B/INN | In the heart of town on the Newfane green, this white-columned, 1834 Greek Revival mansion has rooms and suites that were made for

luxurious romantic getaways, with gas fireplaces and double whirlpool baths. **Pros:** picturesque Vermont location; spacious rooms; trailhead to miles of walking trails on property. **Cons:** little nightlife in these parts; no coffee or tea in rooms; new owner, Delamar Hotels, brings a slight corporate feel. $ *Rooms from: $185 ⊠ 21 West St., Newfane ☎ 802/365–7713 ⊕ www.fourcolumnsvt. com ⇆ 16 rooms* ⦿| *Free breakfast.*

Windham Hill Inn

$$ | **B&B/INN** | The 165 hillside acres of this inn, part of the Relais & Châteaux collection, have views of the West River Valley. **Pros:** West River Valley views; exceedingly cozy spa; farm-to-table gourmet menus. **Cons:** elegant but somewhat bland design; posh, exclusive ambience not for everyone; no coffee or tea in rooms. $ *Rooms from: $219 ⊠ 311 Lawrence Dr., West Townshend ☎ 802/874–4080, 800/944–4080 ⊕ www.windhamhill.com ⇆ 22 rooms* ⦿| *Free breakfast.*

 Activities

Townshend State Park

PARK—SPORTS-OUTDOORS | At this park you'll find a sandy beach and a trail that climbs up a ravine full of small chutes and waterfalls. The hike here leads to views at the summit of 1,680-foot Bald Mountain. ⊠ *2755 State Forest Rd. ☎ 802/365–7500 ⊕ www.vtstateparks. com/townshend.html ⊗ Facilities closed early Sept.–late May.*

Norwich

6 miles north of White River Junction.

On the bank of the Connecticut River, Norwich is graced with beautifully maintained 18th- and 19th-century homes set about a handsome green. Norwich is the Vermont sister town to sophisticated Hanover, New Hampshire (home of Dartmouth College), across the river.

GETTING HERE AND AROUND

Most attractions are off Interstate 91; the town sits a mile to the west.

 Sights

★ **Montshire Museum of Science**

MUSEUM | FAMILY | Numerous hands-on exhibits at this 100-acre science museum explore nature and technology. Kids can make giant bubbles, watch marine life swim in aquariums, construct working hot air balloons, and explore a maze of outdoor trails by the river. Adults will happily join the fun. An ideal destination for a rainy day, this is one of the finest museums in New England. ⊠ *1 Montshire Rd. ☎ 802/649–2200 ⊕ www. montshire.org ⊠ $17 mid-June–early Sept., $15 early Sept.–mid-June.*

 Activities

Lake Morey Ice Skating Trail

ICE SKATING | For the most fun you can have on skates, head to America's longest ice-skating trail. From January to March, the frozen lake is groomed for ice-skating, providing a magical 4½-mile route amid forested hillsides. Bring your own skates or rent them at the Lake Morey Resort, which maintains the trail. ⊠ *1 Clubhouse Rd., Fairlee ☎ 800/423–1211 ⊕ www.lakemoreyresort.com.*

 Shopping

King Arthur Flour Baker's Store

FOOD/CANDY | This shop is a must-see for those who love bread. The shelves are stocked with all the ingredients and tools in the company's *Baker's Catalogue,* including flours, mixes, and local jams, and syrups. The bakery has a viewing area where you can watch the products being made, and you can learn to bake them yourself at classes conducted onsite. The store is a fine spot for a quick bite if you're driving along Interstate 91; the timber-frame café serves high-quality sandwiches, salads, soups, and baked items. ⊠ *105 U.S. 5 S* ☎ *802/649–3361* ⊕ *www.kingarthurflour.com.*

Quechee

11 miles southwest of Norwich, 6 miles west of White River Junction.

A historic mill town, Quechee sits just upriver from its namesake gorge, an impressive 165-foot-deep canyon cut by the Ottauquechee River. Most people view the gorge from U.S. 4. To escape the crowds, hike along the gorge or scramble down one of several trails to the river.

◉ Sights

★ Simon Pearce

ARTS VENUE | FAMILY | A restored woolen mill by a waterfall holds Quechee's main attraction: this marvelous glassblowing factory, store, and restaurant. Water power still drives the factory's furnace. Take a free self-guided tour of the downstairs factory floor, and see the amazing glassblowers at work. The store sells beautifully crafted contemporary glass and ceramic tableware. An excellent, sophisticated restaurant with outstanding views of the falls uses Simon Pearce glassware and is justifiably popular. ⊠ *The Mill, 1760 Quechee Main St.* ☎ *802/295–2711* ⊕ *www. simonpearce.com.*

Vermont Institute of Natural Science Nature Center

COLLEGE | FAMILY | Next to Quechee Gorge, this science center has 17 raptor exhibits, including bald eagles, peregrine falcons, and owls. All caged birds were found injured and are unable to survive in the wild. In summer, experience "Raptors Up Close," a 30-minute live bird program that happens three times a day. ✉ *149 Natures Way* ☎ *802/359–5000* ⊕ *www.vinsweb.org* ☒ *$16.*

Restaurants

★ The Mill at Simon Pearce

$$$ | AMERICAN | Sparkling glassware from the studio downstairs, exposed brick, flickering candles, and large windows overlooking the falls of the roaring Ottauquechee River create an ideal setting for contemporary American cuisine—the food alone is worth the pilgrimage. The wine cellar holds several hundred labels. **Known for:** romantic atmosphere; Simon Pearce glassware and pottery; complimentary house-made potato chips. ⑤ *Average main: $28* ✉ *1760 Main St.* ☎ *802/295–1470* ⊕ *www.simonpearce.com.*

Hotels

The Parker House Inn

$$ | B&B/INN | This beautiful 1857 house on the National Historic Register once belonged to Senator Joseph Parker, who also owned the textile mill next door; the riverfront porch offers an especially pleasant view of hot-air balloons taking off in summer. **Pros:** organic Pharmacopia-brand toiletries; spacious rooms; highly picturesque landscape with lazy river. **Cons:** no yard; large parking lot with many tourists adjacent; on main road. ⑤ *Rooms from: $240* ✉ *1792 Main St.* ☎ *802/295–6077, 800/295–6077* ⊕ *www. theparkerhouseinn.com* ⤴ *8 rooms* ⦿| *Free breakfast.*

Quechee Inn at Marshland Farm

$$ | B&B/INN | Each room in this handsomely restored 1793 country home has Queen Anne–style furnishings and period antiques and guests have privileges at the Quechee Club—a private golf, tennis, and ski club—and Wilderness Trails operates from the property. **Pros:** home of Colonel Joseph Marsh, Vermont's first lieutenant governor; spacious grounds; fresh baked cookies every afternoon. **Cons:** some bathrooms are dated; fills up with weddings; lots of flowered upholstery and wallpaper. ⑤ *Rooms from: $287* ✉ *1119 Main St.* ☎ *802/295–3133, 800/235–3133* ⊕ *www.quecheeinn.com* ⤴ *25 rooms* ⦿| *Free breakfast.*

Activities

Wilderness Trails and Vermont Fly Fishing School

FISHING | In summer, Wilderness Trails leads fly-fishing workshops; rents bikes, canoes, kayaks, and paddleboards; and arranges guided canoe, kayaking, and hiking trips. In winter, the company conducts cross-country skiing and snowshoeing treks. ✉ *1119 Quechee Main St.* ☎ *802/295–7620.*

Shopping

Quechee Gorge Village

ANTIQUES/COLLECTIBLES | FAMILY | Hundreds of dealers sell their wares at this antiques-and-crafts mall in a reconstructed barn that also houses a country store and a classic diner. Shops for Cabot, Vermont Spirits Distilling Company, and Whisper Hill neighbor an ice-cream shop and a toy-and-train museum, where a carousel and a small-scale working railroad operate when weather permits. ✉ *573 Woodstock Rd., off U.S. 4* ☎ *802/295–1550* ⊕ *www.quecheegorge.com.*

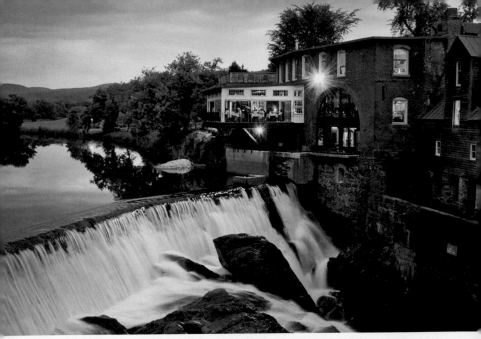

Simon Pearce is a glassblowing factory, store, and restaurant; the factory's furnace is still powered by hydroelectricity from Quechee Falls.

Woodstock

4 miles west of Quechee.

Woodstock is a Currier & Ives print come to life. Well-maintained Federal-style houses surround the tree-lined village green, across the street from a covered bridge. The town owes much of its pristine appearance to the Rockefeller family's interest in historic preservation and land conservation and to native George Perkins Marsh, a congressman, diplomat, and conservationist who wrote the pioneering book *Man and Nature* (1864) about humanity's use and abuse of the land. Only busy U.S. 4 mars the tableau.

ESSENTIALS

VISITOR INFORMATION Woodstock Vermont Area Chamber of Commerce ☎ *802/457–3555, 888/496–6378 ⊕ www. woodstockvt.com.*

Sights

Billings Farm and Museum

FARM/RANCH | FAMILY | Founded by Frederick H. Billings in 1871, this is one of the oldest operating dairy farms in the country. In addition to watching the herds of Jersey cows, horses, and other farm animals at work and play, you can tour the restored 1890 farmhouse, and in the adjacent barns learn about 19th-century farming and domestic life. The biggest takeaway, however, is a renewed belief in sustainable agriculture and stewardship of the land. Pick up some raw-milk cheddar while you're here. ⊠ *69 Old River Rd. ⊹ ½ mile north of Woodstock☎ 802/457–2355 ⊕ www.billingsfarm.org ⊠ $16 ☉ Closed Mar. and Apr.; weekdays Nov.–Feb.*

Marsh-Billings-Rockefeller National Historical Park

HOUSE | Vermont's only national park is the nation's first to focus on conserving natural resources. The pristine 555-acre spread includes the mansion, gardens, and carriage roads of Frederick H. Billings

(1823–90), a financier and the president of the Northern Pacific Railway. The entire property was the gift of Laurance S. Rockefeller (1910–2004), who lived here with his wife, Mary (Billings's granddaughter). You can learn more at the visitor center, tour the residential complex with a guide every hour on the hour, and explore the 20 miles of trails and old carriage roads that climb Mt. Tom. ⌧ 54 Elm St. ☎ 802/457-3368 ⊕ www.nps.gov/mabi 🎫 Tour $8.

🍽 Restaurants

Barnard Inn Restaurant and Max's Tavern
$$$$ | AMERICAN | The dining room in this 1796 brick farmhouse exudes 18th-century charm, but the food is decidedly 21st century. Former San Francisco restaurant chef-owner Will Dodson creates inventive three- and four-course prix-fixe menus with international flavors, or more casual versions at Max's Tavern, also on-site. **Known for:** device-free restaurant; popular for weddings; pond and perennial gardens. ⑤ Average main: $60 ⌧ 5518 Rte. 12, 8 miles north of Woodstock, Barnard ☎ 802/234-9961 ⊕ www.barnardinn.com ۞ Closed Sun. and Mon. No lunch.

Cloudland Farm
$$$$ | AMERICAN | With the table literally on the farm, this restaurant delivers a unique farm-to-table experience that makes it worth the short drive from Woodstock. All ingredients for the seasonal prix-fixe menus come fresh from the farm or local growers, especially Cloudland's own pork, beef, chicken, and turkey. **Known for:** large fireplace in dining room; homemade carrot cake with red wine caramel and carrot jam; bring your own wine or beer. ⑤ Average main: $45 ⌧ 1101 Cloudland Rd., North Pomfret ☎ 802/457-2599 ⊕ www.cloudlandfarm.com ۞ No lunch. Closed Sun.–Wed.

Keeper's Café
$$ | CAFÉ | Creatively prepared, moderately priced organic fare draws customers from all over the region to chef Chris

Loucka's café. In a former general store, the three dining rooms feel relaxed, with local art displayed throughout. **Known for:** PEI mussels with Pernod and Chablis; rosemary garlic Cornish hen; local hangout. ⑤ Average main: $24 ⌧ 3685 Rte. 106, Reading ✛ 12 miles south of Woodstock ☎ 802/484-9090 ۞ No lunch. Closed Sun. and Mon. and Apr.

The Prince and the Pauper
$$ | FRENCH | Modern French and American fare with a Vermont accent is the focus of this candlelit Colonial restaurant off the town green. Three-course prix-fixe meals cost $53, but a less expensive bistro menu is available in the lounge. **Known for:** artwork for sale; complimentary cinema tickets; wine list. ⑤ Average main: $24 ⌧ 24 Elm St. ☎ 802/457-1818 ⊕ www.princeandpauper.com ۞ No lunch.

The Red Rooster
$$$$ | MODERN AMERICAN | The Woodstock Inn's main restaurant can stand on its own as a top-notch culinary destination, thanks in large part to the resources the inn gives the chef, including its own 3-acre garden. On the table this translates into fine-dining versions of Northeastern regional dishes that still keep a rustic, farm flavor. **Known for:** outdoor patio; wine list; seasonal vegetable plates. ⑤ Average main: $36 ⌧ 14 The Green, Burlington ☎ 802/332-6853 ⊕ www.woodstockinn.com.

Soulfully Good
$ | DINER | FAMILY | You'll feel a like neighbor rather than just a customer when dining in one of the two rooms or on the outdoor patio at this light and airy downtown café. Ample sunlight pours in through the large front windows, illuminating the menu of hearty frittatas, waffles, paninis, soups, and salads. **Known for:** buttermilk fried chicken; warm, convivial atmosphere; local, organic sourcing. ⑤ Average main: $10 ⌧ 67 Central St. ☎ 802/457-7395 ⊕ www.soulfullygood.com ۞ Closed Wed. No dinner.

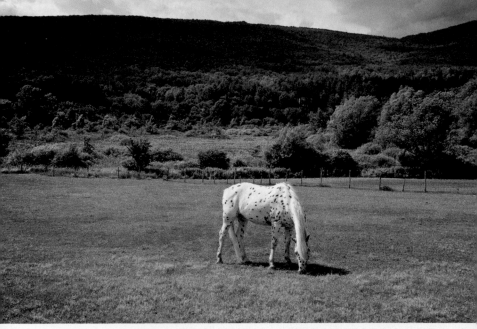

The upscale Woodstock area is known as Vermont's horse country.

★ Worthy Kitchen

$ | AMERICAN | FAMILY | One of Woodstock's liveliest and most popular places to eat, this upscale pub and bistro remains buzzing through most evenings. The chalkboard on the wall lists the hearty menu of American comfort classics given farm-to-table twists, and the craft beer selection is excellent. **Known for:** beer list; social hot spot; burgers with Wagyu beef patties. ⑤ *Average main: $14* ✉ *442 Woodstock Rd.* ☎ *802/457–7281* ⊕ *www.worthyvermont.com* ☉ *No lunch weekdays.*

 ## Hotels

★ The Fan House Bed and Breakfast

$$ | B&B/INN | This charming inn dating to 1840 is as authentic as it gets in Vermont. **Pros:** 300-plus-thread-count linens and down comforters; walking distance to Silver Lake and general store; library nook. **Cons:** no major sights in walking distance; on busy main road; set back and difficult to see from road. ⑤ *Rooms from: $200* ✉ *6297 Rte. 12 N*

☎ *802/234–6704* ⊕ *www.thefanhouse. com* ▭ *No credit cards* ☉ *Closed Apr.* 🛏 *3 rooms* ⑩ *Free breakfast.*

506 On the River

$ | HOTEL | FAMILY | Behind a somewhat bland prefab exterior lies an eclectic boutique experience, thanks in large part to the virtual curiosity cabinet of exotic (or faux exotic) knickknacks stuffed throughout the premises, brought by the Africa-based owners. **Pros:** impressive cocktail menu in bar; patio dining with view of river; lots of activities and space for families. **Cons:** 5 miles west of Woodstock; child-friendly means lots of children; a bit buggy. ⑤ *Rooms from: $199* ✉ *1653 W. Woodstock Rd., Burlington* ☎ *802/457–5000* ⊕ *www.ontheriverwoodstock.com* 🛏 *45 rooms* ⑩ *Free breakfast.*

Kedron Valley Inn

$ | B&B/INN | You're likely to fall in love at first sight with the main 1828 three-story brick building here, the centerpiece of this 15-acre retreat, but wait until you see the spring-fed pond, which has a white sand beach with toys for kids. **Pros:**

wine list; wood-fired Neapolitan pizza; next door to South Woodstock Country Store. **Cons:** 5 miles south of Woodstock; limited cell service; no sights within walking distance. $ *Rooms from: $199* ✉ *4778 South Rd., South Woodstock* ☎ *802/457–1473, 800/836–1193* ⊕ *www. kedronvalleyinn.com* ⊙ *Closed Apr.* ⇦ *16 rooms* ¶⊙¶ *Free breakfast.*

The Shire Riverview Motel
$ | **HOTEL** | Many rooms in this immaculate motel have decks, and most have fabulous views of Ottauquechee River, which runs right along the building. **Pros:** within walking distance of Woodstock's green and shops; sweeping river views; discounted access to Woodstock Recreation Center pool and fitness center. **Cons:** basic rooms; unexciting exterior; not all rooms have river views. $ *Rooms from: $198* ✉ *46 Pleasant St.* ☎ *802/457–2211* ⊕ *shirewoodstock. com* ⇦ *42 rooms* ¶⊙¶ *No meals.*

★ Twin Farms
$$$$ | **RESORT** | Let's just get it out there: Twin Farms is the best lodging in Vermont, and the most expensive, but it's worth it. **Pros:** luxury fit for A-list Hollywood stars, including Oprah Winfrey and Tom Cruise; Japanese furo in woods; onsite spa. **Cons:** steep prices; no children allowed; minimum stays during peak periods and many weekends. $ *Rooms from: $1900* ✉ *452 Royalton Tpke., Barnard* ☎ *802/234–9999* ⊕ *www.twinfarms. com* ⇦ *20 rooms* ¶⊙¶ *All-inclusive.*

★ The Woodstock Inn and Resort
$$$ | **RESORT** | **FAMILY** | A night at the Woodstock Inn, one of Vermont's premier accommodations, is an experience in itself, with a location on Woodstock's gorgeous green that's hard to beat. **Pros:** historic property; perfect central location; one of the best spas in Vermont. **Cons:** posh ambience not for everyone; slightly slick and corporate; very expensive for Vermont. $ *Rooms from: $339* ✉ *14 The Green* ☎ *802/332–6853, 888/338–2745* ⊕ *www.woodstockinn.com* ⇦ *142 rooms* ¶⊙¶ *No meals.*

 Activities

GOLF
Woodstock Inn and Resort Golf Club
GOLF | Robert Trent Jones Sr. designed the resort's challenging course. ✉ *76 South St.* ☎ *802/457–6674, 888/338–2745* ⊕ *www.woodstockinn.com/golf-club* ⛳ *$75 for 9 holes, $95 for 18 holes, weekdays; $95 for 9 holes, $135 for 18 holes, weekends* ▲ *18 holes, 6001 yards, par 70.*

SKIING
Tubbs Snowshoes & Fischer Nordic Adventure Center
SKIING/SNOWBOARDING | The Woodstock Inn's Nordic complex has nearly 25 miles of picturesque groomed cross-country ski trails around Mt. Tom and Mt. Peg. Equipment and lessons are available. ✉ *76 South St.* ☎ *802/457–6674* ⊕ *www. woodstockinn.com* ⛷ *Trail pass: $25.*

 Shopping

ART GALLERIES
Gallery on the Green
ART GALLERIES | This corner gallery in one of Woodstock's oldest buildings showcases paintings by New England artists depicting regional landscapes. ✉ *1 The Green* ☎ *802/457–4956* ⊕ *www.galleryonthegreen.com.*

CRAFTS
Andrew Pearce Bowls
CRAFTS | Son of Simon Pearce, Andrew is making a name in his own right with his expertly and elegantly carved wood bowls, cutting boards, furniture, and artwork. Visitors can watch the carvers at work through windows into the production room. ✉ *59 Woodstock Rd., Taftsville* ☎ *802/735–1884* ⊕ *www.andrewpearcebowls.com.*

Collective
CRAFTS | This funky and attractive shop sells local jewelry, glass, pottery, and clothing from numerous local artisans. ✉ *47 Central St.* ☎ *802/457–1298* ⊕ *www.collective-theartofcraft.com.*

★ Farmhouse Pottery

CERAMICS/GLASSWARE | More and more of James and Zoe Zilian's "studio pottery" is showing up in luxury establishments around the country, even earning the Oprah seal of approval. A visit to the home shop just west of Woodstock shows why, with a rustic but elegant range of stoneware pitchers, enamel jars, linen oven mitts, and beehive salt cellars. Visitors can watch the potters in action through large windows into the production room. ⊠ *1837 W. Woodstock Rd.* ☎ *802/457-7486* ⊕ *www.farmhousepottery.com.*

FOOD

Sugarbush Farm

FOOD/CANDY | FAMILY | Take the Taftsville Covered Bridge to this farm, where you can learn how maple sugar is made and sample as much maple syrup as you'd like. The farm also makes excellent cheeses. ⊠ *591 Sugarbush Farm Rd., off U.S. 4* ☎ *802/457-1757, 800/281-1757* ⊕ *www.sugarbushfarm.com.*

Taftsville Country Store

FOOD/CANDY | East of town, the store sells Vermont cheeses, moderately priced wines, and Vermont-made specialty foods. ⊠ *404 U.S. 4, Taftsville* ☎ *802/457-1135.*

Village Butcher

FOOD/CANDY | This emporium of Vermont edibles has great sandwiches, cheeses, local beers, and delicious baked goods—perfect for a picnic or for lunch on the go. ⊠ *18 Elm St.* ☎ *802/457-2756* ⊕ *www.villagebutchervt.com.*

Woodstock Farmers' Market

OUTDOOR/FLEA/GREEN MARKETS | FAMILY | The indoor market is a year-round buffet of local produce, fresh fish, and excellent sandwiches and pastries. The hot lunch and dinner embrace classic American comfort food. ⊠ *979 Woodstock Rd., aka U.S. 4* ☎ *802/457-3658* ⊕ *www.woodstockfarmersmarket.com.*

SPAS

The Bridge House Spa at Twin Farms

SPA/BEAUTY | A visit to Twin Farms is a trip to another world, and a spa treatment here completes the getaway. The spa at the luxury lodging expounds a philosophy of wellness that goes beyond the realm of massages and skin treatments. Employing an organic product line by Vermont-based Tata Harper and Lunaroma, the spa offers facials, polishes, aromatherapy, massages, and mud wraps that administer a heavenly reboot to your skin and muscles. ⊠ *Twin Farms, 452 Royalton Tpke., Barnard* ☎ *802/234-9999* ⊕ *www.twinfarms.com.*

Spa at the Woodstock Inn and Resort

SPA/BEAUTY | A mesmerizing, 10,000-square-foot, nature-inspired facility, this LEED-certified spa is a world unto itself, with 10 treatment rooms, ultratranquil relaxation area, eucalyptus steam room, and a sophisticated shop stocked with designer bath products. Elegant, minimalist design accentuates the beautiful setting: natural light pours into sparkling dressing rooms and the firelit Great Room, and an outdoor meditation courtyard has a hot tub and a Scandinavian-style sauna. The mood is serene, the treatments varied: start with the 80-minute Himalayan Salt Stone Massage. ⊠ *Woodstock Inn and Resort, 14 The Green* ☎ *802/457-6697, 888/338-2745* ⊕ *www.woodstockinn.com/spa.*

Killington

15 miles east of Rutland.

With only a gas station, a post office, a motel, and a few shops at the intersection of U.S. 4 and Route 100, it doesn't quite feel like the East's largest ski resort is nearby. The village of Killington has suffered from unfortunate strip development along the access road to the ski resort, but the 360-degree views atop Killington Peak, accessible via the resort's gondola, make it worth the drive.

Hotels

Birch Ridge Inn

$ | **B&B/INN** | A slate-covered carriageway about a mile from the Killington ski resort leads to this popular off-mountain stay, a former executive retreat in two renovated A-frames. **Pros:** variety of quirky designs; five-minute drive to the slopes; near Killington nightlife. **Cons:** restaurant closed Sunday and Monday; outdated and tired style; no coffee or tea in rooms. ⑤ *Rooms from: $139* ✉ *37 Butler Rd.* ☎ *802/422–4293, 800/435–8566* ⊕ *www.birchridge.com* ۞ *Closed May* ⇱ *10 rooms* ⦿ *Free breakfast.*

The Mountain Top Inn & Resort

$$$ | **RESORT** | **FAMILY** | This four-season resort hosts everything from cross-country skiing and snowshoeing on 37 miles of trails in the winter to horseback riding, tennis, and swimming and boating in the 740-acre lake throughout the rest of the year. **Pros:** family-friendly vibe; three suites have fireplaces; views of mountains and lake from some rooms. **Cons:** fees for activities can add up; tea/coffeemakers only in suites; limited to no cell service. ⑤ *Rooms from: $325* ✉ *195 Mountain Top Rd., Chittenden* ☎ *802/483–2311* ⊕ *www.mountaintopinn.com* ⇱ *59 rooms* ⦿ *No meals.*

Nightlife

McGrath's Irish Pub

BARS/PUBS | On Fridays and Saturdays, listen to live Irish music and sip Guinness draft at the Inn at Long Trail's pub. ✉ *709 U.S. 4* ☎ *802/755–7181* ⊕ *www.innatlongtrail.com.*

Pickle Barrel Night Club

DANCE CLUBS | During ski season, this club has live music on Friday and Saturday. After 8, the crowd moves downstairs for dancing, sometimes to big-name bands. ✉ *1741 Killington Rd.* ☎ *802/422–3035* ⊕ *www.picklebarrelnightclub.com.*

Wobbly Barn

DANCE CLUBS | Twentysomethings dance at the Wobbly Barn nightclub, open during ski season, and families dig into giant steaks and graze at the salad bar in the restaurant. ✉ *2229 Killington Rd.* ☎ *802/422–6171* ⊕ *www.wobblybarn.com.*

Activities

BIKING
True Wheels Bike Shop

BICYCLING | Part of the Basin Sports complex, this shop rents bicycles and has information about local routes. ✉ *2886 Killington Rd.* ☎ *802/422–3234, 877/487–9972* ⊕ *www.basinski.com/our-stores/true-wheels.*

CROSS-COUNTRY SKIING
Mountain Meadows Cross Country Ski and Snowshoe Center

SKIING/SNOWBOARDING | Right next to Mountain Meadows Lodge on Kent Lake, this center has 34½ miles of trails for cross-country skiing and snowshoeing. ✉ *285 Thundering Brook Rd.* ☎ *802/775–0166* ⊕ *www.xcskiing.net* ⑃ *Trail pass: $19.*

FISHING
Gifford Woods State Park

FISHING | This state park's Kent Pond is a terrific fishing spot. ✉ *34 Gifford Woods Rd., ½ mile north of U.S. 4* ☎ *802/775–5354* ⊕ *www.vtstateparks.com/gifford.html* ۞ *Facilities closed late Oct.–mid-May.*

GOLF
Killington Golf Course

GOLF | At its namesake resort, the course has a challenging layout. ✉ *4763 Killington Rd.* ☎ *802/422–6700* ⊕ *www.killington.com/summer/golf_course* ⑃ *$30 for 9 holes and $50 for 18 holes, weekdays; $45 for 9 holes and $65 for 18 holes, weekends* ⚑ *18 holes, 6186 yards, par 72* ۞ *Closed mid-Oct.–mid-May.*

HIKING

Deer Leap Trail

HIKING/WALKING | This 3-mile round-trip hike begins near the Inn at Long Trail and leads to a great view overlooking Sherburne Gap and Pico Peak. ⊠ *Trailhead off U.S. 4, just east of Inn at Long Trail, Rutland.*

SKI AREAS

★ Killington

SKIING/SNOWBOARDING | **FAMILY** | "Megamountain" aptly describes Killington. Thanks to its extensive snowmaking capacity, the resort typically opens in early November, and the lifts often run into late April or early May. Skiing includes everything from Outer Limits, the East's steepest and longest mogul trail, to the 6½-mile Great Eastern. The 18-foot Superpipe is one of the best rated in the East. There are also acres of glades. Après-ski activities are plentiful, and Killington ticket holders can also ski Pico Mountain—a shuttle connects the two areas. Summer activities at Killington–Pico include mountain biking, hiking, and golf. **Facilities:** 155 trails; 1,509 acres; 3,050-foot vertical drop; 21 lifts. ■**TIP➜ Park at the base of the Skyeship Gondola to avoid the more crowded access road.** ⊠ *4763 Killington Rd.* ☎ *802/422–3261 for snow conditions, 800/734–9435* ⊕ *www.killington.com* ☜ *Lift ticket: $115.*

Pico

SKIING/SNOWBOARDING | When weekend hordes descend upon Killington, locals head to Pico. One of Killington's "seven peaks," Pico is physically separated from its parent resort. Trails range from elevator-shaft steep to challenging intermediate runs near the summit. Easier terrain can be found near the bottom of the mountain's nearly 2,000-foot vertical drop, and the learning slope is separated from the upper mountain, so hotshots won't bomb through it. The lower express quad can get crowded, but the upper one rarely has a line. **Facilities:** 57 trails; 468 acres; 1,967-foot vertical drop; 7 lifts. ⊠ *73 Alpine Dr., Mendon*

☎ *802/422–1330, 802/422–1200 for snow conditions* ⊕ *www.picomountain.com* ☜ *Lift ticket: $79.*

SNOWMOBILE TOURS

Snowmobile Vermont

SNOW SPORTS | Blazing down forest trails on a snowmobile is one way Vermonters embrace the winter landscapes. Rentals are available through Snowmobile Vermont at several locations, including Killington and Okemo. Both have hour-long guided tours across groomed ski trails ($99). If you're feeling more adventurous, take the two-hour backcountry tour through 25 miles of Calvin Coolidge State Forest ($159). ⊠ *170 Rte. 100, Bridgewater Corners* ☎ *802/422–2121* ⊕ *www. snowmobilevermont.com.*

Rutland

15 miles southwest of Killington, 32 miles south of Middlebury.

The strip malls and seemingly endless row of traffic lights on and around U.S. 7 in Rutland are very un-Vermont. Two blocks west, however, stand the mansions of marble magnates. In Rutland you can grab a bite and see some interesting marble, and Depot Park hosts the county farmers' market Saturday 9–2. This isn't a place to spend too much time sightseeing, though.

ESSENTIALS

VISITOR INFORMATION Rutland Region Chamber of Commerce ☎ *802/773–2747, 800/756–8880* ⊕ *www.rutlandvermont. com.*

 Sights

Chaffee Art Center

MUSEUM | Housed in a beautiful mansion, the center exhibits the work of more than 200 Vermont artists. A second location is open downtown on Merchants Row. ⊠ *16 S. Main St.* ☎ *802/775–0356* ⊕ *www.chaffeeartcenter.org* ☜ *Free.*

New England Maple Museum

LOCAL INTEREST | Maple syrup is Vermont's signature product, and this museum north of Rutland explains the history and process of turning sap into syrup. If you don't get a chance to visit a sugarhouse, this is a fine place to sample the different grades and pick up some souvenirs. ⊠ *4578 U.S. 7, Pittsford ⊹ 9 miles south of Brandon* ☎ *802/483–9414* ⊕ *maplemuseum.com* 🎟 *Tour $5.*

Paramount Theatre

ARTS VENUE | The highlight of downtown Rutland is this 838-seat gilded playhouse, an architectural gem dating to 1913. The gorgeous theater presents music, theater, films, and stand-up comedy. ⊠ *30 Center St.* ☎ *802/775–0903* ⊕ *www. paramountvt.org.*

Vermont Marble Museum

MUSEUM | This monument to marble highlights one of the main industries in this region. The hall of presidents has a carved bust of each U.S. president, and in the marble chapel is a replica of Leonardo da Vinci's *Last Supper.* Elsewhere, you can watch a sculptor-in-residence at work, compare marble from around the world, learn about the geological history of the Earth, and check out the Vermont Marble Company's original "stone library." A short walk away is the original quarry, which helped finish the U.S. Supreme Court. ⊠ *52 Main St., off Rte. 3, Proctor* ☎ *800/427–1396* ⊕ *www. vermont-marble.com* 🎟 *$9.*

Wilson Castle

HOUSE | Completed in 1867, this 32-room mansion was built over the course of eight years by a Vermonter who married a British aristocrat. Within the opulent setting are 84 stained-glass windows (one inset with 32 Australian opals), hand-painted Italian frescoes, and 13 fireplaces. The place is magnificently furnished with European and Asian objets d'art. October evenings bring haunted castle tours. ⊠ *2708 West St., Proctor* ☎ *802/773–3284* ⊕ *www.wilsoncastle.com* 🎟 *$12.*

🍴 Restaurants

Little Harry's

$$ | ECLECTIC | Laminated photos of regular customers adorn the tabletops of this restaurant, which locals have packed since 1997, when chef-owners Trip Pearce and Jack Mangan brought Vermont-cheddar ravioli and lamb lo mein to downtown Rutland. The place is "little" compared to the bigger Harry's, near Ludlow. **Known for:** pad Thai; a wide variety of customers; entire menu can be packed to go. Ⓢ *Average main: $22* ⊠ *121 West St.* ☎ *802/747–4848* ⊕ *www. littleharrys.com* ☽ *No lunch.*

🏃 Activities

BOATING
Woodard Marine

BOATING | Rent pontoon boats, speedboats, standup paddleboards, and kayaks at the Lake Bomoseen Marina. ⊠ *145 Creek Rd., off Rte. 4A, Castleton* ☎ *802/265–3690* ⊕ *www.woodardmarine.com.*

HIKING
Mountain Travelers

HIKING/WALKING | This place sells hiking, sporting, and boating equipment; gives advice on local hikes; and rents skis. ⊠ *147 U.S. 4 E* ☎ *802/775–0814, 800/339–0814* ⊕ *www.mtntravelers.com.*

Brandon

15 miles northwest of Rutland.

Thanks to an active group of artists, tiny Brandon is making a name for itself. In 2003 the Brandon Artists Guild, led by American folk artist Warren Kimble, auctioned off 40 life-size fiberglass pigs painted by local artists. The "Really Really Pig Show" raised money for the guild, and has since brought small-town fame to this community through its annual shows. Brandon is also home to the Basin Bluegrass Festival, held in July.

458

ESSENTIALS

VISITOR INFORMATION Brandon Visitor Center ☎ *802/247–6401* ⊕ *www.brandon. org.*

Sights

Brandon Artists Guild

MUSEUM | The guild exhibits and sells affordable paintings, sculpture, and pottery by more than 30 local member artists. ⊠ *7 Center St.* ☎ *802/247–4956* ⊕ *brandonartistsguild.org* ⌦ *Free* ⊘ *Closed Mon. Dec.–Apr.*

Brandon Museum at the Stephen A. Douglas Birthplace

MUSEUM | The famous statesman was born in this house in 1813. He left 20 years later to establish himself as a lawyer, becoming a three-time U.S. senator and arguing more cases before the U.S. Supreme Court than anyone else. This museum recounts the early Douglas years, early town history, and the antislavery movement in Vermont, the first state to abolish slavery. ⊠ *4 Grove St., at U.S. 7* ☎ *802/247–6401* ⊕ *www. brandon.org* ⌦ *Free* ⊘ *Closed Sun. and mid-Oct.–mid-May.*

Restaurants

Café Provence

$$ | **CAFÉ** | Robert Barral, the former executive chef of the New England Culinary Institute, graces Brandon with this informal eatery one story above the main street. Flowered seat cushions, dried-flower window valences, and other hints of Barral's Provençal birthplace abound, as do his eclectic, farm-fresh dishes. **Known for:** Sunday brunch; thin tomato pie; seafood stew. ⑤ *Average main: $23* ⊠ *11 Center St.* ☎ *802/247–9997* ⊕ *www.cafeprovencevt.com* ⊘ *Closed Mon. in winter.*

Hotels

★ Blueberry Hill Inn

$$ | **B&B/INN** | In the Green Mountain National Forest, 5½ miles off a mountain pass on a dirt road, you'll find this secluded inn with lush gardens and a pond with a wood-fired sauna on its bank; there's lots to do if you're into nature: biking, hiking, and cross-country skiing on 43 miles of trails. **Pros:** skis and snowshoes to rent in winter; the restaurant prepares a Vermont-infused, four-course prix-fixe menu most nights; homemade cookies. **Cons:** fills up with wedding parties; no cell phone service; no coffee or tea in rooms. ⑤ *Rooms from: $269* ⊠ *1245 Goshen–Ripton Rd., Goshen* ☎ *802/247–6735* ⊕ *www.blueberryhillinn.com* ⤴ *12 rooms* ⦿ *Free breakfast.*

The Lilac Inn

$ | **B&B/INN** | The best bed-and-breakfast in town has cheery, comfortable guest rooms in a central setting half a block from the heart of Brandon. **Pros:** many rooms have king beds; within walking distance of town; garden gazebo for relaxation. **Cons:** busy in summer with weddings; quaint but tepid traditional design; no coffee or tea in rooms. ⑤ *Rooms from: $169* ⊠ *53 Park St.* ☎ *802/247–5463, 800/221–0720* ⊕ *www.lilacinn.com* ⤴ *9 rooms* ⦿ *Free breakfast.*

Activities

GOLF

Neshobe Golf Club

GOLF | This bent-grass course has terrific views of the Green Mountains. Several local inns offer golfing packages. ⊠ *224 Town Farm Rd.* ☎ *802/247–3611* ⊕ *neshobe.com* ⌦ *$22 for 9 holes, $42 for 18 holes* 🏌 *18 holes, 6341 yards, par 72.*

HIKING

Branbury State Park

HIKING/WALKING | A large turnout on Route 53 marks the trailhead for a moderate hike to the Falls of Lana, a highlight of this park on the shores of Lake Dunmore near the Moosalamoo National Recreation Area. ⊠ *3570 Lake Dunmore Rd.* ⊕ *www. vtstateparks.com/branbury.html* ☎ *$4* ⊗ *Facilities closed late Oct.–late May.*

Mt. Horrid

HIKING/WALKING | For great views from a vertigo-inducing cliff, hike up the Long Trail to Mt. Horrid. The steep, hour-long hike starts at the top of Brandon Gap. ⊠ *Trailhead at Brandon Gap Rte. 73 parking lot, about 8 miles east of Brandon* ⊕ *www.fs.usda.gov/main/gmfl.*

Mt. Independence State Historic Site

HIKING/WALKING | West of Brandon, four trails—two short ones of less than a mile each and two longer ones—lead to some abandoned Revolutionary War fortifications. ⊠ *497 Mount Independence Rd., just west of Orwell, Orwell* ✛ *Parking lot is at top of hill* ☎ *802/948–2000* ⊕ *historicsites.vermont.gov/directory/ mount_independence* ☎ *$5* ⊗ *Closed mid-Oct.–late May.*

PARKS

Moosalamoo National Recreation Area

BIRD WATCHING | Covering nearly 16,000 acres of the Green Mountain National Forest, this area northeast of Brandon attracts hikers, mountain bikers, and cross-country skiers who enjoy the 70-plus miles of trails through wondrous terrain. If there is anywhere to stop and smell the flowers in Vermont, this is it. ⊠ *Off Rtes. 53 and 73* ⊕ *www.moosalamoo.org.*

Middlebury

17 miles north of Brandon, 34 miles south of Burlington.

In the late 1800s Middlebury was the largest Vermont community west of the Green Mountains, an industrial center of river-powered wool and grain mills. This is Robert Frost country: Vermont's late poet laureate spent 23 summers at a farm east of Middlebury. Still a cultural and economic hub amid the Champlain Valley's serene pastoral patchwork—and

the home of top-notch Middlebury College—the town and rolling countryside invite a day of exploration.

⊙ Sights

Edgewater Gallery

MUSEUM | This gallery sits alongside picturesque Otter Creek, and the paintings, jewelry, ceramics, and pieces of furniture inside are just as arresting. Exhibitions in the bright, airy space change regularly, demonstrating the owner's ambition to be more gallery than shop, though all pieces are for sale. A second gallery is across the creek in the Battell Building. ⊠ *1 Mill St.* ☎ *802/458–0098* ⊕ *www. edgewatergallery-vt.com* ☎ *Free.*

Fort Ticonderoga Ferry

TRANSPORTATION SITE (AIRPORT/BUS/FERRY/ TRAIN) | Established in 1759, the Fort Ti cable ferry crosses Lake Champlain between Shoreham and Fort Ticonderoga, New York, at one of the oldest ferry crossings in North America. The trip takes seven minutes. ⊠ *4831 Rte. 74 W, Shoreham* ☎ *802/897–7999* ⊕ *www. forttiferry.com* ☎ *Cars $12, bicycles $2, pedestrians $1* ⊗ *Closed Nov.–Apr.*

Middlebury College

COLLEGE | Founded in 1800, this college was conceived as a more godly alternative to the worldly University of Vermont, though it has no religious affiliation today. The postmodern architecture of the **Mahaney Center for the Arts,** which offers music, theater, and dance performances throughout the year, stands in provocative contrast to the early-19th-century stone buildings in the middle of town. ⊠ *131 College St.* ☎ *802/443–5000* ⊕ *www.middlebury.edu.*

Robert Frost Interpretive Trail

TRAIL | Plaques along this easy 1.2-mile wooded trail bear quotations from Frost's poems. A picnic area is across the road from the trailhead. ⊠ *Trailhead on Rte. 125, 10 miles east of downtown* ⊕ *www. fs.usda.gov/main/gmfl.*

Middlebury Tasting Trail

Among Vermont's craft beer, cider, spirits, and wine explosion, the Middlebury area stands out, with a large cluster of producers with welcoming tasting rooms. Seven, all within a 10-mile radius of the city, have banded together to create to Middlebury Tasting Trail. Find full details at ⊕ www.middtastingtrail.com.

Lincoln Peak Vineyard. Named "Winery of the Year" at the International Cold Climate Wine Competition in 2016, this vineyard is enjoying the fruits of its labor, with an increase in traffic to its tasting room and shop. Enjoy the Frontenac, La Crescent, and Marquette varieties on the postcard-pretty porch overlooking a small pond. ⊠ 142 River Rd. ☎ 802/388-7368 ⊕ www. lincolnpeakvineyard.com ⊘ Closed Mon. and Tues. late Oct.–Dec.; Mon.– Thurs. Jan.–late May.

Otter Creek Brewery. One of Vermont's oldest breweries still knows how to compete with the new generation of start-ups, adopting a fun, summery, colorful tone that invites beer fans to "hop on the bus!" (get it?) at its spacious and chic tasting room. Next to the outdoor patio is a space for lawn games, and a concert series brings live music in the warm weather. ⊠ 793 Exchange St. ☎ 802/388-0727 ⊕ www.ottercreekbrewing.com.

Woodchuck Cider House. This cidery has come a long way since its beginnings in a two-car garage in Proctorsville in 1991, transforming into this $34 million complex that divides its space between a pub, gift shop, and factory. A self-guided tour, with informational signs, includes a look through large windows onto the production floor. ⊠ 1321 Exchange St. ☎ 802/385-3656 ⊕ www.woodchuck. com ⊘ Closed Mon. and Tues.

University of Vermont Morgan Horse Farm
FARM/RANCH | FAMILY | The Morgan horse, Vermont's official state animal, has an even temper, high stamina, and slightly truncated legs in proportion to its body. This farm, about 2½ miles west of Middlebury, is a breeding and training center where in summer you can tour the stables and paddocks. ⊠ 74 Battell Dr., off Morgan Horse Farm Rd., Weybridge ☎ 802/388-2011 ⊕ www.uvm.edu/morgan ⊠ $5 ⊘ Closed late Oct.–Apr.

Vermont Folklife Center
MUSEUM | The redbrick center's exhibits include photography, antiques, folk paintings, manuscripts, and other artifacts and contemporary works that examine various facets of Vermont life. ⊠ 88 Main St. ☎ 802/388-4964 ⊕ www.vermontfolklifecenter.org ⊠ Donations accepted ⊘ Closed Sun. and Mon.

🍴 Restaurants

American Flatbread Middlebury Hearth
$$ | PIZZA | If you love pizza, you're in for a treat. Wood-fired clay domes create masterful thin crusts for innovative, delicious pizzas with a distinct Vermont attitude and an array of locally sourced ingredients. **Known for:** former marble works; fireside dining with earthen oven; local beer and wine. $ Average main: $18 ⊠ 137 Maple St. ☎ 802/388-3300 ⊕ www.americanflatbread.com ⊘ Closed Sun. and Mon. No lunch.

The Bobcat Cafe & Brewery
$$ | AMERICAN | Worth the drive from Middlebury to the small town of Bristol, the Bobcat is fun, funky, and hip—just like the inventive comfort-food menu. Wash your meal down with nearly a dozen excellent house-brewed beers.

Known for: Wednesday-night benefit dinners; busy, sometimes noisy weekends; maple crème brûlée. ⑤ *Average main: $19* ✉ *5 Main St., Bristol* ☎ *802/453–3311* ⊕ *www.thebobcatcafe.com* ⊘ *No lunch.*

Jessica's at Swift House

$$ | AMERICAN | The historical and romantic dining room of the former 19th-century governor's mansion turned inn still serves some of the best meals in town. The fine-dining menu runs the gamut of fish, duck, and rib eye, with a few creative twists. **Known for:** maple crème brûlée; wine list; Vermont cheese board. ⑤ *Average main: $24* ✉ *25 Stewart La.* ☎ *802/388–9925* ⊕ *www.jessicasvermont.com* ⊘ *Closed Mon. and Tues.; also Wed. Jan.–May.*

★ Mary's at Baldwin Creek

$$ | AMERICAN | People drive from the far reaches of Vermont to dine at this farm-to-table restaurant just beyond Bristol, 13 miles northeast of Middlebury. Allow a little extra time to visit the sprawling gardens around the beautiful property; they represent the slow approach to cooking that earned this restaurant its stellar reputation. **Known for:** cream of garlic soup; hand-churned, small-batch ice cream; cooking classes. ⑤ *Average main: $23* ✉ *1868 N. Rte. 116, Bristol* ☎ *802/453–2432* ⊕ *www.innatbaldwincreek.com* ⊘ *Closed Mon. and Tues.*

The Storm Cafe

$$$ | MODERN AMERICAN | There's no setting in town quite like this restaurant's deck, which overlooks Otter Creek Falls at one end of a long footbridge. Even if you're not here in summer, the eclectic, ever-changing menu makes this small café a worthy stop at any time of year. **Known for:** beautiful 19th-century stone mill; banana cream pie; date night. ⑤ *Average main: $25* ✉ *Frog Hollow Mill, 3 Mill St.* ☎ *802/388–1063* ⊕ *www.thestormcafe.com* ⊘ *Closed Mon. No dinner Sun.–Thurs.*

🛏 Hotels

Inn on the Green

$ | B&B/INN | Listed on the National Register of Historic Places, this 1803 inn and its carriage house sit in the center of bucolic Middlebury near the college campus; the inn offers a delicious breakfast, bicycles you are free to use, and Adirondack chairs that are perfect for enjoying the grounds and views. **Pros:** ideal, central location; complimentary continental "breakfast-in-bed"; Aveda hair and skin-care products. **Cons:** some rooms small and close together; typical country-inn design; no coffee or tea in rooms. ⑤ *Rooms from: $169* ✉ *71 S. Pleasant St.* ☎ *802/388–7512, 888/244–7512* ⊕ *www.innonthegreen.com* ⇨ *11 rooms* ⊚ *Free breakfast.*

Swift House Inn

$ | B&B/INN | The 1814 Georgian mansion channels a classic New England style into three buildings on 4 acres of lawns and gardens. **Pros:** attractive, spacious, well-kept rooms; complimentary day pass to Middlebury Fitness Club; some rooms have private decks; on-site restaurant, Jessica's, is one of the best fine-dining options in town. **Cons:** not quite in the heart of town; weak Wi-Fi in some areas; somewhat typical country-inn design. ⑤ *Rooms from: $165* ✉ *25 Stewart La.* ☎ *866/388–9925* ⊕ *www.swifthouseinn.com* ⇨ *20 rooms* ⊚ *Free breakfast.*

⑨ Nightlife

Two Brothers Tavern

$ | BARS/PUBS | Head to this watering hole for pub food a cut above the usual, plus local microbrews on tap in the sports-friendly bar. Look closely at the dollar bills pasted to the ceiling. There's even a marriage proposal up there, along with the answer. Food is served until at least midnight. ✉ *86 Main St.* ☎ *802/388–0002* ⊕ *www.twobrotherstavern.com.*

🛍 Shopping

Danforth Pewter Workshop & Store
CRAFTS | In addition to its handcrafted pewter vases, lamps, and jewelry, this store offers you a front-row seat to the art of pewter spinning in the back workshop. There's also a small museum. ⊠ *52 Seymour St.* ☎ *802/388–0098* ⊕ *www.danforthpewter.com.*

Waitsfield and Warren

32 miles northeast (Waitsfield) and 25 miles east (Warren) of Middlebury.

Skiers first discovered the high peaks overlooking the pastoral Mad River Valley in the 1940s. Today, this valley and its two towns, Waitsfield and Warren, attract the hip, the adventurous, and the low-key. Warren in particular is tiny and adorable, with a general store popular with tour buses. The gently carved ridges cradling the valley and the swell of pastures and fields lining the river seem to keep notions of ski-resort sprawl at bay. With a map from the Sugarbush Chamber of Commerce you can investigate back roads off Route 100 that have exhilarating valley views.

ESSENTIALS
VISITOR INFORMATION Visitor Information Center ☎ *802/496–3409* ⊕ *www.madrivervalley.com.*

🍽 Restaurants

★ American Flatbread Waitsfield
$$ | PIZZA | The organically grown flour and vegetables—and the wood-fired clay ovens that unite them—take the pizza here to another level. In summer, you can dine outside around fire pits in the beautiful valley. **Known for:** maple–fennel sausage pie; homemade fruit crisp with Mountain Creamery ice cream; Big Red Barn art gallery on-site. ⑤ *Average main: $18* ⊠ *46 Lareau Rd., off Rte. 100, Waitsfield* ☎ *802/496–8856* ⊕ *www.* *americanflatbread.com* ⊙ *Closed Mon.– Wed. No lunch.*

Mint
$$ | VEGETARIAN | This creative whole-food-focused vegetarian restaurant blends organic, local produce with influences from Hungary, India, Mexico, Italy, and beyond. The outdoor tables near the Waitsfield covered bridge make it all the more Vermonty. **Known for:** tea selection; lángos, Hungarian fried dough; creative, exotic salads. ⑤ *Average main: $20* ⊠ *4403 Main St., Waitsfield* ☎ *802/496–5514* ⊕ *www.mintvermont.com* ⊙ *Closed Mon. and Tues. No lunch.*

★ Peasant
$$$ | EUROPEAN | The menu may be short in this small, rustic-chic space serving French- and Italian-influenced country fare, but the tastiness is immense, with some of the best pasta dishes in the state. Additional warmth is added by its "peasant family" operation, too, with dad in the kitchen, mom decorating the scene, and daughter running the front of house. **Known for:** unique "Peasant's Prunes" dessert; Vermont pork Bolognese with penne and Asiago; craft cocktail and wine list. ⑤ *Average main: $26* ⊠ *40 Bridge St., Waitsfield* ☎ *802/496–6856* ⊕ *www.peasantvt.com* ⊙ *Closed Tues. and Wed. No lunch.*

Pitcher Inn Dining Room and Tracks
$$$ | AMERICAN | Claiming two aesthetics and one menu, this dining experience offers a posh and pretty upstairs dining room with classic white tablecloths or a stony, subterranean "Tracks," with billiards and shuffleboard on the side. Dishes cover upscale versions of regional classics, with a few international flavors, too. **Known for:** cocktail list with Vermont spirits; duck breast; artisanal cheese board with onion chutney. ⑤ *Average main: $30* ⊠ *275 Main St., Warren* ☎ *802/496–6350* ⊕ *www.pitcherinn.com* ⊙ *Closed Tues. No lunch.*

Hotels

★ The Inn at Round Barn Farm

$$ | B&B/INN | A Shaker-style round barn—one of only five in Vermont—is the centerpiece of this eminently charming bed-and-breakfast set among the hills of the Mad River Valley with resident ducks, squirrels, chipmunks, and songbirds that make it feel like a Disney movie. **Pros:** miles of walking and snowshoe trails; game room with billiard table and board games; gorgeous gardens with lily ponds. **Cons:** no a/c in common areas; fills up for wedding parties; no sights within walking distance. ⑤ *Rooms from: $219* ⊠ *1661 E. Warren Rd., Waitsfield* ☎ *802/496–2276* ⊕ *www.theroundbarn. com* ⤴ *12 rooms* ⑩ *Free breakfast.*

Mad River Barn

$ | B&B/INN | This supposed former bunk house for the Civilian Conservation Corps in the 1930s is now one of the Mad River Valley's chicest accommodations, thanks to extensive renovations in 2013 that transformed it into a rustic farmhouse with an edge of industrial. **Pros:** multiple sized rooms, sleeping up to six people; game room includes shuffleboard, air hockey, foosball, and more; several family suites, with bunkbeds. **Cons:** first floor rooms can suffer noise; lots of weddings in summer can keep it busy and booked; no TVs in rooms. ⑤ *Rooms from: $145* ⊠ *2849 Mill Brook Rd., Waitsfield* ☎ *802/496–3310, 800/631–0466* ⊕ *www. madriverbarn.com* ⤴ *18 rooms* ⑩ *Free breakfast.*

★ The Pitcher Inn

$$$$ | B&B/INN | One of Vermont's three Relais & Châteaux properties, the unique Pitcher Inn has it all including a supremely romantic restaurant and bubbling brook running alongside. **Pros:** exceptional and fun design; across from Warren General Store; complimentary hybrid bikes and access to the Sugarbush Health and Racquet Club. **Cons:** two-night minimum stay on many weekends in peak period; limited to no cell phone service;

restaurant closed on Tuesdays. ⑤ *Rooms from: $500* ⊠ *275 Main St., Warren* ☎ *802/496–6350* ⊕ *www.pitcherinn.com* ⤴ *11 rooms* ⑩ *Free breakfast.*

Activities

GOLF

Sugarbush Resort Golf Club

GOLF | Great views and challenging play are the hallmarks of this mountain course designed by Robert Trent Jones Sr. ⊠ *Sugarbush, 1840 Sugarbush Access Rd., Warren* ☎ *802/583–6725* ⊕ *www. sugarbush.com* ⤴ *$105 for 18 holes, weekdays; $120 for 18 holes, weekends* 🏌 *18 holes, 6464 yards, par 70.*

MULTISPORT OUTFITTER

Clearwater Sports

TOUR—SPORTS | FAMILY | This outfitter rents canoes and kayaks, and leads guided river trips in warmer months. When the weather turns cold, it offers snowshoeing and backcountry skiing tours. ⊠ *4147 Main St., Waitsfield* ☎ *802/496–2708* ⊕ *www.clearwatersports.com.*

SKI AREAS

Blueberry Lake Cross Country and Snowshoeing Center

SKIING/SNOWBOARDING | This ski area has 18 miles of trails through thickly wooded glades. ⊠ *424 Plunkton Rd., East Warren* ☎ *802/496–6687* ⊕ *www.blueberrylakeskivt.com* ⤴ *Trail pass: $14.*

Mad River Glen

SKIING/SNOWBOARDING | A pristine alpine experience, Mad River attracts rugged individualists looking for less polished terrain. The area was developed in the late 1940s and has changed relatively little since then. It remains one of only three resorts in the country that ban snowboarding, and it's one of only two in North America that still has a single-chair lift. Mad River is steep, with slopes that follow the mountain's fall lines. The terrain changes constantly on the interconnected trails of mostly natural snow (expert trails are never groomed).

Telemark skiing and snowshoeing are also popular. **Facilities:** 53 trails; 115 acres; 2,037-foot vertical drop; 5 lifts. ⊠ *62 Mad River Resort Rd., off Rte. 17, Waitsfield* ☎ *802/496–3551* ⊕ *www. madriverglen.com* ⬚ *Lift ticket: $89.*

Sugarbush

SKIING/SNOWBOARDING | FAMILY | A true skier's mountain, Sugarbush has plenty of steep, natural snow glades and fall-line drops. Not as rough around the edges as Mad River Glen, the resort has an extensive computer-controlled system for snowmaking and many groomed trails between its two mountain complexes. This a great choice for intermediate skiers, who will find top-to-bottom runs all over the resort; there are fewer options for beginners. Programs for kids include the enjoyable Sugarbear Forest, a terrain garden full of fun bumps and jumps. At the base of the mountain are condominiums, restaurants, shops, bars, and a health-and-racquet club. **Facilities:** 111 trails; 484 acres; 2,600-foot vertical drop; 16 lifts. ⊠ *102 Forest Dr., Warren* ⊹ *From Rte. 17, take German Flats Rd. south; from Rte. 100, take Sugarbush Access Rd. west* ☎ *802/583–6300, 800/537–8427* ⊕ *www.sugarbush.com* ⬚ *Lift ticket: $119.*

🛍 Shopping

All Things Bright and Beautiful

ANTIQUES/COLLECTIBLES | This eccentric Victorian house is filled to the rafters with stuffed animals of all shapes, sizes, and colors, as well as folk art, European glass, and Christmas ornaments. ⊠ *27 Bridge St., Waitsfield* ☎ *802/496–3997.*

The Warren Store

FOOD/CANDY | This general store has everything you'd hope to find in tiny but sophisticated Vermont: a nice selection of local beer and wine, cheeses, baked goods, strong coffee, and delicious sandwiches and prepared foods. In summer, grab a quick lunch on the small deck by the water; in winter, warm up at the wood stove. Warm, woolly clothing and accessories can be found upstairs. ⊠ *284 Main St., Warren* ☎ *802/496–3864* ⊕ *www.warrenstore.com.*

Montpelier

38 miles southeast of Burlington, 115 miles north of Brattleboro.

With only about 8,000 residents, little Montpelier is the country's smallest capital city, but it has a youthful energy and a quirky spirit that's earned it the local nickname "Montpeculiar." The quaint, historic downtown area bustles by day with thousands of state and city workers walking to meetings and business lunches. The nightlife can't match Burlington's, but several bars, theaters, and cinemas provide ample entertainment. The city is also a springboard for exploring the great outdoors of Central Vermont.

Vermont's capital city is easily accessible from Interstate 89, taking about 45 minutes from Burlington by car through the heart of the Green Mountains. It's also on the main Boston–Montreal bus route. Downtown is flat and easily walkable, but exploring the surrounding hills requires a modest level of fitness as well as a solid pair of shoes or boots, especially during the winter.

◉ Sights

★ Hope Cemetery

CEMETERY | Montpelier's regional rival, Barre, the "Granite Capital of the World," may lack the polish and pedigree of the state capital, but it's home to this gorgeous cemetery filled with superbly crafted tombstones by master stonecutters. A few embrace the avant-garde, while others take defined shapes like a race car, a biplane, and a soccer ball. ⊠ *201 Maple Ave., Barre* ☎ *802/476–6245.*

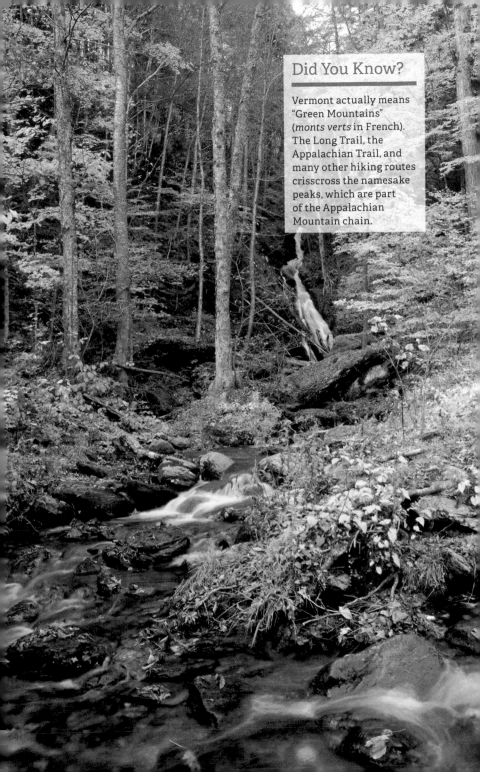

Hubbard Park

HIKING/WALKING | Rising behind the Vermont State House and stretching 196 acres, this heavily forested park offers locals (and their happy, leash-free dogs) miles of pretty trails and wildlife to enjoy. On its highest peak is a romantic stone tower that looks out to 360-degree views of the surrounding mountains. ⊠ *400 Parkway St.* ☎ *802/ 223–7335 Montpelier Parks department* ⊕ *www.montpelier-vt. org* ☒ *Free.*

★ Morse Farm Maple Sugarworks

FACTORY | **FAMILY** | With eight generations of sugaring, the Morses may be the oldest maple family in existence, so you're sure to find an authentic experience at their farm. Burr Morse—a local legend—heads up the operation now, along with his son Tom. More than 5,000 trees produce the sap used for syrup (you can sample all the grades), candy, cream, and sugar—all sold in the gift shop. Grab a maple creemee (soft-serve ice cream), take a seat on a swing, and stay awhile. Surrounding trails offer pleasant strolls in summer and prime cross-country skiing in winter. ⊠ *1168 County Rd.* ☎ *800/242–2740* ⊕ *www.morsefarm.com* ☒ *Free.*

Rock of Ages Granite Quarry

NATURE SITE | Attractions here range from the awe-inspiring (the quarry resembles the Grand Canyon in miniature) to the mildly ghoulish (you can consult a directory of tombstone dealers throughout the country) to the whimsical (an outdoor granite bowling alley). At the crafts center, skilled artisans sculpt monuments and blast stone, while at the quarries themselves, workers who clearly earn their pay cut 25-ton blocks of stone from the sheer 475-foot walls. (You may recognize these walls from a chase scene in the 2009 *Star Trek* movie.) ⊠ *558 Graniteville Rd., off I–89, Graniteville* ☎ *802/476–3119, 866/748–6877* ⊕ *www.rockofages. com* ☒ *Guided tours $5* ⊙ *Closed Sun. and mid-Oct.–mid-May.*

Vermont History Museum

MUSEUM | The collection here, begun in 1838, focuses on all things Vermont—from a catamount (the now-extinct local cougar) to Ethan Allen's shoe buckles. The museum store stocks fine books, prints, and gifts. A second location in Barre, the Vermont History Center, has rotating exhibits with notable photographs and artifacts. ⊠ *109 State St.* ☎ *802/828–2291* ⊕ *www.vermonthistory. org* ☒ *$7* ⊙ *Closed Sun. and Mon.*

Vermont State House

GOVERNMENT BUILDING | The regal capitol building surrounded by forest is emblematic of this proudly rural state. With a gleaming dome and columns of Barre granite measuring 6 feet in diameter, the State House is home to the country's oldest legislative chambers still in their original condition. Interior paintings and exhibits depict much of Vermont's sterling Civil War record. A self-guided tour, available year-round, takes you through the governor's office and the house and senate chambers. Free guided tours run from late June to October. ⊠ *115 State St.* ☎ *802/828–2228* ⊕ *statehouse. vermont.gov* ☒ *Donations accepted* ⊙ *Closed Sun.; also Sat. Nov.–June.*

🍴 Restaurants

★ Down Home Kitchen

$ | **SOUTHERN** | **FAMILY** | This restaurant's North Carolina-born owner brings classic Southern charm to downtown Montpelier, with the best chicken and waffles, fried catfish, collard greens, and cornbread in the state. The atmosphere provides a match, with a long soda fountain serving floats and mint juleps and a central communal wooden table dressed with fresh flowers. **Known for:** Southern hospitality; hearty breakfasts; pies and cakes. ⑤ *Average main: $15* ⊠ *100 Main St.* ☎ *802/225–6665* ⊕ *www.downhome-kitchenvt.com* ⊙ *No dinner Sun.–Thurs.*

Kismet

$$$ | **ECLECTIC** | One of Montpelier's more upscale restaurants, Kismet embraces the farm-to-table philosophy and gives it a shiny gloss and an international flavor. Tranquilly humming in the evening, particularly after State House employees get off work, Kismet buzzes most during its popular weekend brunches. **Known for:** multiple eggs Benedict versions; wine and cocktail list; expensive for Vermont. ⑤ *Average main: $34* ✉ *52 State St.* ☎ *802/223–8646* ⊕ *www.kismetkitchens. com* ۞ *Closed Mon. and Tues. No dinner Sun. No lunch.*

NECI on Main

$$ | **AMERICAN** | Nearly everyone working at this restaurant is a student at the New England Culinary Institute, but the quality and inventiveness of the food is anything but beginner's luck. The lounge downstairs offers the same seasonal menu in a more casual atmosphere. **Known for:** Vermont-inspired tapas platter; dessert buffet; wine list. ⑤ *Average main: $20* ✉ *118 Main St.* ☎ *802/223–3188* ⊕ *www. neci.edu* ۞ *Closed Sun. and Mon. No lunch.*

★ Red Hen Baking Co.

$ | **CAFÉ** | If you're a devotee of artisanal bakeries, it'd be a mistake not to trek the 7-plus miles from Montpelier (15 from Stowe) to have lunch, pick up freshly baked bread, or sample a sweet treat at what many consider Vermont's best bakery. Red Hen supplies bread to some of the state's premier restaurants, including Hen of the Wood, and has varied offerings every day. **Known for:** breads and pastries; local hangout; soups and sandwiches. ⑤ *Average main: $8* ✉ *961 U.S. 2, Suite B, Middlesex* ☎ *802/223–5200* ⊕ *www.redhenbaking.com* ۞ *No dinner.*

Sarducci's

$$ | **ITALIAN** | **FAMILY** | Montpelier's most popular restaurant draws its crowd less for the classic American Italian dishes than for the conviviality, charm, and sizeable portions, not to mention the picturesque Winooski River flowing directly alongside the windows. The pizza comes fresh from wood-fired ovens, while the rest of the menu features your favorite pennes, alfredos, and raviolis, with pleasing tweaks on the old formulas. **Known for:** date night; large gluten-free menu; local favorite. ⑤ *Average main: $18* ✉ *3 Main St.* ☎ *802/223–0229* ⊕ *www.sarduccis. com* ۞ *No lunch Sun.*

The Skinny Pancake

$ | **CAFÉ** | This dine-in creperie makes a great stop for breakfast, lunch, or an easy dinner. The signature crepes go sweet and savory and are filled with fruit, vegetables, and meat from more than a dozen Vermont farms. **Known for:** inventive hot chocolate recipes; Localvore's Dream crepe with chicken, cran-apple chutney, spinach, and blue cheese; Pooh Bear crepe with cinnamon sugar and local honey. ⑤ *Average main: $9* ✉ *89 Main St.* ☎ *802/262–2253* ⊕ *www.skinnypancake.com.*

★ Three Penny Taproom

$ | **ECLECTIC** | This celebrated taproom remains one of the state's best, thanks in large part to its ability to acquire beers few others in the region can. The vibe feels straight out of an artsy neighborhood in Brussels, but with the earthiness of Vermont. **Known for:** darn good burger; top happy-hour hangout in town; premier Vermont and hard-to get brews. ⑤ *Average main: $15* ✉ *108 Main St.* ☎ *802/223–8277* ⊕ *www.threepennytaproom.com.*

 Hotels

Capitol Plaza Hotel

$ | **HOTEL** | Montpelier's only major hotel benefits much from the State House across the street, hosting many of its visiting politicians, lobbyists, and business makers, not to mention tourists seeking a certain quality of accommodation. **Pros:** easy walking distance to all local sights, including bike path; small fitness center; the resident steak house, J.Morgans, serves probably the best cuts in town. **Cons:** somewhat bland design; slight corporate feel; street-facing room may suffer street and bell-tower noise. $ *Rooms from: $192* ✉ *100 State St.* ☎ *802/223–5252, 800/274–5252* ⊕ *www.capitolplaza.com* ⇨ *65 rooms* ⦿ *No meals.*

Inn at Montpelier

$$ | B&B/INN | The capital's most charming lodging option, this lovingly tended inn dating to 1830 has rooms filled with antique four-poster beds and Windsor chairs—all have private (if small) baths. **Pros:** beautiful home; relaxed central setting means you can walk everywhere in town; amazing porch. **Cons:** some rooms are small; somewhat bland, traditional design; no tea or coffee in rooms. $ *Rooms from: $200* ✉ *147 Main St.* ☎ *802/223–2727* ⊕ *www.innatmontpelier.com* ⇨ *19 rooms* ⦿ *Free breakfast.*

Shopping

AroMed

LOCAL SPECIALTIES | Although just a small storefront in downtown Montpelier, this shop counts customers as far away as Hawaii, thanks to owner Lauren Andrew's masterful concoctions of lotions, oils, and aromatics. Her CBD- (cannabidiol-) infused versions are particularly popular. ✉ *8 State St.* ☎ *802/505–1405* ⊕ *www.aromedofvt.com.*

Artisans Hand Craft Gallery

ANTIQUES/COLLECTIBLES | For more than 30 years, Maggie Neale has been celebrating and supporting Vermont's craft community. Her store sells jewelry, textiles, sculptures, and paintings by many local artists. ✉ *89 Main St.* ☎ *802/229–9492* ⊕ *www.artisanshand.com.*

Bear Pond Books

BOOKS/STATIONERY | FAMILY | Old-fashioned village bookstores don't get more cute and quaint than this, and locals work hard to keep it that way by actively embracing the printed word. A community hangout, the nearly 50-year-old shop hosts numerous readings by authors, workshops, and book clubs, as well as a significant section of Vermont writers. ✉ *77 Main St.* ☎ *892/ 229–0774* ⊕ *www.bearpondbooks.com.*

Vermont Creamery

FOOD/CANDY | A leader in the artisanal cheese movement, this creamery invites aficionados to visit its 4,000-square-foot production facility, where goat cheeses such as Bonne Bouche—a perfectly balanced, cloudlike cheese—are made on weekdays. The creamery is in Websterville, southwest of Montpelier. ✉ *20 Pitman Rd., Websterville* ☎ *802/479–9371, 800/884–6287* ⊕ *www.vermontcreamery.com.*

Stowe

22 miles northwest of Montpelier, 36 miles east of Burlington.

★ Long before skiing came to Stowe in the 1930s, the rolling hills and valleys beneath Vermont's highest peak, 4,395-foot Mt. Mansfield, attracted summer tourists looking for a reprieve from city heat. Most stayed at one of two inns in the village of Stowe. When skiing made the town a winter destination, visitors outnumbered hotel beds, so locals took them in. This spirit of hospitality continues, and many of these homes are now country inns. The village itself is tiny—just a few blocks of shops and restaurants clustered around a picture-perfect white church with a lofty steeple—but it serves as the anchor for Mountain Road, which leads north past restaurants, lodges, and shops on its way to Stowe's fabled slopes. The road to Stowe also passes through Waterbury, which is rapidly regenerating thanks to a thriving arts and dining scene.

ESSENTIALS

VISITOR INFORMATION Stowe Area Association ☎ *802/253–7321, 877/467–8693* ⊕ *www.gostowe.com.*

Northern Vermont

👁 Sights

★ Ben & Jerry's Factory

LOCAL INTEREST | FAMILY | The closest thing you'll get to a Willy Wonka experience in Vermont, the 30-minute tours at the famous brand's factory are unabashedly corny and only skim the surface of the behind-the-scenes goings-on, but this flaw is almost forgiven when the samples are dished out. To see the machines at work, visit on a weekday (but call ahead to confirm if they will indeed be in operation). Another highlight is the "Flavor Graveyard," where flavors of yore are given tribute with tombstones inscribed with humorous poetry. Free, family-friendly outdoor movies also play through summer on Friday. ⊠ *1281 Waterbury-Stowe Rd., Waterbury* ☎ *802/882–2047* ⊕ *www.benjerry.com* 🎫 *Tours $4.*

Vermont Ski and Snowboard Museum

MUSEUM | The state's skiing and snowboarding history is documented here. Exhibits cover subjects such as the 10th Mountain Division of World War II, the national ski patrol, Winter Olympians, and the evolution of equipment. An early World Cup trophy is on loan, and one of the most memorable mobiles you'll ever see, made from a gondola and ski-lift chairs, hangs from the ceiling. One recent exhibit, Slope Style, focused on ski fashion from 1930 to 2014. ⊠ *1 S. Main St.* ☎ *802/253–9911* ⊕ *www.vtssm.com* 🎫 *$5* 🕑 *Closed Mon. and Tues.*

🍴 Restaurants

Bierhall

$$ | AUSTRIAN | In 2016, the Von Trapp family finally realized its long-held dream of opening a brewery making Austrian-style lagers on the grounds, and what a brewery it is. Built of thick, massive Vermont wood beams, the cavernous chalet-style space houses a rustic-chic restaurant and bar alongside the beer-making facilities serving Germanic classics, with plenty of beer to wash it down. **Known for:** Bavarian pretzels with beer-cheese dip; chicken schnitzel; Sachertorte and apple strudel. ⑤ *Average main: $20* ⊠ *1333 Luce Hill Rd.* ☎ *802/253–5750* ⊕ *www.vontrapp-brewing.com.*

Cork

$$ | INTERNATIONAL | Pursuing a mission that "the best wines are grown, not made," this natural wine bar meticulously curates an inventory of organic, biodynamic, no-additive, unfiltered, and wild-fermented vintages, either for sale in the small retail section in the front, or complementing upscale bistro dishes and boards in the classy dining room. **Known for:** mostly old-world wines, with some local labels; lots of charcuterie and shareable appetizers; in the heart of Stowe village. ⑤ *Average main: $23* ⊠ *35 School St.* ☎ *802/760–6143* ⊕ *www.corkvt.com* 🕑 *Closed Tues.*

Harrison's Restaurant

$$ | AMERICAN | A lively locals' scene, booths by the fireplace, and creative American cuisine paired with well-chosen wines and regional brews make this place perfect for couples and families alike. The inviting bar is a good spot to dine alone or to chat with a regular. **Known for:** peanut-butter pie; wine and cocktail list; wood fireplace. ⑤ *Average main: $23* ⊠ *25 Main St.* ☎ *802/253–7773* ⊕ *www.harrisons-stowe.com* 🕑 *No lunch.*

★ Hen of the Wood

$$$ | ECLECTIC | Ask Vermont's great chefs where they go for a tremendous meal, and Hen of the Wood inevitably tops the list, thanks to its sophisticated, almost artful, dishes that showcase an abundance of local produce, meat, and cheese. The utterly romantic candlelit setting is riveting: a converted 1835 gristmill beside a waterfall. **Known for:** special occasions and dates; outstanding cooking; wine and cocktail list. ⑤ *Average main: $28* ⊠ *92 Stowe St., Waterbury* ☎ *802/244–7300* ⊕ *www.henofthewood.com* 🕑 *Closed Sun. and Mon. No lunch.*

Continued on page 478

LET IT SNOW

WINTER ACTIVITIES IN VERMONT

by Elise Coroneos

SKIING AND SNOWBOARDING IN VERMONT

Less than 5 miles from the Canadian border, Jay Peak is Vermont's northernmost ski resort.

Ever since America's first ski tow opened in a farmer's pasture near Woodstock in January 1934, skiers have headed en masse to Vermont in winter. Today, 20 alpine and 30 nordic ski areas range in size and are spread across the state, from Mount Snow in the south to Jay Peak near the Canadian border. The snow-making equipment has also become more comprehensive over the years, with more than 80% of the trails in the state using man-made snow. Here are some of the best ski areas by various categories:

GREAT FOR KIDS Smugglers' Notch, Okemo, and **Bromley Mountain** all offer terrific kids' programs, with classes organized by age categories and by skill level. Kids as young as 2 ½ (4 at some ski areas) can start learning. Child care, with activities like stories, singing, and arts and crafts, are available for those too young to ski; some ski areas, like Smuggler's Notch, offer babysitting with no minimum age daytime and evening.

BEST FOR BEGINNERS Beginner terrain makes up nearly half of the mountain at **Stratton,** where options include private and group lessons for first-timers. Also good are small but family-friendly **Bolton Valley** and **Bromley Mountains,** which both designate a third of their slopes for beginners.

EXPERT TERRAIN The slopes at **Jay Peak** and massive **Killington** are most notable for their steepness and pockets of glades. About 40% of the runs at these two resorts are advanced or expert. Due to its far north location, Jay Peak tends to get the most snow, making it ideal for powder days. Another favorite with advanced skiers is Central Vermont's **Mad River Glen,** where many slopes are ungroomed (natural) and the motto is "Ski it if you can." In addition, **Sugarbush, Stowe,** and **Smugglers' Notch** are all revered for their challenging untamed side country.

Mount Mansfield is better known as Stowe.

Stratton Mountain clocktower

NIGHT SKIING Come late afternoon, **Bolton Valley** is hopping. That's because it's the only location in Vermont for night skiing. Ski and ride under the lights from 4 until 8 Wednesday through Saturday, followed by a later après-ski scene.

APRÈS-SKI The social scenes at **Killington, Sugarbush,** and **Stowe** are the most noteworthy (and crowded). Book a seat on the Snowcat that takes intrepid partiers to the Motor Room Bar in Killington, or stop by the always popular Wobbly Barn. For live music, try Castlerock Pub in Sugarbush or the Matterhorn Bar in Stowe.

SNOWBOARDING Boarders (and some skiers) will love the latest features for freestyle tricks in Vermont. **Stratton** has four terrain parks for all abilities, one of which features a boarder cross course. **Mount Snow's** Carinthia Peak is an all-terrain park–dedicated mountain, the only of its kind in New England. Head to **Killington** for Burton Stash, another beautiful all-natural features terrain park. **Okemo** has a superpipe and eight terrain parks and a gladed park with all-natural features. Note that snowboarding is not allowed at skiing cooperative **Mad River Glen.**

CROSS-COUNTRY To experience the best of cross-country skiing in the state, simply follow the Catamount Trail, a 300-mile nordic route from southern Vermont to Canada. **The Trapp Family Lodge** in Stowe has 37 miles of groomed cross-country trails and 62 miles of back-country trails. Another top option is **The Mountain Top Inn & Resort,** just outside of Killington. Its Nordic Ski and Snowshoe Center provides instruction for newcomers, along with hot drinks and lunches when it is time to take a break and warm up.

TELEMARK Ungroomed snow and tree skiing are a natural fit with free-heel skiing at **Mad River Glen. Bromley** and **Jay Peak** also have telemark rentals and instruction.

MOUNTAIN-RESORT TRIP PLANNER

TIMING

■ **Snow Season.** Winter sports time is typically from Thanksgiving through April, weather permitting. Holidays are the most crowded.

■ **March Madness.** Much of the season's snow tends to come in March, so that's the time to go if you want to ski on fresh, nature-made powder. To increase your odds, choose a ski area in the northern part of the state.

■ **Summer Scene.** During summertime, many ski resorts reinvent themselves as prime destinations for golfers, zipline and canopy tours, mountain bikers, and weddings. Other summer visitors come to the mountains to enjoy hiking trails, climbing walls, aquatic centers, chairlift and horseback rides, or a variety of festivals.

■ **Avoid Long Lift Lines.** Try to hit the slopes early—many lifts start at 8 or 9 am, with ticket windows opening a half-hour earlier. Then take a mid-morning break as lines start to get longer and head out again when others come in for lunch.

SAVINGS TIPS

■ **Choose a Condo.** Especially if you're planning to stay for a week, save money on food by opting for a condominum unit with a kitchen. You can shop at the supermarket and cook breakfast and dinner.

■ **Rent Smart.** Consider ski rental options in the villages rather than at the mountain. Renting right at the ski area may be more convenient, but often costs more.

■ **Discount Lift Tickets.** Online tickets are often the least expensive; multi-day discounts and and ski-and-stay packages will also lower your costs. Good for those who can plan ahead, early-bird tickets often go on sale before the ski season even starts.

■ **Hit the Peaks Off-peak.** In order to secure the best deals at the most competitive rates, avoid booking during school holidays. President's Week in February is the busiest, because that's when Northeastern schools have their spring break.

Top left, Killington's six mountains make up the largest ski area in Vermont.
Top right, Stratton has a Snowboard-cross course.

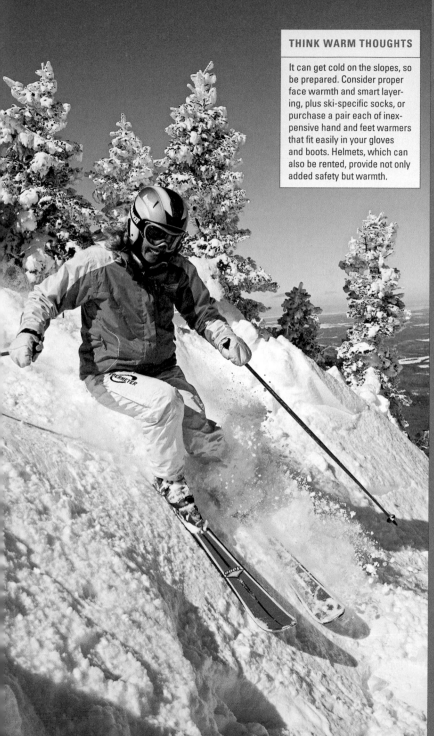

THINK WARM THOUGHTS

It can get cold on the slopes, so be prepared. Consider proper face warmth and smart layering, plus ski-specific socks, or purchase a pair each of inexpensive hand and feet warmers that fit easily in your gloves and boots. Helmets, which can also be rented, provide not only added safety but warmth.

VERMONT SKI AREAS BY THE NUMBERS

Okemo's wide slopes attract snowbirds to Ludlow in Central Vermont.

Numbers are a helpful way to compare mountains, but remember that each resort has a distinct personality. This list is composed of ski areas in Vermont with at least 100 skiable acres. For more information, see individual resort listings.

SKI AREA	Vertical Drop	Skiable Acres	# of Trails & Lifts	Terrain Type ●	■	◆/◆◆	Snowboarding Options
Bolton Valley	1,704	300	71/6	36%	37%	27%	Terrain park
Bromley	1,334	178	47/9	32%	37%	31%	Terrain park
Burke Mountain	2,011	270	50/5	10%	44%	46%	Terrain park
Jay Peak	2,153	385	78/9	22%	39%	41%	Terrain park
Killington	3,050	1509	155/22	28%	33%	39%	Terrain park, Half-pipe
Mad River Glen	2,037	120	54/5	30%	30%	40%	Snowboarding not allowed
Mount Snow	1,700	600	86/20	14%	73%	13%	Terrain park, Half-pipe
Okemo	2,200	667	121/20	31%	38%	31%	Terrain park, Superpipe, RossCross terrain cross park
Pico Mountain	1,967	468	57/7	18%	46%	36%	Triple Slope, terrain park
Smugglers' Notch	2,610	310	78/8	19%	50%	31%	Terrain park
Stowe	2,360	485	116/13	16%	59%	25%	Terrain park, Half-pipe
Stratton	2,003	670	97/11	42%	31%	27%	Terrain park, Half-pipe, Snowboardcross course
Sugarbush	2,600	581	111/16	20%	45%	35%	Terrain park

CONTACT THE EXPERTS

Ski Vermont (☎ *802/223-2439* ⊕ *www.skivermont.com*), a non-profit association in Montpelier, Vermont, and **Vermont Department of Tourism** (⊕ *www.vermontvacation.com*) are great resources for travelers planning a wintertime trip to Vermont.

KNOW YOUR SIGNS

On trail maps and the mountains, trails are rated and marked:

● Beginner   ◆ Advanced

■ Intermediate   ◆◆ Expert

QUÉBEC

Alburg
Swanton
North Hero
Grand Isle
South Hero
Burlington
Shelburne
Richmond
Milton
Fairfax
Saint Albans
Jeffersonville
Johnson
Richford
Enosburg Falls
Jay Peak
North Troy
Newport
Derby Line
Derby Center
Norton
Island Pond
Orleans
Lowell
Barton
Albany
West Burke
Q Burke Mountain
Lyndonville
Lyndon
Concord
Littleton

Smugglers' Notch Resort
Stowe Resort
Bolton Valley Resort
Essex Junction
Stowe
Morrisville
Wolcott
Saint Johnsbury
Danville
Marshfield
Plainfield
Barnet
Wells River
Newbury

Waterbury
MONTPELIER
Barre
West Topsham
Newport

Vergennes
Bristol
Mad River Glen
Sugarbush
Northfield
Chelsea
Bradford
Fairlee

Middlebury
East Middlebury
Hancock
Randolph
East Randolph

Shoreham
Brandon
Bethel
Proctor
Rutland
West Rutland
Poultney
Pico Ski Resort
Killington
Wallingford
White River Junction
Hanover
Lebanon
Woodstock
Hartland
Windsor
Plymouth
Franklin

Granville
West Pawlet
Okemo Mountain Resort
Ludlow
Ascutney
Newport
Claremont
Dorset
Springfield
Chester
Bromley
Manchester
Grafton
NEW HAMPSHIRE
Hillsborough

Stratton
Arlington
Shaftsbury
Jamaica
Westminster
Bellows Falls

Mount Snow
Newfane
Putney
Keene
West Dover
Wilmington
Brattleboro
Bennington
Jacksonville
Pownal
Readsboro

0   10 mi
0   10 km

Vermont Ski Areas

Idletyme Brewing Company

$$$ | AMERICAN | In prime position on the mountain road and the Stowe Recreation Path, this brewpub benefits from the culinary chops of owner Michael Kloeti, of Michael's on the Hill. Add to that a range of Bavarian-style lagers and Vermont IPAs brewed on-site, a large outdoor patio, vegetable garden, and a rich, rustic, chic design, and it's easy to understand what makes it so popular. **Known for:** "brewski" beer flights; ample space for large groups; outdoor Biergarten. ⑤ *Average main: $26* ⊠ *1859 Mountain Rd.* ☎ *802/253–4765* ⊕ *www.idletymebrewing.com.*

Michael's on the Hill

$$$ | EUROPEAN | Swiss-born chef Michael Kloeti trained in Europe and New York City before opening this establishment in a 19th-century farmhouse outside Stowe. The seasonal three-course prix-fixe menus ($45 and $67) blend European cuisine with farm-to-table earthiness, exemplified by dishes such as spice-roasted duck breast and venison *navarin* (ragout). **Known for:** homemade potato gnocchi; wine list; views of Green Mountains and sunsets. ⑤ *Average main: $34* ⊠ *4182 Stowe-Waterbury Rd., 6 miles south of Stowe, Waterbury Center* ☎ *802/244–7476* ⊕ *www.michaelsonthehill.com* ◷ *Closed Tues. No lunch.*

★ Prohibition Pig

$ | AMERICAN | This restaurant and brewery in downtown Waterbury is always packed for a reason: fabulous craft beers, sandwiches, salads, and North Carolina-style barbecue served in an airy and friendly bar and dining room. If you just want a quick bite and a draft, belly up to the tasting-room bar at the brewery in the back, or pop across the street to the Craft Beer Cellar, one of the state's best beer stores. **Known for:** duck-fat fries; "craft" mac and cheese; one of the state's best draft lists. ⑤ *Average main: $15* ⊠ *23 S. Main St., Waterbury* ☎ *802/244–4120* ⊕ *www.prohibitionpig.com* ◷ *No lunch Tues.–Thurs.*

Zen Barn

$$ | ECLECTIC | What's more Vermont than the name "Zen Barn," especially when it includes its own yoga studio in a former hayloft? Add to that an expansive, rustic-chic interior with local art and a stage for live music, an outdoor patio looking out to green fields and mountains, and a menu of eclectic, farm-to-table fare, and the local experience is complete. **Known for:** CBD cocktails; ramen soup; live performances. ⑤ *Average main: $18* ⊠ *179 Guptil Rd., Waterbury* ☎ *802/244–8134* ⊕ *www.zenbarnvt.com* ◷ *Closed Sun. and Mon.*

 # Hotels

Field Guide

$ | HOTEL | This boutique enterprise just north of Stowe village is a whimsically stylish alternative to the town's staid resorts and cadre of inns stuck in ski-chalet mold. **Pros:** waffle kimono robes; seasonal heated pool and hot tub; Trail Suite, with a loft bedroom and view of Stowe's iconic white church. **Cons:** unique style not for everyone; no elevator; no coffee/tea in rooms. ⑤ *Rooms from: $110* ⊠ *433 Mountain Rd.* ☎ *802/253–8088* ⊕ *www.fieldguidestowe.com* ⌗ *30 rooms* ❑ *Free breakfast.*

Green Mountain Inn

$ | B&B/INN | Smack-dab in the center of Stowe Village, this classic redbrick inn has been welcoming guests since 1833; rooms in the main building and the annex feel like a country inn, while the newer buildings refine with added luxury and space. **Pros:** easy walking distance to entire village and main sights; luxury rooms include large Jacuzzis; 300-thread-count Egyptian cotton bedding and Frette bathrobes. **Cons:** farther from skiing than other area hotels; road noise in front of building; no tea in rooms. ⑤ *Rooms from: $169* ⊠ *18 Main St.* ☎ *802/253–7301, 800/253–7302* ⊕ *www.greenmountain-inn.com* ⌗ *104 rooms* ❑ *No meals.*

★ The Lodge at Spruce Peak

$$ | RESORT | At the base of the ski slopes, this lodge would be king of the hill for its location alone, but a stay here also affords many perks including the rustic-meets-contemporary accommodations that run the gamut from studio to three-bedroom units, many with outdoor terraces. **Pros:** mountain views; lots of children's activities; many shops supply all needs. **Cons:** somewhat sterile feel; no separate kids' pool; expensive breakfast. ⑤ *Rooms from: $269 ✉ 7412 Mountain Rd. ☎ 802/253–3560, 888/478–6938 reservations ⊕ www.sprucepeak.com* ⇨ *300 rooms* ⦿ *No meals.*

Stone Hill Inn

$$$ | B&B/INN | A contemporary, romance-inducing bed-and-breakfast where classical music plays in the hallways, Stone Hill has guest rooms with two-sink vanities and two-person whirlpools in front of double-sided fireplaces. **Pros:** perennial gardens with stream; complimentary toboggan and snowshoes; Gilchrist & Soames bathroom amenities. **Cons:** possibly depressing for single people; two-night minimum on weekends and in peak period; no children allowed. ⑤ *Rooms from: $309 ✉ 89 Houston Farm Rd. ☎ 802/253–6282 ⊕ www.stonehillinn. com* ⇨ *9 rooms* ⦿ *Free breakfast.*

Stowe Motel & Snowdrift

$ | HOTEL | FAMILY | The accommodations at this family-owned motel on 14 acres range from studios with small kitchenettes and modern two-bedroom suites warmed by their own fireplaces to rental houses that can sleep 10 or more people. **Pros:** good value for cost; complimentary bikes; 16 acres of landscaped grounds next to river. **Cons:** basic motel-style accommodations; design and furnishings could use an update; occasional road noise. ⑤ *Rooms from: $149 ✉ 2043 Mountain Rd. ☎ 802/253–7629, 800/829–7629 ⊕ www.stowemotel.com* ⇨ *62 rooms* ⦿ *Free breakfast.*

Stoweflake Mountain Resort and Spa

$ | RESORT | With one of the largest spas in the area, Stoweflake lets you enjoy an herb-and-flower labyrinth, a fitness center reached via a covered bridge, and a hydrotherapy waterfall that cascades into a hot tub. **Pros:** walking distances to many restaurants; wide range of rooms; across the street from the recreation path. **Cons:** mazelike layout can make rooms a bit hard to find; uninspired room design; no tea in rooms. ⑤ *Rooms from: $198 ✉ 1746 Mountain Rd. ☎ 800/253–2232 ⊕ www.stoweflake.com* ⇨ *180 rooms* ⦿ *No meals.*

Sun & Ski Inn and Suites

$ | HOTEL | Not many hotels can boast having a bowling alley, but this part-new, part-renovated inn can top even that, adding an 18-hole minigolf course, an indoor pool, and small fitness center. **Pros:** close to the slopes; the family-friendly restaurant is open daily for lunch and dinner; tea/coffeemakers in rooms. **Cons:** not very Vermonty; family friendly can mean lots of children; often two-night minimum stay. ⑤ *Rooms from: $189 ✉ 1613 Mountain Rd. ☎ 802/253–7159, 800/448–5223 ⊕ www.sunandskiinn.com* ⇨ *39 rooms* ⦿ *Free breakfast.*

★ Topnotch Resort

$$$ | RESORT | FAMILY | On 120 acres overlooking Mt. Mansfield, this posh property has a contemporary look, excellent dining options, and one of the best spas in Vermont, which combine to create a world unto itself. **Pros:** ski shuttle will take you directly to the slopes; complimentary tea and cookies every afternoon; American bistro cuisine at the intimate Flannel or tuned-up bar bites at the Roost, the lively lobby bar. **Cons:** boutique style may not be for everyone; no tea in rooms; room rates fluctuate wildly. ⑤ *Rooms from: $350 ✉ 4000 Mountain Rd. ☎ 800/451–8686, 802/253–8585 ⊕ www.topnotchresort. com* ⇨ *91 rooms* ⦿ *No meals.*

★ Trapp Family Lodge

$$$ | **RESORT** | **FAMILY** | Built by the Von Trapp family (of *The Sound of Music* fame), this Tyrolean lodge is surrounded by some of the best mountain views in Vermont and abundant romantic ambience, making it a favorite for weddings. **Pros:** alive with the sound of music; excellent beer brewed on-site; concert series and festivals in warm weather. **Cons:** some sections appear tired and in need of updating; overrun by tourists, especially on weekends; if not an active person, you'll miss half the amenities. $ *Rooms from: $225* ⊠ *700 Trapp Hill Rd.* ☎ *802/253–8511, 800/826–7000* ⊕ *www.trappfamily. com* ➟ *214 rooms* ¡⊙¡ *No meals.*

Nightlife

Doc Ponds

BARS/PUBS | A gastropub from the folks behind the Hen of the Wood restaurant, this place has a diverse beer list. The food's great, too. ⊠ *294 Mountain Rd.* ☎ *802/760–6066* ⊕ *www.docponds.com.*

Matterhorn

DANCE CLUBS | This nightspot hosts live music and dancing on weekends during the ski season. If you'd rather just watch, there's a separate martini bar. ⊠ *4969 Mountain Rd.* ☎ *802/253–8198* ⊕ *www. matterhornbar.com.*

Tres Amigos

MUSIC CLUBS | Inside this Mexican eatery is the Rusty Nail Stage, which rocks with live music and DJs on weekends. ⊠ *1190 Mountain Rd.* ☎ *802/253–6245* ⊕ *www. tresamigosvt.com.*

Performing Arts

Helen Day Art Center

ART GALLERIES—ARTS | Above the local library, Stowe's premier art center hosts impressive rotating exhibitions of contemporary and local art throughout the year, as well as film screenings. It also provides art education to adults and children alike through workshops, lectures, events, and courses. ⊠ *90 Pond St.* ☎ *802/253–8358* ⊕ *www.helenday.com.*

Spruce Peak Performing Arts Center

CONCERTS | Part of the Mountain Lodge complex, this state-of-the-art space hosts theater, music, and dance performances. ⊠ *122 Hourglass Dr.* ☎ *802/760–4634* ⊕ *www.sprucepeakarts.org.*

Activities

CANOEING AND KAYAKING
Umiak Outdoor Outfitters

CANOEING/ROWING/SKULLING | This full-service outfitter rents canoes and kayaks, organizes tours, and sells equipment. It has seasonal outposts at the Waterbury Reservoir and at North Beach in Burlington. ⊠ *849 S. Main St.* ☎ *802/253–2317* ⊕ *www.umiak.com.*

FISHING
The Fly Rod Shop

FISHING | This shop provides a guide service, offers introductory classes, and rents tackle and other equipment. ⊠ *2703 Waterbury Rd., 1½ miles south of Stowe* ☎ *802/253–7346* ⊕ *www. flyrodshop.com.*

HIKING
Moss Glen Falls

HIKING/WALKING | Four miles outside of town, this short hike leads to a stupendous 125-foot waterfall that makes a great way to cool down in summer. ⊠ *615 Moss Glen Falls Rd.* ☎ *888/409–7579 Vermont State Parks* ⊕ *www. vtstateparks.com.*

Mt. Mansfield

HIKING/WALKING | Ascending Mt. Mansfield, Vermont's highest mountain, makes for a challenging day hike. Trails lead from Mountain Road to the summit, where they meet the north–south Long Trail. Views encompass New Hampshire's White Mountains, New York's Adirondacks, and southern Québec. The Green Mountain Club publishes a trail guide. ⊠ *Trailheads along Mountain Rd.* ☎ *802/244–7037* ⊕ *www.greenmountainclub.org.*

★ Stowe Recreation Path

HIKING/WALKING | An immaculately maintained, paved recreation path begins behind the Community Church in town and meanders about 5 miles along the river valley, with many entry points along the way. Whether you're on foot, skis, bike, or in-line skates, it's a tranquil spot to enjoy the outdoors. In autumn, there's a corn maze, and at least four shops along the path rent bikes. ⊠ *Stowe* ⊕ *www.stowerec.org.*

SKI AREA
Stowe Mountain Resort

SKIING/SNOWBOARDING | The name of the village is Stowe, and the name of the mountain is Mt. Mansfield—but to generations of skiers, it's all just plain "Stowe." The area's mystique attracts as many serious skiers as social ones. Stowe is a giant among Eastern ski mountains with intimidating expert runs, but its symmetrical shape allows skiers of all abilities to enjoy long, satisfying runs from the summit. Improved snowmaking capacity, new lifts, and free shuttle buses that gather skiers along Mountain Road have made it all much more convenient. Yet the traditions remain, like the Winter Carnival in January and the Sugar Slalom in April, to name two. Spruce Peak, where you'll find the Adventure Center and the Mountain Lodge, is separate from the main mountain; the peak has a teaching hill and offers a pleasant experience for intermediates and beginners. In the summer, there's a TreeTop Adventure course and an awe-inspiring zipline that extends from the top of the gondola to the bottom in three breathtaking runs. **Facilities:** 116 trails; 485 acres; 2,160-foot vertical drop; 13 lifts. ⊠ *5781 Mountain Rd.* ☎ *802/253–3000, 802/253–3600 for snow conditions* ⊕ *www.stowe.com* ⊠ *Lift ticket: $99.*

SLEDDING
Peacepups Dog Sledding

LOCAL SPORTS | **FAMILY** | This one-man (and multiple-dog) company offers two-hour tours with a team of eight Siberian

huskies. You can ride inside a padded toboggan or learn how to mush and drive on your own. If you prefer to walk the trails yourself, snowshoe rentals are also available. In summer, the trails are open to hiking. Lake Elmore is a roughly 20-minute drive from Stowe. ⊠ *239 Cross Rd., Lake Elmore* ☎ *802/888–7733* ⊕ *www.peacepupsdogsledding.com* ⊠ *$318 for dog sledding tours.*

🛍 Shopping

FOOD AND DRINK
★ Alchemist Brewery and Visitors Center

FOOD/CANDY | The brewery that launched a beer revolution in Vermont with its "Heady Topper" now welcomes guests to its brand-new shop and tasting room. Intense demand still keeps stocks of beer for sale limited. ⊠ *100 Cottage Club Rd.* ☎ *802/882–8165* ⊕ *www.alchemistbeer.com.*

Cabot Cheese Annex Store

FOOD/CANDY | In addition to shelves of Vermont-made jams, mustards, crackers, and maple products, the store features a long central table with samples of a dozen Cabot cheeses. ⊠ *2657 Waterbury–Stowe Rd., 2½ miles north of I–89* ☎ *802/244–6334* ⊕ *www. cabotcheese.coop.*

★ Cold Hollow Cider Mill

FOOD/CANDY | **FAMILY** | You can watch apples pressed into possibly the world's best cider at this working mill and sample it right from the tank. Its store sells all the apple butter, jams and jellies, and Vermont-made handicrafts you could want, plus the legendary 75¢ cider doughnuts. Kids love watching the "doughnut robot" in action. ⊠ *3600 Waterbury–Stowe Rd., Waterbury Center* ✛ *3 miles north of I–89* ☎ *800/327–7537* ⊕ *www.coldhollow.com.*

SPAS

Spa and Wellness Center at Stowe Mountain Lodge

SPA/BEAUTY | This 21,000-square-foot facility has 18 private treatment rooms, a fitness center, and a year-round outdoor pool and hot tub. In addition to the usual array of facials, scrubs, and massages for adults, the spa offers a separate program for kids. ⊠ *Stowe Mountain Lodge, 7412 Mountain Rd.* ☎ *802/760–4782* ⊕ *www. stowemountainlodge.com.*

Spa at Stoweflake

SPA/BEAUTY | One of the largest spas in New England, the Spa at Stoweflake features a massaging hydrotherapeutic waterfall, a Hungarian mineral pool, 30 treatment rooms, and more than 150 treatments like the Bingham Falls Renewal, named after a local waterfall. This treatment begins with a body scrub and a Vichy shower, followed by an aromatherapy oil massage. The spacious men's and women's sanctuaries have saunas, steam rooms, and whirlpool tubs. ⊠ *Stoweflake Mountain Resort and Spa, 1746 Mountain Rd.* ☎ *802/760–1083* ⊕ *www.stoweflake.com.*

Spa at Topnotch

SPA/BEAUTY | Calm pervades the Spa at Topnotch, with its birchwood doors, natural light, and cool colors. Signature treatments include the Mount Mansfield Saucha, a three-stage herbal body treatment, and the Little River Stone Massage, which uses the resort's own wood-spice oil. There's even Rover Reiki (really) for your canine friend. Locker areas are spacious, with saunas, steam rooms, and whirlpool tubs. The indoor pool has lots of natural light. Daily classes in tai chi, yoga, and Pilates are offered in the nearby fitness center. ⊠ *Topnotch Resort and Spa, 4000 Mountain Rd.* ☎ *802/253–6463* ⊕ *www. topnotchresort.com.*

Jeffersonville

18 miles north of Stowe.

Jeffersonville is just over Smugglers' Notch from Stowe but miles away in feeling and attitude. In summer, you can drive over the notch road as it curves precipitously around boulders that have fallen from the cliffs above, then pass open meadows and old farmhouses and sugar shacks on the way down to town. Below the notch, Smugglers' Notch Ski Resort is the hub of activity year-round. Downtown Jeffersonville, once home to an artists' colony, is quiet but has excellent dining and nice art galleries.

Like most places in Vermont, a car is essential to exploring this area. From Burlington, it's about a 45-minute drive along Route 15. Or you can cruise north on Route 108 from Stowe for 30 minutes; however, the road is closed for much of the winter.

◉ Sights

Boyden Valley Winery & Spirits

WINERY/DISTILLERY | On a beautiful stretch of farmland west of Jeffersonville, this winery conducts tours and tastings and showcases an excellent selection of Vermont specialty products and local handicrafts. The winery's Big Barn Red is full-bodied, but the real fun may be in the ice wines, maple crème liqueur, and hard ice cider. ⊠ *64 Rte. 104, Cambridge* ☎ *802/644–8151* ⊕ *www.boydenvalley. com* ⌨ *Tasting $10.*

⑪ Restaurants

158 Main Restaurant and Bakery

$ | AMERICAN | One of the most popular restaurants in Jeffersonville easily earns its accolades with big portions and small prices. The menu features all the classic egg, pancake, and corn-beef-hash dishes a person could wish for at breakfast, and a surprisingly wide-ranging international menu for dinner. **Known for:** $5 Two Egg Basic; Sunday brunch; homemade bread. ⑤ *Average main: $13* ⊠ *158 Main St.* ☎ *802/644–8100* ⊕ *www.158Main.com* ⊘ *Closed Mon. No dinner Sun.*

Hotels

★ **Smugglers' Notch Resort**

$$$ | **RESORT** | **FAMILY** | With five giant water parks for summer fun and just about every winter activity imaginable, including the new 26,000-square-foot indoor "FunZone 2.0," this resort is ideal for families; nightly rates include lift tickets, lessons, and all resort amenities. **Pros:** great place for families to learn to ski; views of several mountains; shuttles to the slopes. **Cons:** not a romantic getaway for couples; extra cost for daily cleaning; very busy during peak season. ⑤ *Rooms from: $322* ⊠ *4323 Rte. 108 S* ☎ *802/332–6841, 800/419–4615* ⊕ *www. smuggs.com* ⊅ *600 condominiums* ⦿l *No meals.*

Activities

KAYAKING

Vermont Canoe and Kayak

KAYAKING | This outfitter rents canoes and kayaks for use on the Lamoille River, and leads guided canoe trips to Boyden Valley Winery. ⊠ *4805 Rte. 15, behind the Family Table* ☎ *802/644–8336* ⊕ *www. vermontcanoeandkayak.com* ⊘ *Closed mid-Sept.–late May.*

LLAMA RIDES

Northern Vermont Llama Co.

LOCAL SPORTS | These llamas carry everything, including snacks and lunches, for half-day treks along the trails of Smugglers' Notch. Reservations are essential. ⊠ *766 Lapland Rd., Waterville* ☎ *802/644–2257* ⊕ *www.northernvermontllamaco.com* ⊡ *$60* ⊘ *Closed early Sept.–late May.*

SKI AREA

Smugglers' Notch

SKIING/SNOWBOARDING | **FAMILY** | The "granddaddy of all family resorts," Smugglers' Notch (or "Smuggs") receives consistent praise for its family programs. Its children's ski school is one of the best in the country—possibly *the* best—and there are challenges for skiers of all levels, spread over three separate areas. There's ice-skating, tubing, seven terrain parks, Nordic skiing, snowshoe trails, and a snowboarding area for kids ages 2½–6. Summer brings waterslides, treetop courses, ziplines, and crafts workshops—in other words, something for everyone. **Facilities:** 78 trails; 300 acres; 2,610-foot vertical drop; 8 lifts. ⊠ *4323 Rte. 108 S* ☎ *802/332–6854, 800/419–4615* ⊕ *www. smuggs.com* ⊡ *Lift ticket: $79.*

Shopping

ANTIQUES

Route 15 between Jeffersonville and Johnson is dubbed the "antiques highway."

Buggy Man

ANTIQUES/COLLECTIBLES | This store sells all sorts of collectibles, including horse-drawn vehicles. ⊠ *853 Rte. 15, 7 miles east of Jeffersonville, Johnson* ☎ *802/635–2110.*

Smugglers' Notch Antiques

ANTIQUES/COLLECTIBLES | In a rambling barn, this shop sells antiques, collectibles, and custom-made furniture from 60 dealers. ⊠ *9 Lanza Dr., Rte 108 S* ☎ *802/644–2100* ⊕ *www.smugglersnotchantiques.com.*

CLOTHING

★ **Johnson Woolen Mills**

CLOTHING | This factory store has great deals on woolen blankets, household goods, and the famous Johnson outerwear. ⊠ *51 Lower Main St. E, 9 miles east of Jeffersonville, Johnson* ☎ *802/635–2271* ⊕ *www.johnsonwoolenmills.com.*

Burlington

31 miles southwest of Jeffersonville, 76 miles south of Montreal, 349 miles north of New York City, 223 miles northwest of Boston.

★ As you drive along Main Street toward downtown Burlington, it's easy to see why this three-college city is often called one of the most livable small cities in the United States. Downtown Burlington is filled with hip restaurants and bars, art galleries, and vinyl-record shops. At the heart is the Church Street Marketplace, a bustling pedestrian mall with trendy shops, crafts vendors, street performers, and sidewalk cafés. To the west, Lake Champlain shimmers beneath the towering Adirondacks on the New York shore and provides the best sunsets in the state. The revitalized Burlington waterfront teems with outdoors enthusiasts who bike or stroll along its recreation path, picnic on the grass, and ply the waters in sailboats and motor craft in summer.

◉ Sights

★ Burlington Farmers' Market

MARKET | Burlington's Saturday farmers' market is an absolute must-see when visiting in summer or fall. Set up in City Hall Park and spilling onto an adjacent street, the market is jam-packed with local farmers selling a colorful array of organic produce, flowers, baked goods, maple syrup, meats, cheeses, and prepared foods. Local artisans also sell their wares, and there's live music on the green. From November to April, the market is held every other Saturday at the University of Vermont's Dudley H. Davis Center. ⊠ *City Hall Park, College and St. Paul Sts.* ☎ *802/310–5172* ⊕ *www. burlingtonfarmersmarket.org* ⚲ *Free.*

★ Church Street Marketplace

MARKET | **FAMILY** | For nearly 40 years, this pedestrian-only thoroughfare has served as Burlington's center of commerce, dining, and entertainment, with boutiques, cafés, restaurants, and street vendors the focus by day, and a lively bar and music scene at night. On sunny days, there are few better places to be in Burlington. ⊠ *2 Church St.* ☎ *802/863–1648* ⊕ *www.churchstmarketplace.com.*

ECHO Leahy Center for Lake Champlain

ZOO | **FAMILY** | Kids and adults can explore the geology and ecology of the Lake Champlain region through the center's more than 100 interactive exhibits, including the newest additions at the Action Lab. The lab's 3-D Water Projection Sandbox manages to make learning about watersheds exciting. You can also get an up-close look at 70 species of indigenous animals, or immerse digitally in the natural world at the 3-D theater, which presents science and nature films every day. ⊠ *1 College St.* ☎ *802/864–1848* ⊕ *www.echovermont.org* ⚲ *$15.*

Ethan Allen Homestead Museum

HISTORIC SITE | When Vermont hero Ethan Allen retired from his Revolutionary activities, he purchased 350 acres along the Winooski River and built this modest cabin in 1787. The original structure is a real slice of 18th-century life, including such frontier hallmarks as saw-cut boards and an open hearth for cooking. The kitchen garden resembles the one the Allens would have had. There's also a visitor center and miles of biking and hiking trails. In warmer months, climb Ethan Allen Tower at the south end of neighboring Ethan Allen Park for stupendous views of Lake Champlain and the Green Mountains. ∎**TIP**➔ **Don't forget mosquito repellent.** ⊠ *1 Ethan Allen Homestead, off Rte. 127* ☎ *802/865–4556* ⊕ *www.ethanallenhomestead.org* ⚲ *$10* ☉ *Closed Nov.–Apr.*

Green Mountain Audubon Nature Center

NATURE PRESERVE | **FAMILY** | This is a wonderful place to discover Vermont's outdoor wonders. The center's 255 acres of diverse habitats are a sanctuary for all things wild, and the 5 miles of trails provide an opportunity to explore the workings of differing natural communities. Events include bird-monitoring walks, wildflower rambles, nature workshops, and educational activities for children and adults. ⊠ *255 Sherman Hollow Rd., 18 miles southeast of Burlington, Huntington* ☎ *802/434–3068* ⊕ *vt. audubon.org* ✉ *Donations accepted.*

Switchback Brewing Co.

WINERY/DISTILLERY | Switchback may not get as much press as other more famous craft Vermont beers, but it's a solid, respected brew that's well worth exploring at the brewery and taproom in Burlington's buzzing South End. In addition to superfresh beer right from the tap and a short but savory menu of bar bites, the space hosts regular events and live music throughout the year. ⊠ *160 Flynn Ave.* ☎ *802/651–4114* ⊕ *www. switchbackvt.com.*

University of Vermont

COLLEGE | Crowning the hilltop above Burlington is the University of Vermont, known as UVM for the abbreviation of its Latin name, Universitas Viridis Montis, meaning the University of the Green Mountains. With nearly 12,000 students, this is the state's principal institution of higher learning. The most architecturally impressive buildings face the main campus green and have gorgeous lake views, as does the statue of founder Ira Allen, Ethan's brother. ⊠ *85 S. Prospect St.* ☎ *802/656–3131* ⊕ *www.uvm.edu.*

★ Waterfront Park

CITY PARK | This formerly derelict industrial district and railroad depot underwent a remarkable transformation in the late '80s and early '90s into a gorgeous stretch of green, with a boardwalk lapped by the lake. It's also a linchpin for a number of sights and facilities, with the Echo Center on the south end, a bodacious skate park on the north, and the Burlington Bike Path running through it all. Sunsets are particularly popular. ⊠ *10 College St.* ☎ *802/864–0123 City of Burlington*

Parks, Recreation & Waterfront ⊕ *www. enjoyburlington.com* ✉ *Free.*

Zero Gravity Brewery

WINERY/DISTILLERY | What started as a single bar tap in a pizza restaurant has turned into one of Burlington's most successful and hippest beers, thanks to frothy gems like Conehead and Green State Lager. Its shiny new brewery in the South End Arts District is always buzzing. Tasty complements include bratwurst, Italian sausage, and crispy cheddar curds. ⊠ *716 Pine St.* ☎ *802/497–0054* ⊕ *www. zerogravitybeer.com.*

 Beaches

North Beach

BEACH—SIGHT | FAMILY | Along Burlington's "new" North End a long line of beaches stretches to the Winooski River delta, beginning with North Beach, which has a grassy picnic area, a snack bar, and boat rentals. Neighboring Leddy Park offers a more secluded beach. **Amenities:** food and drink; lifeguards; parking (fee); showers; toilets. **Best for:** partiers; swimming; walking; windsurfing. ⊠ *North Beach Park, 52 Institute Rd., off North Ave.* ☎ *802/865–7247* ⊕ *www.enjoyburlington.com/venue/ north-beach* ✉ *Parking $8 (May–Oct.).*

 Restaurants

American Flatbread Burlington

$$ | PIZZA | Seating is first-come, first-served at this popular pizza spot, and the wood-fired clay dome ovens pump out delicious and amusingly named pies like "Dancing Heart" (garlic oil, Italian grana padano cheese, toasted sesame seeds) and "Power to the People" (chicken, buffalo sauce, carrots, mozzarella, and blue cheese dressing) in full view of the tables. Fresh salads topped with locally made cheese are also popular. **Known for:** bar run by Zero Gravity Brewery; spacious outdoor seating area; many ingredients sourced from farm 2 miles away. ⑤ *Average main: $18* ⊠ *115 St. Paul St.*

☎ 802/861–2999 ⊕ www.americanflat-bread.com.

A Single Pebble

$$ | **CHINESE** | "Gather, discover, and connect" is the slogan and theme at this intimate, upscale Chinese restaurant on the first floor of a residential row house. Traditional Cantonese and Sichuan style dishes are served family style, and the "mock eel" was given two chopsticks up on the Food Network's *The Best Thing I Ever Ate.* **Known for:** many vegetarian options; fire-blistered green beans wok-tossed with flecks of pork; dim sum on Sunday. ⑤ *Average main: $22* ✉ *133 Bank St.* ☎ *802/865–5200* ⊕ *www. asinglepebble.com.*

Farmhouse Tap and Grill

$$ | **AMERICAN** | The line out the door on a typical weekend night should tell you a lot about the local esteem for this farm-to-table restaurant. Serving only local beef, cheese, and produce in a classy but laid-back style, Farmhouse Tap and Grill provides one of the finest meals in the area. **Known for:** local cheese and charcuterie plates; downstairs taproom or the outdoor beer garden; raw bar. ⑤ *Average main: $20* ✉ *160 Bank St.* ☎ *802/859–0888* ⊕ *www.farmhousetg.com.*

The Great Northern

$$ | **MODERN AMERICAN** | This woody, industrial space benefits not only from being neighbors to Zero Gravity Brewery, but also its location at the heart of Burlington's hippest district, the South End. The menu follows the neighborhood zeitgeist, with foodie-friendly bistro bites for lunch and dinner, a raw bar, and a superpopular brunch on weekends. **Known for:** trendy interior design; artisanal cocktail list; hangout of the young and hip. ⑤ *Average main: $20* ✉ *716 Pine St.* ☎ *802/489–5102* ⊕ *www.thegreatnorthernvt. com* ⊘ *No dinner Sun.*

Guild Tavern

$$$ | **STEAKHOUSE** | Some of Vermont's best steak—all meat is sourced from local farms, dry-aged a minimum of 21 days, and cooked to absolute perfection—can be found roasting over hardwood coals in this tavern's open kitchens. The space itself is also a treat, with antique chicken feeders serving as light fixtures and a soapstone-topped bar in the center. **Known for:** steak for two combo; poutine with hand-cut fries; extensive cocktail list. ⑤ *Average main: $25* ✉ *1633 Williston Rd.* ☎ *802/497–1207* ⊕ *www.guildtavern.com* ⊘ *No lunch.*

★ Hen of the Wood Burlington

$$$ | **MODERN AMERICAN** | The Burlington branch of Hen of the Wood offers a slicker, more urban vibe than its original Waterbury location but serves the same inventive yet down-to-earth cuisine that sets diners' hearts aflutter and tongues wagging. Indeed, many consider this the best restaurant in Vermont, so drop your finger anywhere on the menu and you won't go wrong. **Known for:** mushroom toast; dollar oysters every night 4–5 pm; perfect date night spot. ⑤ *Average main: $30* ✉ *55 Cherry St.* ☎ *802/540–0534* ⊕ *www.henofthewood.com* ⊘ *No lunch.*

★ Honey Road

$$$$ | **MEDITERRANEAN** | This Church Street restaurant may not have won the coveted "Best New Restaurant" Award and "Best Chef Northeast" from the James Beard Foundation, but the mere nomination for both entered it into a golden age, serving arguably the best dinner in Burlington. High expectations are satisfied thanks to its highly creative takes on eastern Mediterranean cuisine, including a selection of sensational mezes. **Known for:** daily Honey Time happy hour with $1 chicken wings; muhammara dip with house-made pita; at the cutting edge of local cuisine. ⑤ *Average main: $45* ✉ *156 Church St.* ☎ *802/497–2145* ⊕ *www. honeyroadrestaurant.com* ⊘ *No lunch.*

Istanbul Kebab House

$$ | **TURKISH** | **FAMILY** | The classics of Turkish cuisine are served with surprising authenticity and maximum deliciousness thanks to the culinary talents of

its Istanbul-raised owners, plus locally sourced produce and meats. The open terrace upstairs offers the only rooftop dining in Burlington. **Known for:** Turkish casseroles (güveç) baked in earthenware bowls; best kebabs in Burlington, if not Vermont; lavash bread made to order. ⑤ *Average main: $19* ✉ *175 Church St.* ☎ *802/857–5091* ⊕ *www.istanbulkebabhousevt.com* ⊗ *Closed Sun.*

Leunig's Bistro and Cafe

$$$ | CAFÉ | This popular café delivers alfresco bistro cuisine with a distinct French flavor, plus a friendly European-style bar and live jazz. Favorite entrées include salade niçoise, *soupe au pistou* (vegetable and white bean soup with Asiago and pesto), and beef bourguignon. **Known for:** crème brûlée; Sunday brunch; outdoor seating on Church Street. ⑤ *Average main: $28* ✉ *115 Church St.* ☎ *802/863–3759* ⊕ *www.leunigsbistro.com.*

Monarch & the Milkweed

$ | AMERICAN | A trendy vibe mixes with exquisite pastries at this café and cocktail bar on the west side of City Hall Park. Buzzing nearly all day, the petite space serves elegant breakfasts by morning, "creative" coffee by day, and artisanal cocktails well into the night, particularly on weekends. **Known for:** CBD sweets; grilled-cheese sandwich; biscuits and gravy. ⑤ *Average main: $13* ✉ *111 Saint Paul St.* ☎ *802/310–7828* ⊕ *www.monarchdthemilkweed.com* ⊗ *No dinner Sun.*

Penny Cluse Cafe

$ | AMERICAN | FAMILY | The lines can be long on weekends to enter this popular breakfast and brunch spot, but it's for a reason. The bright, warm ambience makes a perfect setting for breakfast, brunch, or lunch, with elevated versions of the classic dishes. **Known for:** gingerbread-blueberry pancakes; "zydeco" breakfast with andouille sausage and corn muffins; photo ops for local and visiting politicians. ⑤ *Average main:*

$13 ✉ *169 Cherry St.* ☎ *802/651–8834* ⊕ *www.pennycluse.com* ⊗ *No dinner.*

Trattoria Delia

$$$ | ITALIAN | If you didn't make that trip to Umbria this year, the next best thing is this Italian country eatery around the corner from City Hall Park. The secret to the ambience goes well beyond the high-quality, handmade pasta dishes to the supercozy woody interior, a transplanted sugarhouse from New Hampshire. **Known for:** excellent wine list; wood-grilled prosciutto wrapped Vermont rabbit; primo Italian desserts. ⑤ *Average main: $27* ✉ *152 St. Paul St.* ☎ *802/864–5253* ⊕ *www.trattoriadelia.com* ⊗ *No lunch.*

Waterworks Food + Drink

$$$ | AMERICAN | In an old textile mill on the banks of the Winooski River, this restaurant comes with great views from nearly every table thanks to a glass wall. The expansive bar and dining room adds to the scene with lofty wood-beam ceilings, exposed brick, and a range of American bistro-style dishes. **Known for:** window seats overlooking river; cocktails; classy, upscale ambience. ⑤ *Average main: $25* ✉ *20 Winooski Falls Way, Winooski* ☎ *802/497–3525* ⊕ *www.waterworksvt.com.*

Zabby and Elf's Stone Soup

$ | AMERICAN | The open front, woody interior, and community spirit make Stone Soup a downtown favorite for lunch, especially on warm days. The small but robust salad bar is the centerpiece, with excellent hot and cold dishes—a perfect complement to the wonderful soups and fresh sandwiches. **Known for:** vegetarian dishes; gluten-free baked goods; New York Jewish-style cooking. ⑤ *Average main: $13* ✉ *211 College St.* ☎ *802/862–7616* ⊕ *www.stonesoupvt.com* ⊗ *Closed Sun.*

Burlington's Church Street is an open air mall with restaurants, shops, festivals, and street performers.

 Hotels

Courtyard Burlington Harbor

$$$ | HOTEL | A block from the lake and a five-minute walk from the heart of town, this attractive chain hotel has a pretty bar and lobby area with couches around a fireplace. **Pros:** right in downtown; some of the best lake views in town; across the street from park and lake. **Cons:** lacks local charm; a bit corporate in ambience; fee for self-parking. Ⓢ *Rooms from: $329* ⊠ *25 Cherry St.* ☎ *802/864–4700* ⊕ *www.marriott.com* ⥲ *161 rooms* ⏍ *No meals.*

The Essex

$$ | HOTEL | "Vermont's Culinary Resort," about 10 miles from downtown Burlington, the Essex's open kitchen allows diners to watch and interact with the chefs, and a sprawling spa that incorporates culinary ingredients like salt, honey, lavender, hop oil, and malted barley into the body treatments. **Pros:** daily cooking classes; free airport shuttle; nearby walking trails and golf course. **Cons:** suburban location; somewhat sterile; dated design.

Ⓢ *Rooms from: $275* ⊠ *70 Essex Way, off Rte. 289, Essex Junction* ☎ *802/878–1100, 800/727–4295* ⊕ *www.essexresortspa.com* ⥲ *120 rooms* ⏍ *No meals.*

Hilton Garden Inn

$$$ | HOTEL | One of Burlington's newest hotels, this more playful edition of the Hilton family sits on an ideal location halfway between downtown and the lakefront, putting both in easy walking reach. **Pros:** some rooms have views of the lake; Vermont Comedy Club in the same building; well above average restaurant. **Cons:** uninspired design in rooms; surrounded by busy streets with traffic; small pool. Ⓢ *Rooms from: $309* ⊠ *101 Main St.* ☎ *802/951–0099* ⊕ *www.hiltongardeninn3.hilton.com* ⥲ *139 rooms* ⏍ *No meals.*

★ Hotel Vermont

$$$ | HOTEL | Since opening in 2013, the Hotel Vermont has held the hospitality crown for style and cool, which is showcased in the almost magically spacious lobby, with its crackling wood fire, walls of smoky black Vermont granite, reclaimed oak floors, and local artwork. **Pros:** Juniper restaurant serves excellent cocktails; gorgeous rooms; unbelievable service. **Cons:** luxury doesn't come cheap; view of the lake often blocked by other buildings; additional fee for breakfast and self-parking. $ *Rooms from: $309* ✉ *41 Cherry St.* ☎ *802/651–0080* ⊕ *www. hotelvt.com* ⇌ *125 rooms* ⏹ *No meals.*

The Lang House on Main Street

$$ | **B&B/INN** | Within walking distance of downtown in the historic hill section of town, this grand 1881 Victorian home charms completely with its period furnishings, fine woodwork, plaster detailing, stained-glass windows, and sunlit dining area. **Pros:** family-friendly vibe; interesting location; fantastic breakfast. **Cons:** no elevator; on a busy street; old-fashioned design not for everyone. $ *Rooms from: $219* ✉ *360 Main St.* ☎ *802/652–2500, 877/919–9799* ⊕ *www.langhouse.com* ⇌ *11 rooms* ⏹ *Free breakfast.*

★ **Made INN Vermont**

$$ | **B&B/INN** | Few accommodations in Vermont find a dynamic balance between the traditional inn and trendy boutique spirit, but this eminently charming and quirky 1881 house topped with a cute cupola has done it. **Pros:** excellent location between the University of Vermont and Champlain College; vivacious and involved innkeeper; hot tub out back. **Cons:** bathrooms are private, but not en suite; rooms are modest in size; higher cost than most other inns in town. $ *Rooms from: $259* ✉ *204 S. Willard St.* ☎ *802/399–2788* ⊕ *www.madeinnvermont.com* ⇌ *4 rooms* ⏹ *Free breakfast.*

Willard Street Inn

$ | **B&B/INN** | High in the historic hill section of Burlington, this ivy-covered house with an exterior marble staircase and English gardens incorporates elements of Queen Anne and Georgian Revival styles including the stately foyer, with cherry paneling, and the flower-decked solarium that overlooks the back garden. **Pros:** innkeepers passionate about their job; lots

of friendly attention; complimentary chef-plated breakfast. **Cons:** a tad old-fashioned; walk to downtown can be a drag in winter; no elevator. $ *Rooms from: $175* ✉ *349 S. Willard St.* ☎ *802/651–8710, 800/577–8712* ⊕ *www.willardstreetinn. com* ⇌ *14 rooms* ⏹ *Free breakfast.*

Nightlife

ArtsRiot

MUSIC CLUBS | This unofficial headquarters of the South End Arts District has grown in recent years to include a full-service restaurant serving bistro bites and a concert stage that hosts local and national acts. Every Friday evening in summer, food trucks set up shop in the back parking lot. ✉ *400 Pine St.* ☎ *802/540–0406* ⊕ *www.artsriot.com.*

Citizen Cider

BARS/PUBS | The tiny parking lot out front gets jammed after 5 pm, as the spacious "tasting room" of this hard-cider maker fills with exuberant young, hip professionals and students. Sample cider straight or in a dozen or so cocktails. There's a full bistro menu, too. ✉ *316 Pine St., Suite 114* ☎ *802/497–1987* ⊕ *www.citizencider.com.*

★ Foam Brewers

BREWPUBS/BEER GARDENS | Not much can beat cold beers in Waterfront Park in summer, but this craft brewer makes it extra special with some of the best, and fruitiest, suds in Vermont. Enjoy them on the outdoor patio or inside the funky, fun interior by Russ Bennett, who designed Phish and Bonnaroo festivals. ✉ *112 Lake St.* ☎ *802/399–2511* ⊕ *www.foambrewers.com.*

Higher Ground

MUSIC CLUBS | When you feel like shaking it up to live music, come to Higher Ground—it gets the lion's share of local and national musicians. ✉ *1214 Williston Rd., South Burlington* ☎ *802/652–0777* ⊕ *www.highergroundmusic.com.*

Mule Bar

BARS/PUBS | This Winooski watering hole pours some of the best craft brews from around the state and is a must for aficionados. Outdoor seating and above-average bar bites seal the deal for its young and hip clientele. ✉ *38 Main St., Winooski* ☎ *802/399–2020* ⊕ *www. mulebarvt.com.*

Nectar's

BARS/PUBS | Jam band Phish got its start at Nectar's, which is always jumping to the sounds of local bands, stand-up comics, and live-band karaoke and never charges a cover. Don't leave without a helping of the bar's famous fries and gravy. ✉ *188 Main St.* ☎ *802/658–4771* ⊕ *www.liveatnectars.com.*

Radio Bean

BARS/PUBS | For some true local flavor, head to this funky place for nightly live music, an artsy vibe, and a cocktail. Performances happen every day, but Tuesday night is arguably the most fun, as the Honky Tonk band blazes through covers of Gram Parsons, Wilco, and the like. ✉ *8 N. Winooski Ave.* ☎ *802/660–9346* ⊕ *www.radiobean.com.*

🎬 Performing Arts

★ Flynn Center for the Performing Arts

CONCERTS | It's a pleasure to see any show inside this grandiose Art Deco gem. In addition to being home to Vermont's largest musical theater company, it hosts the Vermont Symphony Orchestra, as well as big-name acts like Neko Case and Elvis Costello. The adjacent Flynn Space is a coveted spot for more offbeat, experimental performances. ✉ *153 Main St.* ☎ *802/863–5966* ⊕ *www. flynncenter.org.*

Vermont Comedy Club

ARTS-ENTERTAINMENT OVERVIEW | Built largely on community fund-raising, this comedy club has become a beloved local institution, inspiring belly laughs with national headliners and up-and-comers,

as well as improv groups and competitions. ✉ *101 Main St.* ☎ *802/859–0100* ⊕ *www.vermontcomedyclub.com.*

Activities

BIKING

★ Burlington Bike Path

BICYCLING | FAMILY | Anyone who's put the rubber to the road on the 7½-mile Burlington Bike Path and its almost equally long northern extension on the Island Line Trail sings its praises. Along the way there are endless postcard views of Lake Champlain and the Adirondack Mountains. The northern end of the trail is slightly more rugged and windswept, so dress accordingly. ✉ *Burlington* ☎ *802/864–0123* ⊕ *www.enjoyburlington. com/venue/burlington-bike-path.*

North Star Sports

BICYCLING | In addition to stocking an extensive supply of sports apparel and accessories, this family-owned shop rents bikes and provides cycling maps. ✉ *100 Main St.* ☎ *802/863–3832* ⊕ *www. northstarsportsvt.com.*

Ski Rack

BICYCLING | Burlington's one-stop shop for winter sports equipment, the Ski Rack also rents bikes and sells running gear throughout the year. ✉ *85 Main St.* ☎ *802/658–3313, 800/882–4530* ⊕ *www. skirack.com.*

BOATING

Burlington Community Boathouse

BOATING | This boathouse administers the city's marina as well as a summertime watering hole called Splash, one of the best places to watch the sun set over the lake. ✉ *Burlington Harbor, College St.* ☎ *802/865–3377* ⊕ *www.enjoyburlington.com/venue/ community-boathouse-marina.*

Community Sailing Center

BOATING | FAMILY | Burlington's shiny new 22,000-square-foot Community Sailing Center has 150 watercraft to rent including kayaks, sailboats, and standup paddleboards for as little as $15 an hour. Private instruction and family lessons are available, as are floating yoga classes. ⊠ *505 Lake St.* ☎ *802/864–2499* ⊕ *www. communitysailingcenter.org* ⊗ *Closed mid-Oct.–mid-May.*

Lake Champlain Shoreline Cruises
BOATING | FAMILY | The trilevel *Spirit of Ethan Allen III,* a 363-passenger vessel, offers narrated cruises, theme dinners, and sunset sails with breathtaking Adirondacks and Green Mountains views. The standard 1½-hour cruise runs four times a day; sunset cruises leave at 6:30 pm on Friday and Saturday. ⊠ *Burlington Boat House, 1 College St.* ☎ *802/862–8300* ⊕ *www.soea.com* ⊠ *From $23.*

True North Kayak Tours
CANOEING/ROWING/SKULLING | This company conducts two- and five-hour guided kayak tours of Lake Champlain that include talks about the region's natural history and customized lessons. ⊠ *25 Nash Pl.* ☎ *802/238–7695* ⊕ *www. vermontkayak.com.*

SKI AREA
Bolton Valley Resort
SKIING/SNOWBOARDING | FAMILY | The closest ski resort to Burlington, about 25 miles away, Bolton Valley is a family favorite. In addition to downhill trails— more than half rated for intermediate and beginner skiers—Bolton offers 62 miles of cross-country and snowshoe trails, night skiing, and a sports center. **Facilities:** 71 trails; 300 acres; 1,704-foot vertical drop; 5 lifts. ⊠ *4302 Bolton Valley Access Rd., north off U.S. 2, Bolton* ☎ *802/434–3444, 877/926–5866* ⊕ *www. boltonvalley.com* ⊠ *Lift ticket: $74.*

⊙ Shopping

With each passing year, Burlington's industrial South End attracts ever greater numbers of artists and craftspeople, who set up studios, shops, and galleries in former factories and warehouses along Pine Street. The district's annual "Art Hop"

in September is the city's largest arts celebration—and a roaring good time.

CLOTHING
April Cornell
CLOTHING | The Vermont designer's flagship store stocks her distinctive floral-print dresses and linens. ⊠ *131 Battery St.* ☎ *802/863–0060* ⊕ *www. aprilcornell.com.*

CRAFTS
Bennington Potters North
CERAMICS/GLASSWARE | Along with the popular pottery line, this store stocks interesting kitchen items. ⊠ *127 College St.* ☎ *802/863–2221* ⊕ *www.bennington-potters.com.*

★ **Frog Hollow**
CERAMICS/GLASSWARE | This nonprofit collective and gallery sells contemporary and traditional crafts, paintings, and photographs by more than 200 Vermont artists and artisans. ⊠ *85 Church St.* ☎ *802/863–6458* ⊕ *www.froghollow.org.*

FOOD
Lake Champlain Chocolates
FOOD/CANDY | This chocolatier makes sensational truffles, caramels, candies, fudge, and hot chocolate. The chocolates are all-natural, made in Vermont, and make a great edible souvenir. Factory tours are available. A retail branch is also on Church Street. ⊠ *750 Pine St.* ☎ *802/864–1807 Pine St., 802/862–5185 Church St., 800/465–5909* ⊕ *www. lakechamplainchocolates.com.*

SPORTING GOODS
Burton
SPORTING GOODS | The folks who helped start snowboarding—a quintessential Vermont company—sell equipment and clothing at their flagship store. A second retail branch is in downtown Burlington, on 162 College Street. ⊠ *80 Industrial Pkwy.* ☎ *802/660–3200, 802/333–0400 College St.* ⊕ *www.burton.com.*

Shelburne

5 miles south of Burlington.

A few miles south of Burlington, the Champlain Valley gives way to fertile farmland, affording views of the rugged Adirondacks across the lake. In the middle of this farmland is the village of Shelburne (and just farther south, beautiful and more rural Charlotte), chartered in the mid-18th century and partly a bedroom community for Burlington. Shelburne Farms and the Shelburne Museum are worth at least a few hours of exploring, as are Shelburne Orchards in fall, when you can pick your own apples and drink fresh cider while admiring breathtaking views of the lake and mountains beyond.

GETTING HERE AND AROUND

Shelburne is south of Burlington after the town of South Burlington, which is notable for its very un-Vermont traffic congestion and a commercial and fast food–laden stretch of U.S. 7. It's easy to confuse Shelburne Farms (2 miles west of town on the lake) with Shelburne Museum, which is right on U.S. 7 just south of town, but you'll want to make time for both.

Sights

Fiddlehead Brewing Company

WINERY/DISTILLERY | There isn't much to the tasting room here, but there doesn't need to be: Fiddlehead only occasionally cans its celebrated beer, making this the best place outside of a restaurant to sample it on tap (and for free). Decide which one you like best and buy a growler to go—or, better yet, take it to Folino's Pizza next door, where the pies are mighty fine. ⊠ *6305 Shelburne Rd.* ☎ *802/399–2994* ⊕ *www.fiddleheadbrewing.com* 🖃 *Free.*

★ Shelburne Farms

COLLEGE | FAMILY | Founded in the 1880s as a private estate for two very rich New Yorkers, this 1,400-acre farm is much more than an exquisite landscape: it's an educational and cultural resource center with a working dairy farm, an award-winning cheese producer, an organic market garden, and a bakery whose aroma of fresh bread and pastries is an olfactory treat. It's a brilliant place for parents to expose their kids to the dignity of farmwork and the joys of compassionate animal husbandry—indeed, children and adults alike will get a kick out of hunting for eggs in the oversize coop, milking a cow, and watching the chicken parade. There are several activities and tours daily, and a lunch cart serves up fresh-from-the-farm soups, salads, and sandwiches. Frederick Law Olmsted, the co-creator of New York City's Central Park, designed the magnificent grounds overlooking Lake Champlain; walk to Lone Tree Hill for a splendid view. If you fall in love with the scenery, arrange a romantic dinner at the lakefront mansion, or spend the night. ⊠ *1611 Harbor Rd., west of U.S. 7* ☎ *802/985–8686* ⊕ *www.shelburnefarms.org* 🖃 *$8.*

★ Shelburne Museum

MUSEUM | FAMILY | You can trace much of New England's history simply by wandering through the 45 acres and 39 buildings of this museum. Some 25 buildings were relocated here, including an old-fashioned jail, an 1871 lighthouse, and a 220-foot steamboat, the *Ticonderoga*. The outstanding 150,000-object collection of art, design, and Americana consists of antique furniture, fine and folk art, quilts, trade signs, and weather vanes; there are also more than 200 carriages and sleighs. The Pizzagalli Center for Art and Education is open year-round with changing exhibitions and programs for kids and adults. ⊠ *6000 Shelburne Rd.* ☎ *802/985–3346* ⊕ *www.shelburnemuseum.org* 🖃 *$25* ☉ *Call for hrs, which vary by season and museum.*

Shelburne Vineyard

WINERY/DISTILLERY | From U.S. 7, you'll see rows and rows of organically grown vines. Visit the attractive tasting room and learn how wine is made. ✉ *6308 Shelburne Rd.* ☎ *802/985–8222* ⊕ *www. shelburnevineyard.com* ☕ *Tasting $7, tour free.*

Vermont Teddy Bear Company

FACTORY | FAMILY | On the 30-minute tour of this fun-filled factory you'll hear more puns than you ever thought possible, while learning how a few homemade bears sold from a cart on Church Street turned into a multimillion-dollar business. Patrons and children can relax, eat, and play under a large canvas tent in summer, or wander the beautiful 57-acre property. ✉ *6655 Shelburne Rd.* ☎ *802/985–3001* ⊕ *www.vermontteddybear.com* ☕ *Tour $4.*

Restaurants

The Bearded Frog

$$ | ECLECTIC | This is the top restaurant in the Shelburne area, perfect for a casual dinner in the bar or a more sophisticated experience in the attractive dining room. At the bar, try the soups, burgers, and terrific cocktails; the dining room serves fresh salads, seared seafood, roasted poultry, grilled steaks, and decadent desserts. **Known for:** $1 pints of Fiddlehead on Fridays; entire menu available to go; many gluten-free, vegetarian, and vegan choices. ⑤ *Average main: $23* ✉ *5247 Shelburne Rd.* ☎ *802/985–9877* ⊕ *www. thebeardedfrog.com* ☾ *No lunch.*

★ The Dining Room at the Inn at Shelburne Farms

$$$ | AMERICAN | Dinner here will make you dream of F. Scott Fitzgerald, as piano music wafts in from the library of this 1880s mansion on the shores of Lake Champlain. **Known for:** possibly best Sunday brunch in area; beautiful gardens; farmhouse cheddar. ⑤ *Average main: $33* ✉ *Inn at Shelburne Farms, 1611 Harbor Rd.* ☎ *802/985–8498* ⊕ *www.shelburnefarms.org* ☾ *Closed mid-Oct.–mid-May.*

Rustic Roots

$$ | AMERICAN | Scuffed wood floors and chunky country tables bring the "rustic" at this converted farmhouse—but not too much. An intimate bar and maroon walls adorned with woodcrafts and art add a touch of elegance, and the French-inspired food is carefully prepared. **Known for:** coffee-maple sausage; pastrami on rye; Bloody Marys. ⑤ *Average main: $21* ✉ *195 Falls Rd.* ☎ *802/985–9511* ⊕ *www. rusticrootsvt.com* ☾ *Closed Mon. and Tues. No dinner Wed., Thurs., and Sun.*

Hotels

Heart of the Village Inn

$ | B&B/INN | Each of the elegantly furnished rooms at this bed-and-breakfast in an 1886 Queen Anne Victorian provides coziness and tastefully integrated modern conveniences. **Pros:** easy walk to shops and restaurants; elegant historical building; hypoallergenic bedding and memory foam mattresses. **Cons:** near to but not within Shelburne Farms; no room service; no children under 12. ⑤ *Rooms from: $189* ✉ *5347 Shelburne Rd.* ☎ *802/985–9060* ⊕ *www.heartofthevillage.com* ⇋ *9 rooms* ⦾ *Free breakfast.*

★ The Inn at Shelburne Farms

$ | B&B/INN | It's hard not to feel like an aristocrat at this exquisite turn-of-the-20th-century Tudor-style inn, perched at the edge of Lake Champlain—even Teddy Roosevelt stayed here. **Pros:** stately lakefront setting in a historic mansion; endless activities; proposal-worthy restaurant. **Cons:** lowest-priced rooms have shared baths; closed in winter; no air-conditioning. ⑤ *Rooms from: $170* ✉ *1611 Harbor Rd.* ☎ *802/985–8498* ⊕ *www. shelburnefarms.org* ☾ *Closed mid-Oct.– mid-May* ⇋ *28 rooms* ⦾ *No meals.*

★ Mt. Philo Inn

$$$ | B&B/INN | Practically on the slopes of Mt. Philo State Park in Charlotte, the 1896 inn offers gorgeous views of Lake Champlain from its outdoor porches and an ideal blend of historical and contemporary boutique decor. **Pros:** walking trail goes directly to Mt. Philo State Park; lots of local stonework incorporated; complimentary breakfast basket includes all the fixings. **Cons:** not walking distance to any sights; rooms too big for just one guest; you cook breakfast yourself. ⑤ *Rooms from: $320* ✉ *27 Inn Rd., Charlotte* ☎ *802/425–3335* ⊕ *www. mtphiloinn.com* ⌁ *4 suites* ✽ *No meals.*

Shopping

The Flying Pig Bookstore

BOOKS/STATIONERY | It should come as no surprise that this bookstore is notable for its whimsy and carefully curated children's section: one of the owners is a stand-up comedian, and the other is a picture-book author. ✉ *5247 Shelburne Rd.* ☎ *802/985–3999* ⊕ *www.flyingpigbooks.com.*

The Shelburne Country Store

CONVENIENCE/GENERAL STORES | As you enter this store, you'll feel as though you've stepped back in time. Walk past the potbelly stove and take in the aroma emanating from the fudge neatly piled behind huge antique glass cases, alongside a vast selection of penny candies and chocolates. There are creemees, of course, but here the specialties are candles, weather vanes, glassware, and local foods. ✉ *29 Falls Rd., off U.S. 7* ☎ *802/985–3657, 800/660–3657* ⊕ *www. shelburnecountrystore.com.*

Vergennes

12 miles south of Shelburne.

Vermont's oldest city, founded in 1788, has a compact downtown area of restored Victorian homes and public buildings, with a few good eateries sprinkled throughout. Main Street slopes down to Otter Creek Falls, where cannonballs were made during the War of 1812. The statue of Thomas Macdonough on the green immortalizes the victor of the Battle of Plattsburgh (1814).

ESSENTIALS

VISITOR INFORMATION Addison County Chamber of Commerce ☎ *802/388–7951* ⊕ *www.addisoncounty.com.*

Sights

Lake Champlain Maritime Museum

MUSEUM | FAMILY | This museum documents centuries of activity on the historically significant lake. Climb aboard a replica of Benedict Arnold's Revolutionary War gunboat moored in the lake, learn about shipwrecks, watch craftsmen work at traditional boatbuilding and blacksmithing, or take a course—for an hour or all day—in boatbuilding, rowing, blacksmithing, or other endeavors. ✉ *4472 Basin Harbor Rd., 7 miles west of Vergennes* ☎ *802/475–2022* ⊕ *www.lcmm.org* ⌁ *$14* ⊙ *Closed mid-Oct.–June.*

Rokeby Museum

FARM/RANCH | A Quaker family farm for nearly two centuries, this National Historic Landmark served as a safe haven for runaway slaves during the days of the Underground Railroad. Join one of the guided house tours, explore the grounds and the historic farm buildings, or set off on the more than 50 acres of hiking trails. ✉ *4334 U.S. 7, Ferrisburgh* ☎ *802/877–3406* ⊕ *www.rokeby.org* ⌁ *$10* ⊙ *Closed Nov.–mid-May.*

⑪ Restaurants

Starry Night Café

$$$ | ECLECTIC | The proprietors of this popular, chic restaurant serve seasonal, farm-to-table cuisine among handcrafted tableware and furniture. A rotating display of works by local artists graces the walls, and the fireside porch, with its views of gardens and trees, is open at least three seasons of the year. **Known for:** handblown glasses; historic buildings, including a covered bridge; date night. ⑤ *Average main: $30* ✉ *5371 U.S. 7, 5 miles north of Vergennes, Ferrisburgh*

🖨 802/877–6316 ⊕ www.starrynightcafe.
com ⊗ Closed Mon. and Tues. No lunch.

Vergennes Laundry by CK

$$ | BAKERY | Once primarily a bakery, and
still mostly looking the part, this rustic-
chic space now helmed by chef Christian
Kruse is pushing three-course dinners
of eclectic international and local fare.
And it's still the top choice in town for
breakfast and brunch, with creative takes
on egg dishes, soups, and sandwiches.
Known for: Chef of the Year by Vermont
Chamber of Commerce; cardamom buns;
Monte Cristo sandwich. ⑤ Average main:
$20 ⊠ 247 Main St. 🖨 802/870–7157
⊕ www.vergenneslaundry.net ⊗ Closed
Mon. and Tues. No lunch Wed.

 Hotels

★ **Basin Harbor Resort & Boat Club**

$$ | RESORT | FAMILY | Set amid 700
acres overlooking Lake Champlain, this
family resort provides luxurious accommodations and a full roster of amenities, including an 18-hole golf course,
60-slip marina, and abundant children's
programs; jacket and tie are required in
common areas after 6 pm late June–
early September. **Pros:** gorgeous lakeside
property; activities galore; wonderful for
families. **Cons:** open only half the year;
not as great for solo travelers; often
booked by corporate groups. ⑤ Rooms
from: $281 ⊠ 4800 Basin Harbor Rd.
🖨 802/475–2311, 800/622–4000 ⊕ www.
basinharbor.com ⊗ Closed mid-Oct.–mid-
May ⭲ 120 units ⧑ Free breakfast.

 Shopping

Dakin Farm

FOOD/CANDY | Cob-smoked ham, aged
cheddar cheese, maple syrup made
on-site, and other well-crafted specialty
foods can be sampled here. You can also
visit the smokehouse and watch the
waxing and sealing of cheeses. ⊠ 5797
U.S. 7, 5 miles north of Vergennes
🖨 800/993–2546 ⊕ www.dakinfarm.com.

Lake Champlain Islands

Lake Champlain stretches more than
100 miles south from the Canadian
border and forms the northern part of
the boundary between New York and
Vermont. Within it is an elongated archipelago comprising several islands—Isle
La Motte, North Hero, Grand Isle, and
South Hero—and the Alburg Peninsula.
Enjoying a temperate climate, the
islands hold several apple orchards and
are a center of water recreation in summer and ice fishing in winter. A scenic
drive through the islands on U.S. 2
begins at Interstate 89 and travels north
to Alburg Center; Route 78 takes you
back to the mainland.

ESSENTIALS

**VISITOR INFORMATION Lake Champlain
Islands Chamber of Commerce** 🖨 802/372–
8400, 800/262–5226 ⊕ www.champlain-
islands.com. **Lake Champlain Regional
Chamber of Commerce** 🖨 802/863–3489,
877/686–5253 ⊕ www.vermont.org.

 Sights

★ **Allenholm Farm**

FARM/RANCH | The pick-your-own apples at
this farm are amazingly tasty—if you're
here at harvesttime, don't miss out.
The farm also has a petting area with
donkeys, miniature horses, sheep, goats,
and other animals. At the store, you can
buy cheeses, dried fruit, homemade pies,
and maple creemees. ⊠ 111 South St.,
South Hero 🖨 802/372–5566 ⊕ www.
allenholm.com 🖙 Free.

Hyde Log Cabin

BUILDING | Built in 1783, this log cabin on
South Hero is often cited as the country's
oldest surviving specimen. It's now
home to the Grand Isle Historical Society.
⊠ 228 U.S. 2, Grand Isle 🖨 802/828–3051
🖙 $3 ⊗ Closed weekdays mid-Oct.–May.

Snow Farm Vineyard and Winery

WINERY/DISTILLERY | Vermont's first
vineyard was started here in 1996; today,

the winery specializes in nontraditional botanical hybrid grapes designed to take advantage of the island's microclimate, similar to that of Burgundy, France. Take a self-guided tour and sip some samples in the tasting room—dessert wines are the strong suit. On Thursday evening, late May–September, you can picnic and enjoy the free concerts on the lawn. ⊠ *190 W. Shore Rd., South Hero* ☎ *802/372–9463* ⊕ *www.snowfarm.com* ☜ *Free* ⊙ *Closed late Dec.–Apr.*

St. Anne's Shrine

RELIGIOUS SITE | This spot marks the site where, in 1665, French soldiers and Jesuits put ashore and built a fort, creating Vermont's first European settlement. Vermont's first Roman Catholic Mass was celebrated here on July 26, 1666. ⊠ *92 St. Anne's Rd., Isle La Motte* ☎ *802/928–3362* ⊕ *www.saintannesshrine.org* ☜ *Free.*

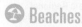 Beaches

Sand Bar State Park

BEACHES | One of Vermont's best swimming beaches is at Sand Bar State Park, along with a snack bar, a changing room, and boat rentals. ⊠ *1215 U.S. 2, South Hero* ☎ *802/893–2825* ⊕ *vtstateparks.com/sandbar.html* ☜ *$4.*

Hotels

North Hero House Inn and Restaurant

$ | B&B/INN | FAMILY | This inn has four buildings right on Lake Champlain, among them the 1891 Colonial Revival main house with a restaurant, pub, and library. **Pros:** resort really gets away from it all; superb lakefront setting; many rooms have screened-in porches. **Cons:** much less to do in winter; two-night minimum on weekends and holidays; relatively bland design. ⑤ *Rooms from: $140* ⊠ *3643 U.S. 2, North Hero* ☎ *802/372–4732, 888/525–3644* ⊕ *www.northherohouse.com* ⊙ *Closed mid-Oct.–Dec.* ⊅ *26 rooms* ⑩ *Free breakfast.*

Ruthcliffe Lodge & Restaurant

$ | HOTEL | If you're looking for an inexpensive summer destination—to take in the scenery, canoe the lake, or go biking—this will do quite nicely as the lodge is on the rarely visited Isle La Motte. **Pros:** inexpensive rates; high-quality restaurant; laid-back vibe. **Cons:** two-night minimum stays on weekends and holiday periods; quite remote; simple, bland design. ⑤ *Rooms from: $142* ⊠ *1002 Quarry Rd., Isle La Motte* ☎ *802/928–3200* ⊕ *www.ruthcliffe.com* ⊙ *Closed mid-Oct.–mid-May* ⊅ *7 rooms* ⑩ *Free breakfast.*

Activities

Alburgh Dunes State Park

PARK—SPORTS-OUTDOORS | This park has one of the longest sandy beaches on Lake Champlain and some fine examples of rare flora and fauna along the hiking trails. ⊠ *151 Coon Point Rd., off U.S. 2, Alburg* ☎ *802/796–4170* ⊕ *www.vtstateparks.com/alburgh.html* ☜ *$4.*

Apple Island Resort

BOATING | The resort's marina rents pontoon boats, rowboats, canoes, kayaks, and pedal boats. ⊠ *71 U.S. 2, South Hero* ☎ *802/372–3922* ⊕ *www.appleislandresort.com.*

Grand Isle State Park

PARK—SPORTS-OUTDOORS | You'll find hiking trails, boat rentals, and shore fishing at Grand Isle. ⊠ *36 E. Shore S, off U.S. 2, Grand Isle* ☎ *802/372–4300* ⊕ *www.vtstateparks.com/grandisle.html* ☜ *$4.*

Hero's Welcome

BOATING | This general store rents bikes, canoes, kayaks, and paddleboards; come winter, they switch to ice skates, cross-country skis, and snowshoes. ⊠ *3537 U.S. 2, North Hero* ☎ *802/372–4161* ⊕ *www.heroswelcome.com.*

Missisquoi National Wildlife Refuge

HIKING/WALKING | On the mainland east of the Alburg Peninsula, the refuge consists of 6,729 acres of federally protected

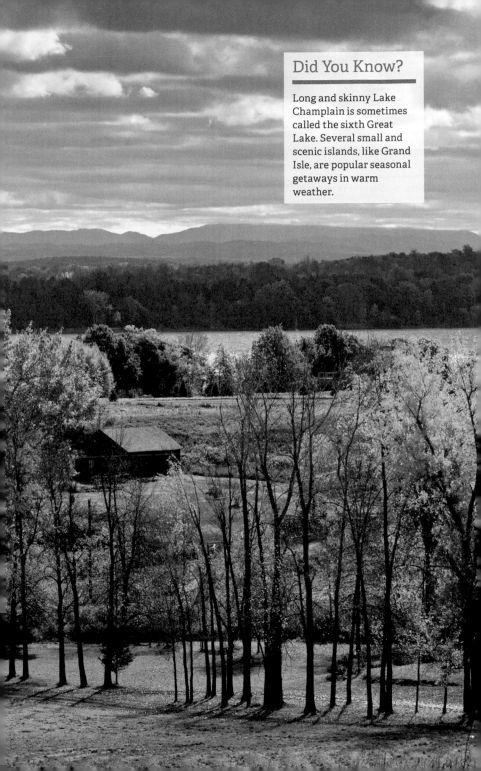

wetlands, meadows, and woods. It's a beautiful area for bird-watching, canoeing, and walking nature trails. ⊠ *29 Tabor Rd., 36 miles north of Burlington, Swanton* ☎ *802/868–4781* ⊕ *www.fws. gov/refuge/missisquoi.*

North Hero State Park

PARK—SPORTS-OUTDOORS | The 399-acre North Hero has a swimming beach and nature trails. It's open to rowboats, kayaks, and canoes. ⊠ *3803 Lakeview Dr., North Hero* ☎ *802/372–8727* ⊕ *www. vtstateparks.com/northhero.html* ⊠ *$4.*

Montgomery and Jay

51 miles northeast of Burlington.

Montgomery is a small village near the Jay Peak ski resort and the Canadian border. Amid the surrounding countryside are seven covered bridges.

GETTING HERE AND AROUND

Montgomery lies at the junction of Routes 58, 118, and 242. From Burlington, take Interstate 89 north to Routes 105 and 118 east. Route 242 connects Montgomery and, to the northeast, the Jay Peak Resort.

 Sights

Lake Memphremagog

BODY OF WATER | Vermont's second-largest body of water, Lake Memphremagog extends 33 miles north from Newport into Canada. Prouty Beach in Newport has tennis courts, boat rentals, and a 9-hole disc-golf course. Watch the sunset from the deck of the East Side Restaurant, which serves excellent burgers and prime rib. ⊠ *242 Prouty Beach Rd., Newport* ☎ *802/334–6345* ⊕ *www. newportrecreation.org.*

 Hotels

★ The INN

$ | B&B/INN | This smart chalet-style lodge comes with tons of character. **Pros:** Trout River views from back rooms; within walking distance of shops and supplies; smart, individually designed rooms. **Cons:** noise from bar can seep into nearby rooms; two-night minimum stay; outside food and alcohol not allowed. ⑤ *Rooms from: $169* ⊠ *241 Main St.* ☎ *802/326–4391* ⊕ *www.theinn.us* ⇆ *11 rooms* ⑩ *Free breakfast.*

Jay Peak Resort

$$ | HOTEL | FAMILY | Accommodations at Jay Peak include standard hotel rooms, suites, condominiums, town houses, and cottage and clubhouse suites. **Pros:** slopes never far away; 60,000-square-foot indoor water park; kids 14 and under stay and eat free and complimentary child care is provided. **Cons:** can get noisy; not very intimate; service can be lackluster. ⑤ *Rooms from: $239* ⊠ *830 Jay Peak Rd.* ☎ *802/988–2611* ⊕ *www. jaypeakresort.com* ⇆ *515 units* ⑩ *Free breakfast.*

Phineas Swann Bed & Breakfast Inn

$ | B&B/INN | The top-hatted bulldog on the sign of this 1880 farmhouse isn't just a mascot: it reflects the hotel's welcoming attitude to pet owners. **Pros:** walking distance from shops and supplies; lots of dogs; each room has different design. **Cons:** decor is a tad old-fashioned; dog theme (and actual dogs) not for everyone; no outside alcohol allowed. ⑤ *Rooms from: $199* ⊠ *195 Main St.* ☎ *802/326–4306* ⊕ *www. phineasswann.com* ⇆ *9 rooms* ⑩ *Free breakfast.*

 Activities

ICE-SKATING

Ice Haus Arena

HOCKEY | FAMILY | The sprawling arena contains a professional-size hockey rink and seating for 400 spectators. You can practice your stick handling, and the rink is open to the public for skating several times a week. There are tournaments throughout the year. ⊠ *830 Jay Peak Rd., Jay* ☎ *802/988–2727* ⊕ *www.jaypeakresort.com* ⬚ *$6.*

SKI AREAS

Hazen's Notch Association

SKIING/SNOWBOARDING | Delightfully remote at any time of the year, this center has 40 miles of marked and groomed trails and rents equipment and snowshoes. ⊠ *1423 Hazen's Notch Rd.* ☎ *802/326–4799* ⊕ *www.hazensnotch. org* ⬚ *Trail pass: $12.*

Jay Peak

SKIING/SNOWBOARDING | Sticking up out of the flat farmland, Jay Peak averages 349 inches of snow per year—more than any other Vermont ski area—and it's renowned for its glade skiing and powder. There are two interconnected mountains, the highest reaching nearly 4,000 feet. The smaller mountain has straight-fall-line, expert terrain that eases mid-mountain into an intermediate pitch. Beginners should stay near the bottom on trails off the Metro quad lift. There are also five terrain parks, snowshoeing, telemark skiing, and a state-of-the art ice arena for hockey, figure skating, and curling. The Pump House, an indoor water park with pools and slides, is open year-round. **Facilities:** 78 trails; 385 acres; 2,153-foot vertical drop; 9 lifts. ⊠ *830 Jay Peak Rd., Jay* ☎ *802/988–2611* ⊕ *www.jaypeakresort. com* ⬚ *Lift ticket: $84.*

St. Johnsbury

16 miles south of East Burke, 39 miles northeast of Montpelier.

St. Johnsbury, the southern gateway to the Northeast Kingdom, was chartered as early as 1786, but really only came into its own after 1830, when Thaddeus Fairbanks invented the platform scale, a device that revolutionized weighing methods. The Fairbanks family's subsequent philanthropic efforts left the city with a strong cultural and architectural imprint. Today "St. J," as locals call it, is the friendly, adventure sports–happy hub of the Northeast Kingdom.

 Sights

★ Dog Mountain

MUSEUM | **FAMILY** | The late Stephen Huneck, an artist and the creator of Dog Mountain, was famous for his colorful folk art sculptures and paintings of dogs. Much more than an art gallery–gift shop, this deeply moving spot even has a chapel, where animal lovers can reflect on their beloved pets. With hiking trails and a swimming pond, this is, first and foremost, a place to spend time with your dog. ⊠ *143 Parks Rd., off Spaulding Rd.* ☎ *800/449–2580* ⊕ *www.dogmt. com* ⬚ *Free.*

★ Fairbanks Museum and Planetarium

MUSEUM | **FAMILY** | This odd and deeply thrilling museum displays the eccentric collection of Franklin Fairbanks, who surely had one of the most inquisitive minds in American history. He built this magnificent barrel-vaulted gallery in 1889 to house the specimens of plants, animals, birds, and reptiles, and the collections of folk art and dolls—and a seemingly unending variety of beautifully mounted curios—he picked up around the world. The museum showcases over 175,000 items, but it's surprisingly easy to feast your eyes on everything here without getting a museum headache. The popular 45-seat planetarium is Vermont's only public planetarium, and there's also the Eye on the Sky Weather Gallery, home to live NPR weather broadcasts. ⊠ *1302 Main St.* ☎ *802/748–2372* ⊕ *www.fairbanksmuseum.org* ⬚ *Museum $9, planetarium $6* ⊙ *Closed early Jan.*

Peacham

TOWN | Tiny Peacham, 10 miles southwest of St. Johnsbury, is on almost every tour group's list of "must-sees." With views extending to the White Mountains of New Hampshire and a white-steeple church, Peacham is perhaps the most photographed town in New England. The movie adaptation of *Ethan Frome,* starring Liam Neeson, was filmed here. The soups and stews are especially tasty at **Peacham Café,** which serves breakfast and lunch. Next door, the **Peacham Corner Guild** sells local handicrafts. ✉ *Peacham* ⊕ *www. peacham.net.*

★ St. Johnsbury Athenaeum

LIBRARY | With its polished Victorian woodwork, dramatic paneling, and ornate circular staircases, this building is both the town library—one of the nicest you're likely to ever come across—and one of the oldest art galleries in the country, housing more than 100 original works, mainly from the Hudson River school. Albert Bierstadt's enormous *Domes of Yosemite* dominates the beautiful painting gallery. ✉ *1171 Main St.* ☎ *802/748–8291* ⊕ *www.stjathenaeum. org* ✉ *Free* ⊗ *Closed Sun.*

 ## Hotels

Rabbit Hill Inn

$$ | B&B/INN | Few inns in New England garner the word-of-mouth buzz that Rabbit Hill seems to from its satisfied guests, but it's no surprise as this inn is full of small pleasures, including 15 acres of gardens and walking trails, a spring-fed pond, and gazebo. **Pros:** game room; several package trips with nearby sights; house-made pastries and tea every afternoon. **Cons:** quite rural setting; lots of flowered upholstery and wallpaper; two-night minimum on weekends (three for some holidays). ⑤ *Rooms from: $225* ✉ *48 Lower Waterford Rd., 11 miles south of St. Johnsbury, Lower Waterford* ⊕ *www.rabbithillinn.com* ⊗ *Closed Apr. and 1st 2 wks of Nov.* ⇨ *19 rooms* ⚬⚬ *Free breakfast.*

NEW
HAMPSHIRE

Updated by
Andrew Collins

 Sights
★★★★★

 Restaurants
★★★☆☆

 Hotels
★★★★☆

 Shopping
★★★★☆

 Nightlife
★★★☆☆

WELCOME TO NEW HAMPSHIRE

TOP REASONS TO GO

★ **The White Mountains:** Great for hiking and skiing, these dramatic peaks and notches are unforgettable.

★ **Lake Winnipesaukee:** Beaches, arcades, boat cruises, and classic summer camps fuel a whole season of family fun.

★ **Fall Foliage:** Head to the Kancamagus Highway in autumn for one of America's best drives, or seek out a less-trafficked route that's equally stunning.

★ **Portsmouth:** Less than an hour's drive from Boston, this small, upbeat American city abounds with colorful Colonial architecture, cosmopolitan dining, and easy access to New Hampshire's only stretch of the Atlantic coastline.

★ **Pristine Towns:** Jaffrey Center, Walpole, Tamworth, Center Sandwich, Bethlehem, and Jackson are among the most charming tiny villages in New England.

1 Portsmouth. Craft brewing and farm-to-table dining.

2 Rye. Home to Millionaires' Row.

3 Hampton Beach. A popular summer destination.

4 Exeter. Cafes and a well-known prep school.

5 Durham. Home of the University of NH.

6 Wolfeboro. The U.S.'s oldest summer resort.

7 Alton Bay. A Lake Winnipesaukee town.

8 Weirs Beach. A center for summertime activity.

9 Laconia. The chief manufacturing hub for the Lakes Region.

10 Meredith. A bustling marina and Main Street.

11 Bristol. Explore Newfound Lake.

12 Holderness. Squam and Little Squam lakes.

13 Center Sandwich. A pretty Lakes Region spot.

14 Tamworth. Churches and Mt. Chocorua.

15 Lincoln and North Woodstock. Neighbors in the White Mountains National Forest.

16 Franconia. Visit ski areas and the Franconia Notch.

17 Littleton. A great supply spot.

18 Bethlehem. A progressive, artsy hamlet.

19 Bretton Woods. A cog railway and ski resort.

20 Bartlett. Ideally located in the White Mountains.

21 Jackson. A storybook New England town.

22 Mt. Washington. Highest peak in the northeastern United States.

23 North Conway. Lots of shopping along Route 16.

24 Kancamagus Highway. One of the nation's first National Scenic Byways.

25 New London. Explore the Lake Sunapee region.

26 Newbury. Host of the nation's oldest crafts fair.

27 Hanover. Home to Dartmouth College.

28 Cornish. Best known for its covered bridges.

29 Manchester. The Granite State's largest city.

30 Concord. The state's capital city.

31 Charlestown. State's largest historic district.

32 Walpole. One of the state's prettiest greens.

33 Keene. Largest city in the state's SW corner.

34 Jaffrey Center. A walkable historic district.

35 Peterborough. A hub since 1760.

VERMONT

North Stratford
Errol
26
3
110
Groveton
2
Lancaster
Berlin
Whitefield
2
Gorham
Mt. Washington
Bretton Woods
17
Bethlehem
22
Littleton
93
18
Twin Mountain
16
19
Lisbon
16
Franconia
21
Jackson
302
302
Glen
Woodsville
Bartlett
20
23
91
Lincoln
Kancamagus Highway
North Conway
WHITE MOUNTAINS
24
Conway
15
White Mountain Nat'l Forest
112
MAINE
North Woodstock
25
118
93
Warren
Tamworth
14
16
153
25A
Center Sandwich
13
Wentworth
Squam Lake
10
Plymouth
Lake Winnipesaukee
Center Ossipee
118
Holderness
12
Hanover
27
Ashland
25
Ossipee
VERMONT
Enfield
New Hampton
10
Meredith
109
16
Bristol
8
Weirs Beach
Sanbornville
Lebanon
89
11
Wolfeboro
6
4
3A
Laconia
11
Plainfield
Grafton
Danbury
9
Alton
7
Grantham
11
Belmont
Alton Bay
Alton
Cornish
Lake Sunapee
Andover
Franklin
11
Milton
Georges Mills
25
Northfield
Farmington
16
28
Claremont
26
New London
93
Newport
North Sutton
Pittsfield
Rochester
Goshen
Newbury
Boscawen
202
16
Dover
31
Charlestown
89
3
30
Northwood
4
Durham
10
CONCORD
5
95
Henniker
93
Northwood
Hillsboro
202
Suncook
Newmarket
Walpole
Stoddard
Hooksett
Epping
Portsmouth
32
Antrim
Goffstown
101
1
Gilsum
9
29
Exeter
4
Rye
Bennington
Manchester
2
Keene
33
New Boston
101
3
Beach
Peterborough
Kingston
Hampton Beach
Marlborough
35
Londonderry
Derry
95
1A
Hinsdale
Troy
Mt. Monadnock
Wilton
Milford
Hudson
91
Jaffrey
Jaffrey Center
202
Greenville
Nashua
Winchester
3
Lowell

MASSACHUSETTS

0   10 mi
0   10 km

New Hampshire's mountain peaks, clear air, and sparkling lakes attract trailblazers, artists, and countless tourists. A varied geography and myriad outdoor activities are part of the draw, but visitors also feel quickly at home in this place of beauty, history, and hospitality. Whether you're seeking adventure or just want to laze on the porch swing of a century-old inn, you'll find ample ways to engage with this rugged, diverse state.

Ralph Waldo Emerson, Henry David Thoreau, Nathaniel Hawthorne, and Louisa May Alcott all visited and wrote about the state, sparking a fervent literary tradition that continues today. It also has a strong political history: this was the first colony to declare independence from Great Britain, the first to adopt a state constitution, and the first to require its constitution be referred to the people for approval. Politically, it remains a fiercely independent swing state that holds some of the earliest election primaries in the country and that's known for both its libertarian and progressive tendencies.

The state's diverse terrain makes it popular with everyone from avid adventurers to young families looking for easy access to nature. You can hike, climb, ski, snowboard, snowshoe, and fish, as well as explore on snowmobiles, sailboats, kayaks, and mountain bikes. New Hampshirites have no objection to others enjoying the beauty here as long as they leave a few dollars behind: it's the only state in the union with neither sales nor income taxes, so tourism brings in much-needed revenue (and tourists can enjoy tax-free shopping).

With a few cities consistently rated among the most livable in the nation, New Hampshire has grown faster than most other northeastern states over the past two decades. The state is gradually developing two distinct personalities: one characterized by rapid urbanization in the southeast and the other by quiet village life in the west and north. Although newcomers have brought change, the free-spirited sensibility of the Granite State remains intact, as does its natural splendor.

MAJOR REGIONS
The **Seacoast,** New Hampshire's 18-mile stretch of coastline, packs in a wealth of scenery and diversions. The honky-tonk of **Hampton Beach** gets plenty of attention—good and bad—but first-timers are

often surprised by the significant portion of the shoreline that remains pristine, especially through the town of **Rye.** This section begins in the regional hub, **Portsmouth;** cuts down the coast to the beaches; branches inland to the prep-school town of **Exeter**; and runs back up north through **Durham** (home to the University of New Hampshire); from here it's a short drive to the Lakes Region.

Throughout central New Hampshire, you'll encounter lakes and more lakes in the aptly named **Lakes Region.** The largest, Lake Winnipesaukee, has 180 miles of coastline and attracts all sorts of water-sports enthusiasts to the towns of **Wolfeboro, Alton Bay, Weirs Beach,** and **Meredith.** Smaller and more secluded lakes with enchanting B&Bs include towns like **Holderness** and **Laconia. Center Sandwich, Tamworth,** and **Bristol** are great bases to explore the surrounding lakes and mountains.

Skiing, snowshoeing, and snowboarding in the winter; hiking, biking, and riding scenic railways in the summer: the Whites, as locals call **The White Mountains,** have plenty of natural wonders. **Mt. Washington,** the tallest mountain in the Northeast, can be conquered by trail, train, or car; other towns with strong railroad ties include **Littleton** and **North Conway. Lincoln and North Woodstock** form a lively resort area, and **Bethlehem, Franconia,** and **Whitefield** are all stunning in their own right. **Bretton Woods, Bartlett,** and **Jackson,** are great ski towns, and the **Kancamagus Highway,** which stretches from Conway to Lincoln and North Woodstock, has been designated a National Scenic Byway.

Quiet villages proliferate in the **Lake Sunapee** region; the lake itself is a wonderful place to swim, fish, or enjoy a cruise. **Hanover,** home to Dartmouth College (founded 1769), retains that true New England college-town feel, with ivy-draped buildings and cobblestone walkways. **New London** is one of the area's main hubs

with several cafés and boutiques, while **Newbury,** on the edge of Mt. Sunapee State Park, is one of the region's outdoor recreation centers. **Cornish,** once the haunt of J.D. Salinger, is where you'll find Cornish-Windsor Bridge, the country's second-longest covered bridge.

New and old coexist in **the Monadnocks and Merrimack Valley,** the state's southwestern region. Here high-tech firms have helped reshape the cities of **Manchester** and **Concord** while small towns in the hills surrounding Mt. Monadnock, southern New Hampshire's largest peak, like **Keene, Jaffrey Center,** and **Peterborough,** celebrate tradition and history. **Charlestown** has the state's largest historic district and **Walpole** has one of the state's loveliest town greens.

Planning

WHEN TO GO
Summer and fall are the best, but also the most popular and expensive, times to visit most of New Hampshire. Winter is a great time to travel to the White Mountains, but most other tourist sights in the state, including museums in Portsmouth and many attractions in the Lakes Region close from late fall until May or June. In summer people flock to beaches, mountain trails, and lakeside boat launches; in the cities, festivals showcase food and beer, music, theater, and crafts. Fall brings leaf peepers, especially to the White Mountains and along the Kancamagus Highway (Route 112). Skiers and snowboarders take to the slopes in winter, when Christmas lights and carnivals brighten the long, dark nights. Spring's unpredictable weather—along with April's mud and late May's black flies—tends to deter visitors. Still, the season has its joys, not the least of which is the appearance, mid-May–early June, of the state flower, the purple lilac, soon followed by the blooming of colorful rhododendrons.

PLANNING YOUR TIME

Some people come to New Hampshire to hike or ski the mountains, fish and sail the lakes, or cycle along backcountry roads. Others prefer to drive through scenic towns, stopping at museums and general stores or small art galleries along the way. Although New Hampshire is a small state, roads curve around lakes and mountains, making distances sometimes much longer than they appear on a map. You can get a taste of the coast, lake, and mountain areas in three to five days; eight days will give you time to make a more complete loop.

AIR TRAVEL

Manchester Boston Regional Airport, the state's largest airport, has nonstop service from more than a dozen U.S. cities. The drive from Boston's Logan Airport to most places in New Hampshire takes one–three hours; the same is true for Bradley International Airport, near Hartford, Connecticut.

BIKE TRAVEL

A safe, scenic route along New Hampshire's seacoast is the bike path along Route 1A, where you can park at Odiorne Point and follow the road 14 miles south to Seabrook. Another pretty route runs from Newington Town Hall to the Great Bay Estuary. There's also a bike path in Franconia Notch State Park, and a mountain-biking center, Great Glen Trails, at the base of Mt. Washington. Many ski areas offer lift services to mountain bikers in summer.

CAR TRAVEL

New Hampshire is an easy drive north from Boston. Many key destinations are near major highways, and local public transit is very limited, so getting around by car is the best way to explore the region. Interstate 93 stretches from Boston to Littleton and on into neighboring Vermont. Interstate 89 will get you from Concord to Hanover and eventually to Burlington, Vermont. To the east, Interstate 95 (a toll road) passes through southern New Hampshire's coastal area between Massachusetts and Maine. Throughout the state, quiet backcountry lanes and winding roads can take a little longer but often reward travelers with gorgeous scenery.

The speed limit on interstate and limited-access highways is usually 65 mph, except in heavily settled areas, where 55 mph is the norm, and on some rural stretches of interstate, where it's 70 mph. On state and U.S. routes, speed limits vary considerably, from 25 mph to 55 mph, so watch signs carefully. The website of the **New Hampshire Department of Transportation** (⊕ *hb.511nh.com*) has up-to-the-minute information about traffic and road conditions.

TRAIN TRAVEL

Amtrak's *Downeaster* passenger train operates between Boston and Portland, Maine, with New Hampshire stops in Exeter, Durham, and Dover.

RESTAURANTS

New Hampshire prides itself on its seafood: not only lobster, but also salmon pie, steamed mussels, fried clams, and fish-and-chips. Across the state you'll find country taverns with both old-school and modern American menus, many of them emphasizing regional ingredients—in smaller hamlets, the best restaurant in town is often inside the historic inn. As in the rest of New England, the state has no shortage of greasy-spoon diners, pizzerias, and pubs that serve hearty comfort fare, but a growing number of contemporary, locavore-driven bistros, third-wave coffee roasters, mixology-minded cocktail bars, and artisanal craft breweries have cropped up in recent years—along with a growing selection of Asian and other ethnic restaurants—especially in Portsmouth, Manchester, and Concord, but also in some surprisingly little towns, such as Keene, Littleton, Bethlehem, and Tamworth. No matter where you go, reservations are seldom required, and dress is casual.

HOTELS

In the mid-19th century, wealthy Bostonians retreated to imposing New Hampshire country homes in the summer. Grand hotels were built across the state, especially in the White Mountains, which at that time competed with Saratoga Springs, Newport, and Bar Harbor to draw the nation's elite vacationers. A handful of these hotel-resorts survive, with their large kitchen staffs and their tradition of top-notch service. And many of those country houses have since been converted into inns. The smallest have only a couple of rooms and are typically done in period style; the largest contain 30 or more rooms and suites and have in-room fireplaces and even hot tubs. You'll also find a great many well-kept, often family-owned motor lodges, particularly in the White Mountains and Lakes regions. In ski areas, expect the usual ski condos and lodges, but most slopes are also within a short drive of a country inn or two. In the Merrimack River valley, as well as along major highways, chain hotels and motels predominate. The state's numerous campgrounds accommodate RVers and tent campers alike. The White Mountains provide an excellent base for camping and hiking. *Hotel reviews have been shortened. For full information, visit Fodors.com.*

What It Costs

	$	$$	$$$	$$$$
RESTAURANTS	under $18	$18–$24	$25–$35	over $35
HOTELS	under $150	$150–$225	$226–$300	over $300

VISITOR INFORMATION

CONTACTS Bike the Whites ☎ 603/356–9025 ⊕ *www.bikethewhites.com.* **Lakes Region Tourism Association** ☎ 603/286–8008, 800/605–2537 ⊕ *www.lakesregion.org.* **Lake Sunapee Region Chamber of Commerce** ☎ 603/526–6575, 877/526–6575 ⊕ *www.lakesunapeenh.org.* **New Hampshire State Parks** ☎ 603/271–3556 ⊕ *www.nhstateparks.org.* **Ski New Hampshire** ☎ 603/745–9396 ⊕ *www.skinh.com.* **Visit New Hampshire** ☎ 603/271–2665, 800/386–4664 ⊕ *www.visitnh.gov.* **White Mountain National Forest** ✉ 71 White Mountain Dr., Campton ☎ 603/536–6100 ⊕ *www.fs.fed.us.* **White Mountains Visitors Center** ☎ 603/745–8720 ⊕ *www.visitwhitemountains.com.*

Portsmouth

47 miles east of Concord; 50 miles south of Portland, Maine; 56 miles north of Boston.

★ More than a quaint harbor town with a long, colorful history, Portsmouth is an upscale community with trendy farm-to-table restaurants, contemporary art galleries, and cultural venues that host nationally recognized speakers and performers. Swank cocktail bars, craft breweries, and late-night eateries create a convivial evening buzz in downtown's Market Square. Settled in 1623 as Strawbery Banke, Portsmouth grew into a prosperous port before the Revolutionary War, during which it harbored many Tory sympathizers. These days, this city of 22,000 has many grand residences from the 18th to the early 20th century; some of them can be found among the restored buildings that make up the Strawbery Banke Museum.

GETTING HERE AND AROUND

Both Interstate 95 and U.S. 1 run through Portsmouth. From the west, take Route 101 and from the north take Route 16. Amtrak runs through Durham, which is a short drive from the coast. Downtown Portsmouth is walkable, though you'll need a car for attractions farther afield.

ESSENTIALS

BUS AND TROLLEY COAST Bus ☎ 603/743–5777 ⊕ *www.coasthus.org.*

BOAT TOURS
Gundalow Company
BOAT TOURS | FAMILY | Sail the Piscataqua River in a flat-bottom gundalow (a type of barge) built at Strawbery Banke. Help the crew set sail, steer the vessel, and trawl for plankton while learning about the region's history from an onboard educator. Passengers are welcome to bring food and beverages. ⊠ *60 Marcy St.* ☏ *603/433–9505* ⊕ *www.gundalow. org* ⊠ *From $28* ◔ *Closed early Oct.– late May.*

Portsmouth Harbor Cruises
BOAT TOURS | Tours of Portsmouth Harbor and the Isles of Shoals, inland-river foliage trips, and sunset cruises are all in this company's repertoire. ⊠ *64 Ceres St.* ☏ *603/436–8084, 800/776–0915* ⊕ *www. portsmouthharbor.com* ⊠ *From $19* ◔ *Closed Nov.–early May.*

Portsmouth Kayak Adventures
ADVENTURE TOURS | FAMILY | Explore the Piscataqua River Basin and the New Hampshire coastline on a guided kayak or standup paddleboard tour. Beginners are welcome (instruction included). ⊠ *185 Wentworth Rd.* ☏ *603/559–1000* ⊕ *www. portsmouthkayak.com* ⊠ *From $45* ◔ *Closed mid-Oct.–May.*

WALKING TOURS
★ Discover Portsmouth
WALKING TOURS | FAMILY | The Portsmouth Historical Society operates this combination visitor center–museum, where you can pick up maps, get the scoop on what's happening while you're in town, and view cultural and historical exhibits. Discover Portsmouth is also the place to learn about self-guided historical tours and to sign up for guided ones. ⊠ *10 Middle St.* ☏ *603/436–8433* ⊕ *www. portsmouthhistory.org* ⊠ *Tours from $15.*

★ Portsmouth Black Heritage Trail
WALKING TOURS | FAMILY | Important local sites in African American history can be seen on the 75-minute guided Sankofa Tour. Included are the African Burying Ground and historic homes of local slave traders and abolitionists. Tours, which begin at the Old Meeting House, are conducted on Saturday afternoons throughout the summer. ⊠ *280 Marcy St.* ☏ *603/570-8469* ⊕ *www.blackheritagetrailnh.org* ⊠ *$20.*

VISITOR INFORMATION
The Portsmouth tourism office (Chamber Collaborative of Greater Portsmouth) is the official government source of visitor info the for entire Seacoast region.

Chamber Collaborative of Greater Portsmouth ⊠ *Portsmouth* ☏ *603/610–5510* ⊕ *www.portsmouthchamber.org.*

◉ Sights

Albacore Park
MILITARY SITE | Built in Portsmouth in 1953, the USS *Albacore* is the centerpiece of Albacore Park. You can board this prototype submarine, which served as a floating laboratory to test an innovative hull design, dive brakes, and sonar systems for the Navy. The visitor center exhibits *Albacore* artifacts, and the nearby Memorial Garden is dedicated to those who have lost their lives in submarine service. ⊠ *600 Market St.* ☏ *603/436–3680* ⊕ *www.ussalbacore. org* ⊠ *$8.*

Fort Constitution State Historic Site
HISTORIC SITE | FAMILY | The original military outpost on the island of New Castle was built on this site in 1631 and rebuilt in 1666 as Ft. William and Mary, a British stronghold overlooking Portsmouth Harbor. The fort earned its fame in 1774, when patriots raided it in one of Revolutionary America's first overtly defiant acts against King George III. Munitions captured here were used against the British at the Battle of Bunker Hill. The structure was renamed Ft. Constitution in 1791; the current ruins date to 1808. The fort commands a great view of nearby Portsmouth Lighthouse. ⊠ *25 Wentworth Rd.* ⊹ *Park at Battery Farnsworth and walk into Coast Guard Station* ☏ *603/271–3556* ⊕ *www.nhstateparks.org* ⊠ *Free.*

0 —————— 6 mi

0 —————— 6 km

New Hampshire Coast

Great Bay Estuarine National Research Reserve

INFO CENTER | FAMILY | Just inland from Portsmouth is one of southeastern New Hampshire's most precious assets. In this 10,235 acres of open and tidal waters, you can spot blue herons, ospreys, and snowy egrets, particularly during the spring and fall migrations. The Great Bay Discovery Center has indoor and outdoor exhibits, a library and bookshop, and a 1,700-foot boardwalk, as well as other trails, which wind through mudflats and upland forest. ⊠ *89 Depot Rd., Greenland* 🕾 *603/778–0015* ⊕ *www.greatbay.org* ⊠ *Free* ☉ *Discovery Center closed Mon. and Tues., weekdays in Oct., and Nov.–Apr.*

Isles of Shoals

ISLAND | FAMILY | Four of the nine small, rocky Isles of Shoals belong to New Hampshire (the other five belong to

Maine), many of them still known by the earthy names—Hog and Smuttynose, to cite but two—17th-century fishermen bestowed on them. A history of piracy, murder, and ghosts suffuses the archipelago, long populated by an independent lot who, according to one writer, hadn't the sense to winter on the mainland. Celia Thaxter, a native islander, romanticized these islands with her poetry in *Among the Isles of Shoals* (1873). In the late 19th century, **Appledore Island** became an offshore retreat for Thaxter's coterie of writers, musicians, and artists. **Star Island** contains a small museum, the Rutledge Marine Lab, with interactive family exhibits. From May to late October you can take a narrated history cruise of the Isles of Shoals, a day trip to Star Island, or a walking tour of Star Island with Isles of Shoals Steamship Company. ⊠ *Barker*

Wharf, 315 Market St. ☎ *800/441–4620, 603/431–5500* ⊕ *www.islesofshoals. com* ⊠ *Cruises from $28.*

John Paul Jones House

BUILDING | **FAMILY** | Revolutionary War hero John Paul Jones lived at this boarding-house while he supervised construction of the USS *America* for the Continental Navy. The 1758 hip-roof building displays furniture, costumes, glass, guns, portraits, and documents from the late 18th century. The collection's specialty is textiles, among them some extraordinary early-19th-century embroidery samplers. ⊠ *43 Middle St.* ☎ *603/436–8420* ⊕ *www.portsmouthhistory.org* ⊠ *$6* ⊙ *Closed early Oct.–late May.*

★ Moffatt-Ladd House and Garden

GARDEN | The period interior of this striking 1763 mansion tells the story of Portsmouth's merchant class through portraits, letters, and furnishings. The Colonial Revival garden includes a horse chestnut tree planted by General William Whipple when he returned home after signing the Declaration of Independence in 1776. ⊠ *154 Market St.* ☎ *603/436–8221* ⊕ *www.moffattladd.org* ⊠ *$8 ($2 garden only)* ⊙ *Closed mid-Oct.–May.*

Prescott Park

ARTS VENUE | **FAMILY** | Picnicking is popular at this 3½-acre waterfront park near Strawbery Banke, whose large formal garden with fountains is perfect for whiling away an afternoon. The park contains Point of Graves, Portsmouth's oldest burial ground, and two 17th-century warehouses. The summerlong Prescott Park Arts Festival features concerts, outdoor movies, and food-related events. ⊠ *105 Marcy St.* ☎ *603/436–2848* ⊕ *www.prescottpark.org.*

★ Strawbery Banke Museum

GARDEN | **FAMILY** | The first English settlers named the area around today's Portsmouth for the wild strawberries along the shores of the Piscataqua River. The name survives in this 10-acre outdoor history museum, one of the largest in New England. The compound has 37 homes and other structures dating from 1695 to 1820, some restored and furnished to a particular period, others used for historical exhibits. Half of the interior of the Shapley-Drisco House (built in 1795) depicts its use as a dry-goods store in Colonial times; its living room and kitchen are decorated as they were in the 1950s, showing how buildings were adapted over time. The Shapiro House has been restored to reflect the life of the Russian-Jewish immigrant family who lived there in the early 1900s. Perhaps the most opulent house, done in decadent Victorian style, is the 1860 Goodwin Mansion, former home of Governor Ichabod Goodwin. Although the houses are closed in winter, the grounds are open year-round, and an outdoor skating rink operates December–mid-March. ⊠ *14 Hancock St.* ☎ *603/433–1100* ⊕ *www.strawberybanke.org* ⊠ *$20* ⊙ *Homes closed Nov.–Apr. except for guided tours on Nov. weekends.*

Warner House

HOUSE | The highlight of this circa 1716 gem is the curious folk-art murals lining the hall staircase, which may be the oldest-known murals in the United States still gracing their original structure. The house, a notable example of brick Georgian architecture, contains original art, furnishings, and extraordinary examples of area craftsmanship. The west-wall lightning rod is believed to have been installed in 1762 under the supervision of Benjamin Franklin. ⊠ *150 Daniel St.* ☎ *603/436–5909* ⊕ *www.warnerhouse. org* ⊠ *$8* ⊙ *Closed Nov.–May and Tues.*

🍴 Restaurants

Annabelle's Natural Ice Cream

$ | **CAFÉ** | **FAMILY** | On sunny days, a stroll around historic downtown Portsmouth isn't complete without a dish or cone of the thick and luscious ice cream doled out at this long-running parlor. Try a dish of maple-walnut, cinnamon spice, or rich

Strawbery Banke Museum includes period gardens and 37 homes and other structures.

French vanilla—the latter is made with golden egg yolks. **Known for:** seasonal flavors like pumpkin pie and peachy peach; fruit sorbets; all-natural ingredients. ⑤ *Average main: $6* ⊠ *49 Ceres St.* ☎ *603/436–3400* ⊕ *www.annabellesicecream.com.*

Black Trumpet Bistro

$$$ | CONTEMPORARY | The acclaimed chef behind this romantic harbor-view restaurant brings the bold flavors of Latin America and the Mediterranean to bear on such eclectic fare as tequila-and-beet-cured salmon, Galician seafood stew, and roast chicken with couscous, olive harissa, and preserved lemon. Chef-owner Mallett belongs to the Heirloom Harvest Project and brings unusual vegetables—sometimes in surprising colors—to the table. **Known for:** plenty of vegetarian options; a lively upstairs wine bar; flourless dark-chocolate torte. ⑤ *Average main: $26* ⊠ *29 Ceres St.* ☎ *603/431–0887* ⊕ *www.blacktrumpetbistro.com* ⊘ *No lunch.*

★ Cava

$$ | TAPAS | Having a meal at this sophisticated little wine and tapas bar down a tiny alley near the downtown riverfront can feel like going on a secret mission, or being ushered into a special dinner party. It has a small exhibition kitchen and bar, and just a handful of tables and chairs, where guests can enjoy stellar food that includes an extensive selection of bocadillos, tapas, and pintxos—from Medjool dates with Serrano and manchego to char-grilled baby octopus—plus a few larger plates, such as paella. **Known for:** one of the state's most interesting wine lists features Spanish cava; authentic Spanish tapas; churros with hot chocolate. ⑤ *Average main: $19* ⊠ *10 Commercial Alley* ☎ *603/319–1575* ⊕ *www.cavatapasandwinebar.com* ⊘ *No lunch.*

Cure

$$$ | MODERN AMERICAN | As its name hints, this buzzy neighborhood bistro in a lively dining room with redbrick walls, beam ceilings, and hardwood floors specializes in cured, brined, and slow-cooked meats, which you can sample through

beautifully presented charcuterie boards, smoked ribs, and slow-roasted Moroccan lamb shank. But take heart if you're less disposed toward red meat—you'll find plenty of creative seafood and veggie dishes on the menu, including gooey lobster mac and cheese. **Known for:** locally sourced ingredients; well-chosen wine list; lively but romantic dining room. $ *Average main: $25* ⊠ *189 State St.* ☎ *603/427–8258* ⊕ *www.curerestaurant-portsmouth.com* ☾ *No lunch.*

Lexie's Joint

$ | **BURGER** | **FAMILY** | What began as a fairly humble and straightforward downtown burger joint has blossomed into a regional mini empire, thanks to the high-quality ingredients, upbeat service, and groovy "peace, love, and burgers"–themed decor. The burgers are reasonably priced and topped with all sorts of goodies, but there are also hot dogs and a few sandwiches, plus plenty of addictive sides. **Known for:** milk shakes with Shain's of Maine homemade ice cream; fried pickles with chipotle aioli; similarly good locations nearby in Durham and Dover. $ *Average main: $7* ⊠ *212 Islington St.* ☎ *603/815–4181* ⊕ *www.peaceloveburgers.com* ☾ *Closed Mon.*

Mombo

$$$ | **INTERNATIONAL** | A short stroll from Strawbery Banke Museum and the pretty gardens of Prescott Park, this romantic restaurant is set in a Colonial red saltbox house with high timber-beam ceilings and wrought-iron chandeliers. In contrast to the historic setting, the food is artfully contemporary and worldly—specialties include jerk-spiced slow-braised oxtail, and pad Thai with sesame-crusted yellowfin tuna and spicy peanuts. **Known for:** elaborate cheese-and-charcuterie plate; international flair; peaceful setting in historic neighborhood. $ *Average main: $28* ⊠ *66 Marcy St.* ☎ *603/433–2340* ⊕ *www.momborestaurant.com* ☾ *Closed Mon. No lunch.*

Profile Coffee Bar

$ | **CAFÉ** | Quick breakfasts and lunches and high-quality coffees and teas are the draw of this contemporary coffeehouse that converts into an intimate venue for live music many evenings (check the website for details). Breakfast sandwiches on Tuscan bread with a variety of fillings are a hit in the morning, while lunch favorites include caprese salads and smoked-salmon sandwiches. **Known for:** snazzy space with lots of natural light; nitro cold brews and Chemex pour overs; tasty snacks and appetizers served at night when there's live music. $ *Average main: $6* ⊠ *15 Portwalk Pl.* ☎ *603/501–1801* ⊕ *www.profilecoffeebar.com* ☾ *No dinner.*

★ Row 34

$$$ | **SEAFOOD** | Set in a gleaming, industrial-chic dining room with tall windows, exposed air ducts, and metal tables and chairs, this contemporary and slightly fancy take on a classic seafood house is the sort of place that's equally appropriate for special celebrations and casual beer-and-oysters happy hours with friends. From tuna tartare to scallop ceviche, you can't go wrong with anything from the raw bar, but also check out the extensive variety of steamed and grilled fare, such as roasted monkfish and grilled salmon collar. **Known for:** fantastic beer selection; $1 raw oysters at happy hour; Sunday brunch. $ *Average main: $27* ⊠ *5 Portwalk Pl.* ☎ *603/319–5011* ⊕ *www.row34nh.com.*

Surf Restaurant

$$$ | **SEAFOOD** | Whether you eat inside the conversation-filled, high-ceilinged dining room or out on the breezy deck, you'll be treated to expansive views of Old Harbour and the Piscataqua River—an apt setting for consistently fresh and tasty seafood. The menu branches into several directions, including lobster rolls, shrimp-pork ramen, and Tuscan-style spaghetti with seafood, but manages everything well, and there's a well-curated wine and cocktail selection to complement your

choice. **Known for:** raw-bar specialties; water views; fresh sushi. ⑤ *Average main: $25* ✉ *99 Bow St.* ☎ *603/334–9855* ⊕ *www.surfseafood.com* ⊗ *No lunch Mon.–Wed.*

Hotels

Ale House Inn
$$ | **HOTEL** | This hip, urbane, craft beer–centric hotel set in a converted Victorian redbrick brewery is directly on the historic riverfront, steps from the city's museums, boutiques, and restaurants. **Pros:** welcome beers from local breweries upon arrival; discounts to several local attractions; bicycles for local jaunts. **Cons:** no breakfast; 12 steps to enter hotel; rooms are a bit cozy. ⑤ *Rooms from: $219* ✉ *121 Bow St.* ☎ *603/431–7760* ⊕ *www.alehouseinn.com* ⟿ *10 rooms* ⊙ *No meals.*

Hotel Portsmouth
$$$ | **HOTEL** | John E. Sise, a wealthy ship merchant, built this downtown Victorian in 1881, and now as a 32-room boutique hotel, it retains its original architectural beauty and charm. **Pros:** handy downtown location; free parking; lounge serving wine, beer, and small bites. **Cons:** breakfast is on the light side; no desks in guest rooms; three-night minimum during busy times. ⑤ *Rooms from: $249* ✉ *40 Court St.* ☎ *603/433–1200* ⊕ *www.thehotelportsmouth.com* ⟿ *32 rooms* ⊙ *Free breakfast.*

Martin Hill Inn
$$ | **B&B/INN** | Plenty of guests fall in love with this yellow 1815 house surrounded by flower-filled gardens, a 10- to 15-minute walk from the historic district and the waterfront. **Pros:** refrigerators in rooms; central location; off-street parking. **Cons:** a little outside the downtown historic district; breakfast is served at a communal table; not suitable for children under 12. ⑤ *Rooms from: $180* ✉ *404 Islington St.* ☎ *603/436–2287* ⊕ *www.martinhillinn.com* ⟿ *7 rooms* ⊙ *Free breakfast.*

★ Wentworth by the Sea
$$$$ | **RESORT** | Nearly demolished to make way for private homes in the 1980s, one of coastal New England's most elegant Victorian grand resorts—where the likes of Harry Truman and Gloria Swanson once vacationed—has been meticulously restored and now ranks among the cushiest golf, boating, and spa getaways in New Hampshire. **Pros:** amenities include an expansive full-service spa, a heated indoor pool, and an outstanding links-style golf course; marina with charters for harbor cruises and deep-sea fishing; dining options include imaginative meals in the Salt Kitchen and Bar, or in the waterfront Latitudes. **Cons:** 10–15-minute drive from downtown Portsmouth; steep rates in summer; large property lacks intimacy. ⑤ *Rooms from: $339* ✉ *588 Wentworth Rd., New Castle* ☎ *603/422–7322, 866/384–0709* ⊕ *www.wentworth.com* ⟿ *161 rooms* ⊙ *No meals.*

Nightlife

BARS
★ Earth Eagle Brewings
BREWPUBS/BEER GARDENS | A true standout among the seemingly endless supply of craft breweries that have popped up along the coast in recent years, this bustling gastropub produces unusual, boldly flavorful ales in the Belgian style, some of them using distinctive botanicals—lemongrass, gingerroot—rather than hops. The food is terrific, there's an airy outdoor beer garden, and musicians perform many evenings. ✉ *165 High St.* ☎ *603/502–2244.*

The Nice
BARS/PUBS | This intimate, hipster-favored bar specializing in colorful '50s-era cocktails (try the refreshing Right-O-Ten with Buffalo Trace bourbon, vermouth, lavender, and balsamic) draws a lively bunch for sipping and socializing. ✉ *Upstairs, 107 State St.* ☎ *603/294–9941* ⊕ *www.theniceportsmouth.com.*

Four of the nine rocky Isles of Shoals belong to New Hampshire; the other five belong to Maine.

Portsmouth Book & Bar

BARS/PUBS | Combine an old-school indie bookstore with a funky café–cocktail bar, set it inside a restored 1817 customhouse, and you've got this endearingly inviting hangout that's popular with everyone from college students to artists to tourists. Live music and readings are offered regularly. ⊠ *40 Pleasant St.* ☎ *603/427–9197* ⊕ *www.bookandbar.com.*

Performing Arts

ARTS VENUES
Music Hall

CONCERTS | Beloved for its acoustics, the 1878 hall presents top-drawer music concerts, from pop to classical, along with dance and theater. The more intimate Music Hall Loft, around the corner, screens art films and hosts lectures by leading writers and artists. ⊠ *28 Chestnut St.* ☎ *603/436–2400* ⊕ *www.themusichall.org.*

Seacoast Repertory Theatre

THEATER | Here you'll find a year-round schedule of musicals, classic dramas, and works by up-and-coming playwrights, as well as everything from a youth theater to drag cabaret nights. ⊠ *125 Bow St.* ☎ *603/433–4472* ⊕ *www.seacoastrep.org.*

Shopping

Market Square, in the center of town, abounds with gift and clothing boutiques, book and gourmet food shops, and exquisite crafts stores.

Byrne & Carlson

FOOD/CANDY | Watch elegant cream truffles, artisanal chocolate, and other fine treats being made in the European tradition at this small shop. ⊠ *121 State St.* ☎ *888/559–9778* ⊕ *www.byrneandcarlson.com.*

Nahcotta

ART GALLERIES | This contemporary design boutique specializes in stylish ceramics, jewelry, glassware, and art. ⊠ *110*

Congress St. ☎ 603/433–1705 ⊕ www. nahcotta.com.

Off Piste

GIFTS/SOUVENIRS | Look to this decidedly quirky, hip emporium for offbeat gifts and household goods—everything from painted buoy birdhouses to irreverent books, games, and mugs. ✉ 37 Congress St. ☎ 603/319–6910.

Piscataqua Fine Arts

ART GALLERIES | This gallery mainly shows works by master woodcutter Don Gorvett, who creates spellbinding scenes of New England's coast, particularly the Portsmouth area. There are also works by some of New England's finest printmakers, including Sidney Hurwitz, Alex deConstant, and Sean Hurley. ✉ 123 Market St. ☎ 603/436–7278 ⊕ www. dongorvettgallery.com.

Portsmouth Farmers' Market

MARKET | FAMILY | One of the best and longest-running farmers' markets in the state showcases seasonal produce along with regional treats such as maple syrup and artisanal cheeses. There's live music, too. It's held Saturday mornings, May–early November. ✉ 1 Junkins Ave. ⊕ www.seacoastgrowers.org.

Rye

8 miles south of Portsmouth.

On Route 1A, as it winds south through Rye, you'll pass a group of late-19th- and early-20th-century mansions known as **Millionaires' Row.** Because of the way the road curves, the drive south along this route is breathtaking. In 1623 the English established a settlement at Odiorne Point in what is now the largely undeveloped and picturesque town of Rye, making it the birthplace of New Hampshire. Today, the area's main draws include a lovely state park, beaches, and the views from Route 1A. Strict town laws have prohibited commercial development in

Rye, creating a dramatic contrast with its frenetic neighbor, Hampton Beach.

GETTING HERE AND AROUND

Interstate 95 and U.S. 1, both west of town, provide the easiest access, but Rye shows its best face from Route 1A, which leads north from Hampton Beach and south from Portsmouth along the coast.

Sights

★ Odiorne Point State Park

NATURE PRESERVE | FAMILY | These 135 acres of protected seaside land are where David Thompson established the first permanent English settlement in what is now New Hampshire. Several nature trails from which you can enjoy vistas of the nearby Isles of Shoals have informative panels describing the park's military history. The rocky shore's tidal pools shelter crabs, periwinkles, and sea anemones. Throughout the year, the **Seacoast Science Center** hosts exhibits on the area's natural history. Its tidal-pool touch tank and 1,000-gallon Gulf of Maine deepwater aquarium are popular with kids. There are also guided nature walks. ✉ 570 Ocean Blvd. ☎ 603/436–8043 ⊕ www.seacoastsciencecenter. org ⊠ Park fee $4 (late May–early Sept., plus spring and fall weekends), Science Center $10.

Beaches

Jenness State Beach

BEACH—SIGHT | FAMILY | Good for swimming and sunbathing, this long, sandy beach is a favorite among locals who enjoy its light crowds and nice waves for bodysurfing. Wide and shallow, Jenness Beach is a great place for kids to run and build sand castles. **Amenities:** lifeguards; parking (fee); showers; toilets. **Best for:** surfing; swimming; walking. ✉ 2280 Ocean Blvd. ☎ 603/227–8722 ⊕ www. nhstateparks.org ⊠ Parking $2/hr May–Sept., $1/hr Apr. and Oct.

Wallis Sands State Beach

BEACH—SIGHT | FAMILY | This family-friendly swimmers' beach has bright white sand, a picnic area, a store, and beautiful views of the Isles of Shoals. **Amenities:** food and drink; lifeguards; parking (fee); showers; toilets. **Best for:** swimming; walking. ⊠ *1050 Ocean Blvd.* ☏ *603/436–9404* ⊕ *www.nhstateparks.org* 🖅 *$15 per car (late May–early Sept.).*

Restaurants

The Carriage House

$$$ | SEAFOOD | Across from Jenness Beach, this elegant cottage serves innovative dishes with an emphasis on local seafood, from raw bar specialties like scallop crudo and littleneck clams on the half shell to roasted cod and tarragon lobster salad. A first-rate hanger steak and lamb stew with eggplant and fry bread round out the menu. **Known for:** classic daily blue-plate specials; Sunday brunch; cozy upstairs tavern with ocean views. $ *Average main: $28* ⊠ *2263 Ocean Blvd.* ☏ *603/964–8251* ⊕ *www.carriagehouserye.com* ☉ *No lunch.*

🏃 Activities

WHALE-WATCHING
Granite State Whale Watch

WHALE-WATCHING | FAMILY | This respected outfitter conducts naturalist-led whale-watching tours aboard the 100-passenger *Granite State.* ⊠ *Rye Harbor State Marina, 1870 Ocean Blvd.* ☏ *603/964–5545, 800/964–5545* ⊕ *www.granitestatewhalewatch.com* 🖅 *$38* ☉ *Closed mid-Oct.–mid-May.*

Hampton Beach

8 miles south of Rye.

This is an authentic seaside amusement center, the domain of fried-dough stands, loud music, arcade games, palm readers, parasailing, and bronzed bodies. The 3-mile-long boardwalk, where kids play games and watch saltwater taffy being made, looks like a relic of the 1940s—indeed, the whole community remains remarkably free of modern franchises. Free outdoor concerts are held on many a summer evening, and once a week there's a fireworks display. An estimated 150,000 people visit the town and its free public beach on the 4th of July, and it draws plenty of people through late September, when its season ends.

GETTING HERE AND AROUND

Interstate 95 is the fastest way to get to Hampton, but the town is best seen by driving along Route 1A, which follows the coast and passes several beaches.

ESSENTIALS

VISITOR INFORMATION Hampton Area Chamber of Commerce ☏ *603/926–8718* ⊕ *www.hamptonchamber.com.*

Sights

Applecrest Farm Orchards

FARM/RANCH | FAMILY | At this 250-acre farm, you can pick your own apples and berries or buy freshly baked fruit pies and cookies, outstanding homemade ice cream, and many other treats. There's also full-service bistro serving quite good farm-to-table fare. Fall brings cider pressing, hayrides, pumpkins, and music on weekends. Author John Irving worked here as a teenager, and his experiences inspired the book *The Cider House Rules.* ⊠ *133 Exeter Rd., Hampton Falls* ☏ *603/926–3721* ⊕ *www.applecrest.com.*

★ Fuller Gardens

GARDEN | Arthur Shurtleff, a noted landscape architect from Boston, designed this late-1920s estate garden in the Colonial Revival style. Away from the beach crowds, it encompasses 1,700 rose-bushes, hosta and Japanese gardens, and a tropical conservatory. ⊠ *10 Willow Ave., North Hampton* ☏ *603/964–5414* ⊕ *www.fullergardens.org* 🖅 *$9* ☉ *Closed Nov.–mid-May.*

Beaches

Hampton Beach State Park

BEACH—SIGHT | **FAMILY** | A long, sandy—but sometimes crowded—strand at the mouth of the Hampton River, this beach has a boardwalk edged by restaurants, attractions, and hotels. There's a year-round visitor center along with multiple picnic areas, an RV campground, and a store (seasonal). **Amenities:** food and drink; lifeguards; parking (fee); showers; toilets. **Best for:** swimming. ⊠ *160 Ocean Blvd.* ☎ *603/227–8722* ⊕ *www.nhstate-parks.org* 🚗 *Parking $15 (late May–early Sept.).*

Restaurants

Ron's Landing

$$$ | **AMERICAN** | Diners enjoy sweeping ocean views from many tables at this casually elegant restaurant that also offers a lighter pub menu in a convivial lounge. Seafood is the top draw here, with steamed mussels and fried whole-belly clams among the favorite starters, and lobster pie and blackened Atlantic salmon top picks among the mains. **Known for:** live music on weekends in the lounge; a variety of preparation options for your fish; close proximity to the beach. ⑤ *Average main: $30* ⊠ *379 Ocean Blvd.* ☎ *603/929–2122* ⊕ *www. ronslanding.com* ⊗ *Closed Mon. and Tues. No lunch.*

Hotels

Ashworth by the Sea

$$ | **HOTEL** | Although this hotel across from the beach has been around for a century, the rooms have a surprisingly bright and contemporary look. **Pros:** center-of-town location; comfortable roof-top bar; open year-round. **Cons:** breakfast not included; books up early in summer; very crowded location. ⑤ *Rooms from: $159* ⊠ *295 Ocean Blvd.* ☎ *603/926–6762* ⊕ *www.ashworthhotel.com* 🚗 *105 rooms* ⑪ *No meals.*

★ Atlantic Breeze Suites

$$ | **HOTEL** | **FAMILY** | The spacious rooms in this contemporary all-suites boutique hotel look either south over the ocean and down along the Hampton Beach shoreline or north over pristine Hampton Salt Marsh Conservation Area, and all have good-size balconies from which to soak up the views. **Pros:** free off-street parking; across the street from the beach; private balconies. **Cons:** books up way in advance in high season; on the north end of the beachfront, a bit of a walk from many restaurants; no pets. ⑤ *Rooms from: $220* ⊠ *429 Ocean Blvd.* ☎ *603/967–4781* ⊕ *www.breezeatthe-beach.com* 🚗 *11 rooms* ⑪ *No meals.*

Nightlife

Hampton Beach Casino Ballroom

MUSIC CLUBS | Despite its name, the ballroom isn't a gambling establishment but rather an 1,800-seat late-19th-century auditorium that has hosted top performers, from the likes of Duke Ellington and Janis Joplin to Trace Adkins and the Beach Boys. ⊠ *169 Ocean Blvd.* ☎ *603/929–4100* ⊕ *www.casinoballroom. com* ⊗ *Closed Dec.–Mar.*

Exeter

9 miles northwest of Hampton, 52 miles north of Boston, 47 miles southeast of Concord.

During the Revolutionary War, Exeter was the state capital, and it was here amid intense patriotic fervor that the first state constitution and the first Colonial Declaration of Independence from Great Britain were put to paper. These days Exeter shares more in appearance and personality with Boston's blue-blooded satellite communities than the rest of New Hampshire—indeed, plenty of locals commute to Beantown. Cheerful cafés, coffeehouses, and shops with artisanal wares make up this bustling town center.

GETTING HERE AND AROUND

Amtrak's *Downeaster* service stops here between Boston and Portland, Maine. By car, Exeter is 9 miles northwest of Hampton on Route 111. Route 101 is also a good way to get to Exeter from the east or west. The town itself is easy to walk around.

ESSENTIALS

VISITOR INFORMATION Exeter Area Chamber of Commerce ☎ *603/772–2411* ⊕ *www. exeterarea.org.*

 Sights

American Independence Museum

HISTORIC SITE | This museum celebrates the birth of the nation. The story unfolds over the course of a guided tour, which focuses on the Gilman family, who lived in the house during the Revolutionary War era. See drafts of the U.S. Constitution and the first Purple Heart, as well as letters and documents written by George Washington and the household furnishings of John Taylor Gilman, one of New Hampshire's early governors. In July, the museum hosts the American Independence Festival, and occasional architectural tours provide a behind-the-scenes look at the two colonial buildings that make up the museum. ⊠ *Ladd-Gilman House, 1 Governor's La.* ☎ *603/772–2622* ⊕ *www.independencemuseum.org* ⊠ *$6* ⊗ *Closed Sun. and Mon. and Dec.–Apr.*

Phillips Exeter Academy

BUILDING | The nearly 1,100 students of this elite prep school give Exeter a certain youthful energy. The grounds, open to the public, resemble an Ivy League university campus. The school's library is one of the masterworks of modernist architect Louis I. Kahn. The Lamont Gallery, in the Frederick R. Mayer Art Center, mounts free contemporary art exhibitions. ⊠ *20 Main St.* ☎ *603/772–4311* ⊕ *www.exeter.edu.*

 Restaurants

The Green Bean

$ | **CAFÉ** | All the soups—think curried butternut squash, spicy corn chowder, and tarragon potato with peas—at this self-serve restaurant are made fresh daily, and the sandwiches, from turkey with cranberry and stuffing to fresh mozzarella with pesto and tomato—are perfect for dunking. Breakfast burritos star in the early morning along with French toast and ham and eggs. **Known for:** large, leafy salads; pretty courtyard seating on warm days; hearty soups. ⑤ *Average main: $9* ⊠ *33 Water St.* ☎ *603/778–7585* ⊕ *www. nhgreenbean.com* ⊗ *No dinner.*

★ Otis

$$ | **MODERN AMERICAN** | Given the caliber of cuisine and the exceptional beverage program of this romantic, urbane restaurant set inside the early-19th-century Inn by the Bandstand, it's remarkable that most main dishes cost under $25—it's a terrific value. The farm-to-table menu here changes often to reflect what's in season, but has featured roasted duck breast with wild mushrooms and a signature dessert of sticky-toffee pudding, with everything always plated beautifully. **Known for:** emphasis on market-fresh, seasonal ingredients; views of charming village center; well-executed craft cocktails. ⑤ *Average main: $22* ⊠ *Inn by the Bandstand, 4 Front St.* ☎ *603/580–1705* ⊕ *www.otisrestaurant.com* ⊗ *Closed Sun. and Mon. No lunch.*

 Hotels

The Exeter Inn

$$ | **HOTEL** | This elegant, ivy-covered Georgian-style redbrick inn on the Phillips Exeter campus has been the choice of visiting parents since it opened in the 1930s. **Pros:** Epoch Restaurant & Bar serves three meals a day; elegant feel; fairly quiet location. **Cons:** a 10- to 15-minute walk from riverfront shopping and dining; fills up fast on fall and spring

weekends; rooms are beginning to show their age. $ *Rooms from: $159* ✉ *90 Front St.* ☎ *603/772–5901* ⊕ *www.theexeterinn.com* ⏎ *46 rooms* ⦿ *No meals.*

★ Inn by the Bandstand

$$$ | B&B/INN | This gorgeously appointed, luxury B&B in the heart of downtown Exeter exudes character and comfort, with individually themed rooms furnished with fine antiques, Oriental rugs, and cushy bedding. **Pros:** convenient downtown location; exceptional dining in Otis restaurant. **Cons:** two- to three-night minimum stay on busy weekends; in a busy part of downtown; rates are a bit steep. $ *Rooms from: $289* ✉ *6 Front St.* ☎ *603/772–6352* ⊕ *www.innbythebandstand.com* ⏎ *8 rooms* ⦿ *Free breakfast.*

Shopping

A Picture's Worth a Thousand Words

BOOKS/STATIONERY | A destination for bibliophiles, this shop sells rare books, town histories, old maps, and antique and contemporary prints. ✉ *65 Water St.* ☎ *603/778–1991.*

Exeter Fine Crafts

CRAFTS | Fine creations by more than 300 of Northern New England's top pottery, painting, jewelry, textile, glassware, and other artisans are available here. ✉ *61 Water St.* ☎ *603/778–8282* ⊕ *www.exeterfinecrafts.com.*

Durham

12 miles north of Exeter, 11 miles west of Portsmouth.

Settled in 1635 and later the home of General John Sullivan, a Revolutionary War hero and three-time New Hampshire governor, Durham was where Sullivan and his band of rebel patriots stored the gunpowder they captured from Ft. William and Mary in New Castle. Easy access to Great Bay via the Oyster River made Durham a maritime hub in the

19th century. Among its lures today are the water, nearby farms that welcome visitors, and the University of New Hampshire, which occupies much of the town's center.

GETTING HERE AND AROUND

By car, you can reach Durham on Route 108 from the north or south and on U.S. 4 from Portsmouth or Concord. The *Downeaster* Amtrak train stops here.

Sights

Museum of Art

MUSEUM | Notable items in this gallery's collection include 19th-century Japanese wood-block prints, Boston expressionist works, and art of New England. ✉ *Paul Creative Arts Center, University of New Hampshire, 30 College Rd.* ☎ *603/862–3712* ⊕ *www.unh.edu/moa* 💰 *Free* 🕙 *Closed Sun. and June–Aug.*

★ Woodman Museum

HOUSE | FAMILY | This campus of four impressive, historic museums consists of the 1675 Damm Garrison House, the 1813 Hale House (home to abolitionist Senator John P. Hale from 1840 to 1873), the 1818 Woodman House, and the 1825 Keefe House, which contains an excellent art gallery with works for sale. Exhibits focus on Early American cooking utensils, clothing, furniture, and Indian artifacts, as well as natural history and New Hampshire's involvement in the Civil War. ✉ *182 Central Ave., Dover* ☎ *603/742–1038* ⊕ *www.woodmanmuseum.org* 💰 *$13.*

Restaurants

Hop + Grind

$ | BURGER | Students and faculty from UNH, whose campus is just a few blocks away, congregate over mammoth burgers with flavorful, original sides (kimchi, fries topped with cilantro-pickled peppers or black-garlic-truffle aioli) and other creative takes on gastropub fare. As the name suggests, this is a hot spot for craft-beer aficionados, who appreciate the long list of options, including a rotating cache of rare and seasonal selections. **Known for:** impressive selection of local craft beers; fun and lively student crowd; malted milk shakes in unusual flavors. $ *Average main: $10* ✉ *Madbury Commons, 17 Madbury Rd.* ☎ *603/397–5564* ⊕ *www.hopandgrind.com.*

Hotels

Three Chimneys Inn

$$ | B&B/INN | This stately yellow structure, which has graced a hill overlooking the Oyster River since 1649, has rooms in the main house and in a 1795 barn. **Pros:** charming, historic ambience; breakfast included; free parking. **Cons:** a long walk (or short drive) into town; restaurant is a bit uneven in quality; books up quickly on fall and spring weekends. $ *Rooms from: $159* ✉ *17 Newmarket Rd.* ☎ *603/868–7800, 888/399–9777* ⊕ *www. threechimneysinn.com* ⮡ *23 rooms* ⦿| *Free breakfast.*

Nightlife

Stone Church

MUSIC CLUBS | Music aficionados head to the Stone Church—an 1835 former Methodist church—for its craft beers, pub grub, and live rock, jazz, blues, reggae, soul, and folk music. ✉ *5 Granite St., Newmarket* ☎ *603/659–7700* ⊕ *www. stonechurchrocks.com.*

Activities

Wagon Hill Farm

HIKING/WALKING | FAMILY | You can hike several trails and picnic at this 139-acre farm that overlooks the Oyster River. The old farm wagon on the top of a hill is one of the most photographed sights in New England. Park next to the farmhouse and follow walking trails to the wagon and through the woods to the picnic area by the water. Sledding and cross-country skiing are winter activities. ✉ *U.S. 4,*

across from Emery Farm ⊕ *www. ci.durham.nh.us/boc_conservation/ wagon-hill-farm.*

Shopping

★ Emery Farm

FOOD/CANDY | FAMILY | In the same family since the 1660s, Emery Farm sells produce in summer (including pick-your-own blueberries), pumpkins in fall, and Christmas trees in winter. The farm shop carries breads, pies, and local crafts, and a café serves sandwiches, ice cream, cider doughnuts, and other light fare. Pumpkin-patch hayrides take place on some weekends in September and October, and May–October children can visit the petting barn. ✉ *147 Piscataqua Rd.* ☎ *603/742–8495* ⊕ *www.emery-farm.com.*

Wolfeboro

40 miles northeast of Concord, 50 miles northwest of Portsmouth.

Quietly upscale and decidedly preppy Wolfeboro has been a resort since Royal Governor John Wentworth built his summer home on the shore of the lake in 1768. The town bills itself as the oldest summer resort in the country, and its center, bursting with tony boutiques, fringes Lake Winnipesaukee and sees a major population increase each summer. The century-old, white clapboard buildings of the Brewster Academy prep school bracket the town's southern end.

GETTING HERE AND AROUND

Enter on the west side of Lake Winnipesaukee on Route 28. Be prepared for lots of traffic in the summertime.

ESSENTIALS

VISITOR INFORMATION Wolfeboro Area Chamber of Commerce ☎ *603/569–2200, 800/516–5324* ⊕ *www.wolfeborochamber.com.*

New Hampshire Lakes Region

Sights

New Hampshire Boat Museum

MUSEUM | FAMILY | Two miles northeast of the town center, this museum celebrates New Hampshire's maritime legacy with displays of vintage wooden boats, models, antique engines, racing photography, trophies, and vintage marina signs. You can also take a 45-minute narrated ride on the lake in a reproduction of a 1928 triple-cockpit HackerCraft ($25; call for times). ⊠ *399 Center St.* ☎ *603/569–4554* ⊕ *www.nhbm.org* ⊠ *$7* ⊙ *Closed mid-Oct.–late May.*

Wright Museum

MILITARY SITE | FAMILY | Uniforms, vehicles, and other artifacts at this museum illustrate the contributions of those on the home front to the U.S. World War II effort. ⊠ *77 Center St.* ☎ *603/569–1212* ⊕ *www.wright-museum.org* ⊠ *$10* ⊙ *Closed Nov.–Apr.*

Beaches

Wentworth State Park

BEACH—SIGHT | FAMILY | Away from the hustle and bustle of Wolfeboro on pretty little Lake Wentworth, this no-frills park features a quiet beach with good fishing, picnic tables and grills, and ballfields. **Amenities:** parking (no fee); showers; toilets. **Best for:** swimming; walking. ⊠ *297 Governor Wentworth Hwy.* ☎ *603/569–3699* ⊕ *www.nhstateparks.org* ⊠ *$4 late May–early Sept.*

Restaurants

East of Suez

$$ | MODERN ASIAN | In a countrified lodge on the south side of town, this friendly restaurant serves creative Asian cuisine, with an emphasis on Philippine fare, such as *lumpia* (pork-and-shrimp spring

With 240 miles of shoreline, Lake Winnipesaukee has something for everyone.

rolls with a sweet-and-sour fruit sauce) and *pancit canton* (panfried egg noodles with sautéed shrimp and pork and Asian vegetables with a sweet oyster sauce). You can also sample Thai red curries, Japanese tempura, and Korean-style flank steak. **Known for:** BYOB policy; banana tempura with coconut ice cream; plenty of vegan options. ⑤ *Average main: $19* ✉ *775 S. Main St.* ☎ *603/569–1648* ⊕ *www.eastofsuez.com* ⊘ *Closed Mon. and early Sept.–late May. No lunch.*

Kelly's Yum Yum Shop

$ | **BAKERY** | **FAMILY** | Picking up freshly baked breads, pastries, cookies, ice cream, and other sweets at Kelly's has been a tradition since 1948. This bakery by the lakefront also has a few savory items, including pizza squares. **Known for:** gingerbread and butter-crunch cookies; pleasant outdoor sidewalk seating; milk shakes. ⑤ *Average main: $6* ✉ *16 N. Main St.* ☎ *603/569–1919* ⊕ *www. myyumyumshop.com.*

 Hotels

★ Pickering House

$$$$ | **B&B/INN** | Following an extensive two-year renovation by innkeepers Peter and Patty Cook, this striking yellow 1813 Federal mansion opened in 2018 as one of New Hampshire's most luxurious small inns. **Pros:** ultracushy rooms; the manager, a founder of prestigious Stonewall Kitchen Cooking School, prepares a lavish breakfast each morning; convenient in-town location. **Cons:** on busy street; among the highest rates in the region; not suitable for children. ⑤ *Rooms from: $385* ✉ *116 S. Main St.* ☎ *603/569–6948* ⊕ *www.pick-eringhousewolfeboro.com* ⬐ *10 rooms* ⦿ *Free breakfast.*

Topsides Bed & Breakfast

$ | **B&B/INN** | Each of the rooms at this quiet, stylish, yet surprisingly affordable retreat captures the allure of a particular region, from Martha's Vineyard to coastal France to British fox-hunting country. **Pros:** handy downtown location; reasonable rates; friendly innkeepers. **Cons:** some rooms up a flight of stairs;

on a busy road; frilly decor may not be to everyone's tastes. ⑤ *Rooms from: $149* ⊠ *209 S. Main St.* ☎ *603/569–3834* ⊕ *www.topsidesbb.com* ⌑ *5 rooms* ❍�‖ *Free breakfast.*

The Wolfeboro Inn

$$ | **HOTEL** | This 1812 inn with a commanding lakefront location is a perennial favorite for Lake Winnipesaukee visitors. **Pros:** lakefront setting; quirky pub with rich history; boat tours are offered on the Winnipesaukee Belle. **Cons:** breakfast not included in rates; Wi-Fi can be spotty; some rooms are a bit compact. ⑤ *Rooms from: $161* ⊠ *90 N. Main St.* ☎ *603/569– 3016* ⊕ *www.wolfeboroinn.com* ⌑ *44 rooms* ❍❖ *No meals.*

Activities

HIKING

Abenaki Tower

HIKING/WALKING | **FAMILY** | A quarter-mile hike to the 100-foot post-and-beam Abenaki Tower, followed by a more rigorous climb to the top, rewards you with a view of Lake Winnipesaukee and the Ossipee mountain range. The setting is particularly photogenic at sunset. ⊠ *Trailhead on Rte. 109, Tuftonboro.*

WATER SPORTS

Scuba divers can explore *The Lady,* a 125-foot-long cruise ship that sank in 30 feet of water off Glendale in 1895.

Dive Winnipesaukee Corp

WATER SPORTS | This operation runs charters out to wrecks, rents boats, and offers scuba equipment rentals, repairs, and sales. ⊠ *Wolfeboro Bay, 4 N. Main St.* ☎ *603/569–8080* ⊕ *www.divewinnipesaukee.com.*

Shopping

Black's Paper Store

GIFTS/SOUVENIRS | **FAMILY** | Browse regionally made soaps, chocolates, maple products, pottery, candles, lotions, potions, yarns, toys, and gifts at this vast

old-fashioned emporium that dates back to the 1860s. ⊠ *8 S. Main St.* ☎ *603/569– 4444* ⊕ *www.blacksgiftsnh.com.*

The Country Bookseller

BOOKS/STATIONERY | **FAMILY** | You'll find an excellent regional-history section and plenty of children's titles at this independent bookstore, where you can do a little reading in the small café. ⊠ *23A N. Main St.* ☎ *603/569–6030* ⊕ *www.thecountrybookseller.com.*

Alton Bay

10 miles south of Wolfeboro.

Lake Winnipesaukee's southern shore is alive with visitors from the moment the first flower blooms until the last maple sheds its leaves. Two mountain ridges hold 7 miles of the shoreline in Alton Bay, which is the name of both the inlet and the town at its tip. Cruise boats dock here, and small planes land year-round on the water and the ice. There's a dance pavilion, along with miniature golf, a public beach, and a Victorian-style bandstand, and you'll find a couple of basic but fun short-order restaurants near the waterfront.

GETTING HERE AND AROUND

You reach Alton Bay from Wolfeboro via Route 28 and Route 28A, which winds along the bay's eastern shoreline. Head briefly west at Route 11 to the dock and small business district.

Restaurants

★ The Crystal Quail

$$$$ | **MODERN AMERICAN** | With just four tables tucked inside an 18th-century farmhouse, this restaurant is worth the drive for its sumptuous meals. Longtime proprietors Harold and Cynthia Huckaby use free-range meats and mostly organic produce and herbs to prepare a daily-changing prix-fixe menu that could feature pheasant pâté, sautéed quail with wild mushrooms, or oat-crusted trout in a beurre blanc sauce. **Known for:** highly personalized service; BYOB wine policy; intimate setting; cash only. $ *Average main: $75* ⊠ *202 Pitman Rd., 12 miles south of Alton Bay, Center Barnstead* ☎ *603/269–4151* ⊕ *www.crystalquail. com* ▭ *No credit cards* ⊘ *Closed Mon. and Tues. No lunch.*

Activities

★ Mt. Major

HIKING/WALKING | About 5 miles north of Alton Bay, a rugged 3-mile trail up a series of granite cliffs leads to the summit of Mt. Major. At the top you'll find a four-sided stone shelter built in 1925, but the real reward is the spectacular view of Lake Winnipesaukee ⊠ *Rte. 11.*

Weirs Beach

17 miles northwest of Alton Bay.

Weirs Beach is Lake Winnipesaukee's center for summertime arcade activity, with souvenir shops, fireworks, the 2,500-seat Bank of New Hampshire outdoor concert venue, and hordes of children—there's even a drive-in theater. Cruise boats also depart from here, and the recently refurbished Winnipesaukee Pier has family-oriented restaurants and other amusements.

GETTING HERE AND AROUND

Weirs Beach is just north of Laconia and south of Meredith on U.S. 3.

Sights

Funspot

AMUSEMENT PARK/WATER PARK | **FAMILY** | The mothership of Lake Winnipesaukee's family-oriented amusement parks, Funspot claims that its more than 500 video games make it the world's largest arcade—there's even an arcade museum. You can also work your way through an indoor miniature golf course and 20 lanes of bowling. Some outdoor attractions are closed in winter. Rates vary depending on the activity. ⊠ *579 Endicott St. N* ☎ *603/366–4377* ⊕ *www.funspotnh.com.*

★ M/S *Mount Washington*

BODY OF WATER | **FAMILY** | The 230-foot M/S *Mount Washington* offers 2½-hour scenic cruises of Lake Winnipesaukee, departing Weirs Beach with stops at Wolfeboro, Alton Bay, Center Harbor, and Meredith depending on the day. Sunset cruises include live music and a buffet dinner, and the Sunday Champagne brunch cruise includes plenty of bubbly. The same company operates the *Sophie C.* ($28), which has been the area's floating post office for more than a century. The boat departs from Weirs Beach with mail and passengers, passing through parts of the lake not accessible to larger ships. The M/V *Doris E.* ($20–$28) has one- and two-hour scenic cruises into Meredith Bay throughout the summer. ⊠ *211 Lakeside Ave., Laconia* ☎ *603/366–5531* ⊕ *www.cruisenh.com* ⊠ *From $32* ⊘ *Closed mid-Oct.–mid-May.*

Winnipesaukee Scenic Railroad

LOCAL INTEREST | **FAMILY** | You can board this scenic railroad's restored cars at Weirs Beach or Meredith for one- or two-hour rides along the shoreline. Special excursions include fall foliage and the Santa train. ⊠ *211 Lakeside Ave.* ☎ *603/745–2135* ⊕ *www.hoborr.com* ⊠ *From $18.*

Beaches

Ellacoya State Park

BEACH—SIGHT | **FAMILY** | Families enjoy this secluded 600-foot sandy beach and park on the southwestern shore of Lake Winnipesaukee. Ellacoya, with views of the Sandwich and Ossipee mountains, is seldom crowded, and its shallow beach is safe for small children. It has sheltered picnic tables and a small campground. **Amenities:** parking (no fee); toilets. **Best for:** solitude; swimming. ⊠ *266 Scenic Rd., Gilford* ☎ *603/293–7821* ⊕ *www.nhstateparks.org* ⊠ *$5 late May–early Sept.*

Activities

GOLF

Pheasant Ridge Golf Club

GOLF | In a bucolic setting frequented by amazing waterfowl, the course here offers great farm and mountain views. ⊠ *140 Country Club Rd., Gilford* ☎ *603/524–7808* ⊠ *$29–$45* 🏌 *18 holes, 6109 yards, par 71.*

SKI AREA

Gunstock Mountain Resort

BICYCLING | **FAMILY** | High above Lake Winnipesaukee, this ski resort has invested millions to increase its snowmaking capacity, and offers plenty of options for beginners as well as slope-side dining. Thrill Hill, a snow-tubing park, has five runs, a lift service, and 21 acres of terrain park. The ski area has 55 trails (24 of them open for night skiing) and 32 miles of cross-country and snowshoeing trails. In summer, the Mountain Adventure Park offers an adrenaline rush with 22 ziplines—the longest at 3,981 feet—an aerial obstacle course, a 4,100-foot mountainside roller coaster, and scenic chairlift rides that access some great hiking routes. There are also mountain-bike trails, Segway tours, and paddleboats. **Facilities:** 55 trails; 2,200 acres; 1,400-foot vertical drop; 8 lifts. ⊠ *719 Cherry Valley Rd., Gilford* ☎ *603/293–4341* ⊕ *www.gunstock.com* ⊠ *Lift ticket $88.*

🛍 Shopping

Pepi Herrmann Crystal

CERAMICS/GLASSWARE | Watch artists at work crafting hand-cut crystal glasses, as well as contemporary tableware, ornaments, and jewelry. ⊠ *3 Waterford Pl., Gilford* ☎ *603/528–1020* ⊕ *www. handcut.com.*

Laconia

9 miles south of Weirs Beach, 27 miles north of Concord.

The arrival of the railroad in 1848 turned the sleepy hamlet of Laconia—then called Meredith Bridge—into the Lakes Region's chief manufacturing hub. Even today it acts as the area's supply depot, a perfect role given its accessibility to both Winnisquam and Winnipesaukee lakes, as well as to Interstate 93. In June the town draws bikers from around the world for Laconia Motorcycle Week.

GETTING HERE AND AROUND

The best way to Laconia is on U.S. 3 or Route 11. Scenic drives from the south include Route 106 and Route 107.

👁 Sights

Belknap Mill

FACTORY | Inside this 1823 textile mill, you can see how cloth and clothing were made almost two centuries ago. Belknap Mill contains operational knitting machines, a 1918 hydroelectric power system, and changing exhibits. ⊠ *Mill Plaza, 25 Beacon St. E* ☎ *603/524–8813* ⊕ *www.belknapmill.org* ⊠ *Free* ⊙ *Closed Sun.*

★ Canterbury Shaker Village

FARM/RANCH | **FAMILY** | Established in 1792, this village flourished in the 1800s and practiced equality of the sexes and races, common ownership, celibacy, and pacifism. The last member of the religious community passed away in 1992. Shakers invented such household items as the clothespin and the flat broom and were known for the simplicity and integrity of their designs. Engaging guided tours—you can also explore on your own—pass through some of the 694-acre property's more than 25 restored buildings, many of them with original furnishings. Crafts demonstrations take place daily. Ask the admissions desk for a map of the many nature trails. The Cafe

View simple yet functional furniture, architecture, and crafts at Canterbury Shaker Village.

offers salads, soups, and baked goods, and sells seasonal vegetables and locally produced maple syrup, and the Shaker Table presents sit-down lunches three days a week. An excellent shop sells handcrafted items. ✉ *288 Shaker Rd., 15 miles south of Laconia via Rte. 106, Canterbury* ☎ *603/783–9511* ⊕ *www.shakers. org* 🍴 *$19 ($10 in early Nov.–early Dec.)* 🕐 *Closed early Dec.–early May.*

Beaches

Bartlett Beach

BEACH—SIGHT | FAMILY | On Lake Winnisquam, this small but pleasant city-run park has a 600-foot-long sand beach. Picnic tables and a playground make Bartlett Beach ideal for families, particularly those with small children. **Amenities:** lifeguards; parking (no fee); toilets. **Best for:** swimming. ✉ *150 Winnisquam Ave.* ⊕ *www. laconianh.gov* 🍴 *Free.*

Restaurants

Tilt'n Diner

$ | DINER | FAMILY | Lakes Region travelers have long been familiar with the flashy pink exterior and neon signage of this convivial 1950s-style restaurant. Specialties include omelets served every possible way, Reuben sandwiches, shepherd's pie, and Southern breakfasts (sausage gravy, biscuits, and baked beans with two eggs). **Known for:** breakfast served all day; retro music and vibe is fun for kids; daily classic blue-plate specials. ⑤ *Average main: $11* ✉ *61 Laconia Rd., Tilton* ☎ *603/286–2204* ⊕ *www.thecman.com.*

Hotels

★ The Lake House at Ferry Point

$$ | B&B/INN | Four miles southwest of Laconia, this gracious red Victorian farmhouse with commanding views of Lake Winnisquam is a wonderfully peaceful retreat with a dock and a small beach. **Pros:** hearty full breakfast included; complimentary use of kayaks; helpful, friendly innkeepers. **Cons:** not within walking distance of dining or shopping; may be a little quiet for some families; two-night minimum most weekends. ⑤ *Rooms from: $200 ⊠ 100 Lower Bay Rd., Sanbornton ☎ 603/637–1758 ⊕ www. lakehouseatferrypoint.com ⤳ 9 rooms ⑩⚊ Free breakfast.*

Meredith

11 miles north of Laconia.

For many years a workaday mill town with relatively little appeal to visitors, Meredith has become a popular summer getaway thanks largely to the transformation in recent years of several historic downtown buildings into Mill Falls, one of the most appealing resort communities on Lake Winnipesaukee. To get the flavor of this bustling town, take a walk down Main Street (just couple of blocks from the lake), which is dotted with intimate cafés, boutiques, and antiques stores. And stroll along the lakefront, where you'll find a bustling marina with some lively dockside restaurants and bars.

GETTING HERE AND AROUND
You can reach Meredith from Interstate 93 via Route 104, or from points south on U.S. 3 (beware that weekend traffic can be very slow in summer). Once in town, it's pretty easy to get around on foot.

ESSENTIALS
VISITOR INFORMATION Meredith Area Chamber of Commerce ☎ *877/279–6121, 603/279–6121 ⊕ www.meredithareachamber.com.*

⊙ Sights

Hermit Woods Winery
WINERY/DISTILLERY | Stop by this airy, contemporary winery in downtown Meredith to sample the light and fruity wines, which are made with local blueberries, apples, cranberries, and honeys as well as imported grapes. Hermit Woods also

makes some excellent hard ciders. Tours of the wine-making facilities, which include a barrel tasting, are available, and you can order cheese, charcuterie, and other treats from the on-site deli to enjoy while sipping vino outside on the sundeck. There's also gift shop with wine-related arts and crafts. ⊠ *72 Main St.* ☎ *603/253–7968 ⊕ www.hermitwoods. com ⬚ Free. Tastings $10, tours $25.*

Meredith Sculpture Walk
PUBLIC ART | FAMILY | Throughout town, especially in parks beside the lake and at the gardens at Mill Falls Marketplace, you'll see colorful contemporary works of outdoor art. They're part of the Annual Meredith Sculpture walk, a year-round juried event featuring 32 distinctive pieces by renowned sculptors. Each June, a new collection of sculptures is installed. For a detailed look, take a free guided tour, offered at 10 am on Wednesday and Saturday, July and August. ⊠ *Meredith* ☎ *603/279–9015 ⊕ www.greatermeredithprogram.com/sculpture-walk.html.*

Restaurants

Canoe
$$ | MODERN AMERICAN | Just a few miles up Route 25 from Meredith in Center Harbor, this contemporary, boathouse-inspired tavern and bistro sits high above Lake Winnipesaukee and has seating in both a quieter dining room and a convivial bar that looks into the open kitchen. It's one of the better eateries in the region for seafood, including wood-fired, bacon-wrapped scallops and a creamy, entrée-size haddock chowder topped with herbs and crushed Ritz Crackers. **Known for:** fun people-watching and conversation at the bar; great selection of wines and local craft beers; salted-caramel brownie sundaes. ⑤ *Average main: $21 ⊠ 232 Whittier Hwy. (Rte. 25), Center Harbor ☎ 603/253–4762 ⊕ www. magicfoodsrestaurantgroup.com ⊗ No lunch Mon.–Thurs.*

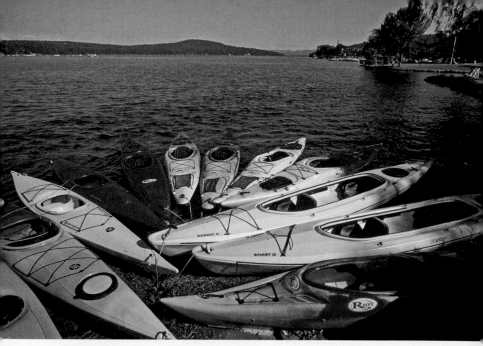

What's your vessel of choice for exploring New Hampshire's Lakes Region: kayak, canoe, powerboat, or sailboat?

Lakehouse Grille

$$$ | AMERICAN | With big windows overlooking the lake and timber posts and ceiling beams, this popular restaurant inside the upscale Church Landing at Mill Falls hotel captures the rustic ambience of an old-fashioned camp dining room. Open for all three meals, this lively spot specializes in classic American favorites with interesting twists, such as eggs Benedict topped with Maine lobster in the morning, and char-grilled steaks, chops, and seafood in the evening. **Known for:** blueberry pie for two with lemon ice cream; farm-to-table cuisine; a lively Sunday jazz brunch. $ *Average main: $27* ⊠ *Church Landing, 281 Daniel Webster Hwy. (U.S. 3)* ☎ *603/279–5221* ⊕ *www.thecman.com.*

 Hotels

★ Mill Falls at the Lake

$$ | HOTEL | You have your choice of four lodgings at this rambling resort: relaxing Church Landing and Bay Point are both on the shore of Lake Winnipesaukee; convivial Mill Falls, across the street, has a swimming pool and a 19th-century mill that now houses more than a dozen shops and restaurants; and Chase House, also across the street, has 21 rooms, all with fireplaces and lake views. **Pros:** activity center offers boat rentals and lake cruises; numerous dining options; impressive spa with heated indoor-outdoor pool. **Cons:** rooms with water views are expensive; some properties aren't directly on the lake; one of the busier spots on Lake Winnipesaukee. $ *Rooms from: $189* ⊠ *312 Daniel Webster Hwy. (U.S. 3)* ☎ *603/279–7006, 800/622–6455* ⊕ *www.millfalls.com* ⊅ *188 rooms* ⊚ *No meals.*

🎭 Performing Arts

Interlakes Summer Theatre

THEATER | During its 10-week season of summer stock, this handsome 420-seat theater presents classic Broadway musicals like *42nd Street, Evita,* and *West Side Story.* ⊠ *1 Laker La., off Rte. 25* ☎ *603/707–6035* ⊕ *www.interlakes-theatre.com.*

★ Winnipesaukee Playhouse

THEATER | Since this critically lauded theater opened in a handsome new red-barn-style venue in Meredith in 2013, it's become one of the top performing arts centers in the region, presenting well-known Broadway shows and original dramas and comedies year-round. ✉ *33 Footlight Circle* 🕾 *603/279–0333* ⊕ *www. winnipesaukeeplayhouse.org.*

Activities

BOATING

Meredith is near the quaint village of Center Harbor, another boating hub that's in the middle of three bays at the northern end of Lake Winnipesaukee.

EKAL

BOATING | At the lakefront activity center at Mill Falls, you can rent standup paddleboards, kayaks, canoes, aqua cycles, and bicycles, and book excursions on a restored 1931 Chris Craft runabout. ✉ *281 Daniel Webster Hwy. (U.S. 3)* 🕾 *603/677–8646* ⊕ *www.ekalactivitycenter.com.*

GOLF

Waukewan Golf Club

GOLF | This beautiful, well-groomed course with undulating fairways and several challenging blind shots has been a local favorite since the late '50s. ✉ *166 Waukewan Rd., Center Harbor* 🕾 *603/279–6661* ⊕ *www.waukewangolfclub.com* 💲 *$30–$55* 🖌 *18 holes, 5828 yards, par 71.*

Shopping

Home Comfort

HOUSEHOLD ITEMS/FURNITURE | This three-floor showroom is filled with designer furnishings, antiques, and accessories. ✉ *Senters Marketplace, 38 Plymouth St. (Rte. 25B), Center Harbor* 🕾 *603/253–6660* ⊕ *www.homecomfortnh.com.*

League of New Hampshire Craftsmen

CRAFTS | Here you'll find wares by more than 250 area artisans who work in everything from stained glass and ceramics to wrought iron and mixed media. There are several other branches around the state. ✉ *Inn at Church Landing, 279 Daniel Webster Hwy. (U.S. 3)* 🕾 *603/279–7920* ⊕ *www.meredith.nhcrafts.org.*

Old Print Barn

ART GALLERIES | This shop carries rare prints—Currier & Ives, antique botanicals, and more—from around the world. ✉ *343 Winona Rd., New Hampton* 🕾 *603/279–6479.*

Bristol

15 miles west of Meredith, 20 miles northwest of Laconia.

The small workaday town of Bristol serves as a base for exploring one of the Lakes Region's greatest treasures: 4,000-acre Newfound Lake, one of the state's deepest and purest bodies of water. You reach the spring-fed lake by driving 2 miles north along Route 3A, passing several beaches. Bristol is also close to popular hiking areas, including 3,121-foot Mt. Cardigan, in nearby Alexandria, and Big and Little Sugarloaf peaks, the trailhead for which is reached along West Shore Road, near the entrance to Wellington State Beach.

GETTING HERE AND AROUND

Bristol lies west of Interstate 93, Exit 23. From Meredith take Route 104 west, and then follow Route 3A north to reach Newfound Lake.

Hotels

Henry Whipple House

$ | **B&B/INN** | About 2 miles south of Newfound Lake in the heart of downtown Bristol, this magnificent turreted Queen Anne house with such original details as bronze fireplaces, chandeliers, and stained-glass windows has five antiques-filled rooms, two with wood-burning fireplaces. **Pros:** elegantly furnished rooms; great value; great breakfasts. **Cons:** books up quickly; two-night minimum in peak periods; not within walking distance of any lakes. ⑤ *Rooms from: $120* ✉ *75 Summer St.* ☎ *603/744–6157* ⊕ *www.thewhipplehouse.com* ⌨ *8 rooms* ⫟⃝ *Free breakfast.*

Activities

★ Wellington State Park
BEACHES | FAMILY | At this picturesque location you'll find the largest freshwater beach in the New Hampshire park system. The 204-acre park offers picnic and fishing areas, numerous hiking trails, and a boat launch. **Amenities:** food and drink; parking (fee); toilets. **Best for:** swimming; walking. ✉ *617 W. Shore Rd., off Rte. 3A* ☎ *603/744–2197* ⊕ *www.nhstateparks.org* ⌨ *$5 mid-May–mid-Sept.*

Holderness

16 miles northeast of Bristol, 8 miles northwest of Meredith.

The tidy small town of Holderness straddles two of the state's most scenic lakes, Squam and Little Squam, both of which have been spared from excessive development but do offer some memorable inns that are perfect for a tranquil getaway. *On Golden Pond,* starring Katharine Hepburn and Henry Fonda, was filmed on Squam, whose quiet beauty attracts nature lovers.

GETTING HERE AND AROUND
You can reach Holderness from either Interstate 93 or Meredith via U.S. 3.

◉ Sights

★ Squam Lakes Natural Science Center
BODY OF WATER | FAMILY | This 230-acre property includes a ¾-mile nature trail that passes by trailside exhibits of black bears, bobcats, otters, mountain lions, river otters, raptors, and other native wildlife. A pontoon boat cruise, one of the center's main attractions, is the best way to tour the waterfront. Naturalists talk about the animals that make their home here, and give fascinating facts about the loon. Children's activities include learning about bugs and wilderness survival skills. The center also operates nearby 1-acre Kirkwood Gardens, which you can stroll through for free. ✉ *23 Science Center Rd.* ☎ *603/968–7194* ⊕ *www.nhnature.org* ⌨ *Trail $20, lake cruise $27* ⊘ *Live-animal exhibits closed Nov.–Apr.*

Restaurants

★ Little Red Schoolhouse
$$ | AMERICAN | FAMILY | Serious fans of lobster rolls flock from both the Lakes Region and the nearby White Mountains to this funky little converted schoolhouse with both screened-in seating and a large outdoor picnic area high on a bluff above the Pemigewasset River. Start off with a cup of lobster bisque or clam chowder before digging into a traditional (lightly dressed, with mayo) or hot-buttered lobster roll—both come on a warm, buttered brioche roll. **Known for:** homemade ice cream and root-beer floats; garlic fries; adjacent gift shop with local crafts and artisanal food products. ⑤ *Average main: $18* ✉ *1994 Daniel Webster Hwy. (U.S. 3), Campton* ☎ *603/726–6142* ⊕ *www.littleredschoolhousenh.com.*

Manor on Golden Pond Restaurant
$$$ | MODERN AMERICAN | Leaded-glass panes and wood paneling set a decidedly romantic tone at this wonderfully atmospheric inn overlooking Squam Lake, whose main dining room is in the manor's original billiards room and retains woodwork from 1904. The menu changes weekly, but has included roasted beets with glazed fennel and orange oil, and locally sourced pork tenderloin with heirloom tomatoes and bacon-onion jam.

Known for: well-chosen wine pairings for every dish; romantic setting overlooking the lake; lavish breakfasts. $ *Average main: $30 ⊠ 31 Manor Dr., at U.S. 3 and Shepard Dr. ☎ 603/968–3348 ⊕ www. manorongoldenpond.com.*

Walter's Basin

$$ | **AMERICAN** | A former bowling alley in the heart of Holderness makes an unlikely but charming setting for meals overlooking Little Squam Lake—local boaters dock right beneath the dining room. Among the specialties on the seafood-intensive menu are steamed mussels with duck sausage, fried whole-belly clams, and Vermont elk meat loaf with mashed potatoes, while sandwiches and salads are among the lighter options. **Known for:** dockside setting; live music in the adjoining Basshole Pub on Thursday nights in summer; lobster BLT sandwiches. $ *Average main: $20 ⊠ 859 U.S. 3 ☎ 603/968–4412 ⊕ www. waltersbasin.com.*

Hotels

Cottage Place on Squam

$ | **RENTAL** | This sweet, old-fashioned compound of cottages and suites on Little Squam Lake is a terrific find—and value—for families, as nearly all units have partial or full kitchens, and many can comfortably sleep up to five guests (there's also a six-bedroom lodge that groups can rent entirely). **Pros:** very affordable; lots of on-site activities, from kayaking to shuffleboard; well-curated shop has fun one-of-a-kind gifts. **Cons:** the retro ambience isn't at all fancy; family popularity might be a turnoff if seeking peace and quiet; no restaurant. $ *Rooms from: $109 ⊠ 1132 U.S. 3 ☎ 603/968–7116 ⊕ www.cottageplaceonsquam.com ⤳ 15 rooms ⦿ No meals.*

Inn on Golden Pond

$$ | **B&B/INN** | The hospitable innkeepers at this comfortable and informal bed-and-breakfast a short distance from Squam Lake make every possible effort

to accommodate their guests—many of whom are repeat clients—from providing them with hiking trail maps to using rhubarb grown on property to make the jam served during the delicious country breakfasts. **Pros:** friendly innkeepers; comfortable indoor and outdoor common spaces; generous full breakfast. **Cons:** not directly on the lake; not especially fancy; can't accommodate pets. $ *Rooms from: $189 ⊠ 1080 U.S. 3 ☎ 603/968–7269 ⊕ www.innongoldenpond.com ⤳ 8 rooms ⦿ Free breakfast.*

★ The Manor on Golden Pond

$$ | **B&B/INN** | A name like this is a lot to live up to, but the Manor succeeds: it's one of the Lakes Region's most charming inns, situated on a slight rise overlooking Squam Lake, with 15 acres of lawns, towering pines, and hardwood trees. **Pros:** fireplaces and Jacuzzis in many rooms; gracious common spaces; there's a small spa, and afternoon tea is served in the library. **Cons:** the top-tier suites are quite expensive; a bit formal for some tastes; not suitable for younger kids. $ *Rooms from: $219 ⊠ 31 Manor Rd., off Shepard Hill Rd. ☎ 603/968–3348, 800/545–2141 ⊕ www.manorongoldenpond.com ⤳ 24 suites ⦿ Free breakfast.*

Squam Lake Inn

$$ | **B&B/INN** | Graceful Victorian furnishings fill the 10 stylishly updated rooms at this peaceful farmhouse inn a short stroll from Squam Lake. **Pros:** secluded and serene setting; plush beds with top-of-the-line bedding; sumptuous gourmet breakfasts included; the location is an easy drive from the area's best shopping and dining. **Cons:** short walk to lake; open only seasonally; two- to three-night minimum on high-season weekends. $ *Rooms from: $219 ⊠ 28 Shepard Hill Rd. ☎ 603/968–4417, 800/839–6205 ⊕ www.squamlakeinn.com ⊗ Closed late Oct.–May ⤳ 10 rooms ⦿ Free breakfast.*

Activities

★ Squam Lakes Association

BOATING | FAMILY | You can rent kayaks, canoes, and standup paddleboards, reserve campsites, enroll kids in education programs, and learn about local wildlife and fishing at this nonprofit organization that's been focused on lake conservation since it formed in 1904. ⊠ *534 U.S. 3* ☎ *603/968–7336* ⊕ *www.squamlakes.org.*

Center Sandwich

12 miles northeast of Holderness.

With Squam Lake to the west, Lake Winnipesaukee to the south, and the Sandwich Mountains to the north, Center Sandwich claims one of the prettiest settings of any Lakes Region community. So appealing are the town and its views that John Greenleaf Whittier used the Bearcamp River as the inspiration for his poem "Sunset on the Bearcamp." The town attracts artisans—crafts shops abound among its clutch of charming 18th- and 19th-century buildings.

GETTING HERE AND AROUND

This rural town is reached from Holderness via Route 113 and Meredith—by way of Center Harbor and Moultonborough, by taking Route 25 to Route 109.

Sights

★ Castle in the Clouds

CASTLE/PALACE | FAMILY | Looking for all the world like a fairy-tale castle, this wonderful mountaintop estate was finished in 1914. The elaborate mansion has 16 rooms, eight bathrooms, and doors made of lead. Owner Thomas Gustave Plant spent $7 million—the bulk of his fortune—on this project and died penniless in 1941. A tour includes the mansion and the Castle Springs water facility on this high Ossipee Mountain Range property overlooking Lake Winnipesaukee; fascinating basement tours are also available. Hiking (and cross-country skiing in winter), and pony and horse rides are also offered, along with jazz dinners many summer evenings on the terrace—with sweeping lake views—at the Carriage House restaurant, which is also open for lunch whenever mansion tours are offered. ⊠ *455 Old Mountain Rd., Moultonborough* ☎ *603/476–5900* ⊕ *www.castleintheclouds.org* ⊠ *$17* ⊘ *Closed late Oct.–mid-May.*

Loon Center

BODY OF WATER | FAMILY | Recognizable for its eerie calls and striking black-and-white coloring, the loon resides on many New Hampshire lakes but is threatened by the gradual loss of its habitat. Two trails wind through the 200-acre Loon Center, which has made great progress in helping to restore the state's loon population; vantage points on the Loon Nest Trail overlook the spot resident loons sometimes occupy in late spring and summer. ⊠ *183 Lee's Mills Rd., Moultonborough* ☎ *603/476–5666* ⊕ *www.loon.org* ⊠ *Free* ⊘ *Closed Sun.–Wed. in winter.*

Restaurants

Corner House Inn

$$ | AMERICAN | In a converted barn adorned with paintings by local artists, this rustic tavern in an 1840s building dishes up classic American fare. Salads made with local greens are a house specialty, but don't overlook the chef's lobster-and-mushroom bisque or the shellfish sauté. **Known for:** live music and storytelling some nights; popular Sunday brunch; extensive list of reasonably priced wines. ⑤ *Average main: $19* ⊠ *22 Main St.* ☎ *603/476–3060* ⊕ *www.cornerhouseinn.com* ⊘ *Closed Tues. No lunch.*

Shopping

Old Country Store and Museum

LOCAL SPECIALTIES | FAMILY | The store has been selling maple syrup, aged cheeses, jams, molasses, penny candy, and other items since 1781. Much of the equipment used in the store is antique, and the free museum displays old farming and forging tools. ⊠ *1011 Whittier Hwy.* ☎ *603/476–5750* ⊕ *www.nhcountrystore.com.*

Activities

BOATING
Wild Meadow Canoes & Kayaks
BOATING | Canoes and kayaks are available here. ⊠ *6 Whittier Hwy., Moultonborough* ☎ *603/253–7536* ⊕ *www.wildmeadowca-noes.com.*

HIKING
Rattlesnake Mountain
HIKING/WALKING | The nearly 500-foot elevation gain of this moderately strenuous but fairly short 2.3-loop trail to the top of Rattlesnake Mountain will get your heart pounding, but the panoramic views over Squam Lake, just to the south, are a satisfying reward. ⊠ *Trailhead on Rte. 113, 6 miles west of Center Sandwich.*

Red Hill
HIKING/WALKING | **FAMILY** | Off Route 25, Red Hill really does turn red in autumn. At the top of this rugged 3.3-mile trail, you can climb a fire tower for 360-degree views of Lake Winnipesaukee and Squam Lake, as well as the White Mountain beyond. ⊠ *Trailhead Red Hill Rd., Moultonborough ✛ 6½ miles south of Center Sandwich.*

Tamworth

13 miles east of Center Sandwich, 20 miles southwest of North Conway.

President Grover Cleveland summered in what remains a place of almost unreal quaintness: Tamworth is equally photogenic in verdant summer, during the fall foliage season, or under a blanket of winter snow. Cleveland's son, Francis, returned and founded the acclaimed Barnstormers Theatre in 1931. One of America's first summer theaters, it continues to

this day. Tamworth has a clutch of villages within its borders, and six historic churches. In the hamlet of Chocorua, the view through the birches of Chocorua Lake has been so often photographed that you may experience déjà vu. Rising above the lake is Mt. Chocorua (3,490 feet), which has many good hiking trails.

GETTING HERE AND AROUND
Tamworth's main village, at the junction of Routes 113 and 113A, is tiny and can be strolled.

Sights

Remick Country Doctor Museum and Farm
FARM/RANCH | **FAMILY** | For 99 years (1894–1993) Dr. Edwin Crafts Remick and his father provided medical services to the Tamworth area and operated a family farm. After the younger Remick died, these two houses were turned into the Remick Country Doctor Museum and Farm. The second floor of the house has been kept as it was when Remick passed away; it's a great way to see the life of a country doctor. Each season, the still-working farm features a special activity such as maple-syrup making. The farm also has hiking trails and picnicking areas. ⊠ *58 Cleveland Hill Rd.* ☎ *603/323–7591, 800/686–6117* ⊕ *www.remickmuseum. org* 🄳 *$5* ⊗ *Closed Sun.; also Sat. early Dec.–early May.*

★ Tamworth Distilling & Mercantile
WINERY/DISTILLERY | Using a 250-gallon copper still constructed in Kentucky, this artisanal distillery set in a stately barn just a short stroll from famed Barnstormers Theatre produces exceptional craft spirits, including Chocorua Straight Rye, Old Hampshire Apple Jack, Von Humboldt's Turmeric Cordial, Tamworth Garden Spruce Gin, and several flavorful cordials. If you're lucky, your stop will include a chance to sample Eau de Musc, a limited-release whiskey infused with an oil extracted from the castor glands of beavers. Distillery tours are available on weekends. ⊠ *15 Cleveland*

Hill Rd. ☎ 603/323–7196 ⊕ www.tam-worthdistilling.com ✉ Tastings $10, tours $25 ⊙ Closed Mon.–Thurs.

Restaurants

Jake's Seafood and Grill

$$ | SEAFOOD | FAMILY | Oars and other nautical trappings adorn the wood-panel walls at this classic New England seafood restaurant between West and Center Ossipee, about 8 miles southeast of Tamworth. The kitchen serves some of eastern New Hampshire's freshest and tastiest fish and shellfish, notably lobster pie, fried clams, and seafood casserole, but you'll also find a full complement of steak, ribs, and chicken dishes. **Known for:** a fish fry on Thursday nights; nostalgic, old-school decor; lobster bakes to go (perfect for picnics). $ *Average main: $19* ✉ 2055 White Mountain Hwy. (Rte. 16), West Ossipee ☎ 603/539–2805 ⊕ www.jakesseafoodco.com.

★ Tamworth Lyceum

$ | CAFÉ | With its timber-beam ceiling, hardwood floors, and quaint little tables, this folksy-looking 1826 former general store–cum–cafe stocks a surprisingly contemporary selection of carefully curated artisanal foods, craft beers, and hip gifts and accessories. The menu carries out the owners' worldly vision, offering delicious quinoa bowls, cage-free-egg–and–cheddar breakfast croissants, and sea-salt avocado toast. **Known for:** gourmet specialty foods and groceries to go; a convivial mix of locals and tourists; an impressive beer, wine, coffee, and tea selection. $ *Average main: $9* ✉ 85 Main St. ☎ 603/323–5120 ⊕ www.tamworthly-ceum.com ⊙ No dinner.

🎭 Performing Arts

★ Barnstormers Theatre

THEATER | Founded in 1931, this highly respected theater company presents dramas and comedies June–August. ✉ 104 Main St. ☎ 603/323–8500 ⊕ www.barnstormerstheatre.org.

Activities

White Lake State Park

PARK—SPORTS-OUTDOORS | FAMILY | The 72-acre stand of native pitch pine here is a National Natural Landmark. The park has a picnic area and a sandy beach, trails you can hike, trout you can fish for, and canoes you can rent. ✉ 94 State Park Rd. ☎ 603/323–7350 ⊕ www.nhstate-parks.org ✉ $5 mid-May–early Sept.

Lincoln and North Woodstock

64 miles north of Concord.

These neighboring towns at the southwestern corner of the White Mountains National Forest and the western end of the Kancamagus Highway (Route 112) form a lively resort base camp, especially for metro Boston families who can make an easy two-hour drive straight up Interstate 93. All sorts of festivals, such as the New Hampshire Scottish Highland Games & Festival in mid-September, keep Lincoln swarming with people year-round. The town itself is not much of an attraction. Tiny North Woodstock maintains a more inviting village feel.

GETTING HERE AND AROUND

Just off Exit 32 of Interstate 93, Lincoln and North Woodstock are connected by Route 112—it's a short drive or pleasant 1-mile stroll between the two.

ESSENTIALS

VISITOR INFORMATION Western White Mountains Chamber of Commerce ☎ 603/745–6621 ⊕ www.western-whitemtns.com.

TOURS

Hobo Railroad

LOCAL INTEREST | FAMILY | Restored vintage train cars take you on 80-minute excursions along the scenic shores of the Pemigewassett River. A Santa Express runs late November–late December. ⊠ *64 Railroad St., Lincoln* ☎ *603/745–2135* ⊕ *www.hoborr.com* ⊠ *$17* ⊘ *Closed Jan.–Apr.*

 Sights

Clark's Trading Post
AMUSEMENT PARK/WATER PARK | FAMILY | Chock-full of hokum, this old-time amusement park is a favorite with families and is perhaps most famous for its half-hour performing bear shows. There are also half-hour train rides over a 1904 covered bridge, a museum of Americana inside an 1880s firehouse, a restored gas station filled with antique cars, circus performers, and an Old Man of the Mountain rock-climbing tower—there's even a mining sluice where you can pan for gems. Tour guides tell tall tales, and vendors sell popcorn, ice cream, and pizza. This unabashedly touristy ensemble also includes a mammoth gift shop and a penny-candy store. ⊠ *110 Daniel Webster Hwy. (U.S. 3), Lincoln* ☎ *603/745–8913* ⊕ *www. clarkstradingpost.com* ⊠ *$22* ⊘ *Closed early Oct.–mid-May.*

★ Lost River Gorge & Boulder Caves
NATURE SITE | FAMILY | Parents can enjoy the looks of wonder on their children's faces as they negotiate wooden boardwalks and stairs leading through a granite gorge formed by the roaring waters of the Lost River. One of the 10 caves they can explore is called the Lemon Squeezer (and it's a tight fit). Kids can also pan for gems and search for fossils, while grown-ups might prefer the attractions in the snack bar, gift shop, and nature garden. Everyone can walk through a fascinating giant man-made birdhouse, venture across a suspension bridge, and climb up into a big tree house. The park offers weekend lantern tours. ⊠ *1712 Lost River Rd., North Woodstock* ☎ *603/745–8720* ⊕ *www. lostrivergorge.com* ⊠ *$21* ⊘ *Closed Nov.–Apr.*

Whale's Tale Waterpark
AMUSEMENT PARK/WATER PARK | FAMILY | You can float on an inner tube along a gentle river, plunge down one of five waterslides, hang five on the Akua surf simulator, or bodysurf in the large wave pool at Whale's Tale. There's plenty here for toddlers and small children. ⊠ *491 Daniel Webster Hwy. (U.S. 3), Lincoln* ☎ *603/745–8810* ⊕ *www.whalestale-waterpark.net* ⊠ *$40* ⊘ *Closed early Oct.–Apr.*

 Restaurants

Woodstock Inn, Station & Brewery
$$ | AMERICAN | FAMILY | This expansive, atmospheric, and wildly popular dining and drinking venue set inside North Woodstock's late-1800s train station is decorated with old maps, historic photographs, and local memorabilia; there are also fun curiosities, such as an old phone booth. The kitchen turns out reliably good pub fare—pizza, burgers, steaks, seafood—and filling breakfasts, and the brewery produces nearly 20 different varieties of year-round and seasonal beers. **Known for:** game room and separate menu for kids; acclaimed craft beers; several different and inviting indoor and outdoor dining areas. Ⓢ *Average main: $18* ⊠ *135 Main St., North Woodstock* ☎ *603/745–3951* ⊕ *www. woodstockinnnh.com.*

 Hotels

Indian Head Resort
$$ | RESORT | FAMILY | This early-20th-century resort identified by its 100-foot-tall observation tower and its lovely setting overlooking Shadow Lake, offers inexpensive and spacious rooms, making it a good choice for families on a budget. **Pros:** reasonable prices; fun, old-school personality; near kid-friendly attractions; a free shuttle to Cannon or Loon Mountain ski areas during ski season. **Cons:** no pets; on busy road 5 miles north of Woodstock; shows a

little wear in places. $ *Rooms from: $172* ⊠ *664 U.S. 3, Lincoln* ☎ *603/745–8000, 800/343–8000* ⊕ *www.indianheadresort.com* ⌦ *148 rooms* ⦿ *Free breakfast.*

Mountain Club on Loon

$$ | **RESORT** | **FAMILY** | With a diverse range of accommodations, including a suite that can sleep 10, and many units with full kitchens, this functional if pretty standard condo-style lodge provides convenient ski-in, ski-out accommodations on Loon Mountain. **Pros:** within walking distance of the lifts; full-service spa; easy proximity to hiking in national forest. **Cons:** very busy on winter weekends; decor is a bit dated; just off a busy road. $ *Rooms from: $159* ⊠ *90 Loon Mountain Rd., Lincoln* ☎ *603/745–2244, 800/229–7829* ⊕ *www.mtnclub.com* ⌦ *235 rooms* ⦿ *No meals.*

Activities

Loon Mountain

SKIING/SNOWBOARDING | **FAMILY** | Wide, straight, and consistent intermediate ski trails prevail at Loon, a modern resort on the western edge of the Pemigewasset River. The most advanced runs are grouped on the North Peak section, with 2,100 feet of vertical skiing. Beginner trails are set apart. There's snow tubing on the lower slopes, and eight terrain parks suitable for all ages and ability levels. In the base lodge are the usual dining and lounging facilities. There are 13 miles of cross-country trails, ice-skating on an outdoor rink, snowshoeing and snowshoeing tours, ziplining, and a rock-climbing wall. **Facilities:** 61 trails; 370 acres; 2,100-foot vertical drop; 11 lifts. ⊠ *90 Loon Mountain Rd., Lincoln* ☎ *603/745–8111* ⊕ *www.loonmtn.com* ⦿ *Lift ticket $88.*

Pemi Valley Moose Tours

TOUR—SPORTS | **FAMILY** | If you're eager to see a mighty moose, embark on a moose-watching bus tour into the northernmost White Mountains. The three-hour trips depart at 8:30 pm late April to mid-October for the best wildlife-sighting opportunities. ⊠ *136 Main St., Lincoln* ☎ *603/745–2744* ⊕ *www.moosetoursnh.com* ⦿ *$32.*

Franconia

16 miles northwest of Lincoln/North Woodstock.

Travelers have long passed through the White Mountains via the spectacular Franconia Notch, and in the late 18th century a town evolved just to the north. It and the region's jagged rock formations and heavy coat of evergreens stirred the imaginations of Washington Irving, Henry Wadsworth Longfellow, and Nathaniel Hawthorne, who penned a short story about the iconic—though now crumbled—cliff known as the Old Man of the Mountain. There is almost no town proper to speak of here, just a handful of businesses just off Interstate 93, aka the Franconia Notch Parkway.

Four miles west of Franconia, Sugar Hill is a village of about 500 people. It's famous for its spectacular sunsets and views of the Franconia Mountains, best seen from Sunset Hill, where a row of grand hotels and mansions once stood.

GETTING HERE AND AROUND

Franconia itself has few services, but is right off Interstate 93 and a good base for visiting many ski areas and the villages of Sugar Hill, Bethlehem, Littleton, Lincoln, and North Woodstock.

ESSENTIALS

VISITOR INFORMATION Franconia Notch Chamber of Commerce ☎ *603/823–5661* ⊕ *www.franconianotch.org.*

Continued on page 547

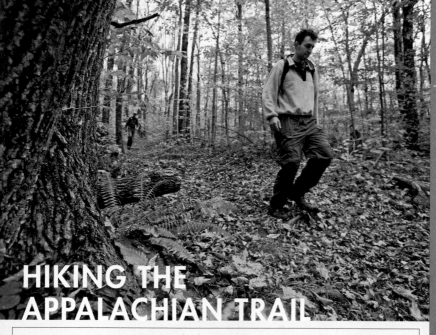

HIKING THE APPALACHIAN TRAIL

Tucked inside the nation's most densely populated corridor, a simple footpath in the wilderness stretches more than 2,100 miles, from Georgia to Maine. The Appalachian Trail passes through some of New England's most spectacular regions, and daytrippers can experience the area's beauty on a multitude of accessible, rewarding hikes.

By Melissa Kim

Running along the spine of the Appalachian Mountains, the trail was fully blazed in 1937 and designed to connect anyone and everyone with nature. Within a day's drive of two-thirds of the U.S. population, it draws an estimated two to three million people every year. Through-hikers complete the whole trail in one daunting six-month season, but all ages and abilities can find renewal and perspective here in just a few hours. One-third of the AT passes through New England, and it's safe to say that the farther north you go, the harder the trail gets. New Hampshire and Maine challenge experienced hikers with windy, cold, and isolated peaks.

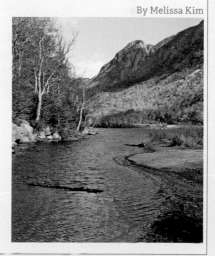

Top, hiking in New Hampshire's White Mountains. Above, autumn view of Profile Lake, Pemigewasset, NH.

ON THE TRAIL

New England's prime hiking season is in late summer and early fall, when the blaze of foliage viewed from a high peak is unparalleled. Popular trails see high crowds; if you seek solitude, try hiking at sunrise, a peaceful time that's good for wildlife viewing. You'll have to curb your enthusiasm in spring and early summer to avoid mud season in late April and black flies in May and June.

With the right gear, attitude, and preparation, winter can also offer fine opportunities for hiking, snowshoeing, and cross-country skiing.

FOLLOW THE TRAIL

Most hiking trails are marked with blazes, blocks of colored paint on a tree or rock. The AT, and only the AT, is marked by vertical, rectangular 2- by 6-inch white blazes. Two blazes mark route changes; turn in the direction of the top blaze. At higher elevations, you might also see cairns, small piles of rocks carefully placed by trail rangers to show the way when a blaze might be obscured by snow or fog.

Scenic U.S. 302 — and the AT — pass through Crawford Notch, a spectacular valley in New Hampshire's White Mountains.

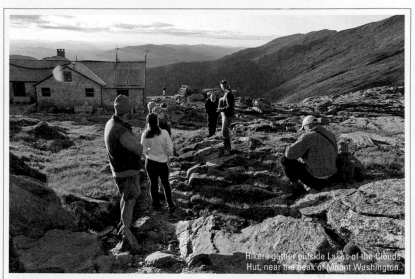

Hikers gather outside Lakes of the Clouds Hut, near the peak of Mount Washington.

TRIP TIPS

WHAT TO WEAR: For clothes, layer with a breathable fabric like polypropylene, starting with a shirt, a fleece, and a wind- or water-resistant shell. Bring gloves, a hat, and a change of socks.

WHAT TO BRING: Carry plenty of water and lightweight high-energy food. Don't forget sunscreen and insect repellent. Bring a map and compass. Just in case: a basic first-aid kit, a flashlight or head-lamp, whistle, multi-tool, and matches.

PLAN AHEAD: In your car, leave a change of clothing, especially dry socks and shoes, as well as extra water and food.

PLAY IT SAFE: Tell someone your hiking plan and take a hiking partner. Carry a rescue card with emergency contact information and allergy details.

BE PREPARED: Plan your route and check the weather forecast in advance.

REMEMBER YOUR BEGINNINGS: Look back at the trail especially at the trail-head and at tricky junctions. If you've got a digital camera, photograph trail maps posted at the trailhead or natural landmarks to help you find your way.

WHERE TO STAY

Day hikers looking to extend the adventure can also make the experience as hard or as soft as they choose. Through-hikers combine camping with overnight stays in primitive shelters, mountain huts, comfortable lodges, and resorts just off the trail.

Rustic cabins and lean-tos provide basic shelter in Maine's Baxter State Park. In Maine and New Hampshire, the Appalachian Mountain Club runs four-season lodges as well as a network of mountain huts for backcountry hikers. A hiker code of camaraderie and conviviality prevails in these huts. Experience a night and you might just find yourself dreaming of a through-hike.

FOR MORE INFORMATION

Appalachian Trail Conservancy
(⊕ www.appalachiantrail.org)

Appalachian National Scenic Trail
(⊕ www.nps.gov/appa)

Appalachian Mountain Club
(⊕ www.outdoors.org)

ANIMALS ALONG THE TRAIL

❶ Black bear

Black bears are the most common—and smallest—bear in North America. Clever and adaptable, these adroit mammals will eat whatever they can (though they are primarily vegetarian, favoring berries, grasses, roots, blossoms, and nuts). Not naturally aggressive, black bears usually make themselves scarce when they hear hikers. The largest New England populations are in New Hampshire and Maine.

❷ Moose

Spotting a moose in the wild is unforgettable: their massive size and serene gaze are truly humbling. Treasure the moment, then slowly back away. At more than six feet tall, weighing 750 to 1,200 pounds, a moose is not to be trifled with, particularly during rutting and calving seasons (fall and spring, respectively). Dusk and dawn are the best times to spot the iconic animal; you're most likely to see one in Maine, especially in and around ponds.

⚠ Black flies

Especially fierce in May and June, these pesky flies can upset the tranquility of a hike in the woods as they swarm your face and bite your neck. To ward them off, cover any exposed skin and wear light colors. You'll get some relief on a mountain peak; cold weather and high winds also keep them at bay.

❸ Bald eagles

Countless bird species can be seen and heard along the AT, but what could be more exciting than to catch a glimpse of our national bird as it bounces back from near extinction? Now it's not uncommon to see the majestic bald eagle with its tremendous wing span, white head feathers, and curved yellow beak. The white head and tail distinguish the bald from the golden eagle, a bit less rare but just as thrilling to see. Most of New England's bald eagles are in Maine, but they are rapidly increasing in population, and can often be seen never rivers and wooded areas, in all six states.

WILDFLOWERS ALONG THE TRAIL

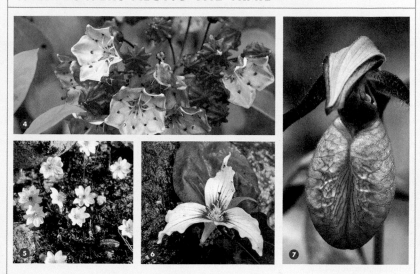

❹ Mountain laurel

The clusters of pink and white blooms of the mountain laurel look like bursts of fireworks. Up close, each one has the delicate detail of a lady's parasol. Blooms vary in color, from pure white to darker pink, and have different amounts of red markings. Connecticut's state flower, mountain laurel flourishes in rocky woods, blooming in May and June. Look for the shrub in southern New England; it's rare along the Appalachian trail in Vermont and Maine.

❺ Mountain avens

A member of the rose family, these showy yellow flowers abound in New Hampshire's White Mountains. You can't miss the large buttercup-like blooms on long green stems when they are in bloom from June through August. So common here, yet extremely rare: the only other place in the whole world where you can find mountain avens is on an island off the coast of Nova Scotia.

❻ Painted trillium

You might smell a trillium before you see it; these flowers have an unpleasant odor that may attract the flies that pollinate it. To identify this impressive flower, look for sets of three: three large pointed blue-green leaves, three sepals (small leaves beneath the petals), and three white petals with a brilliant magenta center. It can take four or five years for a trillium to produce one flower, which blooms in May and June in wet woodlands.

❼ Pink lady slippers

These delicate orchids can grow from 6 to 15 inches high and favor specific wet wooded areas in dappled sunlight. The slender stalk rises from a pair of green leaves, then bends a graceful neck to suspend the paper-thin pale pink closed flower. The slow-growing plant needs help from fungus and bees to survive and can live to be 20 years old. New Hampshire's state wildflower, the pink lady slipper blooms in June throughout New England.

⬤ = Somewhat Common ⬤ = Rare

CHOOSE YOUR DAY HIKE

MAINE
GULF HAGAS, Greenville

Difficult, 8-plus miles round-trip, 6–7 hours

This National Natural Landmark in the North Maine Woods is a spectacular sight for the adventurous day hiker. It involves a long drive on logging roads east from Greenville (see Inland Maine section) to a remote spot and a slippery, sometimes treacherous 8-mile hike around the rim of what's been dubbed Maine's Grand Canyon. Swimming in one of the sparkling pools under a 30-foot-high waterfall and admiring the views of cliffs, cascades, gorges, and chasms in this slate canyon, otherwise unthinkable in New England, will take your breath away.

TABLE ROCK, Bethel

Medium, 2.4 miles round-trip, 2 hours

Maine's Mahoosuc Range is thought to be one of the most difficult stretches of the entire AT, but north of Bethel at Grafton Notch State Park, day hikes range from easy walks in to cascading waterfalls to strenuous climbs up Old Speck's craggy peak. The Table Rock trail offers interesting sights—great views of the notch from the immense slab of granite that gives this trail its name, as well as one of the state's largest system of slab caves—narrow with tall openings unlike underground caves.

NEW HAMPSHIRE
ZEALAND TRAIL, Berlin

Easy, 5.6 miles round-trip, 3.5–4 hours

New Hampshire's Presidential range gets so much attention and traffic that sometimes the equally spectacular Pemigewasset Wilderness, just to its west, gets overlooked. Follow U.S. 302 to the trailhead on Zealand Rd. near Bretton Woods. For an easy day hike to one of the Appalachian Mountain Club's excellent overnight huts, take the mostly flat Zealand Trail over bridges and past a beaver swamp to Zealand Pond. The last tenth of a mile is a steep ascent to the mountain retreat, where you might spot an AT through-hiker taking a well-deserved rest. (Most northbound through-hikers reach this section around July or August.) In winter, you can get here by a lovely cross-country ski trip.

TRAIL NAMES

For through-hikers, doing the AT can be a life-altering experience. One of the trail's most respected traditions is taking an alter ego: a trail name. Lightning Bolt: fast hiker. Pine Knot: tough as one. Bluebearee: because a bear got all her food on her very first night on the trail.

VERMONT
HARMON HILL, Bennington

Medium to difficult, 3.6 miles round-trip, 3–4 hours

This rugged hike in the Green Mountains goes south along the AT where it coincides with the Long Trail, Vermont's century-old "footpath in the wilderness." From the trailhead on Route 9 just east of Bennington, the first half mile or so is strenuous, with some rock and log staircases and hairpins. The payback is the sweeping view from the top; you'll see Mount Anthony, Bennington and its iconic war monument, and the rolling green hills of the Taconics to the west.

STRATTON MOUNTAIN, Stratton

Difficult, 7.6 miles round-trip, 5–6 hours

A steep and steady climb from the trailhead on Kelley Stand Rd. (between West Wardsboro and Arlington) up the 3,940-foot-high Stratton Mountain follows the AT and Long Trail through mixed forests. It's said that this peak is where Benton MacKaye conceived of the idea for the Appalachian Trail in 1921. An observation tower at the summit gives you a great 360-degree view of the Green Mountains. From July to October, you can park at Stratton resort and ride the gondola up (or down) and follow the .75-mile Fire Tower Trail to the southern true peak.

MASSACHUSETTS
MOUNT GREYLOCK, North Adams

Easy to difficult, 2 miles round-trip, less than 1 hour

There are many ways to experience Massachusetts's highest peak (elevation 3,491 feet). From North Adams, follow Route 2 to the Notch Rd. trailheads. For a warm-up, try the Rounds Rock trail (Easy, 0.7 mi) for some spectacular views. Or drive up the 8-mile-long summit road and hike down the Robinson's Point trail (Difficult, 0.8 miles) for the best view of the Hopper, a glacial cirque that's home to an old-growth red spruce forest. At the summit, the impressive **Bascom Lodge**, built in the 1930s by the Civilian Conservation Corps, provides delicious meals and overnight stays (⊕ www.bascomlodge.net).

CONNECTICUT
LION'S HEAD, Salisbury

Medium, 4.1 miles round-trip, 3.5–4 hours

The AT's 52 miles in Connecticut take hikers up some modest mountains, including Lion's Head in Salisbury. From the trailhead on Route 41, follow the white blazes of the AT for two easy miles, then take the blue-blazed Lion's Head Trail for a short, steep push over open ledges to the 1,738-foot summit with its commanding views of pastoral southern New England. Try this in summer when the mountain laurels—Connecticut's state flower—are in bloom.

EXPERIENCE MOUNT WASHINGTON

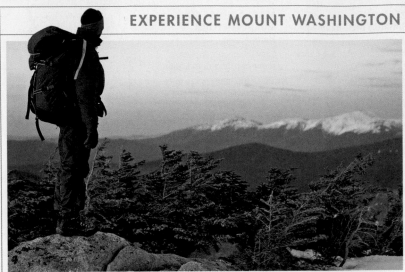

Looking at Mt. Washington from Mt. Bond in the Pemigewasset Wilderness Area, New Hampshire.

Mount Washington is the Northeast's peak of superlatives: worst weather in the world, highest spot in the northeast, windiest place on Earth. It snows in the summer, there are avalanches in winter, and it's foggy 60 percent of the time. Strong 35-mile-per-hour winds are the average, and extreme winds of 100 miles per hour with higher gusts blow year-round. Here, you can literally get blown away.

Explorers, scientists, artists, and botanists have been coming to the mountain for hundreds of years, drawn by its unique geologic features, unusual plants, and exceptional climate.

WHY SO WINDY? The 6,288-foot-high treeless peak is the highest point for miles around, so nothing dampens the force of the wind. Also, the sharp vertical rise causes wind to accelerate. Dramatic changes in air pressure also cause strong, high winds. Add to that the fact that three major storm tracks converge here, and you've got a mountain that has claimed more than 150 lives in the past 175 years.

GOING UP THE MOUNTAIN

An ascent up Mount Washington is for experienced hikers who are prepared for severe, unpredictable weather. Even in summer, cold, wet, foggy, windy conditions prevail. The most popular route to the top is on the eastern face up the Tuckerman Ravine Trail. But countless trails offer plenty of moderate day hikes, like the Alpine Garden Trail, as an alternative to a summit attempt. Start at the Pinkham Notch Visitor Center on Route 16 to review your options.

BACKPACKING ON THE MOUNTAIN

Lakes of the Clouds Hut perches 5,050 feet up the southern shoulder, providing bunkrooms and meals in summer; reservations are required. On the eastern face, the **Hermit Lake Shelter Area** has shelters and tent platforms; to camp here you'll need a first-come, first-served permit from the Visitors Center. Both are operated by the **AMC** (☏ 603/466-2727; ⊕ www.outdoors.org).

NON-HIKING ALTERNATIVES

In the summer, the **Auto Road** (☎ 603/466-3988 ⊕ mtwashingtonautoroad.com) and the **Cog Railway** (☎ 800/922-8825 ⊕ www.thecog.com) present alternate ways up the mountain; both give you a real sense of the mountain's grandeur. In winter, a **SnowCoach** (☎ 603/466-3988 ⊕ mtwashingtonautoroad.com/snowcoach) hauls visitors 4.5 miles up the Auto Road with an option to cross-country ski, telemark, snowshoe, or ride the coach back down.

Sights

★ Flume Gorge

BODY OF WATER | FAMILY | A short but slightly hilly hike to this dramatic 800-foot-long chasm, which has narrow walls that cause an eerie echo from the gorge's running water, is the highlight of this popular state park. A long wooden boardwalk and a series of stairways lead to the top of the falls that thunder down the gorge. The 2-mile loop takes about an hour to complete. The boardwalk begins at the large and modern visitor center, which also has a gift shop, a cafeteria, and a small museum. Among the several somewhat touristy attractions in the western White Mountains, this one is a lot of fun for folks of all ages. ⊠ *Franconia Notch State Park, 852 Daniel Webster Hwy. (U.S. 3)* ☎ *603/745–8391* ⊕ *www.nhstateparks.org* ✉ *$16* ⊗ *Closed late Oct.–mid-May.*

The Frost Place Museum

HOUSE | Robert Frost's year-round home from 1915 to 1920, this is where the poet soaked up the New England life. The place is imbued with the spirit of his work, down to the rusted mailbox in front that's painted "R. Frost" in simple lettering. Two rooms contain memorabilia and signed editions of his books. Out back, you can follow short trails marked with lines from his poetry. This homestead on a peaceful unpaved road will slow you down and remind you of the intense beauty of the surrounding countryside. Poetry readings are scheduled on many summer evenings. ⊠ *158 Ridge Rd.* ☎ *603/823–5510* ⊕ *www.frostplace.org* ✉ *$5* ⊗ *Closed mid-Oct.–Apr.*

New England Ski Museum

LOCAL INTEREST | This small museum lets you travel back in time to see how skiing began as a sport, particularly in New England. Here you can examine artifacts, clothing, and equipment, as well as Bode Miller's five Olympic medals. For lifelong ski enthusiasts, the trip down memory lane will likely evoke warm smiles. ⊠ *Franconia Notch State Park, 135 Tramway Dr.* ⊕ *www.skimuseum.org* ✉ *Free* ⊗ *Closed Apr.–May.*

Old Man of the Mountain

NATURE SITE | FAMILY | This stately profile in the rock high above Franconia Notch crumbled somewhat unexpectedly in 2003. The iconic image had defined New Hampshire, and the Old Man's "death" stunned and saddened residents. Next to Cannon Mountain and overlooking Profile Lake, at the small Old Man of the Mountain Park, you can walk on a short but pretty paved trail to view the mountain face through steel rods that seem to literally put the beloved visage back on the mountain, and you can see photographs and memorabilia related to the history of the Old Man in a small museum and gift shop. ⊠ *Franconia Notch State Park, U.S. 3* ⊕ *www.oldmannh.org* ✉ *Free* ⊗ *Museum and shop closed mid-Oct.–mid-May.*

 Restaurants

★ Polly's Pancake Parlor

$ | AMERICAN | FAMILY | In the Dexter family for multiple generations, Polly's has been serving up pancakes and waffles (from its own original recipe) since the 1930s— the current space dates to 2015 but retains the original country charm. Try the smoked bacon and ham, eggs Benedict, sandwiches on homemade bread, delicious baked beans, and such tempting desserts as raspberry pie. **Known for:** gift shop selling maple products; gingerbread pancakes with blueberries; pretty hilltop setting. ⑤ *Average main: $10* ⊠ *672 Rte. 117* ☎ *603/823–5575* ⊕ *www.pollyspancakeparlor.com* ⊗ *No dinner.*

★ Sugar Hill Inn

$$$$ | MODERN AMERICAN | Inside this romantic 1789 farmhouse inn (the rooms are fantastic, too), you'll find a very elegant dining room where memorable prix-fixe meals ($69–$79) are prepared by one of the region's most accomplished chefs. The menu varies nightly according to what's in season, but examples have included a starter of smoked bluefish pâté with lemon preserve, and an entrée of roasted duck breast with duck-fat potatoes, carrot hash, and demi-glace. **Known for:** lighter à la carte menu in the tavern; artful homemade desserts; a long and impressive international wine list. ⑤ *Average main: $69* ⊠ *116 Rte. 117* ☎ *603/823–5621* ⊕ *www.sugarhillinn. com* ⊗ *Closed Wed. No lunch.*

Hotels

Franconia Inn
$ | RESORT | FAMILY | At this 100-acre family-friendly resort, you can play tennis on four clay courts, soak in the outdoor heated pool or hot tub, hop on a mountain bike, or soar in a glider—the cross-country ski barn doubles as a horseback-riding center in warm weather. **Pros:** nice option for families; packages available that include some meals; outdoor heated pool. **Cons:** a bit remote; historic hotel with some quirks; popularity with families can make it a little noisy for a quiet getaway. ⑤ *Rooms from: $149* ⊠ *1172 Easton Rd.* ☎ *603/823–5542, 800/473–5299* ⊕ *www.franconiainn.com* ⊗ *Closed Apr.–mid-May* ⌚ *34 rooms* ¶⊚¶ *No meals.*

Inn at Sunset Hill
$ | HOTEL | It's all about the view at this striking Victorian inn set high on a ridge in tiny Sugar Hill, its grounds including lovely gardens, a seasonal outdoor pool, and a great little golf course. **Pros:** mesmerizing views; adjacent to excellent 9-hole golf course; serene, relaxing setting. **Cons:** remote area a bit far from restaurants and activities; not a great option for kids; some rooms are shower-only (without tubs). ⑤ *Rooms from: $140* ⊠ *231 Sunset Hill Rd., Sugar Hill* ☎ *603/823–7244* ⊕ *www.innatsunsethill. com* ⌚ *28 rooms* ¶⊚¶ *Free breakfast.*

★ Sugar Hill Inn
$$ | B&B/INN | Although this upscale inn surrounded by neatly manicured gardens dates to 1789, it has a decidedly current

vibe, from its sumptuous rooms with such modern perks as flat-screen TVs and DVD players, refrigerators, and—in deluxe suites—whirlpool tubs, to the superb prix-fixe restaurant serving creative contemporary American fare. **Pros:** several rooms have gas fireplaces and private decks; packages available that combine dining in the fine restaurant; stylish decor. **Cons:** peaceful but somewhat remote setting; books up well ahead on weekends; not a good fit for families. ⑤ *Rooms from: $185* ⊠ *116 Rte. 117, Sugar Hill* ☎ *603/869–7543, 800/548–4748* ⊕ *www.sugarhillinn.com* ⌚ *15 rooms* ¶⊚¶ *Free breakfast.*

Activities

SKI AREAS
Cannon Mountain
SKIING/SNOWBOARDING | FAMILY | The first aerial tramway in North America was built here in 1938, and the view from the top of the 4,080-foot summit is spectacular on a clear day. The ride at this facility in Franconia Notch State Park is free with a ski lift ticket; otherwise it's $18. In winter, you'll find classic New England ski terrain that runs the gamut from steep pitches off the peak to gentle blue cruisers. Beginners may want to head over to the separate Tuckerbrook family area, which offers 13 trails and four lifts. Adventurous types will want to try out the Mittersill area, which has 86 acres of lift-accessed "side country" trails and glades where the snow is au naturel. **Facilities:** 97 trails; 285 acres; 2,180-foot vertical drop; 11 lifts. ⊠ *260 Tramway Dr., off U.S. 3* ☎ *603/823–8800, 603/823–7771 for snow conditions* ⊕ *www.can-nonmt.com* ⊠ *Lift ticket $79.*

Franconia Village Cross-Country Ski Center
SKIING/SNOWBOARDING | FAMILY | The cross-country ski center at the Franconia Inn has more than 40 miles of groomed and backcountry trails and rents skis, boots, and poles. One popular route leads to Bridal Veil Falls, a great spot

for a picnic lunch. You can also enjoy horse-drawn sleigh rides, snowshoeing, snow tubing, and ice-skating on a lighted rink. ⊠ *Franconia Inn, 1172 Easton Rd.* ☏ *603/823–5542, 800/473–5299* ⊕ *www. franconiainn.com/cross_country_ski_center.php* ⊠ *$12.*

🛍 Shopping

Sugar Hill Sampler
LOCAL SPECIALTIES | FAMILY | In this 1815 barn set high on a hill, you'll find an old-fashioned general store filled with quilts, lamps, candles, ornaments, and other crafts, along with gourmet jams, sauces, and condiments. In the back, owner Barbara Serafini has set up a folksy museum with local photos, newspaper clippings, and curiosities—Bette Davis's will among them. ⊠ *22 Sunset Rd., Sugar Hill* ☏ *603/823–8478* ⊕ *www.sugarhillsampler.com.*

Littleton

7 miles north of Franconia.

One of northern New Hampshire's largest towns (this isn't saying much, mind you) is on a granite shelf along the Ammonoosuc River, whose swift current and drop of 235 feet enabled the community to flourish as a mill center in its early days. The railroad came through some time later, and Littleton grew into the region's commercial hub. In the minds of many, it's more a place to stock up on supplies than a real destination itself, but few communities have worked harder at revitalization. Intriguing shops and eateries overlook the river and line Main Street, whose tidy 19th- and early-20th-century buildings suggest a set in a Jimmy Stewart movie.

GETTING HERE AND AROUND
Littleton sits just off Interstate 95. Take Exit 41 to Main Street, where you can explore downtown on foot.

ESSENTIALS

VISITOR INFORMATION Littleton Area Chamber of Commerce ☏ *603/444–6561* ⊕ *www.littletonareachamber.com.*

⊙ Sights

Thayers Inn
HISTORIC SITE | A former grande-dame hotel and still a working—albeit budget-oriented—inn, Thayers also functions as an informal museum. The 35 guest rooms have been upgraded with new linens and furniture, but enough antiques remain to lend it yesteryear charm, and the Olde English Pub on the ground floor is a welcoming spot for a drink or light bite to eat. In the lobby and lining the hall are photos and memorabilia from movie star Bette Davis's huge birthday bash and artifacts of other illustrious guests, including Ulysses S. Grant, Henry Ford, P. T. Barnum, and Richard Nixon. Request a key to climb up to the cupola for a 360-degree view of the town. Two rooms are open to the public: one set up as a guest room from the 1840s, and the other a scene from *Pollyanna*, written by Littleton native Eleanor Hodgman Porter (born 1868). ⊠ *111 Main St.* ☏ *603/444–6469* ⊕ *www.thayersinn.com.*

🍴 Restaurants

★ Schilling Beer Taproom
$ | AMERICAN | With a storybook setting in an converted 18th-century mill overlooking the Ammonoosuc River in downtown Littleton, this craft brewpub offers tasty wood-fired pizzas, bratwurst sandwiches, house-baked soft pretzels, and other fare that pairs well with its distinctive Belgian, German, Scandinavian, and other European ales. The pie topped with prosciutto, pears, chèvre, mozzarella, and beer-caramelized onions is a favorite, best enjoyed with a farmhouse-style saison. **Known for:** indoor and outdoor seating overlooking the river; beer tastings in the adjacent contemporary brewery building; great

pizzas. $ *Average main: $12* ⊠ *18 Mill St.* ☎ *603/444–4800* ⊕ *www.schillingbeer.com.*

★ **Tim-Bir Alley**

$$$ | **MODERN AMERICAN** | Here's a rare find in New Hampshire: an independent restaurant in a contemporary setting that's been serving customers for decades yet still takes its food seriously. The menu changes frequently and uses regional American ingredients in creative ways— on a typical night you might try spiced duck rillettes with pickled radishes and fig jam, or slow-braised, coffee-rubbed lamb breast with chimichurri, fava beans, and spring garlic. **Known for:** stylish yet unpretentious dining room; seasonal farm-to-table cuisine; beautifully plated desserts. $ *Average main: $25* ⊠ *7 Main St.* ☎ *603/444–6142* ⊕ *www.timbiralleyrestaurant.com* ▭ *No credit cards* ⊘ *Closed Mon. and Tues. No lunch.*

 Hotels

Mountain View Grand Resort & Spa

$$ | **RESORT** | **FAMILY** | Casual elegance and stunning views of the White Mountains define this stately yellow wedding cake of a hotel that dates to 1865 and sprawls over 1,700 acres that include a working farm and a well-maintained golf course. **Pros:** full-service spa; dozens of activities; babysitting service and summer camp. **Cons:** breakfast not included in rates; not too many dining options nearby; sometimes fills up with corporate meetings and retreats. $ *Rooms from: $189* ⊠ *101 Mountain View Rd., Whitefield* ☎ *855/837–2100* ⊕ *www.mountainviewgrand.com* ⇶ *144 rooms* ❑ *No meals.*

 Shopping

Little Village Toy and Book Stop

BOOKS/STATIONERY | **FAMILY** | Here you'll find maps or good books about the history of the area, along with unusual children's toys and many adult fiction and nonfiction titles. On the lower level is the League

of New Hampshire Craftsmen's shop, featuring glass, prints, ceramics, fiber, and more. ⊠ *81B Main St.* ☎ *603/444–4869* ⊕ *www.littlevillagetoy.com.*

Bethlehem

5 miles southeast of Littleton.

In the days before antihistamines, hayfever sufferers came by the trainload to this enchanting village whose crisp air has a blissfully low pollen count. Today this progressive, artsy hamlet with fewer than 1,000 residents is notable for its Art Deco Colonial Theatre (which presents indie films and concerts), distinctive galleries and cafés, and stately Victorian and Colonial homes, many of which line the village's immensely picturesque Main Street (U.S. 302), a highly enjoyable locale for an afternoon or evening stroll.

GETTING HERE AND AROUND
U.S. 302 and Route 142 intersect in the heart of this small village center that's easy to explore on foot.

 Sights

The Rocks Estate

FARM/RANCH | **FAMILY** | The estate of John Jacob Glessner (1843–1936), one of the founders of International Harvester, now serves as the 1,400-acre North Country Conservation and Education Center for the Forest Society. Some of the most striking restored buildings here are in the Shingle style. The property is named for the many surface boulders on the estate when Glessner bought it—some were used to erect its rambling rock walls. The Rocks presents natural-history programs and has self-guided tours and hiking trails with excellent views of the Presidential Range. Come winter, cross-country ski trails and a select-your-own-Christmas-tree farm open up. In early spring, watch syrup being made in the New Hampshire Maple Experience Museum. ⊠ *4 Christmas La., Bethlehem*

✢ Off Glessner Rd.🕿 603/444–6228
⊕ www.therocks.org.

Restaurants

The Maia Papaya

$ | CAFÉ | Pause during your stroll through the inviting hamlet of Bethlehem for breakfast, lunch, smoothies, lattes, or homemade chai tea at this endearingly quirky organic café that specializes in vegetarian fare and made-from-scratch baked goods (try not to pass up one of the justly renowned scones). On cool mornings, warm up with the rich and delicious bread pudding French toast; terrific lunchtime options include the artichoke melt panini or the bountiful green salad. **Known for:** plenty of gluten-free and vegetarian options; fruit-filled oat bars; organic oatmeal with local maple syrup. ⑤ Average main: $7 ✉ 2161 Main St., Bethlehem 🕿 603/869–9900 ⊕ www.themaiapapaya.com ⊗ No dinner.

Hotels

★ Adair Country Inn and Restaurant

$$$ | B&B/INN | An air of yesteryear refinement suffuses Adair, a three-story Georgian Revival home that attorney Frank Hogan built as a wedding present for his daughter in 1927—her hats adorn the place, as do books and old photos from the era. **Pros:** home to one of the area's most romantic restaurants; rates include a delicious breakfast and afternoon tea; cross-country skiing and hiking. **Cons:** removed from town; sometimes books up with weddings; closed for a month each fall and spring. ⑤ Rooms from: $229 ✉ 80 Guider La., Bethlehem 🕿 603/444–2600, 888/444–2600 ⊕ www.adairinn.com ⊗ Closed mid-Nov. and Apr. ⇥ 11 rooms ⧖ Free breakfast.

Milburn Inn

$$ | B&B/INN | A relaxing stroll along Main Street from Bethlehem's cluster of inviting restaurants and galleries, this grand 1908 mansion captures the monied ambience of this mountain hamlet's turn-of-the-20th-century heyday. **Pros:** great location; delicious breakfasts featuring fresh baked goods; famous guests have included Thomas Edison and Joe DiMaggio. **Cons:** on a slightly busy road; fills up fast on summer weekends; not an ideal fit for young kids. ⑤ Rooms from: $155 ✉ 2370 Main St., Bethlehem 🕿 603/869–3389, 800/457–9440 ⊕ www.mulburninn ⇥ 7 rooms ⧖ Free breakfast.

🛍 Shopping

★ Marketplace at WREN

ART GALLERIES | WREN (the Women's Rural Entrepreneurial Network) has been an vital force in little Bethlehem's steady growth into a center of artists, craftspersons, and other business owners, many of them women. At WREN's headquarters, there's an outstanding gallery that presents monthly juried exhibits and a retail gift boutique, Local Works, featuring crafts, foods, and other products (it has a second branch at the Omni Mount Washington Hotel). WREN also operates weekly summer farmers' markets in Bethlehem (Saturday 10–2) and Gorham (Thursday 3–7), and offers classes, produces a magazine, and acts as a community business incubator. ✉ 2011 Main St., Bethlehem 🕿 603/869–9736 ⊕ www.wrenworks.org.

Bretton Woods

14 miles southeast of Whitefield, 28 miles northeast of Lincoln/Woodstock.

In the early 1900s private railcars brought the elite from New York and Philadelphia to the Mount Washington Hotel, the jewel of the White Mountains. A visit to this Omni Hotels & Resorts property, which was the site of the 1944 United Nations conference that created the International Monetary Fund and the International Bank for Reconstruction and Development (and the birth of many conspiracy theories), is not to be missed. The area is also known for its cog railway to the summit of Mt. Washington, Bretton Woods ski resort, and access to some of the region's best hiking.

GETTING HERE AND AROUND

Bretton Woods is in the heart of the White Mountains on U.S. 302. A free shuttle makes it easy to get around the resort's various facilities.

Sights

★ Mount Washington Cog Railway

MOUNTAIN—SIGHT | FAMILY | In 1858, Sylvester Marsh petitioned the state legislature for permission to build a steam railway up Mt. Washington. One politico retorted that Marsh would have better luck building a railroad to the moon, but 11 years later the Mount Washington Cog Railway chugged its way up to the summit along a 3-mile track on the mountain's west side. Today it's one of the state's most beloved attractions—a thrill in either direction. A small museum at the base has exhibits about the cog rail, and a casual restaurant offers great views of trains beginning their ascent up the mountain. The full trip takes three hours including an hour spent at the summit. ⊠ *3168 Base Station Rd., 6 miles east of Bretton Woods* ☎ *603/278–5404, 800/922–8825* ⊕ *www.thecog.com* 🎫 *From $72* ⊘ *Closed Dec.–Apr.*

🍴 Restaurants

★ Bretton Arms Dining Room

$$$$ | MODERN AMERICAN | You'll find some of the best upscale cuisine in the area at this Omni Mount Washington Hotel restaurant that offers a far more intimate and romantic experience than the property's Main Dining Room. Locally sourced food features prominently on the menu, which changes regularly but might include *jamón Ibérico* with mustard and manchego cheese, bacon-wrapped Vermont quail, grilled Maine scallops with pork-belly ragout, and beef tenderloin with a bourbon demi-glace.

Known for: hearty breakfasts; thoughtful wine-pairing options for every course; well-curated children's menu. ⑤ *Average main: $40* ⊠ *310 Mt. Washington Rd.* ☎ *603/278–1000* ⊕ *www.omnihotels. com/hotels/bretton-woods-bretton-arms/ dining* ⊘ *No lunch.*

Fabyan's Station

$ | AMERICAN | FAMILY | A model train circles the dining room, a nod to the late 19th century, when 60 trains stopped at this former railroad station every day. Easygoing and family-friendly Fabyan's cooks up delicious pub fare, such as clam chowder, house-smoked ribs, and panfried trout. **Known for:** après-ski drinks; nice craft-beer selection; good kids' menu. ⑤ *Average main: $15* ⊠ *U.S. 302, 1 mile north of ski area* ☎ *603/278–2222* ⊕ *www.brettonwoods.com.*

🛏 Hotels

★ The Notchland Inn

$$$ | B&B/INN | Built in 1862 by Sam Bemis, America's grandfather of landscape photography, the gracious granite manor house conveys mountain charm on a scale seldom seen in this part of the state. **Pros:** Crawford Notch is simply a legendary setting, in the middle of the forest surrounded by mountains; marvelous house and common rooms; outstanding dinners. **Cons:** may seem too isolated for some; books far in advance on summer and fall weekends; not ideal for young kids. ⑤ *Rooms from: $275* ⊠ *2 Morey Rd., Hart's Location* ☎ *603/374–6131, 800/866–6131* ⊕ *www.notchland. com* 🍽 *15 rooms* ⑩ *Free breakfast.*

★ Omni Mount Washington Hotel

$$$ | RESORT | FAMILY | The two most memorable sights in the White Mountains might just be Mt. Washington and this dramatic 1902 resort with a 900-foot veranda, glimmering public rooms, astonishing views of the Presidential Range, and dozens of recreational activities like tubing, sleigh rides, horseback riding, and fly-fishing. **Pros:** incomparable setting and ambience; loads of amenities and dining options; free shuttle to skiing and activities. **Cons:** lots of kids running around the hotel; a bit of a drive from nearest decent-size town; rates can get very steep on summer–fall weekends. ⑤ *Rooms from: $272* ✉ *310 Mt. Washington Hotel Rd., off U.S. 302* ☎ *603/278–1000, 888/444–6664* ⊕ *www. mountwashingtonresort.com* ⤵ *200 rooms* |◎| *No meals.*

🏃 Activities

SKI AREA
★ Bretton Woods

SKIING/SNOWBOARDING | **FAMILY** | New Hampshire's largest ski area is also one of the country's best family ski resorts. The views of Mt. Washington alone are worth the visit, and the scenery is especially beautiful from the Latitude 44° restaurant, open during ski season.

The resort has something for everyone. Steeper pitches, near the top of the 1,500-foot vertical, and 35 glades will keep experts busy, and snowboarders will enjoy the three terrain parks. The Nordic trail system has 62 miles of cross-country ski trails. Both night skiing and snowboarding are available on weekends and holidays. Bretton Woods is also a great place to learn to ski. Trails appeal mostly to novice and intermediate skiers, including two magic carpet lifts for beginners, excellent programs geared to kids, and a children's snowmobile park at the base area as well as plenty of other diversions. Parents can purchase interchangeable family tickets that allow them to take turns skiing while the other watches the kids—both passes come for the price of one. The ski area also offers an adaptive program for anyone with disabilities.

The year-round Canopy Tour ($110) has nine ziplines, two sky bridges, and three rappelling stations. The tour is an exhilarating introduction to flora and fauna of the White Mountains. **Facilities:** 62 trails;

464 acres, 1,500-foot vertical drop; 10 lifts. ✉ *99 Ski Area Rd.* ☎ *603/278–3320, 603/278–1000 for conditions* ⊕ *www. brettonwoods.com* ✉ *Lift ticket $95.*

Crawford Notch State Park

NATIONAL/STATE PARK | **FAMILY** | Scenic U.S. 302 winds southeast of Bretton Woods through the steep, wooded mountains on either side of spectacular Crawford Notch, passing through Crawford Notch State Park, where you can picnic and take a short hike to Arethusa Falls, the longest drop in New England, or to the Silver and Flume cascades. The 5,775-acre park has a number of roadside photo opportunities, plus a visitor center, gift shop, snack bar, and picnic area. ✉ *1464 U.S. 302, Hart's Location* ☎ *603/374–2272* ⊕ *www. nhstateparks.org.*

Bartlett

18 miles southeast of Bretton Woods.

With Bear Mountain to its south, Mt. Parker to its north, Mt. Cardigan to its west, and the Saco River to its east, Bartlett—incorporated in 1790—has an unforgettable setting. Lovely Bear Notch Road (closed in winter) has the only midpoint access to the Kancamagus Highway. There isn't much town to speak of: the dining options listed are actually nearby in Glen. It's best known for the Attitash Ski Resort.

GETTING HERE AND AROUND

U.S. 302 passes though Bartlett, southeast from Bretton Woods and west from Glen, and accesses Attitash Ski Resort.

🍴 Restaurants

Red Parka Steakhouse & Pub

$$ | **AMERICAN** | **FAMILY** | This homey pub decorated with license plates and ski memorabilia has been an institution, especially during winter ski season, since the early 1970s, providing locals and tourists a fun and festive venue for après-ski or-hike socializing. Highlights among the traditional comfort fare include hand-cut steaks and barbecue ribs. **Known for:** live entertainment many evenings; locally sourced all-you-can-eat salad bar; beer served in mason jars. ⑤ *Average main: $22* ✉ *3 Station St., off U.S. 302, Glen* ☎ *603/383–4344* ⊕ *www.redparkapub. com* ⊗ *No lunch.*

White Mountain Cider

$$$ | **MODERN AMERICAN** | Set in a historic cider mill near the Saco River, this rustic yet elegant bistro and adjacent gourmet market and deli presses fresh cider in the fall—it's served with traditional home-made cider doughnuts. But the biggest draw is that it's also the best farm-to-table restaurant in the area, featuring a seasonal menu of eclectic, contemporary dishes, such as burrata with grilled stone fruit and a white balsamic–nasturtium reduction, and five-spice roasted duck with soba noodle salad and plum sauce. **Known for:** flavorful sandwiches and soups in the adjacent market; creative cocktails; friendly, knowledgeable service. ⑤ *Average main: $30* ✉ *207 U.S. 302, Glen* ☎ *603/383–9061* ⊕ *www. ciderconh.com* ⊗ *No lunch in restaurant.*

🛏 Hotels

Attitash Grand Summit Hotel & Conference Center

$$ | **HOTEL** | **FAMILY** | All of the pleasantly furnished rooms at this ski-in, ski-out condo-style resort at the base of Bear Peak have kitchenettes, and many have private balconies with splendid views. **Pros:** outdoor pool and hot tubs; ski-package discounts; kitchenettes in all rooms. **Cons:** generally bland accommodations; facility could use sprucing up; restaurants are a bit meh. ⑤ *Rooms from: $169* ✉ *104 Grand Summit Rd.* ☎ *603/374–1900* ⊕ *www.grandsummitat-titash.com* ⇄ *143 rooms* ⑩ *No meals.*

★ Bernerhof Inn

$$ | **B&B/INN** | Skiers, hikers, and adventurers who favor a luxurious, intimate lodging over a bustling condo resort adore staying in this grand Victorian inn operated with eco-friendly practices and furnished with a mix of fine antiques and period reproductions, along with such modern perks as iPod docks, flat-screen TVs, and—in most cases—double whirlpool tubs; all have electric or gas fireplaces. **Pros:** cooking classes available; full breakfast included; small but wonderfully relaxing spa with massage and body treatments. **Cons:** there's no longer a restaurant on-site; some rooms pick up a little road noise; not good for kids. ⑤ *Rooms from: $154* ✉ *342 U.S. 302, Glen* ☎ *603/383–4200, 877/389–4852* ⊕ *www.bernerhofinn. com* ⇄ *12 rooms* ⑩ *Free breakfast.*

Activities

SKI AREA

Attitash Ski Resort

SKIING/SNOWBOARDING | **FAMILY** | With a vertical drop of 1,750 feet, Attitash Mountain has dozens of trails to explore, and there are more on the adjacent Attitash Bear Peak (vertical drop 1,450 feet). You'll find traditional New England ski runs and challenging terrain alongside wide-open cruisers that suit all skill levels. There are acres of glades, plus a progressive freestyle terrain park. The Attitash Adventure Center has a rental shop, and also offers lessons and children's programs. **Facilities:** 68 trails; 311 acres; 1,750-foot vertical drop; 10 lifts. ✉ *775 U.S. 302* ☎ *800/223–7669* ⊕ *www.attitash.com* 🎫 *Lift ticket $87.*

Jackson

7 miles northeast of Bartlett.

★ Just off Route 16 via a red covered bridge, Jackson has retained its storybook New England character. Art and antiques shopping, tennis, golf, fishing, and hiking to waterfalls are among the draws, as well as the highest concentration of upscale country inns and boutique hotels in the state. When the snow falls, Jackson becomes the state's cross-country skiing capital, and there are also four downhill ski areas nearby—hotels and inns provide ski shuttles. Visit Jackson Falls for a wonderful photo opportunity.

ESSENTIALS
GETTING HERE AND AROUND
Jackson is on Route 16, just north of the junction with U.S. 302 in Glen.

VISITOR INFORMATION Jackson Area Chamber of Commerce ☎ 603/383–9356 ⊕ www.jacksonnh.com.

Sights

Story Land
AMUSEMENT PARK/WATER PARK | FAMILY | This theme park with life-size storybook and nursery-rhyme characters is geared to kids (ages 2–12). The 23 rides include a flumer, a river raft, and the Roar-O-Saurus and Polar Coaster roller coasters. Play areas and magic shows provide additional entertainment. ☒ 850 Rte. 16, Glen ☎ 603/383–4186 ⊕ www.story-landnh.com ☜ $32.

Restaurants

★ Inn at Thorn Hill
$$$ | AMERICAN | This famously romantic inn serves up memorable meals in an intimate dining room, with dim lighting and piano music trickling in from the lounge, and on a heated porch, which has views of the Presidential Range. The menu of complexly flavored regional American fare changes regularly but usually includes a few favorite classic dishes, such as New England clam chowder, braised boneless short ribs with mushroom gravy, and lobster ravioli with a sherry-butter sauce. **Known for:** sweeping mountain views; gracious service; breakfasts from a farm-to-table chalkboard menu. ⓢ Average main: $29 ☒ 42

Thorn Hill Rd. ☎ 603/383–4242 ⊕ www.innatthornhill.com ⊘ No lunch.

Red Fox Bar & Grille
$$ | AMERICAN | FAMILY | Some say this big family restaurant overlooking the Wentworth Golf Club gets its name from a wily fox with a penchant for stealing golf balls off the nearby fairway. Burgers, barbecue ribs, and wood-fired pizzas are on the dinner menu, along with more refined dishes such as seared sea scallops and bourbon steak tips. **Known for:** playroom for kids (and a good children's menu); wood-fired pizzas, steaks, and grills; all-you-can-eat Sunday breakfast buffet. ⓢ Average main: $22 ☒ 49 Rte. 16 ☎ 603/383–4949 ⊕ www.redfoxbarandgrille.com ⊘ No lunch weekdays.

Hotels

Inn at Ellis River
$$ | B&B/INN | Most of the rooms—which are all outfitted with armchairs and ottomans and floral-print duvet covers and featherbeds—in this unabashedly romantic 1893 inn on the Ellis River have fireplaces, and some also have balconies with Adirondack chairs and whirlpool tubs. **Pros:** pretty riverside location; abundantly charming; multicourse breakfasts and afternoon refreshments included. **Cons:** some rooms up steep stairs; not suitable for kids under 12; the least expensive rooms are a bit compact. ⓢ Rooms from: $169 ☒ 17 Harriman Rd., off Rte. 16 ☎ 603/383–9339, 800/233–8309 ⊕ www.innatellisriver.com ☜ 21 rooms ⦿ Free breakfast.

Inn at Jackson
$ | B&B/INN | This homey 1902 Victorian bed-and-breakfast—designed in 1902 by famed architect Stanford White for the Baldwin family of piano fame—is reasonably priced, charmingly furnished, and in the heart of the village. **Pros:** great value considering the charm of the rooms; peaceful setting; wonderful breakfasts. **Cons:** top-floor rooms lack fireplaces; bathrooms are basic and

could use updating; a bit frilly for some tastes. ⑤ *Rooms from: $139* ⊠ *Thorn Hill Rd. and Main St.* ☎ *603/383–4321, 800/289–8600* ⊕ *www.innatjackson.com* ⌒ *14 rooms* ⑩ *Free breakfast.*

★ The Inn at Thorn Hill & Spa

$$ | **B&B/INN** | With a large reception room and sweeping staircase, a deck overlooking the rolling hills around the village, and a common area with a wet bar and a cozy fireplace, this lovely inn—modeled after an 1891 Victorian designed by Stanford White—is breathtaking throughout. **Pros:** superb restaurant; soothing full spa; full breakfast included. **Cons:** rigid peak-season cancellation policy; no children under 16; rooms in carriage house and cottages are a bit less sumptuous. ⑤ *Rooms from: $215* ⊠ *42 Thorn Hill Rd.* ☎ *603/383–4242* ⊕ *www.innatthornhill. com* ⌒ *22 rooms* ⑩ *Free breakfast.*

Wentworth

$$ | **B&B/INN** | **FAMILY** | Thoughtful renovations have given new life and elegance to the 61 guest rooms at this baronial 1869 Victorian, whose amenities include a full spa, a first-rate restaurant, and access to a terrific golf course and cross-country ski trails. **Pros:** discounts at neighboring Wentworth Golf Club; interesting architecture; excellent farm-to-table restaurant. **Cons:** some rooms up steep stairs; two-night minimum many weekends; at a somewhat busy intersection. ⑤ *Rooms from: $219* ⊠ *1 Carter Notch Rd.* ☎ *603/383–9700, 800/637–0013* ⊕ *www.thewentworth. com* ⌒ *61 rooms* ⑩ *Free breakfast.*

Activities

SKI AREAS

★ Jackson Ski Touring Foundation

SKIING/SNOWBOARDING | **FAMILY** | Many experts rate this the best-run cross-country ski operation in the country. That's due to the great advice you get from the attentive staff, and to the 100 miles of groomed trails for skiing, skate skiing, and snowshoeing. The varied terrain offers something for all abilities. Jackson Ski Touring's 80 trails wind through covered bridges and into the picturesque village of Jackson, where you can warm up in cozy trailside restaurants. Lessons and rentals are available. ⊠ *153 Main St.* ☎ *603/383–9355* ⊕ *www.jacksonxc.org.*

Mt. Washington

12 miles north of Jackson.

At 6,288 feet, Mt. Washington is the highest peak in the northeastern United States. The world's highest winds, 231 mph, were recorded here in 1934. You can take a guided bus tour, a drive, or a hike to the summit. A number of trails circle the mountain and access the other peaks in the Presidential Range, but all of them are fairly strenuous and best attempted only if you're somewhat experienced and quite fit. It gets cold up here: even in the summer, you'll want a jacket.

GETTING HERE AND AROUND

Mt. Washington Auto Road heads west from Route 16 about 2 miles north of Wildcat Mountain ski resort and 8 miles south of Gorham.

Sights

★ Mt. Washington Auto Road

MOUNTAIN—SIGHT | **FAMILY** | The drive to the top of the imposing Mt. Washington is among the most memorable White Mountains experiences. Your route: the narrow, curving Mt. Washington Auto Road, which climbs 4,600 feet in a little more than 7 miles. Upon admission to this private road, drivers receive a CD with a narrated tour, along with a bumper sticker that reads, "This car climbed Mt. Washington." The narration is fascinating, and the views are breathtaking. Once at the top, check out **Extreme Mount Washington,** an interactive museum dedicated to science and weather. If you're a bit

The highest peak in New England, Mt. Washington rewards those who drive or hike to the top with spectacular views.

nervous about heights or the condition of your car, it's best to skip driving in favor of a guided bus tour or a ride up the cog railway in Bretton Woods. ⊠ *1 Mt. Washington Auto Rd., at Rte. 16, Pinkham Notch* ☎ *603/466–3988* ⊕ *www.mtwashingtonautoroad.com* 🚗 *Car and driver from $31; guided bus tour $36; museum $2 (free with auto tour)* ⊘ *Closed late Oct.–early May.*

Hotels

Glen House Hotel
$$ | **HOTEL** | The latest of four Glen House hotels that have stood on this site at the base of the Mt. Washington Auto Road since 1852, this upscale three-story retreat opened in 2018 in a Shaker-inspired building whose soaring windows, a yellow clapboard exterior, and simple lines hark back to its predecessors. **Pros:** easy access to Mt. Washington activities; beautifully designed; on-site restaurant and pool. **Cons:** remote area; may be a bit shiny and new for some tastes; limited dining options in the area. ⑤ *Rooms from: $179* ⊠ *979 Rte. 16, Pinkham Notch* ☎ *603/466–3420* ⊕ *www.theglenhouse.com* 🚗 *68 rooms* 🍴 *Free breakfast.*

Activities

All trails to Mt. Washington's peak are demanding and require a considerable investment of time and effort. Perhaps the most famous is the **Tuckerman Ravine Trail,** the path used by extreme skiers who risk life and limb to fly down the face of the steep ravine. The hike to the top can easily take six–nine hours round-trip. Because the weather here is so erratic, it's critical to check weather conditions, to be prepared, and to keep in mind that Mt. Washington's summit is much colder than its base. The average year-round temperature is below freezing, and the average wind velocity is 35 mph.

Great Glen Trails Outdoor Center
SKIING/SNOWBOARDING | **FAMILY** | This outdoor center at the foot of Mt. Washington is the base for year-around outdoor activities. Renowned for its dramatic

28-mile cross-country trail system, Great Glen provides access to more than 1,100 acres of backcountry. Trees shelter most of the trails, so Mt. Washington's infamous weather isn't such a concern. You can travel to the mountain's upper reaches in a Mt. Washington Snow-Coach, a nine-passenger van refitted with triangular snowmobile-like treads. You have the option of skiing or snowshoeing down or just enjoying the magnificent winter view. The center has a huge ski and sports shop, a food court, a climbing wall, and an observation deck. In summer it's the base for hiking, trail running, and biking, and has kayak rentals and excellent tours. ⊠ *1 Mt. Washington Auto Rd., at Rte. 16, Pinkham Notch* ☎ *603/466–3988* ⊕ *www.greatglentrails. com* 🎟 *Trail pass $20, SnowCoach $49.*

Pinkham Notch

HIKING/WALKING | Although not a town per se, scenic Pinkham Notch covers Mt. Washington's eastern side and has several ravines, including the famous Tuckerman Ravine. The Appalachian Mountain Club operates a visitor center that provides year-around trail information to hikers. Guided hikes leave from the center, and you can take outdoor skills workshops there. On-site are an outdoors shop, a lodge with basic overnight accommodations, and a dining hall. ⊠ *AMC Pinkham Notch Visitor Center, 361 Rte. 16, Pinkham Notch* ☎ *603/466–2721* ⊕ *www.outdoors.org/ lodging-camping/lodges/pinkham.*

Wildcat Mountain

SKIING/SNOWBOARDING | Glade skiers will love Wildcat and its 28 acres of designated tree skiing. Runs include some stunning double–black diamond trails; experts can really zip down the Lynx. Beginner skiers, as long as they can hold a wedge, should check out the 2½-mile-long Polecat, which offers excellent views of the Presidential Range. The trails are classic New England—narrow and winding—and the views are stunning. Beginners will find gentle terrain and a broad teaching

slope. For an adrenaline rush, there's a terrain park. In summer you can dart to the top on the four-passenger gondola, hike the many well-kept trails, and fish in the crystal clear streams. **Facilities:** 48 trails; 225 acres; 2,112-foot vertical drop; 5 lifts. ⊠ *Rte. 16, Pinkham Notch* ☎ *603/466–3326, 888/754–9453 for snow conditions* ⊕ *www.skiwildcat.com* 🎟 *$81 weekends.*

North Conway

12 miles south of Jackson, 41 miles east of Lincoln/North Woodstock.

Before the arrival of outlet stores, this town drew visitors for its inspiring scenery, ski resorts, and access to White Mountain National Forest. Today, however, the feeling of natural splendor is gone. Shopping is the big sport, and businesses line Route 16 for several miles. You'll get a close look at them as traffic slows to a crawl here. Take the scenic West Side Road from Conway to Intervale to circumvent the traffic and take in splendid views.

GETTING HERE AND AROUND

Park near the fire station on Main Street and spend half a day visiting the mostly indie shops and restaurants in this part of town.

ESSENTIALS

VISITOR INFORMATION Mt. Washington Valley Chamber of Commerce ☎ *603/356–5701* ⊕ *www.mtwashingtonvalley.org.*

Sights

Conway Scenic Railroad

SCENIC DRIVE | **FAMILY** | Departing from historic North Conway Station, the railroad operates various trips aboard vintage trains. The Notch Train to Crawford Depot (5 hours round-trip) or to Fabyan Station (5½ hours) travels through rugged territory yielding wonderful views. The First Class package includes a three-course lunch in the dining car, but the premium option gets you a seat in the Upper Dome car, which affords the most spectacular views. The Valley Train overlooks Mt. Washington during a 55-minute round-trip journey to Conway or a 1¾-hour excursion to Bartlett. The 1874 station displays lanterns, old tickets and timetables, and other artifacts. Reserve your spot early during foliage season. ✉ *38 Norcross Cir.* ☎ *603/356–5251, 800/232–5251* ⊕ *www.conwayscenic. com* 🖾 *From $18* ⊙ *Closed Dec.–Mar.*

Weather Discovery Center

INFO CENTER | **FAMILY** | Ever wonder what it's like to be in a cabin at the summit of Mt. Washington while 200 mph winds shake the rafters? Find out at this fun, interactive museum, where you can experience simulations of different weather conditions and learn about how weather affects our lives. There's a twice-daily video link (one late morning and one early afternoon) with scientists hard at work at Mount Washington Observatory. ✉ *2779 Main St.* ☎ *603/356–2137* ⊕ *www.mountwashington.org* 🖾 *$2.*

🍴 Restaurants

Delaney's Hole in the Wall

$ | **AMERICAN** | **FAMILY** | This casual tavern has a real fondness for ski history, displaying early photos of local ski areas, old signs and placards, and odd bits of lift equipment. Entrées range from fajitas that come sizzling out of the kitchen to mussels and scallops sautéed with spiced sausage and Louisiana seasonings. **Known for:** après-ski drinks; excellent sushi; watching games on TV in sports-bar section. ⑤ *Average main: $17* ✉ *2966 White Mountain Hwy. (Rte. 16)* ☎ *603/356–7776* ⊕ *www.delaneys.com.*

Table + Tonic Farm Bistro

$$ | **MODERN AMERICAN** | The green-thumb-savvy proprietors of the popular and adjacent Local Grocer natural foods market and café have opened this decidedly hip farm-to-table bistro and bar that

features seasonal fare produced with organic produce and baked goods and boldly flavored cocktails fashioned from house-made shrubs, bitters, syrups, and cordials. Here in this sleek yet rustic dining room you can feast on some of the most interesting cuisine in the Mt. Washington Valley, from grass-fed steak to smoked trout with heirloom tomatoes. **Known for:** healthy breakfast and lunch items in adjacent café and market; creative craft cocktails; house-made organic baked goods. ⑤ *Average main: $22* ✉ *3358 White Mountain Hwy. (Rte. 16)* ☎ *603/356–6068* ⊕ *www.tableandtonic. com* ⊙ *Closed Tues. and Wed. No lunch.*

Hotels

The Buttonwood Inn

$$ | **B&B/INN** | A tranquil oasis in a busy resort area, the Buttonwood sits on Mt. Surprise, 2 miles northeast of North Conway village—close enough to access area dining and shopping, but far away from noise and crowds of downtown. **Pros:** good bedding and amenities; year-round outdoor hot tub and fire pit; 6 acres of peaceful grounds. **Cons:** a bit remote for some; swimming pool is seasonal; some rooms have private baths down the hall. ⑤ *Rooms from: $179* ✉ *64 Mt. Surprise Rd.* ☎ *603/356–2625* ⊕ *www.buttonwoodinn.com* 🡒 *10 rooms* ⏀ *Free breakfast.*

Darby Field Inn

$$ | **B&B/INN** | Most rooms in this unpretentious 1826 farmhouse at the entrance to White Mountain National Park—just off the eastern end of the famously picturesque Kancamagus Highway—have stunning views, and several also have fireplaces. **Pros:** romantic setting; away-from-it-all feel; full country breakfast included with rates. **Cons:** better for couples than families; a drive to other restaurants; sometimes books up with weddings. ⑤ *Rooms from: $165* ✉ *185 Chase Hill, Albany* ☎ *603/447–2181* ⊕ *www.darby field.com* 🡒 *13 rooms* ⏀ *Free breakfast.*

White Mountain Hotel and Resort

$$ | RESORT | FAMILY | Rooms in this upscale contemporary hotel at the base of Whitehorse Ledge have splendid mountain views, and the proximity to White Mountain National Forest and Echo Lake State Park makes you feel farther away from the outlet malls than you actually are. **Pros:** gorgeous natural setting; fitness center and full-service spa; area is great for hiking and biking, and there's also a first-rate golf course. **Cons:** two-night minimum on busy weekends; not within walking distance of town; lacks historic charm. ⑤ *Rooms from: $219* ✉ *2560 West Side Rd.* ☎ *800/533–6301, 603/356–7100* ⊕ *www.whitemountainhotel.com* ⌑ *80 rooms* ⦿ *Free breakfast.*

Activities

FISHING

North Country Angler

FISHING | One of the best tackle shops in the state, North Country offers casting clinics and guided fly-fishing trips throughout the region. ✉ *2988 White Mountain Hwy.* ☎ *603/356–6000* ⊕ *www.northcountryangler.com.*

PARK

Echo Lake State Park

PARK—SPORTS-OUTDOORS | FAMILY | You don't have to be a rock climber to enjoy the views from the 700-foot White Horse and Cathedral ledges, which you can reach via a 1.7-mile road. From the top, you'll see the entire valley, including Echo Lake, which offers fishing, swimming, boating, and, on quiet days, an excellent opportunity to shout for echoes. ✉ *68 Echo Lake Rd., Conway* ☎ *603/356–2672* ⊕ *www. nhstateparks.org* ⦿ *$4 mid-May–mid-Oct.*

SKI AREAS

Cranmore Mountain Resort

SKIING/SNOWBOARDING | FAMILY | This fun-to-ski area has been a favorite with families since it opened in 1938. Most runs are naturally formed intermediates that weave in and out of glades. Beginners have several slopes and routes from the summit; experts must be content with a few short, steep pitches. Snowboarders can explore five different terrain parks. A mountain coaster, a tubing park, a giant swing, and a zipline provide additional entertainment. Night skiing is offered on Saturday and holidays. **Facilities:** 56 trails; 170 acres; 1,200-foot vertical drop; 9 lifts. ✉ *1 Skimobile Rd.* ☎ *800/786–6754* ⊕ *www.cranmore.com* ⦿ *Lift ticket $77.*

Mt. Washington Valley Ski Touring and Snowshoe Foundation

SKIING/SNOWBOARDING | Nearly 30 miles of groomed cross-country trails weave through the North Conway countryside, maintained by this foundation. Membership to the Mt. Washington Valley Ski Touring Club, available by the day or year, is required. Equipment rentals are available. ✉ *279 Rte. 16/U.S. 302, Intervale* ☎ *603/356–9920* ⊕ *www.mwvskitouring. org* ⦿ *From $7.*

Shopping

CLOTHING

More than 120 factory outlets—including L.L. Bean, J. Crew, New Balance, Columbia, Talbots, Polo, Nike, Banana Republic, and American Eagle—line Route 16.

Joe Jones' Sun & Ski Sports

CLOTHING | You'll find outdoor clothing and gear here, as well as that bathing suit you forgot to pack for the hot tub. Joe Jones' also rents gear and clothing. ✉ *2709 White Mountain Hwy.* ☎ *603/356–9411* ⊕ *www.sunandski.com.*

CRAFTS

Handcrafters Barn

CRAFTS | This place stocks the work of 150 area artists and artisans. ✉ *2473 White Mountain Hwy.* ☎ *603/356–8996* ⊕ *www.handcraftersbarn.com.*

Zeb's General Store

CRAFTS | FAMILY | This old-fashioned country store sells specialty foods, crafts, and clothing, as well as a range of products made in New England. ✉ *2675 Main St.* ☎ *800/676–9294* ⊕ *www.zebs.com.*

Kancamagus Highway

36 miles between Conway and Lincoln/ North Woodstock.

In 1937, two old town roads were connected to create this remarkable 35-mile stretch of roadway, winding through some of the state's most unspoiled mountain scenery. Kancamagus (pronounced kank-ah-MAH-gus) was one of the first roads in the nation to be designated a National Scenic Byway. No gas stations, hotels, gift shops, or billboards mar the vistas. There are numerous pulloffs for trailheads leading to memorable hikes, both easy and strenuous, and you'll see one great view after another: the White Mountains, the Swift River, Sabbaday Falls, Lower Falls, and Rocky Gorge. The highest point is just under 3,000 feet, on the flank of Mt. Kancamagus, near Lincoln. On-site or online you can purchase a parking pass ($5 per day or $30 annually) for White Mountain National Forest lots and overlooks.

Sights

★ Kancamagus Highway

SCENIC DRIVE | The section of Route 112 known as the Kancamagus Highway passes through some of the state's most unspoiled mountain scenery—it was one of the first roads in the nation to be designated a National Scenic Byway. The Kanc, as it's called by locals, is punctuated by overlooks and picnic areas, and erupts into fiery color each fall, when photo-snapping drivers really slow things down. In bad weather, check with the White Mountains Visitors Bureau for road conditions. ⊕ *www.kancamagushighway.com.*

⚡ Activities

Boulder Loop Trail

HIKING/WALKING | This 3.5-mile loop trail rises precipitously from the banks of the Swift River to a granite-crowned summit with expansive views, mostly south and west, over the surrounding mountains. The elevation gain of nearly 1,000 feet will give you a nice workout, but even novice hikers in reasonably good shape can make this climb, and the trail is less crowded than many others on the Kanc. The parking area is reached by crossing a quaint covered bridge. ⊠ *Trailhead on Passaconaway Rd., Albany ⊹ Off Rte. 112, next to Covered Bridge Campground* ⊕ *www.fs.usda.gov/whitemountain.*

Lincoln Woods Trail

HIKING/WALKING | FAMILY | This hiking trail off the Kancamagus Highway greatly rewards relatively little effort. Find the trailhead in the large parking lot of the Lincoln Woods Visitor Center, 5 miles east of Lincoln. The trail crosses a suspension bridge over the Pemigewasset River and follows an old railroad bed for 3 miles along the river. ⊠ *Trailhead on Kancamagus Hwy., 5 miles east of I–93, Exit 32* ☎ *603/530–5190* ⊕ *www.fs.usda. gov/whitemountain.*

★ Sabbaday Falls

HIKING/WALKING | FAMILY | The parking and picnic area for Sabbaday Falls, about 15 miles west of Conway, is the trailhead for an easy ½-mile route to this multi-level cascade that plunges through two potholes and a flume. Swimming is not allowed. From the flume, it's possible to continue your hike via a network of several other trails—see the posted map at the parking area for details. There are restrooms on-site. ⊠ *Trailhead on Kancamagus Hwy., 20 miles east of Lincoln, 16 miles west of Conway* ⊕ *www.fs.usda. gov/whitemountain.*

New London

33 miles west of Laconia, 40 miles northwest of Concord.

New London, the home of Colby-Sawyer College (1837), is a good base for exploring the Lake Sunapee region. A campus of stately Colonial-style buildings abuts the vibrant commercial district, where you'll find several cafés and boutiques.

GETTING HERE AND AROUND

You can reach downtown via Interstate 89, Exit 11, and then following Route 114. Mount Sunapee Ski Area offers a ski shuttle to and from many area hotels and inns.

Restaurants

Flying Goose Brew Pub & Grille

$$ | AMERICAN | Offering a regular menu of about a dozen handcrafted beers, including a much lauded black IPA and a heady barleywine as well as a few seasonal varieties—made with hops grown on-site—this restaurant, pub, and solar-powered brewery is a hit with beer connoisseurs. Diners go for the juicy ribs, paper-thin onion rings, fresh-cut steaks, and the burger topped with blue cheese and bacon. **Known for:** addictive white-truffle fries; ciders and gluten-free beer options; live music some evenings. ⑤ *Average main: $19* ✉ *40 Andover Rd., at Rtes. 11 and 114* ☎ *603/526–6899* ⊕ *www.flyinggoose.com.*

Hotels

Follansbee Inn

$ | B&B/INN | Built in 1840, this rambling country inn on the shore of Kezar Lake is the kind of place that almost automatically turns strangers into fast friends. **Pros:** relaxed lakefront setting with 3-mile walking trail; free use of canoes, kayaks, sailboats, rowboats, and bicycles; excellent breakfast. **Cons:** not all rooms have lake views; Wi-Fi can be spotty in places; no restaurants within walking distance. ⑤ *Rooms from: $139*

✉ *2 Keyser St., North Sutton* ☎ *603/927–4221* ⊕ *www.follansbeeinn.com* ⤸ *17 rooms* ❐ *Free breakfast.*

★ The Inn at Pleasant Lake
$$ | B&B/INN | Across Pleasant Lake from majestic Mt. Kearsarge and just a short drive from downtown New London, this 1790s inn has spacious, bright rooms filled with fine country antiques and high-end bedding. **Pros:** lakefront with a small beach; tennis courts; rates includes an outstanding full breakfast and afternoon tea. **Cons:** not within walking distance of town; restaurant closed Monday and Tuesday nights; two-night minimum stay on summer and fall weekends. ⑤ *Rooms from: $219* ✉ *853 Pleasant St.* ☎ *603/526–6271, 800/626–4907* ⊕ *www.innatpleasantlake.com* ⤸ *10 rooms* ❐ *Free breakfast.*

🎭 Performing Arts

New London Barn Playhouse
THEATER | FAMILY | Broadway-style musicals and children's plays are presented here every summer in New Hampshire's oldest continuously operating theater. ✉ *84 Main St.* ☎ *603/526–6710* ⊕ *www.nlbarn.org.*

Newbury

8 miles southwest of New London.

Newbury is on the edge of Mt. Sunapee State Park. The sparkling 6-square-mile lake and the mountain, which rises to an elevation of nearly 3,000 feet, serve as the region's outdoor recreation centers. The popular League of New Hampshire Craftsmen's Fair, the oldest crafts fair in the nation, is held at the base of Mt. Sunapee in early August.

GETTING HERE AND AROUND
From Interstate 89, head south on Route 103A, which follows the eastern shore of Lake Sunapee to Newbury.

◉ Sights

★ The Fells Historic Estate & Gardens
FOREST | John M. Hay, who served as private secretary to Abraham Lincoln and U.S. Secretary of State to Presidents William McKinley and Theodore Roosevelt, built the 22-room Fells on Lake Sunapee as a summer home in 1890. House tours offer a glimpse of late Victorian life on a New Hampshire estate. The grounds, a gardener's delight, include a 100-foot-long perennial garden and a rock garden with a brook flowing through it. Miles of hiking trails can also be accessed on this 83½-acre estate. You can tour the house yourself or on a guided 40-minute tour offered daily at noon. ✉ *456 Rte. 103A* ☎ *603/763–4789* ⊕ *www.thefells.org* ◷ *Apr.–Nov., $10 when house open, $8 when house closed; Dec.–Mar., $5 per household* ⊗ *House closed mid-Oct.–late May.*

Sunapee Harbor
BODY OF WATER | FAMILY | On the west side of Lake Sunapee, this old-fashioned summer resort community has a large marina, a handful of restaurants and shops on the water, a tidy village green with a gazebo, and a small museum. A plaque on Main Street outside the Wild Goose Country Store details some of Lake Sunapee's attributes: it's one of the highest lakes in New Hampshire, for example, and one of the cleanest. Lake Sunapee is home to brook and lake trout, salmon, smallmouth bass, perch, and pickerel. ✉ *Main St. at Lake Ave., Sunapee.*

🏖 Beaches

Mt. Sunapee State Park Beach
BEACH—SIGHT | FAMILY | A great family spot, this beach adjoining an 4,085-acre mountain park has picnic areas, fishing, and a bathhouse, plus access to great hiking trails. You can also rent canoes and kayaks, and there's a campground. **Amenities:** lifeguards; parking (fee); showers; toilets. **Best for:** swimming; walking.

✉ *86 Beach Access Rd.* ☎ *603/763–5561* ⊕ *www.nhstateparks.org* 🏊 *$5 mid-May–mid-Oct.*

🍴 Restaurants

Suna

$$ | MODERN AMERICAN | On a wooded country road just up the hill from Lake Sunapee, this lively little bar and bistro is a great find for a romantic meal or a relaxed bite to eat after a day on the water or hiking or skiing at Mt. Sunapee. The eclectic menu features a mix of classic American and Continental dishes with creative touches—consider starting with the lobster-asparagus flatbread or smoked Gouda tater tots, before graduating to beer-battered fish-and-chips with Creole tartar sauce, or Argentinian-style steak with chimichurri sauce. **Known for:** extensive wine list and craft cocktails; lively après-ski scene in winter; sublime desserts. ⑤ *Average main: $22* ✉ *6 Brook Rd., Sunapee* ☎ *603/843–8998* ⊕ *www.magicfoodsrestaurantgroup.com/suna* ⊙ *Closed Sun. and Mon.*

Wildwood Smokehouse

$ | BARBECUE | The hulking metal smoker outside this Old West–inspired tavern with high pressed-tin ceilings, chandeliers, and red Victorian wallpaper hints at the delicious barbecue served inside. Plates heaped with ribs, beef brisket, pulled chicken, and smoked bratwurst reveal the considerable skill of Wildwood's pit master, and plenty of tasty sides are offered, too, from mac and cheese to dirty rice. **Known for:** pecan pie; "hog wings" (pork shanks in barbecue sauce); popular early evening happy hour. ⑤ *Average main: $16* ✉ *45 Main St., Sunapee* ☎ *603/763–1178* ⊕ *www.wildwoodsmokehousebbq.com* ⊙ *Closed Sun. and Mon.*

Hotels

Sunapee Harbor Cottages

$$ | RENTAL | This cozy compound of six charming, eco-friendly cottages—each sleeping five–eight people and with small but well-equipped kitchens—is a stone's throw from Sunapee Harbor and an easy drive from winter skiing at nearby Mt. Sunapee. **Pros:** ideal for families or friends traveling together; free beach passes; pet-friendly. **Cons:** no maid service; little clothes storage; cottage porches overlook one another. ⑤ *Rooms from: $225* ✉ *4 Lake Ave., Sunapee Harbor* ☎ *603/763–5052* ⊕ *www.sunapeeharborcottages.com* 🛏 *6 cottages* ⦿ *No meals.*

Activities

BOAT TOURS

Sunapee Cruises

TOUR—SPORTS | This company operates narrated afternoon and dinner cruises of Lake Sunapee from June to mid-October. Ninety-minute afternoon cruises on the M/V *Mt. Sunapee* focus on Lake Sunapee's history and the mountain scenery. A buffet dinner is included on the two-hour sunset cruises aboard the M/V *Kearsarge*, a vintage-style steamship. ✉ *Town Dock, 81 Main St., Sunapee Harbor* ☎ *603/938–6465* ⊕ *www.sunapeecruises.com* 🏊 *From $20.*

SKI AREA

Mount Sunapee

SKIING/SNOWBOARDING | FAMILY | This family-friendly resort is one of New England's best-kept secrets. The owners have spent millions upgrading their snow machines and grooming equipment and turning this into a four-season resort. Mt. Sunapee offers over 1,500 vertical feet of downhill excitement, 11 lifts (including three quads), and 66 trails and slopes for all abilities. There are four terrain parks and nine glade trails. In summer, the adventure park features a canopy zipline tour, an aerial challenge course, an 18-hole disc-golf course, miniature golf, and numerous hiking trails. **Facilities:** 66 trails; 233 acres; 1,513-foot vertical drop; 11 lifts. ⊠ *1398 Rte. 103* ☎ *603/763–3500* ⊕ *www.mtsunapee. com* ⊠ *Lift ticket from $85.*

🛍 Shopping

Wild Goose Country Store
GIFTS/SOUVENIRS | FAMILY | On the harbor in Sunapee, this old-fashioned general store carries teddy bears, penny candy, pottery, and other engaging odds and ends. ⊠ *77 Main St., Sunapee* ☎ *603/763–5516.*

Hanover

30 miles northwest of New London, 50 miles north of Walpole.

Eleazar Wheelock founded Hanover's Dartmouth College in 1769 to educate the Abenaki "and other youth." When he arrived, the town consisted of about 20 families. Over time the college and the town grew symbiotically, with Dartmouth eventually becoming the northernmost Ivy League school. Hanover is still synonymous with Dartmouth, but it's also a respected medical and cultural center for the upper Connecticut River Valley.

Plan on spending a day visiting Hanover and to see all the sights on the Dartmouth campus. Shops, mostly of the independent variety but with a few upscale chains sprinkled in, line Hanover's main street. The commercial district blends almost imperceptibly with the Dartmouth campus. Hanover and West Lebanon, with Woodstock, Quechee, and White River Junction across the Connecticut River in Vermont, form something of a two-state vacation destination.

GETTING HERE AND AROUND
Lebanon Municipal Airport, near Dartmouth College, has service from Boston and White Plains, New York, by Cape Air. By car, Interstate 91 and Interstate 89 are the best ways to access the region.

ESSENTIALS
AIRPORT Lebanon Municipal Airport ⊠ *5 Airpark Rd., West Lebanon* ☎ *603/298– 8878* ⊕ *www.flyleb.com.*

VISITOR INFORMATION Hanover Area Chamber of Commerce ☎ *603/643–3115* ⊕ *www.hanoverchamber.org.*

Sights

Dartmouth College
COLLEGE | The poet Robert Frost spent part of a brooding freshman semester at this Ivy League school before giving up college altogether, but the school counts politician Nelson Rockefeller, actor Mindy Kaling, and author Theodor ("Dr.") Seuss Geisel among its many illustrious grads. The buildings clustered around the picturesque green, which is lovely for strolling, include the **Baker Memorial Library,** which houses such literary treasures as 17th-century editions of William Shakespeare's works. The library is also well-known for Mexican artist José Clemente Orozco's 3,000-square-foot murals that depict the story of civilization in the Americas. Free campus tours are available. ⊠ *N. Main and Wentworth Sts.* ☎ *603/646–1110* ⊕ *www.dartmouth.edu.*

Enfield Shaker Museum
MUSEUM VILLAGE | In 1782, two Shaker brothers from Mt. Lebanon, New York, arrived on Lake Mascoma's northeastern side, about 12 miles southeast of Hanover. Eventually, they formed Enfield, the ninth of 18 Shaker communities in the United States, and moved it to the lake's southern shore, where they erected more than 200 buildings. The Enfield Shaker Museum preserves the legacy of the Shakers, who numbered 330 members at the village's peak. By 1923,

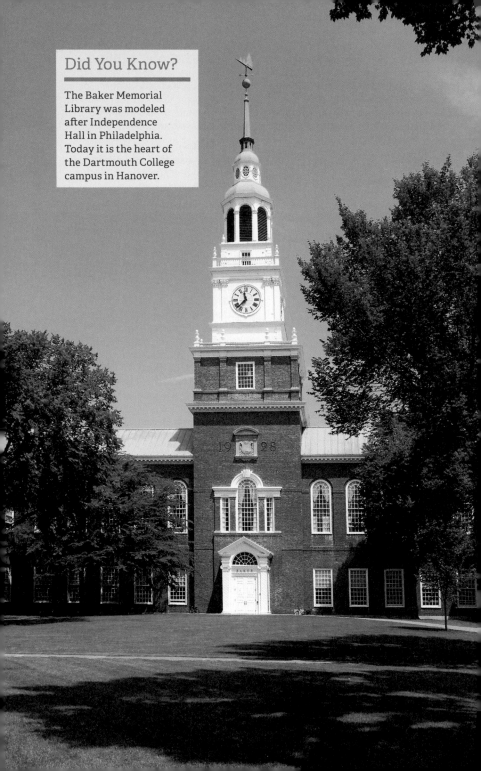

Did You Know?

The Baker Memorial Library was modeled after Independence Hall in Philadelphia. Today it is the heart of the Dartmouth College campus in Hanover.

interest in the society had waned, and the last 10 members joined the Canterbury community, south of Laconia. A self-guided walking tour takes you through 13 of the remaining buildings, among them an 1849 stone mill. Demonstrations of Shaker crafts techniques and numerous special events take place year-round. ⊠ *447 Rte. 4A, Enfield* ☎ *603/632–4346* ⊕ *www.shakermuseum.org* ✉ *$12.*

★ Hood Museum of Art

MUSEUM | Dartmouth's excellent art museum owns Picasso's *Guitar on a Table,* silver by Paul Revere, a set of Assyrian reliefs from the 9th century BC, along with other noteworthy examples of African, Peruvian, Oceanic, Asian, European, and American art. The range of contemporary works—including pieces by John Sloan, William Glackens, Mark Rothko, Fernand Léger, and Joan Miró—is particularly notable. Rivaling the collection is the museum's architecture: a series of austere, copper-roof, redbrick buildings arranged around a courtyard. The museum galleries received ambitious renovation and expansion, completed in early 2019, which includes five new galleries and a striking new entrance designed by the husband-and-wife architectural team of Tod Williams and Billie Tsien (known for the Barnes Foundation in Philadelphia, New York's downtown Whitney Museum, and many other famed works). ⊠ *Dartmouth College, Wheelock St.* ☎ *603/646–2808* ⊕ *hoodmuseum.dartmouth.edu.*

Hopkins Center for the Arts

ARTS VENUE | If the towering arcade at the entrance to the center appears familiar, it's probably because it resembles the project that architect Wallace K. Harrison completed just after designing it: New York City's Metropolitan Opera House at Lincoln Center. The complex includes a 900-seat theater for concerts and film screenings, a 480-seat theater for plays, and a black-box theater for new plays. This is the home of the Dartmouth Symphony Orchestra and

several other performance groups. ⊠ *2 E. Wheelock St.* ☎ *603/646–2422* ⊕ *hop. dartmouth.edu.*

Upper Valley

BODY OF WATER | From Hanover, you can make the 60-mile drive up Route 10 all the way to Littleton for a highly scenic tour of the upper Connecticut River valley. You'll have views of the river and Vermont's Green Mountains from many points along the way. The road passes through groves of evergreens, over leafy ridges, and through delightful hamlets. Grab gourmet picnic provisions at the general store on Lyme's village common and stop at the bluff-top village green in historic Haverhill (28 miles north of Hanover) for a picnic amid the panorama of classic Georgian- and Federal-style mansions and faraway farmsteads. ⊠ *Hanover* ⊕ *www.uppervalleychamber.com.*

🍴 Restaurants

★ Base Camp

$$ | NEPALESE | Arguably the best and definitely the most unusual of the several good ethnic restaurants in greater Hanover, this inviting restaurant in the lower level of a downtown retail-dining complex serves authentic, prepared-to-order Nepalese cuisine. Start with an order of momos (steamed dumplings) bursting with buffalo, paneer-and-spinach, wild boar, or several other fillings, and then try one of the easily shared tarkari (tomato-based) curries or chilies, offered with an extensive variety of meats and vegetables, from goat and duck to sweet potato and mushroom. **Known for:** everything can be prepared from mild to very spicy; plenty of meatless options; helpful, friendly staff. ⑤ *Average main: $19* ⊠ *3 Lebanon St.* ☎ *603/643–2007* ⊕ *www.basecamp-cafenh.com* ⊘ *No dinner Fri. and Sat.*

Lou's Restaurant

$ | AMERICAN | FAMILY | A Hanover tradition since 1948, this diner-cum-café-cum-bakery serves possibly the best breakfast

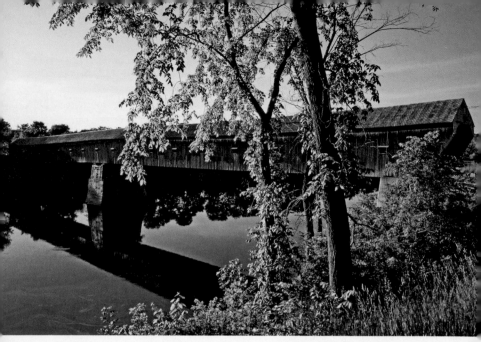

The Cornish–Windsor Bridge is the second-longest covered bridge in the United States.

in the valley, with favorites that include blueberry-cranberry buttermilk pancakes, and sausage-gravy biscuits with two eggs any style. Or just grab a seat at the old-fashioned soda fountain for a juicy burger and an ice-cream sundae. **Known for:** colorful mix of locals and Dartmouth folks; fresh-baked pastries and brownies; breakfast served all day. $ *Average main: $10* ⊠ *30 S. Main St.* ☎ *603/643–3321* ⊕ *www.lousrestaurant.net* ☾ *No dinner.*

Murphy's On the Green

$$ | **MODERN AMERICAN** | Students, visiting alums, and locals regularly descend on this wildly popular pub, which has walls lined with shelves of old books. The varied menu features burgers and salads as well as meat loaf, lobster mac and cheese, and vegetarian dishes like crispy-tofu pad Thai—and there's an extensive beer list. **Known for:** sourcing ingredients from local farms; dinner menu available until 11 pm; lots of veggie options. $ *Average main: $20* ⊠ *5 Main St.* ☎ *603/643–7777* ⊕ *www.murphysonthegreen.com.*

Hotels

Element Hanover–Lebanon

$$ | **HOTEL** | This sleek and well-oufitted outpost of Westin's trendy Element brand is the rare western New Hampshire lodging that feels both urbane and contemporary, with its angular furnishings, supercushy beds, and high-tech features, from keyless room entry to ergonomic work stations. **Pros:** stylish contemporary rooms; great for longer stays; indoor pool and fitness center. **Cons:** short drive from downtown Hanover; lacks the region's Colonial vibe; on a busy road. $ *Rooms from: $159* ⊠ *25 Foothill St., Lebanon* ⊹ *Off Rte. 120* ☎ *603/448–5000, 877/782–0151* ⊕ *www.elementhanover-lebanon.com* ⇗ *120 rooms* ❍❘ *Free breakfast.*

★ The Hanover Inn

$$$ | **HOTEL** | A sprawling Georgian-style brick structure rising six white-trimmed stories above Hanover's main square contains this chichi boutique hotel and is also home to the region's finest restaurant, Pine. **Pros:** center of campus

and town; two excellent restaurants and a fun bar; well-equipped fitness center. **Cons:** breakfast not included; pricey during busy times; books up way in advance many weekends. $ *Rooms from: $249* ✉ *The Green, 2 E. Wheelock St.* ☎ *603/643–4300, 800/443–7024* ⊕ *www.hanoverinn.com* ⥗ *108 rooms* ⑩ *No meals.*

Trumbull House
$$ | **B&B/INN** | The rooms at this white Colonial-style house on 16 acres on Hanover's outskirts have luxurious bedding, feather pillows, writing desks, and other comfortable touches; there's also a romantic guesthouse with a private deck, a whirlpool tub, a refrigerator, and a wet bar. **Pros:** many activities on-site; complimentary access to nearby health club; big breakfast. **Cons:** 3 miles east of town; not well-suited to children; a bit old-fashioned for some tastes. $ *Rooms from: $219* ✉ *40 Etna Rd.* ☎ *603/643–2370, 800/651–5141* ⊕ *www.trumbullhouse. com* ⥗ *6 rooms* ⑩ *Free breakfast.*

Activities

Ledyard Canoe Club
BOATING | On the banks of the Connecticut River, the Ledyard Canoe Club of Dartmouth rents canoes, kayaks, and standup paddleboards by the hour. The club also rents rustic cabins. ✉ *9 Boathouse Rd., below Ledyard Bridge* ☎ *603/643–6709* ⊕ *www.ledyardcanoeclub.org.*

Cornish

22 miles south of Hanover.

Today Cornish is best known for its covered bridges and for having been the home of the late reclusive author J. D. Salinger, but at the turn of the 20th century the village was known primarily as the home of the country's then-most-popular novelist, Winston Churchill (no relation to the British prime minister). His novel *Richard Carvel* sold more than

a million copies. Churchill was such a celebrity that he hosted Theodore Roosevelt during the president's 1902 visit. At that time Cornish was an artistic enclave: painter Maxfield Parrish lived and worked here, and sculptor Augustus Saint-Gaudens set up his studio here, where he created the heroic bronzes for which he is known.

GETTING HERE AND AROUND
About 5 miles west of town off Route 12A, the Cornish–Windsor Bridge crosses the Connecticut River between New Hampshire and Vermont. The Blacksmith Shop covered bridge is 2 miles east of Route 12A on Town House Road, and the Dingleton Hill covered bridge is 1 mile east of Route 12A on Root Hill Road.

◉ Sights

Cornish-Windsor Bridge
BRIDGE/TUNNEL | This 460-foot bridge, 1½ miles south of the Saint-Gaudens National Historic Site, connects New Hampshire to Vermont across the Connecticut River. Erected in 1866, it is the longest covered wooden bridge in the United States. The notice on the bridge reads, "Walk your horses or pay two dollar fine." ✉ *Bridge St.*

★ Saint-Gaudens National Historic Site
GARDEN | In rural Cornish, a small road leads to this historic site that celebrates the life and artistry of Augustus Saint-Gaudens, a leading 19th-century sculptor with major works on Boston Common and in Manhattan's Central Park. You can tour his house (with original furnishings), studio, and gallery, as well as 150 acres of gorgeous grounds and gardens, scattered throughout which are casts of his works. The property has two hiking trails, the longer of which is the Blow-Me-Down Trail. Concerts are held at 2 pm on Sundays in July and August. ✉ *139 Saint-Gaudens Rd., off Rte. 12A* ☎ *603/675–2175* ⊕ *www.nps.gov/saga* ⥗ *$10.*

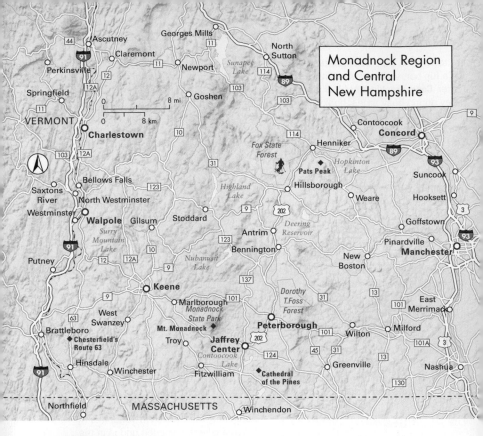

Manchester

45 miles west of Portsmouth, 53 miles north of Boston, 75 miles southeast of Hanover.

With 111,000-plus residents, Manchester is New Hampshire's largest city. The town grew up around the Amoskeag Falls on the Merrimack River, which drove small textile mills through the 1700s. By 1828 Boston investors had bought the rights to the Merrimack's water power and built the Amoskeag Mills, which became a testament to New England's manufacturing capabilities. In 1906 the mills employed 17,000 people and churned out more than 4 million yards of cloth weekly. This vast enterprise served as Manchester's entire economic base; when it closed in 1936, the town was devastated.

Today Manchester is mainly a banking and business center, but many of the old mill buildings have been converted into condos, restaurants, museums, and office space, and both the dining and arts scenes have begun to flourish in recent years. The city has the state's major airport, as well as SNHU Arena, which hosts minor-league hockey games and concerts.

GETTING HERE AND AROUND

The state's largest airport, Manchester-Boston Regional Airport, is a modern, cost-effective, and hassle-free alternative to Boston's Logan Airport, with nonstop service from about a dozen cities. Public transit is impractical for visitors—a car is your best way to get around.

ESSENTIALS

AIRPORT Manchester-Boston Regional Airport ⊠ *1 Airport Rd.* ☏ *603/624–6539* ⊕ *www.flymanchester.com.*

VISITOR INFORMATION Greater Manchester Chamber of Commerce ☏ *603/792–4100* ⊕ *www.manchester-chamber.org.*

 Sights

★ **Currier Museum of Art**

BUILDING | The Currier maintains an astounding permanent collection of works by European and American masters, among them Claude Monet, Edward Hopper, Winslow Homer, John Marin, Andrew Wyeth, and Childe Hassam, and it presents changing exhibits of contemporary art. The museum also arranges guided tours of the nearby Zimmerman House. Completed in 1950, it's New England's only Frank Lloyd Wright–designed residence open to the public. Wright called this sparse, utterly functional living space "Usonian," a term he used to describe several dozen similar homes based on his vision of distinctly American architecture. ⊠ *150 Ash St.* ☏ *603/669–6144* ⊕ *www.currier.org* 🎟 *$15; $25 for Zimmerman House.*

Millyard Museum

LIBRARY | **FAMILY** | In one of the most architecturally striking Amoskeag Mills buildings, state-of-the-art exhibits depict the region's history from when Native Americans lived here and fished the Merrimack River to when the machines of Amoskeag Mills wove cloth. The museum also offers lectures and walking tours, and has a child-oriented Discovery Gallery. There's a very good book and gift shop, too. ⊠ *200 Bedford St.* ☏ *603/622–7531* ⊕ *www.manchesterhistoric.org* 🎟 *$8* ⊗ *Closed Sun. and Mon.*

★ **SEE Science Center**

LOCAL INTEREST | **FAMILY** | The world's largest permanent LEGO installation at minifigure scale, depicting Amoskeag Millyard and Manchester as they looked a century ago, is the star attraction at this hands-on science lab and children's museum. The mind-blowing exhibit, covering 2,000 square feet, is made up of about 3 million LEGO bricks. It conveys the massive size and importance of the mills, which ran a mile on each side of the Merrimack. The museum also contains touch-friendly interactive exhibits and offers daily science demonstrations. ⊠ *Amoskeag Millyard, 200 Bedford St.* ☏ *603/669–0400* ⊕ *www.see-sciencecenter.org* 🎟 *$9.*

 Restaurants

Cotton

$$ | **AMERICAN** | Mod lighting and furnishings lend this restaurant inside an old Amoskeag Mills building a swanky atmosphere, although on warm days you may want to have a seat on the patio, set in an arbor. The farm-to-table-inspired comfort food changes regularly but has featured pan-seared crab cakes, tuna tataki with wasabi aioli, and Delmonico steak with a choice of sauces. **Known for:** entrée-size salads; creative mixed drinks; handsome converted-warehouse setting. ⑤ *Average main: $23* ⊠ *75 Arms St.* ☏ *603/622–5488* ⊕ *www.cottonfood.com* ⊗ *No lunch weekends.*

★ **Red Arrow Diner**

$ | **AMERICAN** | One of New England's most celebrated diners, this bustling downtown greasy spoon has been catering to politicians, students, artists, and everyone in between since 1922. This colorful restaurant, open around the clock, is a friendly place with fresh daily specials as well as such classics as kielbasa-and-cheese omelets and triple-bun Dinahmoe burgers. **Known for:** filling breakfasts; colorful people-watching; house-brewed root beer and cream soda. ⑤ *Average main: $10* ⊠ *61 Lowell St.* ☏ *603/626–1118* ⊕ *www.redarrowdiner.com.*

Republic Cafe & Bistro

$$ | **MEDITERRANEAN** | A key player in downtown Manchester's steady ascendance into a bona fide dining and nightlife hub, this all-day bistro serves artfully prepared Mediterranean fare, with most ingredients sourced within a 50-mile radius. You can make a meal of several small plates—red-lentil cakes, lamb kefta, fig–and–goat cheese flatbreads—or tuck into one of the larger portions, perhaps steak frites or chickpea ragù. **Known for:** stylish, high-ceilinged interior; friendly vibe; first-rate espresso drinks. $ *Average main: $20* ⊠ *1069 Elm St.* ☎ *603/666–3723* ⊕ *www.republiccafe.com.*

Restoration Cafe
$ | **CAFÉ** | Set on the ground floor of a vintage redbrick apartment building on the east side of downtown, this hip café and gathering spot excels both with drinks—everything from nitro cold brews to creative smoothies—and healthy, well-crafted food. At breakfast, consider the egg-cheddar-chive brioche sandwich, while tandoori bowls and rare-seared tuna sandwiches, along with craft cocktails and beers, are popular late in the day; the café closes at 4 most afternoons but is open until 8 on Friday and Saturday evenings. **Known for:** healthy smoothies; sleek industrial vibe; cheerful outdoor patio. $ *Average main: $9* ⊠ *235 Hanover St.* ☎ *603/518–7260* ☉ *No dinner.*

 Hotels

Ash Street Inn
$$ | **B&B/INN** | Each of the five rooms in this striking sage-green 1885 bed-and-breakfast is painted a different color, and all have soft bathrobes, flat-screen satellite TVs, and beds topped with Egyptian cotton linens. **Pros:** stylishly decorated rooms; within walking distance of Currier Museum and many restaurants; complimentary off-street parking. **Cons:** no pets allowed; not a great choice for children; pricey for Manchester. $ *Rooms from: $209* ⊠ *118 Ash St.* ☎ *603/668–9908* ⊕ *www.ashstreetinn.com* ⌁ *5 rooms* ⋈ *Free breakfast.*

★ Bedford Village Inn
$$ | **RESORT** | If you've decided to venture a few miles southwest of Manchester to this lovely manor, you'll be rewarded by comfort, beauty, and sheer luxury. **Pros:** among the most lavish accommodations in the state; gorgeous gardens and grounds; outstanding restaurants and bars. **Cons:** in a suburb outside Manchester; pricey; often booked with weddings on weekends. $ *Rooms from: $219* ⊠ *2 Olde Bedford Way, Bedford* ☎ *603/472–2001, 800/852–1166* ⊕ *www.bedfordvillageinn.com* ⌁ *64 rooms* ⋈ *No meals.*

Manchester Downtown Hotel
$$ | **HOTEL** | Of Manchester's full-service downtown hotels, this 12-story tower has the most central location: a short walk from Amoskeag Mills and the growing cluster of dining options along Elm Street. **Pros:** central downtown location; free airport shuttle; indoor pool and fitness center. **Cons:** there's a fee for parking; unexciting decor; tends to draw a lot of meetings and conferences. $ *Rooms from: $161* ⊠ *700 Elm St.* ☎ *603/625–1000* ⊕ *www.manchesterdowntownhotel.com* ⌁ *252 rooms* ⋈ *No meals.*

 Nightlife

BARS
Backyard Brewery
BREWPUBS/BEER GARDENS | Head to this spacious brewpub, with ample indoor and outdoor seating as well as a pool hall, for some of the more creative craft beers in the region, from hoppy Belgian-style ales to the rich Stone Wall milk stout. There's a full-service food menu, too. ⊠ *1211 S. Mammoth Rd.* ☎ *603/623–3545* ⊕ *www.backyardbrewerynh.com.*

815
BARS/PUBS | A scene-y crowd mixes and mingles at this dimly lighted Prohibition Era–inspired, speakeasy-style cocktail bar with plush arm chairs and sofas and Oriental rugs, and an impressive list of

both innovative and classic cocktails, plus unusual local and international beers. ✉ *825 Elm St.* ☎ *603/782–8086* ⊕ *www.ivotewet.com.*

Performing Arts

THEATERS

The Palace Theatre

CONCERTS | The 1914 Palace, a former vaudeville house, presents musicals and plays, comedy, and concerts throughout the year. ✉ *80 Hanover St.* ☎ *603/668–5588* ⊕ *www.palacetheatre.org.*

Shopping

Bedford Farmers' Market

FOOD/CANDY | **FAMILY** | Held mid-May–late October just outside Manchester, this Saturday market hosts a rich mix of local growers and food purveyors selling seasonal jams, pasture-raised lamb and chicken, homemade treats for dogs and cats, goats' milk soaps and balms, and even New Hampshire wines. There's usually live music, along with activities for children. ✉ *St. Elizabeth Seton Parish parking lot, 190 Meetinghouse Rd., Bedford* ⊕ *www.bedfordfarmersmarket.org.*

Concord

20 miles north of Manchester, 47 miles west of Portsmouth.

New Hampshire's capital (population 43,000) is a small and somewhat quiet city that tends to state business and little else—traditionally, the sidewalks roll up promptly at 6, although downtown has lately experienced an influx of restaurants and bars. Stop in town to get a glimpse of New Hampshire's State House, which is crowned by a gleaming, eagle-topped gold dome.

GETTING HERE AND AROUND

Interstate 93 bisects Concord north–south and is intersected by Interstate 89 and U.S. 202, which becomes Interstate

393 near the city line. Main Street near the State House is walkable, but a car is the best way to explore farther afield.

ESSENTIALS

VISITOR INFORMATION Greater Concord Chamber of Commerce ☎ *603/224–2508* ⊕ *www.concordnhchamber.com.*

Sights

McAuliffe-Shepard Discovery Center

MUSEUM | **FAMILY** | New England's only air-and-space center offers a full day of activities focused mostly on the heavens. See yourself in infrared light, learn about lunar spacecraft, examine a replica of the Mercury-Redstone rocket, or experience what it's like to travel in space—you can even try your hand at being a television weather announcer. There's also a café. ✉ *2 Institute Dr.* ☎ *603/271–7827* ⊕ *www.starhop.com* 💲 *$12.*

New Hampshire Historical Society

LIBRARY | Steps from the state capitol, this museum is a great place to learn about the Concord coach, a popular mode of transportation before railroads. The Discovering New Hampshire exhibit delves into a number of facets of the state's heritage, from politics to commerce. Rotating shows might include locally made quilts or historical portraits of residents. ✉ *30 Park St.* ☎ *603/228–6688* ⊕ *www.nhhistory.org* 💲 *$7* ⊗ *Closed Sun. and Mon.*

Pierce Manse

HOUSE | Franklin Pierce lived in this Greek Revival home before he moved to Washington to become the 14th U.S. president. He's buried nearby. A guided tour covers his life in mid-19th-century historical context. ✉ *14 Horseshoe Pond La.* ☎ *603/225–4555* ⊕ *www.pierce-manse.org* 💲 *$7* ⊗ *Closed Mon. and early Oct.–mid-June.*

★ **State House**

GOVERNMENT BUILDING | The gilded-dome state house, built in 1819, is the nation's oldest capitol building in which the legislature still uses the original chambers. From January through June, you can watch the two branches in action. The Senate has 24 members, and the House house has 400—a ratio of 1 representative per 3,500 residents (a world record). The visitor center coordinates guided and self-guided tours, bookable online or on-site, and displays history exhibits and paraphernalia from presidential primaries. ⊠ *Visitor center, 107 N. Main St.* ☎ *603/271–2154* ⊕ *www.gencourt.state.nh.us/nh_visitor-center/default.htm* ⊠ *Free.*

🍴 Restaurants

Arnie's Place

$ | **AMERICAN** | **FAMILY** | With more than 50 kinds of homemade ice cream—raspberry and toasted coconut are favorites—plus pretty tasty short-order fare like burgers, lobster rolls, hot dogs, and barbecue platters, this casual roadside eatery is perfect for a quick and satisfying bite to eat. You can eat in the small dining room or order at one of five walk-up windows, then grab your grub and head to one of the picnic tables. **Known for:** chocolate shakes; barbecue pulled pork and ribs; soft-serve and traditional ice cream. Ⓢ *Average main: $10* ⊠ *164 Loudon Rd., Concord Heights* ☎ *603/228–3225* ⊕ *www.arniesplace. com* ⊗ *Closed late Oct.–late Feb.*

★ Revival

$$ | **MODERN AMERICAN** | In this handsome, high-ceilinged redbrick building on a downtown side street, foodies and revelers congregate for some of the most creative and accomplished regional American cuisine in the Merrimack Valley. Highlights, in addition to an impressive selection of whiskies and cognacs, might include an artful platter of charcuterie and New England artisanal cheeses, hearty rabbit stew, and seared salmon with pancetta and olive tapenade, but the menu changes often. **Known for:** ingredients sourced from local farms; see-and-be-seen vibe, especially at the bar;

decadent desserts. Ⓢ *Average main: $22* ⊠ *11 Depot St.* ☎ *603/715–5723* ⊕ *www. revivalkitchennh.com* ⊗ *Closed Sun. and Mon. No lunch.*

Hotels

★ The Centennial

$$ | **HOTEL** | The most stylish and romantic hotel in the Merrimack Valley occupies a an imposing brick-and-stone building constructed in 1892 for widows of Civil War veterans, but the interior has been given a head-to-toe makeover: boutique furnishings and contemporary art immediately set the tone in the lobby; pillow-top beds sport luxurious linens and down pillows; and bathrooms have stone floors, granite countertops, and stand-alone showers. **Pros:** sleek redesign of historic structure; smartly designed room and bathrooms; great bar and restaurant. **Cons:** not within walking distance of downtown dining; rooms facing road can get a little road noise; no pets. Ⓢ *Rooms from: $179* ⊠ *96 Pleasant St.* ☎ *603/227–9000* ⊕ *www.thecentennialhotel.com* ⊷ *32 rooms* ⦿ *No meals.*

🎭 Performing Arts

Capitol Center for the Arts

ARTS CENTERS | The Egyptian-motif artwork, part of the original 1927 decor, has been restored in the former Capitol Theatre. Now the Capitol Center for the Arts, it hosts touring Broadway shows, dance companies, and musical acts. ⊠ *44 S. Main St.* ☎ *603/225–1111* ⊕ *www.ccanh.com.*

Charlestown

70 miles northwest of Concord, 37 miles south of Hanover.

Charlestown boasts one of the state's largest historic districts, with about 60 homes—all handsome examples of Federal, Greek Revival, and Gothic Revival architecture (and 10 built before

1800)—clustered about the town center. Several merchants on the main street distribute interesting walking tour brochures of the district.

GETTING HERE AND AROUND
You can reach Charlestown from Interstate 91, but it's best to follow Route 12 north from Keene for the gorgeous scenery.

Sights

Fort at No. 4
HISTORIC SITE | FAMILY | In 1747, this fort 1½ miles north of downtown Charlestown was an outpost on the periphery of Colonial civilization. That year fewer than 50 militiamen at the fort withstood an attack by 400 French soldiers, ensuring that northern New England remained under British rule. Today, costumed interpreters at this living-history museum cook dinner over an open hearth and demonstrate weaving, gardening, and candle making. Each year the museum holds reenactments of militia musters and the battles of the French and Indian War. ✉ 267 Springfield Rd. (Rte. 11) ☎ 603/826–5700 ⊕ www.fortat4.com ☒ $10 ⊗ Closed Mon. and Tues. and Nov.–Apr.

Walpole

12 miles south of Charlestown.

Walpole possesses one of the state's most perfect town greens. Bordered by Elm and Washington Streets, it's surrounded by homes dating to 1790 or so, when the townsfolk constructed a canal around the Great Falls of the Connecticut River, bringing commerce and wealth to the area. The town now has 3,900 inhabitants, more than a dozen of whom are millionaires. Walpole is also home to Florentine Films, documentarian Ken Burns's production company.

GETTING HERE AND AROUND
Walpole is a short jaunt off Route 12, north of Keene.

Restaurants

★ The Restaurant at Burdick's
$$ | FRENCH | Famous artisanal chocolatier and Walpole resident Larry Burdick, who sells his hand-filled, hand-cut chocolates to top restaurants around the country, operates this acclaimed restaurant next door to the shop. With the easygoing sophistication of a Parisian café and incredibly rich desserts, the restaurant features a French-inspired menu that utilizes fresh, often local, ingredients and changes daily. **Known for:** noteworthy wine list; adjacent gourmet grocery with delicious picnic supplies; decadent desserts featuring house-made chocolates and pastries. ⑤ Average main: $22 ✉ 47 Main St. ☎ 603/756–9058 ⊕ www.47mainwalpole.com ⊗ No dinner Sun. and Mon.

Shopping

Boggy Meadow Farm
FOOD/CANDY | FAMILY | At this farm, you can watch the cheese-making process unfold, from the 200 cows being milked to the finer process of cheese making. Boggy Meadow cheeses can be sampled in the store, where you can also order cheese boards, cider doughnuts, and root vegetables. It's worth the trip just to see the beautiful 400-acre farm. ✉ 13 Boggy Meadow La. ☎ 603/756–3300 ⊕ www.boggymeadowfarm.com.

Keene

17 miles southeast of Walpole, 20 miles northeast of Brattleboro, Vermont.

Keene, the largest city in southwestern New Hampshire (population 24,000), has one of the prettiest and widest main streets in the state, with several engaging boutiques and cafés—you can spend a fun few hours strolling along it. Home to Keene State College, the city's atmosphere is youthful and lively, with its funky crafts stores and eclectic entertainment, like the Monadnock International Film Festival, held in April.

ESSENTIALS

VISITOR INFORMATION Greater Keene Chamber of Commerce ☎ *603/352–1303* ⊕ *www.keenechamber.com* **Monadnock Travel Council** ⊕ *www.monadnocktravel. com.*

Sights

Chesterfield's Route 63

BODY OF WATER | For a gorgeous country drive, especially during fall foliage season, head west from Keene along Route 9 to Route 63 (about 11 miles) and turn left toward the hilltop town of Chesterfield. This is an especially rewarding journey at sunset: from many points along the road you can see west out over the Connecticut River valley and into Vermont. The village center itself consists of little more than a handful of dignified granite buildings and a small general store. ✉ *Chesterfield.*

Keene State College

ARTS VENUE | The hub of the local arts community is this bustling college. The permanent collection of the Thorne-Sagendorph Art Gallery includes works by Richard Sumner Meryman, Abbott Handerson Thayer, and Robert Mapplethorpe. ✉ *Thorne-Sagendorph Art Gallery, 229 Main St.* ☎ *603/358–2720* ⊕ *www.keene. edu* ☉ *Gallery closed June–Aug.*

Restaurants

★ Luca's Mediterranean Café

$$ | **MEDITERRANEAN** | A deceptively simple storefront bistro with sidewalk tables overlooking Keene's graceful town square, Luca's dazzles with epicurean creations influenced by Italy, France, Greece, Spain, and North Africa. There's always an extensive selection of small plates, such as almond-crusted fried mozzarella and roasted Brussels sprouts with bacon and honey, plus handmade pastas and complexly flavored grills and

stews. **Known for:** extensive kids' menu; affable but knowledgeable service; great wine list. ⑤ *Average main: $22* ✉ *10 Central Sq.* ☎ *603/358–3335* ⊕ *www. lucascafe.com* ☉ *No lunch Sun.*

Hotels

Chesterfield Inn

$$ | **B&B/INN** | With views of the hill in the distance, the Chesterfield Inn is nestled on a 10-acre farm in the Connecticut River valley. **Pros:** attractive gardens; close to Connecticut River; excellent full breakfast included. **Cons:** no dinner on Sunday; two-night minimum at busy times; remote town that's a 20-minute drive from Keene. ⑤ *Rooms from: $174* ✉ *20 Cross Rd., West Chesterfield* ☎ *603/256–3211* ⊕ *www.chesterfieldinn. com* ⇨ *15 rooms* ⑧ *Free breakfast.*

Fairfield Inn and Suites Keene Downtown

$ | **HOTEL** | You'll encounter a rare urban sensibility at this handsome property set in the early 1900s Goodnow department store on Keene's picturesque Main Street. **Pros:** the bi-level loft suites have two bathrooms; steps from restaurants and shops; decent fitness room. **Cons:** no pool; complimentary breakfast is pretty basic; historic building with quirky layout. ⑤ *Rooms from: $139* ✉ *30 Main St.* ☎ *603/357–7070, 888/236–2427* ⊕ *www. fairfieldinnkeene.com* ⇨ *40 rooms* ⑧ *Free breakfast.*

The Inn at East Hill Farm

$$$ | **RESORT** | **FAMILY** | For those with kids who like animals, East Hill Farm is heaven: a family resort with daylong children's programs on a 160-acre farm overlooking Mt. Monadnock that include milking cows; collecting eggs; feeding the sheep, donkeys, cows, rabbits, horses, chickens, goats, and ducks; horseback and pony rides; hiking and hay rides in summer; and sledding and sleigh rides in winter. **Pros:** agritourism at family resort; activities galore; beautiful setting; no TVs. **Cons:** remote location; noisy dining room; not an ideal choice for adults seeking a romantic retreat. $ *Rooms from: $286* ✉ *460 Monadnock St., Troy* ☎ *603/242–6495, 800/242–6495* ⊕ *www.east-hill-farm.com* ⇆ *65 rooms* ❍ *All-inclusive.*

Nightlife

BREWPUBS
★ Branch and Blade Brewing
BREWPUBS/BEER GARDENS | In this rustic but contemporary taproom with picnic tables and wooden keg tables, you can sample well-crafted local beers, including a sour Gose and potent triple IPA. ✉ *17 Bradco St.* ☎ *603/354–3478* ⊕ *www.bab-brewing.com.*

Performing Arts

ARTS VENUES
Colonial Theatre
CONCERTS | This renovated 1924 vaudeville theater shows art-house movies on the largest screen in town, and also hosts comedy, music, and dance performances. ✉ *95 Main St.* ☎ *603/352–2033* ⊕ *www.thecolonial.org.*

Shopping

Hannah Grimes Marketplace
GIFTS/SOUVENIRS | Shop here for locally made pottery, kitchenware, soaps, greeting cards, toys, and specialty foods. ✉ *42 Main St.* ☎ *603/352–6862* ⊕ *www. hannahgrimesmarketplace.com.*

Jaffrey Center

18 miles southeast of Keene.

Novelist Willa Cather came to Jaffrey Center in 1919 and stayed in the Shattuck Inn, which is now the Shattuck Golf Club. Not far from here, she pitched the tent in which she wrote several chapters of *My Ántonia.* She returned nearly every summer thereafter until her death and was buried in the Old Burying Ground, also the resting place of Amos Fortune, a former slave who bought his freedom in 1863 and moved to town when he was 71. Fortune, who was a tanner, also bought the freedom of his two wives.

GETTING HERE AND AROUND
Jaffrey Center's historic district is on Route 124 and is home to a number of brick buildings and is easily walked in an hour; a car is best for exploring the surrounding countryside.

ESSENTIALS
VISITOR INFORMATION Jaffrey Chamber of Commerce ☎ *603/532–4549* ⊕ *www. jaffreychamber.com.*

Sights

Cathedral of the Pines
MUSEUM | This 236-acre outdoor memorial pays tribute to Americans who have sacrificed their lives in service to their country. There's an inspiring view of Mt. Monadnock and Mt. Kearsarge from the Altar of the Nation, which is composed of rock from every U.S. state and territory. All faiths are welcome; organ music for meditation is played at midday Tuesday–Thursday in July and August. The Memorial Bell Tower, with a carillon of bells from around the world, is built of native stone. Norman Rockwell designed the bronze tablets over the four arches. Flower gardens, an indoor chapel, and a museum of military memorabilia share the hilltop. ✉ *10 Hale Hill Rd., Rindge* ☎ *603/899–3300* ⊕ *www. cathedralofthepines.org.*

Hotels

Benjamin Prescott Inn
$ | **B&B/INN** | Thanks to the dairy farm surrounding this 1853 Colonial house—with its stenciling and wide pine floors—you'll feel as though you're miles out in the country rather than just minutes from Jaffrey Center. **Pros:** reasonably priced; relaxing, scenic grounds; delicious breakfast included. **Cons:** not many amenities; remote setting; not suitable for young children. $ *Rooms from: $129* ✉ *433*

Turnpike Rd. ☎ 603/532–6637 ⊕ www. benjaminprescottinn.com ⇆ 10 rooms ⏐◎⏐ Free breakfast.

★ The Fitzwilliam Inn

$ | B&B/INN | Once a stagecoach stop, the 1786 Fitzwilliam Inn sits on the town green next to the Fitzwilliam Historical Society's Amos Blake House and is a short walk from several antiques dealers. **Pros:** reasonable rates; two inviting on-site dining options; full country breakfast included. **Cons:** some rooms require climbing quite a few stairs; old-fashioned ambience isn't for every taste; least expensive rooms are small. ⑤ Rooms from: $129 ✉ Town Common, 62 Rte. 119, Fitzwilliam ☎ 603/585–9000 ⊕ www.fitzwilliaminn. com ⇆ 10 rooms ⏐◎⏐ Free breakfast.

Activities

Monadnock State Park

PARK—SPORTS-OUTDOORS | The oft-quoted statistic about Mt. Monadnock is that it is America's most-climbed mountain—second in the world after Japan's Mt. Fuji. Whether this is true or not, locals agree that it's never lonely at the top: some days, more than 400 people crowd its bald peak. However, when the parking lot fills up, rangers close the park. Thus, an early morning start, especially during fall foliage, is recommended. Monadnock rises to 3,165 feet, and on a clear day the Boston skyline is visible. Five trailheads branch out into more than two dozen trails of varying difficulty (though all rigorous) that wend their way to the top. Allow three–four hours for any round-trip hike. The visitor center has free trail maps as well as exhibits documenting the mountain's history. In winter, you can cross-country ski along roughly 12 miles of groomed trails on the lower elevations. Note that pets are not permitted in the park. ✉ 116 Poole Rd., off Rte. 124, Jaffrey ☎ 603/532–8862 ⊕ www. nhstateparks.org ⬥ $5.

Shopping

Bloomin' Antiques

ANTIQUES/COLLECTIBLES | Fine art and unusual antiques abound in this quaint shop overlooking the town green. ✉ 3 Templeton Pike, Village Green, Fitzwilliam ☎ 603/585–6688 ⊕ www.bloominantiques.com.

Peterborough

6 miles northeast of Jaffrey Center, 45 miles southwest of Manchester.

Thornton Wilder's play *Our Town* was based on Peterborough. The nation's first free public library opened here in 1833, and the town is home to the country's oldest continuously operating basket manufacturer—it's been making baskets since 1854. The town, which was the first in the region to be incorporated (1760), is still a commercial and cultural hub, drawing big crowds for its theater and concerts in summer. Downtown's charming Depot Square district abounds with distinctive boutiques, galleries, and restaurants. At Putnam Park on Grove Street, stand on the bridge and watch the roiling waters of the Nubanusit River.

GETTING HERE AND AROUND

It's easy to find street parking downtown.

ESSENTIALS

VISITOR INFORMATION Greater Peterborough Chamber of Commerce ☎ 603/924–7234 ⊕ www.peterboroughchamber.com.

Sights

Mariposa Museum

MUSEUM | FAMILY | You can play instruments or try on costumes from around the world and indulge your cultural curiosity at this nonprofit museum dedicated to hands-on exploration of international folk art. The three-floor museum is housed inside a historic Baptist church, across from the Universalist church in the heart

Charming Peterborough was the inspiration for the fictional Grover's Corners in Thornton Wilder's *Our Town*.

of town. The museum hosts workshops and presentations on dance and arts and crafts. ⊠ *26 Main St.* ☎ *603/924–4555* ⊕ *www.mariposamuseum.org* 🍴 *$8* 🕐 *Closed Mon.*

Restaurants

Cooper's Hill Public House

$ | IRISH | Choose a sidewalk table overlooking bustling Depot Square or a table inside the conversation-filled dining room at this lively gastropub adjacent to Peterborough's popular independent cinema and steps from Mariposa Museum. The specialty here is rare whiskies, and there's also a nice selection of wines, craft beers, and other drinks, but don't overlook the consistently excellent Irish-influenced pub fare, including Guinness stew, mushroom-and-kale flatbread, bangers and mash, and terrific burgers. **Known for:** one of the best whiskey selections in the state; ingredients sourced from New England farms; pecan bread pudding. Ⓢ *Average main: $14* ⊠ *6 School St.* ☎ *603/371–9036* ⊕ *www.coopershillpubli-chouse.com* 🕐 *No lunch Mon.–Sat.*

★ Pearl Restaurant & Oyster Bar

$$ | ASIAN FUSION | Don't let the prosaic shopping center setting dismay you— It's worth driving a half-mile south of Petersborough's historic downtown to this sleek, contemporary Asian bistro and oyster bar that serves some of the most flavorful food in southern New Hampshire. Several types of fresh oysters are always available, along with such diverse offerings as ahi tuna poke, Hanoi-style pork spring rolls, Korean barbecue pork, and coconut-veggie rice bowls. **Known for:** creative fusion fare; superb wine list; oysters on the half shell. Ⓢ *Average main: $20* ⊠ *1 Jaffrey Rd.* ☎ *603/924–5225* ⊕ *www.pearl-peterborough.com* 🕐 *Closed Sun. No lunch.*

🛏 Hotels

Birchwood Inn

$ | B&B/INN | Henry David Thoreau slept here, probably on his way to climb Monadnock or to visit Jaffrey or Peterborough. **Pros:** charming restaurant; spacious rooms with elegant antiques; inexpensive. **Cons:**

remote small town; just three rooms; not suited for kids. $ Rooms from: $99 ⊠ 340 Rte. 45, Temple ☎ 603/878–3285 ⊕ www.thebirchwoodinn.com ⤳ 3 suites |⊙| Free breakfast.

★ The Hancock Inn
$$ | **B&B/INN** | This Federal-style 1789 inn in the heart of quaint Hancock, close to the village green, is the real deal—the oldest in the state and the pride of this idyllic town 8 miles north of Peterborough. **Pros:** quintessential Colonial inn in a perfect New England town; many rooms have Jacuzzi tubs and gas fireplaces; excellent restaurant. **Cons:** this tiny town is pretty quiet and remote; some rooms have twin beds; decor might be a little too old-fashioned for some. $ Rooms from: $169 ⊠ 33 Main St., Hancock ☎ 603/525–3318, 800/525–1789 ⊕ www.hancockinn.com ⤳ 13 rooms |⊙| Free breakfast.

The Inn at Crotched Mountain
$ | **B&B/INN** | Three of the nine fireplaces in this rambling 1822 inn are in guest rooms, all of which exude Colonial charm (although several don't have private bathrooms). **Pros:** spectacular country setting; full breakfast; very affordable. **Cons:** too remote for some; the least expensive rooms have shared bathrooms; restaurant only open Saturday nights. $ Rooms from: $120 ⊠ 534 Mountain Rd., Francestown ☎ 603/588–6840 ⊕ www.innatcrotchedmt.com ═ No credit cards ⊙ Closed Apr. and Nov. ⤳ 13 rooms |⊙| Free breakfast.

Jack Daniels Motor Inn
$ | **HOTEL** | **FAMILY** | A welcome exception to the many dowdy, older motels in southwestern New Hampshire, this clean, bright, and handsomely decorated 17-room motor inn just a half-mile north of downtown Peterborough is a terrific find. **Pros:** guests receive free access to local fitness club; one of the only lodgings near downtown Peterborough; continental breakfast. **Cons:** basic motel-style rooms; some street noise; a 10-minute walk from downtown. $ Rooms from: $119 ⊠ 80 Concord St. ☎ 603/924–7548 ⊕ www.jackdanielsmotorinn.com ⤳ 17 rooms |⊙| Free breakfast.

✪ Performing Arts

Monadnock Music
CONCERTS | From early July to late August, Monadnock Music sponsors a series of solo recitals, chamber music concerts, and orchestra and opera performances by renowned musicians. Events take place throughout the area, and some of the offerings are free. ⊠ Peterborough ☎ 603/852–4345 ⊕ www.monadnockmusic.org.

Peterborough Folk Music Society
CONCERTS | The Music Society presents folk concerts by artists such as John Gorka, Red Molly, and Cheryl Wheeler. Concerts are held in the Peterborough Players Theatre and Bass Hall at Monadnock Center. ⊠ Peterborough ☎ 603/827–2905 ⊕ www.pfmsconcerts.org.

★ Peterborough Players
THEATER | **FAMILY** | This first-rate summer (mid-June–mid-September) theater troupe has been performing since 1933, these days presenting seven main-stage productions in a converted 18th-century barn throughout the summer. The Players also present children's shows in July and August. ⊠ 55 Hadley Rd. ☎ 603/924–7585 ⊕ www.peterboroughplayers.org ⊙ Closed mid-Sept.–late June.

⊜ Shopping

Peterborough Basket Company
HOUSEHOLD ITEMS/FURNITURE | At this retail shop of the oldest continuously operating basket manufacturer in the country, which has been a fixture in Peterborough since 1854, you'll find countless varieties of sturdy and handsome woven-hardwood baskets, perfect for stowing everything from picnic victuals to laundry. You'll also find lazy Susans, planters, pet beds, and other smart storage solutions. ⊠ 130 Grove St. ☎ 603/924–3861 ⊕ www.peterborobasket.com.

Chapter 11

INLAND
MAINE

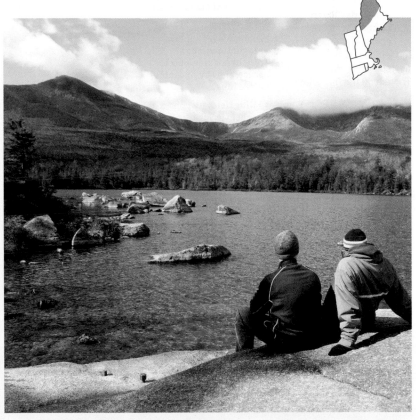

11

Updated by
Mary Ruoff

👁 **Sights**
★★★☆☆

🍴 **Restaurants**
★★★☆☆

🛏 **Hotels**
★★★☆☆

👜 **Shopping**
★★☆☆☆

🍸 **Nightlife**
★★☆☆☆

WELCOME TO INLAND MAINE

TOP REASONS TO GO

★ **Baxter State Park:** Mt. Katahdin, the state's highest peak, stands sentry over Baxter's forestland in its "natural wild state."

★ **Moosehead Lake:** Surrounded by mountains, Maine's largest lake—dotted with islands and chiseled with inlets and coves—retains the rugged beauty that so captivated author Henry David Thoreau in the mid-1800s.

★ **Water Sports:** It's easy to get out on the water on scheduled cruises of large inland lakes; guided or self-guided boating, canoeing, and kayaking trips; and white-water rafting excursions on several rivers.

★ **Winter Pastimes:** Downhill skiing, snowmobiling, snowshoeing, cross-country skiing, and ice fishing are all popular winter sports. You can even go dogsledding!

★ **Foliage Drives:** Maine's best fall foliage is inland, where hardwoods outnumber spruce, fir, and pine trees in many areas.

1 Sebago Lake Area. Less than 20 miles northwest of Portland, the Sebago Lake area bustles with activity in summer.

2 Bridgton. Bridgton is a classic New England town with 10 lakes to explore.

3 Bethel. In the valley of the Androscoggin River, Bethel is home to Sunday River, one of Maine's major ski resorts.

4 Rangeley. This rural area contains long stretches of pine, beech, spruce, and sky, and more classic inns.

5 Kingfield. Just north of Kingfield is Sugarloaf Mountain Resort, Maine's other big ski resort, which has plenty to offer year-round.

6 Greenville. The woodsy town, on Moosehead Lake, is a great base for day trips.

7 Millinocket. The gateway to the premier wilderness destinations of Baxter State Park and the Allagash Wilderness Waterway are, and commercial forestland is open for public recreation. The woodsy town of Greenville, on Moosehead Lake, is a great base for day trips.

Unlike the state's higher-profile coastline, inland Maine is a four-season destination. Natural beauty is abundant here, in the form of mountains, lakes, rivers, and there's an ample supply of classic New England villages.

Sebago and Long lakes, north of Portland and the gateway to the Western Lakes and Mountains region, hum with boaters and watercraft in the summer. Mt. Katahdin, Maine's highest peak and the terminus of the Appalachian Trail, rises in 210,000-acre Baxter State Park, outside Millinocket in the North Woods.

Come winter, ski resorts—including Maine's largest, Sugarloaf and Sunday River, both in the state's western section—wait for large snowfalls (and make it themselves in between). Maine often receives snow when the rest of New England doesn't and vice versa, so track the weather if you're coming for winter sports or to bask in the serenity of a good snowfall.

Rangeley, in western Maine, has been a haven for anglers since the 19th century, but these days this lakes-strewn area is also known for hiking and winter sports. Remote forestland lines most of Moosehead Lake, the biggest natural lake east of the Mississippi River within a single state. Greenville, at its southern end, is the hub. Visitors come to enjoy the lake, explore nearby wilderness locales, and downhill ski.

Wealthy urban "rusticators" began flocking to inland Maine on vacation in the mid-1800s. The legacy of the rusticators and the locals who catered to them lives on at sporting camps still found—albeit in smaller numbers than in days past—on remote lakes and rivers, and through Maine's unique system of licensed outdoor guides. Known as Registered Maine Guides, these well-qualified practitioners lead excursions that might involve kayaking, white-water rafting, hiking, fishing, hunting, canoeing, and moose spotting.

MAJOR REGIONS

The sparsely populated **Western Lakes and Mountains** region stretches north and west, bordered by New Hampshire and Québec. Each season offers different outdoor highlights: you can choose from snow sports, hiking, mountain biking, leaf peeping, fishing, swimming, and paddling. **The Sebago Lake area** bustles with activity in summer. **Bridgton** is a classic New England town, as is **Bethel,** in the valley of the Androscoggin River. Sunday River, a major ski resort nearby, also offers a host of summer activities. The more rural **Rangeley Lakes** area contains long stretches of pine, beech, spruce, and sky, and more classic inns. Just north of **Kingfield** is Sugarloaf Mountain Resort, Maine's other big ski resort, which has plenty to offer year-round.

Much of **The North Woods** is best experienced by canoeing or kayaking, fishing, hiking, snowshoeing, cross-country skiing, or snowmobiling. **Millinocket** is the gateway to Baxter State Park and Allagash Wilderness Waterway, both premier wilderness destinations open for public recreation. The woodsy town of **Greenville,** on Moosehead Lake, is a great base for day trips.

Planning

WHEN TO GO

As a rule, inland Maine's most popular hiking trails and lakeside beaches get busier when the weather gets warmer, but if splendid isolation is what you crave, you can still find it. Summertime is when lodging rates peak and traffic picks up—though rarely jams, outside of a few spots—but the weather makes it a beautiful time of year to visit. Inland Maine gets hotter than the coast in July and August; lakes and higher elevations are naturally cooler. September is a good bet: the weather is more moderate, and the crowds thinner.

Western Maine is the state's premier destination for leaf peepers—hardwoods are more abundant here than on the coast. Peak foliage season runs late September–mid-October.

Maine's largest ski areas can make their own snow—at least one of them opens its doors in mid-November and remains open until May. Inland Maine typically has snow cover by Christmas, so cross-country skiing, snowshoeing, and snowmobiling are in full swing by the end of the year.

Early spring snowmelt ushers in mud season, which leads to black fly season mid-May–mid-June. The flies are especially pesky in the woods but less bothersome in town. Spring is prime time for canoeing and fishing.

PLANNING YOUR TIME

Visitors to inland Maine often spend their entire vacation in the region. That's certainly true of those who come to ski at a resort, fish at a remote sporting camp, or just relax at a lakeside cabin. After a day hike on a mountain trail reached by gravel logging roads, visitors are unlikely

to hurry along to another town. Lodgings and rentals often have minimum stays during peak times. Generally speaking, the farther inland you go, the farther it is between destinations.

GETTING HERE AND AROUND
AIR TRAVEL

Two primary airports serve Maine: Portland International (PWM) and Bangor International (BGR). Portland is closer to the Western Lakes and Mountains area; Bangor is more convenient to the North Woods. Regional flying services, operating from regional and municipal airports, provide access to remote lakes and wilderness areas and offer scenic flights.

CAR TRAVEL

Because Maine is large and rural, a car is essential. U.S. 2 is the major east–west thoroughfare in Western Maine, winding from Bangor to New Hampshire. Interstate 95 is a departure point for many visitors to inland Maine, especially the North Woods. The highway heads inland at Brunswick and becomes a toll road (the Maine Turnpike) from the New Hampshire border to Augusta. Because of the hilly terrain and abundant lakes and rivers, inland Maine can get curvy. Traffic rarely gets heavy, though highways often pass right through instead of around the larger towns, which can slow your trip a bit.

There are few public roads in Maine's North Woods, but private logging roads there are often open to the public (sometimes by permit and fee). When driving these roads, always give lumber-company trucks the right-of-way; loggers must drive in the middle of the road and often can't move over or slow down for cars. Be sure to have a full tank of gas before heading onto private roads in the region.

RESTAURANTS

Fear not, lobster lovers: this succulent, emblematic Maine food is on the menu at many inland restaurants, from fancier establishments to roadside places. Dishes containing lobster are more common than boiled lobster dinners, but look for daily specials. Shrimp, scallops, and other seafood are also menu mainstays, and you may find bison burgers or steaks from a nearby farm. Organic growers and natural foods producers are found throughout the state and often sell their products to nearby restaurants. Pumpkins, blackberries, strawberries, and other seasonal foods make their way into homemade desserts, as do Maine's famed blueberries. Many lakeside resorts and sporting camps have a reputation for good food—some of the latter will even cook the fish you catch.

HOTELS

Well-run inns, bed-and-breakfasts, and motels can be found throughout inland Maine, including some more sophisticated lodgings. At places near ski resorts, peak-season rates may apply in winter and summer. Both hotel rooms and condo units are among the options at the two largest ski resorts, Sunday River and Sugarloaf. Greenville has the largest selection of lodgings in the North Woods region, with elaborate and homey accommodations alike. Lakeside sporting camps, from the primitive to the upscale, are popular around Rangeley and the North Woods; many have cozy cabins heated with wood stoves and serve three hearty meals a day. Conservation organizations also operate wilderness retreats. In Maine's mountains, as on its coast, many small inns don't have air-conditioning. *Hotel reviews have been shortened. For full reviews visit Fodors.com.*

Maine Campground Owners Association

The association's helpful membership directory is available by mail and on its website, which also has an interactive campground map. Many campgrounds have RV spaces and cabin rentals. ☎ 207/782–5874 ⊕ www.campmaine. com.

Maine State Parks Campground Reservations Service

You can get information about and make reservations for 12 state park campgrounds through this service. Note: reservations for Baxter State Park, which is administered separately, are not handled by the service. ☎ 207/624–9950, 800/332–1501 in Maine ⊕ www.campwithme.com.

What It Costs

	$	$$	$$$	$$$$
RESTAURANTS				
	under $18	$18–$24	$25–$35	over $35
HOTELS				
	under $200	$200–$299	$300–$399	over $399

VISITOR INFORMATION

CONTACTS Maine Office of Tourism ☎ 888/624–6345 ⊕ www.visitmaine.com. **Maine Tourism Association** ☎ 207/623–0363, 800/767–8709 ⊕ www.mainetourism.com.

Sebago Lake Area

20 miles northwest of Portland.

The shores of sprawling Sebago Lake and fingerlike Long Lake are popular with water-sports enthusiasts, as are Brandy Pond and many other bodies of water in the area. Several rivers flow into Sebago Lake, linking nearby lakes and ponds to form a 43-mile waterway. Naples, on the causeway separating Long Lake from Brandy Pond, pulses with activity in the summer, when the area swells with seasonal residents and weekend visitors. Open-air cafés overflow with patrons, boats buzz along the water, and families parade along the sidewalk edging Long Lake. On clear days the view includes snowcapped Mt. Washington.

Inland Maine Outdoor Activities

People visit inland Maine year-round for hiking, biking, camping, fishing, canoeing, kayaking, downhill and cross-country skiing, snowshoeing, and snowmobiling.

The Kennebec and Dead rivers, which converge at The Forks in Western Maine, and the West Branch of the Penobscot River, near Millinocket in the North Woods make Maine New England's premier destination for white-water rafting. The Kennebec is known for abundant big waves and splashes; the Dead has New England's longest stretch of continuous white water, some 16 miles. The most challenging rapids are on the West Branch of the Penobscot River, a Class V river on the southern border of Baxter State Park outside Millinocket.

Many outfitters run trips in both the Millinocket region and The Forks. North Country Rivers, based south of The Forks in Bingham, and New England Outdoor Center, outside Millinocket, are leading white-water-rafting outfitters. Guided single- or multiday excursions run rain or shine daily from spring (late April on the Kennebec, May on the Dead and the Penobscot) to mid-October. ■TIP→ Family-friendly rafting trips are available.

Fishing

Maine Department of Inland Fisheries and Wildlife. You can get information about and purchase fishing and hunting licenses by phone and online through this state agency. ☎ 207/287-8000 ⊕ www.mefishwildlife.com.

Guide Services

Maine Professional Guides Association. The association can help you find a state-licensed guide to lead a fishing, hunting, hiking, kayaking, canoeing, white-water rafting, snowshoeing, birding, or wildlife-watching trip. ⊕ www.maineguides.org.

Hiking

Maine Appalachian Trail Club. The club publishes seven Appalachian Trail maps ($8), all of which are bound together in its Maine trail guide ($30). Its interactive online map divides the AT in Maine into 30-plus sections, with photos and information on each. ⊕ www.matc.org.

Maine Trail Finder. The website has trail descriptions, photos, user comments, directions, interactive maps for trails to hike, mountain bike, paddle, snowshoe, and cross-county ski. ⊕ www.mainetrailfinder.com.

Skiing

Ski Maine Association. For alpine and cross-country skiing information. ☎ 207/773-7669 ⊕ www.skimaine.com.

Snowmobiling

Maine Snowmobile Association. The website has contacts and links for about 10,000 miles of local and regional trails, and an excellent statewide map of about 4,000 miles of interconnected trails. ☎ 207/622-6983 ⊕ www.mesnow.com.

White-Water Rafting

Raft Maine Association. An association of four white-water rafting outfitters, the website has information on the companies and Maine's three major white-water rafting rivers—the Kennebec, Penobscot, and Dead. ⊕ www.raftmaine.com.

Western Lakes and Mountains

The Forks

Moxie Pond

Monson

6

201

NEW HAMPSHIRE

27

Stratton

16

Sugarloaf Mountain Resort

Bingham

1

Rangeley Outdoor Sporting Heritage Museum

Wilhelm Reich Museum

Oquossoc

Rangeley

Kingfield

Solon

Rangeley Lakes Trails Center

Rangeley Lake State Park

Wilsons Mills

201

New Portland

Height of Land

4

Phillips

New Vineyard

Skowhegan

17

27

Weld

Farmington

2

95

Andover

26

Grafton Notch State Park

Rumford

Mexico

Wilton

Waterville

Hanover

Dixfield

Chisholm

27

Sunday River

Newry

Locke Mills

Livermore Falls

Bethel

White Mountain Nat'l Forest

2

Bryant Pond

26

Livermore

202

★ **AUGUSTA**

Mt. Abram Ski Resort

Buckfield

4

Turner

v17

Greenwood

Center Lovell

South Paris

Norway

Greene

Waterford

26

Lewiston

Lovell

Harrison

Mechanic Falls

302

Auburn

95

Newcastle

Bridgton

Long Lake

Casco

Fryeburg

Sabbathday Lake Shaker Village

17

Brownfield

Sebago Lake Area

South Casco

Brunswick

Bath

1

Hiram

Sebago Lake State Park

Raymond

295

Kezar Falls

Sabago Lake

Freeport

Boothbay

25

Yarmouth

Georgetown

Standish

302

Falmouth

Gorham

Portland

Casco Bay

Atlantic Ocean

95

4

0   10 mi

0   10 km

GETTING HERE AND AROUND

Sebago Lake, gateway to Maine's Western Lakes and Mountains, is less than 20 miles from Portland on U.S. 302.

ESSENTIALS

VACATION RENTALS Krainin Real Estate ⊠ *1539 Roosevelt Tr., Raymond* ☎ *207/655–5189* ⊕ *www.krainin.com.*

VISITOR INFORMATION Sebago Lakes Region Chamber of Commerce ⊠ *909 Roosevelt Tr., Suite A, Windham* ☎ *207/892–8265* ⊕ *www.sebagolakeschamber.com.*

Sights

Sabbathday Lake Shaker Village

MUSEUM VILLAGE | Established in the late 18th century, this is the last active Shaker community in the world. Several buildings with Shaker furniture, folk art, tools, farm implements, and crafts from the 18th to the early 20th century are open for guided hour-long tours. The structures include the 1794 Meetinghouse, the 1839 Ministry's Shop, where the elders and eldresses lived until the early 1900s, and the 1821 Sister's Shop, where household goods and candies were made. The 1850 Boys' Shop has a free exhibit about Shaker childhood. An exhibit in the 1816 Granary is included with the tour, but tickets are also sold separately. The Shaker Store sells community-produced foods and goods as well as handicrafts by area artisans. If you're visiting the village in late August, don't miss the popular Maine Native American Summer Market and Demonstration. ⊠ *707 Shaker Rd., New Gloucester* ☎ *207/926–4597* ⊕ *www.maineshakers.com* ⊠ *From $7* ⊙ *Closed mid-Oct.–late May.*

Sebago Lake

BODY OF WATER | FAMILY | Year-round and seasonal dwellings, from simple camps to sprawling showplaces, line the shores of Maine's deepest and second-largest lake, the source of Greater Portland's drinking water. ⊠ *Windham* ☎ *207/892–8265* ⊕ *www.sebagolakeschamber.com.*

Sebago Lake State Park

HISTORIC SITE | FAMILY | This 1,400-acre expanse on the north shore of Sebago Lake is a great spot for swimming, boating, and fishing for both salmon and togue. Its 250-site campground is the largest of any of the Maine state parks. Songo Lock State Historic Site, an operational lock along the twisting, narrow Songo River, is a pleasant picnic area. Bicycling along the park's roads is a popular pastime in warm weather. Come winter, the 6 miles of hiking trails here are groomed for cross-country skiing. ⊠ *11 Park Access Rd., Casco* ☎ *207/693–6231* ⊕ *www.maine.gov/sebagolake* ⊠ *Nonresident $8, Maine resident $6.*

Hotels

Migis Lodge

$$$$ | RESORT | FAMILY | Scattered under a canopy of trees along Sebago Lake, the classy pine-panel cottages at this 125-acre resort have fieldstone fireplaces and are furnished with colorful rugs and handmade quilts. **Pros:** massage center in cozy cabin; cookout on resort's private island; evening cocktail hour. **Cons:** pricey; credit cards not accepted; weeklong minimum in peak season (sometimes shorter openings occur). ⑤ *Rooms from: $764* ⊠ *30 Migis Lodge Rd., South Casco* ☎ *207/655–4524* ⊕ *www.migis.com* ⊟ *No credit cards* ⊙ *Closed mid-Oct.–mid-June* ⊅ *35 cottages, 8 rooms* ⑩ *All-inclusive.*

Activities

Sebago and Long lakes are popular areas for sailing, fishing, and motorboating. As U.S. 302 cuts through the center of Naples, at the Naples causeway you'll find rental craft for fishing or cruising.

Songo River Queen II

TOUR—SPORTS | FAMILY | Departing from the Naples causeway, the *Songo River Queen II*, a 93-foot stern-wheeler, takes passengers on one- and two-hour cruises on Long Lake. ⊠ *841 Roosevelt Tr., Naples* ☎ *207/693-6861* ⊕ *www. songoriverqueen.net* ⌂ *From $15.*

Bridgton

8 miles north of Naples, 30 miles south of Bethel.

U.S. 302 becomes Main Street in picturesque Bridgton, which anchors a region whose many lakes and large ponds are popular for boating and fishing. Steps from the tree-lined downtown with its restaurants, galleries, movie theater, and shops, a covered pedestrian bridge leads to 66-acre Pondicherry Park, a nature preserve with wooded trails and two streams. On hot summer days, kids dive off the dock at Highland Lake Beach, just north of Main Street at the lake's southern end. Come winter, visitors hit the slopes at Shawnee Peak.

The surrounding countryside is a good choice for leaf peepers and outdoors lovers. A few miles north, Harrison anchors the northern end of Long Lake. In fall, Fryeburg, 15 miles west on the New Hampshire border, is home to the Fryeburg Fair (⊕ *www.fryeburgfair.org*), the region's largest agricultural fair.

GETTING HERE AND AROUND
From Portland, U.S. 302 runs northwest to Bridgton along the east side of Sebago Lake and the west side of Long Lake. From there it continues west to Fryeburg.

ESSENTIALS
VISITOR INFORMATION Greater Bridgton Lakes Region Chamber of Commerce ⊠ *101 Portland Rd.* ☎ *207/647-3472* ⊕ *www. mainelakeschamber.com.*

Sights

Rufus Porter Museum
MUSEUM | Local youth Rufus Porter became a leading folk artist in the early 1800s, painting landscape and harbor murals on the walls of New England

homes, like this museum's red Cape Cod–style house, which bears unsigned murals by Porter (or one of his apprentices). In 2016, the late-18th-century structure was moved to the museum's new downtown setting, where a circa 1830s dwelling has exhibits about Porter, who also founded *Scientific American* magazine. Early issues are on display, as are some of his inventions and miniature portraits, and there's a video about Porter. ⊠ *121 Main St.* ☎ *207/647-2828* ⊕ *www.rufusporter-museum.org* ⌂ *$8* ⊘ *Closed mid-Oct.– May and Sun.–Tues. June–early Oct.*

Hotels

Noble House Inn
$ | B&B/INN | On a quiet road, this 1903 estate above Highland Lake offers a convenient location, plenty of creature comforts, and a relaxing atmosphere. **Pros:** homemade cookies daily; skiing and golfing packages; distinctive suites. **Cons:** limited lake views; only suites have TVs; cots only fit in some rooms. ⑤ *Rooms from: $170* ⊠ *81 Highland Rd.* ☎ *207/647-3733, 888/237-4880* ⊕ *www. noblehouseinn.com* ⇗ *8 rooms* ⎮⦿⎮ *Free breakfast.*

Activities

Shawnee Peak
SKIING/SNOWBOARDING | FAMILY | Just a few miles from Bridgton, Shawnee Peak appeals to families and to those who enjoy nighttime skiing—trails are lighted except most Sundays. Three terrain parks and seven glade areas offer alternatives to trails and downhill runs. The main base lodge has a restaurant with an expansive deck; the smaller East Lodge has a second-floor bunkhouse. Lodging choices also include Shawnee Peak House and a mountaintop yurt and cabin. Summer visitors can hike and pick blueberries. **Facilities:** 43 trails; 249 acres; 1,300-foot vertical drop; 6 lifts. ⊠ *119 Mountain Rd., off U.S. 302* ☎ *207/647-8444* ⊕ *www. shawneepeak.com* ⌂ *Lift ticket $72.*

Bethel

27 miles north of Bridgton, 65 miles north of Portland.

Bethel is pure New England: a town with white clapboard houses, white-steeple churches, and a mountain vista at the end of every street. The campus of Gould Academy, a college prep school founded in 1836, anchors the east side of downtown. In winter, this is ski country—Sunday River, one of Maine's big ski resorts, is only a few miles north in Newry. On the third weekend in July, Molly Ockett Day, which includes a parade, fireworks, live music, and a frog-jumping contest, honors a Pequawket Indian renowned for her medicinal cures in the early days of white settlement.

GETTING HERE AND AROUND

From the south, both Routes 35 and 5 lead to Bethel, overlapping several miles south of town. Route 5 from Bethel to Fryeburg is especially pretty come fall, with long stretches of overhanging trees. Kezar Lake can be glimpsed as the road passes through tiny Center Lovell. If you're coming to Bethel from the west on U.S. 2, you'll pass White Mountain National Forest.

Head east on U.S. 2 for the 66-mile drive to Rangeley, much of it along Rangeley Lakes National Scenic Byway. From Mexico, go north on Route 17, which winds through the Swift River Valley before ascending to Height of Land overlook. In Oquossoc, continue on Route 4 to Rangeley.

ESSENTIALS

TOURS Mahoosuc Guide Service ⊠ *1513 Bear River Rd., Newry* ☎ *207/824–2073* ⊕ *www.mahoosuc.com.*

VACATION RENTALS Four Seasons Realty & Rentals ⊠ *32 Parkway Plaza, Suite 1* ☎ *207/824–3776* ⊕ *www.fourseasonsrealtymaine.com.*

VISITOR INFORMATION Bethel Area Chamber of Commerce ⊠ *8 Station Pl., off Cross St.* ☎ *207/824–2282, 800/442–5826* ⊕ *www.bethelmaine.com.*

Sights

Artist's Bridge

BRIDGE/TUNNEL | The most painted and photographed of Maine's nine covered bridges can be found on a detour from Newry. Head south on U.S. 2 and then northwest on Sunday River Road (stay to the right at "Y" intersections). ⊠ *Sunday River Rd., 4 miles northwest of U.S. 2, Newry.*

Grafton Notch State Park

NATIONAL/STATE PARK | **FAMILY** | Grafton Notch Scenic Byway along Route 26 runs through Grafton Notch, a favorite destination for viewing fall foliage that stretches along the Bear River Valley 14 miles north of Bethel. It's an easy walk from roadside parking areas to Mother Walker Falls, Moose Cave, and the distinctive Screw Auger Falls, which drops through a gorge, creating pools. Table Rock Loop Trail (2.4 miles round-trip) rewards hikers with views of the mountainous terrain. More challenging is the 7.6-mile round-trip trek along the Appalachian Trail to the viewing platform atop 4,180-foot Old Speck Mountain, one of the state's highest peaks. The Appalachian Trail also traverses the 31,764-acre Mahoosuc Public Land—its two tracts sandwich the park—whose trails offer stunning, if strenuous, backcountry hiking (there are backcountry campsites). In winter, a popular snowmobile trail follows the river through the park. ⊠ *1941 Bear River Rd., Newry* ☎ *207/824–2912 Mid-May–mid-Oct. only, 207/624–6080* ⊕ *www.maine.gov/graftonnotch* ⊑ *Nonresidents $4, Maine residents $3.*

Museums of the Bethel Historical Society

MUSEUM | Start your stroll in Bethel here, across from the Village Common. The center's campus comprises two buildings: the 1821 O'Neil Robinson House and the 1813 Dr. Moses Mason House, both listed on the National Register of Historic Places. The O'Neil Robinson House has changing and permanent exhibits pertaining to the region's history. One parlor room serves as a gift shop with a nice book selection. The Moses Mason House has nine period rooms, and the front hall and stairway are decorated with Rufus Porter School folk art murals. The barn gallery often has changing and traveling exhibits. ⊠ *10 Broad St.* ☎ *207/824–2908, 800/824–2910* ⊕ *www. bethelhistorical.org* 🖾 *O'Neil Robinson free, Moses Mason $5* ⊘ *O'Neil Robinson closed late Oct.–late May, Sun. and Mon. July and Aug., and Sat.–Mon. June and Sept.; Moses Mason closed Sept.– June and Sun.–Wed. July and Aug.*

White Mountain National Forest

FOREST | **FAMILY** | This forest straddles New Hampshire and Maine, with the highest peaks on the New Hampshire side. The Maine section, though smaller, has magnificent rugged terrain. Hikers can enjoy everything from hour-long nature loops to a day hike up Speckled Mountain. The mountain is part of the 14,000-acre Caribou-Speckled Mountain Wilderness Area, one of several in the forest, but the only one entirely contained within Maine. The most popular Maine access to the national forest is via Route 113, which runs south from its terminus at U.S. 2 in Gilead, 10 miles from downtown Bethel. Most of the highway is the Pequawket Trail Maine Scenic Byway, and the section through the forest is spectacular come fall. This stretch is closed in winter but is used by snowmobilers and cross-country skiers. Two of the forest's campgrounds are in Maine; backcountry camping is allowed. ⊠ *Rte. 113, off U.S. 2, Gilead* ☎ *603/466–2713* ⊕ *www.fs.usda.gov/whitemountain* 🖾 *From $5 per car.*

Hotels

Holidae House

$ | **B&B/INN** | Welcoming hospitality keeps guests returning year after year to this charming and affordable downtown bed-and-breakfast. **Pros:** courtesy cordials in parlor; fresh-baked treats in afternoon; blow-up mattresses available. **Cons:** little outdoor space; no mountain views; close to street. ⑤ *Rooms from: $135* ⊠ *85 Main St.* ☎ *207/824–3400, 877/224–3400* ⊕ *www.holidaehouse.com* 🛏 *8 rooms* ⦿⦿ *Free breakfast.*

Activities

CANOEING AND KAYAKING

Bethel Outdoor Adventure and Campground

CANOEING/ROWING/SKULLING | **FAMILY** | On the Androscoggin River, this outfitter rents canoes, kayaks, tubes, standup paddleboards, and a drift boat; leads guided fishing and boating trips; and operates a shuttle service and campground. Maine Mineralogy is based here, with an open-air facility where you can sluice for precious gems. ⊠ *121 Mayville Rd.* ☎ *207/824–4224* ⊕ *www.betheloutdooradventure.com.*

SKI AREAS

Carter's Cross-Country Ski Center

SKIING/SNOWBOARDING | **FAMILY** | This cross-country ski center offers 34 miles of trails for all levels of skiers. Skis, snowshoes, and sleds to pull children are all available for rental. The place also rents lodge rooms and cabins (ski-in) year-round. Carter's has another ski center in Oxford. ⊠ *786 Intervale Rd.* ☎ *207/824–3880 Bethel location, 207/539–4848 Oxford location* ⊕ *www.cartersxcski.com* 🖾 *$15.*

★ Sunday River

SKIING/SNOWBOARDING | **FAMILY** | Once-sleepy Sunday River has evolved into a sprawling resort that attracts skiers from around the world. Stretching for 3 miles, it encompasses eight trail-connected peaks, six terrain parks, and a superpipe. Off-trail "boundary-to-boundary" skiing

One of the Rangeley Lakes, Mooselookmeguntic is said to mean "portage to the moose feeding place" in the Abenaki language.

is allowed, and there's night skiing on weekends and holidays. Sunday River has three base areas and several lodging choices, including condos and two slope-side hotels: the family-friendly Grand Summit, at one of the mountain bases, and the more upscale Jordan Grand, near a summit at the resort's western end. (It's really up there, several miles by vehicle from the base areas, but during ski season there's a shuttle, or you can ski over for lunch.) From the less costly Snow Cap Inn, it's a short walk to the slopes. Maine Adaptive Sports & Recreation, which serves skiers with disabilities, is based at the resort. The main South Ridge Base Lodge is the summer hub, hosting activities that include ziplining, chairlift rides, and mountain and electronic biking. **Facilities:** 135 trails (includes glades); 870 acres; 2,340-foot vertical drop; 15 lifts. ⊠ *15 S. Ridge Rd., off U.S. 2, Newry* ☎ *207/824–3000, 207/824–5200 for snow conditions, 800/543–2754 for reservations* ⊕ *www.sundayriver.com* ⊠ *Lift ticket $105.*

Rangeley

66 miles north of Bethel.

On the north side of Rangeley Lake along Route 4, Rangeley has long attracted anglers and winter-sports enthusiasts. The vastly forested Rangeley Lakes region has 100-plus lakes and ponds linked by rivers and streams. Right behind Main Street, Lakeside Park ("Town Park" to locals) has a large swimming area, a playground, picnic shelters, and a boat launch. Equally popular in summer and winter, Rangeley has a rough, wilderness feel. In late January, the Rangeley Snowmobile Snodeo offers thrilling snowmobile acrobatics, fireworks, a parade, and a cook-off for which area restaurants enter their chilies and chowders.

The western gateway to the region is Height of Land on Route 17, a must-see overlook with distant views stretching to mountains on the New Hampshire border. Rangeley Lake unfolds at an overlook down the road on the opposite side.

Whoopie Pies

When a bill aiming to make the whoopie pie Maine's official dessert was debated in state legislature, some lawmakers countered that the blueberry pie (made with Maine wild blueberries, of course) should have the honor. The blueberry pie won out, but what might have erupted into civil war instead ended civilly, with whoopie pies designated the official state "treat." Spend a few days anywhere in Maine and you'll notice just how popular it really is.

The name is misleading: it's a "pie" only in the sense of a having a filling between two "crusts"—namely, a thick layer of sugary frosting sandwiched between two saucers of rich cake, usually chocolate. It may have acquired its distinctive moniker from the jubilant "yelp" farmers emitted after discovering it in their lunchboxes. The whoopie pie is said to have Pennsylvania Dutch roots, but many Mainers insist that it originated here. Typically, the filling is made with butter or shortening; some recipes add Marshmallow Fluff. Many bakers have indulged the temptation to experiment with flavors and ingredients, particularly in the filling but also in the cake, offering pumpkin, raspberry, oatmeal cream, red velvet, peanut butter, and more.

GETTING HERE AND AROUND

To reach Rangeley on a scenic drive through Western Maine, take Route 17 north from U.S. 2 in Mexico past Height of Land to Route 4 in Oquossoc, then head east into town. Much of the drive is the Rangeley Lakes National Scenic Byway. From Rangeley, Route 16 continues east to Sugarloaf ski resort and Kingfield.

ESSENTIALS

VACATION RENTALS Morton & Furbish Vacation Rentals ✉ *2478 Main St.* ☎ *207/864–9065, 888/218–4882* ⊕ *www.rangeleyrentals.com.*

VISITOR INFORMATION Rangeley Lakes Chamber of Commerce ✉ *6 Park Rd.* ☎ *207/864–5364, 800/685–2537* ⊕ *www.rangeleymaine.com.*

Sights

Height of Land

SCENIC DRIVE | Height of Land is the highlight of Rangeley Lakes National Scenic Byway, with unforgettable views of mountains and lakes. One of Maine's best overlooks, it hugs Route 17 atop Spruce Mountain several miles south of Rangeley's Oquossoc village. On a clear day, you can look west to mountains on the New Hampshire border. There's off-road parking, interpretive panels, stone seating, and a short path to the Appalachian Trail. ✉ *Rte. 17.*

Rangeley Lake State Park

NATIONAL/STATE PARK | **FAMILY** | On the south shore of Rangeley Lake, this 869-acre park has superb lakeside scenery, swimming, picnic tables, a playground, a few short hiking trails, a boat ramp, and a campground. ✉ *1 State Park Rd.* ✦ *Turn on S. Shore Rd. from Rte. 17 or Rte. 4* ☎ *207/864–3858 May–mid-Oct. only, 207/624–6080 for regional state parks office* ⊕ *www.maine.gov/rangeleylake* 🎫 *Nonresident $6, Maine resident $4.*

Rangeley Outdoor Sporting Heritage Museum

MUSEUM | **FAMILY** | Spruce railings and siding on the museum's facade replicate a local taxidermy shop from about 1900. The welcome center inside this popular stop is an authentic log sporting camp from the same period, when grand hotels and full-service sporting lodges drew well-to-do rusticators on long stays. One of the big draws is the exhibit on local flytier Carrie Stevens, whose famed streamer flies increased the region's fly-fishing fame in the 1920s. Displays also include vintage watercraft and Native American birch-bark canoes. ⊠ *8 Rumford Rd., Oquossoc* ☎ *207/864–3091* ⊕ *www.rangeleyhistoricalsociety.org* ⊠ *$5* ⊘ *Closed Nov.–Mar. and Mon. and Tues. Apr.–June, Sept., and Oct.*

Wilhelm Reich Museum

MEMORIAL | FAMILY | The museum showcases the life and work of the Austrian physician, scientist, and writer Wilhelm Reich (1897–1957), who believed that all living matter and the atmosphere contained a force called orgone energy. The hilltop Orgone Energy Observatory exhibits biographical materials, inventions, and equipment used in his experiments, whose results were disputed by the Food and Drug Administration and other government agencies. The observatory deck has magnificent countryside views. In July and August, the museum presents engaging nature programs; trails lace the largely forested 175-acre property, which has two vacation rental cottages. Reich's tomb sits next to one of his inventions. ⊠ *19 Orgonon Cir., off Rte. 4* ☎ *207/864–3443* ⊕ *www.wilhelmreichtrust.org* ⊠ *Museum $8, grounds free* ⊘ *Museum closed Oct.–June and Sun.–Tues.; also closed Wed.–Fri. Sept.*

🍴 Restaurants

Gingerbread House Restaurant

$ | AMERICAN | With a fieldstone fireplace in the main dining room, tables about the deck, and an antique marble soda fountain, there are lots of reasons to stop at what really does look like a giant gingerbread house at the edge of the woods. Serving breakfast and lunch, the latter includes sandwiches and burgers

as well as crab cakes and pesto linguine, but don't miss out on the baked goods and ice cream. **Known for:** hash browns and omelets; garden views; proximity to overlooks and great hiking. ⑤ *Average main: $10* ⊠ *55 Carry Rd., Oquossoc* ☎ *207/864–3602* ⊕ *www.gingerbreadhouserestaurant.net* ⊘ *Closed Apr. and Nov.; Mon.–Thurs. Dec.–Mar.; Mon. and Tues. May, June, Sept., and Oct. No lunch Sun. Sept.–June. No dinner.*

Hotels

Country Club Inn

$ | B&B/INN | FAMILY | Built in 1920 as the country club for the adjacent Mingo Springs Golf Course, this hilltop retreat has sweeping mountain and lake views and plenty of charm. **Pros:** helpful staff; lower no-breakfast rate; sledding hill and outdoor pool. **Cons:** smallish rooms in main building; no TV in rooms; not on Rangeley Lake. ⑤ *Rooms from: $169* ⊠ *56 Country Club Rd.* ☎ *207/864–3831* ⊕ *www.countryclubinnrangeley.com* ⊘ *Closed Nov.–late Dec. and mid-Apr.–mid-May* ➡ *19 rooms* ❙○❙ *Free breakfast.*

The Rangeley Inn

$ | HOTEL | Painted eggshell blue, this historic downtown hotel was built around 1900 for wealthy urbanites on vacation—from the main inn's covered front porch, you step into a grand lobby with polished pine wainscoting and a brick fireplace. **Pros:** free full breakfast in elegant original dining room; nice variety of suites (largest sleeps six); canoeing and kayaking on Hayley Pond. **Cons:** no elevator; tavern only open 3–9; not on Rangeley Lake. ⑤ *Rooms from: $145* ⊠ *2443 Main St.* ☎ *207/864–3341* ⊕ *www.therangeleyinn.com* ⊘ *Closed Nov., Dec., and Apr.* ➡ *42 rooms* ❙○❙ *Free breakfast.*

Activities

BOATING AND FISHING

Rangeley and Mooselookmeguntic lakes are good for canoeing, kayaking, sailing, fishing, and motorboating. Several outfits rent equipment and provide guide service if needed. Lake fishing for brook trout and landlocked salmon is at its best in May, June, and September. The Rangeley area's rivers and streams are especially popular with fly-fishers, who enjoy the sport May–October.

SEAPLANES

★ Acadian Seaplanes

TOUR—SPORTS | In addition to 15-, 30- and 75-minute scenic flights high above the mountains by seaplane, this operator offers enticing "fly-in" excursions. You can travel by seaplane to wilderness locales to dine at a sporting camp, spot moose in their natural habitat, fish, or go white-water rafting on the remote Rapid River. Acadian also provides charter service between the Rangeley area and Portland, Boston, and New York. ⊠ *2640 Main St.* ☎ *207/864–5307* ⊕ *www.acadianseaplanes.com* ⊠ *From $65.*

SKI AREAS

Rangeley Lakes Trails Center

SKIING/SNOWBOARDING | About 35 miles of groomed cross-country and snowshoe trails stretch along the side of Saddleback Mountain. The trail network is largely wooded and leads to Saddleback Lake. You can also fat-tire bike here come winter. A yurt lodge has ski, snowshoe, and fat-bike rentals and a snack bar known for tasty soups. In warmer weather, the trails are popular with mountain bikers, hikers, and runners. ⊠ *524 Saddleback Mountain Rd., Dallas* ☎ *207/864–4309 winter only* ⊕ *www.rangeleylakestrailscenter.com* ⊠ *From $10.*

Kingfield

38 miles east of Rangeley.

In the shadows of Mt. Abraham ("Mt. Abram" to locals) and Sugarloaf Mountain, home to the eponymous ski resort, Kingfield has everything a "real" New England town should have, from historic inns to white clapboard churches. The pretty Carrabassett River slices the village and flows over a dam here.

ESSENTIALS

VISITOR INFORMATION Franklin County Chamber of Commerce ⊠ *615 Wilton Rd., Farmington* ☎ *207/778–4215* ⊕ *www. franklincountymaine.org.*

Sights

Stanley Museum

MUSEUM | Original Stanley Steamer cars built by twin brothers Francis and Freelan Stanley—Kingfield's most famous natives—are the main draw at this museum inside a 1903 Georgian-style former school. Also worth a look are the exhibits about the glass-negative photography business the twins sold to Eastman Kodak, and the well-composed photographs, taken by their sister, Chansonetta Stanley Emmons, of everyday country life at the turn of the 20th century. ⊠ *40 School St.* ☎ *207/265–2729* ⊕ *www.stanleymuseum.org* ⊠ *$4* ☉ *Closed Sun. and Mon. Nov.–Apr. and Mon. May–Oct.*

Activities

SKI AREAS

Sugarloaf Mountain Resort

SKIING/SNOWBOARDING | **FAMILY** | An eye-catching setting, abundant natural snow, and the only above-the-tree-line lift-service skiing in the East have made Sugarloaf one of Maine's best-known ski resorts. Glade areas, four terrain parks, and a border-cross track amp up the skiing options. There are two slope-side

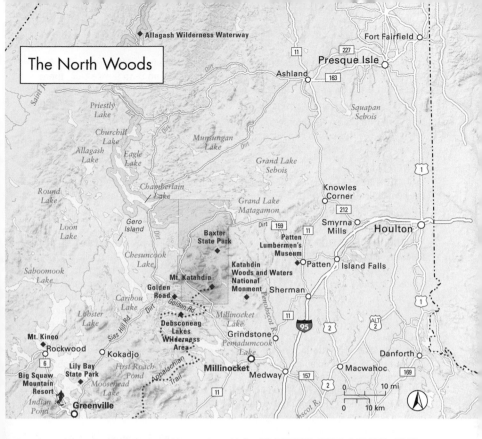

The North Woods

- Allagash Wilderness Waterway
- Fort Fairfield
- Presque Isle
- Ashland
- Priestly Lake
- Churchill Lake
- Munsungan Lake
- Squapan Sebois
- Allagash Lake
- Eagle Lake
- Grand Lake Sebois
- Round Lake
- Chamberlain Lake
- Knowles Corner
- Loon Lake
- Gero Island
- Grand Lake Matagamon
- Smyrna Mills
- Houlton
- Chesuncook Lake
- Baxter State Park
- Patten Lumbermen's Museum
- Saboomook Lake
- Mt. Katahdin
- Katahdin Woods and Waters National Monment
- Patten
- Island Falls
- Caribou Lake
- Golden Road
- Sherman
- Lobster Lake
- Debsconeag Lakes Wilderness Area
- Millinocket Lake
- Mt. Kineo
- Rockwood
- Kokadjo
- Grindstone
- Pemadumcook Lake
- Danforth
- Lily Bay State Park
- First Roach Pond
- Millinocket
- Macwahoc
- Big Squaw Mountain Resort
- Moosehead Lake
- Medway
- Indian Pond
- Greenville

10 mi
10 km

---

hotels and hundreds of slope-side condos and rental homes with ski-in, ski-out access. Sugarloaf Mountain Hotel is in the ski village; the smaller, more affordable Sugarloaf Inn is a bit down the mountain. The Outdoor Center has more than 90 miles of cross-country ski trails, and you can snowshoe and ice-skate. Indoor skateboarding and trampolining are among the many kids-oriented activities. Once at Sugarloaf, you'll find a car unnecessary—a shuttle connects all mountain operations. The ski season runs November–May. In summer you can mountain bike, hike, or zipline; take a moose safari, off-road Segway tour, or pontoon-boat ride; or play golf, either disc golf or a round on what many consider Maine's best golf course. **Facilities:** 162 trails (includes glades); 1,240 acres; 2,820-foot vertical drop; 13 lifts. ⊠ 5092 Sugarloaf Access Rd., Carrabassett

Valley ☎ 207/237–2000, 800/843–5623 for reservations ⊕ www.sugarloaf.com ☜ Lift ticket $95.

Greenville

155 miles northeast of Portland, 70 miles northwest of Bangor.

Greenville, tucked at the southern end of island-dotted, mostly forest-lined Moosehead Lake, is an outdoors lover's paradise. Boating, fishing, and hiking are popular in summer; and in winter, ice fishing, snowmobiling, and cross-country and downhill skiing—you can enjoy both at Big Squaw Mountain ski area just north of town. Greenville has the best selection of shops, restaurants, and inns in the North Woods region. Restaurants and lodgings are also clustered 20 miles north in Rockwood, where the Moose

River flows through the village and—across from Mt. Kineo's majestic cliff face—into the lake.

GETTING HERE AND AROUND

To reach Greenville from Interstate 95, get off at Exit 157 in Newport and head north, successively, on Routes 7, 23, and 15.

ESSENTIALS

VACATION RENTALS Vacasa (Moosehead Lake Cabin Rentals) ☎ 800/251–8042, 207/695–4300 ⊕ www.vacasa.com/usa/Moosehead-Lake.

VISITOR INFORMATION Destination Moosehead Lake ✉ 480 Moosehead Lake Rd. ☎ 207/695–2702 ⊕ www.destination-mooseheadlake.com.

Sights

Gulf Hagas

BODY OF WATER | Called the "Grand Canyon of the East," this National Natural Landmark has chasms, cliffs, four major waterfalls, pools, exotic flora, and intriguing rock formations. Part of the Appalachian Trail Corridor, the slate-walled gorge east of Greenville is located in a remote, privately owned commercial forest, KI Jo-Mary, which allows access to it via gravel logging roads (always yield to trucks). A fee is usually charged at forest checkpoints, where you can also get trail maps and hiking information.

From either parking area you can hike to one of the showcase falls and mostly avoid the difficult rim trail. Start at Head of Gulf parking area for a 3½-mile round-trip hike, a good choice for families with young children, to Stair Falls on the gorge's western end. From the Gulf Hagas parking area, a 3-mile round-trip hike takes you to spectacular Screw Auger Falls on the gulf's eastern end. Gulf hikers who start from this parking area must ford the Pleasant River—usually easily done in summer, but dangerous in high water—and pass through the Hermitage, a stand of old pines and hemlock. A loop route that follows the

rim and the less difficult Pleasant River Tote Trail is an 8- to 9-mile trek; there are shorter loops as well. Slippery rocks and rugged terrain make for challenging progress along the rim trail. ✉ Greenville ✛ From Greenville, travel 11 miles east via Pleasant St., which eventually becomes Katahdin Iron Works Rd., to Hedgehog checkpoint. Follow signs to parking areas: Head of Gulf, 2½ miles; Gulf Hagas, 6½ miles ⊕ www.north-mainewoods.org.

Lily Bay State Park

PARK—SPORTS-OUTDOORS | FAMILY | Nine miles northeast of Greenville on Moosehead Lake, this park has good lakefront swimming, a 2-mile walking trail with water views, two boat-launching ramps, a playground, and two campgrounds with a total of 90 sites. In winter, the entrance road is plowed to access the groomed cross-country ski trails and the lake for ice fishing and snowmobiling. ✉ 13 Myrle's Way ✛ Turn onto State Park Rd. from Lily Bay Rd. ☎ 207/695–2700 ⊕ www.maine.gov/lilybay ▨ Nonresident $6, Maine resident $4.

★ Moosehead Historical Society & Museums

GARDEN | FAMILY | Guides in period costume lead tours of the Eveleth-Crafts-Sheridan Historical House, a late 19th-century Victorian mansion filled with antiques, most of them original to the home. The Lumberman's Museum, with exhibits about the region's logging history, is in the carriage house, and the barn next door houses a re-creation of a one-room schoolhouse and a display on the region's outdoor sporting heritage. You can savor lunch and the architecture of these meticulously maintained buildings from the art-accented Sunken Garden. A mile away in downtown Greenville, the former Universalist Church houses the Center for Moosehead History and Moosehead Lake Aviation Museum. The former has a fine exhibit of Native American artifacts from the Moosehead Lake region, dating from

9,000 BC to the 1700s. The latter focuses on the impact of aviation on the area, from early bush pilots to Greenville's annual International Seaplane Fly-in. ✉ *444 Pritham Ave., Greenville Junction* ☎ *207/695–2909* ⊕ *www.mooseheadhistory.org* ✒ *Eveleth-Crafts-Sheridan Historical House $5, other museums free* ⊙ *Closed early fall–mid-June, except for Lumberman's Museum; contact the society for museums' hrs.*

Mt. Kineo

GOLF COURSE | FAMILY | Accessible primarily by steamship, Mt. Kineo House was a thriving upscale summer resort set below its namesake's 700-foot cliff on an islandlike peninsula jutting into Moosehead Lake. The last of three successive hotels with this name was built in 1884 and became America's largest inland waterfront hotel. It was torn down in 1938, but Kineo remains a pleasant day trip. Mt. Kineo State Park occupies most of the 1,200-acre peninsula, with trails to the summit of the spectacular landmark. You can also play a round on Mt. Kineo Golf Course, one of the oldest courses in New England. There is no road access, but you can take a 15-minute boat trip from Rockwood on the golf course's seasonal shuttle. ✉ *Kineo Dock, Village Rd., Rockwood* ☎ *207/534–9012 for golf course and shuttle, 207/941–4014 for park regional office* ⊕ *www.maine.gov/mountkineo* ✒ *Nonresident $3, Maine resident $2.*

 ## Hotels

★ Appalachian Mountain Club Maine Wilderness Lodges

$$ | RESORT | FAMILY | In Maine's 100-Mile Wilderness, the Appalachian Mountain Club's 75,000 acres includes three historic sporting-camp retreats—Gorman Chairback, Little Lyford, and the rebuilt Medawisla, which reopened in 2017—that have cabins with wood stoves, a bunkhouse (or two), sauna, and a bathhouse with hot showers; Gorman

Chairback and Medawisla have some cabins with private baths. **Pros:** courtesy canoes, kayaks, and standup paddleboards (no boards at Little Lyford); Little Lyford is near Gulf Hagas; made-to-order trail lunch. **Cons:** winter access only by cross-country skis or snowmobile transport (fee) at Little Lyford and Gorman Chairback; no waterfront cabins at Little Lyford; not many courtesy mountain bikes, none at Little Lyford. $ *Rooms from: $204* ✉ *North Woods outside Greenville* ☎ *207/695–3085 AMC Greenville office, 207/358–5187 reservations* ⊕ *www.outdoors.org/lodging/mainelodges* ⊙ *Closed Apr. and Dec. until after Christmas; Little Lyford and Gorman Chairback also closed Nov., 2nd half Mar., and 1st half May* ⌁ *Gorman Chairback: 12 cabins, 1 bunkhouse (sleeps 10); Little Lyford: 10 cabins, 1 bunkhouse (sleeps 12); Medawisla, 9 cabins, 2 bunkhouses (each sleeps 16)* ℗ *All-inclusive.*

★ Blair Hill Inn

$$$ | B&B/INN | Beautiful gardens and a hilltop location with marvelous views over the lake distinguish this 1891 country estate as one of New England's top inns; enjoy cocktails—and that view—from the veranda or the swank cocktail lounge. **Pros:** free concierge plans outdoor excursions; helicopter, Tesla, and electric-car friendly; 21-acre property has stone paths, trout pond, and wooded picnic area; lake views from all but one room. **Cons:** pricey; no direct lake access; fee to use spa sauna and hot tub. $ *Rooms from: $329* ✉ *351 Lily Bay Rd.* ☎ *207/695–0224* ⊕ *www.blairhill.com* ⊙ *Closed Nov.–mid-May* ⌁ *10 rooms* ℗ *Free breakfast.*

Activities

Togue (lake trout), landlocked salmon, smallmouth bass, and brook trout attract anglers to the region from ice-out in mid-May until September; the hardiest return in winter to ice fish.

MULTISPORT OUTFITTERS

Moose Country Safaris & Eco Tours

CANOEING/ROWING/SKULLING | This outfit's offerings include moose-spotting and bird-watching excursions; snowshoe, hiking, and canoe and kayak trips; and tours highlighting waterfalls. ⊠ *191 N. Dexter Rd., Sangerville* ☎ *207/876–4907* ⧠ *Contact for prices.*

Northwoods Outfitters

BICYCLING | You can rent canoes, kayaks, standup paddleboards, camping equipment, ATVs, mountain and fat-tire bikes, snowmobiles, snowshoes, ski equipment, snowboards, and winter clothing here. Northwoods organizes a host of outdoor trips, including open-water and ice fishing, waterfall hikes, snowmobiling and moose-watching (by land or water), and operates a shuttle to remote areas. At the base in downtown Greenville, you can pick up sporting goods, get trail advice, or kick back in the Internet café. ⊠ *5 Lily Bay Rd.* ☎ *207/695–3288, 866/223–1380* ⊕ *www.maineoutfitter.com.*

BOATING

Allagash Canoe Trips

CANOEING/ROWING/SKULLING | Run by a husband and wife, both championship paddlers and Registered Maine Guides, Allagash offers multiday trips on the Allagash Wilderness Waterway, the Moose and St. John rivers, and the East and West branches of the Penobscot River. White-water trips are run on the Kennebec and Dead rivers. You can learn paddling and canoe poling techniques on day-trips. The company also leads winter camping excursions. ⊠ *156 Scammon Rd.* ☎ *207/280–1551, 207/280–0191* ⊕ *www. allagashcanoetrips.com* ⧠ *From $200.*

SEAPLANES

Currier's Flying Service

TOUR—SPORTS | You can take sightseeing flights over the Moosehead Lake region with Currier's from ice-out until mid-October. ⊠ *447 Pritham Ave., Greenville Junction* ☎ *207/695–2778* ⊕ *www.curriersflyingservice.com* ⧠ *From $45.*

SKI AREA

Big Squaw Mountain Resort

SKIING/SNOWBOARDING | FAMILY | A local nonprofit formed to reopen the lower portion of Big Moose Mountain (the resort uses the old name) after it closed for a few years. Back in business since 2013, it operates Thursday–Sunday, holidays, and school-vacation weeks. The summit chairlift, unused since 2004, and the shuttered hotel loom trailside like something out of a Stephen King novel (he's a Mainer, no less), but the mostly intermediate trails on the lower mountain are plenty high enough to wow skiers with views up and down Moosehead Lake, Maine's largest. On a clear day, Mt. Katahdin, the state's highest peak, accents the mountainous horizon. Cheap prices and the spacious, retro-fun chalet lodge draw families. For a fee, ski buffs can summit the mountain via snowcat and ski down ungroomed black diamond trails. The resort also has free trails for cross-country skiing, snowshoeing, and winter biking. **Facilities:** 26 trails; 58 acres; 660-foot vertical drop; 1 lift. ⊠ *447 Ski Resort Rd., Greenville Junction* ☎ *207/695–2400* ⊕ *www.skibigsquaw. com* ⧠ *$30 lift ticket.*

TOURS

Katahdin Cruises

TOUR—SPORTS | The Moosehead Marine Museum runs 3- and 5½-hour afternoon trips on Moosehead Lake aboard the *Katahdin*, a 115-foot 1914 steamship converted to diesel. (The longer trip skirts Mt. Kineo's cliffs.) Also called the *Kate*, this ship carried resort guests to Mt. Kineo until 1938; the logging industry then used it until 1975. The boat and the free shoreside museum have displays about these steamships, which transported people and cargo on Moosehead Lake for a century starting in the 1830s. ⊠ *12 Lily Bay Rd.* ☎ *207/695–2716* ⊕ *www. katahdincruises.com* ⧠ *From $35.*

Millinocket

67 miles north of Bangor, 88 miles northwest of Greenville.

Millinocket, a former paper-mill town with a population of about 4,000, is a gateway to Baxter State Park and Maine's North Woods. Millinocket is the place to stock up on supplies, fill your gas tank, and grab a hot meal or shower before heading into the wilderness. Numerous rafting and canoeing outfitters and guides are based in the region.

GETTING HERE AND AROUND
From Interstate 95, take Route 157 (Exit 244) west to Millinocket. From here follow signs to Baxter State Park (Millinocket Lake Road becomes Baxter Park State Road), 18 miles from town.

ESSENTIALS
VISITOR INFORMATION Katahdin Area Chamber of Commerce ⊠ *1029 Central St.* ☏ *207/723–4443* ⊕ *www.katahdin-maine.com.*

 Sights

Allagash Wilderness Waterway
BODY OF WATER | A spectacular 92-mile corridor of lakes, ponds, streams, and rivers, the waterway park cuts through vast commercial forests, beginning near the northwestern corner of Baxter State Park and running north to the town of Allagash, 10 miles from the Canadian border. From May to mid-October, the Allagash is prime canoeing and camping country. The Maine Bureau of Parks and Lands has campsites along the waterway, most not accessible by vehicle. The complete 92-mile course, part of the 740-mile Northern Forest Canoe Trail, which runs from New York to Maine, requires 7–10 days to canoe. Novices may want to hire a guide, as there are many areas with strong rapids. A good outfitter can help plan your route and provide equipment and transportation. ⊠ *Millinocket* ☏ *207/941–4014 for*

regional parks bureau office ⊕ *www.maine.gov/allagash.*

★ Baxter State Park
MOUNTAIN—SIGHT | FAMILY | A gift from Governor Percival Baxter, this is the jewel in the crown of northern Maine: a 210,000-acre wilderness area that surrounds **Mt. Katahdin,** Maine's highest mountain and the terminus of the Appalachian Trail. Every year, the 5,267-foot Katahdin draws thousands of hikers to make the daylong summit, rewarding them with stunning views of forests, mountains, and lakes. There are three parking-lot trailheads for Katahdin. Depart from the Roaring Branch trailhead for a route that includes the hair-raising Knife Edge Ridge. ■**TIP**→ **Reserve a day-use parking space at the trailheads May 15–October 15.**

The crowds climbing Katahdin can be formidable on clear summer days and fall weekends, so if it's solitude you crave, tackle one of the park's many other mountains. All are accessible from the extensive trail network, and 14 peaks exceed an elevation of 3,000 feet. The Brothers and Doubletop Mountain are challenging daylong hikes; the Owl takes about six hours; and South Turner can be climbed in a morning—its summit has a great view across the valley. A trek around Daicey Pond, or from the pond to Big and Little Niagara Falls, are good options for families with young kids. Another option if you only have a couple of hours is renting a canoe at Daicey or Togue ponds. Park roads are unpaved, narrow, and winding, and there are no pay phones, gas stations, or stores. Camping is primitive and reservations are required; there are 10 campgrounds plus backcountry sites. ■**TIP**→ **The park has a visitor center at its southern entrance, but you can get information, make parking and camping reservations, and watch a video at park headquarters in Millinocket (64 Balsam Drive).** ⊠ *Baxter State Park Rd.* ✛ *Togue Pond Gate (park's southern entrance) is 18 miles northwest of*

There are amazing views from the top of the 5,267-foot-tall Mt. Katahdin.

Millinocket; follow signs from Rte. 157 ☎ 207/723–5140, 207/723–4636 for hiking hotline ⊕ www.baxterstateparkauthority.com ☞ $15 per vehicle; Maine residents free.

Debsconeag Lakes Wilderness Area

NATURE PRESERVE | Bordering the south side of the Golden Road below Baxter State Park, the Nature Conservancy's 46,271-acre Debsconeag Lakes Wilderness Area is renowned for its rare ice cave, old forests, abundant pristine ponds, and views of Mt. Katahdin— there are mesmerizing views along the 5-mile Rainbow Loop. The access road for the Ice Cave Trail (2 miles round-trip) and Hurd Pond is 16 miles northwest of Millinocket, just west of the Golden Road's Abol Bridge. Near here the Appalachian Trail exits the conservancy land, crossing the bridge en route to Baxter. Before hiking, paddling, fishing, or camping in the remote preserve (no fees or reservations required), visit the conservancy's website for directions and other information. The Golden Road accesses are marked. There are trail kiosks and marked trailheads within the preserve. ✉ Golden Rd. ⊕ www.nature. org/maine.

Golden Road

BODY OF WATER | For a scenic North Woods drive, set off on the roughly 22-mile stretch of this private east–west logging road near Baxter State Park northwest of Millinocket. Have patience with ruts and bumps, and yield to logging trucks (keep right!). From Millinocket follow the signs for Baxter State Park from Route 157. This scenic drive begins about 9 miles from town, at the crossover from Millinocket Lake Road to the Golden Road, the latter named for the huge sum a paper company paid to build it.

The North Woods Trading Post, a great stop for takeout and souvenirs and the last place to gas up before Baxter, is at this junction, across from Ambajejus Lake. From here it's 11 miles on the Golden Road to one-lane Abol Bridge, which has a parking area after crossing the bridge. Or stop before it at Abol Bridge Campground, with a restaurant and store. ■TIP→ **Take photos of Baxter's Mt. Katahdin from the footbridge alongside Abol Bridge: this view is famous.** Just beyond the bridge is an access road for Debsconeag Lakes Wilderness Area. From here the Golden Road flows alongside the West Branch of the Penobscot River.

At the western end of the drive, the river drops 70-plus feet per mile through Ripogenus Gorge, giving white-water rafters a thrilling ride during scheduled releases from Ripogenus Dam. The Crib Works Rapid (Class V) overlook is off the Golden Road about 10 miles from Abol Bridge. (Turn right on Telos Road; parking is on the right after the bridge.) For the best gorge views, turn right into McKay Station about a mile after Telos Road. Be cautious on the downhill paths: there's no fencing. To drive across the dam on Ripogenus Lake and view the gorge, return to the Golden Road and continue west three-quarters of a mile to Rip Dam Road, which veers right. Returning to the crossover at the North Woods Trading Post, turn left for Baxter or right for Millinocket. ⊠ *Golden Rd.*

Katahdin Woods and Waters National Monument

NATIONAL/STATE PARK | The day before the National Parks Service Centennial, President Obama named 87,500 acres of Maine's North Woods east of Baxter State Park a national monument. The land was donated by Burt's Bees co-founder Roxanne Quimby's foundation, Elliotsville Plantation, which also gave millions to fund infrastructure and future support of the monument. Currently there is no visitor center, but you can get information at seasonal welcome centers in Millinocket (200 Penobscot Avenue) and Patten (at the Lumbermen's Museum, 61 Shin Pond Road). The monument holds occasional visitor programs. The only access points are from gravel roads. From Stacyville, take Route 11 to Swift Brook Road. From there, you can access the monument's 16-mile Katahdin Loop Road to visit its southern portion. The

road has various scenic viewpoints—several reveal Baxter's Mt. Katahdin—as well as trailheads to short hikes. The land is home to animals such as moose, bald eagles, salmon, and bobcats; rivers, streams, and ponds provide opportunities for paddling and fishing. ⊠ *Millinocket* ✛ *Take Rte. 11 (Katahdin Woods & Waters Scenic Byway) north to Swift Brook Rd.* ☎ *207/456–6001* ⊕ *www.nps.gov/kaww.*

Patten Lumbermen's Museum

MUSEUM | FAMILY | Two reproduction 1800s logging camps are among the 10 buildings filled with exhibits depicting the history of logging in Maine. They include sawmill and towboat models, dioramas of logging scenes, horse-drawn sleds, and a steam-powered log hauler. Exhibits also highlight local artists and history as well as logging-related topics. The museum is a welcome center for nearby Katahdin Woods and Waters National Monument. ⊠ *61 Shin Pond Rd., Patten* ☎ *207/528–2650* ⊕ *www.lumbermensmuseum.org* � *$10* ☉ *Closed mid-Oct.–mid-May and Mon. (except Memorial Day); also closed Tues.–Thurs. late May–June.*

⚡ Activities

MULTISPORT OUTFITTERS
Katahdin Outfitters

BOATING | This company provides gear and shuttles for overnight canoe and kayak expeditions on the Allagash Wilderness Waterway, the West Branch of the Penobscot River, and the St. John River. You can also rent canoes and kayaks from its location just outside Millinocket on the way to Baxter State Park. ⊠ *360 B Bates St.* ☎ *207/723–5700* ⊕ *www.katahdinoutfitters.com* ⊠ *Call for prices.*

★ **New England Outdoor Center** (*NEOC*)
TOUR—SPORTS | FAMILY | With Baxter State Park's Mt. Katahdin rising above the shore opposite both its locations, this business helps visitors enjoy the North Woods. Its year-round home base,

NEOC/Twin Pines on Millinocket Lake, 8 miles from the park's southern entrance, has rental cabins and a restaurant and conducts many guided trips, some within the park. Older renovated log cabins (and a few newer ones) sit beneath tall pines on a grassy nub of land that juts into Millinocket Lake; upscale "green" units (spacious lodges and cozy cabins) are tucked among trees on a cove. Amenities include kayaks and canoes for use on the lake and a recreation center with a sauna.

At the deservedly popular **River Driver's Restaurant,** wood for the trim, wainscoting, bar, and floors was milled from old logs salvaged from local waters. Diners enjoy views of Katahdin from behind rows of windows or from the patio, and your dish may feature farm-to-table fare from the center's own gardens.

In addition to offering a full slate of guided excursions—snowmobiling, fishing, canoe, kayak, hiking, photography, moose-spotting—NEOC rents canoes, kayaks, and standup paddleboards, gives paddling lessons, and rents snowmobiles and fat-tire bikes. Trails for hiking, cross-country skiing (18 miles, groomed), and mountain and fat-tire biking are right on the 1,400-acre property. About 2 miles from Baxter, the seasonal Penobscot Outdoor Center on Pockwockamus Pond is the base for white-water rafting trips on the West Branch of the Penobscot River and home to a wooded campground. There are tent sites as well as canvas tents and simple wood-frame cabins with cots or bunks. A circular fireplace anchors the open-plan base lodge, which sells hot meals and snacks—enjoy your grub in the pub area, around the circular fireplace, hanging by the pool

table, or wherever you're comfortable. A towering window wall reveals glimpses of water through trees, and there are campsites near the water with Katahdin views. Outdoors there's a communal fire pit. ■TIP→ **Nonguests can use showers for $2 after hiking or camping at Baxter.** ⊠ *30 Twin Pines Rd.* ⊹ *From Millinocket Lake Rd., take Black Cat Rd. east 1 mile*☎ *207/723–5438, 800/766–7238* ⊕ *www.neoc.com.*

North Country Rivers

WHITE-WATER RAFTING | From spring to fall, North Country Rivers runs white-water rafting trips on the Dead and Kennebec rivers in The Forks in Western Maine, and on the West Branch of Penobscot River outside Millinocket in the North Woods. North Country's 55-acre resort south of The Forks in Bingham has cabin and bunkhouse rentals, tent and RV sites, a restaurant with a bar, and a store; its Millinocket base is the Big Moose Inn, Cabins & Campground. The outfitter also offers moose and wildlife safaris, rents snowmobiles and kayaks, and has courtesy bikes for resort guests. ⊠ *36 Main St., Bingham* ☎ *207/672–4814, 800/348–8871* ⊕ *www.northcountryrivers.com.*

SEAPLANES

Katahdin Air Service

TOUR—SPORTS | In addition to operating ½- and 1-hour scenic flights over the Katahdin area, this seaplane operator offers fly-in excursions to backcountry locales to picnic at a pond beach, dine at a sporting camp, or moose-watch and bask in nature. It also provides charter service from points throughout Maine to the region's smaller towns and remote areas. ⊠ *1888 Golden Rd.* ☎ *207/723–8378* ⊕ *www.katahdinair.com* ✈ *From $95.*

Chapter 12

MAINE COAST

Updated by
Grace-Yvette Gemmell

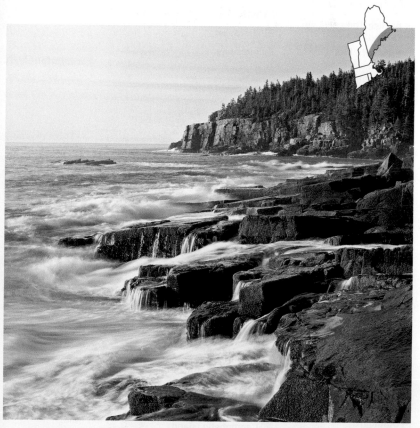

◉ Sights	🍴 Restaurants	🛏 Hotels	🛍 Shopping	🍸 Nightlife
★★★★☆	★★★★☆	★★★★★	★★★☆☆	★★★☆☆

WELCOME TO MAINE COAST

TOP REASONS TO GO

★ **Lobster and Wild Maine Blueberries:** It's not a Maine vacation unless you don a bib and dig into a steamed lobster with drawn butter, and finish with a wild blueberry pie for dessert.

★ **Boating:** The coastline of Maine was made for boaters: whether it's your own boat, a friend's, or a charter, make sure you get out on the water.

★ **Hiking the Bold Coast:** Miles of unspoiled coastal and forest paths Down East make for a hiker's (and a birdwatcher's) dream.

★ **Cadillac Mountain:** Drive a winding 3½ miles to the 1,530-foot summit in Acadia National Park for the sunrise.

★ **Dining in Portland:** With over 250 restaurants and counting, Forest City is a foodie haven with one of the highest per capita restaurant densities in the United States.

1 **Kittery.**

2 **The Yorks.**

3 **Ogunquit.**

4 **Wells.**

5 **Kennebunk and Kennebunkport.**

6 **Biddeford.**

7 **Portland.**

8 **Casco Bay Islands.**

9 **Cape Elizabeth.**

10 **Freeport.**

11 **Brunswick.**

12 **Bath.**

13 **Wiscasset.**

14 **Boothbay.**

15 **Damariscotta.**

16 **Pemaquid Point.**

17 **Port Clyde.**

18 **Monhegan Island.**

19 **Rockland.**

20 **Rockport.**

21 **Camden.**

22 **Belfast.**

23 **Bucksport.**

24 **Bangor.**

25 **Blue Hill.**

26 **Deer Isle.**

27 **Isle Au Haut.**

28 **Bar Harbor.**

29 **Acadia National Park.**

30 **Bass Harbor.**

31 **Schoodic Peninsula.**

32 **Lubec.**

33 **Eastport.**

34 **Campobello Island, Canada.**

Old Town

Newport

egan

Bangor   24

95   9

179

9

191

32
33
34

Machias

Columbia
Falls

193

Bucksport   23

182

Cherryfield

Hancock

Jonesport

Beals
Island

Waterville

Searsport

Ellsworth   25

West Gouldsboro

3

Belfast   22   Castine

1

Blue Hill

Bar Harbor   31

Schoodic
Peninsula

Augusta

Islesboro Blue Hill
Peninusla

Mt.
Desert
Island

28
29

Frenchman Bay

17

21

26   Deer Isle

30

Acadia Nat'l
Park

Waldoboro

20   Camden

Rockport

Bass
Harbor

Northeast
Harbor

1

19   Rockland

Stonington

Newcastle   13   15

Thomaston   27

Isle
au Haut

Penobscot
Bay

2   Wiscasset

Damariscotta

Bath   Boothbay   Port Clyde   17

14   Pemaquid   16

orgetown   Point   18

Monhegan
Island

Atlantic Ocean

As you drive across the border into Maine, a sign reads, "The way life should be." It's a slogan that's hard to argue with once you've spent some time in the Pine Tree State. Here, time stays in step with you, and Mainers take their play just as seriously as their work.

Romantics thrill at the wind and salt spray in their faces on a historic windjammer. Birders fill their notebooks to the brim with new field notes. Families love the unspoiled beaches and sheltered inlets dotting the shoreline—not to mention the numerous homemade-ice-cream stands. Foodies revel in greater Portland's booming restaurant scene, while artists and art lovers find inspiration both on and off the canvas amid art galleries and museums or along the craggy seaboard. Adventure-seekers find many opportunities to kayak and cycle at the Bold Coast and Acadia National Park, whose trails invigorate hikers with their natural beauty. At night, the sky is dark enough to spot rare constellations and experience the magic of auroras.

The Maine Coast is several places in one. Classic New England townscapes with picturesque downtowns mingle with rocky shorelines punctuated by sandy beaches and secluded coves with sweeping views of lighthouses, forested islands, and the wide-open sea. So, no matter what strikes your fancy—a spontaneous picnic on the beach or a sunset cruise with a bottle of local wine, an afternoon exploring hidden tide pools or a dose of culture followed by shopping and dining in town—there's something to suit every disposition.

Counting all its nooks, crannies, and crags, Maine's coast would stretch thousands of miles if you could pull it straight, which means there's always some new, undiscovered territory awaiting you. Stretching north from Kittery to just outside Portland, the Southern Coast is the most popular area, with many top-notch restaurants, museums, and wineries. Don't let that stop you from heading further Down East (Maine-speak for "way up the coast"), where you'll be rewarded with the majestic mountains and rugged coastline of Acadia National Park, as well as the unspoiled, dramatic scenery of the Bold Coast.

MAJOR REGIONS

Stretching north from Kittery to just outside Portland, **the Southern Coast** is Maine's most visited region; miles of sandy expanses and shore towns cater to summer visitors. **Kittery, the Yorks, Wells,** and the **Kennebunks** offer low-key getaways, while **Biddeford**—a stone's throw from **Portland,** Maine's largest city—is on the rise, with charming boutiques and top-notch restaurants. **Ogunquit** is an artists' colony that's giving Provincetown a run for its money. The **Casco Bay Islands** lay just off the coast in various sizes, some are easier to access than others. Beautiful **Cape Elizabeth** is home to Portland Head Light and Winslow Homer's Studio, while **Freeport** is home to the headquarters of L.L. Bean and a lovely harbor.

North of Portland, from Brunswick to Monhegan Island, **the Mid-Coast Region** has a craggy coastline that winds its way around pastoral peninsulas. Its villages boast maritime museums, innovative restaurants, antiques shops, and beautiful architecture. **Brunswick,** while a bigger, more commercial city, has rows of historic brick and clapboard homes and is home to Bowdoin College. **Bath** is known for its maritime heritage. **Wiscasset** has arguably the best antiques shopping in the state. On its waterfront you can choose from a variety of seafood shacks competing for the best lobster rolls. **Damariscotta,** too, is worth a stop for its good seafood restaurants, and you'd be hard-pressed to find better-tasting oysters than those from the Damariscotta River. **Boothbay Harbor** is one of the quaintest towns in the Mid-Coast—and a busy tourist destination come summer, with lots of little stores that are perfect for window-shopping. It's also one of three towns from which you can take a ferry to **Monhegan Island,** which seems to be inhabited exclusively by painters at their easels, intent on capturing the wind-swept cliffs and weathered homes with colorful gardens. **Pemaquid Point** sits at the tip of the Pemaquid Peninsula, while the sleepy town of **Port Clyde** sits at the end of the St. George Peninsula.

Penobscot Bay covers an estimated 1,070 square miles and is home to more than 1,800 islands. It's dramatic natural scenery highlights its picture-perfect coastal towns, which include **Belfast, Rockport, Camden. Rockland** gets lots of attention thanks to a trio of attractions: the renowned Farnsworth Art Museum, the popular summer Lobster Festival, and the lively North Atlantic Blues Festival. **Bucksport** has the stunning Penobscot Narrows Bridge and the Fort Knox historic site. **Bangor** is the unofficial capital of northern Maine.

The large **Blue Hill Peninsula** juts south into Penobscot Bay. Painters, photographers, sculptors, and other artists are drawn to the peninsula; you can find more than 20 galleries on Deer Isle and at least half as many on the mainland. Not far from the mainland are the islands of Little Deer Isle and **Deer Isle. Blue Hill** and **Castine** are the area's primary business hubs. **Isle Au Haut** is only accessible by mail boat, but worth the effort.

Millions come to enjoy **Acadia National Park and Mount Desert Island's** stunning peaks and vistas. **Bar Harbor** is fun to explore, with its many gift shops and restaurants, while **Bass Harbor** offers quieter retreats.

The "real Maine," as some call the region known as **Way Down East,** unfurls in thousands of acres of wild blueberry barrens, congestion-free coastlines, vast wilderness preserves, and a tangible sense of rugged endurance. The landscape of **Schoodic Peninsula's** craggy coastline, towering evergreens, and views over Frenchman Bay are breathtaking year-round Towns on the peninsula include Grindstone Neck, Winter Harbor, and Gouldsboro; the peninsula's southern tip is home to the Schoodic section of Acadia National Park. **Lubec** is a popular destination for outdoor enthusiasts; a popular excursion is New Brunswick's **Campobello Island,** which has the Roosevelt Campobello International Park. **Eastport** is connected to the mainland by a granite causeway; it was once one of the nation's busiest seaports.

Planning

WHEN TO GO

Maine's dramatic coastline and pure natural beauty welcome visitors year-round, but note that many smaller museums and attractions are open only in high season (Memorial Day–mid-October), as are many waterside attractions and eateries.

Summer begins in earnest on July 4th, and you'll find that many smaller inns, B&Bs, and hotels from Kittery on up to Bar Harbor are booked a month or two in advance for dates through August. That's also the case come fall, when the fiery foliage draws leaf peepers. After Halloween, hotel rates drop significantly until ski season begins around Thanksgiving. Bed-and-breakfasts that stay open year-round but are not near ski slopes will often rent rooms at far lower prices than in summer.

In spring, the fourth Sunday in March is designated as Maine Maple Sunday, and farms throughout the state open their doors to visitors not only to watch sap turn into golden syrup but to sample the sweet results.

PLANNING YOUR TIME

You could easily spend a lifetime's worth of vacations along the Maine Coast and never truly see it all. But if you are determined to travel the coast end-to-end, allot at least two weeks at a comfortable pace. Count on longer transit time getting from place to place in summer, as traffic along U.S. 1 can be agonizing in high season, especially in the areas around Wiscasset and Acadia National Park.

GETTING HERE AND AROUND
AIR TRAVEL

Maine has two major international airports, Portland International Jetport and Bangor International Airport, to get you to or close to your coastal destination. Manchester–Boston Regional Airport in New Hampshire is about 45 minutes away from the southern end of the Maine coastline. Boston's Logan Airport is the only truly international airport in the region; it's about 90 minutes south of the Maine border.

BUS TRAVEL

The Shoreline Explorer links seasonal trolleys in southern Maine beach towns from the Yorks to the Kennebunks, allowing you to travel between towns without a car. Concord Coach Lines has

Driving in Coastal Maine

	MILES	TIME
Boston–Portland	112	2 hours
Kittery–Portland	50	50 minutes
Portland–Freeport	18	20 minutes
Portland–Camden	80	2 hours
Portland–Bar Harbor	175	3 hours 20 minutes

express service between Portland and Boston's Logan Airport and South Station. Concord operates out of the Portland Transportation Center (✉ *100 Thompson's Point Rd.*).

Shoreline Explorer

Running late June–Labor Day, the Shoreline Explorer offers seasonal trolley and shuttle service along the southern Maine coast. With links to private trolley operators in Kennebunkport, Ogunquit, and York, the service also provides access to the Amtrak Downeaster at Wells, as well as to the Sanford Regional Airport. Many lines have bicycle racks and wheelchair lifts, as well as stops close to trailheads for hiking. The Shoreline Explorer's Orange Line 5 offers year-round shuttle service with a bike rack from Sanford to Wells. A Day Pass or Multipass can be purchased from the driver. ☎ *207/459–2932* ⊕ *www.shorelineexplorer.com.*

CAR TRAVEL

Once you are here the best way to experience the winding back roads of the craggy Maine Coast is in a car. There are miles and miles of roads far from the larger towns that have no bus service, and you won't want to miss the chance to discover your own favorite ocean vista while on a scenic drive.

TRAIN TRAVEL

Amtrak offers regional service from Boston to Portland via its Downeaster line, which originates at Boston's North Station and makes six stops in Maine: Wells, Saco, Old Orchard Beach (seasonal), Portland, Freeport, and Brunswick.

RESTAURANTS

Many breakfast spots along the coast open as early as 6 am to serve the working crowd, and as early as 4 am for fishermen. Lunch generally runs 11–2:30; dinner is usually served 5–9. Only in larger cities will you find full dinners offered much later than 9, although in larger towns you can usually find a bar or bistro with a limited menu available late into the evening.

Many restaurants in Maine are closed Monday. Resort areas make an exception to this in high season, but these eateries often shut down altogether in the off-season. *Unless otherwise noted in reviews, restaurants are open daily for lunch and dinner.*

Credit cards are generally accepted at restaurants throughout Maine, even in more modest establishments, but it's still a good idea to have cash on hand wherever you go, just in case.

The one signature meal on the Maine Coast is, of course, the lobster dinner. It typically includes a whole boiled lobster with drawn butter for dipping, a clam or seafood chowder, corn on the cob, coleslaw, and a bib. Lobster prices vary from day to day, but generally a full lobster dinner should cost around $25–$30, or about $18–$20 without all the extras.

HOTELS

Beachfront and roadside motels, historic-home B&Bs and inns, as well as a handful of newer boutique hotels, make up the majority of lodging along the Maine Coast. There are a few larger luxury resorts, such as the Samoset Resort in Rockport or the Bar Harbor Inn in Bar Harbor, but most accommodations are simple, comfortable, and relatively inexpensive. You will find some chain hotels in larger cities and towns, including major tourist destinations like Portland, Freeport, and Bar Harbor. Many properties close during the off-season (mid-October–mid-May); those that stay open year-round often drop their rates dramatically after high season. (It is often possible to negotiate a nightly rate

with smaller establishments during low season.) There is a 9% state hospitality tax on all room rates. *Hotel reviews have been shortened. For full reviews visit Fodors.com.*

What It Costs

	$	$$	$$$	$$$$
RESTAURANTS				
	under $18	$18–$24	$25–$35	over $35
HOTELS				
	under $200	$200–$299	$300–$399	over $399

ACTIVITIES

No visit to the Maine Coast is complete without some outdoor activity—on two wheels, two feet, two paddles, or pulling a bag full of clubs.

BICYCLING

Both the Bicycle Coalition of Maine and Explore Maine by Bike are excellent resources for trail maps and other riding information.

Bicycle Coalition of Maine

The well-regarded Bicycle Coalition of Maine provides cyclists with essential touring information like cycling routes, safety tips, where to rent and repair bikes, and annual events. ✉ *34 Preble St., Portland* ☎ *207/623–4511* ⊕ *www. bikemaine.org.*

Explore Maine by Bike

Run by the Maine Department of Transportation, this helpful website includes an exhaustive list of the state's most popular bike routes, as well as other valuable cycling resources. ☎ *207/624–3300* ⊕ *www.exploremaine.org/bike.*

HIKING

Exploring the Maine Coast on foot is a quick way to acclimate yourself to the relaxed pace of life here—and sometimes the only way to access some of the best coastal spots. Many privately owned lands are accessible to hikers, especially way Down East. Inquire at a local establishment about hikes that may not appear on a map.

KAYAKING

Nothing gets you literally off the beaten path like plying the salt waters in a graceful sea kayak.

Maine Association of Sea Kayaking Guides and Instructors

This association lists state-licensed guides and offers information about instructional classes, guided tours, and trip planning. ⊕ www.mainepaddlesports.org.

Maine Island Trail Association

Seasoned paddlers can join the Maine Island Trail Association ($45 individual, $65 family) for a map of and full access to Maine's famous sea trail: more than 200 islands and mainland sites—most privately owned but open to members—on a 375-mile path from the southernmost coast to the Canadian Maritimes. Member benefits include discounts at outfitters and retailers. ⊠ 100 Kensington St., 2nd fl., Portland ☎ 207/761–8225 ⊕ www.mita.org.

VISITOR INFORMATION

CONTACTS Blue Hill Peninsula Chamber of Commerce ☎ 207/374–3242 ⊕ www. bluehillpeninsula.org. DownEast and Acadia Regional Tourism ☎ 207/546–3600, 888/665–3278 ⊕ www.downeastacadia. com. Southern Midcoast Maine Chamber ☎ 207/725–8797 ⊕ www.midcoastmaine. com. State of Maine Visitor Information Center ☎ 800/767–8709 ⊕ www.maine-tourism.com.

Kittery

65 miles north of Boston; 3 miles north of Portsmouth, New Hampshire.

Known as the "Gateway to Maine," Kittery has become primarily a major shopping destination thanks to its massive complex of factory outlets. Flanking both sides of U.S. 1 are more than 120 stores, which attract serious shoppers year-round. But Kittery has more to offer than just retail therapy: head east on Route 103 to the area around **Kittery Point** to experience the great outdoors. Here you'll find hiking and biking trails, as well as fantastic views of Portsmouth, New Hampshire, Whaleback Ledge Lighthouse, and the nearby Isles of Shoals. The isles and the light, along with two others, can be seen from two forts near this winding stretch of Route 103: Fort McClary State Historic Site and Fort Foster, a town park (both closed to vehicles off-season).

GETTING HERE AND AROUND

Three bridges—on U.S. 1, U.S. 1 Bypass, and Interstate 95—cross the Piscataqua River from Portsmouth, New Hampshire, to Kittery. Interstate 95 has three Kittery exits. Route 103 is a scenic coastal drive through Kittery Point to York.

ESSENTIALS

VISITOR INFORMATION

Kittery Visitor Information Center ⊠ Kittery ☎ 888/623–6345 ⊕ www.mainetourism.com.

🍴 Restaurants

Anju Noodle Bar

$ | ASIAN FUSION | With a cozy, open-plan dining area and a laid-back atmosphere, Anju Noodle Bar serves up Asian-fusion dishes such as house-made shredded pork buns, spicy miso ramen, and inspired local seafood dishes. This is one of the few places in the Pine Tree State outside Portland where you'll find fresh and innovative Asian-inspired cuisine done really well. **Known for:** sake heaven; free-style dishes; house-made kimchi. ⑤ *Average main: $15* ⊠ *7 Wallingford Sq., Unit 102* ☎ *207/703–4298* ⊕ *www. anjunoodlebar.com* ⊙ *Closed Mon.*

Chauncey Creek Lobster Pier

$$ | SEAFOOD | FAMILY | From the road you can barely see the red roof hovering below the trees, but chances are you can see the line of cars parked at this popular

outdoor restaurant that has been serving up fresh lobster for more than 70 years. Brightly colored picnic tables fill the deck and enclosed eating areas sit atop the high banks of the tidal river, beside a working pier, which delivers fresh seafood straight to your plate. **Known for:** classic lobster dinners; dog-friendly; ocean-to-plate. Ⓢ *Average main: $23* ⊠ *16 Chauncey Creek Rd.* ☎ *207/439–1030* ⊕ *www.chaunceycreek.com* ⊘ *Closed Columbus Day–mid-May; closed Mon. post–Labor Day–Columbus Day.*

 Activities

HIKING AND WALKING

Cutts Island Trail

HIKING/WALKING | For a peek into the Rachel Carson National Wildlife Refuge, this scenic 1.8-mile upland trail leads into the 800-acre Brave Boat Harbor Division and is a prime bird-watching area. There's a restroom and an information kiosk at the trailhead. The trail is open dawn–dusk year-round; dogs are not allowed. ⊠ *Seapoint Rd.* ☎ *207/646–9226* ⊕ *www.fws. gov/refuge/rachel_carson.*

York Village

8 miles north of Kittery via I–95, U.S. 1, and U.S. 1A.

Spending an afternoon in York village is like going back in time—and you really only need a couple of hours here to roam the historic streets of this pint-size but worthwhile town. One of the first permanent settlements in Maine, the village museums detail its rich history. York is also home to the flagship store of Stonewall Kitchen, one of Maine's signature gourmet-food purveyors; the store has a café and a cooking school. There's also a cluster of vibrant contemporary-art galleries.

GETTING HERE AND AROUND

York is Exit 7 off Interstate 95; follow signs to U.S. 1, the modern commercial strip. From here, U.S. 1A will take you to the village center and on to York Harbor and York Beach before looping back up to U.S. 1 in Cape Neddick.

ESSENTIALS
VISITOR INFORMATION
Greater York Region Chamber of Commerce
✉ *York* ☎ *207/363–4422* ⊕ *www.gate-waytomaine.org.*

Sights

George Marshall Store Gallery

ARTS VENUE | The storefront windows and beadboard trim at the George Marshall Store Gallery (built in 1867) pay homage to its past as a general store, but the focus here is on the present. Changing exhibits, installations, and educational programs focus on prominent and up-and-coming regional artists. ✉ *140 Lindsay Rd.* ☎ *207/351–1083* ⊕ *www.georgemarshallstoregallery.com.*

Museums of Old York

HISTORIC SITE | **FAMILY** | Nine historic 18th- and 19th-century buildings, clustered on York Street and along Lindsay Road and the York River, highlight York's rich history, which dates back to early Colonial times. The Old York Gaol (1719) was once the King's Prison for the Province of Maine; inside are dungeons, cells, and the jailer's quarters. The many period rooms in the Emerson-Wilcox House, the main part of which was built in 1742, display items from daily life here in centuries past, including furniture from the 1600s and an impressive ceramic dishware collection. The 1731 Elizabeth Perkins House reflects the Victorian style of its last occupants, the prominent Perkins family. Start your visit at the museum's visitor center, located at 3 Lindsay Road in the Remick Barn at the corner of U.S. 1A and Lindsay Road in York. ✉ *Visitor center, 3 Lindsay Rd.* ☎ *207/363–1756* ⊕ *www.oldyork.org* 🎟 *From $8.*

Stonewall Kitchen

STORE/MALL | You've probably seen the kitchen's smartly labeled jars of gourmet chutneys, jams, jellies, salsas, and sauces in specialty stores back home. This complex houses the expansive flagship company store, which has a viewing area of the bottling process and stunning gardens. Sample all the mustards, salsas, and dressings you can stand, or have lunch at the café and take-out restaurant. The campus also houses a cooking school where you can join in evening or daytime courses. Reservations are required; most classes are shorter than two hours and cost $55–$80. ✉ *2 Stonewall La., off U.S. 1* ☎ *207/351–2712* ⊕ *www.stonewallkitch-en.com/yorkstore.html.*

Shopping

Gateway Farmers' Market

OUTDOOR/FLEA/GREEN MARKETS | Bring your own bag for morning shopping at the Gateway Farmers' Market, held in the back lot at the Greater York Region Chamber of Commerce in summer (Saturday mid-May–October, 9 am–1 pm), and inside the building in winter (designated Saturdays November–March, 9 am–1 pm). You'll find fresh local produce, lots of baked goods and artisanal breads, local seafood and meat, fresh flowers, and handcrafted items like soaps and candles. It's a good place to gather the makings for a beach picnic or to stock up on holiday gifts. ✉ *1 Stonewall La., off U.S. 1, York* ☎ *207/363–4422* ⊕ *gateway-tomaine.org/farmersmarket/.*

Ocean Fire Pottery

CRAFTS | This artist-owned and -operated studio and gallery features unique wheel-thrown stoneware. Live demonstrations are available daily; call ahead to make sure the studio is open during the off-season. ✉ *23 Woodbridge Rd.* ☎ *207/361–3131* ⊕ *www.oceanfirepottery.com.*

York Harbor

8 miles from Kittery via U.S. 1.

A short distance from the village proper, York Harbor opens to the water and offers many places to linger and explore. The harbor itself is busy with boats of all kinds, while the sandy harbor beach is good for swimming. Much quieter and more formal than York Beach to the north, this area has a somewhat exclusive air. Perched along the cliffs on the north side of the harbor are huge "cottages" built by wealthy summer residents in the late 1800s, when the area became a premier seaside resort destination with several grand hotels.

GETTING HERE AND AROUND

After passing through York Village to York Harbor (originally called Lower Town), U.S. 1A winds around and heads north to York Beach's village center, a 4-mile trip.

Sights

Sayward-Wheeler House

HISTORIC SITE | Built in 1718, the waterfront home was remodeled in the 1760s by Jonathan Sayward, a local merchant who had prospered in the West Indies trade. By 1860 his descendants had opened the house to the public to share the story of their Colonial ancestors. Accessible only by guided tour (second and fourth Saturdays June–October 15, 11–4), the house reveals the decor of a prosperous New England family at the outset of the Revolutionary War. The parlor—considered one of the country's best-preserved Colonial interiors, with a tall clock and mahogany Chippendale-style chairs—looks pretty much as it did when Sayward lived here. ⊠ *9 Barrell La. Ext.* ☎ *207/384–2454* ⊕ *www. historicnewengland.org* ⊠ *$5* ⊘ *Closed mid-Oct.–May.*

Restaurants

Dockside Restaurant

$$$ | SEAFOOD | On an islandlike peninsula overlooking York Harbor, this restaurant has plenty of seafood on the menu. Floor-to-ceiling windows in the stepped modern dining space transport diners to the water beyond—every seat has a water view. **Known for:** "drunken" lobster (sautéed lobster, scallops, shallots, and herbs in an Irish-whiskey cream); beef tenderloin; lively, dockside vibe with spectacular views. ⑤ *Average main: $25* ⊠ *22 Harris Island Rd., off Rte. 103* ☎ *207/363–2722* ⊕ *www.dockside-restaurant.com* ⊘ *Closed Tues. in summer and late Oct.–mid-May.*

Foster's Downeast Clambake

$$$ | SEAFOOD | FAMILY | Save your appetite for this one. Specializing in the traditional Maine clambake—a feast consisting of rich clam chowder, a pile of mussels and steamers, Maine lobster with drawn butter for dipping, corn on the cob, roasted potatoes and onions, and Maine blueberry crumb cake (phew!)—this massive complex provides musical entertainment to go with its belly-busting meals. **Known for:** finger-licking barbecue; classic Maine fare; gatherings for groups of families and friends. ⑤ *Average main: $28* ⊠ *5 Axholme Rd., at U.S. 1A* ☎ *207/363–3255, 800/552–0242* ⊕ *www.fostersclambake.com* ⊘ *Closed early Sept.–late May, and weekdays late May–mid-June.*

Hotels

Inn at Tanglewood Hall

$$ | B&B/INN | This 1880s Victorian "cottage" is a haven of shabby-chic decor and comfort—artfully painted floors, lush wallpaper, and meticulous attention to detail are the fruits of a former designation as a designers' showcase home. **Pros:** authentic historic lodging; short walk to beaches; fireplaces in all rooms. **Cons:** no water views; dated

decor; no pets or children under 12.
⑤ *Rooms from: $200* ✉ *611 York St., York* ☎ *207/351–1075* ⊕ *www.tanglewoodhall. com* ⊅ *6 rooms* ❤ *Free breakfast.*

★ **Stage Neck Inn**
$$$ | **RESORT** | **FAMILY** | A family-run operation that is now in the competent hands of the second generation, this resort hotel takes full advantage of its gorgeous harborside location, with Adirondack chairs, chaise lounges and a fire pit on the surrounding lawns, water views from most guest rooms, and floor-to-ceiling windows in the common spaces. **Pros:** elaborate full-breakfast buffet with scrumptious baked goods; poolside service and snack bar in season; rooms have balconies or deck areas and most have water views. **Cons:** spa is on the smaller side; some rooms have only partial water views; rooms with two beds have doubles rather than queens. ⑤ *Rooms from: $300* ✉ *8 Stage Neck Rd., off U.S. 1A* ☎ *800/340–1130, 207/363–3850* ⊕ *www.stageneck. com* ☉ *Closed 1st 2 wks in Jan.* ⊅ *60 rooms, 1 cottage* ❤ *Free breakfast.*

York Harbor Inn
$$ | **B&B/INN** | A mid-17th-century fishing cabin with dark timbers and a fieldstone fireplace forms the heart of this historic inn, which now includes several neighboring buildings. **Pros:** many rooms have harbor views; close to beaches, scenic walking trails; kid-friendly. **Cons:** rooms vary greatly in style, size, and appeal; no ocean views at the Chapman House; some rooms in need of an update. ⑤ *Rooms from: $200* ✉ *480 York St.* ☎ *207/363–5119* ⊕ *www.yorkharborinn. com* ⊅ *61 rooms* ❤ *Free breakfast.*

 Activities

BIKING
Berger's Bike Shop
BICYCLING | This former auto garage and full-service bike shop rents hybrid bikes for local excursions and sells bikes of all kinds. ✉ *241 York St., York* ☎ *207/363–4070.*

FISHING
For a list of fishing charters, check the directory on the Maine Fishing Guides website (⊕ *www.maineguides.com/ activity/fishing-guides*).

Shearwater Charters
FISHING | Shearwater Charters offers light tackle and fly-fishing charters in the York River and along the shoreline from Kittery to Ogunquit. Bait-fishing trips are also available. Departures are from Town Dock #2 in York Harbor. ✉ *Town Dock #2, 20 Harris Island Rd., York* ☎ *207/363–5324* ⊕ *www.mainestripers.net.*

HIKING AND WALKING
Cliff Walk and Fisherman's Walk
HIKING/WALKING | Two walking trails begin near Harbor Beach. Starting in a small nearby park, the Cliff Walk ascends its granite namesake and passes the summer "cottages" at the harbor entrance. There are some steps, but, as signs caution, tread carefully because of erosion. Fisherman's Walk, on the other hand, is an easy stroll. Starting across Stage Neck Road from the beach, it passes waterfront businesses, historic homes, and rocky harbor beaches on the way to York's beloved Wiggly Bridge. This pedestrian suspension bridge alongside Route 103 (there is minimal parking here) leads to Steedman Woods, a public preserve with a shaded loop trail along the York River estuary's ambling waters. You can also enter the preserve near the George Marshall Store in York Village ✉ *Stage Neck Rd., off U.S. 1A, York.*

York Beach

6 miles north of York Harbor via U.S. 1A.

Like many shorefront towns in Maine, York Beach has a long history entertaining summer visitors. It's easy to imagine tourists adorned in the full-length bathing garb of the late 19th century. Visitors still come here to eat ice cream, enjoy carnival-like novelties, and indulge in the sun and salty sea air.

York Beach is a real family destination, devoid of all things staid and stuffy—children are meant to be both seen and heard here. Just beyond the sands of Short Sands Beach are a host of amusements, from bowling to indoor minigolf and the Fun-O-Rama arcade. Nubble Light is at the tip of the peninsula separating Long Sands and Short Sands beaches. The latter is mostly lined with unpretentious seasonal homes, with motels and restaurants mixed in.

GETTING HERE AND AROUND

It's a scenic 6 miles to York Beach via the loop road, U.S. 1A, from its southern intersection with U.S. 1. Although 2 miles longer, it's generally faster to continue north on U.S. 1A to Cape Neddick and then U.S 1A south to the village center, home to Short Sands Beach. Here U.S. 1A is known as Ocean Avenue as it heads north from York Harbor along Long Sands Beach en route to York Beach village and Short Sands Beach.

A trolley along U.S. 1 links the beaches in summer. You can also get from beach to beach on a series of residential streets that wind around Nubble Point between these beaches.

York Trolley Co

From late June through Labor Day, these bright-red trolleys link Short Sands Beach in York Beach village and nearby Long Sands Beach, running along U.S. 1A, making a number of stops. Maps can be picked up throughout York; fares are $2 one-way, $4 round-trip, cash only (payable to driver upon boarding). You can also connect with a shuttle service to Ogunquit. ⊠ *York* ☎ *207/363–9600* ⊕ *www.yorktrolley.com.*

Sights

★ Nubble Light

HISTORIC SITE | On a small island just off the tip of the cape jutting dramatically into the Atlantic Ocean between Long Sands Beach and Short Sands Beach,

Nubble Light is one of the most photographed lighthouses on the globe. Direct access is prohibited, but the small Sohier Park right across from the light has parking, historical placards, benches, and a seasonal information center that shares the 1879 light's history. ⊠ *End of Nubble Rd., off U.S. 1A, York* ☎ *207/363–3569 (Memorial Day weekend–Labor Day)* ⊕ *www.nubblelight.org.*

York's Wild Kingdom

AMUSEMENT PARK/WATER PARK | FAMILY | Surrounded by forest, this popular zoo has an impressive variety of exotic animals and is home to the state's only white Bengal tiger. There's a nostalgic charm to the amusement park, which offers discounts for kids under 13—the target market, as there are no large thrill rides. Many York Beach visitors come just to enjoy the ocean views from the Ferris wheel and share what's advertised as the "seaboard's largest fried dough." ⊠ *1 Animal Park Rd., off U.S. 1* ☎ *207/363–4911* ⊕ *www.yorkswildkingdom.com* 🍴 *From $15.*

Restaurants

The Goldenrod

$ | AMERICAN | FAMILY | People line the windows to watch Goldenrod Kisses being made the same way they have since 1896—and some 50 tons are made every year. Aside from the famous taffy (there's penny candy, too), this eatery is family oriented, very reasonably priced, and a great place to get ice cream from the old-fashioned soda fountain. **Known for:** laid-back, kid-friendly atmosphere; breakfast served all day; classic American fare, like burgers, hot dogs, and baked dinners. ⑤ *Average main: $10* ⊠ *2 Railroad Ave.* ☎ *207/363–2621* ⊕ *www.thegoldenrod.com* ⊘ *Closed mid-Oct.–mid-May.*

618

618

618

618

 # Hotels

Atlantic House Inn

$ | B&B/INN | FAMILY | In a nicely renovated 1888 beauty, this inn's standard guest rooms feel fresh with designer fabrics, gas fireplaces, and whirlpool tubs. **Pros:** lots of amenities; walk to beach, shops; suites are a good choice for weekly stay; some ocean views. **Cons:** not on beach; lacks public spaces; some rooms have a two-night minimum. $ *Rooms from: $170* ✉ *2 Beach St.* ☎ *207/361–6677* ⊕ *www.atlantichouseinn.com* ⊙ *Closed Nov.–Apr.* ⇆ *16 rooms* ⦵ *No meals.*

Union Bluff Hotel

$$ | HOTEL | This massive, turreted structure still looks much the same as it did when it opened in the mid-19th century, and the proximity to the beach can't be beat—just don your suit and step outside. **Pros:** many spectacular ocean views; in the middle of the action; spacious balconies. **Cons:** rooms lack any charm or character befitting of inn's origins; not for those looking for a quiet getaway; decor in need of an update. $ *Rooms from: $290* ✉ *8 Beach St.* ☎ *207/363–1333* ⊕ *www.unionbluff.com* ⇆ *71 rooms* ⦵ *No meals.*

Ogunquit

8 miles north of the Yorks via U.S. 1.

A resort village since the late 19th century, Ogunquit made a name for itself as an artists' colony. Today it has become a mini Provincetown, with a gay population that swells in summer, and many inns and small clubs cater to a primarily gay and lesbian clientele. The nightlife in Ogunquit revolves around the precincts of Ogunquit Square and Perkins Cove, where people stroll, often enjoying an after-dinner ice cream cone or espresso. For a scenic drive, take Shore Road from downtown to the 175-foot Bald Head Cliff; you'll be treated to views up and down the coast. On a stormy day the surf can be quite wild here.

GETTING HERE AND AROUND

Parking in the village and at the beach is costly and limited, so leave your car at the hotel or in a public parking space and hop the trolley. It costs $1.50 per trip and runs Memorial Day weekend–Columbus Day, with weekend-only service during the first few weeks. From Perkins Cove, the trolley runs through town along Shore Road and then down to Ogunquit Beach; it also stops along U.S. 1.

ESSENTIALS

TRANSPORTATION INFORMATION
Shoreline Explorer ☎ *800/965–5762* ⊕ *www.shorelineexplorer.com/.*

VISITOR INFORMATION Ogunquit Chamber of Commerce ☎ *207/646–2939* ⊕ *www.ogunquit.org.*

 # Sights

Perkins Cove

HISTORIC SITE | FAMILY | This neck of land off Shore Road in the lower part of Ogunquit village has a jumble of sea-weathered fish houses and buildings that were part of an art school. These have largely been transformed by the tide of tourism into shops and restaurants. When you've had your fill of browsing, stroll out along **Marginal Way,** a mile-long, paved footpath that hugs the shore of a rocky promontory known as Israels Head. Benches allow you to appreciate the open sea vistas. Expect heavy foot traffic along the path, even in the off-season. ✉ *Perkins Cove Rd., off Shore Rd.*

Restaurants

Amore Breakfast

$ | AMERICAN | You could hardly find a more satisfying, heartier breakfast than at this smart and busy joint just shy of the entrance to Perkins Cove where a lighthearted mix of retro advertising

Ogunquit's Perkins Cove is a pleasant place to admire the boats (and wonder at the origin of their names).

signs adorn the walls of the bright, open, and bustling dining room. Rest assured you won't find tired standards here—the only pancakes are German potato, and the Oscar Madison omelet combines crabmeat with asparagus and Swiss, topped with a béarnaise sauce. **Known for:** innovative, rotating breakfast menus; bustling, laid-back atmosphere, chock-full of locals; community involvement. ⑤ *Average main: $10* ✉ *87 Main St.* ✚ *At blinking light* ☎ *207/646–6667* ⊕ *www. amorebreakfast.com* ⊘ *Closed mid Dec.– early Apr. No dinner.*

★ Northern Union

$$$ | CONTEMPORARY | From the moment you walk into Northern Union you know you're going to be very good hands. A genuine, welcoming staff and laid-back yet elegant design scheme put you in the mood for a slow, very memorable dinner consisting of seasonally inspired small plates like braised pork belly or duck confit and rotating entrées like seared scallops and lobster fettuccine with spot-on wine pairings that you won't find anywhere else in the area.

Known for: almost everything is made in-house; dishes that can easily be shared; a terrific selection of cold cuts and cheese boards with a local, seasonal bent. ⑤ *Average main: $27* ✉ *261 Shore Rd.* ☎ *207/216–9639* ⊕ *www. northern-union.me* ⊘ *No lunch.*

Wells

5 miles north of Ogunquit via U.S. 1.

Lacking any kind of discernible village center, Wells could be easily overlooked as nothing more than a commercial stretch of U.S. 1 between Ogunquit and the Kennebunks. But look more closely: this is a place where people come to enjoy some of the best beaches on the coast. Until 1980 the town of Wells incorporated Ogunquit, and today this family-oriented beach community has 7 miles of densely populated shoreline, along with nature preserves, where you can explore salt marshes and tidal pools.

GETTING HERE AND AROUND

Just $2 per trip, the seasonal Shoreline Trolley serves Wells Beach and Crescent Beach and has many stops along U.S. 1 at motels, campgrounds, restaurants, and so on. You can also catch it at the Wells Transportation Center when Amtrak's *Downeaster* pulls in.

ESSENTIALS

The Shoreline Trolley is part of the Shoreline Explorer network, which links seasonal trolleys in southern Maine beach towns from York to the Kennebunks, including the Wells area.

VISITOR INFORMATION Wells Chamber of Commerce ☎ *207/646–2451* ⊕ *www. wellschamber.org.*

Sights

Rachel Carson National Wildlife Refuge

NATURE PRESERVE | FAMILY | At the headquarters of the Rachel Carson National Wildlife Refuge, which has 11 divisions from Kittery to Cape Elizabeth, is the Carson Trail, a 1-mile loop. The trail traverses a salt marsh and a white-pine forest where migrating birds and waterfowl of many varieties are regularly spotted, and it borders Branch Brook and the Merriland River. ⊠ *321 Port Rd.* ☎ *207/646–9226* ⊕ *www.fws.gov/refuge/rachel_carson/.*

Beaches

With its thousands of acres of marsh and preserved land, Wells is a great place to spend time outdoors. Nearly 7 miles of sand stretch along the boundaries of Wells, making beachgoing a prime occupation. Tidal pools sheltered by rocks are filled with all manner of creatures awaiting discovery. During the summer season a pay-and-display parking system (no quarters, receipt goes on dashboard) is in place at the public beaches.

A summer trolley serves **Crescent Beach,** along Webhannet Drive, and **Wells Beach,** at the end of Mile Road

off U.S. 1. There is another parking lot, but no trolley stop, at the north end of Atlantic Avenue, which runs north along the shore from the end of Mile Road. Stretching north from the jetty at Wells Harbor is **Drakes Island Beach** (end of Drakes Island Road off U.S. 1). Lifeguards are on hand at all beaches, and all have public restrooms.

Crescent Beach

BEACH—SIGHT | FAMILY | Lined with summer homes, this sandy strand is busy in the summer, but the beach and the water are surprisingly clean, considering all the traffic. The swimming's good, and beachgoers can also explore tidal pools and look for seals on the sea rocks nearby. **Amenities:** food and drink; lifeguards; parking (fee); toilets. **Best for:** swimming. ⊠ *Webhannet Dr., south of Mile Rd.* ☎ *207/646–5113.*

Drakes Island Beach

BEACH—SIGHT | FAMILY | Smaller and quieter than the other two beaches in Wells, Drakes Island Beach is also a little more natural, with rolling sand dunes and access to salt-marsh walking trails at an adjacent estuary. The ice-cream truck swings by regularly in the summer. **Amenities:** lifeguards; parking (fee); toilets. **Best for:** walking. ⊠ *Island Beach Rd., 1 mile southwest of U.S. 1* ☎ *207/646–5113.*

Wells Beach

BEACH—SIGHT | FAMILY | The northern end of a 2-mile stretch of golden sand, Wells Beach is popular with families and surfers, who line up in the swells and preen on the boardwalk near the arcade and snack shop. The beach's northern tip is a bit quieter, with a long rock jetty perfect for strolling. **Amenities:** food and drink; lifeguards; parking (fee); toilets. **Best for:** surfing; walking. ⊠ *Atlantic Ave., north of Mile Rd.* ☎ *207/646–5113.*

Wheels and Waves

STORE/MALL | Rent bikes, surfboards, wet suits, boogie boards, kayaks, and all sorts of outdoor gear at Wheels and Waves. ⊠ *365 Post Rd., U.S. 1* ☎ *207/646–5774* ⊕ *www.wheelsnwaves.com.*

🍴 Restaurants

Billy's Chowder House

$ | **SEAFOOD** | **FAMILY** | Locals and vacationers head to this roadside seafood restaurant in the midst of a salt marsh en route to Wells Beach. The menu features classic seafood dishes like lobster rolls and chowders, but there are plenty of nonseafood choices, too. **Known for:** views of the Rachel Carson National Wildlife Refuge; generous lobster rolls; one of the oldest waterfront restaurants in Wells. $ Average main: $17 ✉ 216 Mile Rd. ☎ 207/646–7558 ⊕ www. billyschowderhouse.com ⊙ Closed mid-Dec.–mid-Jan.

★ Bitter End

$$ | **SEAFOOD** | Pete and Kate Morency, the duo originally behind the ever-popular Pier 77 and the Ramp Bar and Grill in Kennebunkport, are also the masterminds behind this fabulous seafood spot that serves up brilliant, contemporary twists to American and Mediterranean classics, adding healthy spins on staples such as fish-and-chips (think a light turmeric breading and kimchi instead of coleslaw). The fabulous decor consists of an unlikely marriage of old-school American sports memorabilia and something that might be described as shabby ballroom chic—crystal chandeliers hang above old leather boxing gloves, and black-and-white photos of sports icons and an array of shiny trophies (including a retro Miss America cup that has proven a hit with the selfie generation) line the bar amidst a superbly curated bevy of liquors. **Known for:** cuisine fusion and a rotating menu; outdoor seating area with lawn games and a fire pit; a lively happy hour enjoyed by locals and flatlanders alike. $ Average main: $18 ✉ 2118 Post Rd. ☎ 207/360–0904 ⊕ www.bitterend. me ⊙ Closed Tues.

Maine Diner

$ | **DINER** | One look at the 1953 exterior and you'll start craving diner food, but be prepared to get a little more than you bargained for: after all, how many greasy spoons make an award-winning lobster pie? There's plenty of fried seafood in addition to the usual diner fare, and breakfast is served all day. **Known for:** classic Maine diner fare; wild blueberry pie; diner has a vegetable garden, which it uses as much as possible in the creation of its dishes. $ Average main: $15 ✉ 2265 Post Rd. ☎ 207/646–4441 ⊕ www.mainediner.com ⊙ Closed at least 1 wk in Jan.

Spinnakers

$$ | **SEAFOOD** | **FAMILY** | Plenty of seafood shacks dot U.S. 1, but this roadside joint is really worth the stop, even if it's just to grab an ice-cream cone to escape the steady flow of summer traffic. Simple but pleasing contemporary design makes for a cheerful space to enjoy loaded lobster rolls, burgers and sandwiches, and a decidedly unholy lobster poutine consisting of hand-cut fries covered in a delicious mess of local cheese curds and topped with lobster gravy. **Known for:** pick-and-choose seafood basket combos; quick bites that pack a punch and scream Maine; eat in or grab something to go from the takeout window. $ Average main: $18 ✉ 139 Post Rd. ☎ 207/216–9291 ⊕ spinnakers-maine.com ⊙ Closed Mon.

🛏 Hotels

Haven by the Sea

$$ | **B&B/INN** | Once the summer mission of St. Martha's Church in Kennebunkport, this exquisite inn has retained many original details from its former life as a seaside church, including cathedral ceilings and stained-glass windows. **Pros:** unusual structure with elegant appointments; beach towels and beach chairs available; rotating breakfasts that cater to dietary restrictions without compromising taste; nightly happy hour with complimentary appetizers and courtesy sherry, port, and brandy in the main parlor. **Cons:** not an in-town location; distant ocean views;

$50 cancellation fee no matter how far in advance. $ *Rooms from: $260* ✉ *59 Church St.* ☎ *207/646–4194* ⊕ *www. havenbythesea.com* ⏎ *9 rooms, 1 apartment* ⊚ *Free breakfast.*

Kennebunk and Kennebunkport

5 miles north of Wells via U.S. 1.

The town centers of Kennebunk and Kennebunkport are separated by 5 miles and two rivers, but united by a common history and a laid-back seaside vibe. Perhaps best described as the Hamptons of the Pine Tree State, Kennebunkport has been a resort area since the 19th century. Its most recent residents have made it even more famous: the dynastic Bush family is often in residence on its immense estate here, which sits dramatically out on Walker's Point on Cape Arundel. Newer homes have sprung up alongside the old, and a great way to take them all in is with a slow drive out Ocean Avenue along the cape.

Sometimes bypassed on the way to its sister town, Kennebunk has its own appeal. Once a major shipbuilding center, Kennebunk today retains the feel of a classic New England small town, with an inviting shopping district, steepled churches, and fine examples of 18th- and 19th-century brick and clapboard homes. There are also plenty of natural spaces for walking, swimming, birding, and biking, and the Kennebunks' major beaches are here.

GETTING HERE AND AROUND

Kennebunk's main village sits along U.S. 1, extending west from the Mousam River. The Lower Village is along Routes 9 and 35, 4 miles down Route 35 from the main village, and the drive between the two keeps visitors agog with the splendor of the area's mansions, spread out on both sides of Route 35. To get to the grand and gentle beaches of Kennebunk, continue straight (the road becomes Beach Avenue) at the intersection with Route 9. If you turn left instead, Route 9 will take you across the Kennebunk River, into Kennebunkport's touristy downtown, called Dock Square (or sometimes just "the Port"), a commercial area with restaurants, shops, boat cruises, and galleries. Here you'll find the most activity (and crowds) in the Kennebunks.

Take the Intown Trolley for narrated 45-minute jaunts that run daily from Memorial Day weekend through Columbus Day. The $16 fare is valid for the day, so you can hop on and off—or start your journey—at any of the stops. The route includes Kennebunk's beaches and Lower Village as well as neighboring Kennebunkport's scenery and sights. The main stop is at 21 Ocean Avenue in Kennebunkport, around the corner from Dock Square.

ESSENTIALS

VISITOR INFORMATION Intown Trolley ☎ *207/967–3686* ⊕ *www.intowntrolley. com.* **Kennebunk-Kennebunkport Chamber of Commerce** ☎ *207/967–0857* ⊕ *www. gokennebunks.com.*

WALKING TOURS

To take a little walking tour of Kennebunk's most notable structures, begin at the Federal-style Brick Store Museum at 117 Main Street. Head south on Main Street (turn left out of the museum) to see several extraordinary 18th- and early-19th-century homes, including the **Lexington Elms** at No. 99 (1799), the **Horace Porter House** at No. 92 (1848), and the **Benjamin Brown House** at No. 85 (1788).

When you've had your fill of historic homes, head back up toward the museum, pass the 1773 **First Parish Unitarian Church** (its Asher Benjamin–style steeple contains an original Paul Revere bell), and turn right onto **Summer Street**. This street is an architectural showcase, revealing an array of styles from Colonial to Federal. Walking past these grand beauties will give you a real sense of the economic prowess and glamour of the long-gone shipbuilding industry.

For a guided 90-minute architectural walking tour of Summer Street, contact the museum at ☎ *207/985–4802.* You can also purchase a $4.95 map that marks historic buildings or a $15.95 guidebook, *Windows on the Past.*

For a dramatic walk along Kennebunkport's rocky coastline and beneath the views of Ocean Avenue's grand mansions, head out on the **Parson's Way Shore Walk,** a paved 4.8-mile round-trip. Begin at Dock Square and follow Ocean Avenue along the river, passing the Colony Hotel and St. Ann's Church, all the way to Walker's Point. Simply turn back from here.

◉ Sights

Brick Store Museum

MUSEUM | FAMILY | The cornerstone of this block-long preservation of early-19th-century commercial and residential buildings is William Lord's Brick Store. Built as a dry-goods store in 1825 in the Federal style, the building has an openwork balustrade across the roofline, granite lintels over the windows, and paired chimneys. Exhibits chronicle the Kennebunk area's history and Early American decorative and fine arts. Museum staff lead architectural walking tours of Kennebunk's National Historic District by appointment late May–September. ⊠ *117 Main St., Kennebunk* ☎ *207/985–4802* ⊕ *www. brickstoremuseum.org* ✉ *$7* ⊙ *Closed Mon.*

Dock Square

PLAZA | Clothing boutiques, T-shirt shops, art galleries, and restaurants line this bustling square, spreading out along the nearby streets and alleys. Walk onto the drawbridge to admire the tidal Kennebunk River; cross to the other side and you are in the Lower Village of neighboring Kennebunk. ⊠ *Dock Sq., Kennebunkport.*

First Families Kennebunkport Museum

HOUSE | FAMILY | Also known as White Columns, the imposing Greek Revival mansion with Doric columns is furnished with the belongings of four generations of the Perkins-Nott family. From mid-July through mid-October, the 1853 house is open for guided tours and also serves as a gathering place for village walking tours. It is owned by the Kennebunkport Historical Society, which has several other historical buildings a mile away at 125–135 North Street, including an old jail and schoolhouse. ⊠ *8 Maine St., Kennebunkport* ☎ *207/967–2751* ⊕ *www. kporthistory.org* ✉ *$10.*

First Parish of Kennebunk Unitarian Universalist Church

RELIGIOUS SITE | FAMILY | Built in 1773, just before the American Revolution, this stunning church is a marvel. The 1804 Asher Benjamin–style steeple stands proudly atop the village, and the sounds of the original Paul Revere bell can be heard for miles. The church holds Sunday service at 9:30 am in the summer (at 10:30 the rest of the year). ⊠ *114 Main St., Kennebunk* ☎ *207/985–3700* ⊕ *www. uukennebunk.org.*

Kennebunk Plains

NATURE PRESERVE | FAMILY | For an unusual experience, visit this 135-acre grasslands habitat that is home to several rare and endangered species. Locals call it Blueberry Plains, and a good portion of the area is abloom with the hues of ripening wild blueberries in late July; after August 1, you are welcome to pick and eat all the berries you can find. The area is maintained by the Nature Conservancy. ⊠ *Webber Hill Rd., Kennebunk* ✛ *4½ miles northwest of town* ☎ *207/729–5181* ⊕ *www.nature.org.*

Seashore Trolley Museum

MUSEUM | FAMILY | Streetcars were built here from 1872 to 1972, including trolleys for major metropolitan areas—from Boston to Budapest, New York to Nagasaki, and San Francisco to Sydney.

Many of them are beautifully restored and displayed. Best of all, you can take a nearly 4-mile ride on the tracks of the former Atlantic Shoreline trolley line, with a stop along the way at the museum restoration shop, where trolleys are transformed from junk into gems. The outdoor museum is self-guided. ⊠ *195 Log Cabin Rd., Kennebunkport* ☎ *207/967–2712* ⊕ *www.trolleymuseum. org* ⊠ *$12* ⊙ *Closed Sept.–Apr. except 1st 2 weekends in Dec.*

Beaches

Gooch's Beach

BEACH—SIGHT | **FAMILY** | Kennebunk has three beaches, one after another, along Beach Avenue, which is lined with cottages and old Victorians. The most northerly, and the closest to downtown Kennebunkport, is Gooch's Beach, the main swimming beach. Next is stony Kennebunk Beach, followed by Mother's Beach, which is popular with families. There's a small playground and tidal puddles for splashing; rock outcroppings lessen the waves. **Amenities:** lifeguards; parking (fee); toilets. **Best for:** walking; swimming. ⊠ *Beach Ave., south of Rte. 9, Kennebunk.*

Goose Rocks Beach

BEACH—SIGHT | Three-mile-long Goose Rocks, a 10-minute drive north of town, has a good long stretch of smooth sand and plenty of shallow pools for exploring. It's a favorite of families with small children. Pick up a $15 daily parking permit at the Kennebunkport Town Office on Elm Street; the Goose Rocks General Store at 3 Dyke Road; or the Police Department at 101 Main Street. Dogs are allowed (on a leash during the high season), but only before 8 am and after 6 pm. No facilities are available at the beach. **Amenities:** parking (fee). **Best for:** walking. ⊠ *Dyke Rd., off Rte. 9, Kennebunkport* ⊕ *www. visitmaine.com.*

Route 9

For a rewarding drive that goes into the reaches of the coastline on the way to Old Orchard Beach, head out of Kennebunkport on Route 9 to the fishing village of Cape Porpoise. Continuing on Route 9, plan on some beach walking at Goose Rocks Beach or Fortunes Rocks Beach. (A parking permit is a must.) Route 9 then heads past the charming resort villages of Camp Ellis and Ocean Park. Picnic at Ferry Beach State Park; the varied landscapes include forested sections, swamp, beach, a rare stand of tupelo (black gum) trees, and lots of dunes.

🍴 Restaurants

The Kennebunks are chock-full of restaurants and cafés vying for attention. Service and food can be hit-or-miss in this area; often the best meals are those that you pack yourself into a picnic basket to enjoy on one of the area's many sandy beaches.

The Boathouse Restaurant

$$$ | **SEAFOOD** | You can't get more up-close and personal with Kennebunkport's harbor than at this stunning waterside restaurant and bar that serves dressed-up, contemporary takes on classic Maine fare, alongside top-notch cocktails and staples such as perfectly shucked local oysters, fresh scallop ceviche, and hearty clam and corn chowder. The inside spaces are warm and welcoming, with a maritime theme that's not too over-the-top; the outdoor wraparound deck is one of the best spots in town to grab a cocktail and watch the sun set over the Kennebunk River. **Known for:** amazing waterside location; cocktails on the outdoor wraparound deck; great seafood. ⑤ *Average main: $30* ⊠ *21 Ocean Ave., Kennebunkport* ☎ *877/266–1304* ⊕ *boathouseme.com.*

The Burleigh at the Kennebunkport Inn

$$$ | SEAFOOD | Nautical accents give this trendy restaurant a laid-back vibe that is the perfect transition from a day out on the water (or at the beach) to a relaxed end-of-the-day meal. While fresh seafood plays a central role at the Burleigh, you can't go wrong with one of the excellent burgers or pork chops paired with one of the many rotating local craft-beer choices. **Known for:** lobster risotto poached with lemon butter; craft cocktails that will knock you off of your feet; excellent happy hour in the inn's Garden Social Club. ⑤ *Average main: $30* ✉ *One Dock Square, Kennebunkport* ☎ *207/967–2621* ⊕ *kennebunkportinn.com/dining/.*

Duffy's Tavern & Grill

$ | AMERICAN | Every small town needs its own lively and friendly tavern, and this bustling spot is Kennebunk's favorite, housed in a former shoe factory, with exposed brick, soaring ceilings, and hardwood floors; right outside are the tumbling waters of the Mousam River as it flows from the dam. You'll find lots of comfortable standards, like burgers and pizza; the popular fish-and-chips and the tasty onion rings are hand-dipped. **Known for:** lively vibe that brings locals and visitors together; classic pub fare, such as fried calamari and hearty New England clam chowder; handcrafted pizzas. ⑤ *Average main: $16* ✉ *4 Main St., Kennebunk* ☎ *207/985–0050* ⊕ *www. duffyskennebunk.com.*

Mabel's Lobster Claw

$$$ | SEAFOOD | FAMILY | Since the 1950s, Mabel's has been serving lobsters, homemade pies, and lots of seafood for lunch and dinner in this tiny dwelling out on Ocean Avenue. The decor includes paneled walls, wooden booths, and autographed photos of various TV stars (and members of the Bush family), and there's outside seating. **Known for:** paper place mats with illustrated instructions on how to eat a Maine lobster; Lobster Savannah: split and filled with scallops, shrimp, and mushrooms, and baked in a Newburg sauce; take-out window where you can order ice cream and food. ⑤ *Average main: $25* ✉ *124 Ocean Ave., Kennebunkport* ☎ *207/967–2562* ⊕ *www.mabelslobster.com* ⊗ *Closed Nov.–early Apr.*

★ Musette

$$ | MODERN AMERICAN | A welcome addition to the charming village of Cape Porpoise, just 2 miles northeast of Kennebunkport, Musette delivers the same kind of healthy, seasonally inspired fare for which acclaimed chef Jonathan Cartwright is known, but in an unpretentious environment. Classic breakfast and brunch offerings using local ingredients are every bit as appealing as those for dinner, when the mainly seafood menu is dressed up a bit more. **Known for:** community events like yoga on the lawn in summer; best coffee around; à la carte and to-go options. ⑤ *Average main: $24* ✉ *2 Pier Rd., Cape Porpoise* ☎ *207/204– 0707* ⊕ *www.musettebyjc.com.*

★ Ocean Restaurant

$$$$ | SEAFOOD | One of the best seats in town to watch the sun set (or rise) over the Atlantic, the large picture windows at Ocean Restaurant envelope an intimate dining space that features a touch of seaside elegance coupled with captivating, original local art. The menu is chock-full of sheer ambrosial delights, with contemporary takes on classic dishes, such as lobster thermidor, foie gras terrine, coq au vin, and bouillabaisse. **Known for:** equally perfect for a romantic evening or a gathering of friends; gracious, old-world service; ridiculously indulgent desserts that you may want to eat first. ⑤ *Average main: $40* ✉ *208 Ocean Ave., Kennebunkport* ☎ *855/346–5700* ⊕ *capearundelinn.com.*

Pearl Kennebunk Beach and Spat Oyster Cellar

$$ | SEAFOOD | At this classy but cozy seafood-centric restaurant you'll be treated to stellar seasonal fare using ingredients harvested from the Maine coast. Start with craft cocktails at the large, elegant bar and then move to a table close to the

massive stone hearth that is particularly inviting on cooler evenings. **Known for:** excellent happy hour every night featuring fresh seafood; rotating selection of gazpachos; crispy panfried chicken dishes. ⑤ *Average main: $22* ⊠ *27 Western Ave., Kennebunk* ☎ *207/204–0860* ⊕ *www.pearloysterbar.com/pearl-maine* ⊗ *Closed Mon. and Tues.*

★ The Tides Beach Club Restaurant

$$$ | SEAFOOD | This unfussy, beachside dining spot is decorated in soft maritime accents and a crisp color palette, perfect for a relaxing post-beach meal. The menu features lighter seafood fare and salads alongside heartier options, such as lobster rangoons, crispy fried chicken, and burgers, which are complemented by a list of delicious craft cocktails. **Known for:** no dress code—think beach-hair-don't-care chic; perfect for a prebeach bite or postbeach sit-down dining experience; exceptional service that isn't cloying. ⑤ *Average main: $26* ⊠ *254 Kings Hwy., Kennebunkport* ☎ *207/967–3757* ⊕ *tidesbeachclubmaine.com/food/.*

 ## Hotels

★ Bufflehead Cove Inn

$$ | B&B/INN | On the beautiful, saltwater Kennebunk River, where the tides are just as dramatic as on the coast, this gray-shingled B&B sits at the end of a winding dirt road amid fields and apple trees—surprisingly, it's only a five-minute drive from Kennebunkport's Dock Square. **Pros:** pastoral setting with a riverfront location; thoughtful touches, such as a local cheese and wine hour and an excellent selection of books and games; perfect for a serene getaway. **Cons:** two-night minimum stay on weekends; waterside location can mean a need for bug spray; not right in the bustle of the Kennebunks. ⑤ *Rooms from: $200* ⊠ *18 Bufflehead Cove Rd., Kennebunk* ☎ *207/967–3879* ⊕ *www.buffleheadcove.com* ⊗ *Closed mid-Nov.–Apr.* ⚓ *5 rooms,* *1 cottage* ⑩ *Free breakfast.*

★ Cape Arundel Inn and Resort

$$$$ | B&B/INN | This shingle-style 19th-century mansion, originally one of the area's many summer "cottages," commands a magnificent ocean view that takes in the Bush estate at Walker's Point; it's location is just far enough from the bustle of town to truly feel like you've gotten away from it all. **Pros:** exceptional staff that are gracious and discreet; luxurious beds and linens that will make you feel like a spring chicken upon waking; champagne welcome. **Cons:** not for the budget-minded; club-house amenities are ½ mile away from main house; some rooms without ocean views. ⑤ *Rooms from: $500* ⊠ *208 Ocean Ave., Kennebunkport* ☎ *855/346–5700* ⊕ *www.capearundelinn.com* ⊗ *Closed late Dec.–late Feb.* ⚓ *30 rooms* ⑩ *Free breakfast.*

★ The Captain Lord Mansion

$$$ | B&B/INN | Of all the mansions in Kennebunkport's historic district that have been converted to inns, the 1814 Captain Lord Mansion is the stateliest and most sumptuously appointed; distinctive architecture, including a three-story elliptical staircase, gas fireplaces in all guest rooms, and near-museum-quality accoutrements make for a formal but not stuffy setting. **Pros:** beautiful landscaped grounds; bikes for guests; putting green; day-spa services are available for added luxury. **Cons:** not a beachfront location; close proximity to other inns; more of an autumn/winter vibe than what other inns offer in the area. ⑤ *Rooms from: $329* ⊠ *6 Pleasant St., Kennebunkport* ☎ *207/967–3141, 800/522–3141* ⊕ *www.captainlord.com* ⚓ *20 rooms, 1 loft luxury apartment* ⑩ *Free breakfast.*

★ Grace White Barn Inn

$$$ | B&B/INN | For a perfectly romantic, indulgent stay, look no further than the exclusive Grace White Barn Inn, known for its attentive, old-school service and intimate atmosphere. **Pros:** 10-minute walk to the beach; elegant spa offers it all; over-the-top service. **Cons:** prices are steep; not directly on a beach; you

Maine's rocky coastline stretches for about 3,400 miles including Kennebunkport.

pay for what you get here. ⑤ *Rooms from: $340* ✉ *37 Beach Ave., Kennebunk* ☎ *207/967–2321* ⊕ *www.gracehotels. com/whitebarninn* ⤳ *22 rooms, 5 cottages* ⦶ *Free breakfast.*

★ Hidden Pond

$$$$ | RESORT | This unique resort hideaway, tucked away in a wooded, 60-acre enclave near Goose Rocks Beach, includes hiking trails, two pools, a spa, a phenomenal restaurant, and a working farm. **Pros:** use of beach facilities at the nearby Tides Beach Club, its sister property; luxe spa with services offered in individual "tree houses"; guests can cut fresh flowers and harvest vegetables from the property's many gardens; plenty of activities on-site including watercolor painting, children's activities, and fitness classes. **Cons:** steep prices; away from the center of town; no dogs allowed. ⑤ *Rooms from: $500* ✉ *354 Goose Rocks Rd., Kennebunkport* ☎ *207/967–9050* ⊕ *hiddenpondmaine.com* ⊙ *Closed Nov.–May* ⤳ *36 cottages* ⦶ *No meals.*

★ The Inn at English Meadows

$$$ | B&B/INN | A stone's throw from the bustle of Kennebunkport, this charming boutique B&B is housed in a gorgeously restored, historic 1860s farmhouse. **Pros:** luxurious bathroom amenities including rain showers and toiletries by Malin + Goetz; gas fireplaces in many rooms; home-baked goods available throughout the day. **Cons:** not in the middle of town; no water view; limited common spaces. ⑤ *Rooms from: $350* ✉ *141 Port Rd., Kennebunk* ☎ *207/967–5766* ⊕ *englishmeadowsinn.com/* ⤳ *11 rooms* ⦶ *Free breakfast.*

★ Sandy Pines Campground

$$ | RENTAL | The luxe "glamping" (glamorous camping) tents, smart camp carriages, and A-frame hideaway huts on wheels at Sandy Pines Campground deliver every bit as much comfort and luxury as a fine hotel (with a few caveats, including communal bathing areas), but give you a chance to get up close and personal with nature. **Pros:** the glamping areas of Sandy Pines are quiet zones; nightly bonfires under the stars without roughing it; all tents equipped with generous sitting areas that extend outside the tents. **Cons:** expect all that comes with being in nature; glamping tents are not pet-friendly; three-night minimum stay (seasonal). ⑤ *Rooms from: $266* ✉ *277 Mills Rd., Kennebunkport* ☎ *207/967–2483* ⊕ *sandypinescamping. com* ⊙ *Closed mid-Oct.–mid-May* ⋥ *16 units* ⦿ *No meals.*

The Tides Beach Club

$$$$ | B&B/INN | The stately building that now houses the Tides Beach Club is a charming grande dame from the heyday of seaside "cure" retreats during the Gilded Age. Just steps from a long, sandy beach—like its sister property, Hidden Pond—this lively inn is the epitome of laid-back, seaside-chic design, which extends into each of the spacious, bungalowlike rooms that are decorated in rich, feel-good ocean blue and coral hues. **Pros:** use of the common spaces (pools, spa, garden) at the very exclusive Hidden Pond; beach service for a relaxed lunch or dinner on the sand; most of the rooms have ocean views and balconies. **Cons:** definitely will lighten your purse; a lot of activity in and around the inn; not pet-friendly. ⑤ *Rooms from: $550* ✉ *254 Kings Hwy., Kennebunkport* ☎ *207/967–3757* ⊕ *tidesbeachclubmaine. com* ⊙ *Closed Nov.–Apr.* ⋥ *21 rooms* ⦿ *Free breakfast.*

★ The Yachtsman Hotel and Marina Club

$$$$ | HOTEL | These chic new bungalows located smack-dab on the water are a long-overdue addition to Kennebunkport, with their hip beach-vibe design, private lawns that blur the distinction between indoors and outdoors, and harbor views. **Pros:** all rooms have fabulous harbor views; pull-out sofas offer more space in the deluxe harborfront bungalows; large marble showers and luxe toiletries from Malin + Goetz; free shuttle service around town. **Cons:** not on the beach; private lawns aren't exactly private with all the boats passing by; not family-friendly. ⑤ *Rooms from: $499* ✉ *59 Ocean*

Ave., Kennebunkport ☎ *207/967–2511* ⊕ *yachtsmanlodge.com* ⊙ *Closed Dec.– Apr.* ⋥ *30 bungalows* ⦿ *Free breakfast.*

 ## Activities

FISHING

Cast-Away Fishing Charters

BOATING | FAMILY | Half- and fill-day charters are available, as is a two-hour children's charter trip where kids can play lobsterman (or woman) for the day and haul in the traps. ✉ *Performance Marine, 4-A Western Ave., Kennebunk* ☎ *207/284–1740* ⊕ *www.castawayfishingcharters.com.*

BOATING | FAMILY | Lobster-trap hauling trips aboard the *Rugosa* in the scenic waters off the Kennebunks run daily, Memorial Day weekend–early October. ✉ *Nonantum Resort, 95 Ocean Ave., Kennebunkport* ☎ *207/468–4095* ⊕ *www. rugosalobstertours.com.*

WHALE-WATCHING

First Chance

TOUR—SPORTS | FAMILY | This company leads whale-watching cruises on 85-foot *Nick's Chance.* If you don't see a whale, you get a ticket for a free trip. Scenic lobster cruises are also offered aboard 65-foot *Kylie's Chance.* Trips run daily in summer and on weekends in the shoulder season. ✉ *Performance Marine, 4-A Western Ave., Kennebunk* ☎ *207/967–5507* ⊕ *www.firstchancewhalewatch.com.*

★ The Pineapple Ketch

SAILING | FAMILY | Here's a terrific way to get out on the water and see some marine life, aboard a classic 38-foot Down Easter ketch. The captain and crew are knowledgeable and let the passengers guide the direction of both the boat and the tour. Bring your own snacks and beverages, especially for the sunset cruises. ✉ *95 Ocean Ave., Kennebunkport* ☎ *207/468–7262* ⊕ *pineappleketch.com.*

Shopping

Abacus

GIFTS/SOUVENIRS | This shop sells eclectic crafts, jewelry, and furniture. It's a good place to pick up gifts. ⊠ *2 Ocean Ave., at Dock Sq., Kennebunkport* ☎ *207/967–0111* ⊕ *www.abacusgallery.com.*

★ Daytrip Society

GIFTS/SOUVENIRS | The impossibly hip and well-selected array of goods that this modern-design shop stocks makes it an excellent place for both window-shopping and finding gifts for just about anyone on your list (including yourself). A refreshing departure from the rest of the somewhat stodgy gift shops in the village, this boutique is chock-full of eye candy, most of which is also functional. There are many locally sourced and decidedly contemporary products, from hats and jewelry to novelty books, home decor, and scents. Check out Daytrip Jr., its equally hip children's store around the corner. ⊠ *4 Dock Sq., Kennebunkport* ☎ *207/967–4440* ⊕ *www.daytripsociety.com.*

★ Farm + Table

SPECIALTY STORES | This delightful shop is housed in a bright-red Maine barn filled with kitchen items both useful and pleasing to the eye. ⊠ *8 Langsford Rd., Cape Porpoise* ☎ *207/604–8029* ⊕ *www. farmtablekennebunkport.com.*

Maine Art

ART GALLERIES | Showcasing works by artists from Maine and New England, Maine Art has a two-story gallery with a sculpture garden. ⊠ *14 Western Ave., Kennebunk* ☎ *207/967–2803* ⊕ *www. maine-art.com.*

Biddeford

11 miles north of Kennebunkport, 18 miles south of Portland.

Biddeford is waking from a deep sleep, having devolved into something of a ghost town for a good deal of the past

half century. It's a ghost town no more, thanks to chefs and small-business owners who have relocated from Portland; they are giving Biddeford's beautiful old-mill-town architecture a new lease on life. Developers have taken note as well, revamping many of the mill district's historic buildings, including the town's imposing 233,000-square-foot Lincoln Mill. Today, Biddeford is filled with art galleries and quirky boutiques, a distillery, an art school, and top-notch restaurants.

GETTING HERE AND AROUND
From Interstate 95, get off at Exit 2A. U.S. 1 runs right through town.

ESSENTIALS
VISITOR INFORMATION Biddeford-Saco Chamber of Commerce ☎ *207/282–1567* ⊕ *www.biddefordsacochamber.org.*

Sights

Round Turn Distilling

WINE/SPIRITS | There's a reason why all the good craft cocktail bars in Maine stock Bimini Gin, the flagship spirit of this distillery, located in a 150-year-old textile mill on the Saco River. Learn more about the best small-batch gin in the Pine Tree State, and be sure to take a peek at the production area: the distillery uses steam to power its modern steel-and-copper still. The Tasting Room is open Tuesday–Thursday 4–9, Friday and Saturday 2–10, and Sunday noon–6. ⊠ *32 Maine St., Bldg. 13W, Suite 103* ☎ *207/370–9446* ⊕ *www.roundturndistilling.com* ☉ *Closed Mon.*

Restaurants

★ Elda

$$ | **MODERN AMERICAN** | Located in a beautifully restored Main Street building, with high tin ceilings and gorgeous original artworks lining the walls, Elda takes slow food very seriously. Almost all of the ingredients used in the meticulously prepared, seasonally inspired dishes are local, and just about everything on the menu is prepared from scratch in-house. **Known for:** meals often last well over two hours; seafood dishes prepared in unlikely ways (hello, chicken-fried skate); light, flavorful desserts that often incorporate obscure herbs and spices. ⑤ *Average main: $24* ⊠ *140 Main St., Suite 101* ☎ *207/494–8365* ⊕ *www.eldamaine.com* ⊘ *Closed Mon.*

Elements: Books, Coffee, Beer

$ | **CAFÉ** | You could easily while away an entire day at this cozy spot that's part café, part bookstore, and part pub, starting with coffee in the morning to fuel an afternoon of reading, followed by a satisfying brew in the early evening. Pop by for any combination of the three, plus the occasional poetry reading or evening of live local music. **Known for:** part café, part bookstore, part pub; great coffee and beer; live music. ⑤ *Average main: $10* ⊠ *265 Main St.* ☎ *207/710–2011* ⊕ *www. elementsbookscoffeebeer.com.*

★ Palace Diner

$ | **AMERICAN** | Everything about this diner, in an old-fashioned train car just off Main Street, is retro except the food. Hop on a stool at the counter (that's all there is), enjoy the Motown tunes, and tuck into one of the deluxe sandwiches for breakfast or lunch. **Known for:** diner bites that are anything but diner food; delicious fried-chicken sandwich with cabbage slaw and French fries; fantastic collaboration with local chefs from regional restaurants. ⑤ *Average main: $10* ⊠ *18 Franklin St.* ☎ *207/284–0015* ⊕ *www. palacedinerme.com* ⊘ *No dinner* ▭ *No credit cards.*

🛍 Shopping

★ Rabelais Books

BOOKS/STATIONERY | Rabelais Books, whose cheeky slogan is "Thought for Food," is an ode to the art of cooking, drinking, and eating (and writing about it). Get lost in one of the many recipe reference tomes, many of which are very rare, or pick up a book or two for your favorite foodie. Rabelais is located in the massive North Dam Mill complex, which houses a bevy of unique local shops, many featuring products made by local artisans. ⊠ *North Dam Mill Bldg. 18, 2 Main St.* ☎ *207/602–6246* ⊕ *www. rabelaisbooks.com.*

Portland

28 miles from Kennebunk via I–95 and I–295.

★ Maine's largest city may be considered small by national standards—its population is just 66,000—but its character, spirit, and appeal make it feel much larger. It's well worth at least a day or two of exploration, even if all you do is spend the entire time eating and drinking at the many phenomenal restaurants, bakeries and specialty dessert shops, craft cocktail bars, and microbreweries scattered across the city. Work up your appetite roaming the working waterfront and strolling the Eastern Promenade, shopping in the boutiques along the brick streets of the Old Port, or sauntering through the galleries of its top-notch art museum.

A city of many names throughout its history, including Casco and Falmouth, Portland has survived many dramatic transformations, the most recent of which is the massive influx of hipsters and foodies who have opened up artisanal bars and quirky boutiques that are rapidly changing the city's character. Sheltered by the nearby Casco Bay Islands and blessed with a deep port, Portland was a significant settlement right from its start in the early 17th century. Settlers thrived on fishing and lumbering, repeatedly building up the area while the British, French, and Native Americans continually sacked it. Many considered the region a somewhat dangerous frontier, but its potential for prosperity was so apparent that settlers came anyway to tap its rich natural resources.

In 1632 Portland's first home was built on the Portland Peninsula in the area now known as Munjoy Hill. The British burned the city in 1775, when residents refused to surrender arms, but it was rebuilt and became a major trading center. Much of Portland was destroyed again in the Great Fire on July 4, 1866, when a flicked ash or perhaps a celebratory firecracker started a fire in a boatyard that grew into conflagration; 1,500 buildings burned to the ground.

GETTING HERE AND AROUND

From Interstate 95, take Interstate 295 to get to the Portland Peninsula and downtown. Commercial Street runs along the harbor, Fore Street is one block up in the heart of the Old Port, and the Arts District stretches along diagonal Congress Street. Munjoy Hill is on the eastern end of the peninsula and the West End on the opposite side.

ESSENTIALS
RESTAURANTS

America's "Foodiest Small Town" is how one magazine described Portland, which is practically bursting at the seams with fabulous restaurants to rival those of a major metropolis. It's worth it to splurge and try as many as possible while visiting. Fresh seafood, including the famous Maine lobster, is still popular and prevalent, but it is being served up in unexpected ways that are a far cry from the usual bib and butter. There is a broad spectrum of cuisines to be enjoyed, and many chefs are pushing the envelope in their reinventions of traditional culinary idioms. More and more restaurants are using local meats, seafood, and organic produce as much as possible; changing menus reflect what is available in the region at the moment. Even the many excellent food trucks that have popped up across the city—several of which remain open in the off-season—reflect this trend. As sophisticated as many of these establishments have become in the way of food and service, the atmosphere is generally laid-back; with a

few exceptions, you can leave your jacket and tie at home—just not your appetite.
■ TIP➔ Smoking is banned in all restaurants, taverns, and bars in Maine.

HOTELS

As Portland's popularity as a vacation destination has increased, so have its options for overnight visitors. Though several large hotels—geared toward high-tech, amenity-obsessed guests—have been built in the Old Port, they have in no way diminished the success of smaller, more intimate lodgings. Inns and B&Bs have taken up residence throughout the West End, often giving new life to the grand mansions of Portland's wealthy 19th-century merchants. For the least expensive accommodations, you'll find chain hotels near the interstate and the airport.

Expect to pay at least $150 or so per night for a pleasant room (often with complimentary breakfast) within walking distance of the Old Port during high season, and more than $400 for the most luxurious of suites. At the height of summer, many places are booked; make reservations well in advance, and ask about off-season specials.

NIGHTLIFE

Portland's nightlife scene is largely centered on the bustling Old Port and a few smaller, artsy spots on Congress Street. There's a great emphasis on live music from local bands and pubs serving award-winning local microbrews. Several hip bars have cropped up, serving appetizers along with a full array of specialty wines and serious craft cocktails. Portland is a fairly sleepy city after midnight, but you can usually find a couple of bars and restaurants open, even after the clock strikes 12.

PERFORMING ARTS

Art galleries and studios have spread throughout the city, infusing many beautiful, old abandoned buildings and shops with new life. Many are concentrated along the Congress Street downtown

Portland's busy harbor is full of working boats, pleasure craft, and ferries headed to the Casco Bay Islands.

corridor; others are hidden amid the boutiques and restaurants of the Old Port and the East End. A great way to get acquainted with the city's artists is to participate in the First Friday Art Walk, a free self-guided tour of galleries, museums, and alternative-art venues that happens—you guessed it—on the first Friday of each month.

SHOPPING

Exchange Street is great for arts and crafts and boutique browsing, while Commercial Street caters to the souvenir hound—gift shops are packed with nautical items, and lobster and moose emblems are emblazoned on everything from T-shirts to shot glasses.

ACTIVITIES

When the weather's good, everyone in Portland heads outside, whether for boating on the water, lounging on a beach, or walking and biking the promenades. There are also many green spaces nearby Portland, including Crescent Beach State Park, Two Lights State Park, and Fort Williams Park, home to Portland Head

Light. All are on the coast south of the city in suburban Cape Elizabeth and offer walking trails, picnic facilities, and water access. Bradbury Mountain State Park, in Pownal, has incredible vistas from its easily climbed peak. In Freeport is Wolfe's Neck Woods State Park, where you can take a guided nature walk and see nesting ospreys. Both are north of Portland.

Various Portland-based skippers offer whale-, dolphin-, and seal-watching cruises; excursions to lighthouses and islands; and fishing and lobstering trips. Board the ferry to see nearby islands. Self-navigators can rent kayaks or canoes.

TOURS
BUS TOURS
Portland Discovery Land & Sea Tours
BUS TOURS | FAMILY | The informative trolley tours of Portland Discovery detail the city's historical and architectural highlights, Memorial Day–October. Options include combining a city tour with a bay or lighthouse cruise. ⊠ *Long Wharf, 170 Commercial St.* ☎ *207/774–0808* ⊕ *www. portlanddiscovery.com* ✉ *From $19.*

WALKING TOURS
Greater Portland Landmarks

WALKING TOURS | FAMILY | Take 1½-hour walking tours of Portland's historic West End on Friday, July–September, with Greater Portland Landmarks. Tours past the neighborhood's Greek Revival mansions and grand Federal-style homes begin at the group's headquarters and cost $10. You can also pick up maps for self-guided tours of the Old Port or the Western Promenade. ⊠ *93 High St.* ☎ *207/774–5561* ⊕ *www.portlandlandmarks.org* ⊠ *From $10.*

Maine Foodie Tours

SPECIAL-INTEREST | Learn about Portland's culinary history and sample local delights like lobster hors d'oeuvres, organic cheese, and the famous Maine whoopie pie. The culinary walking tours include stops at fishmongers, bakeries, and cheese shops that provide products to Portland's famed restaurants. From summer into early fall, you can also take a chocolate tour, a bike-and-brewery tour, or a trolley tour with a stop at a microbrewery. Tours begin at various locales in the Old Port. ⊠ *Portland* ☎ *207/233–7485* ⊕ *www.mainefoodietours.com* ⊠ *From $29.*

Portland Freedom Trail

SELF-GUIDED | FAMILY | The Portland Freedom Trail offers a self-guided tour of sites associated with the Underground Railroad and the antislavery movement. ⊠ *Portland* ⊕ *www.mainehistory.org/PDF/walkingtourmap.pdf* ⊠ *Free.*

VISITOR INFORMATION

CONTACTS Downtown Portland ☎ *207/772–6828* ⊕ *www.portlandmaine.com.* **Greater Portland Convention and Visitors Bureau** ☎ *207/772–5800* ⊕ *www.visitportland.com.*

The Old Port

★ A major international port and a working harbor since the early 17th century, the Old Port bridges the gap between the city's historic commercial activities and those of today. It is home to fishing boats docked alongside whale-watching charters, luxury yachts, cruise ships, and oil tankers from around the globe. Commercial Street parallels the water and is lined with brick buildings and warehouses that were built following the Great Fire of 1866. In the 19th century, candle makers and sail stitchers plied their trades here; today specialty shops, art galleries, and restaurants have taken up residence.

As with much of the city, it's best to park your car and explore the Old Port on foot. You can park at the city garage on Fore Street (between Exchange and Union Streets) or opposite the U.S. Custom House at the corner of Fore and Pearl Streets. A helpful hint: look for the "Park & Shop" sign on garages and parking lots, and get one hour of free parking for each stamp collected at participating shops. Allow a couple of hours to wander at leisure on Market, Exchange, Middle, and Fore Streets. The city is very pedestrian-friendly. Maine state law requires vehicles to stop for pedestrians in crosswalks.

Sights

Harbor Fish Market

STORE/MALL | A Portland favorite since 1968, this freshest-of-the-fresh seafood market ships lobsters and other Maine delectables almost anywhere in the country. A bright-red facade on a working wharf opens into a bustling space with bubbling lobster tanks and fish, clams, and other shellfish on ice; employees are as skilled with a fillet knife as sushi chefs. There is also a small retail store. ⊠ *9 Custom House Wharf* ☎ *207/775–0251* ⊕ *www.harborfish.com* ⊠ *Free.*

Portland Fish Exchange

FISH HATCHERY | You may want to hold your nose as you take a dip into the Old Port's active fish business at the 20,000-square-foot Portland Fish Exchange. Peek inside coolers teeming

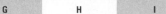

G	**H**	**I**

Edward Payson Park

Washington Ave.

Presumpscot St.

Baxter Blvd.

Veranda St.

295

Eastern Promenade

Casco Bay

Cove St.

Diamond St.

Anderson St.

Hammond St.

North St.

Walnut St.

Montreat St.

Melbourne St.

Quebec St.

Turner St.

Eastern Promenade

Franklin St.

E. Oxford St.

Washington Ave.

Romasco Ln.

Sheridan Ave.

Congress St.

Monument St.

Mountfort St.

Atlantic St.

Munjoy St.

Vesper St.

Morning St.

India St.

Federal St.

Newbury St.

Middle St.

Hancock St.

St. Lawrence St.

Waterville St.

Fore St.

Thames St.

Fort Allen Park

Fish Point

Visitor Information Center

Ocean Gateway Terminal

Portland Harbor

Maine State Pier

TO PEAKS ISLAND

Sights ▼

1. Children's Museum & Theatre of Maine **E6**
2. Eastern Promenade **I5**
3. Harbor Fish Market **G7**
4. Maine Narrow Gauge Railroad Museum **H7**
5. Neal Dow Memorial **D6**
6. Portland Fish Exchange **E8**
7. Portland Museum of Art **E6**
8. Portland Observatory **H6**
9. Tate House Museum **A3**
10. Victoria Mansion **E7**
11. The Wadsworth-Longfellow House **E6**
12. Western Promenade ... **B6**

Restaurants ▼

1. BaoBao Dumpling House **E7**
2. Becky's Diner **E8**
3. Blyth and Burrows **F7**
4. Bolster, Snow & Co. **D6**
5. Drifter's Wife **H6**
6. Duckfat **G7**
7. East Ender **G6**
8. El Rayo Taqueria **F6**
9. Eventide Oyster Co **G7**
10. Five Fifty-Five **E6**
11. Flatbread **G7**
12. Fore Street **G7**
13. Gelato Fiasco **F7**
14. Gilbert's Chowder House **G7**
15. Highroller Lobster Co. **F6**
16. The Holy Donut **G7**
17. The Honey Paw **G7**
18. Hugo's **G7**
19. Local 188 .... **E6**
20. Lolita **H6**
21. Mami **E7**
22. Rose Foods **D4**
23. The Shop at Island Creek Oysters **H5**
24. Speckled Ax Wood Roasted Coffee **E6**
25. Standard Baking **G7**
26. Union **F6**
27. Walter's **F7**
28. Woodford Food and Beverage **D2**

Hotels ▼

1. The Danforth **D7**
2. The Francis **D6**
3. Inn On Carleton **C6**
4. Morrill Mansion **C6**
5. Pomegranate Inn **C7**
6. The Portland Regency Hotel & Spa **F7**
7. The Press Hotel **F6**
8. West End Inn **C6**

G	**H**	**I**

with cod, flounder, and monkfish, and watch fishermen repairing nets outside. ✉ *6 Portland Fish Pier* ☎ *207/773–0017* ⊕ *www.pfex.org* 🔁 *Free.*

Restaurants

Becky's Diner

$ | DINER | FAMILY | You won't find a more local or unfussy place—or one more abuzz with conversation at 4 am—than this waterfront institution way down on the end of Commercial Street. The food is cheap, generous in proportion, and has that satisfying, old-time-diner quality. **Known for:** classic Maine diner food featuring many seafood dishes; very lively atmosphere comingling locals and visitors; parking is easy—a rarity in Portland. $ *Average main: $14* ✉ *390 Commercial St.* ☎ *207/773–7070* ⊕ *www.beckysdiner.com.*

★ Blyth and Burrows

$ | CONTEMPORARY | There are craft cocktails and there is Blyth and Burrows, where the alchemy of spirits is taken to the next level with creative concoctions that include the unholy integration of gorgeous (albeit unusual) ingredients such as absinthe foam, house-made black-lime cordial, blackstrap maple-chipotle syrup, and uncommon liqueurs and spirits. Delicious small plates, like lobster rolls, oysters on the half shell, tenderloin and chimichurri, and local meat and cheese boards keep you from falling under the table. **Known for:** knock-you-under-the-table cocktails; nautical-theme atmosphere filled with antique ships and mermaid figureheads; food that goes well with cocktails. $ *Average main: $12* ✉ *26 Exchange St.* ☎ *207/613–9070* ⊕ *www.blythandburrows.com.*

El Rayo Taqueria

$ | MEXICAN | For some of the best Mexican food in town, head to this fun, hip spot where the flavors are as vibrant as the turquoise, yellow, and fuchsia decor and the guacamole and salsas are made fresh daily. Wash down achiote-seasoned fish tacos or a citrus-and-cumin-marinated chicken burrito with a lemon-hibiscus *refresca* (cold drink) or a house margarita. **Known for:** quick bites such as grab-and-go burritos daily until 11 am; Mexican corn on the cob with chipotle mayo and cotija; a killer key lime pie. $ *Average main: $10* ✉ *26 Free St.* ☎ *207/780–8226* ⊕ *www.elrayotaqueria.com.*

Flatbread

$$ | PIZZA | FAMILY | Families, students, and bohemian types gather at this popular New England chain flatbread-pizza place where two massive wood-fire ovens are the heart of the soaring, warehouselike space; in summer, you can escape the heat by dining on the deck overlooking the harbor. The menu has eight signature pizzas made with fresh, local ingredients, plus weekly veggie and meat specials; everything is homemade, organic, and nitrate-free, and there are delicious local microbrews on tap. **Known for:** unfussy, kid-friendly atmosphere; classic New England setting on a working waterfront; dogs allowed on outside deck. $ *Average main: $18* ✉ *72 Commercial St.* ☎ *207/772–8777* ⊕ *www.flatbreadcompany.com.*

★ Fore Street

$$$ | MODERN AMERICAN | One of Maine's best chefs, Sam Hayward, opened this restaurant in a renovated warehouse on the edge of the Old Port in 1996; today every copper-top table in the main dining room has a view of the enormous brick oven and soapstone hearth that anchor the open kitchen. The menu changes daily to reflect the freshest ingredients from Maine's farms and waters, as well as the tremendous creativity of the staff. **Known for:** Maine mussels oven roasted in garlic and almond butter; desserts to die for including artisanal cheeses, homemade chocolate truffles, and pastries; last-minute planners take heart: a third of the tables are reserved for walk-ins. $ *Average main: $30* ✉ *288 Fore St.* ☎ *207/775–2717* ⊕ *www.forestreet.biz* ⊘ *No lunch.*

★ **Gelato Fiasco**

$ | CAFÉ | FAMILY | Proper Italian gelato and *sorbetto* here come in traditional flavors as well as more offbeat varieties like molasses-peppermint stick, Wild Turkey bourbon, Girl Scout cookie, Vietnamese coffee, and spiked eggnog. There are new flavors every day, along with espresso and other hot drinks. **Known for:** you can try every single flavor before deciding on what you'll get; long lines out the door in the summer; multigenerational bonding spot. ⑤ *Average main: $5* ✉ *425 Fore St.* ☎ *207/699–4314* ⊕ *www. gelatofiasco.com.*

Gilbert's Chowder House

$$ | SEAFOOD | FAMILY | This is the real deal, as quintessential as old-school Maine dining can be. Clam rakes and nautical charts hang from the walls of this unpretentious waterfront diner, and the flavors come from the depths of the North Atlantic, prepared and presented simply: fried shrimp, haddock, clam strips, extraordinary clam cakes, and fish, clam, and seafood chowders (corn, too). **Known for:** family-friendly environment; classic lobster rolls, served on toasted hot-dog buns bursting with claw and tail meat; an ice-cream parlor to round out your meal; chalkboard daily specials. ⑤ *Average main: $19* ✉ *92 Commercial St.* ☎ *207/871–5636* ⊕ *www.gilbert-schowderhouse.com.*

Highroller Lobster Co.

$ | SEAFOOD | Opened in early 2018, this high-energy spot serves lobster numerous ways—in a roll, on a stick, on a burger, over a salad, or even with your Bloody Mary. If you're feeling adventurous, try one of the sauces (lime mayo, curried ketchup, lobster ghee) on your roll, and wash it all down with a beer from the ever-changing menu, which depends on availability from local breweries. **Known for:** origins as a food cart; the lobby pop (a lobster tail on a stick); Highroller whoopie pies baked by the owner's mom. ⑤ *Average main: $15* ✉ *104 Exchange St.* ☎ *207/536–1623* ⊕ *highrollerlobster.com.*

The Holy Donut

$ | CAFÉ | FAMILY | Don't pass up a chance to try these sweet and savory, all-natural, potato-based doughnuts glazed in flavors such as dark chocolate-sea salt, maple, pomegranate, coffee brandy, and chai, or stuffed with delicious fillings like Maine wild blueberries, bacon and cheddar, or ricotta. There are always new inventions, too, like the preposterously wonderful lobster-stuffed doughnut. **Known for:** long lines, but worth the wait; shop closes for the day once all the doughnuts are sold; vegan and gluten-free options are available. ⑤ *Average main: $5* ✉ *7 Exchange St.* ☎ *207/874–7774* ⊕ *www.theholydonut.com.*

★ **Mami**

$ | JAPANESE | Japanese street food takes center stage at this cozy locale. The menu rotates regularly, but you're likely to find uncommon takes on burgers and soba noodles as well as some form of *okonomiyaki*—a savory pancake filled with crazy-delicious flavor and texture combinations. **Known for:** pork-belly skewers; steamed buns; grilled rice balls. ⑤ *Average main: $10* ✉ *339 Fore St.* ☎ *207/536–4702* ⊕ *mamifoodtruck.com* ⊘ *Closed Mon.*

★ **Standard Baking**

$ | BAKERY | FAMILY | You'd be hard-pressed to find a more pitch-perfect bakery in the Pine Tree State, but you'll have to pop by early (or put in an order in advance) to get your mitts on these delectable baked goods. The perfectly airy croissants, crusty baguettes, beguiling tarts, dainty madeleines, and creative breads incorporate locally sourced wheat and are nothing short of revelations. **Known for:** good selection of locally roasted coffees; amazing galettes and brioches; creative scones. ⑤ *Average main: $3* ✉ *75 Commercial St.* ☎ *207/772-5519* ⊕ *www.standardbakingco.com/.*

★ Union

$$$ | **AMERICAN** | **FAMILY** | In the Press Hotel, Union Restaurant has a sophisticated but not stuffy air that is reflected in its menu, which focuses on local ingredients, many of which are foraged and fished, or gathered from its basement greenhouse. Most dishes are modern comfort food; breakfast and brunch are a treat: you'll find maple *pain perdu* served alongside smoked-salmon tartines and classic dishes like eggs Benedict. **Known for:** sustainable ingredients; decadent "chef's table," a multicourse meal with wine pairings and the chef's choice; signature truffle beef pot roast. ⑤ *Average main: $30* ⊠ *Press Hotel, 390 Congress St.* ☎ *207/808–8700* ⊕ *www.unionportland.com.*

Walter's

$$$ | **ECLECTIC** | A fixture in the Old Port since the late 1980s, this relaxed, busy place with a chic modern interior is popular with suits and tourists alike. The seasonal menu nicely balances local seafood and meats with Asian and other international flavors; an inviting bar has a lighter menu. **Known for:** locally sourced ingredients; gluten-free choices; an elegant, warm spot to enjoy dinner with friends or solo at the bar. ⑤ *Average main: $32* ⊠ *2 Portland Sq.* ☎ *207/871–9258* ⊕ *www.waltersportland.com* ⊘ *Closed Sun and Mon. No lunch.*

🛏 Hotels

The Portland Regency Hotel & Spa

$$$ | **HOTEL** | Not part of a chain despite the "Regency" name, this brick building in the center of the Old Port served as Portland's armory in the late 19th century. **Pros:** easy walk to sites; lots of room variety for a hotel; full-service spa with lounges, saunas, steam rooms, hot tub, and an array of luxurious treatments. **Cons:** lower-than-standard ceilings in many rooms; heavy traffic can mean spotty service; not all rooms have noteworthy views. ⑤ *Rooms from: $300* ⊠ *20*

Milk St. ☎ *207/774–4200, 800/727–3436* ⊕ *www.theregency.com* ⇲ *105 rooms* ⦿ *No meals.*

★ The Press Hotel

$$$ | **HOTEL** | **FAMILY** | In a former newspaper building, this boutique hotel is part of the Marriott group—though you'd never guess it, with its pared-down, midcentury-modern aesthetic and fun typography and printing theme throughout that alludes to the building's past. **Pros:** excellent views of the water from the top two floors; sparkling-clean rooms with a modern-design feel; art gallery and excellent public spaces with tasteful furnishings; Frette bed linens and Maine-made Cuddledown comforters and bed throws. **Cons:** right next to the fire department; valet parking can be expensive; some rooms have underwhelming views. ⑤ *Rooms from: $375* ⊠ *119 Exchange St.* ☎ *877/890–5641* ⊕ *www.thepresshotel.com* ⇲ *110 rooms* ⦿ *No meals.*

Nightlife

The Bearded Lady's Jewelbox

BARS/PUBS | This hip, craft cocktail–centric hole-in-the-wall has tons of charm and a speakeasy vibe (indeed, there's no sign on the door). Sip a dainty glass of potent French absinthe, or one of the many creative concoctions on the ever-changing cocktail list. Rotating bar snacks include things like house meatballs, turmeric pickles, and candied popcorn with bacon butter and cayenne pepper. Check out the massive, hand-painted mural on the wall that depicts—you guessed it—some elegant bearded ladies. ⊠ *644 Congress St.* ☎ *207/747–5384* ⊕ *www.thebeardedladysjewelbox.com.*

Bull Feeney's

BARS/PUBS | For nightly specials, plenty of Guinness, and live entertainment, head to Bull Feeney's, a lively two-story Irish pub and restaurant. ⊠ *375 Fore St.* ☎ *207/773–7210.*

Gritty McDuff's Portland Brew Pub

BARS/PUBS | Maine's original brewpub serves fine ales, British pub fare, and seafood dishes. There are between six and eight rotating ales on tap, and there's always a seasonal offering. Come on Tuesday, Saturday, and Sunday nights for live music. ⊠ *396 Fore St.* ☎ *207/772–2739* ⊕ *www.grittys.com.*

★ **Novare Res Bier Café**

BARS/PUBS | At tucked-away Novare Res Bier Café, choose from some three dozen rotating drafts and more than 300 bottled brews. Relax on an expansive deck, munch on antipasti, or share a meat-and-cheese plate. Maine craft beers occupy at least eight of the taps at any given time, and the rest span the globe, with an emphasis on Belgian and Trappist ales. ⊠ *4 Canal Plaza, off Exchange St.* ☎ *207/761–2437* ⊕ *www. novareresbiercafe.com.*

★ **Portland Hunt and Alpine Club**

BARS/PUBS | Scandinavian-inspired small bites and serious craft cocktails drive this hip new locale that includes delicious negronis on tap and excellent charcuterie and seafood boards in an intimate alpine-style hut. Go for the excellent happy hour, weekdays 1–6. ⊠ *75 Market St.* ☎ *207/747–4754* ⊕ *www.huntandalpine-club.com.*

Vena's Fizz House

BARS/PUBS | The old-fashioned soda fountain gets a modern update at Vena's Fizz House, where flavors like raspberry mint, chocolate-covered cherry cordial, and frothy blood orange go into delicious, fizzy "mocktails," while the cocktails feature artisanal ingredients such as peppercorn-bacon bitters, saffron, and ghost pepper. ⊠ *345 Fore St.* ☎ *207/747–4901* ⊕ *www.venasfizzhouse.com.*

 Shopping

ACCESSORIES

★ **Sea Bags**

SPECIALTY STORES | At Sea Bags, totes made from recycled sailcloth and decorated with bright, graphic patterns are sewn right in the store. ⊠ *25 Custom House Wharf* ☎ *207/780–0744* ⊕ *www. seabags.com.*

ART AND ANTIQUES

Abacus

ANTIQUES/COLLECTIBLES | This appealing crafts gallery has gift items in glass, wood, and textiles, as well as fine modern jewelry. ⊠ *44 Exchange St.* ☎ *207/772–4880* ⊕ *www.abacusgallery.com.*

Greenhut Galleries

ANTIQUES/COLLECTIBLES | The contemporary art at this gallery changes with the seasons. Artists represented include David Driskell, an artist and leading art scholar. ⊠ *146 Middle St.* ☎ *207/772–2693, 207/772–2693* ⊕ *www.greenhut-galleries.me.*

BOOKS

Longfellow Books

BOOKS/STATIONERY | This shop is known for its good service, author readings, and excellent selection of new and used books and magazines. Even if you go in looking for something specific, you'll almost certainly stumble on something even better you didn't know about before. ⊠ *1 Monument Way* ☎ *207/772–4045* ⊕ *www.longfellowbooks.com.*

★ **Sherman's Books and Stationery**

BOOKS/STATIONERY | Open since 1886, Sherman's is Maine's oldest book-store chain. The Portland store has an impressive stock of well-selected books interspersed with excellent gift choices, such as stationery, candles, and holiday decor, as well as a fun array of toys. It's a good place to spend a cold or rainy day perusing the selection. ⊠ *49 Exchange St.* ☎ *207/773–4100* ⊕ *www. shermans.com.*

CLOTHING
★ Aristelle
CLOTHING | For the fanciest knickers in downtown Portland and one of the best bra fittings around head to Aristelle, purveyors of elegant undergarments and lingerie, as well as naughty little numbers that would make Bettie Page blush. ⊠ *92 Exchange St.* ☎ *207/842–6000* ⊕ *www. aristelle.com.*

Bliss
CLOTHING | Hip boutique Bliss stocks clothing and accessories by cutting-edge designers, plus jeans by big names like J Brand and Mother. There's also a great selection of Frye boots. ⊠ *58 Exchange St.* ☎ *207/879–7125* ⊕ *www.blissboutiques.com.*

Joseph's
CLOTHING | A smart menswear boutique (and mainstay of the Old Port) that will have you looking suave in no time. ⊠ *410 Fore St.* ☎ *207/773–1274* ⊕ *www.josephsofportland.com.*

★ Judith
CLOTHING | Owned and operated by a former fashion designer, this stunning, well-curated concept boutique features women's apparel, shoes, accessories, and contemporary housewares. ⊠ *131 Middle St.* ☎ *207/747–4778* ⊕ *www. shopjudith.com.*

HOME AND GIFTS
Asia West
HOUSEHOLD ITEMS/FURNITURE | For reproduction and antique furnishings with a Far East feel, head to this stylish showroom on the waterfront. ⊠ *219 Commercial St.* ☎ *207/775–0066* ⊕ *www. asiawest.net.*

Lisa Marie's Made in Maine
GIFTS/SOUVENIRS | Here you'll find an excellent selection of locally sourced items from soaps and candles to dish towels, pottery, and jewelry, all made in the great state of Maine. ⊠ *35 Exchange St.* ☎ *207/828–1515* ⊕ *www.lisamariesmadeinmaine.com.*

Simply Scandinavian
HOUSEHOLD ITEMS/FURNITURE | A gorgeous selection of Scandinavian home and design imports fills this eye-popping boutique, which has two locations right around the corner from each other. ⊠ *19 Temple St.* ☎ *207/874–6768.*

Activities

BIKING
Portland Trails
BICYCLING | **FAMILY** | For local biking and hiking information, contact Portland Trails. The staff can tell you about designated paved and unpaved routes that wind along the water, through parks, and beyond. ⊠ *305 Commercial St.* ☎ *207/775–2411* ⊕ *www.trails.org.*

BOATING
Casco Bay Lines
BOATING | **FAMILY** | Casco Bay Lines operates ferry service to the seven bay islands with year-round populations. Summer offerings include music cruises, lighthouse excursions, and a trip to Bailey Island with a stopover for lunch. ⊠ *Maine State Pier, 56 Commercial St.* ☎ *207/774–7871* ⊕ *www.cascobaylines.com.*

Lucky Catch Cruises
BOATING | **FAMILY** | Set sail in a real lobster boat: this company gives you the genuine experience, which includes hauling traps and the chance to purchase the catch. ⊠ *Long Wharf, 170 Commercial St.* ☎ *207/761–0941* ⊕ *www.luckycatch.com.*

Odyssey Whale Watch
BOATING | **FAMILY** | From mid-May to mid-October, Odyssey Whale Watch leads whale-watching and deep-sea-fishing excursions. ⊠ *Long Wharf, 170 Commercial St.* ☎ *207/775–0727* ⊕ *www. odysseywhalewatch.com.*

Portland Discovery Land & Sea Tours
TOUR—SPORTS | **FAMILY** | For tours of the harbor and Casco Bay in a boat or on a trolley, including an up-close look at several lighthouses, try Portland Discovery Land & Sea Tours. ⊠ *Long Wharf, 170*

Commercial St. ☎ 207/774–0808 ⊕ www. portlanddiscovery.com.

★ Portland Schooner Co.

TOUR—SPORTS | FAMILY | May through October this company offers daily windjammer cruises aboard the vintage schooners *Bagheera, Timberwind,* and *Wendameen.* You can also arrange overnight trips. ⊠ *Maine State Pier, 56 Commercial St.* ☎ 207/766–2500 ⊕ www. portlandschooner.com.

The Arts District

This district starts at the top of Exchange Street, near the upper end of the Old Port, and extends west past the Portland Museum of Art. The district's central artery is Congress Street, which is lined with art galleries, specialty stores, and a score of restaurants and cafés. Parking is tricky; two-hour meters dot the sidewalks, but there are several garages nearby.

◉ Sights

Children's Museum & Theatre of Maine

MUSEUM | FAMILY | Kids can pretend they are lobstermen, veterinarians, shopkeepers, or actors in a play at Portland's small but fun Children's Museum. Most exhibits, many of which have a Maine theme, are hands-on and best for kids 10 and younger. Have a Ball! teaches about the science of motion, letting kids build ramps that make balls speed up, slow down, and leap across tracks. Don't miss the life-size inflatable humpback whale rising to the ceiling at the whale exhibit. The outdoor pirate-ship play area is a great place for a picnic lunch. Camera Obscura, an exhibit about optics, provides fascinating panoramic views of the city; it's aimed at adults and older children, and admission is therefore separate. ⊠ *142 Free St.* ☎ 207/828–1234 ⊕ *www.kitetails.org* ⊠ *From $12.*

Neal Dow Memorial

HOUSE | The mansion, once a stop on the Underground Railroad, was the home of Civil War general Neal Dow, who became known as the "Father of Prohibition." He was responsible for Maine's adoption of the anti-alcohol bill in 1851, which spurred a nationwide temperance movement. Now a museum, this majestic 1829 Federal-style home is open for guided tours that start on the hour. ⊠ *714 Congress St.* ☎ 207/773–7773 ⊠ *$5.*

★ Portland Museum of Art

MUSEUM | Maine's largest public art institution's collection includes fine seascapes and landscapes by Winslow Homer, John Marin, Andrew Wyeth, Edward Hopper, Marsden Hartley, and other American painters. Homer's *Weatherbeaten,* a quintessential Maine Coast image, is here, and the museum owns and displays, on a rotating basis, 16 more of his paintings, plus more than 400 of his illustrations. The museum has works by Monet and Picasso, as well as Degas, Renoir, and Chagall. I.M. Pei designed the strikingly modern Charles Shipman Payson building, which fittingly displays modern art. The nearby L.D.M. Sweat Galleries showcase the collection of 19th-century American art. Special events are held in the gorgeous Federal-style 1801 McLellan House. ⊠ *7 Congress Sq.* ☎ 207/775–6148 ⊕ *www.portlandmuseum.org* ⊠ *$15 (free Fri. 5–9).*

Tate House Museum

HOUSE | Astride rose-granite steps and a period herb garden overlooking the Stroudwater River on the outskirts of Portland, this magnificent 1755 house was built by Captain George Tate. Tate had been commissioned by the English Crown to organize "the King's Broad Arrow"—marking and cutting down gigantic trees, which were shipped to England to be fashioned as masts for the British Royal Navy. The house has several period rooms, including a sitting room with some fine English Restoration chairs. With its clapboard siding still gloriously unpainted, its impressive Palladian doorway, dogleg stairway, unusual clerestory, and gambrel roof, this house will delight all lovers of Early American decorative arts. ⊠ *1267 Westbrook St.* 🕾 *207/774–6177* ⊕ *www.tatehouse.org* 🎫 *$15* ⊗ *Closed Nov.–May.*

Victoria Mansion

HOUSE | Built between 1858 and 1860, this Italianate mansion is widely regarded as the most sumptuously ornamented dwelling of its period remaining in the country. Architect Henry Austin designed the house for hotelier Ruggles Morse and his wife, Olive. The interior design—everything from the plasterwork to the furniture (much of it original)—is the only surviving commission of New York designer Gustave Herter. Behind the elegant brownstone exterior of this National Historic Landmark are colorful frescoed walls and ceilings, ornate marble mantelpieces, gilded gas chandeliers, a magnificent 6-foot-by-25-foot stained-glass ceiling window, and a freestanding mahogany staircase. A guided tour runs about 45 minutes and covers all the architectural highlights. Victorian era–themed gifts and art are sold in the museum shop, and the museum often has special themed events. ⊠ *109 Danforth St.* 🕾 *207/772–4841* ⊕ *www. victoriamansion.org* 🎫 *$16* ⊗ *Closed mid-Jan.–Apr.*

The Wadsworth–Longfellow House

HOUSE | The boyhood home of the famous American poet was the first brick house in Portland and the oldest building on the peninsula. It's particularly interesting, because most of the furnishings, including the young Longfellow's writing desk, are original. Wallpaper, window coverings, and a vibrant painted carpet are period reproductions. Built in 1785, the large dwelling (a third floor was added in 1815) sits back from the street and has a small portico over its entrance and four chimneys surmounting the roof. It's part of the Maine Historical Society, which includes an adjacent research library and a museum with exhibits about Maine life. After your guided tour, stay for a picnic in the Longfellow Garden; it's open to the public during museum hours. ⊠ *489 Congress St.* 🕾 *207/774–1822* ⊕ *www. mainehistory.org* 🎫 *House and museum $15, gardens free* ⊗ *Closed Nov.–Apr.*

 Restaurants

Five Fifty-Five

$$$$ | **MODERN AMERICAN** | Classic dishes are cleverly updated at this classy and very popular Congress Street spot housed in a former 19th-century firehouse with exposed brick and copper accents. The menu changes seasonally to reflect ingredients available from local waters, organic farms, and food purveyors, but the mac 'n' cheese, which boasts artisanal cheeses and shaved black truffles, is a mainstay, as is the signature tasting menu, which starts at $70 and changes frequently. **Known for:** seasonally inspired and locally sourced ingredients; top-notch wine pairings that are worth the splurge; exceptional seafood dishes prepared with sustainable fish. Ⓢ *Average main: $40* ⊠ *555 Congress St.* 🕾 *207/761–0555* ⊕ *www. fivefifty-five.com* ⊗ *No lunch.*

Local 188

$$$ | **SPANISH** | There's an infectious vibe at this eclectic, Spanish-inspired Arts District hot spot that's accentuated by its 2,000-square-foot space, lofty tin ceilings, worn maple floors, and mismatched chandeliers. Regulars chat with servers about which just-caught seafood will decorate the paella or which organic veggies will star in the tortillas, one of several tapas choices. **Known for:** large bar area; some 150 different wines, mostly from Europe; a lively crowd and warm environment. Ⓢ *Average main: $25* ⊠ *685 Congress St.* 🕾 *207/761–7909* ⊕ *www.local188.com* ⊗ *No lunch.*

★ **Speckled Ax Wood Roasted Coffee**
$ | CAFÉ | The Speckled Ax serves up a seriously delicious coffee, whether cold brewed or piping hot with frothy milk. The secret to the richness of the beans is the painstaking roasting process, using a vintage Italian Petroncini roaster fired with local hardwood—ask to take a peek at that contraption while you wait for your drink. **Known for:** pastries and other baked goods; local gathering space; a hip vibe. ⑤ *Average main: $4* ✉ *567 Congress St.* ☎ *207/660–3333* ⊕ *www.speckledax.com.*

Hotels

★ **The Danforth**
$$ | B&B/INN | A stunning showpiece, this stylish inn was one of Portland's grandest Federal-style dwellings when it was built in 1823 on a block known as "Social Corners" for the elaborate parties its owners held in their spacious parlor, and it's located right next to historic Victoria Mansion. **Pros:** gorgeous rooms; basement billiards room; city views from cupola. **Cons:** small windows in some third-floor rooms; short walk to downtown; definitely a splurge. ⑤ *Rooms from: $298* ✉ *163 Danforth St.* ☎ *207/879–8755, 800/879–8755* ⊕ *www.danforthinn.com* ⇨ *9 rooms* ⦿ *Free breakfast.*

Inn on Carleton
$$ | B&B/INN | FAMILY | This 1869 Victorian has a curved mahogany staircase to the third floor, a bay window overlooking the street from the front parlor, and gleaming pumpkin-pine floors. **Pros:** most rooms have electric fireplaces; English garden with fountain; attentive resident innkeeper. **Cons:** no elevator; a short walk to the center of it all; breakfast can be light for some. ⑤ *Rooms from: $210* ✉ *46 Carleton St.* ☎ *207/775–1910, 800/639–1779* ⊕ *www.innoncarleton.com* ⇨ *6 rooms* ⦿ *Free breakfast.*

Performing Arts

Merrill Auditorium
CONCERTS | FAMILY | This soaring concert hall hosts numerous theatrical and musical events, including performances by the Portland Symphony Orchestra and the Portland Opera Repertory Theatre. Ask about organ recitals on the auditorium's huge 1912 Kotzschmar Memorial Organ. ✉ *20 Myrtle St.* ☎ *207/842–0800* ⊕ *portlandmaine. gov/574/Merrill-Auditorium.*

Portland Stage
THEATER | FAMILY | This company mounts theatrical productions on its two stages September–May. ✉ *25-A Forest Ave.* ☎ *207/774–0465* ⊕ *www.portlandstage. org.*

Space Gallery
ART GALLERIES—ARTS | FAMILY | Space Gallery sparkles as a contemporary art gallery and alternative arts venue, opening its doors to everything from poetry readings and art fairs to live music to documentary films. The gallery is open Wednesday–Saturday. ✉ *534–538 Congress St.* ☎ *207/828–5600* ⊕ *www. space538.org.*

● Shopping

ART AND ANTIQUES
Portland Flea-for-All
ANTIQUES/COLLECTIBLES | FAMILY | Friday through Sunday, head to the city's Bayside neighborhood for the Portland Flea-for-All, where you'll find all sorts of vintage eye candy from an-ever rotating array of antiques and artisan vendors—a fun excursion, whether or not you actually buy anything. ✉ *585 Congress St.* ☎ *207/370–7570* ⊕ *www.portlandflea-forall.com.*

Activities

BICYCLING
Bicycle Coalition of Maine

BICYCLING | FAMILY | For state bike trail maps, club and tour listings, or hints on safety, contact the Bicycle Coalition of Maine. Maps are available at the group's headquarters in the Arts District. ⊠ *34 Preble St.* ☏ *207/623–4511* ⊕ *www. bikemaine.org.*

Gorham Bike and Ski

BICYCLING | FAMILY | You can rent several types of bikes, including hybrid and tandem models, starting at $35 per day. ⊠ *693 Congress St.* ☏ *207/773–1700* ⊕ *www.gorhambike.com.*

East End

This neighborhood encompasses Munjoy Hill, the Eastern Promenade, East End Beach, and the Portland Observatory. It's an easy walk to the Old Port, and a great place to watch the harbor goings on, and see the July 4 fireworks.

Sights

Eastern Promenade

HISTORIC SITE | FAMILY | Between the city's two promenades, this one, often overlooked by tourists, has by far the best view. Gracious Victorian homes, many now converted to condos and apartments, border one side of the street. On the other is 68 acres of hillside parkland that includes Ft. Allen Park and, at the base of the hill, the Eastern Prom Trail and tiny East End Beach and boat launch. On a sunny day the Eastern Prom is a lovely spot for picnicking and people-watching. ⊠ *Washington Ave. to Fore St.*

Maine Narrow Gauge Railroad Museum

MUSEUM | FAMILY | Whether you're crazy about old trains or just want to see the sights from a different perspective, the railroad museum has an extensive collection of locomotives and rail coaches, and offers scenic tours on narrow-gauge railcars. The 3-mile jaunts run on the hour and take you along Casco Bay, at the foot of the Eastern Promenade. The operating season caps off with a fall harvest ride (complete with cider), and during the Christmas season there are special Polar Express rides, based on the popular children's book. ⊠ *58 Fore St.* ☏ *207/828–0814* ⊕ *www. mainenarrowgauge.org* ⊠ *Museum $5, train rides $10* ⊘ *Closed Sept.–Apr.*

Portland Observatory

OBSERVATORY | FAMILY | This octagonal observatory on Munjoy Hill was built in 1807 by Captain Lemuel Moody, a retired sea captain, as a maritime signal tower. Moody used a telescope to identify incoming ships, and flags to signal to merchants where to unload their cargo. Held in place by 122 tons of ballast, it's the last remaining historic maritime signal station in the country. The guided tour leads all the way to the dome, where you can step out on the deck and take in views of Portland, the islands, and inland toward the White Mountains. ⊠ *138 Congress St.* ☏ *207/774–5561* ⊕ *www. portlandlandmarks.org* ⊠ *$10* ⊘ *Closed mid-Oct.–late May.*

🍴 Restaurants

Drifter's Wife

$$$ | MODERN AMERICAN | What started out as a cozy spot to sip some of the most stellar natural wines from around the world turned into one of Portland's dining darlings thanks to phenomenal local ingredients incorporated into mouthwatering dishes. This building with a contemporary industrial feel is a most welcoming space, so you may find yourself lingering a little longer than usual over dinner. **Known for:** carefully selected, seasonal menus; local seafood dishes; wines made with natural yeasts and farmed without the use of chemicals. ⑤ *Average main: $30* ⊠ *59 Washington Ave.* ☏ *207/805–1336* ⊕ *www.drifter-swife.com* ⊘ *Closed Sun. and Mon.*

Duckfat

$ | MODERN AMERICAN | Even in midafternoon, this small, hip sandwich shop in the Old Port is packed. The focus here is everyday farm-to-table fare: the signature Belgian fries are made with Maine potatoes cooked, yes, in duck fat and served in paper cones, and standards include meat loaf and the BGT (bacon, goat cheese, tomato). **Known for:** decadent poutine with duck-fat gravy; hopping atmosphere—waits for a table can be long; thick milk shakes prepared with local gelato by Gelato Fiasco. $ *Average main: $12* ✉ *43 Middle St.* ☎ *207/774– 8080* ⊕ *www.duckfat.com.*

★ East Ender

$$ | AMERICAN | FAMILY | The emphasis at this cozy neighborhood restaurant is on the superb food rather than the atmosphere, which isn't surprising, given that the owners formerly served their tasty, no-fuss fare from a truck. Lunch and dinner feature locally sourced, sustainable ingredients in dishes that reflect the seasons; one of the best brunches in town is to be found here Sunday. **Known for:** mouthwatering house-smoked bacon; crispy, thrice-cooked fries; brunch cocktails that incorporate ingredients from local distilleries and house-made cordials. $ *Average main: $24* ✉ *47 Middle St.* ☎ *207/879–7669* ⊕ *www.eastenderportland.com.*

★ Eventide Oyster Co

$ | SEAFOOD | Not only does Eventide have fresh, tasty oysters from all over Maine and New England, artfully prepared with novel accoutrements like kimchi, ginger ices, and cucumber-champagne mignonette, it also serves delicious crudos and ceviches with unique ingredients like blood orange and chili miso. The menu constantly changes, depending on what's in season, so it's best to order a handful of small plates, a glass of bubbly or one of the signature tiki-style cocktails, and, of course, a dozen oysters. **Known for:** brown-butter lobster rolls; a decent selection of alternatives for nonseafood lovers;

teaming up with other local restaurants for special cook-offs and menus. $ *Average main: $15* ✉ *86 Middle St.* ☎ *207/774– 8538* ⊕ *www.eventideoysterco.com.*

The Honey Paw

$ | ASIAN FUSION | Come for the salty wontons, piping-hot broths, and wok-fried noodles; stay for the turntable music, the well-stocked cocktail bar, and the soft-serve ice cream that comes in flavors like honeycomb, magic shell, or caramelized honey. If you order one thing here, make it the lobster toast, topped with a scallop and lobster mousse, radish, lime, and an amazing tarragon emulsion. **Known for:** sister restaurant to Eventide Oyster Co.; house-made noodles; rotating wines on tap and an excellent selection of sake. $ *Average main: $15* ✉ *7 Middle St.* ☎ *207/774–8538* ⊕ *www.thehoneypaw. com* ⊙ *Closed Tues.*

Hugo's

$$$$ | ECLECTIC | Serving the freshest local, organic foods is a priority at Hugo's, and your server is sure to know everything about the various purveyors featured on the menu, which is updated daily and features smartly prepared, seasonally inspired dishes like crispy-skin pork belly and crepe-wrapped arctic char. You can choose five courses with a blind tasting menu for $90 or go à la carte—which could be dangerous, as you may want to try everything on the creative menu. **Known for:** blind tasting menu; an open kitchen; dangerously delicious craft cocktails. $ *Average main: $45* ✉ *88 Middle St.* ☎ *207/774–8538* ⊕ *www.hugos.net* ⊙ *Closed Sun. and Mon. No lunch.*

Lolita

$$$ | TAPAS | Perched on Munjoy Hill near the Portland Observatory, Lolita has a sophisticated bodega vibe, where wood-fired dishes like scallops with hazelnuts and roasted clams are offered alongside charcuterie and cheese boards and plenty of robust wine—the intimate setting makes for a great date night. Or come for a midday snack alone or with a group of friends and pass around a bevy of the many small, tapas-style dishes. **Known for:** delicious cured meats and cheeses; incorporating farm-to-table ingredients; craft cocktails featuring unique bitter blends. $ *Average main: $30* ⊠ *90 Congress St.* ☎ *207/775–5652* ⊕ *www. lolita-portland.com.*

The Shop at Island Creek Oysters

$ | SEAFOOD | This no-fuss counter-service spot, opened by longtime wholesale purveyors of Island Creek Oysters (from Duxbury, MA), serves seriously fresh shellfish and excellent Maine microbrews (and wine) on tap. A clutch of imported, tinned fish and house-made pickled items that pair very well with oysters are also available. **Known for:** laid-back, family-friendly environment; impeccably scrubbed and shucked shellfish; house-made mignonettes. $ *Average main: $10* ⊠ *123 Washington Ave.* ☎ *207/699–4466* ⊕ *www.portland.islandcreekoysters.com* ⊗ *Closed Mon.*

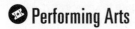 Performing Arts

Mayo Street Arts

ARTS CENTERS | FAMILY | An alternative-arts venue for the innovative and up-and-coming, Mayo Street Arts often features intimate concerts, contemporary exhibitions, and offbeat puppet shows in a repurposed church. ⊠ *10 Mayo St.* ☎ *207/879–4629* ⊕ *www. mayostreetarts.org.*

Shopping

HOUSEHOLD ITEMS/FURNITURE
Angela Adams

HOUSEHOLD ITEMS/FURNITURE | Maine islander Angela Adams specializes in simple but bold geometric motifs parlayed into dramatic rugs (custom, too), canvas totes, bedding, and other home accessories. The shop also carries sleek wood furniture from her husband's woodshop. ⊠ *71 Cove St.* ⊕ *www.angelaadams.com.*

Activities

BIKING
Cycle Mania

BICYCLING | FAMILY | Rent hybrid bikes downtown at Cycle Mania. The $30 per day rate includes a helmet and lock. ⊠ *65 Cove St.* ☎ *207/774–2933* ⊕ *www. cyclemania1.com.*

BOATING
Portland Paddle

KAYAKING | FAMILY | Run by a pair of Registered Maine Guides, Portland Paddle leads introductory sea-kayaking clinics along with guided trips between the Casco Bay islands June through September. Two-hour sunset paddles ($40) are a fave, as are the full-moon standup paddleboard tours ($45). Kayak and SUP rentals are available. ⊠ *Eastern Promenade, East End Beach, off Cutter St.* ☎ *207/370–9730* ⊕ *www.portlandpaddle. net* ⊗ *Closed Nov.–May.*

The West End

A leisurely walk through Portland's West End, beginning at the top of the Arts District, offers a real treat to historic-architecture buffs. The quiet and stately neighborhood, on the National Register of Historic Places, presents an extraordinary display of architectural splendor, from High Victorian Gothic to lush Italianate, Queen Anne, and Colonial Revival.

Sights

Western Promenade

PROMENADE | A good place to start is at the head of the Western Promenade, which has benches and a nice view. From the Old Port, take Danforth Street all the way up to Vaughn Street; take a right on Vaughn and then an immediate left onto Western Promenade. Pass by the Western Cemetery, Portland's second official burial ground, laid out in 1829—inside is the ancestral plot of

For the full Maine experience, try a classic lobster dinner.

poet Henry Wadsworth Longfellow—and look for street parking. ⊠ *Danforth St. to Bramhall St.*

Restaurants

BaoBao Dumpling House

$ | **ASIAN** | **FAMILY** | In a historic town house with traditional Asian decor in Portland's quaint West End, this dumpling house serves deeply satisfying Asian-inspired comfort food in an intimate setting. Start with crispy braised chicken skin with ponzu, cucumber, scallion, and *togarashi* chili, then move on to one of the satisfying dumpling dishes with fillings like lamb, black-bean chili, and peanuts, or thread-cut hake with burdock. **Known for:** dishes integrating local, seasonal ingredients; tap takeovers by local brewmasters; half-priced dumplings Wednesday–Friday 2–4 pm. ⑤ *Average main: $12* ⊠ *133 Spring St., at Park St. in Portland's West End* ☎ *207/772–8400* ⊕ *www.baobaodumplinghouse.com* ⊙ *Closed Mon. and Tues.*

★ Bolster, Snow and Co

$$$ | **MODERN AMERICAN** | In the historic Mellen E. Bolster House, now known as the Francis Hotel, Bolster, Snow and Co. presents food that is a feast for both the eyes and the stomach. **Known for:** eye-popping craft cocktails; homemade breads; house-made noodles. ⑤ *Average main: $25* ⊠ *Francis Hotel, 747 Congress St.* ☎ *207/772–7496* ⊕ *www.bolstersnow. com* ⊙ *Closed Mon. and Tues.*

Hotels

★ The Francis

$$$ | **HOTEL** | In the beautifully restored Mellen E. Bolster House, this charming boutique hotel has a midcentury-modern vibe that seamlessly compliments the building's immaculately preserved historical design elements. **Pros:** bars in rooms; smart spa on second floor; guest rooms feature custom-built furniture. **Cons:** only 15 rooms; some rooms not accessible by elevator; no bathtubs. ⑤ *Rooms from: $300* ⊠ *747 Congress*

St. ☎ 207/772–7485 ⊕ www.thefrancis-maine.com ⇗ 15 rooms ⦿ No meals.

Morrill Mansion

$$ | B&B/INN | FAMILY | This 19th-century town house has tastefully appointed rooms with well-executed color schemes—blue is a favorite hue here—and abundant thoughtful touches like well-stocked snack areas with fresh whoopie pies baked by the innkeeper. **Pros:** close to Arts District; parlors on each floor for relaxing; tea, coffee, and baked treats available throughout the day. **Cons:** not on a grand block; no children under 14; no elevator. ⑤ Rooms from: $200 ⊠ 249 Vaughan St. ☎ 207/774–6900, 888/566–7745 ⊕ www.morrillmansion.com ⇗ 8 rooms ⦿ Free breakfast.

Pomegranate Inn

$$$ | B&B/INN | The classic facade of this handsome 1884 Italianate in the architecturally rich Western Promenade area gives no hint of the splashy, modern (but cozy) surprises within. **Pros:** funky, modern decor; many rooms have gas fireplaces; close to Western Promenade. **Cons:** 15- to 20-minute walk to the Old Port; not pet-friendly; no elevator. ⑤ Rooms from: $329 ⊠ 49 Neal St. ☎ 207/701–1006, 800/356–0408 ⊕ www.pomegranateinn.com ⇗ 8 rooms ⦿ Free breakfast.

West End Inn

$ | B&B/INN | Set among the glorious homes of the Western Promenade, this 1871 Georgian displays much of the era's grandeur, with high pressed-tin ceilings, intricate moldings, ceiling medallions, and a dramatic ruby-red foyer, along with many modern touches, such as Wi-Fi flat-screen TVs in spacious guest rooms, which are either brightly painted or papered with traditional Waverly prints. **Pros:** fireplace library is a cozy place to relax; neighborhood is a historical walking tour; generous breakfast featuring local ingredients. **Cons:** 15- to 20-minute walk downtown; some rooms disproportionately smaller than others in same price

range; some rooms without bathtubs. ⑤ Rooms from: $199 ⊠ 146 Pine St. ☎ 800/338–1377 ⊕ www.westendbb.com ⇗ 6 rooms ⦿ Free breakfast.

Back Cove and Bayside

The Back Cove neighborhood is on the north side of 295 near the city's Back Cove basin, which has a lovely one mile trail around it. It's borders are Forest Avenue to Washington Avenue, and Canco Road to the Cove.

Bordered by Forest Avenue, Marginal Way, Cumberland Avenue, and Franklin Street, Bayside is home to Whole Foods, Trader Joes and the Bayside Trail.

🍴 Restaurants

★ Rose Foods

$ | DELI | FAMILY | The same folks behind the fabulous and consistently tasty Palace Diner in Biddeford have filled a long-neglected gap in Portland's food scene with this pitch-perfect bagel shop. Here you'll find spot-on New York-style bagels with both expected and unusual add-ons, including pastrami nova, chopped liver, and lip-smacking onion frittata. **Known for:** family-friendly, neighborhood environment; house-cured gravlax; general-store-style shop items including books, games, and specialty-food items. ⑤ Average main: $11 ⊠ 428 Forest Ave. ☎ 207/835–0991 ⊕ www.rosefoods.me.

★ Woodford Food and Beverage

$$ | MODERN AMERICAN | The casual, retro vibe at this charming restaurant about 2 miles north of the Old Port makes it worth the journey, as do the superb offerings featuring locally sourced ingredients from land and sea. There's something for everyone on the seafood-focused menu, including steak tartare, classic deviled eggs, croque madames and monsieurs, and burgers. **Known for:** family-friendly environment;

laid back but efficient service; pâté du jour. $ *Average main: $18* ✉ *660 Forest Ave.* ☎ *207/200–8503* ⊕ *www.woodfordfb.com* ☯ *Closed Tues.*

 Nightlife

★ Bayside Bowl

BOWLING | FAMILY | This 12-lane bowling alley sprang out of a survival technique among a group of friends for getting through Maine's harrowing winters. A community-minded locale that often puts on concerts and other events, Bayside Bowl also serves up some seriously delicious cocktails and local craft beers and snacks like poutine, nachos, and fried pickles; the rooftop, which has a food truck that serves killer tacos, has one of the best views of the city (and the sunset) in town. ✉ *58 Alder St.* ☎ *207/791–2695* ⊕ *www.baysidebowl.com.*

 Shopping

ART AND ANTIQUES

Portland Architectural Salvage

HOUSEHOLD ITEMS/FURNITURE | A fixer-upper's dream, Portland Architectural Salvage has four floors of unusual finds from old buildings, including fixtures, hardware, and stained-glass windows, as well as assorted antiques. ✉ *131 Preble St.* ☎ *207/780–0634* ⊕ *www.portlandsalvage.com.*

Casco Bay Islands

The islands of Casco Bay are also known as the Calendar Islands, because an early explorer mistakenly thought there was one for each day of the year (in reality there are only 140 or so). These islands range from ledges visible only at low tide to populous Peaks Island, a suburb of Portland. Some are uninhabited; others support year-round communities, as well as stores and restaurants. Ft. Gorges commands Hog Island Ledge, and Eagle Island is the site of Arctic explorer

Admiral Robert Peary's home. The brightly painted ferries of Casco Bay Lines are the islands' lifeline. There is frequent service to the most populated ones, including Peaks, Long, Little Diamond, and Great Diamond.

There is little in the way of overnight lodging on the islands—the population swells during the warmer months due to summer residents—and there are few restaurants or organized attractions other than the natural beauty of the islands themselves. Meandering about by bike or on foot is a good way to explore on a day trip.

GETTING HERE AND AROUND

Casco Bay Lines provides ferry service from Portland to the islands of Casco Bay.

ESSENTIALS

TRANSPORTATION INFORMATION

Casco Bay Lines ✉ *56 Commercial St., Portland* ☎ *207/774–7871* ⊕ *www.cascobaylines.com.*

Cape Elizabeth

Winslow Homer painted many of his famous oceanscapes from a tiny studio on the rocky peninsula known as Prout's Neck, 12 miles south of Portland. Visitors today navigate a neighborhood of summer homes and a sprawling country-club property for a glimpse of the same dramatic coastline. Follow Route 77 through South Portland (sometimes called "SoPo"), stopping off for bagels and coffee in its hipper residential neighborhoods. In the affluent bedroom community of Cape Elizabeth, a detour along the two-lane Shore Road shows off the famed Portland Head Light and quite a few stunning oceanfront homes.

Sights

★ Cape Elizabeth Light

LIGHTHOUSE | FAMILY | This was the first twin lighthouse erected on the Maine coast in 1828—and locals still call it Two Lights—but half of the Cape Elizabeth Light was dismantled in 1924 and converted into a private residence. The other half still operates, and you can get a great photo of it from the end of Two Lights Road in the surrounding state park of the same name. The lighthouse itself is closed to the public, but you can explore the tidal pools at its base for small, edible snails known as periwinkles, or just "wrinkles," as they're sometimes referred to in Maine. Picnic tables are also available. ⊠ *7 Tower Dr.* ✛ *Off Rte. 77 in Cape Elizabeth. Take Rte. 77 to Two Lights Rd. to Tower Dr.* ☎ *207/799–5871* ⊕ *www.maine.gov/twolights* ⊒ *$7.*

★ Portland Head Light

LIGHTHOUSE | FAMILY | Familiar to many from photographs and the Edward Hopper painting *Portland Head-Light* (1927), this lighthouse was commissioned by George Washington in 1790. The towering, white-stone structure stands over the keeper's quarters, a white home with a blazing red roof, today the Museum at Portland Head Light. The lighthouse is in 90-acre Fort Williams Park, a sprawling green space with walking paths, picnic facilities, a beach and—you guessed it—a cool old fort. ⊠ *Museum, 1000 Shore Rd.* ☎ *207/799–2661* ⊕ *www.portlandheadlight.com.*

Scarborough Marsh Audubon Center

NATURE PRESERVE | FAMILY | You can explore this Maine Audubon Society–run nature center by foot or canoe, on your own or by signing up for a guided walk or paddle. Canoes and kayaks are available to rent and come with a life jacket and map. The salt marsh is Maine's largest and is an excellent place for bird-watching and peaceful paddling along its winding ways. The center has a discovery room for kids, programs for all ages ranging from basket making to astronomy, and a good gift shop. Tours include birding walks. ⊠ *Pine Point Rd., Scarborough* ☎ *207/883–5100, 207/781–2330* ⊕ *www.maineaudubon.org* ⊒ *Free* ⊘ *Closed early Sept.–May.*

★ Winslow Homer Studio

HOUSE | FAMILY | The great American landscape painter created many of his best-known works in this seaside home between 1883 until his death in 1910. It's easy to see how this rocky, jagged peninsula might have been inspiring. The only way to get a look is on a tour with the Portland Museum of Art, which leads 2½-hour strolls through the historic property. ⊠ *5 Winslow Homer Rd., Scarborough* ☎ *207/775–6148* ⊕ *www.portlandmuseum.org* ⊒ *$65* ⊘ *Closed Nov.–mid-Apr.*

Restaurants

★ Bite Into Maine

$$ | SEAFOOD | FAMILY | Hands down Maine's best lobster roll is found at this food truck that overlooks the idyllic Portland Head Light in Cape Elizabeth. Traditional lobster rolls smothered in ungodly amounts of drawn butter are delicious, but you've also got the option to get out of the lobster comfort zone with rolls featuring flavors like wasabi, curry, and chipotle, as well as a toothsome lobster BLT. **Known for:** quick bite; dining with a view over the ocean; always fresh lobster. ⑤ *Average main: $18* ⊠ *1000 Shore Rd.* ☎ *207/289–6142* ⊕ *www.biteinto-maine.com* ⊘ *Closed mid-Oct.–mid-Apr.*

The Lobster Shack at Two Lights

$$ | SEAFOOD | FAMILY | A classic spot since the 1920s, you can't beat the location—right on the water, below the lighthouse pair that gives Two Lights State Park its name—and the food's not bad either. Enjoy fresh lobster whole or piled into a hot-dog bun with a dollop of mayo, or opt for the delicious chowder, fried clams, or fish 'n' chips. **Known for:** seafood boats; family-friendly environment; mini homemade blueberry pies. $ *Average main: $18* ✉ *225 Two Lights Rd.* ☎ *207/799–1677* ⊕ *www. lobstershacktwolights.com* ⊙ *Closed late Oct.–late Mar.*

★ Shade Eatery at Higgins Beach

$$ | **SEAFOOD** | **FAMILY** | This charming neighborhood restaurant and bar just steps from the beach serves up generous, deeply satisfying dishes filled with locally sourced ingredients. Seafood plays a big role in the menu, with unholy lobster rolls filled to the brim with fresh meat, molten cheese, and bacon; fish tacos stuffed with pico de gallo, avocado, and coleslaw; a Portuguese seafood stew; crab cakes; and a delicious scallop ceviche featuring oversized, house-made plantain chips, mango, and jalapeño. **Known for:** family-friendly environment; three-season-porch dining; $1 freshly shucked oysters during happy hour. $ *Average main: $18* ✉ *Higgins Beach Inn, 36 Ocean Ave., Scarborough* ☎ *207/883–6684* ⊕ *www.higginsbeach-inn.com/shade.*

 Hotels

Black Point Inn

$$$$ | **RESORT** | **FAMILY** | Toward the tip of the peninsula that juts into the ocean at Prout's Neck stands this stylish, tastefully updated 1878 resort inn with spectacular views up and down the coast. **Pros:** dramatic setting; geothermally heated pool; discounts in shoulder seasons. **Cons:** non-Atlantic view a little underwhelming with buildings on the horizon; rooms have an older, more stately feel to them; children are asked to only eat in pub area. $ *Rooms from: $490* ✉ *510 Black Point Rd., Scarborough* ☎ *207/883–2500* ⊕ *www.blackpointinn. com* ⊙ *Closed late Oct.–early May* ⇆ *25 rooms* ⋓ *Free breakfast.*

★ Higgins Beach Inn

$$ | **B&B/INN** | Decidedly "new Maine," this lovingly renovated inn with a laid-back, beach-hair-don't care kind of nonchalance is just steps from the surfer's paradise that is Higgins Beach. **Pros:** newly renovated; exceptionally efficient and warm service; small touches that make a difference, such as beach towels and a sparkling water dispenser. **Cons:** no pets allowed; a short walk to the beach; limited common areas. $ *Rooms from: $290* ✉ *34 Ocean Ave., Scarborough* ☎ *207/883–6684* ⊕ *www.higginsbeach-inn.com* ⊙ *Closed Oct.–Apr.* ⇆ *23 rooms* ⋓ *Free breakfast.*

★ Inn by the Sea

$$$$ | **B&B/INN** | With some of the highest-quality, gracious service in the state and a top-notch restaurant that delights at every meal, you'll never want to leave the aptly named Inn by the Sea, which is set on Cape Elizabeth's stunning Crescent Beach. **Pros:** your wish is their command; hands down the most dog-friendly accommodations in Maine; direct access to Crescent Beach with chic beach chairs, towels, and umbrellas at hand; native plants garden; gourmet menu for dogs. **Cons:** a short distance from Portland's food scene; not for the budget-minded; minimum stays in the high season. $ *Rooms from: $580* ✉ *40 Bowery Beach Rd.* ☎ *207/799–3134* ⊕ *www.innbythesea.com* ⇆ *61 rooms* ⋓ *No meals.*

Freeport

17 miles north of Portland via I–295.

Those who flock straight to L.L. Bean and see nothing else of Freeport are missing out. The city's charming backstreets are lined with historic buildings and old clapboard houses, and there's a pretty little harbor on the south side of the Harraseeket River. It's true that many who come to the area do so simply to shop: L.L. Bean is the store that put Freeport on the map, and plenty of outlets and some specialty stores have settled here. Still, if you choose, you can stay awhile and experience more than fabulous bargains; beyond the shops

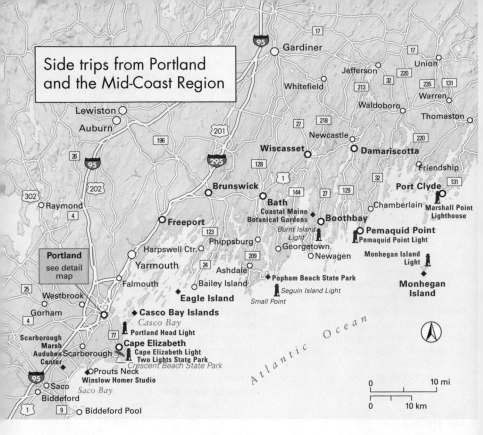

Side trips from Portland and the Mid-Coast Region

are bucolic nature preserves with miles of walking trails and plenty of places for leisurely ambling that don't require the overuse of your credit cards.

GETTING HERE AND AROUND

Interstate 295 has three Freeport exits and passes by on the edge of the downtown area. U.S. 1 is Main Street here.

 Sights

Freeport Historical Society

INFO CENTER | **FAMILY** | Pick up a village walking map and check out the historical exhibits at the Freeport Historical Society, located in Harrington House, a hybrid Federal- and Greek Revival–style home built in the 1830s. Always call ahead when planning a visit. ⊠ 45 Main St. ☎ 207/865–3170 ⊕ www.freeporthistoricalsociety.org.

FARM/RANCH | **FAMILY** | Pettengill Farm The grounds of the Freeport Historical Society's saltwater Pettengill Farm—140 beautifully tended acres along an estuary of the Harraseeket River—are open to the public. It's about a 15-minute walk from the parking area down a farm road to the circa-1800 saltbox farmhouse, which is open by appointment. Little has changed since it was built, and it has rare etchings (called sgraffitti) of ships and sea monsters on three bedroom walls. ⊠ 31 Pettengill Rd. ☎ 207/865–3170 ⊕ www.freeporthistoricalsociety.org ⊠ Free (donations appreciated).

🍴 Restaurants

Harraseeket Lunch & Lobster Co

$$ | **SEAFOOD** | **FAMILY** | Seafood baskets and lobster dinners are the focus at this popular, bare-bones place beside the town landing in South Freeport. Order at the counter, find a seat inside or out, and expect long lines in summer. **Known for:** great seafood; harbor location; picnic table dining. $ *Average main: $18* ✉ *36 S. Main St., South Freeport* ☎ *207/865–4888* ⊕ *www.harraseeketlunchandlobster.com* ▭ *No credit cards* ⊗ *Closed mid-Oct.–Apr.*

Hotels

Harraseeket Inn

$$ | HOTEL | FAMILY | Despite some modern appointments, this large hotel has a country-inn ambience throughout. **Pros:** full breakfast and afternoon tea; elevators and other modern touches; walk to shopping district. **Cons:** additions have diminished some authenticity; some rooms without a garden view; fireplaces only in select rooms. $ *Rooms from: $275* ✉ *162 Main St.* ☎ *207/865–9377, 800/342–6423* ⊕ *www.harraseeketinn.com* ⬏ *84 rooms, 9 town houses* ⥲ *Free breakfast.*

Performing Arts

L.L. Bean Summer Concert Series

CONCERTS | FAMILY | Throughout the summer, L.L. Bean hosts free activities, including concerts, at the L.L. Bean Discovery Park. It's set back from Main Street, along a side street the runs between the company's flagship and home furnishings stores. ✉ *18 Morse St.* ☎ *877/755–2326* ⊕ *www.llbean.com.*

Activities

L.L. Bean Outdoor Discovery Schools

TOUR—SPORTS | FAMILY | It shouldn't come as a surprise that one of the world's largest outdoor outfitters also provides its customers with instructional adventures to go with its products. L.L. Bean's year-round Outdoor Discovery Schools offer courses in canoeing, biking, kayaking, fly-fishing, snowshoeing, cross-country skiing, and other outdoor sports. ✉ *11 Desert Rd.* ☎ *888/552–3261* ⊕ *www.llbean.com/ods.*

Shopping

The *Freeport Visitors Guide* lists the more than 200 stores on Main Street, Bow Street, and elsewhere, including Coach, Brooks Brothers, Banana Republic, J. Crew, and Cole Haan. You can pick it up around town.

★ L.L. Bean

CLOTHING | FAMILY | Founded in 1912 as a mail-order merchandiser after its namesake invented a hunting boot, L.L. Bean's giant flagship store attracts more than 3 million shoppers annually and is open 365 days a year in the heart of Freeport's outlet shopping district. You can still find the original hunting boots, along with cotton and wool sweaters; outerwear of all kinds; casual clothing, boots, and shoes for men, women, and kids; and camping equipment. Nearby are the company's home furnishings store; bike, boat, and ski store; and outlet. ✉ *95 Main St.* ☎ *877/755–2326* ⊕ *www.llbean.com.*

R. D. Allen Freeport Jewelers

JEWELRY/ACCESSORIES | This shop specializes in brightly colored tourmaline and other gemstones mined in Maine. Most of the pieces are the work of Maine artisans. Watermelon tourmaline is a specialty. ✉ *13 Middle St.* ⊹ *2 blocks from L.L. Bean* ☎ *207/865–1818, 877/837–3835* ⊕ *www.rdallen.com.*

★ Thos. Moser Cabinetmakers

HOUSEHOLD ITEMS/FURNITURE | Famed local furniture company Thos. Moser Cabinetmakers sells artful, handmade wood pieces with clean, classic lines. The store has information on tours at the workshop 30 minutes away in Auburn (by appointment only). ✉ *149 Main St.* ☎ *207/865–4519* ⊕ *www.thosmoser.com.*

Brunswick

10 miles north of Freeport via U.S. 1.

Lovely brick and clapboard buildings are the highlight of Brunswick's Federal Street Historic District, which includes Federal Street and Park Row and the stately campus of Bowdoin College. From the intersection of Pleasant and Maine Streets, in the center of town, you can walk in any direction and discover an impressive array of restaurants, as well as bookstores, gift shops, boutiques, and jewelers.

Below Brunswick are Harpswell Neck and the more than 40 islands that make up the town of Harpswell, known collectively as the Harpswells. Route 123 runs down Harpswell Neck, where small coves shelter lobster boats, and summer cottages are tucked away among birch and spruce trees. On your way down from Cook's Corner to Land's End at the end of Route 24, you cross Sebascodegan Island. Heading east here leads to East Harpswell and Cundy's Harbor. Continuing straight south down Route 24 leads to Orr's Island. Stop at Mackerel Cove to see a real fishing harbor; there are a few parking spaces, where you can stop to picnic and look for beach glass or put in your kayaks. Inhale the salt breeze as you cross the world's only cribstone bridge (designed so that water flows freely through gaps between the granite blocks) on your way to Bailey Island, home to a lobster pound made famous thanks in part to a Visa commercial.

GETTING HERE AND AROUND

From Interstate 295 take the Coastal Connector to U.S. 1 in Brunswick. From here Route 24 runs to Bailey Island and Route 123 down Harpswell Neck.

Sights

★ Bowdoin College Museum of Art

ARTS CENTERS | FAMILY | This small museum housed in a stately building on Bowdoin's main quad features one of the oldest permanent collections of art in the United States, comprising paintings, sculpture, decorative arts, and works on paper. The museum often mounts well-curated, rotating exhibitions and has stellar programs for getting children excited about art. ⊠ *245 Maine St.* ☎ *207/725–3275* ⊕ *www.bowdoin.edu/art-museum* ⊠ *Free.*

🍴 Restaurants

★ Cook's Lobster House

$$$ | SEAFOOD | FAMILY | What began as a lobster shack on Bailey's Island in 1955 has grown into a huge, internationally famous family-style restaurant with a small gift shop. The restaurant still catches its own seafood, so you can count on the lobster casserole and the haddock sandwich to be delectable. **Known for:** traditional Maine seafood fare prepared simply; terrific selection of local craft beer and spirits; live music and festive atmosphere in the summer. ⑤ *Average main: $26* ⊠ *68 Garrison Cove Rd., Bailey Island* ☎ *207/833–2818* ⊕ *www.cookslobster.com* ⊘ *Closed early Jan.–mid-Feb.*

★ Frontier

$ | MEDITERRANEAN | There's nothing typical about Frontier, where indie films roll daily, artists and musicians from all over the world share their art, and a globally inspired menu features locally sourced ingredients in recipes culled from diverse cultures. Come for the inspiring events, stay for the delicious food and dangerously terrific cocktails. **Known for:** poblano and fish tacos and other seafood, as well as Mediterranean and Middle Eastern dishes; acting locally and thinking globally; probably one of the very few places you can find fried tomatoes in Maine.

$ *Average main: $15* ⊠ *14 Maine St., Mill 3 Fort Andross* ☎ *207/725–5222* ⊕ *www. explorefrontier.com* ⊘ *Closed Mon.*

Activities

H2Outfitters

KAYAKING | The coast near Brunswick is full of hidden nooks and crannies waiting to be explored by kayak. H2Outfitters, at the southern end of Orr's Island just before the cribstone bridge, is the place in Harpswell to get on the water. It provides top-notch kayaking instruction and also offers half-day, full-day, bed-and-breakfast, and camping trips in the waters off its home base and elsewhere in Maine. ⊠ *1894 Harpswell Island Rd., Orrs Island* ☎ *207/833–5257, 800/205–2925* ⊕ *www.h2outfitters.com.*

Bath

11 miles north of Brunswick via U.S. 1.

Bath has been a shipbuilding center since 1607. The result of its prosperity can be seen in its handsome mix of Federal, Greek Revival, and Italianate homes along Front, Centre, and Washington Streets. In the heart of Bath's historic district are some charming 19th-century homes, including the 1820 Federal-style home at 360 Front Street; the 1810 Greek Revival mansion at 969 Washington Street, covered with gleaming white clapboards; and the Victorian gem at 1009 Washington Street, painted a distinctive shade of raspberry. All three operate as inns. One easily overlooked site is the town's City Hall; the bell in its tower was cast by Paul Revere in 1805.

The venerable Bath Iron Works completed its first passenger ship in 1890. During World War II, BIW (as it's locally known) launched a new ship every 17 days. Not only is it still in production today, BIW is one of the state's largest employers, with about 5,600 workers, who turn out destroyers for the U.S. Navy. (It's a good idea to avoid U.S. 1 on weekdays 3:15–4:30 pm, when a major shift change takes place.) You can tour BIW through the Maine Maritime Museum.

GETTING HERE AND AROUND

U.S. 1 passes through downtown and across the Kennebec River at Bath. Downtown is on the north side of the highway along the river.

Sights

★ Maine Maritime Museum

MUSEUM | **FAMILY** | No trip to Bath is complete without a visit to this cluster of buildings that once made up the historic Percy & Small Shipyard. Plan to spend at least half a day here. In fact, admission tickets are good for two days; there's just that much to see at this museum, which examines the world of shipbuilding and which is the only way to tour Bath Iron Works (June–mid-October). From mid-June through Columbus Day, five nature and lighthouse boat tours cruise the scenic Kennebec River—one takes in 10 lights. The 142-foot Grand Banks fishing schooner *Sherman Zwicker* docks here during the same period. Hour-long tours of the shipyard show how these massive wooden ships were built. In the boat shop, you can watch boatbuilders wield their tools. Inside the main museum building, exhibits use ship models, paintings, photographs, and historic artifacts to tell the maritime history of the region. A separate historic building houses a fascinating lobstering exhibit; it's worth coming here just to watch the 18-minute video on lobstering written and narrated by E. B. White. A gift shop and bookstore are on the premises, and you can grab a bite to eat in the café or bring a picnic to eat on the grounds. ■ **TIP→ Kids ages six and younger get in free.** ⊠ *243 Washington St.* ☎ *207/443–1316* ⊕ *www.mainemariti-memuseum.org* ⊠ *$18, good for 2 days within 7-day period.*

Beaches

Popham Beach State Park

BEACH—SIGHT | FAMILY | This park has bathhouses and picnic tables. At low tide you can walk several miles of tidal flats and also out to a nearby island, where you can explore tide pools or fish off the ledges. It's on a peninsula facing the open Atlantic, between the mouths of the Kennebec and Morse rivers. About a mile from Popham Beach State Park, the road ends at the Civil War–era Fort Popham State Historic Site, an unfinished semicircular granite fort on the sea. Enjoy the beach views at nearby Spinney's Restaurant, or grab a quick bite next door at Percy's Store, which has picnic tables and a path to the beach. **Amenities:** food and drink; lifeguards; parking (no fee); showers; toilets. **Best for:** swimming; walking. ⊠ *10 Perkins Farm La., off Rte. 209, Phippsburg* ☎ *207/389–1335* ⊕ *www.maine.gov/pophambeach* 🎫 *$8.*

Restaurants

Beale Street Barbecue

$ | BARBECUE | Ribs are the thing at one of Maine's oldest barbecue joints, opened in 1996. Hearty eaters should ask for one of the platters piled high with pulled pork, pulled chicken, or shredded beef. **Known for:** fried calamari with habanero mayo served with corn bread; Maine microbrews; "Wild Game Feasts" for take-out. ⑤ *Average main: $17* ⊠ *215 Water St.* ☎ *207/442–9514* ⊕ *www.mainebbq.com.*

No Coward Soul

$$ | PORTUGUESE | An unlikely marriage of traditional Portuguese recipes and hyperlocal Maine ingredients informs the lip-smacking dishes served at this delightful locale with a vintage vibe. While the menu changes almost constantly you can be sure to find Portuguese *bacalhau* (dried and salted cod), carefully curated dishes featuring all sorts of different local meats and seafood, as well as lighter fare, such as seasonally inspired salads and savory soups. **Known for:** killer cocktails; excellent selection of Portuguese wines; moody tunes played on a turntable; terrific fish quenelles. ⑤ *Average main: $23* ⊠ *128 Front St.* ☎ *207/389–4567* ⊕ *www.ncsbath.com* ⊘ *Closed Mon.*

★ Salt Pine Social

$$ | MODERN AMERICAN | This farm-to-table gem of a restaurant serves up a bevy of unique cocktails and creative dishes that pack a powerful punch in terms of texture and flavor combinations. Plenty of local ingredients, including a hefty dose of seafood, informs the menu, though there are also delicious burgers and delicious seasonal vegetable tempura choices. **Known for:** laid-back setting that places the attention on the food; a lively atmosphere fueled by delicious cocktails; house-cured meats and seafood. ⑤ *Average main: $20* ⊠ *244 Front St.* ☎ *207/442–8345* ⊕ *www.saltpinesocial. com* ⊘ *Closed Tues.*

Hotels

★ Kennebec Inn Bed and Breakfast

$$ | B&B/INN | Four immaculate, well-appointed rooms tastefully decorated with maritime touches, luxe bedding and towels, and welcoming common spaces await you at this hidden gem in a historic captain's home—you'll feel like you're at an exclusive retreat. **Pros:** calm and quiet atmosphere make for pure relaxation; delicious, multicourse breakfast you can take at your leisure; knowledgeable, warm innkeeper. **Cons:** only four rooms; a short walk into center of town; no pets. ⑤ *Rooms from: $250* ⊠ *696 High St.* ☎ *207/443–5324* ⊕ *www.kennebecinn. com* 🛏 *4 rooms* ⧖ *Free breakfast.*

Sebasco Harbor Resort

$$$ | RESORT | FAMILY | A family-friendly resort spread over 450 acres on the water near the foot of the Phippsburg Peninsula, this place has a golf course, tennis courts, and a saltwater pool, among a host of other amenities. **Pros:**

good choice for families; perfect location; children's activities; wonderful array of lawn games. **Cons:** no sand beach; heavy traffic and large number of rooms can diminish quality and service; golf fee not included in stay. ⑤ *Rooms from: $320* ⊠ *29 Kenyon Rd., off Rte. 217, Phippsburg* ☎ *877/420–1701* ⊕ *www.sebasco. com* ⊗ *Closed late Oct.–mid-May* ➪ *115 rooms, 23 cottages* ❚◎❙ *Free breakfast.*

Wiscasset

10 miles north of Bath via U.S. 1.

Settled in 1663, Wiscasset sits on the banks of the Sheepscot River. It bills itself "Maine's Prettiest Village," and it's easy to see why: it has graceful churches, old cemeteries, and elegant sea captains' homes (many converted into antiques shops or galleries).

There's also a good wine and specialty foods shop called Treats (stock up here if you're heading north). Pack a picnic and take it down to the dock on Water Street, where you can watch the fishing boats, or grab a lobster roll from Red's Eats or the lobster shack nearby. Wiscasset has expanded its wharf, and this is a great place to catch a breeze on a hot day.

GETTING HERE AND AROUND

U.S. 1 becomes Main Street, and traffic often slows to a crawl come summer. You'll likely have success parking on Water Street rather than Main. It's a good idea to do your driving around Wiscasset very early in the morning and after 7 in the evening when traffic eases a bit. The best way to get around here is on foot.

🍽 Restaurants

Red's Eats

$$ | SEAFOOD | FAMILY | It's hard to miss the long line of hungry customers outside this little red shack on the Wiscasset side of the bridge. Red's is a local landmark famous for its hamburgers, hot dogs,

lobster and crab rolls, and crispy onion rings and clams fried in house-made batters. **Known for:** a whole lobster allegedly goes into each lobster roll; the unholy "Puff Dog," a hot dog loaded with bacon and cheese and deep-fried; long lines in summer. ⑤ *Average main: $20* ⊠ *41 Water St.* ☎ *207/882–6128* ⊟ *No credit cards* ⊗ *Closed mid-Oct.–mid-Apr.*

🛍 Shopping

Edgecomb Potters

CERAMICS/GLASSWARE | Edgecomb Potters is not to be missed: they make vibrantly colored, exquisitely glazed porcelain known all around the country. The store also carries jewelry, glassware, and glass sculptures. ⊠ *727 Boothbay Rd., Edgecomb* ☎ *207/882–9493* ⊕ *www. edgecombpotters.com.*

In the Clover

CLOTHING | There's something charmingly old-school about this pretty boutique with its warm and friendly service and fine displays of women's clothing, accessories, and beauty products. Geared toward elegant but no-fuss women of every age, the shop stocks clothing items such as fine cashmere shawls; pretty but not froufrou lingerie; and sophisticated loungewear as well as a good selection of natural beauty products and fragrances, unique jewelry, and inspiring books. ⊠ *85 A. Main St.* ☎ *207/882–9435* ⊕ *inthecloverbeauty.com.*

★ Rock Paper Scissors

GIFTS/SOUVENIRS | Not your run-of-the-mill gift shop, this well-curated boutique stocks offbeat cards and letterpress stationery, local hand-crafted goods such as blankets, purses, and ceramics, and beautiful, one-of-a-kind objects for the home and kitchen. Stocked to the brim with charming goodies for anyone on your list (including yourself), this shop is decidedly contemporary, with a Scandinavian bent, and is well worth a stop, if only to peruse the gorgeously arranged

Continued on page 665

MAINE'S LIGHTHOUSES
GUARDIANS OF THE COAST By John Blodgett

Perched high on rocky ledges, on the tips of wayward islands, and sometimes seemingly on the ocean itself are the more than five dozen lighthouses standing watch along Maine's craggy and ship-busting coastline.

Marshall Point Light

LIGHTING THE WAY: A BIT OF HISTORY

Portland Head Light

Most lighthouses were built in the first half of the 19th century to protect vessels from running aground at night or when the shoreline was shrouded in fog. Along with the mournful siren of the foghorn and maritime lore, these practical structures have come to symbolize Maine throughout the world.

SHIPWRECKS AND SAFETY

These alluring sentinels of the eastern seaboard today have more form than function, but that certainly was not always the case. Safety was a strong motivating factor in the erection of the lighthouses. Commerce also played a critical role. For example, in 1791 Portland Head light was completed, partially as a response to local merchants' concerns about the rocky entrance to Portland Harbor and the varying depths of the shipping channel, but approval wasn't given until a terrible accident in 1787 in which a 90-ton sloop wrecked. In 1789, the federal government created the U.S. Lighthouse Establishment (later the U.S. Lighthouse Service) to manage them. In 1939 the U.S. Coast Guard took on the job.

Some lighthouses in Maine were built in a much-needed venue, but the points and islands upon which they sat were prone to storm damage. Along with poor construction, this meant that over the years many lighthouses had to be rebuilt or replaced.

LIGHTHOUSES TODAY

In modern times, many of the structures still serve a purpose. Technological advances, such as GPS and radar, are mainly used to navigate through the choppy waters, but a lighthouse or its foghorns are helpful secondary aids, and sometimes the only ones used by recreational boaters. The numerous channel-marking buoys still in existence also are testament to the old tried-and-true methods.

Of the 66 lighthouses along this far northeastern state, 55 are still working, alerting ships (and even small aircraft) of the shoreline's rocky edge. Government agencies, historic preservation organizations, and mostly private individuals own the decommissioned lights.

KEEPERS OF THE LIGHT

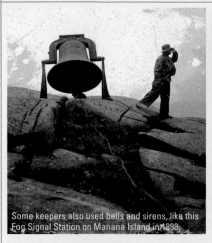

Some keepers also used bells and sirens, like this Fog Signal Station on Manana Island in 1898.

Pemaquid Point's fourth-order Fresnel lens

LIFE OF A LIGHTKEEPER

One thing that has changed with the modern era is the disappearance of the lighthouse keeper. In the early 20th century, lighthouses began the conversion from oil-based lighting to electricity. A few decades later, the U.S. Coast Guard switched to automation, phasing out the need for an on-site keeper.

While the keepers of tradition were no longer needed, the traditions of these stalwart, 24/7 employees live on through museum exhibits and retellings of Maine's maritime history, legends, and lore. The tales of a lighthouse keeper's life are the stuff romance novels are made of: adventure, rugged but lonely men, and a beautiful setting along an unpredictable coastline.

The lighthouse keepers of yesterday probably didn't see their own lives so romantically. Their daily narrative was one of hard work and, in some cases, exceptional solitude. A keeper's primary job was to ensure that the lamp was illuminated all day, every day. This meant that oil (whale or coal oil and later kerosene) had to be carried about and wicks trimmed on a regular basis. When fog shrouded the coast, they sounded the solemn horn to pierce through the damp darkness that hid their light. Their quarters were generally small and often attached to the light tower itself. The remote locations of the lights added to the isolation a keeper felt, especially before the advent of radio and telephone, let alone the Internet. Though some brought families with them, the keepers tended to be men who lived alone.

THE LIGHTS 101

Over the years, Fresnel (fray-NELL) lenses were developed in different shapes and sizes so that ship captains could distinguish one lighthouse from another. Invented by Frenchman Augustin Fresnel in the early 19th century, the lens design allows for a greater transmission of light perfectly suited for lighthouse use. Knowing which lighthouse they were near helped captains know which danger was present, such as a submerged ledge or shallow channel. Some lights, such as those at Seguin Island Light, are fixed and don't flash. Other lights are colored red.

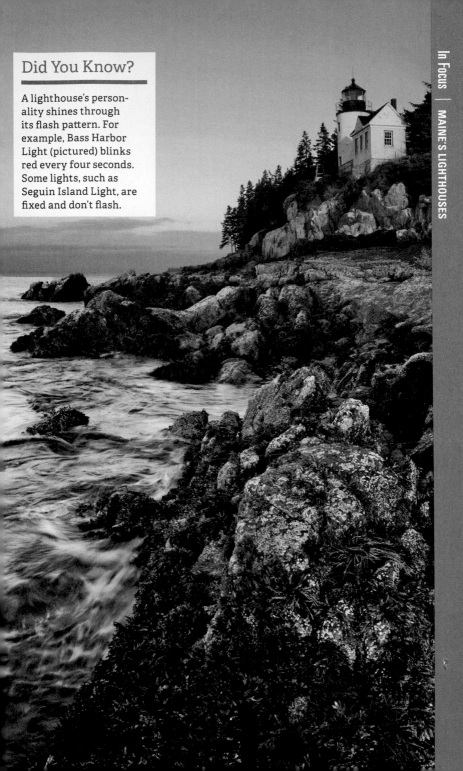

Did You Know?

A lighthouse's personality shines through its flash pattern. For example, Bass Harbor Light (pictured) blinks red every four seconds. Some lights, such as Seguin Island Light, are fixed and don't flash.

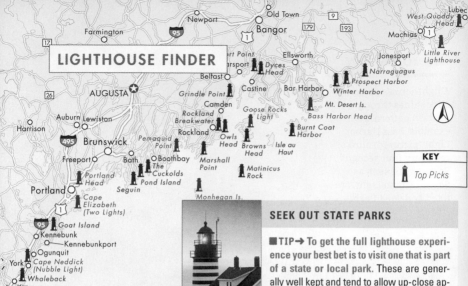

LIGHTHOUSE FINDER

Lubec
West Quoddy Head
Old Town
Newport
Bangor
Farmington
Machias
Little River Lighthouse
AUGUSTA
Ellsworth
Jonesport
rt Point
arsport
Dyces Head
Belfast
Narraguagus
Prospect Harbor
Grindle Point
Castine
Bar Harbor
Winter Harbor
Camden
Goose Rocks Light
Mt. Desert Is.
Rockland Breakwater
Bass Harbor Head
Auburn Lewiston
Rockland
Burnt Coat Harbor
Harrison
Pemaquid Point
Owls Head
Brunswick
Browns Head
Isle au Haut
Freeport
Bath
Boothbay
The Cuckolds
Marshall Point
Matinicus Rock
Portland Head
Pond Island
Seguin
Portland
Cape Elizabeth (Two Lights)
Monhegan Is.
Goat Island
Kennebunk
Kennebunkport
Ogunquit
York
Cape Neddick (Nubble Light)
Whaleback
Kittery
Portsmouth

West Quoddy Head

SEEK OUT STATE PARKS

■ **TIP→** To get the full lighthouse experience your best bet is to visit one that is part of a state or local park. These are generally well kept and tend to allow up-close approach, though typically only outside. While you're at the parks you can picnic or stroll on the trails. Wildlife is often abundant in and near the water; you might spot sea birds and even whales in certain locations (try West Quoddy Head, Portland Head, or Two Lights).

VISITING MAINE'S LIGHTHOUSES

As you travel along the Maine Coast, you won't see lighthouses by watching your odometer—there were no rules about the spacing of lighthouses. The decision as to where to place a lighthouse was a balance between a region's geography and its commercial prosperity and maritime traffic.

Lighthouses dot the shore from as far south as York to the country's easternmost tip at Lubec. Accessibility varies according to location and other factors. A handful are so remote as to be outright impossible to reach (except perhaps by kayaking and rock climbing). Some don't allow visitors according to Coast Guard policies, though you can enjoy them through the zoom lens of a camera. Others you can walk right up to and, occasionally, even climb to the top. Lighthouse enthusiasts and preservation groups restore and maintain many of them. All told, approximately 30 lighthouses allow some sort of public access.

MUSEUMS, TOURS, AND MORE

Most keeper's quarters are closed to the public, but some of the homes have been converted to museums, full of intriguing exhibits on lighthouses, the famous Fresnel lenses used in them, and artifacts of Maine maritime life in general. Talk to the librarians at the **Maine Maritime Museum** in Bath (⊕ www.mainemaritimemuseum.org) or sign up for one of the museum's daily lighthouse cruises to pass by no fewer than ten on the Lighthouse Lovers Cruise. In Rockland, the **Maine Lighthouse Museum** (⊕ www.maine-lighthousemuseum.org) has the country's largest display of Fresnel lenses. The museum also displays keepers' memorabilia, foghorns, brassware, and more. Maine Open Lighthouse Day is the second Saturday after Labor Day; you can tour and even climb lights usually closed to the public.

For more information, check out the lighthouse page at Maine's official tourism site: ⊕ visitmaine.com.

SLEEPING LIGHT: STAYING OVERNIGHT

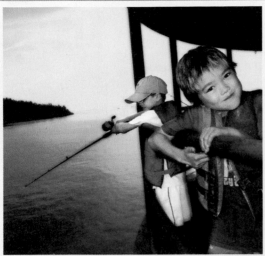

Goose Rocks, where you can play lighthouse keeper for a week.

Want to stay overnight in a lighthouse? There are several options to do so.

■ **TIP→ Book lighthouse lodgings as far in advance as possible, up to one year ahead.**

Our top pick is **Pemaquid Point Light** (*Newcastle Square Vacation Rentals* ☎ *207/563–6500* ⊕ *www.mainecoast-cottages.com*) because it has one of the most dramatic settings on the Maine coast. Two miles south of **New Harbor**, the second floor of the lighthouse keeper's house is rented out on a weekly basis early May through mid-November to support upkeep of the grounds. When you aren't enjoying the interior, head outdoors: the covered front porch has a rocking-chair view of the ocean. The one-bedroom, one-bath rental sleeps up to a family of four.

Situated smack dab in the middle of a major maritime thoroughfare between two Penobscot Bay islands, **Goose Rocks Light** (☎ *203/400–9565* ⊕ *www. beaconpreservation.org*) offers lodging for the adventuresome—the 51-foot "spark plug" lighthouse is completely surrounded by water. Getting there requires a ferry ride from Rockland to nearby **North Haven**, a 5- to 10-minute ride by motorboat, and then a climb up an iron-rung ladder from the pitching boat—all based on high tide and winds, of course. There's room for up to eight people. It's a bit more cushy experience than it was for the original keepers: there's a flat-screen TV with DVD player and a selection of music and videos for entertainment. In addition, a hammock hangs on the small deck that encircles the operational light; it's a great place from which to watch the majestic windjammers and the fishing fleet pass by.

Little River Lighthouse (☎ *877/276–4682* ⊕ *www.littleriverlight.org*), along the far northeastern reaches of the coast in **Cutler**, has three rooms available for rent in July and August. You're responsible for food and beverages, linens, towels, and other personal items (don't forget the bug spray), but kitchen and other basics are provided. The lighthouse operators will provide a boat ride to the island upon which the lighthouse sits.

TOP LIGHTHOUSES TO VISIT

BASS HARBOR LIGHT

Familiar to many as the subject of countless photographs is Bass Harbor Light, at the southern end of **Mount Desert Island.** It is within Acadia National Park and 17 miles from the town of Bar Harbor. The station grounds are open year-round.

CAPE ELIZABETH LIGHT

Two Lights State Park is so-named because it's next to two lighthouses. Both of these **Cape Elizabeth** structures were built in 1828. The western light was converted into a private residence in 1924; the eastern light, Cape Elizabeth Light, still projects its automated cylinder of light. The grounds surrounding the building and the lighthouse itself are closed to the public, but the structure is easily viewed and photographed from nearby at the end of Two Lights Road.

Cape Neddick Light

CAPE NEDDICK LIGHT

More commonly known as Nubble Light for the smallish offshore expanse of rock it rests upon, Cape Neddick Light sits a few hundred feet off a rock point in **York Beach.** With such a precarious location, its grounds are inaccessible to visitors, but close enough to be exceptionally photogenic, especially during the Christmas season.

MONHEGAN ISLAND LIGHT

Only the adventuresome and the artistic see this light, because **Monhegan Island** is accessible by an approximately one-hour ferry ride. To reach the lighthouse, you have an additional half-mile walk uphill from the ferry dock. The former keeper's quarters is home to the Monhegan Museum, which has exhibits about the island. The tower itself is closed to the public.

Portland Head Light

PORTLAND HEAD LIGHT

One of Maine's most photographed lighthouses (and its oldest), the famous Portland Head Light was completed in January 1791. At the edge of Fort Williams Park, in **Cape Elizabeth**, the towering white stone lighthouse stands 101 feet above the sea. The Coast Guard operates it and it is not open for tours. However the adjacent keeper's dwelling is now a museum.

WEST QUODDY HEAD LIGHT

Originally built in 1808 by mandate of President Thomas Jefferson, West Quoddy Head Light sits in **Lubec** on the easternmost tip of land in the mainland United States. The 49-foot-high lighthouse with distinctive red and white stripes, is part of Quoddy Head State Park.

West Quoddy Head Light

array of products on display. ✉ *68 Main St.* ☎ *207/882–9930.*

Sheepscot River Pottery
CERAMICS/GLASSWARE | This shop boasts beautifully glazed kitchen tiles, as well as kitchenware and home accessories, including sinks. Jewelry and other items by local artisans are also on sale. ✉ *34 U.S. 1, Edgecomb* ☎ *207/882–9410* ⊕ *www.sheepscot.com.*

Boothbay

11 miles south of Wiscasset via Rte. 27.

The shoreline of the Boothbay Peninsula is a craggy stretch of inlets, where pleasure craft anchor alongside trawlers and lobster boats. The town of Boothbay comprises the village center, Boothbay Harbor, and East Boothbay. The harbor is like a smaller version of Bar Harbor—touristy, but friendly and fun—with pretty, winding streets and lots to explore. Commercial Street, Wharf Street, Townsend Avenue, and the By-Way are lined with shops and ice-cream parlors. One of the biggest draws here is the stunning Coastal Maine Botanical Gardens, with its beautiful café and gift shop, as well as its famous children's garden.

GETTING HERE AND AROUND
In season, boat trips to Monhegan Island leave from the piers off Commercial Street. Drive out to Ocean Point in East Boothbay for some incredible scenery. Boothbay is 11 miles south of Wiscasset via U.S. 1 and Route 27.

◉ Sights

★ Coastal Maine Botanical Garden
GARDEN | FAMILY | Set aside a couple of hours to stroll among the roses, lupines, and rhododendrons at the 250-acre Coastal Maine Botanical Garden. In the summer, free docent-led tours leave from the visitor center at 1 every day from May–October. The "children's garden" is

a wonderland of stone sculptures, rope bridges, small teahouselike structures with grass roofs, and even a hedge maze. Children and adults alike adore the separate woodland fairy area. The on-site restaurant and café, as well as the bookshop and resource library, are also delightful. It's easy to spend an entire day here and not see everything—be sure to wear comfortable walking shoes. For those less inclined to go by foot, the gardens offer free shuttle service to most spots on the property. ✉ *132 Botanical Gardens Dr., off Rte. 27* ☎ *207/633–8000* ⊕ *www.mainegardens.org* ✉ *$16.*

Restaurants

Boathouse Bistro Tapas Bar and Restaurant
$$ | TAPAS | The multitier rooftop terrace (complete with an outdoor bar) stays crowded all summer at the Boat House Bistro. Austrian-born chef Karin Guerin dishes up tapas-style small plates ranging from mango empanadas to sweet-potato latkes. **Known for:** baked oysters; Spanish-inspired dishes featuring locally caught seafood; a sizeable array of flatbread grillers featuring different toppings. ⑤ *Average main: $22* ✉ *12 The By-Way, Boothbay Harbor* ☎ *207/633–0400* ⊕ *www.theboathousebistro.com* ⊘ *Closed mid-Oct.–mid-Apr.*

🛏 Hotels

Spruce Point Inn
$$ | RESORT | FAMILY | A great base for exploring Boothbay, this lovely seaside inn acts like a resort, while feeling more like you're visiting an old friend's house or a summer home. **Pros:** pet-friendly; family game room; laundry on-site; shuttle by boat to the town center; private boat launch. **Cons:** some private residences close to premises; no indoor pool; golfing access off-site. ⑤ *Rooms from: $250* ✉ *88 Grandview Ave., Boothbay Harbor* ☎ *207/350–9846* ⊕ *www.sprucepointinn. com* ⊘ *Closed mid-Oct.–late Apr.* ⇙ *68 rooms, 5 cottages* ⑩ *No meals.*

Topside Inn

$$$ | B&B/INN | The Adirondack chairs on the immense lawn of this historic hilltop B&B have what is probably the best bay view in town. **Pros:** knockout views; plenty of green space for croquet; easy walk downtown. **Cons:** walls are a bit thin in the annexes; two-night minimum in summer; pets only allowed in the Waters Edge Cottage. ⑤ *Rooms from: $300* ✉ *60 McKown St., Boothbay Harbor* ☎ *207/633–5404* ⊕ *www.topsideinn. com* ⊘ *Closed mid-Oct.–mid-May* ⟿ *25 rooms, 1 suite, 1 cottage* ⊙❘ *Free breakfast.*

Damariscotta

8 miles north of Wiscasset via U.S. 1.

The Damariscotta region comprises several communities along the rocky coast. The town itself sits on the water, a lively place filled with attractive shops and restaurants, as well as some of the best oysters around.

Just across the bridge over the Damariscotta River is the town of Newcastle, between the Sheepscot and Damariscotta rivers. Newcastle was settled in the early 1600s. The earliest inhabitants planted apple trees, but the town later became an industrial center, home to several shipyards and a couple of mills. The oldest Catholic church in New England, St. Patrick's, is here, and it still rings its original Paul Revere bell.

Bremen, which encompasses more than a dozen islands and countless rocky outcrops, has many seasonal homes along the water, and the main industries in the small community are fishing and clamming. Nobleboro, a bit north of here on U.S. 1, was settled in the 1720s by Colonel David Dunbar, sent by the British to rebuild the fort at Pemaquid. Neighboring Waldoboro is situated on the Medomak River and was settled largely by Germans in the mid-1700s. You can still visit the old

German Meeting House, built in 1772. The Pemaquid Peninsula stretches south from Damariscotta to include Bristol, South Bristol, Round Pond, New Harbor, and Pemaquid.

GETTING HERE AND AROUND

In Newcastle, U.S. 1B runs from U.S. 1 across the Damariscotta River to Damariscotta. From this road take Route 129 south to South Bristol and Route 130 south to Bristol and New Harbor. From here you can return to U.S. 1 heading north on Route 32 through Round Pond and Bremen. In Waldoboro, turn off U.S. 1 on Jefferson Street to see the historic village center.

ESSENTIALS

VISITOR INFORMATION Damariscotta Region Chamber of Commerce ☎ *207/563–8340* ⊕ *www.damariscottaregion.com.*

Restaurants

King Eider's Pub & Restaurant

$$ | AMERICAN | FAMILY | This cozy, classic pub right downtown bills itself as having the finest crab cakes in New England. Start with the fresh local oysters that the Damariscotta region is known for, then move on to entrées like steak-and-ale pie, sea-scallop Florentine, or sautéed haddock with chips. **Known for:** live music; special gatherings; classic cocktails such as dark and stormies. ⑤ *Average main: $18* ✉ *2 Elm St.* ☎ *207/563–6008* ⊕ *www.kingeiderspub.com.*

★ Newcastle Publick House

$$ | AMERICAN | FAMILY | In a handsomely renovated historic building, Newcastle Publick House serves delicious comfort food, including fresh oysters, creative flatbreads, and local craft beers, as well as one of the best French onion soups around. There is often live music, making it a great place for a night out on a date or with the entire family. **Known for:** stacked burgers; cozy, old-school atmosphere; gathering place for friendly locals. ⑤ *Average main: $20* ✉ *52 Main*

Maine is the largest lobster-producing state in the United States.

St., Newcastle ☎ 207/563–3434 ⊕ main-eevent.net ⊗ Closed Mon.

Van Lloyd's Bistro

$$ | **AMERICAN** | Packed with funky decor culled from the owners' travels and local antiquing trips, this lively new restaurant serves an eclectic mix of dishes that lean toward a Mediterranean style. Pop in for the excellent happy hour and stay for dishes like pork-belly tortillas, Welsh rarebit, and Angus beef–stuffed grape leaves, or the fantastic Hunter's Plate, which includes a tasty rabbit porchetta. **Known for:** gatherings with friends; predinner drinks; fresh seafood dishes with a twist. ⑤ Average main: $20 ⊠ 85 Parking Lot La. ☎ 207/563–5005 ⊕ www.vanlloyds.com ⊟ No credit cards.

 Hotels

Newcastle Inn

$$ | **B&B/INN** | **FAMILY** | A riverside location, tasteful decor, and lots of common areas (inside and out) make this a relaxing country inn. **Pros:** guests can order beer or wine; suites have sitting areas; water views in many rooms. **Cons:** short walk into the village; not all rooms have water views; some rooms without ample sitting areas. ⑤ Rooms from: $200 ⊠ 60 River Rd., Newcastle ☎ 207/563–5685 ⊕ www.newcastleinn.com ⇨ 14 rooms ⊙ Free breakfast.

Pemaquid Point

10 miles south of Damariscotta via U.S. 1, U.S. 1B, and Rte. 130.

Pemaquid Point is the tip of the Pemaquid Peninsula, bordered by Muscongus and Johns bays. It's home to the famous lighthouse of the same name and its attendant fog bell and tiny museum. Also at the bottom of the peninsula, along the Muscongus Bay, is the Nature Conservancy's Rachel Carson Salt Pond Preserve.

GETTING HERE AND AROUND

From U.S. 1, take U.S. 1B into Damariscotta and head south on Route 130 to Pemaquid Point.

Sights

★ Pemaquid Point Light

LIGHTHOUSE | FAMILY | At the end of Route 130, this lighthouse at the tip of the Pemaquid Peninsula looks as though it sprouted from the ragged, tilted chunk of granite it commands. Most days in the summer you can climb the tower to the light. The former keeper's cottage is now the Fishermen's Museum, which displays historic photographs, scale models, and artifacts that explore commercial fishing in Maine. Also here are the original fog bell and bell house. There are restrooms and picnic tables. ⊠ 3115 Bristol Rd., New Harbor ☎ 207/677–2492 ⊕ www. pemaquidpoint.org ☜ $3.

Restaurants

★ Muscongus Bay Lobster Co.

$$ | SEAFOOD | FAMILY | The food here is practically guaranteed to be fresh: lobsters come in off the boat at one end of the pier, and the restaurant is at the other. Grab a picnic table and be careful not to hit your head on the colorful, dangling wooden buoys. **Known for:** laid-back, BYOB atmosphere; kid-friendly; repeat visitors meet and greet here. ⑤ Average main: $18 ⊠ 28 Landing Rd., Round Pond ☎ 207/529–5528 ⊕ www.mainefreshlobster.com ⊘ Closed mid-Oct.–mid-May.

Round Pond Fisherman's Coop

$$ | SEAFOOD | Sheltered Muscongus Bay is where you'll find this down-home lobster shack, right on the pier with pleasant views of the water. Competition with the neighboring Muscongus Bay Lobster Co. keeps the prices low for fresh-off-the-boat lobster and steamers. **Known for:** BYO drinks and sides; family-friendly; dog-friendly. ⑤ Average main: $18 ⊠ 25 Town Landing Rd., Round Pond ☎ 207/529–5725 ⊘ Closed Labor Day–mid-May.

Activities

Hardy Boat Cruises

BOATING | FAMILY | Mid-May through mid-October, you can take a cruise to Monhegan with Hardy Boat Cruises. The company also offers seal- and puffin-watching trips and lighthouse and fall coastal cruises. Dogs are welcome on the boat for $5. ⊠ Shaw's Wharf, 132 Rte. 32, New Harbor ☎ 207/677–2026 ⊕ www.hardyboat.com.

Port Clyde

5 miles south of Tenants Harbor via Rte. 131.

At the end of the St. George Peninsula, the sleepy fishing village of Port Clyde is a haven for artists, with a number of galleries and a sweeping vista of the ocean that can't be beat. It's also a good spot to spend time nursing a beer or a coffee while waiting for your boat out to Monhegan. Like many places in Maine, lobster fishing is an economic mainstay here. Marshall Point Lighthouse, right in the harbor, has a small museum.

Sights

★ Marshall Point Lighthouse

LOCAL INTEREST | FAMILY | This 31-foot lighthouse, which has been in operation since it was erected in 1858, is perhaps best known as the spot where Forrest Gump concluded his very long cross-country run in the 1994 film adaptation of the book by the same name. Be prepared for sweeping views of the ocean and a resounding "Run, Forrest, run!" coming from visitors taking full advantage of an exceptional photo op. The site also has a small museum and a gift shop, housed in the old lightkeepers' house. ⊠ Marshall Point Rd. ☎ 207/372–6450 ⊕ www. marshallpoint.org.

Monhegan Island

East of Pemaquid Peninsula, 10 miles south of Port Clyde.

If you love rocky cliffs, this is your place. And if you happen to be an artist, you might never leave: there are studios and galleries all over the island. The village bustles with activity in summer, when many artists open their studios. Several shops are open for browsing. You can escape the crowds on the island's 17 miles of hiking trails, which lead to the lighthouse and to the cliffs—bring your camera.

GETTING HERE AND AROUND

Three excursion boats dock here. The boat trip out to Monhegan is almost as exhilarating as exploring the island itself. You'll likely pass by the Marshall Point Lighthouse; be on the lookout for porpoises, seals, puffins, and small whales en route to the island.

Monhegan Boat Line

TRANSPORTATION SITE (AIRPORT/BUS/FERRY/ TRAIN) | FAMILY | The Port Clyde boat landing is home to the *Elizabeth Ann* and the *Laura B,* the mail boats that serve Monhegan Island, about 10 miles offshore. There are three round-trips daily Memorial Day weekend–Columbus Day; one daily in late fall and early spring; and three weekly in the winter. ⊠ *880 Port Clyde Rd., Port Clyde* ☎ *207/372–8848* ⊕ *www.monheganboat.com.*

Sights

Monhegan Island Light

LIGHTHOUSE | FAMILY | Getting a look at this squat stone lighthouse—from land, anyway—requires a slightly steep half-mile walk uphill from the island's ferry dock. The lighthouse was automated in 1959, and the former keeper's quarters became the Monhegan Museum shortly thereafter. Exhibits at the museum have as much to do with life on the island as they do with the lighthouse itself. The tower is open sporadically throughout the

summer for short tours. ⊠ *Lighthouse Hill Rd., ½ mile east of dock, Monhegan* ☎ *207/596–7003.*

Restaurants

Fish House Market

$$ | SEAFOOD | The menu here is focused on fresh, local seafood prepared simply. Order inside the little hut by the water, and when your meal is ready, eat outside at a table inches from the shoreline, lapping up the view of the bay and the lobster boats moored there. **Known for:** BYOB; outstanding fish chowder; lovely waterside location. ⑤ *Average main: $18* ⊠ *98 Fish Beach La., Monhegan* ⊟ *No credit cards.*

Hotels

Island Inn

$$ | B&B/INN | Local works of art are displayed throughout this three-story inn, which dates to 1907; the property has a commanding presence on Monhegan Island's harbor. **Pros:** great food; great view; laid-back atmosphere. **Cons:** a little on the pricey side, but it's on an island after all; no a/c. ⑤ *Rooms from: $250* ⊠ *1 Ocean Ave., Monhegan* ☎ *207/596– 0371* ⊕ *www.islandinnmonhegan.com* ⊗ *Closed Columbus Day–Memorial Day* 🛏 *32 rooms* ❏ *Free breakfast* ⊟ *No credit cards.*

Rockland

25 miles north of Damariscotta via U.S. 1.

This town is considered the gateway to Penobscot Bay and is the first stop on U.S. 1 offering a glimpse of the often-sparkling and island-dotted blue bay. Though once merely a place to pass through on the way to tonier ports like Camden, Rockland now gets attention on its own, thanks to a trio of attractions: the renowned Farnsworth Art Museum, the increasingly popular summer Lobster

Festival, and the lively North Atlantic Blues Festival. Specialty shops and galleries line the main street, and one of the restaurants, Primo (between Camden and the little village of Owls Head), has become nationally famous. The town is still a large fishing port and the commercial hub of this coastal area.

Rockland Harbor bests Camden (by one) as home to the largest fleet of Maine windjammers. The best place in Rockland to view these handsome vessels as they sail in and out of the harbor is the mile-long granite breakwater, which bisects the outer portion of Rockland Harbor. To get there, from U.S. 1, head east on Waldo Avenue and then right on Samoset Road; follow this short road to its end.

GETTING HERE AND AROUND
U.S. 1 runs along Main Street here, while U.S. 1A curves through the residential neighborhood west of the business district, offering a faster route if you are passing through.

FESTIVALS
Maine Lobster Festival
FESTIVALS | FAMILY | Rockland's annual Maine Lobster Festival, held in early August, is the region's largest annual event. About 10 tons of lobsters are steamed in a huge lobster cooker—you have to see it to believe it. The festival, held in Harbor Park, includes a parade, live entertainment, food booths, and, of course, the crowning of the Maine Sea Goddess. ⊠ *Harbor Park, Main St., south of U.S. 1* ☎ *800/576–7512* ⊕ *www. mainelobsterfestival.com.*

North Atlantic Blues Festival
FESTIVALS | FAMILY | About a dozen well-known musicians gather for the North Atlantic Blues Festival, a two-day affair held the first or second full weekend after July 4th. The show officially takes place at the public landing on Rockland Harbor Park, but it also includes a "club crawl" through downtown Rockland on Saturday night. Admission to the festival is $40 at the gate, $75 for a weekend pass. ⊠ *Public Landing, 275 Main St.* ☎ *207/596–6055* ⊕ *www.northatlanticbluesfestival.com.*

VISITOR INFORMATION Penobscot Bay Area Chamber of Commerce ☎ *207/596–0376, 800/562–2529* ⊕ *www.camdenrockland.com.*

Sights

★ Center for Maine Contemporary Art
MUSEUM | The newly minted Center for Maine Contemporary Art is a refreshing departure from the many galleries and museums in the state because it features works exclusively on nautical themes. Expect envelope-pushing exhibitions and impressive public programs. ⊠ *21 Winter St.* ☎ *207/701–5005* ⊕ *cmcanow.org* ⌨ *$8.*

★ Farnsworth Art Museum
MUSEUM | FAMILY | One of the most important small museums in the country, much of the Farnsworth's collection is devoted to Maine-related works of the famous Wyeth family: N. C. Wyeth, an accomplished illustrator whose works were featured in many turn-of-the-20th-century books; his late son Andrew, one of the country's best-known painters; and Andrew's son James, also an accomplished painter, who like his elders before him summers nearby. Galleries in the main building always display some of Andrew Wyeth's works, such as *The Patriot, Witchcraft,* and *Turkey Pond.* The **Wyeth Center,** a former church, shows art by his father and son. The museum's collection also includes works by Fitz Henry Lane, George Bellows, Frank W. Benson, Edward Hopper, Louise Nevelson, and Fairfield Porter. Changing exhibits are shown in the **Jamien Morehouse Wing.** The **Farnsworth Homestead,** a handsome circa-1850 Greek Revival dwelling that's part of the museum, retains its original lavish Victorian furnishings and is open late June–mid-October.

In Cushing, a tiny town about 10 miles south of Thomaston on the St. George River, the museum operates the **Olson House,** which is depicted in Andrew Wyeth's famous painting *Christina's World,* as well as in other works by the artist. It's accessible by guided tour only. ⊠ *16 Museum St.* ☎ *207/596–6457* ⊕ *www.farnsworthmuseum.org* ✉ *$15* ⊗ *Closed Mon. Nov.–May (except Memorial Day); also closed Tues. Jan.–Mar.*

Maine Lighthouse Museum
MUSEUM | FAMILY | The lighthouse museum has more than 25 Fresnel lighthouse lenses, as well as a collection of lighthouse artifacts and Coast Guard memorabilia. Permanent exhibits spotlight topics like lighthouse heroines—women who manned the lights when the keepers couldn't—and lightships. ⊠ *1 Park Dr.* ☎ *207/594–3301* ⊕ *www. mainelighthousemuseum.org* ✉ *$8.*

🍴 Restaurants

★ In Good Company
$$ | MODERN AMERICAN | As the name suggests, this is an excellent spot to slow down and catch up with good friends over a bottle of wine, while savoring seasonally inspired, locally sourced dishes. The creative blend of textures and flavors that come out of the kitchen will charm your senses, a welcome surprise in this intimate space that was formerly a bank. **Known for:** no reservations; excellent wine pairings; pared-down aesthetic with a focus on the food. ⑤ *Average main: $23* ⊠ *415 Maine St.* ☎ *207/593–9110* ⊕ *www.ingoodcompanymaine.com.*

★ Primo
$$$$ | MEDITERRANEAN | Award-winning chef Melissa Kelly and her world-class restaurant have been written up in *Gourmet, Bon Appétit,* and *O* magazines. In this restored Victorian home, upstairs seating has a funky vibe; downstairs is fancier and no matter where you sit, it's farm-to-table here: the restaurant raises its own chickens and pigs, cures its own meats, produces its own eggs, and grows its own fruits and vegetables. **Known for:** house-made pasta; fresh Maine ingredients with Mediterranean influences; consistently excellent; $1 oysters every Sunday. ⑤ *Average main: $40* ⊠ *2 N. Main St.* ☎ *207/596–0770* ⊕ *www.primorestaurant.com* ⊗ *Closed Tues.*

Rockland Cafe
$ | DINER | FAMILY | It may not look like much from the outside, but the Rockland Cafe is one of the most popular eateries in town. It's famous for the size of its breakfasts—don't pass up the fish-cake Benedict. **Known for:** seafood combos; classic liver and onions; lively place for locals to catch up. ⑤ *Average main: $15* ⊠ *441 Main St.* ☎ *207/596–7556* ⊕ *www. rocklandcafe.com.*

Hotels

Berry Manor Inn
$$ | B&B/INN | Originally the residence of Rockland merchant Charles H. Berry, this 1898 shingle-style B&B sits in Rockland's National Historic District. **Pros:** a guest pantry is stocked with drinks, sweets, and treats—there's always pie; within walking distance of downtown and the harbor; some rooms can be combined to create two-room suites. **Cons:** not much of a view; decidedly old-school design; not pet-friendly. ⑤ *Rooms from: $200* ⊠ *81 Talbot Ave.* ☎ *207/596–7696, 800/774–5692* ⊕ *www.berrymanorinn. com* ⤳ *12 rooms* ¶◯| *Free breakfast.*

LimeRock Inn
$ | B&B/INN | Built in 1892 as a private home, the LimeRock is perfectly located in Rockland's National Historic District in the center of town. **Pros:** all rooms have TVs and DVD players; large in-town lot with gazebo; within easy walking distance of the Farnsworth Museum and many restaurants. **Cons:** not on the water; decidedly old-school accommodations; not pet-friendly. ⑤ *Rooms from: $180* ⊠ *96 Limerock St.* ☎ *207/594–2257,*

Windjammer Excursions

Nothing defines the Maine coastal experience better than a sailing trip on a windjammer. These vessels were built all along the East Coast in the 19th and early 20th centuries. Designed primarily to carry cargo, these beauties (most are wood hulled) have a rich past: the schooner *Ladona* served in World War II, while others plied the waters in the lumbering, granite, fishing, and oystering trades or served as pilot boats. They vary in size but can be as small as 46 feet, holding six passengers (plus a couple of crew members), or more than 130 feet, holding 40 passengers and 10 crew members. During a windjammer excursion, passengers are usually able to participate in the navigation, be it hoisting a sail or playing captain at the wheel.

During the Camden Windjammer Festival, held Labor Day weekend, crowds gather to watch the region's fleet sail into the harbor, and most boats are open for tours. The schooner-crew talent show later in the weekend is a bit more irreverent than the majestic arrival ceremony.

A windjammer cruise gives you a chance to admire Maine's dramatic coast from the water. They can run anywhere from one to eight days, and day trips usually involve a tour of the harbor and some lighthouse sightseeing. The price—ranging $230–$1,100, depending on length of trip—includes all meals. Trips leave from Camden, Rockland, and Rockport. You can get information on the fleets by contacting one of two windjammer organizations:

Maine Windjammer Association. ☎ *800/807–9463* ⊕ *www.sailmaine-coast.com.*

Maine Windjammer Cruises. Six handsome vessels offer a variety of cruises. ☎ *207/236–2938, 800/736–7981* ⊕ *www.mainewindjammercruises.com.*

800/546–3762 ⊕ *www.limerockinn.com* ⊅ *8 rooms, 1 cottage* ¶◉¶ *Free breakfast.*

★ Samoset Resort

$$$ | RESORT | FAMILY | Occupying 230 waterfront acres on the Rockland–Rockport town line, this all-encompassing resort offers luxurious rooms and suites with private balconies overlooking the water or the grounds. **Pros:** full-service spa; children's programs; activities from basketball to croquet; the 18-hole course has been ranked among the best in the region. **Cons:** no beach; pool can be overcrowded in summer; high turnover, so service can be spotty. ⑤ *Rooms from: $350* ✉ *220 Warrenton St., Rockport* ☎ *207/594–2511, 800/341–1650* ⊕ *www.samoset.com* ⊅ *254 units* ¶◉¶ *Free breakfast.*

★ 25 Main Hotel

$$$ | HOTEL | With gorgeously designed guest rooms that have an inspired, midcentury-modern vibe, 250 Main has brought a forward-thinking lodging choice to Rockland. **Pros:** immaculately maintained; pet-friendly; complimentary wine-and-cheese hour in the evening. **Cons:** no pool; some traffic noise from the harbor in the morning; only guests are allowed on the roof garden. ⑤ *Rooms from: $350* ✉ *250 Main St.* ☎ *207/594–5994* ⊕ *250mainhotel.com* ⊅ *26 rooms* ¶◉¶ *No meals.*

Walk From Rockport to Camden

For a stunning walk or drive, take the two-lane paved road that winds up and down on its way out of Rockport, with occasional views of the ocean and the village, en route to Camden. Begin at the intersection of U.S. 1 and Pascal Avenue in Rockport. Take a right off U.S. 1 toward Rockport Harbor, then cross the bridge and go up the hill to Central Street. One block later, bear right on Russell Avenue, which becomes Chestnut Street at the Camden town line; take this all the way to downtown Camden.

Lining the way are some of the most beautiful homes in Maine, surrounded by an abundance of flora and fauna. Keep an eye out for views of the sparkling ocean, as well as for Aldermere Farm and its Belted Galloway cows. (These rare cows get their name from the foot-wide white "belt" around their middles.) The walk or drive is beautiful at any time of the year, but in fall it's breathtaking. Like the rest of New England, the coast of Maine gets a large number of fall-foliage "leaf peepers," and the reds and golds of the chestnut, birch, and elm trees along this winding route are especially beautiful.

🏃 Activities

Schooner Heritage

SAILING | FAMILY | This striking windjammer offers three- to six-day cruises and caters to individual wishes. Captain Doug Lee is a storyteller and author of nautical histories. ⊠ North End Shipyard, 11 Front St. ☎ 207/594–8007, 800/648–4544 ⊕ www.schoonerheritage.com.

★ Schooner J. E. Riggin

SAILING | FAMILY | The family-run schooner J. E. Riggin offers real-deal overnight sailing cruises that thoroughly immerse passengers in life on the water. The experience is distinguished from other local cruises by the culinary delights chef Annie concocts using locally sourced ingredients, including vegetables, eggs, and herbs freshly gathered from her own organic garden. Four-day sleeper cruises, with three freshly prepared, organic meals and snacks each day start at $895; it's worth every penny. ⊠ 3 Captain Spear Dr. ☎ 207/594–1875 ⊕ www.mainewindjammer.com.

Schooner Ladona

SAILING | A handsome racing yacht built in 1922 (and rebuilt in 1971), recently restored from nose to tail, the schooner Ladona leads chartered trips lasting from a single afternoon up to six days. All trips include breakfast and lunch, including a traditional Downeast lobster bake and beach barbecue, as well as a selection of wines and ports every evening. ⊠ Rockland ☎ 800/999–7352, 207/594–4723 ⊕ www.schoonerladona.com.

Rockport

4 miles north of Rockland via U.S. 1.

Heading north on U.S. 1, you come to Rockport before you reach the tourist mecca of Camden. The most interesting part of Rockport—the harbor—is not right on U.S. 1. Originally called Goose River, the town was part of Camden until 1891. The cutting and burning of limestone was once a major industry in this area. The stone was cut in nearby quarries and then burned in hot kilns, and the resulting lime powder was used to create mortar. Some of the massive kilns are still here.

One of the most famous sights in Rockport is the **Rockport Arch,** which crosses Union Street at the town line and says "Camden" on the other side. It was constructed of wood and mortar in 1926, demolished in 1984, then rebuilt by popular demand in 1985. The arch has been displayed in a number of movies, including *Peyton Place* and *In the Bedroom.*

GETTING HERE AND AROUND

Rockport is off U.S. 1 between Rockland and Camden. Turn on Pascal Avenue to get to the village center.

🍴 Restaurants

★ 18 Central Oyster Bar and Grill

$$$ | SEAFOOD | The beautiful seaside village of Rockport has come alive with the opening of 18 Central Oyster Bar and Grill, which produces some of the best meals in the Mid-Coast in a cozy spot high above the working harbor. Seasonally inspired, locally harvested seafood with of hint of Southern comfort cooking is the backbone of most of the creative dishes—think fried green tomatoes with crab, chili oil, and microgreens or the crispy fried chicken accompanied by collard greens and heirloom grits. **Known for:** evenly paced, well-balanced dinners transition gracefully from one course to the next; lively atmosphere encouraged by botanically infused cocktails; packed as soon as the door opens for dinner. ⑤*Average main:* $25 ✉ *18 Central St.* ☎ *207/466–9055* ⊕ *www.18central.com* ⊙ *Closed Wed.*

Nina June

$$$ | MEDITERRANEAN | FAMILY | Serving up fresh takes on Mediterranean dishes using seafood harvested from Maine's rocky coast, this lovely trattoria gets just about everything right, from the cheery seaside setting to the family-style meals featuring a constantly changing menu where locally sourced ingredients shine. Everything from the noodles to the pickled veggies are made in-house and the presentation of each dish makes for sheer eye candy. **Known for:** family-style dinners; craft cocktails; harbor views; chef-lead cooking classes. ⑤*Average main:* $26 ✉ *24 Central St.* ☎ *207/236–8880* ⊕ *www.ninajunerestaurant.com* ⊙ *Closed Sun. and Mon.*

Camden

8 miles north of Rockland.

More than any other town along Penobscot Bay, Camden is the perfect picture-postcard of a Maine coastal village. It is one of the most popular destinations on the Maine Coast, and June–September the town is crowded with visitors—but don't let that scare you away: Camden is worth it. Just come prepared for busy traffic on the town's Main Street, and make reservations for lodging and restaurants well in advance.

Camden is famous not only for its geography, but also for its large fleet of windjammers—relics and replicas from the age of sailing—with their romantic histories and great billowing sails. At just about any hour during warm months you're likely to see at least one windjammer tied up in the harbor. Excursions, whether for an afternoon or a week, are best June–September.

The town's compact size makes it perfect for exploring on foot: shops, restaurants, and galleries line Main Street, as well as the side streets and alleys around the harbor. But be sure to include Camden's residential area on your walking tour. It is quite charming and filled with many fascinating old period houses from the time when Federal, Greek Revival, and Victorian architectural styles were the rage among the wealthy; many of them are now B&Bs. The Chamber of Commerce, at the Public Landing, can provide you with a walking map. Humped on the north side of town are the Camden Hills; drive or hike to the summit at the state park to enjoy mesmerizing views of the town, harbor, and island-dotted bay.

GETTING HERE AND AROUND

U.S. 1 becomes Camden's Main Street. Take Route 90 west from U.S. 1 and rejoin it in Warren to bypass Rockland—this is the quickest route south.

ESSENTIALS

VISITOR INFORMATION Penobscot Bay Regional Chamber of Commerce
☎ 207/236–4404, 800/562–2529 ⊕ www.camdenrockland.com.

FESTIVALS

★ Windjammer Weekend

FESTIVAL | FAMILY | One of the biggest and most colorful events of the year is the Camden Windjammer Festival, which takes place over Labor Day weekend. The harbor is packed with historic vessels, there are lots of good eats, and visitors can tour the magnificent ships. ✉ Camden ☎ 800/807–9463 ⊕ www.sailmainecoast.com.

Restaurants

Boynton-McKay Food Co

$ | AMERICAN | FAMILY | At Camden's longtime go-to breakfast and lunch spot, Boynton-McKay's new owners have updated the tried-and-true menu with foodie touches, while staying true to cherished staples. Order one of the ever-changing breakfast skillets, with eggs perched atop veggies and chorizo, or pop by for lunch to grab a slow-cooked brisket sandwich with a side of quinoa salad and avocado. **Known for:** homemade kombucha; weekend brunch; locally roasted coffee. ⑤ Average main: $10 ✉ 30 Main St. ☎ 207/236–2465 ⊕ www.boynton-mckay.com ⊗ Closed Mon. and Tues.

★ Long Grain

$ | ASIAN FUSION | This stylish Asian-fusion eatery places an emphasis on Thai curries and house-made noodles. A very popular restaurant with locals and visitors alike, reservations are essential, though you might be able to squeeze in at the tiny bar without one if you're dining solo and don't mind a little chaos; don't miss the Asian general store in the front of the restaurant, which is stocked with yummy and fun imported items. **Known for:** chef Ravin Nakjaroen is a James Beard nominated chef; consistently excellent delivery; great take-out options. ⑤ Average main: $17 ✉ 20 Washington St. ☎ 207/236–9001 ⊕ www.longgraincamden.com ⊗ Closed Sun. and Mon.

★ Natalie's Restaurant

$$$$ | MODERN AMERICAN | One of the most sought-after dining spots in Camden, Natalie's is the creation of Dutch owners Raymond Brunyanszki and Oscar Verest, who brought in creative chefs to create splurge-worthy dishes in an intimate setting. Located in the cozy and elegant Camden Harbour Inn, the restaurant is fine dining with a distinctly Maine flair, and seasonal ingredients set the tone. **Known for:** phenomenal service with true attention to detail; signature lobster tasting menu; an excellent view overlooking the harbor. ⑤ Average main: $76 ✉ Camden Harbour Inn, 83 Bay View St. ☎ 866/658–1542 ⊕ www.nataliesrestaurant.com ⊗ Closed Sun. Nov.–May. No lunch.

Hotels

Camden Hartstone Inn

$$ | B&B/INN | This 1835 mansard-roofed Victorian home has been turned into a plush, sophisticated retreat and a fine culinary destination. **Pros:** luxury in the heart of town; extravagant breakfasts; some private entrances. **Cons:** not on water; some rooms have slightly dated decor; not all rooms have fireplaces. ⑤ Rooms from: $215 ✉ 41 Elm St. ☎ 207/236–4259 ⊕ www.hartstoneinn.com ⇄ 21 rooms ⑩ Free breakfast.

Lord Camden Inn

$$ | B&B/INN | FAMILY | If you want to be in the center of town and near the harbor, look for this handsome brick building with the bright blue-and-white awnings. **Pros:** large continental breakfast; suitelike "premier" rooms have balconies and sitting areas; mini-refrigerators in rooms. **Cons:** traffic noise in front rooms; no on-site restaurant; decor in many rooms in need of an update. $ *Rooms from: $259* ⊠ *24 Main St.* ☎ *207/236–4325, 800/336–4325* ⊕ *www.lordcamdeninn. com* ⇌ *36 rooms* ❀❀ *Free breakfast.*

★ Norumbega Inn

$$$ | **B&B/INN** | This welcoming B&B is one of the most photographed pieces of real estate in Maine, and once you get a look at its castlelike facade, you'll understand why. **Pros:** eye-popping architecture; beautiful views of both the ocean and the gorgeously maintained, sloping lawn; champagne welcome toast, baked treats and infused waters throughout the day, and after-dinner port and cheese beside a roaring fire; fire pit and lawn games in summer; secret beach within walking distance; ask the innkeepers. **Cons:** stairs to climb; a short distance from the center of town; not dog-friendly. $ *Rooms from: $309* ⊠ *63 High St.* ☎ *207/236–4646, 877/363–4646* ⊕ *www.norumbegainn. com* ⇌ *11 rooms* ❀❀ *Free breakfast.*

★ Whitehall

$$ | **B&B/INN** | **FAMILY** | Although the oldest part of the Whitehall is an 1834 white-clapboard sea captain's home, the bright and cheery design is decidedly contemporary with nostalgic touches here and there; the Millay Room pays homage to the poet Edna St. Vincent Millay, who grew up in the area and read her poetry at the Whitehall, where her career was launched. **Pros:** short walk to downtown and harbor; breakfast entrée choices; beautifully renovated with a design focus. **Cons:** no good water views; walls can be a bit thin; no on-site restaurant. $ *Rooms from: $200* ⊠ *52 High St.* ☎ *207/236–3391, 800/789–6565* ⊕ *www. whitehallmaine.com* ☽ *Closed mid-Oct.– mid-May* ⇌ *41 rooms* ❀❀ *Free breakfast.*

Activities

Heron

SAILING | **FAMILY** | This schooner, which had a cameo in the movie *The Rum Diary*, offers lunchtime sails, wildlife-watching trips, and sunset cruises. ⊠ *Rockport Marine Park, Pascal Ave., Rockport* ☎ *207/236–8605, 800/599–8605* ⊕ *www. sailheron.com.*

★ Mary Day

SAILING | **FAMILY** | Sailing for more than 50 years, the *Mary Day* is the first schooner in Maine built specifically for vacation excursions. Meals are cooked on an antique wood-fired stove. ⊠ *Camden Harbor, Atlantic Ave.* ☎ *800/992–2218* ⊕ *www.schoonermaryday.com.*

Olad

SAILING | Captain Aaron Lincoln runs two-hour trips on both the *Olad* and a smaller sailing vessel, spotting lighthouses, coastal mansions, the occasional seal, and the red-footed puffin cousins known as guillemots. Either boat can also be chartered for longer trips. ⊠ *Camden Harbor, Bay View St.* ☎ *207/236–2323* ⊕ *www.maineschooners.com.*

Windjammer Angelique

SAILING | **FAMILY** | Captain Mike and Lynne McHenry have more than three decades' experience on the high seas. Three- to six-day cruise options aboard the *Angelique* include photography workshops and meteor-watching trips, as well as yoga and wellness excursions. ⊠ *Camden Harbor* ☎ *800/282–9899* ⊕ *www. sailangelique.com.*

Shopping

Camden's downtown area makes for excellent window-shopping, with lots of adorable and sophisticated boutiques stocking a curated assortment of local products. Most shops and galleries are along Camden's main drag. From the harbor, turn right on Bay View, and walk to Main/High Street. U.S. 1 has lots of names as it runs through Maine. Three are within Camden's town limits—it starts as Elm Street, changes to Main Street, then becomes High Street.

Lily, Lupine & Fern

FLOWERS | This full-service florist offers a wonderful array of gourmet foods, chocolates, wines, imported beers, high-quality olive oils, and cheeses. There's a small deck where you can enjoy harbor views and a cup of coffee. ⊠ *11 Main St.* ☎ *207/236–9600* ⊕ *www.lilylupine.com.*

★ Owl and Turtle Bookshop and Cafe

BOOKS/STATIONERY | FAMILY | This pint-size but well-stocked independent bookstore with a cozy café has been serving Camden for over 45 years and frequently hosts author readings and other book-related events. It's closed on Monday. ⊠ *33 Bay View St.* ☎ *207/230–7335* ⊕ *www. owlandturtle.com.*

★ Swans Island

HOUSEHOLD ITEMS/FURNITURE | For gorgeous, handmade blankets, throws, and pillows, as well as wraps and scarves, look no further. All products are made in Maine using natural, heirloom-quality yarns—the expert craftsmanship explains the hefty price tag. ⊠ *2 Bayview St.* ☎ *207/706–7926* ⊕ *www.swansisland-company.com.*

Belfast

13 miles north of Lincolnville via U.S. 1.

Lots of Maine coastal towns like to think of themselves as the prettiest little town in the state, and any judge would be spoiled for choice. Charming Belfast (originally to be named Londonderry) is a strong contender, with a beautiful waterfront; an old and interesting main street rising from the harbor; a delightful array of B&Bs, restaurants, and shops; and friendly townsfolk. The downtown even has old-fashioned street lamps, which set the streets aglow at night.

GETTING HERE AND AROUND

U.S. 1 runs through Belfast as it travels up the coast. From Interstate 95, take U.S. 3 in Augusta to get here. The highways meet in Belfast, heading north. The information center has a large array of magazines, guidebooks, maps, and brochures that cover the entire Mid-Coast. It also can provide you with a free walking-tour brochure that describes the various historic buildings.

ESSENTIALS

VISITOR INFORMATION Belfast Area Chamber of Commerce ☎ *207/338–5900* ⊕ *www.belfastmaine.org.*

Sights

Belfast is a funky coastal town, where the streets are lined with eclectic boutiques, and a decidedly laissez-faire attitude presides. There is still evidence of the wealth of the mid-1800s, when Belfast was home to a number of business magnates, shipbuilders, ship captains, and so on. Their mansions still stand along High Street and in the residential area above it, offering excellent examples of Greek Revival and Federal-style architecture. In fact, the town has one of the best showcases of Greek Revival homes in the state. Don't miss the "White House," where High and Church Streets merge several blocks south of downtown.

Restaurants

Darby's Restaurant and Pub

$$ | AMERICAN | FAMILY | With pressed-tin ceilings, this charming, old-fashioned restaurant and bar—it's been such since the 1890s—is very popular with locals. Pad Thai and chicken with chili and cashews are signature dishes, but the menu also has hearty homemade soups and sandwiches and classic fish 'n' chips. **Known for:** excellent happy hour; gluten-free menu choices; Buddha bowls. $ *Average main: $23* ⊠ *155 High St.* ☎ *207/338–2339* ⊕ *www.darbysrestaurant.com.*

★ **Young's Lobster Pound**

$$$ | **SEAFOOD** | **FAMILY** | Right on the water's edge, across the harbor from downtown Belfast, this corrugated-steel building looks more like a fish cannery than a restaurant, but it's one of the best places for an authentic Maine lobster dinner. You'll see numerous tanks of live lobsters of varying size when you first walk in. **Known for:** "shore dinner": clam chowder or lobster stew, steamed clams or mussels, a 1½-pound boiled lobster, corn on the cob, and chips; family-friendly environment; BYOB. ⑤ *Average main: $25* ⊠ *2 Fairview St., off U.S. 1* ☎ *207/338–1160* ⊕ *youngslobsterpound. webs.com* ⊙ *Takeout only Jan.–Mar.*

Bucksport

9 miles north of Searsport via U.S. 1.

The stunning Penobscot Narrows Bridge, spanning the Penobscot River, makes Bucksport, a town founded in 1763, well worth a visit, even if you only stop while passing through to points north. Fort Knox, Maine's largest historic fort, overlooks the town from across the river. There are magnificent views of the imposing granite structure from the pleasant riverfront walkway downtown.

GETTING HERE AND AROUND

After you pass over the spectacular Penobscot Narrows Bridge onto Verona Island driving north on U.S. 1, you cross another bridge into Bucksport; turn left for downtown and right to continue on the highway. Route 15 heads north to Bangor from here.

◉ Sights

★ **Penobscot Narrows Bridge & Observatory Tower/Fort Knox Historic Site**

HISTORIC SITE | **FAMILY** | An "engineering marvel" is how experts describe the 2,120-foot-long Penobscot Narrows Bridge, which opened in 2006 and which is taller than the Statue of Liberty. It's

certainly beautiful to look at—from the surrounding countryside it pops up on the horizon like the towers of a fairy-tale castle. Spanning the Penobscot River across from Bucksport, the bridge's 437-foot observation tower is the tallest in the world; an elevator shoots you to the top. Don't miss it—the panoramic views, which take in the hilly countryside and the river as it widens into Penobscot Bay, are breathtaking. In summer, the observatory often offers moonrise viewings.

Also here is Fort Knox, the largest historic fort in Maine. It was built between 1844 and 1869, when, despite a treaty with Britain settling boundary disputes, invasion was still a concern—after all, the British controlled this region during both the Revolutionary War and the War of 1812. The fort never saw any real action, but it was used for troop training and as a garrison during the Civil War and the Spanish-American War. Visitors are welcome to explore the many rooms and passageways. Guided tours are given daily during the summer and several days a week in the shoulder seasons. ⊠ *711 Ft. Knox Rd., off U.S. 1, Prospect* ☎ *207/469–6553* ⊕ *www.fortknox.maine-guide.com* ⊠ *Fort from $6* ⊙ *Closed Nov.–Apr.*

Bangor

122 miles north of Portland via I–95, 19 miles north of Bucksport via Rte. 15.

The state's second-largest metropolitan area (Portland is the largest), Bangor is about 20 miles from the coast and is the unofficial capital of northern Maine. Back in the 19th century, the most important product and export of the "Queen City" was lumber from the state's vast north woods. Now, because of its airport, Bangor has become a gateway to Mount Desert Island, Bar Harbor, and Acadia National Park. Along the revitalized waterfront, the American Folk Festival draws big crowds on the last full weekend in August, and an outdoor stage attracts top bands and musicians throughout the summer.

GETTING HERE AND AROUND
Interstate 95 has five Bangor exits: 45–49. U.S. 1A loops up to Bangor from Stockton Springs and Ellsworth, near Bar Harbor, and connects with Interstate 395 on the western side of the Bangor area.

Blue Hill

20 miles east of Castine via Rtes. 166, 175, and 176.

Nestled snugly between 943-foot Blue Hill Mountain and Blue Hill Bay, the village of Blue Hill sits right beside its harbor. About 30 miles from Acadia National Park, Blue Hill makes for a more laid-back base for exploring the Mount Desert Island area, but bear in mind that 30 miles can take at least twice as long to travel with heavy traffic in summertime. Originally known for its granite quarries, copper mines, and shipbuilding, today the town is known for its pottery and the galleries, bookstores, antiques shops, and studios that line its streets. The Blue Hill Fair (⊕ *www.bluehillfair. com*), held Labor Day weekend, is a tradition in these parts, with agricultural exhibits, food, rides, and entertainment. A charming little park with a great playground is tucked away near the harbor downtown.

GETTING HERE AND AROUND
From U.S. 1 in Orland, Route 15 heads south to Blue Hill. To continue north on the highway, take Route 172 north to Ellsworth.

 Restaurants

Arborvine
$$$ | **MODERN AMERICAN** | Glowing gas fireplaces, period antiques, exposed beams, and hardwood floors covered with Oriental rugs distinguish the four candlelit dining areas in this renovated Cape Cod–style house. The seasonal menu features dishes made with organic ingredients that match well with its own beer, like crispy duck with rhubarb and lime glaze, or roasted rack of lamb with a basil-and-pine-nut crust—fresh fish dishes are also superb. **Known for:** fresh seafood dishes; classic New England fare; its adjacent nautical-themed DeepWater Brew Pub serves dishes made with organic ingredients to go with its own beer. ⑤ *Average main: $31* ⊠ *33 Tenney Hill* ☎ *207/374–2119* ⊕ *www.arborvine. com* ⊗ *Closed Mon. No lunch.*

 Hotels

Blue Hill Inn
$$ | **B&B/INN** | One side of this Federal-style inn was built as a home in 1835, but it soon became lodging, adding a wing with a matching facade in the 1850s. **Pros:** plenty of charm; modern suites with kitchens in separate building; 30 miles from Acadia National Park. **Cons:** some narrow stairs and thin walls consistent with historic property; complimentary appetizers each evening if you order wine or spirits; only some rooms have fireplaces. ⑤ *Rooms from: $240* ⊠ *40 Union St.* ☎ *207/374–2844* ⊕ *www. bluehillinn.com* ⊗ *Closed Nov.–mid-May, except for Cape House Suite and Studio* ⇨ *13 rooms* ⊙ *Free breakfast.*

 Shopping

ART GALLERIES
Blue Hill Bay Gallery
ART GALLERIES | This gallery sells oil and watercolor landscapes and seascapes of Maine and New England from the 19th through the 21st century. It also carries the proprietor's own photography. Call ahead in the off-season. ⊠ *11 Tenney Hill* ☎ *207/374–5773* ⊕ *www.bluehillbaygallery.com.*

POTTERY
Rackliffe Pottery

CERAMICS/GLASSWARE | In business since 1969, this shop sells colorful pottery made with lead-free glazes. You can choose between water pitchers, serving platters, tea-and-coffee sets, and sets of canisters, among other lovely items. ⊠ *132 Ellsworth Rd.* ☎ *888/631–3321* ⊕ *www.rackliffepottery.com.*

WINE
Blue Hill Wine Shop

WINE/SPIRITS | In a restored barn at the rear of one of Blue Hill's earliest houses, the Blue Hill Wine Shop carries more than 1,200 carefully selected wines. Coffee, tea, cheeses, and prewrapped sandwiches are also available. ⊠ *138 Main St.* ☎ *207/374–2161* ⊕ *www.blue-hillwineshop.com.*

Deer Isle

16 miles south of Blue Hill via Rtes. 176 and 15.

Reachable by a bridge, Deer Isle thick woods give way to tidal coves. Stacks of lobster traps populate the backyards of shingled houses, and dirt roads lead to secluded summer cottages. This region is prized by artists, and studios and galleries are plentiful.

GETTING HERE AND AROUND

From Sedgwick, Route 15 crosses a 1930s suspension bridge onto Little Deer Isle and continues on to the larger Deer Isle.

VISITOR INFORMATION

CONTACTS **Deer Isle–Stonington Chamber of Commerce** ☎ *207/348–6124* ⊕ *www.deerisle.com.*

Deer Isle Village

16 miles south of Blue Hill via Rtes. 176 and 15.

Around Deer Isle Village, thick woods give way to tidal coves. Stacks of lobster traps populate the backyards of shingled houses, and dirt roads lead to secluded summer cottages. This region is prized by artists, and studios and galleries are plentiful.

Sights

Edgar M. Tennis Preserve

NATURE PRESERVE | Enjoy several miles of woodland and shore trails at the Edgar M. Tennis Preserve. Look for hawks, eagles, and ospreys and wander among old apple trees, fields of wildflowers, and ocean-polished rocks. ⊠ *Tennis Rd., Deer Isle* ☎ *207/348–2455* ⊕ *www.islandheritagetrust.org* 🖾 *Free.*

Haystack Mountain School of Crafts

COLLEGE | Want to learn a new craft? This school 6 miles from Deer Isle Village offers one- and two-week courses for people of all skill levels in crafts such as blacksmithing, basketry, printmaking, and weaving. Artisans from around the world present free evening lectures throughout summer. Tours of the school and studios are available on Wednesday. ⊠ *89 Haystack School Dr., off Rte. 15, Deer Isle* ☎ *207/348–2306* ⊕ *www.haystack-mtn.org* 🖾 *Tours $5.*

Shopping

Nervous Nellie's Jams and Jellies

FOOD/CANDY | Jams and jellies are made right on the property at Nervous Nellie's. There is a tearoom with homemade goodies, and also a fanciful sculpture garden with everything from knights to witches to a lobster and a flamingo. They are the works of sculptor Peter Beerits, who operates Nervous Nellie's with his wife. ⊠ *598 Sunshine Rd., off Rte. 15, Deer Isle* ☎ *207/348–6182, 800/777–6845* ⊕ *www.nervousnellies.com.*

Isle au Haut

6 miles south of Stonington via ferry.

Isle au Haut thrusts its steeply ridged back out of the sea south of Stonington. French explorer Samuel D. Champlain discovered Isle au Haut—or "High Island"—in 1604, but heaps of shells suggest that native populations lived on or visited the island prior to his arrival. The island is accessible only by mail boat, but the 45-minute journey is well worth the effort. Acadia National Park extends to cover part of the island, with miles of trails, and the boat will drop visitors off there in peak season. The island has some seasonal rentals but no inns. With only three stores, you wouldn't think folks would come here to shop, but some do, as the island is home to Black Dinah Chocolatiers (☎ *207/335–5010* ⊕ *www.blackdinahchocolatiers.com*), which makes artful high-end chocolates and has a small café.

GETTING HERE AND AROUND

There's one main road here: it circles the island and goes through the Acadia National Park section. Locals have different names for sections of the road.

Isle au Haut Boat Services (☎ *207/367–5193* ⊕ *www.isleauhaut.com*) operates daily mail-boat ferry service out of Stonington. During the summer season, trips increase from two to five Monday–Saturday and from one to two on Sunday. From mid-June until late September, the boat also stops at Duck Harbor, in the island section of Acadia National Park (it will not unload bicycles, kayaks, or canoes). Ferry service is scaled back in the fall, then returns to the regular or "winter" schedule.

Bar Harbor

34 miles from Blue Hill via Rte. 172 and U.S. 1.

A resort town since the 19th century, Bar Harbor is the artistic, culinary, and social center of Mount Desert Island, and it serves visitors to Acadia National Park with inns, motels, and restaurants. Around the turn of the last century the island was known as a summer haven for the very rich because of its cool breezes. The wealthy built lavish mansions throughout the island, many of which were destroyed in a huge fire that devastated the island in 1947—a good number of those that survived have been converted into businesses. In Bar Harbor, shops are clustered along Main, Mount Desert, and Cottage Streets; take a stroll down West Street, a National Historic District, where you can see some fine old houses.

The island and the surrounding Gulf of Maine are home to a great variety of wildlife: whales, seals, eagles, falcons, ospreys, and puffins (though not right offshore here), and forest dwellers such as deer, foxes, coyotes, and beavers.

GETTING HERE AND AROUND

In Ellsworth, Route 3 leaves U.S. 1 and heads to Bar Harbor. In season, free Island Explorer buses (☎ *207/667–5796* ⊕ *www.exploreacadia.com*) take visitors to Acadia National Park and other island towns. There is also a passenger ferry to Winter Harbor across Frenchman Bay.

ESSENTIALS

VISITOR INFORMATION Bar Harbor Chamber of Commerce ☎ *207/288–5103* ⊕ *www.visitbarharbor.com.*

Sights

★ Abbe Museum

MUSEUM | FAMILY | This important museum dedicated to Maine's indigenous tribes—collectively known as the Wabanaki—is the state's only Smithsonian-affiliated facility and one of the few places in Maine to experience Native culture as interpreted by Native peoples themselves. The year-round archaeology exhibit displays spear points, bone tools, and other artifacts found around Mount Desert Island and exhibits often feature contemporary Native American art, and there are frequent demonstrations of everything from boatbuilding to basket weaving. Call on rainy days for impromptu children's activities. A second location, inside the park at Sieur de Monts Spring, open only during the summer, features artifacts from the earliest digs around the island. ⊠ *26 Mount Desert St.* ☎ *207/288–3519* ⊕ *www.abbemuseum.org* ⊿ *$8.*

Restaurants

★ Burning Tree

$$$ | SEAFOOD | One of the top restaurants in Maine, this easy-to-miss gem with a festive dining room is on Route 3 between Bar Harbor and Otter Creek. The seasonal menu emphasizes freshly caught seafood, and seven species of fish are offered virtually every day—all from the Gulf of Maine. **Known for:** delicious monkfish dishes; Thai-inspired flavors; vegetable dishes using ingredients from own organic garden. ⑤ *Average main: $25* ⊠ *69 Otter Creek Dr., Otter Creek* ✚ *5 miles from Bar Harbor, 7 miles from Northeast Harbor* ☎ *207/288–9331* ☺ *Closed mid-Oct.–mid-June. No lunch.*

★ Havana

$$ | CUBAN | A lively yet intimate spot, Havana serves Latin-inspired dishes paired with robust wines right in the middle of downtown Bar Harbor. In the summer, have a bite on the patio; during winter months, dine in a pleasant indoor space with a modern aesthetic, featuring clean lines and cheery colors. **Known for:** Spanish tortillas; a lively atmosphere fueled by craft cocktails; after-dinner affogato made with MDI ice cream. ⑤ *Average main: $24* ⊠ *318 Main St.* ☎ *207/288–2822* ⊕ *www. havanamaine.com* ☺ *No lunch.*

Mâche Bistro

$$$ | FRENCH FUSION | This lively restaurant serves eclectic French-bistro fare in a hip space with dim lighting and a modern aesthetic. Share some tapas-style appetizers, like the black-truffle salami with truffle-whipped Brie, the duck-confit tartine, or the roasted beets with burrata cheese, or go for something more substantial like steak frites with truffle fries or seared Atlantic scallops with fennel salad, caper relish, and charred onion. **Known for:** lively atmosphere; classic French-bistro fare with a Maine twist; desserts that you'll want to eat first. ⑤ *Average main: $28* ⊠ *321 Main St.* ☎ *207/288–0447* ⊕ *www.machebistro. com* ☺ *Closed Sun. and Mon. No lunch.*

Hotels

Bar Harbor Grand Hotel

$$ | HOTEL | Taking one of the well-appointed, modern rooms in this renovated historic building puts you right in the middle of Bar Harbor, just a stone's throw from lively restaurants, cafés, and gift shops. **Pros:** excellent center-of-town location; breakfast included; good value. **Cons:** street noise; decor could use updates; service can be hit or miss. ⑤ *Rooms from: $245* ⊠ *269 Main St.* ☎ *207/288–5226* ⊕ *www.barharborgrand. com* ☺ *Closed mid-Nov.–Mar.* ⟿ *71 rooms* ⓘⓞⓘ *Free breakfast.*

Bar Harbor Inn & Spa

$$$ | HOTEL | Originally established in the late 1800s as a men's social club, this waterfront inn has rooms spread among three buildings on well-landscaped grounds. **Pros:** views of the beach and harbor; some two-level suites; shore path along the waterfront from the hotel. **Cons:** dated room decor and bathrooms; views often include cruise ships in port; service can be hit or miss. ⑤ *Rooms from: $350* ⊠ *1 Newport Dr.* ☎ *207/288–3351, 800/248–3351* ⊕ *www.barharborinn. com* ☺ *Closed late Nov.–mid-Mar.* ⟿ *153 rooms* ⓘⓞⓘ *Free breakfast.*

Primrose Place

$ | HOTEL | FAMILY | Recently renovated guest rooms at Primrose Place have retained their quaint local charm. **Pros:** centrally located; microwave and refrigerator available for guests in lobby; free parking. **Cons:** two-night minimum in high season; basic rooms; renovated motel-style lodgings are not for everyone. ⑤ *Rooms from: $175* ⊠ *51 Holland Ave.* ☎ *207/288–3771* ⊕ *www.primroseplace-barharbor.com* ⌁ *10 rooms* ⦿ *No meals.*

★ Ullikana Inn

$$ | B&B/INN | FAMILY | Nestled in a quiet spot secluded from the chaos of Bar Harbor proper, this quaint inn has elegant but cozy guest rooms, many of which have fireplaces, snug and sophisticated sitting areas, as well as private balconies overlooking the water. **Pros:** generous gourmet breakfast included; outdoor patio with landscaped gardens; intimate atmosphere; water views; quiet central location. **Cons:** no pool; minimum two-night stay required on weekends; not pet-friendly. ⑤ *Rooms from: $280* ⊠ *16 The Field* ☎ *207/288–9552* ⊕ *www.ullikana.com* ⌁ *10 rooms* ⦿ *Free breakfast.*

★ West Street Hotel

$$$$ | RESORT | Maine has some pretty phenomenal resort destinations in the Kennebunks and on the Mid-Coast, but to enjoy the state's premiere resort experience you'll do best to make the trek all the way Down East to Bar Harbor to stay at the West Street Hotel, where resort culture truly shines. **Pros:** all the expected luxuries of a resort and then some; each floor is equipped with guest pantries filled with snacks and goodies; one of the most tastefully decorated resorts in Maine. **Cons:** it's a trek to get Down East; $25 daily resort fee; dogs allowed, but for an additional $75 per dog per night (two dog limit). ⑤ *Rooms from: $750* ⊠ *50 West St.* ☎ *207/288–0825* ⊕ *www.theweststreethotel.com* ⌁ *85 rooms* ⦿ *Free breakfast.*

★ Wonder View Inn

$$ | HOTEL | FAMILY | On 14 gorgeous, sweeping acres just a stone's throw from downtown Bar Harbor and Acadia National Park, the Wonder View Inn is one of the most pet-friendly properties in town. **Pros:** pet-friendly; microwaves and refrigerators in all rooms; deck with a fire pit surrounded by sweeping views of Acadia. **Cons:** basic rooms; dated interiors; older hotel. ⑤ *Rooms from: $200* ⊠ *50 Eden St.* ☎ *207/288–3358* ⊕ *www.wonderviewinn.com* ☾ *Closed Nov.–Apr.* ⌁ *15 rooms* ⦿ *No meals.*

Activities

AIR TOURS

★ Acadia Air Tours

FLYING/SKYDIVING/SOARING | This outfit runs sightseeing flights over Bar Harbor and Acadia National Park. Most tours run 15 minutes to an hour and range $75–$360 for two people. The romantic sunset tour is $50 extra. ⊠ *1 West St.* ☎ *207/288–0703* ⊕ *www.acadiaairtours.com.*

BICYCLING

Acadia Bike

BICYCLING | FAMILY | Rent mountain bikes and hybrids at Acadia Bike, both good models for negotiating the carriage roads in Acadia National Park. ⊠ *48 Cottage St.* ☎ *207/288–9605, 800/526–8615* ⊕ *www.acadiabike.com.*

Bar Harbor Bicycle Shop

BICYCLING | Rent bikes for anywhere from four hours to a full day at the Bar Harbor Bicycle Shop. ⊠ *141 Cottage St.* ☎ *207/288–3886, 800/824–2453* ⊕ *www.barharborbike.com.*

BOATING

Coastal Kayaking Tours

KAYAKING | FAMILY | This outfitter has been leading trips in the scenic waters off Mount Desert Island since 1982. Rentals are provided through its sister business, Acadia Outfitters, on the same downtown street. Trips are limited to no more than 12 people. The season

Long ramps on Maine's many docks make it easier to access boats at either high or low tide.

is May–October. ⊠ *48 Cottage St.* ☎ *207/288–9605* ⊕ *www.acadiafun.com.*

Downeast Sailing Adventures

BOATING | FAMILY | Take two-hour sailing trips and sunset cruises for $50 per person with six passengers ($50 per person with fewer), or hire a private charter starting at $125 per hour. Boats depart the Upper Town Dock in Southwest Harbor and several other locations. ⊠ *Eagle Lake Rd.* ☎ *207/288–2216* ⊕ *www.downeastsail.com.*

Margaret Todd

BOATING | FAMILY | The 151-foot four-masted schooner *Margaret Todd* operates 1½- to 2-hour trips three times daily among the islands of Frenchman Bay. The sunset sail has live folk music, and the 2 pm trip is sometimes narrated by an Acadia National Park ranger. Trips are $42 and depart mid-May–mid-October. ⊠ *Bar Harbor Inn pier, 19 Cottage St.* ☎ *207/288–4585* ⊕ *www.downeastwindjammer.com.*

WHALE-WATCHING

Bar Harbor Whale Watch Co.

WHALE-WATCHING | FAMILY | This company has four boats, one of them a 140-foot jet-propelled double-hulled catamaran with spacious decks. It's one of two large catamarans used for whale-watching trips, some of which depart at sunset or include a side trip to see puffins. The company also offers lighthouse, lobstering, and seal-watching cruises, as well as a trip to Acadia National Park's Baker Island. Tours run $32–$63 per person. ⊠ *1 West St.* ☎ *207/288–2386, 800/942–5374* ⊕ *www.barharborwhales.com.*

🛍 Shopping

ART

Alone Moose Fine Crafts

ART GALLERIES | The oldest made-in-Maine gallery in Bar Harbor, Alone Moose Fine Crafts offers bronze wildlife sculptures, jewelry, pottery, photography, and watercolors. ⊠ *78 West St.* ☎ *207/288–4229 mid-May–Oct., 207/288–9428* ⊕ *www. finemainecrafts.com.*

Book a Carriage Ride

Riding down one of the park's scenic carriage roads in a horse-drawn carriage is a truly unique way to experience Acadia. You can book a reservation for a ride, late May–mid-October, with Wildwood Stables, located next to Park Loop Road (☎ 877/276–3622). One of the carriages can accommodate wheelchairs.

Eclipse Gallery

ART GALLERIES | Eclipse Gallery carries handblown glass, ceramics, wood and metal furniture, and home decor items like mirrors and lamps. The gallery is open mid-May–October. ✉ *12 Mount Desert St., Suite B* ☎ *207/610–2862* ⊕ *www.eclipsegallery.us.*

Island Artisans

ART GALLERIES | This shop sells basketry, pottery, fiber work, and jewelry created by about 150 Maine artisans. It's open May–December. ✉ *99 Main St.* ☎ *207/288–4214* ⊕ *www.islandartisans.com.*

Native Arts Gallery

ART GALLERIES | Silver and gold Southwest Indian jewelry is a specialty at Native Arts Gallery, open May–October. ✉ *99 Main St.* ☎ *207/288–4474* ⊕ *www.nativeartsgallery.com.*

★ The Rock and Art Shop

BOOKS/STATIONERY | As advertised, there are both "rocks" and "art" for sale at this eclectic family-owned store. There are also taxidermied animals, fossils, home decor and plants, interesting jewelry, and bath products. There are other locations in Bangor, Ellsworth, and just outside Ellsworth off U.S. 1A; here, they're open May–November. ✉ *23 Cottage St.* ☎ *207/288–4800* ⊕ *www.therockandartshop.com.*

SPORTING GOODS
Cadillac Mountain Sports

SPORTING GOODS | One of the best sporting-goods stores in the state, Cadillac Mountain Sports has developed a following of locals and visitors alike. Here you'll find top-quality climbing, hiking, boating, paddling, and camping equipment, and in winter you can rent cross-country skis, ice skates, and snowshoes. ✉ *26 Cottage St.* ☎ *207/288–4532* ⊕ *www.cadillacsports.com.*

Acadia National Park

3 miles from Bar Harbor via U.S. 3.

With about 49,000 acres of protected forests, beaches, mountains, and rocky coastline, Acadia National Park is one of the most visited national parks in America. According to the National Park Service, more than 2 million people visit Acadia each year, and the number is steadily rising. The park holds some of the most spectacular scenery on the Eastern Seaboard: a rugged coastline of surf-pounded granite and an interior graced by sculpted mountains, quiet ponds, and lush, deciduous forests. Cadillac Mountain (named after a Frenchman who explored here in the late 1600s and who later founded Detroit)—the highest point of land on the East Coast—dominates the park. Although rugged, the park also has graceful stone bridges, miles of carriage roads (popular with walkers, runners, and bikers as well as horse-drawn carriages), and the Jordan Pond House restaurant (famous for its popovers).

The 27-mile Park Loop Road provides an excellent overview, but to truly appreciate the park you must get off the main road and experience it by walking, hiking, biking, sea kayaking, or taking a carriage ride. Get off the beaten path, and you can find places you'll have practically all to yourself. Mount Desert Island was once a preserve of summer homes for the very rich (and still is for some), and, partly because of this, Acadia is the first national park in the United States largely created by donations of private land. There are two smaller parts of the park: on Isle au Haut, 15 miles away out in the ocean, and on the Schoodic Peninsula, on the mainland across Frenchman Bay from Mount Desert.

GETTING HERE AND AROUND

Island Explorer buses, which serve the park and island villages June 23–Columbus Day, offer transportation to and around the park. In addition to regularly scheduled stops, they also pick up and drop off passengers anywhere in the park it is safe to stop.

Route 3 leads to the island and Bar Harbor from Ellsworth and circles the eastern part of the island. Route 102 is the major road on the west side.

CONTACTS Island Explorer ☎ *207/667–5796* ⊕ *www.exploreacadia.com.*

ESSENTIALS

A user fee is required May–October. The per-vehicle fee is $25 ($20 for motorcycles) for a seven-consecutive-day pass; you can walk or bike in on a $12 individual pass (also good for seven days); or you can use your National Park America the Beautiful Pass, which allows entrance to any national park in the United States. There are also a few fee-free days throughout the year.

The park is open 24 hours a day, year-round, but roads are closed December–mid-April, except for the Ocean Drive section of Park Loop Road and a small part of the road with access to Jordan Pond.

★ **Acadia National Park** ⊠ *Acadia National Park* ☎ *207/288–3338* ⊕ *www.nps.gov/ acad.*

Mount Desert Chamber of Commerce ⊠ *Northeast Harbor* ☎ *207/276–5040* ⊕ *mtdesertchamber.org.*

Mt. Desert Island Information Center at Thompson Island ⊠ *Bar Harbor*

Caution

Every few years, someone falls off one of the park's trails or cliffs and is swept out to sea. There is a lot of loose, rocky gravel along the shoreline, and sea rocks can often be slippery—so watch your step.

☎ *207/288–3338* ⊕ *www.nps.gov/acad/ planyourvisit/hours.htm.*

◉ Sights

SCENIC DRIVES AND STOPS
★ **Cadillac Mountain**

MOUNTAIN—SIGHT | FAMILY | At 1,530 feet, this is one of the first places in the United States to see the sun's rays at daybreak. It is the highest mountain on the Eastern Seaboard north of Brazil. Hundreds of visitors make the trek to see the sunrise or—for those less inclined to get up so early—sunset. From the smooth summit you have a stunning 360-degree view of the jagged coastline that runs around the island. The only structures at the top are restrooms and a small gift shop, which sells coffee and snacks. The road up the mountain is closed December–mid-May. ⊠ *Cadillac Summit Rd.* ⊕ *www.nps.gov/acad/.*

★ **Park Loop Road**

SCENIC DRIVE | FAMILY | This 27-mile road provides a perfect introduction to the park. You can drive it in an hour, but allow at least half a day, so that you can explore the many sites along the way. The route is also served by the free Island Explorer buses, which also pick up and drop off passengers anywhere it is safe to stop along the route. Traveling south on Park Loop Road toward Sand Beach, you'll reach a small ticket booth, where, if you haven't already, you will need to pay the park entrance fee (May–October). Traffic is one-way from the Route 233 entrance to the Stanley Brook Road entrance

Acadia's Best Campgrounds

Acadia National Park's two main campgrounds, Seawall and Blackwoods, don't have water views, but the price is right and the ocean is just a 10-minute walk from each. The park added a third campground on the Schoodic Peninsula in 2015.

Blackwoods Campground. Located only 5 miles from Bar Harbor, this is Acadia's most popular campground. It is open year-round and well served by the Island Explorer bus system. ⊠ *Rte. 3, 5 miles south of Bar Harbor* ☎ *877/444–6777 for reservations* ⊕ *www.recreation.gov.*

Schoodic Woods Campground. Opened in September 2015, this campground is in the Schoodic Peninsula section of Acadia, meaning you have to take the ferry from Winter Harbor in order to cross over to Mount Desert Island (or drive). It is open May–Columbus Day. ⊠ *Schoodic Loop Road, 1 mile south of Rte. 186, Winter Harbor.*

Seawall Campground. On the quiet western side of the island, Seawall is open late May–September. ⊠ *Rte. 102A, 4 miles south of Southwest Harbor* ☎ *877/444–6777 for reservations* ⊕ *www.recreation.gov.*

south of the Jordan Pond House. The section known as Ocean Drive is open year-round, as is a small section that provides access to Jordan Pond from Seal Harbor. ⊠ *Acadia National Park.*

VISITOR CENTER

Hulls Cove Visitor Center

INFO CENTER | FAMILY | This is a great spot to get your bearings. A large 3-D relief map of Mount Desert Island gives you the lay of the land, and a free 15-minute video about everything the park has to offer plays every half hour. You can pick up guidebooks, maps of hiking trails and carriage roads, and recordings for drive-it-yourself tours—don't forget to grab a schedule of ranger-led programs, which includes guided hikes and other interpretive events. Junior-ranger programs for kids, nature hikes, photography walks, tide-pool explorations, and evening talks are all popular. The Acadia National Park Headquarters, off Route 233 near the north end of Eagle Lake, serves as the park's visitor center during the off-season. ⊠ *25 Visitor Center Rd., Bar Harbor* ☎ *207/288–3338* ⊕ *www.nps.gov/acad.*

🏃 Activities

The best way to see Acadia National Park is to get out of your vehicle and explore on foot or by bicycle or boat. There are more than 45 miles of carriage roads that are perfect for walking and biking in the warmer months and for cross-country skiing and snowshoeing in winter. There are 125 miles of trails for hiking, numerous ponds and lakes for canoeing or kayaking, two beaches for swimming, and steep cliffs for rock climbing.

HIKING

Acadia National Park maintains more than 125 miles of hiking trails, from easy strolls around lakes and ponds to rigorous treks with climbs up rock faces and scrambles along cliffs. Although hiking trails are concentrated on the east side of the island, the west side also has some scenic trails. For those wishing for a longer trek, try the trails leading up Cadillac Mountain or Dorr Mountain; you may also try Parkman, Sargeant, and Penobscot mountains. Most hiking is done mid-May–mid-November; snow falls early in Maine, so

All About Mount Desert Island

With some of the most dramatic and varied scenery on the Maine Coast—and home to Maine's only national park—Mount Desert Island (pronounced "dessert" by locals) is Maine's most popular tourist destination, attracting well over 2 million visitors a year. Much of the approximately 12-by-15-mile island belongs to Acadia National Park. You can take a scenic drive along the island's rocky coastline, whose stark cliffs rise from the ocean. A network of old carriage roads lets you explore Acadia's wooded interior, filled with birds and other wildlife, and trails for hikers of all skill levels lead to rounded mountaintops, providing views of Frenchman and Blue Hill bays and beyond. Ponds and lakes beckon you to swim, fish, or boat, and ferries and charter boats provide a different perspective on the island and a chance to explore the outer islands.

Mount Desert Island has four different towns, each with its own personality. The town of Bar Harbor is on the northeastern corner of the island and includes the little villages of Hulls Cove, Salisbury Cove, and Town Hill. Aside from Acadia, Bar Harbor is the major tourist destination here, with plenty of lodging, dining, and shopping. The town of Mount Desert, in the middle of the island, has four main villages: Somesville, Seal Harbor, Otter Creek, and Northeast Harbor, a summer haven for the very wealthy. Southwest Harbor includes the smaller village of Manset south of the village center. Tremont is at the southernmost tip of the island and stretches up the western shore. It includes the villages of Bass Harbor, Bernard, and Seal Cove. Yes, Mount Desert Island is a place with three personalities: the hustling, bustling tourist mecca of Bar Harbor; the "quiet side" on the western half; and the vast natural expanse of Acadia National Park. But though less congested and smaller, Northeast Harbor and Southwest Harbor are home to inns, campgrounds, restaurants, ferries, galleries, and small museums.

from as early as late November to the end of March, cross-country skiing and snowshoeing replace hiking. Volunteers groom most of the carriage roads if there's been 4 inches of snow or more. ■ TIP→ **You can park at one end of any trail and use the free shuttle bus to get back to your starting point.**

Distances for trails are given for round-trips.

★ Acadia Mountain Trail

HIKING/WALKING | If you're up for a challenge, this is one of the area's best trails. The 2.5-mile round-trip climb up Acadia Mountain is a steep and strenuous 700-foot climb, but the payoff views of Somes Sound are grand. If you want

a guided trip, look into ranger-led hikes for this trail. ✉ *Rte. 102* ☎ *207/288–3338* ⊕ *www.nps.gov/acad.*

★ Ocean Path Trail

HIKING/WALKING | This easily accessible 4.4-mile round-trip trail runs parallel to the Ocean Drive section of the Park Loop Road from Sand Beach to Otter Point. It has some of the best scenery in Maine: cliffs and boulders of pink granite at the ocean's edge, twisted branches of dwarf jack pines, and ocean views that stretch to the horizon. Be sure to save time to stop at **Thunder Hole,** named for the sound the waves make as they thrash through a narrow opening in the granite cliffs, into a sea cave, and whoosh up and out. Approximately halfway between Sand Beach and Otter Cliff, steps lead down to the water, where you can watch the wave action close up. Use caution as you descend (access may be limited due to storms), and also if you venture onto the outer cliffs along this walk. ⊠ *Ocean Dr. section of Park Loop Rd.*

SWIMMING

The park has two swimming beaches, Sand Beach and Echo Lake Beach. Sand Beach, along Park Loop Road, has changing rooms, restrooms, and a lifeguard on duty Memorial Day–Labor Day. Echo Lake Beach, on the western side of the island just north of Southwest Harbor, has much warmer water, as well as changing rooms, restrooms, and a lifeguard on duty throughout the summer. This beach is particularly well suited for small children, as the water remains relatively shallow fairly far out.

Echo Lake Beach

BEACHES | FAMILY | A quiet lake surrounded by woods in the shadow of Beech Mountain, Echo Lake draws swimmers to its sandy southern shore. The lake bottom is a bit muckier than the ocean beaches nearby, but the water is considerably warmer. The surrounding trail network skirts the lake and ascends the mountain. The beach is 2 miles north of Southwest Harbor. **Amenities:** lifeguards; toilets. **Best for:** swimming. ⊠ *Echo Lake Beach Rd., off Rte. 102.*

Sand Beach

BEACHES | This pocket beach is hugged by two picturesque rocky outcroppings, and the combination of the crashing waves and the chilly water (peaking at around 55°F) keeps most people on the beach. You'll find some swimmers at the height of summer, but the rest of the year this is a place for strolling and snapping photos. In the shoulder season, you'll have the place to yourself. **Amenities:** lifeguards; parking; toilets. **Best for:** solitude; sunrise; walking. ⊠ *Ocean Dr. section of Park Loop Rd., 3 miles south of Rte. 3.*

The Early Bird Gets the Sun

During your visit to Mount Desert, pick a day when you are willing to get up very early, around 4:30 or 5 am. Drive with a friend, or a camera with a timer, to the top of Cadillac Mountain in Acadia National Park, and stand on the highest rock you can find and wait for the sun to come up. When it does, have your friend, or your camera, take a photo of you looking at it and label the photo something like, "The first person in the country to see the sun come up today."

Bass Harbor

10 miles south of Somesville via Rtes. 102 and 102A.

Bass Harbor is a tiny lobstering village with a relaxed atmosphere and a few accommodations and restaurants. If you're looking to get away from the crowds, consider using this hardworking community as your base. Although Bass Harbor does not draw as many tourists as other villages, the Bass Harbor Head Light in Acadia National Park is one of the region's most popular attractions and is undoubtedly one of the most photographed lighthouses in Maine. From Bass Harbor, you can hike the Ship Harbor Nature Trail or take a ferry to Frenchboro or Swans Island.

GETTING HERE AND AROUND

From Bass Harbor, the Maine State Ferry Service operates the *Captain Henry Lee*, carrying both passengers and vehicles to Swans Island (40 minutes; $17.50 per person round-trip, $49.50 per car with driver) and Frenchboro (50 minutes; $11.25 per person round-trip, $32.25 per car with driver). The Frenchboro ferry

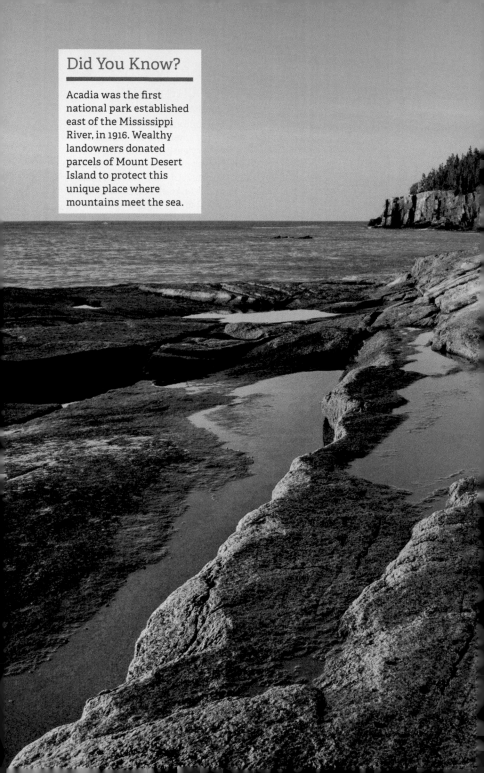

Did You Know?

Acadia was the first national park established east of the Mississippi River, in 1916. Wealthy landowners donated parcels of Mount Desert Island to protect this unique place where mountains meet the sea.

doesn't run daily; a passenger-only ferry on a smaller boat (same price) runs on Fridays, April–November. Round-trip excursions (you don't get off the boat) are $10.

ESSENTIALS

TRANSPORTATION INFORMATION

Maine State Ferry Service ⊠ *45 Granville Rd.* ☎ *207/244–3254* ⊕ *www.maine.gov/ mdot.*

Sights

★ Bass Harbor Head Light

LIGHTHOUSE | Built in 1858, this lighthouse is one of the most photographed lights in Maine. Now automated, it marks the entrance to Bass Harbor and Blue Hill Bay. You can't actually go inside—the grounds and residence are Coast Guard property—but two trails around the facility have excellent views. It's within Acadia National Park, and there is parking. ■ **TIP→ The best place to take a picture is from the rocks below—but watch your step, as they can be slippery.** ⊠ *Lighthouse Rd., off Rte. 102A* ☎ *207/244–9753* ☞ *Free.*

Restaurants

Thurston's Lobster Pound

$$ | SEAFOOD | Right on Bass Harbor, looking across to the village, Thurston's is easy to spot because of its bright yellow awning. You can order everything from a grilled-cheese sandwich, soup, or hamburger to a boiled lobster served with clams or mussels, and dine at covered outdoor tables, or you can buy fresh lobsters to go. **Known for:** family-friendly environment; lobster fresh off the boat; good place to watch sunsets. ⑤ *Average main: $20* ⊠ *Steamboat Wharf, 9 Thurston Rd., Bernard* ☎ *207/244–7600* ⊕ *www.thurstonforlobster.com* ⊘ *Closed mid-Oct.–Memorial Day.*

Schoodic Peninsula

25 miles east of Ellsworth via U.S. 1 and Rte. 186.

The landscape of Schoodic Peninsula's craggy coastline, towering evergreens, and views over Frenchman Bay are breathtaking year-round. A drive through the well-to-do summer community of Grindstone Neck shows what Bar Harbor might have been like before so many of its mansions were destroyed in the Great Fire of 1947. Artists and artisans have opened galleries in and around Winter Harbor. Anchored at the foot of the peninsula, Winter Harbor was once part of Gouldsboro, which wraps around it. The southern tip of the peninsula is home to the Schoodic section of Acadia National Park.

GETTING HERE AND AROUND

From U.S. 1, Route 186 loops around the peninsula. Route 195 runs from U.S. 1 to Prospect Harbor and on to its end in Corea.

Island Explorer

The Island Explorer operates on the Schoodic Peninsula, with bus service from Prospect Harbor, Birch Harbor, and Winter Harbor to anywhere in the Schoodic Peninsula section of the park that's safe to stop. The bus also connects with the Winter Harbor ferry terminal, where you can take a ferry back to Bar Harbor. ⊠ *Winter Harbor* ☎ *207/667– 5796* ⊕ *www.exploreacadia.com.*

ESSENTIALS

VISITOR INFORMATION Schoodic Chamber of Commerce ⊕ *www.acadia-schoodic. org.*

Sights

Within Gouldsboro on the Schoodic Peninsula are several small coastal villages. You drive through Wonsqueak and Birch Harbor after leaving the Schoodic section of Acadia National Park. Near Birch

Harbor you can find Prospect Harbor, a small fishing village nearly untouched by tourism. In Corea, there's little to do besides watch fishermen at work, wander along stone beaches, or gaze out at the sea.

★ Acadia National Park

NATIONAL/STATE PARK | The only section of Maine's national park that sits on the mainland is at the southern end of the Schoodic Peninsula in the town of Winter Harbor. The park has a scenic 6-mile loop that edges along the coast, yielding views of Grindstone Neck, Winter Harbor, Winter Harbor Lighthouse, and, across the water, Cadillac Mountain. At the tip of the point, huge slabs of pink granite lie jumbled along the shore, thrashed unmercifully by the crashing surf, and jack pines cling to life amid the rocks. Fraser Point, at the beginning of the loop, is an ideal place for a picnic. Work off lunch with a hike up Schoodic Head for the panoramic views up and down the coast. During the summer season you can take a passenger ferry ($16 one-way, $26 round-trip) to Winter Harbor from Bar Harbor. In Winter Harbor catch the free Island Explorer bus, which stops throughout the park, but you'll need to take the ferry to get back to Bar Harbor. ⌧ *End of Moore Rd., off Rte. 186, Winter Harbor* ☎ *207/288–3338* ⊕ *www.nps.gov/acad.*

Schoodic Education and Research Center

COLLEGE | In the Schoodic Peninsula section of Acadia National Park, this center offers lectures, workshops, and kid-friendly events about nature. It's worth a drive-by just to see the Rockefeller Building, a massive 1935 French Eclectic and Renaissance-style structure with a stone-and-half-timber facade that served as naval offices and housing. The building now acts as a visitor center after an extensive renovation. ⌧ *9 Atterbury Circle, Winter Harbor* ☎ *207/288–1310* ⊕ *www.schoodicinstitute.org.*

Restaurants

Chase's Restaurant

$ | SEAFOOD | FAMILY | This family restaurant has a reputation for serving good, basic fare—and in this region that means a whole lot of fresh fish. There are large and small fried seafood dinners, as well as several more expensive seafood platters. **Known for:** family-friendly dining; classic Maine fare; no-frills atmosphere. ⑤ *Average main: $10* ⌧ *193 Main St., Winter Harbor* ☎ *207/963–7171.*

Hotels

Acadia's Oceanside Meadows Inn

$ | B&B/INN | FAMILY | A must for nature lovers, this lodging sits on a 200-acre preserve dotted with woods, streams, salt marshes, and ponds; it's home to the Oceanside Meadows Innstitute for the Arts and Sciences, which holds lectures, musical performances, art exhibits, and other events in the restored barn. **Pros:** one of the region's few sand beaches; staff share info about the area over tea; most rooms have water views. **Cons:** need to cross road to beach; decor a bit dated. ⑤ *Rooms from: $185* ⌧ *Rte. 195 Prospect Harbor Rd., Prospect Harbor* ☎ *207/963–5557* ⊕ *www.oceaninn.com* ⊙ *Closed mid-Oct.–late May* ⊅ *15 rooms* �|⊙| *Free breakfast.*

Bluff House Inn

$ | B&B/INN | FAMILY | This cozy, modern inn is on a secluded hillside with expansive views of Frenchman Bay, which you can see from the wraparound porches on each floor; the downstairs porch is partially screened. **Pros:** good value; largest room has sitting area with pull-out couch; picnic area with grill and lobster pots are available. **Cons:** only two rooms have good water views; basic accommodations; off the beaten track. ⑤ *Rooms from: $135* ⌧ *57 Bluff House Rd., off Rte. 186, Gouldsboro* ☎ *207/963–7805* ⊕ *www.bluffinn.com* ⊅ *9 rooms* |⊙| *Free breakfast.*

Way Down East

 Activities

KAYAKING
SeaScape Kayak and Bike

KAYAKING | Led by a Registered Maine Guide, SeaScape's morning and after-noon kayak tours include an island stop and a blueberry snack. The company also rents canoes, kayaks, and bikes from its location in Birch Harbor and welcomes kayakers with disabilities. ⊠ *8 Duck Pond Rd., Winter Harbor* ☎ *207/546–1064* ⊕ *www.seascapekayaking.com.*

 Shopping

ANTIQUES AND MORE
U.S. Bells

ANTIQUES/COLLECTIBLES | Hand-cast bronze doorbells and wind chimes are among the items sold at U.S. Bells. You can also buy finely crafted quilts and wood-fired pottery made by the owner's family. Ask for a tour of the foundry. ⊠ *56 W. Bay Rd., Prospect Harbor* ☎ *207/963–7184* ⊕ *www.usbells.com.*

ART GALLERIES
Lee Fusion Art Glass

ART GALLERIES | Window glass is fused in a kiln to create unusual glass dishware. Colorful enamel accents depict birds, lighthouses, flowers, and designs made from doilies. The store is open June–October. ⊠ *679 S. Gouldsboro Rd., Rte. 186, Gouldsboro* ☎ *207/712–2148* ⊕ *www.leefusionartglass.com.*

Did You Know?

Atlantic puffin colonies were reintroduced to the Maine Coast by the Maine Autobon Society's Project Puffin. Get a closer look at these seabirds and their distinctive beaks on a seasonal puffin cruise from Cutler to Machias Seal Island, the sovereignty of which remains contested between Canada and the United States.

Lubec

*122 miles northeast of Belfast via U.S. 1
and Rte. 189.*

Lubec is one of the first places in the
United States to see the sunrise. A popular destination for outdoors enthusiasts,
it offers plenty of opportunities for hiking
and biking, and the birding is renowned.
It's a good base for day trips to New
Brunswick's Campobello Island, reached
by a bridge—the only one to the island—
from downtown Lubec, so don't forget
to bring your passport. One of the main
attractions there, Roosevelt Campobello
International Park, operates a visitor
center on the U.S. side of the border,
which provides information about the
region, generally; it's in a Whiting general
store and gas station at the corner of
U.S. 1 and Route 189. The village itself
is perched at the end of a narrow strip
of land at the end of Route 189, so you
often see water in three directions in this
laid-back, off-the-beaten-path place.

GETTING HERE AND AROUND

From U.S. 1 in Whiting, Route 189 leads
to Lubec; it's about 13 miles to the village.
You can stock up on groceries in nearby
Machias, just before you hit Whiting, en
route to Lubec. In summer you can take a
water taxi from here to Eastport—about
a mile by boat, but 40 miles by the circui-
tous northerly land route.

◉ Sights

★ West Quoddy Head Light

LIGHTHOUSE | FAMILY | The easternmost
point of land in the United States is
marked by candy-stripe West Quoddy
Head Light. In 1806 President Thomas
Jefferson signed an order authorizing
construction of a lighthouse on this site.
You can't climb the tower, but the former
lightkeeper's house has a museum with
a video with shots of the interior, as well
as displays on Lubec's maritime past;
a gallery displays works by artists who

live or summer in the area. The mystical
2-mile path along the cliffs at Quoddy
Head State Park (one of five trails) yields
magnificent views of Canada's cliff-
clad Grand Manan Island. Whales and
seals—as well as the ubiquitous bald
eagles—can often be sighted offshore.
The 540-acre park has a picnic area with
grills, but sometimes the best place to
take lunch is perched on a rock overlooking the sea. Don't miss the easy, 0.2-mile
bog trail that includes a fascinating array
of subarctic vegetation, including carni-
orous pitcher plants. ☒ *973 S. Lubec Rd.,
off Rte. 189* ☎ *207/733–2180* ⊕ *www.
westquoddy.com* ⌨ *$4.*

🍴 Restaurants

Water Street Tavern and Inn

$$ | SEAFOOD | FAMILY | Perched right on
the water in downtown Lubec, this
favorite local restaurant recently spruced
up its menu, which includes some of the
sweetest scallops you'll ever eat, a very
satisfying burger, and a massive chunk
of chocolate cake. It's also a great place
to grab a drink or a slice of blueberry
pie and a coffee while looking out at
the water from the deck or through the
picture windows. **Known for:** laid-back
atmosphere; there's often live music by
local performers on Thursday; there are
also two cozy suites and three guest
rooms, most with good views of the
water. ⑤ *Average main: $20* ☒ *12 Water
St.* ☎ *207/733–2477* ⊕ *www.watersttav-
ernandinn.com* ⊙ *Closed late-Oct.–Mar.*

🛏 Hotels

★ Peacock House

$ | B&B/INN | Five generations of the
Peacock family lived in this 1860 sea
captain's home before it was converted to an inn. **Pros:** piano and fireplace
in living room; lovely garden off deck;
think-of-everything innkeepers direct
guests to area's tucked-away spots. **Cons:**
not on the water; nestled in the heart of
sleepy Lubec; a short drive to Quoddy

Head State Park. ⑤ *Rooms from: $125* ✉ *27 Summer St.* ☎ *207/733–2403, 888/305–0036* ⊕ *www.peacockhouse. com* ⊘ *Closed Nov.–Apr.* ➴ *7 rooms* ⦿ *Free breakfast.*

Shopping

Monica's Chocolates
$ | |FOOD/CANDY | Taking in all the appetizing scents in this shop is almost enough, but sinking your teeth into one of Monica's truffles, bonbons, crèmes, or caramels is pure heaven. ✉ *100 County Rd.* ☎ *207/733–4500* ⊕ *www.monicas-chocolates.com.*

Campobello Island, Canada

4 miles northeast of Lubec.

A popular excursion from Lubec, New Brunswick's Campobello Island has two fishing villages, Welshpool and Wilson's Beach. The only land route is the bridge from Lubec, but in summer a car ferry shuttles passengers from Campobello Island to Deer Island, where you can continue on to the Canadian mainland.

GETTING HERE AND AROUND
After coming across the bridge from Lubec, Route 774 runs from one end of the island to the other, taking you through the two villages and to Roosevelt Campobello International Park.

Sights

★ Roosevelt Campobello International Park
HOUSE | FAMILY | President Franklin Roosevelt and his family spent summers at this estate, which is now an international park with neatly manicured lawns that stretch out to the beach. You can take a self-guided tour of the 34-room Roosevelt Cottage that was presented to Eleanor and Franklin as a wedding gift. The wicker-filled structure

looks essentially as it did when the family was in residence. A visitor center has displays about the Roosevelts and Canadian-American relations. Eleanor Roosevelt Teas are held at 11 and 3 daily in the neighboring Hubbard Cottage. A joint project of the American and the Canadian governments, this park is crisscrossed with interesting hiking trails. Groomed dirt roads attract bikers. Eagle Hill Bog has a wooden walkway and signs identifying rare plants. ■TIP→ **Note that the Islands are on Atlantic Time, which is an hour later than Eastern Standard Time.** ✉ *459 Rte. 774, Welshpool* ☎ *506/752–2922, 877/851–6663* ⊕ *www.fdr.net* ✉ *Free.*

Restaurants

Family Fisheries
$ | SEAFOOD | FAMILY | Seafood lovers know that fried fish doesn't have to be greasy; that's why people keep heading across the international bridge to eat at this family establishment in Wilson's Beach. The freshest seafood is delivered to the restaurant, where you can bring your own wine (corkage $2) and order fried haddock, scallops, shrimp, or clams, alone or as part of a platter. **Known for:** family-friendly environment; lobsters can be steamed to go; breakfast is served in July and August. ⑤ *Average main: C$15* ✉ *1977 Rte. 774, Wilsons Beach* ☎ *506/752–2470* ⊕ *www.familyfisheries. com* ⊘ *Closed late Oct.–early Apr.*

Eastport

39 miles northeast of Lubec via Rte. 189, U.S. 1, and Rte. 190; 109 miles north of Ellsworth via U.S. 1 and Rte. 190.

Connected by a granite causeway to the mainland at Pleasant Point Reservation, Eastport has wonderful views of the nearby islands, and because the harbor is so deep, you can sometimes spot whales from the waterfront. Known for its diverse architecture, the island city was one of the nation's busiest seaports in the early 1800s.

If you find yourself in town mid- to late summer, you might catch one of a few notable events. For starters, Maine's largest July 4 parade takes place in Eastport—be sure to get downtown early to secure a viewing spot. Then, on the weekend of the second Sunday in August, locals celebrate Sipayik Indian Days at the Pleasant Point Reservation; this festival of Passamaquoddy culture includes canoe races, dancing, drumming, children's games, fireworks, and traditional dancing. And on the weekend after Labor Day, the Eastport Pirate Festival brings folks out in pirate attire for a ship race, a parade, fireworks, cutlass "battles" by reenactors, and other events, including a children's breakfast and a schooner ride with pirates.

GETTING HERE AND AROUND
From U.S. 1, Route 190 leads to the Island City. Continue on Washington Street to the water. In the summer, you can also take a water taxi from here to Lubec—a mile or so by boat, but about 40 miles by land.

ESSENTIALS
VISITOR INFORMATION Eastport Area Chamber of Commerce ☎ 207/853–4644 ⊕ www.eastport.net.

🍴 Restaurants

Chowder House
$ | SEAFOOD | FAMILY | Just north of downtown Eastport, this expansive waterfront eatery sits on the pier next to the ferry dock. Built atop the foundation of an old cannery—it has original details such as wood beams and a stone wall—house specialties include a smoked fish appetizer and seafood pasta in a wine-and-cheese sauce. **Known for:** family-friendly environment; smoked fish appetizers; seafood pasta in a wine-and-cheese sauce. ⑤ *Average main: $17* ⊠ *167 Water St.* ☎ *207/853–4700* ⊕ *www. eastportchowderhouse.org* ⊘ *Closed mid-Oct.–mid-May.*

Dastardly Dick's Wicked Good Coffee
$ | CAFÉ | FAMILY | The coffee isn't the only thing that's wicked good at this local café; homemade pastries, rich soups, and tasty sandwiches are all prepared daily, and the hot chocolate and chai are worth writing home about. **Known for:** local gathering spot; daily soup specials; wicked good baked goods. ⑤ *Average main: $6* ⊠ *62 Water St.* ☎ *207/853–2090* ⊘ *Closed Mon.*

Index

Photo Credits

715

Photo Credits

Clineff (313). Graffizone / iStockphoto (313). libraryimages.net/Flickr, [CC BYND 2.0] (313). Artur Bogacki/Shutterstock (313). Kindra Clineff (314). Kindra Clineff (315). Kindra Clineff (315). Kindra Clineff (316). Kindra Clineff (317). Lise Gagne/ iStockphoto (317). f11photo/Shutterstock (326). jgorzynik/Shutterstock (334). Chapter 8: Rhode Island: Wickedgood | Dreamstime.com (339). Shashwatgupta1998 | Dreamstime.com (350). Denis Jr. Tangney/iStockphoto (352). APCortizasJr / iStockphoto (363). Ken Wiedemann/iStockphoto (373). The Preservation Society of Newport County (386). Carolyn M Carpenter/Shutterstock (386). The Preservation Society of Newport County (386). The Preservation Society of Newport County (387). The Preservation Society of Newport County (388). Library of Congress Prints and Photographs Division (388). Kindra Clineff (389). Frymire Archive / Alamy (389). Library of Congress Prints and Photographs Division (389). Wikimedia Commons (389). Library of Congress Prints and Photographs Division (389). The Preservation Society of Newport County (390). Sergio Orsanigo (391). The Preservation Society of Newport County (391). Travel Bug/Shutterstock (391). Public Domain (399). Leesniderphotoimages | Dreamstime.com (401). rachanon cumnonchai/Shutterstock (404). Kindra Clineff (413). Chapter 9: Vermont: Sean Pavone/Shutterstock (415). Kindra Clineff (423). Kindra Clineff (428). Courtesy of Hildene (434). Simon Pearce (448). Dale Halbur/iStockphoto (450). S. Greg Panosian/iStockphoto (456–457). Fraser Hall / age footstock (465). Dennis Curran / age footstock (471). 2008 Skye Chalmers Photography, inc. (472). Henryk T Kaiser / age fotostock (473). Hubert Schriebl (473). Marcio Silva/iStockphoto (474). Hubert Schriebl (474). SMUGGLERS' NOTCH RESORT/Ski Vermont (475). Okemo Mountain Resort (476). Sean Pavone/Shutterstock (488). Alan Copson / age fotostock (497). Chapter 10: New Hampshire: Denis Jr. Tangney/iStockphoto (501). Public Domain (511). Denis Jr. Tangney/iStockphoto (514). Denis Tangney Jr./iStockphoto (522). Roy Rainford / age footstock (526). Kindra Clineff (528). Jerry and Marcy Monkman/EcoPhotography.com / Alamy (537). Liz Van Steenburgh/Shutterstock (537). Kindra Clineff (538). Mike Kautz, Courtesy of AMC (539). nialat/Shutterstock (540). RestonImages/Shutterstock (540). nialat/Shutterstock (540). jadimages/Shutterstock (541). Ansgar Walk/wikipedia.org (541). J. Carmichael/wikipedia.org (541). rebvt/Shutterstock (541). Matty Symons/Shutterstock (543). Danita Delimont / Alamy (544). Frank Siteman / age fotostock (545). Appalachianviews | Dreamstime.com (557). Luckydoor | Dreamstime.com (566). Jet Lowe/Wikimedia Commons (568). John Greim / age fotostock (579). Chapter 11: Inland Maine: Reddy | Dreamstime.com (581). D A Horchner / age fotostock (593). Kazela/Shutterstock (602). Chapter 12: Maine Coast: Alan Majchrowicz / age fotostock (605). Perry B. Johnson / age fotostock (619). Ray Lewis/Shutterstock (627). Superstock / age fotostock (632) Wolfephoto | Dreamstime.com (647). Michael Czosnek/iStockphoto (658). SuperStock / age fotostock (659). Maine State Museum (660). David CanningsBushell/ iStockphoto (660). Paul D. Lemke/iStockphoto (661). Michael Rickard/Shutterstock (662). Robert Campbell (663). Dave Johnston (663). Casey Jordan (663). Kenneth Keifer/Shutterstock (664). Doug Lemke/ Shutterstock (664). liz west/wikipedia.org (664). Tim Goode/Shutterstock (667). Kindra Clineff (686). Alan Majchrowicz / age fotostock (692–693). Kindra Clineff (695). Ken Canning/iStock (698–699).

About Our Writers: All photos are courtesy of the writers except for the following: Andrew Collins, Courtesy of Fernando Nocedal.

Notes

Notes

Fodor's NEW ENGLAND

Editorial: Douglas Stallings, *Editorial Director*; Margaret Kelly, Jacinta O'Halloran, *Senior Editors*; Kayla Becker, Alexis Kelly, Amanda Sadlowski, *Editors*; Teddy Minford, *Content Editor*; Rachael Roth, *Content Manager*

Design: Tina Malaney, *Design and Production Director*; Jessica Gonzalez, *Production Designer*

Photography: Jill Krueger, *Senior Photo Editor*

Maps: Rebecca Baer, *Senior Map Editor*; Mark Stroud (Moon Street Cartography) and David Lindroth, *Cartographers*

Production: Jennifer DePrima, *Editorial Production Manager*; Carrie Parker, *Senior Production Editor*; Elyse Rozelle, *Production Editor*

Business & Operations: Chuck Hoover, *Chief Marketing Officer*; Joy Lai, *Vice President and General Manager*; Stephen Horowitz, *Director of Business Development and Revenue Operations*; Tara McCrillis, *Director of Publishing Operations*

Public Relations and Marketing: Joe Ewaskiw, *Manager*; Esther Su, *Marketing Manager*

Writers: Seth Brown, Andrew Collins, Mike Dunphy, Grace-Yvette Gemmell, Kim Foley MacKinnon, Mary Ruoff, Laura V. Scheel, and Jane E. Zarem

Editors: Alexis Kelly

Production Editor: Elyse Rozelle

33rd Edition

ISBN 978–1–64097–124–0

ISSN 0192–3412

Library of Congress Control Number 2018958612

SPECIAL SALES
This book is available at special discounts for bulk purchases for sales promotions or premiums. For more information, e-mail SpecialMarkets@fodors.com.

PRINTED IN THE UNITED STATES OF AMERICA

10 9 8 7 6 5 4 3 2 1

About Our Writers

Seth Brown lives in the beautiful Berkshires, where he occasionally performs poetry and comedy. His award-winning humor column The Pun Also Rises runs in the Berkshire Eagle. He is the author of six books including *It Happened In Rhode Island* and *From God To Verse*. Follow him on Twitter @risingpun, where he never talks about travel and mostly makes jokes. He updated the Berkshires and Western Massachusetts chapter of this guide.

Former Fodor's staff editor **Andrew Collins** is based in Mexico City but resides part of the year in a tiny New Hampshire village near Lake Sunapee. A longtime contributor to dozens of Fodor's guidebooks, including Pacific Northwest, Santa Fe, and National Parks of the West, he's also written for dozens of mainstream and LGBTQ publications—*Travel + Leisure*, *New Mexico Magazine*, *AAA Living*, *The Advocate*, and *Canadian Traveller* among them. Additionally, Collins produces the website ⊕ *Love-WinsUSA.com* and teaches travel writing and food writing for New York City's Gotham Writers Workshop.

Born and raised in Burlington, Vermont, **Mike Dunphy** caught the travel bug while studying at the University of Kent in Canterbury, England. Following graduation, he joined the Peace Corps and served as an ESL teacher and trainer in Europe and Turkey for more than 10 years. Returning to the United States, he earned a master's degree in publishing and writing at Emerson College before moving to New York City. There, he successfully built a career as a writer and editor, contributing to CNN, *USA Today*, *Forbes*, *Metro*, *Travel Weekly*, and *Time Out*, among many others. After yet another two-year stint in Europe, he went back to Vermont to become editor in chief of *The Bridge* newspaper in Montpelier. He also teaches article writing, travel writing, and creative nonfiction for Gotham Writers Workshop in New York City. He updated the Vermont chapter. Follow him on Twitter @MikeDDunphy and Instagram @vermontopia.

Originally a hayseed from the Territories, **Grace-Yvette Gemmell's** incurable wanderlust has led her to hang her hat in many offbeat locales, including a haunted house in the Netherlands, a Celtic enclave in Germany, a shoebox on the tiny island of Manhattan, a certain infamous English-language bookshop on Paris's Left Bank, Leopold Bloom's old haunt, and most recently, among the horse chestnuts in Berlin. She's a regular contributor to arts, culture, and travel publications. Grace-Yvette updated the Maine Coast chapter.

Kim Foley MacKinnon, an award-winning Boston-based journalist, loves to explore and write about New England for a number of publications, including the *Food Network*, *Your AAA*, and the *Boston Globe*, among others. She helped update the Fodor's Boston guide and has written or contributed to several other guidebooks. Although much of her work is focused in New England, she also goes farther afield for publications such as *Forbes Travel* and *Cruise Critic*. She updated the Boston chapter this edition. Follow her on Twitter and Instagram @escapewithkim.

As a freelance writer in Belfast, Maine, **Mary Ruoff** covers travel and other subjects. She is an award-winning former newspaper reporter and a graduate of the School of Journalism at the University of Missouri-Columbia. One of her sources on all things Maine is her husband, Michael Hodsdon, a mariner and lifelong Mainer. They enjoy exploring the state with their son, Dima. For this edition, Mary updated the Inland Maine chapter.

Laura V. Scheel updated the Cape Cod, Martha's Vineyard, and Nantucket chapter of this book. She has written frequently for Fodor's since 1999, contributing to multiple guidebooks throughout New England.

 Jane E. Zarem, a freelance travel writer and Connecticut native, is a regular contributor to Fodor's Travel Publications; in addition to updating the Connecticut, Rhode Island, and Travel Smart chapters for this edition, she also covers several islands for *Fodor's Essential Caribbean* and authored (and updated) *Fodor's InFocus: Barbados & St. Lucia*, now in its 5th edition. She also contributed to Fodor's guides focused on adventure vacations, healthy escapes, and weekend travel. Her travel articles, covering much of the globe, have appeared in various print and digital publications over the years—most recently on Afar.com and in Rand McNally's *Getaway* magazine and its Road Atlas. Jane is a member of New York Travel Writers' Association.